Faith in Law, Law in Faith

John Witte, Jr., Robert W. Woodruff Professor of Law, McDonald Distinguished Professor, and Faculty Director of the Center for the Study of Law and Religion at Emory University.

Faith in Law, Law in Faith

Reflecting and Building on the Work of John Witte, Jr.

Edited by

Rafael Domingo
Gary S. Hauk
Timothy P. Jackson

BRILL

LEIDEN | BOSTON

This is an open access title distributed under the terms of the CC BY-NC 4.0 license, which permits any non-commercial use, distribution, and reproduction in any medium, provided the original author(s) and source are credited. Further information and the complete license text can be found at https://creativecommons.org/licenses/by-nc/4.0/

The terms of the CC license apply only to the original material. The use of material from other sources (indicated by a reference) such as diagrams, illustrations, photos and text samples may require further permission from the respective copyright holder.

This is in Open Access with CC-BY-NC funded by the Center for the Study of Law and Religion, Emory University.

The Library of Congress Cataloging-in-Publication Data is available online at https://catalog.loc.gov
LC record available at https://lccn.loc.gov/2024013195

Typeface for the Latin, Greek, and Cyrillic scripts: "Brill". See and download: brill.com/brill-typeface.

ISBN 978-90-04-54617-2 (hardback)
ISBN 978-90-04-54618-9 (e-book)
DOI 10.1163/9789004546189

Copyright 2024 by Rafael Domingo, Gary S. Hauk, and Timothy P. Jackson. Published by Koninklijke Brill NV, Leiden, The Netherlands.
Koninklijke Brill NV incorporates the imprints Brill, Brill Nijhoff, Brill Schöningh, Brill Fink, Brill mentis, Brill Wageningen Academic, Vandenhoeck & Ruprecht, Böhlau and V&R unipress.
Koninklijke Brill NV reserves the right to protect this publication against unauthorized use. Requests for re-use and/or translations must be addressed to Koninklijke Brill NV via brill.com or copyright.com.

This book is printed on acid-free paper and produced in a sustainable manner.

Contents

Foreword   IX
  James T. Laney
Preface and Acknowledgements   XI
Notes on Contributors   XIII

PART 1
Evaluating John Witte's Scholarly Contributions

1   John Witte, Jr. and the Field of Law and Religion   3
      Norman Doe

2   John Witte, Jr. on Christianity and Law   19
      Rafael Domingo

3   John Witte, Jr. and the Study of Legal History   39
      R. H. Helmholz

4   John Witte, Jr.'s Contributions to the Study of Human Rights and Religious Freedom   51
      Nicholas Wolterstorff

5   John Witte, Jr.'s Contributions to the Study of Sex, Marriage, and Family Law   69
      Helen M. Alvaré

6   John Witte, Jr.'s Contributions to Legal and Political Thought   86
      Jonathan Chaplin

7   Building an Interdisciplinary University from the Center Out   113
      Gary S. Hauk

PART 2
Faith and Law in Biblical and Theological Perspectives

8   What Christianity and Law Can Learn from Each Other   135
      Michael Welker

9   Christian Teachings on Obligations   148
     David VanDrunen

10 Law, Christianity, and Good Samaritanism   165
     M. Christian Green

11 Can Laws and Rights Teach? John Witte and the Uses of the Law   184
     Patrick McKinley Brennan and William S. Brewbaker III

12 *Nomos, Agape,* and a Sacramental Jurisprudence   214
     Timothy P. Jackson

13 When Catholicism Was Part of the Common Law: The Influence of the Catholic Intellectual Tradition   235
     Samuel L. Bray

14 The Reception of the Medieval *Ius Commune* in the Protestant Reformation   251
     Mathias Schmoeckel

15 Church Laws as a Means of Ecumenical Dialogue   271
     Mark Hill, KC

16 Bearing Witness to Truth: Christianity at the Crossroads of Race and Law   289
     Brandon Paradise

PART 3
Faith, Law, and Freedom Historically and Today

17 Human Dignity and the Christian Foundations of Law and Liberty   309
     Andrea Pin

18 Calvinism and the Logic of Self-Defense: Rights, Religion, and Revolution   327
     David Little

19 Scriptural Interpretation and the New England Tradition of Rights after the Glorious Revolution: The Example of Cotton Mather   351
     Jan Stievermann

CONTENTS VII

20 Religious Liberty in the Thirteenth Colony   372
    Joel A. Nichols

21 "A Wall of Separation": Church—State Relations in America and Beyond   395
    Daniel L. Dreisbach

22 The Shifting Law and Logic Behind Mandatory Bible Reading in American Public Schools   415
    Mark A. Noll

23 An Integrative Approach to Government Religious Speech   434
    Nathan S. Chapman

24 Freedom of the Church: Religious Autonomy in a Secular Age   455
    Julian Rivers

25 Obeying Conscience: The Commands and Costs of Resisting the Law   479
    Jeffrey B. Hammond

PART 4
Faith, Law, and Family Historically and Today

26 The Legal Basis of the Sacramental Theology of Marriage   501
    Philip L. Reynolds

27 Law, Religion, and Education   515
    Kathleen A. Brady

28 Christianity, Child Well-Being, and Corporal Punishment   540
    Marcia J. Bunge

29 To Ratify or Not to Ratify the UN Convention on the Rights of the Child: Gains and Losses   568
    Mariela Neagu and Robin Fretwell Wilson

30 Faith-Based Family Law Arbitration in Secular Democracies—Is the End Near?   590
    Michael J. Broyde

31   Cosmic Disorder: Angelic Rebellion, the Sin of Sodom, and the Epistle of Jude   615
     Charles J. Reid Jr.

Counting My Blessings: A Response   639
     John Witte, Jr.

Index of Scriptural References   673
Index of Titles   678
Index of Persons   682
Index of Subjects   694

Foreword

In a sense, this foreword has been in the making for more than half a century. It was 1979 when Emory University, which I was privileged to serve as president, received a munificent benefaction from Robert and George Woodruff, at the time the largest gift ever to an American institution. That endowment enabled us to do some things that no other university was doing at the time.

My deep conviction—in fact, my passion—was that the university should be a scene of fertile intellectual conversation, where different disciplines fructify each other's imagination and thought. The university also has a moral calling to work toward the larger common good. My role as president was to plant a seed for such work and to provide some resources. One of the innovations I was most interested in was the conversation between law and religion, two disciplines of study that had grown up together in the earliest universities but had become estranged from each other in recent centuries.

In pursuing this idea of bringing law and religion back into a more constructive dialogue, our good fortune lay in recruiting two young Harvard Law graduates and an eminent Harvard Law professor to Atlanta. Frank Alexander, just starting his distinguished teaching career, started the Law and Religion Program at Emory in 1982. The late, great Harold J. Berman, Emory's first Robert W. Woodruff Professor of Law, brought immediate stature to the enterprise when he joined the faculty in 1985. And a tall, lanky, fresh-faced fellow named John Witte Jr. arrived with Berman as a research associate. Within two years—his high energy, keen intelligence, and very bright promise already abundantly evident—John had become director of the program, now called the Center for the Study of Law and Religion.

I can say without hesitation that all of us associated with Emory have been simply astonished at what has happened in the intervening decades. The range of the work and influence of the center not only has expanded to reach across Emory University, as we had hoped, but, indeed, has stretched around the world. Home to the *Journal of Law and Religion*—the flagship journal in the field—the center has guided the publication of more than 350 books, hosted dozens of major conferences, collaborated with leading scholars on six continents, and inspired the founding of similar centers at other universities. Of all the things I am proud of as president emeritus of Emory, none stands higher than the Center for the Study of Law and Religion.

In many respects, all of the center's achievements reflect the vision and drive of John Witte—not just his executive leadership as director of the center, but his own seminal studies. His laser-like mind, sweeping historical and legal perspective, galvanizing vision, and soaring standards for scholarship, teaching, and collegiality are matched only by his extraordinary appetite for work. He is a prolific writer, from whose keyboard has poured forth a steady torrent of monographs, edited volumes, journal articles, reviews, book chapters, lectures, and op-eds. Not a Johnny one-note, he delves into legal history, constitutional law, historical theology, human rights, marriage, the family, and the shaping of character and moral vision in late modern societies. He has a gift for making all of this deep and broad learning accessible to a wide readership.

This volume appropriately pays tribute to John's remarkable career. A few years ago, Emory conferred on him the Robert W. Woodruff Professorship of Law—the highest accolade for a faculty member at Emory and the title first held by his mentor, Hal Berman. John now has in every sense succeeded Hal, and I can well imagine how proud he would be, as am I. All of us who care about the overarching purposes of education and the conversation between these two fundamental aspects of human life—law and religion—are in John's debt.

James T. Laney
President Emeritus, Emory University

Preface and Acknowledgements

For several decades, the work of John Witte Jr. as scholar, teacher, public lecturer, and project leader, has been among the most influential in the English-speaking world in the field of law and religion in general, and in the study of law and Christianity in particular. A Harvard Law School graduate, Witte is Robert W. Woodruff Professor of Law, McDonald Distinguished Professor of Religion, and director of the Center for the Study of Law and Religion at Emory University. He has published some three hundred articles, eighteen journal symposia, and forty-five books, and his writings have appeared in fifteen languages. Witte has delivered more than four hundred public lectures throughout the world, including, recently, the Gifford Lectures at Aberdeen, and he has taught more than eight thousand law students since his Emory debut in 1985. He has led a score of international research projects on faith and democracy; religion and human rights; marriage, family, and children; and Christianity and law, together yielding more than two hundred new volumes. Witte also (co-)edits four book series in law and religion for Cambridge, Eerdmans, Brill, and Aranzadi as well as the flagship periodical in the field (and a Cambridge imprint), the *Journal of Law and Religion*.

This volume, *Faith in Law, Law in Faith*, evaluates and elaborates Witte's wide-ranging scholarly contributions in thirty-one original chapters written by leading law professors, historians, theologians, and ethicists. Part I evaluates Witte's contributions to his main areas of scholarly focus and collaboration—law and religion in Abrahamic perspective, with a particular focus on law and Christianity; legal history in the Western legal tradition, particularly in the Reformation and early modern period; human rights and religious freedom viewed in historical, comparative, and constitutional perspectives; the history, law, and theology of marriage, family, and children; and major themes of legal and political theory.

The next three parts offer fresh reflections on Witte's signature topics of "faith, freedom, and family." Part II offers biblical and theological perspectives on fundamental questions of justice and mercy, love and forgiveness, covenant and community, race and reconciliation, and the sources and uses of church law and state law over time and across jurisdictions. Part III explores the biblical, philosophical, and historical foundations of human rights and religious freedom in the Western legal tradition and takes up vexing constitutional issues of separation of church and state, religious autonomy, prayer in schools, public religious expression, and private conscientious objections. Part IV samples the wide field of marriage and family law, with close case studies of the history of marital sacrament; children's rights, education, and (corporal) discipline; faith-based arbitration of family disputes; and biblical debates about sexual relations and marriage. The introduction and conclusion situate this volume in the field of law and religion and map a few of the frontiers for further study.

We editors are grateful for the erudition and cooperation of the thirty-three contributors to this volume—a few of them Witte's former students, and almost all of them collaborators in scholarly projects and publications that Witte has led since the mid-1980s. We are also delighted to have the foreword by Rev. Dr. James T. Laney, former president of Emory University, who inspired the creation of the Emory Center for the Study of Law and Religion in 1982 and appointed Witte as director in 1987. Several Center members have contributed generously to the creation of this volume, especially Whittney Barth, executive director, and Amy Wheeler, chief of staff. We are also grateful for the financial support of the Center's most generous benefactor over the years, the McDonald Agape Foundation and its president and chairman, Peter McDonald.

Two persons who have had an immense and permanent influence on John should be mentioned—his great mentor and the father of the field of law and religion, the late Harold J. Berman; and John's indispensable life partner, Eliza Ellison. John's career—and, thus, this book—would not have been the same without them.

We have enjoyed our collaboration with Lauren Danahy and Akiko Hakuno at Brill in bringing this volume to press and making it available in open access format that ensures global distribution. Finally, we are grateful to Professors Javier Martínez Torrón, Mark Hill KC, and their colleagues in the International Consortium of Law and Religion Studies for hosting the presentation of this volume in honor of John Witte's 65th birthday in 2024.

We would be remiss, of course, if we did not also express our personal and profound thanks to our friend, colleague, and, in some ways, exemplar, John Witte. For many years, he has seasoned his steadfast encouragement of our own scholarship with incisive suggestions, gentle grace, modesty, and humor. The field of law and religion in general would be poorer without John's contributions, and so would our own scholarly life. It is therefore a deep joy to have collaborated in publishing this tribute to John and his enduring legacy.

Rafael Domingo, Gary S. Hauk, and Timothy P. Jackson

Notes on Contributors

Helen M. Alvaré
is the Robert A. Levy Endowed Chair in Law and Liberty at Antonin Scalia Law School, George Mason University.

Kathleen A. Brady
is Senior Fellow and McDonald Distinguished Fellow at the Center for the Study of Law and Religion, Emory University.

Samuel L. Bray
is the John N. Matthews Professor of Law at the University of Notre Dame Law School.

Patrick M. Brennan
is the John F. Scarpa Chair in Catholic Legal Studies and Professor of Law at Villanova University Charles Widger School of Law.

William S. Brewbaker III
is Dean and Professor of Law at the University of Alabama School of Law.

Michael J. Broyde
is Professor of Law and director of the SJD Program at the Emory University School of Law and Berman Projects Director at the Emory Center for the Study of Law and Religion.

Marcia J. Bunge
is Professor of Religion and the Drell and Adeline Bernhardson Distinguished Endowed Chair at Gustavus Adolphus College (USA) and Extraordinary Research Professor at North-West University (South Africa).

Jonathan Chaplin
is a Fellow of Wesley House, Cambridge, where he contributes to the Centre for Faith in Public Life.

Nathan S. Chapman
is the Pope F. Brock Professor of Law at the University of Georgia School of Law.

Norman Doe
is Professor of Law and Director of the Centre for Law and Religion at Cardiff Law School, Cardiff University.

Rafael Domingo
is Álvaro d'Ors Professor of Law at the University of Navarra.

Daniel Dreisbach
is Professor in the Department of Justice, Law, and Criminology at American University.

M. Christian Green
is a Senior Fellow at the Center for the Study of Law and Religion, Emory University.

Jeffrey B. Hammond
is Associate Professor of Law at the Thomas Goode Jones School of Law, Faulkner University.

Gary S. Hauk
is University Historian Emeritus of Emory University and Senior Editor at the Emory Center for the Study of Law and Religion.

R. H. Helmholz
is the Ruth Wyatt Rosenson Professor Emeritus of Law at the University of Chicago Law School.

Mark Hill KC
is Global Visiting Professor and Distinguished Fellow, University of Notre Dame London Law Programme and Honorary Professor at Cardiff University.

Timothy P. Jackson
is the Bishop Mack B. and Rose Stokes Professor Emeritus of Theological Ethics at the Candler School of Theology, Emory University.

James T. Laney
served as President of Emory University from 1977 to 1993 and as the United States Ambassador to the Republic of Korea from 1993 to 1997.

David Little
is a Research Fellow at the Berkeley Center of Georgetown University, retired in 2009 as the T. J. Dermot Dunphy Professor of the Practice in Religion, Ethnicity, and International Conflict, Harvard Divinity School.

Mariela Neagu
is a former Head of the National Authority for Children's Rights in Romania and is Postdoctoral Researcher at the Centre on Skills, Knowledge, and Organisational Performance (SKOPE) at the University of Oxford.

Joel A. Nichols
is Interim Dean and Mengler Chair in Law at the University of St. Thomas School of Law, in Minnesota.

Mark A. Noll
formerly the Francis A. McAnaney Professor of History at the University of Notre Dame, is Research Professor of History at Regent College, an affiliate of the University of British Columbia.

Brandon Paradise
is Associate Professor of Law and Professor Dallas Willard Scholar at Rutgers Law School, and McDonald Distinguished Fellow at the Emory University Center for the Study of Law and Religion.

Andrea Pin
is Full Professor of Comparative Public Law at the University of Padua and a Senior Fellow at the Center for the Study of Law and Religion, Emory University.

Charles J. Reid Jr.
is Professor of Law at the University of St. Thomas School of Law, in Minnesota.

Philip L. Reynolds
is the Charles Howard Candler Professor Emeritus of Medieval Christianity and the Aquinas Professor Emeritus of Historical Theology at the Candler School of Theology, Emory University.

Julian Rivers
is Professor of Jurisprudence at the University of Bristol Law School.

Mathias Schmoeckel
is Professor and Executive Director of the Institute of German and Rhenish Legal History and Civil Law at the University of Bonn.

Jan Stievermann
is Professor of the History of Christianity in North America at the University of Heidelberg.

David VanDrunen
is Robert B. Strimple Professor of Systematic Theology and Christian Ethics at Westminster Seminary California.

Michael Welker
is Senior Professor of Systematic Theology and Director of the Research Center for International and Interdisciplinary Theology at the University of Heidelberg.

Robin Fretwell Wilson
is the Roger and Stephany Joslin Professor of Law at the University of Illinois College of Law, Chicago.

Nicholas P. Wolterstorff
is the Noah Porter Professor Emeritus of Philosophical Theology at Yale University.

PART 1

Evaluating John Witte's Scholarly Contributions

∴

CHAPTER 1

John Witte, Jr. and the Field of Law and Religion

Norman Doe

1   Early Influences on John Witte

To understand the evolution of John Witte's interest in law and religion, it is necessary to explore its early origins.¹ His Dutch parents immigrated to Canada in 1953; family and faith were crucial to his early life in Ontario. He explains: "I am a Christian believer, and I have been a member of a Christian family from the very beginning. My parents ... were of the Christian Reformed faith. I was brought up in that tradition, catechized both at home and at church, sent to Reformed primary and secondary schools, and imbued with the idea that Christianity is the fundamental part of life."²

Witte attended Calvin College, a liberal arts college founded in Grand Rapids, Michigan, by the Reformed Church. Among his many teachers, he studied with the philosophers H. Evan Runner and Nicholas Wolterstorff (later of Yale Divinity School); these both taught him "to discern the religious sources and commitments implicit or explicit in historical and modern ideas and institutions," such as law and politics,³ and he later collaborated with them around their shared interest in Christian approaches to human rights.⁴ At Calvin College, Witte majored in history, philosophy, and biology—indeed, he took the Medical College Admission Test, the Law School Admission Test, and the Graduate Record Examinations. While these gave him considerable latitude in choosing a career, Witte decided upon a future in law; he explains: "the field of

---

1 This chapter draws on Norman Doe, "An Introduction to the Work of John Witte, Jr.," in John Witte, Jr., *Faith, Freedom, and Family New Essays on Law and* Religion, ed. Norman Doe and Gary S. Hauk (Tübingen: Mohr Siebeck, 2021), 1–17.
2 Interview with John Witte, Jr., May 6, 2015, Handong International Law School, Pohang, South Korea, https://www.johnwittejr.com/uploads/5/4/6/6/54662393/handong_interview _2015.pdf (hereafter Handong Interview), 1.
3 John Witte, Jr., Heidelberg Lecture, "Promotionsfeier der Theologischen Fakultät," University of Heidelberg, February 8, 2017, lecture on receiving Dr. Theol., *Honoris Causa* (hereafter Heidelberg Lecture), 3.
4 Interview with John Witte, Jr., Institute of Sino-Christian Studies, Hong Kong, August 9, 2019, https://www.johnwittejr.com/uploads/9/0/1/4/90145433/witte_interview_christinaty _human_rights_and_culture_r_.pdf (hereafter Hong Kong Interview), 2 and 13.

law was the place where I could find an interesting venue for exploring some of the deep questions about the role that Christianity played in shaping civilization." He graduated with the degree of bachelor of arts (BA) in 1982.[5]

Then came the plan to pursue a doctor of jurisprudence (JD) and/or a doctor of philosophy (PhD) degree. Witte's preference was to study law and history at Yale Law School and the Yale history department with the Reformation scholar Steven Ozment (1939–2019). Ozment left Yale for Harvard, however, and Harvard had no joint JD/PhD program with the history department. So, with "the dilemma of where to go," Witte "wrote to Harold J. Berman at Harvard Law School, whose work I had read at some length as a college student, and asked what I should do." Witte recalls, with typical admiration and respect, that Berman "was very generous in responding with a hand-written two-page letter, inviting me to come work with him." It was, for Witte, "a deep privilege to sit at the feet of a great master who was wrestling with some of the fundamental questions of law and religion in the Western tradition." Indeed, Berman was "a man who had sacrificed much for the sake of coming to the Gospel, accepting it notwithstanding his Jewish upbringing and with the result of eventual ostracism by his family. Berman worked me very hard, forty hours a week, during the time I was going to law school; my Dutch Calvinist work ethic carried me in that context." Witte wrote his thesis on the scientific revolution and the law.[6]

Berman (1918–2007) continued to be a major influence on Witte. They worked together closely for over twenty years. Berman, the "twentieth-century master of the idea of law and revolution," taught Witte "the importance of mapping the shifting belief systems in the evolution and revolutions of the Western legal tradition." Berman himself had been influenced as a student by his own mentor, Eugen Rosenstock-Huessy (1888–1973). It was the work of Rosenstock-Huessy on change and continuity consequent upon revolution that Berman invoked in his treatment of legal transformations attendant upon, for example, the Papal Revolution of the twelfth and thirteenth centuries, the Lutheran revolution of the sixteenth, the English Revolution of the seventeenth, and the French and American revolutions of the eighteenth.[7] A key aspect of Witte's work, therefore, shaped by these formative experiences, is unravelling the idea of legal development—transformation and reformation.

---

5 Handong Interview, 2.
6 Handong Interview, 1.
7 Handong Interview, 8–10. See, for example, Harold J. Berman, *Law and Revolution: The Formation of the Western Legal Tradition* (Cambridge, MA: Harvard University Press, 1983); Harold J. Berman, *Law and Revolution II: The Impact of the Protestant Reformations on the Western Legal Tradition* (Cambridge, MA: Harvard University Press, 2006); see also his *Faith and Order: The Reconciliation of Law and Religion* (Grand Rapids: Eerdmans, 1993).

Indeed, Witte dedicated a book to Berman, whom he describes as his "mentor, colleague, and friend."⁸

Another early influence on Witte was Herman Dooyeweerd (1894–1977), the Dutch professor of jurisprudence at the Vrije Universiteit, Amsterdam (1926–65). As Witte recalls, for Dooyeweerd the "founding metaphors and motifs or fundamental law ideas" both anchored and transformed "the basic ideas and institutions of a given civilization," such as in the Christianization of Rome, the Middle Ages, the Protestant Reformation, and the French Revolution.⁹ Witte edited lectures that Dooyeweerd delivered in 1937 in Amsterdam—and in his introduction to the volume, Witte unpacks brilliantly the originality of Dooyeweerd as a Christian thinker who used biblical and Christian teachings to understand law, politics, society, and "the natural, voluntary, and contractual social institutions" between "the individual and the state," that is, between the public and the private spheres.¹⁰ Witte later took up Dooyeweerd's complex Christian theory of rights, and summarizes it in his collected works.¹¹

Of both Berman and Dooyeweerd, Witte sums up: "Those two big figures had a deep influence on me early in my scholarly life." What he took from them "was the idea that there are fundamental seams, transformative moments, watershed periods" throughout history—and he builds on this idea, particularly with regard to his keen interest in "the consequences of what happens when there is a bend in the stream" or "fundamental shift" in juridical change.¹²

---

8   John Witte, Jr., *Law and Protestantism: The Legal Teachings of the Protestant Reformation* (Cambridge: Cambridge University Press, 2002). See also John Witte, Jr., and Frank S. Alexander, eds., *The Weightier Matters of the Law: Essays on Law and Religion in Tribute to Harold J. Berman* (Atlanta: Scholars Press, 1988); John Witte, Jr., "A Conference on the Work of Harold J. Berman," *Emory Law Journal* 42 (1993): 419–589; John Witte, Jr., "In Praise of a Legal Polymath: A Special Issue Dedicated to the Memory of Harold J. Berman (1918–2007)," *Emory Law Journal* 57 (2007): 1393–643; and John Witte, Jr., and Christopher J. Manzer, introduction to Harold J. Berman, *Law and Language: Effective Symbols of Community*, ed. John Witte, Jr. (Cambridge: Cambridge University Press, 2013), 1–35.
9   Handong Interview, 10.
10 Herman Dooyeweerd, *A Christian Theory of Social Institutions*, ed. John Witte, Jr., trans. Magnus Verbrugge (Toronto: Paideia Press, 1986).
11 See chapter 16 of *Faith, Freedom, and Family: New Essays on Law and Religion*, ed. Norman Doe and Gary S. Hauk (Tübingen: Mohr Siebeck, 2021).
12 Handong Interview, 10. See, for example, his overviews of major eras and shifts in law and religion in chapters 4, 14, 24, and 37 of *Faith, Freedom, and Family* as well as in his introduction to John Witte, Jr. and Frank S. Alexander, eds., *Christianity and Law: An Introduction* (Cambridge: Cambridge University Press, 2008), 1–32; and his introductions to his monographs *The Reformation of Rights: Law, Religion, and Human Rights in Early Modern Calvinism* (Cambridge: Cambridge University Press, 2007); *The Sins of the Fathers: The Law and Theology of Illegitimacy Reconsidered* (Cambridge: Cambridge University Press,

In terms of scholars, a third influence on Witte was another Dutchman, the theologian Abraham Kuyper (d. 1920), whose impact continues; Witte says: "Kuyperian thinking remains an important orientation for me" in terms of

> a set of intellectual habits and methodological instincts ... particularly the basic respect for Scripture, tradition, reason, and experience; the emphasis on social pluralism and sphere sovereignty, and the wariness of political, ecclesiastical, or any other kind of monism or monopoly in social organization and authority structuring; the appetite for covenant thinking; the insistence that everyone operates with a basic worldview [of] beliefs, values, or metaphors.[13]

Witte's continuing admiration for Kuyper work is evident in several scholarly works, which include the lectures and articles Witte produced for the centennial conference on Kuyper's Stone Lectures at Princeton Theological Seminary in 1998[14] and his receipt of the Kuyper Prize at Princeton University in 1999.[15]

2   The Concept of Law and Religion in the Thought of John Witte

In the four decades since Witte's move from Harvard to Emory, he has produced a torrent of books, articles, and lectures, all while administering the Center for the Study of Law and Religion, teaching more than eight thousand law students, and convening seminal international conferences. The bedrock for all this energy, exploration, and endeavor is Witte's rich and powerful understanding of "law and religion." It has three streams, which Witte himself explains as follows. The first is the *dialectical interaction* of law and religion: "Religion gives law its spirit and inspires its adherence to ritual, tradition, and justice." Equally,

---

2009); *From Sacrament to Contract: Marriage, Religion, and Law in the Western Tradition,* 2nd ed. (Louisville, KY: Westminster John Knox Press, 2012); *Sex, Marriage, and Family in John Calvin's Geneva,* 2 vols. (Grand Rapids: Eerdmans, 2005, 2022); and John Witte, Jr., Joel A. Nichols, and Richard W. Garnett, *Religion and the American Constitutional Experiment,* 5th ed. (Oxford: Oxford University Press, 2016).

13 Hong Kong Interview, 1–2. Kuyper had also been prime minister in the Netherlands from 1901 to 1905. See further chapters 1, 2, and 10 of *Faith, Freedom, and Family.*

14 John Witte, Jr., "The Biology and Biography of Liberty: Abraham Kuyper and the American Experiment," *Religion, Pluralism, and Public Life: Abraham Kuyper's Legacy for the Twenty-First Century,* ed. Luis Lugo (Grand Rapids: Eerdmans, 2000), 243–62.

15 John Witte, Jr., "God's Joust, God's Justice: The Revelations of Legal History," *Princeton Theological Seminary Bulletin* 20 (1999): 295–313.

"law gives religion its structure and encourages its devotion to order, organization, and orthodoxy." Moreover, while each discipline is distinct, "Law and religion share such ideas as fault, obligation, and covenant and such methods as ethics, rhetoric, and textual interpretation. Law and religion also balance each other by counterpoising justice and mercy, rule and equity, discipline and love." This interaction gives the two disciplines vitality and strength: "Without law at its backbone, religion slowly crumbles into shallow spiritualism. Without religion at its heart, law gradually crumbles into empty, and sometimes brutal, formalism." Law and religion also "cross-over and cross-fertilize each other": *conceptually* (for example, sharing such concepts as sin and crime, covenant and contract, righteousness and justice, and mercy and equity); *methodologically* (sharing, for example, hermeneutical methods to interpret texts, casuistic methods of argument, systematic methods to organize doctrines, forensic methods of sifting evidence and rendering judgments); and *institutionally* (for example, through multiple relations between both political and ecclesiastical officials and offices).[16]

The second stream of thought in law and religion might be styled *the religiosity of secular laws,* the idea that "the laws of the secular state retain strong religious dimensions." "Every legitimate legal system ... has what Harold Berman calls an 'inner sanctity,' a set of attributes that command the obedience, respect, even reverence of both political officials and political subjects." Like religion, "law has authority" (it is "decisive or obligatory"); "law has tradition" (for example, in precedent, principles, and practices); and "law has liturgy and ritual" (for example, courtroom procedure, professional pageantry, and legislative language").[17] These commonalities between law and religion may differ in origin and purpose (temporal and spiritual), but they exist profoundly in substance and form. These are products of the centuries-long interaction of law and religion in the Western tradition, Witte shows in several writings.[18]

The third stream is *the juridical character of religion*: "Religion maintains a legal dimension, an inner structure of legality, which gives religious lives and religious communities their coherence, order, and social form." Importantly,

> Legal habits of the heart structure the inner spiritual life and discipline of religious believers, from the reclusive hermit to the aggressive zealot. Legal ideas of justice, order, judgment, atonement, restitution, responsibility, obligation, and others pervade the theological doctrines of

---

16 Heidelberg Lecture, 1–2. See further chapter 1 of *Faith, Freedom, and Family.*
17 Heidelberg Lecture, 2. See further chapter 11 of *Faith, Freedom, and Family.*
18 See esp. chapters 4–9, 14–15, 25–29, and 34–37 of *Faith, Freedom, and Family.*

countless religious traditions. Legal structures and processes ... define and govern religious communities and their distinctive beliefs and rituals, mores, and morals.[19]

However, law and religion may be in tension: as "every major religious tradition has known both theonomism and antinomianism—the excessive legalization and the excessive spiritualization of religion," so "every major legal tradition has known both theocracy and totalitarianism—the excessive sacralization [and] secularization of law." Equally, as "every major religious tradition strives to come to terms with law by striking a balance between the rational and the mystical, the prophetic and the priestly, the structural and the spiritual," so it is that "every major [secular] legal tradition struggles to link its formal structures and processes with the beliefs and ideals of its people."[20]

These are inspirational understandings of the relationship between law and religion. But they come at a high price. Their pursuit, study, and substantiation all clearly necessitate an interdisciplinary expertise—the specialist knowledge and methods of jurists and theologians, of historians and sociologists, and of philosophers and political theorists. So, how does Witte see himself within this multifaceted field of law and religion? He says, "I am not a philosopher, political theorist, ethicist, or theologian, though I dabble in these fields. I am a lawyer and legal scholar, focused on the history of law and religion." He works, therefore, "largely as an historian," tapping into "the wisdom of the Protestant and broader Christian traditions on fundamental questions of law, politics, and society." He is not a politician seeking "to hammer out political platforms," nor a litigator pressing constitutional cases. However important that work is for the law and religion field, that is "just not my vocation," Witte writes.[21] Indeed, "I have long felt that my calling is to be an historian." "In college and certainly in law school, I became interested in the Protestant Reformation as a ... transformative moment in the history of the West, and the influence the Protestant reformers had ... on law, politics, and society."[22] Witte links this calling to his earlier experiences: "My parents and pastors taught me from the beginning

---

19 Heidelberg Lecture, 1–2.
20 Heidelberg Lecture, 3. See also John Witte, Jr., "The Interdisciplinary Growth of Law and Religion," in *The Confluence of Law and Religion: Interdisciplinary Reflections on the Work of Norman Doe*, ed. Frank Cranmer et al. (Cambridge: Cambridge University Press, 2016), 247–61; "The Study of Law and Religion in America: An Interim Report," *Ecclesiastical Law Journal* 14 (2012): 327–54; and afterword to *Leading Works in Law and Religion*, ed. Russell Sandberg (London: Routledge, 2019), 197–205.
21 Hong Kong Interview, 3.
22 Handong Interview, 2, 11–12.

that Law and Gospel belong together, that Scripture goes hand in hand with tradition, and that historical experience has deep meaning [and] purpose for those who have eyes to see and ears to hear." "I have translated all this schoolboy instruction into a commitment to studying the history of law and religion in the Western tradition."[23] Witte also has a deep respect for modern legal historians, contributing to several volumes to honor their scholarship.[24]

3 The Methods of John Witte as a Scholar of Law and Religion

The methods Witte uses as a historian of law and religion are broadly triadic: "I try to study this history with three 'R's' in mind," he says: "*retrieval* of the religious sources and dimensions of law in the Western tradition, *reconstruction* of the most enduring teachings of the tradition for our day, and *reengagement* of an historically informed religious viewpoint with the hard legal issues that now confront church, state, and society." At the same time, Witte bears three "I's" in mind; he explains: "Much of my historical work is *interdisciplinary* in perspective, seeking to bring the wisdom of religious traditions into greater conversation with law, the humanities, and the social and hard sciences." Moreover, "it is *international* in orientation, seeking to situate American and broader Western debates over interdisciplinary legal issues within a comparative historical and emerging global conversation." Also, there is the interfaith aspect: "it is *interreligious* in inspiration, seeking to compare the legal teachings of [Roman] Catholicism, Protestantism, and Orthodoxy," and "sometimes" those of Judaism, Christianity, and Islam.[25]

However, Witte's methods make particular demands on the ethics of scholarship. As such, he recognizes five responsibilities that attach to the Christian

---

23 Heidelberg Lecture, 3.
24 See, for example, John Witte, Jr. et al., eds., *Texts and Contents in Legal History: Essays in Honor of Charles Donahue* (Berkeley, CA: Robbins Collection, 2016); John Witte, Jr. et al., eds., *The Equal Regard Family and Its Friendly Critics: Don Browning and the Practical Theological Ethics of the Family* (Grand Rapids: Eerdmans, 2007); Witte and Alexander, *The Weightier Matters of the Law*; John Witte, Jr., "Hugo Grotius and the Natural Law of Marriage: A Case Study of Harmonizing Confessional Differences in Early Modern Europe," in *Studies in Canon Law and Common Law in Honor of R. H. Helmholz*, ed. T. L. Harris (Berkeley, CA: The Robbins Collection, 2015), 231–50; John Witte, Jr., "Canon Law in Lutheran Germany: A Surprising Case of Legal Transplantation," in *Lex et Romanitas: Essays for Alan Watson*, ed. Michael Hoeflich (Berkeley: University of California Press-Robbins Collection, 2000), 181–224. See further chapters 11–13, 17–24, and 35–37 of *Faith, Freedom, and Family*.
25 Heidelberg Lecture, 3.

scholar. First, *stewardship*: "As a scholar, one critical responsibility is to be a good steward of the wisdom, knowledge, and methodology that you acquired in your profession and to maintain and develop it, to continue to teach it to the next generation, to prepare the next generation of scholars to stand and succeed you." Second, *discipline*: "If your Christian vocation is to be a scholar, be the very best scholar and teacher you can be." Third, *accessibility*: scholars should express themselves "in and on the terms that anyone can understand." Fourth, *influence*: "Christian scholars ... must try to find ways of reforming and improving their profession or discipline to accord better with what the faith teaches," finding themes "where the Christian tradition has had or can have notable influences." Fifth, *engagement*: "Christian scholars have different ways to engage the community, the polity, and public debate." On one hand, "One can simply produce scholarship, write it, teach it, lecture about it, and equip other specialists to take the work and run with it. That is a lot of what I do. I do [not] spend a lot of time doing the litigation, lobbying, and legislative work that are a natural outgrowth of what I do." On the other hand, scholars may engage in "legal debates about faith, freedom, and family: they participate in cases, they craft legislation, they work hard ... with the other leaders of the culture" on "hard questions"—through op-eds, debates, television, and other media: "That is equally important and responsible Christian scholarship."[26]

Witte has a deep appreciation of the horizons open to Christian scholars of law and religion and the fields in which they may live out these responsibilities of stewardship, discipline, accessibility, influence, and engagement. First, there is the field of secular law. On one hand, Witte accepts the "common sentiment" that Christian faith and the legal profession may be "incompatible" or at least "in tension." Quoting Luther's claim, *Juristen, böse Christen* (Jurists are bad Christians), Witte accepts that law is often seen as "a grubby, greedy, and ugly profession, and some of that is true." However, law is "fundamental," one of the "universal solvents of human living," for "a society without law would quickly devolve into hell itself." And so "we need Christians at work in the law."[27] For example, as to secular law, Christian lawyers have a part to play in the field of human rights on the basis that: these are "natural gifts of God"; "human beings are created in the image of God"; and "God has given us the gifts of [for example] companionship of other humans."[28] Witte himself has

---

26 Handong Interview, 10–11.
27 Ibid., 15–16. See also, for example, John Witte, Jr., "What Christianity Offers to the World of Law," *Journal of Law and Religion* 32 (2017): 4–97. See further chapter 2 of *Faith, Freedom, and Family*.
28 Hong Kong Interview, 9–10.

led in several important projects on Christianity and human rights,[29] following these with studies on perspectives of other religious traditions globally.[30]

Witte also considers that Christian scholars of law and religion may contribute to ecumenism and inter-Christian dialogue. One challenge is for "Catholic, Protestant, and Orthodox Christians to develop a rigorous ecumenical understanding of law, politics, and society" and "together to work out a comprehensive new ecumenical 'concordance of discordant canons' that draws out the best of these traditions, that is earnest about its ecumenism, and that is honest about the greatest points of tension." For Witte, "few studies would do more both to spur the great project of Christian ecumenism and to drive modern churches to get their legal houses in order. Law is at the backbone of the church, and at the foundation of Christian solidarity."[31] This thinking bore fruit in the work of an ecumenical panel whose statement of principles of Christian law was launched at the 11th Assembly of the World Council of Churches in 2022 as an instrument for greater unity among Christians worldwide—and Witte and the Center for the Study of Law and Religion at Emory have provided invaluable support to this, including Witte's sharing his aspirations at a meeting of the panel in Oxford in 2018.[32]

A related challenge that Witte advances, "perhaps the greatest of all," is "to join the principally Western Christian story of law, politics, and society known in North America and Western Europe with comparable stories ... in the rest of the Christian world," in the Global South and East—Africa, Korea, China, India, Philippines, Malaysia, and beyond, where "rich new indigenous forms and norms of law, politics, and society are also emerging, premised on very

---

29 See, for example, John Witte, Jr., "Christianity and Human Rights," *Journal of Law and Religion* 30 (2015): 353–495; John Witte, Jr. and Frank S. Alexander, eds., *Christianity and Human Rights: An Introduction* (Cambridge: Cambridge University Press, 2010); and John Witte, Jr., ed., *Christianity and Democracy in Global Context* (Boulder, CO: Westview Press, 1993).

30 See, for example, John Witte, Jr. and Johan D. van der Vyver, eds., *Religious Human Rights in Global Perspective: Legal Perspectives* (Dordrecht: Martinus Nijhoff Publishers, 1996); John Witte, Jr. and Michael J. Broyde, eds., *Human Rights in Judaism: Cultural, Religious, and Political Perspectives* (New York: Jason Aronson Publishers, 1998); John Witte, Jr. and M. Christian Green, eds., *Religion and Human Rights: An Introduction* (New York: Oxford University Press, 2012); John Witte, Jr. and Michael Bourdeaux, eds., *Proselytism and Orthodoxy in Russia: The New War for Souls* (Maryknoll, NY: Orbis Books, 1999); and John Witte, Jr. and Richard C. Martin, eds., *Sharing the Book: Religious Perspectives on the Rights and Wrongs of Proselytism* (Maryknoll, NY: Orbis Books, 2000).

31 Heidelberg Lecture, 4–6.

32 John Witte, Jr., foreword to *Church Laws and Ecumenism*, ed. Norman Doe (Abingdon: Routledge, 2020), vii–ix.

different Christian understandings of theology and anthropology." "It would take a special form of cultural arrogance for Western and non-Western Christians to refuse to learn from each other."[33] Once more, Emory has helped to promote this vision in several ways, including a host of published studies.[34]

The same applies to interfaith dialogue. Under the direction of Witte, the Emory center has convened "deep conversations between and among Christians, Jews, and Muslims, sometimes Eastern religions too, on fundamental legal, political, and social questions."[35] Likewise, "Christian scholars have been among the leaders of [the] global law and religion movement," with growing numbers of Jewish and Muslim scholars, and specialists in Asian and traditional religions who "have already learned a great deal from each other" and "cooperated in developing richer understandings of … legal and political subjects." This "comparative and cooperative interreligious inquiry into fundamental issues of law, politics, and society needs to continue," especially in a world today of "increasing interreligious conflict and misunderstanding" struggling "to discover from within and impose from without proper, responsible, and effective legal constraints on religious fundamentalism, extremism, and terrorism."[36] Once again, Witte's call for more comparative religious law studies has been heard and acted upon.[37]

4   Testing the Contribution of John Witte to Law-and-Religion Scholarship

Responses to the scholarship and leadership of John Witte in the field of law and religion provide an appropriate forum in which to test the extent and

---

33   Heidelberg Lecture, 4–6.
34   For example, the contribution of Emory Center member Johan D. van der Vyver, "African Traditional Religion and Indigenous Perspectives on the Environment," in *Law, Religion and the Environment in Africa*, ed. M. Christian Green (Stellenbosch: Sun Media, 2020), 333–42. See further John Witte, Jr. and Frank S. Alexander, eds., *Modern Christian Teachings on Law, Politics, and Human Nature*, 2 vols. (New York: Columbia University Press, 2005). The Cambridge Studies on Christianity and Law series that Witte edits and the Routledge Law and Religion Series that I edit include several commissioned several studies on "great Christian jurists in world history" from across the Christian world. See further chapter 3 of *Faith, Freedom, and Family*.
35   Hong Kong Interview, 3–4.
36   Heidelberg Lecture, 4.
37   See, for example, Norman Doe, *Comparative Religious Law: Judaism, Christianity, Islam* (Cambridge: Cambridge University Press, 2018); and Norman Doe, *Christian Law: Contemporary Principles* (Cambridge: Cambridge University Press, 2015).

value of his contribution to this field. The quantity and quality, the breadth and depth, and the written and oral genres of Witte's work are breathtaking. His publications have appeared in fifteen languages—including Chinese, Korean, Polish, and German. He has delivered more than 350 public lectures—at schools, research institutes, and academic conferences in North America, Europe, Israel, Japan, Hong Kong, South Korea, and South Africa. He has given dozens of high-profile endowed lectures—including the Brauer Lectures at Chicago, the Franke Lectures at Yale, the Meador Lectures at Virginia, the Beatty Lectures at McGill, the Lofton Lecture at Melbourne, the Steinmetz Lecture at Duke, the McDonald Lecture at Oxford, the Pennington Lecture at Heidelberg, the Jefferson Lectures at Berkeley, the Cunningham Lectures at Edinburgh, the Tikvah Lecture at Princeton, and the Gifford Lecture at Aberdeen. His leadership in the field is evidenced in his position as series editor of the Cambridge Studies in Law and Christianity, as coeditor of the *Journal of Law and Religion*, as an editorial board member of, *inter alia*, the *Ecclesiastical Law Journal* and the *Journal of Church and State*, and as series editor of the *Emory Studies in Law and Religion*. In his editorial work, he himself explains that: "I have been working hard ... on themes of Christianity and law across the world today, as part and product of a broader effort to build a vast new library of books not only in law and Christianity, but also in law and each of the other axial world religions."[38]

The extent to which Witte collaborates with others across the world is further evidence of his inspirational leadership in the field. Witte's zeal for collaboration not only functions at the professional level. He also thrives on and stimulates friendship, fellowship, and fun inherent in collegial work, especially through his now well-known roundtables, which he has convened in dozens of universities around the world. This is nowhere better seen in recent years than in the preparatory work and roundtables in Atlanta and London to advance a coedited volume, under the leadership of Mark Hill KC, on Christianity and criminal law. Hill himself—a distinguished ecclesiastical judge and leader in the renaissance of the study of English ecclesiastical law and the wider field of law and religion—also has a genius for inspiring a sense of community among scholars, including bridging the experiences of practice and scholarship. The

---

[38] Heidelberg Lecture, 3. See, for example, John Witte, Jr. and Gary S. Hauk, eds., *Christianity and Family Law: An Introduction* (Cambridge: Cambridge University Press, 2017); Norman Doe, ed., *Christianity and Natural Law: An Introduction* (Cambridge: Cambridge University Press, 2017); and Rafael Domingo and John Witte, Jr., *Christianity and Global Law* (London: Routledge, 2020). The Emory Center has commissioned a score of other such "introductions" to Christianity and law for publication in the Routledge Law and Religion Series and the Cambridge Studies in Christianity and Law series.

energy that Hill and Witte brought to this collaboration is evident in the fruit it yielded and in the enduring friendships it stimulated.[39]

How have Witte's published studies been received? Of his books on law and religion, human rights, and religious freedom, four may be selected here as ground-breaking. *Law and Protestantism: The Legal Teachings of the Lutheran Reformation* (Cambridge, 2002) provides an account of the eventual recognition of the need for norms in Lutheran ecclesial and earthly life, and the transformative impact of Lutheran theological ideas on the secular laws of Germany and Scandinavia. *God's Joust, God's Justice* provides a powerful case for the study of law and religion.[40] *The Reformation of Rights* explains how early modern Calvinism (anticipating the Enlightenment) contributed to the development of constitutional law, the rule of law, human rights, and religious freedom; it shows that the Calvinists from the sixteenth to the eighteenth century articulated a religious understanding of rights and liberties bounded by responsibilities and duties, all in a covenantal framework. *The Blessings of Liberty* documents and defends the essential interdependence of human rights and religious freedom from antiquity until today and the Christian roots and routes of rights developments in the Western legal tradition on both sides of the Atlantic. In this book, Witte answers both modern Christian critics who see human rights as a betrayal of Christianity and modern secular critics who see Christianity as a betrayer of human rights.

There are also those works on faith, freedom, and family, topics treated "separately and together, historically and today, in the West and beyond."[41] For example, of his books, *From Sacrament to Contract* explores how Lutheran, Calvinist, and Anglican reformers replaced the traditional Roman Catholic idea of marriage as a sacrament with a new idea of the marital household as a social estate, covenant, or little commonwealth to which all are called—clerical and lay alike. *The Sins of the Fathers* is "in some sense a plea against the stigmatization of the other, especially the bastard as that person is called in this tradition. My adopted brother was a bastard, and that book was dedicated to his memory. It is … a troubling story about Christian brutality and charity

---

39 Mark Hill, Norman Doe, R. H. Helmholz, and John Witte, Jr., eds., *Christianity and Criminal Law* (London: Routledge, 2020). The roundtable at London (October 2018) also allowed new friends to hear the power of Witte's preaching at the Temple Church, London (prominent in the genesis of Magna Carta and mother church of the common law).

40 This was later abridged and translated as John Witte, Jr., *The Foundations of Faith, Freedom, and the Family*, trans. H. Ohki and Y. Takasaki (Tokyo: Seigakuin University Press, 2008) (Japanese edition).

41 Heidelberg Lecture, 3.

at once." What Witte describes, on its publication, as his "biggest, fattest, most ambitious scholarly book" is *The Western Case for Monogamy over Polygamy*, which "broke open a lot of historical material that nobody has ever seen and that tells the story that really has not been told before in the Western tradition", "excruciatingly difficult to write," and taking five years.[42]

Book reviews are an obvious barometer to test opinion about Witte's contribution to the field. A typically balanced review is of his *Church, State, and Family*, a book of equal ambition and achievement. The reviewer, himself a distinguished scholar of law and religion, writes: "The first six chapters provide a rollercoaster ride through history, visiting the teachings on sex, marriage and family life by those who have shaped the family teachings of the Western legal tradition"—these chapters alone "would be more than enough to mandate [the book's] inclusion on reading lists and bookshelves." However, chapter 7 (as Witte states) reconstructs traditional teaching into "a multidimensional theory of the marital family sphere, with natural and spiritual poles, and with social, economic, communicative and contractual dimensions radiating between these poles." The remaining chapters apply this theory to "several hard issues born of the modern sexual revolution," such as defects in religious approaches to children's rights; the case against polygamy; arguments for and against the use of faith-based family laws in modern liberal democracies (he proposes a shared jurisdictional model); and equality within marriage, which, Witte argues, is "not well served by legal equality between all forms of marriage, or by its wholesale abolition." In the conclusion, Witte calls for "radical same-sex marriage and LGBTQ advocates [to] stop viewing religious liberty as the enemy" and for Western churches and other religions "to rein in their anathemas and actions against same-sex marriage in public life and instead focus on improving the culture of marital life more broadly." The reviewer concludes: "Whether you agree with Witte's assessment or not, this is a book which needs to be read. Impressive and epic in scope yet providing an integrated and focused argument, it is a work of first-rate scholarship"—in sum, writes the reviewer, it is "a definitive work" and sets "a high benchmark."[43]

---

42   Handong Interview. See also John Witte, Jr., *Church, State, and Family: Reconciling Traditional Teachings and Modern Liberties* (Cambridge: Cambridge University Press, 2019). On these volumes and their critics, see further chapters 35 and 37 of *Faith, Freedom, and Family*.

43   The quotations are from *Church, State, and Family*, xiv, 365, and 377. The reviewer is Russell Sandberg: *Ecclesiastical Law Journal* 22 (2020): 260–63.

5 The Legacy of John Witte

The legacy of Witte to date is formidable. Of the work of the Emory center, Witte says: "It has been deeply gratifying to see the growing interest in law and religion study around the world." In the 1980s, "we were almost alone; now fifty-five centers and institutes of law and religion have popped up on campuses around the globe." Then "there was only a small handful of journals and books"—now there are twenty-seven periodicals with more than seventeen hundred books on law and religion published worldwide in the past twenty years. In the United States, virtually all law schools now have a basic course on religious liberty or church-state relations, a growing number also have courses in Christian, Jewish, and Islamic law, and some consider religion in such courses as legal ethics, legal history, jurisprudence, law and literature, legal anthropology, comparative law, environmental law, family law, and human rights. Therefore, religion is no longer a "hobbyhorse" of lone scholars or religiously chartered law schools. Rather, "Religion now stands alongside economics, philosophy, literature, politics, history, and other disciplines as a valid and valuable conversation partner with law."[44] It was a particular delight and honor for the Centre for Law and Religion at Cardiff Law School—the establishment of which, in 1998, was inspired by the work of the Emory center—to welcome Witte to mark the thirtieth anniversary of the LLM in Canon Law in 2021 when in the Fall of 2022 he delivered the keynote address on metaphors and the law.[45]

For so many of these achievements, Witte has rightly received a host of honors—yet another sign of the esteem with which he is held globally. At Emory Law School, he has been recognized on twelve separate occasions (from 1992–93 to 2011–12) as the Most Outstanding Professor and in 1994 received the Emory University Scholar/Teacher Award. In 1995, the United Methodist Foundation for Christian Higher Education awarded him the Most Outstanding Educator Award for all Methodist-affiliated Schools, and that same year he received the Max Rheinstein Fellowship and Research Prize from the Alexander von Humboldt-Stiftung, in Bonn. In 1998 the Black Law Students Association at Emory Law School presented him with its Professor of the Year Award,

---

44 Heidelberg Lecture, 4.
45 In 2008 Witte also attended the tenth anniversary of the establishment of the Cardiff Centre for Law and Religion, and in 2017 he attended a symposium that helped to inspire the publication of R. Sandberg, ed., *Leading Works in Law and Religion* (London: Routledge, 2018), and on the same visit delivered a magisterial lecture to mark five hundred years since the Reformation—later published as "From Gospel to Law: The Lutheran Reformation and its Impact on Legal Culture," *Ecclesiastical Law Journal* 19 (2017): 271–91.

and in 1999, Princeton Theological Seminary presented him with the Abraham Kuyper Prize for Excellence in Theology and Public Life. Further honors followed in this century, including the National Religious Freedom Award from the Council for America's First Freedom (2008); the James W. C. Pennington Award from the University of Heidelberg (2016); the Harry Krause Lifetime Achievement Award in Family Law from the University of Illinois (2016); and a Doctor of Theology degree (*honoris causa*) from the University of Heidelberg (2017). Witte was listed in 2018 among the top law-and-religion scholars worldwide, second only to Stanford's Michael McConnell in stature.[46] These are, all of them, extraordinary honors.

What of the future? Witte has a particular project in mind. First, typically, he looks to the past: "For two thousand years, Christians have wrestled with the place of Scripture in the evolving legal cultures around them" and "the fundamental questions of faith, freedom, and family, of politics, law, and society." "It takes a special form of arrogance to simply ... offer one's own normative perspective uninformed by the tradition." Second, therefore, "it might be wise to try to distill this into a more systematic [and] normative form"—namely, a modern "Christian jurisprudence." Third, it will be a jurisprudence that is "authentic," "engages the hard legal questions," "is accessible to insiders and outsiders," and "tries to distill the two-thousand-year tradition [into] a form that other people might be able to profit from and build upon." Fourth, in other words: "In my more audacious moments, I feel the pull to try to write a modern Summa, Institutes, or Dogmatics on Christian Jurisprudence." Fifth, he admits: "I am sure pride is part of this," but "to answer the fundamental questions of law, politics, and society with power, precision, and prescription" is "maybe my calling ... to say more."[47]

In 2021, Witte's collection of recent articles and book chapters was published under the title *Faith, Freedom, and Family: New Essays on Law and Religion*. This eight-hundred-page volume contains a wealth of studies that reflect and bring together in a single accessible volume the fundamentals of Witte's work in this field. All the elements of the story we have seen thus far in this chapter are to be found in the studies unfolding there. All the labor of research, all the deep thinking, all the tireless honoring of the past and recalibrating what it teaches for the hard issues of today are set out there. Part one, on "Faith," has three studies that map in general terms the field of law and religion—its educational value, its use of metaphor, and its Christian contribution. Several

---

46 Rex Ahdar, ed., *Research Handbook on Law and Religion* (Cheltenham: Edward Elgar Publishing, 2018), 5.
47 Handong Interview, 11–12.

chapters explore in a long historic perspective what faith in law means, and how particular scholars have given shape to the field of law and religion, ancient and modern. Part two, on "Freedom," offers selected studies on the history of religious freedom, the Protestant Reformation of rights, resistance, and revolution as well as natural law and natural rights. Part two also takes up the contributions of several scholars to our understanding of human rights and religious freedom; the reach is national, international, and global, the method evaluative and sometimes critical. Part three, on "Family," focuses on sex, marriage, and family life with insights from scripture and history, law and theology, politics and society, and a response to his reviewers in this field.

6   Conclusion

All in all, it is clear that Witte has been shaped personally in his interest in law and religion by his family and his faith, and advantaged by the ample academic freedom and institutional support that he has enjoyed at Emory. The intellectual influences upon him were many, but he generously recognizes those of Berman, Dooyeweerd, and Kuyper. His move from Harvard to Atlanta was a watershed moment—there he has helped to bring together a vibrant community of talents. The responsibility of the directorship of the Emory Center for the Study of Law and Religion has, indeed, stimulated a profound and rich understanding of law and religion around notions of the dialectical interaction between them, the religiosity of secular law, and the juridical character of religion. In all this, Witte is a historian of law and religion. His methods are to retrieve, reconstruct, and reengage these disciplines with the challenging issues of today, with interdisciplinary, international, and interreligious elements. Not only does Witte offer a work ethic for the Christian scholar in this field around ideas of stewardship, accessibility, and engagement but he also provides a challenging agenda for ecumenism and greater interfaith dialogue. His studies on religion, human rights, and religious freedom have been ground-breaking, bringing into clear relief the contribution of Reformation thinkers as they anticipate Enlightenment approaches to law and religion. His work—recognized by his academic peers globally and from many disciplines—has been an inspiration to many and will continue to shape this discipline.

CHAPTER 2

John Witte, Jr. on Christianity and Law

Rafael Domingo

1   Introduction: John Witte as a Christian Jurist

John Witte's entire life and vast intellectual output have been marked by one fundamental fact: he is first and foremost profoundly Christian. Witte's Christianity determines his being, his character, his status as a leading scholar, and all his academic work. As a Christian, Witte knows and feels himself to be a child of God, made in God's image, regenerated by the waters of baptism, and called upon to participate in this world in the royal, prophetic, and priestly mission of Christ through his work as a historian and jurist, his dedication to his family and friends, and his commitment to liberty and the communities in which he lives. This vocational, radical, and transformative Christian identity suffuses not only Witte's person but also his work, which form an unbreakable unity. Witte cannot be understood apart from his academic work, nor can the work be understood apart from the man, just as a self-portrait cannot be understood without the artist.[1]

To speak of Christianity and law in John Witte—or of law and Christianity; the words can be reversed, because their influence is reciprocal—is to speak of every one of the thousands of pages that Witte has written in the history of law, marriage, family, children, the relationship between law and religion, human rights, religious freedom, and political and social philosophy.[2] That is why this chapter, to a certain extent, is all-encompassing, because even when Witte approaches other topics and religions, he does so from the analogies and perspectives of Christianity. It is also his own Christianity that has prompted Witte's interest in and love for other religions, which he in no way sees as competitors, but rather as sister faiths (especially Judaism and Islam) or as admirable treasures full of human and divine wisdom (Greco-Roman thought,

---

1   See the two extensive interviews conducted with Witte on "Freedom and Order: Christianity, Human Rights, and Culture" (August 2019) and "Christianity and Law" (May 2015), published in John Witte, Jr., *Faith, Freedom, Family: New Essays on Law and Religion*, ed. Norman Doe and Gary S. Hauk (Tübingen: Mohr Siebeck, 2021), 691–732.
2   See "Bibliography of John Witte Jr., 1981–2021," in *Faith, Freedm, and Family*, 733–62.

Buddhism, Confucianism, Hinduism, and Indigenous traditions).[3] The fact is that every Christian is a *homo religiosus*, a being open to transcendence and in a permanent quest for truth, before being properly a *homo Christianus* by baptismal grace.

Witte's Christianity is anchored in the Protestant Reformed tradition, and heavily influenced by the well-known Dutch pastor, theologian, and politician Abraham Kuyper (1837–1920),[4] who, within Calvinism, emphasized the sovereignty of Christ over salvation, the world, and indeed all of creation. Thus, words such as "creation," "sovereignty," and "covenant" echo with a special musicality in Witte's writings.[5] As Witte himself states:

> Kuyperian thinking remains an important orientation for me. It provides a set of intellectual habits and methodological instincts—particularly the basic respect for scripture, tradition, reason, and experience; the emphasis on social pluralism and sphere sovereignty and the wariness of political, ecclesiastical, or any other kind of monism or monopoly in social organization and authority structuring; the appetite for covenant thinking; and the insistence that everyone operates with a basic worldview, a basic set of founding beliefs, values, or metaphors, even if they remain mostly implicit.[6]

Over time, Witte, without abandoning his roots, has opened up toward a more interdenominational and ecumenical Christianity, and has broadened his capacity to admire and embrace not only the best of all the families of Protestantism, but also many other aspects of Roman Catholicism and Orthodox

---

3 See, for example, Don Browning, M. Christian Green, and John Witte, Jr., eds. *Sex, Marriage, and Family in World Religions* (New York: Columbia University Press, 2006); John Witte, Jr. and Johan D. van der Vyver, eds., *Religious Human Rights in Global Perspective*, 2 vols. *Legal Perspectives* (Dordrecht: Martinus Nijhoff Publishers, 1996); and John Witte, Jr. and M. Christian Green, eds., *Religion and Human Rights: An Introduction* (New York: Oxford University Press, 2012).

4 See John Witte, Jr., introduction to Abraham Kuyper, *On Charity & Justice*, ed. Matthew J. Tuininga (Bellingham, WA: Lexham Press, 2022). See also idem, "Abraham Kuyper on Family, Freedom and Fortune," in *Faith, Freedom, and Family*, 199–214.

5 See, esp., John Witte, Jr., *The Reformation of Rights: Law, Religion, and Human Rights in Early Modern Calvinism* (Cambridge: Cambridge University Press, 2007); idem, *The Blessings of Liberty: Human Rights and Religious Freedom in the Western Legal Tradition* (Cambridge: Cambridge University Press, 2021); idem, *Church, State, and Family: Reconciling Traditional Teachings and Modern Liberties* (Cambridge: Cambridge University Press, 2019); and John Witte, Jr. and Eliza Ellison, eds., *Covenant Marriage in Comparative Perspective* (Grand Rapids: Eerdmans, 2005).

6 *Faith, Freedom, and Family*, 694.

Christianity.⁷ This explains why both ecumenical and interreligious dialogues flow so naturally with him, because of his understanding of Christian unity. Witte feels a deep attraction for everything that is good within Christianity, as well as beyond it, and he bases this on a healthy regard for the creation order, common grace or general revelation, and natural law. This attraction to all denominations and traditions is not in any way a matter of eclecticism, nor of doctrinal relativism. His work exudes conviction and love of tradition, but also openness to the future. He is also aware of the sins of the Christian tradition, both inside and outside the church.

Although Witte's Christianity is a precondition for understanding his intellectual production, it is not a sufficient condition. Witte's Christianity must be considered along with what we could call his "fundamental intuition." Behind all great scholars usually lie one or a few major intuitions that mark their intellectual trajectory. Intuitions in the strictest sense of the term are lights in our understanding acquired without recourse to conscious reasoning.⁸ Intuitions are sources of inspiration, with which we fully identify because they show us an attractive path to follow. That is why sometimes intuitions are not expressed in literal words, but in metaphors, of which Witte is so fond.⁹ When these intuitions mature in the soul, they end up turning into intentions and these, in turn, evolve into major research projects.

Intuitions are the point of departure and driving force of all serious academic research. We come back to them time and time again throughout our academic lives, just as we return to our birthplace and family home. These intuitions may be original or shared, often reach beyond our own area of knowledge and, every now and then, shed new light on an old idea, opening up a new horizon for knowledge. The intuition of Friedrich Carl von Savigny (1779–1861) and his historical school of jurisprudence, for instance, was to underscore the connection between history and law and to understand the latter as a product of "the spirit of the people" (the *Volksgeist*).¹⁰ Hans Kelsen

---

7   See, for example, John Witte, Jr. and Frank S. Alexander, eds., *Modern Christian Teachings on Law, Politics, and Human Nature*, 2 vols. (New York: Columbia University Press, 2005); John Witte, Jr. and Michael Bourdeaux, eds., *Proselytism and Orthodoxy in Russia: The New War for Souls The New War for Souls* (Maryknoll, NY: Orbis Books, 1999).

8   On intuition, see Jacques Maritain, *The Degrees of Knowledge*, trans. Gerald B. Phelan, repr. ed. (Notre Dame: University of Notre Dame Press, 2011 [1995]), esp. 263–70.

9   See John Witte, Jr., "Law, Religion, and Metaphor," in *Faith, Family and Freedom*, 37–55, esp. 39.

10 Friedrich Carl von Savigny, *Vom Beruf unserer Zeit für Gesetzgebung und Rechtswissenschaft* (Heidelberg: Mohr und Zimmer, 1814); in English, *Of the Vocation of Our Age for Legislation and Jurisprudence* (Kitchener, Ont: Batoche, 1999); and Friedrich Carl von Savigny, *System des heutigen römischen Rechts*, 3rd ed. (Berlin: De Gruyter, 2019).

(1881–1973) had the intuition of purifying law of all extraneous political elements in order to develop a true science of law on the basis of a fundamental norm (*Grundnorm*).[11] John Rawls (1921–2002), for his part, understood "justice as fairness," within the framework of a society of free citizens holding equal basic rights. Therein lay his fundamental intuition.[12]

The intuition that has marked Witte's academic life, which he shared with his mentor Harold J. Berman (1918–2007),[13] is that law and religion have more in common than is apparent at first sight: that law has a religious dimension and religion a juridical one.[14] Religion and law share origins, principles, values, rites, customs, rituals, formalities, methods, concepts, and hierarchies, and they depend on each other. When this interaction is culturally hidden or even manipulated, religion is diluted into ethereal spiritualism, and law is reduced to coercive regulatory imposition. But when law and religion are held in healthy dialectical relation, each side is improved by the other, and society and its core institutions are best positioned to achieve justice, peace, order, and freedom.[15]

This fundamental intuition that Witte shares with Berman—his beliefs about "faith in law, and law in faith," as this book's title captures it—is very old, even pre-Christian, as Witte recognized already in his earliest published work, in 1981.[16] His work has consisted in part in excavating this enduring intuition,

---

11 Hans Kelsen, *Reine Rechtslehre. Einleitung in die rechtswissenschaftliche Problematik* (Leipzig: F. Deuticke, 1934; 2nd ed., 1960). The second edition was translated into English by Max Knight: Hans Kelsen, *The Pure Theory of Law* (Berkeley: University of California Press, 1967).

12 John Rawls, *A Theory of Justice*, rev. ed. (Cambridge, MA: The Belknap Press of Harvard University Press, 1999), and John Rawls, *Justice as Fairness: A Restatement* (Cambridge, MA: Harvard University Press, 2001).

13 Harold J. Berman, *The Interaction of Law and Religion* (Nashville, TN: Abingdon Press, 1974).

14 John Witte, Jr., ed., "A Conference on the Work of Harold J. Berman," in *Emory Law Journal* 42 (1993): 419–589.

15 See, esp., John Witte, Jr. and Christopher Manzer, introduction to Harold J. Berman, *Law and Language: Effective Symbols of Community*, ed. John Witte, Jr. (Cambridge: Cambridge University Press, 2013), 1–35; idem, "Harold J. Berman," in *Great Christian Jurists in American History*, ed. Daniel L. Dreisbach and Mark A. Hall (Cambridge: Cambridge University Press, 2019), 230–44.

16 See Witte's very first publication reflecting this: "Hellenic Philosophy of Law: Essential Terms," in *The Association for the Advancement of Christian Scholarship: Academic Paper Series*, No. 1 (Nov. 1981): 1–34. He has returned to Greco-Roman sources often in his work on the history of the family, human rights, and religious freedom. See, for example, John Witte, Jr., *From Sacrament to Contract: Marriage, Religion, and Law in the Western Tradition*, 2nd ed. (Louisville, KY: Westminster John Knox Press, 2012), 17–30; idem, *The Sins of*

and applying it with new insights and overtones in a pluralistic and secularized society. To highlight this intuition's long lifespan, one only needs to point out that the Latin word for law (*ius*) is derived from the god Jupiter, or that the ancient Romans used the word *sacramentum* to refer to judicial processes in ancient legal times,[17] many centuries before Christianity began using the same expression to refer to the signs instituted by Christ by which divine grace is dispensed to humans. During the Middle Ages, divine law was both religious and juridical, as Thomas Aquinas and the great glossators and commentators on canon, civil, and feudal law all confirmed.[18] In the modern age, Gottfried Wilhelm Leibniz (1646–1716) insisted on this connection because he saw law and religion as having a common structure, a common vocabulary, a common formalism, and a shared interest.[19] Yet it is true that this idea has been lost in our secular age and has needed to be relaunched in a different context.[20] Witte has devoted all his efforts to this endeavor since beginning his career at the Center for the Study of Law and Religion at Emory University after completing his legal studies at Harvard Law School with Berman, before both of them moved to Emory in 1985.

For forty years, Witte has been applying and developing this fundamental intuition about law and religion in various fields of legal history, in line with his personal convictions and abilities, but above all with his deepest experiences: his attachment to Protestantism, his love for his family and friends, and his respect for human rights. Witte substantiates all of these commitments with the triad *faith, freedom, and family*.[21] By way of example, the happy yet sad experience of the life and death of his brother Ponkie (1964–1980), who was born out of a nonmarital relationship and adopted by Witte's parents, was the

---

the Fathers: The Law and Theology of Illegitimacy Reconsidered (Cambridge: Cambridge University Press, 2009), 49–72; idem, *The Western Case for Monogamy Over Polygamy* (Cambridge: Cambridge University Press, 2015), 101–43; and idem, *The Blessings of Liberty: Human Rights and Religious Freedom in the Western Legal Tradition* (Cambridge: Cambridge University Press, 2021), 23–27.

17 See Franz Wieacker, *Römische Rechtsgeschichte* I (Munich: Beck, 1988), no. 15, pp. 310–40, with bibliography. See also Olga Tellegen-Couperus, *Law and Religion in the Roman Republic* (Leiden: Brill, 2012) and Rafael Domingo, *Roman Law: An Introduction* (London: Routledge, 2018).

18 See John Witte, Jr. and Rafael Domingo, eds., *The Oxford Handbook of Christianity and Law* (Oxford: Oxford University Press, 2023), esp. chaps. 6–8.

19 See Gottfried Wilhelm Leibniz, *The New Method of Learning and Teaching Jurisprudence*, trans. Carmelo Massimo de Iuliis (Clark: Talbot Publishers, 2017), pt. 2, para. 4, p. 33.

20 Charles Taylor, *A Secular Age* (Cambridge, MA: The Belknap Press of Harvard University Press, 2007).

21 *Faith, Freedom, and Family.*

force that drove Witte to write one of his more beautiful and important books in defense of children's rights: *The Sins of the Fathers*.[22] This is probably Witte's freshest and most creative book, or at least the one that reflects his innermost personality. It has so far been translated into Chinese (2011) and Korean (2022).

In other chapters of this volume honoring Witte, distinguished scholars Norman Doe, Helen Alvaré, R. H. Helmholz, Nicholas Wolterstorff, and Jonathan Chaplin address the subject of Witte's contribution to the history of law (especially the relationship between Protestantism and law), family law and human rights, politics, and the relationship between law and religion itself. In this chapter, I focus on the relationship between Christianity and law as such, as part of a specific project that integrates and transcends these other, specific fields in which Witte has stood out as an author. Out of necessity, because Witte's work must be taken as a whole, I will refer to these other topics, adding cross references.

2   Relations between Christianity and Law as an International Project

Witte has become one of the most outstanding global scholars in the study of the relationship between Christianity and law as a great branch of the massive three-millennium-old tree of law and religion. This project is "interdisciplinary, interdenominational, and international," as Witte usually categorizes it,[23] and right now more than fifteen hundred Protestant, Roman Catholic, and Orthodox scholars (jurists, theologians, philosophers, historians, and sociologists) are contributing to it. Underlying this project is the idea that the relationship between Christianity and law is not merely accidental but inherent, with metahistorical significance and permanent value for the development of humanity.

A great lover of triads, Witte turns to them to explain the project. "I try to study this history with three "r's" in mind—retrieval of the religious sources and dimensions of law in the Western tradition, reconstruction of the most enduring teachings of the tradition for our day, and reengagement of a historically informed religious viewpoint with the hard legal issues that now confront church, state, and society."[24] Witte believes that Christians must regain a leading role in public life not in a dogmatic or nostalgic way, but "fully equipped

---

22   *The Sins of the Fathers*, XI–XIV.
23   John Witte, Jr., *God's Joust, God's Justice* (Grand Rapids: Eerdmans, 2006), X–XI, 4–9; and unpublished lecture on receiving an honorary doctorate in theology at the University of Heidelberg, Feb. 8, 2017.
24   Witte, *God's Joust, God's Justice: Law and Religion in the Western Tradition*, X.

with the revitalized resources of the Bible and the Christian tradition in all their complexity and diversity."[25]

Just as you have to excavate before building a house, Witte has embarked on his project by initiating a deep international and interdisciplinary conversation on the mission of Christianity in the secular era, especially in the field of law, to ensure that the project is underpinned by solid foundations. At a time when many intellectuals advocate a public space free from religion, Witte is arguing that Christian values and principles should be democratically restored to public life. This is how he puts it:

> The easy notions of a public reason that brackets all comprehensive doctrines and that brackets especially religious discourse about fundamental matters of the state is giving way to a more realistic and inclusive epistemology. Even early architects of religion-free public reason, like John Rawls and Jürgen Habermas, began to realize that a de-theologized discourse, a bleached and bland public reason, could not work in debates about such fundamental institutions as marriage and family life. Christians and persons of other faiths, as a consequence, are invited back into the conversation.[26]

To channel the project, in 2015 Witte founded and began directing the Cambridge Studies in Law and Christianity Series, which to date includes more than thirty published books.[27] Witte is also a frequent contributor to other collections, such as the Routledge Series on Law and Religion, edited by Norman Doe,[28] and works from other important presses, including Oxford University Press and Mohr Siebeck, which have taken on individual titles. Some of this project's results and reviews have been published in the Cambridge University Press *Journal of Law and Religion*, edited by the Center for the Study of Law and Religion at Emory. Last but not least, a major instrument for disseminating this great project has been *The Canopy Forum*, an online publication published by the Emory center. The McDonald Agape Foundation has been instrumental in launching this project, especially by funding scholarships for research

---

25 Ibid., 464.
26 John Witte, Jr., "Christianity and Law: Interview, May 2015," in *Faith, Freedom, and Family*, 726.
27 Information available at: https://www.cambridge.org/core/series/law-and-christianity/6D77992447E6BD14E748AE05E137D92B.
28 Information available at: https://www.routledge.com/Law-and-Religion/book-series/LAWRELIG. In this series, of the twenty-two published titles, nine have been directed or commissioned by Witte.

fellowships and projects among bright young scholars who have been working with Witte and his center colleagues.

Witte uses a broad definition of Christianity that encompasses the three major Catholic, Protestant, and Orthodox branches, as well as various denominations within them. To date, the Orthodox world is the most underrepresented in the law-and-religion field, thus fulfilling the old Latin adage that law indeed comes from the West, just as light comes from the East: *ex Oriente, lux; ex Occidente, ius.*[29] Witte has worked hard in his projects to include Orthodox voices alongside other Christian views.

As could not be otherwise in a project of this quality and ambition, Witte refers to law in its broadest sense, which is also the one that best captures its meaning. Law is a regulatory social order of justice, powers, rights, and freedoms, exercised and maintained by institutions that exercise authority individually or collectively, and that affect local, national, international, and global private and public human relations.

The key to understanding the relationship between Christianity and law is that law precedes Christianity in time, but Christianity elevates the very idea of law to a new dimension, which is the dimension of love. Christianity assumed and adopted Jewish and Roman law, but effected a profound spiritualization of law: *ius Evangelio praecedit, Evangelium autem ius elevat* (law precedes the Gospel, but the Gospel elevates law). In the same way that light blinds and harms us when we look too closely, however, so too the relationship between law and Christianity can be blinding when religion comes too close to law, or when law tries to conquer the religious space illegitimately, contravening Christ's own mandate: "Give therefore to Caesar the things that are Caesar's and to God the things that are God's" (Matthew 22:21; Mark 12:17; Luke 20:24).[30]

Witte has approached this massive project in law and Christianity from three different perspectives: one that we could call merely relational, another biographical, and a third jurisprudential.[31] Though operating in different stages of his work, these different perspectives coincide in time and are cumulative and mutually supportive. They are not closed but rather interdependent perspectives, as exemplified by the works coedited by Witte—*Christianity and*

---

29   See Rafael Domingo, *Ex Roma ius* (Cizur Menor, Navarra: Thomson Reuters Aranzadi, 2005).
30   See further Rafael Domingo, *God and the Secular Legal System* (Cambridge: Cambridge University Press, 2016).
31   John Witte, Jr., "What Christianity Offers to the World of Law," in *Faith, Freedom, and Family*, 57–66.

Family Law, which takes a biographical approach, and *Christianity and Global Law*, which addresses both the relational and biographical perspectives.[32]

3 The Relational Perspective

From the relational perspective, Witte has sought to map the historical, conceptual, categorical, and dogmatic ties between Christianity and law, both as ideas and in their most varied institutional forms and ramifications. That is why the titles of books written from this relational perspective usually include the word "Christianity" (or some denominational version of it) followed by the conjunction "and."

This relational perspective was strongly consolidated with the publication of his early book on *Christianity and Democracy in Global Context*, which is a collection of the speeches given by renowned speakers (Desmond M. Tutu, Harold Berman, Richard John Neuhaus, Bryan Hehir, and Jean Bethke Elshtain, among others) at a four-day international conference convened by the Emory center in 1991.[33] With a foreword by former U.S. President Jimmy Carter, who maintained strong academic ties with Emory University for four decades, the book examines Christianity's positive and negative influences in shaping and consolidating democracies. The conclusion one draws from reading it, in line with Jacques Maritain's stance, is that democracy was morally and legally enhanced when it became symbiotically related to Christianity.[34]

Early modern Protestantism first embraced the democratic ideal; centuries later, modern Roman Catholicism followed suit, especially with the Second Vatican Council, but above all with John Paul II, who applauded the idea of civic participation and collaboration and peaceful succession among rulers.[35] On the other hand, the tie between Orthodox Christianity and democracy is much weaker, and perhaps this partly explains why Orthodox-majority countries have lagged behind in the process of democratic transformation.

---

32 John Witte, Jr. and Gary S. Hauk, eds., *Christianity and Family Law: An Introduction* (Cambridge: Cambridge University Press, 2017); Rafael Domingo and John Witte, Jr., eds., *Christianity and Global Law* (London: Routledge, 2020).

33 John Witte, Jr., ed., *Christianity and Democracy in Global Context* (Boulder, CO: Westview Press, 1993; repr. ed. London: Routledge, 2019).

34 See Jacques Maritain, *Christianity and Democracy* (San Francisco: Ignatius Press, 2012), and *The Rights of Man and the Natural Law* (San Francisco: Ignatius Press, 1986, repr. 2011).

35 See John Paul II, *Encyclical Letter Centesimus Annus*, no. 46 (Vatican City: Libreria Editrice Vaticana, 1991).

Witte's analysis of the relational perspective of law and Christianity matured and gained new momentum with the publication of his monographs on *Law and Protestantism: The Legal Teachings of the Lutheran Reformation* (2002), *Sex, Marriage, and Family in John Calvin's Geneva* (2006), and *The Reformation of Rights: Law, Religion, and Human Rights in Early Modern Calvinism* (2007). As R. H. Helmholz's chapter herein elaborates, these volumes zeroed in on how classic Protestantism related to law, and what contributions the Reformation movements made to the transformation of public, private, penal, and procedural law and legal theory in European lands and their colonies.

While the relationship of Protestantism and law has continued to occupy him as a scholar,[36] Witte took a much broader, pan-Christian and interdisciplinary view in *Christianity and Law: An Introduction* (2008), a volume coedited with his colleague and friend Frank Alexander. This marked the start of what we could call his expansion phase. In this volume, prestigious scholars from the fields of law, history, philosophy, and theology—including Luke Timothy Johnson, Brian Tierney, R. H. Helmholz, Don S. Browning, Michael J. Perry, David Novak, David Little, and Norman Doe, among others—analyzed the connections between law and Christianity in the different branches of legal knowledge, ranging from canon and natural law to contract, criminal, and procedural law. This volume constituted Witte's roadmap for the coming years, as he eventually turned each chapter of the book into a new volume that further studied the relationship between Christianity and law in each specific area of law. Witte personally oversaw his areas of expertise and commissioned other experts to edit the remaining volumes.[37]

First, Witte edited a volume on *Christianity and Human Rights* (2010), again with Frank Alexander. The book was prefaced by South African Archbishop Desmond Tutu, whose opposition to apartheid in his country resulted in his receiving the Nobel Peace Prize in 1984. "I can testify that our own struggle for justice, peace, and equity would have floundered badly had we not been inspired by our Christian faith and assured of the ultimate victory of goodness

---

36 See, for example, John Witte, Jr. and Amy Wheeler, eds., *The Reformation of the Church and the World* (Louisville, KY: Westminster John Knox Press, 2017); and forthcoming volumes, *Sex, Marriage, and Family in John Calvin's Geneva 2: The Christian Household* and *A New Reformation of Rights: Calvinist Contributions to Modern Human Rights*.

37 See, for example, Norman Doe, ed., *Christianity and Natural Law: An Introduction* (Cambridge: Cambridge University Press, 2017); Daniel Crane and Samuel Gregg, eds., *Christianity and Market Regulation: An Introduction* (Cambridge: Cambridge University Press, 2021); Jeffrey B. Hammond, and Helen Alvaré, eds., *Christianity and the Laws of Conscience: An Introduction* (Cambridge: Cambridge University Press, 2021); and Pamela Slotte and John D. Haskell, eds., *Christianity and International Law: An Introduction* (Cambridge: Cambridge University Press, 2021).

and truth, compassion and love against their ghastly counterparts," the Archbishop declared.[38] Human rights are not a Christian invention, yet neither are they a creation of the Enlightenment. Rather, they derive from a combination of Jewish, Greek, and Roman teachings with the new and radical teachings of Christ based on the love of every human being with the same love of God. Christianity has illuminated the concepts of dignity, equality, freedom, compassion, and democracy that underlie the modern human rights paradigm, and it has deepened them with its insights into sanctity and grace.

In 2017, Witte and his friend and colleague Gary Hauk coedited the aforementioned study on *Christianity and Family Law*,[39] which analyzes the contribution of Christian thinkers from Saint Paul to John Paul II in shaping the doctrine and law of marriage and the family. It is undoubtedly one of the volumes where the inseparable unity between law and Christianity in the West is most evident, as Witte has shown in several other monographs, not least his *Sins of the Fathers, From Sacrament to Contract, The Western Case for Monogamy over Polygamy,* and *Church, State, and Family.*[40] Three years later, in 2020, Witte published two more coedited volumes—one with Mark Hill, Norman Doe, and Dick Helmholz on the relationship between Christianity and criminal law,[41] and the other with me on Christianity and global law, understood as a law beyond international law, where state interest and cooperation between states give way to a deeper, fuller human solidarity.[42] Several other volumes in this series of introductions to Christianity and law are in print, most of them with forewords or chapters by Witte, engaging Christianity and freedom, natural law, justice and agape, private law, church law, international law, the laws of conscience, market regulation, migration, and taxation.[43] Forthcoming in this series are new studies on Christianity and the law of alternative dispute resolution, capital punishment, child law, constitutional law, disability law, education law, evidence law, environmental law, health law, intellectual property law, labor and employment law, legal ethics, poor law, and social-welfare law.

Once the project had expanded and been applied to a broad variety of fields of law, Witte decided to embark on a major review, recapping the best of Christianity's influence on law in a new, more comprehensive global work *The*

---

38 Desmond M. Tutu, "The First Word: To Be Human Is to Be Free," in Witte and Alexander, *Christianity and Human Rights*, 1–7, at 6.
39 *Christianity and Family Law*.
40 See the chapter by Helen Alvaré herein.
41 Mark Hill, Norman Doe, R. H. Helmholz, and John Witte, Jr., eds., *Christianity and Criminal Law* (London: Routledge, 2020).
42 *Christianity and Global Law*. On the idea of global law, see Rafael Domingo, *The New Global Law* (Cambridge: Cambridge University Press, 2010).
43 See list of introductions in Witte, "What Christianity Offers to the World of Law."

Oxford Handbook of Christianity and Law.[44] In this collection, which he and I coedited, more than sixty experts from five continents address the relationship between Christianity and law from a historical, theological, juridical, and philosophical perspective. The work sums up Witte's four decades of work on this subject and, at the same time, is a new roadmap for studying this fertile relationship of Christianity of law historically and in our current age of secularization and globalization. Witte has come back to the ground he excavated thirty years ago and started work on a great building with solid foundations. There is still a long way to go, however.

Witte is also working on a multiyear project with his German colleague, the Heidelberg theologian Michael Welker, on the roles of law, religion, the market, family, health care, the military, and other institutions in character building—a project featuring, among other things, the civic and educational function of law.[45] Law in accordance with justice distills moral values, thus contributing to the moralization of modern liberal societies. Hence the need to draw up a basic civil morality for modern liberal societies and to analyze the appropriate instruments, mechanisms, and procedures for cultivating and enforcing morality.

4 The Biographical Perspective: the Idea of the Christian Jurist

The second perspective from which Witte analyzes the relationship between Christianity and law is biographical. This is no longer just a matter of putting together two ideas and analyzing similarities, differences, and reciprocal influences and connections throughout history, but of ascertaining how Christianity and law are forged and intertwined in the minds and hearts of specific Christian jurists, philosophers, and theologians who, with their writings and actions, have guided law along the paths of justice. In essence, this biographical perspective is a projection of Witte's own experience as a Christian jurist. Christianity is not a passing fashion, but rather touches upon an essential part of every person's being as well as supernatural being. *Ius ex persona oritur*, we could say in the manner of the classics: "law comes from the person."[46]

---

44 *The Oxford Handbook of Christianity and Law*.
45 See, for example, John Witte, Jr. and Michael Welker, eds., *The Impact of the Law on Character Formation, Ethical Education, and the Communication of Values in Late Modern Pluralistic Societies* (Leipzig: Evangelische Verlagsanstalt, 2021).
46 Domingo, *The New Global Law*, XVI.

Witte knows better than anyone that Martin Luther had condemned jurists as "bad Christians" (*Juristen böse Christen!*),⁴⁷ yet Witte's own experience as a Christian jurist is much more decisive than the impulsive reformer's whimsical cry. On this question, Witte prefers to side with Jimmy Carter, who, when asked about this question, answered, "It is a matter of what we Christians are going to do about democracy" and its law.⁴⁸ Indeed, the relationship between Christianity and law has a strong biographical content that cannot be ignored.

The category of Christian jurist encompasses any Christians who have devoted themselves to the cause of justice in its broadest sense and have had a significant impact on law and the legal system. Being a Christian jurist does not necessarily entail having a law degree or having practiced law; rather, it involves having made an important contribution to law that has enlightened legal systems and political communities with Christian values. John Paul II, for example, never studied law. Even so, during his lifetime he was called "the Pope of human rights" and was awarded an honorary doctorate in law by the University of La Sapienza.⁴⁹ Something similar can be said of the philosopher Jacques Maritain, whose contribution to the Universal Declaration of Human Rights makes him worthy of the title of Christian jurist.⁵⁰ One could cite many more such examples: Isidore of Seville, Thomas Aquinas, Catherine of Siena, John Calvin, Martin Luther King Jr., Oscar Romero, and many others.

This biographical approach is based on the empirical fact that specific human beings, flesh and blood, are behind the significant developments and reforms of law, as is also the case in empirical science. Just as the history of the theory of relativity would not have begun in 1905 without the Swiss patent-office clerk Albert Einstein, so the concept of constitutional courts would not have taken hold in Western Europe in the 1920s without the Austrian-American jurist Hans Kelsen.

The biographical approach has great potential for the study of law and legal history because it shows both the complexity and ambiguity and even the accidental nature of historical and modern legal systems. What lies behind legal documents and rules are facts and, beyond them, people. The who of the

---

47   The phrase was popularized before Luther, though it is attributed to him. See Michael Stolleis, "Juristenbeschimpfung, oder, "Juristen – böse Christen," in *Politik – Bildung – Religion. Hans Maier zum 65. Geburtstag*, ed. Theo Stammen et al. (Paderborn: Schöningh, 1996), 163–70.
48   Jimmy Carter, foreword to *Christianity and Democracy in Global Context*, xv.
49   Rafael Domingo, "John Paul II," in *Law and Christianity in Poland: The Work of Great Jurists*, ed. Franciszek Longchamps de Bérier and Rafael Domingo (London: Routledge, 2022), 247–62.
50   William Sweet, "Jacques Maritain," in *Great Christian Jurists in French History*, ed. Olivier Descamps and Rafael Domingo (Cambridge: Cambridge University Press, 2019), 387–403.

person always prevails over the what and the how. To the extent that critical legal actors are Christians, the law and legal systems that they shape are, of necessity, imbued and permeated with their Christian values and beliefs. The reason is that legal systems are simultaneously a whole in themselves and thus, to a degree, self-sufficient, but also a part of and thus interdependent with other parts of society. Christian jurists participate not only in legal institutions and the church but also in many other institutions in their societies, thus carrying their faith into those other systems.

John Witte has used this biographical approach to the study of law and Christianity throughout his many monographs on the history of family law, religious freedom, and human rights. He has returned again and again to retrieve and reconstruct the work of many of the "legal titans" of the Christian tradition, as he calls them—especially Lactantius, Augustine, and Chrysostom among the Church Fathers; Gratian, Lombard, Hostiensis, Raymond of Peñyafort, and Aquinas in the Middle Ages; Luther, Melanchthon, Calvin, Beza, Althusius, Cranmer, Hooker, and Vitoria in the Reformation era; Grotius, Coke, Selden, Blackstone, Adams, Madison, Jefferson, and Story among the early moderns; and Kuyper, Dooyeweerd, Maritain, Brunner, King, Niebuhr, and their modern progeny. One of Witte's strengths has been to read these historical figures in and on their own terms and in their own contexts, but then to extract enduring lessons from their writings for the ongoing legal challenges of the tradition and of our day.

In 2005, Witte began to extend this biographical approach with an eventual eye to creating a multivolume and multiauthored series on Great Christian Jurists in World History. He began with the publication of *The Teachings of Modern Christianity on Law, Politics, and Human Nature*, in which—again in collaboration with Frank Alexander—he brought together a series of outstanding essays on central modern Roman Catholic, Protestant, and Orthodox Christian figures in the world of the relationship between Christianity and law.[51] But it was really in 2015, with the appearance of the Cambridge Studies in Law and Christianity Series, that Witte expanded this project, commissioning volumes from legal historians around the world, which he has published in this Cambridge series (on the first millennium, England, Spain, France, the Netherlands, and the United States), in Norman Doe's Law and Religion Series with Routledge (on Italy, the Nordic countries, Russia, Latin America, and Poland), and with Mohr Siebeck (on Germany) and Federation Press (on Australia).[52] In

---

51   John Witte, Jr. and Frank S. Alexander, eds., *Modern Christian Teachings on Law, Politics, and Human Nature*, 2 vols. (New York: Columbia University Press, 2005).
52   See list in *Faith, Freedom, and Family*, 62–64.

this biographical project, Witte has written specific chapters on jurists (Johann Oldendorp, John Calvin, Johannnes Althusius, John Selden, Abraham Kuyper, and Harold Berman),[53] coedited the book on German jurists in collaboration with Mathias Schmoeckel,[54] but above all set up teams, collected financial support, coordinated with publishing houses, and written forewords (for the Polish, Russian, Latin American, and Italian volumes).

Such an extensive project, in which the methodology has been steadily polished with experience and experimentation, and which involves so many different people, has inevitably produced mixed results. In each volume, one can criticize whether a particular jurist deserves the status of Christian in the strict sense, even whether the person chosen deserves the status of jurist. There are also notable absences; for example, Thomas More should have been included among the English jurists. Overall, however, and with ever greater success, most legal historians have risen and responded to this idea of reappraising the biographical perspective to legal history and appreciating the expansive category of a "Christian jurist."

The fact that the project is divided into geographical areas and nations, rather than chronologically, apart from the volume on the first millennium, is also open to criticism. But Witte has mapped the path as he has gone along. Instead of outlining in advance a perfect methodology, which does not exist, and then applying it, what he has done is to explore the issues, analyze them, and gradually polish the methodology over time. Law, like cooking, entails a lot of artistry, and this can only be learned by practicing. The highly visible result is manifest and has served to let outsiders know what is happening with law and Christianity in each country studied. The strong language barriers and the local nature of law are two further real obstacles that only a global project like this one is capable of overcoming. While the project has prompted strong criticism from conventional legal historians, this is outweighed by the amount of support the project enjoys and the promise that it holds as it opens ever wider frontiers of law and Christianity.[55]

---

53 See reprinted collection in *Faith, Freedom, and Family*, 119–228.

54 Mathias Schmoeckel and John Witte, Jr., eds., *Great Christian Jurists in German History* (Tubingen: Mohr Siebeck, 2020).

55 See, for example, Christoph J. H. Meyer, "Was von christlichem Recht und Juristenleben übrigblieb." Book review of Orazio Condoerlli and Rafael Domingo, eds., *Law and the Christian Tradition in Italy* (2020), in *Rechtsgeschichte—Legal History. Zeitschrift des Max-Planck-Instituts für Rechtsgeschichte und Rechtstheorie* 29 (2021): 302–06. For a very positive approach, however, see Kyle C. Lincoln: Review of Rafael Domingo and Javier Martínez-Torrón, eds., *Great Christian Jurists in Spanish History* (2018), in *Bulletin of Medieval Canon Law* 38 (2021): 452–57.

5   The Jurisprudential Perspective: Toward a Christian Jurisprudence

The third perspective from which Witte addresses the relationship between Christianity and law endeavors to build a general jurisprudential framework, based on Christian values, for a pluralistic society. Following in the footsteps of his mentor, Harold Berman, who at the end of his academic career devised an "integrative jurisprudence," Witte is seeking theoretically to integrate and harmonize the Christianity-law relationship by creating a narrative suitable for a pluralistic, post-Christian society.[56] No modern jurist has trodden this path yet, but, if I may say so, Witte's subconscious has already prompted him to work on it. One only has to read the reflective conclusions of his latest historical books—reflections that are ever more extensive, ever more theoretical, and transcending the main historical topic of the book.[57] One glimpses a change of focus in Witte's intellectual project—from "retrieval" of the relationships of Christianity and law and the teachings of great Christian jurists to "reconstruction" of a Christian jurisprudence for our modern day.

Witte is a man of synthesis, an intellectual cartographer, adept at generating new understandable paradigms. He knows how to create narratives and convincingly explain religious and, in particular, Christian phenomena to anyone familiar with the world of the transcendent. He demonstrated this with his studies on Protestantism and law, as well as with his histories of marriage, family, and children, and of religion, human rights, and religious freedom.[58] He is now on a relentless quest for a new paradigm between faith and law, between Gospel and culture in the context of a pluralistic and highly secularized society. After reflecting and heading such a large group of people for so many years, Witte now intends to offer the world a more personal and all-encompassing theoretical reflection on the relationship between law and Christianity. He does not aspire to be a theologian or a philosopher, which he is not, but a legal theorist of the relationship between Christianity and law in its broadest sense within the framework of the relationship between religions and law.

Witte judges that the necessary protection of nonbelievers and secular thought is not a sufficient reason to erect a Berlin Wall between law and religion, particularly between Christianity and law, as if their relation were a taboo subject. Any exclusion of religion from the public sphere will always be

---

56   John Witte, Jr., "Law and Religion: The Challenges of Christian Jurisprudence," *St. Thomas Law Journal* 2 (2005): 439–52; and idem, "The Integrative Christian Jurisprudence of Harold Berman," in *Faith, Freedom, and Family*, 215–28.
57   See, for example, *The Blessings of Liberty*, 290–303.
58   See chapters by Helen Alvaré, Nicholas Wolterstorff, and Jonathan Chaplin herein.

artificial, because law has an unavoidable religious dimension. In the West, this religious dimension is mainly Judeo-Christian. It is not surprising that, in his acceptance speech upon receiving an honorary doctorate in theology from the University of Heidelberg, Witte used the metaphor of the cathedral to refer to law: "The law is like a massive medieval cathedral, always under construction, always in need of new construction. It stands at the center of the city, at the center of matters spiritual and temporal, at the center of everyone's life."[59] If, up to now, Witte has been occupied, as a historian of law, with telling us the story of how this cathedral was built, it now seems that he himself wants to participate in its design and construction, putting his best talents at its service.

As Witte is so fond of triads,[60] some of which I have already mentioned, I will venture to turn to them in this initial phase of this new, more theoretical perspective in order to encourage Witte to continue along this path. In addition to the triads he has already generated, I offer four more that I think capture Witte's thinking, and which I gladly submit for consideration and critique.

6   Christianity, Community, Culture

Christianity provides a unique metadimensional Trinitarian paradigm for the law, one that illuminates all the legal aspects from within and without. If the revelation of God as Father, Son, and Holy Spirit (Matthew 28:19) is the central mystery of Christian faith and the center of the whole of reality, this mystery must enlighten all human existence and dimensions, including the legal realm.

The doctrine of the Trinity understands God relationally. The Triune God is certainly a unique and absolute unity, the Absolute One, whose three divine persons manifest the pure communication of love, the most profound depths of free self-giving. Each divine person freely gives the plenitude of love to the others, glorifying them.[61] This revealed truth serves to illuminate a united and diverse political community; the greater the diversity, the greater the unity, and the greater the unity, the greater the diversity. This sense of communal inclusion, which does not exclude other communities but rather affirms that all are part of a global community, calls for a cultural change. Our Western

---

59   Witte, lecture on receipt of honorary doctorate; and idem, "Afterword: The Cathedral of the Law," in idem, *God's Joust, God's Justice*, 466–67.
60   On Witte's triads, see Gary S. Hauk, foreword to *Faith, Freedom, and Family*, xix.
61   See John Witte, Jr., "Law, Religion, and Metaphor," in idem, *Faith, Freedom, and Family*, 37–55, esp. 53–55.

secularized culture has often promoted fragmentation, territorialization, and exclusionary nationalism.

7 Creation, Covenant, Conscience

Creation occupies a central place in Witte's thought. It is a manifestation of God's infinite love, which permeates the entire universe, and most particularly the human being, made specifically in God's image and likeness (Genesis 1:27). Creation establishes a covenant between God and humankind over the created order. A covenant institutes a more solid and permanent framework than a contract, because the covenant includes the natural order of creation and assumes a conceptual framework of truths that cannot be altered by mere human consent. God does not enter into contracts, but God does enter into covenants. Moreover, every human contract that respects the natural order and puts God as a witness becomes a covenant (for example, marriage). Conscience is a divine light within human beings that helps them to interpret God's will in every covenant.[62] This creation-covenant-conscience triad clashes with a world vision based on mere chance without creation, where human liberty is reduced to simple freedom of choice without respecting the natural order, and the conscience is mistaken for personal conviction without a recognition of prior truths.

8 Law, Liberty, Love

Christianity has elevated law, liberty, and love to a new divine order. Law cannot be reduced to pure legalism because justice reaches all dimensions of reality and participates in the same created order (*ius divinum*). Liberty is a gift of God to fulfill our obligations to God, to ourselves, to others, and to the universe as such. Liberty is the necessary, though not sufficient, condition for fully loving God and, in God, all creatures and the created universe. Law's mission is to protect this liberty as one of the most precious divine gifts,[63] as it is to protect and impart justice: without justice there is no love, and love perfects justice by imbuing it with charity. This triad of love, liberty, and law is in direct

---

62   John Witte, Jr., "Covenant Liberty in Puritan New England," in *Jurisprudenz, Politische Theorie und Politische Theologie*, ed. Frederick S. Carney, Heinz Schilling, and Dieter Wyduckel (Berlin: Duncker & Humblot, 2004), 169–89.

63   *The Blessings of Liberty*, 290–303.

opposition to the triad that reduces law to legalism, freedom to arbitrariness, and love to personal satisfaction.

9 Sovereignty, Society, Solidarity

Witte employs a broad concept of sovereignty, inherited from Kuyper, which can be applied to God, to the nation-state, to the smaller political community, and to all institutions (family, church, school, business) and power structures that order society according to the principles of liberty and justice. Witte conceives society as a network of relationships and institutions united by the bonds of cooperation and solidarity, a solidarity born of the sharing of all human beings in the one and only image of a Triune God. This law of human solidarity, without excluding the rich variety of persons, cultures, and peoples, assures us that all men and women are truly brothers and sisters.

10 Evaluation and Impact

As I have indicated, Witte's work on Christianity and law is a reflection of his own life—a deeply Christian man, educated in the Protestant Reformed tradition, in love with history and law, and committed to the challenges of his time. Following the example of his mentor, Harold Berman, Witte has placed his faith at the service of the ideals of justice and law. Witte can be defined as a Christian jurist who has devoted himself primarily to the study of the relationship between law and religion from a historical perspective. He has done so primarily in the area of the influence of Protestantism, especially in the early stages of its first reformers—and, by extension, in the areas of human rights, religious freedom, and marriage and the family, which he has traced from classical and biblical sources to the latest legal developments.

Over time, Witte has spearheaded a bold and far-reaching project that aims to encompass the relationship between law and Christianity as such, in which more than five hundred scholars from five continents are collaborating, making him one of the leading scholars in the field. He is working on this contribution from three perspectives: a purely relational one, a biographical one, and a jurisprudential one. Despite having already borne much fruit, the project still requires greater methodological clarity and maturity. Witte is an instinctual and experimental thinker; he maps the scholarly and methodological path as he goes along, letting his sources and intuitions guide and inspire him. What he still needs to produce is an extensive programmatic series of publications that create a paradigm for the study of the relationship between Christianity and law in modern pluralistic societies. His article entitled "What Christianity Offers to the World of Law" is only a first draft of that bigger effort.[64] Witte knows this and is working on it. The theoretical and jurisprudential part is fundamental to consolidate and complete his life-long project. This theoretical part could be based on the four alliterative triads that I now suggest, inspired by Witte's works: a) Christianity, community, culture; b) creation, covenant, conscience; c) law, liberty, love; and d) sovereignty, society, solidarity.

---

64   *Faith, Freedom, and Family*, 57–66.

CHAPTER 3

John Witte, Jr. and the Study of Legal History

R. H. Helmholz

John Witte, Jr. came to Emory University in 1985 directly after his graduation from Harvard Law School. That change of venue has mattered to him, and also to us in assessing Witte's own contributions to the field of legal history. He had made the move together with Harold J. Berman, whose famous work *Law and Revolution* (1983) had made a case for recognizing the medieval canon law as the first truly developed European legal system. Witte had done research for that book, helping its author put its argument together. It was a good start and a happy one. The work dealt with legal history, and it had an impact on the scholarly consensus of the course of Western legal history. Witte, along with many others, has continued to make appreciative use of its contents.[1] In the years that have followed, however, he has also gone beyond what he learned in completing that assignment—far beyond.[2] Quite apart from his organizational skills and the many scholarly conferences on subjects involving legal history which he has organized, his own record of scholarship and publication on this subject has been noteworthy. There is a great deal of it. Some of it is corrective, some of it looks both forward and backward, and all of it is of interest. Every piece of it is the product of patient research clearly and engagingly presented. This chapter takes up four of what its compiler believes are Witte's most significant contributions to the field of legal history.

It should be said first, however, that the honoree of this volume did not forget his obligations to Berman. In 2013, six years after Berman's death, Witte published a book that Berman had begun but not finished. It was *Law and Language: Effective Symbols of Community*. In 2002, Witte had described him as his

---

1 See, for example, his introduction in John Witte, Jr. and Frank Alexander eds., *Christianity and Law: An Introduction* (Cambridge: Cambridge University Press, 2008), 5, where Witte described it as a one of the four "massive transformations of the Western Legal Tradition." See also his "The Integrative Christian Jurisprudence of Harold J. Berman," in *Great Christian Jurists in American History*, ed. Daniel Dreisbach and Mark Hall (Cambridge: Cambridge University Press, 2019), 230–44.
2 The best account of this aspect of Witte's career known to me is Norman Doe's foreword to John Witte, Jr., *Faith, Freedom, and Family: New Essays on Law and Religion*, ed. Norman Doe and Gary S. Hauk (Tübingen: Mohr Siebeck, 2021), XVII–XXI.

"mentor, friend, and colleague,"[3] and finishing a work that touched upon law's history, a project Berman had not been able to complete, was a recognition of the debts he owed to his mentor. By then, however, he was more than a pupil. He had also gone beyond the projects Berman had initiated. In particular, he had taken a step to help fill a gap to which Berman had once remarked wistfully: there had been "a time not long ago when a good lawyer was required to know the story of the development of European legal institutions."[4] Helping to keep that knowledge alive, and in fact to advance it, has been one of Witte's achievements.

1 Human Nature in Legal History

The first advance has been in treating the Protestant reformers as human beings—able and strong men, to be sure, but also subject to human frailties. Most men and women are capable of growth—or at least change—over the course of their lifetimes. These changes extend even to important matters, and they are not necessarily equivalent to backsliding. It may seem strange to discover that Witte's recognition of this obvious feature of human life is an important contribution to legal history, but it is. It provides a corrective to what has become an all too common habit among historians—identifying a participant in the religious development of the sixteenth century with a single characteristic. Martin Luther is probably the best example of the more balanced view that has marked Witte's treatment of the most prominent among the reformers. It has been too easy for historians to focus on two significant events in Luther's life. First, he publicly burned the papal lawbooks, that is the *Corpus iuris canonici*, which contained the law of the church, and he never repented having done so. Indeed, he seems to have been proud of it. Second, he is known for endorsing the Latin phrase that equated good lawyers with bad

---

3   John Witte, Jr., *Law and Protestantism: The Legal Teachings of the Lutheran Reformation*. (Cambridge: Cambridge University Press, 2002), XVII. See also Harold Berman, *Law and Revolution, II: The Impact of the Protestant Reformations on the Western Legal Tradition* (Cambridge, MA: Harvard University Press, 2003), 187–89.

4   Harold J. Berman, *Law and Revolution: The Formation of the Western Legal Tradition: The Formation of the Western Legal Tradition* (Cambridge, MA: Harvard University Press, 1983), 7. See also Russell Sandberg, "The Time for Legal History: Some Reflections on Maitland and Milsom Fifty Years On," *Law & Justice* 180 (2018): 21–37.

Christians. *Bonus Jurista Malus Christa*.[5] It has been a natural step, therefore, to portray him as an enemy of the traditional law of the church.

In one sense, this is correct. Luther did remain a critic of several parts of the church's law throughout his life. However, he also came to recognize the worth of many of the rules that were stated in the canon law. Witte's discussion of the reasons for his change of mind on the subject is exemplary. One explanation for it was that he found himself besieged by queries from his supporters. They came from many sides, asking him for clear answers to their own difficult problems. As Witte put it, Luther was "not at all comfortable with his role as de facto Protestant pope."[6] He did not want that to take place. So he took stock. The world as it is has always required legal rules, and Luther came to recognize the worth of many of the rules found in the substantive canon law. Much of the medieval church's law, including papal decretals, actually provided "a valid and valuable source of Christian equity and justice."[7] It is true that Luther always remained a vocal critic of exercise of the papal power of dispensation, particularly where it was exercised to permit what would otherwise have been an unlawful or immoral act. However, he also came to recognize the worth of much of what was found in traditional canon law. He grew into this position—learning from experience one might say—and in this he was acting in in a way most of us do. A strength of John Witte's treatment of Luther is attributable to his demonstration of the reformer's ability to moderate his views as he grew older. Witte put it pithily in the title to one of his chapters: "Perhaps jurists are good Christians after all."[8]

His treatment of the other great reformer, John Calvin, is different in its coverage from that devoted to Luther, but it is equal in its recognition of the complexity of human nature and consequent actions. It is contained in a volume published in 2007 devoted to the subject of the history of religious liberty and human rights in Calvinist thought, and it begins appropriately with Calvin himself. About this reformer's role in its recognition and implementation, past authors have disagreed sharply. Some have praised him as a champion of religious liberty. He was "pioneer of the freedom of conscience

---

5 See, for example, *Law and Protestantism*, 119; Courtney Kenny, "Bonus Jurista Malus Christa," *Law Quarterly Review* 19 (1903): 328–34.
6 *Law and Protestantism*, 69.
7 Ibid., 83.
8 Ibid., 119. The innovative character of Witte's contribution to this subject is recognized in Heikki Pihlajamäki and Risto Saarinen, "Lutheran Reformation and the Law in Recent Scholarship," in *Lutheran Reformation and the Law*, ed. Virpi Mäkinen (Leiden: Brill, 2006), 2–3.

and human rights."⁹ Others have done the reverse. In their view, Calvin was "as undemocratic and authoritarian as possible."¹⁰ His treatment of Michael Servetus—burned for heresy with Calvin's approval in Geneva—has long been a particular black mark on this great reformer's reputation.

Witte admitted the existence of contradictions in Calvin's thought, but he showed that when fully understood, they were much less stark than critics have allowed. He noted first that Calvin lived in an age of "bombast and hyperbole that typified sixteenth-century humanist literature."¹¹ Strong statements and strong actions were the order of the day. Roughly speaking, Calvin's record, including his condemnation of Servetus, should also be viewed in a comparative light. It should also be divided into two halves, an early and a late period. In the first, writing as a theologian rather than as a jurist, he focused his attention on spiritual liberty of the individual and also on political liberty. In the second, from the late 1540s till his death in 1564, his thinking on the subject matured. He learned from experience. The two periods should therefore be considered in that light. In the second, Calvin had assumed the direction of Geneva's church and much of its government. This left less room for the recognition of individual liberty in his writing, required as he then was to face "the hard realities of Genevan ecclesiastical and political life."¹² Who does not recognize the humanity inherent in this situation? Our minds change, sometimes slightly, sometimes greatly, over the course of our lives. So did Calvin's. Our beliefs are also colored by the duties we assume. So were Calvin's. Throughout, however, his penchant was always "for orderliness and moderation."¹³ It was the stable feature that linked the two periods in Calvin's life.

2 Surprises in Legal History

A second strength of Witte's historical work, related to but not identical with the first, is the attention he has always paid to the works of little-known lawyers among early Protestants. This has sometimes revealed surprising results, and

---

9   John Witte, Jr., *The Reformation of Rights: Law, Religion, and Human Rights in Early Modern Calvinism* (Cambridge: Cambridge University Press, 2007), 39, here referring specifically to the views of Emile Doumergue and Walter Köhler, but also giving additional examples.
10 Ibid., 40; referring specifically to the views of Ernst Troeltsch, but also giving other examples.
11 Ibid., 41.
12 Ibid.
13 Ibid., 52.

it has always enlarged our understanding of what we learn from discussions of the thought of Luther and Calvin. Theologians and historians of religion, often those from Germany, have made occasional use of the works of some of these men, particularly with theologians like Philip Melanchthon (1497–1560), but it has not been common for legal historians to do so, and Witte's patient examination of his contribution to the field of law and history has yielded significant results.[14] Witte has also dealt with examples of the role in shaping the law which emerged from the Reformation played by many jurists, such as Johann Oldendorp (ca. 1480–1567), Melchior Kling (1504–71), and Johannes Schneidewin (1519–69). Their work has been forgotten by most historians of the period, but it is given its due in Witte's hands.

He went even further in his research of the subject, investigating the careers and work of some now quite obscure figures. Among them were *reformateurs* like Wenceslaus Linck of Nürnberg and Wolfgang Capito of Strassbourg. These men effectively curtailed the hold the medieval church's law had exercised on significant subjects, as by helping to end clerical immunity from civil responsibility in courts of law or by asserting a freedom from payment of taxation. A further example of Witte's treatment of a largely unknown figure is that of Johann Eberlin von Günzburg. He spoke out strongly against the place of papal dispensations in the received canon law, together with its excessive use of excommunication.[15] And that led to concrete results. Further examples are those of Argula von Grumbach and Johann Apel, who reacted strongly against the requirement of celibacy among the clergy, treating it as though its principal effect was to encourage them to take concubines. The careers and writings of reform-minded critics like these have demonstrated something of the scope of the attacks on the received canon law during the early years of the Reformation, and Witte was right to call their influence to the attention of legal historians. Many lawyers, acting alone or together with men in holy orders, were involved in this movement, and it has been Witte's accomplishment to bring their accomplishments into Reformation history.

Witte has also been patient in exploring the other side—the men and the factors that worked toward the retention of the canon law, despite its connection with the papacy. The medieval canon law was more difficult to dislodge

---

14 For these references, see *Law and Protestantism*, 60–63; see also John Witte, Jr., "The Good Lutheran Jurist Johann Oldendorp (ca. 1486–1567)," in *Great Christian Jurists in German History*, ed. Mathias Schmoeckel and John Witte, Jr. (Tübingen: Mohr Siebeck, 2020), 80–98.

15 See, for example, Susan Groag Bell, "Johan Eberlin von Günzburg's 'Wolfaria': the First Protestant Utopia," in *Church History* 36 (1967): 122–39.

from practice in Protestant lands than has traditionally been supposed. The scope and the reasons for its retention were the theme of Witte's contribution to a volume on the fate of canon law in Protestant lands.[16] His chapter in it opened with a quotation from the famous Hugo Grotius stating that the canon laws had "acquired the force of law" in the Netherlands despite their apparent origin from the papacy. As it had turned out, this was also true elsewhere. Some of what was found in the medieval canon law was abandoned or altered, but most of it nevertheless continued to be treated as a valid source of law in most Protestant lands.

How can this have been? It seems contrary to common sense to link Protestant lawyers with Catholic canon law. The continued connection between them has been, however, a result of scholarship of the past fifty years, and in making that connection John Witte has pulled an oar. Closer examination of legal records, including those from Scotland, Germany, England, and Scandinavia, has shown that by the sixteenth century, canon law had worked its way into the law accepted throughout Europe, and it proved virtually impossible to dislodge.[17] Together with Roman law, it provided rules that had long governed many aspects of legal practice—the *ius commune*—and a large part of them remained in force *faute de mieux*. The world of polemics and the world of law are not identical.

This surprising result calls attention to an error in jurisprudence. Retention of the canon law in Protestant court practice is better understood by recognizing that it is a mistake to think of sixteenth-century jurisprudence in terms of legal positivism. Positivism holds that the test of a law's validity depends upon its recognition in the commands of the lawmaker. That was not the view taken by the classical jurists, however, and we must make room for their assumptions, not ours. Custom was then a valid source of law, for example, and in

---

16 John Witte, Jr., "The Plight of Canon Law in the early Dutch Republic," in *Canon Law in Protestant Lands*, ed. Richard Helmholz (Berlin: Duncker & Humblot, 1992), 135–64; see also Witte, "Canon Law in Lutheran Germany: A Surprising Case of Legal Transplantation," in *Lex et Romanitas: Essays for Alan Watson*, ed. Michael Hoeflich (Berkeley, CA: Robbins Collection, 2000), 181–24.

17 See the review of the subject by Hector MacQueen, in a book review published in *Savigny-Stiftung Zeitschrift für Rechtsgeschichte, Kan. Abt.* 80 (1994): 582–85. See also Mia Korpiola, "Lutheran Marriage Norms in Action: The Example of Post-Reformation Sweden, 1520–1600," in Mäkinen, *Lutheran Reformation and the Law*, 131–69.

sixteenth-century Europe, the canon law had become something like a custom. Its contents could be accepted and applied for that reason.[18]

We must recognize also that most of the substantive canon law had little to do with the papacy. The law of tithes, wills and trusts, defamation, marriage and divorce, charity, elections, court procedure, and evidence stood on their own. Their contents could be used even if they had been stated in a papal decretal found in the *Corpus iuris canonici*. Some of them, it is true, were thought to require amendment. The reach of the prohibited degrees in matrimonial law provides an example. However, that could be accomplished without rejecting the basic law on other parts of the canon law, and in fact here change was also achieved in Catholic lands by the decrees adopted at the Council of Trent. It amounted to amendment, not rejection of the received law. So it could happen, although it seems ironic, that many Protestant lands followed the medieval law on the subject more closely than was true in Catholic areas of Europe, where the decree *Tametsi* amended the medieval canon law by adding a requirement that to be valid, a marriage had to have been contracted in the presence of the parish priest. Witte has not been alone in tracing both the retention and the development of the medieval canon law on subjects like the continued use of the canon law in Protestant lands, but he has made significant contributions to it. His work has played a part in a real advance.

3   Natural Rights in Legal History

A third historical subject to which Witte has made significant contributions has become a topical and controversial one—the history and current status of legal rights. He has published at least four books related to this subject, and he has organized groups to meet in order to uncover the religious and historical elements of this subject. A result of his initiative has been the production of a collection of seventeen separate essays devoted to natural rights—one called *Christianity and Human Rights: An Introduction*. Witte's introduction to that volume contains a valuable summary of its contents together with a strong statement of his own belief in the importance of religiously motivated contributions to this subject. However, it is not one-sided in its assessment. His

---

18   The contemporary reasoning that lay behind the real but limited acceptance of the canon law is well explained in an Irish report: *Le Case de Commenda* (CP 1611), Davies 68, 80 Eng. Rep. 552.

introduction to that volume begins with a Dickensian flare. The opening words of *Tale of Two Cities*: "It was the best of times. It was the worst of times"—and so, Witte believes, has been the long history of human rights rooted in the law of nature. For every "springtime of hope" in their recognition, there has also been a "winter of despair" when one regards modern developments, but that is not unique to our times. There have always been ups and downs in the historical record of human rights. There have also been false steps. What Witte's initiative has added to that record is a recognition of the importance, indeed the necessity, of considering the religious dimension to the subject's history. Human rights did not begin with the Enlightenment.[19] It is appropriate that his work is recognized in the most recent assessments of this subject.[20]

The place of religion in the creation of human rights has been one of the consistent themes of his scholarship. Both the chapters of the 2010 volume and Witte's introduction begin with the Christian Bible. It is good to be reminded of its contents. The Ten Commandments, for example, have provided "an organizing framework for the understanding of fundamental religious and civil rights" (p. 17). The New Testament also contains statements of a "radical Christian message of human equality." If the realities of life in the first centuries of the Christian era did not always match these calls, as for instance in securing what we now recognize as women's rights, that does not render religion irrelevant in their recognition today. In this, Witte is no Pollyanna. Often recognition of religion's importance has been limited to the importance of the correct religion, and thus becomes a means of denying human rights to those whose religious views differ from those of the majority. Still, it is worthy of note that the sixteenth-century reformers "all began their movements with a call for freedom from the medieval Catholic Church" (p. 26). Today their successors would be required to acknowledge that even the Catholic Church has endorsed the concept of religious freedom, acknowledging its importance in the decrees of the Second Vatican Council (1962–63).[21]

In one particular, Witte's familiarity with and interest in the history of all forms of Christianity has been of particular use in advancing our understanding

---

19 Ibid., 40: "The Enlightenment inherited many more rights and liberties than it invented, and many of these were of Christian origin."

20 For appreciation of Witte's contributions, see, for example, Rachel Johnston-White, "A Moral Language of our Time? Human Rights and Christianity in Historical Perspective," *Contemporary European History* 31 (2022): 155–66, at 157; and the index in Norman Doe, ed., *Christianity and Natural Law: An Introduction* (Cambridge: Cambridge University Press, 2017), 261.

21 See, for example, *Dignitatis humanae* (1965), in *Decrees of the Ecumenical Councils, Volume II*, ed. Norman Tanner (London: Sheed & Ward, 1990), 1001 et seq.

of Western law's past. That is in the role played by the law of nature. A generation ago, natural law was widely perceived as an exclusive preserve of Roman Catholic doctrine. Its utility for Catholics was drawn most often from the writing of Thomas Aquinas, whose great treatise contains a statement that a human law that is contrary to the law of nature could not be a true law,[22] and the application of natural law in the Catholic effort to hold back the flood tide of contraception played a part in cementing the impression that natural law was "a Catholic preserve."

Whether or not that was a fair assessment of today's situation, it is far from an accurate description of the history of the subject. It served many purposes. It was expressly invoked in great matters: for example, to justify the Dutch rejection of the rule of Philip II, king of Spain.[23] However, its relevance was not reserved for such great events. At Witte's initiative, a conference and subsequent volume exploring the place of the law of nature within other legal traditions was held.[24] A scholarly success, it surveyed the positive place which that source of law had played in many forms of Christianity. The Lutheran, Anglican, Orthodox, and Reformed traditions embraced it in earlier centuries. Even the leaders of Baptist churches had sometimes appealed to it as a source of guidance and justification.[25] What this contribution to the historical record proved was that before the middle of the nineteenth century, natural law was accepted as a matter of course by virtually all European lawyers, including some of the most able and best-known Protestants. In other contributions to the subject, Witte had shown that Hugo Grotius was only one among the many Protestant jurists who accepted and made ordinary use of the law of nature.[26] We do not know, of course, what the future of that subject will be in our own day. Some predict its revival in the service of the common good.[27] If such a revival actually occurs, it will find support in the historical work of this volume's honoree.

---

22 *Summa Theologiae*: 1a2ae. 95, 2, Blackfriars ed. (London: Blackfriars Press, 1966), 104–05: "Si vero aliquo a lege naturali discordet, jam non erit lex, sed legis corruptio."
23 John Witte, Jr., "Natural Rights, Popular Sovereignty, and Covenant Politics: Johannes Althusius and the Dutch Revolt and Republic," *University of Detroit Mercy Law Review* 87 (2010): 565–627, at 565.
24 See Doe, *Christianity and Natural Law*, XII–XIV.
25 See Paul Goodliff, "Natural Law in the Baptist Tradition," in Doe, *Christianity and Natural Law*, 140–61; at 160, the author concludes that the historical appeals to liberty of conscience have drawn upon both biblical and natural law sources.
26 See, for example, *Law and Protestantism*, 140–75, carefully exploring its place in the works of Johannes Eisermann and Johann Oldendorp in order to cement the point.
27 For example, Adrian Vermeule, *Common Good Constitutionalism: Recovering the Classical Legal Tradition* (Cambridge: Polity Press, 2022).

4 The Future in Legal History

Some of Witte's best work has concerned the history of the law of marriage and the family. The book which he and Robert Kingdon published on matrimonial law and its enforcement in Calvin's Geneva is easily the leading work on that subject.[28] It is thorough, interesting, and full of insights. The collection of his essays contained in the recent *Faith, Freedom, and Family*, a work edited by Norman Doe and Gary S. Hauk, contains a collection of thirteen of his articles on the subject. They cover a wide range. Some of them have been mentioned above, but one of them has not. It concerns the future of a subject that has roots in the past: the subject of plural marriage—in other words polygamy.

Polygamy has not been high on the agenda of many modern reformers in this field.[29] However, so much has changed in society's attitude towards sexuality and marriage during the past sixty years that it is far from impossible that this subject will arise. Indeed, it seems likely. Who in the mid-twentieth century could have supposed that sodomy would come to be recognized as a constitutionally protected human right? But it has happened. Of course, polygamy is not sodomy, but like sodomy, it can be a matter of choice for men and women. With some reason, many object that if polygamy becomes lawful, women will be the losers in the end, but it is possible to answer that dealing with that problem is simply a matter of fixing upon a sensible public policy to curb abuses. The possibility also leads to the adoption of an approach like that taken by Judge Richard Posner.[30] He treats the prohibition of polygamy as a taboo, concluding that many women might sensibly prefer a plural marriage with a rich man over an exclusive marriage with a poor man. He then asks: why should women not have the ability to make that choice? He appears to think they should.

An answer to Posner's question is the subject of one of Witte's most impressive books: *The Western Case for Monogamy over Polygamy*. It is notable for eschewing Posner's theoretical approach, tracing instead the actual history of polygamy from its early acceptance to its gradual abandonment in Judaism, its later history in Europe, and then its similar history in the United States among adherents of the Church of Jesus Christ of Latter-day Saints. Instead of speculation about possibilities, Witte relies on the history of the subject for what it tells us about the subject. The past contains lessons, ones we should heed.

---

28 *Sex, Marriage, and Family in John Calvin's Geneva*, vol. 1 (Grand Rapids; Eerdmans, 2005).
29 See, for example, Russell Sandberg, *Religion and Marriage Law: The Need for Reform* (Bristol: Bristol University Press, 2021).
30 Richard Posner, *Sex and Reason* (Cambridge, MA: Harvard University Press 1992), 253–60.

We learn that polygamy was tolerated in the Hebrew Bible. Its acceptance was attributed, at least in part, to necessity. The Bible started with God's direction that the earth be filled with men and women (Genesis 1:28), or as in the story of Abraham, Sarah, and Hagar (Genesis 16:2). Polygamy served that purpose. But gradually the earth was filled, the practice was first restricted and then forbidden, both by the commands of Roman emperors and those of Jewish leaders themselves, the most influential of whom was Rabbi Gershom ben Judah (960–ca. 1040). What may have been a necessity, or at least a possibility, in primitive times had become a vice with the passage of time and changes in society. The medieval canon law forbade it, as did secular law in Western lands during the Middle Ages and beyond.

For Witte, this history matters. The pattern has been repeated more than once. Some early Protestants had also experimented with permitting polygamy. Even Luther had once recognized it as an alternative in the absence of any possibility of divorce.[31] Henry VIII seems also to have considered it as a possibility. However, after the death of the "first generation of heady Protestant reform," the Continental movement's leaders reversed course. They "came down hard on polygamy." The leaders and the law of the Church of England did the same. By act of Parliament in 1604 polygamy became a felony.[32] A chapter in Witte's book—"The English Case against Polygamy"—gives the significant details, although it also exhibits an admirable completeness, shown by his coverage of counter examples like the later arguments in favor of plural marriage advanced by John Milton.[33]

Other examples of the normal pattern—initial inclination toward acceptance of polygamy followed later by its rejection—are found in the works of Enlightenment thinkers and, of course, the history of the Mormons in the American West during the nineteenth century. Witte's book pays ample attention to them. In each case, early willingness to admit the possibility of plural marriage gave way in time to its prohibition. The obvious exception is Islamic law. The influx of immigrants from Muslim lands makes its influence a possibility, although it is represented in Witte's book by a picture of three Muslim women holding up a sign that reads "Say No to Polygamy" (p. 442). Of course,

---

31 Witte, *The Western Case for Monogamy Over Polygamy* (Cambridge: Cambridge University Press, 2015), 212.
32 1 Jac. I, c. 11. See also his "Prosecuting Polygamy in Early Modern England," in *Texts and Contexts in Legal History: Essays in Honor of Charles Donahue*, ed. John Witte, Jr., Sara McDougall, and Anna di Robilant (Berkeley CA: Robbins Collection, 2016), 429–48.
33 *The Western Case for Monogamy Over Polygamy*, 330–35.

the book's subject is the history of Western law, and that is what the book describes. It is part of our history, one from which we can and should learn.

The justification for dealing with monogamy in the context of evaluating Witte's scholarship on legal history is that it demonstrates, almost better than any other facet of his work, the importance that legal history has occupied in his thought and his work. Starting with his partnership with Hal Berman, he has followed a historical trail. And he has widened it. The subject of polygamy demonstrates both the insights legal history provides and the respect Witte has for them. He does not favor its revival. That is clear enough. But he does not find or seek support for his view in a theoretical approach—feminist, economic, or social—as fashionable as they are. He finds what he needs in the historical record. Many times tried but always rejected after a trial: that is what our legal history reveals about polygamy, and that has convinced Witte that it would be a mistake to begin yet another such adventure.[34] History matters.

5 Conclusion

This essay began by recalling Witte's arrival at Emory University in the company of Harold Berman. In the years that followed, many reviews and books have been published in praise of Berman's scholarship,[35] and Witte was an editor of one of them. Berman had sought to integrate the study of law and religion. He demonstrated the need for the return to taking account of one of the vital characteristics of the study of law, one that had been prominent in earlier centuries—its religious roots. Witte has been faithful to that insight, and as this essay has shown, he has also gone beyond it, enriching it in (at least) four distinct ways. His career is an advertisement for the merits of beginning with an able mentor, especially one who will also become a friend.

---

34 See also John Witte, Jr., *From Sacrament to Contract: Marriage, Religion, and Law in the Western Tradition,* 2nd ed. (Louisville, KY: Westminster John Knox Press, 2012), 325–30.
35 See John Witte, Jr. and Frank S. Alexander, eds., *The Weightier Matters of the Law: Essays on Law and Religion: A Tribute to Harold J. Berman* (Atlanta, GA: Scholars Press, 1988); and Howard O. Hunter, ed., *The Integrative Jurisprudence of Harold J. Berman* (Boulder, CO: Westview Press, 1996).

CHAPTER 4

John Witte, Jr.'s Contributions to the Study of Human Rights and Religious Freedom

Nicholas Wolterstorff

1   Introduction

For the past thirty-five years, John Witte has been actively involved in the study of human rights and religious freedom. He has directed several major international projects and conferences on "religious foundations of American constitutionalism," "Christianity and democracy in global context," "religious human rights in global perspective," "the problem and promise of proselytism" and "what's wrong with children's rights?"—deep collaborative explorations of human rights and religious freedom featuring a range of interdisciplinary, interreligious, and international perspectives. He has contributed a number of edited volumes and journal symposia on these topics and related ones.[1]

Witte's more significant and enduring contribution to this topic, however, has come in a series of monographs: *Religion and the American Constitutional Experiment*; *God's Joust, God's Justice*; *The Reformation of Rights*; *Church, State, and Family*; *Faith, Freedom, and Family*; and *The Blessings of Liberty*. Witte also has published several articles that anticipate his sequel volume, *A New Reformation of Rights: Calvinist Contributions to Modern Human Rights*.[2]

---

[1] See, especially, John Witte, Jr., ed., *Christianity and Democracy in Global Context* (Boulder, CO: Westview Press, 1993; repr. ed. London: Routledge, 2019); John Witte, Jr. and Johan D. van der Vyver, eds., *Religious Human Rights in Global Perspective: Legal Perspectives* (Dordrecht: Martinus Nijhoff Publishers, 1996); John Witte, Jr. and Michael Bourdeaux, eds., *Proselytism and Orthodoxy in Russia: The New War for Souls* (Maryknoll, NY: Orbis Books, 1999); John Witte, Jr. and Richard C. Martin, eds., *Sharing the Book: Religious Perspectives on the Rights and Wrongs of Proselytism* (Maryknoll, NY: Orbis Books, 2000); John Witte, Jr. and Frank S. Alexander, eds., *Christianity and Human Rights: An Introduction*. With Frank S. Alexander. *Christianity and Human Rights: An Introduction* (Cambridge: Cambridge University Press, 2010); and John Witte, Jr. and M. Christian Green, eds., *Religion and Human Rights: An Introduction* (New York: Oxford University Press, 2012).

[2] See, especially, John Witte, Jr. and Justin J. Latterell, "Between Martin Luther and Martin Luther King: James Pennington and the Struggle for 'Sacred Human Rights' Against Slavery," *Yale Journal of Law and Humanities* 31 (2020): 205–71.

In this chapter I divide my analysis of John Witte's contribution to the study of human rights and religious freedom into two main parts. In the first part, I analyze the intrinsic significance of Witte's contribution; in the second part, I highlight its polemical significance.

2 The Intrinsic Significance of Witte's Contribution

The nineteenth-century English poet Gerard Manley Hopkins introduced the term "inscape" into the English language.[3] What Hopkins called the inscape of a thing was its particular distinctiveness—the distinctiveness of a particular tree, for example, of a particular melody, of a particular plowed field. He writes of the grief he felt when a tree in his garden was cut down and its inscape destroyed.[4]

Some things are bland; there is little if anything distinctive about them. Not so for Witte's writings on the topic at hand; taken together, they have a very definite inscape. Let me describe some of that inscape, beginning with the genre of his writings on the topic.

3 The Genre of Witte's Contribution

The general topic of human rights and religious freedom can be treated in a number of different ways. One's treatment of the topic might have the character, for example, of advocacy, arguing for the importance of human rights and religious freedom. Though there are eloquent passages of such advocacy in Witte's writings, passages in which he vigorously engages naysayers of various sorts,[5] his writing on the topic does not have the overall character of advocacy.

One could also treat it as a philosophical topic: what are human rights, how are they grounded, what is religious freedom, and what accounts for the right

---

3 The term was Hopkins's translation of a term that he found in the medieval philosopher/theologian Duns Scotus: *haecceitas*, literally, "thisness."

4 Hopkins used the term "inscape" in many of the writings included in John Pick, ed., *A Hopkins Reader* (Oxford: Oxford University Press, 1953). The reference to the inscape of the tree is on page 46 of that volume.

5 See, especially, John Witte, Jr., *Faith, Freedom, and Family: New Essays on Law and Religion*, ed. Norman Doe and Gary S. Hauk (Tübingen: Mohr Siebeck, 2021), 427–56 (challenging human rights skeptics Nigel Biggar and Samuel Moyn); and John Witte, Jr. and Joel A. Nichols, "'Come Now Let Us Reason Together': Restoring Religious Freedom in America and Abroad," *Notre Dame Law Review* 92 (2016): 427–50 (challenging First Amendment critics).

to freedom of religion? That, too, is not how Witte treats the topic; he is not, by profession, a philosopher—though, that said, there are a good many philosophical passages in his writings, these being invariably probing and perceptive.[6]

Again, one could treat the topic as one of intellectual history: what have philosophers and other theorists in the Western intellectual tradition said about the nature and grounding of human rights in general, and about the nature and grounding of the right to religious freedom in particular? That, too, is not how Witte treats the topic; he is not, by profession, an intellectual historian—though, in this case too, there are many passages in his writings in which he presents and engages what theorists across the centuries have written on the topic. He is, de facto, an intellectual historian.

Primarily, though, Witte is a *legal* historian. He treats the topic, human rights and religious freedom, primarily as a topic in legal history. What interests him is the way human rights in general, and the right to religious freedom in particular, have figured in the concrete, often messy reality of constitutions, charters, compacts, laws, judicial decisions, and the like in the West. The subtitle of his recent book, *The Blessings of Liberty,* is "Human Rights and Religious Freedom in the Western Legal Tradition."

In the introduction to *The Blessings of Liberty,* Witte, explaining that he writes as "a legal historian, not a Christian theologian or philosopher," says: "Folks in my legal discipline operate closer to the ground than many high-flying human rights theorists at work today."[7] This makes it sound as if theorists, such as philosophers, deal with the same matter as legal historians, the difference being that whereas philosophers fly high over the terrain, legal historians fly low. That seems to me misleading. Later in the same passage, Witte writes: "We legal historians ... dig out and document how, over many centuries, our legal forebears gradually developed, by fits and starts, an ever wider set of rights categories ... to map and deal with the complex interactions between and among persons, associations, and authorities." Exactly. But philosophers don't describe this same terrain from higher up. They do not join historians in dealing with the "nitty-gritty, concrete complexity of the law on the books and law in action." Only when giving examples to illustrate their theories do they take note of "the law on the books and law in action."[8]

---

6 See, especially, John Witte, Jr., *The Reformation of Rights: Law, Religion, and Human Rights in Early Modern Calvinism* (Cambridge: Cambridge University Press, 2007), 321–45; and John Witte, Jr., *The Blessings of Liberty: Human Rights and Religious Freedom in the Western Legal Tradition* (Cambridge: Cambridge University Press, 2021), 290–303.
7 *The Blessings of Liberty,* 11.
8 Ibid.

4 The Centrality of Religion in Witte's Contribution

Let me move on from these comments about the genre of Witte's contribution to highlight some of the salient features of its content. It is my impression—I have not counted the pages—that over the course of his prodigiously productive career as a legal historian, Witte has written more extensively about human rights in the Western legal tradition than about any other aspect of the tradition. And what strikes one at once, when reviewing his essays and monographs on the topic, is that, almost always, religious freedom figures prominently in the discussion. It would be possible to write about human rights in the Western legal tradition and say little or nothing about religious freedom; some writers have done exactly that. Not so Witte.

Why is this? Is it because he happens to be personally interested in religion? Witte identifies himself in his writings as a Christian. Is it because he is a Christian that he so consistently brings religion into the picture?[9] Is it a matter of personal interest on his part? Is it like someone who has taken, say, a personal interest in freedom of assembly and who then expresses that interest by writing essays and monographs in which freedom of assembly figures prominently in their history of human rights?

No doubt the fact that Witte regularly brings religious freedom into the picture when discussing the history of human rights is a reflection of his personal interests. But we would overlook one of the most salient aspects of the inscape of his work if we thought it was no more than that. The following passage opens *The Blessings of Liberty*:

> For the past thirty years I have been writing on the history, theory, and law of human rights and religious freedom. My main arguments have been (1) that religion has long been a critical foundation and dimension of human rights; (2) that religion and human rights still need each other for each to thrive; and (3) that robust promotion and protection of religious freedom is the best way to protect many other fundamental rights today, even though religious freedom and other fundamental rights sometimes clash and need judicious balancing.[10]

In short, it's not just Witte's personal interest in religion that accounts for the prominence of religious freedom in his writings. It's the subject matter itself that accounts for that prominence. Writing about human rights in the

---

9   See further the chapter by Rafael Domingo herein.
10 *The Blessings of Liberty*, XI.

Western legal tradition *calls for* highlighting the role of religious freedom in that tradition.

Parenthetically, it's not only when discussing human rights that Witte highlights the importance of religion; the same is true of his treatment of other segments of legal history. Witness, for example, his main books on family and marriage law: *Sex, Marriage, and Family Life in John Calvin's Geneva* (Eerdmans, 2005), *The Sins of the Fathers* (Cambridge, 2009), *From Sacrament to Contract: Marriage, Religion, and Law in the Western Tradition* (Westminster John Knox Press, 2nd ed., 2012), *The Western Case for Monogamy over Polygamy* (Cambridge, 2015), *Faith, Freedom, and Family*, and *Church, State, and Family*.[11] The role of religion in the Western legal tradition, both as a shaper of that tradition and as shaped by that tradition, is a scarlet thread that runs throughout Witte's work.

When one reviews the totality of Witte's writings on human rights and religious freedom, another feature that jumps out as distinctive of its content is the combination of fine-grained detail in some of his monographs with a big sweeping picture in others. Witte is a master of both the granular and the global, of both the small and the large. Three examples of Witte's gift for deeply researched, detailed studies of some segment of the Western legal tradition are these: *The Reformation of Rights*; *Law and Protestantism: The Legal Teachings of the Lutheran Tradition* (Cambridge, 2002); and *Religion and the American Constitutional Experiment*. Three examples of his gift for comprehensive surveys are *God's Joust, God's Justice*; *Faith, Freedom, and Family*; and his most recent attempt at pulling it all together, *The Blessings of Liberty*.

5   The Rhetorical Form of Witte's Contribution

From discussing what is distinctive about the genre and content of Witte's contribution to the study of human rights and religious freedom, let us move on to its rhetorical form. Whether he is conducting a granular study of some segment of the Western legal tradition or presenting a comprehensive survey of human rights and religious freedom in the tradition, Witte always tells a story.

Some historical writing takes the form of describing what life was like at some time and place in the past. In such writing, nothing much happens; there are, at most, mininarratives. Simon Schama's description of life in the Netherlands in the seventeenth century, *The Embarrassment of Riches*, is a masterful

---

11   See further the chapter by Helen M. Alvaré herein.

example of that sort of historical writing. Other historical writing takes the overarching form of narrative. Happenings are reported, one thing happening after another.

A subset of narratives in general consists of those that take the rhetorical form of *stories*. What I mean by a *story* is a narrative that does not just tell one thing after another but tracks a development. The historian singles out some aspect of culture or society—be it in the past or in the present—and then tells the story of how that came about, the story of that development.

Witte's writing about human rights and religious freedom in the Western legal tradition tells a story, a story both rich in detail and comprehensive in scope. It's the story of how the "rich latticework"—his phrase—of human rights and religious freedom that we in the West currently enjoy came about. The story tells of the complex interplay among constitutions, laws, and judicial decisions; it tells of the formulation of abstract principles in constitutions, of laws putting those abstract principles into practice, and of judicial decisions interpreting those principles and laws.

Witte identifies six main components of the American version of this rich latticework: liberty of conscience, free exercise of religion, religious pluralism, religious equality, separation of church and state, and no establishment of religion. He writes: "These six principles—some ancient, some new—appeared regularly in the debates over religious liberty and religion-state relations in the eighteenth century.... They remain at the heart of the American experiment today—as central commandments of the American constitutional order and as cardinal axioms of a distinct American logic of religious liberty."[12]

There are high points in the story—*primus inter pares* of the high points in Witte's story being the Magna Carta and the legislation and judicial decisions that it spawned, or the First Amendment to the United States Constitution, and the new religious freedom experiment it unleashed. And there are low points, too, which he takes up: places and times when rights and liberties were constricted, especially for religious dissenters and outsiders, or for American slaves who were reduced to chattel, or women who were subordinated and deprived of their rights. And as with any good story, there are subplots, twists and turns, fits and starts.

Aristotle remarked, in his *Poetics*, that in a good piece of fiction, the storyline has a quality of probability about it, sometimes even inevitability. Given these characters and this situation, it's likely that things would turn out as they did,

---

12   *The Blessings of Blessings,* 139, and elaborated in John Witte, Jr., Joel A. Nichols, and Richard W. Garnett, *Religion and the American Constitutional Experiment,* 5th ed. (Oxford: Oxford University Press, 2022), 59–92.

perhaps even inevitable. Over and over, in the story Witte tells, things might well have gone differently. The constitutions and charters might never have been adopted, the legislative applications might have taken a very different form, judges might have rendered decisions quite different from those they did render. Over and over, happenstance.

Paired with the bright story Witte tells about the emergence of our rich latticework of rights and liberties is a dark story, a story of oppression, domination, prejudice, and discrimination. Religious liberty clauses appear in constitutions and charters because, in the social context from which they emerge, there was a history of violations of rights and constrictions of liberty. Religion cases come before courts because some person or group of persons feels aggrieved; they believe they have been deprived of what they have a right to. Among the many admirable features of the story Witte tells is that the dark side of the story receives full attention; it is never obscured or hurried past.

To conclude my description of the intrinsic significance of Witte's contribution to the study of human rights and religious freedom—my description of its inscape—let me return to his thesis concerning the significance of the right to religious freedom for the recognition of human rights in general. He writes: "The right to religious freedom has long been a foundational part of the gradual development of human rights in the Western tradition, and today it is regarded as the cornerstone in the edifice of human rights.... [F]reedom of religion embraces ... freedom of conscience, exercise, speech, association, worship, diet, and evangelism; ... freedom of religious and moral education, and freedom of religious travel, pilgrimage, and association with coreligionists abroad."[13] This is just the beginning of Witte's list of the rights attendant on the right to freedom of religion both for individuals and for religious groups.

6 The Polemical Significance of Witte's Contribution

We have been considering the intrinsic significance of Witte's contribution, its inscape. Let us move on to its extrinsic significance. A full description of its extrinsic significance would, of course, pinpoint the significance of Witte's contribution to the field of legal history: where, for example, has he made pathbreaking contributions, where has he expanded or corrected the work of others, etc. Since I am myself not a legal historian but a philosopher, I will leave it to Witte's colleagues in the field of legal history to discuss this aspect of the

---

13   *The Blessings of Liberty*, 6.

significance of his work.[14] Let me remark, however, that, accustomed as I am to dealing with abstractions, I have found it fascinating to observe how the ideas of human rights and religious freedom have been embedded, over the centuries, in laws, constitutions, judicial decisions, and the like. Embedded in life. It's something like the difference between theorizing about personality types and engaging with human beings who fit those types.

What I can do is pinpoint some of the polemical significance of Witte's contribution. The story Witte tells, about the emergence and employment of the idea of human rights, has competitors. He writes: "The history of Western rights is still very much a contested work in progress ... , with scholars still sharply divided over the roots and routes of rights and liberties. Every serious new historian of human rights over the past century has tended to focus on a favorite period or person."[15] Witte then lists the authors of thirteen narratives competing with his own.

Most of the competing narratives are told by intellectual historians rather than legal historians. Witte presents them, however, not as narratives concerning the idea of human rights in the *intellectual* history of the West but as narratives concerning the idea of human rights in the history of the West generally. A signal contribution of Witte's work is that it makes clear that telling the full story of human rights in the West requires that one attend not only to its intellectual history but to its legal history as well. There is a lesson in this for those of us who are theorists: do not assume that it is theorists who gave birth to such fundamental ideas as the idea of human rights; it may instead have been practitioners of one sort or another.

The point is well made by one of Witte's colleagues in the field of legal history, the historian of medieval law and jurisprudence Charles J. Reid Jr. In the course of discussing the employment of the idea of human rights by the canon lawyers of the twelfth and thirteenth centuries, Reid asks why so many historians instead trace the emergence of the idea to the philosophers of the fourteenth century. The answer, he says, is that these historians, being "conditioned to expect that the most significant debates over rights will be found in philosophical treatises of scholars like Aquinas, Scotus and Ockham, simply have not sufficiently considered juristic sources."[16]

Witte does not directly engage, in any detail, most of the thirteen alternative narratives that he lists. One that he does engage in some detail is the narrative

---

14 See further the chapter by R. H. Helmholz herein.
15 *The Blessings of Liberty*, 16.
16 Charles J. Reid, Jr., "The Canonist Contribution to the Western Rights Tradition: An Historical Inquiry," *Boston College Law Review* 33, no. 1 (Dec. 1991): 37–92, at 39.

that, for some time now, has been dominant—the narrative which claims that it was thinkers of the European Enlightenment—in particular, Hobbes and Locke—who innovated the idea of natural subjective rights.[17] Rather than mentioning that Witte's work has polemical significance and leaving it at that, let me give some "body" to this dimension of its significance by briefly presenting that alternative narrative and then pointing out how Witte's work undermines it. Before I do so, however, let me present another narrative that has enjoyed considerable currency, especially in neo-Thomist circles, and point out how Witte's work undermines that narrative as well.

Some preliminary comments about terminology are called for. Prominent in the two narratives that I will present is the distinction between *subjective rights* and *objective right*. A subjective right is a right that one *possesses*, a right that one *has*: one's right to practice one's religion freely, for example, or one's right to not be demeaned. Objective right, on the other hand, is right action: doing the right thing: the right thing for a burglar to do is to return what he stole.

Equally prominent is the distinction between *positive* subjective rights and *natural* subjective rights. A positive subjective right is a right that one has on account of its having been bestowed on one by some human action: some law, some promise, etc. A natural subjective right is a right that one has whether or not it has been bestowed on one, a right that one has "in the nature of things."

In the literature, one finds the term "human right" often used interchangeably with the term "natural right." (It appears to me that Witte uses the terms interchangeably).[18] It is my own view that the terms should not be used interchangeably. A human right is a right one has just by virtue of being a human being. But there are rights one has "in the nature of things" that are not, in that sense, human rights—for example, the right of a child to be treated in certain ways by its parent(s). This is a right possessed by a certain kind of human being, viz., a child, not by human beings in general. Be that as it may, because the two terms are regularly used interchangeably in the literature I will do so as well in what follows.

Each of the narratives that I will present affirms that the idea of objective right goes back into antiquity. What they claim is that it was only centuries

---

17 Another narrative that Witte engages in detail is that of Samuel Moyn, *The Last Utopia: Human Rights in History* (Cambridge: Cambridge University Press, 2010); and Moyn, *Christian Human Rights* (Philadelphia: University of Pennsylvania Press, 2015). See Witte, *Faith, Freedom and Family*, 441–56 (chapter titled "'A New Black Mass': Evaluating Samuel Moyn's Account of the 'Myth' of Human Rights").

18 He sets out a taxonomy of rights in *The Reformation of Rights*, 33–37 and further in Witte and Green, *Religion and Human Rights*, 3–21.

later that writers systematically employed the distinctly different idea of *natural subjective* rights.

7 The Narrative of Subjective Rights as Beginning in the Late Middle Ages

The narrative that I mentioned as popular especially in neo-Thomist circles holds that it was the late medieval nominalist philosopher William of Ockham (1265–1347) who first systematically employed the idea of natural subjective rights, initially in the course of defending his fellow Franciscans against attacks on the order by Pope John XXII. The most influential proponent of this narrative was the French legal theorist and philosopher Michel Villey, who, from the mid-1940s to the mid-1980s, published a voluminous and influential body of writings on the history of the idea of subjective rights.

To understand how and why Ockham employed the idea of natural subjective rights in his dispute with the pope, some background is necessary.[19] After the death of Saint Francis (1226), disagreements arose among his followers as to what exactly their vow of poverty consisted of. On September 28, 1230, Pope Gregory IX issued a bull, *Quo elongati,* in which he declared that the Franciscans could use the things they needed but were not to own anything, either individually or communally. Disagreements continued. So on August 14, 1279, Pope Nicholas III issued a bull, *Exiit,* in which he defined Franciscan poverty more precisely. He wrote: "In temporal things we have to consider especially property, possession, usufruct, right of use and simple factual use," adding that "the life of mortals requires the last as a necessity but can do without the others."[20] He declared that the Franciscans had given up right of possession and right of use (*usus juris*) but retained factual use (*usus facti*). In this, they were following Christ and the apostles, who also had no rights of possession or use, only factual use.

In late 1322, Pope John XXII created a furor. For several years he had been having trouble with the Franciscans over the nature of their poverty and had

---

19   I base what follows mainly on two sources: part two of Brian Tierney, *The Idea of Natural Rights: Studies on Natural Rights, Natural Law, and Church Law 1150–1625* (Grand Rapids: Eerdmans, 1997); and John Moorman, *A History of the Franciscan Order from its Origins to the Year 1517* (Oxford: Clarendon Press, 1968). I present Villey's narrative somewhat more fully than I do here in Nicholas Wolterstorff, *Justice: Rights and Wrongs* (Princeton, NJ: Princeton University Press, 2008), 45–50. Some sentences in my presentation here are taken from that earlier presentation.

20   Quoted in Tierney, *The Idea of Natural Rights,* 94.

become quite hostile. On December 8, 1322, he issued a bull, *Ad conditorem*, in which, claiming to be interpreting the bull Nicholas had issued, he ingeniously argued as follows. The factual use of things, which Nicholas had assigned to the Franciscans, has to be understood as a *licit* use, and a licit use of something is a *rightful* use of it. One's use of something that is not a rightful use on one's part is a violation of justice. So the factual use of things by the Franciscans implies the right of using those things. Now when it comes to things that perish in the using—food, for example—it is absurd to suppose that one can separate a right of using from a right of owning. Only the owner of something can rightly destroy it, as one does when one swallows a piece of bread. So the Franciscans, whatever they may say, have not really renounced all right of ownership and all right of use, retaining only factual use. John then tightened the screws. He declared that Christ and the apostles also did not merely use things but had rights of possession and use, and that the Franciscans would henceforth be judged as heretical if they denied this. And he declared that from now on the church would no longer own the things the Franciscans used; ownership would be turned over to the order. Like it or not, the Franciscans would be owners.

The Franciscans were stung, and several undertook to answer John, William of Ockham preeminent among them. His response went as follows. "Every right of using is either a natural right or a positive right."[21] Now when Nicholas said that the Franciscans had given up every right of using, he must have had positive rights in mind, since there were no laws, regulations, or anything else of the sort bestowing rights of using on the Franciscans. John claimed to be doing no more than interpreting the bull Nicholas had issued. Accordingly, when John spoke of the right of using and the right of possession, he should be interpreted as also having positive rights in mind.

So consider John's claim that the Franciscans did in fact retain rights of property and of use. The Franciscans obviously had no positive rights of ownership and use; they had renounced it all. What they had not renounced was the *natural* right of using what was given them. That right cannot be renounced. "It is licit to renounce property and the power of appropriating but no one can renounce the natural right of using."[22] In short: the Franciscans "have no positive right, but they do have a right, namely, a natural right."[23]

Villey's interpretation of the significance of Ockham's response to the pope was that Ockham's employment of the idea of natural subjective rights marked the beginning of the calamitous displacement of the traditional idea of justice

---

21 Quoted in ibid., 121.
22 Quoted in ibid., 164.
23 Quoted in ibid., 122.

as objective right order by the new-fangled idea of justice as subjective rights. Villey left no doubt that he firmly embraced the then-standard neo-Thomist picture of medieval philosophy as reaching its apogee in Aquinas and plunging downhill from there, with Ockham being especially culpable for introducing the individualist ways of thinking that led to the calamities of the Reformation, Descartes, and the Enlightenment. Villey's own contribution to this declinist narrative was his development of the thesis that it was Ockham who first systematically employed the idea of subjective rights in general, and of natural subjective rights in particular, and that it was his nominalism that made this development possible. "William of Ockham, founder of nominalism, an individualist philosophy ... , enemy of the pope and convicted of heresy according to many, may be called the founder of subjective rights."[24]

Villey's defense of this interpretation of the significance of Ockham's employment of the idea of subjective rights came in two main parts. First, he argued that it was indeed Ockham who first systematically employed the idea of subjective right; before Ockham, not even the concept of *positive* subjective rights had been systematically employed, so he claimed.[25] Ockham was the first to employ it systematically; and he did so in the context of arguing for the existence of *natural* subjective rights. "Subjective rights from their origin and still today are conceived of as natural rights," wrote Villey.[26] Before Ockham, it was only the idea of objective right that was systematically employed.

To defend this sweeping claim, Villey engaged in extensive analyses of the writings of ancient and medieval authors, with special emphasis on the ancient Latin jurists. To those of us who are not antecedently resistant to the thought that the ancient jurists might have employed the idea of subjective rights, Villey's interpretations of the Latin texts often come across as willfully contorted. Here is one example. The Roman jurist Ulpian famously defined the virtue of being just as *suum ius cuique tribuere* (giving to each what is rightly his). The formula seems obviously to employ the idea of a subjective right, that is, a right that a person possesses. Not so, argued Villey. Stoicism was the philosophical context of Roman juristic thought, and the Stoics thought of justice in terms of objective right order. So what Ulpian must have meant by a person's *ius* (right) was simply a person's share in the goods distributed by a right social order.

The second part of Villey's defense of his interpretation consisted of arguing that it was Ockham's nominalism—his rejection of universals and his

---

24   Quoted in ibid., 27–28.
25   It's hard to understand the declarations of popes Nicholas and John as not making claims about subjective rights!
26   Quoted in Tierney, *The Idea of Natural Rights*, 20.

insistence that reality consisted of particulars—that made it possible and plausible for him to introduce the concept of a subjective right and to employ it systematically in his writings. Brian Tierney summarizes Villey's claim thus:

> The modern idea of subjective rights ... is rooted in the nominalist philosophy of the fourteenth century, and it first saw the light of day in the work of William of Ockham. Ockham inaugurated a "semantic revolution" when he transformed the traditional idea of objective natural right into a new theory of subjective natural rights. His work marked a "Copernican moment" in the history of the science of law.[27]

In Villey's words: "It is the whole philosophy professed by Ockham that is the mother of subjective right."[28]

Even a casual reading of Villey's argumentation on this point makes clear that it comes to little more than attribution of guilt by association: subjective rights are rights possessed by individuals, and Ockham's nominalist metaphysics contained only particulars; so it was Ockham's nominalism that inspired his innovative employment of the idea of subjective rights. Villey left no doubt that, in his view, what was true in Ockham's case remains true: the idea of subjective rights has its home in individualistic ways of thinking.

8 The Narrative of Rights as Beginning in the Enlightenment

The alternative to his own narrative that Witte engages at some length in a number of his writings can be presented more briefly, since it is more familiar and also much less complex than the Villey narrative. It's the claim, as mentioned earlier, that thinkers of the European Enlightenment innovated the idea of natural subjective rights. Some of those who espouse this narrative exhibit no knowledge of the Villey narrative;[29] others do know of it but hold that Hobbes and Locke were ignorant of medieval thought and newly innovated the idea.

It was in the course of developing the foundations of modern political liberalism that they employed the idea. We can take Locke as typical.[30] Imagine,

---

27   Ibid., 14.
28   Quoted in ibid., 30.
29   Leo Strauss, *Natural Right and History* (Chicago: University of Chicago Press, 1953).
30   I discuss Locke's views somewhat more expansively than I do here in Nicholas Wolterstorff, *Understanding Liberal Democracy: Essays in Political Philosophy* (Oxford: Oxford

says Locke, a group of persons living in a "state of nature," that is, in the situation of not being subject to any legitimate government. The persons in such a situation would have rights and duties—*subjective* rights and duties. Some of their rights might be positive rights, bestowed on them by some act of their fellows, such as a promise. But some would be natural rights. The most fundamental of these would be what Locke calls "perfect freedom"—that is, the natural right "to order their actions, and dispose of their possessions and persons as they think fit, within the law of nature."[31] By "within the bounds of the law of nature" Locke meant, within the bounds of natural rights and duties.

Now suppose that in the state of nature someone violates the law of nature and wrongs another person. Then two additional rights, constituting what Locke calls "the executive power," come into play. Everyone has the natural right to protect themselves, by force if necessary, to punish anyone who wrongs them, and to demand reparations; and anyone who agrees with the injured party that he has been wronged has the natural right to assist him in exercising those rights.

Locke observed that it takes little knowledge of human beings to see that where there is no government, the enjoyment of these rights is precarious. The weak and the dull are susceptible to being wronged by the strong and the clever; partiality leads people to charge that they have been wronged when they have not been; anger leads them to punish excessively; etc. So groups of people living in a state of nature get together and form a contract to establish a state for the purpose of remedying these disadvantages. They jointly "delegate" (Locke's word) to the state their natural right personally to protect themselves and their natural right personally to punish and exact reparations from those who wrong them, and they promise to comply with the laws, directives, and judicial decisions that the state issues pursuant to achieving the purposes for which it was formed. They have a natural duty to keep that promise.

The social individualism of Locke's way of thinking is unmistakable. In an article well-known in legal circles—"Obligation: A Jewish Jurisprudence of the Social Order"—Robert Cover, an esteemed professor in Yale Law School and himself Jewish, wrote: "The story behind the term 'rights' is the story of social contract. The myth postulates free and independent if highly vulnerable human beings who voluntarily trade a portion of their autonomy for a measure of collective security.... [T]he first and fundamental unit is the individual

---

University Press, 2012), 259–65. A few sentences in the text above are taken from that earlier discussion.
31   Locke's *Second Treatise of Government*, §4.

and 'rights' locate him as an individual separate and apart from every other individual."[32]

Cover's words suggest, but he does not actually say, that what was originally true remains true: the idea of natural subjective rights originated within individualist ways of thinking, and it remains the case that it is within such ways of thinking that the idea has its home. What Cover's words suggest, Joan Lockwood O'Donovan makes explicit: "the modern liberal concept of rights belongs to the socially atomistic and disintegrative philosophy of 'possessive individualism.'"[33]

The narrative told by Villey concerning natural rights in the late medieval period, and the narrative told by O'Donovan and many others concerning natural rights in the Enlightenment, are both declinist narratives: the traditional idea of natural objective right was calamitously displaced by the new-fangled idea of natural subjective rights. Further, the ways of thinking that these two narratives identify as culprits are remarkably similar. In Ockham's case, it was his metaphysical particularism; in the case of Locke and his cohorts, it was their social atomism.

9 Witte's Story Undermines the Alternative Narratives

I have said nothing, up to this point, about the actual content of Witte's contribution, other than noting that, in the story he tells, human rights and religious freedom have been persistently and inextricably intertwined. To show how his story undermines the two competing narratives that I have summarized, along with the others, we must now have some of that content before us.

In the introduction to *The Blessings of Liberty*, Witte gives a preview of what he will discuss in the nine highly detailed chapters that follow. No need for an extensive summary of the story Witte tells; for our purposes here, it will suffice to quote some sentences from his previews of the first three chapters, along with some sentences from his summaries of these chapters.[34]

---

32 *Journal of Law and Religion* 5 (1987): 65–74, at 66.
33 Joan Lockwood O'Donovan, "Natural Law and Perfect Community: Contributions of Christian Platonism to Political Theory," *Modern Theology* 14, no. 1 (Jan. 1998), 19–42, at 20. O'Donovan makes the point more elaborately in her essay "The Concept of Rights in Christian Moral Discourse," in *A Preserving Grace: Protestants, Catholics, and Natural Law*, ed. Michael Cromartie (Grand Rapids: Eerdmans, 1997), 143–61.
34 I will not follow the usual practice of putting these somewhat lengthy quotations in block indent format.

Witte writes: "Chapter 1 retrieves and reconstructs the gradual emergence of rights and liberties in the teachings of the Bible, classical Roman law, and medieval canon and civil law." Summarizing his discussion in the chapter, he writes: "For Western jurists and judges, rights talk was a common way to define and defend the law's protection, support, limitations, and entitlements of persons and groups in society as well as the proper relationships between political and other authorities and their respective subjects.... Lawyers since classical Roman and medieval times used rights ideas and terms."[35]

"Chapter 2 zeroes in more closely to offer a lengthy study of the development of rights and liberties in the Anglo-American legal tradition from Magna Carta, in 1215, to seventeenth-century England and its colonies leading up to the American Revolution." He concludes the chapter with these sentences: "The American constitutional founders, like the liberal Enlightenment philosophers, inherited many more rights than they contributed. What they contributed more than anything was a philosophical defense of these rights that transcended particular religious premises and a constitutional system of governance that allowed for a much broader, if not universal, application."[36]

"Chapter 3 retrieves the long-deprecated teachings of the Protestant Reformation concerning natural law and natural rights, and reconstructs the Reformers' role in the development of human rights, religious freedom, and democratic revolution in early modern Protestant lands. Lutherans, Anabaptists, and Calvinists alike made notable contributions to the expansion of public, private, penal, and procedural rights and liberties." Opening his discussion in Chapter 3 Witte writes: "Some view human rights as a dangerous invention of the Enlightenment, predicated on a celebration of reason over revelation, of greed over charity, of nature over scripture, of the individual over the community, and of the pretended sovereignty of humanity over the absolute sovereignty of God." He wryly adds: "While such skepticism might make for good theology in some Protestant circles today, it is not good history."[37]

In short, the systematic employment of the idea of natural subjective rights did not begin with the philosophers of the European Enlightenment. Centuries before the Enlightenment, the Reformers were employing the idea. Nor did it begin with William of Ockham. It goes back to the canon lawyers of the twelfth and thirteenth centuries, and back beyond them to the jurists of ancient Rome and to Jewish and Christian scripture.

---

35   Ibid., 8, 72.
36   Ibid., 8, 75.
37   Ibid., 8, 76.

The story Witte tells not only undermines these alternative stories of origins. It also undermines the claim that employment of the idea of natural human rights is intrinsically connected to a philosophy of possessive individualism; the Reformers were not possessive individualists. And it undermines the claim that employment of the idea of natural human rights is intrinsically connected to philosophical nominalism. The Roman jurists, and the canon lawyers of the twelfth and thirteenth centuries, were not nominalists.

It's true that someone whose life orientation is that of possessive individualism may well find the language of rights useful for his purposes: he will insist loudly and exclusively on his rights. But I have argued philosophically that, rather than this being the home use of rights language, it is an abuse of the language of rights.[38] When someone comes into my presence, not only do I have rights vis-à-vis them but they have rights vis-à-vis me. The situation is symmetrical. And as for the supposed individualism of rights: it is sufficient to observe that social entities also have rights—families, schools, groups, corporations, etc. Philosophical reflection yields the same results as Witte's historical studies.

10 Witte's Story Undermines the Claim That Religion Does Not Merit Special Protection

Witte's work has an important additional dimension of polemical significance—additional to the fact that it undermines a wide swath of alternative narratives of human rights. The millennia-long story Witte tells about the persistent interweaving of human rights with religious freedom constitutes a powerful case against the claim one hears nowadays that religion deserves no special protection.

About the discussions that led to the U.S. Bill of Rights, Witte writes: "One key to the enduring success of [the] American experiment in religious freedom lies in the eighteenth-century founders' most elementary insight—that religion is special and needs special constitutional protection." Witte notes that this claim, that religion is special and needs special protection, is questioned nowadays by a considerable number of political philosophers and legal theorists. Religion "has become obsolete in our post-establishment, postmodern, and post-religious age, these critics argue. Religion, they say, is too dangerous,

---

38 See Nicholas Wolterstorff, *Journey toward Justice* (Grand Rapids: Baker Academic. 2013), chap. 10.

divisive, and diverse in its demands to be accorded special constitutional protection."[39]

Alluding to his own research, Witte replies: "too many of these critical arguments fail to appreciate how dearly fought religious freedom has been in the history of humankind, how imperiled religious freedom has become in many parts of the world today, and how indispensable religious freedom has proved to be for the protection of other fundamental human rights in modern democracies." Then, after acknowledging that religion has been responsible for many evils, he composes an eloquent articulation of the contribution religion makes to the flourishing of individuals and the common good. Religions "deal uniquely with the deepest elements of individual and social life."[40]

We would be much the poorer in our knowledge of the history of human rights and religious freedom, and in our grasp of their importance, had John Witte not devoted his prodigious skills and energy to exploring the legal history of rights and freedoms in the West.

---

39 *The Blessings of Liberty*, 156, 163.
40 Ibid., 166.

CHAPTER 5

John Witte, Jr.'s Contributions to the Study of Sex, Marriage, and Family Law

Helen M. Alvaré

1   Introduction

Today, the importance of the family to individual and social thriving is well known. It is a subject continually and prolifically investigated by scholars in the myriad areas influencing family relations and functioning: sociology, law, culture, anthropology, medicine, and economics, to name some of the leading arenas. The inverse dynamic is also better known: the relationship between family fragility or breakdown and the decline of individual and social welfare.

At the same time, especially in many of the most prosperous nations, even long-held and bedrock family norms and patterns are queried and challenged. Given general agreement about the individual and social importance of the family, it therefore becomes quite important to know which norms and patterns conduce to individual, familial, and social strength, and which should be resisted or altered.

Not surprisingly, in this environment of significant flux and challenge respecting received traditions, there exists suspicion or even disdain for the roles that history and religion—perhaps especially Christianity—have played in shaping tradition. Both are frequently charged with possessing an insufficient regard for human rights and freedom in the arenas of sex, marriage, and parenting. Furthermore, because of the many forces shaping personal and social choices and outcomes in these arenas, there is a tendency to feel dispirited even about the possibility of understanding contemporary problems, let alone how to promote specific laws, values, and practices that might ameliorate family life, especially in situations affecting vulnerable individuals and groups.

It is against this backdrop that one can reflect upon the immense scale of Professor Witte's contributions to the fields of sex, marriage, and family law. At a time of mistrust of historical antecedents of, and religious influences upon, current laws in these areas, Witte provides appealing reasons to consult historical and religious subjects. He shows that these can illuminate our contemporary legal and cultural situations and choices. And he further proposes that some might be not only legitimate but *fruitful* sources for fair-minded, freedom-loving, and compassionate twentieth- and twenty-first-century reflection and enactment. One might call this service that Witte performs a kind of "ressourcement"—an investigation of the wisdom and missteps of the past in order to assist the present. Furthermore, at a time of discouragement about how to assist individuals and families to make choices more conducive to long-run happiness, stability, and freedom—given the myriad and complex factors influencing family welfare—Witte shows that diverse fields of knowledge can and do work together to offer rational and viable ways forward.

Perhaps just as important, always and everywhere—in every book and article he has written and edited, and every conference and volume he has organized—Witte models the tone, methods, and intellectual and personal virtues that should inform family law scholarship going forward if it is to serve human flourishing, particularly of the most vulnerable. He never falls prey to temptations to serve other agendas or fashions—whether political or ideological or religious—even during moments in history when heated controversies are swirling in each of these spheres.

Today, nearly every leading public and private institution in the Western world has demonstrated a preoccupation with questions about sex, marriage, and family law. Scholars have consequently produced innumerable books and articles on pertinent subjects. But even in this crowded field, the accomplishments of John Witte stand out. In order to consider his contributions, and simultaneously to offer some ways forward for future scholarship, this chapter does the following: first, it addresses the historical, religious, and interdisciplinary contents of Witte's work, from time to time stopping to highlight particularly impressive but likely to be overlooked contributions. Second, I consider those personal and intellectual virtues he demonstrates, and through which he drives family law scholarship toward a higher level, providing emerging scholars a template for a career they can take pride in.

It is impossible fully to tease apart Professor Witte's historical, religious, and interdisciplinary accomplishments. There is considerable overlap. Still, it is possible to begin by highlighting several particularly valuable features of each without undue repetition.

2 History

For readers who might otherwise be inclined to associate human progress only with more contemporary developments, Witte's scholarship helps them to grasp that one might better understand, evaluate, and even assist the present in light of its antecedents. Along with his coeditors in *Sex, Marriage, and Family in World Religions*, he asserts boldly that one cannot know how to evaluate the many changes in these arenas "or how to think about the future if we do not understand the role of the world religions in shaping attitudes and policies toward sex, marriage, and family in the past."[1]

In his historical presentations, Witte takes advantage of an important epistemological principle: that understanding is better advanced by the use of distinctions, not merely descriptions. Thus, he presents historical family law and culture in ways that help readers understand *by distinction* the sex, marriage, and family regimes that the West has today chosen for itself—including what it has retained from the past, what it has rejected and replaced, and what it has altered.

His historical tours are prolifically and impeccably sourced and nonideological. They offer marvelous detail, while also performing the difficult task of summarizing very large shifts and developments that have unfolded over thousands of years of Western history. He might begin with pre-Christian, Jewish, Greek, and Roman materials, then move to the introduction of Christianity, to medieval canon law, and to the Reformation, the Enlightenment, European colonization, and onward to today. Sometimes he proceeds chronologically, sometimes according to leading figures or ideas, and sometimes by way of some combination of these approaches. Altogether, his encyclopedic coverage allows the reader to understand not only myriad discrete matters, but also how and why ideas spread or failed to spread, why older ideas were rejected in favor of newer, and, throughout, to see advances or declines in respect for the dignity of different members of the family, and family groups.

One note here about Witte's capacity to take immense volumes of sources and developments and then briefly but accurately summarize them. This is an underappreciated feat, but immensely helpful to students and scholars alike. They may possess less-than-detailed knowledge about a particular development or historical period or thought-leader in the areas of sex, marriage, and family, but cannot devote time to arrange the basics in order, even as they require the material for purposes of building their own new scholarship. Witte is aware that he is attempting to offer summaries that comprehend and distill a massive amount of material while remaining accurate, but he seems to do it with ease. In the introduction to his volume *From Sacrament to Contract*, for example, he states that its "principal topical foci are Christian theological

---

1 Introduction to Don S. Browning, M. Christian Green, and John Witte, Jr., eds., *Sex, Marriage, and Family in World Religions* (New York: Columbia University Press, 2006), XVII (italics original).

norms and Western legal principles of marriage and family life. Its principal geographical focus is Western Europe and its extension overseas to America. Its principal goal is to uncover some of the main theological beliefs that have helped to form Western marriage law in the past, and so to discover how such beliefs might help to inform Western marriage law in the future."[2]

Imagine aspiring to trace the entire subject of Christianity's influence in family law.[3] Or characterizing the most prominent five models of marriage over the last two millennia, and their influences upon current Western marriage law.[4] Imagine accurately characterizing the meaning of marriage throughout history and nations as Witte does: "For marriage is one of the great mediators of individuality and community, revelation and reason, tradition and modernity. Marriage is at once a harbor of the self and a harbinger of the community, a symbol of divine love and a structure of reasoned consent, an enduring ancient mystery and a constantly modern invention."[5] Imagine summarizing the classical foundations of Western marriage laws and customs in thirteen pages. Or the "biblical foundations" of the same in twenty-one pages.[6] Professor Witte manages.

At the same time—exhibiting the scholarly virtues elaborated upon below—he acknowledges that his surveys are not the last word. In his and Philip L. Reynolds's *To Have and to Hold: Marrying and Its Documentation in Western Christendom, 400–1600*, they write that the text is "not a comprehensive survey of the forms and norms of marriage formation and documentation in pre-modern Christian Europe; the surviving evidence is too scattered and spotty, and it is subject to too many different methods of interpretation, to make such a claim." Instead, it is "a fair representation of the range of customs, laws and practices surrounding the formation and documentation of marriages in pre-modern Europe and the range of legal, social, and religious modes of scholarly analysis that can be responsibly applied to the documentary evidence that has survived."[7]

Professor Witte can accomplish these highly useful summaries because he has first gone into the woods—often in the company of leading experts he has

---

2 John Witte, Jr., *From Sacrament to Contract: Marriage, Religion, and Law in the Western Tradition*, 2nd ed. (Louisville, KY: Westminster John Knox Press, 2012), 1.
3 See John Witte, Jr. and Gary S. Hauk, eds., *Christianity and Family Law: An Introduction* (Cambridge: Cambridge University Press, 2017).
4 *From Sacrament to Contract.*
5 Ibid., ix.
6 Ibid., 17–30, and 31–52.
7 Philip L. Reynolds and John Witte, Jr., eds., *To Have and to Hold: Marrying and Its Documentation in Western Christendom, 400–600* (Cambridge: Cambridge University Press, 2009), x.

assembled—and examined individual trees for a great deal of time, and then stepped back to consider the forest, while also often looking across nations, religions, and historical periods.

Returning to a consideration of Witte's substantive use of history, one of his signal contributions is to paint a nuanced and carefully sourced picture of Western nations' turning away from explicitly religious and communal conceptions of, and influences upon, sex, marriage, and family law, toward more individualist, subjectivist, and privatized schemes. He shows how Western lawmaking regarding marriage was once shaped by the theological beliefs and principles of Christianity—which had itself relied upon Jewish, Greek and Roman sources—later the Church Fathers, then Roman Catholic canon law, Reformation theology, and the contractarian ideas of the Enlightenment. He describes how, during the twentieth and twenty-first centuries, the state and not the church became the principal external authority governing marriage and family life. At this time, movements arose toward recognizing far more marital pluralism and private ordering. Both within and outside marriage, there developed a focus upon autonomy, privacy, individual sexual gratification, equal protection, and personal happiness.

Witte paints a rich picture showing how these twentieth- and twenty-first-century shifts ultimately instantiated the "contractarian model" of marriage, a body of ideas launched during the Enlightenment, "elaborated theoretically in the nineteenth century, but not implemented legally until the twentieth century." While this model was too radical for earlier times, he writes, it "anticipated much of the agenda for the transformation of marriage law in the twentieth century" respecting "privacy, equality and sexual autonomy."[8] One can see this clearly in Western nations' recent lawmaking and cultural transformations respecting divorce, prenuptial contracts, same-sex marriage, and nonmarital sex.

Witte assesses both what is gained and what is lost by the ascendancy of the contractarian model, and helps us understand current misgivings about the present array of family laws and practices, even as much progress has been made toward fairer treatment of women, children, and persons who identify as LGBTQ. He writes that Enlightenment contractarian notions of marriage were designed to improve it, not abandon it, and were a reaction against "paternalism, patriarchy and prudishness."[9] Later, however, he writes, the rise of the contractarian model during "the 1950s forward, seems calculated to break the preeminence of the traditional family and the basic values of the Western legal

---

8 *From Sacrament to Contract*, 11.
9 Ibid., 314–15.

tradition that have sustained it."[10] He often addresses how vulnerable members of the family suffer most from the consequences of this transition, by way of abortion, nonmarital births, divorce, and poverty, and how the contractarian model can neglect the relationship between family functioning and social welfare. Some elements of the model even pose risks to democracy, freedom, and social justice as well.

Even as Witte's conclusions on these matters enjoy support from interdisciplinary and empirical sources, it is no small amount of scholarly confidence and pluck that is required to question the degree of subjectivity and individualism characterizing our contemporary handling of sex, marriage, and parenting *and* to suggest that this approach has harmed the less privileged to a greater degree.

Witte also relies upon history not only to "to take stock of the dramatic transformation of marriage and family life in the world today"[11] but also to mine it for wisdom that might assist current problems, as well as to highlight its missteps and later course corrections. This is a contribution to peace of mind. Many political and cultural voices are inclined to conclude that present problems are both unprecedented and insurmountable. But in Witte's work, there is neither nostalgia for the past nor unmitigated approval of the present. In short, he evaluates legal and cultural stances both then and now according to the same measure: which assist individual, familial, and social flourishing, especially of the oppressed or weak? This contrasts with contemporary inclinations toward uncritical acceptance of Enlightenment contractarian notions—and rejection of earlier sex, marriage, and family norms—on the grounds that current convictions about human rights and freedoms are unquestionably superior.

Witte observes accurately that family transformations "on a comparable scale to those we face today have been faced before,"[12] respecting matters both large and small. He discusses, for example, the changing balance between the private and social aspects of marriage, the shifting interrelationships between church and state, the wisdom of broad sexual license, the ramifications of multiple forms of family, the distinctions between annulment and divorce, the wisdom of waiting periods before entering marriage, and whether to maintain proportionality between the stringency of processes for entering or leaving marriage.

Looking at one of these smaller matters as an example of mining the past to serve the present—waiting periods between obtaining a marriage license

---

10   Ibid., 309.
11   Preface and acknowledgements to Reynolds and Witte, *To Have and to Hold*, xiv.
12   *From Sacrament to Contract*, 326.

and marriage—many states are shortening or eradicating such periods. Witte notes, however, that there might be wisdom available from the past. John Calvin, for example, "took seriously the need for a delay between betrothals and weddings." This allowed "others to weigh in on the maturity and the compatibility of the couple, to offer them counsel and commodities, and to prepare for the celebration of their union and their life together thereafter."[13] This becomes important today in light of the observed disadvantages of conceiving marriage as so private that couples do not feel themselves supported by, nor answerable to, any social norms.

Similarly, earlier insights about the implications of polygamy might also have purchase today at a time when arguments in its favor are gaining some traction in popular and scholarly fora. Witte assists the current conversation by discovering that the rational case against polygamy is at least as old as ancient Judaism. He reminds us that the Hebrew word for a co-wife was "trouble."[14] He also unearths longstanding convictions that polygamy disadvantages the "leftover" men—which can affect the peace of the larger society. It also harms children and, particularly, those women who are very young and/or pressured to marry.

But Witte is also willing to criticize past "wisdom." For example, in his discussion of older laws concerning "illegitimacy" in *The Sins of the Fathers*, he observes the unfairness of punishing children for their parents' giving birth to them outside of marriage, and lauds the later twentieth-century Supreme Court decisions ending such children's legal disabilities. At the same time, and according to the same metric—children's human rights and adults' responsibilities to children—he notes that recent sharp rises in nonmarital births have led to a variety of social, emotional, financial, and cognitive difficulties for the children involved.[15] Regarding not only nonmarital births but also similarly complex and delicate familial problems, Witte offers this balanced observation about the need for more enlightened solutions: "We cannot be blind to the patriarchy, paternalism, and plain prudishness of the past. Nor can we be blind to the massive social, psychological, and spiritual costs of the modern sexual revolution."[16] In short, he concludes that the past has some wisdom for

---

13 John Witte, Jr., "Marriage Contracts, Liturgies, and Properties in Reformation Geneva," in Reynolds and Witte, *To Have and to Hold*, chap. 13.
14 John Witte, Jr., *The Western Case for Monogamy Over Polygamy* (Cambridge: Cambridge University Press, 2015), 35.
15 Ibid., 160–61, 175.
16 *From Sacrament to Contract*, ix.

us regarding the good of marital childbearing, but not necessarily regarding the *means* used to attempt to curb it.

Witte's conviction that history is an indispensable lens through which to assess current choices respecting sex, marriage, and parenting is complemented by his equally strong conviction that we cannot assess current changes in family law "or how to think about the future if we do not understand the role of the world religions in shaping attitudes and policies toward sex, marriage, and family in the past."[17] I turn now to his work concerning the influence that religions have exerted upon family law and culture, and their potential to provide assistance in our time.

3 Religion

Professor Witte's body of work about the historical association between religions and sex, marriage, and family law and culture in the West reveals persistent religious influence even through the period when the crafting and administration of family law moved from ecclesiastical to civil realms. He demonstrates religions' direct and indirect influence upon law and culture, with special attention to Christianity. His masterful work *From Sacrament to Contract* sets forth in historical order the leading religious, theological, and intellectual ideas that shaped Western law concerning sex, marriage, and the family,[18] and charts the decisive moves away from religious sway in more recent decades.

Witte carefully describes legal regimes in which church and state have overlapping or separate jurisdictions or aims. These accounts implicitly pose to the contemporary mind the question whether—given the likelihood that church *and* state will *always* possess significant interests in the well-being of spouses and children—church and state today might find grounds for both separation of powers and cooperation.

It should be briefly noted here that Witte does not treat "religion" or even particular religions as monoliths. He rather writes about and organizes volumes about myriad religions, and notes disputes *within* religions, from their beginnings to today. For example, he helped organize and edit a volume that treated, *inter alia*, the rise of "situation ethics," the "womanist" and other

---

17 Browning, Green, and Witte, *Sex, Marriage, and Family in World Religions*, XVII (italics original).
18 *From Sacrament to Contract*, 1.

African-American critiques, and disputes over same-sex unions, all within the Christian tradition.[19]

Witte also anticipated a more recent willingness by some lawmakers and scholars to look to religious ideas and practices for assistance with significant problems affecting sex, marriage, and parenting dilemmas. In his *Church, State, and Family*, and his and Steven M. Tipton's edited volume, *Family Transformed: Religion, Values, and Society in American Life*, for example, the authors "pay[] particular attention to the role that religious ideas, institutions, and practices have played in the drama of the modern family, and ... judge[] their potential to shape its future direction."[20]

Witte also defends religions against highly generalized accusations that they have not and do not respect modern notions of human rights, particularly freedom, and equality between the sexes and between heterosexuals and homosexuals. Relying upon historical and religious primary sources, Witte proposes instead that the contemporary West, more than it realizes, has benefited from religious teachings and principles. He writes that "by 1650, Christians of various types had already defined, defended, and died for every right that would appear a century and a half later in the United States Bill of Rights or in the French Declaration of the Rights of Man and of the Citizen."[21] He also opines that "a good case has been made that modern human rights norms still need religious and moral sources and sanctions to be fully cogent and effective even in our post-establishment and post-modern secular politics."[22] This is because so-called neutral, objective, and value-free arguments "rest[] ultimately on a foundation of fundamental beliefs and values." At the same time, he observes, ideas claimed to be purged of religious influences "are becoming [in some cases] as fundamentalist about the cogency and correctness of their ideas, methods, and arguments as Christian and other religious fundamentalists of the past."[23]

Regarding the particular matter of Christianity's respect for women, volumes edited together with Gary S. Hauk and Steven M. Tipton highlight scholarship contextualizing Saint Paul's exhortations about the place of

---

19 Luke Timothy Johnson and Mark D. Jordan, "Christianity," in Browning, Green, and Witte, *Sex, Marriage, and Family in World Religions*, 77–149, at 138–47.
20 See John Witte, Jr., *Church, State, and Family: Reconciling Traditional Teachings and Modern Liberties* (Cambridge: Cambridge University Press, 2019); and Steven M. Tipton and John Witte, Jr., eds., *Family Transformed: Religion, Values, and Society in American Life* (Washington, DC: Georgetown University Press, 2005), 1.
21 *The Western Case for Monogamy Over Polygamy*, 25.
22 Ibid., 25–26.
23 Ibid.

women in marriage, so that they might be more fairly understood as progress for women against the backdrop of the first century.[24] To the Galatians, for example, Paul wrote that "there is neither Jew nor Greek, there is neither slave nor free person, there is not male and female; for you are all one in Christ Jesus" (Gal. 3:27–28). And to the Ephesians he wrote, "As the church is subordinate to Christ, so wives should be subordinate to their husbands in everything. Husbands, love your wives, even as Christ loved the church and handed himself over for her" (Eph. 5:24, 25). Regarding these passages, the final chapter opines: "But on the whole, the earlier Jesus movement and the authentic Pauline letters seriously challenged the honor-shame family patterns of antiquity. They did this by celebrating male servanthood rather than male dominance, by applying the golden rule and neighbor love to relationships between husband and wife, by requiring males to renounce their sexual privileges with female slaves and young boys, and by elevating the status of women."[25]

Witte also highlights how, later in the history of Christianity, John Calvin led reforms to the laws of Geneva that punished sexual felonies (including rape), initiated new protections for abused wives and widows, demanded the faithfulness of husbands and not only wives, promoted the education of children (so that they could come to know God through reading the scriptures), and provided sanctuary to nonmarital, abandoned, and abused children.[26]

At the same time, Witte does not fail to criticize what he judges to be harmful Christian influences affecting families and the law. Regarding the law of "illegitimacy," for example, he writes that even as ignoring the well-being of nonmarital children is "liberty run wild," the "historical doctrine of illegitimacy was a Christian theology of sin run amuck."[27] And he harshly criticizes those laws and policies inflicted upon Indigenous peoples in the name of progress, civilization, and Western Christianity.[28]

A particularly admirable accomplishment of Witte's writings about religion and the family is his engaging an ecumenical and interfaith array of religious scholars in conversation directed to promoting the common good.[29] This is a

---

24 Don S. Browning, "The World Situation of Families: Marriage Reformation as a Cultural Work," chapter 13 in Tipton and Witte, *Family Transformed*, 277–78; and Gary S. Hauk, "Jesus and St. Paul," chapter 2 in Witte and Hauk, *Christianity and Family Law*, 48–49.
25 Browning, "The World Situation of Families," 278.
26 Don S. Browning, foreword to John Witte, Jr. and Robert M. Kingdon, *Sex, Marriage and Family in John Calvin's Geneva*, vol. 1 (Grand Rapids; Eerdmans, 2005), XXIII and 1.
27 *The Sins of the Fathers*, 8.
28 *The Western Case for Monogamy Over Polygamy*, 426.
29 See, for example, Browning, Green, and Witte, *Sex, Marriage, and Family in World Religions*.

signal contribution toward harmony in a world that continues to experience religious clashes, within and between religions and nations. In the course of these conversations—whether between the covers of a book or across a table at a conference—scholars, listeners, and readers can not only appreciate what is insightful and constructive about other faiths, but also learn to acknowledge religions' mutual debts. They can also better understand the significance of their *own* religion's choices by comparison with others'. Witte has facilitated these understandings especially among Protestants, Catholics, and Jews, but also among these denominations and Eastern religions.[30]

4   Interdisciplinarity

In his own writings, and by assembling teams of interdisciplinary scholars, Professor Witte fashions presentations of issues or historical periods that take into account the many different factors operating on sex, marriage, and family law in the past and the present. As noted above, because an array of philosophical, theological, sociological, economic, and other factors, together, influence behaviors and laws concerning the family, any account of relevant history, developments, laws, and practices should incorporate insights from these various fields. Witte does this very intentionally, repeatedly, and thoroughly. In an afterword to a law-review symposium, for example, he writes that it was intended to "bring the enduring wisdom of religious traditions into greater conversation with the modern disciplines of law, health, public policy, social science, and the humanities."[31]

In addition to engaging with varying intellectual domains, Witte engages other important axes in his interdisciplinary endeavors, including time, an interfaith array of religions (as noted above), and geography. He will often, for example, focus upon a specific subject or practice—for example, marriage, divorce, sexual norms, nonmarital births, polygamy, or nonmarital sexual relations—and explore its constants and its changes over long periods of time. At other times, as in *Sex, Marriage, and Family in World Religions*, he not only coordinates multiple subject matters according to a variety of religions

---

30   See ibid., and John Witte, Jr. and Frank S. Alexander, eds., *The Teachings of Modern Protestantism on Law, Politics, and Human Nature* (New York: Columbia University Press, 2007); and John Witte, Jr. and Frank S. Alexander, eds., *The Teachings of Modern Roman Catholicism on Law, Politics, and Human Nature* (New York: Columbia University Press, 2007).

31   John Witte, Jr., "Exploring the Frontiers of Law, Religion, and Family Life," *Emory Law Journal* 58, no. 1 (2008–09): 87.

but also allows multiple religions to understand their points of agreement and difference. He might also use a global lens to assist individual countries to enlarge and improve the terms of their debates over even neuralgic issues of sex and family.[32] Additional benefits of exploring sex, marriage, and family along so many axes include the anthropological insights—and associated potential solutions to problems—that can emerge from such a multifaceted view of human nature and familial relations across so many varying sources and periods.

Witte's interdisciplinary investigations—again, whether between the covers of an edited book, or in his own writing, or at one of the many conferences he organizes—yield important fruits. First, they often demonstrate the way in which the disciplines of reason and religion might work together. Second, they might yield a more complete approach to explaining a series of events or even solving a complex problem. In what follows, I explore each of these outcomes.

First, in his own work, and also in his collaborations with others, Witte helps to illuminate that religious teachings incorporate a practical rationality, as against a regularly voiced suspicion that faith is devoid of or incompatible with reason. As he and his coauthors state in *Sex, Marriage, and Family in World Religions*, "[r]eligious traditions almost always combine in subtle ways naturalistic, legal, moral, and metaphysical levels of thinking and reasoning"[33]—thus the overlap between biblical teachings about sex, marriage, and parenting, and many of the observations of the Greek philosophers. Religions might also, for example, incorporate into their analyses complementary observations regarding utilitarian reasoning, human rights, or scientifically measurable observations. Witte points out that on these grounds there even emerged some overlaps and synergies between Christian and Enlightenment stances about nonmarital sex, divorce, and polygamy.

The complementarity of faith and reason also features prominently in Witte's discussion of polygamy, during which he observes that bans on polygamy predated Christianity and persisted through the Protestant Reformation and even after Western nations disestablished Christianity. Secular bases for such bans were not identical to the grounds of Christian condemnations, but featured more than a few similarities.

A second advantage of Witte's interdisciplinary projects is their yielding a more *complete* approach to explaining events or even solving a complex problem. This is because an interdisciplinary lens not only respects reality—the existence of multiple and varying forces upon laws and practices concerning

---

32 Reynolds and Witte, *To Have and to Hold*, xiv.
33 Browning, Green, and Witte, *Sex, Marriage and Family in World Religions*, xxiii.

sex, marriage, and parenting—but avoids telling simplistic stories. Interdisciplinarity avoids the tendency visible in more than a few contemporary accounts of the family—from all political sides—to interpret the family and its historical trajectory through narrow lenses, whether as a story of oppression moving toward liberty, or as the progressive liberation from religious influences, or through some other lens that fails to acknowledge *all* of the actual forces at work. Instead, Witte's work provides varying, overlapping, richer, and ultimately truer accounts of history by acknowledging and mining a wide variety of events and fields, which together affect the laws and practices concerning sex, marriage, and parenting.[34] This is particularly evident in his and Steven Tipton's edited volume, *Family Transformed*. The volume considers the impacts on the family of law, biology, technology, the economy, labor participation, and civil rights, among other arenas. It also proposes how these disciplines might shed light upon how to ameliorate thorny family problems.

A further noteworthy element of Witte's interdisciplinary approach is his ability to gather and attain cooperation and innovation among leading scholars from each of the relevant disciplines. He is able to foster unusual amounts of collegial trust among experts that, whatever the subject at hand may be, it will be approached with reliable sources, empirical validity, scholarly expertise, and—just as important—good will, even in the midst of competing views. This method produces scholarship on which students and later scholars can rely with equanimity.

5 Virtues

Professor Witte demonstrates overlapping scholarly and personal virtues that further commend his work not only to fellow scholars and the discipline, but also to society and to the ages. First, he makes bold to question the outcomes of the turn to subjectivity, to adults' individualism, and to notions of freedom that tend more toward license and less adult responsibility. And despite the potential for friction in such a project, he performs this work with careful language, respect for the evidence, and an "apt and cheerful"[35] manner. Witte has charted this course during a period of family law and family-law scholarship when relatively few intellectuals in high places are willing to question the

---

34 Witte and Kingdon, *Sex, Marriage, and Family in John Calvin's Geneva*, XVIII.
35 John Witte, Jr., "An Apt and Cheerful Conversation on Marriage," in *A Nation Under God? Essays on the Fate of Religion in American Public Life*, ed. R. Bruce Douglass and Josh Mitchell (Lanham, MD: Rowman & Littlefield, 2000), 91–110.

status quo. His work, therefore, encourages other scholars to look at the evidence and paves a safer path for all to do so, both now and in the future.

Second, Witte regularly evaluates the state of law and culture respecting sex, marriage, and parenting from the perspective of vulnerable parties. In *The Sins of the Fathers*,[36] for example, he sets forth the robust evidence that children reared without the stable presence of their parents suffer disadvantages, on average, in many domains, even as he decries "illegitimacy" law as a cruel means of discouraging nonmarital parenting.

In a convincing contribution to both religious and civic thinking about nonmarital births, he offers a close reading of both Jewish and Christian interpretations of scripture to show that the weight of scripture is against the doctrine of illegitimacy.[37] This will come as a surprise to many. Even as illegitimacy distinctions historically served the desire of the church to strengthen marriage as the only place for sex and procreation, and to protect children by assuring two parents' attention, the early Church Fathers denounced the disadvantaging of children even as they preached against nonmarital sex.[38]

Further attending to the vulnerable, Witte considers the fraying or breaking of family ties as disproportionately burdening the poor and disadvantaged minorities, whether through abortion, nonmarital births, or divorce. He points out how the wealthy can cushion the negative consequences of family decline while poorer groups and even societies suffer under its weight.[39]

A third signal virtue of Witte's writing is his evenhanded treatment of positions emerging from the so-called right or left. His work is a living expression of Saint Paul's admonition that "whatever is true, whatever is honorable, whatever is just, whatever is pure, whatever is lovely, whatever is gracious, if there is any excellence and if there is anything worthy of praise, think about these things" (Philippians 4:8). Titles of several of his works easily illustrate this virtue. There is his coedited volume *The Equal Regard Family and Its Friendly Critics*,[40] and his chapter titled "An Apt and Cheerful Conversation on Marriage."[41] There is also the subtitle to his *Church, State, and Family* book—*Reconciling Traditional Teachings and Modern Liberties.* Even more noteworthy is how Witte manages

---

36 *The Sins of the Fathers.*
37 Ibid., 11–47.
38 Ibid., 27–47.
39 Ibid., 160–61.
40 John Witte, Jr., M. Christian Green, and Amy Wheeler, eds. *The Equal Regard Family and Its Friendly Critics: Don Browning and the Practical Theological Ethics of the Family* (Grand Rapids: Eerdmans, 2007).
41 Witte, "An Apt and Cheerful Conversation on Marriage."

to hew to this method even while treading on minefields like nonmarital births, polygamy, same-sex marriage, abortion, and divorce.

A fourth virtue that Witte's work displays is the use of complete, detailed, and primary sources and accounts in service of all investigations and conclusions. This obviously supports other virtues apparent in both his methods and content. The use of excellent sources, for example, will tend to fair assessments of a subject, as mentioned just above. His methods stand in contrast to some family-law scholarship that neglects influential but disliked historical figures in favor of preferred figures, or neglects primary sources in favor of secondary summations or characterizations more suited to the author's prior commitments.

An excellent example of close reading of primary sources is his and Philip Reynolds's *To Have and to Hold*. One chapter, for example, considers rare examples of dower charters during the twelfth century from two dioceses in France.[42] Witte also contributes a chapter that examines marriage contracts in Reformation Geneva.[43] Overall, as Witte and Reynolds write, the text examines "how, why, and when pre-modern Europeans documented their marriages—through deeds, settlements, and charters, through the depositions used in episcopal and consistory courts, and through other surviving indicia of the couple's agreement to marry."[44] It considers the function of documentation in the process of marrying and what the surviving documents say about how premodern Europeans understood it. It looks closely at the documents' assignments of property rights as between a husband and a wife. This research is an excellent example of how a meticulous consideration of primary sources can act as a window into the broader matter of the state of marriage and relations between the sexes at a particular point in history in a particular place. Such documents indicate what freedom of action was permitted to betrothed men and women as compared with rights asserted by their parents, what property rights women possessed over against the husband and his family, and what were the separate or overlapping domains and relative strengths of the church and the state regarding marriage.

There are more occasions of Witte's exacting consideration of primary, even mundane, sources as important tools for capturing the interplay of law and

---

42 Laurent Morelle, "Marriage and Diplomatics: Five Dower Charters from the Regions of Laon and Soissons, 1163–1181," in Reynolds and Witte, *To Have and to Hold*, chap. 5.

43 John Witte, Jr., "Marriage Contracts, Liturgies, and Properties in Reformation Geneva," in Reynolds and Witte, *To Have and to Hold*, chap. 13.

44 Witte and Reynolds, *To Have and to Hold*, ix.

culture respecting some aspect of the family. Concerning inter- and intrafamilial relations, for example, he examines the details of diriment and prohibitive impediments to marriage contracts in medieval Roman Catholic canon law. On the matter of the state and society's changing culture and beliefs respecting nonmarital childbearing, there is his review of medieval canon law's hierarchy of illegitimates and legitimates. And there is his detailed examination of sometimes small but important shifts in law to soften treatment of children born outside of their parents' lawful marriages. This includes looking at the use of legal tools including putative marriage and adoption, and distinguishing more kindly social views of such children from disapproval of their parents' behavior.

Witte brings this same level of exacting research to his treatment of both constancy and change over long periods of history concerning myriad elements of law and culture respecting sex, marriage, and the family. A nonexhaustive list includes his treatment of arranged marriages, secret marriages, marriage licenses, betrothal and engagement practices, banns of marriage, clandestine and oral contracts, penalties for fornication, adultery, and incest, wife and child abuse, alimony, annulment, divorce, coverture, dower, prenuptial contracts, impediments of blood or affinity, consummation, and church consecration of marriages.

A notable practice complementing Witte's complete, evenhanded, meticulous, and primary-sourced investigations is his coverage—in his own writing and his edited volumes—of both the major "household names" and the less-well-known historical figures shaping the law and culture of sex, marriage, and parenting throughout Western history. Not every student or even scholar would have encountered the work of Henry Home, Lord Kames of Scotland, a leading figure in the Scottish Enlightenment. And while all would have heard of King Henry VIII in connection with the founding of the Anglican Church, very few would be familiar with Thomas Becon's and Martin Bucer's influence upon sixteenth-century Anglican theology.

An additional virtue characterizing Witte's methods is his realism combined with modesty and even "cheerfulness" respecting proposed solutions to notoriously difficult dilemmas affecting sex, marriage, and parenting. This is quite difficult, as suggested above, given the wide diversity of influences upon many family behaviors, the anger and controversy that attend many family issues, and potentially entrenched cultural, political, or religious forces. But Witte acknowledges and respects all of this, while simultaneously offering compassionate and helpful prescriptions *and* recognizing that the law can be an insufficient and blunt instrument. In a world awash with law reviews and other publications suggesting sometimes sweeping legal remedies for a wide variety of complex problems, Witte's methodological habit of exhibiting modesty regarding what the law can accomplish is refreshing and realistic. It also explicitly leaves open the possibility that families, civil society, and religions can play important roles in solving various problems plaguing family life.

Professor Witte's suggestions at the conclusion of his volume on nonmarital children are a good example. He disclaims the "neo-puritan path" of legally sanctioning nonmarital sexual relationships while supporting "aggressive" paternity and maternity suits, "stiff payments of child support," and even tort suits by children whose parents have abandoned or abused them. He concludes: "[g]overnment has no business policing the consensual sex of able adults. But a single impulsive act of conceiving a child should trigger a lifetime of responsibilities to care for that child."[45] Witte also leaves room for nonstate actors. "[W]e need to find creative new ways of re-engaging our families and neighborhoods, our worship centers and schools, our charities and voluntary associations int eh great task of responsible sex and childrearing."[46]

Finally, no discussion of the work of John Witte could be complete—or should likely even *begin*—without highlighting those personal virtues that infuse both his substantive and procedural accomplishments: his unfailingly gracious, hospitable demeanor, his measured and accurate speaking, his generosity in bringing new scholars along and introducing them to experienced scholars, and his convening colloquies and presentations that allow accomplished scholars to meet in an atmosphere of good will and fair play.

6   Conclusion

Family law can be a daunting scholarly arena today. The subjects of sex, marriage, and parenting are innately complex and increasingly controversial. It is easy to write and publish provocative pieces proposing even dramatic breaks with past norms and practices. It is far harder to hew a path that soberly consults and harmonizes history, religion, and myriad empirical sciences, defers to the needs of children and other vulnerable persons, and remembers that the family is inescapably both private and public, both sacred and secular. Professor Witte's body of work more than successfully navigates this path, and inspires not only emerging but also more experienced scholars to follow in his footsteps.

---

45   *The Sins of the Fathers*, 177.
46   Ibid., 178.

CHAPTER 6

John Witte, Jr.'s Contributions to Legal and Political Thought

Jonathan Chaplin

1 Introduction

John Witte's voluminous corpus has been occupied primarily with a cluster of closely linked concrete legal and constitutional questions, especially church-state relations, religious freedom, family and marriage, and the religious dimensions of human rights and constitutional democracy. These have been accompanied and undergirded by detailed historical forays into, especially, the contributions of the Protestant Reformation to these questions, cumulatively amounting to a substantial independent contribution to the history of political thought.

Witte's work also presupposes a broad stance on a recurring question in political theory, namely, the determination of the scope of state authority. While most lawyers do not trouble themselves much with this question, Witte is keenly aware of its importance. The state is the body authorized to make and enforce public laws and to oversee an array of private-law relations, concerning religion or anything else. Arguably, every law implies some sort of claim about the scope of state authority. When we ask, why is *this* law proscribing, prescribing, or permitting *that* kind of action?, we implicitly ask why the law-making body ordering that class of actions takes itself to be authorized to do so, and whether that assumption is valid both factually as a matter of law and normatively as a matter of principle. Witte's work speaks powerfully to the issue as it manifests itself in the state's interface with religion, at a time when the reach of state authority is extensive:

> The modern state, for better or worse, continues to reach deeply into virtually all aspects of modern life—through a vast network of laws and regulations on education, healthcare, family, zoning, taxation, workplace, food safety, nondiscrimination, charity, and more. Interaction between

the state and religious individuals and groups is inevitable, as is increased interaction among religious groups in our pluralistic society.[1]

The question of the scope of state authority is not only a question about the democratic legitimacy of state authority. For even if we have resolved that issue—for example, by pointing to the outcome of an election or, more fundamentally, to a constitutional provision mandating that governments be popularly elected or to a preamble asserting the supreme authority of "the people"—the matter of how far the writ of democratic authority may run has not yet been resolved. It is a cardinal assumption of a constitutional democracy that not everything a democratically elected government does or seeks to do is necessarily conducive to the public good, or even licit. The question of the scope of state authority cannot be resolved entirely within the fields of either constitutional doctrine or democratic theory, but requires appeal to a broader normative political (and, as will become clear, social) theory. Examining the implications of Witte's work for the question of state authority can serve as a window on his broader contributions in this field.

Witte has not yet elaborated at length what his own general understanding of the scope of state authority is, although elements of his view frequently surface in his writings. In a symposium on his book *Church, State, and Family*, I observed that this book does not offer an extended account of the scope of state authority with regard to family and marriage, but rather invokes a series of interlocking and mutually reinforcing norms to justify state action in particular cases of family regulation.[2] That also seems true of his other writings. This is not a criticism, for Witte writes as a legal historian specializing in American law, not as a legal philosopher or political theorist. And, in any case, a general conception of state authority can be credibly constructed only on the basis of extensive empirical evidence of actual state lawmaking, of the kind Witte supplies in abundance. But the lacuna invites the question of what a

---

1 John Witte, Jr., Joel A. Nichols, and Richard W. Garnett, *Religion and the American Constitutional Experiment*, 5th ed. (Oxford: Oxford University Press, 2022 [2000], 307. And: "Few religious bodies—and, indeed, few believers—can now avoid contact with the state's pervasive network of education, charity, welfare, child care, healthcare, family, construction, zoning, workplace, taxation, security, and other regulations. Today's governments not only enact and enforce laws, but they also make grants, extend loans, confer licenses, enter contracts, and control access to the civic and economic arenas. And so, both confrontation and cooperation with the modern welfare state are almost inevitable for any organized religion whose adherents and agencies venture beyond quiet worship to public engagement" (ibid., 355).
2 "The Role of the State in Regulating the Marital Family," in Book Review Symposium, *Journal of Law and Religion* 34 (2019): 509–19.

fuller statement of his assumed conception of state authority might look like. I acknowledge that, in responding to even one theme in such a capacious and creative body of work as John Witte's, it seems churlish to ask for more. Yet he has himself stated his aspiration to present a more systematic account of his legal and political thought, so I am delighted to be able to cheer him on in that task!

The first part of this chapter highlights five themes in early Calvinism that Witte has lifted up and put to work in his own legal and political thinking. The second part continues the story by highlighting Witte's deployment of four central Neo-Calvinist political principles, and showing how they are operative in his contemporary treatments of state authority. The conclusion briefly summarizes his chief contributions.

2 Early Calvinist Inspirations

Witte's extensive writings on the Reformation's impact on law and politics have substantially reinforced the claim that there is such a thing as "Protestant political thought."[3] He has added valuable grist to the mill of those who hold that such thought, in its early manifestations, is not a mere reprising of scholastic political thought, nor that, in the modern period, it is a mere accommodation to secularizing Enlightenment thought. On the contrary, Protestantism has been an original generative source for modern Western political thought and practice. Witte's historical writings—especially those on (European) Lutheranism, Anglicanism, and Calvinism and (American) Puritanism—have sharpened our awareness of the Protestant distinctiveness of these traditions,

---

3 Notably, John Witte, Jr., *The Reformation of Rights: Law, Religion and Human Rights in Early Modern Calvinism* (Cambridge: Cambridge University Press, 2007); id., *Law and Protestantism: The Legal Teachings of the Lutheran Reformation* (Cambridge: Cambridge University Press, 2002); id., *God's Joust, God's Justice: Law and Religion in the Western Tradition* (Grand Rapids: Eerdmans, 2005); id., *The Blessings of Liberty: Human Rights and Religious Freedom in the Western Legal Tradition* (Cambridge: Cambridge University Press, 2021), chaps. 1–5; id., *From Sacrament to Contract: Marriage, Religion, and Law in the Western Tradition*, 2nd ed (Louisville, KY: Westminster John Knox Press, 2012), chaps. 5–7; id., *Faith, Freedom, and Family: New Essays in Law and Religion*, ed. Norman Doe and Gary S. Hauk (Tübingen: Mohr Siebeck, 2021), chaps. 4–8, 15; id., "The Biography and Biology of Liberty: Abraham Kuyper and the American Experiment," in *Religion, Pluralism and Public Life: Abraham Kuyper's Legacy for the Twenty-First Century*, ed. Luis E. Lugo (Grand Rapids: Eerdmans, 2000), 243–62 (an expanded version of which appears as chap. 6 of *Reformation of Rights*). See also John Witte, Jr. and Frank S. Alexander, eds., *Modern Protestant Teachings on Law, Politics, and Human Nature* (New York: Columbia University Press, 2007).

while also deepening our appreciation of the deep diversity in what has nevertheless been a rancorous family.

While Witte's views on the role of the state draw eclectically from many historical and modern Christian and secular sources, his own affinities lie particularly with sixteenth- and seventeenth-century Calvinism, notably the thought of Calvin, Beza, Althusius, Milton, and the Puritans, and its modern rendition in Dutch Neo-Calvinism. Witte is drawn to these Calvinist thinkers, it seems, in part because they offer accounts that are both deeply grounded in distinctively Protestant convictions and capable of being elaborated in applicable constitutional principles—that is, ones lawyers can work with, as opposed to mere theological or ethical platitudes that cut no ice on matters of positive law. It is hardly surprising that Calvinism, founded by a civil lawyer, turned out more than its fair share of legal thinkers. But it is the cogency, not only the concreteness, of Calvinist arguments that Witte is drawn to, even when he departs from their substantive conclusions. In this section I offer my own interpretive reading of five abidingly significant insights he finds in such sources, accentuating how they speak to questions of state authority.[4]

First, Calvinist thinkers operate with a more pronounced distinction between ecclesial and political spheres than other Reformation thinkers, yet without lapsing into an Anabaptist dichotomy of church and world that would counsel Christian withdrawal from the exercise of (coercive) state authority. Witte draws particular attention to the way in which the Reformation served to roll back the jurisdictional overreach of the late medieval Roman Catholic Church.[5] By the early sixteenth century, the church was still exercising extensive authority over matters of marriage, family, property, and criminal law that, Calvinist thinkers judged, properly belonged to secular civil authorities.[6] A major consequence of the Reformation was that many such matters came to be removed from ecclesiastical jurisdiction and transferred to civil authorities (albeit, initially, ones that were required to be "godly"). It is worth noting that such areas had come to be included within church jurisdiction in the Middle Ages because, under the model of the *corpus Christianum*, it was assumed that church and state were populated by identical constituencies, even while ruled by two distinct authorities. The church, then, was no less "public" than the state, and so was entitled to exercise authority over many temporal matters

---

4   This reading inevitably passes over many other valuable insights he has retrieved from Calvinism and other sources and exploited to good contemporary effect.
5   Lutherans agreed on that point.
6   "Secular" in the sense of pertaining to matters of justice "of this age" (the *saeculum*), not "secularist" in the sense of closed to divine revelation.

that were somehow implicated in its specific sacerdotal remit (*res mixta*). While there were numerous turf wars in the Middle Ages over the precise boundaries of the respective jurisdictions of church and state, the Reformation inflicted eventually fatal damage on the assumption that memberships of church and state were coterminous.[7] "Public" now came to be seen as a wider category than "ecclesial," and "public authority" more clearly demarcated from church authority.

Second, within the civil realm, Calvinist thinkers offer more complex and compelling accounts than other Reformation streams of thought about the proper balance between claims of state authority, on one hand, and personal and social liberty on the other. The demand for freedom from ecclesial control of spiritual affairs naturally led to demands for greater freedom in civil affairs. The Reformation is often charged with unleashing the emergence of individualism, and some later strands certainly did. But, as Witte amply shows, the clamor for greater personal liberty in spiritual and civil matters was no casting off of social and political obligation, only its recalibration in the light of Luther's radical recovery of "the freedom of the Christian."[8] Thus, we see Calvinist thinkers affirming *both* the high priority of personal and associational liberties and rights, especially religious ones, *and* the solemn duty of political authorities, under God, to promote (coercive) civil justice across a whole society, in ways that would indeed curtail illicit claims to liberty.

Normatively, authority and freedom are not pitted against each other. Here Calvinist thought stands apart from forms of Lutheranism that so pitted them. It diverges even further from stands of liberalism that proceed from an imagined individual natural liberty in a hypothetical state of nature. Given such a baseline, the obliging force of political authority then appears as a problem to be solved, usually by some account of consent. Rather, as Witte shows, for Calvinists, while political authority is ultimately grounded in divine authority, so are the liberties and rights of the people; these are not the gift of the state.[9] A Christian tradition which produced the heretical and authoritarian theory of the divine right of kings also generated the radically liberating idea of the divine rights of citizens. Institutional authority and personal liberty are

---

7   "Eventually," because the assumption lingered on for decades after the Reformation. See Richard Hooker, *Of the Laws of Ecclesiastical Polity*, ed. Arthur Stephen McGrade (Cambridge: Cambridge University Press, 1989), 130.
8   Martin Luther, "The Freedom of a Christian" [1520], in *Luther: Selected Political Writings*, ed. J. M. Porter (Philadelphia: Fortress Press, 1974), 25–35.
9   *Reformation of Rights*, esp. chaps. 3, 4.

simultaneously constituted and limited by the requirements of a God-given order of justice that, in turn, must be specified in the rule of just law.

Calvinist thinkers did not, moreover, construe individual liberty and rights as incompatible with the state's complementary remit to promote public virtue. The task of the state is not confined to the negative, remedial function of enforcing a minimum threshold of civil order by restraining violence, disorder, theft, and so forth. The law could never be salvific, but it could and should prompt the virtuous public behavior necessary for the good order of society.[10] While Witte excludes from the scope of state authority today any remit actively to promote religion, and affirms a wide suite of modern liberties, he rejects the liberal egalitarian claim that the state should or could be neutral toward rival conceptions of the human good. On the contrary, he appears to endorse a limited version of state "perfectionism,"[11] as I think Kuyper did. It would be interesting to know whether and how Witte might elaborate such a defense.[12]

Third, Calvinist thinkers flesh out the content of justice in terms of principles of natural law that, while importantly clarified and deepened by scripture, are yet in principle accessible to all, even those whose reasoning faculties have been corrupted by sin. While Luther pitted freedom against law (except "the law of Christ," the moral demand of love), Calvin and his followers construed law as central to the larger ordering sovereignty of God over all human life, a sovereignty intended to promote the human good as well as God's glory. Calvin revived the standing of both natural and positive law in the early Protestant movement. In various historical studies, Witte shows how natural-law principles, and some of their outworkings in constitutional law and political institutions, continued to carry substantial public weight in Western polities, long after the time when the Bible could be cited as a shared public authority.[13]

Fourth, Calvinist thinkers accorded a much higher place to popular political participation than other strands of Reformation thought. Lutheranism and Anglicanism, for example, concentrated extensive spiritual and temporal

---

10   See *Faith, Freedom, and Family*, chap. 5.
11   See my "The Role of the State in Regulating the Marital Family," 511–12. See John Witte, Jr., introduction to John Witte, Jr. et al., eds, *The Impact of the Law on Character Formation, Ethical Education, and the Communication of Values in Late Modern Pluralistic Societies* (Leipzig: Evangelische Verlagsanstalt GmbH, 2021), 15–30.
12   An interesting conversation partner here would be fellow Kuyperian Nicholas Wolterstorff, who claims that Saint Paul offers grounds only for a protectionist, not a perfectionist, view of the state. Wolterstorff does not, however, deny that a perfectionist role might be defended on other grounds. See *The Mighty and the Almighty: An Essay in Political Theology* (Cambridge: Cambridge University Press, 2012), 101–02.
13   See, for example, *The Blessings of Liberty*, chap. 4.

authority in monarchs or princes, leaving them more vulnerable to authoritarian lapses (such as Tudor and Stuart Erastianism). Witte shows how Puritan covenant theology was a decisive influence here.[14] The Puritans argued that the "covenant of works," long deemed to have been made with Abraham and applying principally to the people of Israel (and codified in Torah), was in fact first made with Adam and thus embraced all humans. It was "a natural relation in which all persons participated," defining "every person's role, rights, and responsibilities in the unfolding of God's plan."[15] Puritans also transformed the "covenant of grace," formerly seen as a unilateral act of divine mercy, into a "bargained contract involving acts of divine will and human will."[16] Witte has observed how these advances proved decisive in paving the way for the later affirmation of a general freedom of religious conscience. But he also shows how they generated novel concepts of social, ecclesial, and political covenants that proved formative for Western politics.

The *social* covenant, for example, established the bonds of a society in which all were bound to display public virtue and contribute to the common good, and all were entitled to benefit from the services supplied by a variety of charitable and educational associations.[17] Every member shared in the responsibility to sustain a morally virtuous community, and the provision of many public goods was not exclusively, or even primarily, a direct duty of government. The social covenant, which Witte describes as "a recipe for both associational liberty and social pluralism,"[18] thus also worked against the state's assuming tasks that could be performed by other agents. Althusius had earlier developed a rich account of multiples types of covenantally constituted public and private bodies, each one exemplifying a functionally specific instance of "symbiotic association" and offering a distinctive contribution to the public good.[19] Such a model has the effect of simultaneously mandating and distributing authority

---

14 See "Biography and Biology," an extended account of which appears as chap. 5 of *Reformation of Rights*, and a brief summary of which is found at *Religion and the American Constitutional Experiment*, 37–42.
15 "Biography and Biology," 253.
16 Ibid., 253.
17 Ibid., 256.
18 Ibid., 257.
19 *Reformation of Rights*, 181–96. For a creative contemporary application of such a "consociational" model, see Luke Bretherton, *Resurrecting Democracy: Faith, Citizenship, and the Politics of a Common Life* (New York: Cambridge University Press, 2015), chap. 7; and Luke Bretherton, *Christ and the Common Life: Political Theology and the Case for Democracy* (Grand Rapids: Eerdmans, 2019), chap. 12.

within political institutions, and of circumscribing such authority by affirming the independent authority of other institutions.

The Puritan *political* covenant implied, in the first instance, a clearer jurisdictional separation of church and state than early Calvinists, such as Calvin and Beza, had been prepared to countenance. For the Puritans, "church and state were the two principal seats of authority within the broader social community, each formed by a further covenant among those who had already joined the social covenant."[20] Construed as "two separate covenantal associations, two coordinate seats of godly authority and power in society," each bore "a distinctive calling and responsibility, and ... a distinctive polity and practice that could not be confounded."[21] At the same time, church and state were to "cooperate in the achievement of the covenant ideals of the community," the state providing material and moral aid to the church,[22] and the church both teaching the faith and making available its own resources for the benefit of the wider community.[23]

In America, several of these forms of mutual service were later scaled back significantly, having been judged to run afoul of either the Free Exercise Clause or the Establishment Clause (some of these curtailments Witte endorses, others not).[24] By contrast, another momentous upshot of the Puritan political covenant—its democratic implications—expanded in significance. In the political covenant, the people themselves, not only God and ruler, were seen as party to the covenant by which state authority is grounded and circumscribed.[25] This tripartite covenant proved to be a crucial feeder for later liberal social-contract theories founded on popular consent. Such theories, in turn, facilitated the institution of a system of representative democracy based (in time) on universal adult franchise.[26]

---

20   "Biography and Biology," 257.
21   Ibid., 258. Thus, for example, "Political officials ... were prohibited from holding ministerial office, from interfering in internal ecclesiastical government, from performing sacerdotal functions, or from censuring the official conduct of a cleric who was also a citizen of the commonwealth" (258).
22   For example, by provision of public lands, the collection of tithes, the granting of tax exemptions, or the imposition of Sunday or blasphemy laws (ibid., 258).
23   "Biography and Biology," 259. For example, by making their buildings available for public uses such as education and the registration of births, marriages, and deaths.
24   The scaling back is extensively documented in *Religion and the American Constitutional Experiment*.
25   "Biography and Biology," 258–61.
26   Ibid., 261. See also John Witte, Jr., ed., *Christianity and Democracy in Global Context*, repr. ed. (London: Routledge, 2018 [1993]).

Fifth, the Calvinist recognition that human sinfulness tainted not only personal life but also social institutions—an early anticipation of "structural sin"[27]—led them to establish an array of structural safeguards against the abuse of authority in church and state. For the Puritans, these included term limits, a separation of powers, a federal distribution of authority, legal codification (to make the law clear and accessible to all), democratic election, and the demand that officials be people of faith and virtue. Witte shows that many such ideas were formative on the design of early state and federal constitutions in America.[28]

All five Calvinist insights carry implications for the scope of state authority. The first both *legitimates* the application of state authority in certain matters of public order that fall outside the unique spiritual jurisdiction of the church, and equally *proscribes* the state from intruding into those areas of spiritual jurisdiction. The second resists authoritarian construals of state authority by insisting that the same order of civil justice underwriting such authority simultaneously hedges it around with robust individual and associational rights that are not concessions of the state but objective demands to which the state must defer. It also affirms a role for state law in fostering virtuous behavior conducive to the public good. The third implies that determining what justice requires is not the exclusive preserve of those appointed to be (or at least claiming to be) mediators of special divine revelation, but is in principle available to all, thereby democratizing the process by which public normativity was determined. The fourth lays the foundation for the claim that the exercise of governmental authority must be accountable to the people in whose name it is exercised, even if not simply responsive to every popular demand. This point also amounts to the claim that while democracy never guarantees just laws, it is a significant inhibitor of governmental acts that might ride roughshod over the people's fundamental rights and interests. The fifth tempers the exercise of the will of both people and government by erecting a lattice of constitutional safeguards against potential abuses of authority.[29]

---

27 Or, more correctly, a revival of the Augustinian idea that a society can be misshapen by its disordered loves.

28 "Biography and Biology," 260–01.

29 The fourth and fifth points loom large in Reinhold Niebuhr's distinctively Protestant account of democracy in *The Children of Light and the Children of Darkness: A Vindication of Democracy and a Critique of Its Traditional Defenders* (New York: Charles Scribner's Sons, 1944).

3   Kuyperian Trajectories, Then and Now

When we turn to the modern Calvinist sources on which Witte draws, we find substantial continuity with earlier sources, but also striking evolutions. Pride of place here goes to the late nineteenth- and early twentieth-century century Dutch Neo-Calvinist church leader, theologian, institution builder, and politician Abraham Kuyper.[30] Witte deploys Kuyperian insights selectively, and critically, for his own purposes, acknowledging that it is "increasingly a background orientation" rather than an explicit focus.[31] He usually deploys such insights without announcing them as such, not least because they can be and have been grounded in alternative sources, religious and secular. Indeed, very likely he has himself struck upon many such insights in quite other sources. For example, his championing of associational liberty echoes many Tocquevillian themes. In any thinker, we need to distinguish what philosophers of science call the "context of discovery" (the route by which an idea was encountered) and the "context of justification" (the arguments supporting it). So I make no claim that these discrete Kuyperian insights are *uniquely* Kuyperian or even Calvinist. I do think, however, that when we put together the full package of such insights, we find a model that discloses the special charisms of such origins.

It is important to note that Witte often draws on Kuyperian insights for their relevance to the American context, a task made easier by the fact that Kuyper himself spoke enthusiastically of the formative impact of Calvinism on America.[32] We might say that, for Witte, Neo-Calvinism (whatever its flaws) serves as one highly instructive working example of what Calvinist legal and political thought might look like when it encountered the radically altered conditions of a modernity already experiencing advanced secularization and pluralization.[33] In what follows, I take my cue from the four central constitutional principles that Witte notes were appreciated by Kuyper as having been most fully realized in America, and which Witte himself commends: freedom of religion; a broader defense of liberties and rights; associational liberty; and

---

30   For an accessible introduction to Kuyper's thought, see, for example, Jessica R. Joustra and Robert J. Joustra, eds., *Calvinism for a Secular Age: A Twenty-First Century Reading of Abraham Kuyper's Stone Lectures* (Downers Grove, IL: InterVarsity Press, 2022).

31   *Faith, Freedom, and Family*, 694.

32   See Kuyper, *Lectures on Calvinism* (Grand Rapids: Eerdmans, 1931), chap. 3. However, Witte critiques Kuyper's flattering account of the American tradition ("Biography and Biology," 251–53).

33   Hence the apt title of James E. Bratt's biography of Kuyper: *Abraham Kuyper: Modern Calvinist, Christian Democrat* (Grand Rapids: Eerdmans, 2013).

political pluralism.[34] I indicate how these principles serve as orientations for his treatments of concrete contemporary issues where the scope of state authority is implicated, devoting most attention to the first principle (coupled with the second) and the third (coupled with the fourth).

4   State Authority and Religion

The first principle is a robust commitment to the protection of freedom of conscience and religion, of its various forms of public manifestation, and of its outworking in a regime of "confessional pluralism" in which many religious and secular visions are protected, and in some cases harnessed, in the public realm.[35] These commitments in turn imply "the presumptive equality of all faiths before the law, the disestablishment of religion, and the basic separation of the offices and operations of church and state."[36] Kuyper takes the tradition forward here by radicalizing ideas already anticipated in later Puritan thought. Thus, against the Dutch Reformed Church (Hervormde Kerk) of his day, he explicitly rejected the earlier Calvinist and Presbyterian principle that the state had a duty to enforce true faith and offer special privileges to the true church. His motto was "a free church in a free state,"[37] under which banner he campaigned tenaciously for a state recognition of confessional pluralism in many sectors of Dutch society. The upshot was a theological model of church-state relations allowing clear jurisdictional differentiation between them, but also many forms of constructive cooperation—modern renditions of the "mutual service" between the two bodies applauded by the Puritans. This did not, however, preclude Kuyper from holding that there might still be a recognition of God in the constitution, and that the state might maintain laws

---

34   *Faith, Freedom, and Family*, 695–98; see also chap. 10 therein. Witte expounds Kuyper's account of these principles more fully in "The Biography and Biology of Liberty."

35   Witte, *The Blessings of Liberty*; and Witte, Nichols, and Garnett, *Religion and the American Constitutional Experiment*. It is worth noting that the specific modern religious freedoms that most contemporary religious commentators, including Witte, endorse are much closer to what Witte identifies in the latter book as the evangelical stream in early America than to the Puritan one (ibid., 42–46).

36   *Faith, Freedom, and Family*, 696. See also "Biography and Biology," 245. Elsewhere, Witte lists the six "essential liberties" widely recognized in early America: liberty of conscience; free exercise of religion; religious pluralism; religious equality; separation of church and state; and no establishment of a national religion (*Religion and the American Constitutional Experiment*, 2).

37   *Lectures on Calvinism*, 99.

against blasphemy or in support of sabbath observance, conclusions to which Witte is unfavorable.

With great erudition, Witte has traced the historical lineage of these contemporary commitments in the United States, enumerated their detailed legal implications, analyzed their shifting constitutional standing in recent decades, warned of their political and legal fragility, and offered remedies where they are inadequately codified or implemented. Welcoming the new era in America's experiment with religious freedom since 2012, he cites favorably these illustrations of the Supreme Court's strengthened protection:

> [T]he Court has rejected establishment clause challenges to local legislative prayers and to a large memorial cross standing prominently on state land. It has strengthened the autonomy of religious organizations in making labor and employment decisions. It has insisted that religious and nonreligious schools and students receive state aid equally as a matter of free exercise rights. It has enjoined several public regulations, including certain Covid-related restrictions, that discriminated against religion. It has strengthened the constitutional and statutory claims of religious individuals and groups to exemptions from general laws that burdened conscience. It has insisted that death row inmates have access to their chaplains to the very end. And the Court has even allowed the collection of money damages from government officials who violated individuals' religious freedom.[38]

I will not interrogate these specific examples, but simply note their importance for the question of how state authority is circumscribed. Witte celebrates the new era as, overall, a welcome advance in protecting religious freedom. Implicitly, he takes it as evidence of a significant improvement in the (American) state's "religious literacy." It reveals that the state is learning better how to recognize the forcefulness, distinctiveness, pervasiveness, and particularity of religious claims and identities in the public realm, and of the variegated social and institutional forms in which they need to manifest themselves. A narrow strict separationism, by contrast, misconstrues religion as a matter of private individual conscience. Ironically, this could lead both to an underestimation of the scope of state authority (for example, by leaving some religious claims unvindicated) and to an overestimation of it (for example, by imposing improper burdens on religious associations).

---

38 *Religion and the American Constitutional Experiment*, 6.

But the state's heightened religious literacy does not amount to an improper endorsement of religion. Rather it shows the state's enhanced awareness of religion's true character both as a universal human impulse and as a powerful public reality that cannot be marginalized, about which the state cannot be blind, and that shapes the state's performance of its own task. This is a particularly clear example of an important wider consideration. It shows that the determination of the scope of state authority is necessarily bound up with the state's ability properly to identify the highly complex fabric of the public realm which it is tasked to oversee. The state can govern justly only that which it knows truthfully (even though that truth is fiercely contested in democratic debate).

The point is borne out in relation to the second Kuyperian principle Witte alludes to: the need for a broader defense of liberties and rights, beyond religious ones.[39] While Witte does not set out a general theory of liberties and rights, he does allude illuminatingly to many different kinds of liberties and rights throughout his corpus. More than many other defenders of religious liberties and rights, he shows how these are enmeshed in a mutually supporting array of other indispensable liberties and rights that demand realization, even as they must be judiciously balanced against each other and against a range of duties, powers, and other legal relations.[40] Here he demonstrates the importance of not just religious literacy but a broad rights literacy.

This is especially clear in his work on the family (on which more below), and on human rights. His writings on human rights avoid the abstractness and otherworldliness often plaguing purely philosophical or theological defenses of them.[41] Witte robustly vindicates the concept of human rights against religious critics who decry them as, at bottom, mere assertions of subjective human will, lacking any intrinsic limitation. Yet his wide-ranging work in this area cumulatively shows how human rights are not infinitely inflatable moral claims. Rather, they have been progressively incorporated into positive legal codes that, however imperfectly formulated, serve as highly specific benchmarks for the proper discharge of state authority—its use *and* its restraint. He shows how the legal specification of many human rights applies pressure on state officials to lend exceptional weight to certain fundamental human interests

---

39   *Faith, Freedom, and Family*, 697.
40   See, for example, John Witte, Jr., "Ordered Freedom: Herman Dooyeweerd's Emerging Theory of Rights," in *Faith, Freedom, and Family*, 315–34.
41   See, for example, *Faith, Freedom, and Family*, chaps. 17, 18, 23, 24. John Witte, Jr., introduction to John Witte, Jr. and Frank S. Alexander, eds, *Christianity and Human Rights: An Introduction* (Cambridge: Cambridge University Press, 2010), 8–43; John Witte, Jr., introduction to John Witte, Jr. and Johan D. van der Vyver, eds, *Religious Human Rights in Global Perspective: Religious Perspectives* (The Hague: Martinus Nijhoff, 1996), xvii–xxxv.

that have proved especially vulnerable to state excess or neglect, notably the interests of women, children, vulnerable minorities, or political dissidents.[42] Such a lending weight might demand either active intervention to protect vulnerable interests (the introduction of child-protection laws, for example), or simply inaction: to protect life and liberty, often all that the state has to do is do no harm.

Witte is fully aware that many legal rights are not human rights, that all rights must be continually balanced against other rights and against duties, and that they can be promulgated and enforced only by competent lawmaking authorities. But he shows compellingly how embedding a special class of human rights in law has today become one indispensable means of determining the proper scope of state authority. As he puts it, human rights have become "the *jus gentium* of our times."[43] A proper grasp of human rights has become an essential part of the rights literacy that the state, and its citizens, need.

Let me now return to Witte's treatment of religious freedom, which attends to just the kind of complexity and concreteness alluded to. Witte amply documents the past record of constitutional and judicial confusion on the public place of religion in America, especially the lamentable absence of consistency in much Supreme Court Establishment Clause jurisprudence.[44] Against such a background, we can say that one of Witte's most significant contributions to an account of the scope of state authority is the formulation of an "integrated understanding of the First Amendment religion clauses." He captures it thus:

> The free exercise clause ... outlaws government *proscriptions* of religion—governmental actions that unduly burden the conscience, unduly

---

[42] Witte's work on the legal standing of Islamic sharia councils is an instructive case study of this concern. See, for example, *Faith, Freedom, and Family*, chap. 32; John Witte, Jr., *Church, State, and Family: Reconciling Traditional Teachings and Modern Liberties* (Cambridge: Cambridge University Press, 2019), chap. 10; Joel A. Nichols and John Witte, Jr., "National Report United States of America: Religious Law and Religious Courts as a Challenge to the State," in *Religious Law and Religious Courts as a Challenge to the State: Legal Pluralism in Comparative Perspective: Proceedings of the 35th Congress of the Society of Comparative Law in Bayreuth, September 10–12, 2015*, ed. Uwe Kischel (Tübingen: Mohr Siebeck, 2015), 83–111.

[43] *Reformation of Rights*, 342.

[44] "Few areas of law remain so riven with wild generalizations and hair-splitting distinctions, so given to grand statements of principle and petty applications of precept, so rife with selective readings of history and inventive renderings of precedent. Few areas of law hold such a massive jumble of juxtaposed doctrines, methods, and rules" (*Religion and the American Constitutional Experiment*, 304). It is, he thinks, approaching greater consistency today (ibid., 305).

restrict religious action and expression, intentionally discriminate against religion, or invade the autonomy of churches and other religious bodies. The establishment clause, in turn, outlaws government *prescriptions* of religion—actions that coerce the conscience, unduly mandate forms of religious action and expression, intentionally discriminate in favor of religion, or improperly ally the state with churches or other religious bodies. Both the free exercise clause and the establishment clause thereby provide complementary protections to the first principles of the American experiment—liberty of conscience, free exercise of religion, religious pluralism, religious equality, separation of church and state, and no establishment of religion.[45]

Further, he observes (commenting on the Establishment Clause) that such an understanding allows for a clearer account of the "mutual service" that should pertain between state and religion today:

> The distinction between religious and political authorities and institutions does not require the exclusion from the public square of faith or of the faithful; it permits healthy and productive cooperation in the pursuit of public goods like education, healthcare, and social welfare. The healthy secularity that the establishment clause, correctly interpreted, promotes means that government officials have no constitutional business interfering in the internal affairs of peaceable and voluntary religious groups, and also means that religious officials have no constitutional business converting the offices of government into instruments of their mission and ministry.[46]

This is a bold and promising account which I strongly endorse.[47] However, as Witte would undoubtedly concede, it leaves unresolved important general questions about the scope of state authority. I mention just two.

---

45 Ibid., 7; see also 305.
46 Ibid, 307. Further: "Government has no business funding, sponsoring, or actively involving itself in the liturgy, worship, or core religious exercises of a particular religious school, group, or official. Religious groups have no business drawing on government sponsorship or direct funding for their core religious activities. Nor do religious groups have any constitutional business insisting that government cede or delegate to them core political responsibilities. All such conduct violates the principle of separation of church and state and is properly outlawed by the establishment clause" (307).
47 I argue the case for the disestablishment of the Church of England in similar terms in *Beyond Establishment: Resetting Church-State Relations in England* (London: SCM, 2022).

One is whether religion should continue to be regarded as "special" by the state (as distinct from by religious adherents). Witte echoes the claim of many religious commentators that religious freedom, as the "first freedom," rightly enjoys a special constitutional standing:

> The founders understood that religion is more than simply another form of speech and assembly, of privacy and autonomy; it requires and deserves separate constitutional treatment. The founders thus placed freedom of religion *alongside* freedom of speech, press, and assembly, giving religious claimants special protection and restricting government in its interaction with religion.[48]

The claim to the specialness of religion can come in two forms, and Witte seems to endorse both. One is that, as a matter of historical fact, religious freedom has served as an "icebreaker" for the law's subsequent recognition of many other civil freedoms, such as freedom of speech and freedom of association. This is partly a story about the journey of religious and other freedoms in the West.[49] Another is that religious freedom can claim a certain normative primacy over others, insofar as the freedom to express convictions and hold identities that are most fundamental to human life can be seen to undergird and mandate claims to protection of many other deep human concerns. This is a claim about the universality of the specialness of religion. It implies a rejection of the suggestion that religious freedom claims are merely Western constructions that carry less weight in other cultures.

Others claim that according religion special status in law risks releasing religion from the critical scrutiny that its dark sides demand,[50] or that religious claims are in any case adequately accommodated under other constitutional protections, such as freedom of conscience, speech, expression, and association.[51] The U.S. debate is framed by the fact that religion is indeed accorded elevated constitutional status in the First Amendment. The jurisprudential trend in much of Europe, however, has been toward generic protection, as seen in the emergence of the legal formula of "freedom of religion *or* belief," and

---

48   *Religion and the American Constitutional Experiment*, 343–44. See also ibid., 203–05.
49   Witte contrasts the chronology of rights affirmations in Catholicism (where religious rights came last) with that in Calvinism (where they came first). *The Reformation of Rights*, 330.
50   *Religion and the American Constitutional Experiment*, 350.
51   See, for example, Jocelyn McClure and Charles Taylor, *Secularism and Freedom of Conscience* (Cambridge, MA: Harvard University Press, 2011); and Cécile Laborde, *Liberalism's Religion* (Cambridge, MA: Harvard University Press, 2017), chap. 2.

the assessment of conscientious nonreligious belief claims in the same terms as those of religious claims. Debate is ongoing as to whether this is causing a general weakening of religious claims.[52] It shows, again, that determining the scope of state authority presupposes a correct identification, and naming, of the societal realities which the state is called upon to oversee and order accordingly.

The second question is how the state is to resolve conflicts between apparently competing equality claims, both those within the field of religious equality and those between religious equality and other forms of equality. Regarding the first, suppose the state does affirm the use of Christian (or other) prayers in the official business of a state legislature or local government (as distinct from permitting on-site voluntary prayers, but outside official business). As Witte notes, in U.S. law this might be justified on the grounds of either free exercise or history and tradition.[53] Interestingly, he defends the latter on democratic, rather than traditionalist, grounds: "So long as private parties are not coerced into participating in or endorsing this religious iconography, and so long as government strives to be inclusive in its depictions and representations, there is nothing wrong with a democratic government reflecting and representing the traditional religious values and beliefs of its people."[54]

Critics might suggest that such a decision nevertheless breaches the Establishment Clause. It might implicate the state, if not in "coercing the conscience" of nonprofessing legislators (they could step outside), then at least in "improperly allying the state" with (or endorsing) one faith over others.[55] Against that concern, permitting local legislative prayers might be thought justifiable by appeal to the principle of a vertical distribution of authority across different tiers of government. The argument might be that, up to a point, such tiers are at liberty to apply the Establishment Clause differently, perhaps by enjoying a margin of appreciation in balancing this constraining clause against the more permissive principles of federalism and localism. But how would one go about balancing the two principles, each of which has robust independent legitimacy?

---

52 See *Faith, Freedom, and Family*, chaps. 8, 9.
53 *Religion and the American Constitutional Experiment*, 227–28, 285–89, 351–54.
54 Ibid., 352.
55 There is a growing European debate over how far "tradition" is being invoked to conceal an entrenched privilege enjoyed by a "Christian (or Christian-secular) hegemony," to the detriment of minorities. See Sophie Anne Lauwers, "Religion, Secularity, Culture? Investigating Christian Privilege in Western Europe," *Ethnicities* 23, no. 3 (June 2022): 403–25. Witte is fully aware of the importance of religious freedom for minorities; see *Faith, Freedom, and Family*, chap. 22.

Or take a case where the claims of religion seem to run up against other dimensions of the state's commitments to equality.[56] Suppose, for example, that the state may indeed mandate equal access for religious schools to state aid, so as to avoid discrimination against religion.[57] Critics might counter that this could skew public funding toward middle-class districts where private religious schools mostly flourish, thereby disadvantaging poorer families and neighborhoods. How is the claim to equal *religious* treatment to be balanced against the (presumably?) equally important principle of *social* equality? And might not the federal principle also permit differential regimes of religious school funding across different states or localities; and if not, why not?[58]

In both examples, the question is why state authority imposes equal treatment in one case but not the other. A full answer would require a broader account of the principle of the political equality of all citizens, its differentiated applications across a range of instances of law and public policy, and, widening the lens, how the state's satisfaction of equality claims is to be balanced against a range of other equally if not more compelling state duties.

I do not at all suggest there are easy answers to these questions, nor imply that the prudential application of broad principles of religious freedom will always generate neat resolution in concrete cases.[59] Certainly, Witte's "integrated understanding"—no government proscriptions of or prescriptions of religion—offers a substantial advance in clarifying the permissible scope of state authority in this area. I merely offer two remarks on the clarificatory task.

---

56 The primary conflict here in recent decades, of course, has been between religious equality or liberty claims and claims regarding sex and gender.
57 See *Religion and the American Constitutional Experiment*, chap. 9.
58 Champions of religious freedom do not, of course, always agree on specific cases. In June 2023, an Oklahoma school board voted to approve an online Catholic public charter school that would serve K-12 students across the state, which would make it the nation's first publicly funded religious charter school; see Nuria Martinez-Keel, "Oklahoma Board Approves Nation's First State-Funded Catholic School," *USA Today*, Jun. 5, 2023. Witte's co-author Richard Garnett defends the decision on the grounds that governments "may not discriminate against religious institutions that are otherwise eligible for public benefits and contracts"; see Richard Garnett, "Oklahoma Catholic Charter School Passes Constitutional Muster," *National Review*, Jun. 13, 2023. John Inazu, by contrast, holds that governments are *entitled* to fund religious charter schools, but not *required* to; see John Inazu, "Did Oklahoma Just Violate the Establishment Clause?," substack.com, Jun. 16, 2023.
59 Witte observes that part of the "back-and-forth" on such questions "is typical of any area of constitutional law in action, particularly when it also involves larger questions of federalism, separation of powers, and the nature of judicial review." *Religion and the American Constitutional Experiment*, 278.

One is that, while a more fully articulated account of state authority would not dissolve tensions about the state's role in religion, it might serve to bring them into useful conversation with parallel tensions across the many other dimensions of the state's task where the balancing of multiple complex demands also comes with the territory. Could the case of religious freedom prompt new expressions of sector-specific literacy that might be useful for state regulation of, for example, the business, health, or environmental sectors (or vice versa)?

The other is that Witte's work clearly points up how the constraints arising from constantly shifting historical and political contexts preclude full consistency in the application of state authority in this area. Witte rightly criticizes, for example, the "unrealistic and ahistorical spirit" of strict separationism in regard to religion and education.[60] Even if we could secure broad agreement on an integrated understanding of state authority vis-á-vis religion, these First Amendment border disputes are, in any case, going to be thrashed out agonistically in particular contexts, with rival protagonists employing, or weighting, different principles differently in pursuit of competing intuitions about desirable outcomes. To have that sobering conclusion elaborated across different policy sectors would itself be a useful exercise.[61]

5   State Authority, Nonstate Associations, and Subnational Bodies

The next Kuyperian principle I want to highlight as one of Witte's important contributions is his robust affirmation of associational liberty—what Kuyper called sphere sovereignty.[62] This is the notion that "standing between the state and the individual, there are many other spheres, structures, or institutions of

---

[60]   *Religion and the American Constitutional Experiment*, 279. And: "Accommodating old religious traditions in modern American public life can sometimes be a bit messy or clumsy. It is always tempting to start over, especially when standing at a clean blackboard, opening a new document, or starting the first page of a new law review article. But as Justice Souter reminded us, 'The world is not made brand new every morning'" (ibid., 353).

[61]   Adrian Vermeule's reflections on the role of "determination" (*determinatio*) in the application of natural-law principles, in his case mostly within administrative law, may be instructive here. He presents a fairly sanguine reading of judicial consistency in this area. See Adrian Vermeule, *Common Good Constitutionalism* (London: Polity, 2022); and Cass R. Sunstein and Adrian Vermeule, *Law and Leviathan: Redeeming the Administrative State* (Cambridge, MA: Harvard University Press, 2020).

[62]   *Faith, Freedom, and Family*, 697. On Puritan and civic republican defenses of a generic associational plurality ("structural pluralism"), see *Religion and the American Constitutional Experiment*, 70–71.

authority and liberty [family, church, corporation, school, union, and other voluntary associations] that are important parts of how to order liberty and structure the rule of law in a given society."[63] The legal rights and powers of such associations are not creations of the state (even where it offers legal forms that recognize them). Independent associations should be seen as *jurisgenerative*.

Witte's extensive work on marriage and family, as two tightly related forms of human association, has made a major contribution to this theme.[64] *Church, State, and Family*, for example, documents how the unique standing of the marital family, as a foundational association for the whole of society, has evolved historically, and argues cogently and at times controversially for a particular set of rights and duties attaching to it. Such rights and duties reflect what he identifies as the six dimensions of the marital family: natural, communicative, spiritual, social, economic, and contractual.[65] These "multidimensional" rights and liberties are not simply asserted by the wills of the separate members but arise from the network of relations (marriage, parenthood, childhood) that constitute a multidimensional association displaying a wide array of inherent needs, interests, capacities, and freedoms (albeit, assuming very different forms in particular instances and across different cultures). The liberty of this association is given by its ontology—a point of general importance for a theory of associations.

Most of Witte's other contributions in this area arise from his extensive and detailed work on the rights and autonomy of religious associations, especially schools, and churches or other worshipping communities.[66] The liberty of such bodies is, in part, a natural and necessary outworking of individual freedom of religion, since the individual pursuit of religious goals, whether worship, proclamation, social service, or education, typically requires corporate outworking.[67] To this extent, Witte's account converges with liberal accounts that derive associational rights from individual rights. But his account of religious associations also shows the limits of such liberal accounts. For the

---

63 *Faith, Freedom, and Family*, 696. See also "Biography and Biology," 246.
64 See, for example, *Faith, Freedom, and Family*, chaps. 25–37.
65 *Church, State, and Family*, chap. 7.
66 See, for example, *Religion and the American Constitutional Experiment*, chaps, 9, 10, 12.
67 "Just as every person has the right to seek religious truth and to cling to it when it is found, so religious communities have the right to teach and hold to their own doctrines. Just as every person ought to be free from official coercion when it comes to religious practices or professions, so religious institutions are entitled to be free to govern their own internal affairs without state interference. Just as every person has the right to select their own religious teachings and authorities, religious organizations have the right to select their own ministers and teachers" (*Religion and the American Constitutional Experiment*, 339).

corporate pursuit of even individual goals also demands *sui generis* rights to associational self-governance that cannot be derived wholly from the rights of individual members. These corporate rights are essential if associations are to be able to set and sustain their religious identities and purposes, free from fear that individual members might invoke state authority to subvert these identities or purposes on the grounds that they breach their supposed individual rights. As Witte puts it: "Ensuring that religious organizations retain rights *as organizations* to discharge their own appropriate authority and exercise their own appropriate jurisdiction is a core part of religious freedom."[68] Thus, religious associations must be free "to organize, structure, and govern themselves in accordance with their religious mission, character, and commitments," and this in two distinct ways.

> First, they voluntarily structure themselves internally in ways that conform to their religious beliefs or desires—or simply accord with what they think will be an effective governance model. Second, religious groups are required to structure themselves for external purposes in a legally sanctioned form so that they may enjoy the rights, benefits, and protections of secular legal status.[69]

Witte underlines the importance of establishing the correct legal form so that religious associations are treated, as far as possible, in accordance with their self-chosen identity rather than being forced to modify it merely for reasons of compliance.[70] He is alert to the ongoing worry regarding "the extent to which the state is defining and shaping the religious structure or merely reflecting (sometimes poorly) the preexisting religious structures that communities of faith have voluntarily created."[71]

---

68 Ibid., 310.
69 Ibid., 311.
70 Religious associations "have the right to be free from undue government interference with, influence over, or control of their internal activities. When religious organizations choose to participate in governmental programs and benefits, they should be allowed to do so equally without the establishment clause acting as an obstacle. When they choose to assist in providing social services, even using government funds, they should be allowed to do so fairly but on their own terms, so long as they do not violate the free exercise rights of the users of their services. When they resort to civil courts for resolution of internal disputes, their internal decisions about internal matters should be respected" (*Religion and the American Constitutional Experiment*, 339–40).
71 Ibid., 313. See also Julian Rivers's chapter herein, on the limitations of a jurisdictional approach to religious autonomy.

This conception of associational autonomy could usefully be generalized in two ways in the construction of a fuller account of the scope of state authority. First, it might be broadened to include many more (perhaps all) "expressive associations," including many committed to nonreligious beliefs or identities. Associational religious freedom naturally extends into a general "expressive freedom of association."[72] Arguably, all the following claims of corporate religious freedom noted by Witte apply prima facie to nonreligious expressive associations:

> churches that seek to keep their property from a dissident faction; religious schools that seek to hire like-minded believers and fire those who fall aside; voluntary religious student groups that wish to share facilities and funds on an equal basis with nonreligious groups; nonprofit social service organizations that seek to serve vulnerable members of society while holding true to their core beliefs; and even for-profit organizations and entities that seek to participate in the economic marketplace without sacrificing their convictions.[73]

If so, that might have a bearing on whether the state should regard religious associational rights as special.

Second, expressive associational freedom is but one instance of a generic associational freedom essential to a healthy civil society. The state must facilitate, via a variety of legal and policy instruments, a broad regime of protection and support for multiple independent associations pursuing any number of licit purposes. As Witte has shown, expressive freedom itself rests upon the ability of the association to exercise an array of other associational rights and powers, such as the right to legal personality (necessary for standing), to determine its internal constitution, to own and dispose of property, to enter into employment, service, or other contracts, to choose a location, and to pursue any purposes consistent with its articles of association (where it has them).

While the legal dimensions of this theme have not yet penetrated far into mainstream social and political theory, it only takes a moment's thought to see how essential such an array of rights and powers is to the proper functioning of bodies like businesses, universities, trade unions, professional associations,

---

72   William A. Galston, *Liberal Pluralism: The Implications of Value Pluralism for Political Theory and Practice* (Cambridge: Cambridge University Press, 2002), chap. 10. See also John Inazu, *Confident Pluralism: Surviving and Thriving through Deep Difference* (Chicago: University of Chicago Press, 2016), chap. 2.

73   *Religion and the American Constitutional Experiment*, 341.

voluntary bodies, cultural organizations, and many more. Critically, the legally sanctioned forms in which such bodies structure themselves require that the state, again, accurately identify and defer to the entities it is engaging with and not force them into a mold that would skew those identities. Thus, for example, to offer to a university a legal structure designed primarily for a commercial enterprise, or incrementally to manipulate it—for example by perverse financial incentives—to mimic such an enterprise would be an improper exercise of state authority.

A defense of the rights of religious associations would, then, be strengthened were it shown to be one instance of a generic theory of associational rights with wider implications for determining the scope of state authority.[74] Such a theory would need to be attentive to the ontology of many distinct types of association. There would, of course, be many commonalities across such associations that might be reflected in shared legal forms—for example, associations of different types being grouped into a single category of charities for tax purposes, or elements of corporate law applying to both for-profit enterprises and social enterprises. But there would be other distinctive elements of associations that the state would need to attend to if its authority were to be exercised appropriately and justly.[75] For example, the importance of a legal distinction between a marriage and a privately ordered contract is demonstrated cogently in *Church, State, and Family* (chapter 11). This is not because the state is bound to prefer Christian or traditional marriage, but because it has duties to protect the rights of weaker parties, typically women and children, that might be rendered vulnerable if regulated merely under easily dissoluble interindividual contracts. The importance of a distinction between an expressive and a nonexpressive association is also clear from Witte's argument that associations established primarily to advance religious (or other conscientious) purposes may need specific exemptions not required by others.

---

[74] A significant debate in political theory emerging today concerns how claims to associational autonomy can be reconciled with the claim of the state to "democratic sovereignty." "Pluralists," such as those who, like Witte, champion "corporate religious liberty," sometimes find themselves at odds with "democratic sovereigntists," such as liberal egalitarians like Laborde, in *Liberalism's Religion*, chap. 5. The latter argue that, however much the state may defer to associational autonomy, only it retains the final authority to determine the precise legal scope of such autonomy. Witte's work on sharia councils shows that he broadly accepts this latter claim, but his work on religious associations shows he would argue for wider associational autonomy than many liberal egalitarians.

[75] U.S. lawyers will know the fine-grained distinctions between different kinds of association recognized in U.S. law. On the options for religious bodies, see *Religion and the American Constitutional Experiment*, 311–15.

Again, the point applies generally: just as the state's proper discernment of the societal realities it oversees requires religious literacy when ordering religious matters, so it requires a general associational literacy when ordering the broad range of matters pertaining to many types of association (religious or otherwise). Otherwise it risks neglecting, mistreating, or flattening them.

So far I have considered the state's role in protecting the integrity and self-governance rights of associations. Witte is aware, too, that associational liberty serves broader societal purposes beyond the protection of these internal features. One purpose is to facilitate the emergence of organized conduits for the forming and flowering of individual capacities, protecting "important opportunities for the individual to flourish in externally guided but self-chosen ways."[76] A second purpose is to acknowledge that free, self-governing centers of social power, other than the state, act as "bulwarks against state tyranny," preserving the independence of civil society against improper state intrusion and, by restraining the state, supporting the effectiveness of the rule of law.[77] These purposes have been amply treated by theorists of civil society, associative democracy, and moral pluralism.[78] This work is relevant in disclosing how individual associations function with larger, complex associative matrices that, as important components of public space, may also require legal protection and support. A third societal purpose, still to be adequately acknowledged in the mainstream, is to protect the unique qualities of religious associations, allowing them to offer contributions to the common good that might not otherwise be forthcoming. As Witte puts it:

> [A] healthy understanding of [religion-state] separation enhances and promotes authentic pluralism in society by safeguarding and even celebrating religious organizations' distinctiveness. In turn, when the law recognizes and vindicates the independence and autonomy of religious institutions, it further empowers and enables them to contribute in a variety of ways to the common good and to the flourishing of all persons.... [R]eligious groups and activities deserve to be free precisely because

---

[76] *Faith, Freedom, and Family*, 696. "Plural social institutions must remain strong for the individual to have places to flourish" (697).

[77] Ibid., 696–97. Businesses are not typically included in most definitions of civil society, but the point does not affect my argument at this point.

[78] See, for example, Paul Hirst, *Associative Democracy: New Forms of Economic and Social Governance* (Amherst: University of Massachusetts Press, 1994); Nancy L. Rosenblum, *Membership and Morals: The Personal Uses of Pluralism in America* (Princeton: Princeton University Press, 1998); and Don E. Eberly, ed., *The Essential Civil Society Reader: The Classic Essays* (Lanham, MD: Rowman & Littlefield, 2000).

they are religious, precisely because they engage in sectarian practices, precisely because they sometimes take their stand above, beyond, and against the cultural mainstream, thereby providing leaven and leverage for the polity to improve.[79]

Associational liberty is a question of the relation between the state and non-state bodies. It gives rise to one kind of pluralism. Importantly, Witte distinguishes this from a very different kind, political pluralism, by which he means the principle of a vertical distribution of political authority across several tiers—what Kuyper calls "orderly federalism."[80] The two senses are blended in the thought of Althusius. As Witte shows, Althusius developed a highly original account of "symbiotic association" in which successive tiers of public authority are built up from below by popular consent, partly on the basis of private bodies, such as families and corporations.[81] But given the extent and complexity of state authority today, it is highly important to distinguish the two senses. Associational liberty is the liberty of bodies that are not part of the state and that are constituted to pursue a wide array of purposes distinct from the unique purposes of the state. Political pluralism calls for a particular distribution of authority across different tiers of a single body, the state, which, in all its manifestations and via all its organs, pursues those unique purposes.

Distributing political authority vertically is a typically Calvinist method for ensuring that political power is widely dispersed among office-holders, who, sinners like the rest of us, will always be tempted to concentrate power in their own hands. Kuyper praises the federal principle at work in the formation of the Dutch Republic; and Witte imagines that Kuyper would have celebrated the principle's codification in the Tenth Amendment of the U.S. Constitution, which "reserves to the states all powers not specifically given to the federal government, as well as to the critical role of state and local governments in sharing the governance of the nation."[82] Vertical distributions of political authority have not been an explicit focus of Witte's work on contemporary issues, although their implications for the regulation of religion crop up in several of his writings.[83]

---

79 *Religion and the American Constitutional Experiment*, 357, 359.
80 *Faith, Freedom, and Family*, 697.
81 *Reformation of Rights*, chap. 3.
82 *Faith, Freedom, and Family*, 697.
83 On religion and education, for example, he notes, with seeming approval, that "state and local legislatures have used the Court's relaxed establishment clause scrutiny and greater deference to local lawmaking as an invitation to experiment anew with religion and education" (*Religion and the American Constitutional Experiment*, 279).

A fuller defense of such a vertical distribution would be a valuable addition to a contemporary Kuyperian-inspired account of the scope of state authority, not least because Kuyper's successors both in the Netherlands and, more surprisingly, in North America have not devoted much thought to it.[84] Herman Dooyeweerd, for example, writing under a unitary Dutch state, construed the vertical distribution of authority as a prudential matter for the central government to decide pursuant to its task of promoting public justice across the nation as a whole. While he attributed a principled sphere sovereignty to many *nonpolitical* authorities (families, churches, trade unions, and so forth), he attributed only a contingent autonomy to *subnational* tiers of political authority, the scope of which, he thought, was properly determined by the national state.[85] Such a view might be thought to stand in tension with the historical process by which most federations have been formed, namely, on the basis of the consent of the federating bodies which thought themselves to enjoy an original political sovereignty which was then pooled.[86] Few American Kuyperians have lent support to reactionary states' rights movements, but many have expressed alarm at the massive expansion of federal power in the modern period. So it is an interesting question whether a Kuyperian-inspired account of state authority could come up with any original proposals regarding the just balancing of national, state, and local authorities.[87]

6   Conclusion

I have interpreted John Witte's contribution to legal and political thought primarily through the lens of his readings of early and modern Calvinist sources; there are other possible lenses. I identified five principles arising from early Calvinism and four from Neo-Calvinism that seem to serve broadly to orient his constructive work in these fields. I have also shown how both also presuppose certain commitments in the field of social, and especially associational,

---

[84] His followers in the United States and Canada have concentrated mostly on issues of religious freedom, confessional and associational pluralism, and social justice, saying little about the federal dimensions of these nations' polities.

[85] See Jonathan Chaplin, *Herman Dooyeweerd: Christian Philosopher of State and Civil Society* (Notre Dame, IN: University of Notre Dame Press, 2011), 263–64.

[86] See Nicholas Aroney, "Federalism: A Legal, Political, and Religious Archaeology," in *Christianity and Constitutionalism*, ed. Nicholas Aroney and Ian Leigh (New York: Oxford University Press, 2022), 303–24.

[87] Canadian Kuyperians have, for example, been foremost in campaigning on behalf of self-governance rights for First Nations communities.

theory. At various points I have gestured toward issues that invite further clarification, elaboration, and integration in possible future work in these areas. The unifying thread in these assessments has been the question, arising in political theory, of the proper scope of state authority on religious and more general matters. This is not the only, perhaps not the primary, question in political theory, but it is one that pervades many others. We are broadly familiar with the family of positions in liberal political theory on state authority (classical liberal, liberal egalitarian, libertarian, and so forth). Much has also been written on the parallel array of stances within Catholicism (various iterations of Thomism, liberation theology, integralism, and more). It seems to me that one of Witte's major contributions has been to point toward one authentic contemporary iteration of a characteristically Protestant theory of the state. This is marked by a robust defense of individual rights and liberties, of an associational and federal pluralism, and of a broad and multidimensional conception of the public good, all held in a distinctive equipoise.[88] Such a conception shares many particular features with the state as understood in several modern liberal democracies, while diverging from secular liberal views on a number of particulars. But it contrasts with secular liberalism in grounding these features in a conception of the state seen as teleologically ordered to justice and the public good, and covenantally constituted so as to pursue them. As John Witte moves further in his journey from "retrieval" to "reconstruction" (as Rafael Domingo puts it), the prospect of him further elaborating such a Protestant theory is an enticing one.[89]

---

88 I offer sketches of such a theory in *Faith in Democracy: Framing a Politics of Deep Diversity* (London: SCM, 2021), and "Justice: Constitutional Design and the Purpose of the Political Community," in Aroney and Leigh, *Christianity and Constitutionalism*, 367–87.

89 In "The Role of the State in Regulating the Marital Family," I suggest some possible conversation partners in that future task (519). Another is the Adrian Vermeule of *Common Good Constitutionalism*. This book has proved highly controversial, not only because of its content but also because its author is a prominent and bullish advocate of "Catholic integralism" (albeit not in that book). Such integralism is incompatible with Witte's commitments to equal religious liberty and disestablishment, but Vermeule's proposal that the purpose of the state is the promotion of the "common good" (as understood in "the classical legal tradition") seems partly convergent with Witte's position.

CHAPTER 7

Building an Interdisciplinary University from the Center Out

Gary S. Hauk

In one of the more recent, and perhaps the most personally revelatory, of his long list of books published over the past forty-some years, John Witte, Jr. recalls that as a child and adolescent growing up in Canada, he played a lot of soccer.[1] Or, at least, he played enough to be sufficiently skillful as a center halfback to be in the thick of things much of the time. Playing offense as well as defense, he had opportunities to score but also to steal the ball from opponents. What gave him as much pleasure as anything, he remembers, was the joy of passing the ball at just the right moment to enable a teammate to score. This assist counted almost as much as if John had scored the goal himself. Toting up stats at the end of the season, he took great pride in the number of his assists.

Comparing this sporting activity to his professional life, John reflected in this recent essay that he still finds satisfaction as a kind of intellectual center halfback. In his work as a teacher, scholar, and director of an influential academic center, joy often comes in passing the ball—in this case, suggesting a dissertation topic for a student, inviting a colleague for a visiting lectureship, or collaborating on a book. All of these initiatives involve fellow scholars—teammates—in probing the relationship of law and religion.

This game has been going on much longer than regulation—some forty years—and by now the score has been run-up to ridiculous numbers. And along the way, John Witte has made more assists than statisticians can adequately tabulate.

The playing field for much of this fun has been Emory University, where John served from 1987 to 2022 as director of what is now called the Center for the Study of Law and Religion (CSLR). In 2022, he stepped away from day-to-day administration of the center and appointed a new executive director while

---

[1] John Witte, Jr., "Assists and the Legal Profession," in id., *Table Talk: Short Talks on the Weightier Matters of Law and Religion* (Leiden: Brill, 2023).

continuing as the faculty director and chair of an advisory board that oversees strategic directions and policies.

The center was the brainchild of James T. Laney, who served as president of Emory from 1977 to 1993. Trained as an ethicist and committed to the highest standards of academic excellence, he aimed to make Emory a beacon of higher purpose in academia. In his view, the university should instill in students "the kind of moral vision that transcends parochial interests and nurtures the sympathy and understanding necessary for moral judgment." Universities, in his thinking, should educate the heart as well as the mind—deepening students' humanity as well as expanding their intellectual horizons. Graduates should leave the university to build and serve a saner, more resilient, more firmly founded civil society. Laney's firm conviction, he said, was that "the university should be a scene of fertile intellectual conversation, where different disciplines fructify each other. The university also has a moral calling to work toward the larger common good."

Impelled by that exalted image of the university, Laney encouraged interdisciplinary teaching and scholarship. Building bridges between the schools and departments across the campus, he thought, would foster collaboration, deepen understanding, and unveil new insights. Most important, cross-fertilization would nurture commitments to the common weal beyond the campus. The Law and Religion Program, as it was then called, was founded in 1982 as one of the first Emory initiatives in response to this vision. Witte became its director in 1987 and would later acquire distinguished titles as Robert W. Woodruff Professor of Law and McDonald Distinguished Professor of Religion.

The CSLR website declares the center's intention to probe the religious dimensions of law, the legal dimensions of religion, and the interaction of legal and religious ideas and institutions. Now offering six advanced-degree programs, numerous cross-listed courses, and dozens of student and postdoc fellowships, the center over the years has brought together scores of Emory faculty, hundreds of students and fellows, and thousands of conference participants from around the world. Luminaries such as President Jimmy Carter (the University Distinguished Professor at Emory since 1982), Archbishop Desmond Tutu (a Robert W. Woodruff Visiting Professor at Emory in the 1990s), and the Dalai Lama (the Presidential Distinguished Professor at Emory) have graced the center's lecterns. Dozens of research projects have made CSLR the hub of a global network of some sixteen hundred scholars. It is truly a steeple of excellence on the Emory campus.

1   The Roots of Cross-disciplinary Scholarship

The vision for such fruitful interdisciplinary study actually inspired Emory leaders as far back as 1952, when the University recruited Ernest Cadman Colwell to establish the Graduate Institute for the Liberal Arts (ILA). Colwell knew what he was doing. An Emory alumnus twice over (college and theology), he had been president of the University of Chicago, whose prestigious Committee on Social Thought offered a model for the ILA. Wags joked that the acronym ILA stood for "I'll learn anything." But the faculty of the ILA worked with absolute seriousness of purpose. The programs of the institute relied on the collegiality of faculty members in quite different departments. Religion consorted with literature. Women's studies brought together departments of English, sociology, anthropology, and history. African American studies spanned the humanities and social sciences. Some of these programs, such as African American studies and women's studies, in time became freestanding departments offering their own PhD degrees.

Laney intended ambitiously to expand this interdisciplinary work beyond the liberal arts into the professional schools. If scholars in religion and literature could collaborate, why couldn't faculty members in the schools of law and theology, or business and medicine, or theology and nursing. Academic deans, recruited to fulfill this ambition, soon structured their budgets and degree programs to chart the path forward. (Even before the Laney administration, the law school had experimented in this vein by appointing Jonas Robitscher in 1971 as the Henry R. Luce Professor of Law and the Behavioral Sciences; he served on the faculty of both the law school and the medical school until his death in 1981. Witte was appointed in 1993 as the first Jonas Robitscher Professor of Law, a title he held until his appointment as Robert Woodruff Professor of Law in 2014.)

The program in law and religion became the pioneer in this endeavor. By good fortune, a young attorney named Frank Alexander, sporting JD and MTS degrees from Harvard, had returned to his native South to practice law. For him the law was a form of ministry, a means to serve as well as to understand concepts common to both law and religion—concepts like fault, justice, freedom, and responsibility. Laney had met Alexander years before, when Alexander was an undergraduate at the University of North Carolina at Chapel Hill, and in the spring of 1981, Alexander accepted an invitation to teach at Emory Law School. The next year, with Laney's encouragement, he established a joint-degree program with courses cross-listed in the schools of law and theology.

Alexander did not have to carry the program alone for long. Having attracted the munificent gift of $105 million from brothers Robert and George Woodruff in 1979—at the time the largest gift in American philanthropic history—Laney and the Emory board of trustees established the Robert W. Woodruff Professorships to lure the foremost scholars in the world to Emory. One of the first to arrive was Harold Berman, Alexander's mentor at Harvard Law School. An expert in the law of the Soviet Union, Berman had become interested in comparative and international law, but finally turned to the subject that would define his legacy. In 1974 he published *The Interaction of Law and Religion*, which shaped the field for the next half century. He followed this with a pathbreaking, two-volume work on *Law and Revolution* (Harvard, 1983 and 2003), which went on to be published in fourteen languages.

Nearing mandatory retirement from Harvard in the mid-1980s, Berman welcomed Laney's offer to extend his career at Emory as the first Woodruff Professor of Law and as a fellow in the Law and Religion Program. There he continued his teaching and scholarship for twenty-two more years, until his death in 2007. He also served as a fellow at the Carter Center, which had been established in affiliation with Emory by former President Carter.

Berman brought to Emory another Harvard Law School protégé, John Witte, Jr., who arrived in 1985 as "a stowaway in Hal Berman's briefcase," as Witte once put it. In time, Witte would succeed Berman as Woodruff Professor of Law and as a leader in the field of law and religion. Beginning life at Emory as a research fellow for Berman, Canada-born Witte stepped out of academia briefly to practice law before receiving his own invitation from President Laney in 1987 to join the Emory Law School faculty and direct the center. Thus began John's long game of making shots on goal and, to Emory's great benefit, passing the ball to colleagues for innumerable assists.

Under his direction, the center grew from a small joint-degree curriculum with a few courses into a full-fledged academic powerhouse sponsoring groundbreaking research, teaching hundreds of students each year, hosting international conferences, and issuing an ever-flowing stream of publications. He has hosted dozens of roundtable conferences around the world and delivered hundreds of public lectures on six continents, including the 2022 Gifford Lectures.

2 Overcoming the Skeptics

If the result of all this labor has been to enliven and extend the field of law and religion to other campuses around the world, the effect on the home campus has been no less leavening. To carry out its mission, CSLR has had to overcome a level of skepticism that seemed to greet the very mention of religion in postwar academic circles in the United States. After Sputnik, American higher education increasingly became captive to the hard sciences and quantitative methods, as the humanities increasingly were pushed to the margins—none more so than religion. The thesis that Western society had become secularized meant that scholarship focused on religion carried little prestige outside of seminaries and divinity schools. Religion as a facet of history, sociology, and literature—let alone health, commerce, and law—had lost its luster.

In law schools especially, skeptics thought of examining modern law through a religious lens as an antiquated and misguided enterprise, something that had been undertaken in medieval universities but was made obsolete by modern positivism. Worse, perhaps, in this view, the enterprise distracted professors and students from the real aim of professional education, which is to prepare good lawyers for the nuts-and-bolts activities of keeping a rule-of-law society operating with airtight contracts, smooth-running judicial processes, and clear and comprehensive legislation. The connection of religion to the law was only of historical interest.

Of course, at the very moment when the Law and Religion Program was being established at Emory, religion come to the fore on the world stage. American politicians on the conservative end of the political spectrum in the late 1970s and 1980s began calling America to claim and return to what they perceived as the nation's Christian foundation. In some ways this was not much different than Martin Luther King Jr. quoting Amos and President Carter quoting Micah while exhorting Americans to righteousness and justice. Religion had played a role in American public life forever.

Meanwhile, on the other side of the world, religious leaders like Archbishop Desmond Tutu were denouncing the oppressive apartheid regime in South Africa, while Pope John Paul II was giving hope to reforming believers and nonbelievers alike that the Soviet hegemony over Eastern Europe would crack and collapse. Astonishingly, 1991 recorded not only the repeal of South African apartheid laws but also the lowering of the Soviet flag over Moscow, thanks in no small part to the influence of religion on people's understanding of what makes for a just society.

3 Law and Religion Take Center Stage at Emory

That landmark year also provided the occasion for Emory's Law and Religion Program to prove its mettle at home. Witte, Alexander, and colleagues in Emory's Candler School of Theology and the law school had undertaken a multiyear project to examine "Christianity and Democracy in Global Context." Eight hundred participants from around the world gathered at Emory, joined by five hundred Emory students, alumni, faculty, and staff members. President Carter delivered the opening address, Archbishop Tutu offered closing comments, and the conference put the Emory program on the map. People wanted to know how new democracies owed their planting and later flowering to religious inspiration and movements. How could religious communities nurture a richer harvest of democracy in the future? What were the prospects of growth in formerly barren fields around the world, and what role, if any, would churches play?

The conference proceedings, edited by Witte and published as *Christianity and Democracy in Global Context* (Westview, 1993), precipitated a flood of publications in the years to come. In a telling ratification of the interdisciplinary vision for Emory, five of the eighteen chapters in the book were written by Emory faculty members not in the law school, while University Professor Carter wrote the foreword and Visiting Professor Tutu the postscript. That amounts to seven "assists" from Witte to his Emory teammates and a dozen more to players around the world.

A second major project launched by Witte brought to Emory several other leading human-rights scholars. Building on the conference on Christianity and democracy, the center broadened its focus to include Jewish and Muslim contributions to cultivating and protecting religious freedom and human rights in Europe, Africa, and the Americas. Another international conference brought Tutu back to campus, where he was joined by Martin E. Marty, the eminent University of Chicago church historian, and John T. Noonan Jr., judge of the U.S. Ninth Circuit Court of Appeals and prolific author on legal and religious matters. Fifty other speakers and eight hundred conference attendees filled out the conversations. A variety of publications resulted, most notably a two-volume, fifteen-hundred-page anthology on *Religious Human Rights in Global Perspective* (Martinus Nijhoff, 1996).

This project also introduced the Emory community to an international faculty star, who for the next three decades would add his own luster to the center and the Emory law firmament. Johan D. Van der Vyver had burnished his reputation on human rights as a professor in South Africa, first at Potchefstroom University and later at the University of Witwatersrand, where he was an outspoken opponent of apartheid. Coming to Emory in 1990–91 as a visiting distinguished professor, he was appointed to the I. T. Cohen Professorship of International Law and Human Rights in 1995. That same year, President Carter appointed him as a fellow in the Human Rights Program of the Carter Center.

Witte and Van der Vyver would team up for the next two decades to steer several more seminal projects on proselytism, religious liberty in Russia, and children's rights. Witte dedicated his volume on *The Blessings of Liberty* to Van der Vyver in celebration of his sixty years of teaching. (Van der Vyver passed away in his home in South Africa in May 2023, after concluding another year of teaching.)

4 Expanding beyond the Christian Paradigm

As the 1990s deepened, Witte and the Law and Religion Program began to find at Emory a congenial culture for what they were trying to do. A survey of faculty members throughout the university in the early 1990s found that, contrary to what had been happening among U.S. academics in the 1970s, more than half of Emory faculty members considered religion to be an important aspect of their research or scholarship. This was true whether they were humanists, social scientists, or natural scientists, and whether they were in the school of business, law, medicine, nursing, public health, or theology. Clearly there were opportunities for the Law and Religion Program to build collaborative relationships and draw on intellectual and financial resources throughout the university for future programming.

One of the earliest collaborative partners and advocates was in the Emory College Department of Religion. David Blumenthal, now retired as the Jay and Leslie Cohen Professor of Judaic Studies, remarks that "law as a *religious* category" is crucial in Judaism; that is, law and religion are two sides of the same coin of daily life. So it was natural for him to say yes when invited to join the Emory conversations on law and religion in the 1980s. Having joined the Emory faculty in 1976, Blumenthal was an early advocate of cross-disciplinary scholarship and a stalwart participant in the program on law and religion.

He also was instrumental in bringing to Emory two prolific contributors to the center's efforts. The first of those was Michael J. Broyde, who was both a rabbi with degrees from Yeshiva University and a lawyer educated at the New York University School of Law. Recruited to Emory College in 1991, Broyde also taught as an adjunct in the law school, where he moved three years later. Witte laid out a welcome mat at the door of the Center for the Study of Law and Religion, where Broyde established the Law and Judaism Program in 1996.

About the same time, Blumenthal was introducing Witte to Abdullahi Ahmed An-Naim, an outspoken and intellectually powerful Muslim human-rights advocate from Sudan. An exile from his homeland, where he had become involved in the push for freedom, equality, and human rights against the regime then in power, An-Naim came to Emory after teaching at UCLA and the University of Saskatchewan, then serving as a fellow at the Center for the Study of Human Rights at Columbia University and as executive director of Human Rights Watch/Africa in Washington, DC.

An-Naim's book *Toward an Islamic Reformation: Civil Liberties, Human Rights and International Law* (Syracuse, 1990), set the course of his work for the next three decades. His method was to go back to the sources of his faith, stripped of centuries of legal and cultural accretion, and to suggest ways to live by those simple teachings. His central claim was that the Qur'an and Hadith of the Prophets were better than humanly created sharia as a guide to faithful living. Now the Charles Howard Candler Professor of Law, Emeritus, at Emory Law School, An-Naim has directed three major explorations of various dimensions of human rights in Islamic context, among other projects.

5 Keeping the Team Together and the Game Alive

John Witte's ability as an academic leader may derive in part from that youthful joy that he found playing center halfback decades ago. Gathering a constellation of productive and pathbreaking academics in law and religion has required him to have not only the kind of intellect that is the coin of the realm in academia but also personal qualities that instill friendship and loyalty. In a recent collection of his essays titled *Faith, Freedom, and Family* (Mohr-Siebeck, 2021), he expatiates on "the three things people will die for"—the three f-words in the title. To these three I would add "friendship," which is a layer of the bedrock of his way of being in the world. He cultivates friendship the way a rose gardener tends to bushes and blooms. That has been true as well of his nurturing of relationships within the Center for the Study of Law and Religion and across the university. With possible rare exceptions (and I know of none), the colleagues whom he has recruited as academic collaborators he counts also as friends—a sentiment no doubt reciprocated.

During the first two decades of leading the center, John and others laid the groundwork for the long-term fulfillment of President Laney's vision of a more structured program in law and religion. What began as a two-person administrative operation—Witte and a part-time assistant—in a faculty office on the fifth floor of the law school building grew into a major academic enterprise. An entire suite on the third floor of the Emory Law School now houses six full-time staff, seven faculty members, and the Harold J. Berman Library as well as space for student interns. Any given year also brings a flock of postdocs who receive financial support and teaching opportunities as they leaven the intellectual community.

The center's growth has been fueled largely by external funding chased down by Witte and some of his colleagues. Most significant was a grant of $3.2 million in 2000 from The Pew Charitable Trusts that Witte landed with the strong support of Rebecca S. Chopp, Emory's provost at the time (she would go on to become dean of the Yale Divinity School and then president, successively, at Colgate University, Swarthmore College, and the University of Denver before retiring in 2019). Pew had already given more than a million dollars to support the center's projects on democracy, proselytism, human rights, and religious freedom, and the foundation's leadership liked the hefty academic return they got on these investments. Pew picked the Emory Law and Religion Program to become one of the nation's "centers of excellence" in interdisciplinary religious study, along with centers at Princeton, the University of Southern California, and Yale. A five-year grant committed Emory to an in-kind match of $1.6 million and a subsequent ten-million-dollar permanent endowment, which still generates operating funds for the center. As part of the transaction, the Law and Religion Program took on its current name, the Center for the Study of Law and Religion.

The Pew grant came in part as recognition of how deeply and widely religion as a subject suffused the work of scholars throughout Emory University, not only in the humanities and professions but also in the social sciences and natural sciences. Indeed, a university strategic plan five years later, in 2005, made "religions and the human spirit" a key theme for development over the next ten years.

More funding would follow over the next two decades—some twenty-five million dollars, including generative grants from the Lilly Endowment, the Ford Foundation, the Henry Luce Foundation, the John Templeton Foundation, the Consciousness Development Foundation, the Judy and Michael Steinhardt Foundation, the Fieldstead Institute, the FUNVICA Foundation, and the Social Science Research Network, among others.

Individual benefactors have proved munificent as well. One of the most consistent and personally engaged was Alonzo L. McDonald, a 1948 Emory College alumnus and later member of the Emory Board of Trustees. This former McKinsey CEO had also served as an ambassador and White House chief of staff under President Carter. A devout Christian who converted to Roman Catholicism late in life, McDonald had long been interested in scholarship that promised to deepen Christian faith. Through his McDonald Agape Foundation, he underwrote programs and scholars not only at Emory but also at Oxford, Cambridge, Heidelberg, Harvard, Yale, Chicago, Georgetown, Duke, and Hong Kong. His sole criteria seemed to be scholarly excellence and productivity. One of his favorite lines was "Perfection is tolerated." Impact was critical.

McDonald-funded work has culminated in more than eighty volumes on law and Christianity, including thematic introductions to Christianity and law commissioned and coedited by Witte on themes of human rights, freedom, natural law, justice and agape, family law, private law, church law, international law, and more. Another series, on great Christian jurists in world history, ambitiously presents fresh case studies on law and religion through the lives of a thousand of the most important Christian legal minds of the past two millennia. Chapter authors and book editors in both series hail from six continents.

Again—tote up the number of assists here, and the stat board begins to light up.

6   Engaging New People at Emory

After stepping down as director of the center in 1987, Frank Alexander remained active as a faculty member teaching law and religion but also worked closely with Witte in various ways. They ran two or three roundtable conferences each year and published volumes together: *Modern Christian Teachings on Law, Politics, and Human Nature* (3 vols., Columbia, 2006); *Christianity and Law: An Introduction* (Cambridge, 2008); and *Christianity and Human Rights* (Cambridge, 2010). But as Alexander began shifting his work to issues of housing and community development, Witte had the good fortune of finding a new collaborator in a brilliant and creative Spanish legal scholar, Rafael Domingo, who joined the center in 2012.

Witte recounts that he received a call out of the blue from Joseph Weiler, director of the Strauss Institute at New York University School of Law. Weiler said that Domingo had just finished a fellowship there and was interested in continuing his scholarly focus on law and Christianity at Emory. Was there room? Witte said there was, and thus did Domingo come to Atlanta, to the delight of his center colleagues.

Tenured as a young man at the University of Navarra, in Spain, where he served as dean of the law school for a time, Domingo has attacked the keyboard with a vengeance, authoring three books and editing five others in his first six years at Emory. Now the Spruill Family Professor of Law and Religion, he adds special expertise in Roman law and European legal history, along with a relentless work ethic. He is also charting new territory by examining the emerging "global law" and, most creatively, exploring the role of God and religion in modern legal systems, the connections between spirituality and the professions, and the spirit of the law beyond its letter.

A second arrival at the center, in 2013, was a return. Silas W. Allard had first come to Emory as the sort of student that the center had been designed to attract. A graduate of the University of Missouri, where he won awards for leadership and was engaged in human rights advocacy, he earned his JD and MTS degrees from Emory in 2011. After clerking for two years at the Court of International Trade, in New York, Allard returned to the center as managing director of the center and managing editor of the *Journal of Law and Religion*. Most intensely interested in migration, he has coedited a volume of essays on legal, theological, philosophical, and sociological perspectives on migration, an increasingly prevalent, worldwide phenomenon. Noting that "there are more people on the move today than at any point in human history," Allard underscores the "profound implications" that this phenomenon has for both legal systems and people whose faith calls them to show hospitality.

Other alumni of the center continue to play a part in its ongoing scholarship and teaching. Justin Latterell arrived at Emory to pursue a PhD in religion and wrote his dissertation under the direction of Witte and CSLR Senior Fellow Steven M. Tipton, of the theology school, with a focus on secularization and the intersection of religion, ethics, and law. After completing his degree, Latterell stayed on as a McDonald Fellow and, eventually, director of academic programs at the center and book-review editor for the *Journal of Law and Religion*.

Terri Montague earned her JD and MTS degrees from Emory in 2014 after serving for three years as the first president and CEO of Atlanta's BeltLine, a three-billion-dollar community development project. After a term as adviser to the U.S. Department of Housing and Urban Development, Montague returned to CSLR in 2021 as a McDonald Senior Fellow and senior lecturer in law.

Farther from Emory but still closely associated with the work of the center, Witte has coauthored with Joel A. Nichols and Richard Garnett the preeminent monograph on U.S. constitutional law on religion, *Religion and the American Constitutional Experiment*, now in its fifth edition from Oxford University Press. Nichols earned JD and MDiv degrees from Emory in 2000, eventually joining the faculty at Pepperdine Law School. He is now dean and the Mengler Chair in Law at the University of St. Thomas School of Law in St. Paul, Minnesota.

Other alumni/ae whose careers Witte has helped lay the foundation for include:
- Bernice King, who earned her MDiv and JD degrees in 1990; she is the daughter of the Rev. Dr. Martin Luther King Jr. and CEO of the King Center in Atlanta, which carries on King's work to create "the Beloved Community."
- Sara Toering, who earned MDiv and JD degrees from Emory in 2006; she was the first person to be awarded the prestigious Robert W. Woodruff

Fellowship in both the theology school and the law school and currently serves as general counsel for the Center for Community Progress, in Atlanta.
- Matthew J. Tuininga, who earned his PhD in religion at Emory in 2014 working with CSLR faculty, and taught at Emory, Oglethorpe University, and the University of the South (Sewanee) before joining the faculty of Calvin Theological Seminary in 2016.
- Audra Savage, JD (Columbia), who completed her LLM (2014) and SJD (2018) degrees at Emory and held a CSLR postdoctoral fellowship in religion and human rights before her appointment in 2021 as assistant professor of law at Wake Forest Law School.
- Major Coleman, PhD (Chicago), set to complete his SJD in 2023, recently appointed as assistant professor of law at North Carolina Central Law School.
- M. Christian (Christy) Green, JD/MDiv (1995), who went on to earn a PhD from the University of Chicago. As an independent scholar, she publishes widely on religion and human rights, religion and the environment, religious developments in Africa, and religion and the family. She is special content editor of the *Journal of Law and Religion* and is a member of the journal's international editorial board.
- Eric Wang, a Robert W. Woodruff Fellow in Emory Law School, is already a rising star in law and religion. A *summa cum laude* graduate of Princeton University, he studies theology, labor, and industrialization through the writings of leading progressive theorists, such as Walter Rauschenbusch, Abraham Kuyper, and Lyman Abbott.

7 New Projects

With fresh investments and infusions of strong scholars, CSLR in the 2000s and 2010s embarked on a series of projects focused on faith perspectives of the family. Most notable for involving distinguished faculty members from around Emory was the five-year project on "Sex, Marriage, and Family and the Religions of the Book" (2001–06). This comprehensive study delved into how Christianity, Judaism, and Islam have shaped laws governing sex, marriage, and family life. The bitter culture wars over gender and sexuality, gay marriage, and abortion provided the context for charting the complexities of faith in relation to family law. Codirected by Witte and Don S. Browning, a visiting Woodruff Professor from the University of Chicago and renowned scholar of interdisciplinary family studies, the project drew Emory faculty from different departments—not only An-Naim, Blumenthal, and Broyde but also chaired professors from different colleges and schools at Emory who would become leading senior fellows in the center over the next two decades These included Luke Timothy Johnson, Woodruff Professor of New Testament and Christian Origins; Frances Smith Foster, Candler Professor of Literature and Women's Studies; Mark D. Jordan, then Candler Professor of Religion before his appointment as Niebuhr Professor of Divinity at Harvard; Anita Bernstein, Sam Nunn Professor of Law; Timothy P. Jackson, Stokes Professor of Theology and Christian Ethics; Carol M. Hogue, Terry Professor of Public Health; and Philip L. Reynolds, Candler Professor of Medieval Theology and Aquinas Professor of Historical Theology. They convened every Wednesday afternoon for a semester to survey this vast field of inquiry and plan their individual and collective work. They then met subsequently for one long weekend every semester for three years to moot drafts of new books. Thirty-seven volumes resulted, and hundreds of scholars participated in the nineteen public forums and two international conferences sponsored by the project.

As this project moved toward publication, CSLR embarked on another one under the rubric "The Child in Law, Religion, and Society" (2005–10). This interdisciplinary exploration brought into sharp relief issues of childrearing, children's rights, education, child abuse, poverty, homelessness, juvenile delinquency, violence, and public policy responses. Directed by Witte and Martin Marty, this project also drew on a range of Emory scholars, including Martha Fineman, Woodruff Professor of Law; Brooks Holifield, Candler Professor of American Church History; and Robyn Fivush, Candler Professor of Psychology. Similarly productive, the project yielded thirteen public forums and twenty-four volumes.

The third major project in this series was on "Faith-Based Family Laws in Pluralistic and Democratic States" (2008–13), led by An-Naim, Broyde, and Christy Green. Funded by the Ford Foundation and the Social Science Research Network, this project offered a rich comparative study of religious family laws in various parts of Africa and the West. A comprehensive website, a score of public forums in African lands, and a journal symposium resulted.

While guiding these projects and directing the center, Witte continued his own prodigious pace of publication, with forty-five books, three hundred articles, and eighteen journal symposia to his name, on topics ranging from human rights to marriage, from family law to constitutional law, and from the Protestant Reformation to the transmission of values in late modern pluralistic societies.

8   From Player-Coach to Mainly Coach

By the time CSLR was ready to celebrate its twenty-fifth anniversary, in 2007, the global landscape had changed so much that new questions loomed. The modern welfare state, which had grown up under the influence of religion, was eroding: how should a more secular, pluralist society address needs of the underprivileged? The shock of 9/11 generated anti-sharia and anti-Muslim movements: how should religious leaders and lawmakers respond? The Catholic Church was rocked by revelations of clerical sexual abuse: what would result from this crisis? New biotechnologies were blurring the lines between humans and machines: what did religious ethics have to say about this? As CSLR scanned the horizon for challenges that would occupy future generations of people of faith under the law, what should the center tackle next?

In typical fashion, the center used its silver anniversary, in 2007, to organize another international conference, this time on the future of law and religion. A veritable who's who in the field of law and religion—Robert Bellah, the great sociologist of religion at UC Berkeley; Kent Greenawalt, the Christian legal theorist at Columbia; Jean Bethke Elshtain, the eminent feminist political theorist at Chicago; Douglas Laycock, the nation's leading scholar and advocate of religious liberty; and David Novak, a renowned Jewish philosopher from Toronto—joined other luminaries and Emory scholars to celebrate what the achievements of CSLR and to illuminate a path forward. Part of their collective recommendation was for the center to stay the course while planting new fields. The study of faith, freedom, and family in the Abrahamic traditions should remain perennial staples: "rather like portraits, landscapes, and triptychs," as Martin Marty put it; "your 'studio' of law and religion has to have these." At the same time, he suggested, it might be time to "turn another leaf in your center's work."

9   The Pursuit of Happiness—and Marriage

One new "turning of the leaf" was to begin exploring the relationship of law to non-monotheistic religions, such as Buddhism. Beginning in 1996, Emory had developed a special relationship with Tenzin Gyatso, the 14th Dalai Lama. That relationship had led to unique collaborations between Emory and Tibetan institutions, including a study-abroad program for Emory undergraduates in Dharamsala, India, and interdisciplinary research and teaching among various college departments and professional schools at Emory. Capitalizing on these relationships, and anticipating a visit of His Holiness to the campus as

Presidential Distinguished Professor in the fall of 2010, CSLR launched a four-year project to explore the meaning of that marvelous phrase in the Declaration of Independence, "life, liberty, and the pursuit of happiness." Just what did "the pursuit of happiness" entail? What did it require and make possible? What were the legal and religious dimensions of the term? Even the Dalai Lama was interested in the question, as the title of his 1998 book indicated: *The Art of Happiness: A Handbook for Living*.

Launched in 2007 with support from the John Templeton Foundation, and directed by Philip L. Reynolds, the "happiness project" produced many weekends of conferences, many days' worth of lectures, the usual shelf of books, and a raft of new interdisciplinary courses on the Emory campus. The climax was an international conference with the Dalai Lama as the keynote speaker. The conference also brought him into conversation with leaders from other faith traditions: Lord Jonathan Sacks, chief rabbi of the United Kingdom; Bishop Katharine Jefferts Schori, presiding bishop of the Episcopal Church; and Professor Seyyed Hossein Nasr of George Washington University, a renowned scholar of Islam. Other interlocutors included internationally prominent Buddhist teachers, psychologists, sociologists, historians, and legal scholars. Several of the conference presentations were turned into essays and published in the *Journal of Law and Religion*, which is housed at Emory.[2]

Reynolds not only guided this project but also exemplifies the kind of generative collaboration that might be deemed one of Witte's "assists." Arriving at the Candler School of Theology in 1992, Reynolds retired thirty years later. In addition to collaborating on the happiness project, he edited a volume in the Cambridge University Press series on great Christian jurists and became a senior fellow at CSLR. He once remarked that he considered these CSLR projects "the 'most university-like' activities of my time at Emory. The opportunity to learn from professors in other fields, and to acquire skills in critical conversation with experts in just about *any* field of academe, was hugely valuable. Above all, though, this experience was sheer intellectual and collegial *pleasure*. Sometimes I'd withdraw for a few moments from the conversation and reflect that to be *here*, engaged in *this*, was a rare privilege and an unanticipated blessing."[3]

One of the results of Reynolds's CSLR engagement is a volume he edited with Witte titled *To Have and to Hold: Marrying and Its Documentation in Western Christendom, 400–1600* (Cambridge, 2007). Spanning more than a millennium

---

2 Volume 29, number 1, February 2014.
3 "A Conversation with Philip Reynolds," Sep. 7, 2021, https://cslr.law.emory.edu/news/releases/2021/09/philip-reynolds-feature.html#.Y_UJ1hPMKDw.

of history and practices from Iceland to Florence and North Africa, the book gathers thirteen chapters by scholars writing about the foundations of Western marriage and the practices that made it a cornerstone of civil society.

With Witte's encouragement, Reynolds picked up another project on marriage that had long occupied his scholarly labors. Reynolds had begun this work in 1989 as a study of marriage in scholastic theology. Over the succeeding decades, the focus expanded and led to his first book, *Marriage in the Western Church: The Christianization of Marriage During the Patristic and Early Medieval Periods*. After arriving at Emory, he expanded the focus yet again, delving into the Reformation and the Counter-Reformation, including the detailed record of the proceedings of the Council of Trent. With a mammoth accumulation of materials to work with, Reynolds imagined having to publish his study in two volumes; Witte urged one. Organizing his massive study with exquisite refinement, Reynolds published *How Marriage Became One of the Sacraments: The Sacramental Theology of Marriage from its Medieval Origins to the Council of Trent* (Cambridge Studies in Law and Christianity, 2016). At more than a thousand pages in length, this book is his magnum opus and won him the Haskins Medal from the Medieval Academy of America. In a review of the book, Professor Wolfgang P. Müller, of Fordham University, neatly and correctly infers the "close professional ties" between Reynolds and Witte that helped to shape and sustain the production of this massive and comprehensive work. Reynolds later said, "That the monograph was not only completed but also published owes a great deal to my esteemed colleague, John Witte. John insisted that I ought to complete the work as a single book. And once that job was done, he was my persistent advocate in getting the oversized book published."[4]

10   And Then the Children

Like Philip Reynolds, Timothy P. Jackson is now retired from the theology school at Emory, where he was the Bishop Mack B. and Ruth Stokes Professor of Theological Ethics. He connected easily with CSLR. In 2003–04 the center hosted a series of forums under the rubric of "The Child in Law, Religion, and Society," bringing together, again, Jimmy Carter and Martin Marty along with former CDC director and smallpox eradicator William Foege and Habitat for Humanity founder Millard Fuller as well as Emory law professor Martha Fineman. Jackson, as a senior fellow in the center, found ample material

---

4   Philip L. Reynolds, personal communication to the author, April 8, 2023.

with which to build on his scholarship on Christian charity and the tensions between justice and love. With Witte's encouragement, he edited one of the first volumes to come out of the forum on the child. This was *The Morality of Adoption: Social-Psychological, Theological, and Legal Perspectives* (Eerdmans, 2005). He followed this with *The Best Love of the Child: Being Loved and Being Taught to Love as the First Human Right* (Eerdmans, 2011).

Jackson recalls that in conversation, John Witte has often commented on "the luxury of discipline"—the marvelous freedom scholars have to shape their academic endeavors according to their best energies and most compelling interests. "The phrase has inspired my own efforts," says Jackson, "especially my *Mordecai Would Not Bow Down: Anti-Semitism, the Holocaust, and Christian Supersessionism*, the unfolding themes of which I discussed with John at length." Remarking on Witte's own superb discipline as a scholar, and playing on the sobriquet of singer James Brown as "the hardest-working man in show business," Jackson calls Witte "the hardest working man in the nomos business," leading by example. Picking up John's own recollection of his days playing soccer, Jackson calls him "the Lionel Messi of the Law and Religion pitch: capable of moving deftly and tirelessly amid extremely complex lines and of both scoring points and creatively feeding others' goal production."

11   New Frontiers, New Forums, New Leaders

As the end of the second decade of the twenty-first century loomed, Witte and others in CSLR began to think about planning more deliberately for the next phase of work. Particularly urgent was the question about how to sustain the kinds of intra-university connections that had been forged over the previous decades. New leaders of the law school had less interest in the center and more in emerging fields, such as environmental law and health care law. Changing leadership of the university likewise meant changing priorities. External funding was harder to reel in. More seriously, early advocates of interdisciplinary scholarship and stalwart partners of the center were retiring from Emory. On the other hand, a promising younger generation was maturing and looking for opportunities. It was time to rethink the organization and directions of the center.

One new direction was digital publishing. The rising cost of print publication and the limited reach of print materials made digital publication logical. The center's website was loaded with information, videos, and downloadable lectures. But new platforms were needed to reach nonacademic audiences with thoughtful pieces that were more than an op-ed but less than a heavily footnoted journal article. In 2019 the center recruited John Bernau, a newly minted PhD in sociology from Emory with extensive experience in digital scholarship to build these new platforms.

The first, launched in October 2019, was *Canopy Forum*, which announced "a new direction in law and religion." This online journal aims to enhance public discourse about the critical issues dividing contemporary societies, from war to poverty, climate change, migration, sectarian tension, and resource scarcity. One example of its wading into controversies of the moment was the extended series of essays by Emory scholars of various stripes regarding the intersection of religion, law, and public health during the Covid-19 pandemic. In some ways, the creation of *Canopy Forum* a few months before the beginning of the pandemic prepared the center for adapting to what was to come—a much greater dependence on digital tools, remote learning, and virtual forums. Here the presence of the Emory Center for Digital Scholarship offered both resources and examples of how to proceed. This marked a turn to new ways of expanding the audience for the work of the center—without the cost, logistical complexity, and long preparation for traditional conferences and symposia.

Organizationally, too, the center was transitioning. Having moved to more online programming and publications, the center was no longer hosting the kind of large public events that had filled the calendar earlier. Turning to new and younger scholars on campus and new residential fellows to teach and offer online programming, the center sought to continue building a stronger virtual community around the world. Witte himself, who had carried the administrative ball so ably for thirty-five years, wanted to devote more time to scholarship and teaching. He thus stepped away from administration to become faculty director of the center's advisory board, leaving daily operations and supervisory work to a new executive director.

The center found that new executive director after a nationwide search in 2022. Whittney Barth, a graduate of Miami University, Harvard Divinity School, and the University of Chicago Law School with experience in higher education as well as litigation, arrived in August 2022. Announcing the choice of Barth by the search committee, Witte said, "Whittney brings to the job a brilliant mind, rich academic experience, a learned pen, a generous heart, superb organizational strengths, and the refined legal skills needed to navigate bureaucratic complexities."

It's hard to say whether this hand-off of responsibilities is an assist from Witte to Barth or from Barth to Witte. In some sense it allows John to take on still more ambitious production of the scholarship that has marked his career for four decades. In any case, more goals surely are in sight.

Other changes in the center resulted from two years of analysis, discussion, and peering into the future. A strategic plan completed in 2018 called for new programs "to anticipate and analyze issues before they become politically and culturally hot." The center would continue to focus on law, religion, and human rights, the place of religion in liberal democracies, and the role of law in the Abrahamic religions. But new labor was contemplated.

To begin, the area of law, religion, and jurisprudence would lift up the interest of scholars like Rafael Domingo, who was exploring the interconnections between law and spirituality, and a project led by Michael Welker, a theologian at Heidelberg and a CSLR senior fellow, who with Witte would study the roles of institutions in late modern pluralistic societies in shaping morality, character, and virtue. A second new research area—social justice—would address the role of law and religion in perpetuating or redressing social inequities, inequalities, and injustices, particularly for migrants, refugees, the poor, unemployed, disabled, and incarcerated. The third new area—law, religion, and health—called for focusing on issues of health care and public health: bioethics and the regulation of healthcare; religious opposition to health care interventions; conscience exemptions for healthcare providers; and religious law and doctrine pertaining to healthcare decision-making.

Significant, too, were two programs that returned the center to putting scholarship into action. The early days of the center had offered students practicums in law clinics and other settings throughout Atlanta, as well as workshops for lawyers and religious leaders. In 2015 CSLR launched a four-year Restoring Religious Freedom Project under the direction of Mark Goldfeder, the Spruill Family Senior Fellow in Law and Religion. This project offered hands-on experience to students wanting to explore the prominent area of religious-freedom law. And in 2021, a grant from the Lilly Endowment allowed the center to begin an intensive project on law and ministry, directed by Shlomo Pill, Justin Latterell, and John Bernau. Recognizing that few religious leaders receive training to handle the many legal issues that affect their work, the project aimed to develop resources to help leaders of every kind of religious organization deepen their understanding of the law.

In all of these new directions and appointments, Witte not only has provided a bright and guiding light but also has sought to ensure that the original vision for the center—as a place of interdisciplinary, international, and interfaith scholarship and conversation—not only would be maintained but also would advance. The questions that will engage the center's faculty and fellows in the coming years are laid out, and the foundation appears firm. Preparing for its fifth decade, the Center for the Study of Law and Religion appears well positioned to carry on the legacy of those early pioneers in the field, who envisioned a way to help religious practitioners and legal professionals better understand each other's contributions to civil society. Two great solvents of human experience—as Witte likes to call them—both law and religion show no signs of diminishing in importance. In the United States, religious disputes continue to percolate through state and federal courts, while elsewhere in the world a resurgence in fundamentalisms augurs further questions about the role of religion in creating the laws of society. The mutual influence of law and religion seems as inextricable today as ever.

PART 2

Faith and Law in Biblical and Theological Perspectives

∴

CHAPTER 8

What Christianity and Law Can Learn from Each Other

Michael Welker

John Witte and I first met in 1998, at the Princeton Theological Seminary conference on "Abraham Kuyper's Legacy for the 21st Century." Max Stackhouse, influential ethicist and director of the Abraham Kuyper Center for Public Theology, had organized this event. It was to deal with his legacy. John wrote: "[Kuyper] was a formidable theologian and philosopher, journalist and educator, churchman and statesman of extraordinary accomplishment. ... He founded the Free University of Amsterdam, ... was a minister of justice and finally prime minister of the Netherlands."[1] Kuyper was able not only to penetrate the multisystemic configuration of pluralistic societies, but also to partially shape it.

After this conference, John's and my academic cooperation developed and, along with it, our friendship. Very likely, a contributing factor was my interest in understanding multisystemic configurations in societies, cultures, and academic fields in order to overcome simplistic, often dualizing perspectives on societal, cultural, and religious realities. My postdoctoral work on the mathematician, physicist, and philosopher Alfred North Whitehead and work on the sociologists Talcott Parsons and Niklas Luhmann had been decisive for opening up my thinking. However, there was a second area where John's and my interests touched. My lectures on the topic "Law and Gospel" had drawn me into more intense work with the biblical traditions and the development of biblical law codes over the centuries and under different political pressures by several global powers.[2] I moved from a primarily philosophically oriented theology to a biblical orientation in theology and, at the same time, to a theological realism.

---

1 John Witte, Jr., "Abraham Kuyper on Family, Freedom, and Fortune," in John Witte, Jr., *Faith, Freedom, and Family: New Studies in Law and Religion*, ed. Norman Doe and Gary S. Hauk (Tübingen: Mohr Siebeck, 2021), 199–214, at 199.
2 Lectures held at the universities of Tübingen in 1983/84; Münster in 1988; Heidelberg in 1992 and 1996.

With this background, the encounter with John Witte's work and our projects of cooperation became a wonderful source of inspiration and encouragement. A continuous topic in our conversation that John put repeatedly into the focus of our attention was the question: Can there be such a thing as a "Christian jurisprudence," open for cooperation with other religions and secular worldviews? In the following contribution to honor him on his sixty-fifth birthday, I propose an answer to this question.

In the first part, I show that theology should listen to the work of legal scholars. I did so in Münster, when Werner Krawietz, from the faculty of law, and I held a doctoral seminar over four semesters at the end of the 1980s. Then, with John Witte, the concentration on the area of law became more focused for me. I was impressed by his immense body of work and by the work of his mentor, Harold Berman, and his attempt to identify "the weightier matters of the law."[3] In the first part of this chapter, I deal with impulses from Berman and Witte. Theology should learn from law!

In the second part, I add specifically *theological* "weightier matters of the law" according to the biblical traditions, and explain the relevance of including them in the interdisciplinary cooperation between law and religion. Setting out from Matthew 23:23, I explore systematic interconnections between the care for justice, the care for mercy, and the care for faith. I argue that content-based theology can and should be of interest to law scholars.

The third part unfolds the power of the divine Spirit as a Spirit of justice, freedom, truth, peace, and benevolence—a gigantic package of the good. This part first addresses what Joseph Weiler termed "a Christophobia in Europe," and asks why it may have developed, and why it is necessary to counter it in what is known as the enlightened public, in the academy, and in the areas of law and even of theology. Doing so will bring about consequences for a meaningful relation between law and Christian religion and will sensitize us to the fact that we need attention to the working of the multimodal divine Spirit. Christology and pneumatology are crucial in a self-critical and mutually inspiring dialogue between law and religion.

---

3 Harold Berman, "The Weightier Matters of the Law," an address to the opening of Vermont Law School, Royalton, Vermont (Royalton Press, 1974), 1–10; Berman, "The Moral Crisis of the Western Legal Tradition and the Weightier Matters of the Law," *Criterion* 19, no. 2 (1980): 15–23. See also John Witte, Jr., "The Integrative Christian Jurisprudence of Harold J. Berman," in *Faith, Freedom, and Family*, 215–28; John Witte, Jr. and Frank S. Alexander, eds., *The Weightier Matters of the Law: Essays on Law and Religion: A Tribute to Harold J. Berman* (Atlanta, GA: Scholars Press, 1988).

1 "The Weightier Matters of the Law"

Harold Berman (1918–2007), one of the great American jurisprudential "polymaths" (so John Witte), has often spoken, even in publication titles, of "the weightier matters of the law," that is, of what is most important or significant about the law. He had, not explicitly but in effect, taken up Matthew 23:23: "You have neglected the weightier matters of the law."

In speaking of the weightier matters of the law, Berman has in mind a crisis of the contemporary legal system in the West. Violent social, economic, and political transformations "have put a tremendous strain upon traditional legal institutions, legal values, and legal concepts in virtually all countries of the West." As central problems, Berman identifies attacks on the autonomy of law, on the professional training of its representatives, and on the quality and integrity of legal scholarship in its university training. He laments the loss of confidence in law as a coherent whole, as a *corpus juris*, and the flight into a pragmatism held together only by common techniques of jurisprudence. He sees confidence weakened or even shattered in a historically shaped "growth of law," in an inner logic in its evolution, in its sovereignty vis-à-vis politics, and in its power to transcend social and political upheavals and even revolutions.[4]

How can firm convictions and postulates be regained? The law, he says, is entitled to structural integrity, to a confidence in its continuity and permanence, to an appreciation of its religious roots, and to the recognition that its qualities transcend the claims of the other social systems. All this, Berman argues, must be recovered in an "integrative jurisprudence."

In his attempt to work for a such a renewal, Berman became a "pioneer of the study of law and religion"[5] in the last three decades of his career. "Berman remained an ecumenical Christian throughout his adult life, although he remained proud of his Jewish heritage: 'God made me both root and branch,' he often said, referring to Paul's description of Jews and Christians in Romans 9–11. While he worshipped regularly in the Episcopal Church, he loved to attend Russian Orthodox services when in Russia."[6]

In his book *Faith and Order: The Reconciliation of Law and Religion*,[7] Berman wrote, "[I]f we wish law to stand, we shall have to give new life to the essentially religious commitments that give it its ritual, its tradition, and its

---

4 Harold Berman, *Law and Revolution: The Formation of the Western Legal Tradition* (Cambridge, MA: Harvard University Press, 1983), 33, 37–39, 44.
5 *Faith, Freedom, and Family*, 215.
6 Ibid., 217.
7 Harold J. Berman, *Faith and Order* (Grand Rapids, MI: Eerdmans, 1993).

authority—just as we shall have to give new life to the social, and hence the legal, dimensions of religious faith."[8] Over the years, he warned, as Witte later paraphrased him, that "[w]ithout religion, law tends to decay into empty formalism. Without law, religion tends to dissolve into shallow spirituality."[9]

These strong statements stand in some tension with Berman's affirmation that the era of dualism is waning, that we are entering an "age of synthesis."[10] John Witte praised Berman's monumental work that "helped to launch the modern law-and-religion movement, now comprising several hundred law professors and dozens of centers, programs, journals, and associations around the world."[11] Mildly critical, however, he added, "A streak of mystical millenarianism colors Berman's legal historical method—much of it already conceived while he was a young man witnessing the carnage of World War II. ... Historical periods and patterns are rather too readily equated with providential plans and purposes. The doctrine of God becomes ever more diffuse, even faintly pantheistic."[12] But Witte also recalled, "Toward the end of his life, Berman emphasized the role of the Holy Spirit in bringing about this global reconciliation."[13]

At this point, a deeper biblical perspective on the weightier matters of the law and a more differentiated account of the complex working of the Holy Spirit—its working beyond mystical hopes for all sorts of global integrations—seems appropriate.

2 Biblical Perspectives on the Weightier Matters of the Law

The full text of Matthew 23:23, contains three key words which define these "weightier matters of the law"—justice, mercy, and *pistis* [faith]. They are central terms that go back to the Hebrew Bible, where they are embedded in biblical law codes that partly overlap with secular law codes. A striking example of the structure of such a law code can be found in the Book of the Covenant, Exodus 20–23, a text which many scholars date back to 900–700 BCE. This text contains a clear pursuit of legal and judicial justice linked to moral and religious concerns. At its core are codified laws. They are bracketed by legal

---

[8] Ibid., 13, and jacket description (taken from *Faith, Freedom, and Family*, 221).
[9] *Faith, Freedom, and Family*, 222; elaborated in Harold J. Berman, *The Interaction of Law and Religion* (Nashville: Abingdon Press, 1974), 31–47.
[10] Berman, *Interaction of Law and Religion*, 110–18.
[11] *Faith, Freedom, and Family*, 226; see also "The Educational Values of Studying Law and Religion," in ibid., 21–36.
[12] Ibid., 225.
[13] Ibid., 224.

regulations concerning what I term "the mercy code of the law," and that in turn is surrounded by further provisions concerning faith and the knowledge and worship of God.

2.1 *Justice, the First of the Weightier Matters of the Law, Is of the Utmost Importance in the Book of the Covenant*

The codified articulation of laws and the concern for justice are elemental to the Book of the Covenant. *A multitude of the laws mentioned in this book have a conditional sentence structure that shows the interest in a legislative and judicial regulatory technique.* "If someone does x so that y occurs, he shall do or suffer z." The interest is clearly in fixing typical conflicts in law in order to limit them, regulate the harm done and suffered, and prevent future conflicts. The guiding ideas are restoration of the situation before the conflict, if possible, compensation of the damage, or increase of restitution as a punishment in case of greater damage or to deter future crimes. However, there is not only the case-oriented increase of punishments but also the reduction of punishments in legal thinking that takes place in an effort to achieve just calibration, such as the compensation in view of murder and manslaughter (Exodus 21:12–14).

Several important legal ideas or principles can be identified in this so-called archaic legal system. These principles become particularly clear when we consider the example of the *lex talionis* (Exodus 21:23–25), which is often regarded as inglorious. In cases involving particular injuries sustained in a physical altercation, legal judges are instructed, "If anything happens to you, you shall give life for life, eye for eye, tooth for tooth, hand for hand, foot for foot, burn for burn, wound for wound, welt for welt." The formula "an eye for an eye, a tooth for a tooth" has usually been misunderstood as an instruction to retaliate that feeds on an injured, subjective sense of justice whose demands for retribution can never be satisfied. It would lead to the escalation of feuds and the promotion of permanent relations of conflict. In contrast, however, the *lex talionis* aims to limit the mechanism of blood vengeance and the escalation of revenge and retaliation: "*Only* one eye for an eye." Thus, the law is an important step toward limiting and reducing conflict in a long process of striving for more humane legal development.

In the process, judicial lawmaking and legal culture accomplish a tremendous cultural feat. *By legislating and judicially recording interpersonal conflicts, they are treated as past conflicts that have, in principle, already been resolved. This creates legal sobriety and security of expectation.*

The effort to formulate, refine, promulgate, and codify just laws—to use and test them in *thinking about and teaching about law and in judicial legal practice*—is a major task in all political and cultural contexts of life. When the fulfillment of this task is hindered not only individually but also institutionally, or even by political and religious authorities, serious crises occur.

A strong signal of such a crisis was sent out in 2021 by the worldwide outrage over the brutal murder of the African American George Floyd by white police officers in Minneapolis. In his powerful sermon at the funeral service for George Floyd in Houston, on June 4, 2020, Rev. Al Sharpton drew particular attention to the continuing failure of the legal system to address racism, and to the use of violence, including in the police, the judicial system, and politics. Justice and equal rights for all people—this is what we must stand up and fight for![14] The fact that Matthew 23:23 mentions *justice first and foremost* as "most important in the (biblical) law" points to the fact that without an honest culture of law and law-abiding jurisdiction, religion, morality, and politics also degenerate, especially when they condone or even support the failure of law.

Harold Berman's strong plea for the autonomy and systematic and systemic stability of law is exceedingly important. However, in this context, the interdependencies of justice with mercy and faith—emphasized by Matthew and many other biblical traditions, not least the biblical law corpora—need to be addressed as well.

2.2 The Power of Mercy in Biblical Law[15]

Talk of mercy and mercy laws as well as the mercy code of the law sounds not only antiquated but downright offensive to many contemporary ears. Together with the still-common talk of protecting the weaker or even the weak, these expressions belong to the feudal world of lordship and servility, which we still keep present with the terms "pleas for mercy" and "pardon." They seem to contradict an ethos of equality and equal treatment in accordance with fundamental rights, the protection of minorities, the rule of law, the welfare state, and efforts to transform moral rights into juridical rights in the context of protecting human rights.

The fact that biblical traditions and religious-liturgical language often pair the terms justice and mercy, or law and mercy, seems to indicate that they belong to a past time and world. However, commitment to the rights of the economically and socially disadvantaged is not just a special theme of the legal system; rather, it is a *structural* theme for a legal system committed to

---

[14] I am grateful to Christine Böckmann, who alerted me to this sermon.
[15] In this part I pick up thoughts that I delivered as the Alonzo L. McDonald Lecturer in 2013 at the Emory Center for the Study of Law and Religion published as Michael Welker, "The Power of Mercy in Biblical Law," *Journal of Law and Religion* 29, no. 2 (2014): 225–35.

respecting and promoting a just legal order that takes seriously the social functions of justice and the interrelationship of legal security, freedom, and peace.

Actually, the laws of mercy impact biblical legal culture in many ways. The collection of rules termed "casuistic law," for legal and judicial treatments of conflicts, is, as mentioned earlier, framed by laws of mercy. On one side they are laws for the treatment of male slaves and female slaves (Exodus 21:1–11), and on the other side a collection of laws intended to benefit the acutely or chronically economically and socially disadvantaged, namely, widows, orphans, the poor, foreigners, and, again, slaves (Exodus 22:20–23:12). Many of these laws are appellative; they belong to what is called "apodictic law."

What do the laws of mercy aim at? In the slave laws, they limit the duration of slavery (slavery is a matter of course in the ancient world) to six years, and they normatively state that slaveholders must not exploit the slaves' labor on the Sabbath.

In general, the laws of mercy cultivate the expectation that those who are privileged will withdraw their own claims—even to the point of relinquishing their legally guaranteed rights—in favor of the disadvantaged and distressed, and that this will translate into creative action on their behalf. I have suggested that in such cases we speak of a "free, creative withdrawal of self for the benefit of the neighbor."[16] It should be emphasized that this is a creative movement in favor of other people, not a withdrawal that merely leaves them alone.

Here a stark contrast to natural law becomes obvious. Whereas the laws of mercy advance the rights of the disadvantaged, the precepts of natural law for all living beings to live honorably, to injure no one, and to grant to each their own perhaps seem to make for equal status; in fact, however, the right of the fittest is supported, since all natural life must live at the expense of other life.[17]

The laws of mercy are of central importance not only in family life but also in the areas of medicine, care institutions, education, social policy, and migration policy. The establishment of this right in law and in judicial and political practice brings with it enormous evolutionary thrusts for legal culture.

1. The establishment of mercy laws directly affects juridical law, strengthening and challenging its competence. On one hand, no case can fall outside the scope of the law; no person, however weak, poor, and miserable, can fall outside this scope. On the other hand, the systemic orientation of law toward the inclusion of the disadvantaged requires the constant

---

16   Ibid.
17   See the detailed discussion of natural law in Michael Welker, "A Magnum Opus" (review of *Faith, Freedom, and Family*), *Journal of Law and Religion* 28, no. 1 (2023): 108–17.

renewal of the culture of law and its progress toward the universalization of the claims of justice.

2. The law of mercy also has an enormous impact on the identity of individuals and on moral communication. The people who are able to experience and exercise a free and creative self-restraint for the benefit of others go beyond the perspectives of indispensable self-preservation. They go beyond what the biblical traditions call a mere fleshly existence. The law of mercy underpins the values of social welfare, freedom, and equality. It fulfills an important political function, enabling the law to become a moral teacher in the establishment of justice.

3. Furthermore, the law of mercy helps deal with a painful paradox that plagues all legal and moral development. Societies want to improve their laws and their justice, and they want to cultivate and refine their interpersonal morality. How can they carry out this difficult but necessary task of transforming and improving normative capacities without destroying the binding force of their laws and the security of expectations they provide? The protection and improvement of the living conditions of the disadvantaged provide an orienting regulative, a measure for the establishment and perfection of an equality-oriented justice, freedom, and social peace.

4. The aforementioned slave law has a particularly dramatic impact on legal evolution. It is not only momentous for the existence of slaves, who may be treated as potentially free men, not as "talking tools" (Marcus Terentius Varro), and may claim certain protective rights. It also *revolutionizes the function of the law in general, which is now not only an instrument of acute conflict management, but an instrument of social transformation with long time perspectives and the claim to individual and collective long-term memory.* It thus touches on the third group of laws, which explicitly focuses on religious issues.

2.3 *Pistis—and the Crucial Role of Faith for the Law*

As pointed out with regard to the structure of the Book of the Covenant, before and after the laws of mercy there are series of regulations dealing with the organization of the common relationship with God, with worship (Exodus 20:22–21:11 and 23:13ff.). They speak of places and times of worship gatherings. We know little about the cultic arrangements of the time outside sacred buildings and spaces. And yet the clues that the laws of the Book of the Covenant and the other biblical legal corpora offer make it clear that the cultic public ascribed to itself the status of a people freed from slavery in Egypt by God's "mighty hand and outstretched arm." This is linked to formulas highly relevant to the law of mercy that are also found in other legal corpora: "You yourselves were strangers in Egypt," and "You yourselves know how it feels to be a stranger."

The behavior and self-understanding of the community before God is shaped by God's dramatic historical interventions in the life of the community. These experiences of God go far beyond (possible) concrete experiences of the cultic public. Even those who were never in Egypt can be addressed as slaves freed by God's hand. They can be incorporated into a web of public collective imaginings that far exceed the realm of personally accessible experience.

Why was the double identity (You were strangers, but now you are free) not simply abandoned? Why were the associated legal and moral impositions of the laws of mercy not rejected? Why did Israel joyfully accept the ascription of such a historical identity reaching so far back, and a life spread over broad time horizons? How did the law come to function as the vehicle of a far-reaching culture of memory and expectation? A whole complex of statutory and legal concerns must be appreciated in the search for an answer to these questions. In contemporary German law, they can be captured in the formulas "eternity clause" or "eternity guarantee" (§ 79 Abs. 3 GG), a guarantee of continuity for fundamental constitutional decisions that, learning from traumas of the past, seek to permanently ward off devastating antihuman political and legal developments. Here, in this third dimension of Matthew's "weightier matters of the law," several aspects of Harold Berman's concern for these matters are articulated.

They can also be recognized in formulas of the inviolability of human dignity. "In a legal order of relative values, human dignity is an absolute value. The only one."[18] "Günter Dürig has ... emphasized as the content of the guarantee of dignity that 'every human being (is) a human being by virtue of his/her spirit, which sets them apart from impersonal nature and enables them by their own decision to become conscious of themselves, to determine themselves and to shape themselves and the environment.'"[19] The development of the concepts of fundamental rights and of universal human rights is rooted in the absolute value of inviolable human dignity. What does the biblical *pistis* contribute to the support of this demanding legal culture?

With recourse to the historical experiences founded in God's activity, the biblical laws reveal the religious—at least civil-religious—foundations of the

---

18 Josef Isensee, "Menschenwürde: die säkulare Gesellschaft auf der Suche nach dem Absoluten," *Archiv für öffentliches Recht (AöR)* 131 (2006): 175.

19 Günter Düring, "Der Grundrechtssatz von der Menschenwürde," [in *AöR* (1956), 125] in Klaus Stern, § 16 Menschenwürde, in *Leitgedanken des Rechts, Festschrift Paul Kirchhof*, vol. 1, ed. Hanno Kube et al. (Heidelberg: C. F. Müller, 2013), 169–80, at 172.

postulates of human dignity and human rights. They commit to a culture of remembrance and expectation, not limited in space and time, with regard to the formative power of religion and law. Universal expectations of connection defy contrary experiences and developments. God's work is remembered biblically as a liberating and saving work and is always hoped for anew. The common history is grasped as a transition from hardship, suffering, and distress to experiences of liberation and freedom. Shared feelings of gratitude and joy are given greater weight than feelings of loss and powerlessness. *An individual and social sense of power permeates and reshapes opposing experiences.*

The differentiated basic presentation of "You have been strangers and slaves—and now you are free" leads to a rich experience of identity and awareness of the depth of the human person. A multitude of individual and shared empathic discoveries is thus released, an indispensable source and support for legal, political, medical, scientific, and educational efforts to develop and unfold an ethos of justice, equality, and freedom. What can be and what has to be added to these rich perspectives on the weightier matters of the law by addressing Jesus Christ and the Spirit of Christ?

3 The Law and the Spirit of Christ—Divine and Human: Some Impulses for a Christian Jurisprudence

In 2003, the South Africa-born Orthodox Jew and professor of international law and the European Union at the NYU School of Law, Joseph Weiler, published a book in several languages, *A Christian Europe: Passages of Exploration*. He provocatively diagnosed a "Christophobia" in Europe and beyond. This Christophobia, he argued, blocks engagement with Europe's cultural and spiritual foundations as well as with its cultivation and further creative development.[20]

Together with other colleagues, he bemoaned that the final draft of the Constitution of the European Union, a treaty of some seventy thousand words, did not include a single word about God, Christ, or Christianity. In October 2022 he gave the inaugural lecture of the 2022/23 John Paul II Lectures under the title: "A Non-Christian Europe—Is It Possible?"

We should not only associate this Christophobia with difficulties to relate a genuinely Christian orientation to other religions or secular cultures and to gain and keep respect in academic orbits. The sad fact that even many Christian

---

20   Joseph Weiler, *Ein christliches Europa: Erkundungsgänge* (Salzburg: Anton Pustet, 2004), esp. 75ff; see also Michael Welker, *God the Revealed: Christology* (Grand Rapids: Eerdmans, 2013), 28–31.

theologians pay only lip service to Christology and Trinitarian theology and are content with a more or less metaphysical theism, or in recent times with an ecologically motivated romanticism of nature, is rooted in basic problems with Christology. Without a thorough understanding of the divine Spirit, the divinity of Christ is simply incomprehensible. A most impressive human Jesus and a numinous "Lord" fall apart. Intellectual insecurity and fear of being accused of ecclesial and cultural triumphalism block an honest access to confessing Christ and admitting a genuinely Christian identity.

But it is not only an insufficient Christology with no clear relation to the Holy Spirit that causes difficulties for even thinking of a "Christian jurisprudence." There are also severe problems with a theology of the law, particularly in the Protestant church families that hold the theology of Paul and of the reformers indebted to him in high respect.

They are confused by tensions between Paul's assertions. On one hand, there are statements such as, "We have in the law the embodiment of knowledge and truth" (Romans 2:20); "the law is holy, and the commandment is holy and just and good" (Romans 7:12); "the law is spiritual" (Romans 7:14); "the law of the Spirit of life in Christ Jesus" (Romans 8:2). On the other hand, there is Paul's talk about "the law of sin and death" (Romans 8:2), and "the power of sin is the law" (1 Corinthians 15:56).

The confusion caused by these statements dissolves when we see that the law indeed fights against injustice, untruth, oppression, hostility, and hate, and is therefore good, but that it can itself come under the power of sin and then promote injustice, untruth, oppression, hostility, and mutual hate, and therefore is sinful. This means that it is necessary to differentiate between the good law and the law under the power of sin. The perception that the law can fall under the power of sin is relevant in the reflection on what is needed to strengthen it. The search for and affirmation of the weightier matters of the law cannot remain content with a good professional education of future lawyers, with stable legal institutions, with support and respect for the law in the broader society and culture, and with a widespread trust in the law's regulating powers. The interdependencies of justice, mercy, and faith as the weightier matters of the law are minimum markers to protect the law against distortions not only from the outside but also from the inside. But even they are not sufficient.

What does Christianity, what does Christian theology and Christian faith assert when they concentrate on the cross of Christ? Why do many Christian churches place the cross of Christ in the center of their places of worship? A long theological tradition with towering figures like Paul, Luther, and Bonhoeffer emphasized the revelation of the merciful and the cosuffering God revealed at the cross. The biblical witnesses, however, emphasize a second central message, namely, *that the cross reveals God's merciful judgment in the world under the power of sin.* Jesus is crucified in the name of the global power Rome, with strong support of the reigning religion, with reference to the Mosaic law and the Roman law, with the moral support of public opinion. Here we see the law in its political, religious, legal, and moral dimensions corrupted by the powers of sin. A differentiated alliance of powers cooperates against the revelation of God and God's attempt to mediate beneficial divine gifts for the common good of humankind.[21]

Two observations about the work of the Spirit are crucial in dealing with the situation of the multidimensional law in distress and in self-endangerment. One shows the modesty of the presence of the resurrected Jesus Christ after Easter and the inconspicuousness of his so-called kingly, priestly, and prophetic offices. In continuity with his pre-Easter life, this king is a brother, a friend, and even an innocent outcast. He mediates to his witnesses the powers of healing, salvific education, and reconciliation. This priest directs us in the inconspicuous power of his Spirit toward God with the greeting of peace, thanksgiving for and the breaking of the bread, the opening of the scriptures, and the assembling of the community. This prophet opens—in the power of his Spirit—our eyes to the abyss of sin, lies, and betrayal, but also to truth, true justice, and true freedom and peace.[22]

The other observation is that of the outpouring of Christ's Spirit after his resurrection. Here we encounter Christ's elevated and saving life in discontinuity with his pre-Easter life. We encounter *the working of the multimodal Holy Spirit, a Spirit of justice, a Spirit of freedom, a Spirit of truth, a Spirit of peace, and a Spirit of benevolence and love.*[23] This divine Spirit is so much richer than an all-uniting, all-relating, all-integrating power. It challenges monohierarchic, patriarchal, gerontocratic, and chauvinist secular and religious powers and organizations (see Joel 3 and Acts 2). This Spirit—which works in a revelatory way as the Spirit of Christ, but also works in a nonexclusivist way from other religious and nonreligious traditions—provides a blissful yet self-critical guidance in the dialogue and cooperation between law and religion.

---

21 See Welker, *God the Revealed*, 185–91.
22 Ibid., 235–43, 277–94, 304–13.
23 See Michael Welker, *In God's Image: An Anthropology of the Spirit: The 2019/20 Gifford Lectures*, trans. Douglas W. Stott (Grand Rapids: Eerdmans, 2021. See Rom. 8:10 (justice); 2 Cor. 3:17 (freedom); 2 Thess. 2:13 and John passim (truth); Rom. 14:17 and Gal. 5:22 (peace); the whole NT (love and benevolence).

4 Summary

What can religion and law, law and Christianity, learn from each other? My first answer was: Religion in general and Christianity in particular should carefully study the "weightier matters of the law." They should hold legal thought and good juridical practice in the highest respect. They should not blur this respect with vague moral and religious interests and emotions.

My second answer was that in the dialogue of law and religion, the insights and rationalities of a religious law which connects justice, mercy (care for the powerless and excluded), and faith (relation to truth / the divine) should be perceived and valued. The legal and the religious perspectives on "the weightier matters of the law" should be brought into conversation and mutual enrichment.

My third answer turned to specific Christian and broader biblical perspectives. It deals with the problem that juridical and religious laws can become corrupted by the powers of sin and generate systemic distortions. Here the deeper orientation toward the cross of Christ and toward other totalitarian catastrophes in human history should alert us to whatever dangerous religious and political-legal triumphalisms develop. Moreover, an appreciation of the divine Spirit of justice, freedom, truth, peace and co-creaturely benevolence should illuminate the interaction and cooperation of law and religion. According to the biblical traditions (especially Joel 3 and Acts 2), the divine Spirit overcomes monohierarchic, patriarchal, and gerontocratic societal structures and all sorts of nationalistic and chauvinist limitations. It helps to meet the continuing challenge for free societies presented by such manifestations of power over the ages up to today.

CHAPTER 9

Christian Teachings on Obligations

David VanDrunen

Covenant is an immensely rich concept, both historically and constructively. Ancient Near Eastern rulers entered into covenants to organize and regulate their political life. The Hebrew scriptures, through a complex appropriation and modification of the covenant forms of their ancient Near Eastern neighbors, describe several covenants that God entered with human partners as well as a number of intrahuman covenants. The New Testament interprets this Old Testament teaching and presents the new covenant in Christ as its culmination. This biblical material has in turn prompted many Jewish and Christian thinkers to develop theologies of covenant in their elaboration of religious doctrine. The idea of covenant has also played important roles in the Western legal and political traditions.

It should be no surprise that covenant has been an important theme in the scholarship of John Witte, Jr. Even his origins may have disposed him to this topic from an early age: Witte was raised in the Dutch Reformed tradition, and Reformed Christianity, more than any other Christian tradition, has emphasized the biblical covenants as an organizing topic of theology. Witte would became a scholar of law and religion, and few concepts play a more promising role in the intersection and integration of law and religion than covenant. Moreover, given the appearance of covenant in a number of different religious and legal traditions, it has prospect for the sort of fruitful engagement across confessional divides that Witte has sought to cultivate for decades at Emory University's Center for the Study of Law and Religion.

It is truly an honor to contribute to his *Festschrift*. I have long regarded him as a model scholar. He not only is a prolific and accomplished writer but also is dedicated to excellence in teaching and is a master collaborator and encourager. It's the last of these qualities that I appreciate most of all. Despite the fact that Witte moves in the highest echelons of the academic world and I teach at a small and relatively obscure theological seminary, he has encouraged me, offered me otherwise inaccessible opportunities, and promoted my work for nearly two decades now. I am profoundly grateful for these things and offer this chapter as a small token of thanks.

I first survey what Witte has contributed to recent scholarship on covenant. Then I offer some of my own reflections on covenant related to Witte's work and seeking to build on it. I conclude that covenant continues to be an important concept for the fields of political theology and law and religion, although charting its contemporary practical implications in increasingly secular societies is a difficult endeavor.

1 John Witte's Scholarship on Covenant

Witte's work on covenant has addressed the topic in two primary contexts: marriage and political association. The former focus seems to appear more frequently in his writings, and so I discuss this first.

Witte has often written about the biblical, and particularly Old Testament, roots of considering marriage as a covenantal relationship. He notes that earlier parts of the Old Testament canon don't treat marriage as a covenant in any direct way. But as we reach the prophetical literature, this idea takes on great theological and practical importance. As Witte explains, several prophets—particularly Isaiah, Jeremiah, Ezekiel, Hosea, and Malachi—analogize the marriage relationship to God's covenant relationship with Israel. Israel's unfaithfulness to Yahweh was like marital infidelity that threatened to dissolve their bond. This conception of marriage as a covenant became most explicit in Malachi, which refers to a woman being the companion and wife of her husband "by covenant" (2:14).[1]

Witte is not an Old Testament scholar by specialty, of course, and his writing on these matters makes generous use of other scholars' work. But Witte has added his own constructive reflections on what this covenantal dimension contributes to an understanding of marriage. For one, it confirms several things evident elsewhere in scripture. It confirms the presentation of marriage as a monogamous union of one man and one woman in Genesis 2. It also confirms God's participation in each marriage as well as the procreative function of marriage. Further, it confirms God's laws for marriage formation already present in the natural and Mosaic laws. But the covenant metaphor, according to Witte, also added new dimensions to Mosaic regulations about marriage and exemplified the spirit of those regulations. It drew individual marriages

---

1 See, for example, John Witte, Jr., *From Sacrament to Contract: Marriage, Religion, and Law in the Western Tradition*, 2nd ed. (Louisville: Westminster John Knox, 2012), 39–43; John Witte, Jr., *God's Joust, God's Justice: Law and Religion in the Western Tradition* (Grand Rapids: Eerdmans, 2006), 377; John Witte, Jr. and Joel A. Nichols, introduction to *Covenant Marriage in Comparative Perspective*, ed. John Witte, Jr. and Eliza Ellison (Grand Rapids: Eerdmans, 2005), 16–18; and John Witte, Jr., *Church, State, and Family: Reconciling Traditional Teachings and Modern Liberties* (Cambridge: Cambridge University Press, 2019), 228–30.

into the larger covenantal relationship God had made with Israel and pointed to a new egalitarian ethic in which husbands were to be just as faithful to their wives as their wives were to be to them.[2]

Witte has devoted great attention to the development of the law and theology of marriage in the West, an area in which he has made many of his most important contributions to scholarly learning. One of his favorite areas of interest is how the Protestant Reformation transformed Western marriage policy and law. According to Witte, Martin Luther and the Lutheran Reformation added new dimensions to the theology and practice of marriage, many of them related to their two-kingdoms doctrine. For Lutherans, marriage was an institution of the earthly kingdom. In his early work, John Calvin largely followed Luther. But although he never rejected this Lutheran precedent, "Calvin's mature theology of marriage was grounded in the biblical doctrine of covenant."[3] In a number of works, Witte has outlined this rich covenantal conception of marriage developed by Calvin and continued in later Reformed writers.[4]

Although primarily a *historian* of the law and theology of marriage, Witte also keeps a keen eye on contemporary debates and contributes wise interventions on the future course of marriage and family law. Among the developments that piqued his interest a couple of decades ago was the fledgling movement to recognize "covenant marriage" in several American states. The idea was to give prospective couples two legal options, either to pursue a merely contractual marriage that is easy to enter and easy to leave or to choose a covenantal marriage that requires premarital counseling and sets a high bar for divorce.[5] In more recent work, however, Witte has acknowledged that despite this movement's promising start, it failed to get far off the ground.[6]

Witte has also directed his legal-historical attention to the importance of covenant for political association. Here again he has found the most evidence for this within the Reformed tradition. In several works, especially *The Reformation of Rights*, Witte has examined numerous early Reformed texts—many

---

2   See, for example, *From Sacrament to Contract*, 43–45; and *Church, State, and Family*, 230–32.
3   *From Sacrament to Contract*, 185; see also John Witte, Jr. and Robert M. Kingdon, *Sex, Marriage, and Family in John Calvin's Geneva*, vol. 1, *Courtship, Engagement, and Marriage* (Grand Rapids: Eerdmans, 2005), 490.
4   See, for example, *From Sacrament to Contract*, 184–212; *God's Joust*, 378–80; Witte and Kingdon, *Sex, Marriage, and Family*, 482–90; John Witte, Jr., *The Western Case for Monogamy Over Polygamy* (Cambridge: Cambridge University Press, 2015), 245–53; and *Church, State, and Family*, 85–105.
5   See, for example, *God's Joust*, 364–68; and Witte and Nichols, introduction to *Covenant Marriage*, 1–5.
6   See *Church, State, and Family*, 312–14.

of them not widely known—and explained how the idea of covenant enabled important thinkers to navigate the weighty political challenges their communities faced. Viewing political association through a covenantal lens carried a number of benefits, but perhaps above all these Reformed thinkers believed it provided a bulwark against tyranny—and remedies when facing it. Among the figures Witte has surveyed on political covenants are Christopher Goodman, Theodore Beza, Johannes Althusius, John Milton, and the New England Puritans.[7]

As Witte has shown that early Reformed theologians drew their covenantal perspective on marriage from scripture, so he also demonstrates the biblical inspiration for their covenantal perspective on politics and law. They believed that political covenants of their own day were parallel to intrahuman Old Testament covenants, in which Israelite kings pledged their submission to God's law and to the people's liberties.[8] Witte is aware of how such convictions problematize the idea of religious liberty. He has argued, however, that the New England Puritans' idea "of a liberty of covenant, while initially exclusivist, eventually became the basis for a robust theory of confessional pluralism."[9]

John Witte has amassed a treasure of historical scholarship on the importance of covenant in biblical literature and especially in the Western legal and political tradition. While immensely valuable in its own right, this scholarship raises pressing questions about its relevance for contemporary law, politics, and marriage—and this may be putting it lightly, given the religious fragmentation and increasing secularity of our own day. In the rest of this chapter, I seek to extend and engage some of these important conversations that Witte has instigated. I do so as a Reformed theologian, for whose own work on ethics and political theology the covenant idea has been crucial.

2 Intrahuman Covenantal Relationships: Initial Reflections

There are many kinds of human relationships. What makes *covenantal* relationships different from others? One characteristic of covenantal relationships is that they are designed to be long-term. There would be no point in establishing

---

7 See, especially, John Witte, Jr., *The Reformation of Rights: Law, Religion, and Human Rights in Early Modern Calvinism* (Cambridge: Cambridge University Press, 2007), 122 (Goodman), 122–41 (Beza), 187–203 (Althusius), 223 (Milton), and 287–314 (the New England Puritans). For related discussions, see, for example, *God's Joust*, 143–60, 350–51; and John Witte, Jr., *The Blessings of Liberty: Human Rights and Religious Freedom in the Western Legal Tradition* (Cambridge: Cambridge University Press, 2022), 60, 102, 115–16.

8 See, for example, *The Reformation of Rights*, 122, 125, 188–91; and *The Blessings of Liberty*, 20.

9 *The Reformation of Rights*, 288.

a covenant to govern a temporary relationship between two strangers meeting in the wilderness. They may wish to make an exchange—say, a little food for a piece of clothing—but no covenant is necessary when they have no plan to interact again. In Genesis 14, the awkward meeting of Abraham and the king of Sodom may be a good illustration of this, especially as we begin to think about these issues theologically. This king and Abraham had joined forces in a local war, each for his own purposes (14:8–16). Afterwards, the two met, and arguably the king of Sodom tried to formalize a relationship with Abraham (14:21). But Abraham clearly wanted little to do with him and kept their relationship to a minimum by agreeing only to settle immediate needs. He tidied up accounts and refused any future commitments (14:22–24). Abraham was willing to enter committed, long-term relationships with political authorities, as considered below, but not with the king of Sodom, surely because of Sodom's despicable moral character, which Genesis 18–19 depicts.[10]

Some human relationships can be short-term and meet only immediate needs. But we also need long-term relationships. One common and useful form of longer-term relationship is *contract*. In contracts, the parties agree to discharge certain obligations in the future, ordinarily with the understanding that enforcement mechanisms stand behind them. The difference between contractual and covenantal relationships doesn't necessarily concern the substance of the obligations or the reality of enforcement. The essential difference is that covenants involve swearing an oath to God. Covenants invoke God to witness the agreement and even to enforce it. Covenants therefore have a solemnity and weightiness that contracts don't, even though violating the latter may entail painful temporal consequences.

Contracts and covenants, then, are different kinds of long-term relationships. This raises the question of why a covenantal relationship would ever be

---

10 David Novak calls this a "commercial transaction." See *The Jewish Social Contract: An Essay in Political Theology* (Princeton: Princeton University Press, 2005), 44. Novak's work on intrahuman covenants as rooted in divine-human covenants has been very helpful and stimulative for my own work over the years. Many of my conclusions are similar, although not identical, to his. Acknowledging Novak's contribution here seems especially fitting since I have heard John Witte express his appreciation for Novak's work as well, and Novak has contributed to several of Witte's projects. See, for example, David Novak, "Religious Human Rights in Judaic Texts," in *Religious Human Rights in Global Perspective: Religious Perspectives,* ed. John Witte, Jr. and Johan D. van der Vyver (The Hague: Martinus Nijhoff, 1996), 175–202; David Novak, "Law and Religion in Judaism," in *Christianity and Law: An Introduction,* ed. John Witte, Jr. and Frank S. Alexander (Cambridge: Cambridge University Press, 2008), 33–52; and David Novak, "The Judaic Foundation of Rights," in *Christianity and Human Rights: An Introduction* (Cambridge: Cambridge University Press, 2010), 47–63.

desirable or advantageous. The simple answer is that some long-term relationships are much more serious than others. There's no infallible way to prevent the violation of any human agreement, but we feel the need for special measures to impress the *gravitas* of certain kinds of relationships upon the parties and to heighten the odds that they'll discharge their obligations. Calling God to participate in a relationship certainly serves these ends.[11] Nevertheless, precisely because of the weightiness of such arrangements and the high bar for entering them, we don't want every relationship to be covenantal. I don't want or need a covenantal relationship with the employee who sells me a cup of coffee at a restaurant off the highway while I'm driving across the country. I don't even need or want one with the pest-control company that sprays the exterior of my house every couple of months—a contractual relationship works perfectly well. Such relationships serve good purposes in the course of human life and cause inconvenience when something goes wrong, yet in the big picture not much is at stake. But that's not true for at least a small number of relationships. The uniting of people into a political community and the uniting of two people in marriage are obvious examples. As discussed above, these are the kinds of relationships that have drawn John Witte's attention in his work on covenant.

Establishing covenantal relationships in a limited number of areas of life may seem theoretically attractive, but it raises further questions, which are necessarily theological in nature. Perhaps most serious: On what grounds are human beings justified in invoking God to witness and enforce relationships of their own making? Why isn't this presumptuous? Why isn't it a form of blasphemy, a misuse of God's name in violation of the Decalogue? What gives us authority to put God under obligation? Even if there's a satisfactory response to this problem, at least one other big question remains: Can people of different religious convictions enter covenants with each other? Such people don't share the same ideas about the "God" they invoke,[12] and presumably mutual agreement on the terms of a covenant is essential to its validity. The potential contemporary usefulness of covenant surely depends greatly on the answer to this question.

The Old Testament uses covenantal language and imagery when describing some political and marital relationships. This practice indicates, for those of us who acknowledge the Old Testament's authority, that there is theological justification for entering political and marital covenants in certain circumstances. It's worth exploring why this is the case, which in turn may provide insight

---

11   See Novak, *The Jewish Social Contract*, 211.
12   Ibid., 34–35.

about the usefulness of the covenant idea today. I begin by reflecting on political covenants and will focus mostly on them, although I'll also address marital covenants toward the end of this chapter.

3 Political Covenants

I return to the first of the big questions raised above: On what grounds are human beings justified in invoking God to witness and enforce relationships of their own making? The basic answer I propose is that human parties are justified in establishing political covenants when such covenants emerge between people who are already together in covenant with God and when such covenants serve to advance that covenant with God.[13] Before proceeding further, I should note that covenants may take different forms. In the Old Testament there are divine-human covenants and intrahuman covenants, and these are necessarily different in some respects. But there are also different kinds of divine-human covenants and different kinds of intrahuman covenants, reflected in the relative strength of the covenanting parties or the kinds of obligations each party has. I need not provide further details here, but the discussion below presumes such differences.[14] Now back to the point above: intrahuman political covenants are justified when grounded in and advancing a covenant that God has already made with both parties.

The first two intrahuman political covenants in the Old Testament are those between Abraham and Abimelech, king of Gerar, in Genesis 21 and between Isaac and Abimelech (II?) in Genesis 26. Both covenants involved oaths (21:23–24, 31–32; 26:28–31). As we read these accounts in the context of Genesis, we find that despite Abraham's and Isaac's many differences with Abimelech, they had one very important thing in common: they were all human partners of the covenant God made in Genesis 8:21–9:17, what I will call the *Noahic covenant*. God made this covenant with Noah as the father of a renewed humanity after the great flood, and with his offspring after him (9:8–9). The text also states that God made it with all living creatures of the earth for all future generations (9:10, 12, 15–16). It's a truly universal covenant, extending even to the earth itself and the broader natural order (8:21–22; 9:13, 17). The implications are clear: all

---

13   Novak offers a similar answer. See, especially, his distinction between "master" covenants and "derivative" covenants in *The Jewish Social Contract*, 33–34.
14   For a useful summary of the different kinds of covenants in scripture and in the ancient Near East, see Scott W. Hahn, *Kinship by Covenant: A Canonical Approach to the Fulfillment of God's Saving Promises* (New Haven: Yale University Press, 2009), 29.

CHRISTIAN TEACHINGS ON OBLIGATIONS 155

human beings (along with all animals) together are the party with whom God covenants. Abraham, Isaac, and Abimelech, therefore, shared a covenantal bond as fellow humans.[15]

There are compelling reasons to interpret their covenants in Genesis 21 and 26 in light of this preexisting covenantal bond. To begin, scholars have noted that the covenants of Genesis 21 and 26 are *parity* covenants. That is, Abraham and Isaac covenanted with Abimelech as equals.[16] Their mutual participation in the Noahic covenant is part of the explanation for this. For one thing, the Noahic covenant put all human beings in their place, for in it God, the superior, covenanted with humans, the inferior.[17] This implied a fundamental equality of humility among all humans. But the Noahic covenant also acknowledged the equal dignity of all human beings. They're all divine image-bearers, and their blood is of equivalent value (9:6).

This organic connection between the Noahic covenant and the intrahuman covenants of Genesis 21 and 26 provides some reason to think that the legitimacy of the latter rests in the former. But surely intrahuman covenanting can't be justified merely on the ground of mutual participation in the Noahic covenant. The additional element necessary is that intrahuman covenants must advance the Noahic covenant's purposes. Humans can have confidence invoking God's name to witness and enforce their own covenants if such covenants promote covenantal responsibilities that God has already given them.

What are the Noahic covenantal responsibilities? The account of the Noahic covenant doesn't mention many, but one of them comes in poetic form: "Whoever sheds the blood of man, by man shall his blood be shed, for God made man in his own image" (9:6).[18] To put it simply, the human community ought to enforce justice against wrongdoers and restore peace where there's conflict. And this was indeed a central purpose of the covenants in Genesis 21 and 26. Abraham and Abimelech had had a serious dispute in Genesis 20, which

---

15 For detailed discussion of this Noahic covenant, including a defense of distinguishing the covenant with Noah here *after* the great flood from the covenant with Noah *before* the flood (Genesis 6:18), see David VanDrunen, *Divine Covenant and Moral Order: A Biblical Theology of Natural Law* (Grand Rapids: Eerdmans, 2014), chap.2. That volume is part of the Emory University Studies in Law and Religion, under the general editorship of John Witte, Jr.

16 See, for example, Hahn, *Kinship by Covenant*, 43.

17 As Novak puts it, "The most either of them can ever be is a covenanted, junior partner of God. Only then can they become equal partners with each other." See *The Jewish Social Contract*, 46.

18 Scripture quotations are from The ESV Bible (The Holy Bible, English Standard Version), copyright © 2001 by Crossway, a publishing ministry of Good New Publishers. Used by permission. All rights reserved.

they resolved, albeit through a rather frigid encounter. When Abimelech later approached Abraham to propose an intimate covenantal bond, he professed interest in maintaining just relations between them and their posterity (21:23). In his response, Abraham noted that Abimelech's servants had stolen from him, a wrong remedied through the covenant (21:25–31).[19] Likewise, Genesis 26 sets Isaac's covenant with Abimelech in the context of a long-standing quarrel. Their covenant aimed to prevent future "harm" and maintain "peace" (26:29). Thus, I believe David Novak is correct to say: "As for Abraham and Abimelech, what they are doing in their covenant is extending God's universal justice into their own particular political situation…. The conditions of the covenant, which Abraham and Abimelech did make for themselves, have moral authority because they are modeled on the original Noahide covenant Abraham and Abimelech did not make for themselves."[20]

Before reflecting further on political covenants grounded in the Noahic covenant, I pause for an interlude. The Old Testament describes other intrahuman political covenants that are crucially different from those of Abraham and Isaac with Abimelech. I think especially of covenants that the people of Israel established with some of their kings—David (1 Samuel 5:3; 1 Chronicles 11:3), Asa (2 Chronicles 15:12–14), and Joash (1 Kings 11:17; 2 Chronicles 23:3, 16)—in which they made various commitments to each other and to the Lord. These intra-Israelite covenants weren't grounded in the Noahic covenant as the covenants of Abraham and Isaac with Abimelech were. The former pledged, for example, that Israel would be the Lord's people (1 Kings 11:17; 2 Chronicles 23:16) and that any Israelites who failed to seek the God of Israel would be put to death (2 Chronicles 15:13). The Israelite people had no inherent right to make themselves God's special people, nor did any Israelite have an inherent right to execute a person for failure to worship properly. Nor did the Noahic covenant give Israelites or anyone else such authority.

But another covenant functioned to ground these intra-Israelite political covenants in a way analogous to how the Noahic covenant grounded the intrahuman covenants in Genesis 21 and 26, namely, the Mosaic covenant established at Sinai and later renewed in Deuteronomy. In this covenant, God declared that Israel would be his "treasured possession among all peoples" (Exodus 19:5). This covenant also commanded that idolaters should be executed (for example, Exodus 22:20). Hence, when later Israelite kings and people made the covenants they did, they committed themselves to be the

---

19 See Daniel I. Block, *Covenant: The Framework of God's Grand Plan of Redemption* (Grand Rapids: Baker Academic, 2021), 109.
20 Novak, *The Jewish Social Contract*, 45–46.

sort of people God had already made them at Sinai. When they invoked God's name, they weren't blaspheming by trying to coerce God to enforce their own projects. Rather, these intra-Israelite covenants were justified inasmuch as they advanced God's own project in the Mosaic covenant.

This interlude isn't a digression, since it raises important constructive questions and also prompts some engagement with issues raised by John Witte's scholarship. As mentioned above, Witte has noted how many early Reformed political writers viewed political association through the lens of covenant. In doing so, they analogized their contemporary political covenants with the political covenants between Israelite kings and people. Witte's historical work is certainly accurate, but did these early Reformed thinkers have good grounds for this analogy? If my preceding analysis of Old Testament covenanting is on solid footing, the answer seems to be negative. The Israelite kings and people covenanted with each other in response to the prior covenant God had made with Israel. But early modern European kings and people couldn't look back to any covenant God had made with them. God never established France, for instance, as his special people, as he established Israel at Sinai. The intra-Israelite political covenants were thus a problematic precedent for sixteenth- and seventeenth-century political covenants.

As Christians, of course, early Reformed writers could look back to the New Testament and claim to be covenanted with God through the *new covenant*. Should these Reformed thinkers have appealed to the new covenant as precedent for their political covenants, then? This too would have been problematic. In the New Testament, the new-covenant community wasn't a political nation but a church. Christ gave his church apostles, prophets, evangelists, pastors, and teachers (Ephesians 4:11), but no magistrates. He gave his church the keys of the kingdom of heaven (Matthew 16:18–19), but no sword of justice that magistrates possessed (Romans 13:4). The covenants of Abraham and Isaac with Abimelech enacted the requirements of the Noahic covenant in which all three participated, and the covenants of Israelite kings and people enacted the requirements of the Mosaic covenant in which they all participated. But entering a *political* covenant does not and cannot enact the requirements of the new covenant.

This isn't to say that early Reformed writers were wrong in their desire to view political association of their own day through a covenantal lens. In my judgment, however, they should have considered the Noahic covenant the foundation for their own political covenanting. In turn, this implies that they should have regarded the political covenants of Genesis 21 and 26, rather than those between Israelite kings and people, as proper biblical precedent. God put the Noahic covenant into place until the end of the world as we know it

(Genesis 8:22), and thus it was no less relevant background for understanding God's governance of human affairs in early-modern Europe than it was in the days of Abraham and Isaac. Since there was no other supervening biblical covenant to regulate the political affairs of early-modern Europeans (which implies a *disanalogy* with Old Testament Israelites living under the supervening Mosaic covenant), Reformed writers should have recognized the Noahic covenant rather than the Mosaic covenant as politically normative.[21]

These concerns aren't simply theoretical. One major practical difference between viewing the Noahic covenant as foundational and viewing the Mosaic covenant as foundational is whether those entering a political covenant constitute a special people holy to the Lord. Covenanting under the auspices of the Mosaic covenant, the Israelites properly considered themselves such a people. The Mosaic law promulgated detailed regulations for right worship and their coercive enforcement. This provided justification for what we today would call rejection of religious liberty in their political covenants (as observed above, for example, in 2 Chronicles 15:13). But the Noahic covenant established no particular people as a special people holy to the Lord, nor did it give instructions for right worship and its enforcement. It thus provides no justification for seeking uniformity of religious belief and practice in political covenants established under its auspices.

Religious liberty is another prominent topic in John Witte's scholarship, as explored elsewhere in this volume. I suggest that regarding the Noahic covenant as foundational for political covenants provides excellent theological rationale for supporting a broad measure of religious freedom.[22] Or from another angle: those already convinced of the good of religious liberty should find it attractive to view the Noahic covenant as politically foundational.

Of course, this was not the mindset of early Reformed writers. Like most of their contemporaries in other Christian traditions as well, they considered their political communities Christian nations, or at least as communities that ought to be Christian nations. They sought toleration for their own worship when under hostile governments but didn't think of broad religious liberty as a political ideal.

---

21 One important early modern Protestant figure who used the Noahic covenant as a foundation for legal, political, and social life was English jurist John Selden. See discussion of his views in John Witte, Jr., *Faith, Freedom, and Family: New Essays in Law and Religion*, ed. Norman Doe and Gary S. Hauk (Tübingen: Mohr Siebeck, 2021), chap. 9 ("The Integrative Christian Jurisprudence of John Selden").

22 For detailed defense of this claim, see David VanDrunen, *Politics after Christendom: Political Theology in a Fractured World* (Grand Rapids: Zondervan Academic, 2020), chap.7.

When a particular community decided to make a real-life political covenant under Reformed inspiration—I think specifically of the Scottish National Covenant of 1638—it followed the spirit of the Mosaic covenant rather than the Noahic covenant. The signers, representing both civil and ecclesiastical constituencies, swore to oppose "Papistry" and to embrace and defend Reformed Christianity in their realm.[23]

As a self-identifying confessional Presbyterian, I acknowledge the Scottish Presbyterians as among my spiritual forebears. Yet I must regard their conception of political covenant as inconsistent with a biblical covenant theology, and thus inconsistent with their own deepest convictions. The Reformed tradition would do well to dissent from this part of its legacy, in my judgment.

4 The Prospects for Contemporary Political Covenants

The previous section leaves open the question whether viewing political association through a covenantal lens is helpful for Christians and others in our present day. Since religious liberty is now quite widely affirmed (though hardly uncontroversial), my preceding comments may suggest initial grounds for an affirmative answer. Nevertheless, those preceding comments also raise a puzzling question: how can people who *aren't* united by a common religious confession enter valid covenants with each other? If they don't share the same conception of the "God" whom their covenant oath invokes, how can the different parties have confidence in each other's understanding of the terms and commitment to observe them? This was the second of the big questions I raised in my initial reflections on intrahuman covenants.

This question takes us back to the political covenants Abraham and Isaac made with Abimelech. These biblical stories indicate that political covenants can indeed be valid between parties of different religions and also indicate the

---

23   On the National Covenant generally, see, for example, *Dictionary of Scottish Church History & Theology*, ed. Nigel M. de S. Cameron et al (Downers Grove, IL: InterVaristy, 1993), 620. A different but relevant example may be the Afrikaners, who emerged from and developed their own version of Dutch Reformed Christianity. Their self-understanding as a covenanted people seems to have contributed to the inseparability of their commitments to their religion and to their national identity, with many complicated and tragic implications for the history of South Africa. For related discussion, see Jonathan Neil Gerstner, *The Ten Thousand Generation Covenant: Dutch Reformed Covenant Theology and Group Identity in Colonial South Africa, 1652–1814* (Leiden: Brill, 1991), especially chap. 11. See also, generally, Hermann Giliomee, *The Afrikaners: Biography of a People*, expanded ed. (Charlottesville: University of Virginia Press, 2009).

conditions for this validity. I'll first explain why I believe these two claims are true and then reflect on what this suggests for our contemporary context.

Did Abraham and Abimelech share a common religion? The most plausible evidence for an affirmative answer is probably in the opening verses of Genesis 20. Abraham was on the move, as he often was, and he sojourned in Gerar, where Abimelech was king. Afraid for his safety, Abraham presented his wife Sarah as his sister, and Abimelech promptly took her into his harem. At this point "God came to Abimelech in a dream by night" (20:3). In context, it's clear that this is the same God as the one described throughout Genesis. God informed Abimelech that Sarah was Abraham's wife, Abimelech protested his innocence since Abraham had told him otherwise, and God acknowledged his ignorance but instructed Abimelech to return Sarah to Abraham, upon pain of death (20:3–7). Abimelech, it seems, had a relationship with the same God whom Abraham worshiped.

But on further reflection, it's doubtful that Abraham and Abimelech truly shared a common religion. Earlier narratives in Genesis describe an intimate relationship that God established with Abraham by covenant oath, through which he promised to make his offspring numerous and a blessing to all nations of the earth, to which promises Abraham clung by faith (Genesis 15: 17). Genesis communicates that no other individual or people enjoyed such a privilege. Polytheistic idolatry was presumably the default religious orientation of the day. Even Abraham had been an idolater (see Joshua 24:2). Genesis 20 gives no indication that Abimelech had any intimate fellowship with Abraham's God or even that their nocturnal encounter concerning Sarah had any precedent. It's unlikely that Abimelech thought of Abraham's God as anyone other than one deity among others. Abraham and Abimelech didn't share a common faith.

Yet they entered a covenant in Genesis 21, in which they both swore oaths. This demands explanation, and it seems to lie in an important detail in Genesis 20: the "fear of God" existed in Gerar under Abimelech's reign. Following the revelation that Sarah was actually Abraham's wife, Abimelech confronted Abraham and accused him of doing "things that ought not to be done" (20:9). Abraham offered a rather half-hearted defense, explaining that he thought, "There is no fear of God at all in this place, and they will kill me because of my wife" (20:11). The context makes evident that Abraham was wrong in this suspicion. Gerar was not the sort of place that kills husbands to steal their wives. There was fear of God in this place.

What is fear of God, in this context? As in several other Old Testament texts, it seems to represent respect for a divine power higher than oneself, under whose judgment one stands. As such, this fear of God restrained those who had it from certain egregious acts of injustice, and the lack of it explained the egregious acts of others (for example, Exodus 1:17; 18:21; Deuteronomy 25:17–19).[24] Abimelech didn't share Abraham's faith, but he had some respect for the divine. What exactly that meant we can't know. But it was such that Abimelech could recognize that "God" was with Abraham and propose that Abraham "swear to me here by God" that he would deal honestly with him in the future (21:22–23). Abraham agreed, and they "both" swore oaths (21:31).

It would be interesting to know what names for God each of their oaths used. The text tells us that after Abimelech departed, Abraham "called there on the name of the LORD [YHWH], the Everlasting God" (21:33). This was God's special covenant name, which Abimelech never uttered and presumably didn't know. But even if they called God by different names, reflecting their different religions, they were able to swear oaths to promote mutual peace and justice. Abraham and Abimelech weren't spiritual kin, but neither were they moral strangers. As Novak has put it, they occupied "a common moral universe."[25] Covenants such as theirs didn't aim to bring utopia but to promote relatively and provisionally livable societies. And that seems to be precisely the goal the Noahic covenant suggests is appropriate.[26]

So what about our own day? It isn't immediately obvious what contemporary occasions might call for covenants in political communities that already have a settled and functioning constitutional order. The situation of Abraham sojourning with his large household of servants in the city-state of Gerar seems exceedingly distant from the politics of my own country, the United States, and of many other countries. But we can leave it open for now as to whether there may be occasions in which associations within the contemporary American constitutional order might enter political covenants. Of course, the United States continues to negotiate and enter *treaties* with other countries. This is pertinent to note since "treaty" and "covenant" are arguably synonyms. Some English translations of scripture use "treaty" to translate the common Hebrew word for "covenant" when it describes what I've called a political covenant. So I pose this question: Is the contemporary United States the kind of place qualified to enter covenants, either among its own people or with other countries? The fitting way to ask the question, in terms of preceding discussion, is whether the contemporary United States is a place that fears God.

I have my doubts. Many people do regard the United States as a religious country, although such claims seem true only on a relative basis, in comparison to more secularized places, such as Western Europe. But even if the

---

24 See VanDrunen, *Divine Covenants*, 157–61.
25 Novak, *The Jewish Social Contract*, 42–43.
26 Ibid., 47.

United States can be deemed religious by some plausible measure, this is hardly equivalent to the "fear of God" among Gentiles in the Old Testament. Are the American people marked by a deep sense of accountability before the divine judgment? Does respect for the divine play a major role in constraining Americans from egregious acts of injustice? It's difficult to imagine an impartial observer claiming this, even if the divine is understood in a theologically imprecise way, as the narrative in Genesis 20–21 appears to allow. Most religious Americans seem to recognize a much gentler and indulgent God than the one Abimelech feared. Sexual and materialistic self-fulfillment and construction of one's own identity surely characterize American culture and drive moral choices more than awe before the divine judgment. Perhaps there are countries in the world today that can be characterized as God-fearing. I don't know. Or perhaps there are small-scale political associations within the United States that are God-fearing and might find occasion to covenant with each other for limited purposes.

Yet I don't mean to communicate despair about the United States. To judge a place as lacking in the fear of God is simply to say that it's no Gerar.[27] It doesn't mean that it's Sodom either, or Amalek, which swept behind Israel when they came out of Egypt and cut off the weaker people lagging behind because Amalek "did not fear God" (Deuteronomy 25:17–18). Viewing American political association through a contractual lens—somewhere between a trustful covenantal lens and a deeply suspicious transactional lens—may be the best we can do. But it's better than the worst we could do.

5 Marital Covenants

If there is a strongly viable place for covenants as a means for social organization in today's world, marital covenants are likely the better candidate. Perhaps this is why John Witte has spent more time writing about them than about political covenants. In this final section of the chapter, I offer a few brief reflections on the subject.

Although it may be disagreeable to some readers, I believe it's proper to consider marital covenants, like political covenants, under the auspices of the Noahic covenant. It's true, as Witte has discussed, that the Old Testament prophets frequently analogized God's relationship to Israel to marriage, and

---

27 Gerar itself was far from ideal. Abimelech, thinking Sarah was unmarried, "took" her (Genesis 20:2). Abimelech wouldn't have killed Abraham if she were his wife, which was good, but what he did still sounds like violence against women.

that Paul did the same with Christ's relationship to the church (Ephesians 5:22–33). Nevertheless, scripture identifies the origin of marriage in the creation order (Genesis 1:28; 2:20–25). After the great flood, the Noahic covenant reestablished this order, including the primitive commission to be fruitful and multiply (9:1, 7). Marriage isn't a Jewish or Christian institution but a *human* institution, even though the understanding and practice of marriage varies from one religious culture to another.

Marital covenants can thus be justified on similar grounds to political covenants. What right do a man and woman have to invoke the name of God when entering into a marriage relationship by their own choice? The answer is that God has established marriage as a good and necessary human relationship, and he has confirmed its ongoing importance by way of covenant. Thus, when couples swear by God's name to enter into a marital covenant, they advance God's own covenantal purposes. The man and woman already share a preexisting covenant relationship with God, and on that basis can covenant with each other to promote its requirements.

Marital covenants have no greater theoretical legitimacy than political covenants, but there are practical reasons to think that the former have greater prospects than the latter for meeting the criteria of validity. One reason is simply that marital covenants involve a much smaller number of parties, at least in our own day, when heads of state don't speak personally on behalf of a community as ancient potentates did. That is, a head of state who genuinely fears God can't enter an international treaty or covenant on the basis of the integrity of her personal oath. Many political communities today may be simply too big or too democratically conceived to make covenants between them viable. But not so with marriage. A second reason is that shared religious conviction is one of the most common things that bring marriage partners together, and some religions require their adherents to marry only within the faith. To put it another way, individuals who fear God, and who fear God in the same way, tend to find each other and marry. Many couples, of course, lack the sort of religious beliefs that would make legitimate covenanting possible. But for many others their shared conviction will make their oaths mutually comprehensible and thus their obligations mutually clear.

In the face of easy divorce and broader breakdown of the family in much of the world, the potential usefulness of viewing marriage as covenantal is rather obvious. The fledgling covenant-marriage movement in the United States may have fizzled in a strictly legal sense, but there's nothing stopping families and other nonpolitical bodies from promoting and recognizing marital covenants. The state may view marriage as only a legal contract, but couples and their supporting communities can treat it much more profoundly, for what it truly is.

6   Conclusion

I write this chapter with great appreciation for John Witte, Jr. and his contribution to contemporary thinking about covenant. It's with some regret that I can't offer a more enthusiastic assessment of the prospects for covenant in our present cultural moment, but as I believe Witte would agree, covenant by itself cannot heal an ill society. Making covenants, in fact, presumes a certain moral health already present in those who make them. If and when Western societies begin to heal from their focus on individual self-fulfillment, and begin to gain (or regain) a sense of the fear of God, perhaps political and marital covenanting can be both a beneficial result of that healing and an instrument for its continuation and sustenance.

CHAPTER 10

Law, Christianity, and Good Samaritanism

M. Christian Green

1   Introduction: Good Samaritans or Good Preachers

It should be evident that no book of reflections on a scholar of law and religion of John Witte's caliber could do without an examination of the core ethical teachings contained in the story of the Good Samaritan. A consummate biblical passage on law and religion and a linchpin of Christian ethics in so many ways, the story comes in Jesus's response to a query from a lawyer. The parable, contained in the Gospel of Luke, is prefaced with the following exchange:

> And behold, a lawyer stood up to put him to the test, saying, "Teacher, what shall I do to inherit eternal life?" He said to him, "What is written in the law? How do you read?" And he answered, "You shall love the Lord your God with all your heart, and with all your soul, and with all your strength, and with all your mind; and your neighbor as yourself." And he said to him, "You have answered right; do this, and you will live."[1]

Jesus's response is a recitation of the Great Commandment, whose meaning should have been all but self-evident to early followers of Jesus. The lawyer, however, follows his question with a second. As the account in the Gospel of Luke reads, "But he, desiring to justify himself, said to Jesus, 'And who is my neighbor?'"[2] This question is the crux of the Good Samaritan story.

We are left to wonder at the lawyer's reported motive of self-justification. Did he ask the question in earnest, or was he playing the devil's advocate? Was the lawyer a sophist seeking to appear smart by one-upping the Lord? Was he seeking to exculpate or excuse himself rhetorically from his own failures to live up to the Great Commandment? Was the lawyer engaged in a sort of hypocritical virtue signaling, perhaps obscuring his own ability to be more judicious than just, more righteous than right, or perhaps just a grumpy pragmatist in

---

1 Luke 10:25–28; all biblical quotations are from the Revised Standard Version, unless noted otherwise.
2 Luke 10:29.

© M. CHRISTIAN GREEN, 2024 | DOI:10.1163/9789004546189_011
This is an open access chapter distributed under the terms of the CC BY-NC 4.0 license.

suggesting that there should be some parsing of the parameters of the agapic love that Jesus was recommending for humanity?

With the parable of the Good Samaritan that Jesus offers in response, he takes the lawyer's question seriously—offering not only an answer but also some marching orders.

Jesus replied:

> "A man was going down from Jerusalem to Jericho, and he fell among robbers, who stripped him and beat him, and departed, leaving him half dead. Now by chance a priest was going down that road; and when he saw him he passed by on the other side. So likewise a Levite, when he came to the place and saw him, passed by on the other side. But a Samaritan, as he journeyed, came to where he was; and when he saw him, he had compassion, and went to him and bound up his wounds, pouring on oil and wine; then he set him on his own beast and brought him to an inn, and took care of him. And the next day he took out two denarii and gave them to the innkeeper, saying, 'Take care of him; and whatever more you spend, I will repay you when I come back.' Which of these three, do you think, proved neighbor to the man who fell among the robbers?" He said, "The one who showed mercy on him." And Jesus said to him, "Go and do likewise."[3]

"Go and do likewise." "Do this and you will live." These are compelling commands. They do not seem to admit of ambiguity or afford permission to opt out. And yet the story of the Good Samaritan continues to raise questions of interpretation, as much now as when it was first uttered.

What we know of the parable is that the Good Samaritan is a Samaritan, perceived as an enemy and outsider by Jews, and yet in this instance traveling in their land. The victim was traveling from Jerusalem to Jericho, perhaps a Jewish priest returning home to Jericho from the temple, possibly with some collected funds to take to his community. Alternatively, he might have been a man of commerce, heading to Jericho to profit from its activities as an ancient trading center. We don't really know much about him, but he was clearly a victim of a crime, seemingly harmed through no fault of his own. The priest and the Levite passed the man by, the subsequent speculation being that they might have perceived him as dead and feared defilement from handling the corpse. They weren't so much bystanders to the crime, but they were witnesses

---

3   Luke 10:31–38.

after the fact. Even so, they were bystanders to his ultimate plight and yet did nothing. It was the outsider and stranger who was the "upstander" who acted to come to his aid.

The point of this chapter in the present volume is to take up the question of where the story of the Good Samaritan figures into the study of law and religion—and particularly in the work of John Witte. After all, the concept of the Good Samaritan, as it has entered the law, is a concept that shows up very early in the first-year American law school curriculum, including the torts, contracts, and criminal law sources that Witte has taught to law students for decades, alongside courses on legal history, law and religion, and human rights. One learns particularly in the first-year torts class about "Good Samaritan laws," intended to protect from legal liability those who render assistance.

For many students, the idea that someone who helps could be the subject of a lawsuit is something of a shock. But if one looks more comparatively and internationally, one learns that there are places in the world where there is no "duty to rescue." There are also places, such as most of Europe and Latin America, where there is a "duty to rescue." And then there are places, like the United States, the United Kingdom, Australia, and many parts of Canada—basically much of the Anglo-American legal world—where there are "Good Samaritan" laws. In these Anglo-American areas, people may welcome rescuers—but they may also try to sue them; hence the need for legal protection in the Good Samaritan laws. The standard comparison has been that the Anglo-American world is just more individualistic, libertarian, and adversarial in its legal system,[4] even when it comes to Good Samaritans, in contrast to the more communitarian ethic that prevails in many European nations and their New World manifestations in French Catholic Quebec, New England states with Puritan legacies (Massachusetts and Vermont), Lutheran Midwestern states (Minnesota and Wisconsin), and the far-flung and often Spanish Catholic-influenced states of Washington, California, and Florida—all of which have retained the "duty to rescue" standard.[5]

---

4   The status of the United States as a libertarian outlier was first brought home to me in reading a well-known book by a frequent Witte associate, Professor Mary Ann Glendon, who for decades taught comparative law and other topics at Harvard Law School, Witte's legal alma mater. See Mary Ann Glendon, *Rights Talk: The Impoverishment of Political Discourse* (New York: Free Press, 1991). Indeed, it was almost certainly Witte who recommended the book to me.
5   I mention religion because it is worth thinking about whether these states' orientations—particularly those that recognize a "duty to rescue"—coincide with religious principles. However, it is beyond the scope of this essay to conduct a full inquiry. As a native of Louisiana, I do

Another international area influenced by the parable of the Good Samaritan is the field of international human rights law, where there has been debate over the past few decades about the "responsibility to protect." The responsibility to protect (R2P) was a doctrine undergoing development in the early 1990s, when I was John Witte's student. It emerged in response to the genocides in Rwanda and Yugoslavia, which were themselves redolent of the earlier genocide of the Holocaust.[6] The experience of the Holocaust, or Shoah, was in many ways the genesis of the modern international human rights regimes in the Universal Declaration of Human Rights, and the many covenants, treaties, declarations, and resolutions that followed.[7] The development of international human rights laws was the global community's response to the central question of the Good Samaritan story: And who is our neighbor? To whom are we responsible? Whom must we protect? What is our responsibility to come to the aid of our global neighbors? These questions were central in the Rwandan and Bosnian conflicts, and they are equally central to the conflicts in Syria and the Russian aggression against Ukraine. These have been key questions of international human rights law as it has sought to respond to past, present, and future genocides of peoples and cultures.

In this context, it is not surprising that the story of the Good Samaritan made its way into several of John Witte's early articles on law, religion, and human rights. There, Witte writes: "In desperate circumstances, it is sometimes better to be a Good Samaritan than a good preacher, to give food and comfort before sermons and catechisms."[8] But what does this really mean? In this chapter, I examine the Good Samaritan and related themes through the work of John Witte, drawing further inspiration from the great minds of two friends and teachers that Witte and I were blessed to share: the late Don S. Browning and Jean Bethke Elshtain. These reflections range from the ethics of bystanders to the kindness of strangers and the proper balance of charity and justice in the

---

find it interesting that Louisiana, which retains the Civil Code, has cast off the French and Spanish commitment to a duty to rescue. There is probably a story there.

6 A key book in the "Responsibility to Protect" debates was written by another Harvard professor, now diplomat, Samantha Power. See Samantha Power, *A Problem from Hell: America and the Age of Genocide* (New York: Basic Books, 2002).

7 See Johannes Morsink, *The Universal Declaration of Human Rights: An Endangered Connection* (Washington, DC: Georgetown University Press, 2018); and Johannes Morsink, *The Universal Declaration of Human Rights: Origins, Drafting, and Intent* (Philadelphia: University of Pennsylvania Press, 2000).

8 John Witte, Jr., "Law, Religion, and Human Rights," *Columbia Human Rights Law Review*, 28, no. 1 (1996): 11. See also John Witte, Jr., introduction to *Religious Human Rights in Global Perspective: Religious Perspectives*, ed. John Witte, Jr. and Johan D. van der Vyver (Leiden: Martinus Nijhoff, 1996), XVII–XXXV.

modern social welfare state. The common denominator is the ongoing challenge raised by the story of the Good Samaritan for law, religion, and ethics.

2   "You Know, There Really Are No Bystanders": Good Samaritan Ethics and the Great Commandment

If the ethics of the Good Samaritan is about knowing and responding compassionately to the circumstances of one's neighbor, it is first necessary to see the neighbor and to see them as falling within the circle of one's concern. Interestingly, toward the end of the first decade of the twenty-first century, at exactly the time that the internet and social media were connecting people within and around the world's nations more than in any previous era, when surveillance systems and technologies were increasingly allowing us to witness crimes, genocides, and the most mundane lives and circumstances of others in ways that only Foucault with his panopticon could imagine,[9] there was an inexplicable epidemic of horrendous lapses by modern-day Levites and Pharisees among us. The sick slumped and died before cameras in hospitals, the elderly and babies were left unattended in streets, and we were just beginning to see that police body, cruiser, and street cameras would be the silent sentinels to law enforcement abuses and surveillance of the public—at least until they were released to the public's horror.[10] We would soon see, often through others' smartphone cameras, atrocities against citizens that would launch civil wars and citizen protests in places like Syria, Hong Kong, Iran, and even U.S. streets following incidents of police brutality.[11] Satellites, our "eyes in the sky," would

---

9   Michel Foucault, *Discipline and Punish: The Birth of the Modern Prison*, trans. Alan Sheridan (New York: Vintage Book, 1995), chap. 3.

10 For examples of some troubling headlines from the times—and at a time when Witte and I were contemplating a project on humanitarianism, no less—see the following: Peter Applebome, "The Day the Traffic Did Not Stop in Hartford," *The New York Times*, Jun. 8, 2008; Anemona Hartocollis, "Video of a Dying Mental Patient Being Ignored Spurs Changes at Brooklyn Hospital, *The New York Times*, Jul. 2, 2008; and Keith B. Richburg, "An Injured Toddler Is Ignored and Chinese Ask Why," *The Washington Post*, Oct. 19, 2011. On police cameras, see, for example, Frej Klem Thomsen, "The Ethics of Police Body-Worn Cameras," *Moral Philosophy and Politics*, Jun. 20, 2020.

11 See, for example, "Arab Spring: The First Smartphone Revolution," *The Economic Times*, Nov. 30, 2020; Matt J. Duffy, "Smartphones in the Arab Spring," *International Press Institute Report* (2011): 53–56; Jacob Granger, "Voice for the Voiceless: Smartphones Are the Weapon of Choice to Tell Stories from the Syrian Civil War," Journalism.co.uk, Jun. 6, 2019; and "What You Should Know about the Smartphone Revolution in Iran," *Article 19*, Jun. 9, 2016.

reveal authoritarian prison camps, mass graves after genocides, terrorist compounds as drone weapons delivered their payloads. A counterterrorism mantra of the time instructed us: "See Something, Say Something."[12] But as the older saying goes, "there are none so blind as those who will not see."[13] With these new technologies, we have much more to see, even as bystanders, and many more opportunities to respond in a Good Samaritan way—or not.

There has been a lot to see in recent years, but our ethics have not always risen to the occasion. How to think about the ethics of bystanders in a Samaritan sense was the focus of some work that I did under the leadership and direction of a mutual friend I shared with John Witte, the late and great Don Browning. Specifically, in a seminar that convened over several years on the "Moral and Spiritual Formation of Children," led by Elizabeth Marquardt, another scholar inspired by Witte's work on marriage, family, and children in law,[14] I produced a paper titled, "'There but for the Grace': The Ethics of Bystanders to Divorce."[15] The paper departed from my own memories as a child of being part of the "divorce culture" generation as no-fault divorce took hold in the United States in the 1970s and 1980s.[16] While my parents never divorced, the parents of many friends did—and in ways that seemed threatening even to those of us whose parents stayed together.

In writing about bystanders to divorce, a key question was whether I had any basis (or maybe "standing") in legal terms to be bothered by the sad circumstances of the families of others. Was it any of my business? What reason could I have for being affected by other people's family troubles and dissolutions? Wouldn't my being sad about it make it even worse for childhood friends who had to shuttle between parents and divide their holidays? Was I a stakeholder of sorts—or merely a bystander—to the tragedies of others? Perhaps I should keep my discomfort and anxiety about my own familial stability to myself, be grateful for my blessings, and keep a silent, stiff upper lip.

The concept of the bystander and the appropriate response to the travails of others also became connected in my mind to the Good Samaritan. Surely,

---

12   Jen Chung, "MTA Updates Famous 'See Something, Say Something' Campaign with Real NYers Who Saw Something, Said Something," *Gothamist*, Mar. 21, 2016.
13   The phrase is said to be based on Jeremiah 5:21: "Hear this, O foolish and senseless people, who have eyes, but do not see, who have ears, but do not hear."
14   See Elizabeth Marquardt, *Between Two Worlds: The Inner Lives of Children of Divorce* (New York: Random House, 2005).
15   M. Christian Green, "'There but for the Grace': The Ethics of Bystanders to Divorce," *Propositions* (New York: Center for Public Conversation, 2012).
16   See Barbara Dafoe Whitehead, *The Divorce Culture: Rethinking Our Commitments to Marriage and Family* (New York: Vintage, 1998).

the parable of the Good Samaritan should have something to say about how to be an "upstander" and not just a bystander in a world marked by tragedy. After all, the "bystander effect," as it has come to be called in the social sciences, also had a troubling legacy. It was best memorialized in the story of *New York Times* editor A. M. Rosenthal of the rape and murder of Kitty Genovese in New York in 1964.[17] As the story went, dozens of Genovese's neighbors—thirty-eight in total, it was said—failed to respond to her screams and intervene to save her from her attacker. (A later documentary film produced by Genovese's brother, in fact, revealed that many bystanders had come forward at the time to report the crime to police).[18] The "bystander effect" came to stand for a supposed tendency among people to do nothing in aid of their neighbors in distress out of a sense that someone else would take care of it. In that sense, the bystander was the opposite of the Good Samaritan—really the very antithesis.

But the pernicious origins of the bystander effect did not stop me from delving into all manner of social contagion, social network, and cultural trauma theories to understand the ethics of bystanders. It seemed that there were many theories concerning social forces by which the bystander could be deterred from action. So it was like a pinprick in my burgeoning bystander ethics balloon when Witte's and my mentor, Don Browning, turned to me after the presentation and said, "You know, from a Christian perspective, there really are no bystanders." What? Really? Not after I spent twenty minutes and many pages propounding them. I felt deflated, but also defiant. I bristled. I was getting my inner Cain on. What Browning seemed to imply was that the Christian religion assumes a very high level of responsibility for others—that we ultimately cannot and probably never should try to erect a bystander barrier to others. "Am I my brother's (or sister's) keeper?" The story of the Good Samaritan seems to say, definitively: Yes.

Browning's reminder that "there are really no bystanders" in Christianity is also reminiscent of an observation at the core of the thought of a thinker who has played a central role in the legal and theological development of John Witte—namely, John Calvin. Calvin puts the point squarely in his *Institutes of the Christian Religion*, observing:

> We are not our own: let us therefore not set it as our goal to seek what is expedient for us according to the flesh. We are not our own: in so far as we can, let us forget ourselves and all that is ours.

---

17 See A. M. Rosenthal, *Thirty-Eight Witnesses: The Kitty Genovese Case* (New York: Skyhorse, 2016).
18 *The Witness*, film, dir. James D. Solomon, exec. prod. William Genovese (2015).

Conversely, we are God's: let us therefore live for Him and die for Him. We are God's: let His wisdom and will therefore rule all our actions. We are God's: let all the parts of our life accordingly strive toward Him as our only lawful goal.[19]

"We are not our own." It's a powerful statement—and one that has many implications for human agency toward our neighbors in this world. It counsels a "relativization," as we say in ethics, of the self in relation to others. It is a strong basis for what theologian H. R. Niebuhr called "the responsible self."[20]

Calvin's observation, in turn, is redolent of the Great Commandment as expressed in John 13:34: "I give you a new commandment, that you love one another. Just as I have loved you, you also should love one another."[21] If we are to strive for God and to love God, then clearly we must love one another. In such a theology, there clearly can be no bystanders. Even to posit that there could be bystanders—that is, people who are not in fact standing by or with their fellow humans but standing separate and apart from and unaffected by their suffering—is to separate oneself from others and thus from God. In short, as Jesus admonishes the priest and the Levite in the parable—it is sin. In that context, the Good Samaritan is not an exceptional individual—a bystander who happened to become an upstander. The Good Samaritan is no mere exemplar of an occasional grace. The Good Samaritan is who Christians are called to be. The exception is to be the rule.

3 "One Deals with What One Is Dealt": Charity, Justice, and the Good Samaritan State

Becoming a Good Samaritan bystander is not easy for striving Christian individuals—and it may be even harder for aspiring Christian states. At the collective level of the state, the Good Samaritan story implicates another key discussion in Christian ethics—namely, the debate over the relationship between charity and justice. In considering this debate in light of the Good Samaritan story, I am guided by memory of a remark from another mutual acquaintance whom John and I shared: Jean Bethke Elshtain. Elshtain and I once exchanged

---

19 John Calvin, *Institutes of the Christian Religion*, ed. John T. McNeill, trans. Ford Lewis Battles, Library of Christian Classics (Philadelphia: Westminster, 1960 [1559]), 3.7.1.
20 H. R. Niehbuhr, *The Responsible Self: An Essay in Christian Moral Philosophy* (New York: Harper & Row, 1963).
21 John 13:34, New Revised Standard Edition.

a series of commiserations about personal and familial health issues and the challenges they posed. Therein, Elshtain, a good Midwestern Lutheran, and thus a partaker of the same Reformation traditions that shaped John Witte,[22] remarked resolutely: "One deals with what one is dealt."

Upon hearing this, my initial reaction was much the same as that of another fellow student to whom I recounted the story: "That's so Jean!" It was no doubt dripping with abundant truth and human experience, even though it sounded a little harsh. But wait, subsequent reflection counseled, "What does this mean?" "One deals with what one is dealt." It is a statement at once hopeful and fatalistic. Life deals us many things. Not all are within our control. But some things are. They may even be, at least partially, our fault. They may even be the result of sin. There is hope in our capacity to deal. But what happens when that capacity falls short? Must we individually pull ourselves up by our own tattered bootstraps? Will a Good Samaritan step in to assist and offer the kindness of a stranger? Or is there some collective responsibility—maybe even a responsibility of a Christian or Good Samaritan state that those around a person in distress should share?

This question of the relationship of charity and justice in the Good Samaritan state is a good question to ask of the work of John Witte, particularly his studies of the development of "poor-relief" laws (*Armenordnungen*) in Europe under the Protestant Reformation. Indeed, these laws to do with poor relief and proper allocation of resources from the community chest in the "Church Ordinance" laws, dating back to 1522, are some of the earliest effects of the reformers on law.[23] The sort of charity expressed in these poor-relief laws was one of the real achievements of Reformation law in an early modern European world in which many were still condemned to lives that were, in the immortal words of Thomas Hobbes, "solitary, poor, nasty, brutish, and short."[24] It is interesting that the "solitary" and "poor" parts often get lopped off this phrase in popular parlance. Is it an attempt in subsequent capitalist societies to evade the communal responsibility to care for those who are less well off? What responsibility does a Good Samaritan-informed Christian state have to ameliorate and assist those whose lives would otherwise be "nasty, brutish, and short"?

---

22   See, for example, Jean Bethke Elshtain's wonderful remarks, titled "Does Luther Make Sense?" at Reformation Day at Emory University's Candler School of Theology on November 11, 2009, available in audio recording at https://archive.org/details/podcast_reformation-day-2009_does-luther-make-sense_1000091636127.

23   John Witte, Jr., *Law and Protestantism: The Legal Teachings of the Lutheran Revolution* (Cambridge: Cambridge University Press, 2002), 184.

24   Thomas Hobbes, *Leviathan* (1651) I, XIII, 9.

The problem of charity and justice is that individual acts of charity do not always add up to the structural and systematic change necessary to do justice. And the kindness of strangers often flows most readily to those who are not too strange—that is, to those who are not of a different sex, race, ethnicity, nationality, or socioeconomic class from the potential patron or benefactor. Charity, a theological virtue ("And now abideth faith, hope, charity, these three; but the greatest of these is charity"),[25] may be written on the human heart in a natural law sense, but as perceived and enacted by humans it is also subject to the distortions of sin that are present in human societies. In recognizing that tendency toward sin, the Reformation thinkers likely inserted a needful corrective into Christian ethics. Witte describes this evolution in the reformer Philip Melanchthon:

> "Our nature is corrupted by original sin," Melanchthon wrote, echoing Luther' s doctrine of total depravity. "Thus the law of nature is greatly obscured." This, too, was a decided departure from conventional teaching. Medieval writers recognized that all individuals have an innate or natural knowledge of good and evil, which they sometimes called "synderesis." Through proper discipline, a person could come to understand and apply this knowledge and so do good and avoid evil. A person must use reason to apprehend the natural law. He must use conscience to apply it in concrete circumstances. Thus, for example, through the exercise of reason a person apprehends and understands the principle of love of neighbor; through the exercise of conscience he connects this principle with *the practice of aiding the poor and helpless* or of keeping his promises."[26]

As Witte observes of Melanchthon's reconstruction of natural law for Protestant understandings, "For many medieval writers, reason was a cognitive or intellectual faculty, conscience a practical or applicative skill. Melanchthon, like Luther, would have none of this fine casuistry. God planted a perfect natural knowledge of the nature of good and evil in our minds. But our sin keeps us from apprehending or applying it without distortion."[27]

Reformation thought on charity underwent further refinement at the hands of the German jurist Johannes Eisermann. As Witte notes:

> [I]n a Christian commonwealth, charity must be prized and churlishness scorned. "Even though men are of private estate, they are not excused

---

25   1 Corinthians 13:13, King James Version.
26   *Law and Protestantism*, 124–25.
27   Ibid., 125.

from helping others," Eisermann argued. This is the plain instruction not only of nature but especially of Scripture. We must "exhort delightfully in hospitality, rendering to none evil for evil, for we are commanded to feed [even] our enemies if they are hungry, to give them drink if they are thirsty, and thereby heap burning coals on their head and thus provoke them to do likewise." In giving charity, "man is a veritable god to his fellow man."[28]

Eisermann drafted laws on poor relief, but he was no redistributive socialist and, in fact, was a staunch defender of private property, by Witte's account.[29] There were limits to private charity, most notably the need attend to one's own responsibilities and not fall into destitution. Witte characterizes Eisermann's thought and legislation on the subject thus:

> Though saints and sinners alike deserve charity, a person of modest means must be discriminating in dispensing it. One's own family and dependents deserve closest care. Beyond that, only the worthy poor should be served—orphans, widows, the aged, the sick. The unworthy poor—the lazy beggar, the itinerant mendicant, the loitering vagabond—must work for their alms or be banished if they refuse. Eisermann's insights were part of a whole industry of new Evangelical reflections on poverty and charity.[30]

Witte further quotes Eisermann himself on the moral underpinnings of these new laws that Witte describes as the "core of a very active Christian welfare state." Eisermann observed:

> It is the duty of the magistrate to restore the decayed, gather the dispersed, recover the lost, reform the disordered, punish the evil, enlarge the common good, *relieve the poor*, defend the orphan and the widow, promote virtue, administer justice, keep the law, demonstrate that he is the father of the country, hold the people's commitment to him as if they were his own children, embrace godliness faithfully and with his whole heart, perform all that is profitable or necessary among the people, according to his duty, no less than if God Himself were present.[31]

28　Ibid., 149.
29　Ibid., 149.
30　Ibid., 150.
31　Ibid., 151–52.

So, "saints and sinners alike"—but also a distinction between the "worthy" and "unworthy" poor. It's the latter point that sticks a bit in the craw. Were there really "deserving and undeserving poor"? Were human magistrates to determine who was "worthy" or "unworthy" in the sight of God?

In a sense, they were, for Witte describes how the Reformation lawyers had a particular theology behind their law—one that rejected what they saw as excessive spiritualization of both poverty and charity in the church that they were protesting. As Witte observes:

> The Lutheran reformers rejected traditional teachings of both the spiritual idealization of poverty and the spiritual efficaciousness of charity. All persons were called to work the work of God in the world, they argued. They were not to be idle or to impoverish themselves voluntarily. Voluntary poverty was a form of social parasitism to be punished, not a symbol of spiritual sacrifice to be rewarded. Only the worthy local poor deserved charity, and only if they could not be helped by their immediate family members, the family being the "first school of charity." Charity, in turn, was not a form of spiritual self-enhancement. It was a vocation of the priesthood of believers. Charity brought no immediate spiritual reward to the giver. Instead, it brought spiritual opportunity to the receiver. The Evangelical doctrine of justification by faith alone undercut the spiritual efficacy of charity for the giver. Salvation came through faith in Christ, not through charity to one's neighbor. But the Evangelical doctrine of the priesthood of all believers enhanced the spiritual efficacy of charity for the receiver. Those who were already saved by faith became members of the priesthood of all believers. They were called to love and serve their neighbors charitably in imitation of Christ. Those who received the charity of their neighbors would see in this personal sacrificial act the good works brought by faith, and so be moved to have faith themselves.[32]

As Witte further notes of the reformers and their theology of charity,

> They translated their belief in the spiritual efficacy of the direct personal relationship between giver and receiver into a new emphasis on local charity for the local poor, without dense administrative bureaucracies.... The "redemptive charity" that the reformers had in mind came more in the direct personal encounter between the faithful giver and the grateful

---

32   Ibid., 193–94.

receiver, not so much in the conventional notion that the receiver should experience and receive charity within a Church institution.[33]

In later centuries, these Reformed Protestant concepts of charity would undergo some modification in the context of modern administrative states, while also sticking to core beliefs, including concepts of the "worthy" or "deserving" poor. In Witte's writing on the public theology of the nineteenth-century neo-Calvinist theologian and journalist Abraham Kuyper, who served as prime minister of the Netherlands in the early years of the twentieth century, one sees the worthy and unworthy poor distinction still in play. Witte writes, "Like Calvin, Kuyper commended work and condemned idleness, championing the Protestant teaching that God calls all persons to a 'vocation' that best suits their natural abilities and gifts. But 'if anyone is not willing to work, let him not eat.'"[34] At the same time, Witte further observes of Kuyper's theology of poor relief, "All Christians were to serve the poor, needy, orphans, and sojourners in their midst, for 'as much as you do it to the least of these you do it to me,' Jesus had said (Matt. 25:45). And the church itself was to maintain the diaconate to collect and distribute alms to the 'deserving poor'—those who, despite their best efforts, still needed help."[35]

Even so, Witte notes—as Kuyper did in his time—that new challenges were testing understandings of "vocation" and the "worthy" or "deserving poor." As Witte describes the tenor of Kuyper's times:

> Yet, the gusts and gales of Dutch industrialization were posing profound new socioeconomic changes and challenges to the Netherlands and much of the West. Now that employers had access to newfound steam power, electricity, and machinery, many enterprises no longer needed as much manual labor, or were growing too large to heed local labor concerns. With open trade, population growth, and foreign workers intensifying competition, Dutch workers were finding it harder to get and keep their jobs. The old systems of guilds that had long guarded local craftsmen's interests were giving way to more *laissez-faire* business practices that left many workers with lower wages, longer working hours, and harder working conditions. Many workers were forced to sign easily

---

33 Ibid., 194.
34 John Witte, Jr. and Eric Wang, "Abraham Kuyper and Reformed Public Theology," *International Journal of Reformed Public Theology* 6, no. 2 (2020): 10–11 (citing 2 Thessalonians 3:10); pagination is to SSRN copy found at: https://papers.ssrn.com/abstract=3959072.
35 Witte and Wang, "Abraham Kuyper and Reformed Public Theology," 11.

terminable contracts, and later lost their jobs or began to slide into poverty. The Industrial Revolution, Kuyper wrote, stripped workers of a "sense of security" in life. In response, workers in Kuyper's day were picketing and striking, boycotting goods, sabotaging factories, and joining trade unions that endorsed violence. Kuyper labeled the new challenges of industrialization, labor, unemployment, and poverty as "*the* social question" that needed the urgent attention of all spheres of life, including notably the state.[36]

In the context of such broad and sweeping social transformation, reliance on individual or institutional charity for sustenance was likely to lead to disasters. Charitable endeavors by individuals and organizations might make a dent in social welfare, but they could not provide for it entirely. This is where the Samaritan ethic needed an accompanying social ethic.

The challenge for Christian leaders of Kuyper's time was how to properly allocate the responsibilities of families, churches, and the state—each within their "sphere sovereignty"—to address these new concerns that were both spiritual and structural.[37] As Witte describes the result:

> Against both socialists who sought to dismantle property rights and market structures and capitalists who downplayed market problems and impoverished workers, Kuyper outlined new roles for church and state in confronting "the social question." In "normal" situations, Kuyper wrote, the church was to assume responsibility for assisting the poor with their spiritual and material needs.... Thus the church was not only to share the Gospel, but also to implement a diaconate funding system wherein alms were collected from all and discretely donated to those in need. Miserly charity was insulting, and ad hoc philanthropy was inadequate to meet the biblical commands to love and care for our neighbors.[38]

36　Ibid., 11.
37　On sphere sovereignty, see, for example, Abraham Kuyper, *Our Program: A Christian Political Manifesto* (Bellingham, WA: Lexham Press, 2015); Abraham Kuyper, *Charity & Justice* (Bellingham, WA: Lexham Press, 2022); Herman Dooyeweerd, *The Struggle for a Christian Politics*, ed. D. F. M. Strauss (New York: Paideia, 2012), also in *The Collected Works of Herman Dooyeweerd*, Series B, Vol. 17 (New York: Paideia Press). See also Jonathan Chaplin, *Herman Dooyeweerd: Christian Philosopher of State and Civil Society* (Notre Dame: University of Notre Dame Press, 2022).
38　Witte and Wang, "Abraham Kuyper and Reformed Public Theology," 12.

The problems of too "miserly charity" and too "ad hoc philanthropy" persist—along with problematic divisions of "worthy" and "unworthy" and "deserving" and "undeserving" in the "new normals" of our circumstances today. Many of us are dealing with what we are dealt, but it is not clear (if it has ever been) that we are being dealt equitably or are equally capable of dealing in the new gusts and gales.

4 "No Fault of Their Own": Charitable Choices and Challenges

A United States Department of the Treasury fact sheet reads: "The American Rescue Plan will change the course of the pandemic and deliver immediate and direct relief to families and workers impacted by the COVID-19 crisis *through no fault of their own*."[39] Through no fault of their own. It's a phrase one hears frequently in connection with government spending—especially after collective disasters such as natural disasters and dreadful pandemics. It's also a phrase one hears from "fiscally conservative" politicians to defend social spending that is necessary, whatever their ideological proclivities against "welfare" and "socialism" and toward downsizing government. Politicians often have a soft spot for social spending when the recipients are victimized by forces "through no fault of their own." The challenge tends to come when the recipients are seen as complicit in their circumstances.

In U.S. politics, the relationship between government spending and charitable giving, particularly by religious organizations, has an interesting recent history. When I began my studies with John Witte in the 1990s, the 1992 election of a Democratic president, Bill Clinton, was followed by a Republican revolution in the midterm elections, in which Congress, led by the Speaker of the House, then the Georgia congressman Newt Gingrich,[40] enacted numerous reforms on fiscal responsibility, personal responsibility (welfare), tax credits for children and marriage, and job creation and wage enhancement. It was a conservative program in American political terms, and it would likely have met with strong approval from Protestant Reformation forebears. There was even talk of "devolution of powers" from the federal government to the states that seems inspired by Kuyperian and Dooyeweerdian sphere sovereignty.

Further changes to the system of charity and social welfare came just a few years later with the "charitable choice" provisions under President Clinton,

---

39 United States Department of the Treasury, "Fact Sheet: The American Rescue Plan Will Deliver Immediate Economic Relief to Families," Mar. 18, 2021 (emphasis added).
40 See Newt Gingrich et al., *Contract With America* (New York: Times Books, 1994).

by which the government was permitted to purchase social services from religious providers.⁴¹ The charitable choice provisions raised questions from those who thought they might violate separation of church and state, favor particular religious denominations, or condition service recipient benefits on subscription or conversion to a faith. Faith-based providers, in turn, raised questions about diminution of their prophetic message, interference with religious autonomy, and excessive entanglement with government. The U.S. Supreme Court has largely taken a permissive perspective on charitable choice despite these complaints from various sides, and the permissive view seems likely to continue, and perhaps to expand, in the near future, given the primacy of the Free Exercise Clause over the Establishment Clause and affirmative, nondiscriminatory aid to religious individuals and groups in the Court's recent jurisprudence.⁴²

"Compassionate conservatism" became the term for the continuation of this charitable-choice impulse under the administration of President George W. Bush.⁴³ But circumstances changed, in many respects, with the Great Recession of 2008. This was a global economic recession that touched lives the world over, but in the United States, it gave rise to the Tea Party movement, which began as a fiscally conservative movement concerned to lower taxes and reduce the federal debt, but which became a volatile movement of libertarian, conservative, and populist forces, all of which ultimately wanted much less government in people's lives. Their fiscal concerns might have meshed with some of the Protestant reformers' concerns for efficient management of the community chest and national resources, but without the moral underpinnings of concern for neighbor love and social welfare. These new conservative movements were all about liberty—but not always about love. And by the time of President Donald Trump, they were calling for "deconstruction of the administrative state" in a way that would presumably have shocked the *Obrigkeit* of old.

Throughout most of these recent programs— the "Contract With America," "charitable choice," and "compassionate conservatism"—there has been some preservation of distinction between those who are worthy or unworthy of social welfare assistance. The Personal Work and Responsibility Act of 1996

---

41 For discussion of the charitable-choice provisions, see Carl Esbeck, "Charitable Choice and the Critics," *N.Y.U. Annual Survey of American Law* 57, no. 1 (2000): 17–33; and Stanley Carlson-Thies, "Charitable Choice: Bringing Religion Back into American Welfare," *Journal of Policy History* 13, no. 1 (2001): 109–32.
42 See Carl Esbeck, "Charity for the Autonomous Self" (review essay), *Journal of Law and Religion* 32, no. 1 (2017): 185–96.
43 Marvin Olasky, *Compassionate Conservatism: What It Is, What It Does, and How It Can Transform America* (New York: Free Press, 2000).

and other welfare reforms enacted under President Clinton led to the conscientious resignation of some program officials, as the work requirements—particularly for single mothers—were seen as onerous in a society that lacked affordable childcare options and at a time when the intact, two-parent family seemed largely to be eroding. After the terrorist attacks of September 11, 2001, the international distractions of the global war on terror largely displaced the domestic policy on social welfare and the family that had occupied the last decades of the twentieth. Sustained attention to the concerns about how to balance charity and justice in the care of society's most vulnerable fell, to some extent, by the wayside.

As the twenty-first century moved on, the rise of the internet and the effects of global economic recessions in 2001 and 2008 led to social and technological revolutions in work and at home. Entire industries were being displaced or upended in the new millennium. Scientists began to issue increasingly urgent calls for global attention to climate change. Political polarization and rising authoritarianism abroad weakened societies and their safety nets. The COVID-19 pandemic was a great leveler in some respects, since it prompted the shutdown of entire societies, but it also underscored social, political, and economic problems and dramatic inequalities in health and well-being, even in advanced nations. The effects of these large phenomena may be no one's fault in particular, but they are surely what we are being dealt, and the key question is who, between the private charitable and public governmental sectors, will lead in addressing them.

5   Being Good Samaritans and Charitable Bystanders in Today's Sociopolitical Sphere

In an introduction to a recent volume on Abraham Kuyper's social and political thought, titled *On Charity & Justice*, John Witte recites at one point a little Calvinist catechism that strikes this reader for thinking of how to be a Good Samaritan and a charitable bystander in today's world. I divide it in half here in order to make specific reflections. It is a nice blend of the theological and political, the individual and the collective and what we are called to do in order to "Go and do likewise."

First, Witte observes of the Calvinist tradition, particularly as carried forth in a *semper reformanda* way by Kuyper and others:

> Instead of assuming that natural human life was lawlessly "brutish, nasty, and short," they emphasized the natural restraints of God's law written

on all hearts and God's common grace, which "shines on all that's fair." Instead of seeing natural rights as pathways to a self-interested pursuit of life, liberty, and property of the sovereign individual, they saw rights as opportunities to discharge divine duties set out in the Decalogue and other moral laws.⁴⁴

In this way, the tradition cautions against "naturalization" of plights of poverty, otherness, and victimization and recommends postures of abundance, solidarity, and agency. The Good Samaritan gave of his time and treasure in a way that the self-interested sovereignty of the priest and Levite, keen to preserve their purity and distance, did not. Where the priest and Levite saw inconvenience and possibly even contagion in the plight of the man by the road, the Good Samaritan saw the opportunity to discharge divine love toward a stranger.

Second, Witte sees in the Calvinist legal, social, and political order certain features that can encourage this Good Samaritan behavior. Witte observes:

> Instead of seeing constitutions as social and government contracts between individuals designed to protect individual rights, they treated constitutions as divinely modeled covenants between rulers, people and God, designed to protect human and associational rights, to break up and bracket political power, and to encourage and celebrate godly values.⁴⁵

We see ongoing discussion today over who should take responsibility for the vulnerable among us. Some argue for a robust public sphere, by which we come together collectively as a society to create governments and social structures that will meet people's needs and assure the general welfare. Others argue that this sort of assurance only comes about when we have a strong private sphere, where people have "skin in the game" by having ownership of property that they can then use to benefit others through charitable acts and arrangements. Others propose public-private partnerships as a hybrid to get the job done. What all of these arrangements depend on are systems of law and rule of law to provide for and protect these arrangements.

---

44   John Witte, Jr., "Abraham Kuyper: Always Reforming," in *Abraham Kuyper on Charity & Justice*, ed. Matthew J. Tuininga (Bellingham, WA: Lexham Press, 2022), XXXIII–LXVII, reprinted with updates as "Abraham Kuyper on Family, Freedom, and Fortune," in John Witte, Jr., *Faith, Freedom, and Family: New Essays on Law and Religion*, ed. Norman Doe and Gary S. Hauk (Tübingen: Mohr Siebeck, 2021), 199–214, at 205.

45   Ibid., 205.

Finally, Witte points to a set of rights that are often categorized as civil and political rights, but which can also be essential to defending social welfare rights and to coming to the aid of our neighbors in distress, whether at home or abroad.

> Instead of seeing free speech, free exercise, or free assembly as individual rights limited only by the rights of others and the boundaries of treason, Calvinists saw them as constitutional expressions of the biblical teaching that all persons are called by Christ to be prophets, priests, and sovereigns in the world, with duties to speak, serve, and rule with others in the creation and protection of a godly public.[46]

Much as there was problematic "rights talk" when Mary Ann Glendon wrote about it in 1991—the very year that I became John Witte's student—there is arguably problematic "liberty talk" today. Some of our freedoms of speech, exercise of religion, and association have become cudgels in the hands of authoritarian and antidemocratic forces today. There are new calls for free speech that seem to depend on the silencing of others. Some castigate new social media, which, even though they carry certain risks of hate speech and incitement of insurrection in some contexts, have been used in others as tools for uncovering human rights violations, exercising important associational freedoms to organize, and coming together in revolutions to topple bad regimes and empower new democratic movements to support good ones. In the current context, these constitutional freedoms can indeed produce prophets—the original "See Something, Say Something" folks. And when people's skills of seeing something and saying something are cultivated. They are likely to do something, even something risky, like coming to the aid of a stranger as a Good Samaritan.

---

46   Ibid.

CHAPTER 11

Can Laws and Rights Teach? John Witte and the Uses of the Law

Patrick McKinley Brennan and William S. Brewbaker III

1   Introduction

The default mode of thinking about law today supposes that law is an empty vessel into which policy preferences can be poured and given social effect without regard to their justice, rightness, or goodness. This "instrumental view of law—the idea that law is a means to an end—is taken for granted in the United States, almost a part of the air we breathe."[1] Understood as merely an instrument, law can be manufactured as desired and then invoked, threatened, manipulated, enforced, and utilized, with force if necessary, in furtherance of endless ends.

The dominance of the instrumental understanding of law was not inevitable. It succeeded a conversation in which "law was widely understood to possess a necessary content and integrity that was, in some sense, given or predetermined. Law was the right ordering of society binding on all."[2] To be sure, there was never a time in which there was just one version of the noninstrumental understanding of law; there were always many ways of understanding human law's relation to natural law, natural right(s), the common good, the Logos, divine law, the Ten Commandments, the Great Commandment, and so forth. Nor did the noninstrumental understandings of law preclude consideration of whether laws were workable in practice.[3] What the noninstrumental versions, variously expressed, had in common that categorically distinguished them from the instrumental view, however, was the judgment that "law was not entirely subject to our individual or group whims or will"[4] because, definitively,

---

1   Brian Tamanaha, *Law as a Means to an End: Threat to the Rule of Law* (Cambridge: Cambridge University Press, 2006), 1.
2   Ibid.
3   See Thomas Aquinas, *Summa Theologiae* [hereinafter ST] I–II, q.94, a. 5, trans. English Dominican Fathers (New York: Benziger Bros., 1947–48) ("additions" to natural law); ibid. at q. 96, a. 2 (need for law to be "possible ... according to the customs of the country"); ibid. at q. 95, a. 1 ad 2 (discussing comparative institutional competence of judges and legislators).
4   Ibid.

law had by nature a *purpose*. Not merely an empty core to be filled up by whatever desires prevailed in the political and legal processes, law was essentially, though always imperfectly in practice, an ordering to a lived reality that was aimed at the good of the persons it ordered.

John Witte's wide-ranging work engages questions about the *purpose* of human law at many points, but especially in its resuscitation of the Reformed Protestant doctrine of "the uses of the law." This chapter begins by setting out Witte's historical analysis of the uses of the law and proceeds to his application of the doctrine to contemporary criminal law. With the uses model of law thus in view, the chapter then asks in a sustained way what we are to make of Witte's programmatic contention that "human rights and their vindication help the law achieve its basic uses in this life."[5] One coauthor (Brewbaker) offers a qualified Protestant agreement with Witte's analysis of uses of law as a vindicator of human rights, while the other coauthor (Brennan) advances a qualified disagreement with the claim that law is rightly understood as an instrument for settling contests between human rights and the right of the state.

This chapter's critical engagement of Witte's way of situating rights vis-à-vis law in the long arc of the Western conversation welcomes Witte's judgment that "secular political philosophy does not and should not have a monopoly on the nurture of human rights."[6] It embraces also his judgment that "avowedly secular values are not inherently more objective, in an epistemological sense, than their religious counterparts."[7] It draws appreciatively, furthermore, on his argument that rights emerged from Christian and other religious reflection on fundamentals of human dignity, human community, and the freedom of individuals and groups to form and act upon their beliefs about the divine.[8] Respecting Witte's judgment that "rights and liberties depend upon fundamental beliefs for grounding, limitation, and direction,"[9] and discerning and navigating characteristic differences between Protestant and Catholic understandings of individual and group liberties in relation to the common good, we press the question of what room and substance Witte gives to the "common good," a term he uses frequently, in the "human rights regime[s]"[10] he commends. Having done so, we conclude by asking in a suggestive way whether Witte might agree that establishing friendship, which Thomas

---

5   John Witte, Jr., *The Blessings of Liberty: Human Rights and Religious Freedom in the Western Legal Tradition* (Cambridge: Cambridge University Press, 2022), 298.
6   Ibid., 300.
7   Ibid., 301.
8   Ibid., 6–7.
9   Ibid., 11.
10   Ibid., 300.

Aquinas understood to be "the principal intention of human law,"[11] should be understood as in some sense the *telos* or purpose of human law.

2 The Protestant Doctrine of the Uses of the Law

The theology of the Protestant Reformation is sometimes summarized under five headings: (1) *sola scriptura*—scripture alone as the ultimate authority; (2) *sola fide*—salvation by faith alone; (3) *sola gratia*—salvation by grace alone; (4) *solus Christus*—salvation through Christ alone (affirming the priesthood of the believer); and (5) *soli Deo gloria*—the glory of God as the sole goal of life. Although this formulation came along hundreds of years after the Reformation itself, it remains a helpful summary of Reformation distinctives.

It is no surprise that the question of the uses of the law would arise in the context of a Christian theological system bearing these emphases. The question of how to rightly interpret Old Testament law in the New Testament era was, of course, an old one. That said, the Reformation's "new" teaching that one's own works were not a cause of one's justification before God raised new questions. Granted, all agreed that the "law was a tutor to lead us to Christ" (Galatians 3:24), but if one's works play no part in one's justification, and, indeed, if "all who rely on the works of the law are under a curse" (Galatians 3:10), the question whether and, if so, how the law had any continuing use in the life of the believer took on great urgency. The doctrine of the uses of the law provided an answer—or rather, a family of answers—to that question.[12]

In a well-known essay, Witte provides a fine summary of the Reformed doctrine of the uses of the law, including a historical survey that shows the various points of disagreement among its interpreters. Witte's summary first addresses the question of what law we are talking about when we speak of the uses of the law. As Witte argues, the law in question is the divine moral law, which, the reformers believed, God "has written ... on the hearts of all persons, rewritten ... in the pages of Scripture, and summarized ... in the Ten Commandments."[13] The uses of this law, as summarized by Witte, are as follows: "First, the law has a *civil* use to restrain persons from sinful conduct by threat of

---

11   *ST* I–II, q. 99, a.2.
12   See John Witte, Jr., "The Three Uses of the Law: A Protestant Source of the Purposes of Criminal Law?," in Witte, *God's Joust, God's Justice: Law and Religion in the Western Tradition* (Grand Rapids: Eerdmans, 2006), 268–76, for a summary of various forms the doctrine took.
13   Ibid., 264.

divine punishment.... Threatened by divine sanctions, persons obey the basic commandments of the moral law."[14] The basic commandments include the commands "to obey authorities, to respect their neighbor's person and property, to remain sexually continent, [and] to speak truthfully of themselves and their neighbors."[15] This use is appropriately named the civil use because the effect of obedience to these basic commands is to create a "public morality" that "benefits sinners and saints alike ... by allow[ing] for a modicum of peace and stability in this sin-ridden world."[16]

The moral law's second use is *theological*. The moral law serves as a mirror into which the sinner can look, as Luther put it, "to reveal his sin, blindness, misery, wickedness, ignorance, hate, contempt of God."[17] The law provides sinners with an accurate picture of themselves and their hopelessness apart from Christ's grace. As Calvin puts it, "[A]fter [the sinner] is compelled to weigh his life in the scales of the law, he is compelled to seek God's grace."[18]

Finally, the moral law has an *educational* use. It "teach[es] those who have already been justified 'the works that please God.'"[19] We have seen that the civil law helps reinforce public morality by threat of divine punishment. To be sure, the law's educational function does something similar with respect to these same basic expectations of external morality. However, for the Christian, the use of the law goes even further, teaching believers "not only the 'public' or 'external' morality that is common to all persons, but also the 'private' or 'internal' morality that is becoming only of Christians."[20]

---

14   Ibid., 265.
15   Ibid., 265.
16   Ibid., 265 (quoting Calvin). It is worth noting that this aspect of law helps "establish friendship" in the sense discussed in the final section of this chapter.
17   Ibid., 266 (quoting Luther).
18   Ibid., 266 (quoting Calvin). Witte's account includes an additional, less familiar, aspect of the theological use of the law: "[T]he moral law has a *theological* use to condemn sinful persons for their violations of the law. Such condemnation ensures both the integrity of the law and the humility of the sinner" (ibid., 265). What Witte means by the "integrity of the law" is somewhat unclear. He says "The violation of the law is avenged, and the integrity—the balance—of the law is restored by the condemnation of those who violate it" (ibid., 266). Perhaps he means something similar to what he quotes Melanchthon as saying later in the essay, when Melanchthon is speaking about the "reasons for criminal punishment." Melanchthon says: "God is a righteous being, who out of his great and proper goodness created rational creatures to be like him. Therefore, if they strive against him[,] the order of justice requires that he destroy them. The first reason for punishment then is the order of justice in God" (ibid., 277).
19   Ibid., 266 (quoting Calvin).
20   Ibid., 266 (citing Calvin: "As a teacher, the law not only coerces them against violence and violation, but also cultivates in them charity and love. It not only punishes harmful acts

3   Witte's Modest Historical Claim

Witte's contribution in the essay noted above is to connect the Reformed "uses" doctrine to contemporary legal thought by making a claim about Anglo-American criminal law: "The new theological doctrine of the uses of moral law that emerged out of the Reformation had a close conceptual cousin in the new legal doctrine of the purposes of criminal law that [later] came to prevail in early modern England and America."[21] Like the theologians' teaching about the uses of the law, the account of the purposes of the criminal law that gradually emerged also found three purposes: "(1) deterrence or prevention; (2) retribution or restitution; and (3) rehabilitation or reformation—the classic purposes of criminal law that every law student still learns today."[22] Not only are there three purposes, but Witte argues further that "[t]he definition of the deterrent, retributive, and rehabilitative purposes of the criminal law bears a striking resemblance to the definition of the civil, theological, and educational uses of the moral law."[23] Like the civil use of the divine law, deterrence involves the criminal law's role in "coercing persons to adopt ... an external, public, or civic morality."[24] Like the theological use of the divine law, state punishment "can induce the sinner to repent from his evil, confess his sin, and seek God's forgiveness."[25] Indeed, Witte notes, this aspect of criminal law was "one of the principal early rationales for the establishment of penitentiaries in England and America—to give prisoners the solitude and serenity necessary to reflect on their crime and seek forgiveness for it."[26]

Finally, Witte argues, criminal law's oft-mentioned rehabilitative function resembles the educational use of the divine moral law. Criminal law can "restore in the community a knowledge of and respect for the requirements

---

of murder, theft, and fornication, but also prohibits evil thoughts of hatred, covetousness, and lust.")

21   Ibid., 276–79.
22   Ibid., 280.
23   Ibid., 280.
24   Ibid., 281.
25   Ibid., 284.
26   Ibid., 283. As noted above, note 20, Witte argues that the theological use also involves offenses against the integrity of the divine law. This point connects more closely to the idea of retribution in the criminal law, but less clearly to the standard treatments of the Reformed three uses doctrine. Witte makes a point of the connection between retribution and this sort of justice. See *God's Joust, God's Justice*, 282–83.

of moral law."²⁷ Indeed, for some jurists, Witte argues, its purpose went even further, teaching citizens "a more expansive private morality of avoiding fault and evil."²⁸ Witte cites as examples of this more expansive private morality the establishment of religion and punishment of heresy, blasphemy, and Sabbath violations, together with obligations to help the poor and the criminalization of a wide variety of sexual immorality.²⁹ The alleged analogy between the law's role in calling Christians to a higher morality and the criminal law's teaching function may sound more persuasive to modern ears than it would have in times closer to the Reformation. As Witte himself shows in later work, the reformers drew a distinction between laws that prescribed specific church teaching and those that merely established basic public order. It seems quite possible that they would have regarded the laws characterized here as "a more expansive private morality" as merely aspects of basic social order.³⁰

To be clear, Witte is not arguing "that the Protestant theological doctrine of the three uses of moral law was *the* source of the modern Anglo-American legal doctrine of the purposes of criminal law,"³¹ merely that "the close analogies between the structure and content of these theological and legal doctrines reflect ample doctrinal cross fertilization between them."³²

4 Contemporary Applications

Witte's historical claim is relatively modest. Nonetheless, it leads him to notice some important theological continuities between the Reformed theologians and the early modern jurists who formulated the threefold purposes of criminal law. These continuities stand in stark contrast with contemporary assumptions about the nature and purposes of laws in general.

The ideas that Witte sees as holding the older system together are: (1) "the theory of natural and moral law," (2) "the traditional anthropological assumption that human beings and human communities are at once saintly and sinful, *simul iustus et peccator*," and (3) "the traditional moral theory of government

---

27 Ibid., 284.
28 Ibid., 284.
29 See ibid., 284.
30 See John Witte, Jr., *The Reformation of Rights: Law, Religion, and Human Rights in Early Modern Calvinism* (Cambridge: Cambridge University Press, 2007), 64–65.
31 Ibid., 286.
32 Ibid., 287.

which helped to integrate the three purposes of criminal law and punishment."[33] These three ideas suggest that law has a transcendent source, that human beings are capable of both immoral conduct and reformation, and that the state has a connection, however problematic, to divine ordering. In contemporary American life, on the other hand, "the state is seen solely as a representative of the people, not a vice-regent of God."[34] It "has no higher role to play than to mediate among the conflicting private desires and selfish interests of its citizens ... [and] has no legitimate role in shaping those desires."[35] Liberalism, while it "has many great virtues,"[36] threatens to become self-defeating: "The moral relativism underlying liberalism's neutrality tends to corrode all values, even liberalism's own values of individual dignity and rights."[37] Witte argues that criminal law cannot succeed without a sense that its norms have a source beyond the whim of those who happen to be in charge.

In later writings, Witte broadens his approach to the uses of the laws. Rather than make the limited historical claim recounted above in connection with the criminal law, he suggests a more direct link between the old Reformed accounts of the uses of the [divine moral] law and the functions of [civil] law more generally. In a recent book, he notes in passing that the "basic uses" of the [civil] law include "the civil use of keeping peace, order, and constraint among its citizens even if by force; the theological use of driving one to reflect on one's failings and turn to better ways of living in community; and the educational use of teaching everyone the good works of morality and love that please God, however imperfect and transient that achievement inevitably will be in the present age."[38]

Even more striking is his argument, to which we will direct primary attention, that "human rights and their vindication help the law achieve its basic uses in this life."[39] Rights and their recognition, Witte seems to suggest, help

---

33   Witte, "Three Uses," in *God's Joust, God's Justice*, 289. Regarding the third item, "the state is seen solely as a representative of the people, not a vice-regent of God.... The cardinal teaching of liberalism ... is that government should be morally neutral, showing no preference among competing concepts of the good" (*God's Joust, God's Justice*, 288–89). See also ibid., 290 (discussing the rejection of the formative state and John Stuart Mill's harm principle.)
34   Ibid., 289.
35   Ibid., 290.
36   Ibid., 290.
37   Ibid., 290.
38   *The Blessings of Liberty*, 298.
39   Ibid.

the law keep the peace, help us reflect on our failings, and even help teach us good works of morality and love.

5   Why Witte Is Right: a Protestant Endorsement (with Reservations)

5.1   *Why Witte May Be Wrong*

Before discussing why Witte may be correct in his claims about rights and the uses of the law generally, let us begin by noting some possible objections to Witte's thesis about human rights and the uses of the law. A first objection relates to the rhetorical invocation of the uses-of-the-law framework in the context of modern law. Recall that the framework was first developed to describe the functions of the *divine moral law* in the life of a community (the civil use) and in the lives of individual believers (the theological and educational uses). One might doubt whether the theologians who formulated the uses doctrine would be confident that insights about how divine moral law functions can be assumed to apply equally to the laws human beings make.

Witte's original article does not present this question. As discussed above, Witte's earlier works merely make the modest historical claim that early modern jurists' understanding of the purposes of criminal law was a "close conceptual cousin" of the Reformed understanding of the three uses of the divine moral law. From there, as recounted above, Witte makes a number of compelling observations about the criminal law's implicit dependence on extralegal norms about government authority and human conduct.[40]

The more recent assertions about the uses of civil law, however, are not qualified in the same way. Rather, Witte assumes there is at least an analogical relationship between the purposes of civil law generally and the uses outlined in the old Reformed doctrine. This argument is least controversial with respect to the civil use of the law. Few would deny that one of civil law's most important functions is to safeguard a degree of social peace and stability. The reformers argued that fear of divine punishment was the active agent in securing peaceful social life. Of course, they might well have expected that state authorities would be the most likely agencies of divine punishment (at least in this life), so there might be little practical difficulty in arguing for the validity of a civil use of the civil law. Still, even this extension of the doctrine becomes less plausible as applied to laws other than those dealing with crimes and, perhaps, torts.[41]

---

40   See supra text accompanying notes 26–34.
41   For example, the "secondary rules" that H. L. A. Hart identifies in *The Concept of Law*. See H. L. A. Hart, *The Concept of Law*, 3rd ed. (Oxford: Oxford University Press, 2012), 79–99.

In a similar vein, one could agree with Witte that civil law might have a theological use in that it could possibly lead someone to "reflect on [their] failings"[42] and thus seek God's forgiveness. While it seems implausible that modern lawmakers have this purpose in mind, it is still possible that civil law—again primarily criminal and tort law—could have such an effect, regardless of the human lawgiver's specific intentions.

The biggest challenges to extending the uses doctrine to civil law arise with the educational use of the law. We have already seen that, at least on some accounts, the divine moral law is intended to teach the believer a higher gospel morality that would not be expected of unconverted sinners. Civil law, however, is usually seen as an expression of the external morality that conduces to public order, not a set of aspirational norms for living the most virtuous possible human life. Even so, it may be fair to say that the civil law may serve as a guardrail that helps keep persons from gross sins and thus please God more than they otherwise might.

Perhaps the fairest reading of Witte's more recent use of the uses of the law is simply as a broad categorical gesture meant more as an observation about the effects laws generally have than as an extension of divinely revealed truth. Following the Reformation jurists, Witte's earlier characterization of the three uses extended the meaning of "law" from its primary meaning (divine moral law) to a secondary meaning (civil law). Perhaps the concept of theological use could similarly be extended from the reformers' primary meaning (leading the sinner to seek God's grace) to a more secular secondary meaning ("turn[ing the citizen] to better ways of living in community").[43] Similarly, its educational use may be merely teaching the "good works of morality and love."[44]

Regardless of how we understand Witte's intentions, however, he clearly assumes some degree of correspondence between the norms of any given state's civil law and the divine moral law. This creates an important difficulty. The problem is not just that the demands of moral virtue may be greater than the law's requirements, but, more fundamentally, that the laws of any given real-world government are likely to be perverse in some, and perhaps many,

---

42 *The Blessings of Liberty*, 298.
43 Ibid., 298.
44 Ibid. The full quotation, however, refers to "pleasing God" in a way that undercuts this reading: "Rights and their vindication help the law achieve its basic uses in this life—[including] ... the educational use of teaching everyone the good works of morality and love that please God, however imperfect and transient that achievement inevitably will be in the present age" (ibid).

respects. This is not to doubt that laws generally have an expressive function.⁴⁵ It is rather to question the morality expressed in those laws that actually exist.

One need not look far for examples of laws that pretty much everyone agrees taught the wrong thing. Whether or not they deserved to be called law or actually constituted law in some metaphysical sense, laws authorizing some human beings to enslave others in the American South and elsewhere, Jim Crow laws in America and apartheid laws in South Africa, and—most famously in law school jurisprudence courses—Nazi laws, helped build a cultural context in which pernicious norms could be maintained and rationalized.

Saint Augustine gives us reason to believe that even though these examples may be aberrations, that the disconnect between law and (true) morality will always be a question of degree and not kind. On one hand, the natural law is written on the heart of human beings and cannot be entirely erased. Therefore, laws in general usually reflect norms approximating genuine justice in many if not most cases. On the other hand, the laws of any given community are shaped by its loves, which are disordered to the extent that they are not ordered by the love of God. The more disordered the loves, the more we may expect the laws to miss the mark; the less disordered the community's loves, the better the laws are likely to be.

So the best we can say about the educational effects of any system of real-world civil laws is that it will teach a vision of the good life that is ordered by the community's loves. No community—not even the church, says Augustine!⁴⁶—has its loves entirely in order this side of heaven. The more misshapen those loves are, the worse the laws, and the worse the ensuing education will be.

5.2   Why Witte Is (Mostly) Right

Witte not only claims that civil law serves a threefold purpose analogous to the Reformation's three uses, but he also makes a more specific claim for human rights: "'human rights,' he argues, 'and their vindication help the law achieve its basic uses in this life.'"⁴⁷

My coauthor [Brennan] will argue later in this chapter that Witte is mostly wrong about this claim for a number of familiar reasons that might be summarized under the familiar theoretical heading "the priority of the good over the right." I [Brewbaker] argue here that even if Witte is arguably wrong in theory, he may nevertheless be right in practice.

---

45   See, for example, Cass R. Sunstein, "Law's Expressive Function," *The Good Society* 9, no. 2 (1999): 55–61.
46   See Herbert A. Deane, *The Political and Social Ideas of St. Augustine* (New York: Columbia University Press, 1963), 99–100 (citing sources).
47   *The Blessings of Liberty*, 298.

The defense is not original with me. It turns out to be, on my reading, the case that Witte makes for himself. Witte concedes a number of theoretical (and theological) critiques of rights and rights discourse:

> I agree with Christian skeptics who criticize the utopian idealism of some modern rights advocates, the reduction of rights claims to groundless and self-interested wish lists, the monopoly of rights language in public debates about morality and law, and the dominant liberalism of much contemporary rights talk.... I further acknowledge that some rights and liberties recognized today are more congenial to scripture, tradition, and Christian experience than others.[48]

At the same time, however, he argues that "a good number of contemporary ... rights have deep roots in the Western Christian tradition and remain worth affirming and advocating."[49] He also notes that "Christians from the start have claimed their rights and freedoms first and foremost in order to discharge the moral duties of the faith."[50]

Most relevant to the point at hand, he asserts that "[r]ights claims can reflect and embody love of God and neighbor" and can provide "the opportunity and accountability necessary to learn and discharge ... moral duties."[51] Rights claims call our attention to the respect that is due our neighbor: "To insist on the rights of self-defense and the protection and integrity of one's body or loved ones, or to bring private claims and support public prosecution of those who rape, batter, starve, abuse, torture, or kidnap you or your loved ones is, in part, an invitation for others to respect the divine image and 'temple of the Lord' that each person embodies."[52] While Witte acknowledges that rights may sometimes be acknowledged in form but denied in substance,[53] he notes that rights-conferring enactments, such as the U.S. Civil Rights Act of 1964 and the Voting Rights Act of 1965, have served important educational purposes as well as providing means of redress.[54]

---

48 Ibid., 296.
49 Ibid., 296 (mentioning family laws that confer rights on spouses, parents, and children; social welfare rights, free speech rights, contract rights, criminal procedural rights, freedom of conscience, and free exercise of religion). See *The Blessings of Liberty*, 296–97.
50 Ibid., 297.
51 Ibid.
52 Ibid. (citing 1 Cor. 3:16).
53 See Witte's discussion of Robert Franklin in *The Blessings of Liberty*, 294.
54 Indeed, Witte opens *The Blessings of Liberty* by calling the Civil Rights Act of 1964 and the Voting Rights Act of 1965 "some of the most remarkable human rights documents [the world] had ever seen" (ibid., 1).

Still, one might argue (as my coauthor does later in this chapter)[55] that one must have some basis for specifying the content of abstract rights and for distinguishing between "good rights" and "bad rights." Witte acknowledges this problem,[56] but nevertheless argues that "rights should remain part of Christian moral, legal, and political discourse, and that Christians should remain part of broader public debates about human rights and public advocacy for their protection and implementation."[57] The gap between Witte and his critics may ultimately be a self-conscious difference in ambition: Witte is proposing a course of prudent action rather than a theoretical or theological statement of faith. As he writes in the introduction to *The Blessings of Liberty*, Witte sees himself "as a Christian jurist and legal historian, not a Christian theologian or philosopher."[58] He sees legal rights and liberties as emerging over time through a process that includes acts and customs of civil society as well as the acts and customs of those holding political or judicial office.[59] Witte asks the practical question, "What should we do next?" rather than seeking to offer a comprehensive account of political and legal morality.

That said, what grounds Witte's project? If he is unwilling to offer a thick theoretical/theological defense of human rights, what gives him the confidence to urge his fellow Christians to include rights claims in their moral, legal, and political discourse and to "remain part of broader public debates about human rights"?[60]

Witte has not (to my knowledge) answered this question in express terms, but I will offer three possible justifications. Witte is, among other things, a Reformed exponent of the natural law tradition.[61] Legal academics often focus, understandably enough, on natural law jurisprudence and its ongoing attempts to refine our understanding of the details and implications of the natural law. On this understanding, natural law looks like the development of a set of arguments from first principles. However, natural law can also be seen as a *fact* about human nature. It just is the case that the moral law is written on the heart,[62] and if that is true, this fact provides hope (though by no means any guarantees) as we engage in the process of political and legal deliberation about our common life. We can expect our discourse to produce some quantity of true "middle axioms" (statements that occupy space somewhere

---

55   See the next section herein.
56   *The Blessings of Liberty*, 299–300.
57   Ibid., 296.
58   Ibid., 12.
59   Ibid., 11–12.
60   Ibid., 296.
61   See, for example, ibid., 76–104.
62   See Romans 2:15.

between foundational moral principles and discrete rules that decide concrete questions) because human beings know (even if we tragically also suppress)[63] moral truth to some degree. And this is the case even when a given individual's proclaimed belief system provides no adequate foundation for the moral truths he asserts.

Witte's intellectual background is also worth noting at this point. Witte is a graduate of Calvin University, which is affiliated with the Christian Reformed Church and is known for its insistence that faith commitments ground intellectual and cultural life. Calvin's tradition draws perhaps most famously (though by no means exclusively) on the Dutch Reformed tradition, whose most famous representative is probably Abraham Kuyper.

One of the ideas for which Kuyper is justly famous is the notion of *common grace*. Although Kuyper's account of the topic is complex and multifaceted, he affirms that God, in his sovereignty, is committed not only to the flourishing and salvation of the elect, but equally to the realization of all the good potential of the world he has made. As a result, even where special, saving grace is absent in the lives of individuals, there is "'a temporal restraining grace, which holds back and blocks the effects of sin' so that humankind's full flowering, for which God created us, is not frustrated."[64] Nicholas Wolterstorff (a Calvin faculty member prior to his appointment at Yale) provides a helpful summary taken from a remarkable collection edited by Witte and Frank Alexander:

> God's common grace is to be seen at work in the inward life of humankind wherever "civic virtue, a sense of domesticity, natural love, the practice of human virtue, the improvement of the public conscience, integrity, mutual loyalty among people, and a feeling for piety leaven life." It is to be seen at work in the outward existence of humankind "when human power over nature increases, when invention upon invention enriches life, when international communication is improved, the arts flourish, the sciences increase our understanding, the conveniences and joys of life multiply, all expressions of life become more vital and radiant, forms become more refined and the general image of life becomes more winsome."[65]

---

63 See Romans 1:18 ("For the wrath of God is revealed from heaven against all ungodliness and unrighteousness of men, who by their unrighteousness suppress the truth").

64 Nicholas Wolterstorff, "Abraham Kuyper," *The Teachings of Modern Christianity on Law, Politics, and Human Nature*, vol. 1, ed. John Witte, Jr. and Frank S. Alexander (New York: Columbia University Press, 2006), 311 (quoting Kuyper).

65 Ibid. 311, quoting James D. Bratt, ed., *Kuyper: A Centennial Reader* (Grand Rapids: Eerdmans, 1988), 181.

Kuyper believes in a doctrine of progress of a particular kind: "[T]he ongoing development of humanity is contained in the plan of God. It follows that the history of our race resulting from this development is not from Satan nor from man but from God and that those who reject and fail to appreciate this development deny the work of God in history."66 It is not that humanity can never take a wrong turn, or that humanity's fall into sin has not slowed down the process of realizing the potential of the created order; rather, a sovereign God can be counted upon ultimately to realize his good intentions for creation in the various spheres of human life and culture, and he does this through the insights of those outside his salvation as well as those within it.

Something like this confidence in God's ultimate vindication of the world he has made may be underwriting Witte's insistence that "rights should remain part of Christian moral, legal, and political discourse," even in the face of the difficulties with rights talk that he forthrightly acknowledges.67 Kuyper sees a world in which human life involves centuries of "constant change, modification, [and] transformation in human life."68 At the same time, unless human life is merely "an endless, unvarying repetition of the same things," these developments must be directed toward something: "Though it pass through periods of deepening darkness, this change has to ignite ever more light, consistently enrich human life, and so bear the character of perpetual development from less to more, a progressively fuller unfolding of life."69 Witte's confident admonition toward Christian engagement in human rights discourse and advocacy may owe something to a Kuyperian faith in God's sovereign action in the world.

Witte also seems to think that Christians have an important role to play in disciplining debate about human rights. Even though human beings "just know" something about the moral order because, whether they acknowledge it or not, the natural law is written on their hearts, Witte also argues that Christians have theoretical contributions to make. According to Witte, Protestant thought "avoids the limitless expansion of human rights claims by grounding [human rights] norms in the creation order, divine callings and covenant relationships."70 Human rights' origins stem from built-in features of the natural order like family, church, and state and the nature of the human person as one who has a distinct vocation of service to fulfill. Grounding human rights in

---

66   Bratt, *Kuyper: A Centennial* Reader, 175.
67   *The Blessings of Liberty*, 296.
68   Bratt, *Kuyper: A Centennial* Reader, 174.
69   Ibid.
70   John Witte, Jr., introduction to John Witte, Jr. and Frank S. Alexander, eds., *Christianity and Human Rights: An Introduction* (New York: Cambridge University Press: 2010), 32.

these created structures helps identify principled limitations on the particular entitlements that may be passed off as human rights.

Finally, like it or not, rights talk is the dominant mode of political discourse in the contemporary West. Jefferson Powell has argued persuasively that, as a practical matter, American society is unlikely to be rendered more just by abandoning its focus on rights. The American political community, Powell claims, is "constituted by the very individualism expressed in rights talk."[71] As a result, rights talk is the natural political vernacular of our political discourse and, thus, the natural vocabulary for expressing concerns about social justice and social peace. Witte's argument appeals to something very much like Powell's insight. The fact that rights imply correlative duties permits rights discourse to be seen as a conversation about what we owe to each other—that is, what it means to work out our love of God and neighbor in public.

6   Why Witte May Be Wrong: a Catholic Critique (with Important Points of Agreement)

6.1   *Law's Nudging and Teaching*

Witte has asked us to think of civil or human law in part in terms of its educational use. The opposing view, as Witte appreciates, is the idea of *law as a policeman*, an idea that has been in English-language jurisprudential circulation since Hobbes proposed a law-giving Leviathan that maintained public order by threats indifferent to any positive view of human living. When Oliver Wendell Holmes Jr. popularized his "bad man" view of law, he was drawing on, even as he criticized, John Austin's jurisprudential thesis that law just is the command of the sovereign backed by the threat of force. Under this view, law serves "to keep people from acting in ways that harm others (or their property); in operating as a negative constraint, law is not concerned with inculcating a positive view of the way people should live and flourish together."[72]

The inadequacy of the policeman approach to law has been the focus of the work of John Noonan. "Constraint by the threat of force is no doubt

---

71   H. Jefferson Powell. "The Earthly Peace of the Liberal Republic," in *Christian Perspectives on Legal Thought*, ed. Michael W. McConnell, Robert F. Cochran Jr., and Angela C. Carmella (New Haven, CT: Yale University Press, 2001), 85–86.

72   Cathleen Kaveny, *Law's Virtues: Fostering Autonomy and Solidarity in American Society* (Washington, DC: Georgetown University Press, 2012), 19.

characteristic of a legal system. But," Noonan contends, "two other functions, neglected by Austin, are equally characteristic: to channel and to teach."[73] Noonan first elaborates law's channeling function:

> By marking out certain types of agreement as privileged—contracts in general, marriage in particular, corporations and trusts in Anglo-American law—the legal system affords ways in which human energies and material resources may be pooled and increased. In [H. L. A.] Hart's amendment of Austin, this function is performed by power-creating rules. But his emphasis is wrong. The human beings attracted, by the legal privileges attached, to enter a contract or form a marriage are not so much given power to have legal consequences follow their agreement as they are brought to enter cooperative relationships where almost everything will depend not on power and sanction but on reciprocal trust and good will; the legal system has not provided power so much as directions for acting in harmony—a musical script, not a set of batons.[74]

Trusts, estates, and even simple contracts for the sale of goods exemplify law's channeling function, but marriage does so in a most salient way because, on all accounts, "marriage is a keystone of our social order."[75]

The laws of marriage and the family have long been one of Witte's principal areas of scholarly focus, and, as he has shown, the law of marriage continues today to channel human choices and preferences: "The modern Western state does not require its citizens to get married, but it does 'nudge' in that direction. It provides state marital licenses, tax and social security incentives, spousal evidentiary and health care privileges, and hundreds of additional federal and state benefits and incentives."[76] The state's nudge toward marriage does not purport to set out a template for living the most virtuous life possible, but, by incentivizing choice in the direction of a particular form of cooperative relationship, it does inculcate through "a musical script, not a set of batons," a positive view of the way people should live and flourish together.

---

73   John T. Noonan Jr., *Persons and Masks of the Law: Cardozo, Holmes, Jefferson, and Wythe as Makers of the Masks* (Berkeley: University of California Press, 1976), 12.
74   Ibid.
75   Obergefell v. Hodges, 576 U.S. 644, 669 (2015).
76   John Witte, Jr., *The Western Case for Monogamy Over Polygamy* (Cambridge: Cambridge University Press, 2015), 463.

Unlike when Noonan was writing about marriage's channeling function in the 1970s, the content of the "musical script" has become the subject of the most radical cultural contestation, and in 2015, in *Obergefell v. Hodges*, marriage was redefined for U.S. constitutional purposes as a "two-person union,"[77] not a three- or four-person union, without regard to whether the two are of the opposite sex. Today, however, the limitation of marriage to two-person unions is on the block. The new question being agitated at the level of constitutional law concerns whether the definition of marriage should now be expanded from two-person unions to polygamous (whether polyandrous or polygynous or both) unions. Appreciating marriage law's channeling function, polygamists and their allies wish to see marriage redefined yet again.[78]

This latest call for a legal redefinition of marriage has in turn called forth considerable resistance from Witte in 465 pages of dense history and argument in *The Western Case for Monogamy Over Polygamy*. Although his argument leads him to conclude that "The constitutional case for polygamy is weak compared to the cases supporting the liberalization of other traditional sex, marriage and family laws,"[79] Witte acknowledges with resignation that "There may come a time that the West will more readily accept polygamy as a valid marital option that is licensed and regulated by the state."[80] We return to this possible eventuality and Witte's response to it below.

Related to the channeling or nudging function of law, but distinct from it on Noonan's analysis, is its teaching function: "Teaching—the main activity of appellate judges; for what else are 95 percent of their written opinions?— is even harder to accommodate within an Austinian or Hartian reduction. Teaching is, necessarily, person to person, informing and evoking. It cannot be equated with Pavlovian conditioning as an exercise in applied force."[81] Law's teaching addresses, and its success depends on how it addresses, the population as a whole, as Noonan explains:

> Addressing both Holmes's bad man (a real but not very typical representative of the population) and also the larger audience made up of the uncertain, the confused, the conforming, and the aspiring, the documents composed by constitution writers, legislators, and judges are educative. Their success is far more by persuasion that they are right than

---

77 *Obergefell*, at 666.
78 *The Western Case for Monogamy*, 6–8, 19–20, and 444–46.
79 Ibid., 464.
80 Ibid., 465.
81 Noonan, *Persons and Masks*, 13.

by coercion. To think of law as a science of power, unlocked by a key, badly obscures this function.[82]

The documents teach, as do the practices of enforcing them, and together these teachings carry the authority of the state.

The teaching function of law is a two-edged sword, however, because duly ratified constitutions and procedurally proper statutes alike are sometimes very useful instruments in teaching "the wrong thing."[83] "Always and everywhere the law teaches," but "What, then, should be its lessons?"[84]

A perverse pedagogy of law to which Noonan devoted instructive analysis is slavery, which existed, Noonan shows, not just by the brute power of negative constraint but also by what law taught. "Control statutes and status statutes together were indispensable to the creation and maintenance of the institution"[85] of slavery, and while enforcement of the statutes with the strong arm of the state sometimes occurred, of course, Noonan's insight was that the institution depended on a world of concepts controlled by lawyers who used them to teach the public a *doctrine*: "[T]he legislators and courts of Virginia presented a doctrine on the morality of slavery. They taught that it was good. In the pedagogy of the law, slaves were identified with the soil—the literal foundation of prosperity in the colony—or, generically, with property. As long as the teaching of the lawgivers was accepted, slavery could not be criticized without aspersion on the goodness of wealth itself."[86]

What Noonan called "the teaching of the lawgivers" about the goodness of slavery is no longer accepted, but its repudiation, like the laws that entrenched what needed repudiating, was not effected by turning an on-off switch to off. There have been questions to be asked and answered at every turn, from *Dred Scott*, the Civil War, and the Reconstruction Amendments through *Brown v. Board of Education*, *Cooper v. Aaron*, the Birmingham jail, the Civil Rights Act of 1964, and Selma, down to the present and continuing debate about the propriety of race-based affirmative action in higher education. In his "Letter from Birmingham Jail" (1963), Rev. Dr. Martin Luther King Jr. quoted Saint Augustine for the proposition that "an unjust law is no law at all," as he urged and defended peaceful disobedience of statutes still in force that taught a

---

82   Ibid.
83   See discussion at IV.A.
84   Kaveny, *Law's Virtues*, 29.
85   Noonan, *Persons and Masks*, 35 (emphasis added).
86   Ibid., 41. Interestingly, lawyers creating and enforcing law that protected property, even where the "property" was human, seemed to enjoy the support of Locke's teaching that a purpose of government was to protect property. See Noonan, *Persons and Masks*, 35.

degrading doctrine about the worth and dignity of some people based on their skin color. Contending that those statutes should be disobeyed "because they are morally wrong" and are *therefore* no *law* at all, King denied that procedural pedigree gave good and sufficient reasons to follow statutes that taught the inferiority of Blacks and separated Blacks from whites and others. Doing so, King took a noninstrumental view of law.

But if procedural pedigree cannot guarantee legal status—that is, if due process and specifically legislative process as such cannot create law, but only what Justice Samuel Chase in *Calder v. Bull* (1798) referred to as "An ACT of the Legislature"—in the morally serious matter of race, can it nonetheless do so in the morally serious matter of marriage? Writing in the context of marriage and possible legal recognition of polygamy, Witte observes, "In a democratic polity, the judgment of whether the state should nudge for or against certain behavior—let alone outright prescribe or proscribe it—rests ultimately with the people."[87] Perhaps, but the story is more complicated because sometimes "the people" in a democratic polity are overruled by judges giving effect to constitutional "rights," some of them not even enumerated in the text of the Constitution, as Witte appreciates. Because the Supreme Court in *Obergefell* has found a right, indeed a "fundamental right," to same-sex marriage, it is timely to ask whether by parity of reasoning it ought to find a right, indeed a fundamental right, to polygamous marriage?[88] As we emphasized above, it is Witte's pointed contention that "human rights and their vindication help the law achieve its basic uses in this life."[89]

6.2   Rights Conflicts?

With respect to racial discrimination by law, "the people," we now agree, were "morally wrong," dead wrong. With respect to marriage, though, Witte does not argue that legalized polygamy would be morally wrong; instead, he rests on the following comparison, quoted above, to areas in which the courts have reached liberalizing conclusions: "The constitutional case for polygamy is weak compared to the cases supporting the liberalization of other traditional sex, marriage, and family laws; there are just too many serious concerns about harms and rights on the other side."[90] Witte thus concludes *The Western Case for*

---

87   *The Western Case for Monogamy*, 463.
88   "All of [the] traditional natural law arguments against same-sex relations are seriously disputed today, and their erosion has helped topple traditional Western laws against sodomy, same-sex unions, and in some places same-sex marriage. But none of these traditional natural law arguments applies to polygamy": *The Western Case for Monogamy*, 452.
89   Text at note 7.
90   *The Western Case for Monogamy*, 464–65.

Monogamy Over Polygamy as follows: "The West can now simply and politely say to the polygamist who bangs on its door seeking admission or permission to practice polygamy: 'No thank you; we don't do that here,' and close the door firmly."[91]

In the courts of the United States, however, such an answer will not suffice. When litigants attacking legislative limitation of marriage to two-person unions press the question in properly presented cases, one of which the Supreme Court will eventually need to take, the existence of the law being challenged will be the starting point, not the end point, for as Chief Justice John Roberts wrote in dissent in *Obergefell*: "Proper reliance on history and tradition of course requires looking beyond the individual law being challenged, so that every restriction on liberty does not supply its own constitutional justification."[92] The history and tradition of limitation of marriage to two-person unions will then be subject to judicial analysis according to familiar precedents, and those precedents, for their part, structure the judicial inquiry in terms of whether the right in question is fundamental, in which case the legislative restriction will stand only if it meets the demanding requirements of strict scrutiny, in which case the availability of a mere rational basis will be enough for the courts to sustain the law against challenge.

Under this familiar judge-made body of law, it is the job of courts to recognize individual rights, on one hand, but also, on the other hand, to allow them to be trumped or overridden when (1) there is a "compelling governmental interest" and (2) the government can show that the challenged law is the "least restrictive alternative." The familiarity of this line of analysis can obscure the startling fact that what are said by the courts to be "rights" sometimes turn out not to be rights full stop at all; they collapse (or are suppressed) when government can establish to the court's satisfaction its own countervailing and prevailing right. On this judicial way of proceeding, which we owe above all to Holmes, both sides have rights, with the result that *conflict*, between individual rights and the right of government, is baked in from the start.[93] This mode of analysis that takes conflict as given, in a way redolent of the starting points of social contractarian analysis from Hobbes and Locke to Rawls and his disciples, is so familiar to American lawyers as to seem almost inevitable.

Jamal Greene's recent work is a telling recent case in point. It takes the conflict for granted, calls for the multiplication of rights claims, and concludes

---

91 Ibid., 465.
92 *Obergefell*, at 698 (Roberts, C. J., dissenting).
93 Jamal T. Greene, *How Rights Went Wrong: Why Our Obsession with Rights Is Tearing America Apart* (Boston: Mariner, 2021), 56–57, 85–86.

with a call for judicial "judgment" among the conflicting claims.[94] Greene's eagerness "to balance the different interests at stake is a product" once again "of viewing law and rights in instrumental terms, seen as supporting particular interests or ends rather than constituting ends in themselves."[95] It is the product of understanding law to be merely an empty vessel. But is this instrumental approach correct? Is it true, more specifically, that conflict between individual rights and government's rightful jurisdiction cannot honestly be avoided?

Adrian Vermeule thinks not, in work that has been garnering much critical attention and merits consideration for the light it can shed on Witte's understanding of law as a vindicator of rights.[96] On the familiar view sketched above, "[t]he implicit premise," Vermeule observes, "is that the interests of 'government' as representative of the political collective, on the one hand, and the rights of individuals, on the other, are opposed and must be balanced against each other. It is," Vermeule continues, "implicitly but unmistakably, a utilitarian and aggregative conception of rights."[97] To this, Vermeule proposes an alternative which he styles the common-good or classical approach. This approach lays claim to the latter title, on Vermeule's account, because it was the way the courts usually reasoned about rights until Progressivism rather successfully entrenched the conflict model bequeathed to us by Holmes. On the classical model, according to Vermeule, rights do not arise in a way that can put them essentially at odds with the interests rightly to be defended by the state, and this is because "rights exist to serve, and are delimited by, a conception of justice that is itself ordered to the common good."[98]

On the classical, common-good model, as Vermeule explains, "[r]ights, properly understood, are always ordered to the common good and that common good is itself the highest individual interest. The issue is not balancing or override by extrinsic considerations, but internal specification and determination of the right's proper ends and, therefore, its proper boundaries or limits."[99] When the common good enters into the very definition of rights themselves and guides their determination, there looms no moment of conflict at which any true rights of persons can be overridden or trumped. "[T]he classical legal tradition has a rich account of rights, rooted in the basic idea of *ius* as what is

---

94 Ibid., 86.
95 Tamanaha, *Law as a Means*, 218.
96 Criticism of Vermeule's work in this area tends to be passionate, as in Leon Wieseltier, "Christianism," *Liberties: A Journal of Culture and Politics* 2, no. 3 (Spring 2022): 326, at 356–63.
97 Adrian Vermeule, *Common Good Constitutionalism* (Boston: Polity, 2022), 166.
98 Ibid., 24.
99 Ibid., 167.

due to each.... It is definitely not," Vermeule emphasizes, "that the common good 'overrides' rights; rather it defines their boundaries all along."[100]

On the classical view developed since the twelfth century and drawn upon by Vermeule, what is due to each includes a limited realm of freedom or liberty, and each of these little realms is what is sometimes called a *subjective right*.[101] Correctly understood, as Dominic Legge asserts, such subjective rights "are not set over against the common good, as if an increase in the common good necessitated a diminishment of individual liberty. Rather," as Legge elaborates, "that individuals be secure in their liberties as citizens—that they 'possess rights'—is precisely an aspect or dimension of the common good, and the protection of those rights in law is a means for securing the common good of a just republic."[102] Questions about how broad these zones of liberty should be will be the foci of political disagreement and decision-making, but the distinctive mark of the classical approach is that the common good will provide the ultimate criterion of judgment.[103]

Taking the common good as the end to which all law is rightly ordered, the classical view allows for a range of institutional allocations of decision-making authority. Unlike the regnant Holmesian model, the classical view does not make public authority intrinsically suspect, a constant threat to individual rights; such authority is, instead, presumptively at the service of the common good in which the individual's flourishing in part consists.[104] On one hand, then, the classical view takes no a priori position on the proper scope of judicial review; on the other, "the political morality of the common good itself includes role morality and division of functions."[105]

In our system, Vermeule contends, the principal responsibility for identifying the requirements of the common good has been lodged in legislatures

---

100   Ibid., 24.
101   Witte, introduction to *Christianity and Human Rights*, 18–19.
102   Dominic Legge, OP, "Do Thomists Have Rights?,"*Nova et Vetera* 17 (2019): 127–47, at 146. Witte stresses the error of thinking that subjective rights as such were a modern invention. See Witte, *Blessings of Liberty*, 14–75. On Aquinas's defense of subjective rights as required for the sharing of goods vital to the common good, see Russell Hittinger, *The First Grace: Recovering the Natural Law in a Post-Christian World* (Wilmington, DE: ISI Books, 2003), 270–71.
103   The difficulties of determining the common good and zones of individual liberty were familiar to premodern Christian political theorists. See, for example, James Hankins, *Virtue Politics: Soulcraft and Statecraft in Renaissance Italy* (Cambridge, MA: Belknap Press, 2019), 342–50.
104   Vermeule, *Common Good*, 29.
105   Ibid., 43.

through the police powers or their equivalents, with courts properly interfering with legislative judgments only when they can be said to be arbitrary:

> [R]ights (as *ius*) are intrinsically ordered to the common good, but the common good is not given in a fixed, identical form for all polities at all times.... The common good, then, is itself subject to public *determinatio* or concretization, as are the rights that flow from the common good. Because of the basic structure of determination, judges would defer to the legislative specification within broad boundaries of reasonableness.... Judges, in this framework, ask whether the public *determinatio* has transgressed the broad boundaries of reason and become 'arbitrary'—a word frequently invoked in the caselaw. The closest analogue in modern law is probably to (forgiving versions of) arbitrariness review under the Administrative Procedure Act.[106]

Administrative lawyers today tend to associate arbitrariness review under the Administrative Procedure Act (APA) with *Overton Park* and "hard look" review, but arbitrariness review under the APA as originally understood "was a sort of lunacy test."[107] On the classical account of the role morality of courts vis-à-vis legislatures as constituted in our system, then, it would be fair to say that courts should defer to legislative determinations of rights unless they are fairly describable as lunatic.[108]

6.3 *Why Witte May Be Wrong*

The classical, common-good understanding of rights recently popularized by Vermeule is just as contestable as the competing understandings against which it contends, whether Holmes's, Greene's, or anyone else's. It remains, then, to situate Witte's work on the use of law to vindicate rights in the contest among competing versions in which the common-good version is now receiving so much attention, and Witte's own methodological reflections provide a starting point.

---

106   Ibid.
107   Martin Shapiro, *Who Guards the Guardians: Judicial Control of Administration* (Athens: University of Georgia Press, 1988), 56.
108   The use American courts traditionally made of the natural law (law of nature) was not to the contrary, as Richard Helmholz, on whom Vermeule relies, has demonstrated. See Richard Helmbolz, *Natural Law in Court: A History of Legal Theory in Practice* (Cambridge, MA: Harvard University Press, 2015).

It is a signature of all Witte's work that it celebrates human freedom as "a unique gift of God to all human creatures."[109] Witte cautions, though, that he "support[s] the positive law of rights and liberties today more out of utility than ideology. In my view," Witte continues, "rights *laws* over time and across cultures have proved to be useful *instruments* to promote and protect the good life and the good society; to impose and enforce limits on the power of states, churches, and other authorities; and to enable and equip persons to carry out their vocations and duties to God, neighbor, and self."[110] These instruments, Witte contends, "have traditionally provided a forum and focus for subtle and sophisticated philosophical, theological, and political reflections on the *common good* and our common lives."[111] The recognition of rights and liberties in law emerged not in a laboratory or classroom but in the authoritative resolution of these reflections across the spectrum of human living, as Witte's historical work shows in splendid detail:

> acts become behaviors; behaviors become habits; habits yield customs; customs produce rules; rules beget statutes; statutes require procedures; procedures guide cases; statutes, procedures, and cases get systematized into codes; and all these forms of legality are eventually confirmed in national constitutions, if not in regional conventions and international covenants.[112]

Acknowledging that this "bottom-up approach to [rights] sometimes produces blurrier lines of reasoning; more slippage between principles, precedents, and practices; [and] provisional and sometimes messier recommendations and prescriptions for church, state, and society," Witte expresses the hope that "it also makes for an account and defense of human rights and religious freedom that is more realistic, rigorous, and resilient over time and perhaps even across cultures."[113] Resisting the claims and criticisms of philosophically and theologically motivated critics of human rights who "often have one or two key definitions or forms of rights in mind—sometimes with labels such [as] 'natural,' 'universal,' 'human,' 'fundamental,' or 'unalienable,' rights,"[114] Witte criticizes

---

109 *The Blessings of Liberty*, 11.
110 Ibid., 11 (emphasis added).
111 Witte, introduction to *Christianity and Human Rights*, 41 (emphasis added).
112 *The Blessings of Liberty*, 11–12.
113 Ibid., 12.
114 Ibid.

such "lofty theoretical heights"¹¹⁵ for losing sight of what "[w]e lawyers deal with [in] the routine corners and concerns of public and private life."¹¹⁶

On the ground where lawyers and legislators work, though, it is not only possible but characteristically human to ask about any assertion, "Is this true? Is this right? Or, when warranted, is this at least probably true, probably right?" The ability to answer "probably" precludes any excuse for trying not to answer at all, especially when laws of general applicability are being made on the basis of the answer.

On the Catholic understanding of the human person (articulated here by Bernard Lonergan), "every person is an embodiment of natural right. Every person can reveal to any other his natural propensity to seek understanding, to judge reasonably, to evaluate fairly, to be open to friendship."¹¹⁷ So, unless and to the extent we interdict such questions, we can seek understanding by asking and answering the questions, "Do individuals (and groups) sometimes have rights that must be limited by government on the basis of government's interests that are somehow *inimical* to those antecedent human rights? Or, instead, do individual (and group) rights, subjective rights, emerge only as determinations of justice ordered to the common good, such that any apparent conflict between government and the governed is only contingent (the result of incorrect understanding or judgment) and not intrinsic and necessary (as it was for Holmes)?"

Witte denies that "rights constitute a freestanding system of morality" and denies also that they "render Christian moral and religious teachings superfluous," contending instead that "human rights are 'middle axioms' of political discourse. They are a means to the ends of *justice* and the *common good*."¹¹⁸ The italicized terms bring Witte's approach within the broad rhetorical ambit of the classical approach, and on the classical understanding, as we have seen, the common good was the flourishing of a political community and itself the

---

115   Ibid.
116   Ibid., 11.
117   Bernard Lonergan, "Natural Right and Historical Mindedness," in *A Third Collection: Papers by Bernard J. F. Lonergan, SJ*, ed. Frederick J. Crowe (New York: Paulist Press, 1985), 170, 182. Witte's work follows the standard narratives according to which, roughly, neo-Thomist developments culminated in the Second Vatican Council's "transform[ing] the Catholic Church's theological analysis toward human rights and democracy": Witte, introduction to *Christianity and Human Rights*, 24. The opposing or at least complexifying views are developed in Russell Hittinger, "Two Modernisms, Two Thomisms: Reflections on the Centenary of Pius X's Letter against the Modernists," *Nova et Vetera* 5 (2017): 843–80; and John Rao, *Removing the Blindfold: Nineteenth-Century Catholics and the Myth of Modern Freedom* (Kansas City, MO: Angelus Press, 2014), 155–76.
118   *The Blessings of Liberty*, 300 (emphasis added).

individual's highest interest, and as such provided the criterion for determining subjective rights. On the competing modern understanding, by contrast, the common good amounts to no more than an aggregation of individual interests, and as such is not available in advance to determine subjective rights. Subjective rights, on this understanding, are free agents of a sort, unordered to the common good, and law is just their unassuming instrument.[119] Which of these two is Witte's understanding?

Although Witte laments "the libertarian accents that still too often dominate our rights talk today,"[120] and asserts that "[w]e need not accept the seemingly infinite expansion of human rights discourse and demands,"[121] what remains programmatically unclear in Witte's work is the *criterion (or criteria) of judgment* being brought to bear to justify excluding some rights claims from legal vindication. The closest he seems to come to an answer leaves a hole—to be filled in, but by whom?—in the center: "[T]he norms that rights instantiate depend upon the visions and values of human communities for their content and coherence—or, what the Catholic philosopher Jacques Maritain described as 'the scale of values governing [their] exercise and concrete manifestation.'"[122] Is it enough that the resulting legal apparatus be in "dialectical harmony"[123] with its informing sources? As Stuart Hampshire observed, the age's dominant political liberalism, largely accepted by Witte, tends to admit as reasonable and harmonious only what is judged to be so by the standards of liberalism itself.[124]

---

119 On the classical view, "Human flourishing, including the flourishing of individuals, is itself essentially, not merely contingently, dependent upon the flourishing of the political communities (including ruling authorities) within which humans are always born, found, and embedded. This is not at all to say, of course, that the individual should be absorbed into the political community or subjected to it; that is the opposite error of the one the libertarian commits. The end of the community is ultimately to promote the good of individuals, but common goods are real as such and are themselves the highest goods for individuals": Vermeule, *Common Good*, 29.
120 *God's Joust, God's Justice*, 111.
121 *The Reformation of Rights*, 343. Nigel Biggar, *What's Wrong with Rights?* (Oxford: Oxford University Press, 2020), 150, questions the basis on which Witte accepts some "liberal" rights claims but rejects others.
122 *The Blessings of Liberty*, 300 (internal citation omitted).
123 *God's Joust, God's Justice*, 5.
124 Michael J. White, *Partisan or Neutral? The Futility of Public Political Theory* (Lanham, MD: Rowman & Littlefield, 1997), 168.

6.4 *No Avoiding Decisions for or against the Good*

Witte the historian is correct that there were rights and liberties before liberalism, and he is also correct that (*pace* Samuel Moyn) Christians contributed mightily to the development of subjective rights of individuals and of groups in the Western legal tradition.[125] When the courts finally decide whether the Constitution of the United States should be interpreted to invalidate state limitation of marriage to two-person unions, the Supreme Court will not speak in terms of morally good and morally bad; it will speak in terms of whether there is a fundamental right that trumps legislation to the contrary. What Chief Justice Roberts wrote of the majority opinion vindicating those seeking same-sex marriage in *Obergefell* will be true of polygamists in some such future case: "The majority's driving themes are that marriage is desirable and petitioners desire it."[126] If the Supreme Court were to defer to legislative resolution against polygamists' desires (unless such resolution could be said to be arbitrary in the sense of lunatic), it would be content to deny polygamists their desire because the classical approach does not imagine that it is law's duty to liberate people "from the unchosen bonds of tradition, family, religion, economic circumstances, and even biology."[127] A Supreme Court operating according to the classical account would not let desire cloaked as a right trump legislative judgment, in the form of an exercise of the police power, of what is good for the populace. Refusing to relegate the good to private judgment[128] and refusing, moreover, to "instrumentalize[] law in the service of the relentlessly liberationist project" and "use it as a tool for extrinsic ends that warp its true nature,"[129] the classical understanding would put law in service of marriage understood as a naturally given institution in need of legally adequate specification by the legislature. "A civil specification that distorts the essence of the natural institution would be unreasonable and arbitrary, from the standpoint of common good constitutionalism."[130]

Neutrality about the good is an illusion that should fool no one, as Witte himself attests: "Serious public and political arguments about the fundamentals of

---

125 *The Blessings of Liberty*, 14–44.
126 *Obergefell*, at 699 (Roberts, C. J., dissenting).
127 Vermeule, *Common Good*, 22.
128 On the reduction of what is good to private judgment, see Alasdair MacIntyre, "The Privatization of the Good," *Review of Politics* 52 (1990): 344–61.
129 Vermeule, *Common Good*, 120.
130 Ibid., 132. The civil specification would develop subjective rights in part on the basis of natural human powers. See D. C. Schindler, *The Politics of the Real: The Church Between Liberalism and Integralism* (Steubenville, OH: New Polity, 2021), 132–37.

life and the law do not occur under a 'fictitious scrim of value neutrality.'"[131] Even while Bruce Ackerman denies that we "can *know* anything about the good,"[132] every legitimate act of government takes some position, explicit or implicit, on goods and the common good specifically. Judicial discourse about rights is no exception to the need to be partisan about that in which the good life for individuals or communities consists. Witte has done us a great service in advancing understanding of how rights claims, functioning as a contemporary *ius gentium*,[133] have advanced juridical resolution of which goods will be taught, nudged, licensed, or forbidden by the state.

As a Christian, however, Witte knows that the highest ideal is not doing justice by enforcing rights, however that might look, and so Witte's rights talk, as he repeatedly acknowledges, is only penultimate as it leaves room (in Noonan's expression) for "Augustine's sublime fusion in which ... justice is defined as 'love serving only the one loved,'"[134] perhaps in terms of friendship, a concept never thematized in Witte's work. Openness to friendship was one aspect of the natural right of which Lonergan said "every person is an embodiment."

7 From "Uses" and "Rights" to Friendship?

In asking whether the Old Law contains moral precepts, Thomas Aquinas answers, in language we quoted in part in the introduction, that "just as the principal intention of human law is to create friendship between man and man, so the chief intention of the Divine law is to establish man in friendship with God."[135] For Thomas, friendship is an analogical term, and the sort of friendship he has in mind for human law to establish is civic friendship, about which Aristotle wrote, "It also seems that friendship holds cities together and that legislators take it more seriously than justice."[136] Aquinas does not say very much about civic friendship, but it seems to occupy a place not far removed

---

131 John Witte, Jr., *Church, State, and Family: Reconciling Traditional Teachings and Modern Liberties* (Cambridge: Cambridge University Press, 2019), 362 (quoting Lenn Goodman).
132 Bruce Ackerman, *Social Justice in the Liberal State* (New Haven: Yale University Press, 1980), 368.
133 *The Blessings of Liberty*, 299. See also *The Reformation of Rights*, 342, on the place of the "transcendent principles of the *ius naturale*" in informing this *ius gentium*.
134 Noonan, *Persons and Masks*, xx.
135 Aquinas, *Summa Theologiae*, I–II, q. 99, a. 2.
136 Aristotle, *Nicomachean Ethics*, trans. C. D. C. Reeve (Indianapolis: Hackett Publishing, 2014), 1155a.

from his account of the common good.[137] In speaking of friendship, Thomas may be personalizing the common good and, perhaps, opening up space for an account of the common good that is more hospitable to a discourse of rights.[138]

If Catholics sometimes feel a visceral aversion to the individualism of rights talk, Protestants may experience similar feelings of aversion to the collectivist overtones of common-good talk, especially given their emphasis on human fallenness. Introducing the notion of friendship may provide some space for common ground. Colin Gunton has written that freedom is "something we confer ... on each other by the manner of our bearing to one another."[139] Presumably it is the gift of not expecting that every action any one person takes will be for the (perceived) benefit of every other person; there need not be congruence at every moment between individual action and the interest of the group; common-goodism is not collectivism. Friendship includes the conferral of a zone of independence and freedom within which to respond to one's own understanding of who God is calling one to be. As we know from personal experience, the respect that friends show to each other includes the grant of this sort of freedom.

Law, including legal rights, is at least in part about establishing this sort of freedom. Law is modest in its ambitions because lawgivers and judges cannot read the hearts of their fellow citizens, because lawgivers and judges are also fallen creatures, because laws must be calibrated to the moral capacities of the communities they govern, and so on. Civic friendship is reinforced when citizens are appropriately protected from oppression and wrongdoing,[140] when there is general public order, and when citizens are left to live "each man under his own vine and his own fig tree."[141] The Catholic, more than the Protestant, will characteristically affirm that it is of the essence of friendship that the friend

---

137   Compare *ST* I–II q.90, a. 2 ad 3 (the "last end" of the law is the common good), with ibid., q. 99, a. 2 ("the principal intention of human law is to create friendship between man and man")

138   See John Finnis, "Reason, Authority, Friendship," in *Reason in Action: Collected Essays Volume I* (Oxford: Oxford University Press, 2011), 110, 122; James V. Schall, "The Totality of Society: From Justice to Friendship," *The Thomist* 20 (1957): 1, 16–24.

139   Colin E. Gunton, *The One, The Three, and the Many* (Cambridge: Cambridge University Press, 1993), 64.

140   *The Blessings of Liberty*, 297–98.

141   See Micah 4:4: "[T]hey shall sit every man under his vine and under his fig tree, and no one shall make them afraid." (ESV). This phrase was famously quoted in the letter from George Washington "To the Hebrew Congregation in Newport, Rhode Island," August 18, 1790.

desires and seeks the good of the other, including in and through the political order, though subject to various side constraints, such as subsidiarity.[142]

Even just in finding ways to talk together about law, rights, community, and God, as Witte has magisterially invited us to do, we are engaged in what Witte's mentor, Harold Berman, called "communification," the working out of sympathetic bonds of community through mutual understanding of our sameness and similarity amid difference.[143] And that process of communification, in which each person can show himself or herself open to friendship, is one in which we can discover that we are one another's equals. Our attentiveness to human equality, an attentiveness that runs through Witte's work,[144] provides in turn an opportunity to recognize that goods, sometimes vindicated in law through rights claims, are "realizable as much in the lives of other human beings as in my own life."[145]

---

142 In addition, the Catholic will be quick to specify the supernatural virtue of charity as that by which those receiving and possessing that grace may achieve its proper ends; see Patrick McKinley Brennan, "The Forgiveness of Love in Charity: Getting Conversationally Opened Up," in *Christianity, Ethics, and the Law: The Concept of Love in Christian Legal Thought*, ed. Zachary Calo, Joshua Neoh, and A. Keith Thompson (New York: Routledge, 2023), 198, 230–33.

143 John Witte, Jr., introduction to Harold Berman, *Law and Language: Effective Symbols of Community*, ed. John Witte, Jr. (Cambridge: Cambridge University Press, 2013), 16.

144 Witte develops the Protestant basis of human equality in *God's Joust*, 60–61; see also *The Blessings of Liberty*, 33, and John Witte, Jr., foreword to John E. Coons and Patrick M. Brennan, *By Nature Equal: The Anatomy of a Western Insight* (Princeton: Princeton University Press, 1999), XXIII.

145 John Finnis, "Discourse, Truth, and Friendship," in *Reason in Action: Collected Essays Volume I* (Oxford: Oxford University Press, 2011), 48.

CHAPTER 12

Nomos, *Agape*, and a Sacramental Jurisprudence

Timothy P. Jackson

1   Introduction

John Witte, Jr. asks, "What would our public and private laws look like if we worked hard to make real and legally concrete the biblical ideals of covenant community or sacramental living?"[1] No one in his generation has done more to sustain and deepen the Western tradition of wedding jurisprudence and religious faith than John Witte. In this essay, I respond to and honor Professor Witte's corpus by exploring how, for believers, law relates to autonomy and theonomy, justice and love. More specifically, I briefly examine the relation of law and faith in four contexts: (1) the pre-Christian writings of Plato and Aristotle; (2) the pre-Christian writings of Moses and the Prophets; (3) the early Christian writings of Matthew, Mark, Luke, John, and Paul; and (4) the late Christian or post-Christian writings of Martin Luther, Immanuel Kant, Søren Kierkegaard, and Friedrich Nietzsche.

This rapid romp through authors and eras generates two main historical observations and one central normative contention. My first observation is not controversial: Athens and Jerusalem (and Wittenberg) have displayed a shifting pattern of emphasis on transcendence and immanence, ideality and practicality. Greece and Israel (and Germany) have faced similar challenges to keeping an initially theocentric vision of law from being transformed into various forms of subjectivism and will to power. My second observation is more contested but increasingly widely accepted: law (*nomos*) and unconditional love (*agape*) are not implacable adversaries but dialectical partners, even as are the Old and New Testaments. Instead of law being dead and inflexible rules in tension with the living and personal spirit of neighbor love, law is love made incarnate in space and time. What is highly disputed is my normative contention that, while there is value in both supernaturalism and naturalism, we ought to give decided priority to the former. More concretely, we ought

---

1 John Witte, Jr., "What Christianity Offers to the World of Law," in id., *Faith, Freedom, and Family: New Essays on Law and Religion*, ed. Norman Doe and Gary S. Hauk (Tübingen: Mohr Siebeck, 2021), 60.

© TIMOTHY P. JACKSON, 2024 | DOI:10.1163/9789004546189_013
This is an open access chapter distributed under the terms of the CC BY-NC 4.0 license.

to distance eudaimonism and related forms of pragmatic voluntarism and reimagine Christian jurisprudence in light of the sacraments.

2 Plato and Aristotle

Plato and Aristotle are usually held to represent Greek eudaimonism, and so they do, broadly construed. Both are concerned with human flourishing and the living of a virtuous life in community. The differences between Glaucon's brother and the Stagirite are also rightly emphasized, however. Plato accents the transcendence of the forms and the supernatural character of a singular good as the source and illuminator of all reality, such that human development—of both self and polis—is directly dependent on relation to the divine. In *The Laws*, Plato makes clear his abiding axiological priorities:

> They are correct laws, laws that make those who use them happy. For they provide all the good things. Now the good things are two fold, some human, some divine. The former depend on the divine goods, and if a city receives the greater it will also acquire the lesser. If not, it will lack both.[2]

Just laws for Plato "are said to be from Zeus and the Pythian Apollo."[3]

In Aristotle's more empirical approach to virtue, human development is more a matter of the unfolding of an immanent and natural potential, rather than of communion with a Holy Other. Both Plato and Aristotle reject bodily gratification, physical beauty, money, and prestige as the highest good,[4] but in Aristotle there is a palpable shift from theology as primal to anthropology. He writes: "Now some thought that apart from these many goods [pleasure, wealth, and honour] there is another which is good in itself and causes the goodness of all these as well."[5] He clearly has Plato and his school in mind, but he rejects their theory of a universal, self-subsistent good: "of honour, wisdom, and pleasure, just in respect of their goodness, the accounts are distinct and diverse. The good, therefore, is not something common answering to one

---

2 Plato, *The Laws*, trans. Thomas L. Pangle (Chicago: University of Chicago Press, 1988), 631b.
3 Ibid., 632d, p. 11.
4 See Plato, *The Laws*, 631c, and *Euthydemus*, 281d2–e1; and Aristotle, *The Nicomachean Ethics* (335–22 BCE), trans. David Ross, revised J. L. Ackrill and J. O. Urmson (Oxford: Oxford University Press, 1984), 1095a12–b30, pp. 4–7.
5 Aristotle, *The Nicomachean Ethics*, 1095a26–27, p. 5.

Idea."⁶ Instead, Aristotle moves the discussion to multiple intrinsic goods and rational contemplation as humanity's highest achievement.

Still, the difference between the two greatest Greek thinkers should not be overstated. Both see human nature as part of a providentially ordered cosmos and as having the capacity for excellence as well as decadence. Yet in Plato, the well-ordered soul and the well-ordered city require ascending apprehension of and transformation by the Highest. One cannot understand justice without comprehending supernatural goodness:[7]

> Therefore, say that not only being known is present in the things known as a consequence of the good, but also existence and being are in them besides as a result of it, although the good isn't being but is still beyond being, exceeding it in dignity and power.[8]
>
> At all events, this is the way the phenomena look to me: in the knowable the last thing to be seen, and that with considerable effort, is the *idea* of the good; but once seen, it must be concluded that this is in fact the cause of all that is right and fair in everything ... and that the man who is going to act prudently in private or in public must see it.[9]

In Aristotle, in contrast, a descent into one's own psychic depths is the first thing needful, thus accent falls on self-cultivation and temporal relationships that allow one to grow and thrive.

> Now, a human being is by nature a compound of superior and inferior, and everyone accordingly should conduct their lives with reference to the superior part of themselves.[10]
>
> If happiness is activity in accordance with virtue, it is reasonable that it should be in accordance with the highest virtue; and this will be that of the best thing in us.... the life according to reason is the best and pleasantest, since reason more than anything else *is* man.[11]

---

6   Ibid., 1096b24–b25, pp. 9–10.
7   Nicholas White emphasizes this point in "Plato's Concept of Goodness," in *A Companion to Plato*, ed. Hugh H. Benson (Oxford: Blackwell, 2006), 356.
8   Plato, *The Republic*, trans. Allan Bloom (New York: Basic Books, 1968), 509b, p. 189.
9   Ibid., 517b–c, p. 196.
10 Aristotle, *The Eudemian Ethics*, trans. Anthony Kenny (Oxford: Oxford University Press, 2011), 1249b9–11, p. 148.
11 Aristotle, *The Nicomachean Ethics*, 1177a, p. 263, and 1178a, p. 266.

The most essential relationship, without which life is not worth living, is friendship (*philia*) that cultivates excellence and fosters contemplation in both parties.[12] Virtue, for Aristotle, is far from narcissism or mere self-interest. In *The Nicomachean Ethics*, he allows that "we call those acts just that tend to produce and preserve happiness and its components for the political society." But, for all the emphasis on reciprocal friendship as important to personal flourishing, "justice, alone of the virtues, is thought to be 'another's good', because it is related to our neighbor; for it does what is advantageous to another, either a ruler or a co-partner."[13]

Aristotle writes: "We maintain ... that the divine is the eternal best living being, so that the divine is life unending, continuous, and eternal."[14] Nevertheless, his references to an "unmoved mover" that forever contemplates its own thought do not denote a single, personal Deity in the usual theistic sense. In spite of the line quoted immediately above, Stephen Menn contends:

> Aristotle has no word like 'God' with a capital 'G': he believes in many gods and divine things, and they are not all unmoved movers.... Aristotle never uses the phrase 'the unmoved mover' to pick out just one being (or even to pick out the many movers of the heavenly spheres), and that phrase would not express the essence of the beings it applies to. When he wants to express more adequately the essence of his single first principle, he calls it not 'god' or 'unmoved mover', but '*nous*' [Reason or intellect] or '*noêsis*' [thinking or intellectual apprehension], or the Good. He never says that it is a form, and it does not seem to be a substance or a being in any stronger sense than other substance are, but its activity is needed for the actual existence of an ordered world.[15]

Although Aristotle sometimes calls his first principle "the good," its singularity is dubious, and "it" seemingly does not care about individuals and cannot return love in the usual sense. Aristotle states: "It would be ridiculous to reproach God for not returning love in the same way he is loved, and similarly for a subject to reproach his ruler. The role of a ruler is to receive, not to give, love, or at least to give it in another way."[16] Even more emphatically, the Philosopher declares

---

12   Aristotle, *The Eudemian Ethics*, 1236a–b.
13   Ibid., 1129b13–1130a6, pp. 108–09.
14   Aristotle, *Metaphysics*, trans. Richard Hope (Ann Arbor: University of Michigan Press, 1968), 1072b30, p. 260.
15   Stephen Menn, "Aristotle's Theology," in *The Oxford Handbook of Aristotle*, ed. Chiristopher Shields (New York: Oxford University Press, 2012), 422–23.
16   Aristotle, *The Eudemian Ethics*, 1238b26–29, p. 122.

that god is "too grand to think of anything else except himself."[17] A god will self-contemplate but will lack the virtues of justice and love, including friendship,[18] since these imply needs to be met, evils to be resisted, or limits to be overcome. As Aristotle concludes near the end of *Eudemian Ethics*, "God is not a superior who issues commands,"[19] since a god is self-sufficient and neither wants anything from us nor wishes anything for us. There is a First Cause of the universe, which has no temporal beginning or end, but it/they do not interact with human beings in particularized ways. Thus, Aristotle must look to human nature for substantive ethical and political guidance.

Plato and Aristotle both extol for human beings the four cardinal virtues of justice, temperance, prudence, and courage, but for Plato they are much more dependent on piety and an intuition of the divine good that finally outstrips verbal reasoning. For Plato, *nomos* is higher than *nous*, and *eros* is not fulfilled by either self-love or friendship. Plato, too, affirms many gods, but for him, again, the good is a coherent and conscious divinity that supersedes the others and can be apprehended by and act to transform persons. The Platonic Good warrants being spelled with an upper case "G" and is a (indeed, the) moral agent and craftsman—Plato calls him "father"[20]—whereas Aristotle's divine reality seems more like an amoral energy or energies, or even an impersonal event.

3 Moses and the Prophets

Leap now a little under a thousand miles in space, from Athens to Jerusalem, and a little over a thousand years back in time, from ca. 375 BCE to ca. 1400 BCE. See the metaphysical continuity in reverse. The biblical conception of truth and goodness evident in Moses and the Prophets begins with the righteousness of God, as in Plato, and moves on to a sinful humanity's need for divine grace to restore its relation and resemblance to the Highest. God is the giver of law and the agent and measure of virtue, which is identified with holiness rather than happiness:

> Who is like you, O LORD, among the gods?
> Who is like you, majestic in holiness,
> awesome in splendor, doing wonders?

---

17   Ibid., 1245b19, p. 139.
18   Ibid., 1245b15, p. 139.
19   Ibid., 1249b13, p. 148. This line is cited by Stephen Menn in "Aristotle's Theology," 452n5.
20   Plato, *Timaeus*, trans. Robin Waterfield (Oxford: Oxford University Press, 2008), 28c, p. 17.

> You stretched out your right hand;
>   the earth swallowed them.
> In your steadfast love you led the people whom you redeemed;
>   you guided them by your strength to your holy abode.
>
>   EXODUS 15:11–13[21]

> Then God spoke all these words, "I am the LORD your God, who brought you out of the land of Egypt, out of the house of slavery; you shall have no other gods before me. You shall not make for yourself an idol, whether in the form of anything that is in heaven above or that is on the earth beneath or that is in the water under the earth."
>
>   EXODUS 20:1–4

> "Speak to all the congregation of the Israelites and say to them: You shall be holy, for I the LORD your God am holy."
>
>   LEVITICUS 19:2

Human beings are made in the image of God (Genesis 1:27), but specific divine mandates are required to guide and rectify human life. Although negative prohibitions constitute the majority of the Ten Commandments, restraint of evil is not the sole purpose or content of the Torah. In its widest sense, Torah is the very heart and mind of God and analogous to the eternal Law (*nomos*) of Plato and the original Word (*logos*) of the Gospel of John. As such, Torah precedes the original sin (Genesis 3:1–7) and even the creation of the temporal world, including humans. It is already a reduction of the biblical meaning of "law" when it is identified exclusively with prudential scruples or even robust moral rules. This is the first step to tying law too closely to human flourishing and alienating it from the full holiness of God. Unfallen human beings needed instruction from God (for example, Genesis 2:16–17), and even pristine human nature was never self-sufficient, ethically or religiously. To suggest otherwise is, again, to eat pridefully from the tree of knowledge. It is to embrace a subjectivism in which humanity constitutes or controls good and evil, thus eclipsing theology with anthropology and promoting personal or political efficacy as the font and measure of jurisprudence rather than the "steadfast love" of God (*hesed*). As recounted and celebrated in Genesis 24:27, Exodus 15:13, Job 10:12, Isaiah 63:7, and numerous Psalms, that love is generous, just, and productive, not merely constraining or remedial.

---

21 All biblical quotations are from the New Revised Standard Version Updated Edition. See https://www.biblegateway.com/versions/New-Revised-Standard-Version-Updated-Edition-NRSVue-Bible/.

We are told repeatedly in Hebrew scripture, especially in Isaiah, that Yahweh loves *tsedaqah* (righteousness) and *mishpat* (justice). The terms are used so frequently together that they can be read as a hendiadys. A hendiadys is the expression of an idea by the use of two usually independent words connected by the conjunction "and" (as "sound and fury" or "nice and warm") instead of the usual combination of independent word and its modifier (as "furious sound" or "nicely warm"). *Tsedaqah* denotes doing right by another in light of one's relationship with them. According to Isaiah 51:6, 8, Israel's deliverance from exile is a divine act of *tsedaqah*. Quite often, *tsedaqah* seems primarily an aretological term. It frequently refers, that is, to a disposition of character, a question of virtuous motive or identity. Yahweh acts to fulfill an obligation to His people on the basis of long-standing care and commitment, what I have called God's holiness. Psalm 33 demonstrates also, however, that righteousness is a principle of world order that God wrote into the universe in creating it.

Mishpat, for its part, is a power word, describing the decisive acts of Yahweh.[22] To my ears, it usually has more deontological overtones, referring to a form of action—as in "just judgment" or "fair dealing." In any event, the righteousness and justice associated with Yahweh's reign underscore Yahweh's commitment to protect the marginalized and vulnerable. Psalm 9:7–9, 18 explicitly links the throne of Yahweh with righteousness and justice demonstrated in care for the oppressed. Psalm 146 concludes with the affirmation that Yahweh reigns forever (146:10). This is the capstone of praise for the Maker of the cosmos who protects the oppressed, hungry, prisoners, blind, alien, orphan, and widow (146:6–9).

How do *tsedaqah* and *mishpat* relate to *hesed*? Scripture tells us that Yahweh fills the earth with *hesed* (unfailing love). *Hesed* is a saving word, according to many commentators, and is thus linked with God's deliverance of Israel—but, as we have seen, so is *tsedaqah*. The word *hesed* almost defies translation into English and has been rendered as covenant love, loving-kindness, covenant-fidelity, steadfast love, loyalty, and mercy. It is, according to the title of a book that studies the term, "faithfulness in action."[23] The term refers to Yahweh's

---

22 See John Goldingay, *The Theology of the Book of Isaiah* (Downers Grove, IL: InterVarsity Press, 2014), 20–22.

23 Katharine Doob Sakenfeld, *Faithfulness in Action* (Minneapolis: Fortress, 1985). On *hesed* in the marital covenant, see John Witte, Jr., *From Sacrament to Contract: Marriage, Religion and Law in the Western Tradition*, 2nd ed. (Louisville, KY: Westminster John Knox Press, 2012), 44–45; and more fully id. "The Covenant of Marriage: Its Biblical Roots, Historical Influence, and Modern Uses," INTAMS *Review on Marriage and Spirituality* 18 (2012): 147–65.

self-giving commitment made under no obligation (like Rahab's protection of the Israelite spies in Joshua 2:4–12), a commitment that God continues to make as a legal obligation, even though it is costly and the partner proves to be unworthy.

To the extent that human beings are called to reflect God's *hesed* in their lives (see Psalm 42:8, Isaiah 16:5, and Hosea 6:6), Greek flourishing is a nonstarter. Eudaimonism must strike Moses and the Prophets as akin to rulers who "give judgment for a bribe" and priests who "teach for a price" (see Micah 3:11). Like everybody, the Jews want exoneration and happiness, but they are divinely edified as to means and ends. Yahweh is the key to both. To speak anachronistically, for the Jews, eudaimonism in ethics is like sliding head first into first base in baseball: it seems natural and prudent, but it actually slows you down and can lead to injury. We need grace and conviction to resist the temptation, follow the Coach, and keep running. Even Daniel, for all his loyalty to God and relativizing of worldly powers, seems to take a misstep in tying his faith so closely to the "reward" of resurrection (Daniel 12:13). Judaism upheld moral monotheism for centuries without being motivated by an afterlife.

4 The Gospels and Saint Paul

Moses's motif of theocentric holiness is also the foundation of the New Testament, with divine grace now taking the primary form of Jesus Christ:

> Therefore prepare your minds for action; discipline yourselves; set all your hope on the grace that Jesus Christ will bring you when he is revealed. Like obedient children, do not be conformed to the desires that you formerly had in ignorance. Instead, as he who called you is holy, be holy yourselves in all your conduct, for it is written, "You shall be holy, for I am holy."
> 1 PETER 1:13–16

> Finally, brothers and sisters, we ask and urge you in the Lord Jesus that, as you learned from us how you ought to live and to please God (as, in fact, you are doing), you should do so more and more. For you know what instructions we gave you through the Lord Jesus.... God did not call us to impurity but in holiness. Therefore whoever rejects this rejects not human authority but God, who also gives his Holy Spirit to you.
> 1 THESSALONIANS 4:1–7

> Bear one another's burdens, and so fulfill the law of Christ.
> GALATIANS 6:2

Sanctification is growth in holiness rather than increase in happiness. The main spiritual point in both the Hebrew Bible and the New Testament is to obey and please God, rather than to prosper and fulfill oneself. What makes Jesus such a compelling figure is that in him, the God-man, theology and anthropology meet. For him, nonetheless, God the Father alone is good and demands obedience, including the surrender of material wealth and its donation to the poor (Matthew 19:16–22). Law and Gospel are one in focusing on personal atonement and self-sacrifice, as evinced in the theocentricity of the three theological virtues of faith, hope, and love. Faith is faith in God's faith, hope is hope for God's hope, and love is love for God's love. Divine love (*agape*) is "the greatest of these," according to Paul (1 Corinthians 13); and, in my judgment, it is characterized by three interpersonal features: (1) unconditional willing of the good for the other, (2) equal regard for the well-being of the other, and (3) passionate service open to self-sacrifice for the sake of the other.[24] The cardinal virtues are not at odds with the theological, but they are not identical to them either. The suffering and death of Christ on the cross is the end for many of us of any plausible religious eudaimonism in the West, but, as we have seen, eudaimonism was never central to Moses and Judaism. And Greek philosophy was arguably on its way to overcoming it until the fateful (but not ineluctable) turn of Aristotle that essentially naturalized happiness.

The abiding tendency among Christian exegetes to read the New Testament, especially Paul's epistles, as pitting Law against Gospel is a tragic mistake. New Testament *nomos* (like Hebraic *Torah*) is regularity and reliability, covenant fidelity translated into a particular context and in a repeatable form. It is no more antithetical to *agape* than is taking an oath on the Bible to speak the truth in court. The oath is a concrete expression of love of neighbor that willingly binds heart and mind in and through specifics. Similarly, God's choosing the Jewish people to be "a light unto the nations" (Isaiah 42:6) is a means for God to love the entire world, even as God's incarnating in Jesus is an expression of Torah for all of humanity, especially Gentiles. God uses the tribe of Israel to overcome tribalism, even as God employs the individual Jesus to overcome individualism.

Christian obedience is not the drill of living in accord with God's commands or natural laws out of fear of divine or human sanctions or in anticipation of

---

24 See Timothy P. Jackson, *The Priority of Love: Christian Charity and Social Justice* (Princeton: Princeton University Press, 2003).

personal profit; it is, rather, participation in God's own holiness, valuable for its own sake. What is key is not our moral development but God's service and companionship. When Jesus says to Martha, "I am the resurrection and the life" (John 11:25), it is to his incarnate fellowship with God that he is referring, a fellowship that both requires and overcomes death. This is why self-abnegation and gratitude, rather than happiness and dignity, are central in Christian ethics. The more God-consciousness the more self-consciousness, and one's character and ethical skills are no doubt enhanced by fidelity to God, but such enhancement is not the motive. To repeat, the four cardinal Greek virtues are natural and anthropocentric, whereas the three theological virtues are supernatural and theocentric. Piety, not prudence, is paramount for Plato, the Prophets, Paul, and even for patience anticipating the Parousia.

"You shall be holy as I am holy," saith the Lord (Leviticus 19:2). The question of piety revolves around God as the subject of theology and morality rather than the object. What is primary is *imitatio Dei* touched by divine grace, not *amor sui* moved by human will. The Ten Commandments first appear in Exodus, when the Jews are on the run in an alien land. The prime inspiration of the commandments is to carry God close to oneself and one's people, rather than to cultivate personal happiness or temporal fulfillment. It's a question of means and ends. Human law and love are like salt and light that serve purposes outside of themselves and must be traced back to their divine origin (see Matthew 5:13–16).[25] Virtues themselves are secondary to communion with and promotion of the Good.

5 Luther, Kant, and Nietzsche

If the Platonic Good or the Judeo-Christian God does not exist, then Immanuel Kant is the best we can do; if some form of classical theism is true, then Immanuel Kant is our worst temptation. The first line of Section I of Kant's *Groundwork of the Metaphysics of Morals* (1785) makes the salient point: "It is impossible to think of anything at all in the world, or indeed even beyond it, that could be considered good without limitation except a *good will.*"[26] Kant would have us focus on rational agency or "autonomy" as "the ground

---

25 See also John Witte, Jr., "Three in One: Emil Brunner's Christian Natural Defense of the Family," in *Faith, Freedom, and Family*, 564.

26 Kant, *Groundwork of the Metaphysics of Morals*, in *The Cambridge Edition of the Works of Immanuel Kant: Practical Philosophy*, trans. and ed. Mary J. Gregor (Cambridge: Cambridge University Press, 1996), 4:393, p. 49.

of the dignity of human nature and of any rational nature."[27] For Kant, the only unqualifiedly good thing is the good will, and there is no question that first of all and most of the time he means the good *human* will. He explicitly distinguishes a "holy will" from a "human will."[28] For the traditional Jew and the Christian, in contrast, the prime task is to will the Good, which reposes in a Holiness infinitely above and beyond us. The good will based in human freedom or to will the Good as commanded and empowered by a transcendent God—that is the divide: either autonomy, being self-lawed (from *auto* + *nomos*), or theonomy, being God-lawed (from *theos* + *nomos*).

From its inception, American democracy stood on the twin pillars of biblical Christianity and Enlightenment humanism, a melding of Pilgrim and Puritan faith, on one hand, and of Deistic rationalism, on the other. In addition to the *Groundwork*, Kant's *Critique of Pure Reason* and *Critique of Practical Reason*, published in 1781 and 1788, respectively, helped to kick out the first of those pillars and to tip the Western intellectual balance toward Deistic rationalism. Kant's thought is the decisive next step taken by Enlightenment humanism following Martin Luther's promotion of the secular and rejection of the *imitatio Christi*. The Protestant Reformation was a necessary corrective to the selling of indulgences and the corruption of the papacy, and a valorizing of human reason and will was the furthest thing from Luther's intention. A profound elevation of "the human" and "the natural" ensued, nonetheless—an elevation historically associated with Wittenberg, Germany. As Søren Kierkegaard notes:

> Luther understood the problem thus: No man can endure the anxiety [*Angst*] that his striving will decide his eternal salvation or eternal damnation. No, no, says Luther, this can only lead to despair or to blasphemy. And therefore (note this!), therefore it is not so (Luther apparently alters New Testament Christianity because otherwise mankind must despair). You are saved by grace; be assured, you are saved by grace—and then you strive as well as you can.
>
> This is Luther's variation of the matter. I will not speak here of the swindle concocted by a later Protestantism. No, I will stand by this Lutheran principle. My objection is this: Luther should have let it be known that he reduced Christianity.

---

27 Ibid., 4:436, p. 85.
28 Ibid., 4:414, p. 67.

Furthermore, he ought to have made it known that his argument: "otherwise we must despair"—is actually arguing from the human side. But, strictly speaking, this argument is without foundation when the question is what the New Testament understands by Christianity; strictly speaking, the fact that Luther could argue thus shows that for him Christianity was not yet unconditionally sovereign, but that this sovereignty, too, has to yield under the assumption that "otherwise a man must despair."[29]

Kant gave Luther's human "sovereignty" one more turn of the screw, and God all but dropped out of the dynamics of practical reason. According to Kant, the moral law declares that we ought to become perfect, with our virtue and our happiness in complete accord, but manifestly such perfection is not possible in this life alone. Because "ought" implies "can," however, we must postulate that God exists as a metaphysical guarantor of personal immortality, so that "ought" can indeed imply "can" in an endless afterlife.[30] Note that it remains the case, for Kant, that our noumenal selves do the willing in Heaven, so divine grace is relegated to a kind of Deistic life insurance policy. Luther wanted to destroy the idea of works righteousness by making fulfillment of God's law humanly *impossible*, but in fact he made the fulfillment *unnecessary*, at least for the elect. Instead of eternal and divine law indicting us and throwing us back on God's grace, as Luther intended and as both the Pilgrims and the Puritans affirmed, Luther's teachings opened the door to "naturalizing" ethics and making it amenable to our finite powers of mind and heart, lest we become pitiable. Our good will is all that matters, not our striving or actual existential obedience to the Heavenly Father. In this way, Lutheran total depravity paradoxically morphed into Kantian personal autonomy: we Kantians give *ourselves* the law, and the categorical imperative is to respect *our own persons, rather than the Persons of the Trinity*.

After Kant, it did not take long for Friedrich Nietzsche to announce that neither commands from above nor commands from within have any moral credibility. Nietzsche's elegantly simple insight was that, especially in the wake of the death of the Eternal Lord, no temporal authority, including human

---

29 Søren Kierkegaard, *Søren Kierkegaard's Journals and Papers*, vol. 3, ed. Howard V. Hong and Edna H. Hong, assisted by Gregor Malantschuk (Bloomington: Indiana University Press, 1975), XI^1 A 297 n.d., 1854, pp. 101–02.

30 Kant, *Critique of Practical Reason*, in *The Cambridge Edition of the Works of Immanuel Kant: Practical Philosophy*, 5:124–32, pp. 239–46.

reason and volition, can withstand the acids of genealogical deconstruction. With Kant's passing, the already moribund Deistic God effectively expired. Hence, even as theology had to yield to humanist ethics, so humanist ethics had to yield to a pragmatic aesthetics: all we have are natural drives and the epic beauty of our own will to power. Even as Luther judged that the only way to avoid despair and/or blasphemy was to reduce New Testament Christianity, so Nietzsche maintained that the only way to avoid nihilism and/or hypocrisy was to reduce Enlightenment humanism. This meant going back to paganism and embracing healthy instinct and the survival of the fittest as the sole "truth" of our condition. Luther fled from receiving pity into the arms of a forgiving Jesus Christ; Nietzsche fled from giving pity and found his prototype in an unforgiving Cesare Borgia.[31]

The movement from Luther to Kant to Nietzsche made over God in our image, now called *der Übermensch*. The movement was neither intentional nor unavoidable, but it helps us see the problematic status of morality sans the Deity. Without God, action is just acting; with God, just acting is unjust action. This is a pithy way of saying that human beings must find the source and content of goodness outside of themselves. On this, Moses, Socrates, and Jesus agree. As important as autonomy can be in some limited contexts, it becomes an idol when elevated to a primary ethical and religious fount or ideal. Creatures do not create themselves and have neither the capacity nor the authority to be purely self-lawed; *pace* Kant, voluntary self-affirmation and rational consistency are not enough for virtue. One might be consistently perverse, as were antisemitic Jews who fought for the Nazis. *Malgré lui*, Martin Luther's advocacy of *sola fide* and "the priesthood of all believers" led to the supplanting of theonomy in favor of autonomy. His "freedom *of* a Christian"[32] became freedom *from* Christianity as imitation of the Highest. Now we are the masters of our own life and death, and the resultant legal positivism finds it impossible to prohibit direct-abortion-on-demand and active-euthanasia-on-demand. These are simply "our right to choose." Nietzsche merely added that might undeniably *makes* right.

Kierkegaard calls Kant "my philosopher" and himself observes that "Christianity, as it is in the New Testament, focuses on man's will; everything turns on

---

31 Nietzsche, *Beyond Good and Evil*, in *Basic Writings of Nietzsche*, trans. and ed. Walter Kaufmann (New York: Random House, 1966, 1967, 1968), sect. 197, p. 298.
32 See discussion of Luther's original teachings on freedom and order in John Witte, Jr., *Law and Protestantism: The Legal Teachings of the Lutheran Reformation* (Cambridge: Cambridge University Press, 2002), 87–117, and later amplifications in id. "The Freedom of a Christian: Martin Luther's Reformation of Law & Liberty," *Evangelische Theologie* 74 (2014), 127–35.

that, on transforming the will."[33] But Kierkegaard makes it clear that the transformation in question is modeled on and moved by a righteousness outside the human will. "Kant thought that man was his own legislator (autonomy); that is, subjecting himself to the law that he gives to himself. Properly understood, that is to postulate lawlessness or experimentation.... Not only is there no law that I give myself as a maxim, it is the case that there is a law given me by a higher authority."[34] For Kierkegaard, the governing reality behind morality is eternal *theos* not temporal *nous*, and the demanding call is to imitation of the Second Person of the Trinity rather than to self-legislation according to reason. Kant is Kierkegaard's philosopher but not his theologian. Being fundamentally Arminian, SK holds that the grace of the Holy Spirit is required to transform the human will but that grace is not irresistible. We must consent to being gifted by the Spirit in following Christ, which means being willing that our will be eclipsed. We have these words from Christ to his Father: "not my will but Thine be done" (Luke 22:42). But, even more chillingly, we hear the Son's cry on the cross: "*Eli, Eli lema sabachthani?*"—"My God, my God, why have you forsaken me?" (Matthew 27:46). To be loved by God is not merely to be transformed; it is to be broken.

Here is Kierkegaard's definitive word for Kantians on will: "Only a man of will can become a Christian, because only a man of will has a will that can be broken. But a man whose will is broken by the unconditioned or by God is a Christian.... A Christian is a man of will who no longer wills his own will, but with the passion of his crushed will—radically changed—wills another's will."[35] A Kierkegaardian Christian must, by Kantian lights, be guilty of heteronomy, having the determination of one's will outside of oneself. Kantian virtue, in turn, must strike a Kierkegaardian Christian as glittering vice, failing to give divine credit where it is due. In Kant, God effectively drops out as lawgiver, and it is all about the cultivation of our own powers via being self-lawed: *eudaimonia* as dignity, *arete* as autonomy.

I dub Kant rather than Nietzsche the Christian's "worst temptation," because Kant is a quite "reasonable" elaboration of Luther and the Reformation. Nietzsche, on the other hand, is too derisively explicit in his rejection of biblical faith to be appealing to Christians, but he is nevertheless waiting with a smile at the end of the Kantian road to a naturalized philosophy. Again, I am not claiming that the regression from Luther to Kant to Nietzsche

---

33 Søren Kierkegaard, *Papers and Journals: A Selection*, trans. Alastair Hannay (London: Penguin, 1996), 54 XI 2 A 86, p. 618.
34 Ibid., 50 X 2 A 397, p. 467.
35 Kierkegaard, *Papers and Journals*, 55 XI 2 A 436, p. 646.

is inevitable—cultural history is not that deterministic—but I do contend that each figure was a pivotal step toward the valorizing of biology and social Darwinism we see today.

6 Jurisprudence in Light of the Sacraments

If Plato is correct that one can understand justice only by first comprehending the transcendental Good, then political science cannot be separated from theology. If Moses and Jesus are right, and law must be grounded in the steadfast love of God and neighbor (*hesed* and *agape*), then jurisprudence cannot be detached from theology either. Not everyone is a Platonist, a Jew, or a Christian, so how should a diverse and democratic society think about the relation between religious faith and politics, economics, and law?

I subscribe to what I have called, "the Emory School," led by faculty in the Candler School of Theology—including Jon Gunnemann, Steven Tipton, Brooks Holifield, Carol Newsom, Philip Reynolds, Brent Strawn, and myself—as well as by Witte and his mentor, Harold J. Berman. This perspective offers a middle way between two dominant institutional voices in contemporary America. On one hand is what I somewhat playfully call "the Harvard (Divinity) School," which, as a rule, so accommodates liberal pluralism as either to surrender distinctive Christian creeds and behaviors altogether or to claim to translate them into neutral, secular terms. On the other hand is "the Duke (Divinity) School," which generally embraces the sectarian option, circles its theological wagons, and encourages the Christian church to withdraw from the wider fallen world, lest it be corrupted. The Emory School, in contrast, strives to retain its distinctive Christian identity and behavior but also constructively to engage the larger cultural surround.

More specifically, I reject the segregation of different cultural spheres—for example, religion, politics, and law—as though they are or can be autonomous and nonoverlapping. Instead, I advocate the principled application of religious beliefs and practices to all aspects of life, including jurisprudence, such that conscience is respected and ecclesial power is limited *as a matter of theological conviction itself.* I endorse an individual believer and citizen in using any religious resource to settle pressing social questions. If one judges scripture or the commands of God to prohibit elective abortion or chattel slavery as immoral, for example, one has the right (and perhaps the duty) to say so in public and to promote the relevant laws and policies. In turn, sacred texts and prayerful inspirations can and should be brought to bear on these same moral matters by those who disagree. The civic challenge to all concerned is to give justifying arguments in support of normative positions.[36]

Broad constitutional restrictions on what the state may do either to restrict or to empower the exercise of religion should remain or be put in place. The state ought not to establish a particular religion as the national orthodoxy, for instance, or require statements of faith for voting rights. Moreover, the question of whether there is a God and what God's will for creatures may be should be left to individual conscience, rather than settled *a priori* by standing governmental dictate. But these are the metarules of the democratic game, and they do not predetermine particular moves within the game. In the American context, the metarules were themselves an expression of religious tolerance and the desire to check centralized power. Ongoing respect, for both belief and unbelief, must be enacted in the process of debate and decision, which may or may not involve prudent compromise. Within that process, private citizens, elected officials, lawyers, and appointed judges and justices are entirely at liberty to bring theological reasons and emotions to bear on all contested issues. Religious believers may be outargued and/or outvoted, but they should not be silenced in advance.

John Rawls notwithstanding, there is no guaranteed or prestateable "overlapping consensus" and no nonmetaphysical "public reason" that permits (much less requires) religious premises and precepts to be evacuated from the public domain. There is no justification, liberal or otherwise, for the muzzling of religious discourse in political, economic, and legal contexts. The state may prohibit coercion and fraud, but this stricture is applicable to any mode of speech or action, religious or nonreligious. To assert otherwise is not merely to disestablish a national church, it is to exclude faith from a society's collective life in a way neither just nor loving. It is, indeed, to violate the conscience of the responsible believer by forcing her to betray her identity and not speak or vote her mind. A religion that can be privatized without loss is certainly not

---

36   See further Timothy P. Jackson, "The Return of the Prodigal: Liberal Theory and Religious Pluralism," in *Religion and Contemporary Liberalism,* ed. Paul Weithman (Notre Dame, IN: University of Notre Dame Press, 2017), 182–217. See comparable views in John Witte, Jr., *Church, State, and Family: Reconciling Traditional Teachings and Modern Liberties* (Cambridge: Cambridge University Press, 2019) and John Witte, Jr., Joel A. Nichols, and Richard W. Garnett, *Religion and the American Constitutional Experiment,* 5th ed. (Oxford: Oxford University Press, 2022).

biblical, since biblical faith requires us to love all neighbors and to care actively for the weak and vulnerable.[37]

What does Christian jurisprudence look like when it is fully delivered from eudaimonism and the will to power, as well as from a bogus "liberalism"? How does it appear when seen, instead, through the lens of the sacraments, the sacraments being our most immediate interaction with the goodness of God? The traditional Roman Catholic sacraments can be grouped under three headings: (a) initiation, which includes baptism, confirmation, and the Eucharist; (b) healing, which includes penance and last rites; and (c) service, which includes holy orders and marriage. John Witte observes:

> Many ... aspects of social intercourse had been governed by the Catholic Church's canon law and organized in part by the church's seven sacraments. Lutheran jurists used the Ten Commandments, instead of the seven sacraments, to organize the various systems of positive law. They looked to the state, instead of the church, to promulgate and enforce these positive laws on the basis of the Ten Commandments and the biblical and extrabiblical sources of natural law and morality.[38]

Indeed, Martin Luther rejected all but two of the Catholic sacraments—baptism and the Lord's Supper—as well as much of the medieval canon law they supported. Others have extensively researched the relation between the Protestant Reformation, secularization, and the rise of the modern nation-state,[39] so, rather than offering further remarks on this score, let me say a few words about how all seven sacraments are relevant to the understanding of law.

(1) For Christians, the universal human need for *baptism*, the washing away of original sin, is a source of what might be called negative unity. Saint Paul observes that "through the law comes the knowledge of sin" (Romans 3:20),

---

37 See John Rawls, *Political Liberalism* (New York: Columbia University Press, 1993); see also my *Political Agape: Christian Love and Liberal Democracy* (Grand Rapids: Eerdmans, 2015), esp. chap. 4.

38 Witte, "Faith in Law: The Protestant Reformation of Law and Politics," in *Faith, Freedom, and Family*, 81.

39 Joseph R. Strayer writes: "The modern state, wherever we find it today, is based on the pattern which emerged in Europe in the period 1100 to 1600." He contends that the most important test or criterion of such a state is "a shift in loyalty from family, local community, or religious organization to the state and the acquisition by the state of a moral authority to back up its institutional structure and its theoretical legal supremacy." See Strayer, *On the Medieval Origins of the Modern State* (Princeton: Princeton University Press, 1970), 12 and 9.

but the reverse is also true: knowledge of sin impacts our understanding of law. Paul declares that "all have sinned and fall short of the glory of God," so those who believe "are now justified by [God's] grace as a gift, through the redemption that is in Christ Jesus" (Romans 3:23–24). This realization ought to occasion humility and mercy, especially in making legal judgments about others. The fact that we are all fallible and capable of admitting this should condition our conception of legal punishment and rehabilitation as well.

(2) *Penance* is rightly a part of condign retribution and reform, in addition to fines or loss of liberty. As is often pointed out, a penitentiary is ideally a place where criminals go to be penitent, not merely to be incarcerated.[40] Legal sanctions must address the whole person as a unity of body and soul, fallible but bearing a conscience as well as a record. Just as God's love created space and time so that a law-governed world might exist and intelligent beings evolve, so the penal system should give criminals time and space to reflect and repent. They may decline to do so, but that is between them and God.

(3) Another sad occasion for solidarity is the inevitability of death, as acknowledged in the giving of *last rites*. Mortality, like fallibility, is a tie that ought to bind us in sympathy to all sentient beings. The dissolution of the image of God in death, contrasted with the dignity and sanctity of life, moves the Roman Catholic Church to reject capital punishment.[41] The last rites we give to others, including the most extreme lawbreakers, should be an honoring of the *imago Dei*, rather than its destruction. No temporal authority has the right directly and lethally to target a defenseless human life, no matter how guilty of transgression that life might be. For such a life still bears a sacred worth that is a gift of God and ought to be inviolable. If justice gives each person their due, how differently will that due be calculated if we judge human lives to be the intentional creation of a loving Deity, as opposed to the pointless upshot of random mutation and natural selection? The scientific debate continues on these matters, and no legislative fiat should preclude the affirmation of theistic evolution as the background to *last rites*.

(4) *Holy orders*, the ordination of priests and bishops, confer the sacramental power to baptize, confirm, witness marriages, absolve sins, and consecrate the Eucharist. They also convey to bishops the authority to ordain. The men taking holy orders vow celibacy for life. I find in holy orders an analogical key to the proper understanding of lawyers, judges, and justices. Lawyers are the ordained priests of the law with special powers to administer it for the

---

40 See Witte on penitentiaries, or *Zuchthausen*, in "The Uses of Law for the Formation of Character," in *Faith, Freedom, and Family*, 114.
41 See the *Catechism of the Catholic Church*, 2nd ed., #2267.

common good. Like bishops, judges and justices have still higher authority to enforce and interpret the law, as in passing sentences and deciding constitutional issues. While lawyers, judges, and justices hold offices not open to all, they are not themselves the law but rather servants of the law that comes from God and must be affirmed by the people. Just as individual consciences must decide whether to join the Body of Christ, private citizens are the jurors who pronounce on the guilt and innocence of peers. Finally, just as priests and bishops pledge chastity to better serve God, so lawyers, judges, and justices ought to forgo profiteering from their roles. You cannot serve God and mammon or *nomos* and *eros*.

(5) In the sacrament of *marriage*, the vows are plausibly seen as divine *nomos* binding and transmuting *eros*, which is a preferential and self-interested love, while *agape* is universal and self-sacrificial. The marital pledge of constancy must transform erotic love into something less variable and subjective by grounding it in *agape* as more kenotic and eternal. This is a model of how God incarnates law which is lost, of course, when marriage is secularized. In addition to alienating Christians from the *imitatio Christi*, Luther helped usher in a rather ambivalent attitude toward matrimony. As Scott Hendrix has noted, "in one sense marriage was demoted because it ceased to be a sacrament; but in another sense its status was elevated because it was deemed equal to or superior to celibacy."[42] Although Luther himself valued marriage as a covenant of fidelity, it has become for many in the West a purely contractual relation accompanied by "no-fault" divorce.

(6) *The Eucharist* signals even more graphically divine love's way with the world. All sacraments are instruments and expressions of God's steadfast love for fallen creatures—"an outward and visible sign of an inward and spiritual grace," as the Lutheran and Anglican catechisms put it. In John 6:54–56, Jesus Christ informs his disciples: "Those who eat my flesh and drink my blood have eternal life, and I will raise them up on the last day, for my flesh is true food, and my blood is true drink. Those who eat my flesh and drink my blood abide in me and I in them." What are we to make of this apparently cannibalistic ritual? The original disobedient eating in the Garden of Eden can be undone only by a second obedient eating after the Garden of Gethsemane. This holy anthropophagy is necessary not because Christ is a masochist but because we human beings are sadists and masochists, sadists and masochists whose bloodlust will be satisfied in no other way. This is how the kenotic law of theonomy redeems

---

42 Scott Hendrix, "Luther on Marriage," *Lutheran Quarterly* 14 (2000): 335–50, at 335.

the lawlessness of autonomy. If baptism is a kind of spiritual chemotherapy to destroy the uncontrolled cancer of sin, Holy Communion functions like a blood transfusion—more specifically, a stem cell transplant—given subsequently by *Christus Donator* to the patient. All we can be is grateful.

(7) In *confirmation*, a bishop or priest blesses a consenting person, saying: "Be sealed with the gifts of the Holy Spirit." In this way, the person becomes a full member of the church guided by the inner presence of the Spirit. I treat confirmation last among the sacraments, because it highlights the fact that theonomy itself is a gift of divine grace that must be freely accepted. God is our Creator and Governor, but God would respect individual consciences to the extent that this is compatible with love and justice. I cannot transgress the Ten Commandments of the Bible with psychic impunity, even as I cannot violate the ordinances of a sovereign nation against theft and murder with legal impunity. But a wise church and state allow for some forms of conscientious objection, the right to opt out of some forms of ecclesial and civic membership and activity. Not all should be compelled to be congregants or combatants, for example, even in a Catholic Church or a just war.

7   Conclusion

Are we God-lawed and -loved, with a call to holiness from on high, the Platonic and biblical vision? Are we self-lawed and -loved, with an imperative for happiness from within, the Kantian vision with roots in Aristotle? Is the reality of our situation a third alternative in which theocentric and anthropocentric accounts of law and love are illusory, the Nietzschean vision? I have agreed with John Witte in endorsing the first scenario. I have been much harder on Luther than Witte is,[43] but I have otherwise followed his lead in imagining what jurisprudence might look like if enacted sacramentally.

The possibility of theonomy means we are not condemned to be forever buffeted between crude self-annihilation and crass self-aggrandizement. We are made in the image of a holy God, whose grace delivers us from our absurdity and guilt. Because our life is a gift and our sins are forgiven, we need not begin with the pursuit of happiness or end in despair. We can love because we

---

43   Like many, including Witte, I am deeply troubled by Luther's violent tirade against the Jews in "On the Jews and Their Lies" (1543). See my *Mordecai Would Not Bow Down: Anti-Semitism, the Holocaust, and Christian Supersessionism* (Oxford: Oxford University Press, 2021), chap. 4.

are loved (1 John 4:19). This is the final meaning of the sacraments; thus, I have gestured toward a Christian sensibility in which the key to *lex et veritas* is *caritas*, and the foundation of *nomos kai agathos* is *agape*. As John Witte's mentor, Harold Berman, reminds us, "the ultimate purpose of human law is to create conditions in which love of God and love of neighbor may flourish."[44]

---

44 Harold J. Berman, "Law and Logos," *DePaul Law Review* 44 (1994): 143–66, at 143.

CHAPTER 13

When Catholicism Was Part of the Common Law: The Influence of the Catholic Intellectual Tradition

Samuel L. Bray

John Witte has written extensively on the influence of the Protestant thought on the development of Western law—from the magisterial Reformations of the sixteenth century until our day.[1] Others have written on the adage that "Christianity is part of the common law."[2]

This chapter considers a related question that has been not so much studied: What is the influence of the Catholic intellectual tradition on the common law? That question asks about the relationship between two things, and each requires definition. "The common law" refers to the legal tradition that was developed in England and subsequently transplanted into many other lands, from Australia to Nigeria to the United States.[3] I will focus here on the aspect of the common law that has judges finding and articulating what the law is.[4] As used in this chapter, "the common law" is capacious enough to include both law and equity.

"The Catholic intellectual tradition" is a late-twentieth-century term that began to be widely used only in the 1990s, shortly after the term "Catholic social teaching" gained widespread currency. The former term is a kind of intellectual

---

1 See, for example, John Witte, Jr., *Law and Protestantism: The Legal Teachings of the Lutheran Reformation* (Cambridge: Cambridge University Press, 2002); id., *The Reformation of Rights: Law, Religion, and Human Rights in Early Modern Calvinism* (Cambridge: Cambridge University Press, 2007); John Witte, Jr. and Frank S. Alexander, eds., *The Teachings of Modern Protestantism on Law, Politics, and Human Nature* (New York: Columbia University Press, 2007). See further the chapters by R. H. Helmholz and Nicholas Wolterstorff herein.
2 See Stuart Banner, "When Christianity Was Part of the Common Law," *Law and History Review* 16 (1998): 27–62.
3 On its origins, see Sir John Baker, *An Introduction to English Legal History*, 5th ed. (Oxford: Oxford University Press, 2019), 25–43; on its spread around the world, see Christian R. Burset, *An Empire of Laws: Legal Pluralism in British Colonial Policy* (forthcoming 2023); and on its theory, see Gerald J. Postema, *Bentham and the Common Law Tradition*, 2nd ed. (Oxford: Oxford University Press, 2019), 3–78.
4 See, for example, Stephen E. Sachs, "Finding Law," *California Law Review* 107 (2019): 527–81; and *James B. Beam Distilling Co. v. Georgia*, 501 U.S. 529, 549 (1991) (Scalia, J., concurring in the judgment).

marketing device, a way of bundling together certain ideas and attitudes in a convenient package.⁵ Although the term is late modern, its referent is a much older tradition. "The Catholic intellectual tradition" is a way of organizing a certain set of concerns that matter to a Catholic university, including the University of Notre Dame, to whose faculty I belong.

In setting out the animating concerns of this tradition, I will lean on an acute unpublished analysis by Professor John Cavadini, who described "the integration of reason and revelation" as "one hallmark—perhaps the main one—of the Catholic intellectual tradition."⁶ This integration is not settled at a particular moment but is, Professor Cavadini says, "an ongoing 'dialectic between faith and reason.'"⁷ The revelation to which he refers is preeminently the revelation of Jesus Christ in the scriptures. As further discussed below, this integration of reason and revelation is also pervasive in Protestant thought.

In addition to these definitions, one more preliminary point is necessary. The question considered in this chapter is broader than the influence upon the common law of the *ius commune*, a blend of Roman and canon law that spread throughout Europe in the late Middle Ages. The degree of that influence has long been debated, and the leading recent analyses are by Professor Dick Helmholz.⁸ Although the *ius commune* can be seen as an example or outworking

---

5 See David Paul Deavel, "Preface: The Catholic Intellectual Tradition," *Logos: A Journal of Catholic Thought and Culture* 24 (Fall 2021): 5–20, at 6.
6 J. C. Cavadini, "Eight Modest Theses on 'The Catholic Intellectual Tradition,'" unpublished manuscript dated May 17, 2022. See below, note 59. It is standard for analyses of the Catholic intellectual tradition to emphasize the interplay of faith and reason. "The two major principles that undergird" the Catholic intellectual tradition are said to be "the unity of all knowledge and the complementarity of faith and reason": Deavel, "Preface: The Catholic Intellectual Tradition," 8. The "common criteria" of the Catholic intellectual tradition are "a complicated link between faith and reason": Mary Ellen O'Donnell, "The Catholic Intellectual Tradition: A Classification and a Calling," in *The Catholic Studies Reader*, ed. James T. Fisher and Margaret M. McGuinness (New York: Fordham University Press, 2011), 58. The tradition's "fare" is "wherever faith and understanding are seeking each other": John C. Haughey, *Where Is Knowing Going?: The Horizons of the Knowing Subject* (Washington, DC: Georgetown University Press, 2009), 69. See also Pope John Paul II, *Fides et Ratio—Encyclical Letter, John Paul II* (1998), ¶ 59 (referring to "the great tradition of Christian thought which unites faith and reason").
7 Cavadini, "Eight Modest Theses on 'The Catholic Intellectual Tradition.'"
8 See R. H. Helmholz, *The Ius Commune in England: Four Studies* (Oxford: Oxford University Press, 2001); R. H. Helmholz, *Roman Canon Law in Reformation England* (Cambridge: Cambridge University Press, 1990); and R. H. Helmholz, "Magna Carta and the *ius commune*," *University of Chicago Law Review* 66 (1999): 297–371.

of the Catholic intellectual tradition,[9] it does not exhaust that tradition. The dialectic between faith and reason is not irreducibly legal. The question here, therefore, is how the common law was influenced not specifically by the *ius commune* but more broadly by the Catholic intellectual tradition.

With these preliminaries noted, we can return to the question with which this chapter began. As soon as the question is asked, we run headlong into a problem, one you might be tempted to see as an impasse. Much of what we call the common law was developed from the late sixteenth through the early nineteenth centuries. It was developed by the great judges of those centuries, judges such as Coke, Hale, and Mansfield. During these centuries, Roman Catholic belief and worship were proscribed in England. In fact, one could not be a judge or a lawyer appearing in court without taking the Oath of Supremacy.[10] Although the oath required by King James I (VI of Scotland) was defended as requiring only political allegiance,[11] after the Restoration office holders were specifically required to affirm Protestant teaching on points like transubstantiation and the invocation and adoration of saints. Moreover, the principal doctrinal formulary of the Church of England includes an article that expressly states: "The Bishop of *Rome* hath no jurisdiction in this Realm of *England.*"[12] Common lawyers knew what jurisdiction meant. They knew what it meant to say that the bishop of Rome did not have any.

There were recusants, but they were typically on the margins of power. Edmund Plowden, the sixteenth-century lawyer whose work was influential for later thinking about the equity of the statute,[13] was a Catholic. But that fact limited his opportunities for promotion.[14]

---

9   See Helmholz, *The Ius Commune in England*, 26 (noting Saint Augustine's rationale for sanctuary within a church building, and the shifting rationale in later canon law).

10 See, for example, David Lemmings, *Professors of the Law: Barristers and English Legal Culture in the Eighteenth Century* (Oxford: Oxford University Press, 2000), 41n.64; and Alexandra Walsham *Charitable Hatred: Tolerance and Intolerance in England, 1500–1700* (Manchester, UK: Manchester University Press, 2006), 59–62.

11 This was, however, hotly debated. On Bellarmine's rejoinder, see Stefania Tutino, *Empire of Souls: Robert Bellarmine and the Christian Commonwealth* (Oxford: Oxford University Press, 2010), 117–58.

12 "The Thirty-Nine Articles of Religion," in *The Book of Common Prayer: The Texts of 1549, 1559, and 1662*, ed. Brian Cummings (Oxford: Oxford University Press, 2011), 684.

13 See James Edelman, "The Equity of the Statute," in *Philosophical Foundations of the Law of Equity*, ed. Dennis Klimchuk, Irit Samet, and Henry E. Smith (Oxford: Oxford University Press, 2020), 352; and Samuel E. Thorne, introduction to *A Discourse upon the Exposicion & Understanding of Statutes With Sir Thomas Egerton's Additions*, ed. Samuel E. Thorne (San Marino, CA: Huntington Library, 1942), 3, 55–56, 79–83.

14 See "Plowden, Edmund (c. 1518–1585)," *Oxford Dictionary of National Biography*, Jan. 3, 2008: "The family tradition that Elizabeth once offered Plowden the office of lord

In other words, the common law was by and large developed by people who had taken an oath not to follow the commands of the bishop of Rome. Does that mean the question in this chapter is a feint? Is the answer that there was in fact no influence of the Catholic intellectual tradition on the common law?

That answer would be too fast. There are three distinct ways we can speak of an influence of the Catholic intellectual tradition on the common law. These are inheriting, conversing, and generating.

We can start with *inheriting*. The common law has no date of enactment or ratification. Instead, it relies heavily on custom,[15] and much of that custom can be traced to the medieval period. Fundamental structures of the common law—such as the writs, the jury, and the steady war on restraints against alienation of real property—go back to the Year Books and the late medieval law of England.[16]

We should not think that each of these had a theological origin. But they were often given theological justifications. For example, Lord Coke explained various rules about the jury, grounding them in practicality—what he called "expedition of justice"—and in custom, for he said "in this case usage and ancient course maketh law."[17] But why twelve members for the jury? He noted various places where there were twelve decision makers in English law, and then trotted out this justification: "And that *number of twelve* is much respected in *holy writ*, as 12 *apostles*, 12 *stones*, 12 *tribes*, &c."[18]

---

chancellor if he would renounce Catholicism is probably unfounded, but it is a fair reflection of his reputation as a lawyer, despite the disabilities caused by his faith." See also Geoffrey de C. Parmiter, "Edmund Plowden and the Woolsack: A Query," *Law & Justice* 134 (2000): 29–37 (finding the question close). Plowden's recusancy did not prevent Lord Coke from commending him as "of great Gravity, Knowledge Integrity": Sir Edward Coke, "Part Ten of the *Reports*: Preface," in *The Selected Writings and Speeches of Sir Edward Coke*, vol. 1, ed. Steve Sheppard (Indianapolis, IN: Liberty Fund, 2003), 343.

15 See *Bracton on the Laws and Customs of England*, vol. 2, trans. and rev. Samuel E. Thorne (Cambridge, MA: Belknap Press, 1968), 19; and Oliver Wendell Holmes Jr., *The Common Law*, ed. Mark DeWolfe Howe (Cambridge, MA: Belknap Press of Harvard University Press, 1963), 5.

16 See, for example, F. W. Maitland, *The Forms of Action at Common Law: A Course of Lectures* ed. A. H. Chaytor and W. J. Whittaker (Cambridge: Cambridge University Press, 1909).

17 Edward Coke, *The First Part of the Institutes of the Laws of England or, A Commentary Upon Littleton*, 16th ed., ed. Francis Hargrave and Charles Butler (London, 1809), 155a, § 234.

18 Ibid. To a late-modern reader, such biblical and theological references may seem mere embellishments, but that would understate their apparent force for judges and lawyers such as Lord Coke. A more promising approach might be thinking of them as enabling a decision maker to choose an option. See Richard M. Re, "Precedent as Permission," *Texas Law Review* 99 (2021): 907–49.

The common law inherited many other things, we could say, from the Catholic intellectual tradition. One is the chancellor's conscience. Before Chancery was known as a court of equity, it was known as a court of conscience, and that language has never gone out of equity.[19] But what is this conscience? It was sometimes said to be the conscience of the inequitable litigant. As Lord Chancellor Ellesmere famously put it, "The Office of the Chancellor is to correct Mens Consciences for Frauds, Breach of Trusts, Wrongs and Oppressions, of what Nature soever they be, and to soften and mollify the Extremity of the Law, which is called *Summum Jus*."[20] Even more often it is said to be the conscience of the chancellor, of the judge wielding equity.[21] Equity's conscience has been traced to scholastic theology.[22]

That, then, is the first mode of influence. The common law inherited concepts, habits, and more from what we could call, with a little anachronism, the Catholic intellectual tradition.

The second mode of influence is *conversing*. If we look at the reports from the Courts of King's Bench and Common Pleas, we will not find many Catholic theologians being expressly cited.[23] But citations can overstate influence, and they can also understate influence. Here I will only be suggestive, but I will note new and largely unexplored terrain for legal scholars.

In the past three decades there have been major developments in the historiography of early modern Protestant Europe. The old idea that the Reformation was a rupture from natural theology or scholasticism as a theological method has been debunked. Taken as a whole, the Reformation was not a break from natural law, or from canon law, or from large swathes of the work of

---

19 Samuel L. Bray and Paul B. Miller, "Getting into Equity," *Notre Dame Law Review* 97 (2022): 1763–99; Henry E. Smith, "Equity as Meta-Law," *Yale Law Journal* 130 (2021): 1123–30; P. G. Turner, "Rudiments of the Equitable Remedy of Compensation for Breach of Confidence," in *Equitable Compensation and Disgorgement of Profit*, ed. Simone Degeling and Jason N. E. Varuhas (Oxford: Hart Publishing, 2017), 239, 240, 260–61, 266–69, 274–75.

20 See, for example, The Earl of Oxford's Case, 21 Eng. Rep. 485, 486 (Chancery 1615). For discussion, see Samuel L. Bray and Paul B. Miller, "Christianity and Equity," in *The Oxford Handbook of Christianity and Law*, ed. John Witte, Jr. and Rafael Domingo (Oxford: Oxford University Press, 2023); and D. Ibbetson, "A House Built on Sand: Equity in Early Modern English Law," in *Law & Equity: Approaches in Roman Law and Common Law*, ed. E. Koops and W. J. Zwalve (Leiden: Martinus Nijhoff, 2014), 55–78.

21 On the complexity of conscience in the late fifteenth- and early sixteenth-century Chancery, see Sir John Baker, *The Oxford History of the Laws of England: Volume VI, 1483–1558* (Oxford: Oxford University Press, 2002), 39–48.

22 Richard Hedlund, "The Theological Foundations of Equity's Conscience," *Oxford Journal of Law and Religion* 4 (2015): 119–40.

23 But see, for example, *The Case of Modus Decimandi*, 77 Eng. Rep. 1424, 1428 (Common Pleas 1608).

the scholastic theologians.²⁴ These points of continuity were aided by the continued use of Latin by scholars throughout early modern Europe.²⁵ In England, Latin was used along with English for the Articles of Religion, for convocation records, and for canon law, including the Canons of 1604 (which remained in force until the twentieth century).

For the first two centuries of the Reformation and Counter-Reformation, there was a huge traffic in ideas across the emerging confessional divide.²⁶ Catholic and Protestant scholars read and responded to each other, and that was true in England as well as elsewhere. To give one instance from the early to middle sixteenth century, Christopher St. German supported the Henrician Reformation and battled in print with Thomas More.²⁷ St. German also

---

24   See, for example, Gerald Bray, "Canon Law and the Church of England," in *The Oxford History of Anglicanism, Volume 1: Reformation and Identity c. 1520–1662*, 168–185, ed. Anthony Milton (Oxford: Oxford University Press, 2017); Bray and Miller, "Christianity and Equity"; Richard H. Helmholz, ed. *Canon Law in Protestant Lands* (Berlin: Duncker & Humblot, 1992); W. J. Torrance Kirby, "Richard Hooker's Theory of Natural Law in the Context of Reformation Theology," *Sixteenth Century Journal* 30 (1999): 681–703; Richard A. Muller, *After Calvin: Studies in the Development of a Theological Tradition* (Oxford: Oxford University Press, 2003); Richard A. Muller, *The Unaccommodated Calvin: Studies in the Foundation of a Theological Tradition* (Oxford: Oxford University Press, 2001); Carl R. Trueman and R. Scott Clark, eds., *Protestant Scholasticism: Essays in Reassessment* (Carlisle: Paternoster, 1999); and Witte, *Law and Protestantism*. For a recent general assessment, see Maarten Wisse, "Reformed Theology in Scholastic Development," in *The Oxford Handbook of Reformed Theology*, ed. Michael Allen and Scott R. Swain (Oxford: Oxford University Press, 2020), 57–73.

25   See, for example, Stephen Mark Holmes, "The Title of Article 27(26): Cranmer, Durandus and Pope Innocent III," *Journal of Ecclesiastical History* 64 (2013): 357–64, at 363: "Common sources and habits of mind, aided by the common use of Latin, remained among the scholars of the different Christian factions of late sixteenth- and seventeenth-century Europe, and the overthrow of an Anglo-Catholic historiography of the English Reformation should not obscure continuities in early British Protestantism." See also Anthony Grafton, *World Made by Words: Scholarship and Community in the Modern West* (Cambridge, MA: Harvard University Press, 2009); and Dirk van Miert, "Language and Communication in the Republic of Letters: The Uses of Latin and French in the Correspondence of Joseph Scaliger," *Bibliothèque d'Humanisme et Renaissance* 72 (2010): 7–34.

26   Many examples could be given, but one is chronology, the study of historical dates. Professor Anthony Grafton notes that "Kepler and other chronologers tried to construct a chronological Republic of Letters—a virtual realm where Calvinists, Lutherans, and Catholics could discuss the dates of Jesus's life in a calm and constructive way." Anthony Grafton, "Chronology, Controversy, and Community in the Republic of Letters: The Case of Keplar," in *World Made by Words*, 133. "To some extent," Grafton adds, "they managed it." Ibid.

27   See Ian Williams, "Christopher St German: Religion, Conscience and Law in Reformation England," in *Great Christian Jurists in English History*, ed. Mark Hill and R. H. Helmholz (Cambridge: Cambridge University Press, 2017), 69–92, at 72–76.

popularized Aristotelian equity in England, and seems to have relied heavily on Jean Gerson.²⁸

But it was not merely a phenomenon of early modern English jurists reading medieval scholastics. Consider an example taken from the western side of the Atlantic. Writing about Protestant scholasticism at Harvard from 1636 to 1700, Professor Scott McDermott has said:

> education at early Harvard ... remained substantially within the tradition of the medieval arts curriculum of European universities. Indeed, texts by Calvinist scholastics like Johann Heinrich Alsted and Bartolomeus Keckermann, themselves heavily influenced by Aristotelian Catholic scholasticism, were supplemented with books written by Catholics like Eustachius a Sancto Paulo. That the founders of Massachusetts Bay, within the first decade of its settlement, made it a priority to establish a college in which the scholastic tradition could be taught suggests that [other scholars are] wrong to dismiss the confluence of Calvinist and Catholic thought in this period.²⁹

If that was the education that colonial judges were getting, how could it not influence their work?

Nor was this kind of curriculum limited to North America. Long after the Ninety-Five Theses and the Council of Trent, scholastic authors were central to the curriculum of the English universities.³⁰ It was said of an ambitious student who studied at Queens' College, Cambridge, in the second decade of the seventeenth century, that he "devoured the schoolmen, Scotus, Ockham, and Aquinas"; was "much affected" by Calvin; and had Aristotle for his "tutelary

---

28 See J. L. Barton, introduction to *St. German's Doctor and Student*, ed. F. T. Plucknett and J. L. Barton (London: Selden Society, 1974), XXIII–XXIV, XLIV–XLVII.

29 Scott McDermott, "The Opening of the American Mind: Protestant Scholasticism at Harvard, 1636–1700," in *Catholicism and Historical Narrative: A Catholic Engagement with Historical Scholarship*, ed. Kevin Schmiesing (Lanham, MD: Rowman & Littlefield, 2014), 19–45, at 21. I am grateful to Layne Hancock for this source. On Alsted, see Howard Hotson, *Johann Heinrich Alsted 1588–1638: Between Renaissance, Reformation, and Universal Reform* (Oxford: Oxford University Press, 2000); on Keckermann, see Joseph S. Freedman, "The Career and Writings of Bartholomew Keckermann (d. 1609)," *Proceedings of the American Philosophical Society* 141 (1997): 305–64; on Eustachius, see Roger Ariew, "'Le meilleur livre qui ait jamais été fait en cette matière': Eustachius a Sancto Paulo and the Teaching of Philosophy in the Seventeenth Century," in *Teaching Philosophy in Early Modern Europe: Text and Image*, ed. Susanna Berger and Daniel Garber (Cham: Springer, 2021), 31–46.

30 For a sketch, see John Twigg, *The University of Cambridge and the English Revolution 1625–1688* (Woodbridge, UK: Boydell Press, 1990), at 207 and n2.

saint."³¹ "Studying the *Summa* while the barber was cutting his hair, he blew away the hairs which fell on the page and carried on reading."³²

Or consider Sir Matthew Hale, chief justice of the Court of King's Bench (1671–1676). Fifteen volumes of Francisco Suárez's work were in his library, and he "had studied them carefully already early in his life."³³ Later in life, Hale would spend his Sunday evenings reading and writing massive compendia of notes on theology and the Bible, which remain unpublished and have been given almost no attention by legal scholars.³⁴ And he wrote religious poetry.³⁵ Such avocations should not surprise us. Hale was the author not only of *The History of the Common Law of England* but also of a *Treatise of the Nature of Laws in General and Touching the Nature of Law*. In this latter work, he appealed to philosophers and theologians, mostly Christian, but also Jewish and Muslim. When discussing "the doctrine of Christian philosophers" on the divine influence on human understanding, he refers to two thirteenth-century bishops, Robert Grosseteste of Lincoln and William Auvergne of Paris; and two Franciscans, Adam de Marisco and Roger Bacon.³⁶ Hale then remarks with approbation on the continuity between their views on this point and the later views of "the Roman councils and Schoolmen."³⁷ Matthew Hale shaped the common law, and theology—including scholastic theology—shaped Matthew Hale.

More needs to be done in tracing these lines of influence. Yet when the influence of the Catholic intellectual tradition on the common law is shown, we as contemporary lawyers and legal scholars will still be free to decide its valence. For some late moderns, the imprint of Christian theology will mar the

---

31   Sarah Bendall, Christopher Brooke, and Patrick Collinson, *A History of Emmanuel College, Cambridge* (Woodbridge, UK: Boydell Press,1999), 216.
32   Ibid. The student was John Preston, later master of Emmanuel College, Cambridge.
33   Gerald J. Postema, introduction to Matthew Hale, *On the Law of Nature, Reason, and Common Law: Selected Jurisprudential Writings*, ed. Gerald J. Postema (Oxford: Oxford University Press, 2017), XXII.
34   David S. Sytsma, "Matthew Hale as Theologian and Natural Law Theorist," in Hill and Helmholz, *Great Christian Jurists in English History*, 170.
35   See Robert C. Evans, Stephen Paul Bray, and Christina M. Garner, "The 'Christmas Poems' of Sir Matthew Hale: Brief Preface and Annotated Texts," *The Ben Jonson Journal* 20 (2013): 95–125.
36   Matthew Hale, *Treatise of the Nature of Laws in General and Touching the Law of Nature*, in Hale, *On the Law of Nature, Reason, and Common Law: Selected Jurisprudential Writings*, 76. For their opinions, Hale cites John Selden's *De jure naturali et gentium juxta disciplinam Ebraeorum*. For an introduction to Selden's work, see Harold J. Berman and John Witte, Jr., "The Integrative Christian Jurisprudence of John Selden," in *Great Christian Jurists in English History*, 139–61.
37   Ibid.

common law. For others, it may be a reason for skepticism about narratives that pit modernity and faith against one another.

Those, then, are the first two modes of influence: inheriting and conversing. A third is *generating*.

If we are going to think of how the common lawyers were influenced, we need to get into their minds and think of how they saw the world. At the time of the Reformation, the Roman side obviously claimed the mantle of catholicity. But so did the Protestant side. Indeed, the Reformation was, in important respects, a debate about what catholicity consisted in.[38] One side emphasized the connection to the ancient see of Rome, which carried forward the apostolic authority of Saint Peter. The other side emphasized other ecclesiological *loci* that also had patristic and medieval roots, whether general councils called by Christian princes or regional forms of episcopal governance, such as synods.

The Roman and non-Roman sides both appealed to the scriptures and invoked the tradition of the early church.[39] Each side thought that it would win the argument if it could only show that the other side had—to use a Newmanesque word long before its time—"developed" the doctrine. All agreed that whoever had not changed or augmented the deposit of faith was the truly catholic side.[40]

So in Paris and Rouen, on the French side of the English Channel, the Catholic intellectual tradition was proceeding apace. And on the other side of the

---

[38] See, for example, *An Apology or Answer in Defence of The Church Of England: Lady Anne Bacon's Translation of Bishop John Jewel's Apologia Ecclesiae Anglicanae*, ed. Patricia Demers (Cambridge: Modern Humanities Research Association, 2016), 55–59. As Stephen Hampton notes, Suárez's *Defensio Fidei Catholicae* was written as "a rejoinder to James I's claim that he was entitled to call himself a catholic Christian." Stephen Hampton, "Confessional Identity," in *The Oxford History of Anglicanism, Volume 1: Reformation and Identity c. 1520–1662*, 210, 211.

[39] See Diarmaid MacCulloch, *Thomas Cranmer: A Life* (New Haven: Yale University Press, 1996), 617: "To define Cranmer as a reformed Catholic is to define all the great Continental reformers in the same way: for they too sought to build up the Catholic Church anew on the same foundations of Bible, creeds and the great councils of the early Church." For homiletic examples, see Katrin Ettenhuber, "The Preacher and Patristics," in *The Oxford Handbook of the Early Modern Sermon*, ed. Hugh Adlington, Peter McCullough, and Emma Rhatigan (Oxford: Oxford University Press, 2012), 35–53. Jewel's Challenge Sermon in 1559, for example, argued that transubstantiation was "newly deuised" and not found in the scriptures or the ancient church. Torrance Kirby, "John Jewel at Paul's Cross: A Culture of Persuasion and England's Emerging Public Sphere," in *Defending the Faith: John Jewel and the Elizabethan Church*, ed. Angela Ranson, André A. Gazal, and Sarah Bastow (University Park: Pennsylvania State University Press, 2018), 53.

[40] See Owen Chadwick, *From Bossuet to Newman*, 2d ed. (Cambridge: Cambridge University Press, 1987), 1–2, 13.

Channel, in London and Canterbury—by the lights of the English bishops and jurists—the Catholic intellectual tradition was also proceeding apace. The jurists in the Church of England considered themselves Catholic. The preface to the 1662 Book of Common Prayer says the revisers rejected any proposed changes that would strike at the doctrines and practices "of the whole Catholick Church of Christ."[41] The Church of England, including in its members the common law judges, prescribed the regular recitation of the Apostles' Creed, Nicene Creed, and Athanasian Creed. These creeds refer, respectively, to "The holy Catholick Church";[42] "one Catholick and Apostolick Church";[43] and "the Catholick Faith" and "the Catholick Religion."[44] The Prayer for All Sorts and Conditions of Men, which is ordered for use four days a week, includes a petition for "the good estate of the Catholick Church."[45] Similar references can be found in the canons of the Church of England,[46] Bishop John Jewel's *Apology*,[47] and Richard Hooker's *Laws of Ecclesiastical Polity*.[48]

In other words, if we are going to try to understand the jurists who developed the common law, we will find that they publicly identified themselves as "Catholic," in the sense of being part of the universal church.[49]

---

41 *The Book of Common Prayer, 1662*, in *The Book of Common Prayer: The Texts of 1549, 1559, and 1662*, at 210.
42 Ibid., 247, 255.
43 Ibid., 392.
44 Ibid., 257, 258, 259.
45 Ibid., 268. This prayer was a new composition, added in 1662.
46 Canons of 1571, in *The Anglican Canons, 1529–1947*, ed. Gerald Bray (Woodbridge, UK: Boydell & Brewer, 1998), 196–199 (no. 6, requiring preachers to teach nothing "but that which is agreeable to the doctrine of the Old Testament and the New, and that which the catholic fathers and ancient bishops have gathered out of that doctrine"); Canons of 1603 (1604), in *The Anglican Canons, 1529–1947*, at 342–343 (no. 55, giving a bidding prayer that begins: "Ye shall pray for Christ's holy catholic church, that is, for the whole congregation of Christian people dispersed throughout the whole world, and especially for the churches of England, Scotland and Ireland").
47 See, for example, Jewel, *Apology*, 131–42.
48 See, for example, Richard Hooker, *Of the Laws of Ecclesiastical Polity: The Folger Library Edition of the Works of Richard Hooker*, vol. 1, ed. Georges Edelen (Cambridge, MA: Belknap Press of Harvard University Press, 1977), bk. 3.1, at 194–206; see also Richard Hooker, "A Learned Discourse of Justification, Workes, and How the Foundation of Faith Is Overthrowne," in *Tractates and Sermons: The Folger Library Edition of the Works of Richard Hooker*, vol. 5, ed. Laetitia Yeandle and Egil Grislis (Cambridge, MA: Belknap Press of Harvard University Press, 1990), 83, 155.
49 There was, of course, continuing contestation about the meaning of catholicity and the value of patristic tradition. See, for example, Anthony Milton, *Catholic and Reformed: The Roman and Protestant Churches in English Protestant Thought 1600–1640* (Cambridge: Cambridge University Press, 1995), 150–56; and Jean-Louis Quantin, "Perceptions of

Consider, for example, *Thomas v. Sorrell* (1673/4). A plaintiff proceeding on behalf of the king sought £450 in damages from a person accused of selling wine at a tavern in Stepney in violation of a statute. The case was referred by the Court of King's Bench to Exchequer Chamber, where a leading opinion was given by Sir John Vaughan, chief justice of the Court of Common Pleas (1668–1674). Chief Justice Vaughan's opinion is a widely cited classic, exploring at length the royal prerogative to grant dispensations from legal prohibitions. He relies on sources that are squarely within the Catholic intellectual tradition.

At the beginning of his opinion, Chief Justice Vaughan knows that he needs to clear away misconceptions about the distinction between *malum in se* and *malum prohibitum*, so he starts with first principles, including the point that acts are not in themselves wrong without some kind of law that is being controverted. In this argument he appeals to the scholastic theologians: "And so all the schoolmen agree, that actus qua actus non est malus."[50]

Chief Justice Vaughan's argument continues, and he cites not only Bracton, Coke, and Selden, but also Saint Paul, Edward Stillingfleet, Hugo Grotius, and Francisco Suárez.[51] His appeal to Suárez is especially interesting. Vaughan needs to argue that a royal dispensation can be given not only to named and known individuals, but also to a corporate body that will have new members in the future. In the case at hand, that corporate body was the Company of Vintners in the City of London. Chief Justice Vaughan writes:

> That a dispensation may he granted to a body corporate or aggregate, as well as to private persons, Suarez de Legibus, which Mr. Attorney cited in this case, and is in truth a most learned work, is very express.
>
> Dispensation autem per se primo versari potest circa personam privatam, quia solum est particularis exceptio à Communi Lege; potest etiam ferri circa communitatem aliquam quae sit pars majoris communitatis, sicut uni Religioni, Ecclesiæ aut Civitati conceditur privilegium, per quod excipitur à Lege Communi. Potest etiam concedi toti communitati pro uno Actu, vel pro certo tempore per modum suspensionis. This last must be understood where the dispensator is the intire law-maker.

Christian Antiquity," in *The Oxford History of Anglicanism, Volume 1: Reformation and Identity c. 1520–1662*, 280–97.

50   Thomas v. Sorrell, 124 Eng. Rep. 1098, 1100 (Exchequer Chamber 1673/4).
51   These references appear in the marginal annotations in the edition in Vaughan's Reports; some references first appear in the 1706 corrected edition. See Edward Vaughan, *The Reports and Arguments of that Learned Judge, Sir John Vaughan*, 2nd corr. ed. (London, 1706), 330.

> And accordingly dispensations are as frequently granted by the Pope, from whom the use of dispensations was principally derived to us, to bodies corporate, that is, to religious orders, as to private persons, as is apparent in the Bullaries, if any will consult them; but I forbear citing them, because they are forreign authorities.[52]

Thus the chief justice of the Court of Common Pleas could appeal to a Jesuit scholastic as an authority and praise him for his learning, which he does for no other authority quoted in the opinion. Chief Justice Vaughan declines to cite "forreign authorities," but Suárez does not seem to him similarly remote. For this leading common law judge, the learning of Suárez was not foreign law.

The only remaining question is whether Chief Justices Vaughan and Hale were idiosyncratic. To answer that question with painstaking proof would require a book, not the conclusion to an essay. So consider the critical view of Andrew Amos. He served on an English criminal law commission, was a member of the council reforming the laws of India, and became the Downing Professor of the Laws of England at Cambridge. Early in his legal career, in 1825, Amos published an edition of Sir John Fortescue's *De laudibus legum Angliæ*. Amos included a lengthy note on the first chapters, calling them "replete with exploded opinions of philosophy, antiquated definitions of law, and strained applications of Scripture."[53]

Amos was clear-eyed about what he did not like in the English judges, namely, "the nature of the studies which principally engaged their attention."[54] What were those studies? Amos tells us:

> theological learning was a favorite pursuit of the most eminent legal characters of this country. Sir E. Coke's poetical advise to students respecting the study of the Scriptures is well known. Sir Thomas More gave lectures, when a young man, upon St. Augustine['s] "de civitate De" in St. Lawrence' church: Clarendon wrote reflections and contemplations upon the Psalms of David; and Burnet observes in his Life of Hale, that a person who should read the compositions upon the subject of divinity, which that Judge wrote, would imagine that the study of theology had occupied most of his time and thoughts. Fortescue informs us, in a subsequent part of his treatise, how much the reading of the Scriptures was blended with that of Law,

---

52   Thomas v. Sorrell, 124 Eng. Rep. at 1107.
53   Fortescue, *De Laudibus Legum Angliæ: The Translation into English*, ed. A. Amos (Cambridge, 1825), 4, note a.
54   Ibid., 6.

in the Inns of Court.... Not less remarkable is the strong tincture which the minds of our ancient lawyers imbibed from the Aristotelian philosophy: Sir John Dodderidge who died a Justice of the King's Bench, A.D. 1628, in a treatise called "The English Lawyer" expounds the law of England according to the doctrines of the schoolmen, treating each subject with reference to its material, formal, efficient and final cause: A commission of sewers is viewed in the same fourfold light by Sir E. Coke in his reports, and he considers the creation of a corporation as taking place conformably to Aristotle's notions respecting the origin of bodies in nature: The great deference paid by lawyers to the authority of that philosopher is very apparent from Plowden's observations, at the conclusion of his report of the case of Eyston and Studd; and the impressions which the jurisprudence of the country has received from this circumstance are still very discernible.... It is also observable, that the writings of the civilians had a material influence in forming the opinions of the legal profession in this country.[55]

The conclusion is inescapable that the common law judges, such as Coke, Ellesmere, Hale, and Vaughan, had all the hallmarks of what today would be called the Catholic intellectual tradition.[56] Later luminaries of the common law could be added, including Mansfield, Blackstone, Story, and Lushington.[57]

Recall that Professor Cavadini summarizes the Catholic intellectual tradition in eight theses.[58] The first seven are simply the intellectual tradition of the Western church. The eighth refers to "one specific example" of how the

---

55   Ibid., 4–5.
56   See Deavel, "Preface: The Catholic Intellectual Tradition."
57   See, for example, S. M. Waddams, *Law, Politics and the Church of England: The Career of Stephen Lushington 1782–1873* (Cambridge: Cambridge University Press, 1992); Wilfred Prest, "William Blackstone's Anglicanism," in *Great Christian Jurists in English History*, at 213–35. This does not, of course, mean that they are above critique, from outside as well as from within the Catholic intellectual tradition. For example, John Finnis, "Blackstone's Theoretical Intentions," in *Philosophy of Law: Collected Essays*, vol. 4 (Oxford: Oxford University Press, 2011), 189, 208 (noting that in William Blackstone's work the theories of law's relation to nature that were advanced by "Aquinas, Hooker, and St German have all disappeared and have not been replaced" [footnote omitted]).
58   The theses are quoted with Professor Cavadini's permission (citations omitted):
    1. One hallmark—perhaps the main one—of the Catholic Intellectual Tradition is its integration of reason and revelation—
    2. Where "revelation" is not reducible to or derivative from "reason," but can only be accepted by faith and each revealed truth[] is called a "mystery"—
    3. While yet revelation does not replace reason, but is hospitable to reason, such that reason "seeks to understand" what it has received in faith.

tradition could be worked out; it does not purport to limit the tradition's scope.[59] In other words, the hallmarks of the Catholic intellectual tradition characterize leading thinkers before the Reformation as well as after its inception, in both Catholic and Protestant countries. It would be unimaginable to read the works of Saint Augustine and Francisco Suárez, along with the works of Richard Hooker and Johann Oldendorp, and not find in all of them "the integration of reason and revelation."[60] If I could put the point even more expansively, what Professor Cavadini describes as the hallmarks of the Catholic intellectual tradition are simply the hallmarks of *Mere Christianity*. And perhaps, dear reader, you are aware of who wrote that book.

Allow me to put this a little more crisply. If we were to say the Catholic intellectual tradition means the *Roman* Catholic tradition, then there would be

---

4. Therefore this "quest to understand," while it avoids reducing what is believed to something discoverable by reason alone, is not isolated or sequestered from the rest of the conversations reason has—
5. First because the common currency of intellectual discourse—e.g. what "language" is, what "beauty" is, what "knowledge" is, what a "human being" might be, etc.—must be invoked in order to have a coherent, rational conversation—this is the level of philosophy—
6. And second because the various disciplines are always developing and their very results pose questions which would only be questions if there is something that transcends their respective methodologies (for example, the status of human death and its relationship to sin requires some understanding of what a human being might be (a conversation that must be philosophically governed) and what sin might be (a theological conversation because it involves revelation)[)].
7. Thus we talk, not about a settled integration between "reason" and "revelation" valid for all time, but an ongoing "dialectic between faith and reason," an ongoing quest for integration that is open ended.
8. Catholic Social Teaching is one specific example of this way of thinking about the Catholic Intellectual Tradition.

Cavadini, "Eight Modest Theses on 'The Catholic Intellectual Tradition.'"

59 On Catholic social teaching, see, generally, *Catholic Social Teaching: A Volume of Scholarly Essays*, ed. Gerard V. Bradley and E. Christian Brugger (Cambridge: Cambridge University Press, 2019).

60 See, for example, W. J. Torrance Kirby, "Reason and Law," in *A Companion to Richard Hooker*, ed. Torrance Kirby (Leiden: Brill, 2008), 251–71; A. S. McGrade, "Classical, Patristic, and Medieval Sources," in *A Companion to Richard Hooker*, 51–87; Witte, *Law and Protestantism*, 154–168; and John Witte, Jr., "The Good Lutheran Jurist Johann Oldendorp (ca. 1486–1567)," in *Great Christian Jurists in German History*, ed. Mathias Schmoeckel and John Witte, Jr. (Tübingen: Mohr Siebeck, 2020). Professor Diarmaid MacCulloch described Hooker's *Laws* as "a work which grounded its assault on its opponents on axioms from Aristotle, Plato and the medieval scholastics, rather than getting straight down to satisfyingly direct insults": Diarmaid MacCulloch, "Richard Hooker's Reputation," *The English Historical Review* 117 (2002): 773–812, at 781.

some influence on the common law. That influence would have two modes: inheriting and conversing. But in this view, the Catholic intellectual tradition would still have been viewed by the great common law judges as something apart. They could see it from where they stood. But it was in the distant past or in the distant present, across the waters of the English Channel.

Yet the contours of this intellectual tradition are not specifically Roman Catholic.[61] All the great English jurists I mentioned would find themselves squarely within what could be called the Catholic, or catholic, intellectual tradition. In fact, given the cross-confessional argument and pollination in the early modern period, across the republic of letters, it is plausible to think that sharply demarcated "Catholic" and "Protestant" intellectual traditions are from a later time. Perhaps that time is even as late as the nineteenth century, with the rise of German universities and a resurgent papacy marked by skepticism of modernity.[62] Such an inquiry, however, lies beyond the scope of this chapter. Also beyond this chapter's scope is another nineteenth-century development, namely the argument by codifiers in the United States that the common law was too "Catholic."[63]

In short, if we recognize a broader referent for the Catholic intellectual tradition, one that encompasses at least Western Christianity, the boundaries of the concept will prove less anachronistic. And then, once we allow the common law judges to fit within this tradition, the question asked at the start of this chapter receives a dramatic answer. We are face to face with the vast influence of Christianity on the common law.

This influence is no longer as visible on the surface of the law. Yet it still runs deep. Many of our most cherished concepts, including ideas of equality and human rights, are gifts in considerable part from this intellectual tradition.[64]

---

61 See *supra* notes 6 and 58.
62 See, generally, Thomas Albert Howard, *Protestant Theology and the Making of the Modern German University* (Oxford: Oxford University Press, 2006); and John W. O'Malley, *Vatican I: The Council and the Making of the Ultramontane Church* (Cambridge, MA: Belknap Press of Harvard University Press, 2018). For an eighteenth-century episode of divergence, see Richard H. Popkin, "Skepticism and the Counter-Reformation in France," *Archiv für Reformationsgeschichte* 51 (1960): 58–87.
63 See Kellen Funk, "Sect and Superstition: The Protestant Framework of American Codification" (draft under review).
64 See John Witte, Jr., "A New Calvinist Reformation of Rights" (The Gifford Lectures 2022); John Witte, Jr. and Frank S. Alexander, eds., *Christianity and Human Rights: An Introduction* (Cambridge: Cambridge University Press, 2010); Witte, *The Reformation of Rights*; and Witte, *Law and Protestantism*. For a twentieth-century case study, compare Christopher McCrudden, "Where Did 'Human Dignity' Come from? Drafting the Preamble to the Irish Constitution," *American Journal of Legal History* 60 (2020): 485–535, with Samuel Moyn,

It is true that the participants of the tradition have often failed to live up to its insights and imperatives.[65] Yet those very failures make all the more astonishing the gifts that this tradition has given to the modern world.[66] No one has taught all these lessons better, showing that "time and tradition can be teachers for those who learn to listen,"[67] than the wise, warm, and extravagantly learned scholar to whom this essay is dedicated, Professor John Witte.

Acknowledgments

I am thankful for comments from Gerald Bray, Christian Burset, Kellen Funk, Layne Hancock, and Richard Helmholz.

"The Secret History of Constitutional Dignity," *Yale Human Rights & Development Law Journal* 17 (2014): 39–73.

65 Desmond M. Tutu, "The First Word: To Be Human Is to Be Free," in Witte and Alexander, *Christianity and Human Rights*, 1–7.

66 See Tom Holland, *Dominion: How the Christian Revolution Remade the World* (New York: Basic Books, 2021).

67 John Witte, Jr., foreword to id., *God's Joust, God's Justice: Law and Religion in the Western Tradition* (Grand Rapids: Eerdmans, 2006), ix–x.

CHAPTER 14

The Reception of the Medieval *Ius Commune* in the Protestant Reformation

Mathias Schmoeckel

1 Introduction

John Witte has written extensively on the influence of the Protestant Reformations on the laws of church and state—in Lutheran, Reformed, Anglican, and Anabaptist communities alike.[1] Indeed, the new faith communities born of the early "reformations" needed rules to govern at least baptism, the Eucharist, worship, charity, burial, family life, education, clerical marriage, and the like, all of which were theologically reformed very early on. Protestant leaders, therefore, turned to the classic medieval canon and Roman law on which they were raised, even though they criticized it and sought to reform it in accordance with their new ideals. This effort at reformation and repurposing the law applied not to the classic sources of canon law and civil law (known collectively as the *ius commune*) but also local legal traditions (known as the *ius particulare*).

Besides crafting new ecclesiastical ordinances (*Kirchenordnungen*), especially those introduced by Johannes Bugenhagen (1485–1558),[2] the new churches needed laws to administer local church offices, church courts (consistories), and church visitations to local communities. Protestants had to clarify which rules of traditional law, especially ecclesiastical law, remained valid and which had to be abandoned. After Martin Luther's excommunication and burning of the canon law books in 1520, eatly Protestants certainly could

---

[1] See especially John Witte, Jr., *Law and Protestantism: The Legal Teachings of the Lutheran Reformation* (Cambridge: Cambridge University Press, 2002); John Witte, Jr. and Robert M. Kingdon, *Sex, Marriage, and Family in John Calvin's Geneva* (Grand Rapids: Eerdmans, 2006); John Witte, Jr., *The Reformation of Rights: Law, Religion, and Human Rights in Early Modern Calvinism* (Cambridge: Cambridge University Press, 2007); id., *Faith, Freedom, and Family: New Essays on Law and Religion*, ed. Norman Doe and Gary S. Hauk (Tübingen: Mohr Siebeck, 2021); id., *Raíces protestantes del Derecho*, trans. and ed. Rafael Domingo (Madrid: Aranzadi, 2023).

[2] Anneliese Sprengler-Ruppenthal, "Kirchenordnungen II. Evangelische," *Theologische Realenzyklopädie* (*TRE*), vol. 18 (Berlin: de Gruyter, 1989), 607–707.

no longer accept medieval Catholic canon law as a whole, which was the foundation of the pope's authority.

In Wittenberg, Lutheran leaders debated how to a reevaluate these inherited legal traditions and to build a new foundation of a Protestant legal order, including a new theory of legal sources. Other Protestants at the University of Basel worked out their own Protestant legal formulations. In France, the increasingly Protestant law schools, such as the one at Bourges, continued and intensified the debates that had started in Germany, and giving rise to new emphasis on different legal traditions and sources, and often leading to dramatic legal changes. This transformation slowly led to a new perspective with regard to the influence of history as well.

2   Wittenberg

2.1   *Luther's Rejection of Canon Law*

When Luther was confronted with his imminent excommunication by the Bull *Exsurge Domine* on December 12, 1520,[3] he burned the papal bull containing the declaration of excommunication, adding to the fire with several books of the Roman Catholic Church, especially the canon law books, such as the *Decretum Gratiani*,[4] and some books on penance. Luther's position was well justified, since he had started to study canon law and, throughout his life, understood it quite well. Already in his tract addressing the Christian nobility, Luther denied the authority of ecclesiastical law completely and wrote that it should not be taught anymore. Especially in matters of faith and justification, he rejected the applicability of law in general, because he regarded faith as God's free gift, which could not be bought by human actions: obeying the law and practicing good deeds according to the theory of indulgences of his time would not purchase salvation.

For Luther, furthermore, the papal decretals that comprised the bulk of canon law after Gratian's *Decretum* only intended to prove the command of the pope, who wanted to dominate even Christian councils. Luther could certainly not accept any law which was founded on the authority of the pope. He argued in a quite compelling way that accepting the contents of one decretal

---

3   See Witte, *Law and Protestantism*, 53ff.
4   For Luther's texts in the following, see Mathias Schmoeckel, *Das Recht der Reformation* (Tübingen: Mohr Siebeck, 2014), 67–90, with further references to secondary literature; id., "Der Einfluss der Reformation auf die Kanonistik: Kontroversen um die Rechtsquellenlehre und das 'gemeine Recht,'" *Proceedings of the Thirteenth Congress of Medieval Canon Law*, Monumenta Iuris Canonici, series C: subsidia, vol.14 (Città del Vaticano: P. Kardinal Erdö/Sz. Anzelm Suzromi, 2010 [2011]), 707–30.

invariably included acceptance of the pope's legislative power. However well-founded the decisions of the decretals might be, the useful contents of the law could not be an argument in their favor for Luther.[5] All laws issued by the church were, according to Luther, a work of the devil.[6]

There was one possible exception, though, for the oldest tradition of canon law, which Gratian himself had "read." Luther rebuked Gratian not because he rejected his theories, but because he found them rather outdated. He conceded that Gratian had acted in good faith, but that his results were insufficient. Particularly in marital law, Luther found several examples to prove the insufficiency of Gratian's canon law. Against the arguments of the law professors in Wittenberg, some of them close friends, Luther wanted to stop all teaching of canon law in the university classrooms.

Philipp Melanchthon, Luther's colleague and eventual successor, at first followed Luther's harsh rejection of canon law, arguing that popes had no right to enact laws. But in the 1530s he changed his position in this respect as well. In a lecture on the ancient *Canones Apostolorum*, he accepted its contents as the first version of Christian ecclesiastical law.[7] In his "Apologia" of the *Confessio Augustana*, he even argued by drawing on canon law.[8] He criticized the writings of canon lawyers rather than canon law itself. Of course, this might just have been a strategy to persuade the other side.

But unlike Luther, Melanchthon was prepared to listen to his fellow professors in the Wittenberg law faculty.[9] Canonists and other lawyers, such as Henning Göde (1450–1521), Christoph Scheurl (1481–1542), Hieronymus Schürpf (1481–1554), Melchior Kling (1504–1571), and later Matthaeus Wesenbeck (1531–1586) and Eberhard von Weyhe (1553–1633), were prominent spokesmen for the necessity of canon law. In 1528 Justus Jonas the Elder (1493–1555) argued for a re-introduction of canon law lectures in Wittenberg. Schürpf and Kling argued in their publications that use of the canon law was inevitable, particularly in the fields of marital[10] and procedural law, at least as long there was no

---

5   See Wilhelm Maurer, "Reste des Kanonischen Rechtes im Frühprotestantismus," ZRG KA 82 (1965): 190–253, 192ff.
6   For Luther's thoughts on the sources of law, see Witte, *Law and Protestantism*, 74.
7   Wilhelm Maurer, "Reste des Kanonischen Rechtes im Frühprotestantismus," ZRG KA 82 (1965): 190–253, at 219.
8   See Jaroslav Pelikan, "Verius servamus canones," *Studia Gratiana* 11 (1969): 367–87, 384ff.; and Witte, *Law and Protestantism*, 72.
9   Suggested by Isabelle Deflers, *Lex und ordo* (Berlin: Duncker & Humblot, 2005), 133ff.
10 Heiner Lück, "Beiträge ausgewählter Wittenberger Juristen zur europäischen Rechtsentwicklung und zur Herausbildung eines evangelischen Eherechts während des 16. Jahrhunderts," *Reformation und Recht* (2017): 73–109.

contradiction to their new theology.[11] Protestant lawyers would have to know canon law as long as there was no new authority in the field.[12]

In the end, this opinion prevailed in Wittenberg. Canon law remained useful for many subjects, therefore, including ecclesiastical law. As Johann Oldendorp pointed out, canon law was inevitable for the establishment of law courts and their trials.[13] The University of Wittenberg kept a chair dedicated to canon law, mostly the *primus ordinarius*, and continued canon law courses. In the same way, Melchior Kling had to bring back canon law in order to establish a new Protestant marital law according to Martin Luther's new concepts.[14] Canon law continued to inspire some lawyers in this academic tradition,[15] such as Justus Henning Boehmer (1674–1749). In theory, at least, the *Decretum Gratiani* can be seen as a subsidiary source of law in German Protestant churches until today.[16]

2.2 Melanchthon's Veneration of Roman Law

While Luther categorically rejected canon law, he slowly gained some respect for Roman law from his colleagues in Wittenberg. He appreciated it as the concretization of natural law and an expression of human reasonability. He argued that Roman law contained a wealth of experience, particularly for secular issues. Although the ancient Romans had been heathens, they had developed great skills, superior to those of all modern lawyers. He could not find any discrepancies between Roman law and his theology. Roman law could claim validity not only until today, in his view, but even until the day of the last judgment. He advised students to learn Roman law.

---

11 Rudolf Schäfer, "Die Geltung des kanonischen Rechts in der evangelischen Kirche Deutschlands von Luther bis zur Gegenwart. Ein Beitrag zur Geschichte der Quellen, der Literatur und der Rechtsprechung des evangelischen Kirchenrechts," ZRG KA 36 (1915): 165–413, 203f., on Schürpf and Kling.

12 See also *Law and Protestantism*, 72.

13 Friedrich Merzbacher, "Johann Oldendorp und das kanonische Recht," *Für Kirche und Recht. Festschrift für Johannes Heckel*, ed. S. Grundmann (Cologne: Böhlau Verlag, 1959), 222–49.

14 *Law and Protestantism*, 72; id. *God's Joust, God's Justice: Law and Religion in the Western Tradition* (Grand Rapids: Eerdmans, 2005o, 346ff.; and Johannes Heckel, *Lex charitatis*, 2d ed., ed. Martin Heckel (Cologne: Böhlau, 1973), 144ff.

15 See Udo Wolter, "Die Fortgeltung des kanonischen Rechts und die Haltung der protestantischen Juristen zum kanonischen Recht in Deutschland bis in die Mitte des 18. Jahrhunderts," in *Canon Law in Protestant Lands*, ed. R. H. Helmholz (Berlin: Duncker & Humblot, 1992), 13–48.

16 Johannes Heckel, "Das Decretum Gratiani und das deutsche Evangelische Kirchenrecht," *Studia Gratiana* 3 (1955): 483–537, at 523, on the validity of canon law based on ecclesiastical tradition; and Mathias Schmoeckel, *Grundfragen des Evangelischen Kirchenrechts* (Tübingen: Mohr Siebeck, 2023).

Melanchthon intensified his affections for Roman law and became its fervent admirer, especially after 1525. Together with the court astrologer Johannes Carion in 1543, Melanchthon published a "Chronic," in which he referred to the emperor Lothar (III of Supplinburg), who had ordered the adoption of Roman law in the courts of the Empire;[17] afterwards Irnerius had rekindled Roman jurisprudence. As no such enactment can be found, this report has since become known as the Lotharian Legend. This new idea soon spread to Italy, where the Lotharian Legend was used to prove the validity of the Roman law in its integrity, as otherwise the use of every rule in the following centuries and in the different territories would have to be demonstrated in order to prove its customary validity.[18]

Apparently, Melanchthon did not want to establish the authority of Roman law based on mere custom as had been the tradition of the Roman Empire, but he preferred a written enactment. For Melanchthon, the *ratio scripta* gave Roman law the legitimacy that he wanted. Indeed, he said, now Roman law could be regarded as the indication of God's own law, like the Decalogue—written guidelines for society and its morals, which would teach humanity justice. Just like God's commandments, Roman law had to be proclaimed; thanks to written forms it could become known. Justinian's codification and the order of Emperor Lothar III guaranteed the validity of the Roman law in its entirety. This is how Melanchthon wanted to assure that nobody could deny the authority of Roman law.[19]

Melanchthon regarded Roman law as the quintessence of human reason, so that no hesitation regarding its validity could be tolerated. Melanchthon venerated Roman law as the oracle of nations, which should teach humanity the exact contents of equity or *aequitas*. In 1538 he characterized ancient Roman law as true philosophy, particularly because of its harsh punishment of crimes.

---

17 Johannes Carion, *Chronica* (Wittenberg, 1533), 186. Melanchthon's role as editor was known only later, and his influence on its contents only in the twentieth century. In his later writings, Melanchthon continued to use this argument in order to legitimize the use of Roman law.

18 See Mathias Schmoeckel, "Lotharische Legende," *HRG* vol. 3, 2nd ed. (Berlin: 2015), 1056–58.

19 See Guido Kisch, *Melanchthons Rechts- und Soziallehre* (Berlin: de Gruyter, 1967), 144f.; James Q. Whitman, *The Legacy of Roman Law in the German Romantic Era: Historical Vision and Legal Change* (Princeton: Princeton University Press, 1994), 26ff.; Peter Oestmann, "Kontinuität oder Zäsur—zum Geltungsrang des gemeinen Rechts vor und nach Hermann Conring," *Kontinuitäten und Zäsuren in der Europäischen Rechtsgeschichte, Rechtshistorische Reihe* 196 (1999): 191–210; and Schmoeckel, "Lotharische Legende." On the argument of ratio scripta, see Alejandro Guzmán, "Ratio scripta," *Ius Commune Sonderhefte* (1981), who emphasizes the humanist influence.

In its humanity and the richness of its rules, it was superior to all other laws. Moreover, it was in accordance with all other information on natural law, so that the Decalogue could even be regarded as its summary: Roman laws are seen as deduced from natural knowledge, as the rays of divine wisdom, also comprised by the Decalogue and, therefore, provided always with good consequences. Melanchthon's readers had to assume that Roman law was nothing but a longer version of divine natural law. Studying Roman law could accordingly help one to learn about Christian virtues, just like texts from the Bible and the writings of the Church Fathers.

Evidently, Melanchthon taught the lawyers of Wittenberg to venerate Roman law. Roman law was not only reasonable, but the most equitable, sound, and realistic law of all. Everybody should be taught civil law from childhood onwards. Roman law was useful for enhancing the power of the Holy Roman Empire, for ignoring the authority of the pope and the church, and for granting the freedom of testimony and property. So it was as useful politically as it was economically.[20] Humanists agreed on the dignity of the imperial law as the heir of antiquity. Obviously, Roman law could be attractive for a great part of modern society.

But of course, even Roman law could claim authority only as long it did not contradict Protestant theology or tradition and their understanding of justice and equity. According to Luther's idea of a prerogative, abstract *Lex Christi*, even Roman law could only be applied if it had been accepted from the perspective of Protestant theology,[21] but this could generally be assumed. Nor did Melanchthon negate the concurrence between canon law and the particular law of the land in principle. He instead opened a large field for lawyers to seek to fulfill the standards of Protestant theology. For everything that had been banned in canon law, Roman law now offered a substitute. This was necessary to close evident lacunae in the present law system, to find solid foundations for the judiciary, and to provide lawyers with a new approach to jurisprudence. Where the rejection of canon law was carried out in a stricter way than in Wittenberg—for example, in Basel—the remaining chairs of the law faculty were

---

20 For the exception of usury by, for example, the first banks, the "Monte di Pietà," see Heribert Holzapfel, *Die Anfänge der Montes Pietatis (1462–1515)* (Munich: Lentner Verlag, 1903; repr. Brussels, 2002).
21 For love of neighbor especially, see Hartwig Dieterich, *Das protestantische Eherecht in Deutschland bis zur Mitte des 17. Jahrhunderts, Jus Ecclesiasticum*, no. 10 (Tübingen: Mohr Siebeck, 1970), 45.

dedicated to Roman law only.[22] In many instances Roman law had to close the lacunae left by the abandonment of canon law.

In the end, Melanchthon's enthusiasm for Roman law helped Protestant lawyers to concentrate on the *Corpus iuris civilis*,[23] whereas the research on the *Corpus iuris canonici* remained more in the background. Even in questions of affiliation, the French Calvinist François Hotman (1524–1590)[24] did not want to recur to canon law. He admitted the discrepancy between canon law and Roman law, but preferred to use Roman law.[25] The same approach can be found even in the new Protestant marital law.[26] In order to reintroduce divorce, the ordinances of the Roman emperors could be used. Roman law studies became the dominant field of jurisprudence in Protestant universities. This tradition remained valid until Savigny and his nineteenth century historical school of law. This element is certainly more than a Protestant bias. Nevertheless, the eminent progress of German jurisprudence until the nineteenth century had been influenced by this tradition.

3.3 *Rediscovery of Saxon Law*

While Luther abhorred canon law and criticized Roman law as a wilderness, he was rather fond of Saxon law. The Saxon reformers were affected by some regionalism, which they particularly used for public teaching.[27] In the view of humanists, all times had their own laws, so that the *Sachsenspiegel*, or "Mirror of the Saxons" (probably from around 1220)[28]—a collection of Saxon customs—could be regarded as the very image of Saxon tradition. Luther could even equate it with the Old Testament: what Moses had been for the Jews in the collection of ancient Jewish law, Eike von Repgow had been for

---

22   See Rudolf Thommen, *Geschichte der Universität Basel 1532–1632* (Basel: Nabu Press, 1889), 20; on the connection between confession and dogmatic bias in this faculty, see Christoph Strohm, *Calvinismus und Recht* (Tübingen: Mohr Siebeck, 2008), 168ff.

23   Equally, Whitman, *The Legacy of Roman Law*, 32ff., 232, where Roman law is envisaged as "vector of rationalization."

24   See Donald R. Kelley, *François Hotman: A Revolutionary's Ordeal* (Princeton: Princeton University Press, 1973); and Mathias Schmoeckel, "François Hotman," in *Great Christian Jurists in French History*, ed. Rafael Domingo and Olivier Descamps (Cambridge: Cambridge University Press, 2019), 149–72.

25   François Hotman, *De Gradibus Cognationis et Affinitatis: Libri duo* (Paris, 1547), 16f.

26   Anneliese Sprengler-Ruppenthal, *Gesammelte Aufsätze zu den Kirchenordnungen des 16. Jahrhunderts* (Tübingen: Mohr Siebeck, 2004), 202–50, 221ff., 373.

27   Gerald Strauss, *Law, Resistance, and the State: The Opposition to Roman Law in Reformation Germany* (Princeton: Princeton University Press, 1986), 198ff.

28   Peter Landau, "Der Entstehungsort des Sachsenspiegels. Eike von Repgow, Altzella und die anglo-normannische Kanonistik," *Deutsches Archiv* 61 (2005): 73–101.

Germany in the *Sachsenspiegel*. This comparison was not meant to lessen the significance of the Pentateuch, but it indicated rather Luther's esteem for the Saxon law tradition. Moses's "writings" had provided a formidable law for his society, but it did not hold the authority of God's own law, the Decalogue. None of these laws was perfect, but had to ensure the prosecution of crimes by the government. In the same way, the "Mirror of the Saxons" helped to deter the population from committing crimes. Luther supposed the Saxon law tradition to be easier to handle in court, but he wanted to leave the decision about the best source of law to the lawyers.

Even Philipp Melanchthon, in spite of his particular veneration for Roman law, developed some ideas that were open to the use of Saxon law. Fundamentally, he rejected lay judges and jurors; he demanded that the deciding members of the court should have received a university education. They should act publicly, to demonstrate the law to the people. This necessarily demanded some training. In his *Loci communes*, he particularly demanded the necessity of public punishment. He did not want to prescribe to lawyers how to handle legal procedure. But he clearly preferred a trial in public, which could educate the population. Moreover, he preferred easy and short procedures to long and learned debates. This was, of course, the character of the courts in the Saxon tradition. For this reason, he preferred the procedural rules of the "Mirror of the Saxons."

There was a noticeable movement at the University of Wittenberg to prefer the local legal tradition to "foreign" laws. The lawyers tried to argue that neither canon nor Roman law had ever been acknowledged in Saxony,[29] so that Saxon law was the only option. For the same reason, other scholars worked on the textual tradition of the "Mirror of the Saxons" and its glosses. In 1542, a professor at the University of Wittenberg, Melchior Kling (1504–1571) offered his prince, the Elector of Saxony, a new, systematically ordered version of the "Mirror of the Saxons." He worked on the edition until his death, and his sons could finish the new edition only in 1572.[30] Kling divided the material into four parts, distantly inspired by the ancient Roman lawyer Gaius. But from the beginning, he underlined the importance of orality in legal procedure. Contrary to Roman

---

29 See Strauss, *Law, Resistance, and the State*, 99ff.

30 Melchior Kling, *Das Gantze Sechsisch Landrecht mit Text und Gloss/ in eine richtige Ordnung gebracht/ durch Doctor Melchior Klingen von Steinaw/ an der Strassen/ itzo zu Halle, Doch mit dieser Erklerunge/ das er den Stenden/ die das Sechsisch Recht gebrauchen/ nicht genugsam/ Sondern der Alte Sachssenspiegel/ sonderlich Doctor Christoff Zobels/ welcher wol erklert/ dabey sein mus/ Wie in Epistola dedicatoria erhebliche und genugsame ursachen angezeiget werden sollen* (Leipzig, 1572); a second edition followed in 1577, a third in 1600.

law procedure, the necessity to resolve matters on the day of the trial helped to settle cases quickly, which would help poorer people in particular. He admitted the existence of some reasons and forms for swift justice, even in the *ius commune*, but this only proved that this general difference was not essential, and that Saxon law remained superior.

In the same way, Matthias Coler (1530–1587) argued for the superiority of the "Mirror of the Saxons" over Roman law in the field of court procedure. This argument can be found again in the writings of Matthew Wesenbeck and others. The orality and concentration of Saxon legal procedure on the days of public trial were more convincing than material law issues.

Konrad Lagus (c.1500–1546)[31] wrote an exhaustive manual on Saxon law around 1537, which was published only in 1597 by Joachim Gregorii von Pritzen (1527–1599).[32] Lagus presented the Saxon ways of legal procedure according to the principles of the *ius commune*. He thus wanted to integrate the advantages of Roman law, such as the differences between property (*dominium*) and possession (*possessio*), as well as between the protection of possession by "possessory" or "petitory" actions. As he wanted to combine the advantages of the different legal traditions, he referred to them only from time to time.

An addition called *Ein kurtzer und nützlicher Process* (A short and useful trial), according to the customs of the city of Magdeburg, was added, probably by the editor, Joachim Gregorii. He wanted to prove that the book was in accordance with the Saxon law court trials of the first and second instance. He even claimed to have learned this as a student of Martin Luther and Melanchthon, as well as of Hieronymus Schürpf and Melchior Kling. The orality of the Saxon legal procedure was to be preferred to other laws. He therefore concentrated on the Saxon law tradition alone, instead of comparing it to other laws. So he presented the Saxon procedure from the first legal action until the sentence of appeal. Following him, Hermann Conring, Justus Henning Boehmer, and Christian Thomasius also praised the simplicity of German legal procedure.[33]

---

[31] On him, see Hans Erich Troje, "Konrad Lagus (ca. 1500–1546)." On the use of the loci as a method, see "Melanchthon in seinen Schülern," *Wolfenbütteler Forschungen*, no. 73, ed. Heinz Scheible (Wiesbaden: Harrasowitz Verlag, 1997), 255–83.

[32] See Roderich von Stintzing and Ernst Landsberg, eds., *Geschichte der Deutschen Rechtswissenschaft*, vol. 1 (Munich: Oldenbourg, 1880), 304n1.

[33] See Knut Wolfgang Nörr, *Naturrecht und Zivilprozeß: Studien zur Geschichte des deutschen Zivilprozeßrechts während der Naturrechtsperiode bis zum beginnenden 19. Jahrhundert* (Tübingen: Mohr Siebeck,1976), 11ff. Many authors valued Saxon law, even Conring: see Hermann Conring, "De Nomothetica/Über die Gesetzgebung," th. 64, trans. A. Paul, ed. H. Mohnhaupt, *Prudentia legislatoria*, Bibliothek des Deutschen Staatsdenkens (Munich: C. H. Beck, 2003), 7–87, at 75.

Other benefits were seen in Saxon law as well. Compared to Roman law, the Saxon law in general could be seen as the lord, whereas civil law had to remain the servant.[34] Even the apparent differences had the advantage of giving the authors more freedom to choose the best solution.

In the end, it was not only the advantages of the ancient "German procedure" that recommended the use of Saxon law, but also the greater freedom the lawyers gained by it. Lawyers had to find a way of combining the different legal traditions and could determine the new criteria according to their convictions. The more the "Mirror of the Saxons" offered alternatives, the more scholars were free to establish the necessities of a modern legal order.

The tradition of Roman imperial law might have been venerated, but claiming the intellectual improvements of Saxon law gave the lawyers of the Saxon Protestant universities the liberty and autonomy to separate from the Holy Roman Empire and its old legal traditions. Saxon law even gave the lawyers of the University of Wittenberg a foundation to find arguments against the emperor. The research into the German law tradition was meant to increase the autonomy of Protestant lawyers against the imperial lawyers.[35] Those motives were admitted by editors like the important Melchior Goldast von Heiminsfeld (1578–1635).

3   University of Basel

Since its beginning in the fifteenth century, the University of Basel had been a place of canon law teaching. Peter of Andlau had been a famous canon law professor.[36] Students could obtain a lic.jur.—degree in canon law; for a *doctor iuris utriusque*, students had to study ten years.[37] In 1529, the Reformation was introduced in the university and city of Basel, and it was probably the Protestant theologian Johannes Oekolampadius who reorganized the

---

34   Hans Erich Troje, "Gemeines Recht und Landesbrauch in Bernhard Walthers (1516–1584) Traktat 'De iure protomiseos'," in *Studien zur europäischen Rechtsgeschichte: Festschrift für Helmut Coing zum 28 Februar 1972* (Frankfurt am Main: Klostermann, 1972), 151–69, at 165.

35   Donald R. Kelley, *Foundations of Modern Historical Scholarship* (New York: Columbia University Press, 1970), 242, on the example of Dumoulin and Cujas for the antiquarians—and consequently for the Protestants.

36   Ernst Staehelin, "Die Universität Basel in Vergangenheit und Gegenwart," *Archiv für das schweizerische Unterrichtswesen* 45 (1959/60): 1–23, at 13.

37   Hans Rudolf Hagemann, "Jurisprudenz und Rechtsleben in den ersten Jahrzehnten der Universität Basel," *Gestalten und Probleme aus der Geschichte der Universität Basel*, ed. Ernst Staehelin et al. (Basel: Helbing & Lichtenhahn, 1960), 29–54, at 32.

university. In the law school, only the teaching of Roman law, consisting of the courses on the Institutes, the Pandects, and the Codex, justified three chairs dedicated to these subjects.

The University of Basel had known a discussion on the prevalence of Roman or canon law since the first years of the sixteenth century. Guido Kisch published short tracts on this question from Johann Ulrich Surgant (from 1502) over texts from Thomas Murner (1518 and 1519), Claudius Cantiuncula (1522 and 1534) as well as Johannes Sichardus (1528 and 1530).[38] In Basel, Bonifacius Amerbach, a friend of Erasmus of Rotterdam, continued to lecture on Roman law and used the authority of Philipp Melanchthon to underscore the authority of Roman law.[39]

Another discussion concerned the medieval authors of *ius commune*. Humanism in theology meant to discredit the old authors since the Church Fathers, but could law be continued without the authorities of medieval jurists Bartolus de Saxoferrato and Baldus de Ubaldis? In Basel, like the humanists from Lorraine, Claudius Cantiuncula (Claude Chansonnette, 1490–1560), who taught Roman law from 1518 to 1524, thought the old authorities indispensable. Bonifacius Amerbach started his teaching in 1524 with his famous *Defensio interpretum iuris civilis*. The old authors should not be regarded according to their Latin, but with regard to their qualities as lawyers.

4 France

4.1 *Triumph of Roman Law*

Domenico Maffei was speaking of the "return of Roman law in France" already in the sixteenth century.[40] Of course, Roman law had been present in the French universities since the thirteenth century. In southern France, the Roman law tradition (*pays du droit écrit*) was regarded as the decisive legal tradition. But even in northern France, in the provinces of the *coutumes*, the authority of Roman law, at least as a theory, had been recognized.[41] The progress of jurisprudence in the sixteenth century led to the triumph of Roman law

---

38 Guido Kisch, "Die Anfänge der Juristischen Fakultät der Universität Basel 1459–1529," *Studien zur Geschichte der Wissenschaften in Basel* 15 (1962): 327–38.
39 Guido Kisch, *Melanchthons Rechts- und Soziallehre* (Berlin: De Gruyter, 2019), 214–20, with Melanchthon's tracts on *De Irnerio et Barolo iurisconsultis oratio* [1537].
40 Domenico Maffei, *Gli inizi dell'umanesimo giuridico* (Milan: Giuffrè, 1956), 182ff.
41 Piano Mortari, *Diritto romano e diritto nazionale* (Milan: Giuffrè, 1962), 8. The references for the following can be found in Mathias Schmoeckel, *Das Recht der Reformation in Frankreich* (Tübingen: Mohr Siebeck, 2023).

in French law faculties on different levels. In the work of the greatest French lawyers of this age, such as, among others, Jacques Cujas (1522–1590), Francois de Connan (1508–1551), André Tiraqueau (1488–1558),[42] François-Éguinaire Baron (1495–1550), and Denis Godefroy (1549–1622), the Roman law tradition continued to achieve famous new works, commentaries, and manuals of Roman law destined to advance the jurisprudence of the time. Certainly, Roman law dominated in the faculties as the chief subject of education. But the achievements of the professors can be found on different levels, namely, in establishing new sources, new historical insights into the history of Roman law, and a dogmatic perspective.

But the French discussion of this time is marked moreover by the difference of standpoints. In his *Antitribonien ou discours d'un grand et renomme iurisconsulte de notre temps sur l'estude des loix*, written in 1567 and published in 1603,[43] François Hotman (1524–1590), the most famous Calvinist lawyer of France, challenged the traditional authority of Roman law for France.[44] He argued that it had never been enacted in France. Although there had been kings of France for at least eight hundred years, Roman law had been taught in the kingdom for only the past three hundred years. In contrast to Melanchthon, he did not invent a law establishing the authority of Roman law. Instead, he compared the ancient Roman law, referring to the *paterfamilias* or the Roman slaves, in order to show the difference in contemporary law. He did not want to deny the scientific value of Tribonian's achievement. The *Corpus iuris civilis* should be studied for its academic achievements, but Europe's law had been re-invented by Irnerius and Gratian. France, however, needed a new legislation.

4.2   A Critical Use of Canon Law

Traditionally, France was regarded as a country void of canon law since the Protestant Reformation; only much later authors, such as Louis de Thomassin (d'Eynac, 1619–1695), returned canon law to the kingdom.[45] In reality, however, canon law held an important place in practice and within the faculties at the beginning of the sixteenth century. The rather classical canon lawyer Pierre Rebuffe (1487–1557) already questioned the authority of the church in France,

---

42   Giovanni Rossi, *Incunaboli della modernità. Scienza giuridica e cultura umanistica in André Tiraqueau (1488–1558)* (Turin: Giappichelli, 2007), 238–51, on discretionary power of judges.

43   Ralph E. Giesey, "When and Why Hotman Wrote the Francogallia," *Bibliothèque d'humanisme et Renaissance* 29 (1967): 581–611.

44   Kelley, *Francois Hotman*, 125.

45   Jean Gaudemet, *Les Sources du droit canonique, VIIIe–XXe siècle* (Paris: CERF, 1993), 197.

much in favor of the competence of the royal courts.⁴⁶ Charles Dumoulin (1500–1566) taught that canon law was applicable only in the territories where the pope had the right of legislation.

In France, however, canon law and papal constitutions could not deviate from French law.⁴⁷ This was based on the Pragmatic Sanction, enacted in Bourges in 1438, which established the independence of the Gallic church, confirmed in the Concordat of Bologna in 1516. François Le Douaren (1509–1559) was a little more permissive in admitting the applicability of the *Decretum*, whereas he thought the decretals to be worse, and the *Liber Sextus*, according to him, had never been accepted in France. Right from the beginning, therefore, the French discussion of canon law concentrated on its applicability in France rather than on its evaluation from a theological perspective. François Hotman, however, rejected canon law: it would lead to the ruin of all law, he thought.⁴⁸ Only the *Decretum Gratiani* could be regarded as acceptable.⁴⁹

Increasingly, the history of church law became a major argument in the religious debate. The search for the original church, therefore, was used to question the legitimacy of the authority of the Roman Church in secular matters. Protestant lawyers like the French Calvinist Pierre Pithou (1536–1596) turned their interest to early canon law with the intention of proving what the law of the first Christians and the first church had been. If this original form of Christian law did not know the pope and his privileges, then his claim for superiority could be rejected. From this perspective, the first church constituted an ideal to which the modern church should revert, and it was up to historians to determine its true and original character. Together with his three brothers, Pithou belonged to the most eminent humanists of France. Pierre and François Pithou reedited the *Corpus iuris canonici* in 1587, as well as the late-antique *Legum Romanarum et mosaicarum collation*. This was also a means to defend Gallican liberties.

Other authors worked on the traditional liberties of the Gallican church. Pithou's publication, *Les libertez de l'eglise gallicane*, is considered to be the

---

46 Howell A. Lloyd, "Constitutional Thought in Sixteenth-Century France: The Case of Pierre Rebuffi," *French History* 8 (1994): 259–75.

47 Brigitte Basdevant-Gaudemet, *Histoire du droit canonique et des institutions de l'église latine xvᵉ–vxᵉ siècle* (Paris: Economica, 2014), 211f., 467–70, 475.

48 On this perspective, see Rodolphe Dareste, *Essai sur François Hotman* (Paris: Nabu Press, 1850), 28ff., 36.

49 Mario Turchetti, *Concordia o tolleranza? François Bauduin (1520–1573) e i "monnoyers"* (Geneva: Librairie Droz, 1984), 129, 320ff.

classic summary of this position.[50] In his *Ecclesiae Gallicanae in schismate status*, published in 1594, he collected the arguments for French independence, drawing on historical developments. François Le Douaren's[51] 1557 publication *De sacris Ecclesiae ministeriis & beneficiis libri octo*[52] became famous. How should the priest in the country be paid? Le Douaren used history to establish a system which even Lutherans could accept.

In 1550 a scandal ensued concerning the beneficiaries of clerics in France: did they have to pay their levies to the king or to the pope? The king favored the thought of quitting the Roman Church altogether, following the English example. He asked Dumoulin to write an opinion proving that the payment belonged to the kingdom. Dumoulin's book on the administration of beneficiaries and the apostolic datary was written for this purpose. In the end, pope and king maintained their alliance, and Pierre Lizet, president of the Parlement of Paris, started a persecution for heresy against Dumoulin, who for the rest of his life could no longer safely stay in France. Obviously, canon law was not ignored in France, but the literature flourished in order to strengthen the French position against the pope.

4.3 The Coutumes as the Essential French Law

In the sixteenth century, France developed a new esteem for its own legal tradition. In 1517, Barthélemy de Chasseneuz (Chassaneus, Chassené, 1480–1541), published his *Commentaria in consuetudines ductus Burgundiae*, a commentary on the *coutume* of Burgundy. The *Commentaria* also used the *ius commune* tradition for new humanistic inspirations.[53]

However, Charles Dumoulin's work on the *Coutume de Paris*, which he published with his commentaries in 1552, became much more famous. In 1540 Dumoulin had converted to Protestantism. This inspired France to a new

---

50 Donald R. Kelley, "'Fides Historiae,' Charles Dumoulin and the Gallican View of History," *Traditio* 22 (1966): 347–402, http://www.jstor.org/stable/27830814, 352n14.

51 Olivier Descamps, "Le Douaren, François," in *Dictionnaire historique des juristes français XIIe–XXe siècle*, ed. Patrick Arabeyre (Paris: PUF, 2007), 630f.; Maximilian Herberger, *Dogmatik. Zur Geschichte von Begriff und Methode in Medizin und Jurisprudenz* (Frankfurt am Main: Vittorio Klostermann, 1981), 260.

52 Kelley, "'Fides historiae,'" 361, on Franciscus Duarenus, "De sacris ecclesiae ministeriis ac beneficiis libri octo," *Opera omnia* (Lucca, 1768), 185ff.

53 Patrick Arabeyre, "Entre priscus docendi stylus et nova docendi methodus. Visions renaissantes du panthéon des juristes français," *Historia et Ius* 8 (2015), 1–16, at 10; Bruno Méniel, L'humanisme juridique est-il un humanisme? Le cas du Catalogus gloriae mundi de Barthélemy de Chasseneuz, "L'Humanisme juridique. Aspects d'un phénomène intellectuel européen," in *Esprit des lois, Esprit des lettres*, vol. 14, ed. L.-A.Sanchi (Paris: X. Prévost, 2022), 257–73.

interest in its own local laws and influenced legal ideas in France as well as its colonies.[54] Dumoulin himself was called the Papinien François. He did not ignore the *ius commune* but emphasized the French development in contrast to the Italian tradition. His treatment of legal history was meant to prove the greatness of France and the independence of French law and its sources.

The French discussion was marked by a progressing national sentiment.[55] The Parlement of Paris, the highest court of the central part of the French kingdom, debated whether Roman law had to be considered the supreme law of the Christian tradition, or whether France's own law tradition, especially the *coutumes*, had to be preferred.

In Bourges the debate started as to whether the Breton François Le Douaren, when called to the Parlement of Paris in 1547, should be succeeded by a specialist of Roman law or French legal history. By choosing François Baudouin (1520–1573), the faculty chose a specialist on both as a compromise.

François Hotman (1524–1590) once again defended a more radical position, not so much in his *Antitribonien* but in his *Francogallia* of 1573, a reaction to the St. Bartholomew's Day Massacre. Hotman defined France by drawing on its history, equating the Gauls of Vercingetorix with the Franks of Clovis. He found an essential identity in these epochs, so that he spoke only of "Franco-Gallia," which at the same time underlined the difference from the Romans. For Hotman, the Gauls and the Franks had never surrendered their original liberty to the Romans. The *Lex Salica* was considered as a means to save the royal independence and the essential form of the kingdom (*regni Francogalliae constituendi forma*). Comparing Gaulish and Frankish legal history, Hotman established general traits of the French kingdom, mostly in order to limit royal power. He considered the Merovingian *placita,* just as the *curia regis,* as independent institutions that initiated the French courts of law and the administration of the realm. In the end, since the beginning of the realm, *curators*, alongside the king, had administered the kingdom. For this reason, the king could not be identical with the kingdom, just as a captain could not be confounded with his ship. Since the late Middle Ages, royal powers were limited by principles and the competence of magistrates, such as the lawyers of the Parlement of Paris.

---

54   François-Olivier Martin, *Histoire de la coutume de la prévôté de Paris, Vol. 1: Introduction, l'état des personnes, la condition des biens; Vol. 2: La propriété et les droits réels* (Paris: Forgotten Books, 1922, reprint 1995).

55   Jean-Louis Thiereau, "L'alliance des lois romaines avec le droit Français," in *Droit Romain, jus civile et droit français,* Études d'Histoire du Droit et des Idées Politiques, vol. 3, ed. Jacques Krynen (Toulouse: Presses de l'Université des Sciences Sociales de Toulouse, 1999), 347–74, at 355.

In the following decades, French nationalism became more important. French replaced Latin as the language of law in legal literature, legislation, and jurisprudence. Eminent historians and editors, such as the brothers Pithou and their *Leges Visigothorum*, helped to question the established authorities of *Corpus iuris canonici* and *Corpus iuris civilis*[56] in France. The discussion later asked whether all *coutumes* were equal in importance or just in their rank, or if some were more important.

This generation used law, in particular Roman law, to unify the kingdom and to develop ideas to protects the kingdom's legal institutions as well as the citizens. It has been regarded for a long time as the Golden Age of French law.[57]

5 Amalgamation

5.1 *Canon Law and Its Inherent Qualities*

In Saxony, Eberhard von Weyhe (1553–1633) started a new approach for defining the applicability of Roman and canon law, which many followed. Although historical research would show that popes never had any right of legislation,[58] he wanted to accept the inherent quality of canon law, especially in cases not regulated by Roman law. So he tried to determine general criteria for the applicability of the different laws. Matters in which canon law was still necessary could be found particularly in the laws of succession, obligations, and votes, as well as in family law. It was wrong to assume that modern jurisprudence could be based on Roman law alone. The old papal law, therefore, still had to be studied, amended, and taught.

A professor in Altdorf, Konrad Rittershausen (1560–1613),[59] developed simple rules to determine the application of canon law:

---

56 Brigitte Basdevant-Gaudemet, "Pithou, François," "Pithou, Nicolas," and " Pithou, Pierre," in Arabeyre, *Dictionnaire historique des juristes français XIIe–XXe siècle*, 627–29; Kelley, *Foundations of Modern Historical Scholarship*, 250ff.; on the instrumentalization of legal history in the contest of confessions, see Christoph Strohm, *Calvinismus und Recht* (Tübingen: Mohr Siebeck, 2008), 320ff.

57 Winfried Dotzauer, *Deutsche Studenten an der Universität Bourges. Album et liber amicorum* (Meisenheim am Glan: Hein, 1971), 43.

58 Eberhard à Weyhe, *De controversia an jus Pontificium siue Canonicum, meritò & licitè, in scholis, & foro fidelium, locum obtinere, doceri, obseruari, ac Publice priuataeque utilitatis, denique humanae necessitatis gratia, ipsius commercium fidelibus concedi possit?* (Wittenberg, 1588), D1ᵛ.

59 On Rittershausen, see Johann August Ritter von Eisenhart, "Rittershausen, Konrad," in *Allgemeine Deutsche Biographie*, vol. 28 (Leipzig: Duncker & Humblot, 1889), 698–701.

- Canon law should be applied whenever civil law—he was referring to the Roman law tradition here—was unclear;[60] otherwise, Roman law should prevail.
- Canon law could be used to supplement Roman law—for example, in marital matters, contracts, obligations (*in pactis, stipulationibus,* and *Emphyteusi*), usury, beneficiaries, testaments, tithes (*decimis*), oaths, and all questions of legal procedure.
- When *ius civile* conflicted with *ius canonicum*, Roman law should be followed in secular matters, but canon law in ecclesiastical courts, particularly in Roman Catholic countries.
- But with regard to religious questions, canon law was regarded as more useful in many countries.
- In case of doubt, nobody should assume a discrepancy between civil and canon law.

In the end, all major matters of canon law could be cited in Protestant courts, at least in a supplementary way.

Christian Thomasius (1655–1728), law professor in Halle, worked on a synthesis of these different strategies to legitimize the use of canon law. He published a commentary on Giovanni Paolo Lancilotti's handbook of canon law written by the famous law professor from Wittenberg, Caspar Ziegler (1621–1690). This manual, first published in 1713, was dedicated to canon law instruction in Protestant universities. Thomasius pleaded in many instances for the applicability of canon law not only in universities but also in court. Students needed to know canon law more than even the local ordinances of their territories or Roman law. Of course, canon law had some disadvantages, but judges, professors, and students needed to be informed about the shortcomings of law. Students should be warned of the prejudice that canon law had been abandoned, and rather should recognize its persistent benefit.

Other authors, however, were less inclined to admit the use of canon law. Hermann Conring (1606–1681) wrote a short tract against the heresy of "Hildebrand" (Pope Gregory VII), evident in Gregory's *Dictatus Papae*. As this could be seen as the basic program for the legislation of the following popes, Conring asserted that the Roman Catholic Church, as well as its law, had become heretical themselves. In his famous publication on the history of

---

60   Cunrad Rittershusius, *Differentiarum juris civilis et canonici seu pontificii libri Septem, Utriusque Iuris Studiosis apprimè utiles & necessarij* (Strasbourg, 1618), 18f.: The first principle is that, when things are obscure or dubious in civil law, they have to be defined by canon law, and the canons have to be observed.

German law, *De origine iuris Germanici*,[61] he used the complaints of medieval popes about deficiencies of German law practice to prove that canon law had hardly ever been introduced to Germany. Once again, historical arguments were used to prove what should be regarded as the present law of the land.

Many authors followed him, such as Samuel Stryk (1640–1710). Even more radically, the Prussian Johannes Brunnemann (1608–1672) regarded canon law only as the law of the Roman Catholic Church, which could only exceptionally be used outside, if its admission to the law of the land could be proved. In the end, canon law could still be applied when useful. Luther's resentment, though, continued to dominate the official opinion.

5.2 The Natural Law School

In the quest for a new law, many Protestant authors used the natural law approach advised by Melanchthon. Of course, the uses and conceptions of natural law changed tremendously. Still, legal uses were inevitable. Lutheran and Calvinist authors knew canon law quite well and used this tradition for those subjects in which canon law traditionally had prevailed, the laws establishing hierarchy, procedure, ecclesiastical order, family and criminal law, but also ethical corrections of civil law, such as the validity of contracts and good faith.

Grotius's description of the law of nature, his *De iure belli ac pacis libri tres* of 1615, contained, therefore, many subjects taken from the canon law tradition.[62] The Protestant background of the natural law authors of the seventeenth and eighteenth centuries was known in their time. The German Jesuit Ignaz Schwarz (1690–1763)[63] wrote an extensive book on the confessional prejudices of these natural law authors. As Grotius slowly came to dominate the new international public law,[64] this was one way in which the natural law tradition gradually modernized the European legal order.

---

61   See Frank L. Schäfer, *Juristische Germanistik. eine Geschichte der Wissenschaft vom einheimischen Privatrecht* (Frankfurt am Main: Klostermann, 2008), 59 ff.

62   James Muldoon, "Hugo Grotius, Medieval Canon Law and the Creation of Modern International Law," in Proceedings *of the Ninth International Congress of Medieval Canon Law*, ed. Martin Bertram (Berlin: De Gruyter, 1992), 1157–64; idem, "The Contribution of the Medieval Canon Lawyers to the Formation of International Law," *Traditio* 28 (1972): 483–97.

63   See Harald Dickerhof, *Land, Reich, Kirche im historischen Lehrbetrieb an der Universität Ingolstadt (Ignaz Schwarz 1690–1763)* (Berlin: Duncker & Humblot, 1971), 35; on this work, 132ff.

64   Björn Florian Faulenbach, "Rolle und Bedeutung der Lehre in der Rechtsprechung der Internationalen Gerichtshöfe im zwanzigsten Jahrhundert," in *Rechtshistorische Reihe* (Frankfurt am Main: Peter Lang, 2010), 407.

6   Conclusion

For most matters, Roman law as well as canon law were too important in the *ius commune* tradition, which had been developed from the thirteenth century onward, to be neglected or forgotten. The offices of magistrates, the hierarchy of functionaries, legal procedure, public finance, family, and criminal and international law could not be conceived without the pioneering influence of canon law. Protestant reform, however, gave cause to reconsider the importance of these traditional sources of law: it provided lawyers with good reason to re-evaluate canon law, which had assumed an increasingly dominant position in the Middle Ages. European Protestants developed a new admiration for Roman law, as well as new reasons to honor the local legal tradition, which until the sixteenth century had hardly any dignity.

Due to the humanistic assumption that all ages needed their own laws, both canon law and Roman law—notwithstanding their internal and dogmatic values—could be seen as examples of good law, but no longer as contemporary law. The more dominant the national laws became, the less ancient and medieval legal traditions could be regarded as fundamental for the state. Instead, these subjects became part of history, while the local tradition was regarded as a way to understand national legislation.

In France, François Baudouin (1520–1573),[65] from Artois, argued in his *De Institutionae historiae universae*, from 1561,[66] that truth had to be established with respect to the history of any subject. Laws could not be understood by ignoring their historical background. Law experts had to know history in order to understand the rules.[67] For this reason, the legal historian Roderich von Stintzing (1825–1883) regarded Baudouin as "the first legal historian," who had helped to use legal history for the recognition of law.[68] Two years later, Jean Bodin (1529/30–1596) published his *Methodus ad facilem historiarum cognitionem*.[69] Instead of fallible human evaluation, a sound recognition of law

---

65   Alain Wijffels, "Baudouin, François," *Dictionnaire historique des juristes français*, 69f.; Mario Turchetti, *Concordia o tolleranza?*, 200; Gary W. W. Jenkins, *Calvin's Tormentors: Understanding the Conflicts That shaped the Reformer* (Ada, MI: Baker Academic, 2017), 94f.
66   See Michael Erbe, *François Baudouin (1520–1573)* (Genève: Gütersloher Verlagshaus, 1984), 110ff.
67   Kelley, *Foundations of Modern Historical Scholarship*, 118.
68   Roderich von Stintzing, *Geschichte der Deutschen Rechtswissenschaft* (Munich: Oldenbourg, 1880), 382.
69   For this book, see Sara Miglietti, *Jean Bodin, une pensée en mouvement. Étude des variants entre les deux redactions de la Methodus (1566, 1572)*, *Nouvelle Revue du Seizième Siècle* (Geneva: Librairie Droz, 2022).

needed precise knowledge of the local, temporal, and cultural environment. This would help to establish true historiography. This approach presupposed a true nature of each people, based on its history, geography, and even climate. In the eighteenth century, history became, in the perspective of Romanticism, a way to eliminate the individual factor. So when Savigny developed his ideas on the historic school of law, his intention was to scrutinize legal history, Roman and canon law, and the national particularities, in order to distinguish finally obsolete law, confined to history, from the current law of the land.

CHAPTER 15

Church Laws as a Means of Ecumenical Dialogue

Mark Hill, KC

> Through the comparative study of the various juridical instruments of the Churches ... it is possible to explore critically the extent to which different Christian traditions share common principles in their canons and other instruments of internal governance.
> —His All Holiness Bartholomew I, Archbishop of Constantinople, Ecumenical Patriarch

∴

John Witte, a Canadian by birth and a Calvinist by nurture, has wandered somewhat from his nation and denomination in his scholarly and spiritual life. His academic output is marked by the catholicity of his interests, and the breadth and depth of his research. Both personally and through the center he has led with such distinction at Emory University, he has taught and published on every conceivable area where religion and law converge, hence the richness of this Festschrift. For pedestrian scholars, such as myself, with more limited horizons and less exotic habitats, a single subject must suffice. This chapter therefore has a narrower topic and a shorter reach. It considers the significance of the law and polity of different Christian traditions and draws on the work of the Colloquium of Anglican and Roman Catholic Canon Lawyers, supplemented more recently by the activities of the Panel of Experts in Christian Law. The cumulative effect of this study has identified certain universal principles of Christian law which can be deployed to deepen and to give greater traction to the current ecumenical endeavor, something now recognized at the highest level in the World Council of Churches.[1]

The purpose of the law for Christian communities is much the same today as it was in the days of the early church: to regulate the functioning of the

---

1 See, in particular, Norman Doe, "The Ecumenical Value of Comparative Church Law: Towards the Category of Christian Law," *Ecclesiastical Law Journal* 17 (2015): 135–69. See also Norman Doe, ed., *Church Laws and Ecumenism: A New Path for Christian Unity* (London: Routledge, 2021).

community of faith and the conduct of its component members by a combination of commands, prohibitions, and permissions. The law may appear only to be concerned with order and discipline,[2] but in truth it touches upon spiritual, theological, pastoral, and evangelistic concerns at the heart of the Christian faith. In a speech to mark the fiftieth anniversary of the Society for the Law of the Eastern Churches, Pope Francis stated:

> Many of the theological dialogues pursued by the Catholic Church, especially with the Orthodox Church and the Oriental Churches, are of an ecclesiological nature. They have a canonical dimension too, since ecclesiology finds expression in the institutions and the law of the Churches. It is clear, therefore, that canon law is not only an aid to ecumenical dialogue, but also an essential dimension. Then too it is clear that ecumenical dialogue also enriches canon law.[3]

Law ought not to be seen as a negative and oppressive legalistic instrument: as applied ecclesiology, it contributes to sustaining and expressing the freedom of all God's children.[4] The integrity of a church, or indeed any secular institution, depends upon certain beliefs and behavior being common to all its members.[5] Christ himself instructed his apostles to bind and to loose, and thus the apostles began a process of lawmaking for the Christian church.[6]

1   Common Vision

The World Council of Churches' Faith and Order Commission paper, *The Church: Towards a Common Vision* (2013), which was twenty years in

---

2 See, by way of example, Mark Hill, "Due Process as a Principle of Anglican Canon Law," in *The Right to Due Process in the Church; A Comparative Ecclesiastical Approach*, ed. Rik Torfs (Leuven: Peeters, 2014), 15.
3 "Udienza ai partecipanti al Convegno promosso dalla Società per il Diritto delle Chiese Orientali," Sep. 19, 2019, https://press.vatican.va/content/salastampa/it/bollettino/pubblico/2019/09/19/0714/01466.html.
4 Robert Ombres, OP, "Why Then the Law?" *New Blackfriars* 55 (1974): 296–304. See also Norman Doe, "Towards a Critique of the Role of Theology in English Ecclesiastical and Canon Law," *Ecclesiastical Law Journal* 2 (1992): 328–46.
5 For a discussion of the theology of canon law, see Robert Ombres, OP, "Faith, Doctrine and Roman Catholic Canon Law," *Ecclesiastical Law Journal* 1, no. 4 (1989): 33–41.
6 See, by way of example, the rules relating to the conduct of worship prescribed by Saint Paul in his first epistle to the Corinthians.

preparation, represented an extraordinary ecumenical achievement in ecclesiology.[7] However, it did not explicitly consider church law, whether as a help to ecumenism or as a hindrance. The Christian church has no single humanly created system of Christian law.[8] Rather, each institutional church has its own regulatory system of law, order, or polity[9] dealing typically with ministry, governance, doctrine, worship, ritual, property, and finance. Each regulatory system is the servant of that church. It facilitates and orders its life, mission, and witness and binds the faithful in duties and rights for the maintenance of ecclesial communion. It translates the church's theological self-understanding into norms of conduct.

Common Vision was intended to encourage further reflection in the church for discerning the next steps toward visible unity: "agreement on ecclesiology has long been identified as the most elemental theological objective in the quest for Christian unity."[10] Similarly, a key pursuit of comparative church law must be the systematic search for visible juridical unity through exposure of similarities between the regulatory systems of churches, and their articulation as shared principles of law. This juridical unity, and the common action it stimulates, is an elemental aspect of ecumenism. Juridical convergence is, to borrow from *Common Vision*, one of the "aspects of ecclesial life and understanding which has been neglected or forgotten." Church law is the product of theological reflection; it translates theology into practical norms of action; and its pastoral quality is evident in its service of the community of the faithful seeking to enable and order life in witness to Christ.[11] That *Common Vision* does not refer explicitly to, or consider, church regulatory systems and their place in ecumenism is perhaps related to the historical position of the Faith and Order Commission that church law is about difference, not similarity.[12] This emphasis is misplaced: law and its ecumenical study is fertile ground for convergence. The absence of any explicit discussion in *Common Vision* of the

---

7   World Council of Churches, *The Church: Towards a Common Vision*, Paper No. 214 (Geneva: WCC Publications, 2013), preface, VIII. This paper is referred to hereafter as *Common Vision*.
8   For a magisterial study of the subject, see Norman Doe, *Christian Law* (Cambridge: Cambridge University Press, 2012).
9   Hereafter the term "law" is adopted as a convenient shorthand incorporating also the terms "order" and "polity" adopted by some denominations to describe their regulatory instruments.
10 *Common Vision*, foreword, and preface.
11 See Norman Doe, "Juridical Ecumenism," *Ecclesiastical Law Journal* 14 (2012): 195–234.
12 "The Ecumenical Movement and Church Law," Document IV.8 (1974); see Doe, *Christian Law*, 1–2.

role of church law impoverished its treatment of normativity in church life. Regulatory instruments seek to order and facilitate ecclesial life. The value of law can only be fully understood, and its potential realized, when it is properly perceived as facilitative and shorn of the myth that it is exists, not to serve the church, but to constrain and inhibit.

2   The Sources, Forms, and Purposes of Church Law

For *Common Vision*, the church has a threefold mission: to proclaim the Gospel, administer the sacraments and worship, and give pastoral service. The regulatory instruments of churches echo this theological standpoint. They provide that each institutional church is an autonomous community that exists to preach the Gospel, to administer sacraments and worship, and to provide pastoral service.[13] In the Protestant tradition, a Lutheran church is a national or local assembly of the faithful shaped by authoritative Reformation texts and its "biblical foundations"; as "part of the whole Church of Christ," its objects include to "declare the teachings of the prophets and apostles and seek to confess in our time the faith" and to engage in "worship and Christian service."[14] For *Common Vision*, all Christians share the conviction that scripture is normative: church laws similarly indicate the importance of holy scripture and tradition operating with other regulatory entities which also shape church life normatively.[15] For instance, the Roman Catholic Church has a Code of Canon Law (1983) which recognizes custom and often presents canons themselves as derived from divine law.[16]

While *Common Vision* uses words importing juridical concepts, it does not explain those terms as juridical in form and theological in context. Anglican laws contain "principles, norms, standards, policies, directions, rules, precepts, prohibitions, powers, freedoms, discretions, rights, entitlements, duties, obligations, privileges and other juridical concepts."[17] For some Lutheran churches, a precondition to membership is acceptance of the constitution and bylaws.[18]

---

13   Doe, *Christian Law*, chap. 1.
14   The Reformation texts include the Augsburg Confession (1530) and Formula of Concord (1577).
15   See Doe, *Christian Law*, chap. 1.
16   Code of Canon Law 1983 of the Latin Church, cc. 24, 207, 331, 1249.
17   *The Principles of Canon Law Common to the Churches of the Anglican Communion*, 2nd ed. (2022; hereafter, *Principles of Canon Law*), Principle 4.5.
18   Lutheran Church of Great Britain, *Rules and Regulations*, Congregations, 1.

3   The Faithful and Lay Officers

For *Common Vision*, the church universal consists of Christ's followers (the people of God), with obligations of responsibility. Each institutional church has its own membership, for which faith in Christ is essential.[19] The faithful share communion (*koinonia*), a key concept in ecumenism embracing participation, fellowship, and sharing. The juridical norms of churches reflect these propositions. Juridical systems seek to facilitate and order the communion of the faithful associated together in a church. Each church has a membership in which there is a fundamental equality, but with a distinction between the laity and the ordained. The Roman Catholic faithful constitute the "people of God," and each one "participates in their own way in the priestly, prophetic and kingly office of Christ" in order "to exercise the mission which God entrusted to the Church to fulfil in the world"; but "by divine institution, among Christ's faithful there are ... sacred ministers [and] others called lay people"; but all enjoy "a genuine equality of dignity and action."[20] Christian churches regulate admission to membership. Churches have elaborate norms on the functions of the faithful. For instance, Orthodox must "uphold Christian values and conduct" and "respect" the clergy; they are "obliged to take part in the divine services, make confession and take holy communion regularly," "observe the canons," "carry out deeds of faith", "strive for religious and moral perfection," and be "an effective witness" to the faith; their rights include participation in, for example, the parish meeting, if in "good standing."[21]

4   Ordained Ministers

Common Vision has a detailed discussion of ordained ministry: patterns of ministry; authority and ministry; and the principle of oversight. Juridical analysis is valuable as it discloses convergence in terms of principle and action. The triple function of the ministry (word, sacrament, guidance), is given by Christ to the church to be carried out by some of its members for the good of all.[22] Juridical analysis yields extensive consensus in principle and practice. Suitable, qualified persons may be called to and ordained or otherwise "set apart" for ministry, which is understood across the traditions to be of divine institution.

---

19   *Common Vision*, paras. 7, 12, 14, 16, 18, 19, 21, 23, 27.
20   Code of Canon Law, cc. 205, 207, 208.
21   Russian Orthodox Church, *Statutes*, XI.3; GOAA, *Regulations*, Art. 18.
22   *Common Vision*, para. 20.

Ordination itself is the process by which the vocation of individuals to serve as ministers is recognized and by which they are set apart for ministry.

For *Common Vision*, ministers assemble and build up the Body of Christ by proclaiming and teaching the Word of God, by celebrating the sacraments, and by guiding the community in its worship, its mission, and its caring ministry.[23] All authority in the church comes from its head, Jesus Christ, who shared his authority with the apostles and their successors.[24] The norms of Christian churches reflect the authority, functions, and lifestyle of ordained ministers as envisaged in *Common Vision*. Ministers are accountable for the exercise of their ministry to competent authority as prescribed by law.[25] Clerical oversight is addressed in the laws of Christian churches, and is exercised principally by an ordained minister, usually in collaboration with others.

5 Institutional Ecclesiastical Governance

For *Common Vision*, Christ is the source of authority in the church. However, churches differ about who is competent to make final decisions. Regulatory instruments provide concrete evidence of the commitment of churches to these ideas and of different approaches to the location of authority (subsidiarity). A church may have an episcopal, presbyterian, congregational, or other form of government as required or permitted by its conception of divine law, with Christ as the head of the church universal in all its manifestations. Governance is exercised through a hierarchical system of international, national, regional, and local institutions. The authority which an institution has at each level varies between the traditions and their doctrinal position. In the Catholic and Orthodox churches the highest authority is an international institution: the pope and/or college of bishops, or a patriarch and holy synod. Authority descends to national, regional, and local institutions (such as a diocesan synod or a parish council). In the Congregational and the Baptist traditions, authority resides primarily in the local church (and is shared by laity and ministers) and ascends (for limited purposes of common action) to regional, national, and international institutions.

Churches generally organize themselves on the basis of regional and local territorial units. Catholics, Orthodox, and Anglicans have dioceses (each led by a bishop). In the Protestant tradition, Lutheran churches have dioceses or synods and, within these, districts or circuits. Roman Catholic, Orthodox, and

---

23 Ibid., para. 19.
24 Ibid., para. 48.
25 Doe, *Christian Law*, 93–101.

Anglican dioceses are divided into parishes. In the Reformed, Presbyterian, Congregational, and Baptist models, regions and districts are typically composed of circuits, congregations, and local churches. In turn, each local unit has its own assembly for governance. A Methodist circuit meeting is the focal point of the working fellowship of the churches in the circuit, overseeing their pastoral, teaching, and evangelistic work.[26] Among Christian traditions, the local church may be subject to the control or direction of regional and national institutions but nevertheless enjoy autonomy within its own sphere.

Common Vision recognizes that when the church comes together to take counsel and make important decisions, there is need for someone to summon and preside over the gathering for good order and to facilitate the process of promoting, discerning, and articulating consensus.[27] Christian traditions provide for international oversight and leadership, with varying degrees of authority attached to it, in juridical norms applicable to global ecclesial communities which either constitute or are constituted by an institutional church. In the Roman Catholic Church, with the pontiff, the College of Bishops exercises power over the universal church, and its decrees, if confirmed by the pope, are to be observed by all the faithful.[28] However, at the international level the institutions of the Anglican Communion (for example, the Lambeth Conference), Lutheran World Federation (Assembly, Council, and Secretariat), World Methodist Council, World Communion of Reformed Churches (General Council), and Baptist World Alliance (Congress), exercise no coercive jurisdiction over their autonomous member churches.

6 Church Discipline and Conflict Resolution

Christian churches acknowledge the fact of sin among believers, its often-grievous impact, and the need for self-examination, penitence, conversion, reconciliation, and renewal. Whatever the theological position of churches, the juridical instruments recognize the capacity of the faithful to engage in wrongdoing, and each church has norms to address such conduct, to resolve internal disputes, and to maintain church discipline. Christian churches share basic ideas about the nature and purpose of ecclesiastical discipline. Typically discipline in the church is an exercise of that spiritual authority which Jesus has appointed in his church. The ends contemplated by discipline are the

---

26 Methodist Church of Great Britain, *Constitutional Practice and Discipline*, Deed of Union 1(III) and SO 61.
27 *Common Vision*, paras. 54–57.
28 Code of Canon Law, cc. 336–48, 360–61 and 754.

maintenance of the purity of the church, the spiritual benefit of the members, and the honor of Christ. All members and ministers of a church are subject to its government and discipline, and are under the jurisdiction and care of the appropriate church courts in all matters of doctrine, worship, discipline, and order in accordance with the rules and regulations from time to time applying. Discipline is to correct the offender and to protect the reputation and resources of the church. It is not considered to be punitive. The instruments of churches commonly provide for the settlement of disputes by means of procedure short of formal judicial process.[29] Every effort must be made by the faithful to settle disputes amicably, and recourse to church courts and tribunals is a last resort.

Most churches have a system of courts or tribunals for the enforcement of discipline and formal and judicial resolution of ecclesiastical disputes at international, national, regional, and/or local levels. They are established by competent authority, administered by qualified personnel, and tiered as to original and appellate jurisdiction, and they exercise such authority over members as is conferred on them by law.[30] Judicial process may be composed of informal resolution, investigation, or a formal hearing, as may be prescribed by law, including an appeal. Disciplinary procedures at trial must secure fair, impartial, and due process on the basis of natural justice. The parties, particularly the accused, have the right to notice, to be heard, to question evidence, to silence, to an unbiased hearing, and, if appropriate, to appeal.[31] Christian churches assert their inherent right to impose spiritual and other lawful censures, penalties, and sanctions upon the faithful, provided a breach of discipline is established objectively. Sanctions must be lawful, and just churches may enable removal of sanctions on the basis of forgiveness, leading to the restoration of the full benefits of ecclesial association.[32]

7 Doctrine and Worship

Common Vision proposes that proclamation of the faith is an integral action of the church, as is unity in and protection of the apostolic faith.[33] Churches

---

29 See, by way of example, Mark Hill, "Mediation: An Untapped Resource for the Church of England?" *Ecclesiastical Law Journal* 13 (2011): 57–77.
30 Doe, *Christian Law*, 164–71.
31 Mark Hill, "Due Process as a Principle of Anglican Canon Law," 15.
32 Doe, *Christian Law*, 182–86.
33 *Common Vision*, para. 37.

consider doctrine as the teaching of the church on matters of faith and practice. Various norms have developed. The doctrine of a church is rooted in the revelation of God as recorded in holy scripture, summed up in the historical creeds, and expounded in instruments, texts, and pronouncements issued by ecclesiastical persons and institutions with lawful authority to teach. Doctrinal instruments include catechisms, articles of religion, confessions of faith, and other statements of belief.[34] The doctrines of a church may be interpreted and developed afresh by those persons or institutions within it with competence to do so, to the extent and in the manner prescribed by the law of that church. For all Christian traditions, proclamation of the Word of God is a fundamental action of the church and a divine imperative incumbent on all the faithful for the evangelization of the world. Each church has a right to enforce its own doctrinal standards and discipline, and the faithful should not publicly manifest, in word or deed, a position contrary to church doctrine; those who do so may be subject to correction by means of disciplinary process.[35]

Christian churches may develop liturgical texts or other forms of service for the public worship of God, provided these are consistent with the Word of God and church doctrine. The forms of service for worship may be found in a book of rites or liturgy (Catholic and Orthodox),[36] a book of common prayer (for example, Anglican),[37] orders of worship (Lutheran), a directory of worship (for example, Presbyterian), and other service books lawfully authorized for use. The faithful must engage in regular attendance at divine worship, and the administration of worship is subject to supervision by designated church authorities.[38]

8   Rites of Passage

Common Vision identifies several ecumenical challenges with regard to ritual: who may be baptized; the presence of Christ in the Eucharist and its relation to his sacrifice on the cross; chrismation or confirmation; and those who do not affirm baptism and Eucharist but do affirm that they share in the church's sacramental life.[39] The legal evidence substantiates the differences in approaches

---

[34]   Doe, *Christian Law*, 188–94.
[35]   *Principles of Canon Law*, Principle 53.
[36]   Code of Canon Law, cc. 2, 455, 826, 838: the pope has authority over the formulation of liturgical texts.
[37]   *Principles of Canon Law*, principles 54–55.
[38]   Doe, *Christian Law*, 224–32.
[39]   *Common Vision*, para. 40.

among the traditions in terms of the classification of some rites as sacraments. Most churches have norms on marriage, and some on confession and funerals. *Common Vision* recognizes growing convergence among churches about baptism as "the introduction to and celebration of new life in Christ and of participation in his baptism, life, death and resurrection."[40] Juridical instruments echo these theological propositions. In Catholic law, baptism (infant or adult) is the gate to the sacraments and constitutes a rebirth as children of God configured to Christ.

According to *Common Vision*, a dynamic and profound relation exists between baptism and the Eucharist. The juridical unity among Christian churches may be articulated in a number of principles. The Eucharist, Holy Communion, or Lord's Supper, instituted by Christ, is central to ecclesial life, and the faithful should participate in it regularly. It is administered by ordained persons or those otherwise lawfully deputed, normally in a public church service or, exceptionally, at home, such as to the sick. A church by due process may exclude from admission to the sacrament those whom it judges unworthy to receive it. These norms are found in the Catholic, Orthodox, and Anglican churches as well as the Lutheran, Methodist, Presbyterian, and Baptist traditions. Other rites which *Common Vision* does not deal with include marriage. Churches have complex norms on marriage, which is defined typically as a lifelong union between one man and one woman, instituted by God for the mutual affection and support of the parties.[41] To be married validly in church, the parties must satisfy the conditions prescribed by church law and must have been instructed in the nature and obligations of marriage.[42]

9 Ecumenical Relations

Common Vision invites leaders, theologians, and faithful of all churches to seek the unity for which Jesus prayed.[43] Currently, some denominations identify the church of Christ exclusively within their own community; some see in others

---

40 *Common Vision*, para. 41.
41 Code of Canon Law, c. 1055; Evangelical Lutheran Church of South Africa, *Guidelines*, 7.2–7.8.
42 Code of Canon Law, cc. 1057–64; *Principles of Canon Law*, Principle 71. When the *Principles* were revised in 2022, in consequence of the approval of same-sex marriage in several provinces of the Anglican Communion, it proved impossible to find a common principle as to who may marry whom: see the preamble to the text of the previous iteration of principle 70.
43 *Common Vision*, para. 8, citing John 17:21.

a real but incomplete presence of the church; some have joined covenant relationships; some believe the church to be located in all communities that present a convincing claim to be Christian; others maintain that Christ's church is invisible and cannot be adequately identified.[44] Juridical instruments inform both members and the public more generally about a church's commitment to and participation in ecumenism. Some churches have well-developed ecumenical norms; others less so. While the church is divided denominationally, each denomination teaches that there is one, holy, catholic, and apostolic church, and that the denomination is a portion, member or branch of it, or else that the church universal subsists in it. Ecumenism seeks the restoration of visible Christian unity—a divine imperative—and its goal is full ecclesial communion. A church must promote ecumenism through dialogue and cooperation, protect the marks of the church universal, and define what ecclesial communion is possible. Ecumenical activity is generally in the keeping of a central authority, but ecumenical duties may be given to the local church and to ordained ministers. Ecumenical norms may enable interchange of ministers, the sharing of the sacraments, mixed marriages, and sharing of property. But such norms are usually in the nature of exceptions to general rules, which confine such facilities to the enjoyment of the faithful within the ecclesiastical tradition which created those norms. Norms may also enable church members to share in spiritual activities, such as common prayer, spiritual exercises, and funerals, and in mission and social justice initiatives.[45]

10 Church Property and Finance

In its discussion of the church and society, *Common Vision* makes no mention of the temporal assets of the churches—their property and finances—and the uses of these. This too is a fertile ground to identify juridical unity among the separated churches. Christian churches commonly assert their right to acquire, own, administer, and dispose of property (which may be held at the international, national, regional, or local level, depending on the church in question).[46] Places of worship should be dedicated to the purposes of God, and the activities carried out in relation to sacred property should not be inconsistent with the spiritual purposes which attach to that property. Oversight of the administration of property vests in a competent church authority, and a periodic

---

44 *Common Vision*, para. 10.
45 Doe, *Christian Law*, 304–08.
46 Ibid, 310–19.

appraisal of its condition may be the object of a lawful visitation. A church has the right to make rules for the administration of its finances. The civil law on financial accountability should be complied with, and each ecclesiastical unit, through designated bodies, should prepare an annual budget for approval by its assembly. The faithful must contribute financially to church work, and church officers should encourage the faithful in this. A church should insure its property against loss, remunerate ministry, and make financial provision for ordained ministers who are in ill health and who retire.

11 Church, State, and Society

Christian churches have norms on the authority of the state in its own secular sphere of governance, the institutional separation of the church from the state, the requirement on the church to comply with state law, the involvement of its members in political activity, the promotion of human rights, and the engagement with society in charitable, welfare, educational, and other activity. These juridical facts find a direct echo in theological propositions found in *Common Vision*, which observes that it is appropriate for believers to play a positive role in civic life, but not to collude with secular authorities in sinful and unjust activities. Church laws provide that the state is instituted by God to promote and protect the temporal and common good of civil society—functions fundamentally different from those of the church. There should be a basic separation between a church and the state, but a church should cooperate with the state in matters of common concern. Churches (or entities within them) may negotiate the enactment of state laws specifically devoted to them, and enter agreements with the state and civil authorities to regulate matters of common concern.[47] The faithful may participate in politics to the extent permitted by church law—clergy in some churches cannot hold office involving the exercise of civil power. The faithful should comply with state law, but disobedience by the faithful to unjust laws may be permitted. Also, the faithful should not resort to state courts unless all ecclesiastical process is exhausted.

Common Vision sees religious freedom as one of the fundamental dimensions of human dignity, and Christians should seek to respect that dignity and to dialogue with others to share the Christian faith.[48] The exercise of religious freedom is particularly important in so far as the advance of a global secular culture provides challenges for the church, as does a radical decline in

---

47 Norman Doe, *Law and Religion in Europe* (Oxford: Oxford University Press, 2011), esp. chap. 4.
48 *Common Vision*, para. 60.

membership and concomitant perceptions of irrelevance. Church law has the potential to convert promotion of human rights and religious freedom into norms of action for the faithful. Also, the state should recognize, promote, and protect the religious freedom of churches corporately and of the faithful individually, as well as freedom of conscience. *Common Vision* proposes that the first attitude of God to all creation is love. So, as God intends the church to transform the world, a constitutive aspect of evangelization is the promotion of justice and peace.[49] Church regulatory systems are invaluable in translating exhortations such as these into action. Each church recognizes for itself a responsibility to promote social justice and engage in charitable activity in wider society. Churches present engagement in social responsibility as a function of faith and law.

12   Developing Principles of Christian Law

Assessing the ecclesiological content of *Common Vision* from the standpoint of church law, as summarized above, emphasized the importance of identifying clear principles of Christian law. Ecumenical Patriarch Bartholomew[50] commended the work of the Panel of Experts in Christian Law,[51] comparing the legal systems of different ecclesial traditions and inducing from them common principles of law. The panel's *Statement of Principles of Christian Law*, issued in 2016, corrected the historic deficit in the ecumenical enterprise, which had previously neglected the potential of church law as a unifying force for global Christianity. Canonical principles are an integral part of the legal thought of Patriarch Bartholomew, and in his address he reiterated that the ancient canons contain the guiding and fundamental principles on which all legislative work of the church, created by changing ecclesiastical circumstances, must be based. His remarks are equally applicable beyond the Eastern Churches to all other Christian ecclesial traditions, past and present, which see church laws as applying or containing principles which themselves are foundational, theological in content, and reflective of a church's self-understanding.[52]

---

49   *Common Vision*, para. 59.
50   In his keynote address to the 24th International Congress of the Society for the Law of the Eastern Churches, Rome, September 2019.
51   See Mark Hill, "Christian Law: An Ecumenical Initiative," *Ecclesiastical Law Journal* 16 (2014): 215–16.
52   For a detailed exposition of the historic development of principles in legal history, see Norman Doe, "The Evolution of Principles of Christian Law," in Doe, ed., *Church Laws and Ecumenism: A New Path for Christian Unity* (London: Routledge, 2021), chap. 1.

The methodology for the formulation of the principle of Christian law replicated two earlier ventures. In a bilateral ecumenical context, the Colloquium of Anglican and Roman Catholic Canon Lawyers used the category of principles of law in its work. Established in 1999, the colloquium seeks to compare the respective legal systems of the two communions, meets annually, publishes its proceedings,[53] and has addressed such topics as clerical discipline, initiation into the church, authority in the church, ecumenical cooperation, orders and primacy, ministry, marriage, bishops, and liturgy.[54] The impetus for this bilateral colloquium came in large part from the deployment of the concept of principles of canon law to enhance unity between the member churches of the Anglican Communion. Based on a comparative study of the laws of each autonomous Anglican church,[55] the Anglican Communion Legal Advisors Network published at the Lambeth Conference in 2008 a document titled *The Principles of Canon Law Common to the Churches of the Anglican Communion*.[56] In 2009, the Anglican Consultative Council commended the *Principles* for study in all provinces, and encouraged provinces to use the network as a central resource in dealing with legal issues in those provinces.[57] A second edition of the *Principles*[58] was launched at the Lambeth Conference in 2022, the result of a collaboration between the Centre for Law and Religion at Cardiff University, the Ecclesiastical Law Society, and the Anglican Consultative Council. Reading groups, held online across the globe, suggested revisions in the light of intervening developments. The principles were redrafted, and examined by a committee, which then consulted globally with legal experts from various provinces. The second edition was launched at the Lambeth Conference in August 2022.[59]

---

53   Norman Doe, ed., *The Formation and Ordination of Clergy in Anglican and Roman Catholic Canon Law* (Cardiff: Centre for Law and Religion, 2009), 155.
54   See Mark Hill, "A Decade of Ecumenical Dialogue on Canon Law: Report on the Proceedings of the Colloquium of Anglican and Roman Catholic Canon Lawyers 1999–2009," *Ecclesiastical Law Journal* 11 (2009): 284–38.
55   Norman Doe, *Canon Law in the Anglican Communion* (Oxford: Oxford University Press, 1998).
56   Published by the Anglican Communion Office, London, 2008. It had one hundred macroprinciples and about six hundred microprinciples in eight parts: church order; Anglican Communion; government; ministry; doctrine and liturgy; rites; church property; and ecumenism.
57   ACC-14, Resolution 14.20.
58   https://ecclawsoc.org.uk/principles-resources/.
59   In February 2023, the Anglican Consultative Council met in Accra, Ghana, and passed a resolution which "commends the *Principles* to the Churches of the Anglican Communion

In November 2013, an invited panel of experts met in Rome, at my invitation as convenor. Participants attended in their personal capacities, not as representatives of their denominations, and on the basis of their expertise in the church law, church order, or church polity of particular Christian churches: Anglican, Baptist, Catholic, Lutheran, Methodist, Orthodox, Presbyterian, and Reformed. Its aim was to explore how these churches share common principles in their regulatory instruments, and how these principles contribute creatively to ecumenism. The panel coalesced around the following propositions: (1) there are principles of church law and order common to the churches studied, and their existence can be factually established by empirical observation and comparison; (2) the churches contribute through their laws to this store of principles; (3) the principles have a strong theological content and are fundamental to the self-understanding of Christianity; (4) they have a living force and contain within themselves the possibility of development and articulation; and (5) they demonstrate a degree of unity among churches, stimulate common Christian actions, and should be fed into the global ecumenical enterprise to enhance fuller visible unity. The panel concluded that a consideration of church law may provide a new medium for the ecumenical enterprise: namely, that law (an element of the self-understanding of churches) should be conceived as an instrument for global ecumenism. Thus, in 2014 the panel set about drafting a formal response to *Common Vision*,[60] and began a process leading in 2016 to an agreed-upon *Statement of Principles of Christian Law Common to the Component Churches*. The statement has ten sections: churches and their laws; the faithful; ordained ministry; church governance; church discipline; doctrine and worship; rites; ecumenism; church property; and church and state relations.[61] In November 2017, in Geneva, the panel presented Dr. Odair Mateus, director of the World Council of Churches Faith and Order Commission, with a copy of the *Statement of Principles*.[62] Subsequently, panel members road-tested the statement at ecumenical events in Uppsala, Cardiff, and Amsterdam in 2018, and in London, Melbourne, Sydney, and Oslo in 2019. At a private audience in the Apostolic Palace, Rome, on September 19, 2019,

---

for study and use" and encourages all the member churches to keep their canons under review in the light of them: ACC-18, Resolution 3(d).

60 *Common Vision*.
61 For the full statement of principles, see Doe, *Church Laws and Ecumenism*, Appendix II.
62 Mark Hill and Norman Doe, "Principles of Christian Law," *Ecclesiastical Law Journal* 19 (2017): 138–55. Dr. Mateus then proposed an ongoing consultative partnership between the Panel and the Commission: see Doe, *Church Laws and Ecumenism*, 24.

Pope Francis pronounced, for the first time in papal history, that church law is not only an aid to ecumenical dialogue but also an essential dimension of it.[63]

On September 2, 2022, at Karlsruhe, Germany, at the 11th Assembly of the World Council of Churches, a workshop was held on the *Statement of Principles*, chaired by Professor Norman Doe, at which I spoke together with Fr. Aetios (Dimitrios Nikiforos), Grand Ecclesiarch at the Ecumenical Patriarchate of Constantinople. Participants then discussed its value, sharing their reaction to and experiences of using the statement, from as far afield as India, Australia, the United States, the Netherlands, Germany, Luxembourg, and Switzerland. The proposal, adopting words of the ecumenical patriarch, was agreed *nem con* that this "World Council of Churches workshop commends the *Statement of Principles of Christian Law* for study and use as an essential element of the ecumenical movement."

13 Conclusion

The routine and mundane exercise of comparing the legal frameworks of different Christian churches reveals that there are profound similarities among the basic elements of the normative regimes of governance across various ecclesiastical traditions. This is not altogether surprising: juridical unity is often based on the practice of churches in adopting a common source for shaping their laws (chiefly scripture). From these similarities, by simple scientific method, may be induced common principles of Christian law. Regulatory systems of churches shape and are shaped by ecclesiology. These systems also tell us much about convergence in action, based on common norms of conduct, as well as the commitment of churches to ecumenism. While dogmas may divide churches, the widespread similarities among their norms of conduct produce regulatory convergence. This reveals that the juridical norms of the faithful, whatever their various denominational affiliations, link Christians through their encouragement of common forms of action. As laws converge, so does behavior. These similarities among the norms of conduct of different Christian churches indicate that their faithful engage in the visible world in much the same way. Comparing church law-order-polity systems (themselves forms of applied ecclesiology) enables the articulation of principles of law-order-polity common to the churches. Laws link Christians in common action and, as

---

63 "Udienza ai partecipanti al Convegno promosso dalla Società per il Diritto delle Chiese Orientali."

Common Vision itself states, "common action" is "intrinsic to the life and being of the Church."[64]

The study of church law brings a new vibrancy to ecclesiological and ecumenical scholarship. Professor John Witte, Jr. has written clearly in this vein. As he put in a recent tribute to our mutual friend and colleague Professor Norman Doe:

> Law is at the backbone of Christian ecclesiology and ecumenism. Despite the deep theological differences that have long divided Christian churches and denominations—over the Bible, the Trinity, the sacraments, justification by faith, clerical celibacy, women's ordination, natural law, and so much more—the church universal has always been united in its devotion to and need for church law. From the earliest instructions of St. Paul and the *Didache* for the new churches to the elaborate codes of canon law and books of church discipline in place today, the Christian church has been structured as a legal entity. The church depends upon rules, regulations, and procedures to maintain its order, organization, and orthodoxy; its clergy, polity, and property; its worship, liturgy, and sacraments; its discipline, missions, and diaconal work; its charity, education, and catechesis; its publications, foundations, and religious life; its property, governance, and interactions with the state and other social institutions. Still today, every church, whether an individual congregation or a global denomination, has law at its backbone, balancing its spiritual and structural dimensions, and keeping it straight and strong especially in times of crisis.
>
> The church laws themselves, of course, vary greatly in form and function over time and across the denominations and regions of the world. Some church laws are written, others are customary. Some are codified, others more loosely collected. Some are mandatory, others probative or facilitative. Some are universal canons, others are local and variant. Some are drawn from the Bible, others go back to ancient Roman law and the Talmud. Some church laws deal with the essentials of the faith, others with the adiaphora. Some are internally created by the church's own government, others are externally imposed or induced by the state. Some church laws are declared by ecclesiastical hierarchies, others are democratically selected. Some churches maintain elaborate tribunals and formal procedures, others use informal and conversational methods of enforcement. But, for all this variety, church law is a common and

---

64   *Common Vision*, para. 61.

necessary feature of church life, and an essential dimension of ecclesiology and theology.[65]

With the combined endorsement of the World Council of Churches and Professor John Witte, Jr., juridical ecumenism has at last found an honored place in the comparative study of church laws.

Acknowledgments

I am grateful to Professor Norman Doe, Director of the Centre for Law and Religion at Cardiff University, for his input into this chapter. An earlier version of this paper appeared as Mark Hill, "The Regulation of Christian Churches: Ecclesiology, Law and Polity," *Theological Studies* 72, no. 1 (2016).

---

65 John Witte, Jr., "Law at the Backbone: The Christian Legal Ecumenism of Norman Doe," *Ecclesiastical Law Journal* 24 (2022): 194–208. See also id., "Norman Doe, Master Comparativist in the Field of Law and Religion," in *The Confluence of Law and Religion: Interdisciplinary Reflections on the Work of Norman Doe,* ed. Frank Cranmer et al. (Cambridge: Cambridge University Press, 2016), 247–61.

CHAPTER 16

Bearing Witness to Truth: Christianity at the Crossroads of Race and Law

Brandon Paradise

It is a privilege to contribute this essay in honor of John Witte, Jr. I distinctly remember my first conversation with John. I was then a relatively new member of the academy who had grown weary of an intellectual landscape that seemed dominated by liberal technocratic theories that aimed to provide morally and religiously neutral solutions to enduring social justice issues. Although critical race theory (CRT) offered deeper and more candid engagement with the nature of enduring social justice issues, in the end, critical theory's postmodern, deconstructive approach to truth undermined the moral truths needed to ground social justice claims. In other words, in its skepticism of objective truth and in its tendency to reduce law to power and interests, critical theory appeared unable to persuasively explain why its own claims should be accepted as true and just. In contrast to both liberal and critical race theories, the teachings of Martin Luther King Jr. and the African American Christian tradition that undergirded the King-led wing of the Black freedom movement engaged the deep and complex nature of racial injustice while retaining a focus on truth. But despite Christianity's role in the Black freedom movement and the religion's ability to offer deep critical engagement without surrendering truth claims, the legal academy, with its predominantly secular outlook, with rare exceptions appeared largely unaware of or even indifferent to the African American Christian tradition. Put bluntly, in my judgment, both liberal scholarship and CRT seemed largely at best apathetic and at worst hostile toward Christianity. I perceived a calling to help bring the resources of the Christian tradition to bear on race and law scholarship. But for a young, untenured professor, this was not an easy calling to follow. It was clear that several senior colleagues did not see the value or point of scholarship at the nexus of Christianity, race, and law.

In this context, coming to know John was a great source of encouragement. A prolific Christian scholar with an impressive body of work, including over 40 books, 280 articles, and the editorship of 17 journal symposia, he held the directorship of Emory's Center for the Study of Law and Religion. The center has sponsored a magnificent body of Christian legal scholarship that has made significant inroads against the ideal of a religiously neutral scholarship. Throughout his career, John has consistently criticized the notion of a religiously neutral scholarly discourse, arguing that Christianity, in particular, and religion in general can positively shape a legal culture that fosters the common good while respecting pluralism.

In our first conversation, John spoke of Christian scholars not hiding their light under a bushel and encouraged my calling. In the years since, he has been far more than a source of encouragement. Expressing confidence in my work at the intersection of race, law, and Christianity, he welcomed me as a McDonald Distinguished Fellow at the Emory center. More recently, he entrusted me to lead a funded symposium project on the topic of "Christianity, Law and Racial Justice: Shaping the Future." (I invited John's former student and fellow McDonald Distinguished Fellow and Senior Lecturer, Terri Montague, to join as project co-lead). Because of John's vision and support and Terri's efforts as project co-lead, fourteen scholars, including Terri and me, gathered at Emory to discuss papers on race, law, and Christianity. Underscoring the significance of the meeting, the Rev. Dr. Bernice King—one of Martin Luther King Jr.'s daughters—and Dr. Cornel West offered rich remarks highlighting the importance of bringing the Christian tradition to bear on race and law. The conference proceedings will culminate in the publication of a collaborative symposium edition of the *Journal of Law and Religion* and *Political Theology*. Thanks to John's support, we will soon see a significant step toward the aim of creating a robust scholarly discourse on Christianity, race, and law.

In celebration of John's work, this chapter seeks to show that beyond the concrete support he has given to developing the field of Christianity, race, and law, John's scholarship— especially his conception of rights—navigates between contextual and objective conceptions of law while maintaining a steadfast commitment to moral truth appropriate to Christian scholarship at the intersection of race and law. In particular, the chapter argues that John's capacious understanding of law and religion and his mapping of the interaction between the two, as well as his arguing for the positive contribution that religious values can make to the development of rights and law, align with critical race theory's historical approach to law and its emphasis on incorporating the perspectives of people of color. However, unlike CRT's skepticism of the existence of objective truth, John's historical, contextual approach to rights as middle axioms of political discourse envisions grounding rights in moral truths. The chapter argues that this conception of rights can enable scholarship at the intersection of Christianity, race, and law to continue CRT's emphasis on the historical, contextual nature of rights while being faithful to Christianity's commitment to the existence of moral truth.

The chapter also raises questions inspired by John's celebration of pluralism and his emphasis on a robust dialogue among and within diverse moral communities as a way of securing moral truth and justice. In the spirit of critical race theory, the chapter argues that unequal power relations among communities cast doubt on whether a robust and open debate is possible and, assuming that such a debate takes place, whether such debate is sufficient to secure truth and justice. As a field that should be sensitive to the impact of power on determining which community's voice is heard and whose interests are reflected in law and legal policy, scholars working at the intersection of Christianity, race, and law would rightly be skeptical of placing faith in debate as a means of securing truth. On the other hand, John's celebration of pluralism rightly guards against Christian triumphalism and intolerance. The chapter accordingly concludes with the following suggestion. While Christian scholars should welcome robust debate, CRT persuasively argues that power and interests often drive law and legal reasoning on issues of race. Drawing on the thought of Martin Luther King Jr., the chapter argues that truth and the Christian virtue of agape love are bound up with one another. Moreover, it is by adopting truth and love as ways of life that truth is secured. In contrast to CRT, the right response to the ethic of interests that dominates questions of race and law is a firm stand for an ethic of truth and love that refuses to return untruth for untruth.

1 An Expansive View of Law and Religion and the Inevitable Interaction of the Two

As this first section explains, John offers a capacious understanding of both "law" and "religion" that captures their interaction as an inevitable feature of collective life. Moreover, under this broad understanding of law and religion, incorporating religious values into law and lawmaking helps to better align law with the fundamental beliefs that animate actual people and communities.

John has advocated against narrow understandings of "law" and "religion" that render the two mutually unintelligible.[1] Under the narrow view, "law" is limited and identified with the rules and statutes that govern a society, while religion is understood as "a body of doctrines and exercises designed to guide private conscience and the voluntary religious society."[2] In contrast, on

---

[1] John Witte, Jr., "Law, Religion, and Human Rights," *Columbia Human Rights Law Review* 28, no. 1 (19896): 1–31, at 3.
[2] Ibid., 3.

the broadest view, "law consists of all norms that govern human conduct and all actions taken to formulate and respond to those norms."[3] On this understanding, the customs, processes, and rules of churches, corporations, and other associations qualify as law.[4] Like law, religion can be broadly understood. On the broadest view, "religion embraces all beliefs and actions that concern the ultimate origin, meaning, and purpose of life, of existence."[5]

Building on the foregoing broad understanding of "law" and "religion," John has noted a variety of ways in which law and religion are related. They are conceptually related; for example, they employ analogous concepts, such as redemption and rehabilitation, sin and crime, covenant and contract, and righteousness and justice).[6] They have developed analogous hermeneutical methods, employing, among other things, logical, ethical, evidentiary, and rhetorical methods that bear a family resemblance.[7] Church-state relations institutionally link law and religion vis-à-vis the centuries-long dialectic among jurists, theologians, and philosophers that form our approach to the relationship between church and state.[8] Moreover, among other things, lawyers and clergy both mediate conflicts and serve society, thus professionally linking law and religion.[9]

The above links and interactions between law and religion render the two dependent upon and even "dimensions" of one another.[10] As a permanent feature of human life, religion will inevitably shape law and rights, as these latter receive their content and their enforcement from more fundamental beliefs, including religious beliefs as values.[11]

Building upon the idea that law and religion inevitably interact, John has argued for including religious values in legal scholarship and lawmaking. In addition, rather than intervening in disciplines, such as critical race theory and critical legal studies, that reject the Enlightenment ideal of law as objective and neutral, John has made the case for including religious values in fields, such as human rights, where some see comprehensive views like religion as incompatible with certain liberal ideals, including the idea that legal reasoning and argument should be presented in terms that all reasonable people

---

3   Ibid., 3–4.
4   Ibid., 4.
5   Ibid., 4.
6   Ibid., 5.
7   Ibid., 6.
8   Ibid., 6–7.
9   Ibid., 7.
10 Ibid., 7.
11 Ibid., 2, 30.

can accept.¹² Finally, as John has noted, even massively influential proponents of so-called bracketing of religious values, including the philosophers Jürgen Habermas, John Rawls, and Richard Rorty, ultimately reversed course to conclude that religious values should be welcome in democratic deliberation.¹³ Thus, while powerful opposition to religious values in law, lawmaking, and legal scholarship continues to exist, thanks to John and the work of likeminded scholars today there is more discursive space for religious values than when the so-called secularization thesis—that religious values and the importance of religion would continue to diminish in advanced societies—enjoyed wide support.

2   Religious Values and the Still-Emerging Field of Christianity, Race, and Law

The greater discursive space that religion enjoys today made my own work of analyzing the marginalization of the African American Christian tradition in critical race theory (CRT) implicitly easier than it might have been at the height of the secularization thesis.¹⁴ In this respect, historical conditions have converged to enable modes of scholarly work at the intersection of Christianity, law, and race in a way that may not have been possible in the not-too-distant past. Moreover, John's own work and the immense body of Christian scholarship produced during his leadership of Emory's Center for the Study of Law and Religion has helped to legitimate legal scholarship that takes religion

---

12   In a coauthored paper with Justin Latterell, John asserts that "[p]luralism now outshines strict secularism as a discursive ideal for modern democracies." See John Witte, Jr. and Justin J. Latterell, "Christianity and Human Rights: Past Contributions and Future Challenges," *Journal of Law and Religion* 30 (2015): 353–85, at 383. It is unclear, however, if John and his coauthor mean to include the United States among the democracies in which pluralism has eclipsed strict secularism. Although the United States Supreme Court has moved away from strict secularism's corollary, strict separationism, and toward accommodation of religion, as far as I can tell, American life remains divided between those who would include religious values in lawmaking processes and those who favor strict secularism. See Christian Joppke, "Beyond the Wall of Separation: Religion and the American State in Comparative Perspective," *International Journal of Constitutional Law* 14 (2016): 984–1008, at 1004; Gregory A. Smith, "In U.S., Far More Support Than Oppose Separation of Church and State," Pew Research Center, Oct. 28, 2021), 12, https://www.pewresearch.org/religion/2021/10/28/in-u-s-far-more-support-than-oppose-separation-of-church-and-state/.
13   Witte and Latterell, "Christianity and Human Rights," 383.
14   Brandon Paradise, "How Critical Race Theory Marginalizes the African American Christian Tradition," *Michigan Journal of Race & Law* 20 (2014): 117–211.

and religious values seriously. I now describe the context in which the still-emerging field of Christianity, race, and law scholarship seeks to incorporate religiously grounded norms into race and law scholarship. Specifically, I now all too rapidly describe relevant features of CRT and my previous work analyzing the marginalization of the African American Christian tradition in race and law scholarship.[15]

Perhaps most significantly, CRT rejects the "Enlightenment ideal of law ... as an autonomous, ahistorical phenomenon capable of and appropriately understood by objective, rational, and neutral analysis" in favor of the view that law is historical and contingent.[16] CRT's understanding of the historical, contingent nature of law enables it to expose how unequal racial power and white supremacy structure law and legal institutions and thereby inscribe and perpetuate racial subordination. Moreover, rather than aspiring toward what it takes to be the unobtainable ideals of objectivity and neutral analysis, CRT emphasizes the necessity of understanding law and racial subordination through the perspectives of people of color.[17] Put differently, insisting that issues of race and law are shaped by the political and cultural forces at work in broader social life, as a means of addressing racial subordination, CRT argues that law and legal analyses ought to incorporate the perspectives of people of color.

In light of CRT's commitment to developing work based upon the perspectives of Black people, in prior work I sought to understand why "religiously grounded normative arguments" played a marginal role in CRT "despite the prominence of the Black church in the civil rights movement, the still central role of faith for many African Americans, and CRT's commitment to addressing racial subordination from the perspectives of Black people."[18] I also note the African American Christian tradition's absence from a list of intellectual movements, "including liberalism, law and society, feminism, Marxism, poststructuralism, critical legal theory, pragmatism, and nationalism," that prominent CRT scholars credit as shaping CRT.[19] Despite the marginal role of the African American Christian in CRT, I argue that developing a body of scholarship "grounded in the normative resources of the African American Christian tradition" is consistent with "CRT's emphasis on the importance of developing

---

15 Ibid., 117–211.
16 Ibid., 156–57.
17 Ibid., 120.
18 Ibid., 120.
19 Ibid., 122–23, quoting Mari Matsuda et al., *Words That Wound: Critical Race Theory, Assaultive Speech, and the First Amendment* (Boulder, CO: Westview Press, 1993), 6.

a body of legal scholarship that 'looks to the bottom' and reflects the normative perspectives of communities of color."[20]

3 Rights and Truth in Law and Religion and CRT

Rejection of the ideal of law as autonomous and objective and developing wholly according to internal resources, in favor of a view of law as porous and influenced by the fundamental beliefs, such as religious values, that prevail in a society raises questions about the significance and nature of rights. In particular, if, as John Witte argues, law inevitably incorporates religious values or, as CRT argues, ought to include the perspectives of people of color, rights should not be understood as the objective products of legal reason alone.

For some, the conclusion that extralegal values and forces shape law and rights calls the very value of rights into question. Indeed, John and CRT have defended rights against, respectively, fellow Christian thinkers—such as Stanley Hauerwas, Patrick Parkinson, and Helen Alvaré—and the rights-trashing of CRT's ideological ally, Critical Legal Studies (CLS). Against Hauerwas's worry that rights discourse threatens to distract from and cheapen the deeper moral claims required to adequately address injustice and fulfill the Christian vision of life, Parkinson's worry that accepting human rights may mean adopting liberal values, and Alvaré's worry that equality-based rights claims threaten religious liberty, John asserts that "rights and their vindication help the law achieve" the civil use of securing peace and order, the theological use of fostering self and community improvement, and "the educational use of teaching everyone the good works of morality and love that please God, however imperfect and transient that achievement inevitably will be in the present age."[21] Similarly, CRT defends rights against CLS's claim that rights discourse "legitimate[s] an illegitimate perception of law" by concealing the law's status as a "legitimating tool of underlying hierarchy."[22] In contrast, CRT argues that CLS's critique of rights neglects the important role that "rights play[] in the struggle against racial subordination."[23]

---

20 Ibid., 124 (footnotes omitted).
21 John Witte, Jr., *The Blessings of Liberty: Human Rights and Religious Freedom in the Western Legal Tradition* (Cambridge: Cambridge University Press, 2022), 292–93, 298.
22 Paradise, "How Critical Race Theory Marginalizes the African American Christian Tradition," 155.
23 Ibid., 156.

Accordingly, John and CRT each defend the value of rights, though as means and not ends in themselves. CRT identifies rights as a means of carrying out an antisubordination agenda, whereas John sees rights as promoting the three uses of the law described above. In addition to sharing the view that rights are means rather than ends, both see rights as artifacts of political discourse.[24]

However, on the question of truth, John and CRT draw different lessons from their common view that rights are essentially political. Whereas in identifying law and rights with politics CRT arguably (and notoriously, in the eyes of some) reduces law to power,[25] John assumes that law and rights are directed to securing moral truth and justice.[26] Perhaps reflecting his Christian commitments, John is confident that there is more to reality than politics and interests. Moral truth and moral value exist, however historically conditioned and imperfectly we may approximate them. Thus, in the context of human rights but with a logic that applies to other rights,[27] John writes:

> human rights are "middle axioms" of political discourse. They are a means to the ends of justice and the common good. But, the norms that rights instantiate depend upon the visions and values of human communities for their content and coherence—or, what the Catholic philosopher

---

24 Witte, *The Blessing of Liberty*, 301. Devon W. Carbado and Cheryl I. Harris, "Intersectionality at 30: Mapping the Margins of Anti-Essentialism, Intersectionality, and Dominance Theory," *Harvard Law Review* 132 (2019): 2193–239, at 2212.

25 See Darren Lenard Hutchinson, "Critical Race Histories: In and Out," *American University Law Review* 53 (2004): 1187–1215, at 1189–90 for a discussion rejecting criticisms that CRT is nihilistic but acknowledging that in adopting postmodern deconstructionism while making positive claims of racial justice, "Critical Race Theorists inhabit an admittedly contradictory space." See Kenneth B. Nunn, "'Essentially Black': Legal Theory and the Morality of Conscious Racial Identity," *Nebraska Law Review* 97 (2018): 287–333, at 305–06, for a discussion of postmodern skepticism in CRT.

26 Witte, *The Blessings of Liberty*, 300–01.

27 For purposes of this chapter, I assume that John's understanding of the interaction of law and religion renders enacted, positive rights permeable and subject to and the product of political forces and thus, like human rights, a form of political discourse. However, it bears noting that John analogizes human rights to the *ius gentium* (the international common law), which in the West historically sat between natural law (laws of reason and conscience) and civil law (enacted positive law of a particular community), thus distinguishing human rights and positive law. See John Witte, Jr., "A Dickensian Era of Religious Rights: An Update on Religious Human Rights in Global Perspective," *William & Mary Law Review* 42 (2001): 707–70, at 722–23. It is also worth noting that in calling human rights "middle axioms of our discourse," John implies that higher (natural law) and lower (civil law) axioms constitute a part of a single, perhaps somewhat continuous political discourse. Ibid. 722–23.

Jacques Maritain described as "the scale of values governing [their] exercise and concrete manifestation."[28]

Accordingly, because religious values inevitably inform the "visions and values of human communities" that provide the content and coherence of the norms that rights seek to make real, religion and religious values aid in the development of rights and their implementation as means of securing justice and the common good.[29]

As middle axioms of political discourse, rights are best understood as contextual and time-bound constructs that rest on more fundamental norms, including religious values that may be universal, even if they come to be known through the unfolding of history. Understanding rights as contextual and time-bound is thus to understand law and lawmaking as embedded, situated, and influenced by the forces and values of the society that a legal regime governs. But as John understands it, this historical, contextual approach does not deny that law and rights should be rooted in moral truth and transcendent values. To the contrary, he writes positively of moral truth and moral and metaphysical knowledge.[30]

In contrast to a vision of rights as middle axioms of political discourse that ought to approximate and be grounded in more fundamental beliefs and moral truths, critical race theorists tend to deploy a postmodern, deconstructive methodology that is skeptical of mind-independent truth claims.[31] Moreover, as seen in Derrick Bell's highly influential interest-convergence thesis, in which racial progress and regress occur insofar as they align with white interests, CRT frequently portrays law as predicated upon (even perhaps reducible to) power and interests rather than moral or ethical ideals.[32] However, while CRT correctly claims that disparate racial power is essential to understanding American law, CRT flounders to the extent that it expresses skepticism toward

---

28 Witte, *The Blessings of Liberty*, 399, quoting Jacques Maritain, introduction to UNESCO, *Human Rights: Comments and Interpretations* (New York: Columbia University Press, 1949). See also Witte, "A Dickensian Era of Religious Rights, 722–23.
29 See, generally, Witte, *The Blessings of Liberty* for a detailed historical discussion of the contribution of religious values in the development of rights. See Witte, "Law, Religion, and Human Rights," 3–8, 30 for a discussion of the inevitable interaction between law and religion.
30 See Witte, *The Blessings of Liberty*, 298–300.
31 Nunn, "'Essentially Black,'" 305–06.
32 Derrick Bell, "Brown v. Board of Education and the Interest-Convergence Dilemma," *Harvard Law Review* 93 (1980): 518–33, at 523.

"truth."³³ Put bluntly, one cannot deny the possibility of truth while asserting truth claims of one's own regarding the nature of racial justice.

4 Rights, Power, and Truth in the Emerging Discipline of Christianity, Race, and Law

A key question for the emerging field of Christianity, race, and law concerns the relationships among rights, power, and truth. This part offers three interrelated approaches to this question. First, it attempts to rapidly capture why scholarship examining race and law from the perspective of the Christian tradition should generally reject CRT's skepticism of truth itself while also embracing CRT's insights into how power and interests shape American law and the law's role in racial subordination. Second, the section argues that John Witte's conception of human rights as middle axioms of political discourse offers a promising avenue for how scholarship at the intersection of Christianity, race, and law can understand the impact of power on rights while nonetheless seeking to ground rights on moral truths. Finally, the section evaluates how John's and CRT's understandings of their foci on, respectively, grounding rights in truth and justice and ending racial subordination sharpens a challenge facing race and law scholarship that draws on the Christian tradition: how to remain faithful to the Christian commitment to moral truth while adequately grappling with CRT's insight that racial power profoundly shapes and even drives issues of race and law.

4.1 *Rejecting Epistemic Relativism*

Although understandings about the nature of truth and how human beings apprehend moral and theological truths vary across Christian traditions, such variations do not need to be addressed here. For purposes of this discussion, the key point is that, notwithstanding such complexity, Christianity generally rejects CRT's tendency toward epistemic relativism. In fact, even the most cursory review of Christian scriptures strongly and unambiguously aligns Christianity with the existence of truth.³⁴ Indeed, passages too numerous to list

---

33 For fuller discussion, see Paradise, "How Critical Race Theory Marginalizes the African American Christian Tradition," 157n171.

34 It bears noting that the postmodern philosophy underlying CRT's skepticism of truth has also influenced some contemporary Christian theologians. However, for reasons I cannot explain here, postmodern Christian theology may not be a coherent project. As Orthodox theologian David Bentley Hart has implied, postmodern theology may entail a contradiction in terms: "the project of constructing a post-metaphysical theology is

affirm the existence of truth. As illustrative examples, consider the following statements attributed to Christ himself: "I am the way; I am truth and life";[35] "when the Spirit of truth comes he will lead you to the complete truth";[36] and "you will come to know the truth, and the truth will set you free."[37] In fact, the Christian scriptures implicitly portray skepticism of truth itself as standing in opposition to Christianity and playing a part in Christ's crucifixion. Thus, in his encounter with Pontius Pilate, Jesus says, "all who are on the side of truth listen to my voice."[38] Pilate, expressing uncertainty about the nature of truth and perhaps implying that truth is relative or subjective, replies, "What is truth?"[39]

Christianity is not just confident in the existence of truth; it identifies truth with God himself and with the highest Christian virtue, love.[40] Thus, in general, race and law scholarship anchored in the Christian tradition will retain a commitment to truth. Yet, as noted above, it is also clear that power profoundly shapes how American law treats questions of race and law. The emerging field of Christianity, race, and law therefore faces the challenge of maintaining CRT's careful attention to the impact of racial power on American law and legal institutions, while simultaneously upholding an unambiguous commitment to the existence of truth.

4.2 *Rights: Integrating Truth and Political Discourse*

John's conception of rights as middle axioms of political discourse is, I believe, capable of accommodating CRT's habit of identifying rights and law with the sphere of politics and power relations while avoiding the philosophical skepticism into which CRT often falls. As the very phrase "middle axioms of political discourse" implies, rights are something more than mere politics, but they are not themselves fundamental moral truths, though they may be based on such truths.[41] Thus understood, we can (with CRT) remain attentive to the impact

---

somewhat preposterous.... [It's] like post-atmospheric air." See https://www.youtube.com/watch?v=hPN7aG522YM.

35   John 14:6 (The New Jerusalem Bible [NJB]).
36   John 16:13 (NJB).
37   John 8:32 (NJB).
38   John 18:37 (NJB).
39   John 18:38. (New International Version [NIV]).
40   See and compare John 14:6 and 1 Cor. 13:6 (NJB).
41   In the context of human rights, John has stated that "rights lie halfway between the local civil laws of a particular political community and the higher laws maintained by religious or philosophical communities." See John Witte, Jr., "Freedom and Order: Christianity, Human Rights, and Culture: A Chinese Conversation with John Witte, Emory University (August 9, 2019), https://www.johnwittejr.com/uploads/9/0/1/4/90145433/witte_interview_christinaty_human_rights_and_culture_r_.pdf. Although this statement implies that

of politics and power on both the formation and application of rights while nonetheless seeking to ground rights in fundamental moral truths.

Although understanding rights as middle axioms would enable the discipline of Christianity, race, and law to give focus to both power and truth, as mentioned above, understandings of the complicated nature of truth and its apprehension vary across the Christian tradition. A practical implication, then, is that Christian scholars taking up questions of race and law may offer different approaches to the grounding of rights in fundamental truths. We leave the task of developing what these approaches might be to scholars writing from the particular Christian traditions from which such varied views can be developed, and instead we turn to John's work and CRT for lessons that can inform future work. As we now see, John emphasizes a robust, inclusive discourse as the ordinary means of securing truth and justice, whereas, reflecting the influence of standpoint theory, CRT emphasizes listening (and even deference) to the perspectives of people of color.[42]

4.3 *Robust Inclusive Debate versus Standpoint Theory*

It is helpful to recall that John's defense of the place of religious values in law and legal scholarship is primarily a reaction against liberal theories that wish to bracket religious values and exclude them from the public square. In John's view, incorporating religious values makes law and rights more efficacious by better aligning law with the fundamental beliefs of the citizenry. In contrast, CRT is focused on showing how—contrary to the liberal, Enlightenment ideal of law as neutral and objective—law is in fact shaped by broader power relations that facilitate and further racial subordination. CRT asserts that by rejecting neutrality and objectivity and looking to the perspectives of people of color, law can better address racial injustice. With these different agendas in mind, I now briefly describe how John and CRT propose to pursue their respective visions.

Perhaps reflecting the importance of "discourse" in the phrase "middle axioms of political discourse," John endorses philosopher Lenn E. Goodman's view that morality and justice are discerned through a "historical process —an actual debate among actual people who have actual lives and actual beliefs,

---

John may distinguish human rights from civil rights in local political communities, at least on questions of racial justice, for reasons I cannot offer here, I believe human rights and civil rights closely overlap and in some cases should or do entirely converge. For additional, related discussion see note 27 above.

42 Randall L. Kennedy, "Racial Critiques of Legal Academia," *Harvard Law Review* 102 (1989): 1745–1819.

hopes, fears, plans and needs."[43] In pluralist societies like our own, such a debate "sharpens a society's values," enabling participants to "learn and evaluate the contours—and limits—of their own moral teachings."[44] This historical process of rigorous and candid debate (as opposed to abstract thought experiments, such as the veil of ignorance) provides the basis for justice as a "concept and as an institutional reality."[45]

In contrast, CRT is skeptical that a robust, inclusive discourse will secure racial justice. In particular, given the unequal distribution of power among groups and their unequal influence over our society's institutions, discourse alone is unlikely to secure justice. Perhaps more important, at least with respect to race, law and legal institutions do not reflect ideals of justice so much as they do racial interests. Hence, as discussed above, Derrick Bell's interest-convergence thesis posits that law facilitates racial progress when perceived white self-interests align with Black interests.[46] In addition, rather than positing that a robust, interracial dialogue is the best means of identifying the nature of racial subordination or its solution, CRT emphasizes looking to the bottom and privileging the perspectives of people of color. Specifically, according to "standpoint epistemologies" that have influenced CRT, people of color and others at the bottom have "access to understanding about oppression that others cannot have."[47] CRT thus suggests that on matters of racial justice, deference should be given to the perspectives of people of color.

Setting aside the epistemological asymmetry that standpoint theory entails, CRT's skepticism of truth itself raises questions about why the perspectives of people of color should be considered true. Moreover, even if we ignore the question of truth, it is unclear why deference would be given to minority voices, given CRT's claim that power and interests rather than moral considerations drive issues of race and law. Notwithstanding the foregoing questions,

---

43   Witte, *The Blessings of Liberty*, 301.
44   Ibid., 301–02.
45   Ibid., 302.
46   See note 32 above.
47   Robert S. Chang, "Toward an Asian American Legal Scholarship: Critical Race Theory, Post-Structuralism, and Narrative Space," *California Law Review* 81, no. 5 (1993): 1243–1323, at 1280. Reflecting the importance of standpoint epistemology, Athena Mutua includes as a tenet of CRT "recognition of both the experiential knowledge and critical consciousness of people of color in understanding law and society." Athena D. Mutua, "The Rise, Development and Future Directions of Critical Race Theory and Related Scholarship," *Denver Law Review* 84 (2006): 329–94, at 354.

the deference for which CRT calls is clearly distinct from a robust debate among proponents of differing views.

While the status of truth in CRT arguably undermines any argument that could be made on behalf of deference to perspectives of color, for reasons alluded to above, CRT casts doubt on the notion that robust debate will secure moral truth on questions of race and law. Specifically, given the unequal distribution of power among groups and their unequal influence over our society's institutions, even if we assume the view that rational analysis (and therefore debate) enables us to better approximate truth, CRT's claim that interests and power rather than truth and justice drive law may prove correct. In other words, it may be that in our society, the interests of the powerful tend to eclipse truth and justice and therefore the specific requirements of racial justice. However, as the next part argues, even if in our society interests tend to prevail over justice, the Christian tradition and the thought of Martin Luther King Jr. suggest that the solution to the reduction of law to power and interests is the elevation of truth, not the embrace of a philosophical outlook that abandons truth and thereby undermines the foundations of justice claims.

5 Overcoming Reductionism: Preserving Truth through Agape Love

This final part tentatively suggests that taken together, John's work and CRT indicate that scholarship at the intersection of race, law, and Christianity should take seriously Martin Luther King Jr.'s understanding that fostering a society and legal system capable of being faithful to truth entails a turn to the Christian virtue of agape love and the corresponding capacity to rise above the racial interests that CRT sees as driving issues of race and law. As a result, it may be possible to escape the reduction of race and law issues to power and politics.

It is fitting to begin this brief discussion with a statement about King's fundamental outlook on moral truth and epistemic skepticism. As King scholar and Black church historian David V. Lewis notes, "[f]or King, any 'relative attitude' toward truth or 'right and wrong' constituted a revolt 'against the very laws of God himself.'"[48] Moreover, "[w]hen King spoke of the arc of the moral universe bending toward justice, he also had in mind the long arc of truth, for

---

48 Lewis V. Baldwin, *The Arc of Truth: The Thinking of Martin Luther King, Jr.*, Kindle edition (Minneapolis: Fortress Press, 2022), 67, quoting Clayborne Carson, Peter Holloran, and Ralph E. Luker, eds., *The Papers of Martin Luther King, Jr.* (Berkeley: University of California Press, 1992–2014), 2:252.

love and justice were for him dimensions and/or expressions of the activity of truth."[49] King also lamented the onset of postmodernism and its rejection of absolute truth.[50] On the other hand, King held that perceptions of truth could vary among individuals and groups, and that "truth is the whole."[51] In this respect, King embraced a notion of "experiential truth" that (without embracing epistemic skepticism) can accommodate CRT's claim that victims of racism possess experiential knowledge that nonvictims do not.[52] But King nonetheless maintained an unambiguous commitment to the existence of objective truth.

In addition, consistent with a historicized, contextual vision of rights that are nonetheless grounded in moral truths, King rejected a "static" conception of truth in favor of truth as an "unfolding process."[53] This dynamic, historical conception of truth allowed for "new truths" or discovery and learning.[54] Indeed, for King, this historical, dynamic approach to truth accords with his understanding of revelation. Specifically, God is truth, and God is continuously working and revealing Himself in history; truth is therefore progressively revealed in history.[55]

For King, love, which is bound up with truth, is the ultimate key to reality. It is, in the language of philosophy, the highest good.[56] With Gandhi, King believed that commitment to truth entails a commitment to love and, therefore, nonviolence.[57] As important, truth, love, and nonviolence are not mere propositions or principles of discourse. They constitute a way of life in which a person stands and comes into a more complete, fuller sense of truth, love, and nonviolence.[58] Moreover, in contrast to embracing the sufficiency of an analysis focused on power relations and interests, King believed that an ethic of interests was the greatest threat to lives lived according to truth.[59] He held

---

49 Baldwin, *The Arc of Truth*, XVIII.
50 Ibid., 68.
51 Ibid., 69, quoting Martin Luther King Jr., *Stride Toward Freedom: The Montgomery Story* (New York: Harper, 1958), 101.
52 Ibid., 70.
53 Ibid., 69.
54 Ibid., 69.
55 Baldwin, *The Arc of Truth*, 80, quoting Carson, Holloran, and Luker, *The Papers of Martin Luther King, Jr.*, 6:78, 118.
56 Baldwin, *The Arc of Truth*, 89.
57 Ibid., 89.
58 Ibid., 10, 48, 89.
59 Ibid., 89–91.

that living according to truth requires people to put agape love—an ethic of seeking the good of others—at the center of their lives.[60]

If CRT is correct that the perceived self-interests of white Americans drive issues of race and law, it goes without saying that actors who work to implement such interests have not put agape love at the center of their lives, for love seeks the good of others. On the other hand, CRT's embrace of postmodern philosophy and its destabilization of moral truth claims violates one of King's cardinal principles—that the end is preexistent in the means.[61] Applied in the context of democratic deliberation and legal scholarship, King's view that means and ends are inseparable entails that the moral truth of ending racial subordination will not be achieved by the means of abandoning moral truth itself. To the contrary, following King, the means of denying objective truth in favor of reducing law and rights to interests prefigures the end that, on issues of race, law and rights will continue in the morally impoverished condition that CRT describes.

Although for King truth and love are ultimately to be achieved as a way of life and therefore require a moral transformation of individuals and ultimately collective life,[62] King values reason as a way of apprehending truth.[63] Moreover, because he identifies truth with the "whole," it is clear that King would welcome John's vision of an inclusive, robust debate among different moral communities. On the other hand, King does not limit the identification of truth to discursive reason but identifies with Gandhi's notion that truth is also obtained through practical experimentation, including the belief that experience demonstrates that violent means have failed to produce a better world.[64]

However, it is important to note that historically, rights and moral insight have sometimes occurred in the wake of bitter, even violent struggle, as John's work attests.[65] Although rights have sometimes developed or even expanded in the wake of violence, one can question whether violence was necessary. One can even examine the degree to which newly articulated or granted rights have been honored. But here we can set these questions aside. To the extent that we are engaged in democratic deliberation and legal scholarship, we are ostensibly engaged in achieving change through persuasive rather than military power. But as King's work as a minister and human rights activist

---

60   Ibid., 91.
61   King, "Love, Law, and Civil Disobedience," in *A Testament of Hope*, 45.
62   Baldwin, *The Arc of Truth*, 1.
63   Ibid., 89.
64   Paradise, "How Critical Race Theory Marginalizes the African American Christian Tradition," 202.
65   Witte, *The Blessings of Liberty*, 76–104.

demonstrates, democratic engagement is not necessarily limited to discourse alone. As a result, if the emerging discipline of Christianity, race, and law takes King's teachings seriously, while it should resist the impulse to answer such brute-interest seeking with denials of objective truth, future work should examine what it means not only to draw on the Christian tradition but also to see scholarship as a vehicle of ministry that bears witness to truth within a larger context of democratic life.

6 Conclusion

This chapter has argued that John Witte, Jr.'s capacious vision of the field of law and religion, his defense of welcoming religious values in lawmaking and legal scholarship, and his understanding of rights as middle axioms of political discourse can inform the theoretical foundation of the emerging field of Christianity, race, and law. In particular, John's work has helped to create discursive space for religious values in legal scholarship and articulates a historicized, contextual conception of rights that can incorporate CRT's teachings on the importance of power and interest to issues of race and law, while simultaneously preserving the commitment to moral truth that is essential to mainstream Christian thought. The chapter has also argued that, in light of CRT's work showing that race and law issues are more frequently shaped by power and interests than by rational analysis, Martin Luther King Jr.'s understanding that truth is apprehended through a way of life and not discourse alone is a helpful complement to relying on robust debate among different moral communities as a means of securing truth and justice.

PART 3

Faith, Law, and Freedom Historically and Today

CHAPTER 17

Human Dignity and the Christian Foundations of Law and Liberty

Andrea Pin

> There are no *ordinary* people.
> You have never talked to a mere mortal.
> [I]t is immortals whom we joke with,
> work with, marry, snub, and exploit.[1]

∴

1 Introduction

Two opposite narratives have been built around the complex relationship between law and Christianity in historical perspective. On one hand stand those who see modernity and postmodernity as a rupture from the previous ages. Michel Villey and Paolo Grossi are two of the most prominent thinkers who have embraced this hermeneutic of rupture, noticing a steady decline in the interrelationship between law and Christianity through the centuries. Through different paths, and each at its own pace, most legal and political systems of the West would have distanced one from the other.[2] On the other hand stands another line of impressive scholars, including Harold Berman and Brian Tierney, who have dug into the ground of contemporary legal thinking, uncovering and retrieving the religious sources of today's Western legal thought.[3]

---

1 C. S. Lewis, *The Weight of Glory* (New York: Harper One, 1949), 46.
2 Michel Villet, *La Formation de la Pensée Juridique Moderne* (Paris: PUF, 2006); and Paolo Grossi, *Mitologie Giuridiche della Modernità* (Milano: Giuffré, 2001, 2005, and 2007).
3 Harold J. Berman, *Law and Revolution: The Formation of the Western Legal Tradition* (Cambridge, MA: Harvard University Press, 1983); id., *Law and Revolution II: The Impact of the Protestant Reformations on the Western Legal Tradition* (Cambridge, MA: Harvard University Press, 2003); and Brian Tierney, *Religion, Law and the Growth of Constitutional Thought, 1150–1650* (Cambridge: Cambridge University Press, 1982).

This strand of thinking traces back in history notions and mechanisms that still shape the law.

Within the academic circles that read the trajectory of legal history as a rupture from the past, scholars are also divided between those who mourn the end of Christian culture and those who welcome secularization. Some have read the legal developments of modernity as the progressive liberation of humankind from Christian shackles. In Christopher McCrudden's mocking terms, "the bare bones of an 'orthodox' narrative" of rupture would be that "in the beginning was the Enlightenment which led to the American and French Revolutions, which led in turn to the adoption of human rights as a necessary part of modernity."[4] On the other extreme of the academic spectrum that believes in this rupture, some complain that modernity lost most of the values that the premodern era cherished. Opinions vary also about the degree to which the contemporary age has betrayed or is in keeping with its origins. The scholars who believe that the Western world is almost irredeemable because it lost connection with its ancestry disagree with those who are of the view that the break from the past is not sufficient. However, whether this sort of scholars mourn the past, celebrate postmodernity, or want to push secularization further, they all agree on a basic fact: the end of Christendom, as Chantal Delsol recently called it. In a few words, they all believe that our age has repudiated the four components of Christian civilization: truth, hierarchy, authority, and constraint.[5]

John Witte, Jr.'s scholarship hardly fits with either the camp of those nostalgic about the past or those who hail secularization. He is safely within the field of those who believe that there is a strong and healthy connection between the past and the present—that contemporary ideas about the law, legal values, and politics in the West are imbued with the past. Despite this positive reading of history, however, he has never turned a blind eye to what he believes to be among the fundamental legal challenges of our time, nor has he overlooked the flaws and the shortcomings of the Christian legacy. Sometimes he has been explicitly critical of the Christian tradition—his tradition—when he believed that it was wrong. But he has always tried to keep a bird's eye on contemporary developments by looking at them in light of the longstanding tradition. He has not simply argued that contemporary Western civilization owes a lot of its achievements to its religious past—that religion occupies a primary place in the genealogy of rights. His scholarship rather sheds light on

---

4 Christopher McCrudden, "Human Rights Histories," *Oxford Journal of Legal Studies* 35 (2015): 179–212, at 182.
5 Chantal Delsol, *La Fin de la Chrétienté* (Paris: Les Éditions du Cerf, 2021), 17.

contemporary issues precisely by taking a look at the past.[6] For Witte, the past does not always have a normative dimension; but it is always teaching us something. In his capable hands, legal history—especially the kind that combines religious and secular perspectives on laws—has a hermeneutic value, not a justificatory one.[7]

Faith and the family in the West have drawn much of Witte's attention for a conjunction of reasons, some of which this chapter investigates. Faith and family are among the main pillars on which he has built much of his understanding of Christianity and the Western legal tradition. As Witte has persuasively shown, they are the social, cultural, and legal environments in which human beings find meaning and a place for themselves as well as for those around them. In a nutshell, they are the primary institutions through which human beings become self-aware and aware of others, as they respond to the very basic human need to belong and to experience loving and being loved.[8]

Witte's studies in religion and the family have thus contributed to an increasingly neglected aspect of the crucial constitutional notion of human dignity: the need for humans to socialize and create bonds. By looking at what protects, nurtures, and educates human beings, Witte has in fact uncovered the relational angle of human dignity.

This chapter identifies the standard narrative of modernity and secularization on human dignity and how Witte's scholarship challenges that narrative. To exemplify—and criticize—the conflict between a secular and a religious reading of human dignity, the chapter then briefly considers post-World War II's constitutional settings and the judicial reasoning that has authorized euthanasia in some jurisdictions in recent years. After focusing on the key role of religion and family in nurturing a sense of the dignity of human beings, the chapter concludes with observing that Witte's scholarship stands out for its compelling arguments in favor of religions and the family without being blindly complacent about either.

---

6 McCrudden, "Human Rights Histories," 180.
7 John Witte, Jr., introduction to *Christianity and Human Rights: An Introduction*, ed. John Witte, Jr. and Frank S. Alexander (Cambridge: Cambridge University Press, 2010), 13. See further id., *God's Joust, God's Justice: Law and Religion in the Western Tradition* (Grand Rapids: Eerdmans, 2006), 1–30, 460–65, setting out his theory of history.
8 See esp. John Witte, Jr., *From Sacrament to Contract: Marriage, Religion, and Law in the Western Tradition*, 2nd ed. (Louisville, KY: Westminster John Knox Press, 2012); id., *Church, State, and Family: Reconciling Traditional Teachings and Modern Liberties* (Cambridge: Cambridge University Press, 2019). See further the chapter herein by Helen M. Alvaré.

2 God, Dignity, and Modernity: Challenging the Mainstream

With the rise of dignity as a key legal concept in the twentieth century, a stream of scholarly and judicial rumination on this topic has almost flooded the field of constitutional studies. Such a pervasive concept has not led to a shared understanding of human dignity, however. Many commentators now believe that human dignity has become a sort of signpost—a symbol that refers to the essence of human beings but largely fails to capture it.[9] Instead of simplifying and clarifying the debate about rights and the necessity of protecting them, narratives of human dignity now abound, often conflict, and even contradict each other, blurring the contents and contours of the concept as well as of the human rights that the notion is supposed to cover.

A large consensus has developed around the belief that the notion of dignity has sidelined religion, putting human beings at the center of the legal and political edifice and depriving legal reasoning of a transcendent dimension. In her influential book, Catherine Dupré embraces the usual—if not the standard—narrative about the historical development of dignity, which largely overlaps with the one criticized by McCrudden. In her view, dignity took off slowly but steadily with the birth of modernity in Europe: intellectual titans prepared the ground for the widespread awareness about the necessity of protecting human beings that arose from the ashes of World War II. Dupré identifies the pivotal figures and moments of the multicentury legal journey that dignity as a legal concept underwent, from Pico della Mirandola to the French Revolution and Immanuel Kant. She argues that it was largely because of the contribution of these thinkers and the cultural and political turmoil that decapitated the French king, that the concept of dignity acquired a new, modern meaning. Perhaps even more important, through this journey the concept took on a secularized, horizontal meaning and was deprived of its once largely transcendent value. "[D]ignity does not proceed from God, it is not a quality given by God to man as a divine creation and creature," she writes. On the contrary, "dignity proceeds from man's inner worth and his unique ability to set his own ends, namely, to make his own laws."[10] This understanding of dignity is traceable within Pico's *De Dignitate Hominis* (1496), which magnified the capacity of individuals to make their own destiny, and later peaked with Immanuel Kant, whom also John Rawls celebrated as the main innovator in

---

9   Christopher McCrudden, "Human Dignity and Judicial Interpretation of Human Rights," *European Journal of International Law* 19 (2008): 655–724, at 678.
10 Catherine Dupré, *The Age of Dignity: Human Rights and Constitutionalism in Europe* (Oxford: Hart, 2015), 35.

the development of the subject. For Rawls, Kant clarified that "the ground of dignity is the capacity to make universal law and to act from the principle of autonomy. This autonomy reflects the autonomy (or the supremacy) of pure practical reason."[11]

This reading of dignity does not just make the reference to God useless. Such a narrative of secularization even rules out any divine foundation or reading of dignity as plainly incompatible with its modern and contemporary developments. In fact, for Catherine Dupré, "a constitutional definition of human dignity" becomes "ontologically incompatible with a religious definition." This is not just a matter for philosophers and theologians to debate. "This incompatibility," she writes,

> goes to the heart of European constitutionalism, which is based on the paradigm that democracy is about taking the ultimate political power away from God and his or her representative on earth to give it to human beings. It is the rejection of God from the political equation that historically made it possible to turn human beings into citizens and actors in their political destiny.[12]

In a few words, by choosing constitutions, modernity repudiated God and human submission to Him.[13]

3   Misunderstanding History, Law, and Religion

Reading legal history as a clash between a religious understanding of dignity that praised passivity and submission to God, on one hand, and a horizontal, purely immanent reading of dignity that liberated humankind, on the other, is dubious from a biblical point of view. As Rabbi Joseph Soloveitchik once noted, the idea of human beings as submissive hardly squares with the Jewish Bible: when the Psalmist praises God for having made man "a little lower than the angels," crowning him with honor and dignity, he celebrates "man's capability of dominating his environment and exercising control over it."[14] Even

---

11   John Rawls and Barbara Herman, *Lectures on the History of Moral Philosophy* (Cambridge, MA: Harvard University Press, 2000), 210.
12   Dupré, *The Age of Dignity*, 19.
13   Remo Bodei, *Dominio e Sottomissione* (Bologna: il Mulino, 2019), 221.
14   Joseph P. Soloveitchik, *The Lonely Man of Faith* (New York: Random House, 1965 and 2006), 14–15.

the selection of pivotal figures that would have heralded the modern, secular understanding of human dignity is debatable. As Michael Rosen noted, the "Kantian man is not cut off from God by an act of proud disobedience against a perceived tyrant, but, to the contrary, is essentially tied to him."[15]

Understanding modern dignity purely in secular and horizontal terms also betrays the complexities and dismembers the holistic approach that projected the idea of human dignity on a global scale in the second half of the twentieth century. In the early 1950s, Charles Malik, a member of the committee that drafted the Universal Declaration of Human Rights and an outspoken supporter of the idea of including human dignity within the text, asked himself "What is the ultimate trouble with the world today?"—only to reply, "It is the loss of the dimension of transcendence."[16]

Pitting modernity against premodernity under the prism of secularization is misleading also from a legal point of view, as it hardly squares with the reality of written constitutions that first employed the notion of human dignity. The document that has garnered the reputation for kicking off the success of dignity as a constitutional concept after World War II is the Basic Law of the German Federal Republic (1949), which is still in force and famously enshrines the concept of human dignity in Article 1. Interestingly, the Preamble to the Basic Law begins by stating that Germans were "Conscious of their responsibility before God and man." The best known instantiation of human dignity as a constitutional concept thus did not pit a secular against a religious reading of dignity, but actually hosted both.

The divorce between the transcendent and the material dimension of human dignity eventually happened in several jurisdictions. But this process developed rather late in modernity and postmodernity, and selectively picked some aspects of the notion while overlooking others. In British as well as Canadian courts, for instance, there is evidence of the dissociation between the secular and religious component of dignity in cases that have dealt with euthanasia and assisted suicide.[17] The religious component of dignity is often expressed through the notion of "sanctity" and identifies the intangibility of human life. Sanctity is thus juxtaposed to the concept of dignity, which signifies

---

15 Michael Rosen, *The Shadow of God* (Cambridge, MA: Belknap Press of Harvard University Press, 2022), 193.
16 Charles Malik, "The Near East: The Search for Truth," *Foreign Affairs* 30 (1952): 255–64, at 264.
17 *Airedale NHS Trust v Bland* [1993] AC 789; *R (on the application of Nicklinson and another) (Appellants) v Ministry of Justice (Respondent), et al* [2014] UKSC 38; *Rodriguez v British Columbia* [1993] 3 SCR 519; *Carter v Canada* [2015] 1 SCR 331.

the human right to make fundamental decisions about oneself, including the control over one's bodily life.

The selective narrative that pits sanctity against dignity is both the cause and the consequence of the scholarship that pits modern and postmodern rights against those of earlier times.[18] Distinguishing sanctity from dignity, in fact, magnifies the gap between an understanding of dignity as untouchable and one that prizes individual autonomy, thereby corroborating the impression that Western legal history translates in terms of dissociation between the secular and the religious planes.

John Witte's viewpoint could not be further from this approach. He does not survey history—and especially legal history—looking for signs of human liberation from legal constraints and from servitude to God. Using a metaphor, he has insisted that the Western tradition has seen the *genesis* of rights "in the accounts of human nature and natural order," as taught by religious and nonreligious texts of antiquity. The *exodus* phase marked the transition of "primordial rights and liberties in the gradual development of public, private, penal, and procedural rights and liberties for individuals and groups set out in legal, canonical, and other authoritative texts." Finally, the *deuteronomy* "of rights and liberties in modern times" peaked with the Universal Declaration of Human Rights in 1948.[19]

What Witte particularly values in the long historical process that led human societies into modernity and then postmodernity, however, is the insistence on human liberty. A great deal of his scholarship, after all, focuses on the historical roots of liberty as modernity understands it. In particular, he acknowledges the historical importance of Protestantism in calling "for full freedom ... freedom of the individual conscience ... freedom of political officials from clerical power and privilege.... 'Freedom of the Christian' was the rallying cry of the early Protestant reformation."[20] The problem, of course, is what the West has made of such a great deal of liberty.

---

18   Timothy P. Jackson, *Political Agape: Christian Love and Liberal Democracy* (Grand Rapids: Eerdmans, 2015), 88–95, reflects on the dissociation between "sanctity" and "dignity" and links sanctity back to religious thinking. See further the chapter by Timothy P. Jackson herein.

19   John Witte, Jr., *The Blessings of Liberty* (Cambridge: Cambridge University Press, 2021), 290.

20   John Witte, Jr., *Faith, Freedom, and Family: New Essays on Law and Religion,* ed. Norman Doe and Gary S. Hauk (Tübingen: Mohr Siebeck, 2021), 67.

4 The Image of God and the Nature of Man

Assisted suicide and euthanasia are particularly thorny issues. It is therefore little or no surprise that it was within such contexts that a gap between sanctity and dignity developed. After all, the sense of untouchability of human life and the need to pursue the self-determination of the individual were probably bound to collide in such areas. The emphasis on personal autonomy and the necessity of clearing the way for individuals to make their own independent choices, however, is traceable much more widely.

The issue of autonomy has occupied gigantic intellectuals of the twentieth century, such as Joseph Raz. Raz argued that, although distinctions can be drawn between liberalism and individualism, the two historically "grew together." In fact, he added, "people's well-being is promoted by having an autonomous life."[21] In the twenty-first century, Francis Fukuyama similarly noted that "[l]iberal societies confer rights on individuals, the most fundamental of which is the right to autonomy, that is, the ability to make choices."[22] Nowadays, influential constitutional theories often understand rights as instrumental to individual autonomy. Rights—the argument goes—would leverage "the importance for autonomous persons of being able to choose one's intimate partners, utter one's political views, and control what happens to one's body, and take ... the importance of these interests as the reason for protecting them."[23]

For the detractors of such a logic, the emphasis on the autonomy of human beings and the process of secularization have developed hand in hand to the extent that they have become indissociable. The shift from a transcendent to a horizontal notion of dignity complements an individualized version of dignity, and together they make up the hallmark of late modernity and postmodernity. "[P]lacing the individual in the centre of political attention" would be a characteristic of our times, and would have "contributed to the emergence of the self-centered individuals."[24] The contemporary legal language, loaded with an endless and ever-expanding list of rights and extreme individualism, would belong to a secularized world.

---

21   Joseph Raz, *The Morality of Freedom* (Oxford: Oxford University Press, 1986), 17 and 198.
22   Francis Fukuyama, *Liberalism and Its Discontents* (New York: Farrar, Straus, and Giroux, 2022), 1.
23   Kai Moeller, *The Global Model of Constitutional Rights* (Oxford: Oxford University Press, 2012), 57.
24   J. H. H. Weiler, "Deciphering the Political and Legal DNA of European Integration: An Exploratory Essay," in *Philosophical Foundations of European Union Law*, ed. Julie Dickson and Pavlos Eleftheriadis (Oxford: Oxford University Press, 2012), 158.

John Witte has taken issue with both these narratives throughout his scholarly work.[25] By uncovering the legacy of key legal and political concepts and institutions, he has shed light not just on the limits of pitting modernity and postmodernity against the past, but also on how lively and useful the past is for understanding and living a full life in the twenty-first century. He is neither optimistic because the West abandoned religion and the moral values and traditions that come with it, nor pessimistic because those values cannot be retrieved. Without any nostalgia for the past, he has provided his readers and the public with fresh perspectives on which battles are worth fighting—and which resources the West still has in its pocket. On two resources he has put special attention, often emphasizing their mutual relationships: faith and the family.

5 The Secular Legacy of Christianity

John Rawls famously addressed the place of religion in the public sphere later in his life, when he argued that religiosity could survive modernity and postmodernity, but needed to be confined to specific precincts. In his view,

> Political liberalism does not dismiss spiritual questions as unimportant, but to the contrary, because of their importance, it leaves them for each citizen to decide for himself or herself. This is not to say that religion is somehow "privatized"; instead, it is not "politicized" (that is, perverted or diminished for ideological ends). The division of labor between political and social institutions, on the one hand, and civic society with its many and diverse associations (religious and secular), on the other, is fully maintained.[26]

What Rawls appended to his earlier theories has actually been at the forefront of Witte's scholarship. But Witte's argument is more daring and comprehensive than Rawls's later belief. Witte does not simply argue that social life must accept religious people and religiosity as part of society, lest such individuals be cut off from it. He rather argues that there should be room for religious people, and for Christians in the West in particular, because there is room—and, in fact, need—for religion and its spirit in today's legal discourse.

---

25 Witte, *The Blessings of Liberty*, 291.
26 John Rawls, *The Law of Peoples with "The Idea of Public Reason Revisited"* (Cambridge, MA: Harvard University Press, 2003), 127.

Witte indirectly calls on Christians *qua* Christians to participate at a time when the dominant liberalism can become harmful. On a variety of levels, Christianity in the West can stimulate personal and social awareness, especially about one specific fact: that human beings are relational. They do not simply focus on themselves. They partake in a bigger picture, and Christianity can remind them of this. Faith can nurture among people a sophisticated sense of their "moral duties" toward the transcendent and of the "duties of love" toward the neighbor. Taking care of people means heeding their call as well as the call that comes from God, as Witte clarified when he wrapped up his spectacular legal analysis of the Protestant Reformation. He then emphasized Martin Luther's view that "[f]reedoms and commandments, rights and duties, belong together in Luther's formulation. To speak of one without the other is ultimately destructive. Rights without duties to guide them quickly become claims of self-indulgence. Duties without rights to discharge them quickly become sources of deep guilt."[27]

This mutually sustaining framework of horizontal human relationships among peers and a vertical dynamic with their creator does not simply suggest a Christian twist to contemporary legal systems. It is not an intellectual tool that tries to reconcile modern and postmodern Christians with the place they inhabit while causing no harm to the rest of the society by balancing modern rights with Christian duties. Thanks to his excavations in legal history, Witte has persuasively argued that rights claims themselves can be seen as embodying love of God and neighbors.[28] Rights, after all, are the offspring of centuries-long intellectual developments that are rooted in religious thinking, which have given legal substance to the duty to take care of oneself and of anyone else. Religious values have morphed into a web of legal claims and devices. Legal systems of the West are not just capable of accommodating religious needs: they exude religious culture.

John Witte's line of reasoning does not defend Christianity against modernity. He is actually defending modernity and postmodernity by reclaiming its true nature. Witte thus does not subscribe to the idea that liberalism failed as a political and philosophical project,[29] or that the language of rights should

---

27 John Witte, Jr., *Law and Protestantism: The Legal Teachings of the Lutheran Reformation* (Cambridge: Cambridge University Press, 2002), 302.
28 *The Blessings of Liberty*, 297.
29 Patrick J. Deneen, *Why Liberalism Failed* (New Haven: Yale University Press, 2018).

be rejected[30] or replaced with a focus on the common good.[31] Such theories are critical of the logic, the language, and the institutional frameworks that modernity generated, as they would inevitably harm traditional communities and values. In Patrick Deneen's words, "the underpinnings of our inherited civilized order—norms learned in families, in communities, through religion and a supporting culture—would inevitably erode under the influence of the liberal social and political state."[32]

On the contrary, Witte's argument is that there is room to improve the status of Western civilization by retrieving its religious roots. In his work, arguing in favor of religion and for a public role of religions is defending modernity, not undermining it or fantasizing about an alternative universe where Pico, the French Revolution, or Kant never materialized. Retrieving the true nature of liberalism is retrieving a role for religions. Religion and modernity should not be pitted one against the other—they can mutually sustain each other.

Make no mistake. John Witte's understanding of faith and the legal and political institutions that it brought about does not equate to a blank check for religious discourse and institutions. Religion does not always shed light on darkness—it may also project darkness, blinding people to their own experience and to people's dignity. His appraisal of the religious contribution to secular law and to the Western world more broadly includes what he has called a healthy "hermeneutic of confession:" a process through which religions take responsibility for the horrible, painful mistakes that they made in the past and may continue to make.[33]

Professor Witte calls for religious people to engage in such a hermeneutic of confession, as he once made it plain when he explained how he came to reflect on the longstanding tradition of penalizing illegitimate children:

> "Bastards have no place in this assembly of the Lord; even to the tenth generation none of his descendants may enter here." That was the startling admonition that I heard from the pulpit of the conservative Protestant church of my youth. These harsh words ... were intoned gravely as the final public step of banishing a single woman and her illegitimate child from our church. Even as a youth, I remember being shocked.... How could the church banish this little baby and withhold from him the

---

30 Nigel Biggar, *What's Wrong with Rights?* (New York: Oxford University Press, 2020).
31 Adrian Vermeule, *Common Good Constitutionalism* (Cambridge: Polity Press, 2022).
32 Deneen, *Why Liberalism Failed*, XII.
33 Witte, introduction to *Christianity and Human Rights*, 13.

sacrament of baptism? [W]hat would come of my little foster-brother, Robert, given his illegitimate birth? Surely, he would be banished soon, too. I remember being terrified.[34]

This painful memory cuts across two decisive aspects of John Witte's scholarship: the role of faith and that of family, the institutions around which the life of people has gravitated for millennia. Borrowing from the marvelous Neibuhr brothers, Witte's scholarship on faith and the family is a profound reminder that "we cannot make individual liberty as unqualifiedly the end of life as our ideology asserts,"[35] because "[w]e have not chosen to be social beings, immeasurably dependent on our fellows, nor have we chosen our culture; we have come to consciousness in a society and among established human works."[36]

6 Communities of Faith

One of the reasons for being optimistic about the future of religions in postmodern times is their necessity. If globalization and the global market of the twenty-first century are gone by now, what has remained is the mentality that they shaped. Michael Sandel's exploration of what he has called the *Tyranny of Merit* describes a social structure that is obsessed with economic success, career achievements, and social recognition[37]—a toxic environment that measures human worthiness by purely horizontal metrics. Although Sandel targets the United States, many more are the countries and societies that fit the picture quite perfectly.

In an atmosphere saturated with competition, there is hardly a more important institution than religion and religiosity. The late Chief Rabbi Jonathan Sacks put it adamantly when he wrote in the early 2000s that

> the global market tends to reduce all things to economic terms. Religion offers a different kind of solace. It speaks of the dignity of the person and the power of the human spirit. It tells us that we are more, or other,

---

34 John Witte, Jr., *The Sins of the Fathers: The Law and Theology of Illegitimacy Reconsidered* (Cambridge: Cambridge University Press, 2009), XI.

35 Reinhold Niebuhr, *The Irony of American History* (1952), Italian trans. *L'Ironia della Storia Americana*, ed. Alessandro Aresu (Milano: Bompiani, 2012), 174.

36 H. Richard Niebuhr, *Christ and Culture* (San Francisco: Harper, 1996), 250.

37 Michael J. Sandel, *The Tyranny of Merit* (New York: Farrar, Straus, and Giroux, 2020), 12–13.

than what we earn or what we buy. In the fast-moving world economy there are winners and losers. Life takes on a ruthless, Darwinian struggle for survival. Religion reminds us that there are other sources of self-worth. We are not necessarily set against one another in a win-or-lose competition.[38]

John Witte's decades-long defense of religion and religious freedom is analogously based on anthropological premises. In Witte's writing, religion gives shape to the personal and collective quest for truth and meaning—from an intellectual as well as existential point of view. Religion provides people with a moral compass. It proposes to them a virtuous life. Most interestingly, it provides people with a transcending social context—a dimension that the early stage of dignity in the twentieth century had crystal clear. Religious institutions cannot subsist as self-centered: religions connect generations, cut across time and space, and project themselves and their peoples to a plane that is beyond human control.

What makes the contribution of religions to human dignity so unique is both their horizontal and their vertical components. Their horizontal aspect surfaces in their institutions: they have legal orders; they set obligations and rights; they have judicial procedures; they devise ways of redress against injustice. But all these aspects find roots in their vertical component—in their reference to the ultimate being.

Witte's scholarship is extremely careful in keeping both the vertical and horizontal components of religions within the picture. He certainly values religious legal orders and their institutional dimensions more broadly—but he never embraces a merely cultural understanding of religion and religious values. Religions' importance and relevance are inseparable from their vertical claim. They are statements about what is worth pursuing, living, and dying for.

His focus on the transcendent dimension of religion is also critical because it embeds the importance of personal liberty—one of the most necessary and yet difficult achievements among religions. It is only by respecting and valuing personal liberty that religions can nurture the vertical dimension that constitutes them. Understanding them as cultural infrastructures betrays their role and overlooks the importance of personal freedom in embracing or denying religious truths: religions can force people into their horizontal dimension, but certainly not into their vertical one.

---

38   Jonathan Sacks, *The Dignity of Difference* (London: Bloomsbury, 2002), 39.

7   The Secular Meaning of Family

One of the main preoccupations that have kept John Witte busy for decades is the role of the family in historical and contemporary societies. He is interested in protecting the family for the goods it embeds, nurtures, and aspires to achieve, as "the essential components of family life and the ethical and cultural values that they represent are among the most salient questions in modern Western culture and liberal societies."[39] Neither an ethereal institution detached from reality, nor a culturally shaped particular deprived of spiritual or legal significance, the family is the cornerstone of polities.

Balancing freedom with belonging is also one of Witte's core preoccupations within the field of family law. The contractual component of marriage, about which he has written so frequently, is much more than a metaphor. The idea of contract within marriage fleshes out two necessary components of marriage: the personal adhesion to a set of obligations and rights, and the participation in a partnership that has its own rules, habits, priorities, and goods.[40] Freedom does not saturate marriage relations; but it is the only way to access them.

Witte's magnum opus against polygamy is a pivotal example of his efforts to retrieve a conceptually thick understanding of family that does not overlook the importance of liberty.[41] He acknowledges that "exponential changes in modern Western family laws have been, in no small part, valiant efforts to bring greater freedom, choice, and equality to public and private life."[42] While developments in the United States and in the West more generally have expanded the notion of marriage and family, Witte's tour de force survey from antiquity to modernity's option for monogamy forcefully argues that the notions of marriage and family have boundaries. They simply do not stretch as much as the notion of freedom suggests they should. Freedom itself, he argues, must not be taken in an abstract way. Polygamous marriages are hardly the offspring of free wills of individuals that encounter each other and match on equal grounds. They are born of unequal partners and generate slavery.

Marriage is just one—big—piece of a broader picture in Witte's body of scholarship on family. Protecting family as such means protecting the very

---

[39]   Joseph E. David, *Kinship, Law, and Politics: An Anatomy of Belonging* (Cambridge: Cambridge University Press, 2020), 105.
[40]   John Witte, Jr., *Church, State and Family* (Cambridge: Cambridge University Press, 2019), 215–18.
[41]   John Witte, Jr., *The Western Case for Monogamy Over Polygamy* (Cambridge: Cambridge University Press, 2015).
[42]   *Church, State and Family*, 2.

possibility of human peaceful coexistence and mutual love among people outside the family. As Jonathan Sacks once noted:

> The universality of moral concern is not something we learn by being universal but by being particular. Because we know what it is to be a parent, loving our children, not children in general, we understand what it is for someone else, somewhere else, to be a parent, loving his or her children, not ours. There is no road to human solidarity that does not begin with moral particularity by coming to know what it means to be a child, a parent, a neighbour, a friend. We learn to love humanity by loving specific human beings. There is no short-cut.[43]

As an institution, the family does a critical job in making individuals reach beyond themselves. It fosters mutual care, appreciation, and respect within and across generations. It makes us discover and savor dependency. If contemporary understandings of dignity prioritize individual rights and autonomy,[44] families make it possible for human beings to discover that human dignity is not atomistic. The institution of family pushes us to understand our relational component in a very concrete, physical way: one that connects the intellect with the body, encompassing the wholeness of humanity. It is no surprise that Witte's book on the legal development of the practice and institution of adoption ends with a reminder: "children do much better when born and raised in intact marital homes."[45]

Because of its critical importance, the family needs protection—from both a cultural and a legal point of view. As Witte argued, "[h]uman families ... need broader communities and narratives to stabilize, deepen, and exemplify" their "natural inclinations and rational norms. They need models and exemplars of love and fidelity, trust and sacrifice, and commitment and community to give these natural teachings further content and coherence.... [T]hey depend ultimately on positive laws and procedures when needed."[46] After all, religion, family, and policies live or perish together, forming a triad within which people learn their own dignity, the dignity of others, and the normative dimension of dignity itself.

---

43   Sacks, *The Dignity of Difference*, 58.
44   Nicholas Aroney, "The Social Ontology of Human Dignity," in *The Inherence of Human Dignity, Foundations of Human Dignity*, vol. 1, ed. Angus J. L. Menuge and Barry W. Bussy (London: Anthem Press, 2021), 166.
45   *The Sins of the Fathers*, 184.
46   *Church, State and Family*, 9.

8 Conclusion: John the Heretic

John Witte's scholarly devotion to legal studies about Christianity and the family is rooted in an understanding of legal, political, and social life that values these subjects as fundamental for the survival and well-being of humans in the West. Almost certainly, he would agree that "law and public policy exist *for the protection and flourishing of persons.*"[47] Although very broad in its scope, this might sound as a typically conservative, even traditionalist, statement. Interestingly enough, however, Witte couples this view with a fairly optimistic view of the trajectory of law. If faith and family were among the cornerstones of Christianity and its law, they can also play a pivotal role today, as today's law is so indebted to the past.

In Witte's thinking there is no place for nostalgia. There is, however, a substantial amount of preoccupation. In his works he seems to argue that the law is not a self-sufficient framework that operates independently from human beings. Actually, law relies on human institutions and the willingness to keep up with fundamental values. Witte has insisted that the law in the West has not simply put boundaries and vested rights; it has also created obligations, stimulated care for others, and prompted individuals and groups to develop mutual relationships based on trust. John Witte's multidimensional understanding of human beings encourages an understanding of law that is also complex and multifaceted, and that invites collaborations among human beings. Law does not just provide goods; it also expects people to pursue justice and good for themselves and others.

Not being nostalgic does not mean being naive. John Witte is not convinced that legal progress is ineluctable and that the arc of history spontaneously and effortlessly bends toward justice without the need for people to bend it. In Witte's thinking, the future of Christianity and Western societies at large is in the hands of Christians themselves, as long as they accept living—and are accepted—as "members of pluralistic societies."[48] Thinkers like Rawls and Habermas put themselves to work at some point, he noted, to show that contemporary societies are capable of transcendency and of being able to accept religious discourse. Witte himself has shown why and how this is possible and even necessary.

---

47 O. Carter Snead, *What It Means to Be Human* (Cambridge, MA: Harvard University Press, 2020), 65.
48 *The Blessings of Liberty*, 301.

When Jeremy Waldron embarked on an analysis of John Locke's understanding of equality and its Christian roots, he was not driven merely by historical curiosity. "Our thinking—he wrote—is undeniably entangled with the issues of the day, and large parts of it ... are more or less inseparable from context, understandings, and political stakes that would not survive transposition to another time and place.... But we are also conscious that part of our discussion addresses something enduring."[49] John Witte, Jr. went beyond Waldron. He did not simply explore the past because there are permanent issues that make the past interesting to study. His works showcase that there is a legal and institutional continuity between today's West and its past–and that the West has made value-loaded choices, which is necessary to uncover to move forward.

How to move forward is a theme that John Witte, Jr. has been deeply concerned with, and to which he has contributed in his own way. Professor Witte has provided his readers with a vast array of considerations of a kind that, as he maintains, makes him "a Christian jurist and legal historian, not a Christian theologian or philosopher."[50] He seems very distant from the approach of legal and political theorists of the caliber of Carl Schmitt. Schmitt famously shed light on the religious legacy of the contemporary constitutional toolkit when he argued that constitutional concepts were secularized theological concepts that Christianity developed through the centuries. But Schmitt found continuity in concepts, not in Christianity. John Witte, on the contrary, believes that Christianity has a future—and that the future of the West is deeply intertwined with it.

Interestingly enough, for Witte, the future of Christianity in the West does not lie primarily in a smarter conceptualization of rights, freedoms, or the relationship between church and state. The future largely depends on social institutions—notably including religion and the family. Secular laws should protect such institutions, because these are the hubs within which human life meets its meaning, purpose, and unfolds, making human dignity thus tangible and visible.

Joseph Weiler once noted that through the "notion of human dignity ... [w]e all ask explicitly, or otherwise, what is the meaning of our being, of our existence. Of course, it is up to each of us, through our actions and emotions,

---

49   Jeremy Waldron, *God, Locke, and Equality* (Cambridge: Cambridge University Press, 2002), 8.
50   *The Blessings of Liberty*, 11.

to give meanings to our lives."[51] John Witte would probably agree with these words. He has forcefully argued that, by making room for religions and the family, the West can make room for the institutions that keep that question alive.

51　J. H. H. Weiler, "United in Fear—The Loss of Heimat and the Crises of Europe," in *Legitimacy Issues of the European Union in the Face of Crisis: Dimitris Tsatsos in Memoriam*, ed. Lina Papadopoulou et al. (Baden-Baden: Nomos, 2017), 362.

CHAPTER 18

Calvinism and the Logic of Self-Defense: Rights, Religion, and Revolution

David Little

1   Introduction

One of John Witte's distinctive contributions to the study of law and religion, among many others, is fixing attention on the role of rights and religion in the history of resistance and revolution in the Western tradition. To some degree, his views run against the stream. Scholars like Leo Strauss have, as Witte says, famously asserted that before the Enlightenment, the word "right" was used exclusively in an objective sense to mean "rightly ordered" as part of a hierarchical system of social and political status and duty. Only when "secular thinkers," such as Thomas Hobbes and John Locke, came along did the idea of "subjective rights," understood as individual or personal entitlements representing a radical challenge to hierarchical order, gain acceptance.[1] Other scholars, Witte points out, have long believed that "early modern Calvinist theories of resistance provided important counterweights to the political absolutism of Jean Bodin, James I, and their followers," but they have "usually overdrawn the distinction between Calvinist and other Protestant traditions of resistance, and have ignored the theories of fundamental rights and social contract developed by early modern Calvinist writers."[2]

Against such accounts, Witte calls attention to a "Protestant logic of revolution" that "was built in part on the familiar legal doctrine of legitimate self-defense,"[3] and that existed well in advance of the Enlightenment and outside of Calvinism, even if many Calvinists were among its most enthusiastic advocates. It is that logic, he claims, that has "driven French, Dutch, Scottish, and English revolutionaries in the sixteenth and seventeenth centuries to throw off their tyrannical oppressors in protection of their fundamental rights. It was in

---

1   John Witte, Jr., *The Reformation of Rights: Law, Religion, and Human Rights in Early Modern Calvinism* (New York: Cambridge University Press, 2007), 20–21.
2   John Witte, Jr., *Faith, Freedom, and Family: New Studies in Law and Religion*, ed. Norman Doe and Gary S. Hauk (Tübingen: Mohr Siebeck, 2021), 288–89.
3   Ibid., 346.

part that same tradition that early American revolutionaries appealed to when they called their countrymen to arms against British tyranny."[4]

In a perceptive, if here and there incomplete, synopsis of a complicated history, Witte identifies key aspects of the premodern European religious "tradition of resistance, revolution, and even regicide against any tyrant who pervasively violates the people's fundamental rights."[5] He begins by making the important point that "resistance and revolution against tyranny was no Calvinist invention,"[6] since the key ideas have broad resonance in ancient biblical, Greek, and Roman settings, not to mention Roman Catholic and other Protestant circles. He then refers to the way Lutherans and later Calvinists, in particular, went on to develop and variously implement the Protestant logic of revolution, which he describes as follows:

> Defense of oneself and of third parties against attack, using proportionate and even deadly force and violence when necessary, was an ancient legal teaching. When a person is unjustly attacked by another, the victim has the right to defend himself or herself—to resist, either passively by running away, or actively by staying to fight with proportionate force. Other parties, particularly relatives, guardians, or caretakers of the victim, also have the right to intervene to help the victim—again, passively by assisting escape, or actively by repelling the assailant with force. Early modern Calvinists argued by analogy that magistrates who exceed their authority forfeit their political office and become simply like any other private persons. If magistrates and their agents use force to implement excessive authority, their victims may rise up in passive or active resistance, using mortal force when necessary. The right to communal revolt was thus, in part, the individual right of self-defense writ large.[7]

Without elaborating, Witte links the biblical idea of covenant to the right of self-defense. Early modern Calvinists, he says, believed that political society, adopting what amounts to a contract theory of government, results from a solemn agreement among God, rulers, and people on the model of the ancient Israelite covenant. God agrees to protect and bless rulers and a people so long as they obey the laws of God and nature. Rulers, for their part, agree to obey the laws and defend "the people's essential rights, particularly those rooted in

---

4 Ibid., 346.
5 Ibid., 344ff.
6 Ibid.
7 Ibid., 344–45.

the Bible," while the people, in turn, consent to follow the laws "by electing and petitioning their rulers and by honoring and obeying them, so long as the rulers honored God's law and protected the people's rights."[8] If the people, or members thereof, should violate the laws, rulers may rightfully punish them; similarly, if rulers should violate the laws and become tyrants, the people may properly use force to resist and remove them from office, if necessary, and even condemn them to death, if convicted.

2 The Logic of Self-Defense

Witte's reference to a "Protestant logic of revolution ... built in part on the familiar legal doctrine of legitimate self-defense" is worth considering in some detail. The words suggest a common set of ideas having a certain rational structure and some features and implications that underlie the animating beliefs and activities of a substantial number of important revolutionary movements in Europe and America from the sixteenth to the eighteenth century.

To begin with, we must underscore, as Witte does, that this set of ideas was neither a Calvinist nor a broadly Protestant invention, even if deployed in a distinctive way by Protestants. The right of self-defense has found acceptance as a moral and legal standard across numerous non-Protestant and non-Western religious, philosophical, and cultural traditions from ancient times on.[9] This discovery has led one scholar to the following conclusion: These traditions all "have in common that they generally consider the person acting in self-defense to be morally and legally justified [and] none of these traditions considers the right of self-defense to be a boundless license to violence. Instead, concepts such as imminence of attack, necessity, ... proportionality of defense, and [right] intent are invoked across very different traditions to circumscribe the parameters of legitimate defense."[10]

Several things are presupposed: "Right of self-defense" means that persons, simply as such, and individually or collectively, are morally and legally entitled to use reasonable or defensive force to protect themselves or others against arbitrary force; "reasonable or defensive force" means employing the least amount of force, *administered without malice*, that is *necessary* and *proportional* to resist an *imminent* arbitrary attack; "arbitrary force" means (at a

---

8 Ibid., 345.
9 Jan Arno Hessbruegge, *Human Rights and Personal Self-Defense in International Law* (New York: Oxford University Press, 2017), 27–47.
10 Ibid., 30.

minimum) deliberately inflicting death, serious injury, or severe pain or suffering, or forcibly depriving of or neglecting basic survival needs primarily for self-serving or manifestly unfounded reasons. These stipulations guarantee that the right of self-defense is "not a boundless license to violence"; indeed, they are what prevent a use of force from becoming an arbitrary act.[11]

Beginning in the twelfth century, canon lawyers and Roman Catholic thinkers adapted and expanded on these characteristics as a basis for the use that Calvinist revolutionaries would put them to later on. Most important, the Catholic thinkers anchored the right of self-defense in a broad theory of subjective natural rights. Though the idea of subjective rights was clearly present in Roman law, it was not closely linked to the notion of natural law as it was by the canonists[12] and, after them, by William of Ockham and members of the conciliar movement.[13] A belief in subjective natural rights posited in all persons a sphere of personal liberty, "a zone of human autonomy," generated by an inward "power" or "faculty" possessed by every individual and taken to be guided by reason[14] that inspired a new exhilarating sense of personal and corporate empowerment.

Whereas in Roman law the idea of subjective rights was "rarely, if ever," "used to describe the right of a citizen against the state,"[15] that usage began to blossom with the advent of new thinking in the twelfth century. For the canonists, "all persons," according to natural law, "held a right to defend themselves from attack or depredation. If they had no such right, [they] would have been subject to indiscriminate violence or worse.... This way of thinking about rights stood behind the widely recognized power to resist a tyrannical

---

11 There is extensive philosophical discussion of the right of self-defense well-summarized in "Self-Defense," *Stanford Encyclopedia of Philosophy*, https://plato.stanford.edu/entries/self-defense. The article emphasizes the difficulty of explaining the grounds and limits of the right, but succeeds only in showing that the difficulties pertain to how inadvertent attackers or innocent bystanders should be treated. The difficulties do not apply to clear examples of arbitrary attack (as defined above), such as a mortal attack, cited in the article, that is motivated by personal jealousy and only avertable by a lethal response. While the treatment especially of innocent bystanders must always be considered, the focus of this article is the exercise and justification of self-defense in response to what are claimed to be clear instances of arbitrary attack. See David Little, "The Right of Self-Defense and the Organic Unity of Human Rights," *Journal of Law and Religion* 36, no. 3 (2021): 459–95.
12 Charles Donahue Jr., "*Ius* in Roman Law," in *Christianity and Human Rights: An Introduction*, ed. John Witte, Jr. and Frank S. Alexander (New York: Cambridge University Press, 2010), 78. See, also Brian Tierney, *The Idea of Natural Rights: Studies on Natural Rights, Natural Law, and Church Law, 1150–1625* (Atlanta, GA: Scholars Press, 1997), 58–77.
13 Tierney, *Idea of Natural Rights*, chaps. 7 and 9.
14 Ibid., 99–100, 173–75, 198–200.
15 Donahue, "*Ius* in Roman Law," 78.

ruler," even to the point of tyrannicide.[16] Canonists also held, within limits, that private property could not willfully be seized by a ruler, and possessing it thereby represented "a basic right held by the individual."[17] On the other hand, all rights to private property were themselves subject to the prior rights of the needy, who in extreme circumstances might not permissibly be denied a claim to survival.[18]

Ockham and the conciliarists, such as Jean Gerson, Jacques Almain, Nicholas of Cusa, and others, supported and developed these positions. Ockham believed the right of self-defense against arbitrary attack, and the claim of the poor *in extremis* to the "superfluities of the rich" in the name of survival, to be two "inalienable natural rights" that stood as everlasting limitations on the power of rulers,[19] and other conciliarists expanded on the rights to security and survival.[20] Gerson declared the right of self-defense to be imprescriptible, and went on to apply it explicitly to a social body, the church. "Since it would be licit for one single person to repel force with force in case of violence attempted by a true pope against life or chastity ... why in a similar case should it not be so permitted to the whole church?"[21]

Furthermore, basing their arguments on the right of self-defense, conciliarists made an important contribution to political theory. They held a view about the origins of political society later shared by John Locke: all persons, according to the law of nature, are assumed to be entitled to defend themselves, forcibly, if necessary, against threats to safety and survival. The problem was that they inclined to use force arbitrarily, not defensively. They wantonly attacked others in the service of their own interests or exercised force maliciously and excessively in protecting themselves, resulting in an endemically violent and chaotic state of affairs. To deliver themselves from this "fallen" condition, they banded together and agreed to entrust to a ruler the primary responsibility of administering force in accord with defensive standards, thereby guaranteeing their rights to safety and survival better than they could do if left to themselves.

> Far more more decisively than their predecessors, [the conciliarists] insist[ed] that political authority is not merely derived from but inheres in the body of the people.... [The] people only delegate and never alienate

---

16 R. H. Helmholz, "Human Rights in the Canon Law," in Witte and Alexander, *Christianity and Human Rights*, 103.
17 Ibid.
18 Ibid., 101.
19 Tierney, *Idea of Natural Rights*, 75, 194, 183.
20 Ibid., chaps. 9 and 10.
21 Ibid., 233.

their ultimate power to their rulers, and [therefore] the status of a ruler can never be that of an absolute sovereign, but only that of a minister or official of the commonwealth.[22]

It is in this way that conciliarists made "deeply influential contributions to the evolution of a radical and constitutionalist view of the sovereign State."[23] The fundamental objective of the state is to protect by means of representative government and the constitutional regulation of sovereign power the basic rights of all to security and survival against the ever-present threat of arbitrary abuse.

Nevertheless, there remains a deep "ambiguity inherent in the whole Conciliar position." On one hand, there is a "representative ideology," a "populist side," to their thinking, which holds that authority in both church and state "derives solely from the common agreement and consent of subjects,"[24] and respects subjective rights by permitting the individual exercise of self-defense against arbitrary attacks on the part of a pope or other ruler,[25] and by encouraging popular participation in political life in order to protect rights to security and survival. On the other hand, it was hard for most conciliarists to shed altogether the hierarchical principle. Although the traditional system of the three estates—clergy, nobles, and people—was ideally sensitive to the needs of the people, there was a strong tendency to assert that final authority for reigning in or deposing a ruler, not to mention determining other political and legal matters, lay not chiefly with the people, but with the two upper estates, the clergy and nobles. That was so, as John Mair put it, in order that "no element of passion shall intrude."[26] The implication was that the "lower orders" cannot be trusted, after all, to control themselves and act according to the conditions of defensive force if threatened with arbitrary force, just as they cannot in general be trusted to function politically in ways that best protect their other rights. We may call this reaction *political paternalism*, which comes to this: All persons are free to exercise their natural rights so long as they are directed by their political superiors to know how best to do that.

---

22   Quentin Skinner, *The Foundations of Modern Political Thought: The Reformation*, 2 vols. (Cambridge: Cambridge University Press, 1978), 2:119–20.
23   Ibid., 115.
24   John B. Morrall, *Political Thought in Medieval Times* (New York: Harper & Bros., 1962), 128–29.
25   Tierney, *Idea of Natural Rights*, 232–33.
26   Skinner, *Foundations of Modern Political Thought*, cited at 2:123. See also Morrall, *Political Thought in Medieval Times*, 128–29.

There is another reaction that introduces a second kind of ambiguity. It concerns conflicting tendencies in conciliar thought regarding the role of religion in the justification and enforcement of rights. One on hand, subjective natural rights are, from the beginning, not thought of as "derived specifically from Christian revelation or from some all-embracing natural-law theory of cosmic harmony, but from an understanding of human nature itself as rational, self-aware, and morally responsible. This understanding endured as the basis of many later natural rights theories, both medieval and modern."[27] Since natural rights, as enforceable entitlements, are justified by natural reason and not religious belief, they are appropriately enforced on natural, not religious, authority, and people may be held accountable to them whether Christian or not. What best binds a people together politically is not religion but a common belief in natural rights; therefore, it is necessary to enforce only rights, not religion.

In line with such thinking, conciliarists proposed to limit the authority of both church and state by carefully distinguishing their respective jurisdictions and functions according to constitutionally determined "laws and statutes," as Gerson put it.[28] The two societies are each self-sufficient in their own right. Church officials have no authority or aptitude for interfering in worldly matters, including the administration of physical force, suggesting very different responsibilities for the two institutions.[29] Whereas the state, concerned with "outward matters"—the material security and survival of human beings—may exercise its authority by employing "outward weapons"—physical force and coercion—the church, concerned with "inward" spiritual beliefs and the practices that manifest them, may exercise its authority by employing only "spiritual weapons"—nonviolent forms of persuasion and discipline.

Such reflections might have opened the door to ideas of freedom of religious belief and practice, especially against the background of medieval Catholic thought on the subject. Though not a proponent of natural rights, Thomas Aquinas, for example, hinted at such a position in defending a right to uncoerced belief. In the nature of human reasoning, he argued, "unwilling belief is an impossibility. The only valid act of faith is that which proceeds from a free, interior choice." Accordingly, it is thoroughly improper, he concluded, to compel people outside the church, such as Jews, Muslims, and pagans, to join.[30] To

---

27   Tierney, *Idea of Natural Rights*, 76.
28   Cited in Matthew Spinka, *John Hus and the Council of Constance* (New York: Columbia University Press, 1965), 19.
29   Skinner, *Foundations of Modern Political Thought*, 2:114–23.
30   Eric D'Arcy, *Conscience and Its Right to Freedom* (New York: Sheed and Ward, 1961), 153–56.

be sure, he qualified his claim, asserting that Christian apostates and heretics, as distinct from nonbelievers, might, like anyone guilty of breaking a contract, be legally punished for their deviance because they had broken a pledge to be good Christians. However far-fetched that particular claim, Thomas had successfully introduced thoughts about the distinction between belief and physical coercion that would be hard for natural rights thinkers to ignore.[31]

On the other hand, conciliarists like Gerson may have written eloquently about "evangelical liberty," but they "could not conceive of anything like a modern right to religious freedom."[32] The three objectives of the conciliar movement, made clear in the Council of Constance (1414–1418), were to end papal schism, reform the church, and defend the faith, especially against the heresies of John Wyclif and Jan Hus. The third ambition led to the public execution of Hus in 1415, leaving no doubt about conciliar commitments to enforcing orthodoxy to the fullest extent of the law. Such a reaction may be described as *religious paternalism*, which amounts to this: All persons have a right by nature to follow conscience, so long as they are directed by their religious superiors to discover what conscience truly teaches.

A deep dilemma lies at the heart of the logic of self-defense as it was worked out in the late Middle Ages by people like the canonists, Ockham, and the conciliarists, and that dilemma has to do with the whole idea of subjective natural rights. Ordinary persons, in the face of arbitrary force, are free by nature to take the law into their own hands, but, in doing so, are liable to go too far and use force arbitrarily themselves. Because they cannot be trusted, the only solution is for them to agree to submit to a governing authority designed to restrain force and to protect ordinary persons' rights to security and survival. The dilemma is how far the governing representatives ought to go in trusting ordinary people to know the best way to protect their rights. The dilemma, as we mentioned, has both political and religious dimensions.

---

31 Though there is not much evidence that this important implication was drawn out by the conciliarists, it was clearly perceived later by Bartolomeo de las Casas, the sixteenth-century Dominican missionary to Central America, in defending the natural rights of the local Indians against the depredations of the conquistadores. "The whole of Las Casas' life's work was inspired by the conviction that the Indians could be converted only by peaceful persuasion without any violence or coercion." "Las Casas resembled Ockham in frequently appealing to canonistic texts in order to defend a doctrine of rights." Tierney, *Idea of Natural Rights*, 272, 276.

32 Ibid., 214.

3 Calvinism and Revolution

Though, as we said, Calvinist leaders were by no means the only ones to invoke the logic of self-defense in the cause of revolution, they were important exemplars. Their efforts to encourage and support the use of force to end the rule of one government and start a new one—our definition of revolution—in France, the Netherlands, Scotland, England, and America in the sixteenth through the eighteenth centuries were profoundly consequential.

Lutherans undoubtedly made an important contribution. Martin Luther himself, along with Philip Melanchthon, introduced key arguments in favor of resistance to the Holy Roman Emperor, Charles V, and the popes of the time who encouraged imperial efforts to impose a Catholic order throughout premodern Europe. There were occasional appeals to natural law and reason as the basis for resistance and to canon and civil law provisions for limiting the emperor's authority to work his will, and toward the end of Luther's life he became an impassioned advocate of forcible resistance in the name of defending and maintaining what he regarded as the true religion.[33]

But with one exception, Lutherans did not dwell extensively on the role of natural rights to security and survival or to constitutional reform in favor of wider popular participation in government. That exception was expressed eloquently in the Magdeburg Confession of 1550, where, in response to the oppressive demands of the emperor, the leaders of that small Lutheran city in Saxony formally protested. They complained against forcibly "eradicating true doctrine and worship" and endangering "life and limb," "wife and child," and the "local liberties of the people." They called upon lesser magistrates and citizens "to stand up to such superiors" and "protect themselves and their people," exercising "their rights to defend themselves" under the "universal" and "natural" "law of legitimate self-defense."[34]

It was the Calvinists, starting with John Calvin himself,[35] who drew inspiration more elaborately than most Lutherans from the conciliar tradition, thereby applying and developing the logic of self-defense to a greater extent than Lutherans did. This conclusion is not surprising since, as an adolescent,

---

33 W. D. J. Cargill Thompson, "Luther and the Right of Resistance to the Emperor," in *Church, Society, and Politics*, ed. Derek Baker (Oxford: Basil Blackwell, 1975), 159–202.

34 Drawn from David Little, "Religion and the Justification of Rights," *Journal of Law and Religion* 36, no. 1 (2023), 148, citing John Witte, Jr., *The Blessings of Liberty: Human Rights and Religious Freedom in the Western Legal Tradition* (Cambridge: Cambridge University Press, 2022), 87–88.

35 For Witte's treatment of Calvin, see esp. *The Reformation of Rights*, 39–80, and *Faith, Freedom, and Family*, 139–54.

Calvin spent part of his education in a school heavily influenced by John Mair, a Scottish conciliarist.[36] The key evidence is Calvin's strong emphasis on natural rights and their relation to the activities of civil government. He refers frequently to the "natural rights" of persons, "the common rights of humankind," the "rights of a common nature," the "equal rights and liberties of all," as well as the "rights of citizenship," and property and marital rights, among others.[37] Josef Bohatec, the great Calvin scholar, summarizes them as the "original natural rights of freedom," which, for Calvin, are enumerated in both Tables of the Decalogue and serve as the basis for the primary responsibility of government.

> God has equipped rulers with the full authority that the rights of each individual to person and property not be denied, for these rights are goods bestowed by God. The authorities protect these rights through laws, which therefore must be made firm and durable, and all trace of arbitrariness avoided.... The subjective rights of freedom have no strong security if they are not supported by the authorities and legislation.[38]

Although he would change his views later, Calvin, in his 1540 *Commentary on Romans*, published when he was thirty-one, states that, according to Paul, the rights to be enforced by the governing authorities are restricted to the Second Table of the Decalogue, to "that part of the law which refers to human society." Paul "makes no mention here ... of [enforcing] the worship of God," but addresses only political affairs. "Since magistrates are the guardians of peace and equity, all who desire that every individual should preserve his rights and ... live free from injury must defend to the utmost of their power the order of the magistrates."[39]

Elsewhere, Calvin indicates that equity is a crucial part of the natural law that "God has engraved upon human minds," and that "equity alone must be

---

[36] There is scholarly controversy over how exactly this influence occurred. As a young man, Calvin attended the College de Montagu in Paris, where John Mair, a Scottish conciliarist, was an influential teacher, but whether Calvin actually studied with him is unknown. Whatever the specific source of influence, the ideas of the movement were certainly in the air, and undoubtedly shaped Calvin's thinking.

[37] Witte, *Reformation of Rights*, 34–35.

[38] Josef Bohatec, *Calvins Lehre von Staat und Kirche* (Aalan: Scientia, 1961), 94–95 (my translation).

[39] John Calvin, *Epistles of Paul the Apostle to the Romans and Thessalonians* (Grand Rapids, MI: Eerdmans, 1976), 285–86.

the goal and the rule and the limit of all [temporal] laws."[40] He means two things by "equity." First, "that everyone's rights should be safely preserved," implying that "not only are those thieves who secretly steal the property of others, but those also who seek for gain from the loss of others, accumulate wealth by unlawful practices, and are more devoted to their private advantage than to equity."[41] Second, it is a "fair apportioning" of what is owed to those in need,[42] that "no one should swallow up like some abyss, what belongs to him, but that he be beneficent to neighbors, and that he may relieve their indigence by his abundance."[43] In his *Commentary on the Psalms*, Calvin leaves no doubt about the political and legal implications. "A just and well-regulated government will be distinguished for maintaining the rights of the poor and the afflicted ... [since] kings and judges ... are appointed to be the guardians of the poor, and ... in resisting wrongs that are done to them."[44]

Calvin is serious here about the jurisdiction of law and government extending only to the security and survival of citizens and *not* to belief and worship. "The whole of [Paul's] discussion [in Romans 13] concerns the civil government. Those, therefore, who bear rule over human consciences attempt to establish their blasphemous tyranny from this passage in vain."[45] When these comments are combined with other statements—also later revoked—favoring religious freedom for "all peaceable believers, including Catholics, Jews, and Muslims" that were included in the 1536 edition of Calvin's *Institutes*, it is plausible to conclude that the idea of a conceptual gap between belief and compulsion present in Thomas's thought and incipient in the conciliar tradition and after had some effect on the young Calvin.

His commitment to justifying rights on grounds of natural reason is also evident in comments like this: "We observe in all human minds universal impressions of a certain civic fair dealing and order.... While people dispute among themselves about individual sections of the law, they agree on the general

---

40 John Calvin, *Institutes of the Christian Religion*, ed. John T. McNeill, trans. Ford Lewis Battle, 2 vols. (Philadelphia: Westminster Press, 1960), bk. 4, chap. 20, para. 16, 1504.
41 Calvin, *Commentary on Exodus* 20:20, cited in David Little, "Economic Justice and Progressive Taxation," in *Reformed Faith and Economics*, ed. Robert L. Stivers (Lanham, MD: University Press of America, 1989), 79.
42 Calvin, *Commentary on Second Corinthians*, 8:14, cited in Little, "Economic Justice," 79.
43 Calvin, *Commentary on Second Thessalonians*, 3;12, cited in Little, "Economic Justice," 79.
44 Calvin, *Commentary on the Psalms*, 82:3, cited in Little, "Economic Justice," 73.
45 Calvin, *Epistles of Paul the Apostle on Romans*, 13:5, 283.

conception of equity.... This is ample proof that in the arrangement of this life no person is without the light of reason."[46]

To be sure, Calvin altered or, better, complicated these views as the result of his deep involvement in the public administration of sixteenth-century Geneva over roughly twenty years. In the face of the growing challenges inside and outside Geneva, represented most acutely by the attacks of Michael Servetus on the doctrine of the Trinity in 1553, Calvin came to believe there was need to extend the jurisdiction of the civil magistrate beyond Second Table social offenses to matters of religious belief and worship, prescribed in the First Table. He now called for the civil enforcement of "the outward worship of God" and "sound doctrine of piety and the position of the Church,"[47] claiming that "no government can be happily established unless piety is the first concern," and "that those laws are preposterous which neglect God's right and provide only for human life."[48] To establish religion by bringing both Tables of the Decalogue under the control of the state was obviously to limit the rights of citizens not only religiously but also politically and economically. It meant overshadowing appeals to natural reason common to all citizens as the basis for law and policy with parochial appeals to Christian scripture and Reformed theology. In short, it meant that Calvin moved strongly in the direction of religious paternalism.

These complications affected Calvin's theory of the church and state and, eventually, his thoughts on revolution. Building on the conciliarists, he was a dedicated constitutionalist in his political thinking, believing that "every commonwealth rests upon laws and agreements," preferably written,[49] that are regarded as fundamental to the protection of the "freedom of the people," a favorite phrase, defined by the "original natural rights of freedom" that individual members all share. He also agreed that polyarchic, representative governments "compounded of aristocracy and democracy"[50] are better than monarchies. Monarchs rarely live up to what is just and right or "know how much is enough," showing that human "fault and failing causes it to be safer and more bearable for a number to exercise government." The pluralization and separation of power introduces "certain remedies against tyranny," as

---

46 Calvin, *Institutes*, bk. 2, chap. 2, para. 13, 272. See also his discussion of "certain ideas of justice and rectitude ... implanted by nature in the hearts of all persons," in Calvin, *Epistles of Paul the Apostle on Romans*, 2:14–15, 47–49.
47 Calvin, *Institutes*, bk. 4, chap. 20, para. 2, 1487.
48 Ibid., bk. 4, chap. 20, para. 9, 1495.
49 Calvin's *Homilies on 1 Samuel,* cited in Herbert D. Foster, "Political Theories of the Calvinists," *Collected Papers of Herbert D. Foster* (Privately Printed, 1929), 82.
50 Calvin, *Institutes*, bk. 4, chap. 20, para. 8, 82.

"when magistrates and estates have been constituted [who] have the power to keep the prince to his duty and even to coerce him if he attempt anything unlawful."[51] So does popular representation: "The best condition of the people [is] when they can choose, by common consent, their own shepherds, for when any one by force usurps the supreme power, it is tyranny."[52] Or: "kingship by hereditary right does not seem to be in accordance with liberty; a well-ordered government is one derived from a general vote."[53]

Again building on conciliar thinking, Calvin applied these same ideas to the church. There is a similar emphasis on polyarchic, representative church order, involving the pluralization and separation of power and popular participation. There is also, in theory at least, the same stark differentiation of authority and jurisdiction between church and state as the conciliarists affirmed on paper. "The church," said Calvin, "does not have the right of the sword to punish or compel, not the authority to force; not imprisonment, nor the other punishments which the magistrate commonly inflicts…. The church does not assume what is proper to the magistrate; nor can the magistrate execute what is carried out by the church."[54] The problem was that when it came to putting things into practice, Calvin, like the conciliarists, reneged on theory and seriously blurred the lines between the institutions by putting the state to work in the service of the church—by arranging, that is, for the state to enforce the First as well as the Second Table of the Decalogue.

As Calvin's ideas on church and state spread across much of Europe, and eventually to the New World, some of his followers, who propounded those ideas, predictably encountered ardent, often violently aggressive opposition from the established political and religious authorities. How and on what grounds should Calvinists defend themselves against the "tyranny" they encountered? Was their primary concern the defense of common natural rights to security and survival of "all the people," grounded in "the light of reason," and including the freedom to believe and worship as conscience dictated? Or was their paramount concern, instead, to defend the right to establish true religion in place of false religion, and thereby to give special protection to the rights of fellow Calvinists over everybody else? Was their task, in short, to seek to enforce only the Second Table by itself, or the First and Second Tables together? What is more, Calvinists faced a second question concerning what kind of government they should be defending. In order best to protect the people and their rights,

---

51   Calvin's *Homilies on 1 Samuel*, cited in Foster, "Political Theories of the Calvinists," 82.
52   Calvin's *Commentary on Micah*, 5.5.
53   Calvin, *Institutes*, book 4, chap. 20, para. 31, 1518.
54   Ibid., book 4, chap. 11, para. 3, 1215.

should monarchy be eliminated altogether, or simply restrained constitutionally, either by modifying or strengthening the traditional estates system, or by further pluralizing and separating political power and increasing popular representation?

Calvin provided some guidance in addressing these questions, but much of it was quite ambiguous, confirming his reputation as "a master of equivocation."[55] His followers would frequently exploit the ambiguities and take positions different from the master. Calvin accepted the personal right of self-defense as legally permissible, though he suggested that it was unbecoming for Christians to exercise it. Commenting on Jesus's rebuke to Peter to put his sword away as described in Matthew 26:52, he says, "if any man resist a robber, he will not be liable to public punishment, because the laws arm him against one who is the common enemy of mankind." But still, he emphasizes that the strict conditions of defensive force are difficult to comply with. "Excessive wrath must be laid aside, and hatred, and desire of revenge, and all irregular sallies of passion, that nothing tempestuous may mingle with the defense. As this is a rare occurrence, ... Christ properly reminds his people of the general rule, that they should entirely abstain from using the sword."[56]

Calvin's attitude toward collective self-defense is somewhat less hesitant, though there is similar worry about the potential excesses of any use of defensive force. It is both "natural equity" and the "nature of the office" that entitle magistrates to "restrain the misdeeds of private individuals" and "to defend by war" "dominions entrusted to their safekeeping" "anytime they are under attack." At the same time, they must avoid "giving vent to their passions," or

---

55   Skinner, *Foundations of Modern Political Thought*, 2:192. Skinner's elegant phrase is a much more accurate summary of Calvin's thinking than his "unequivocal" suggestion that Calvin himself added nothing distinctive to Protestant revolutionary ideas and simply cribbed without remainder from "radical Conciliarist thought" and Lutherans (2:321, 323). See also Skinner, "The Origins of the Calvinist Theory of Revolution," in *After the Reformation*, ed. Barbara Malament (Philadelphia: University of Pennsylvania Press, 1980). It is true, as we have said, that Calvin borrowed from conciliarists and Lutherans, but he added a strong, if variable, concern for natural rights and constitutional, representative government, which his followers developed beyond his original suggestions. Skinner has correctly been criticized by Carlos Eire in *War Against the Idols* (Cambridge: Cambridge University Press, 1986), 302–10, but Eire overemphasizes the religious reasons for Calvinist revolutionary behavior and ignores the reasons based on "natural equity," natural reason, and constitutional considerations. Moreover, Skinner is himself not entirely consistent. At 2:214, he properly refers to the equivocal character of Calvin's thought: "There are signs that Calvin begins to modify his doctrine of passive obedience at the end of the 1550s, and started to move towards the acceptance of the constitutional theory of resistance."

56   Calvin's *Commentary on Matthew*, 26:52.

being "seized with hatred" or "with implacable severity," and when faced with attack, "let them not accept the occasion ... unless they are driven to it by necessity," and "everything else [has been] tried" before taking up arms. Above all, let magistrates "be led by concern for the people alone," and "not for their own advantage."[57]

When it came to revolutionary action, Calvin's hesitancy involved more than just his sensitivity to the conditions of defensive force. In numerous places, he cautioned against popular rebellion of any kind, reminding readers of Paul's admonition, in Romans 13:1–2, that everyone be subject to governing authorities. That is so although citizens be "cruelly tormented by a savage prince" or "greedily despoiled by one who is avaricious or wanton," or even "vexed for piety's sake by one who is impious and sacrilegious,"[58] because "a wicked ruler is the Lord's scourge to punish the sins of the people," and it is therefore "our fault that this excellent blessing of God is turned into a curse."[59] In that spirit, he had "opposed rioting, unregulated iconoclasm and individual resistance, all of which he associated with social disorder."[60]

However, such thinking was, especially toward the end of Calvin's life, in severe tension with countervailing thoughts that were accentuated by the plight of his followers in neighboring France at the hands of the hostile Catholic monarchy there. Calvin had long held that lesser magistrates "appointed to restrain the willfulness of kings," such as ephors for Spartan kings, tribunes for Roman consuls, or, "as things now are," the three estates for the French monarchy, might use force in defense of "the freedom of the people."[61] With the mounting abuses heaped upon his Huguenot followers, he spoke with a new intensity, renouncing in no uncertain terms any reluctance he may have had previously about the right of lesser magistrates to take up arms against "the fierce licentiousness of kings."[62]

He was still, for the most part, a political paternalist, usually opposing any action initiated outside established constitutional authority. However, he began entertaining new, quite rebellious thoughts in the early 1560s. On one occasion, he supported the assassination by a private citizen of a French

---

57   Calvin, *Institutes*, bk. 4, chap. 20, paras. 11 and 12, 1499–501.
58   Ibid., bk. 4, chap. 20, para. 29, 1516.
59   Calvin's *Commentary on Romans*, 13:3, 282.
60   Bruce Gordon, *Calvin* (New Haven: Yale University Press, 2009), 321.
61   Calvin, *Institutes*, bk. 4, chap. 20, para. 31, para. 1519.
62   Ibid.

official turned against the Huguenots, "reflecting his growing acceptance that such acts could be legitimate."[63]

As we would expect, Calvin showed special concern for Second Table violations and the natural rights grounds on which the violations stand condemned. In particularly graphic language, he called attention to what some "dictatorships and unjust authorities" do: they "drain the common people of their money, and afterward lavish it on insane largesse," as well as "exercise sheer robbery, plundering houses, raping virgins and matrons, and slaughtering the innocent." Such atrocities, he declared, arouse an "inborn feeling [always present] in human minds to hate and curse tyranny as much as to love and venerate lawful kings."[64]

Again, as we would expect, he also addresses First Table violations, hinting, along the lines of his radicalized thinking of the 1550s and early 1560s, at open rebellion. If evil rulers "command anything against [God], let it go unesteemed." Christians, he continues, "ought not be concerned about all that dignity which magistrates possess; for no harm is done when it is humbled before that singular and truly supreme power of God." Like Daniel, Christians ought to refuse obedience to rulers who issue "impious edicts," since by uttering such commands, a ruler has "exceeded his limits" and "abrogated his power." Indeed, further reflecting on Daniel in his commentary, published in 1561, Calvin proclaims that rather than obey magistrates who rebel against God, "we ought, rather, utterly to defy them," or, literally, "to spit on their heads."[65] Such claims rest undoubtedly on scriptural grounds, though it remains unclear from these sentiments how far Calvin means for disobedience to go. If force is to be used, is it simply to defend the right to follow conscience, or is it to vanquish false religion and impose the true faith? As Calvinism spread, these would be serious issues.

4   The French Connection

Though Quentin Skinner in his *Foundations of Modern Political Thought* argues, misleadingly, that "there are virtually no elements in the [Calvinist theory of revolution that] are specifically Calvinist at all," his account of the historical

---

63   Gordon, *Calvin*, 327; see also 312 and the reference to W. Nijenhuis, "The Limits of Civil Disobedience in Calvin's Last-Known Sermons," *Ecclesia Reformata: Studies on the Reformation*, vol. 2 (Leiden: Brill, 1994), chap. 4, discussing Calvin's *Homilies on Samuel I and II*.
64   Calvin, *Institutes*, bk. 4, chap. 20, para. 24, 1512.
65   Cited in Calvin, *Institutes*, bk. 4, chap. 20, para. 1519n54.

setting and essential nature of French Calvinist, or Huguenot, contribution is otherwise a useful guide.[66] As we know, Skinner is partly right: Calvin did not invent the logic of self-defense or the way it would be interpreted and applied by his followers. However, he did in fact develop a consequential approach, combining appeals to natural rights and natural reason, including (if inconsistently) the right of free conscience and the right to constitutional and representative government, with appeals to the Bible and Christian history and doctrine, in a way that would be distinctively influential. That becomes apparent in the thought of two Calvinist thinkers associated with the Huguenot movement—Theodore Beza and Philippe du Plessis Mornay.

Skinner correctly locates the growth of the Huguenot minority and the role of these men in the context of "the growth of absolutism" in sixteenth-century Europe. Absolutism provoked increasing resentment among the upper classes "that the apparatus of government" of the Valois monarchy "had become more centered around the court and person of the king," leading to "the atrophying of the legal and representative elements in the constitution at that time"[67] and the dismantling of "the feudal pyramid of legal rights and obligations."[68] In 1576, the eminent political theorist Jean Bodin abandoned his earlier reservations about untrammeled political sovereignty and answered the bourgeoning Huguenot threat by becoming "a virtually unyielding defender of absolutism, demanding the outlawing of all theories of resistance and the acceptance of a strong monarchy as the only means of restoring political unity and peace."[69]

The August 24, 1572, St. Bartholomew's Day Massacre, in which thousands of Huguenots were slaughtered and thousands more exiled by royal troops and mobs of sympathizers, was a grisly manifestation of the violent hostility toward perceived threats that could result from an absolutist ideology. François Hotman, a humanist scholar and converted Calvinist, was the first to respond. He published his *Francogallia* in 1573, declaring that some rebellions "are just and even necessary," particularly when "a people oppressed by a savage tyrant begs assistance from a lawful assembly of citizens."[70] But while he expanded on Calvin's thoughts about the importance of lesser magistrates in leading revolutions, and about the excellence of polyarchic, representative government, he completely ignored the significance of natural rights, not to mention

---

66   Skinner, *Foundations of Modern Political Thought*, 2:321.
67   Ibid., 2:255.
68   Ibid., 2:264.
69   Ibid., 2:284.
70   Julian H. Franklin, *Constitutionalism and Resistance in the Sixteenth Century: Three Treatises by Hotman, Beza, and Mornay* (New York: Pegasus, 1969), 84.

the relevance of scripture and doctrine. Besides, his historical work was "frequently tendentious and inaccurate," as his opponents regularly charged.

What the Huguenots needed was a firmer, more convincing foundation for taking up arms against tyranny. Theodore Beza, Calvin's successor in 1564 and author of *Right of Magistrates* (1574), and Philippe Mornay, a soldier, diplomat, theologian, political adviser, and author of *Vindication of Liberty against Tyrants*, came to the rescue. While they gave considerable attention to scripture and doctrine and to the role of First Table considerations in the reasons and goals of revolution, they accentuated appeals, in Beza's words, to the "general and universal rule of equity and rectitude" that is "based on maxims and common principles that have remained ... despite the fall" into sin, and that "is so definite and firm that nothing clearly contrary and repugnant to it should be found proper and valid among humanity."[71] Among other things, Beza, as Witte points out, asserted rights to free speech and political petition. "Beza insisted that to criticize, petition, or sue a magistrate for political failings was not to be discourteous, let alone disobedient. The magistrate 'suffers no injustice if he is constrained to do his duty.'"[72] When a sovereign becomes a tyrant by lying to his people, "the people justly asserts its rights against him."[73]

Mornay is even more explicit. Claiming that "no one is a king by nature," and that "the rights of the people" precede any agreement with the king, he assumes a condition of "natural liberty,"[74] and explains it as follows: "We are all 'free by nature, born to hate servitude ... and [we] possess this freedom as one of our natural rights, as 'a privilege of nature'" that can never be denied.[75] As Skinner says,

> Like Locke a century later, the Huguenots [informed by Beza and Mornay, among others] assume that amongst the things we may be said to have the freedom and thus the right to dispose of within the bounds of the laws of nature are those properties ... which are intrinsic to our personalities, and in particular our lives and liberties, ... which everyone may be said to possess in a prepolitical state.[76]

---

71 Beza, *Right of Magistrates*, 124–25.
72 Witte, *Faith, Freedom and Family*, 303–04.
73 Ibid., 306–07.
74 Philippe Mornay, *Vindication of Liberty against Tyrants*, in Marshall, *Constitutionalism and Resistance in the Sixteenth Century*, 169.
75 Skinner, *Foundations of Modern Political Thought*, 2:327.
76 Ibid., 2:329.

A fundamental principle of both Beza and Mornay is that governments are established to protect the people's rights.[77] They are designed to moderate the temptation of human beings to disrespect and disregard the natural rights to security and survival of one another and thereby degrade the full enjoyment of equal rights for all. It is for that reason that people contract or "covenant" with rulers. There is a contract or covenant with God, as we shall see, but it also applies to a purely political or secular agreement which, in Beza's words, amounts to "a mutual oath between the king and the people."[78] Both men reject the idea that a sovereign is in any way above the law, but is rather an "agent" of the people and serves, together with the lesser magistrates elected by the people, and similar to the ephors, consuls, and estates mentioned by Calvin, in a polyarchic representative system.[79]

In regard to the right of self-defense, Beza acknowledges the New Testament emphasis on nonviolence and recommends, as an initial response to tyranny, "prayers united with repentance," since evil rulers are "most often an evil or scourge sent by God for the chastisement of nations." But he goes on to "deny that it is illicit for peoples oppressed by notorious tyranny to make use of lawful remedies,"[80] and proceeds to condone "legitimate self-defense against a tyrant," though only according to the conditions of defensive force: "that the tyranny has become thoroughly obvious"; that "there is no recourse to arms until all other remedies have been tried"; and that "there is careful consideration not only of what is permitted but of what is expedient [proportional?], lest the cure be worse than the disease."[81]

Mornay concurs. "In the first place, nature instructs us to defend our lives and also our liberty, without which life is hardly life at all.... To fight back is not only permitted, but enjoined, for it is nature herself that seems to fight here."[82] "What is more at war with nature than for a people to promise that it will put chains and fetters on itself, will put its throat beneath the knife, and will do violence to itself?" "Between the king and people there exists a mutual obligation which, whether civil or only natural, explicit or tacit, cannot be superseded by

---

77 For a discussion of Beza, see Witte, "Rights, Resistance, and Revolution in the Western Tradition," in *Faith, Freedom, and Family*, chap. 15, and more fully Witte, *The Reformation of Rights*, 81–142.
78 Skinner, *Foundations of Modern Political Thought*, 2:331.
79 Ibid., 2:332–35.
80 Beza, *Right of Magistrates*, in Marshall, *Constitutionalism and Resistance in the Sixteenth Century*, 104–05.
81 Ibid., 130–31.
82 Mornay, *Vindication of Liberty against Tyrants*, in Marshall, *Constitutionalism and Resistance in the Sixteenth Century*, 187–88.

any other compact, or violated in the name of any other right, or rescinded by any act of force."[83]

Beza is clear, and Mornay agrees, that tyranny, at bottom, equals arbitrary rule: "Right is anything I like."[84] When it comes to spelling out the tyrannical acts, they are for the most part less explicit. Mornay concludes that "kings are neither owners nor usufructuaries of the royal patrimony," and "are even less able to claim the private property of individuals as their own, or the public property owned by individual municipalities,"[85] implying that violations of such statements would constitute acts of tyranny against the Second Table of the Decalogue. Beza says almost nothing about the Second Table, and they both allude more to First Table violations, raising the question of the role of force in regard to religious belief and practice.

Beza is the more explicit. He is sensitive to the objection that because "religion is a matter of conscience," it "may not be coerced" or "established by arms," but he proceeds to reject outright the claim that resort to arms is "so opposed and repugnant to [religion] that [it] can have no place whatsoever in religious matters."[86] Reason and scripture, he claims, teach that the "true end of all rightly ordered government" is "the glory of God," and since that "religion is planted by the Spirit of God along, through the Word," "it is the duty of a prince who would convert his subjects from idolatry or superstition to true religion" to "provide and enforce good edicts against those who, from pure stubbornness, would resist the establishment of true religion." It follows, he thinks, that princes who impose idolatry and false belief are guilty of "flagrant tyranny" that may be opposed in accord with the conditions of defensive force for the purpose, it appears, not of defending the principle of free conscience, but of replacing false with "true religion."[87]

Though Mornay spends less time on the subject, he agrees, for the most part, with Beza. Like Beza, he believes that the people make an original covenant with God besides the covenant they make with their ruler. Accordingly, the first covenant promises that, along with supporting the people's welfare, ruler and people will "maintain God's glory," no doubt defined as Beza would, and the assumption is that violations by ruler (or people) of the first covenant are as grievous as violations of the second, and equally worthy of a defensive use of

---

83   Ibid., 185.
84   Ibid., 117.
85   Ibid., 179.
86   Ibid., 133.
87   Ibid., 134–35.

force.[88] There is evidence that when he was in the Netherlands, "he went from town to town, saying that religion ought to be preached—not forced upon the people," since "truth never resorts to violence."[89] But he makes no allowance for such thinking in the *Vindication,* and it may be concluded that, on balance, Mornay shared with Beza the spirit of religious paternalism, though he may have been more hesitant about it than Beza.[90]

They both also tended toward political paternalism, giving lesser magistrates, and not the people at large or individual citizens, the exclusive right to initiate defensive force against tyrants, though both, interestingly, made an important exception. In the case of a tyrant who, as Beza says, "would seize dominion without title, or has already usurped it—whether [the tyrant] comes from without or arises from within," private citizens should first appeal to lesser magistrates, but if those magistrates should fail to respond, "each private citizen should exert all his strength to defend the legitimate institutions of his country, and to resist an individual whose authority is not legitimate because he would usurp, or has usurped dominion in violation of the law."[91] Mornay says the same thing.[92]

However, in the case of a ruler "who has been avowed by his people, [he] may abuse his dominion, and still retain his authority over private subjects because the obligation to him was contracted by common consent and cannot be withdrawn and nullified at the pleasure of a private individual. Were it otherwise, infinite trouble would ensue, even worse than the tyranny itself, and a thousand tyrants would arise on the pretext of suppressing one."[93] Mornay agrees with Beza that the people, as a whole or as individual citizens, have no recourse whatsoever to take up arms against a "titled" ruler other than to appeal to the lesser magistrates. "The commonwealth is so little entrusted to private individuals that they, rather, are entrusted to the care of the notables

---

88 Ibid.
89 Paul T. Fuhrmann, "Philip Mornay and the Huguenot Challenge," in *Calvinism and Political Order*, ed. George L. Hunt (Philadelphia: Westminster Press, 1965), 57; see ibid., 50 and 55 for evidence of a theocratic impulse in Mornay's thought.
90 "Mornay fought Catholicism verbally, in writing, and on the battlefield, but there is no indication that he ever used his authority to keep people from exercising the Catholic religion." Ibid., 63.
91 Beza, *Right of Magistrates*, in Marshall, *Constitutionalism and Resistance in the Sixteenth Century*, 107.
92 "The law of nature, the law of peoples, and civil law command us to take up arms against tyrants without title, nor is there any legal scruple to detain us.... Therefore, when this kind of tyranny occurs, anyone may act to drive it out, including private individuals." Mornay, *Vindication of Liberty against Tyrants*, 188.
93 Beza, *Right of Magistrates*, 109.

and magistrates and are in effect their wards."[94] What is to be done if the notables and magistrates, in turn, ignore the abuses perpetrated by a titled ruler against the people is not addressed.

5 Conclusion

As John Witte understands, supported as he is by Brian Tierney, Quentin Skinner, and others, revolutionary thought in the West has historical roots much older than the Enlightenment, roots that are deeply embedded in Western Christian thought and practice. Of course, the elemental ideas are even older and of much wider acceptance, but it was Western European Christians—first the conciliarists and their predecessors in the twelfth through the fifteenth centuries, and then the Protestants, particularly the Calvinists, in the sixteenth through the eighteenth centuries—in whom the ideas germinated and were developed and put into practice with great consequence.

The key inspiration was understanding the right of self-defense as the linchpin in a system of subjective natural rights. The idea that persons, individually and in groups, were by nature equally entitled to use force to protect themselves and others against imminent, unwarranted attacks, so long as they did it with due restraint and without malice, laid a radically novel foundation for government. Governments are necessary because uncontrolled self-enforcement is likely to lead to more, not less, unwarranted attacks. But governments are also under new management. Their primary obligation is now to protect the equal rights to life and livelihood of all persons within their care in accord with the conditions of defensive force, and to find ways in designing and administering the government to represent adequately the sovereignty of the people grounded in such an understanding. This obligation set a standard of paramount importance. So long as a government complied, it was legitimate and should be obeyed. When it did not, it lost its legitimacy and might be subject to revolutionary overthrow.

That the movements nurturing and promoting this logic of self-defense—conciliarists and and their predecessors, Protestants and particularly Calvinists—were Christian movements was both motivating and perplexing. Motivating because these rights, naturally available to all human beings,

---

94   Mornay, *Vindication of Liberty against Tyrants,* 195. See Skinner, *Foundations of Modern Political Thought,* 2:331, for a confirmation of this conclusion in the thought of Beza and Mornay: "the right to hold the king to his promises can never by a property of the people as a whole," but only to appointed officials.

regardless of race, creed, or gender, were also seen as sacred in character, as ordained by the Christian God, and, therefore, as something worth dying for. Perplexing because of the temptation to see these rights not as equally available to all, but as the special entitlement of Christians, and as requiring special Christian oversight in interpreting how they should be protected and enforced by earthly governments.

Different phases of the revolutionary tradition managed the tensions in different ways. The conciliarists developed an impressive theory of natural rights built up around the "greatest of rights"—the right of self-defense—and combined it with remarkably modern ideas about representative government and constitutionalism. That included the sharp separation of ecclesiastical and political authority, and might, in turn, have led to notions of the disestablishment of religion and freedom of conscience implicit in natural-rights reasoning. Nevertheless, they pulled back in horror from such implications, and eagerly enlisted the state in persecuting heretics like Jan Hus. Similarly, their ideas about representative government and popular sovereignty might have pushed them beyond the rather conventional confidence they placed in the estates system, but it did not.

John Calvin displayed the same kind of ambivalence toward natural rights and representative government. He gave much more attention to natural rights than he has been given credit for, including provision for an "inborn feeling in human minds to hate and curse tyranny," which underlay his willingness to lend vigorous support to the Huguenot cause in France. Early on, he flirted with the implication of conciliar thinking, limiting the jurisdiction of the state to "outward matters," and going so far as to favor a doctrine of freedom of conscience. He was a dedicated constitutionalist and, in theory, vigorously stood for the sovereignty of the people and representative government. On the other hand, he came to his belief in the right of rebellion late in life. He distinctly reversed himself on religious freedom and eventually took on the unmistakable image of a religious paternalist, and that development, in turn, strongly modified his commitment to popular sovereignty, since it awarded special consideration to the religiously orthodox.

There is something of the same ambivalence, again, in the Huguenot case on the part of Theodore Beza and Philippe Mornay. They are different in that they both develop the logic of self-defense more extensively than the conciliarists or Calvin, and spend more time on the role of natural rights in revolution and as the foundation of a well-ordered government. They both appear to give special preference to Christian control in government, though Mornay, at least, shows some hesitancy about enforcing religion to the same degree as Calvin and Beza. Both Mornay and Beza refer at length to the importance of popular sovereignty, though neither carries the discussion very far in respect to what that means in detail.

The rest of the story, to be told elsewhere, will apply the same analysis to key authors writing in defense of the Dutch Revolt, the Scottish Reformation, the Puritan Revolution, and the American Revolution.

CHAPTER 19

Scriptural Interpretation and the New England Tradition of Rights after the Glorious Revolution: The Example of Cotton Mather

Jan Stievermann

In the current history wars, New England Puritanism once again serves as the mythic origin of either the exceptional greatness of the United States or American evils such as white Christian nationalism. Whenever John Witte has treated the New England tradition, he has made a self-conscious attempt to avoid these pitfalls. Witte's goal has never been to make out the Puritans as heroic founding fathers of modern democracy, whose understanding of rights and freedom directly corresponded or teleologically led to ours. Nor has it been his intention to exculpate the Puritans for any of their shortcomings and the wrongs they undoubtedly committed, even if measured by their own standards. At the same time, Witte has always pushed back against presentist misrepresentations and vilifications of the Puritans. In the respective chapters of *The Reformation of Rights* (2007) and *Religion and the American Constitutional Experiment* (5th ed. 2022), among other publications, he aimed to reconstruct how the "'fundamental ideas' of Puritan Calvinism"—of "conscience, confession, community, and commonwealth"—importantly contributed "to the genesis and genius of the American experiment" with "religious, ecclesiastical, associational, and political liberty."[1] These Puritan ideas, in turn, were informed by complex traditions of Christian, specifically Protestant Reformed, theology and jurisprudence that the first settlers brought to the New England colonies, where these ideas would subsequently mesh, but also partly clash, with new Enlightenment theories of individual liberty and natural rights.

By making this argument, Witte has been one of the leaders in a modest but significant movement to reevaluate the political thought of New England Puritan leaders that is mostly found in their religious writings. What connects

---

1 John Witte, Jr., *The Reformation of Rights: Law, Religion, and Human Rights in Early Modern Calvinism* (Cambridge: Cambridge University Press, 2007), 319. See further id., *The Blessings of Liberty: Human Rights and Religious Freedom in the Western Legal Tradition* (Cambridge: Cambridge University Press, 2021), chap. 4 ("'A Modest Mild and Equitable Establishment of Religion': Religious Freedom in Massachusetts, 1780–1833").

Witte's work to the studies of J. F. Cooper, Michael Winship, J. S. Maloy, David Hall, and Adrian Weimer, among others, is their shared insight that the wellspring of Puritan conceptualizations of the body politic is their ecclesiology, specifically their covenantalism. Drawing on their inheritance of Reformed federalism, New England Puritans, as Witte puts it, viewed church and state as two independent but interlocking "covenantal associations within a broader covenantal community." Membership in each came with inherent rights but also duties. "Each was separate from the other in their forms and functions, offices and officers, but mutually responsible to see that all served the common good in accordance with the terms of the social covenant."[2] For this reason, as Maloy notes, "democratic ideas and practices in ecclesiastics had theoretical ramifications for politics" and could be transferred from one sphere to the other.[3] In practice, the Puritans engaged in "daring revision of church government that eliminated any central authority," and accorded exceptional participatory privileges to those deemed worthy of membership. This went along with legal reforms that put New England far ahead of the mother country and "a remaking of civil government that limited central state powers."[4] Just as the New England Way in church polity was enshrined in individual church covenants and the Cambridge Platform, the Puritans also codified rights to legal personality and political freedoms in compacts or constitutions, notably the Massachusetts Body of Liberties. These helped to engender, as Witte has emphasized, an American tradition of constitutionalism and insistence on guaranteed rights under a limited government that would crucially inform the American Founding.[5]

The following chapter seeks to further the conversation on Puritanism's contribution to that tradition in two ways. First, it extends the historical scope. Witte and others have given most attention to early New England. Most recently, Adrian Weimer examined the post-Restoration period, when Puritans responded to the absolutist ambitions of Charles II by crafting what she calls a "potent regional constitutional culture," which was "marked by wariness of metropolitan ambition, defensiveness about civil and religious liberties, and a

---

2 *Reformation of Rights*, 17.
3 J. S. Maloy, *The Colonial American Origins of Modern Democratic Thought* (Cambridge: Cambridge University Press, 2008), 86, 113.
4 David D. Hall, *A Reforming People: Puritanism and the Transformation of Public Life in New England* (New York: Knopf, 2011), 4 and XI. See also Michael Winship, *Godly Republicanism: Puritans, Pilgrims, and a City on a Hill* (Cambridge, MA: Harvard University Press, 2012). On Congregational church polity, see J. F. Cooper, *Tenacious of Their Liberties: The Congregationalists in Colonial Massachusetts* (New York: Oxford University Press, 1999).
5 *Reformation of Rights*, 2.

conviction that self-government was divinely sanctioned."[6] I look at the crucial transitional period after the Glorious Revolution, when colonial leaders had to negotiate new charters, navigate a growing religious pluralism, and give fresh meaning to the inherited notions of their rights and liberties in the contexts of an increasingly integrated British Empire as well as the early Enlightenment. In so doing, as I argue, they further developed New England's "constitutional culture" in significant ways.

Second, I extend the scope of textual source material and pay special attention to biblical commentaries and writings on church history as important but often overlooked genres through which Puritan authors expressed their political thought. My case study is Cotton Mather (1663–1728), who is widely acknowledged as the leading churchman and theologian of third-generation Puritanism in Massachusetts, but has also been much misunderstood and maligned as the exemplary embodiment of all Puritan wrongs, in particular their religious bigotry and persecuting spirit.

Against such stereotypical views, I demonstrate that Mather derived from his interpretations of the Bible and history a changed view of the two covenantal associations, how they ought to relate to each other, and who can enter them and enjoy their privileges. In contrast to his forebears, Mather's understanding implied a stricter—if by no means complete—separation of state and church. In conversation with Reformed theologians and Whig theorists, he found in the scriptures far-reaching notions of political liberty, separation of powers, and checks and balances within a mixed-government framework, as well as a divine right of resistance to tyrants. However, it should be noted upfront that Mather's understanding of political liberties sharply diverges from that of modern liberal democracies, in that he assumed a hierarchical society with different estates and graded privileges as well as differing duties. Mather took it for granted that only freeholding white men should enjoy the full extent of the English freedoms he touted, while those of women and servants would be restricted. And although Mather criticized the transatlantic slave trade and, in some ways, resisted the ongoing racialization of Africans and Indians as naturally inferior peoples, he never challenged the institution of slavery. Instead, he tacitly accepted the growing number of bondsmen in the colonies, focusing on their religious education and emphasizing their duty to be obedient to Christian masters, rather than calling for their emancipation

---

6 Adrian C. Weimer, *A Constitutional Culture: New England and the Struggle Against Arbitrary Rule in the Restoration Empire* (Philadelphia: University of Pennsylvania Press, 2023), 3.

in resistance to the worst form of tyranny.[7] In this important respect, Mather failed to go beyond his time and the self-interest of the white, male, elite group to which he belonged, and, really, follow the logic of his theological and political thought to what now seems its obvious conclusions.

Yet in other regards, Mather was willing to call into question what had been consensual in the world he grew up in, notably when it came to religious qualifications for full civic rights. He concluded that a truly biblical Christianity demanded a much more expansive understanding of religious freedom than the original architects of the Massachusetts Bay had allowed. Mather would come to promote *"Liberty of Conscience"* as "the Native Right of Mankind," as he put it in his 1718 ordination sermon for the Baptist Elisha Callender,[8] while advocating comprehensive and tolerant Protestant establishments for both Old and New England. A rising British Empire committed to these principles, Mather hoped, would be a champion in what he saw as the Protestant cause of liberty, locked in apocalyptic battle with the forces of Antichristian tyranny.

Cotton Mather came of age in a world dramatically changed from that of his grandfathers, John Cotton and Richard Mather, who had been among the founders of the Massachusetts Bay and principal architects of the so-called New England Way in church polity. Back in England, the Stuart Restoration of 1660 put out of reach, at least for the foreseeable future, the Puritan dream of a truly reformed national church and ushered in a most trying period for Dissenters. Post-Restoration Puritans continued to see themselves as the representatives of Protestantism in England and to strive for a renewed and comprehensive Church of England. However, under a reestablished High Church and the Clarendon Code (1661–65), nonconformist ministers were pushed to the sidelines of ecclesial and political life, and thousands lost their livelihoods and suffered imprisonment. Especially for the hotter sorts of Protestants, the "Romish" sympathies of Charles II and the openly acknowledged Catholicism of James II, along with the absolutist tendencies of the Stuarts, raised the specter of tyranny akin to Catholic France.

Across the ocean in New England, the fears of popery and arbitrary government were compounded by Stuart efforts to integrate and control the hitherto fairly independent colonies much more fully. The Puritans of Massachusetts lived in constant fear that their experiment with a Congregational church

---

7 On this, see my "The Genealogy of Races and the Problem of Slavery in Cotton Mather's 'Biblia Americana,'" in *Cotton Mather and Biblia Americana—America's First Bible Commentary: Essays in Reappraisal*, ed. Reiner Smolinski and Jan Stievermann (Tübingen: Mohr Siebeck, 2010), 515–76.

8 Mather, *Brethren Dwelling Together in Unity* (Boston, 1718), 37.

polity might be terminated together with their far-reaching political autonomy and privileges. Most importantly, these included the annual free election of the governor, as well as of the Council of Assistants and the town delegates that together made up the bicameral General Court. As a legislative body, the General Court had established with the 1641 Massachusetts Body of Liberties a comprehensive legal code that offered, at the time, truly exceptional guarantees of individual rights and procedural due process (even though certain rights, notably suffrage, were enjoyed only by freemen who were also church members), while also enshrining Mosaic law in its regulations of the commonwealth's religious and moral life.

Just as Cotton Mather turned twenty-one, New England's worst fear became a reality when the First Charter of Massachusetts (1630) was revoked by James II in 1684. Subsequently, Massachusetts was integrated into the Dominion of New England, ruled by a royally appointed governor, Sir Edmund Andros, and his handpicked council. The Puritan panic over Andros's autocratic regime was exacerbated by his introduction of Anglicanism, which many saw as the portent of a looming counterreformation in case of a Catholic succession to the English throne. At this critical point, or so it seemed to young Cotton Mather, the hand of providence intervened, making the English parliamentary opposition rise up in order to prevent such a succession and end Stuart absolutism. In what came to be known as the Glorious Revolution of 1688/89, William of Orange and his wife, Mary, were invited to ascend the throne, while James II was forced into exile. As news of these events reached British North America, upheavals ensued in several parts, including Massachusetts. In April 1689, Bostonians rose up and arrested without bloodshed the provincial government under Andros. Historians have reconstructed that Mather played an important part in Boston's Glorious Revolution, and he is considered the principal author of the anonymously published pamphlet *The Declaration, Of Gentlemen, Merchants, and Inhabitants of Boston* (1689), which served as a semiofficial statement, articulating the main grievances of Massachusetts citizens and legitimizing their open resistance against royal authority.[9] The *Declaration of Gentlemen* has been recognized by David Levin and Rick Kennedy as a landmark document of New England that anticipates many of the arguments held forth by the patriots during the Revolutionary crisis, including those in Thomas Jefferson's 1776 Declaration of Independence.[10]

---

9 See Kenneth Silverman, *The Life and Times of Cotton Mather* (New York: Harper & Row, 1984), 62–72.
10 David Levin, "Cotton Mather's Declaration of Gentlemen and Thomas Jefferson's Declaration of Independence," *New England Quarterly* 50 (1977): 271–79; Rick Kennedy, "*Eleutheria*

A closer look reveals that the *Declaration of Gentlemen* combines an older and broader Reformed tradition of thinking about a divine right of resistance with a specifically English Whig ideology, as it had developed during the English Civil War, the exclusion crisis of 1679–81, and the Glorious Revolution. The language of the *Declaration* specifically shows the influence of Continental Calvinist theologians, such as Theodore Beza, but also Scottish and English Puritan divines who had justified their revolt against Charles I based on concepts of a political covenant among God, ruler, and the people informed by different rights and mutual duties. Despotic rulers who violate the terms of the covenant—most egregiously by infringing upon the religious rights of their subjects to live according to scriptural rules—may be legitimately resisted without violating God's command to obey rightful authorities. In Mather's argument, these basic assumptions are inflected by Whig ideas about how "a general moral decay of the people … would invite the intrusion of evil and despotic rulers" to intrude upon the inherited freedoms of English Protestants, and more specifically, how, in Robert Middlekauff's apt summary, this entailed a constant danger of "the encroachment of executive authority upon the legislature, the attempt that power always made to subdue the liberty protected by mixed government."[11]

Thus, the *Declaration* speaks of the unlawful nullification of the Old Charter and the Body of Liberties under false pretenses, and interprets it at once as part of a *"Popish Plot,"* aiming at "no less than the execution of the Protestant Religion," and as part of a larger attempt by the Stuarts to extirpate English liberty across the realm. The king had imposed an "Absolute and Arbitrary" regime on Massachusetts, with "Sr. Edmund Andros" as a provincial tyrant. Together with a council of self-serving cronies, the governor had arrogated the power "to make Laws and raise Taxes as he pleased," raised dues, and illegally revoked land titles in a way that clearly denied the traditional "Priviledges of *English* men," going back to "the *Magna Charta*." Persons who "did but peaceably object against the raising of Taxes without an Assembly" were fined and imprisoned without due process and in violation of *"Habeas Corpus."* Given

---

(1698): Cotton Mather's History of the Idea of Liberty That Links the Reformation to the Glorious Revolution and the American Revolution," in *Revolution as Reformation: Protestant Faith in the Age of Revolution, 1688–1832*, ed. Peter C. Messer and William Harrison Taylor (Tuscaloosa: University of Alabama Press, 2021), 28–39.

11   Robert Middlekauff, *The Glorious Cause: The American Revolution, 1763–1789*, rev. ed. (New York: Oxford University Press, 2005), 51. On the intersections between Whig ideology and post-Restoration Puritanism with its continuing hopes to transform England into a truly reformed nation, see Mark Goldie, *Roger Morrice and the Puritan Whigs: The Entring Book, 1677–1691* (Woodbridge, UK: Boydell Press, 2016).

these flagrant violations of the political contract, resistance was justified in the eyes of the "Almighty God," who, as the *Declaration* concludes "hath been pleased to prosper the noble undertaking of the Prince of *Orange*, to preserve the three Kingdoms from the horrible brink of Popery and Slavery," and who was meting out just punishment against "those *worst of men*, by whom English Liberties have been destroy'd."[12]

The dark days of the Andros regime and the turmoil of the Glorious Revolution were foundational experiences for Mather that profoundly influenced his political and ecclesiological thinking. As much as he would celebrate William's victory over Stuart tyranny and publicly defend the New Charter that his father, Increase, negotiated with the new king, Cotton Mather remained conflicted about the results of the Glorious Revolution on both sides of the Atlantic. He applauded the guarantee of a Protestant succession, the Bill of Rights (1689), and the system of "king in parliament" that evolved in England. Yet, for the rest of his life, he would remain fearful not only of Stuart plots but also of creeping tendencies toward royal absolutism among the new monarchs, especially under Mary and Anne. He was simultaneously thankful for and disappointed by the Act of Toleration (1691), which broadly guaranteed freedom of religion for all Trinitarian Protestants in England, but failed to put Dissenters on equal footing with members of the Church of England. They continued to be excluded from certain rights—including the right to hold office and enter universities—and continued to be vulnerable to further encroachments, depending on the religious tendencies of king and parliament. Although the New Charter for the reorganized Province of Massachusetts restored land titles and other basic freedoms, it severely curtailed the colony's political autonomy and democratic rule by implementing a royal governor out of the reach of popular control. The Assistants were transformed into the Governor's Council, to be selected by the king's representative to serve not only as his council for advice but also as the upper house of the Massachusetts Court. The governor had to approve and could veto all laws proposed by the legislature, and he had the power to convene, prorogue, and dissolve the General Court. Most significantly, for Mather, the New Charter broke the back of Congregationalism's political ascendancy, by removing full church membership as a qualification for the suffrage and replacing it by property ownership. Moreover, Massachusetts now had to exercise inner-Protestant toleration. Initially Cotton Mather mourned the loss of the old New England Way and, to a certain extent, would

---

12 *The Declaration, Of the Gentlemen, Merchants, and Inhabitants of Boston, and the Countrey Adjacent. April 18th* (Boston, 1689), no pag.

continue to look back to the days of the Old Charter with nostalgia. Yet he quickly adjusted.

1 Mather and Protestant Liberty

Locally, Mather attempted to make the best of the situation post-1691, seeking to work the system from within for what he perceived as the common good, while also monitoring and criticizing perceived transgressions of the powers that be. With a view to the larger Empire, Mather, in conversation with a new generation of Dissenting theologians as well as English political theorists and historians, became a strong and vocal advocate of a comprehensive understanding of Protestant liberty. He embraced a new identity as a loyal subject of the English crown and provincial citizen of the British Empire, whose identity he defined in contrast to the "popery" and political despotism of France or Spain. In line with this Whig version of imperial ideology, Mather saw the British as especially blessed by God with far-reaching political rights and religious freedoms.[13] But these privileges also needed to be jealously protected against popular corruption, royal overreach, as well as a power-hungry party of High Church Anglicans determined to oppress Dissenters. Mather's most detailed and sophisticated articulations of these idea(l)s can be found in his writings on history and church history as well as his biblical interpretations, notably his mammoth commentary on all the books of scripture, *Biblia Americana* (1693–1728), which he failed to publish during his lifetime, but which is now being made available in a critical edition.[14]

Mather saw the story of British Protestantism as part of a larger struggle between the forces of true Christian liberty and Antichristian tyranny spanning the postapostolic period to Christ's triumphant return. Like so many other Protestant exegetes, Mather believed that the course and millennial telos of

---

13 Owen Stanwood has argued that the Boston revolutionaries of 1689, "[r]eacting against the centralizing tendencies of the Stuart kings," adopted a specific, religiously inflected version of English "country ideology" to their own purposes." What made the outlook of these "American Whigs" like Mather specific is how it fused fears of arbitrary government and concerns for public virtue and local freedoms with panic over a "diabolical popish plot" and "apocalypticism." See Stanwood, *The Empire Reformed: English America in the Age of the Glorious Revolution* (Philadelphia: University of Pennsylvania Press, 2011).

14 See the ongoing edition: *Biblia Americana: America's First Bible Commentary: A Synoptic Commentary on the Old and New Testaments*, Gen. ed. Reiner Smolinski and Jan Stievermann, 10 vols. (Tübingen: Mohr Siebeck, 2010–). Citations from the *Biblia* are cited parenthetically, using the abbreviation BA.

church history was encoded in the Book of Revelation. In his extensive annotations on Revelation in the *Biblia Americana*, Mather frequently finds occasion to discuss the nature and development of Antichristian tyranny, as, for instance, in an essay-length entry on Revelation 9, in which Mather expounds the vision of the trumpets with the help of *The Judgments of God upon the Roman Church* (1689) by the Low Church Anglican exegete Drue Cressener. Here Mather argues that the spirit of Antichristian tyranny began to creep into the church as early as Constantine's reign, when Christianity became the established religion of the Roman Empire. The *"Christian Emperours"* were quickly "running into the *Tyranny* of the Heathen Princes" by governing the church with "a Spirit of *Persecution* towards Dissenters." This opened the door for the corruption of primitive Christianity by "horrible *Idolatries*, and *Superstitions*, and *Impieties*," because now fallible emperors and ecclesial councils became the ultimate authority in matters of faith, rather than the rules of scripture freely debated by pious Christians. Constantine's reign also ushered in the *"Tyranny* of the *Roman Church"* (BA 10:547). The reign of the Antichrist proper began in the fifth century, when the Western Roman Empire crumbled and the bishop of Rome asserted and expanded not only his spiritual but also his temporal power. The "Finishing Stroke of this Churchwork," Mather thought, was made when Pope Boniface assumed "the Title of, *Universal Bishop*. A. C. 606." With this, the *"Ecclesiastical* Authority" of Rome "became far more Absolute than ever the *Imperial* had been." At least in theory, the princes of all the kingdoms that succeeded the Western Empire ruled by the grace of the pope, who also claimed for himself the right to appoint bishops across these realms. Together princes and bishops began to exercise what Mather calls *"A Tyranny over Conscience*; The Forcing of Men against their *Conscience*, to submitt unto the *Roman Authority*, in Points of Faith and Worship" (BA 10:546–47). Just as the Pope made himself de facto the head of the church, arrogating the place of Christ, worldly princes everywhere in Europe, influenced by spirit of Antichristian tyranny, tended toward despotic rule over their peoples, thereby denying the ultimate Lordship of God. With the onset of the Reformation the reign of Antichrist had started to enter its final period, but spiritual and temporal tyranny would not be finally vanquished until the onset of the millennium, when the pristine church would be restored and liberty would prevail.

As Mather outlined in his anonymously published *Eleutheria* (1698), post-Reformation England had seen a constant struggle between what he—employing biblical allusions—called the party of the Eleutherians, or friends of true Christian liberty, and their opponents, the Idumeans. The latter, in Mather's interpretation, represented the Romanizing "Party in the Church of *England* which *hates to be Reformed*" and which, due to the nation's sins, had, again and again, prevailed since the days of Edward VI, seeking to counteract the "*Reformation of Doctrine*, in the very *Essential Points* of the *Grace of God*," and effectually stopping "the *Reformation of Discipline*." Under the Stuarts, this party had gained the upper hand and "procured those *Laws* to be Enacted against *Conscientious Dissenters*." Relying on the power of tyrannical rulers to further their own interests, the Idumeans had taught the divine right of kings and supported royal absolutism at the expanse of Parliament and the rule of law.[15]

An Eleutherian, according to Mather, was "any man who desires the *Reformation* of the *Church*, to be carried on by the *Rules* of the Lord Jesus Christ." Since the days of the Elizabethan compromise, such true Protestants were mostly found among the Puritan movement and the Dissenters, but also many conformists could be counted among them. What united the Eleutherians, for all their differences, was a shared concern for the essentials of the gospel and the evangelical conviction that true faith was a gift of grace that must be voluntarily embraced. This made them convinced that forced conversions or "Persecution for Conscience sake is a very Unchristian or Antichristian Symptom." Politically, everyone worthy of the name Eleutherian had "the heart of a true *Englishman* in him, for the *Constitution* of the *State*," that guaranteed "Government without *Slavery*, in *Spirituals* or *Temporals*."[16] They favored a system of checks-and-balances with a strong representative legislature, so "That no illegal, despotick, and *arbitrary Government* may be imposed upon the brave *English Nation*: LIBERTY and PROPERTY is their cognizance." Mather believed that the Nonconformists who originally fled from the persecution of the Idumeans into the "*American Wilderness*, now known by the Name of NEW-ENGLAND," in order to "pursue the *Designs* of a *Scriptural Reformation*, and enjoy the Spiritual *Blessings* of a *Reformed State*," had been the best of the "ELEUTHERIANS."[17] But since then, the colonies had also become a battlefield of the two contending parties, and during the Andros regime the cause of liberty had almost come to ruin. This view of New England history is also reflected in Mather's famous *Magnalia Christi Americana* (1702), especially his biographies of the governors. For instance, he painted Simon Bradstreet and William Phips as defenders of religious and political liberty against the tyranny of the Dominion government.

---

15 *Eleutheria, or, An idea of the Reformation in England and a history of non-conformity in and since that Reformation* (London, 1698), 76, 67, 70–71.
16 *Eleutheria*, 105, 60, 105.
17 *Eleutheria*, 59, 76.

Mather was convinced that the friends of liberty in Old and New England had the Bible on their side. In particular, Mather, in line with Reformed tradition, looked to the Old Testament for precedents of government that reflected God's will or defied it. Rick Kennedy has been the first to study this political dimension of Mather's Christian Hebraism.[18] When discussing the story of Joseph in Egypt in the *Biblia Americana*, for instance, Mather emphasized how the Jewish patriarch came to establish tyranny in Egypt and sinfully stripped "the *Egyptians* of those *Rights*, which all the Innocent Part of Mankind have a Natural Claim to." Joseph's despotism clearly ran counter to "the *Way of Governing* in the praceding Histories of the Bible," specifically when one considered what was told about the original and exemplary form of government instituted by Moses and how much of "a *Republican Strain* there appears in it" (BA 1:1111–13). Most clearly articulated in a series of entries on Exodus 18–19, Mather's understanding of the Mosaic government bespeaks the influence of early modern theories of Hebrew republicanism as well as English Whig theories of mixed government.[19] At Exodus 19:6, he commented that "the ancient *Form of Government* among the People of God," as settled by Moses after the exodus, was covenantal in nature. It derived from and corresponded with the covenant Israel had entered into with the "God of Heaven," who "would in a very peculiar and visible Manner bee the *King* of that People." He had "obtained their Election, and Submission, whereby they explicitly putt themselves under his Government." God "thereupon claimed all the *Rights of Majesty*, in Determining their *Lawes*, their *Wars*, and their *Officers*" (BA 2:260). The power of the officers, therefore, was derived from a three-way political compact among them, the people, and their God. It was predicated on the condition that they would govern in a way that answered to the laws of the divine covenant.

More specifically, Mather argued that the form of government instituted by Moses combined in its constitution elements of monarchy, aristocracy, and democracy. It featured a separation into judicative, legislative, and executive branches, and was organized in a multitiered fashion, starting with local magistrates and judges at the village level and rising up all the way to the state level. In the beginning, Moses was the "Chief Civil Magistrate," or head of the governing council, which judged "the most *Weighty Causes*" and decided "the most *Important Affayrs* of the Kingdome" in conjunction with the "Elders" or "Senate of Seventy." According to Mather's Hebraist sources, this senate (the Great

---

18 In the following section, I build on Kennedy's *The First American Evangelical: A Short Life of Cotton Mather* (Grand Rapids: Eerdmans, 2015), 54–58.

19 See Eric Nelson, *The Hebrew Republic: Jewish Sources and the Transformation of European Political Thought* (Cambridge, MA: Harvard University Press, 2010).

Sanhedrin), was an elective body chosen by "*Representatives* and *Governours of the Tribes*" and the "*Officers* and *Judges*" or "Captains," who administered and adjudicated local affairs. Quite possibly, the Mosaic form of government had already been a bicameral one like those of England or Massachusetts. For some scriptural passages suggested that the "Senate of the Seventy" was complemented and balanced by a "*Publick Council & Congregation of all the People*," a "*Parliament*" comprised of the "Captains of Thousands, the Seventy Seniors, and all the Chief of the People" (BA 2:257–58).

Later on, Moses's position as "Chief Magistrate" would be filled by other tribal chiefs and judges, before God eventually appointed kings for Israel. At 1 Samuel 8:7, Mather emphasized that the demand for a king was in response to a growing corruption of the people and its representatives, who were undermining the laws of the divine covenant. Yet the introduction of a stronger executive could not stop the loss of godliness and, in the long run, even exacerbated it. "Afterwards, when Saul, and when David, came *Arbitrarily* to do those things, which were formerly done by the Direction of God immediately," Mather commented, "the Loss was growing yet more Irretrievable," especially when the monarchy became hereditary and further expanded its power at the expense of the other branches of government (BA 3:270). To Mather, the Bible did not depict monarchy as inherently problematic. However, by highlighting the grievous crimes of even the greatest kings, David and Solomon, scripture taught that no mortal and sinful man must reign absolutely, lest kingship degenerate into tyranny. Monarchical rule had to be limited by God's laws and always needed to respect the natural rights and liberties of the people. And it must be balanced and checked by a representative body. Among the modern nations, Mather thought, the English people had been especially blessed by having a constitutional system that came closest to this divinely ordained model. However, English liberty was precarious and always under threat from the machinations of the "IDUMEANS."

Accordingly, Mather hailed every new monarch upon their ascension to the throne, just as he would try to establish good relations with every new governor of Massachusetts in the hope that they would rule in accordance with the "*Republican Strain*" of the Bible and the tradition of English liberty. Yet there was a pessimistic strand in his political thinking, reminiscent of the English Commonwealth men. Like them, Mather feared that due to the sinful nature of humans there was always a tendency toward corruption, the arrogation of power, and encroachment on rights. In a series of entries on Romans 13, Mather thus reflected on the conditions of and limitations to the Pauline command, "Let every soul be subject unto the higher powers." Especially significant is a lengthy entry on this passage derived from the annotations in John

Locke's *Paraphrase and Notes on the Epistles of St. Paul* (1705–07), which are, in turn, informed by his *Two Treatises on Government* (1689). In Robert E. Brown's illuminating analysis, Locke and Mather found in Paul "a universal theology of government," which, in accordance with Mosaic precept, asserted that all magistrates have their power from God.[20] Hence, they must rule according to, as Mather cited Locke, "the end for which God gave it, (that is) the good of the people sincerely pursued according to the best of the skill of those who share that power." Even if they personally are ungodly men, earthly rulers are owed allegiance, and Christian citizens must not resist their authority, as long the rulers respect the basic terms of the political covenant.[21] But unlike the modern "IDUMEANS" of England, Paul taught no doctrine of passive submission. Christians must not forgo "those due rights, which by the law of nature, or the constitutions of their country, belonged to them." The Pauline command of subjection applied only to "Magistrates having and exercising a *lawful* Power." If the powers that be continue to break the law and infringe upon those "due rights," Christians, by implication, have a right to resist them. And when Paul spoke of the duty to render one's dues, he did not determine "*who it was, to whom any of these, or any other Dues of Right, belonged.... For that he leaves them to be determined by the Lawes and Constitutions of their Countrey*" (*BA* 9:157). In other words, citizens could monitor their rulers and hold them accountable with regard to whether or not they conducted themselves in accordance with the law and the national constitution, which alone entitled them to their dues and obedience. Mather would have found Locke's reading of Romans 13 supportive of the position he had taken during Boston's Glorious Revolution and expressed in the *Declaration of Gentlemen*.

2 Mather and Religious Freedom

Cotton Mather's interpretation of religious freedom was arguably even more daring. It fundamentally called into question any form of religious coercion—including the model of a Congregational establishment implemented by the founders of Massachusetts Bay—not simply for pragmatic reasons but on

---

20 I here draw on Brown's "Bible Politics and Early Evangelicalism: Scriptural Submission and Resistance in Nonconformist Commentary," in *The Bible in Early Transatlantic Pietism and Evangelicalism*, ed. Ryan Hoselton et al. (University Park: Pennsylvania State University Press, 2022), 91–108, esp. 102–03.

21 John Locke, *A Paraphrase and Notes on the Epistles of St. Paul*, vol. 2, ed. Arthur Wainwright (Oxford: Clarendon Press, 1988), 586–87.

theological and scriptural grounds. Convinced that the New Testament provided a clear-enough model of primitive Christianity, Mather's grandfathers had primarily understood religious freedom as the freedom to realize what they regarded as a truly evangelical church order and form of worship. They did recognize liberty of conscience and the right to interpret the scriptures for oneself as worthy of protection, countenancing a relatively high degree of theological debate and diversity of opinions. However, as evinced in the expulsion of Anne Hutchinson and Roger Williams or the bloody suppression of the Quakers, this freedom found its limits where its outward expression was seen as violating the fundamentals of the faith and endangering orderly church life. The original Congregational establishment was based on an ideal of church-state relations that prescribed a separation in terms of their respective jurisdiction, but still involved close coordination and cooperation. Under the First Charter, in Witte's formulation, the "separation of church and state did not connote disestablishment of the dominant religion or the toleration of other religions."[22]

Under the New Charter, Congregationalism remained privileged, in that each parish and township was required to maintain at least one Congregational minister for whose support the state levied a tax on every citizen. However, Massachusetts now had to allow other Protestants to establish themselves and exercise their religion freely. Furthermore, political rights were no longer tied to Congregational church membership. Mather was surprisingly quick to see God's purpose behind these profound changes. By the early 1690s he had become a true champion of religious voluntarism. On Luke 14:23 ("compel them to come in") Mather noted in his *Biblia Americana* that this part of Jesus's parable had falsely served as a proof text to justify religious coercion. Like the Lord Jesus, the fathers of the primitive church had been convinced that "Men should not be *compelled* by any external Violence unto the Profession of the *Faith*." Rightly understood, the compulsion spoken of in this verse noted "only a sweet *Force* from Heaven upon the Minds & Wills of Men, which accompanies the Perswasion of the Faithful Ministers of the Gospel" (BA 7). But when the church rose to power this understanding was distorted. In his commentary on Revelation 9, Mather minced no words when describing the imposition of conformity and persecution in the post-Constantinian church as indicative of the rise of Antichrist. In assuming "*The Power of giving Law to the Consciences of Men in Disputable Matters*," he wrote, "The Christian Emperours [were] playing over again, the Game of *Tyranny*, that had been plaid by the *Pagans*, when

---

22   John Witte, Jr. and Joel A. Nichols, *Religion and the American Constitutional Experiment*. 5th ed. (New York: Oxford University Press, 2022), 27.

those *Martyrs* were *sacrificed* (BA 10:547). The sixteenth- and seventeenth-century Protestant reformers, including his forebears, had started to push back against this spiritual tyranny, but failed to realize evangelical liberty to its fullest extent.

Mather's engagement for that cause reflected his beliefs in the coming eschatological repristination of the primitive church, but also his concerns as he looked across the ocean. What he saw was a new wave of religious persecutions against European Protestants in Catholic territories, most dramatically in France after the revocation of the Edict of Nantes in 1685, which to him was indicative of the last raging of Antichrist. This made him fearful that, the Act of Toleration notwithstanding, English Dissenters on both sides of the Atlantic might have to face more hardships. For instance, eligibility for public office was still dependent on adherence to the Anglican communion. Between 1689 and 1702, the requirement to take the oaths and submit to tests was extended to beneficed clergy, members of the universities, lawyers, schoolteachers, and preachers. Criticizing these and other measures, Mather began to advocate for more robust protections of the full civic rights of nonconforming Protestants across the three kingdoms—no matter whether the establishment was Anglican as in England, Presbyterian as in Scotland, or Congregationalist as in Massachusetts. A "Christian by Non-conformity to this or that Imposed *Way of Worship*, does not break the Terms on which he is to enjoy the Benefits of *Humane Society*," he argued in a 1692 sermon before the governor and General Court, and hence has "a Right unto his Life, his Estate, his Liberty, and his Family," and should not be limited in his "*Political Capacity*."[23]

After the turn of the century, Mather's pleas for religious freedom became more emphatic, as Tories and High Church Anglicans under Queen Anne worked to further reinforce uniformity, for example by a bill to outlaw Occasional Conformity (1711) and the Schism Act of 1714, which targeted dissenting academies. As the imperial system tightened, Mather, like many of his fellow New Englanders, became increasingly worried that an "Anglicization" of the colonies would also step up the pressure for conformity there. In this situation, Mather—in dialogue with similar ideas by other Dissenters but also Latitudinarian bishops in favor of a "Broad Church"—promoted a comprehensive national church for England. To further "the Common Protestant Cause, Religion, and Interest in this Nation, and consequently in all other Nations and Countries," he wrote in *Eleutheria*, the Church of England was in need "of enlarging its Foundations, and consequently of taking in the Nonconformists,

---

23 Mather, *Optanda: Good men described, and good things propounded* (Boston, 1692), 44.

and making them constituent Parts of the Church with her self." Under such a comprehensive establishment, "Nonconformists" ought to be "on the same Foundation" with Conformists, ecclesiastically and politically.[24]

The Hanoverian succession of 1714 and the Whig Party's subsequent rise to supremacy entailed a growing influence of the Low Church faction in the Church of England that was readier to accommodate Dissenters. However, by that time the idea of a comprehensive church establishment for England was also dead. Still, Mather did not walk back any of his demands for religious liberty and also applied them to the situation in New England, past and present.

In chapter 13 of *Parentator*, the biography of his father published in 1724, he tells the exemplary story of how Increase Mather allegedly changed his mind on religious freedom. By means of that story, Cotton was able to at once celebrate the original Puritan project of creating a church-polity built on "The Faith and Order of the Gospel" "with all possible Purity," and to repudiate the founders' interpretation of the relation between church and state. Late in life, said Cotton Mather, Increase came to understand that the founders' zeal for ecclesial purity misled them into giving too much coercive power to the magistrate in religious matters: "Toleration was decried, as a Trojan horse profanely and perilously brought into the City of GOD." *Parentator* speaks of the "Unhappy Laws" against dissidents that sprang from the sometime "Bitter Spirit" of intolerance in the early days, and that produced some "Extremity" and "Unadvised and Sanguinary Things … particularly, the Rash Things done unto the Quakers."[25] Similarly, in *Brethren Dwelling in Unity*, Mather had expressed his regret over the persecution of Baptists in early New England.[26] For the members of any established church "to Punish Men, in their Temporal Enjoyments, because in some religious Opinions they Dissent from them, … is a Robbery, whereof he could not but say, *It appears to me Unreasonable*." Coercion only gave rise to sinful hypocrisy.[27]

---

24 *Eleutheria*, 117, 59. Mather's ideas for a comprehensive national church offering inner-Protestant toleration and consisting of a federation of assemblies with large discretionary freedoms to regulate the circumstantials of governance and worship, resembles those articulated by some English Dissenters, notably Mather's correspondent Edmund Calamy's. See the introduction to the second part of Calamy's *Defense of Moderate Conformity* (1704), part 2, 1–94. However, Mather had a much more elastic definition of the adiaphora.
25 Cited from *Two Mather Biographies: Life and Death and Parentator*, ed. William J. Scheick (Bethlehem, PA: Lehigh University Press, 1989), 115.
26 *Brethren Dwelling Together in Unity*, 39.
27 *Two Mather Biographies*, 116.

This chapter in *Parentator* also shows how Cotton Mather's mature position on these issues was crucially informed by his extended studies of the relevant New Testament texts and testimonies of the early church. Worked out over hundreds of pages in his *Biblia Americana*, these studies became distilled into his later published works. Jesus Christ himself would never have advocated the suppression or persecution of false believers, Mather now argued. Not once did he so much as imagine the possibility of his followers silencing the Sadducees or Pharisees. Rather, as Mather glosses on the parable of the wheat and the tares (Mathew 13:24–30) in *Parentator*, it was "the Declared Will of our SAVIOUR, That the Tares must have a Toleration" until His return.[28] Therefore, the modern officers of His church should not take it upon themselves to tear out perceived tares in the search for purity on this side of the millennium. Hence, Mather arrived at a version of biblical primitivism that idealized the apostolic, pre-Constantinian church also for its reliance on a voluntary promotion of the faith and abstinence from force.[29]

With regard to the issue of enforcing religious uniformity, Mather arrived at the conclusion that under the gospel dispensation, the Jewish laws regulating uniform worship and observance had been abrogated. The founders of the New England Way had mistaken these laws as prophetic types to be literally fulfilled in the future church, functioning as models for its internal discipline and relation to temporal power. Men like John Cotton had called for the magistrate to enforce both tables of Mosaic law and thus, like the pious kings of Israel, to punish and suppress blasphemers, apostates, and false prophets, as much as adulterers, murderers, and false witnesses. Ascribing his own insight to Increase again, Cotton writes in *Parentator*: "He became sensible, That the Example of the Israelitish Reformers, Inflicting Penalties on False Worshippers, would not Legitimate the Proceedings among the Christian Gentiles." The Jewish kingdom built in the promised land of Canaan had to be understood as a spiritual type. Its antitype, Christ's kingdom, was not of this world, or at least not fully, until the Parousia. Writes Mather: "The Christian Religion brings us not into a Temporal Canaan; it knows no Designs; it has no Weapons, but what are purely Spiritual."[30] Ironically, Cotton Mather thus approached Roger Williams's position in his famous debate with John Cotton.[31]

---

28 *Two Mather Biographies*, 115.
29 See also *Eleutheria*, 23.
30 *Two Mather Biographies*, 116. See also *Optanda*, 43.
31 See Reiner Smolinski, "'The Way to Lost Zion': The Cotton-Williams Debate on the Separation of Church and State in Millenarian Perspective," in *Millennial Thought in America: Historical and Intellectual Contexts, 1630–1860*, ed. Bernd Engler, Joerg O. Fichte, and Oliver Scheiding (Trier: WVT, 2002), 61–96, esp. 72.

In contrast to his forebears, Mather argued that the office of the magistrate in the Christian state should be confined to policing the second table of the Mosaic Law and thus to keeping the peace and upholding general Christian morality. This power of the civil magistrate, as he wrote in *Eleutheria*, to regulate "any disorder" also extended to the church, but only insofar as that disorder "shall have a direct influence on the *State*." Hence, the notion of a *"National Church Government"* was to be "recognized as no more than an *Human* and a *Civil* Policy *circa Sacra*."[32] Matters of doctrine or worship practice ought to be out of bounds for the state. Like Roger Williams, or William Penn for that matter, Mather included in the disorders to be suppressed by the magistrate gross "Blasphemies and Attempts to Poison People with Atheism and Profaneness," but he did so not because such actions violated conformity. Rather, they must be checked by the magistrate, as he now argued, because they "Destroy the Ligaments of Humane Society." Yet anyone, including Catholics and Jews, ought to enjoy full civic liberties as long as they are loyal and law-abiding subjects who do not seek to seek to undermine the Protestant state-church. Arguing for a de facto secular definition of citizenship, Mather proclaims in *Parentator*, "that a Good Neighbour and a Good Subject, has a Claim to all his Temporal Enjoyments before he is a Christian."[33] Mather's arguments thus reflect the growing influence of Enlightenment philosophies, most significantly that of Locke, which conceived of innate and inalienable natural rights: "Liberty of Conscience" to Mather is now as much a "Native Right of Mankind," as a person's "Right unto his *Life*, and all the Comforts of it." These rights should be fully enjoyed by every law-abiding *"Good Subject."*[34] Nevertheless, Mather still insisted that the state ought to function as a protector and supporter of Protestant religion, as long as that cooperation with the churches was broad-based enough. The government must not impose a particular version of Protestantism.

Eventually, these theological deliberations led Mather to call for a reform of church polity in Massachusetts that mirrored his plan for a comprehensive Church of England. In his handbook for candidates for the ministry, *Manuductio ad Ministerium* (1726), Mather proclaimed that in New England, Protestants

---

32   *Eleutheria*, 58. Compare, again, Calamy's *Defense of Moderate Conformity* (1704), part 2, esp. 29–30, 89–94.

33   *Two Mather Biographies*, 116. See also *Brethren Dwelling in Unity*, 37. Here Mather also clarifies his positions on Catholics. He argues for toleration as long as there are no efforts to work against Protestantism. Such efforts ought to be checked by the magistrate: "The *Papist* also whose declared Principle it is, to *Persecute* as soon as he shall be uppermost ought certainly so far to be mortified as to be kept *uncapable* of exerting his own execrable principle" (37–38).

34   Mather, *Brethren Dwelling in Unity*, 37.

of all stripes should enjoy the freedoms of worship, ecclesial self-government, and forming "Sacred Corporations." He even proposed that all Protestant churches should equally partake in the "Priviledges and Advantages of the *Evangelical Church-State*."[35] It is not entirely clear whether this meant that Mather challenged the system of parochial Congregationalism, as it had developed since the 1690s, or whether he thought of further accommodations for other Protestant churches. We know that since the turn of the century he had supported court decisions that enabled Baptists and others to be exempted from the duty to pay the parochial church taxes for the Congregational ministry and instead use tithes for the upkeep of their own clergy.[36] However, in practice the required registration and formal incorporation could be difficult to obtain, especially for small religious communities. So maybe Mather was advocating a more generous handling of this existing system of exemption. But his language is broad enough to allow for the possibility that he was ready to move beyond that model toward a kind of general Protestant establishment.

Mather's definition of what counted as Protestantism became quite elastic. Mather's exegetical work did not shake his inherited belief that Congregationalism was the most scriptural form of church organization and government. When he published his apologetic account of New England Congregationalism, *Ratio Disciplinae*, in 1726, he reaffirmed that conviction while, at the same time, distancing himself from what now appeared as a rather embarrassing case of provincial hubris on the part of those founders, who saw the New England Way as an immediate anticipation of Christ's millennial church. Decades of scrutinizing the New Testament Epistles and the Book of Acts seem to have deepened Mather's awareness of the uncertain scriptural basis of many of the finer points of ecclesial polity and liturgy that the Protestant churches had traditionally quarreled about. These debates were irresolvable by biblical or rational arguments, but ultimately the differences on which they turned did not really matter that much in Mather's mature view.

Such differences, as he asserted in *Malachi* (1717), were to be counted among the "Lower and Lesser points of Religion" that did not pertain to salvation: "They are not External Rites and Forms, that will distinguish, The People of GOD. The Kingdom of GOD comes not with the Observation of such things as those. No; 'Tis a People found in various Rites, and in various Forms," Mather boldly proclaimed. Rather, they "are All that cordially embrace our Everlasting MAXIMS of PIETY, and Live unto GOD upon them, in whatever Subdivision of

---

35   Mather, *Manuductio ad Ministerium. Directions for a Candidate of the Ministry* (Boston, 1726), 126.

36   See, for instance, his reflections on how the advantages of the *"Church State"* ought to be made available to all Protestants in *Brethren Dwelling Together in Unity*, 28–29.

Christianity, they are to be met withal." For years, Mather labored on distilling these "Everlasting MAXIMS of PIETY" from the Scriptures. Combining the fundamental doctrines of God and Christ with "Real and Vital PIETY," these maxims contained what Mather considered the core of the Christian faith necessary unto salvation. Eventually, he reduced these to three, so that being a true Christian consisted in the "Fearing of God, and in Prizing of His CHRIST, and in Doing of Good unto Men." A demonstrable devotion to these scriptural maxims made one a true Christian, which in Mather's mind was identical with being a true Protestant. At the same time, these scriptural maxims marked the outer boundaries of Mather's definition of Protestantism and thus limited who, in his mind, ought to enjoy the full ecclesiastical privileges of the *"Evangelical Church-State"* he envisioned. This excluded not only Catholics but also Quakers, Deists, and other groups that did not subscribe to a fundamentally "orthodox" understanding of the doctrine of God or of Christ's redemptive work.[37]

On this side of the millennium, Protestants should love one another and work together as much as possible to advance the kingdom. They should also, as Mather emphasizes in his later works, practice pulpit exchange and table fellowship: "And let the Table of the Lord have no Rails about it, that shall hinder a Godly *Independent*, and *Presbyterian*, and *Episcopalian*, and *Antipedobaptist*, and *Lutheran*, from sitting down together there."[38] Mather believed that the Second Coming was not far off. In conjunction with it, he, like many Puritans and Pietists, expected an eschatological revival, which would enable the completion of the Reformation, the overcoming of remaining differences on adiaphoric matters, and the spread of evangelical liberty to the far ends of the world.

3   Conclusion

Together with other recent studies, John Witte's works have encouraged us to appreciate anew how the "Puritan teachings on liberties of covenant and covenants of liberty were one fertile seedbed out of which later American constitutionalism grew." Witte has pointed to the afterlife of "Puritan constitutional ideas … among various Enlightenment Liberal and Civic Republican schools of

---

37 Mather, *Malachi Or, The Everlasting Gospel, preached unto the Nations* (Boston, 1717), 51. On Mather's project of uniting Protestants under his Maxims of Piety, see my "A 'Syncretism of Piety': Imagining Global Protestantism in Early Eighteenth-Century Boston, Tranquebar, and Halle," *Church History* 89, no. 4 (Dec. 2020): 829–56.

38 Mather, *Manuductio*, 127, 115.

American political thought in the later eighteenth and nineteenth centuries."[39] As I hope to have demonstrated, looking at Cotton Mather's political theology, which he developed in his biblical interpretations and historical writings, helps us better understand the crucial but understudied period of transition in the New England tradition from the "classical" age of seventeenth-century Puritanism to the prerevolutionary period of the mid-eighteenth century. The continuities to the more religiously and socially conservative Revolutionaries are especially strong, as evinced, for example, by the writings of New England's own John Adams. In *A Dissertation on the Canon and Feudal Laws* (1765), Adams paid homage to the Puritan ideas of guaranteed rights, mixed government, rooted in a consensual compact and limited by law, which we have found so fully articulated by Mather. Adams noted, too, that his forebears, while generally loyal to the king, had always acknowledged a divine right of resistance against tyrants. Indeed, Mather's reading of Romans 13 in many ways anticipates Jonathan Mayhew's widely cited refutation of a Christian duty of passive resistance in *A Discourse Concerning Unlimited Submission and Non-resistance to the Highest Powers* (1750). Likewise, Mather's principled critique of all forms of religious coercion looks forward to Elisha Williams's famous *Essential Rights and Liberties of Protestants* (1744), while Mather's propositions for a broad-based Protestant establishment in many ways resemble the religious provisions of the Massachusetts Constitution of 1780, or what Patrick Henry envisioned for postrevolutionary Virginia in his *A Bill Establishing a Provision for Teachers of the Christian Religion* (1784). Thus, Mather represents an "establishmentarian" model that aimed to reconcile religious freedom with a vision of Protestant Christendom. This model would still have significant support in the early republic, but ultimately lost out against the radical separationist paradigm shared by Jeffersonians and Baptists alike.

---

39 *The Reformation of Rights*, 318.

CHAPTER 20

Religious Liberty in the Thirteenth Colony

Joel A. Nichols

As a college senior in the mid-1990s, I was exploring graduate programs and talked with John Witte, Jr. about the possibility of attending Emory University to join the law and religion program.[1] He was persuasive, encouraging me to attend and to come study with him and his colleagues there. When I began as a first-year law student that next year, Professor Witte was my criminal law professor. He promptly called on me on the very first day, interrogating me extensively and socratically in a class of some ninety students. While I recall the stress of being "on call" that first time and wondering if I'd merely stumbled around the material, I remember even more strongly crossing paths with Professor Witte in the parking lot when leaving school that same day. Our brief conversation went like this: "Nice work today in class, Joel," he said with a smile. That sort of kindness, connected to his expectation of excellence and academic rigor, has remained a hallmark of our nearly thirty-year relationship.

During my time at Emory, I was fortunate to work as John's research assistant for four years. This included an early invitation, even while a student, as a full participant in a roundtable discussion of religious liberty with international scholars—and then a nudge to publish a solo article as part of that endeavor. In later years, John's encouragement never ended, even as our professor-student relationship pivoted into collaboration and occasional coauthorship.

For this volume, I'm honored to contribute a chapter that bridges our long relationship. What follows is drawn primarily from research for my MDiv honors thesis (and, yes, John was one of my readers!). But this work also evidences strong overlap with my partnership with John in more recent years on religious

---

1 An earlier version of this chapter originally appeared as chapter 12 of *Disestablishment and Religious Dissent: Church-State Relations in the New American States, 1776–1833*, edited by Carl H. Esbeck and Jonathan J. Den Hartog (Columbia: University of Missouri Press, 2019). Reprinted by the permission of the University of Missouri Press. It is adapted, in part, from "Religious Liberty in the Thirteenth Colony: Church-State Relations in Colonial and Early National Georgia," *New York University Law Review* 80, no. 6 (2005): 1693–772.

© JOEL A. NICHOLS, 2024 | DOI:10.1163/9789004546189_021
This is an open access chapter distributed under the terms of the CC BY-NC 4.0 license.

liberty, including the role that history plays in our current understandings and applications of core ideas.

∴

1   Religious History

From its founding in 1732, Georgia was a place of both religious tolerance and religious pluralism. Early Georgians valued liberty of conscience and free exercise of religion, direct but nonpreferential governmental support for religion, and nondiscrimination based on religion.[2] These multiple principles of religious liberty found in the colonial charter stemmed from the necessity of recognizing divergent religious beliefs and religious faiths.[3] A mixture of religious adherents was welcomed, and the various faiths were not asked to conform to or support the Church of England. This pluralism served as an ameliorating feature helping to render "reality milder than the law" with respect to church-state relations.[4] There was a gradual movement toward recognizing the value of disestablishment, and even when, in 1758, the Church of England became the official church in the colony, the establishment was, in practice, a weak (or "soft") establishment with limited real ecclesiastical presence.

Georgia's religious pluralism was so accepted that it was seen as unremarkable at the time, and relations among religious groups were relatively harmonious. Aside from the prohibition against Catholics, it appears that itinerant preachers were welcome in Georgia, especially after the Revolution and especially in the frontier regions. During the period of establishment in the colonial period, 1758–1776, dissenters still played a prominent role in civic life.[5]

At Georgia's founding, the trustees of the colonial corporation decided against establishing an official church, but they sent an Anglican minister with

---

2   Allen D. Candler, ed., *The Colonial Records of the State of Georgia* (Atlanta: Franklin-Turner, 1907) 13:257–58.
3   John Witte, Jr., Joel A. Nichols, and Richard W. Garnett, *Religion and the American Constitutional Experiment*, 5th ed. (New York: Oxford University Press, 2022), 29–34, 60–71, 74, 84, 91.
4   Hugh Trevor-Roper, "Toleration and Religion after 1688," in *From Persecution to Toleration: The Glorious Revolution and Religion in England*, ed. Ole Peter Grell, Jonathan I. Israel, and Nicholas Tyacke (New York: Oxford University Press, 1991), 389, 400.
5   Rev. John J. Zubly, letter, Savannah, GA, July 11, 1773, *Proceedings of the Massachusetts Historical Society* 8 (1865): 216.

the first group of colonists in November 1732—the first in a line of rapid turnover.[6] Parishes struggled to attract ministers, both before and after the 1758 establishment of the Church of England. Further, the numerical strength of the Anglican church remained surprisingly low throughout the entire eighteenth century.[7] For example, in 1748 there were 388 dissenters and only 63 Anglicans in Savannah, with as few as 200 practicing Anglicans in the whole of Georgia by the end of the proprietary period (1752).[8] That number seems implausibly low, but there are no other reliable estimates. What does seem sure is that the Church of England was not the strong force that established churches were in South Carolina and Virginia. By the turn of the century, when the Church of England in the newly independent United States had been renamed the Protestant Episcopal Church, it had gone from the preferred religion of the colonial founders to the legally established religion to merely one of many diverse religious groups.

There was surprising variation in religious groups in Georgia. Jews were present from the inception of the colony, such that one-fourth or one-fifth of Savannah's citizens were Jewish at the end of the first year. The Jewish community continued throughout the period up to the Revolution, with Georgia granting the congregation a charter of incorporation and land for a new synagogue.[9]

Two groups of Lutherans settled in Georgia, known commonly as the Salzburgers (so named because they generally emigrated from Salzburg in modern Austria) and Moravians. The trustees convinced the pietistic and persecuted Salzburgers to immigrate by stressing free exercise of religion and offering to fund their migration.[10] The Salzburgers settled in their own community

---

6   Henry Thompson Malone, *The Episcopal Church in Georgia, 1733–1957* (Atlanta: Protestant Episcopal Church in the Diocese of Atlanta, 1960), 5–6, 24–42; and Junius J. Martin, "Georgia's First Minister: The Reverend Dr. Henry Herbert," *Georgia Historical Quarterly* 66, no. 2 (1982): 113–18. See, for example, William R. Cannon, "John Wesley's Years in Georgia," *Methodist History* 1 (1963): 1.

7   Reba Carolyn Strickland, *Religion and the State in Georgia in the Eighteenth Century* (New York: Columbia University, 1939), 15–34, 52–53.

8   Malone, *Episcopal Church in Georgia*, 25; Edwin Scott Gaustad, *Historical Atlas of Religion in America* (New York: Harper & Row, 1962), 8.

9   See, generally, Saul Jacob Rubin, *Third to None: The Saga of Savannah Jewry, 1733–1983* (Savannah: S. J. Rubin, 1983); B. H. Levy, "The Early History of Georgia's Jews" in *Forty Years of Diversity: Essays on Colonial Georgia*, ed. Harvey H. Jackson and Phinizy Spalding (Athens: University of Georgia Press, 1984), 163; and Edmund S. Morgan, *Roger Williams: The Church and the State* (New York: W. W. Norton, 1967), 51.

10   George Fenwick Jones, *The Salzburger Saga: Religious Exiles and Other Germans along the Savannah* (Athens: University of Georgia Press, 1984), 4, 9.

(Ebenezer) and continued to increase, reaching as many as twelve hundred by the early 1770s.[11] In 1735 two groups of Moravians arrived and stayed in Savannah (instead of possessing their land grant).[12] Numbering no more than thirty, the pacifist Moravians did not stay long. Because of their conscientious objection to military service, Moravians ceased coming to Georgia, and those already in Georgia eventually moved to Pennsylvania.[13]

Scottish Presbyterians began arriving in early 1736, coming more for land than to escape religious persecution. By 1755 Savannah's Presbyterian population founded the Independent Presbyterian Church, with John J. Zubly serving as minister to patrons in and outside of Savannah.[14] Other Presbyterians from the older colonies settled in the frontier regions of Georgia and petitioned the legislature for land grants, although they did not form any churches that we know of. These Presbyterians also petitioned the governor and the Council (the upper house of the colonial legislature) in 1765 to grant fifty thousand acres for immigrants from Ireland. Settlers that arrived as late as 1769 were granted land and funds by the Council, with grants limited to Protestants.[15]

Congregationalists arrived in 1752, coming to Georgia because of the availability of land, and were soon joined by others from New England.[16] By 1771 their geographic area boasted about 350 white inhabitants and 1,500 slaves, and Congregationalists controlled about one-third of Georgia's wealth.[17] After some hardship, the Congregational Church reconstituted itself and became strong enough to incorporate under the 1789 incorporation law.[18]

---

11   Harold E. Davis, *The Fledgling Province: Social and Cultural Life in Colonial Georgia, 1733–1776* (Chapel Hill: University of North Carolina Press, 1976), 16–17; George Fenwick Jones, *The Georgia Dutch: From the Rhine and Danube to the Savannah, 1733–1783* (Athens: University of Georgia Press, 1992), 38–39, 48; and *Colonial Records of Georgia*, 5:674.

12   Wallace Elden Miller, "Relations of Church and State in Georgia, 1732–1776" (PhD diss., Northwestern University, 1937), 184–88; and *Colonial Records of Georgia*, 2:81, 29:143. See also Jones, *Georgia Dutch*, 49–51; and Miller, "Relations," 188–90.

13   Strickland, *Religion and the State in Georgia*, 76–78; Davis, *Fledgling Province*, 18; and Jones, *Georgia Dutch*, 52–53. On the Moravians leaving Georgia, see *Colonial Records of Georgia*, 21:364–65, 404–5, 503–5, 4:22–23.

14   Miller, "Relations," 194–95; Orville A. Park, "The Georgia Scotch-Irish," *Georgia Historical Quarterly* 12, no. 2 (1928): 115; and Ernest Trice Thompson, *Presbyterians in the South* (Richmond, VA: John Knox Press, 1963), 37.

15   Strickland, *Religion and the State in Georgia*, 117–18.

16   Allen P. Tankersley, "Midway District: A Study of Puritanism in Colonial Georgia," *Georgia Historical Quarterly* 32, no. 3 (1948): 149; and Strickland, *Religion and the State in Georgia*, 115–16.

17   Davis, *Fledgling Province*, 22, 201.

18   James Stacy, *History and Published Records of the Midway Congregational Church: Liberty County, Georgia* (Spartanburg, SC: Reprint, 1979), 45; and Horatio Marbury and William H.

There was a halting Quaker presence in Georgia. While Quaker settlers were explicitly contemplated by the 1732 charter, no families arrived until 1767, when a group from Pennsylvania was given land grants. After the Revolution, these Quakers eventually migrated to Ohio, spurred by internal strife and opposition to slavery.[19]

By the late 1790s, Baptists gained large numbers of adherents through revivalism. Sustained growth and the presence of a Baptist church did not take hold until the early years of the revolutionary period.[20] By 1793, however, Baptists were the most numerous denomination in the state, and they grew in influence as well as numbers.[21] There were also Black Baptist churches in Georgia, including the largest Baptist church after the War of Independence at Savannah, which climbed to around seven hundred members by 1800.[22]

Methodism was slower to come to Georgia than to other parts of the United States.[23] The first Methodist societies were not present until the mid-1780s, when there were only seventy members in the state. In just a few years, Methodism grew to more than eleven hundred members, with rapid expansion during the 1790s and beyond.[24]

Catholics were always few in number, and their exclusion had both religious and political motives. Both the charter and the continuing use of oaths were

---

Crawford, eds., *Digest of the Laws of the State of Georgia* (Savannah: Seymour Woohopter & Stebbins, 1802), 144–45.

[19] Alex M. Hitz, *The Wrightsborough Quaker Town and Township in Georgia* (Bulletin of Friends Historical Association) (1957): 10–12, reprinted in Robert Scott Davis, Jr., ed., *Quaker Records in Georgia: Wrightsborough 1772–1793* [Friendsborough, 1776–77] (Augusta, GA: Augusta Genealogical Society, 1986): 2–4.

[20] J. H. Campbell, *Georgia Baptists: Historical and Biographical* (Macon: J. W. Burke, 1874), 1–2; and Jesse Mercer, *History of the Georgia Baptist Association* (Washington, GA: Georgia Baptist Association, 1979), 13–18. See also Robert G. Gardner et al., *A History of the Georgia Baptist Association, 1784–1984* (Atlanta: Georgia Baptist Historical Society, 1988), 12.

[21] Gardner, *History of Georgia Baptist Association*, 41.

[22] Ronald W. Long, "Religious Revivalism in the Carolinas and Georgia from 1740–1805" (PhD diss., University of Georgia, 1968), 117; and Gardner, *History of Georgia Baptist Association*, 17.

[23] Frederick E. Maser and Howard T. Maag, eds., *The Journal of Joseph Pilmore, Methodist Itinerant, For The Years August 1, 1769 to January 2, 1774* (Philadelphia: Message, 1969), 180–81. See also Warren Thomas Smith, *Preludes: Georgia, Methodism, the American Revolution* (Atlanta: Methodist Administrative Services, 1976), 18; and Alfred Mann Pierce, *A History of Methodism in Georgia, February 5, 1736–June 24, 1955* (Atlanta: North Georgia Conference Historical Society, 1956), 27.

[24] Maser and Maag, *Journal of Joseph Pilmore*, 37–38; George G. Smith, *The History of Georgia Methodism from 1786 to 1866* (Atlanta: A. B. Caldwell, 1913), 26–29; Pierce, *History of Methodism in Georgia*, 34–38, 56–57, 59; and Warren Thomas Smith, *Preludes*, 22–27.

largely effective against Catholicism, as the largest number reported in Georgia over the first twenty years was four, in 1747.[25] The trustees tried to prevent Catholics from obtaining land and canceled grants when the grantees were found to be Catholic, and they prevented any Catholics from inheriting land through will, deed, or trust.[26] Catholics continued to struggle for legal equality after the Revolution, and little is known about their actual numbers.[27]

The relative equality of the Protestant dissenting groups alongside the then-established Anglican church at the time of Revolution can be seen in the 1773 report by Zubly: "[I]n the present house of Representatives, a third or upwards are dissenters, & most of the churchmen of moderate principles." With such political clout in the hands of dissenters, we may believe Zubly when he reports that "[t]here has been little or no altercation between the church & dissenters."[28]

2 Beginnings: A Haven for Dissenting Groups

After years of urging by South Carolinians, Great Britain relented in deciding to establish a series of settlements to the south of South Carolina for protection against the Spanish, French, and Native Americans in Florida. The initial impetus for settling Georgia in the late 1720s was to provide a haven for debtors languishing in English jails. By the time of the Crown's grant of a charter in 1732, the underlying goals for the colony had expanded to include "all unfortunates," and colonial Georgia quickly became a haven for European groups that had been persecuted because of religion.[29] This religious pluralism was due to explicit guarantees of religious liberty in Georgia's initial charter.[30]

---

25 Strickland, *Religion and the State in Georgia*, 43.
26 *Colonial Records of Georgia*, 1:319, 550, 2:230, 271; and Strickland, *Religion and the State in Georgia*, 81.
27 Correspondence of Henry Laurens, of South Carolina, microformed on "Materials for History Printed from Original Manuscripts," 39–45 (Frank Moore, ed., 1861); and Georgia Constitution of 1777, Article VI (1785), reprinted in Francis Newton Thorpe, *Federal and State Constitutions, Colonial Charters, and Other Organic Laws of the States, Territories, and Colonies Now or Heretofore Forming the United States of America* 2 (1909): 773.
28 Zubly, letter, Savannah, July 11, 1773, 216.
29 E. Merton Coulter, *Georgia: A Short History* (Chapel Hill: University of North Carolina Press, 1960), 16; E. Merton Coulter and Albert B. Saye, eds., *A List of the Early Settlers of Georgia* (Athens: University of Georgia Press, 1949); Davis, *Fledgling Province*, 31–32; Strickland, *Religion and the State in Georgia*, 115; *Colonial Records of Georgia*, 38:120; and *Collections of the Georgia Historical Society*, 3 (1873), 167.
30 *Charter of Georgia* (1732), reprinted in Thorpe, *Colonial Charters*, 773.

King George II issued a charter to the corporate trustees of the colony of Georgia on June 9, 1732. The charter makes explicit the "liberty of conscience" for *all* persons, including Catholics, but "free exercise" of religion is granted to all persons *except* Catholics. There is no establishment of the Church of England in the charter. Indeed, the charter makes no mention of the need to spread Christianity through evangelism (which was standard in previous American colonial charters). The only invocation of the divine is a statement that the success of the colony will depend upon the blessing of God. There is an implicit acknowledgment of the religious pluralism that would soon exist in the colony through an allowance for the possibility of affirmation, in lieu of oath swearing, for the "persons commonly called quakers." There is no conscientious objection clause, since one of the founding purposes was to provide a defensive buffer for South Carolina against the Spanish and others. Finally, the text of the charter is only the starting point for religious liberty in Georgia, for it provides that the corporation behind the venture should make laws "fit and necessary for and concerning the government of the said colony, and not repugnant to the laws and statutes of England."[31]

During this proprietary period, the government provided direct support to religion in several ways. The salaries for Anglican ministers initially came primarily from the Society for the Propagation of the Gospel in Foreign Parts (SPG), whereas the corporate trustees set aside glebe lands and provided indentured servants to work those lands, from which the proceeds would go to support the church and the ministry. While these glebes were not specifically designated for the Church of England, they were so used in fact.[32]

Aside from the glebes and moneys from the SPG, Anglican ministers were paid out of a general grant by Parliament, from donations by individuals designated to Georgia for "religious uses," and by a twenty-pound stipend the British government made payable to every Anglican minister who went to the colonies.[33] The trustees took additional actions to support religion in the colony: providing clothing and supplies for the traveling evangelist George Whitefield, funding the construction of parsonages and churches, and arranging for a catechist in Savannah to educate the children in religious matters.[34]

When the SPG discontinued paying the salary of the rector of Christ Church parish in Savannah, in 1771, Parliament provided seventy pounds to the rector

---

31 Thorpe, *Colonial Charters*, 765, 772–74.
32 Ibid., 45–54; Strickland, *Religion and the State in Georgia*, 47–48, 53; and *Colonial Records of Georgia*, 2:148–49, 200–2, 509–10.
33 *Colonial Records of Georgia*, 3; and Strickland, *Religion and the State in Georgia*, 45, 51.
34 *Colonial Records of Georgia*, 19:394–96, 29:200, 31:25, 27, 3:51, 135, 141, 165.

each year, as well as providing funds for two schoolmasters.[35] Additionally, the Georgia legislature provided money for ministers through a tax on liquor, applied to liquor purchases by Anglicans and dissenters alike.[36]

Direct governmental support for religion was strikingly not limited to the Church of England. The Salzburgers petitioned the trustees for a grant of glebe land in the 1740s, receiving five hundred acres and other direct support for their church, including paint and oil for constructing churches; an altar cloth, vestments, a chalice, and other articles for use in services; and money to help build houses for their ministers.[37]

In 1741 the trustees directed that marriages should be performed according to the canons of the Church of England. However, the Salzburgers were exempt from this requirement, provided their clergy obtained licenses from a magistrate. Salzburger ministers were not allowed to marry Englishmen without permission from civil officials, unless there was no English minister available. In the royal period (1752–1776), the governors were given power to grant marriage licenses and charged with ensuring that marriages conformed to rites of the Church of England, securing a colonial law to that effect, if possible. However, such a law was never passed in Georgia.[38]

Education in Georgia was somewhat haphazard and occurred under the auspices of the government, the churches, and sometimes a combination of the two.[39] For example, the Anglican church maintained a direct role in the education of children in Savannah, even though the schools were officially run by the civil government. The Salzburgers provided education for the young of their community, with religion playing a role in the curriculum and instruction.[40] An attempt was made by the touring evangelist George Whitefield to create a college for further education. This never came to fruition because various patrons added conditions to funding, including one by the Archbishop of Canterbury that the college would always be led by a member of the Church of

---

35 Ibid., 34:124, 161–62, 218.
36 Strickland, *Religion and the State in Georgia*, 112–13; *Colonial Records of Georgia*, 28:24, 26.
37 Compare Strickland, *Religion and the State in Georgia*, 70–71, 76, with *Colonial Records of Georgia*, 26:164, 6:255; see also Davis, *Fledgling Province*, 207–12, 22:299.
38 Strickland, *Religion and the State in Georgia*, 69, 123. See also *Colonial Records of Georgia*, 34:296.
39 Strickland, *Religion and the State in Georgia*, 92–99, 176–79.
40 Davis, *Fledgling Province*, 236, 239–40; *Colonial Records of Georgia*, 34:69–70, 298–99, 483; and Henry Melchior Muhlenberg, *The Journals of Henry Melchior Muhlenberg*, ed. Theodore G. Tappert and John W. Doberstein (Camden, ME: Picton Press, 1945), 669.

England and the liturgy used at the college would always be Anglican.[41] These conditions conflicted with Whitefield's vision that the college would rest upon "a broad bottom, and no other."[42] While Whitefield did not give up on his plans, he died before any alternative could be secured.[43]

3 Royal Colony Status: Retaining "Space" for Dissenters

In 1752, due to financial pressures, the trustees surrendered their interests to George II, and the royal period began.[44] This period also marked a movement toward greater favoritism of the Church of England by the Crown and its colonial supporters. It was not until October 1754 that the president of the corporation received the royal decree to turn over power to the governor and the Council. The transfer of power little touched matters of religion. Not all appointed Council members were required to be Anglicans.[45] All those appointed took oaths and met religious tests, including allegiance to the king and rejection of transubstantiation, the latter excluding Catholics from office.[46] However, there is some evidence that the insistence upon oath taking was not strictly enforced, for by 1773 as many as one-third of the Assembly were dissenters, and there is no record of any dissenters being excluded.[47] The Georgia legislature did try to liberalize its policies on oaths in 1756, but that attempt was overturned by the Privy Council in 1759 because dissenters in England did not enjoy a similar exemption.[48] The governor and the Council continued the practice

---

41 See George Whitefield, *The Works of the Reverend George Whitefield* (London: Edward & Charles Dilly, 1771), 3:475–79; and Peter Y. Choi, *George Whitefield: Evangelist for God and Empire* (Grand Rapids: Eerdman's, 2018), 194–232.
42 Whitefield, *Works of Whitefield*, 3:481–82.
43 Long, *"Religious Revivalism"*, 206–7; *Georgia Gazette*, Jan. 31, 1770.
44 *Colonial Records of Georgia*, 2:523–25.
45 W. Keith Kavenaugh, ed., "Transfer of the Government of Georgia from a President and Assistants to a Royal Governor and Council, October 13, 1754," *Foundations of Colonial America: A Documentary History* (New York: Chelsea House, 1973) 3:1835–36, 1839. See also *Colonial Records of Georgia*, 7:183.
46 Kavenaugh, "Transfer of the Government," 1838. See, for example, *Colonial Records of Georgia*, 34:66, 295.
47 "Estate of Lucretia Triboudite, Feb. 27, 1770," in *Inventories of Estates*, book F, Reel 40/33, 448–50 (Georgia Department of Archives and History); Zubly, letter, Savannah, July 11, 1773, 214, 216; *Colonial Records of Georgia*, 7:12–13, 15, 335–36.
48 *Colonial Records of Georgia*, 18:158–59, 16:111, 126; William L. Grant and James Munro, eds., *Acts of the Privy Council of England, Colonial Series* (London: HMSO, 1908–12), 4:407–8.

of the trustees and were generous with dissenters—especially regarding land grants for church construction and glebes.[49]

The formal establishment of the Anglican church in Georgia was a three-year process. In 1755 a bill to establish the Church of England was passed by the Assembly (the lower house of the legislature), but failed to pass the Council (which was appointed by the king and included one dissenter and one dissenter sympathizer).[50] Two years later, the Assembly proposed a similar bill, and again the Council did not approve it.[51] The Assembly tried again the following year and succeeded in overcoming the opposition of two prominent dissenting groups: the Salzburgers and a Congregationalist community. The latter had urged the Assembly to remember that the colony was founded as "an Asylum for all sorts of Protestants to enjoy full Liberty of Conscience Prefferable [sic] to any other American Colonies."[52]

When this third bill went to the Council—which was composed entirely of Anglicans, except for two dissenters—it stalled until the bill was amended in a way that omitted the words "Church of England" and substituted instead the phrase "to establish the Worship of God in the Province of Georgia."[53] Because some on the Council feared this phrasing would establish religion too broadly, the Assembly met in conference with the Council to create a compromise. The final bill functionally established the Church of England, but omitted any express mention of the Church of England as established, or of Anglicanism as the "official religion of the colony." It mentioned the phrase "Church of England" only in the title and preamble.[54] This third bill passed within fourteen days of its introduction.[55]

---

49   *Colonial Records of Georgia*, 7:183, 293, 388, 588, 749, 8:111; Strickland, *Religion and the State in Georgia*, 124.

50   *Colonial Records of Georgia*, 13:66. See also 16:55, 62, 65.

51   *Colonial Records of Georgia*, 13:156–157, 159, 16:180–81.

52   "Unsigned Letter in Favor of Ottolenghe, Without Date, Read in Committee (Jan. 15, 1759)," SPG Archives, series C, AM.8, #1 (Misc. Docs. Ga., 1758–84), microformed on *Society for the Propagation of the Gospel in Foreign Parts, American Material in the Archives of the United Society for the Propagation of the Gospel* (Micro Methods, 1964), at reel C2, 2; *Colonial Records of Georgia*, 13:257–58.

53   "Ottolenghe Letter," Jan. 15, 1759.

54   "Ottolenghe Letter," Jan. 15, 1759, 4–5. The *Colonial Records* say that the Assembly portion of the conference committee consisted of six members and not three (contrary to the report of Ottolenghe's letter). *Colonial Records of Georgia*, 13:294, 16:287.

55   *Colonial Records of Georgia*, 13:248, 260–61, 265–66, 270, 274, 277–78, 291–95, 298, 305, 16:266–68, 272–73, 277–79, 282–84, 287–88, 297; "Ottolenghe Letter," Jan. 15, 1759.

The 1758 Act divided Georgia geographically into eight parishes.[56] Ministers and rectors were authorized to sue and be sued in the church's name, were endowed with the cure of all souls in their parish, and were given possession of all the Anglican church property in the parish—including houses of worship, cemeteries, glebe lands, and any other church realty. The law also established a system for election of church wardens and vestrymen, charged with caring for and governing the churches. All freeholders or taxpayers in a parish were entitled to vote, and the only requirement for serving as a vestryman or church warden was to be an inhabitant of the parish (and a freeholder, in the case of church wardens).[57]

The rector, wardens, and vestrymen were empowered to raise money in their parishes by taxes "on the estate, real and personal," of all people within the parish. These tax revenues not only covered church expenses but were also for the general well-being of the community. Ministers and rectors were forbidden from exercising "any ecclesiastical law or jurisdiction whatsoever." This was an important jurisdictional separation for non-Anglicans, who feared the power of canon or ecclesiastical courts common in England.[58] Part of the general tax revenue of Georgians also went to support Anglican ministers. Ironically, most of the ministerial salary paid by the colonists came not from the 1758 act but from taxes on alcohol.[59] The lack of a religious test for vestrymen and church wardens was a clear victory for dissenters. Historical records, though scarce, indicate that at least some non-Anglicans were elected as vestrymen and church wardens.[60]

The royal instructions to the governor of Georgia provide additional insight into the control over religion in this period. Governors were instructed to ensure that God was worshipped in accordance with the rites of the Church of England and that ministers were assigned, churches were built, and glebes were maintained. The governor was to grant licenses to perform marriages and probate wills, and he was required to see that vice was punished. The governor was given the authority to appoint an Anglican minister to a benefice when a parish became vacant.[61] In practice, however, the appointment of ministers was largely done by a vestry's appeal to the SPG in England.[62]

---

56 *Colonial Records of Georgia*, 18:690.
57 Kavenaugh, "Transfer of the Government," 3:2309, 2311.
58 Kavenaugh, "Transfer of the Government," 3:2312, 2314.
59 Strickland, *Religion and the State in Georgia*, 112–13.
60 *Georgia Gazette*, Jul. 12, 1769 (listing John Rae as vestryman); Muhlenberg, *Journals of Muhlenberg*, 625, 630, 644.
61 See *Colonial Records of Georgia*, 34:3ff. (1754), 245ff. (1758), 390ff. (1761), 424ff. (1761).
62 Davis, *Fledgling Province*, 204.

Immediately after the passage of the 1758 act, the Georgia Assembly passed a bill empowering constables to enforce the peace on Sundays in Savannah. Ministers of the Church of England and many others were exempted from being selected as a constable, which was akin to jury duty.[63] If a person was not exempt and failed to serve as constable when selected, he was required to pay ten pounds sterling to the parish.

If a man did serve as a constable in Savannah (and only Savannah, it appears), he was to "attend, aid, and assist the church wardens" in preventing "tumults from Negroes and other disorderly people." Even more striking is the language requiring constables to "take up and apprehend all such persons who shall be found loitering or walking about the streets and compel them to go to *some place* of divine worship."[64] This directive to compel attendance at a church service, and not specifically at the Anglican service, underscores the strength of competing religious groups—at least Protestant groups—even after establishment.

Four years later, in 1762, the Georgia legislature outlawed the sale of most goods and services on "the Lord's Day." Church wardens and constables of each parish were authorized to roam the streets twice each Sunday, during worship time, to ensure compliance.[65] There are no records that indicate that a fine was ever imposed, evidencing a general solicitude for religion and Sabbath quietude rather than support specifically for the Church of England.

While the establishment of the Anglican church was not particularly onerous for dissenters, disputes did occasionally arise. The most prominent clash regarding religious liberty in royal Georgia centered on whether dissenters would have to pay fees to the Anglican rector and sexton when they used the services of the church in burying their dead.[66]

Reverend Samuel Frink was a convert to Anglicanism who had grown up the son of a Congregational minister in New England. Seeking to increase his income, Frink took the side of the Church of England as the established church and sought to incorporate privileges he deemed appropriate to that

---

63 See act of March 27, 1759, *Foundations of Colonial America*, 3:2062–66.
64 *Foundations of Colonial America*, 3:2065 (Section XI) (emphasis added).
65 The law further stated that violators must be prosecuted within ten days after committing the offense and that a person was entitled to treble damages if he was prosecuted and acquitted. Act of March 4, 1762, *Foundations of Colonial America: A Documentary History*, 3:2314–17 (Section II).
66 To some extent, though, the disagreements were mostly a personal squabble between the two leading ministers of Savannah. For more on Zubly, see Joel A. Nichols, "A Man True to His Principles: John Joachim Zubly and Calvinism," *Journal of Church & State* 43, no. 2 (2001): 297.

status. His theory was that any fees paid for the utilization of religious services at the Anglican church should be paid to the Church of England and its minister—none other than himself. The Assembly had designated an appropriate schedule of fees for the performance of certain tasks, including bell ringing and grave digging, by the Anglican sexton at funerals and burials. Frink sought to enforce payment of the fees even when the Anglican sexton did not perform the duties, bringing a lawsuit in 1769 against a leading Presbyterian, Reverend John J. Zubly, who had arranged a funeral for a pauper.[67] At the trial in the Court of Conscience, the jury brought in a verdict in favor of Frink. The judge quickly affirmed the decision, claiming that the sexton had a right to fees for burials anywhere in the parish, and thus dissenters had no right to a bell of their own.[68]

The judgment infuriated the editor of the *Georgia Gazette*. Reporting the case in editorial fashion, the newspaper decried the ruling as biased against dissenters and counter to the "FREE exercise" of religion guaranteed by "the charter of this province."[69] Zubly, too, was outraged by the decision. Publishing letters addressed to Frink, Zubly protested the injustice of paying fees to a sexton and rector for work that they never performed.[70] Zubly's primary concern was the precedent of the case—that it might to be used to assess fees against dissenters all across Georgia.[71] Provincial legislators introduced bills to address the matter, but the bickering over bells and cemeteries was interrupted before final action was taken. Rather, the interests of the colony were consumed by the deteriorating relations with England. The controversy sufficiently subsided that Zubly could later write, "We now bury in the same Ground unmolested, & pay no fees except to the sexton, which I have consented to pay whenever his attendance should be required, & not otherwise."[72]

Another dispute between Anglicans and dissenters centered on licenses to perform marriages. Governor Henry Ellis (1758–60) had altered marriage

---

67   Frink also brought a lawsuit against the captain of a ship for having his Presbyterian mate buried in Savannah according to the same protocol. Davis, *Fledgling Province*, 204, 224–25.
68   Davis, *Fledgling Province*, 226; *Georgia Gazette*, May 10, 1769.
69   *Georgia Gazette*, May 10, 1769. This was a historical error by the editor, as the provincial charter had been superseded by royal charter and only liberty of conscience was protected—not free exercise.
70   Randall M. Miller, ed., *"A Warm & Zealous Spirit": John J. Zubly and the American Revolution, a Selection of His Writings* (Macon, GA: Mercer University Press, 1982), 86–88.
71   Indeed, Frink proceeded with at least one other suit against a recently widowed female dissenter. Miller, *"Warm & Zealous Spirit,"* 90. There are no historical records incidating a court appearance on the matter.
72   Zubly, letter, Savannah, July 11, 1773, 217.

licenses upon request to authorize dissenters (instead of an Anglican rector) to perform weddings. Governor James Wright (1760–76), however, would not grant this courtesy, apparently thinking it not within his power. Reverend Frink therefore allowed Reverend Zubly to perform ceremonies on licenses made out to Frink, but Zubly declined any fee payment from the betrothed couple. Frink soon tired of endorsing licenses to Zubly with no benefit, save Frink's ability to boast that he was the only licensed minister in the parish. So Frink changed the relationship such that Zubly was to charge a fee and give half of the money to Frink. This provoked Zubly to cease seeking endorsements from Frink. Zubly stubbornly continued to perform marriage ceremonies even though he lacked government sanction.[73] Meanwhile, the Lutheran Salzburger ministers at Ebenezer continued to perform marriages between couples of their own flock in accord with their rites, and could perform marriages among non-Salzburgers in accord with the rites of the Anglican church.[74]

Thus, as the Revolution approached, there was increased debate among religious groups about the proper role of government in religion, especially resentment concerning preferences vested in the established religion. The Revolution cut short this discussion. Yet it would take several years of evolving legal formulations for Georgia to work out a more nuanced and evenhanded position on these matters.

4 Three Constitutions: Revolution and Beyond (1777–1798)

Revolutionary feelings took hold only slowly in Georgia. In 1774 Georgia sent no delegates to the First Continental Congress, notably irritating the other colonies.[75] The following year, Georgia did send five delegates to the Second Continental Congress. Only a few months later, in February 1776, the colonists conclusively wrested control of the government from the royal governor, James Wright, who had been under house arrest.[76] A state Provincial Assembly met and promulgated a short document on April 15, 1776,[77] which was the "first written fundamental document ever made by Georgians." It was not so much a constitution as a "short text of eight rules and regulations," designed to be

---

73 Zubly, letter, Savannah, July 11, 1773, 218.
74 Strickland, *Religion and the State in Georgia*, 123.
75 Franklin Bowditch Dexter, ed., *The Literary Diary of Ezra Stiles, D.D., L.L.D. President of Yale College* (New York: Charles Scribner's Sons, 1901), 544–46.
76 Coulter, *Georgia: A Short History*, 118–26.
77 This document is reproduced in Allen D. Candler, ed., *The Revolutionary Records of the State of Georgia* (Atlanta: Franklin-Turner, 1908) 1:274–77.

temporary and contingent upon developments in the Second Continental Congress and the exigencies of the time.[78] The document made no mention of religion, but merely set down rules for keeping the peace until such time as a fuller form of governance could be constructed.

Upon official receipt of the Declaration of Independence on August 10, 1776, Archibald Bulloch, who had been named by the state's temporary republican government as president and commander-in-chief of Georgia, convened the Provincial Assembly to read the document, begin securing delegates, and call a constitutional convention. The convention met in Savannah from October 1, 1776, to February 5, 1777, and resulted in the adoption of the Constitution of the State of Georgia.[79] The bulk of the 1777 constitution addressed structural governmental concerns, resulting in the formation of legislative and executive branches, the latter consisting of both a council and a weak governor. It addressed religion in Article 56: "All persons whatever shall have the free exercise of their religion; provided it be not repugnant to the peace and safety of the State; and shall not, unless by consent, support any teacher or teachers except those of their own profession."[80]

This provision echoed some of the more tolerant sentiments of the 1732 charter. It apparently subsumed liberty of conscience in the text "free exercise of their religion." It also began to disestablish religion—although there was neither a formal statement of disestablishment of the Church of England nor a measurable level of religious agitation or malcontent expressed at the Georgia convention. Government financial support for religion persisted, but persons were not forced to contribute money to the religion of others. The 1777 constitution did retain the "peace and safety of the State" proviso, which could result in government control over religious practices that were harmful to others.[81]

While Catholics and non-Christians were guaranteed free exercise of religion, they were excluded from serving as representatives in the Assembly. Only persons "of the Protestant religion" were eligible to serve in that capacity.[82] This policy actually was an advance for the period—especially when coupled with the lack of religious test for voters.[83] The other explicit mention of religion in the constitution was the exclusion of clergy of all denominations from

---

78 Coulter, *Georgia: A Short History*, 129.
79 Cynthia E. Browne, *State Constitutional Conventions from Independence to the Completion of the Present Union, 1776–1959, a Bibliography* (Westport, CT: Greenwood Press, 1973), 8:43.
80 Georgia Constitution of 1777, Article LVI, reprinted in Thorpe, *Colonial Charters*, 784.
81 Georgia Constitution of 1777, Article LVI, reprinted in Thorpe, *Colonial Charters*, 784.
82 Georgia Constitution of 1777, Article VI (1785), reprinted in Thorpe, *Colonial Charters*, 779.
83 Georgia Constitution of 1777, Article IX.

holding a seat in the legislature.[84] Such an exclusion was common in state constitutions for many years.[85]

There is no mention of "God" or "Almighty" anywhere in the 1777 constitution—not even in the preamble. This omission stands in contrast to a number of other state constitutions at the time. Nor is there any mention of religion in the provision for education, which simply reads: "Schools shall be erected in each county, and supported at the general expense of the State, as the legislature shall hereafter point out."[86] Finally, the 1777 constitution made some allowance for Quakers and Anabaptists, whose beliefs did not allow them to swear oaths.[87] Such individuals were allowed to affirm, instead of swear, in denoting their allegiance to Georgia.[88] However, the document did not make such an allowance for persons being sworn into state offices.[89]

The 1777 constitution, similar to its progeny, made no mention of conscientious objection for pacifism—despite the fact that a town of Quakers had settled in Wrightsborough. Rather than a right to conscientious objection from military service, Georgia—like other states and even the federal government—chose to deal with the matter by legislative discretion rather than by constitutional right. In 1778 Georgia excused persons from military service for reasons of conscience, but it imposed double taxation for exercising such a choice.[90] The exemption was discontinued in 1792 for three years and then reinstated. During this three-year interim, Quakers were allowed to pay an additional 25 percent tax for conscientious objection. From 1784 to 1792, clergy were unconditionally exempt.[91]

One other feature of the 1777 constitution touches on religion—that of the renaming of parishes. Newly designated as counties, the geographic areas received nonreligious appellations in place of their old titles, which had been based upon saints and tied to the 1758 establishment of the Church of England.[92]

---

84   Georgia Constitution of 1777, Article LXII.
85   See, for example, Anson Phelps Stokes, *Church and State in the United States* (New York: Harper, 1950), 1:622–28.
86   Georgia Constitution of 1777, Article LIV, reprinted in Thorpe, *Colonial Charters*, 784.
87   Georgia Constitution of 1777, Article XIV ("Every person entitled to vote shall take the following oath or affirmation, if required, viz....").
88   Georgia Constitution of 1777, Article XIV.
89   Georgia Constitution of 1777, Article XXIV.
90   *Colonial Records of Georgia*, 19:96.
91   Marbury, *Georgia Digest* 356, 359–60.
92   Georgia Constitution of 1777, Article IV, reprinted in Thorpe, *Colonial Charters*.

The 1777 constitution left open the possibility of a state tax to support religion of each person's "own [religious] profession." In 1782 an attempt at such a statute was introduced in the Assembly that provided for the establishment of churches and schools. Nothing came of this. Two years later, another attempt was made to pass a bill to promote religion and piety by granting certain rights and material aid to religious societies and schoolhouses.[93] In 1785, however, a funding measure found success. The Georgia legislature passed a bill allowing tax monies to be used in each county "[f]or the regular establishment and support of the public duties of Religion."[94] The law proclaimed that the "regular establishment and support [of the Christian religion] is among the most important objects of Legislature [sic] determination."[95]

The Georgia Baptist Association sent a lengthy remonstrance (probably authored by Silas Mercer) to the legislature, decrying the 1785 bill and protesting the intervention of the government in religious affairs: "[R]eligion does not need such carnal weapons as acts of assembly and civil sanctions, nor can they be applied to it without destroying it." The Baptist Association was also worried that passage of one such law might lead to others of an even more intrusive nature—including laws that would lead "to the establishment of a particular denomination in preference and at the expense of the rest." The state's role was, rather than passing laws supporting religion, to support morality generally and to ensure that "all are left free to worship God according to the dictates of their own consciences, unbribed and unmolested."[96]

The 1785 act guaranteed "all the different sects and denominations of the Christian religion ... free and equal liberty and Toleration in the exercise of their [r]eligion," and confirmed all the "usages[,] rights, [i]mmunities and privileges ... usually ... held or enjoyed" by religious societies.[97] Each county with at least thirty heads of families was to select a minister of a church of its choosing to whom state tax dollars would flow. The tax rate was set at four pence on every hundred pounds' valuation of the property owned by church members. Upon receipt of the tax revenue, the sum would be paid from the state treasury directly to the minister. When the population grew sufficient to warrant another church, at least twenty heads of families could petition to be

---

93   Candler, *Revolutionary Records*, 141, 465; *Journal of the General Assembly, House* (Jan. 21, 1784–Aug. 15, 1786), 9, 11, 19, 53–54.
94   *Colonial Records of Georgia*, 19:395–98; *Journal of the General Assembly, House* (Jan. 21, 1784–Aug. 15, 1786), 161, 167, 227, 233, 248, 266.
95   *Colonial Records of Georgia*, 19:395.
96   Samuel Boykin, *History of the Baptist Denomination in Georgia* (Atlanta: Jas P. Harrison, 1881), 1:262, 263.
97   *Colonial Records of Georgia*, 19:397–98.

recognized as a separate church and its minister receive a proportionate share of tax dollars.

The only evidence of implementation of the 1785 act is an advertisement in the *Georgia Gazette* on January 26, 1786. The advertisement urged all Episcopalians in Chatham County to register with their church wardens so that their numbers might be determined for submitting an application of the tax monies from the treasury.[98] There is no other known implementation, and the law was subsequently superseded by an article concerning religious freedom in the 1798 constitution.[99]

5 New Constitutions

Following ratification of the United States Constitution in late 1788, Georgians revisited their state constitution. The legislature appointed three individuals from each county, and they drafted a proposed constitution from November 4 through 24, 1788. Copies were circulated throughout the state.[100] The people then elected delegates who convened to consider the document. The delegates made so many alterations as to necessitate a second convention. So in April 1789, a second constitutional convention met and completed the document. It was ratified on May 6, 1789.[101] Unfortunately, there are no extant records or journals of the two conventions.[102]

The 1789 constitution provided for a bicameral legislature and a stronger executive. The major clause on religion was shortened to read: "All persons shall have the free exercise of religion, without being obliged to contribute to the support of any religious profession but their own." The "peace and safety" provision was happily dropped, possibly due in part to James Madison's prominent fight in Virginia to remove similar language from the Virginia Declaration of Rights. There was no clause on the disestablishment of religion, and citizens

---

98 *Georgia Gazette*, Jan. 26, 1786.
99 Georgia Constitution of 1798, Article IV, Section 10, reprinted in Thorpe, *Colonial Charters*, 791.
100 Walter McElreath, *A Treatise on the Constitution of Georgia* (Atlanta: Harrison, 1912), 86–87.
101 John N. Shaeffer, "Georgia's 1789 Constitution: Was It Adopted in Defiance of the Constitutional Amending Process?," *Georgia Historical Quarterly* 61, no. 4 (1977): 339; Coulter, *Georgia: A Short History*, 173; and Fletcher M. Green, *Constitutional Development in the South Atlantic States, 1776–1860: A Study in the Evolution of Democracy* (Getzville, NY: William S. Hein, 2015), 127–28.
102 Browne, *State Constitutional Convention*, 43; and Green, *South Atlantic States*, 127–28.

were presumably still subject to being compelled to support their own religion should the 1785 act be enforced.

Other changes regarding church-state relations found their way into the 1789 constitution in more subtle ways. The requirement of professing the Protestant faith as a prerequisite for public office dropped out, but the exclusion of clergy "of any denomination" from membership in the General Assembly was retained. As a further acknowledgment of the religious pluralism in the state, the opportunity to affirm rather than swear to the oath of office was extended to members of the state Senate and House of Representatives as well as to the governor. Although the foregoing concession was primarily an accommodation to the Quakers, the right of conscientious objection from military service was still omitted. Another notable omission was the removal of any mention of education in the constitution, whether public or private schools. Finally, the 1789 constitution still did not mention God or "the Almighty" in its preamble or in its text. The latter continued to run counter to many other states.[103]

A nonreligious issue of great importance in the 1789 constitution was the provision for a convention to revise the document just five years later.[104] So in 1795 (a year late), delegates met and made several amendments to the constitution that entered into force without popular ratification. But no mention was made of religious issues. The delegates further provided for another constitutional convention to be held just three years later.[105]

The *Journal* from this 1795 convention shows that a delegate moved that "Rev. Mr. Mercer be requested to offer up a Prayer to the Supreme Being." Mercer complied.[106] This is potentially important because sources indicate this was probably Silas Mercer, a Baptist preacher present at both the 1795 and 1798 constitutional conventions. Sources conflict on the number of Baptists at these two conventions. Their influence on the issue of disestablishment is not

---

103 Georgia Constitution of 1789, Article I, Sections 1, 3, 7, 18; Article II; Article IV, Section 5, reprinted in Thorpe, *Colonial Charters*, 785.
104 Georgia Constitution of 1789, Article IV, Section 8.
105 See, generally, *Journal of the Convention of the State of Georgia, Convened at Louisville, on Monday, May 3d, 1795, for the Purpose of Taking into Consideration, the Alterations Necessary to be Made in the Existing Constitution of this State. To Which Are Added, Their Amendments to the Constitution* (Augusta: A. M'Millan, 1795) (hereafter cited as *1795 Journal*). The amendments are reprinted in Thorpe, *Colonial Charters*, 790, and they touch on such matters as length of service for a senator, method of gubernatorial election, date of meeting of the assembly, reapportionment of representation in the lower house, and place of the capital of the state (moved to Louisville).
106 *1795 Journal*, 4.

certain but likely material.[107] Other than the one statement about prayer, the 1795 *Journal* has no discussion of religion.

The 1798 constitutional convention met amid increasing tensions over fair representation between the growing number of upcountry settlers and the longstanding inhabitants of the coastal cities. The new constitution retained the formal structure of the old, but allowed for more flexibility in designating new counties and more allowance for representation to meet the crisis over voter apportionment. Delegates provided enough changes that the document is considered a new constitution instead of merely amendments to the earlier one, as first contemplated. The 1798 constitution proved stable enough to last Georgia until the eve of the Civil War.

The *Journal* of the 1798 convention reveals only hints at the mindset of the delegates, and external historical sources are not illuminating regarding the rationale for the presence or absence of various provisions. The first mention of religion is on the opening day. The delegates resolved that "the Convention will attend divine service tomorrow [Wednesday, May 9, 1798] at 11 o'clock, in conformity to the proclamation of the President of the United States."[108] This was in response to President John Adams's call for a day of fasting and prayer over the threat of war with France.

With the 1789 constitution (as amended in 1795) serving as a template, sections were read aloud and then agreed upon or amended by delegates present. The 1798 constitution lengthened the religion clause, providing for a fuller range of religious liberty and disestablishment. Article IV, Section 10, provided:

> No person within this State shall, upon any pretence, be deprived of the inestimable privilege of worshipping God in a manner agreeable to his own conscience, nor be compelled to attend any place of worship contrary to his own faith and judgment; nor shall he ever be obliged to pay tithes, taxes, or any other rate, for the building or repairing any place of worship, or for the maintenance of any minister or ministry, contrary to what he believes to be right, or hath voluntarily engaged to do. No one

---

107 *1795 Journal*, 3–4. Silas Mercer's son Jesse Mercer was also a Baptist minister reputedly at this convention, though his name does not appear in the *Journal*. A "James Mercer" is mentioned in the *Journal*, but the relation of these men is unclear. See *1795 Journal*, 4. James Mercer may have been Jesse Mercer's uncle, though about his same age. See C. D. Mallary, *Memoirs of Elder Jesse Mercer* (New York: John Gray, 1844), 18. Another source proclaims that three Baptist ministers (Silas Mercer, Benjamin Davis, and Thomas Polhill) were present at this 1795 convention. Boykin, *Baptist Denomination in Georgia*, 1:263.

108 *Journal of the Convention of the State of Georgia* (Louisville, 1798), 2 (hereafter cited as *1798 Journal*).

religious society shall ever be established in this State, in preference to another; nor shall any person be denied the enjoyment of any civil right merely on account of his religious principles.[109]

The drafters chose to elaborate in some detail their intentions regarding religion, rather than invoking the commonly used terms of art such as "free exercise" and "liberty of conscience." Thus, an individual's freedom to worship, and to worship according to his or her conscience, was made sacrosanct. Noncompulsion in matters of religion was secured. Disestablishment took the form of a guarantee that an individual was not required to pay monetary support for a place of worship, minister, or ministry contrary to that individual's beliefs. The principle of nonpreferential treatment of religions was constitutionalized and was linked to governmental nonestablishment of any one religious group. This, however, left open the possibility of nonpreferential government aid to religion in general. All religious tests were ended.

The 1798 *Journal of the Convention* sheds little light on this expanded section. The previous religion clause was read (by an unnamed person), and then "it was moved to amend the same by Mr. [Jesse] Mercer [a Baptist minister and Silas's son,] as follows.... On the question thereupon, it was agreed to."[110] Other than this short paragraph, no mention is made of the religion clause. Although the 1798 *Journal* gives no additional information to indicate authorship of the religion clause, it has long been speculated that Silas Mercer, the prominent Baptist minister previously mentioned, was behind it.[111] There is no textual support for this other than the singular statement from the 1798 *Journal* quoted above and that the completed clause moved Georgia closer to Baptist understanding of the relationship between church and state. It appears that seven or more Baptists, including Mercer, attended the convention, which would have meant that seven of sixty-eight delegates were Baptists.[112] The measurable Baptist presence lends to the plausibility of Baptist influence on the religious freedom section.

---

109   Georgia Constitution of 1798, Article IV, Section 10.
110   *1798 Journal*, 21.
111   William Bacon Stevens, *A History of Georgia, from Its First Discovery by Europeans to the Adoption of the Present Constitution in MDCCXCVIII* (Philadelphia: E. H. Butler, 1859), 2:501. Stevens asserted that section of Constitution "securing religious liberty of conscience, in matters of religion, was written by the Rev. Jesse Mercer." See also *1798 Journal*, 28.
112   Boykin, *Baptist Denomination in Georgia*, 263; and Spencer B. King Jr., *Baptist Leaders in Early Georgia Politics*, 5 *Viewpoints: Georgia Baptist History* 45 (1976). This would have meant that Baptists comprised 10 percent of the convention, or four times the percentage of Baptists in the overall state population at the time.

The 1798 constitution contained additional provisions touching on religion. First, the option of affirmation instead of oath swearing was retained for the offices of governor, senator, and representative.[113] Second, the ban on clergy holding seats in the legislature was discontinued.[114] Finally, the 1798 constitution retained some notable omissions from its predecessors: no mention of education (let alone private religious education), no reference to God or a deity in the preamble or elsewhere, and no mention of conscientious objection to military service.

With the adoption of the 1798 constitution, Georgia set in place the elements of modern religious freedom: free exercise was guaranteed to all, the state was to have no single established church and no preference among religions, clergy were not excluded from public or political life, oaths or affirmations were allowed for discharging public duties or holding public office, there were no religious tests, and no one could be forced to support a minister or church unless they agreed to its tenets.

6 Conclusion

Religious pluralism was the norm in colonial Georgia as dissenters and persecuted groups came to the new colony, often lured by the promise of land and tranquility to worship in accord with conscience. As evidenced by its policies regarding glebes and education, the proprietary colonial government did not show significant favoritism among religious groups—at least for those Protestant faiths with sufficient adherents. Even when the royal government established the Church of England in 1758, the relationship between religion and the Crown did not change markedly. Georgia's Anglican establishment was a "soft" establishment, as the laws relating to establishment were weakly enforced and were, in practice, more for the maintenance of the welfare of the poor and needy than for the promulgation of the Christian gospel. Because religion and morality were seen as important in civil society, the authorities were willing to foster and aid religion whenever possible. This continued even after the Revolution, with the passage of the rather striking 1785 act that provided

---

113   Georgia Constitution of 1798, Article I, Section 18–19; Article II, Section 5.
114   When the section that excluded ministers of all denominations from the legislature came up for discussion, it was initially retained with no discussion in the *Journal*. However, the following day, "Mr. [James] Simms" from Columbia County proposed to amend the exclusion by including practicing attorneys in the exclusion; the amendment passed. *1798 Journal*, 12. No further move was made on the offending section until the following day, when the convention struck the entire section from the constitution. *1798 Journal*, 16.

for direct governmental support of religion through collection and redistribution of tax dollars. While there is little record of enforcement of the 1785 act, its text was not limited to the Protestant Episcopal Church. Apparently never implemented generally, the statute was repealed by the 1798 constitution.

Georgia was explicitly founded as a Protestant Christian colony, but its founders and charter alike readily accorded all its new inhabitants a good measure of religious liberty. Liberty of conscience was promised to all, and free exercise to all except Catholics and non-Christians. These seminal principles seem to have held sway throughout eighteenth-century Georgia, and citizens were free to observe their own religious beliefs and practices relatively unmolested—even after an established church was instituted. The principles of liberty of conscience and free exercise later evolved into the modern disestablishment formulations put forth by dissenters as the flegling state progressed through three constitutions.

Viewed collectively, the record indicates that most early Georgians thought there should be close cooperation between church and state, with no clear preference for only one Protestant denomination. Early Georgia was a place with respect for religion and religious differences; a place that experimented with a soft establishment of the Church of England, only to move away from the idea after less than twenty years; and a place that believed government had a direct role to play in fostering religion and morality generally. With the adoption of the 1798 constitution, the state took a material step toward adopting the view of Baptists and other Protestant dissenters, whereby the support of each church was entirely voluntary for those who adhered to its doctrines and engaged with its practices.

CHAPTER 21

"A Wall of Separation": Church—State Relations in America and Beyond

Daniel L. Dreisbach

Few metaphors in American letters have had a greater influence on law and policy than Thomas Jefferson's "wall of separation between Church & State."[1] In our own time, the "wall of separation" has been accepted by many Americans as a pithy, authoritative expression of the First Amendment prohibition on laws "respecting an establishment of religion." Leading twentieth-century jurists embraced this figurative phrase as a virtual rule of constitutional law and as an organizing theme of church-state jurisprudence. In *Everson v. Board of Education* (1947), the U.S. Supreme Court was asked to interpret the First Amendment's nonestablishment provision. "In the words of Jefferson," the justices famously declared, the First Amendment "clause against establishment of religion by law was intended to erect 'a wall of separation between church and State.' ... That wall must be kept high and impregnable. We could not approve the slightest breach."[2] The following term, in *McCollum v. Board of Education* (1948), Justice Hugo L. Black asserted that the justices had "agreed that the First Amendment's language, properly interpreted, had erected a wall of separation between Church and State."[3] The "wall of separation" has become the *locus classicus* of the notion that the First Amendment mandates a strict separation between religion and the civil state.

Even at the Supreme Court, however, the metaphor has not been received uncritically. In *McCollum*, Justice Stanley F. Reed denounced the Court's reliance on the metaphor. "A rule of law," he protested, "should not be drawn from a figure of speech."[4] More than a decade later, in the 1962 school prayer case,

---

1   Thomas Jefferson to the Danbury Baptist Association, Jan. 1, 1802, in *The Papers of Thomas Jefferson*, ed. Julian P. Boyd et al., 45 vols. to date (Princeton, NJ: Princeton University Press, 1950–), 36:258 [hereinafter *Papers of Jefferson*].
2   *Everson v. Board of Education*, 330 U.S. 1, 16, 18 (1947).
3   *McCollum v. Board of Education*, 333 U.S. 203, 211 (1948).
4   *McCollum*, 333 U.S. at 247 (Reed, J., dissenting).

Justice Potter Stewart similarly cautioned his judicial brethren. The Court's task in resolving complex constitutional controversies, he opined, "is not responsibly aided by the uncritical invocation of metaphors like the 'wall of separation,' a phrase nowhere to be found in the Constitution."[5] The following term, in the 1963 school prayer case, Stewart reiterated his concern that the nuance and complexity of the "First Amendment cannot accurately be reflected in a sterile metaphor which by its very nature may distort rather than illuminate" the issues before the Court.[6] In 1985, then Justice William H. Rehnquist, writing in dissent, assailed the Court's reliance on the metaphor: "There is simply no historical foundation for the proposition that the Framers [of the First Amendment] intended to build the 'wall of separation' that was constitutionalized in *Everson*.... The 'wall of separation between church and State' is a metaphor based on bad history, a metaphor which has proved useless as a guide to judging. It should be frankly and explicitly abandoned."[7] In the years that followed, the Court appealed less frequently to the metaphor, although there were occasional efforts to rehabilitate its use in church-state jurisprudence. Justice John Paul Stevens, writing in dissent, warned in 2002 that "[w]henever we remove a brick from the wall that was designed to separate religion and government, we increase the risk of religious strife and weaken the foundation of our democracy."[8] Twenty years later, Justice Sonia Sotomayor, also writing in dissent, bitterly complained that "[t]his Court continues to dismantle the wall of separation between church and state that the Framers fought to build."[9]

What is the source of this figure of speech, and how did this symbol of strict separation between church and state become so influential in American legal and political thought? More important, what are the consequences of its ascendancy in church-state law, policy, and discourse? What should the student of church-state relationships and the interplay between religion and civic life make of this architectural metaphor? Has it illuminated or obfuscated understandings of the prudential and constitutional relationship between church and state, the sacred and the secular? Finally, what has John Witte, Jr. contributed to our understanding of this metaphor? These are among the questions considered in this chapter.

---

5 *Engel v. Vitale*, 370 U.S. 421, 445–446 (1962) (Stewart, J., dissenting).
6 *Abington School District v. Schempp*, 374 U.S. 203, 309 (1963) (Stewart, J., dissenting).
7 *Wallace v. Jaffree*, 472 U.S. 38, 106, 107 (1985) (Rehnquist, J., dissenting).
8 *Zelman v. Simmons-Harris*, 536 U.S. 639, 686 (2002) (Stevens, J., dissenting).
9 *Carson v. Makin*, 596 U.S. __, __ (2022) (Sotomayor, J., dissenting).

1   The Wall That Jefferson Built

Thomas Jefferson was inaugurated the third president of the United States on March 4, 1801, following one of the most bitterly contested elections in American history. Candidate Jefferson's religion, or the alleged lack thereof, emerged as a critical issue in the campaign. His Federalist foes, led by the incumbent president John Adams, vilified him as an infidel or even an atheist. The campaign rhetoric was so vitriolic that, when news of Jefferson's election swept across the country, housewives in New England were seen burying family Bibles in their gardens or hiding them in wells because they expected the Holy Scriptures to be confiscated and burned by the new administration in Washington.[10] (As strange as this reaction sounds, these fears resonated with pious Americans who had received alarming reports of the French Revolution, which Jefferson was said to support, and the widespread desecration of religious sanctuaries and symbols in France. By the mid-1790s, the revolution in France had turned bloody and anti-Christian.)

One pocket of support for the Jeffersonian Republicans in Federalist New England was found among the Baptists. At the dawn of the nineteenth century, Jefferson's Federalist opponents dominated New England politics, and the Congregationalist church still enjoyed legal favor in Connecticut and Massachusetts.[11] The New England Baptists, who supported Jefferson, were outsiders—a beleaguered religious and political minority in a region where a Congregationalist-Federalist axis dominated political life. As religious dissenters, the Baptists were drawn to Jefferson because of his renowned commitment to religious liberty. The Baptists were hoping the new president would bring to the nation the same spirit of religious liberty he had championed in his native Commonwealth of Virginia.

---

10   Dumas Malone, *Jefferson and His Time*, vol. 3, *Jefferson and the Ordeal of Liberty* (Boston: Little, Brown and Co., 1962), 481; David Saville Muzzey, *Thomas Jefferson* (New York: Charles Scribner's Sons, 1918), 207–08; and Albert Jay Nock, *Jefferson* (New York: Harcourt, Brace and Co., 1926), 238.

11   See Robert J. Imholt, "Connecticut: A Land of Steady Habits," in *Disestablishment and Religious Dissent: Church-State Relations in the New American States, 1776–1833*, ed. Carl H. Esbeck and Jonathan J. Den Hartog (Columbia: University of Missouri Press, 2019), 327–50; and John Witte, Jr. and Justin Latterell, "The Last American Establishment: Massachusetts, 1780–1833," in Esbeck and Den Hartog, *Disestablishment and Religious Dissent*, 399–424.

On New Year's Day, 1802, President Jefferson penned a missive to the Baptist Association of Danbury, Connecticut.[12] The Baptists had written to the president in October 1801, congratulating him on his election to the "chief Magistracy in the United States." They celebrated his zealous advocacy for religious liberty and chastised those who had criticized him "as an enemy of religion[,] Law & good order because he will not, dares not assume the prerogative of Jehovah and make Laws to govern the Kingdom of Christ."[13]

Although the Danbury Baptists had not asked the president to issue a religious proclamation, Jefferson told his advisers that he wanted to use his reply to the Baptists to address a controversy that had arisen early in his administration. The controversy concerned his refusal to continue the practice of presidents Washington and Adams and many state chief executives of designating days for public prayer, fasting, and thanksgiving.[14] The president was eager to explain his position on the matter because his Federalist detractors had called for religious proclamations and then smeared him as an enemy of religion when he declined to issue them.

In a carefully crafted reply, endorsing the persecuted Baptists' aspirations for religious liberty, the president wrote:

> Believing with you that religion is a matter which lies solely between Man & his God, that he owes account to none other for his faith or his worship, that the legitimate powers of government reach actions only, & not opinions, I contemplate with sovereign reverence that act of the whole American people which declared that *their* legislature should "make no law respecting an establishment of religion, or prohibiting the free exercise thereof," thus building a wall of separation between Church & State. [A]dhering to this expression of the supreme will of the nation in behalf of the rights of conscience, I shall see with sincere satisfaction the progress of those sentiments which tend to restore to man all his natural rights, convinced he has no natural right in opposition to his social duties.[15]

---

12   The story of Jefferson's correspondence with the Danbury Baptist Association is recounted in Daniel L. Dreisbach, *Thomas Jefferson and the Wall of Separation between Church and State* (New York: New York University Press, 2002).
13   The Danbury Baptist Association to Thomas Jefferson, Oct. 7, 1801, in *Papers of Jefferson*, 35:407–08.
14   See Jefferson to Levi Lincoln, Jan. 1, 1802, in *Papers of Jefferson*, 36:256–57.
15   Jefferson to the Danbury Baptist Association, Jan. 1, 1802, in *Papers of Jefferson*, 36:258.

Jefferson thus allied himself with the Baptists in their struggle to enjoy the rights of conscience as a natural, inalienable right and not merely as a favor granted, and subject to withdrawal, by the civil state.

What does the historical record reveal about Jefferson's views on the prudential and constitutional relationship between church and state? Far more has been written about Jefferson's church-state record than can be summarized in a short chapter, but it is worth asking whether the wall is used today in ways that its architect would recognize and endorse? Are modern constructions of the "wall of separation" consistent with Jefferson's policies and practices as a public official?

Jefferson's record on church-state matters does not always point in the same direction. As president, he famously invoked the wall apparently to support his decision to discontinue the practice of his presidential predecessors in issuing religious proclamations. This suggests that he embraced a separationist construction of the First Amendment. Throughout his long public career, however, including two terms as president, he pursued policies incompatible with the "high and impregnable" wall the modern Supreme Court has attributed to him. The same Jefferson who, as president, invoked a "wall of separation" when declining to issue a religious proclamation also, as governor of Virginia, issued a proclamation appointing "a day of publick and solemn thanksgiving and prayer to Almighty God."[16] As a member of the Virginia legislature in the late 1770s, he is credited with framing bills that authorized "Appointing Days of Public Fasting and Thanksgiving" and "Punishing Disturbers of Religious Worship and Sabbath Breakers."[17] Moreover, after ratification of the First Amendment and without raising constitutional objection, "Jefferson's administration provided money [from the federal treasury] for at least one missionary school and, pursuant to a treaty, funded the construction of a Catholic Church and the

---

16   "Proclamation Appointing a Day of Thanksgiving and Prayer," Nov. 11, 1779, in *Papers of Jefferson*, 3:178.

17   *Report of the Committee of Revisors Appointed by the General Assembly of Virginia in MDC-CLXXVI* (Richmond, Va.: printed by Dixon & Holt, 1784), 59–60; *Papers of Jefferson*, 2:555–56. These bills were part of a legislative package in Virginia's revised code that included Jefferson's "Bill for Establishing Religious Freedom." All three bills were apparently framed by Jefferson and sponsored in the Virginia legislature by James Madison. See Daniel L. Dreisbach, "A New Perspective on Jefferson's Views on Church-State Relations: The Virginia Statute for Establishing Religious Freedom in Its Legislative Context," *American Journal of Legal History* 35 (1991): 172–204.

salary of a priest."[18] Critics of strict separation revel in the irony that Jefferson pursued policies that apparently breeched the "wall of separation."

Jefferson's wall is often described as a representation of a universal principle on the prudential and constitutional relationship between religion and the civil state. Jefferson's record, to the contrary, indicates that the wall had less to do with the separation between religion and *all* civil government than with the separation between the national and state governments on matters pertaining to religion (such as official proclamations for days of public prayer, fasting, and thanksgiving). Recall that the same Jefferson who declined to issue a religious proclamation as president issued a religious proclamation as the governor of Virginia.[19] The "wall of separation" was a metaphoric construction of the First Amendment; and Jefferson said time and again that the First Amendment imposed its restrictions on the national government only.[20] In other words, Jefferson's wall separated the national regime on one side from state governments and religious authorities on the other.

How did this wall, limited in its jurisdictional application, come to exert such enormous influence on American jurisprudence? Jeffersonian partisans were drawn to the political principle of separation between religion and politics in the campaign of 1800 to silence the Federalist clergy who had denounced candidate Jefferson as an infidel or atheist. In the Danbury letter, with its metaphoric formulation, Jefferson deftly transformed the political principle into a constitutional principle of separation between church and state by identifying the figurative language of separation with the text of the First Amendment. The constitutional principle was eventually elevated to constitutional law by

---

18   Nathan S. Chapman, "Forgotten Federal-Missionary Partnerships: New Light on the Establishment Clause," *Notre Dame Law Review* 96, no. 2 (2020): 697.

19   Jefferson's commentary on religious exercises, such as those called for in religious proclamations, suggests that he placed the wall between the federal government and state governments. In his Second Inaugural Address, delivered in March 1805, Jefferson wrote:
>   In matters of Religion, I have considered that its free exercise is placed by the constitution independent of the powers of the general [that is, federal] government. I have therefore undertaken, on no occasion, to prescribe the religious exercises suited to it: but have left them, as the constitution found them, under the direction & discipline of the state or church authorities acknowledged by the several religious societies.

Jefferson, Second Inaugural Address, Mar. 4, 1805, in *Papers of Jefferson*, 45:654. In a letter to the Reverend Samuel Miller in early 1808, Jefferson sounded the same theme: "Certainly no power to prescribe any religious exercise ... has been delegated to the general [that is, federal] government. It must then rest with the states, as far as it can be in any human authority." Jefferson to the Reverend Samuel Miller, Jan. 23, 1808, in *Thomas Jefferson: Writings* (New York: Library of America, 1984), 1187.

20   See, for example, "Jefferson's Fair Copy" of "The Kentucky Resolutions of 1798," before Oct. 4, 1798, in *Papers of Jefferson*, 30:544–45.

the Supreme Court in the mid-twentieth century,[21] effectively re-creating First Amendment doctrine.

2 The Metaphor Enters Public Discourse

By late January 1802, Jefferson's letter to the Danbury Baptists began appearing in New England newspapers,[22] but it soon slipped into obscurity. When was Jefferson's metaphor "rediscovered," and how did it attain prominence in church-state discourse? The letter was not accessible to a wide audience until it was reprinted in the first major collection of Jefferson's papers, published in the mid-nineteenth century.[23]

The phrase "wall of separation" entered the American legal lexicon in the U.S. Supreme Court's 1879 ruling in *Reynolds v. United States*. Opining that the missive "may be accepted almost as an authoritative declaration of the scope and effect of the [first] amendment thus secured," the Court reproduced a flawed transcription of the Danbury letter's central paragraph.[24] The metaphor, it would seem, is not what drew the Court to this text. Chief Justice Morrison R. Waite, who authored the opinion, was apparently drawn to another clause in Jefferson's letter, but he declined to edit the lengthy sentence in which it appeared to exclude the figurative phrase. Jefferson's statement that the powers of civil government reach men's actions only and not their opinions was key to the Court's reasoning. The *Reynolds* Court was focused on the *legislative* powers of Congress to criminalize the Mormon practice of polygamy and was apparently drawn to this passage because of the mistranscription of "*legitimate* powers of government" as "*legislative* powers of government." But for this erroneous transcription, the Court might have had little or no interest in the

---

21 See John Witte, Jr., "That Serpentine Wall of Separation," *Michigan Law Review* 101, no. 6 (2003): 1869–1905, at 1903.
22 See, for example, *American Citizen and General Advertiser* (New York), Jan. 18, 1802, 2; *American Mercury* (Hartford, CT), Jan. 28, 1802, 3; *The Centinel of Freedom* (Newark, NJ), Feb. 23, 1802, 3; *Constitutional Telegraphe* (Boston), Jan. 27, 1802, 2; *Independent Chronicle* (Boston), Jan. 25, 1802, 2–3; *New Hampshire Gazette* (Portsmouth), Feb. 9, 1802, 2; *Rhode-Island Republican* (Newport), Jan. 30, 1802, 2; *Salem Register*, Jan. 28, 1802, 1; and *The Sun* (Pittsfield, MA), Feb. 15, 1802, 4.
23 *The Writings of Thomas Jefferson*, ed. Henry A. Washington, 9 vols. (Washington, DC: Taylor and Maury, 1853–54), 8:113–14. Virtually all twentieth-century anthologies of Jefferson's works reproduced Washington's flawed transcription of the Danbury letter.
24 *Reynolds v. United States*, 98 U.S. 145, 164 (1879).

Danbury letter, and the wall metaphor might not have entered the American legal lexicon.

Nearly seven decades later, in the landmark *Everson* case, the Supreme Court "rediscovered" the metaphor and elevated it to constitutional doctrine. Citing no source or authority other than *Reynolds*, Justice Hugo L. Black, writing for the majority, invoked the Danbury letter's "wall of separation" passage in support of his strict separationist construction of the First Amendment prohibition on laws "respecting an establishment of religion." Black did not simply reference the figurative phrase, he graphically characterized the First Amendment wall as "high and impregnable," not allowing "the slightest breach."[25] Like *Reynolds*, the *Everson* ruling was replete with references to history, especially the roles played by Jefferson and Madison in the Virginia disestablishment struggles in the tumultuous decade following independence from Great Britain. Jefferson was depicted as a leading architect of the First Amendment, even though he was in France when the measure was drafted by the first federal Congress in 1789.[26]

Black and his judicial brethren also encountered the metaphor in briefs filed in *Everson*. In a lengthy discussion of history supporting the proposition that "separation of church and state is a fundamental American principle," an amicus brief filed by the American Civil Liberties Union (ACLU) quoted the clause in the Danbury letter containing the "wall of separation" image. The ACLU warned that the challenged state statute, which provided state reimbursements for the transportation of students to and from parochial schools, "constitutes a definite crack in the wall of separation between church and state. Such cracks have a tendency to widen beyond repair unless promptly sealed up."[27]

The trope's current fame and pervasive influence in popular, political, and legal discourse date from its rediscovery by the *Everson* Court. Shortly after the ruling was handed down, the metaphor began to proliferate in books and articles. In a 1949 best-selling anti-Catholic polemic, *American Freedom and Catholic Power* (Beacon Press), Paul Blanshard advocated an uncompromising political and legal platform favoring "a wall of separation between church and state."[28] Protestants and Other Americans United for the Separation of Church and State (today known by the more politically correct name of "Americans

---

25 *Everson*, 330 U.S. at 18.
26 See *Everson*, 330 U.S. at 13.
27 Brief of the American Civil Liberties Union as *Amici Curiae* at 8, 12, 34, *Everson v. Board of Education*, 330 U.S. 1 (1947).
28 Paul Blanshard, *American Freedom and Catholic Power* (Boston: Beacon Press, 1949), 305.

United for Separation of Church and State"), a leading strict separationist advocacy organization, wrote the phrase into its 1948 founding manifesto. Among the "immediate objectives" of the new organization was "[t]o resist every attempt by law or the administration of law further to widen the breach in the wall of separation of church and state."[29]

In the cases following *Everson*, the Supreme Court continued to cite Jefferson's figurative phrase frequently and favorably. Indeed, the Court essentially "constitutionalized" Jefferson's phrase, subtly substituting his figurative language for the literal text of the First Amendment. The metaphor gained currency in not only judicial rulings but also the broader church-state discourse. Use of the metaphor peaked again during the controversies surrounding the school prayer cases of the early 1960s. The Court's reliance on the Jeffersonian metaphor prompted critiques of the justices' uses of history in general and the wall metaphor in particular.[30] Justice Rehnquist's scathing repudiation of the metaphor in *Wallace v. Jaffree* (1985), reinforced by several works of scholarship calling into question the Court's use of history,[31] was followed by a slow retreat from reliance on the metaphor in First Amendment rulings. The metaphor, however, remains a popular trope in academic and polemical discourse.

3 The Trouble with Metaphors in the Law

Metaphors are a valuable literary device. They enrich language by making it dramatic and colorful, rendering abstract concepts concrete, condensing complex concepts into a few words, and unleashing creative and analogical insights. But their uncritical use can lead to confusion and distortion. At its heart, metaphor compares two or more things that are not, in fact, identical. A metaphor's literal meaning is used nonliterally in a comparison with its subject. While the comparison may yield useful insights, the dissimilarities between the metaphor and its subject, if not acknowledged, can distort or pollute one's understanding of the subject. Metaphors inevitably graft onto their subjects

---

[29] Joseph Martin Dawson, *Separate Church and State Now* (New York: Richard R. Smith, 1948), Appendix B, 209.

[30] See Daniel L. Dreisbach, "*Everson* and the Command of History: The Supreme Court, Lessons of History, and Church-State Debate in America," in *Everson Revisited: Religion, Education and Law at the Crossroads*, ed. Jo Renee Formicola and Hubert Morken (Lanham, MD: Rowman and Littlefield, 1997), 23–57.

[31] See, for example, Robert L. Cord, *Separation of Church and State: Historical Fact and Current Fiction* (New York: Lambeth Press, 1982); and Philip Hamburger, *Separation of Church and State* (Cambridge, MA: Harvard University Press, 2002).

connotations, emotional intensity, and/or cultural associations that transform the understanding of the subject as it was known premetaphor. If attributes of the metaphor are erroneously or misleadingly assigned to the subject and the distortion goes unchallenged, then the metaphor may reconceptualize or otherwise alter the understanding of the underlying subject. The more appealing and powerful a metaphor, the more it tends to supplant or overshadow the original subject, and the more one is unable to contemplate the subject apart from its metaphoric formulation. Thus, distortions perpetuated by the metaphor are sustained and magnified.

After two centuries, Jefferson's figurative phrase remains controversial. The question debated is whether the wall illuminates or obfuscates the constitutional principles it metaphorically represents.

Proponents argue that the metaphor promotes private, voluntary religion and freedom of religion in a secular polity. The wall, defenders say, graphically and concisely conveys First Amendment principles. It prevents religious establishments, discourages corrupting entanglements between civil governmental and ecclesiastical authorities, and avoids sectarian conflict among religious denominations competing for government favor and aid. An impenetrable barrier prohibits not only the formal recognition of, and legal preference for, one particular church (or sect) but also all other forms of government assistance for religious objectives. A regime of strict separation, defenders insist, is the best, if not the only, way to promote religious liberty, especially the rights of religious minorities.

Opponents counter that the graphic metaphor has been a source of much mischief because it reconceptualizes—indeed, misconceptualizes—First Amendment principles. Given the nature of metaphors, reliance on this extraconstitutional figure of speech as a substitute for the text of the First Amendment almost inevitably reimagines, if not distorts, constitutional principles governing church-state relationships. Although the "wall of separation" may felicitously express some aspects of First Amendment law, it misrepresents or obscures others. Critics contend that the metaphor misrepresents constitutional principles in several important ways.

First, the trope emphasizes *separation* between church and state—unlike the First Amendment, which speaks in terms of the nonestablishment and free exercise of religion. "Separation of church and state" and the First Amendment concept of "nonestablishment" are often used interchangeably today; however, in the lexicon of the late eighteenth and early nineteenth centuries, the expansive concept of "separation" was not identical to the narrow institutional concepts of "nonestablishment" and "disestablishment." Many advocates of disestablishment or nonestablishment (and liberty of conscience), such as evangelical dissenters, did not necessarily embrace more expansive conceptions of "separation," because they feared a strict separation could lead to a divorce of religion's beneficent influences from public life and policy. Many in the founding generation, including evangelical Baptist dissenters, would have viewed such a divorce with alarm, because they believed religion was indispensable to their experiment in republican self-government insofar as religion informed the public ethic and nurtured the civic virtues necessary for self-government to succeed.

Second, a wall is a bilateral barrier that inhibits the activities of both the civil government and religion—unlike the First Amendment, which imposes restrictions on civil government (that is, Congress) only. In short, a wall not only prevents the civil state from intruding into the religious domain but also prohibits religion from influencing civil government. The various First Amendment guarantees were entirely a check or restraint on civil government, specifically on Congress. The free press guarantee, for example, was not written to protect the civil state from the press; rather, it was intended to protect a free and independent press from control by the national government. Similarly, the religion provisions were added to the Constitution to protect religion and religious institutions from corrupting interference by the national government and not to protect the civil state from the influence of religion. As a bilateral barrier, however, the wall unavoidably restricts religion's ability to influence civic life, and, thus, it necessarily exceeds the limitations explicitly imposed by the First Amendment. Reimagining the First Amendment as a "wall of separation," critics say, transforms a constitutional provision intended to limit civil government into a constitutional mandate to restrict religion's reach into public life.

In application, certain conceptions of separation have not only imposed an extraconstitutional restraint on religion but also dangerously granted the civil state de facto powers over religion. Having assumed the separation of church and state, the state has then exercised the prerogative to specify the legitimate jurisdictions of both the church and the state. The civil state, in order to determine that which is permissible or impermissible pursuant to the principle of separation, has presumed to define what is "religion" and what are the appropriate realm, duties, and functions of the "church" in a civil society. Yale University law professor Stephen L. Carter has denounced the state's construction of a "single-sided wall" that confines, indeed imprisons, the community of faith, but imposes few corresponding restraints on the civil state's ability to interfere with religion and religious institutions. The state, often acting through its judges, "decides when religion has crossed the wall of separation.... Unsurprisingly, then, religion is often found to have breached the wall, whereas the state almost never is."[32] "[I]n its contemporary rendition," Carter continues in even more forceful language, separation of church and state "represents little more than an effort to subdue the power of religion, to twist it to the ends preferred by the state."[33] The result is that the First Amendment is transformed from being explicitly and exclusively a restriction on the powers of civil government to being a grant of power to the state to define and, ultimately, confine the place of religion in society.

Herein lies the danger of this metaphor, critics contend. All too often the wall is used to separate religion from public life, thereby promoting a religion that is essentially private and a state that is strictly secular. The "high and impregnable" wall described in *Everson* and its progeny has been used to inhibit religion's ability to inform the public ethic, deprive religious citizens of the liberty to participate in politics armed with ideas informed by their spiritual values, and infringe the right of religious communities and institutions to extend their faith-based ministries into the public square on the same terms as their secular counterparts. The wall has been used to restrain the religious voice in the public marketplace of ideas and to segregate faith communities behind a restrictive barrier.

4   Witte and the Wall

Recognizing its significance for church-state law, policy, and discourse, John Witte, Jr. has been attentive to the diverse uses and interpretations of the "wall of separation." He has focused on the metaphor in essays and reviews,[34] as well as considered its implications in more general analyses of church-state

---

32   Stephen L. Carter, *God's Name in Vain: The Wrongs and Rights of Religion in Politics* (New York: Basic Books, 2000), 79–80.

33   Ibid., 78.

34   See, for example, Witte, "That Serpentine Wall of Separation"; Witte, "The New Freedom of Public Religion: Thomas Jefferson's metaphor of 'a wall of separation between church and state' has become for many the source and summary of American religious freedom," *Sightings* (Martin Marty Center, The University of Chicago Divinity School, Oct. 9, 2003); Witte, "Facts and Fictions about the History of Separation of Church and State," *Journal of Church and State* 48, no. 1 (2006): 15–46; Witte, "Church and State: Exploring the Superstitions behind the Wall of Separation," *The Lutheran* (Sep. 2008): 14–18; Witte and Justin J. Latterell, "Beyond the Separation of Church and State in America," *Oasis* 14 (2012): 73–78; and Witte, "The Shifting Walls of Separation Between Church and State in the United States," in *The Most Sacred Freedom: Religious Liberty in the History of Philosophy and America's Founding*, ed. Will R. Jordan and Charlotte C. S. Thomas (Macon, GA: Mercer University Press, 2016), 103–20. See also Witte, "The Metaphorical Bridge Between Law

jurisprudence.³⁵ How has he assessed uses of the wall in judicial and academic literature? What has he contributed to the scholarship on the propriety and utility of the "wall of separation" in constitutional jurisprudence? Much of the scholarship on this topic tends to be partisan, emphasizing either the benefits or the dangers of the metaphor. Witte, by contrast, has been measured and balanced in his analysis, recognizing both the promises and the perils that Jefferson's figurative phrase poses for church-state jurisprudence.

Witte has been careful to place the rhetoric and policies of church-state separation in their appropriate historical contexts. He has surveyed conceptions of the separation principle in Western thought over the course of two millennia, giving careful consideration to how they have informed expressions of church-state separation in American political culture and jurisprudence.

Witte's analysis of religious liberty in the American experience highlights six principles of the "essential rights and liberties" of religion: liberty of conscience, free exercise of religion, religious pluralism, religious equality, separation of church and state, and disestablishment of religion.³⁶ These "first principles" capture the bold features and subtle distinctions of the innovative American experiment. They were featured prominently in the political discourse of the founding era, incorporated into many state and federal constitutions of the age, and "remain at the heart of the American experiment today."³⁷ These concepts, as Witte amply illustrates from primary sources, were invested with multiple, sometimes overlapping, meanings and layers of meaning. He readily concedes that, given the diverse theological and political perspectives and communities represented in the late eighteenth century, there was no

---

       and Religion," *Pepperdine Law Review* 47, no. 2 (2020): 435–62 (discussion of metaphors in the law).

35 See, for example, Witte, "The Theology and Politics of the First Amendment Religion Clauses: A Bicentennial Essay," *Emory Law Journal* 40, no. 2 (1991): 489–507; Witte, "The Essential Rights and Liberties of Religion in the American Constitutional Experiment," *Notre Dame Law Review* 71, no. 3 (1996): 371–445; Witte, "From Establishment to Freedom of Public Religion," *Capital University Law Review* 32, no. 3 (2004): 499–518; and Witte, "Back to the Sources? What's Clear and Not So Clear about the Original Intent of the First Amendment," *Brigham Young University Law Review* 47, no. 4 (2022): 1303–83. See also John Witte, Jr., Joel A. Nichols, and Richard W. Garnett, *Religion and the American Constitutional Experiment*, 5th ed. (Oxford: Oxford University Press, 2022); and T. Jeremy Gunn and John Witte, Jr., eds., *No Establishment of Religion: America's Original Contribution to Religious Liberty* (Oxford: Oxford University Press, 2012).

36 John Witte, Jr., *Religion and the American Constitutional Experiment: Essential Rights and Liberties*, 1st ed. (Boulder, CO: Westview Press, 2000), 37; and Witte, "Back to the Sources?," 1308–17.

37 *Religion and the American Constitutional Experiment*, 1st ed., 37.

consensus on the definitions, priority, interdependence, and policy implications of these six defining principles. Moreover, even within communities, there were disagreements over the definition and scope of a principle or tension between the goals and applications of two or more principles. This is as true of conceptions of separation of church and state as the other principles. Nonetheless, calling attention to these principles, notwithstanding competing interpretations of their meaning, scope, and application, invites consideration of the diverse interests and values that informed discussions of religious liberty in the founding era. Witte believes that separation of church and state must remain a valuable, vital principle of the American experiment, so long as it is used prudentially and balanced with other founding principles of religious liberty.[38]

This sets the stage for Witte's assessment of the separation principle, including Jefferson's architectural formulation of it. Not everyone who uses or endorses the language of separation agrees on its meaning. In our own time, for example, civil libertarians, secular humanists, theologically liberal mainline Protestants, and even evangelical Southern Baptists are all likely to endorse the "separation of church and state," but they almost certainly hold discordant views on the meaning and application of that principle to law and public policy. Witte brings much-needed clarity to the conversation by identifying and describing five distinct understandings of church-state separation in the American founding and in church-state discussions continuing to the present day.[39]

First, the principle of separation of church and state protects the church from the civil state. This vision of separation is concerned with, inter alia, protecting the autonomy and purity of the church (and religious societies, more generally), as well as religious exercise and expression, from control and interference by government authorities.

Second, the principle protects the state from the church. This understanding of separation arguably informed, in part, the common practice for much of American history of prohibiting clergy from holding public offices. This interpretation is reflected in our own time by federal tax laws disallowing tax-exempt religious organizations from participating in political campaigns or endorsing political candidates.[40]

---

38 See Witte, "Shifting Walls," 104. See also Witte, "That Serpentine Wall of Separation," 1904.
39 Witte, "Shifting Walls," 104–15; "Facts and Fictions," 28–34; and "That Serpentine Wall of Separation," 1889–91.
40 Witte, "Shifting Walls," 108.

Third, the separation principle protects the individual's liberty of conscience from intrusions by either the church or civil state or both conspiring together. Witte notes that Jefferson's figurative language has often been deployed in the service of a strict separationist construction of the First Amendment, but, he argues, Jefferson's letter to the Danbury Baptists actually "tied the principle of separation of church and state directly to the principle of liberty of conscience."[41] "[R]eligion," Jefferson wrote, "is a matter which lies solely between Man & his God." And the First Amendment, with its "wall of separation," was an expression "in behalf of the rights of conscience," which, Jefferson hoped, would "tend to restore to man all his natural rights." Jefferson's formulation, Witte concludes, "assured individuals of their natural right of conscience, which could be exercised freely and fully to the point of breaching or shirking social duties."[42]

Fourth, the principle protects "individual states from interference by the federal government in governing local religious affairs."[43] This jurisdictional understanding, affirming federalism, denied the federal government authority over religion and protected state governments from interference by the federal government in matters pertaining to religion. For much of American history, each state was free to structure church-state arrangements in accordance with its own laws.[44] State governments, in other words, could establish, disestablish, or selectively favor or disfavor specific religious sects without interference by the federal regime. Witte pushes the boundaries of the "jurisdictional view" even further, showing its application beyond state actors and in the service of other essential principles of religious liberty: "The individual's jurisdiction over religion was protected by the constitutional principle of liberty of conscience. The church's jurisdiction was protected by the constitutional principle[s] of free exercise and free association."[45]

Fifth, the principle has been used to separate "religion from public life altogether."[46] This strict separationist view, Witte concedes, "was the most novel, and most controversial, understanding of separation of church and state in the

---

41 Ibid., 108–09.
42 Ibid., 109. See also Witte, "That Serpentine Wall of Separation," 1896–97.
43 "Shifting Walls," 110.
44 The Supreme Court incorporated the First Amendment free exercise and nonestablishment of religion provisions into the Fourteenth Amendment's due process of law clause in *Cantwell v. Connecticut*, 310 U.S. 296, 303 (1940) and *Everson v. Board of Education*, 330 U.S. 1, 15 (1947), respectively, thereby making these provisions applicable to state and local authorities.
45 Witte, "That Serpentine Wall of Separation," 1891.
46 Witte, "Shifting Walls," 111.

young American republic,"[47] and few Americans of the era embraced its more radical implications. This understanding of separation found more adherents in the nineteenth century; and, in the mid-twentieth century, it gained significant influence when the Supreme Court adopted a strict separationist reading of the First Amendment—an interpretation that the Court said was buttressed by Jefferson's wall. Witte cautions those tempted to attribute to Jefferson a strict separationist perspective, reminding them that "Jefferson's views on the separation of church and state are considerably more nuanced than this simple wall metaphor would have us believe."[48] Witte also emphatically rejects that separation of church and state has ever "meant that America was committed to the secularization of society or the privatization of religion."[49]

He further observes that today, unlike Jefferson's day, the civil state is such an expansive and "intensely active sovereign" that a "complete separation is impossible. Few religious bodies can now avoid contact with the state's pervasive network" of laws, regulations, policies, and social welfare programs in carrying out their ministries.[50] This makes it imperative that the modern civil state, with its expansive reach, balance separationist policies with principles of liberty of conscience, free exercise of religion, religious equality, and the like. Although the Supreme Court favored a strict separationist position in *Everson* and its progeny, in more recent years the Court has taken a more relaxed approach to church-state relations; and this, Witte opines, has "ultimately served to enhance religious freedom in America rather than contract it."[51]

Again, Witte emphasizes that separation of church and state is only one principle essential to the American experiment in religious liberty. The separation principle, he has said, must be balanced with other essential principles he has identified. "When viewed in isolation, the principle of separation of church and state serves religious liberty best when it is used prudentially, not categorically. Separationism needs to be retained, particularly for its ancient insight of protecting religious bodies from the state and for its more recent insight of protecting the consciences of religious believers from violations by government or religious bodies."[52] The separation principle, however, must be "contained, and not used as an anti-religious weapon in the culture wars of the public square, the public school, or the public court. Separationism must be viewed as a shield, not a sword in the great struggle to achieve religious

---

47   Ibid., 112.
48   Ibid., 104.
49   Witte and Latterell, "Beyond the Separation of Church and State in America," 73–78.
50   Witte, "From Establishment to Freedom of Public Religion," 517.
51   Witte, "Shifting Walls," 116.
52   Ibid., 117.

freedom for all. A categorical insistence on the principle of separation of church and state in its fifth and strictest sense avails us rather little."[53] A zealous, rigid adherence to the separation principle, he warns,

> runs afoul of other constitutive principles of the First Amendment—particularly the principles of liberty of conscience and religious equality. The [Supreme] Court must be at least as zealous in protecting religious conscience from secular coercion as protecting secular conscience from religious coercion. The Court should be at least as concerned to ensure the equal treatment of religion as to ensure the equality of religion and non-religion. It is no violation of the principle of separation of church and state when a legislature or court accommodates judiciously the conscientious scruples of a religious individual or the cardinal callings of a religious body. It is also no violation of this principle when government grants religious individuals and institutions equal access to state benefits, public forums, or tax disbursements that are open to non-religionists similarly situated.[54]

To do otherwise, Witte concludes, would privilege what Justice Stewart called "a religion of secularism."[55]

Turning his attention to the architectural formulation of separation made famous by Thomas Jefferson, Witte notes that the "wall of separation" was not Jefferson's invention. The metaphor has deep roots in Western thought, featuring in church-state discourse for at least five hundred years. There has been no consensus, however, regarding the purposes of this barrier. Some commentators have championed a wall as a prudential, indeed an essential, fixture of church-state relationships. Others have denounced walls of separation as obstacles to healthy, cooperative relations between church and state. Witte illustrates the diverse understandings and uses of the separation principle by drawing attention to various historical constructions of the wall. The examples he highlights, in addition to Jefferson's wall, include:

The Anabaptists, who believed they were in the world but not of the world,[56] rejected the close identification of civil state and church that had been prevalent in Western Christendom since the reign of Constantine. Although they

---

53   Ibid., 117–18.
54   Ibid., 119.
55   *Abington School District*, 374 U.S. at 313 (Stewart, J., dissenting).
56   Anabaptists took to heart biblical admonitions that Christians should "be not conformed to this world" (Romans 12:2) but remain "separate" from the world and its temptations. See also Schleitheim Confession of Faith (1527), art. 6.

believed the civil state was instituted and ordained by God and is "necessary in the 'world,' that is, among those who do not heed or obey Christ's teachings, it is not necessary among the true disciples of Christ."[57] Small, self-sufficient, and self-governing Anabaptist communities thus avoided participation in, and interaction with, the civil state. Describing their perspective, Witte references a letter written by the Dutch Anabaptist leader Menno Simons (1496–1561) mentioning a *Scheidingsmaurer*—a "separating wall" or "wall of separation"— between the realms of the true church and a fallen, outside world.[58]

Richard Hooker (1554–1600), the sixteenth-century Anglican divine and apologist for the Elizabethan settlement, described "walles of separation between ... the *Church* and the *Commonwealth*" in his magnum opus, *Of the Laws of Ecclesiastical Polity*.[59] Both revelation and reason, he argued, supported the organic identity of church and state, as coextensive aspects of a unified Christian society. He believed, further, that "the episcopal form of government was best for the Church of England, and that Church and state were two aspects of the same commonwealth, a commonwealth in which both were rightly under the monarch."[60] Hooker rejected the Puritan notion of church and commonwealth as two distinct and perpetually separated corporations, divided by "walls of separation" that denied the crown its divine prerogative to rule over both the church and the commonwealth.[61]

The seventeenth-century colonial advocate for religious liberty and founder of Rhode Island, Roger Williams (1603?–1683), championed a "hedge or wall of separation" to safeguard the purity of Christ's church from the corrupting wilderness of the world. Williams was a spiritual or theological separatist whose relentless quest was to separate the true church from theological impurity and the unclean world. He adamantly rejected the idea of a national church because it improperly combined regenerate and unregenerate members of society. Where there was an established church, Williams instructed

---

57 Hans J. Hillerbrand, "An Early Anabaptist Treatise on the Christian and the State," *Mennonite Quarterly Review* 32 (1958): 30–31.

58 See Witte, "Facts and Fictions," 21–22; "That Serpentine Wall of Separation," 1881–82; and *Religion and the American Constitutional Experiment*, 1st ed., 15. Witte indirectly references a letter from Menno Simons to "J.V." [perhaps Johannes Voetius, a Dutch jurist], December 1548, cited in Dreisbach, *Thomas Jefferson and the Wall of Separation between Church and State*, 73.

59 Richard Hooker, *Of the Laws of Ecclesiastical Polity: Books VI, VII, VIII*, ed. P. G. Stanwood, vol. 3, of *The Folger Library Edition of The Works of Richard Hooker*, ed. W. Speed Hill (Cambridge, MA: Belknap Press of Harvard University Press, 1981), 320.

60 Kenneth Scott Latourette, *A History of Christianity* (New York: Harper and Brothers, 1953), 812.

61 See Witte, "Facts and Fictions," 25.

congregations to be separated from it in order to maintain spiritual purity. Drawing on the imagery of Isaiah 5:5–6, Williams lamented in a 1644 tract that, when a gap is opened "in the hedge or wall of separation between the garden of the church and the wilderness of the world, God hath ever broke down the wall itself, removed the candlestick, and made His garden a wilderness, as at this day." If God's church or garden is to be restored, he continued, "it must of necessity be walled in peculiarly unto Himself from the world."[62] Williams recommended this wall, not to protect the outside world (including the civil polity) from religious influences, but to preserve the religious purity of the separated church from corrupting external influences.

The eighteenth-century Scottish radical Whig reformer, James Burgh (1714–1775), advocated building "an impenetrable wall of *separation* between things *sacred* and *civil*" in order to prevent the church from "getting too much power into her hands, and turning religion into a mere state-engine."[63] Burgh was a man of faith, as well as a man of reason. He brought to his writings a dissenter's zeal for religious toleration and a profound distrust of established churches. Burgh thought religion was a matter between God and one's conscience; and he contended that two citizens with different religious views are "both equally fit for being employed, in the service of our country."[64] He warned that state establishments of religion corrupt church officers (whose comfortable reliance on the civil state encourages pride, indolence, and impiety) and ultimately destroy true spirituality and profane religion. For this reason, Burgh proposed building "an impenetrable wall of *separation*."[65]

These examples come from different eras; and each of these walls, as Witte points out, served a purpose different from the others.

---

62 Roger Williams, "Mr. Cotton's Letter Lately Printed, Examined and Answered," in Perry Miller, *Roger Williams: His Contribution to the American Tradition* (1953; reprinted in New York: Atheneum, 1962), 98.

63 [James Burgh], *Crito, or Essays on Various Subjects*, 2 vols. (London, 1766, 1767), 2:119 (emphasis in the original); *Crito*, 1:7.

64 *Crito*, 2:68.

65 *Crito*, 2:119 (emphasis in the original). See generally Witte, "Facts and Fictions," 27–28. Jefferson's wall is most similar to Burgh's, and it is the wall Jefferson is most likely to have encountered in his reading. Although he might have encountered Hooker's wall in his reading, it is unlikely that he was familiar with Menno's or Williams's uses of the metaphor.

5 Conclusion

John Witte reminds us that "separation of church and state" and its attendant "wall of separation" formulation have long been a part of Western thought and discourse. Although mindful of the criticisms of "separationism," he makes a compelling case that the separation principle has made a valuable contribution to religious liberty in the American experience. He explicates the principle's multifarious understandings and applications in church-state law, policy, and discourse, acknowledging that some applications have protected private and public religion and others have inappropriately restricted religion in public life. Benjamin Cardozo once counseled: "[m]etaphors in law are to be narrowly watched."[66] Witte similarly urges Americans to be attentive to both the uses and abuses of Jefferson's figurative language. Moreover, the separation principle, he argues, must be construed in conjunction with other essential principles of religious liberty, especially liberty of conscience, free exercise of religion, and religious equality.

---

66   *Berkey v. Third Ave. Ry. Co.*, 244 N.Y. 84, 94, 155 N.E. 58, 61 (1926).

CHAPTER 22

The Shifting Law and Logic Behind Mandatory Bible Reading in American Public Schools

Mark A. Noll

In its memorable decision *Abington v. Schempp*, from 1963, the U.S. Supreme Court ruled that daily Bible readings in Pennsylvania's public schools amounted to "unconstitutionality under the Establishment Clause." Neither allowing for use of the Catholic Douay translation as an alternative to the Protestant King James Version nor a provision for students to excuse themselves from the exercise could obscure the "sectarian" character of the ceremony or its "pervading religious character." The First Amendment's prohibition of religious establishments, as applied to the states by the Fourteenth Amendment, demanded religious "neutrality," which the religious character of the daily Bible readings violated. Without this ban, the Court foresaw that "the breach of neutrality that is today a trickling stream may all too soon become a raging torrent."[1] Only eleven years earlier, however, the trickling stream had not seemed nearly so threatening when the Supreme Court dismissed an appeal of a decision by New Jersey's highest tribunal allowing that state's provision for daily Bible readings in public schools to continue.[2] Yet when, in 1952, the New Jersey court elaborated at length to justify the practice and when, in 1963, the Supreme Court wrote even more extensively to declare it unconstitutional, the original logic that had supported Bible reading in public schools for so much of American history in so many of the states had almost vanished.

The purpose of this contribution to a Festschrift that could not be more well deserved is, first, to spell out the logic widely accepted in the founding era concerning the fate of democratic republics and, then, how that logic led instinctively to the practice of daily Bible readings in schools as tax-supported public education began in the new United States. This chapter shows, second, how that logic gradually lost focus as the practice was debated in and out of court from the mid-1850s to nearly the present. Third, it notes briefly why a higher logic led some defenders of the Bible as a divinely given book to argue that it should *not* be read in the public schools. The chapter closes by expressing an

---

1 Abington School District v. Schempp, 374 U.S. 203, 222–24 (1963).
2 Doremus v. Board of Education, 342 U.S. 429 (1952).

opinion about the contemporary United States, where conventional political wisdom is now so greatly different from the earliest days of the republic.

1 The Founding Logic

In two related articles, John Witte has identified with clinical precision the founders' conceptual reasoning that would later lead to daily Bible readings in tax-supported schools.³ His careful consideration of the Massachusetts Constitution of 1780 and the concerns of its principal author, John Adams, set out what might be called the New England variant of standard revolutionary political theory—that is, the moral calculus of democratic republicanism. By the second half of the eighteenth century, American patriots with virtual unanimity held that to survive, a republic required virtuous citizens. They also believed that to nurture virtuous citizens, nothing was more important than religion. With equal certainty, they posited that religious nurture could not be entrusted to the inherently corrupting pattern of Old-World religious establishments. The New England variant that Adams advocated held that a carefully constrained establishment—what he called "slender" or "moderate and equitable"—could avoid the evils of Britain's state church while allowing religion to encourage republican virtue in the citizenry.⁴

In Witte's summary, "Adams was convinced that the establishment of one common public religion among a plurality of freely competing private religions was essential to the survival of society and the state." Then, quoting from statements made at widely separated points in Adams's life, Witte explains that while Adams stood resolutely for free religious exercise, he also insisted that citizens in a republic "must just as certainly begin by 'setting religion at the fore and floor of society and government…. [I]t is religion and morality alone which can establish the principles upon which freedom can securely stand.'

---

3   John Witte, Jr., "'A Most Mild and Equitable Establishment of Religion': John Adams and the Massachusetts Experiment," in *Religion and the New Republic: Faith in the Founding of America*, ed. James H. Hutson (Lanham, MD: Rowman & Littlefield, 2000), 1–40; John Witte, Jr. and Justin Latterell, "The Last American Establishment: Massachusetts, 1780–1833," in *Disestablishment and Religious Dissent: Church-State Relations in the New American States, 1776–1833*, ed. Carl H. Esbeck and Jonathan J. Den Hartog (Columbia: University of Missouri Press, 2019), 399–424.
4   On Adams's qualifications, see Witte, "A Most Mild and Equitable Establishment," 18–19. For religious contributions to Revolutionary republican theory, see Mark A. Noll, *America's God: From Jonathan Edwards to Abraham Lincoln* (New York: Oxford University Press, 2002), chap. 5 ("Christian Republicanism").

A common 'religion and virtue are the only foundation, not only of republicanism and of all free government, but of social felicity under all governments and in all the combinations of human society.'"[5]

Although some in New England, like the Baptist leader Isaac Backus, objected that *any* form of establishment brought inevitable corruption, Adams's reasoning prevailed. It was reflected at several points in the state's new constitution from 1780, especially Article III of the "Declaration of the Rights of the Inhabitants of the Commonwealth of Massachusetts":

> As the happiness of a people, and the good order and preservation of civil government, essentially depend upon piety, religion, and morality; and as these cannot be generally diffused through a community but by the institutions of the public worship of God, and of public instructions in piety, religion, and morality: Therefore, to promote their happiness, and to secure the good order and preservation of their government, the people of this commonwealth have a right to invest their legislature with power to authorize and require ... [the agencies of local government] to make suitable provision, at their own expense, for the institution of the public worship of God, and for the support and maintenance of public Protestant teachers of piety, religion, and morality.[6]

Other New England constitutions—newly written, as in Vermont and New Hampshire, or taken over from a colonial charter, as in Connecticut—repeated much of the Massachusetts formula. But so also did a few states not in New England (Delaware, Georgia, and Maryland) echo in their new constitutions at least some of the same.[7]

Virginia is regularly portrayed as moving completely in the opposite direction. Yet the leaders who constructed that state's new government were just as committed as their New England peers to the moral logic of republican government, but without the New England variant. Patrick Henry hoped to see a multiple-church establishment or "general assessment," where taxpayers designated their taxes to the religious bodies of their own choice. As is well known, James Madison's skillful maneuvering frustrated Henry's plan. Yet in

---

5 Witte, "A Most Mild and Equitable Establishment," 16.
6 Quoted here from Daniel L. Dreisbach and David Mark Hall, *The Sacred Rights of Conscience: Selected Readings on Religion Liberty and Church-State Relations in the American Founding* (Indianapolis: Liberty Fund, 2009), 246.
7 Esbeck and Den Hartog, *Disestablishment and Religious Dissent*, 302–03 (Vermont), 334 (Connecticut), 357 (New Hampshire), 45 (Delaware), 235–36 (Georgia), and 318 (Maryland).

arguing for Virginia's famous Statute for Religious Freedom, which outlawed any form of church establishment, Madison agreed that religion was an indispensable foundation for a stable republic. Madison, Thomas Jefferson, and their supporters stood rather with Isaac Backus in contending that religious establishments of any kind inevitably corrupted public life and thus undermined the republic that Henry's proposal was supposed to protect.[8]

It is worth pausing to underscore how pervasive the moral calculus of democratic republicanism remained for more than half a century. Founders might differ on the wisdom of even "slender" church establishments, as illustrated by Adams and Henry versus Madison and Backus, but they agreed on what they thought would secure political freedom, stability, and responsibility: a democratic republic required a moral citizenry, and religion provided the essential grounding for that morality.

So it was expressed by the Confederation Congress in 1787, when it passed the Northwest Ordinance for organizing the opening frontier: "Religion, morality and knowledge being necessary to good government and the happiness of mankind, schools and the means of education shall forever be encouraged."[9]

So it was articulated even more memorably in 1796, when George Washington's Farewell Address specified "religion and morality" as the "indispensable supports" for "political prosperity." In this address he raised a rhetorical question: "Can it be, that Providence has not connected the permanent felicity of a nation with its virtue?" He answered by reasoning to another rhetorical query: "'Tis substantially true, that virtue or morality is a necessary spring of popular government. The rule indeed extends with more or less force to every species of free government. Who that is a sincere friend of it, can look with indifference upon attempts to shake the foundation of the fabric?"[10]

Thomas Jefferson, who resisted any extension of New England influence, especially church establishments, nonetheless regularly affirmed his belief in the republican calculus. When, early in the new century, a correspondent explained why he "considered Christianity as the *strong ground* of Republicanism," Jefferson himself wrote to another correspondent first to qualify, but then to confirm: "the Christian religion when divested of the rags in which they [the domineering clergy] have inveloped [*sic*] it, and brought to the original

---

8   See Carl H. Esbeck, "Disestablishment in Virginia, 1776–1802," in Esbeck and Hartog, *Disestablishment and Religious Dissent*, 145, 150–52.
9   "An Ordinance for the Government of the Territory of the United States North-West of the Ohio River," in Dreisbach and Hall, *Sacred Rights of Conscience*, 238.
10 "Farewell Address" (Sept. 19, 1796), *Washington: Writings* (Library of America), ed. John Rhodehamel (New York, 1997), 972, 971.

purity and simplicity of its benevolent institutor, is a religion of all others most friendly to liberty, science, and the freest expression of the human mind."[11]

A generation later, Joseph Story's highly regarded *Commentaries on the Constitution*, from 1833, provided a magisterial restatement of conventional republican theory. Story fully supported the separation of church and state as defined by the First Amendment, but he also took for granted that, "The promulgation of the great doctrines of religion," which included cultivation of "all the personal, social, and benevolent virtues," could "never be a matter of indifference in any well ordered community." So fundamental did Story consider the relationship between religion and the health of American society that he was prepared to make a further assertion: "Indeed, in a republic, there would seem to be a peculiar property in viewing the Christian religion, as the great basis, on which it must rest for its support and permanence, if it be, what it has ever been deemed by its truest friends to be, the religion of liberty."[12]

Circumstances, emphases, and conceptions of political well-being did change as the nation's history unfolded. But at least through the time of Story's *Commentaries*, almost no controversy surrounded John Adams's foundational conception of the requirements for a successful republican government.

2   The Logic Applied to Public Schools[13]

On the basis of that consensus, it was an entirely natural step that, when tax-supported public education began, influential Americans instinctively concluded that readings from the Bible were an ideal means to secure the future of the republic. If morality in the citizenry was essential for a republic to flourish, what better way to inculcate that morality than by prescribing instruction for as many children as possible from a repository of moral teaching almost universally respected. (It is important to remember that, until the

---

11   Benjamin Rush to Jefferson, Aug. 22, 1800; and Thomas Jefferson to Moses Robinson, Mar. 23, 1801; in *Jefferson's Extracts from the Gospels*, ed. Dickinson W. Adams, *The Papers of Thomas Jefferson*, Second Series (Princeton: Princeton University Press, 1983), 318, 325.

12   Joseph Story, *Commentaries on the Constitution* (1833), cited from *The Founders' Constitution*, 5 vols., eds. Philip B. Kurland and Ralph Lerner (Chicago: University of Chicago Press, 1987), 5:108a, 108b.

13   My treatment of state court decisions in all that follows depends heavily on the superb accounts in two books by Steven K. Green, *The Bible, the School, and the Constitution: The Clash That Shaped Modern Church-State Doctrine* (New York: Oxford University Press, 2012), and, especially, *The Second Disestablishment: Church and State in Nineteenth-Century America* (New York: Oxford University Press, 2010).

rise of a significant Catholic population in the 1830s, "religion" in the early United States effectively meant Protestant Christianity and "the Bible" meant the Protestants' King James Version.[14])

Between the adoption of the Massachusetts Constitution in 1780 and Justice Story's summary of U.S. Constitutional logic in 1833, however, three significant changes did affect the application of republican logic.

First, John Adams's New England variant of that logic was discarded. In a process extending over two generations, with Massachusetts the last to fall into line the same year that Story published his *Commentaries*, the states came to agree with Virginia in considering any tax support for the churches as compromising the separation of church and state.

In a second development that is more difficult to chart specifically, the nation's conventional wisdom about human nature began to shift. As recently documented by historian Robert Tracy McKenzie, the movement was from realism to optimism.[15] Isolated quotations are not proof positive, but they do suggest an evolution of conventional wisdom—from, that is, George Washington ("The motives which predominate most in human affairs is [sic] self-love and self-interest") and Alexander Hamilton ("Men are ambitious, vindictive, and rapacious") to Andrew Jackson ("I have great confidence in the intelligence, and virtue, of the great body of the American people") and the nation's first widely recognized historian George Bancroft ("The Spirit of God breathes through the combined intelligence of the people").[16] Shifting opinions about human morality inevitably affected the moral calculus of democratic republicanism. If traditional views about the threat of sin gave way to confidence in innate human capacities, the "religion" necessary to preserve republican freedom became less explicitly Christian and more generically humanistic.

The third important development was the beginning of tax-supported common schooling. In the new United States, citizens mobilized at different times

---

14 If documentation is needed, see Mark A. Noll, *America's Book: The Rise and Decline of a Bible Civilization, 1794–1911* (New York: Oxford University Press, 2022), 99–100 and *passim*.
15 Robert Tracy McKenzie, *We the Fallen People: The Founders and the Future of American Democracy* (Downers Grove, IL: InterVarsity Press, 2021). The quotations that follow are among the many highlighted in this insightful book.
16 George Washington to James Madison, Dec. 3, 1784: https://founders.archives.gov/documents/Madison/01-12-02-0320; Alexander Hamilton, *The Federalist No. 6* (Nov. 14, 1787): https://founders.archives.gov/documents/Hamilton/01-04-02-0156; *The Papers of Andrew Jackson, Vol. VI, 1825–1828*, eds. Harold Moser and J. Clint Clifft (Knoxville: University Tennessee Press, 2002), 143; George Bancroft, "The Office of the People in Art, Government, and Religion" (Address at Williamstown College, Aug. 1835); and https://www.swarthmore.edu/SocSci/rbannis1/AIH19th/Bancroft.html.

to replace the colonial educational structures that had leaned heavily on official sponsorship by individual Protestant denominations. But wherever those initiatives took place, they inevitably included daily readings from the King James Bible as part of the curriculum. Moreover, until the number of Catholics rose rapidly from the 1830s, almost no one objected.

Historian David Komline has shown that the "common school awakening" in the United States occurred with strong religious backing that came from representatives of the Protestant denominations who agreed to subordinate their theological differences for a broader educational goal. To such ones it seemed obviously "nonsectarian" when such differences were set aside so that the Bible they all trusted could serve a public purpose.[17] Quakers spearheaded New York City's Society for Establishing a Free School (1805). Many local programs with leaders from many denominations adopted the English Quaker Joseph Lancaster's system of older children instructing younger children (ca. 1800–1835). The generically evangelical Thomas Gallaudet featured general biblical instruction at his Connecticut Asylum for the Education of Deaf and Dumb Persons (1817). In the 1820s the moderately evangelical Congregationalist Emma Willard set up the Troy Female Seminary in Troy, New York; Unitarians founded the Round Hill School in Northampton, Massachusetts; and two conservative evangelical Congregationalist sons of the late Yale College president Timothy Dwight began a short-lived academy in New Haven that included Black as well as white students. During the 1830s New York City expanded its tax-supported educational systems under leaders from many Protestant denominations; Massachusetts established its system with Unitarians in the lead; and the parallel development in Ohio was supported by Congregationalists (including Lyman Beecher), Methodists, Universalists, "Christians" (especially Alexander Campbell), and even Roman Catholics (particularly Bishop John Baptist Purcell).

Yet despite educational developments marked by an extraordinary diversity of sponsorship and a multitude of different ways to collect taxes, organize levels of instruction, and train teachers, the panoply of early common schools in the United States uniformly provided regular instruction (usually more than simple reading) from the King James Bible. That instruction inevitably

---

17 David Komline, *The Common School Awakening: Religion and the Transatlantic Roots of American Public Education* (New York: Oxford University Press, 2020). I have summarized and augmented Komline's superb research in order to explain why required Bible readings in tax-supported schools continued unabated when, in the middle decades of the nineteenth century, public reliance on scripture otherwise began to decline. See Noll, *America's Book*, chap. 14, "The Common School Exception."

involved a mixture of religious and secular assumptions, which at the time bothered almost no one. Crucially, for the tangled legal history that began in the 1850s when Catholic parents did protest tax-supported required use of the Protestant Bible, the rationale for using the supposedly nonsectarian Bible had been clearly spelled out *before* common schools came into existence.

An early instance was provided by Benjamin Rush, a signer of the Declaration of Independence and the new nation's foremost physician. In 1786 Rush published a plan for the Pennsylvania legislature to establish a tiered statewide system of tax-supported schools, a plan his title designated as "the Mode of Education, Proper in a Republic." Rush began with an explicitly Christian rehearsal of the standard republican calculus: "The only foundation for a useful education in a republic is to be laid in RELIGION. Without this, there can be no virtue, and without virtue there can be no liberty, and liberty is the object and life of all republican governments.... [T]he religion I mean to recommend in this place, is the religion of JESUS CHRIST." To Rush, it was obvious why "a Christian cannot fail of being a republican," since "every precept of the Gospel inculcates those degrees of humility, self-denial, and brotherly kindness, which are directly opposed to the pride of monarchy and the pageantry of a court." To operationalize this reasoning, Rush proposed instruction from the scriptures. This proposal grew directly from his conception of good government: "there is no book of its size in the whole world, that contains half so much useful knowledge for the government of the states, or the direction of the affairs of individuals as the Bible."[18] Although Rush's pamphlet would be reprinted several times, his imprimatur was not required either to promote Bible reading in common schools or to explain the republican purpose behind the reading.

One of the clearest statements concerning both republican purpose and the Bible appeared in 1848 from Horace Mann, a leading pioneer of American public education who had gained a national reputation through his service as secretary of the Massachusetts State Board of Education. Mann's way of positioning the Bible in the schools occupied a central place in his lengthy twelfth "annual report on education," from 1848. In effect, Mann hoped to sustain John Adams's New England variant of the republican calculus, but with public

---

18 Benjamin Rush, *A Plan for the Establishment of Public Schools and the Diffusion of Knowledge in Pennsylvania: To Which Are Added Thoughts upon the Mode of Education, Proper in a Republic, Addressed to the Legislature and the Citizens of the State* (Philadelphia: Thomas Dobson, 1786), 15–18.

schools replacing the church.[19] Significantly for what came later, Mann did not so much defend Bible reading as such, but explain why the practice should support general republican values rather than anything specifically Christian.

From first to last, that support dominated Mann's rationale. Instead of using Bible reading to evangelize, and certainly instead of dispensing with it altogether, Mann thought that "all sensible and judicious men, all patriots, and all genuine republicans" would agree that "those articles in the creed of republicanism which are accepted by all, believed in by all, and which form the common basis of our political faith, shall be taught to all." Such education would naturally stress how to prevent "immoralities and crimes [that] break over all moral barriers, destroying and profaning the securities and sanctities of life." For emphasis, he expressed his great satisfaction that an earlier Massachusetts law had spelled out the vision so fully: "our law explicitly and solemnly enjoins it upon all teachers, without any exception, 'to exert their best endeavors to impress on the minds of children and youth committed to their care and instruction the principles of piety, justice, and a sacred regard to truth, love to their country, humanity, and universal benevolence, sobriety, industry, and frugality, chastity, moderation, and temperance, and those other virtues which are the ornament of human society, and the basis upon which a republican constitution is founded.'"[20]

If, however, Mann sounded like a reprise of Rush, two aspects of his report anticipated later American history. First was his messianic confidence in what public education could accomplish, and accomplish without Christian conversion or the agency of the Holy Spirit. Rather, "it is the opinion of our most intelligent, dispassionate, and experienced teachers, that we can, in the course of two or three generations, and through the instrumentality of good teachers and good schools" produce a much better "state of society," and do so "without any miracle, without any extraordinary sacrifices or, costly effort, but only by working our existing common-school system with such a degree of vigor as can easily be put forth, and at such an expense as even the poorest community can easily bear."[21] Without pausing to mark the transition, this hopeful Unitarian had taken up the advocacy of John Adams, who had also been a Unitarian, but one worrying about natural human tendencies. In contrast, Mann expressed

---

19   On Mann's self-consciousness in substituting public education for church establishment, see Nathan S. Rives, *The Religion-Supported State: Piety and Politics in Early National New England* (Lanham, MD: Lexington, 2022).
20   Horace Mann, "Report for 1848," in *Annual Reports on Education by Horace Mann* (Boston: Lee and Shepard; NY: Lee, Shepard, and Dillingham, 1872), 700, 704, 736–37.
21   Ibid., 708.

great confidence in the capacity of common schooling to do for the republic what Adams had thought only a "just and equitable" church establishment could accomplish.

A second aspect of Mann's report involved a confusing use of terms—"religion," "Christianity," "sectarian," and "nonsectarian"—that, when later disaggregated, would lead to the *Schempp* decision that removed the Bible reading he so ardently defended. After Mann quoted the Massachusetts law about the "virtues ... upon which a republican government is founded," he immediately asked a rhetorical question, "Are not these virtues and graces part and parcel of Christianity?" Yet elsewhere in the report, he took pains to insist that he wanted nothing that could be identified with anything specifically Christian. Certainly there should be no establishment of religion. Moreover, the question about what exactly "religious truth is" should be left "to the arbitrament, without human appeal, of each man's reason and conscience." Again, because "our public schools are not theological seminaries," they are not allowed to teach anything about what "is essential to religion or to salvation."[22] In other words—and lumping together the terms of endless battle in later legal controversies—Mann held that the Massachusetts practice "founds its morals on the basis of religion; it welcomes the religion of the Bible.... But here it stops ... because it disclaims to act as an umpire between hostile religious opinions."[23] But, realistically, could the Protestants' revered version of scripture function as a truly nonsectarian guide for public morality?

In one of the earliest legal challenges to daily Bible readings, a Massachusetts court in 1859 simply reiterated the republican argument without Mann's excess baggage. The court took up the question whether a schoolteacher had been in his rights to strike an eleven-year-old Catholic student on the hand for thirty minutes with a rattan stick for failing to recite the Lord's Prayer and the Ten Commandments in the language of the King James Version.[24] The youth, Thomas Whall, had been counseled by his parents and his priest to refuse because of their objection to the required use of the Protestant Bible. The court's judgment exonerated the teacher and sanctioned the practice by leaning heavily on the ability of local school boards to determine their own procedures ("The authority of a parent cannot justify the disobedience, by a child, of

---

22 Ibid., 736 ("virtues and graces"), 718–20 (opposition to establishment), 723 ("each man's reason"), 729 ("essential to religion or salvation").
23 Ibid., 729–30.
24 For insightful treatment of this case in the wider sweep of the nineteenth century, see John T. McGreevy, *Catholicism and American Freedom: A History* (New York: W. W. Norton, 2003), 7–11.

the regulations of a school"). But it also went out of its way to state explicitly that such Bible readings were justified, not only because of Article III in the 1780 Massachusetts Declaration of Rights, but because they were essential for a free society: "Our schools are the granite foundation on which our republican form of government rests." The Bible, the court explained further, was "the book best adapted from which to 'teach children and youth the principles of piety, justice, and a sacred regard to truth, love to their country, humanity, and a universal benevolence, sobriety, moderation and temperance, and those other virtues which are the ornaments of human society, and the basis upon which a republican constitution is founded.'"[25]

Yet like Mann's extensive 1848 report, this brief judgment from 1859 equivocated on what would become a stress point in later judicial considerations. It claimed that the Bible was in the public schools not "for the purpose of teaching sectarian religion, but a knowledge of God and of his will, whose practice is religion." If "the Bible [meaning the King James Version] has long been in our public schools, ... no scholar is requested to believe it, none to receive it as the only true version of the laws of God."[26] The judgment seemed to be saying several things that did not cohere: (a) The Bible reveals God's will. (b) God's will is the basis for republican virtue, which is why the Bible is mandated for use in common schools. (c) But public school pupils do not have to believe that it is God's will for them as individuals.[27] As reasons for keeping the Bible in common schools multiplied and legal reasoning verged toward judicial doublespeak, focus on the moral calculus of democratic republicanism was bound to waver.

3   The Logic Diluted

The Massachusetts police court that rendered the 1859 *Commonwealth v. Cooke* decision was not the first to adjudicate whether required readings from the King James Version should be allowed in tax-supported schools. That distinction

---

25   Commonwealth v. Cooke, 7 Am. Law Register 417 (Ma. Police Court, 1859), 417, 421, 423.
26   Ibid., 423.
27   This ruling was brought to a close by a quotation from the Gospel of Mark (3:25) that Abraham Lincoln in that very year made famous (if "a house be divided against itself, that house cannot stand") and by a proposition that later court decisions would reverse: if the religious convictions of a single child's parent were able to overturn the decision of a properly authorized agency of Massachusetts government, it would violate "that heretofore impassable gulf which lies between *Church and State*." *Commonwealth v. Cooke*, 424, 425.

belonged to the Maine Judicial Supreme Court, which five years earlier had been asked to rule on the right of a local school committee to mandate such readings and to expel students who would not participate. This Maine ruling included the ambiguities concerning "religion," "Christianity," "sectarian," and "nonsectarian" visible in Horace Mann's report and soon to appear in the 1859 Massachusetts ruling. More importantly for the republican logic of the founding era and the implementation of that logic through Bible readings, the decision also began the process of subordinating attention to the moral logic of democratic republicanism.

As in Massachusetts, the challenge in Maine came from a Roman Catholic family objecting to readings from the King James Version; as also in the later case, historical anti-Catholic instincts played an obvious role in the decision.[28] The Maine court opined at length on procedure, specifically concluding that the rights of a duly established local school superseded the rights of the Catholic parent who had sued ("A law is not unconstitutional, because it may prohibit what one may *conscientiously think* right, or require what he may *conscientiously* think wrong"). But when it turned to why it was good for schools to require Bible readings, reasoning wandered. Early in their ruling, the judges affirmed that "the entire book is the noblest monument of style, of thought, of beauty, of sublimity, of moral teaching, of pathetic narrative, the richest treasury of household words, of familiar phrases, of popular illustrations and associations, that any language every possessed." Later in their ruling they praised the King James Bible: this "particular version ... from the idiomatic English of the translation, and the sublime morality of its teachings, furnishes the best illustration which the language affords of pure English undefiled, and is best fitted to strengthen the morals and promote the virtues which adorn and dignify social life."[29]

Along the way the court did remember that Maine's legislature had mandated a provision coming closer to the republican calculus: "all the instructors of youth" should diligently teach "the principles of morality and justice, and a sacred regard for the truth; love to their country, humanity and universal benevolence; sobriety, industry, and frugality; chastity, moderation, and temperance; and all other virtues, which are the ornaments of human society." But that judgment was also compromised by the concession that students did not have to believe what they were required to read: "No theological doctrine

---

28 For the anti-Catholic environment in Ellsworth, Maine, see John T. McGreevy, *American Jesuits and the World: How an Embattled Religious Order Made Modern Catholicism Global* (Princeton: Princeton University Press, 2016), 36–41.

29 Donahue v. Richards, 38 Me. 379 (1854), 380, 383, 401–02.

was taught.... The truth or falsehood of the book in which the scholars were required to read, was not asserted.... The Bible was used merely as a book in which instruction was given."[30]

And so it would go until *Schempp* in 1963. In the famous "Cincinnati Bible War" of 1869–1870, defenders of daily readings from the King James Version again mixed and matched their arguments. In an effort to end strife among the city's majority Protestant population, its large Catholic minority, and a rising number of Jews, the Cincinnati Board of Education in the summer of 1869 voted to eliminate Bible readings. When an ad hoc group of Protestants filed suit to reverse the decision, the Superior Court of Cincinnati scheduled four days of arguments at the end of November to consider the suit. A large book of four hundred pages brought those arguments to the public.

Lawyers defending the practice came closer to articulating the founders' republican calculus than others who would follow in their path. They cited specifically the provision of the 1787 Northwest Ordinance that provided for "schools and the means of education" to support the "religion, morality, and knowledge" required for "good government and the happiness of mankind." They hammered even more on the school board's error in disregarding a paragraph from Ohio's revised constitution of 1852: "Religion, morality and knowledge ... being essential to good government, it shall be the duty of the General Assembly to pass suitable laws, to protect every denomination in the peaceable enjoyment of its own mode of public worship and to *encourage schools and the means of instruction.*" While attorneys for the board stressed "every denomination," the plaintiff's lawyers emphasized the civil purpose of this provision: "Compliance with the teachings and requirements of the Christian religion is all that is necessary to make a perfect citizen.... The recognition of religion and God necessarily implies the recognition of the Holy Bible."[31]

From this point forward, defenders of Bible reading regularly offered a more diffuse rationale, sometimes convincing the courts, sometimes not. In 1898 the Michigan supreme court allowed readings to continue from a book of scripture selections. Most of the arguments in this case focused on sectarianism, constitutional free exercise, and the meaning of worship. Only offhand references echoed the republican calculus, as when the judgment referred to "the moral precepts of the Ten Commandments ... which are intended to inculcate good morals," or when one of the judges dissenting from the decision explained

---

30   Ibid., 399 (both quotations).
31   *The Bible and the Public Schools: Arguments in ... the Superior Court of Cincinnati, with the Opinions and Decisions of the Court* (Cincinnati: Robert Clark, 1870), 9 (Northwest Ordinance), 39, 290–321 (1852 Constitution), 150 ("Bible").

why the Northwest Ordinance's language concerning "religion, morality, and knowledge" did not give the right to "teach ... religion in the public schools."[32]

Only a few years later, the Nebraska Supreme Court ruled the other way. In this 1902 decision, a parent from Gage County complained that his children were being required to take part in daily exercises that included Bible reading and sometimes the singing of gospel songs. Court records show that the state superintendent of education defended the practice by quoting from the clause in Nebraska's constitution that echoed the reasoning of the 1780 Massachusetts Declaration of Rights: "religion, morality, and knowledge" were described as "being essential to good government." Yet Justice John Joseph Sullivan, speaking for a unanimous court, upheld the complaint by repeating arguments that were now being heard much more frequently. In the court's judgment, daily readings from the King James Version constituted a "sectarian" imposition. Moreover, forcing children to participate in a sectarian variety of "religious worship" violated the Nebraska constitution's guarantee of religious liberty to all, and thus threatened the "public" character of Nebraska's educational system.

The arguments defending Bible reading provided by state superintendent William Jackson, which the court rejected, were noteworthy for their variety. He did eventually hint at the republican calculus ("No more complete code of morals exists than is contained in the New Testament which reaffirms and emphasizes the moral obligations"), along with an effort to distinguish what was moral from what was religious ("The Bible teaches the highest morality apart from religious instruction")—yet only after wandering further afield: "The Bible surely cannot be considered as falling within the category of sectarian books.... The Bible is the rarest and richest book in the department of thought and imagination ... the greatest classic of our literature."[33]

A similar potpourri of arguments defending the practice came from Illinois justice John Hand, who dissented when, in 1910, the state supreme court ruled that since required daily Bible readings and hymn singing constituted "worship," they were not allowed. In protest, Justice Hand contended that Illinois had long recognized the need for youth to embrace principles of justice and morality in order to preserve a safe society. But unlike arguments extending back to Horace Mann, he also defended the particularly religious character of scripture by citing Justice Story from an 1844 ruling: "Where can the purest principles of morality be learned so clearly or so perfectly as from the New Testament? Where are benevolence, the love of truth, sobriety, and industry

---

32   Pfeiffer v. Board of Education, 118 Mich. 560 (1898), 561, 571.
33   State ex rel. Freeman v. Scheve, 65 Neb 853 (1902), Jackson quoted at 855–56.

so powerfully and irresistibly inculcated as in the sacred volume?"[34] For this jurist, it was inconceivable to separate desirable civic purpose from traditional Christian belief.

Into the recent past, even as the Constitutional arguments were strengthened against Bible readings, the older pattern of catch-as-catch-can defenses continued. In its landmark *Schempp* ruling from 1963, the Supreme Court expounded at great length on why the practice constituted a "sectarian" breach of "neutrality." Along the way, it provided only a cursory summary of the argument offered by defenders of the practice—that, in the Court's summary, the daily exercise contributed to "the promotion of moral values, the contradiction to the materialistic trends of our times, the perpetuation of our institutions and the teaching of literature."[35] By contrast, when, in 1950, the New Jersey Supreme Court had affirmed the practice in a unanimous judgment, it expatiated at some length on why Bible reading in public schools had still, as of that year, been approved in more states than it had been disallowed. With a concern absent from the U.S. Supreme Court's decision of 1963, the New Jersey jurists also linked their judgment (upheld by the U.S. Supreme Court in 1952) to what they viewed as the all-out competition of the Cold War. Their ruling is worth extensive quotation in order to illustrate the many arguments enlisted to defend the practice so shortly before it would be ruled unconstitutional.

> While it is necessary that there be a separation between church and state, it is not necessary that the state should be stripped of religious sentiment. It may be a tragic experience for this country and for its conception of life, liberty and the pursuit of happiness if our people lose their religious feeling and are left to live their lives without faith. Who can say that those attributes which Thomas Jefferson in his notable document called "unalienable rights" endowed by the Creator may survive a loss of belief in the Creator? The American people are and always have been theistic.... The influence which that force contributed to our origins and the direction which it has given to our progress are beyond calculation. It may be of the highest importance to the nation that the people remain theistic, not that one or another sect or denomination may survive, but that belief in God shall abide. It was, we are led to believe, to that end that the statute was enacted; so that at the beginning of the day the children should

---

34 For a thorough discussion of People ex. rel. Ring v. Board of Education, 92 N.D. 251, 254–56 (ILL. 1910), see Green, *Second Disestablishment*, 321–24. Justice Hand quoted Supreme Court Justice Story from Vidal v. Girard's Executors, 43 U.S. 127 (1844).

35 Abington School District v. Schempp, 374 U.S. at 223.

pause to hear a few words from the wisdom of the ages and to bow the head in humility before the Supreme Power. No rites, no ceremony, no doctrinal teaching; just a brief moment with eternity.... It may be that the true perspective engendered by that recurring short communion with the eternal forces will be effective to keep our people from permitting government to become a manmade robot which will crush even the Constitution itself. Our way of life is on challenge. Organized atheistic society is making a determined drive for supremacy by conquest as well as by infiltration. Recent history has demonstrated that when such a totalitarian power comes into control it exercises a ruthless supremacy over men and ideas, and over such remnants of religious worship as it permits to exist. We are at a crucial hour in which it may behoove our people to conserve all of the elements which have made our land what it is. Faced with this threat to the continuance of elements deeply imbedded in our national life the adoption of a public policy with respect thereto is a reasonable function to be performed by those on whom responsibility lies.[36]

Echoes of the republican calculus are difficult to find in this judgment. Instead, the New Jersey justices emphasized the need to hold absolutism at bay, general theistic traditions and religious feelings, and a desire that students pause for "a brief moment with eternity." The link between the Bible and the moral calculus of democratic republicanism, which had been so strong with Horace Mann and the Massachusetts Police Court, and which had survived piecemeal long thereafter, had faded away.

4   A Higher Logic?

Before attempting final comments on this history, a brief word is in order to document a different strand of American legal-religious reasoning—voices that agreed with the *Schempp* Court in holding that devotional Bible readings should not be required in public schools, but because they wanted to preserve an explicitly Christian understanding of the scriptures. These individuals worried that recommending Bible readings for their political utility undermined the singular importance that Christian believers should ascribe to the theological uniqueness of scripture.

John Witte has catalogued an extensive roster of Massachusetts residents who, in debates leading to the new constitution of 1780, objected to the

---

36   Doremus v. Board of Education, 5 NJ 435 (N.J. 1950) 75 A.2d 880

perpetuation of even a "slender" establishment. Some repeated James Madison's contention that any form of establishment inevitably corrupted public life, but some also worried about the effect on personal faith. According to one protest, it was "intirely [sic] out of the power of the legislature to establish a way of Worship that shall be agreeable to ... the minds of individuals, as it is a matter that solely relates to and stands between God and the Soul before whose Tribunal all must account each for himself."[37]

The most unusual intervention in the Cincinnati Bible War of 1869 had come from an attorney, Stanley Matthews, who argued in favor of banning the readings. Yet Matthews, who would later be appointed to the U.S. Supreme Court by his friend James A. Garfield, spoke as a friend of traditional Christianity, repeatedly stressing, "I am a Calvinist Protestant. I believe in the doctrines of election and predestination.... [The Bible is] a sacred book in the highest sense of the terms."[38] But then Matthews reversed the logic expressed by many defenders of the practice. Precisely *because* he valued Christian truth so highly, he did not want its transmission handed over to civil authorities. An image from the Old Testament underscored his reasoning: "Let no unholy hands be laid upon the sacred ark." The religious education children most needed was not ethics for citizenship, "not merely ... the learning of abstract morals." Instead, "the duties of a religious life" could only be found "in the Gospel of God our Savior, and the scheme of redemption for a lost and sinful race as revealed in the person and work of the God-Man, Christ Jesus, and held forth in the instructions, and services, and means of grace, and living oracles, committed to the keeping of the church of the living God, as his kingdom on the earth."[39] The responsibility for *that* religious training belonged to parents and the churches. In Matthews's view, doctrinal fidelity remained far more important than civic utility.

Early in the twentieth century J. Gresham Machen, another conservative Presbyterian, followed Matthews. Against fellow believers who complained that state court decisions against Bible readings were ruining the republic, Machen fulminated:

> I am opposed to the reading of the Bible in public schools.... [S]uch presentation is opposed to the Christian religion at its very heart. The relation between the Christian way of salvation and other ways is not a relation between the adequate and the inadequate or between the perfect and the imperfect, but it is a relation between the true and the false.

---

37   Witte, "A Most Mild and Equitable Establishment," 23–24 (quotation from the Town of Dartmouth, 23).

38   Stanley Mathews for the board, in *The Bible and the Public Schools*, 207, 228,

39   Mathews, in *The Bible and the Public Schools*, 257.

> The minute a professing Christian admits that he can find neutral ground with non-Christians in the study of "religion" in general, he has given up the battle and has really, if he knows what he is doing, made common cause with that synchronism which is today ... the deadliest enemy of the Christian faith.[40]

To Americans who agreed with Matthews and Machen, opponents of required Bible readings were entirely correct to view them as "sectarian worship." To those who defended the nonsectarian or secular functions of the exercise, opponents called not for the separation of church and state but for the rescue of the holy from the profane. Their reasoning nicely complicates a debate that all too often has been caricatured as Christian America versus secular America.

5   Opinion

The secondary or derivative question posed by the history sketched here is whether mandatory readings from the Protestant King James Bible have been a good way for Americans to promote the personal virtue without which republics fail. The answer must certainly be "no." Citizens in the early United States relied on this expedient because, having left behind the props of European Christendom, they feared for the future of a democratic republic. With near unanimity they agreed that the Bible, the divinely revealed Word of God, was uniquely capable of encouraging the virtue without which republics failed. Yet in short order, many also realized that imposing the Protestant Bible could only be justified by insisting on its moral, civic, and nonsectarian purposes. (Some jurists, nonetheless, long continued to include Christian reverence for scripture alongside their republican, cultural, and traditional arguments for the practice, even as a few Christians denounced it for turning a book of divine salvation into a utilitarian tool for civic health.) Confusion between reasons for respecting the Bible as God's Word and reasons for putting it to use to promote republican virtue prepared the way for later courts to view the practice as sectarian and, with the *Schempp* Supreme Court, to rule it unconstitutional for violating religious neutrality. In addition to constitutional reasoning, the nation's manifest religious pluralism, eventually including "no religion," has

---

40   J. Gresham Machen, "The Necessity of the Christian School," in *Forward in Faith* (Educational Convention Year Book, 1933); quoted here from *J. Gresham Machen: Selected Shorter Writings*, ed. D. G. Hart (Phillipsburg, NJ: Presbyterian & Reformed, 2004), 170–71.

rendered it impossible to make the sacred text of one of the nation's religions a mandated foundation of public schooling for all.

But what of the primary or foundational question? Was John Adams wrong when, out of his concern for the American republic, he defended a "slender" church establishment—or when Horace Mann, for the same reason, applied the New England variant of republican political theory to common schools? Were they correct in worrying about their republic falling prey to the corrupting excesses of democracy?

The answer to these questions depends on how one now evaluates prospects for the American republic. In the twenty-first century, where the founders' realistic view of human nature no longer commands general assent, there exists no agreed-upon framework to account for the clashing pursuit of differently defined individual rights. A sober view of the nation's history must also recognize that many severe impediments (especially racial and economic impediments) have undermined the republican ideal of liberty and justice for all; these impediments have also frustrated the ability of citizens to act with altruistic public virtue even if they wanted to. Moreover, republican worries seem justified in a political climate where advocacy from the Left focuses on what government should do and from the Right on what it should not do, but with neither Left nor Right stressing the duty of citizens to develop the internal moral character that could subordinate personal advantage to the public good.

In the scope of human history, the American republic is still a short-lived experiment. Already in its history it was once saved from dissolution by the force of arms rather than by the restraint of public virtue. Some may conclude that the nation's future is secure despite current difficulties. By contrast, my reading of American history leads me to agree with John Adams that, in fact, "the good order and preservation of civil government essentially depend upon piety, religion, and morality." I cannot, however, specify a plan for implementing this wisdom that would be allowable under the Constitution's wholesome requirements for maintaining both liberty and religious impartiality. I am therefore left with the kind of commendation and uncertainty with which John Witte ended his study of the 1780 Massachusetts constitution: "the balance that the Supreme Court has struck in favor of a complete disestablishment of religion can ... no longer serve a people so widely devoted to a public religion and a religious public. Somewhere between extremes, our society must now find a new constitutional balance—with Adams's efforts serving as a noble instruction."[41]

---

41   Witte, "A Mild and Equitable Establishment," 31.

CHAPTER 23

An Integrative Approach to Government Religious Speech

Nathan S. Chapman

1   Introduction

Measured by lack of judicial consensus, one of the hardest questions the modern Supreme Court has faced is what limits, if any, the Establishment Clause places on government religious speech. The Court has decided dozens of cases about government-sponsored prayers and religious symbols, and although some relatively stable patterns can be divined from the holdings, the justices have never settled on a test, principle, or even rationale to guide officials, litigants, and lower courts. From the beginning, the Court drew a line between government-sponsored prayers in public schools (impermissible) and chaplain prayers before legislative sessions (permissible). Eventually, a majority of the Court decided that the touchstone in cases involving religious symbols was whether a reasonable observer would think the government was endorsing religion. Although the Court has recently said it has abandoned the endorsement test, it continues to evaluate government-sponsored religious symbols by whether they express support for religion.[1] The question of the government's religious speech has been a mess from the beginning, and the Court does not appear to have marked a path out of it.[2]

Through more than three decades of profuse and trenchant scholarship on the historical and intellectual underpinnings of the rights of religious freedom, John Witte has illuminated a more complete, complex, and coherent way forward. Embracing an "integrative" approach that merges positivist, naturalist, and historicist jurisprudence, Witte has explored not only the text and historical context of the First Amendment, but also its natural rights background and

---

1   American Legion v. American Humanist Association, 139 S. Ct. 2067, 2082–83, 2089–90 (2019).
2   John Witte, Jr., Joel A. Nichols, and Richard W. Garnett, *Religion and the American Constitutional Experiment*, 5th ed. (Oxford: Oxford University Press, 2022), 301.

its place in the long tradition of American constitutionalism.[3] One of Witte's key insights has been that the purpose of the religion clauses was to protect religious liberty, understood as the confluence of multiple overlapping principles, including separation, disestablishment, equality, free exercise, pluralism, and liberty of conscience.[4] While Witte has never thoroughly applied this powerful analytical toolkit to the question of government religious speech, his account of religious liberty does suggest a solution. Without disregarding the importance of the tradition of separation of church and state, he argues that where conceptions of separation would drive religion from the public sphere, they should be subordinate to the principle of religious liberty.[5] This analysis would seem to resolve the question of religious speech: in short, it is of no constitutional moment. If speech comes with coercion, then the problem is the coercion, not the speech. If the speech is not coupled with coercion, then it simply does not raise a constitutional concern.

I generally agree with Witte's approach and with these conclusions,[6] but I have one hesitation. Perhaps we have reached too hastily the conclusion that mere speech can never interfere with religious liberty. Might there be a form of government religious speech that does not involve strong pressure to participate in religious exercise but nevertheless violates the religious liberty protected by the Establishment Clause? My tentative answer is yes: the Establishment Clause prohibits speech that amounts to a threat of religious discrimination. My hope is that this chapter builds constructively upon the notion of religious liberty, and the integrative approach to jurisprudence, that Witte has persuasively shown and persistently modeled in his scholarship for many decades.

2   The Question

The Supreme Court's diverse and inconsistent decisions have made it difficult to pin down the precise legal question. Scholars generally sort the cases

---

3   John Witte, Jr., "The Integration of Religious Liberty," *Michigan Law Review* 90 (1992): 1363–83; and Witte, Nichols, and Garnett, *American Constitutional Experiment*, 1–128.

4   John Witte, Jr., "The Essential Rights and Liberties of Religion in the American Constitutional Experiment," *Notre Dame Law Review* 71 (1996): 371–445, at 376.

5   John Witte, Jr., "Facts and Fictions about the History of Separation of Church and State," *Journal of Church & State* 48 (2006): 15–45, at 42.

6   Nathan S. Chapman and Michael W. McConnell, *Agreeing to Disagree: How the Establishment Clause Protects Religious Diversity and Liberty of Conscience* (Oxford: Oxford University Press, 2023), 157–72.

into categories by outcome and perceived factual distinctions: government-sponsored speech in public schools is usually unconstitutional, presumably because school children are impressionable; government-sponsored prayers before a legislative session are usually constitutional because of tradition; and short expressions of ceremonial Deism and displays of religious symbols are a toss-up. These categories generally make sense, but the reasoning and outcomes within and across them are inconsistent. The categorizations are really conclusions that obscure more than they reveal about the underlying conceptual question.

This chapter asks the question underlying all of these cases: what limit, if any, does the Establishment Clause place on what the government may communicate, and why? Communication includes straightforward speech and writing, as well as the use of symbols or even, perhaps, the message conveyed by an action. In this sense, the question captures the range of forms of communication that are recognized, and often protected, by the Free Speech Clause when performed by a private party. Put in terms of free speech jurisprudence, the question is whether the Establishment Clause places any content-based, or perhaps viewpoint-based, restrictions on the government's communication.

The justices appear to agree that the clause forbids government religious speech in a setting that coerces participation or indoctrination. This is the minimum doctrinal reading of the Court's cases involving prayer, Bible reading, and Ten Commandments displays in public school rooms and events. Some justices have maintained that compulsion should be the only limit on government speech, but the Court as a whole has consistently rejected coercion as the sole touchstone of government religious speech. The trouble is that the justices have never settled on another test.

For a time, a majority of the justices appeared to embrace the view that the government violates the Establishment Clause when a reasonable observer would conclude that its conduct or speech has the effect of "endorsing" religion.[7] The Court has even applied this test to cases involving prayer at public school events.[8] But the endorsement test was never stable. The justices who embraced it consistently disagreed about its application to specific cases, leading to incoherent and inconsistent results. Other justices have offered various permutations on the endorsement test, but none have yet to gain the same purchase.[9]

---

7 County of Allegheny v. Greater Pittsburgh ACLU, 492 U.S. 573 (1989).
8 Santa Fe Indep. Sch. Dist. v. Doe, 530 U.S. 290 (2000).
9 Witte, Nichols, and Garnett, *American Constitutional Experiment*, 301.

The Court has recently purported to provide an alternative approach to religious symbols cases, and separately declared that it has rejected the endorsement test. Both of those claims are dubious. The Court's recent methods are entirely consistent with the endorsement test, and, though the cases were, in my mind, rightly decided, they have done nothing to even acknowledge, much less address, the disestablishment limits on government speech.

In *American Legion v. American Humanist Association*, the Supreme Court held that longstanding war memorials in the shape of a Latin cross do not violate the Establishment Clause.[10] The decision is laudable for reaching broad agreement about religious displays that have been on government property for a long time.[11] But it did nothing to eliminate confusion about what the Establishment Clause prohibits the government from saying or why. In fact, the Court's analysis may have made things worse. Although the Court said that it was not basing its judgment on whether the cross amounted to an endorsement of Christianity,[12] its entire analysis boiled down to whether the original context and the passage of time had sufficiently drained what is plainly a Christian symbol of its religious content.[13] On this basis, the Court concluded that old religious displays generally do not violate the Establishment Clause. The necessary implication, of course, is that some religious symbols (to say nothing of straightforward religious speech) *may* violate the Establishment Clause. Underneath a surface of broad agreement about the result remains a cacophony of views about what the Establishment Clause forbids.

In *Kennedy v. Bremerton School District*, the Court held that a public school violated the Free Speech and Free Exercise Clauses when it fired a football coach for praying publicly at the fifty-yard line after games.[14] Although the Court claimed that it had already abandoned the endorsement test,[15] the holding did not rely on that assertion. The Court determined that the prayers were attributable to the coach in his individual capacity, and therefore protected. Since the school was not responsible for the prayers, the Establishment Clause—implemented by whatever test—simply did not apply. In fact, the Court made it clear that it was not unsettling any of its prior school-prayer decisions.[16] While the case helpfully clarifies the rights of school employees

---

10   139 S.Ct. 2067 (2019).
11   Michael W. McConnell, "No More (Old) Symbol Cases," *Cato Supreme Court Review* (2018–19): 91–118.
12   139 S. Ct., 2082–83.
13   Ibid., 2089–90.
14   142 S. Ct. 2407 (2022).
15   Ibid., 2427.
16   Ibid., 2430.

to engage in private religious exercise, it says absolutely nothing about what the Establishment Clause might prohibit the government from noncoercively saying, or why.

The question is not going to disappear. Consider some examples of straightforward government religious speech that is not obviously coercive. The official motto of the United States is "In God We Trust," and it appears on U.S. currency.[17] Adults and children alike routinely pledge allegiance "to the Flag of the United States of America, and to the Republic for which it stands, one Nation under God." Some government entities are named for sectarian religious beliefs, such as Los Angeles, California, and Corpus Christi, Texas.

The government occasionally goes further. President Ronald Reagan declared 1983 the "Year of the Bible," asserting that "[t]here could be no more fitting moment than now to reflect with gratitude, humility, and urgency upon the wisdom revealed to us in the [Bible]" and "encourag[ing] all citizens, each in his or her own way, to reexamine and rediscover its priceless and timeless message"?[18] Government-designated clergy members offer prayers before a variety of events, such as the presidential inauguration, legislative sessions, and Supreme Court hearings ("God save this honorable Court"). Could the government go even further? Could the state of Texas declare that a personal relationship with Jesus Christ is the path to spiritual salvation? Or could the state of Michigan print on its official seal that "There is no God but Allah, and Muhammad is his messenger"? Would religious confessionalism satisfy the Establishment Clause so long as the state does not coerce observers into religious faith or practice?

Whatever limits the Establishment Clause places on religious symbols derives from the limits it places on speech more generally. The challenge posed by symbols is that they are usually more vague or multivalent than words. But the difference is one of degree, not of kind. Speech can be vague, too. When Reagan declared that wisdom was "revealed to us in the Bible," was he attributing such revelation to God, or to human authors, the way "wisdom is revealed" in secular texts from Plato to Shakespeare? Does encouraging citizens to

---

17 Several states have similar mottos that appear on their official flags. Florida's is "In God We Trust." Colorado's is "Nil sine Numine" (Nothing without the Divine). The motto of the territory of American Samoa is "Samoa, Muamaua Le" (Samoa, let Atua [God or the gods or the ancestors] be first). Kentucky's is "Deo gratium habeamus" (Let us be grateful to God). Ohio's is "With God, all things are possible." South Dakota's is "Under God the people rule." Troy Brownfield, "The 50 State Mottos, Ranked," Mar. 25, 2019, https://www.saturdayeveningpost.com/2019/03/the-50-state-mottos-ranked.

18 Ronald Reagan, "Presidential Proclamation 5018," Feb. 3, 1983, https://reaganlibrary.gov/archives/speech/proclamations-february-3-1983.

explore the Bible "each in [their] own way[s]" endorse Christianity or encourage intellectual and moral curiosity?

Whatever vagueness there might be, deliberate or otherwise, in speech, it is inherent, and often compounded, with symbols. Perhaps judicial prudence would suggest drawing a line of administrability between government speech and religious symbols—whatever outright speech the Establishment Clause may prohibit. But such a line would be the product of judicial prudence, not the Establishment Clause. Sometimes courts underenforce constitutional norms because of concerns about the separation of powers, federalism, or institutional competence. And sometimes they overenforce them, especially if violations are hard to detect. Indeed, as we shall see, overenforcement may be one of the stronger arguments for policing noncoercive government speech.

Knowing that the Establishment Clause prohibits the communication of X does not, of course, resolve the constitutionality of any given communication. Regardless whether the communication is with words, symbols, or both, or whether it is written, spoken, broadcast locally or widely, there will always be a crucial question of interpretation or semiotics: what does this speech or speech-act or symbol mean? What does it communicate? The proper hermeneutic for that analysis is itself a question of law. Whose opinion about the meaning matters, and why? The government's? The claimant's? Some hypothetical objective observer? Only once the meaning of the government's communication is settled can the constitutional rule be applied to determine whether the communication violates the Establishment Clause. This chapter does not have space to fully address these issues, but it is important to recognize that they are logically posterior to the foundational question, which is what sort of communication does the Establishment Clause prohibit, and why?

It is also worth distinguishing the Establishment Clause issue from the question of standing. A federal court has constitutional authority only to decide "cases or controvers[ies]" in which the claimant has standing to sue, which requires the claimant to show a unique and concrete injury.[19] Some justices have argued that cases involving mere religious speech, without any coercion, do not give the vast majority of claimants standing to sue because symbols do not create a concrete injury: the only injury is emotional.[20] It is important to keep standing conceptually discrete from the merits question, for it is logically and legally possible for the Establishment Clause to prohibit more than anyone would have standing to challenge.

---

19 Lujan v. Defenders of Wildlife, 504 U.S. 555, 563 (1992).
20 American Legion, 139 S. Ct. at 2098–2103 (Gorsuch, J., concurring in the judgment).

3 Witte's Contribution to the Question

A hallmark of John Witte's scholarship is the judicious implementation of what he calls an integrative approach to law. This approach is a way of judgment, of discerning both what the law is and what it ought to be, that seeks to marry disparate sources of law, and sometimes divergent legal principles, to provide a coherent approach to understanding and evaluating legal questions.

As defined by Witte's mentor and friend Harold Berman, "integrative jurisprudence is a legal philosophy that combines the three classical schools: legal positivism, natural-law theory, and the historical school." The idea is that "each of these three competing schools has isolated a single important dimension of law, and that it is both possible and important to bring the several dimensions together into a common focus."[21] In contrast to modern positivism, now so dominant among scholars, integrative jurisprudence considers both morality and the historical trajectory of the law within a political community. In contrast to a jurisprudence that gives pride of place to the judge's moral sentiments, it considers natural law to be the universal norms that provide the basis for a political community's particular solutions to problems of justice, fairness, and peace. And in contrast to originalism, it recognizes that "law is an ongoing historical process, developing from the past into the future."[22] Integrative jurisprudence brings the habits of mind of Aquinas and Althusius, Story and Savigny into the twenty-first century.

Witte has rarely discussed the theory of integrative jurisprudence, but his work consistently applies it. In an early book review, he praised the authors for taking an integrative approach to the religion clauses.[23] Witte demonstrated the power of the approach in a 1996 article that laid the basis for what became the standard one-volume work on the history and doctrine of the religion clauses (now coauthored with Joel Nichols and Richard Garnett). With a politically, philosophically, and theologically sensitive account of the late eighteenth century, Witte showed that the overarching historical purpose of the religion clauses was to protect an American conception of religious liberty that combines "a variety of principles," namely "liberty of conscience, free exercise, pluralism, equality, separation, and disestablishment."[24] These

---

21 Harold J. Berman, "Toward an Integrative Jurisprudence: Politics, Morality, and History," *California Law Review* 76 (1988): 779–801; and Jerome Hall, "From Legal Theory to Integrative Jurisprudence," *University of Cincinnati Law Review* 33 (1964): 153–205.
22 Berman, "Integrative Jurisprudence," 795.
23 Witte, "Integration," 1363.
24 Witte, "Essential Rights and Liberties," 376; and Witte, Nichols, and Garnett, *American Constitutional Experiment*, 59–92.

principles together form a shield of "religious liberty for all" that integrates the natural rights of religious liberty, the implementation of those rights through positive law, and the history, tradition, and trajectory of religious liberty in the American constitutional tradition.

A challenge for integrative jurisprudence is reconciling, or perhaps choosing among, sources or principles of law in tension with one another. Unlike pure positivism, an integrativist cannot simply dismiss contrary claims of morality or the lived experience of society. Witte identifies this problem, and a possible solution, in an essay devoted to understanding the historical, and proper, role of arguments for religious liberty from the principle of church-state separation. Contrary to Philip Hamburger's claim that separation of church and state was not an important feature of American religious liberty contestation in the late eighteenth century,[25] Witte shows that Americans frequently deployed various (sometimes inconsistent) conceptions of church-state separation. But contrary to some strict separationists (including some members of the Supreme Court), he argues that separation was never an end in itself: it was always in service of the broader principle of equal religious liberty. On this basis, he praises the Court's use of separationist arguments "to extend the ambit of religious liberty, especially for minority faiths," but he also chides the Court for invoking the concept to "erode the province of religious liberty by effectively empowering a single secular party to veto popular laws touching religion that cause him or her only the most tangential constitutional injury." In those cases, it seems, the principle of separation is in conflict with principles of free exercise, liberty of conscience, and pluralism; a categorical requirement of separation would shut down various forms of governmental accommodation of religion. When principles conflict, courts should remember that each of them "serves religious liberty best when it is used prudentially not categorically."[26]

Witte has not given sustained attention to the problem of government religious speech, but his work touching on the issue suggests he does not think it threatens the essentials of religious liberty. In several pieces, he offers a characteristically subtle and insightful analysis of the caselaw, culling the often-inconsistent Supreme Court decisions for "rules of thumb" to guide courts, lawyers, and officials through the jurisprudential thicket.[27] This suggests that

---

25 Philip Hamburger, *Separation of Church and State* (Cambridge, MA: Harvard University Press, 2004).
26 Witte, "Facts and Fictions," 42.
27 Witte, Nichols, and Garnett, *American Constitutional Experiment*, 289–307; and John Witte, Jr. and Nina-Louisa Arold, "Lift High the Cross?: Contrasting the New European and American Cases on Religious Symbols on Government Property," *Emory International Law Review* 25 (2011): 5–55.

he accepts the Court's jurisprudence, as a form of positive law, to govern the issue. Yet elsewhere he casts doubt on the validity of the decisions that invalidate religious symbols for "endorsing" religion. Mere offense to observers, he thinks, should not be the basis for an Establishment Clause violation. Instead, offended observers should exercise "prudence in seeking protection from public religion" by "clos[ing] [their] eyes to the city crucifix that offends" or "cover[ing] [their] ears to the public prayer that [they] can't abide."[28] Witte seems to agree with the justices who think that noncoercive government religious speech simply raises no questions under the establishment clause.

This view is amply supported by American practice before the middle of the twentieth century. There is little evidence that Americans before then believed that disestablishment forbade the government from sponsoring certain forms of religious speech, whether through government chaplains, the expression of faith by officials, the use of "ceremonial Deism," or the incorporation of religious symbols into government architecture and design.[29]

Yet there are countercurrents in the history of disestablishment sounding in the principles of equality, liberty of conscience, pluralism, and separation that together comprise religious liberty. In the first government-religious-speech case, *Engel v. Vitale*, the Supreme Court invalidated a New York law requiring public-school officials to begin the school day with a scripted prayer. The Court pointed to political disputes in England over the Book of Common Prayer and the view of the American founders that "one of the greatest dangers to the freedom of the individual to worship in his own way lay in the Government's placing its official approval upon one particular kind of prayer or one particular form of religious services."[30] The following year, the Court leaned heavily on the principles of separation and religious equality (styled "neutrality"), distilled from nearly fifteen years of Establishment Clause decisions, to declare that the Establishment Clause forbids laws that have the purpose or effect of advancing religion. On the basis of this rule, the Court invalidated state laws that required devotional Bible reading in public schools.[31] From there, it was not such a stretch to invalidate a state law requiring the passive display of the

---

28 Witte, "Fact and Fiction," 44–45.
29 Chapman and McConnell, *Agreeing to Disagree*, 157–61; and Stephanie Barclay, Brady Earley, and Annika Boone, "Original Meaning and the Establishment Clause: A Corpus Linguistic Analysis," *Arizona Law Review* 61 (2019): 505–60.
30 Engel v. Vitale, 370 U.S. 421, 429 (1962).
31 Abington Sch. Dist. v. Schempp, 374 U.S. 203, 222–23 (1963).

Ten Commandments in public-school classrooms.[32] At about the same time, the Court upheld the practice of employing a chaplain to offer prayers before a legislative session.[33] The extension of the school-prayer decision to passive displays, coupled with a contrary approach in legislative prayer cases, prompted the justices to propose various doctrinal tests for government religious speech. As we shall see, many of those tests are based on concerns that are familiar from the history and tradition of religious liberty in the United States, embodied in principles of separation, pluralism, equality, and liberty of conscience.

Witte's approach provides guidelines for a more thorough evaluation of the religious-speech tests proposed by justices over the past four decades. First, history and tradition matter. The long history of government religious speech with few to no complaints counsels strongly in favor of understanding the Establishment Clause to place no limits on noncoercive speech. Second, positive law counts, too. The Court has invalidated a variety of noncoercive forms of government religious speech, and those decisions are still good law. Third, there are multiple important and interlocking principles that together inform the religious liberty protected by the religion clauses. Each of them reflects an important value the Constitution sought to implement. Fourth, each of those principles can be exaggerated and should be understood not as categorical requirements but rather valid to the extent that they support religious liberty. A Wittean, integrative approach to the religion clauses would consider whether the subsidiary principles, in light of the history and practice of religious liberty in the American tradition, support a conception of religious liberty that might prohibit some forms of noncoercive government religious speech.

4 Religious Speech Tests Proposed by the Supreme Court

The Supreme Court has sometimes evaluated government religious speech by an Establishment Clause doctrine or method that applies generally to all government conduct, and sometimes by a rule that focuses on the content of the government communication. Before turning to the speech-specific tests, it is worth considering how the Court's holistic approaches to the Establishment Clause have contributed to the confusion surrounding the issue.

---

32 Stone v. Graham, 449 U.S. 39 (1980).
33 Marsh v. Chambers, 463 U.S. 783 (1983).

4.1 *Non-Speech-Specific Approaches to the Establishment Clause*

The secular-purpose requirement. Until recently, the Court has held that a law, including one that authorizes or requires religious speech or symbols, must have a sufficiently secular purpose.[34] The requirement does not directly answer the question about the content of government speech; it focuses instead on the government's objectives, whatever the content of the law or government-sponsored communication. The secular-purpose requirement does not have a strong basis in the original understanding of the religion clauses or the traditional understanding of disestablishment. At the founding, an establishment consisted principally of the unequal distribution of rights, privileges, and immunities on the basis of religious belief and practice to promote religious conformity. It also often entailed government control over religious doctrine, clergy, and institutions.[35] I know of no instance in which a law or policy was considered to be part of an establishment merely because the government's purpose was to promote religion or one religion over another without including an unequal distribution of legal rights and privileges.

In light of the history of disestablishment, the secular-purpose requirement was perhaps best understood as a prophylactic heuristic to avoid the end of a religious establishment (induced religious conformity) by avoiding its beginnings (a purpose to promote such conformity). The only Supreme Court decisions invalidating government religious communications for lack of a secular purpose involved public-school classrooms or events with a high risk of religious conformity.[36] The Court has recently repudiated the secular-purpose requirement without overruling any of the cases applying it, which suggests that those cases may now be best understood to rest upon a concern about coercion, not illicit government purposes.[37] If so, in addition to having little support in the history and tradition of religious liberty, the secular-purpose requirement now has little support in positive law.

The history and tradition of government practice. The Supreme Court has recently abandoned the purpose-and-effects test in favor of history and tradition: the Court determines whether government action violates the Establishment Clause by comparing it to past government conduct that was understood

---

34   Lemon v. Kurtzman, 403 U.S. 602, 613 (1971).
35   Michael W. McConnell, "Establishment and Disestablishment at the Founding, Part I: Establishment of Religion," *William & Mary Law Review* 44 (2003): 2105–208.
36   Santa Fe Indep. Sch. Dist. v. Doe, 530 U.S. 290 (2000) (prayer before football game); Wallace v. Jaffree, 472 U.S. 38 (1985) (period of silence for meditation); and Stone v. Graham, 449 U.S. 39 (1980) (Ten Commandments displays in classrooms).
37   Kennedy v. Bremerton, 142 S. Ct. 2407, 2427 (2022).

to violate the clause.[38] The approach smacks more of traditionalism than originalism,[39] and on first blush shares Witte's commitment to integrating positivism, natural law, and historical jurisprudence. A simplistic application of this approach might conclude that mere religious speech would never violate the Establishment Clause: there are few examples of officials (to say nothing of courts) concluding that mere religious speech violates the Establishment Clause (or comparable state norms of disestablishment) in the early Republic, the nineteenth century, or the early twentieth century. The exceptions, like President Jefferson's and President Madison's reticence about declaring a national day of thanksgiving, prove the rule. History and tradition largely permit mere government religious speech.

Yet an integrative jurisprudence does not simply rubber-stamp the past. It also considers the positive law and the moral principles underlying that law. The Court's decisions invalidating government religious speech are part of the positive law of the land. And perhaps for good reason—the Court has consistently pointed to historically grounded principles of equality, pluralism, and liberty of conscience in religious-speech cases. An integrative approach should take those concerns seriously and seek to synthesize them with the weight and trajectory of history, and with the norms of constitutional law and judicial review more broadly.

4.2 Rules against Specific Kinds of Government Speech

No endorsement of religion. Members of the Supreme Court have proposed various rules against specific kinds of government speech. The rule that has gained the most support, serving as the basis of several decisions, is the rule against government endorsement of religion. The question is whether "the challenged governmental action is sufficiently likely to be perceived by adherents of the controlling denominations as an endorsement, and by the non-adherents as a disapproval, of their individual religious choices."[40]

The government rarely endorses religion in so many words, so applying the test ordinarily requires interpretation of government speech, conduct, and symbols. This entails a close analysis of the physical setting of the speech and its historical and immediate political context to determine whether a reasonable

---

38 Kennedy, 142 S. Ct. at 2427; and Town of Greece v. Galloway, 572 U.S. 565, 576 (2014).
39 Marc DeGirolami, "The Traditions of American Constitutional Law," *Notre Dame Law Review* 95 (2020): 1123–81.
40 Allegheny County v. Greater Pittsburgh ACLU, 492 U.S. 573, 597 (1989).

observer would interpret the speech as endorsement or disapproval of their religious beliefs.[41]

The rationale for the endorsement test sounds in several of the core principles of religious liberty. "Endorsement," the Court writes, "sends a message to nonadherents that they are outsiders, not full members of the political community, and an accompanying message to adherents that they are insiders, favored members of the political community."[42] The rule seeks to implement principles of equality, pluralism, separation, and liberty of conscience. It prevents the government from announcing a preference for one religious belief or group over others (including those who reject religion). The doctrine seeks to ensure that the government treats religions equally (none of them get preference), acknowledges the reality—and perhaps the good—of religious pluralism, ensures strict separation of church and state, and protects the conscience of members of the religious majority and dissenters who would prefer their government to remain silent on religious matters. All of these principles are vital for a robust regime of religious liberty.

But the endorsement test is unfortunately at odds with other principles of religious liberty, with the historical and traditional understanding of religious liberty in the United States, and with the ordinary principles of constitutional law. Some government religious expressions facilitate the exercise of religion, sometimes in a way that is respectful of pluralism, such as an ecumenical ceremonial prayer. Some, such as holiday religious displays, allow members of the public to see their religious beliefs respected and acknowledged in the public sphere. Indeed, it is impossible for the government to treat religions entirely equally. Many examples of government religious speech are longstanding, and eliminating them now from the public sphere would strike some as unduly hostile toward religion. Even with respect to new forms of religious speech, the government cannot be entirely neutral. Some religious groups believe the government has an affirmative duty to honor God; if the government were mute about the divine, members of those groups would rightly conclude that they were outsiders.

The endorsement test is also at odds with the history and tradition of religious liberty in the United States. As discussed above, there is little evidence that Americans believed that government endorsement of religion, without

---

41 Ibid., 620 (Blackmun, for a plurality).
42 Lynch v. Donnelly, at 688 (O'Connor, J., concurring in the judgment); see also ibid., 701 (Brennan, J., dissenting) ("The effect on minority religious groups, as well as on those who may reject all religion, is to convey the message that their views are not similarly worthy of public recognition nor entitled to public support.").

legal enforcement, was inconsistent with disestablishment. The only well-known examples are when Presidents Jefferson and Madison departed from the practice of presidents before and since by declining to declare a day of thanksgiving and prayer. By contrast, state and federal governments from the founding to the present have routinely engaged in religious expression that could be understood to endorse religion.

The endorsement test is also a constitutional anomaly. The history and tradition of religious liberty in the United States has focused on ensuring that the government does not distribute different legal rights, privileges, and immunities on the basis of religious belief (or nonbelief) or practice. The endorsement test, however, protects hypothetical observers from the psychological or emotional experience of feeling like "an outsider," of not being able to "take pleasure in seeing the symbol of their belief given official sanction and special status."[43] That is, it protects them from feeling like their religious status somehow affects their political status in the community—even when it has absolutely no effect on their legal rights, privileges, and immunities. Such protection is not only unusual for religious liberty, it is a constitutional idiosyncrasy. No other constitutional restriction on governmental power has been implemented by a doctrine that prohibits the government from making observers feel like it has exceeded that power. Such a doctrine gives individual claimants extraordinary power over democratically enacted laws and policy that have no tangible effect on their beliefs or conduct. Moreover, whatever some observers may feel or believe about their political status as a result of government religious speech, judicial intervention only makes matters worse by either validating that belief (yes, you are right to feel like an outsider) or rejecting it (no, you aren't); it exacerbates political alienation without eliminating genuine threats to the freedom to believe and exercise religion according to one's own conscience.

As discussed above, the Court has never truly repudiated the endorsement test. In *American Legion*, the Court articulated what it suggested was a new rule for symbols cases: symbols that have been in the landscape for a sufficient amount of time, without generating political controversy, are presumptively valid. But to articulate this rule, the Court applied a vague form of ... the endorsement test. It considered the history and tradition of war memorial crosses generally, and the specific history of the Bladensburg cross, to determine that time and secular use had drained the cross of its religious meaning. The *American Legion* rule creates a useful default rule for longstanding religious displays, but that rule is nothing more than a generalized conclusion

---

43   Ibid., 701n7 (Brennan, J., dissenting).

based on an inquiry into the public meaning of longstanding religious symbols. Indeed, it is little different than the way that Justice O'Connor, the progenitor of the endorsement test, evaluated what she considered to be examples of ceremonial Deism. "In God We Trust" on the currency and "God save this honorable Court" in the courtroom were not properly understood as endorsements of religion, she concluded, because they had become secularized through use and ubiquity.[44]

The endorsement test protects feelings, not religious belief and exercise. But maybe there is a better justification for the test. Perhaps it operates as a prophylactic against official discrimination or reasonable fears of discrimination on the basis of religion. Under this theory, the endorsement test overenforces the Establishment Clause, but for a good reason: official discrimination is often difficult, if not impossible, to detect, but concerns about future discrimination may affect religious liberty by creating an incentive for dissenters to change their religious beliefs or conduct to avoid discrimination.

Assuming the best case for the endorsement test is that it serves as a prophylactic against religious-exercise-altering official discrimination, the test is still not the best way to police that concern. There are plenty of ways the government may endorse religion without threatening discrimination. Prohibiting such endorsement therefore overenforces the Establishment Clause in the teeth of the history and tradition of religious liberty and general constitutional jurisprudence.

No endorsement of sectarian religion. Justice Scalia championed a permutation of the endorsement test "where the endorsement is sectarian, in the sense of specifying details upon which men and women who believe in a benevolent, omnipotent Creator and Ruler of the world are known to differ (for example, the divinity of Christ)."[45] This test would allow endorsement of religion in general, and even of monotheism, but not the endorsement of a doctrine unique to a religious denomination.[46] This rule seeks to blend the American tradition of government religious speech with concerns about equality and pluralism. Permitting the government to invoke generic religious norms, Scalia thought, promotes social unity by drawing on beliefs and practices shared by most Americans.

---

44 Elk Grove Unified School District et al. v. Newdow et al., 542 U.S. 1, 37 (2004) (O'Connor, J., concurring).
45 Lee v. Weisman, 505 U.S. 577, 641 (1992) (Scalia, J., dissenting).
46 McCreary County, 545 U.S. 844, 909 n.12 (2005) (Scalia, J., dissenting) ("The Establishment Clause prohibits the favoring of one religion over another.").

From the standpoint of those who favor the endorsement test, however, the problem with this approach is that endorsements of generic religion will still make those who object to monotheistic religion feel like outsiders. Even worse, it will also ostracize believers who find invocations of a generic God to be offensive. The test even fails as an attempt to blend American history and contemporary religious pluralism. There are plenty of instances of sectarian government speech throughout history, and today there are a panoply of nonmonotheistic views of religion. The rule also requires courts to make theological judgments about what sort of speech is sufficiently generic, a delicate task for which they are ill-equipped. And although it rules out less government speech than the endorsement test does, the no-sectarian-speech test still prohibits speech that likely has no effect on religious beliefs and practices.

No taking a position on religious questions. The Supreme Court has also said the Establishment Clause prohibits the government from "appearing to take a position on questions of religious belief."[47] The Court subsequently subsumed this concern into the endorsement test, basing it on the same rationales. Professor Andrew Koppelman, however, has offered a more robust defense of a similar rule in the name of neutrality: "The Establishment Clause forbids the state from declaring religious truth,"[48] from declaring "any particular religious doctrine to be the true one," and from enacting "laws that clearly imply such a declaration of religious truth."[49] The state may treat religion, and the private exercise of religion and search for religious truth, to be human goods, but it may not take sides. Koppelman offers a variety of justifications for this rule, many of which sound in founding-era principles of religious liberty, including the state's incompetence to discover religious truth, the risk of political controversy, and the risk that state support will corrupt religion.[50] Koppelman argues that this rule is consistent with the American tradition of religious neutrality: as America has grown more religiously pluralistic, the government's religious speech has likewise become more ecumenical. American pluralism now limits the government to communicating that religion in general is, or might be, a good thing.

I share many of Koppelman's concerns about the government taking a position on religious truth, but it is not clear that the rule is either necessary or sufficient to protect religious liberty. America is certainly more religiously

---

47 Allegheny County, 492 U.S. at 594.
48 Andrew Koppelman, *Defending American Religious Neutrality* (Cambridge, MA: Harvard University Press, 2013), 6.
49 Ibid., 3
50 Ibid., 6, 46.

pluralistic than it used to be, and there is little doubt that its official religious speech is more pluralistic, either in the aggregate or because it is deliberately ecumenical. So it is unclear why the appropriate institution for enforcing religious neutrality is the judicial system rather than the ordinary political process. And a rule against "taking a position" on religious truth will underprotect religious liberty in many cases and overreach in others. A mayor may make it clear that he favors one religious group over others without taking a position on religious truth, but that preference would make outsiders fear discrimination more than if he had simply declared the religion to be true. By contrast, when the federal government holds a national prayer breakfast, it plainly signals a belief in God (which is a position on religious truth), but it is unlikely that the event will make anyone worry that their legal rights depend on their prayer habits.

The rule against taking a position on religious truth can also be difficult to apply. Consider President Reagan's declaration of the "year of the Bible." The declaration recognizes the Bible's various secular merits while carefully avoiding a position on religious questions like whether the Bible reveals religious truth and whether it was divinely inspired. Consider, too, the symbols cases. Koppelman admits they are hard because they "lie precisely on the line between permitted ceremonial Deism and forbidden state endorsement of religion."[51] The reason they are hard, though, is because symbols, standing alone, do not declare religious *truth*. They trade on religious ideas, but vaguely so. It is unclear whether they are simply acknowledging religion's role in society, attempting to transform a religious message, or making a point that is adjacent to a religious practice. Does a war-memorial cross represent the Christian belief that Christ's death was a self-sacrifice with spiritual dimensions, or does it trade on the Christian tradition to make a broader point about the value of service members' self-sacrifice? The latter takes a position on moral truth— the self-giving of service members is a valuable contribution to our society— but not about religious truth. Koppelman thinks prayers offered by legislative chaplains are plainly unconstitutional because they require officials to choose the chaplains, thus "decid[ing] disputed points of theology."[52] But legislatures and other government bodies can and do choose chaplains without opining on theology by adopting a religiously neutral procedure for people to offer invocations.[53] And even if the government selected a chaplain from one faith tradition, it is unclear why that would amount to a declaration of religious truth

---

51 Ibid., 75.
52 Ibid., 76.
53 Town of Greece, 572 U.S., 1816.

rather than an attempt to accommodate the members of the legislative body (or the military, or the prison, etc.) who would like to pray along with that chaplain. The principle is attractive, but it is difficult to administer and is subtly distinct from the core concern of the Establishment Clause to avoid the use of governmental rights and privileges to induce religious conformity.

No proselytization. Justice Kennedy generally maintained that religious speech is problematic only when it is accompanied by coercion, but he also suggested that "[s]peech may coerce in some circumstances." For example, he said that the Establishment Clause "forbids a city to permit the permanent erection of a large Latin cross on the roof of city hall" because "such an obtrusive year-round religious display would place the government's weight behind an obvious effort to proselytize on behalf of a particular religion."[54] The idea seems to be that proselytization, or perhaps "an obvious effort to proselytize," amounts to the sort of coercion the Establishment Clause prohibits. Kennedy never teased out this line of thought, but he seemed to be suggesting that even permanent symbols may affect religious liberty by directly affecting an observer's religious beliefs and exercise.

But what would make proselytization problematic? As John Locke noted long ago, proselytization, without the application of force, is just an appeal to reason. The magistrate, he argued, has the same access to persuasion by argumentation as anyone else.[55] Some might respond that the government has greater resources, more money, more ability to hold the observer's attention than other people do. Yet large corporations, including religious organizations, have great resources too. What makes governmental proselytization, or at least the reasonable belief that the government is proselytizing, different?

The difference is that the government has a monopoly on the lawful exercise of force. The government alone can withhold public rights and privileges based on one's response to its message. The government's effort to proselytize, depending on the circumstances, may reasonably be understood as a threat to rights and privileges on the basis of religious beliefs and exercise. A tacit threat, unlike mere endorsement or a declaration of religious truth, could reasonably induce an observer to change his or her religious beliefs or practices to avoid discrimination.

---

54 Allegheny County, 492 U.S., 661 (Kennedy, J., concurring in part and dissenting in part).
55 John Locke, *A Letter Concerning Toleration and Other Writings*, ed. Mark Goldie (Indianapolis: Liberty Fund, 2010), 13, Online Library of Liberty, https://oll.libertyfund.org/title/goldie-a-letter-concerning-toleration-and-other-writings.

5 Toward an Integrated Approach: No Threats of Religious Discrimination

The justices' attempts to articulate an Establishment Clause limit on government religious speech have sought to implement many of the principles of religious liberty—separation, equality, liberty of conscience, religious pluralism—but they have ignored the overarching concern of the religion clauses: *equal liberty*. The historical and traditional acceptance of the vast majority of government religious speech does not mean that none of it violates the Establishment Clause, but it ought to be a clue that Americans generally have not considered it to be inconsistent with the clause's purpose. The clause was meant to end specific sorts of laws and practices because they had the purpose and effect of inducing religious conformity. The question, then, for those who seek to integrate the positive law, the natural law norms of religious liberty, and the tradition of religious liberty in the United States is, what kind of religious speech might directly affect private religious belief and practice.

A tentative answer is lurking within the rules already on offer: mere government speech (whether in word or symbol) violates the Establishment Clause when it threatens discrimination with respect to legal rights and privileges on the basis of religion. The reason is that such a threat could reasonably induce someone to change their religious membership, belief, or exercise to avoid official discrimination. Whether the threat is understood to be coercive itself, or to rely on future coercion, what matters is that it is likely to induce religious conformity, and that is the evil, the mischief, that the Establishment Clause was meant to prohibit.

Much more needs to be done to flesh out the rule. For instance, must the government intend to threaten discrimination? Or is it sufficient for a reasonable observer to infer such a threat? What sorts of evidence ought to be necessary to prove that a communication amounts to a threat of discrimination? Must there be evidence of past discrimination, or some action in addition to the message?

For now, it is sufficient to identify several merits of the threat-of-discrimination test. First, it brings the religious-speech doctrine into line with the Court's approach to the Establishment Clause. The Court has struggled to articulate a religious-speech doctrine. Even the justices who favor the coercion test have admitted that some forms of mere speech might be sufficient to violate the Establishment Clause, but they have struggled to explain what it is about such speech that is problematic, or how to identify it. The problem addressed by the threat test is the same as the problem addressed by the coercion test; it simply acknowledges that threats, though themselves not formally coercive, have the same effect of inducing private parties to change their religious exercise. As Witte and others have shown, that has always been the core concern of federal and state disestablishment and free-exercise provisions.

Second, the threat test coheres with, and supplements, the Court's approach to discrimination in free-exercise cases. The Court has long made it clear that official discrimination in favor of one religion violates the Establishment Clause, while official discrimination against one religion violates the Free Exercise Clause. Although the Court has spoken of these rules as reinforcing equality or neutrality, it has often missed the underlying rationale for religious equality or neutrality: discriminatory treatment affects religious choice. Restricting rights and privileges to one religious group, or to those who hold a particular religious belief, creates an incentive for outsiders to change their religious beliefs and practice. It is the enemy of religious freedom and its natural byproduct, religious pluralism.

Third, restricting the Establishment Clause limits on religious speech to speech that conveys a threat of religious discrimination bring the religious-symbols doctrine into line with the ordinary rules of standing. There is currently a gap between the religious-symbols doctrine and the ordinary standing doctrine: a claimant may challenge a government religious symbol for endorsing religion when the symbol causes the claimant no individualized or concrete injury. A claimant who is threatened with religious discrimination, however, would have such an injury. A symbol alone may rarely be enough to establish a threat, but if it were, a member of the threatened group would have standing to sue.

A threat-of-discrimination test would not eliminate all of the difficult features of the endorsement test. Cases would still require fact-intensive inquiries into the meaning of government communications, and reasonable jurists would still disagree about its application in hard cases. But any test of government speech would require such an inquiry, including whatever test the Court applied in *American Legion*. A threat test, however, would greatly reduce the scope of the inquiry. Rather than looking for whether a government is endorsing some relatively vague religious concept, idea, or group, judges would focus on a much sharper inquiry that plays to their strengths: has the government, or an official, threatened to engage in a specific form of *conduct*.

6 Conclusion

Although the threat-of-discrimination test itself does not have deep roots in the American tradition of religious liberty, it operates as a prophylactic rule to enforce the most central norm of disestablishment: the government may not prefer one religion or religious group in the distribution of rights and privileges. This is the norm embodied in the first religious liberty provision of the U.S. Constitution—the No Religious Test Clause—and given wider, more universal ambit in the Establishment Clause. A threat-of-discrimination test is one sensible way to integrate the religious principles that John Witte has identified as the foundation of the tradition of American religious liberty with the caselaw and the ongoing American experience with religious pluralism.

CHAPTER 24

Freedom of the Church: Religious Autonomy in a Secular Age

Julian Rivers

1   Introduction

The global COVID-19 pandemic resulted in unprecedented legal restrictions on acts of collective religious worship across the whole world. These restrictions generated considerable conflict, even violence, in many countries. In a report released late in 2022, the Pew Research Center found that in 23 percent of the 198 countries surveyed, authorities had used physical means (that is, arrests and prison sentences) to enforce restrictions on religious groups.[1] In many ways, existing government restrictions and social hostilities were simply exacerbated by the pandemic. Minorities who are already subject to discrimination were subjected to additional discriminatory policing. Old prejudices found newer manifestations, as, for example, in the extent to which Jewish people were blamed for spreading the virus in many countries. But the report also contains evidence of new levels of tension. In over a third of the world's countries, one or more religious groups defied pandemic-related public health rules, and in a quarter, religious groups started litigation or spoke out publicly against the measures. A common cause of complaint was the sense of injustice in being made subject to restrictions from which some secular social activities—deemed "essential" by governments—were exempt.

The COVID-19 pandemic provides an important case-study in the legal protection of religious group autonomy under pressure. It enables us to see how arguments from autonomy fare in the context of litigation, and to consider how best to give those arguments legal expression under modern conditions. In some respects, the case law generated by the pandemic is far from ideal. The pandemic itself developed rapidly, resulting in an unprecedented volume and pace of regulatory change as governments sought to impose and then lift restrictions. The factual matrices giving rise to litigation had often changed even in the context of expedited processes, rendering the points of law in

---

[1] Pew Research Center, "How COVID-19 Restrictions Affected Religious Groups Around the World in 2020," Nov. 29, 2022.

dispute moot or merely "academic." On the occasions where judgment was reached, it was often brief and simply intended to explain in outline any temporary measures ordered by the judge. Some have even questioned whether legal doctrine had any influence at all on intuitive responses conforming to a common pattern of judicial deference to governments.[2]

Nevertheless, looking at the case law through the lens of religious group autonomy immediately reveals a rather surprising point. In recent decades, such arguments have found their most common application in the context of the employment of ministers of religion.[3] At the very least, religious groups cannot be held to the same standards of religious nondiscrimination as secular employers. Having a particular religion or belief is a central qualification. Other protected characteristics of antidiscrimination law are not far behind—think of male-only and celibate vocations to the priesthood. Beyond the specific context of nondiscrimination, a good case can be made that the entire modern employment law framework inappropriately distorts the nature of the relationship between a minister and his or her religious group, colorfully indicated by the claim that a minister works for God, not the church. Such arguments can be found in a number of jurisdictions, but they have arguably made the most headway in the United States, where the Supreme Court has established extensive immunities for religious groups from secular scrutiny of employment decisions.[4]

However, arguments based on religious group autonomy barely figured in the COVID-19 judgments of the Supreme Court. On the other hand, in the United Kingdom, where the "ministerial exception" is rather more limited, arguments from group autonomy were at the forefront of claims made by religious litigants. In the main Scottish case, the argument made considerable headway. However, the difficulties the judge had in applying it are instructive for the nature and content of that principle more generally, and indeed help explain its absence in the U.S. context. We shall see that religious group autonomy in its strong, "jurisdictional" form is hard to sustain as a principle of modern

---

2 Mark L. Movsesian, "Law, Religion and the COVID-19 Crisis," *Journal of Law and Religion* 37 (2022): 9–24.

3 See, above all, the seminal work of Douglas Laycock, "Towards a General Theory of the Religion Clauses: The Case of Church Labor Relations and the Right to Church Autonomy," *Columbia Law Review* 81 (1981): 1373–417; and id., "Church Autonomy Revisited," *Georgetown Journal of Law and Public Policy* 7 (2009): 253–78.

4 *Hosanna-Tabor Evangelical Lutheran Church and School v. EEOC*, 565 US 171 (2012); *Our Lady of Guadalupe School v. Morrissey-Berru*, 140 S. Ct. 2049 (2020). For a comparative introduction, see Pamela Slotte and Helge Årsheim, "The Ministerial Exception—Comparative Perspectives," *Oxford Journal of Law and Religion* 4, no. 2 (2015): 171–98.

liberal democratic constitutionalism. Legal doctrines which attempt to protect religious group autonomy sooner or later reach their limits. One should not conclude from this that arguments based on religious group autonomy need to be abandoned. On the contrary, they are essential to the legal and social anchoring of civil liberty. But religious group autonomy needs to be recast as a principle of organizational self-government under law. Everything turns on the question of the law to which religious groups are rightly subject.[5]

Such a move is easier to make in the European context, where fundamental constitutional rights are typically understood to trigger proportionality analyses. These seek to balance the interests of claimants and the public interest.[6] Yet even here there is a need for further doctrinal development. When courts undertook proportionality analyses in relation to COVID-19 restrictions, they did so primarily by reference to the substantive interests at stake, such as the religious imperative to gather in person for collective prayer, worship, and the administration of sacraments on one hand, and the risk of the transmission of disease on the other. Religious group autonomy conceived as a principle of self-government adds another layer of complexity. The proper question is not simply whether restrictions on collective acts of worship are justifiable given the balance of interests at stake, but whether the degree to which religious authorities are subject to state regulation in balancing the interests at stake for themselves is justifiable. Proportionality analysis, or balancing, needs to be applied in a way which is sensitive to the relative expertise and legitimacy of the parties before the court.

This idea is familiar enough when courts are reviewing the decisions of legislatures and executive agencies. Indeed, such arguments figured significantly in cases where courts found pandemic restrictions warranted. Understood as a principle of self-government, religious group autonomy demonstrates that such arguments cut both ways. Theological expertise and ecclesiastical legitimacy are also relevant to proportionality analysis, and these point to a narrowing of the scope of governmental powers.

---

5   An exploration of the range of possible judicial oversight in relation to religious ministers, appropriately framed in this way, is Paul Billingham, "The Scope of Religious Group Autonomy: Varieties of Judicial Examination of Church Employment Decisions," *Legal Theory* 25, no. 4 (2019): 244–71.
6   In the context of the ministerial exception, see Emma Svensson, "Religious Ethos, Bond of Loyalty, and Proportionality—Translating the 'Ministerial Exception' into 'European,'" *Oxford Journal of Law and Religion* 4, no. 2 (2015): 224–43.

2   Religious Groups and COVID-19 Restrictions before the U.S. Supreme Court

COVID-19 cases before the U.S. Supreme Court appeared on the "shadow docket" of listings for injunctive relief, and in some cases no majority reasoning was offered. Nevertheless, they quickly became mired in the politics of judicial appointments. In the early cases, before the death of Ruth Bader Ginsburg in 2020, the Court consistently ruled 5–4 in favor of governmental restrictions, Chief Justice John Roberts siding with the Democrat-appointed four on grounds of deference to government discretion in responding rapidly to an unprecedented public health crisis.[7] Nevertheless, powerful dissents, such as that of Justice Brett Kavanaugh in the *Calvary Chapel* case, were an indication of future change. In that case, the state of Nevada had provoked the understandable frustration of religious groups by subjecting businesses such as casinos to a 50 percent occupancy limit, but religious meetings to a fifty-person cap. Once Justice Amy Coney Barrett had taken up her appointment, the balance of power shifted, and religious groups started to record wins.[8]

Quite apart from the controversy triggered by a topic which has so quickly become enmeshed in wider culture wars, legal scholars have debated vigorously whether the approach of the new Republican majority represents a departure from, or development in, the Supreme Court's previous case law. As is well known, that case law is dominated by the problematic interaction between the Free Exercise and Establishment Clauses of the First Amendment, which itself reflects the complex relationship between liberty and equality. Case law from the 1960s onward had suggested that regulations burdening the free exercise of religion—even facially neutral provisions—should be subjected to "strict scrutiny," a very demanding test.[9] In order to trigger strict scrutiny, there needed to be some discriminatory treatment of religion, such as an exception, targeting, or animus.[10] But in *Employment Division v Smith*, the Court controversially held that neutral and generally applicable provisions were presumptively constitutional, subject only to "rational basis review," a very easy test to satisfy.[11] In

---

[7]   *South Bay United Pentecostal Church v. Gavin Newsom*, 590 U.S. _ (2020); *Calvary Chapel Dayton Valley v. Steve Sisolak*, 591 U.S. _ (2020); *Danville Christian Academy v Beshear*, 592 U.S. _ (2020).

[8]   *Roman Catholic Diocese of Brooklyn v. Andrew M. Cuomo*, 592 U.S. _ (2020); *South Bay United Pentecostal Church v. Gavin Newsom*, 590 U.S. _ (2021); *Tandon v Newsom*, 593 U.S. _ (2021).

[9]   *Sherbert v Verner*, 374 U.S. 398 (1963).

[10] *Church of the Lukumi Babalu Aye v City of Hialeah* 508 U.S. _ 520 (1993).

[11] *Employment Division v Smith*, 494 U.S. 872 (1990).

theory, this generated a two-stage analysis, first determining the appropriate standard of review, then applying that standard to the restriction on free exercise to determine whether it is justified. However, in practice, debates around free exercise of religion since *Smith* have been preoccupied with the first stage, settling (or unsettling) the boundary between "strict scrutiny" cases, which religious persons or groups almost always win, and "rational basis" cases, in which they almost always lose.

The COVID-19 cases concerned complex regulatory regimes in which collective religious worship has been one of a range of social activities subjected to restriction. The doctrinal question is whether the shift from rational basis to strict scrutiny tests in the Court's COVID-19 decisions represents an application of *Smith*, a departure, or a limit. One could take the view that both the liberal and the conservative approaches are simply applications of *Smith* in which the justices disagree on the facts. The question is basically one of nondiscrimination. If religious groups have been subjected to standards which are common to a range of nonreligious social activities, and there is some rational basis for the set of restrictions applied to that set of activities, then the regime as a whole passes constitutional muster. But there is plenty of scope for disagreement as to whether religious groups *have* been subjected to the same standards. It all depends on the choice of the comparators. Conservatives could typically point out that religious worship was subjected to stricter standards than, say, retail businesses, and liberals could typically point to similar restrictions on concerts and cinemas. Egregious cases of antireligious discrimination—as, for example, in the decision by the mayor of Washington, DC, to proscribe outdoor religious gatherings while promoting political rallies—were relatively rare.[12]

However, the COVID-19 cases did not simply reduce to arguments about the most appropriate secular comparators. In his dissent in *Calvary Chapel*, Justice Kavanaugh sought to restructure the problem by requiring state authorities to justify the absence of religious groups from any regime of exemptions. He preserved the two-stage structure of Smith but held that the exclusion of religious groups from the most privileged secular category would then trigger the need for "substantial justification" based on a "compelling reason." The comparator still returned at the second stage, since the presence of a less-regulated secular analogue would cast doubt on the legitimacy of the purported justification, but it played a much less significant role. This approach creates a strong presumption against the exclusion of religious groups from the "most favored"

---

12   *Capitol Hill Baptist Church v Muriel Bowser* 496 F. Supp. 3d 284 (D.D.C. 2020).

category of organizations.[13] In *Tandon v Newsom*, a majority of the Court expressly adopted this approach, but in a subtly modified form.[14] The basic idea was still that once a state is willing to make some exceptions to a prohibition, religious persons and groups may not be treated any worse than the most favored category of exceptions, unless there is a compelling state interest for doing so. But the question of the comparator was once again foregrounded by focusing on the existence of more favored secular analogues which undermine state interests to a sufficiently similar degree.

"Most favored nation" approaches to religious liberty work well enough in cases of individual conscience. If a state is willing to allow a man an exception to a no-beards rule for medical reasons, it cannot treat religious reasons for wearing a beard as having any lesser status. It is the mere existence of the beard which undermines the state interest in hygiene, regardless of the reason for wearing one. But it is not obvious how such theories operate in the context of a spectrum of different activities and restrictions. The fact that one is allowed to leave one's house to buy food is relevant to the prohibition on leaving to attend an act of religious worship only if in some sense the activities are comparable in the threat they pose to public health. It would be no argument that restrictions on public worship are not unconstitutional because people can still pray and sing at home with the members of their family. That fact is simply irrelevant. Perhaps the more plausible view is that *Smith* was only ever intended to address cases of individual conscience in relation to identical acts and omissions, and not core activities of religious groups. On this account, the COVID-19 cases demonstrate the limits of *Smith* rather than either an application or a departure.

From a European perspective, the U.S. Supreme Court COVID-19 case law in relation to collective worship suffers from two connected weaknesses. First, there is a familiar structural point. In theory, both strict scrutiny and rational basis review allow for balancing, which is to say a consideration of competing reasons for and against restrictions on liberty. However, they each approach that exercise with the scales heavily weighted. This in turn throws all the emphasis back on the earlier, comparator stage, in which the search is for a presumptive rule to determine the case. This bifurcation between religious liberty

---

13 The analogy of "most favored nation status" was drawn from Douglas Laycock, "The Remnants of Free Exercise," *Supreme Court Review* 1 (1990): 49–50.

14 Luray Buckner, "How Favored Exactly? An Analysis of the Most Favoured Nation Theory of Religious Exemptions from Calvary Chapel to Tandon," *Notre Dame Law Review* 97, no. 4 (2022): 1643–67. An alternative route to a similar outcome is offered by Mark Storslee, "The COVID-19 Church-Closure Cases and the Free Exercise of Religion," *Journal of Law and Religion* 37 (2022): 72–95.

restrictions which are very easy and almost impossible to justify has its defenders in terms of ease of application and reliability of outcome—although the experience with the COVID-19 cases rather belies those claims. Proportionality analysis sits more evenly between the two. Politically, it represents a more consensual approach to the reconciliation of competing value judgments. Where presumptions and burdens operate, they do so far more subtly. Although the stages of evaluation within proportionality analysis are clearly separated, they are amenable to application in a more flexible, less rule-like, manner. This point is of central importance as we seek to integrate perspectives from religious group autonomy.

More specifically, the influence of *Smith* unhelpfully prioritizes comparability with secular activities. COVID-19 regulations severely restricted acts of collective religious worship which were in many cases central to the religious life and obligations of worshippers. The question is whether such restrictions are inherently justified or not, given what was at stake in terms of public health. An excessive restriction is not cured because other, nonreligious activities are treated equally badly. There is undoubtedly a place for comparators in the process of justification, but the question is better framed as one of civil liberty rather than nondiscrimination. This not only requires careful tailoring to minimize intrusion into the collective life of the religious group, but it also requires account to be taken of internal measures to reduce risk. Indeed, construed as a positive obligation as well as a negative limit on intervention, it requires governments to encourage and promote responsible internal decision-taking. The nuanced review which this requires can be facilitated by the more flexible approach offered by proportionality.[15]

3   Religious Group Autonomy and COVID-19 in British Courts

Strong accounts of religious group autonomy can be found in both English and Scottish litigation by religious groups challenging COVID-19 restrictions. The English cases never reached court, because on two occasions restrictions were lifted before the cases were heard. In the early stages of the first national lockdown (imposed from March 26, 2020) there was initial acceptance of the need for immediate and drastic measures until the implications of the new disease should be clearer. Indeed, many churches adopted stricter restrictions than

---

15   This point is implicit but clearly present in Kathleen A. Brady, "COVID-19 and Restrictions on Religious Worship: From Nondiscrimination to Church Autonomy," *Fides et Libertas* (2021): 23–41.

those legally imposed, which included exceptions for funerals, broadcasting acts of worship, and the provision of essential voluntary or public services.[16] However, as the government started to develop its planned easing of restrictions, and it became apparent that lifting restrictions on acts of collective religious worship was not a high priority, several church leaders started joint legal action.

Their pre-action letter[17] put the claim to church autonomy in the strongest possible terms:

> Rather, our clients' concern is that, as a matter of principle, the imposition of appropriate anti-epidemic measures in the Church is ultimately a matter for Church authorities rather than secular state authorities.
>
> Whatever difficulties may sometimes arise in drawing a precise boundary between temporal and ecclesiastical matters, there is no doubt, and has never been any doubt, that closure and opening of churches for services and rites is a matter for ecclesiastical authorities and not for temporal ones.

The letter went on to refer to "self-regulation" on the part of the church and to emphasize the extreme importance of the constitutional "principle of Church autonomy."

Taken literally, these claims were vastly overinflated. They suggest that even Parliament has no constitutional competence to impose any restrictions on religious groups acting within their own sphere. This would turn them into fully autonomous legal systems—islands of immunity within the common law—which could be invited to regulate their actions for the common good, but not legally required to do so. However, the argument was never refined or tested, because the government responded by inviting the church leaders to roundtable discussions, and soon afterwards collective worship was permitted with social distancing and other health measures in place.[18]

Under the second national lockdown, in autumn 2020, collective worship was once again prohibited in England and Wales. Although the prohibition proved to be relatively brief, it was long enough for legal proceedings to be revived and presented in a more developed form, although, once again, the

---

16 Health Protection (Coronavirus, Restrictions) (England) Regulations 2020, reg. 5(6).
17 Letter before claim of May 28, 2020, CC-Resource-Misc-Judicial-Review-Opening-Churches-200529.pdf (christianconcern.com).
18 Permission was refused for an expedited hearing on June 26; the prohibition on opening for public worship was lifted on July 4.

case did not reach the point of trial. The argument combined formal with substantive considerations.[19] Formally, it was argued that the relevant section of the Public Health (Control of Disease) Act 1984, under which restrictions were imposed, was very broadly phrased.[20] According to familiar arguments based on the principle of legality, broad statutory empowerments do not authorize governmental interferences with fundamental rights—in this case, the autonomy and independence of religious institutions. Such restrictions would need specific provision in primary legislation. Alternatively, it was argued that the regulations failed to survive a proportionality test, which applied by virtue of the Human Rights Act 1998. The formal arguments therefore combined with straightforward substantive ones arguing that the government had inadequately balanced competing interests in freedom of religion or belief and public health.

This argument is no longer based on religious group autonomy. The claimants clearly accepted, as they had to, that Parliament has the authority to make law regulating religious worship. Moreover, they accepted that state authorities, including administrative and judicial bodies, are competent to assess the balance of interests between churches and the general public. Far from presenting a radical claim based on group autonomy, it adopted familiar formal and substantive arguments for collective religious liberty. It was therefore no different from other judicial review actions, including one brought by the chairman of a Bradford mosque. These, too, failed in part and in other respects ran out of time, albeit with strong hints from the judges concerned that the claimants would ultimately have failed in substance as well.[21]

The Scottish government had not closed places of worship during the second national lockdown; however, early in 2021, at the start of the third lockdown, the roles reversed. While places of religious worship were allowed to remain open for collective worship elsewhere, in Scotland they were closed. This continued until, on March 24, 2021, legal action resulted in a ruling from Lord Braid in the Outer House of the Court of Session that in some respects the

---

19   See https://christianconcern.com/wp-content/uploads/2018/10/CC-Resource-Misc-Judicial-Review-Church-Bundle-Permission-20201123.pdf.

20   The Coronavirus Act 2020 s. 52 and Schedule 22 contained more precise powers to prohibit or restrict events, gatherings, or entry to premises. In the event, it was not used to ban religious gatherings, and it is no longer in force.

21   *R (Hussain) v Secretary of State for Health and Social Care* [2020] EWHC 1392 (Admin); *R (Dolan) v Secretary of State for Health and Social Care* [2020] EWCA Civ 1605; *R (Hussain) v Secretary of State for Health and Social Care* [2022] EWHC 82 (Admin). See also the Privy Council decision in *Maharaj v Attorney General of Trinidad and Tobago* [2022] 3 WLR 309.

restrictions were unlawful.[22] The Scottish government decided not to appeal, and full restrictions were lifted.

Lord Braid's extensive discussion of church autonomy took as its starting point the agreement between both parties on the basic constitutional principle that the church (and religious groups more widely) has exclusive jurisdiction in spiritual matters, while the state has exclusive jurisdiction in civil matters. He accepted that the Church of Scotland Act 1921 is declaratory of a centuries-old constitutional tradition, found most notably in the General Assembly Act 1592 and the 1707 Articles of Union with England, that the church has "the right and power subject to no civil authority to legislate, and to adjudicate finally, in all matters of doctrine, worship, government and discipline in the church."[23] It is significant that the articles in which those words are found are not *authorized* by Act of Parliament but *recognized* as declaratory of the constitutional position, making the mutual independence of church and state deeper than the sovereignty of Parliament. Section 1 of the act even makes a sustained effort to entrench it against future change.

The problem lay in determining on which side of the line a general prohibition on collective worship lay. As Lord Braid rightly concluded, the question is unanswerable. On one hand, it is harder to imagine a greater interference with the right of the church to determine its own forms of worship than to ban it altogether. On the other hand, the protection of the public health of all citizens is surely a civil matter, fully within the competence of government. Lord Braid pointed out that it was a logical consequence of the argument from autonomy that only the church could have the power to order the closure of a church building for any reason, including public health reasons. If a religious group refused to do that, the government would be powerless. That was an unacceptable conclusion for him. In any case, the petitioners conceded that the state could legitimately order a 24/7 curfew on the streets surrounding the church if such a draconian measure were unavoidable. This would of course have the effect of making worship impossible in fact, although not prohibited in law.

The fact that the argument from church autonomy was made and considered in the strongest possible terms proved fatal to its success. In order to achieve autonomy in relation to worship, the claimants were forced to argue that the geographical space within which worship takes place has to be treated as an island of independent jurisdiction, immune from state regulation. The state

---

22 *Revd. Dr. William Philip v Scottish Ministers* [2021] CSOH 32. For a discussion of the constitutional aspects, see Jamie McGowan, "Public Health, Proportionality and the 'Freedom of the Halie Kirk': On Philip v Scottish Ministers," *Public Law* (2022): 454–553.

23 Church of Scotland Act 1921, Schedule 1, para. IV.

might lawfully be allowed to take action on the land surrounding the building, which would have the coercive effect of preventing the church from making use of its powers, so long as it did not claim normative authority over those powers. There are intriguing echoes here of medieval doctrines of sanctuary.

One might think that this rather overstates the problem. After all, the Scottish government was not attempting to tell churches and religious groups how to worship; they simply proscribed the gathering for any sort of worship. What the church has exclusive jurisdiction over is the *mode* of worship. It would, admittedly, be unconstitutional of the Scottish government to display any sort of theological preference for one form of worship or another, but they did not do that.

However, this move does not solve the problem. To start with, the ban on collective worship was, in one perspective, very clearly a preference for one type of worship over another, since the Scottish government took comfort from the fact that people could still engage in acts of worship online. The question of whether worshipping online is an acceptable substitute for the physical presence of the worshipper is a theological one which stimulated debate within many Christian denominations. Moreover, it would be easy to imagine circumstances in which government policy might touch in a more nuanced way on what is and is not permissible as a matter of worship. One only needs to consider acts such as the consumption of wine from a common cup, or, indeed—an example at stake in the Scottish litigation—the legality of a ban on singing.

In the end, two basic points determined Lord Braid's rejection of a jurisdictional approach to church autonomy. On one hand, if the state ordered the closure of every church in the land without good reason, that would be straightforwardly unconstitutional. On the other hand, restrictions on worship could not be unlawful if they pursued a legitimate state purpose. So the case turned on the potential justification of policies by reference to accepted public goods. Having reached that point, the adoption of proportionality analysis was inevitable. The main factor leading to his finding that the restrictions were disproportionate was the willingness of the Scottish government to open indoor jury centers in cinemas. The government had failed to explain why they had preferred the right to a fair trial over the right to freedom of religion or belief.[24] In the end, then, the resort to a comparator to undermine a purported secular justification brought his reasoning close to that of U.S. courts.

---

24 *Philip*, [114]–[116].

The Scottish litigation shows that jurisdictional approaches to religious group autonomy represent a high-risk argumentative strategy. Whenever the public interest and the law in which it is cast demand state intervention in a religious matter, courts are bound to determine the question in favor of the state, and there is no further argument to be had.[25] The scope of the "spiritual" domain risks being defined merely negatively, as the residue of the noncivil. Thankfully, Lord Braid did not leave the matter there, but instead recognized that limitations of fundamental rights (including freedom of worship) may be justified only if they are proportionate, which is to say the least necessary means to achieve some competing public interest, on condition that the burden on the exercise of those rights is justified in the circumstances. However, it is not immediately obvious how arguments from religious group autonomy should figure within proportionality analyses. To see this, we have to make a considerable detour into its origins and nature.

4 The Origins and Nature of Religious Group Autonomy: from "Jurisdiction" to "Self-Government under Law"

Scholars of law and religion, especially those with an interest in historical dimensions of their subject, such as John Witte, Jr., whose work we honor with this volume, have regularly reminded their modern readers of the origins of civil liberty in the plural structure of European society.[26] Christianity was distinctive among religions in positing an institutionalized distinction between church and government. In 494, Pope Gelasius I famously claimed that Christian society was governed by two swords, not one.[27] The church had a rightful

---

25 See *Percy v Board of National Mission of the Church of Scotland* [2005] UKHL 73, [2006] 2 AC 28.
26 See especially his monographs: *God's Joust, God's Justice: Law and Religion in the Western Tradition* (Grand Rapids: Eerdmans, 2005); *The Reformation of Rights: Law, Religion, and Human Rights in Early Modern Calvinism* (Cambridge: Cambridge University Press, 2007); *Church, State, and Family: Reconciling Traditional Teachings and Modern Liberties* (Cambridge: Cambridge University Press, 2019); *Faith, Freedom, and Family: New Essays on Law and Religion,* eds. Norman Doe and Gary S. Hauk (Tübingen: Mohr Siebeck, 2021); *The Blessings of Liberty: Human Rights and Religious Freedom in the Western Legal Tradition* (Cambridge: Cambridge University Press, 2021); and *Religion and the American Constitutional Experiment,* 5th ed. (Oxford: Oxford University Press, 2022).
27 Gelasius I, "Letter to Emperor Anastasius," reproduced in part in Oliver O'Donovan and Joan Lockwood O'Donovan, *From Irenaeus to Grotius: A Sourcebook in Christian Political Thought* (Grand Rapids, MI: Eerdmans, 1999), 179.

place alongside the emperor in ordering society for the common good.²⁸ The doctrine of two kingdoms was given substantial institutional expression after the reforms of the Catholic Church in Latin-speaking Western Europe initiated by Pope Gregory VII in the late eleventh century.²⁹ Combined with the rediscovery and renewed study of Justinian's sixth-century Digest of Roman Law, this had the effect of generating the first recognizably modern rational bureaucracy. The Catholic Church of the late medieval period was an institution directed not only to the pursuit of "spiritual" ends in any narrow sense, but also to the regulation of many areas of social life with significance for faithful Christian living. It had mechanisms for the generation of new law, institutions for adjudication and enforcement, as well as sanctions such as penance and excommunication, which could combine with social ostracism to produce an effective deterrent. Medieval society was characterized by a plurality of institutions and jurisdictions, but the doctrine of two fundamental institutions facilitated the expansion of church and civil government—we can hardly talk of the "state" at this point—to exercise oversight over all others. Manor courts and monastic orders might be more or less independent of kings and bishops but were in no position ultimately to resist such oversight.

The fact that medieval Europeans could think in terms of two distinct social institutions operating according to two distinct branches of the *ius commune*—canon law and civil law—inevitably generated intense scrutiny over questions of competence and jurisdiction. The conflicts between church and state are well known, expressed most vividly in the career and demise of Thomas Becket, first the compliant lord chancellor and then the intransigent archbishop of King Henry II. It could also produce the memorable first article of Magna Carta from the pen of Archbishop Stephen Langton: "the church in England shall be free and have its rights undiminished and its liberties unimpaired." This was not religious liberty in the modern sense; it was a bid for the jurisdictional autonomy of the Catholic Church based on a theory of political authority which descended from God, through the pope and church, to civil rulers.³⁰

---

28 The idea that the church was uniquely tasked with the rational administration of welfare can be found already in the writings of Ambrose of Milan (339–397). For its longer-term impact, see, for example, Larry Siedentop, *Inventing the Individual: The Origins of Western Individualism* (London: Penguin, 2015).

29 Harold J. Berman, *Law and Revolution: The Formation of the Western Legal Tradition* (Cambridge, MA: Harvard University Press, 1983).

30 The classic account of medieval debates between "descending" and "ascending" theories of authority is Walter Ullmann, *Principles of Government and Politics in the Middle Ages*, 2nd ed. (London: Methuen, 1966).

Modern conditions of religious and nonreligious diversity call into question the legitimacy of any appeal to the belief that the church (or one particular church) represents the people of God on earth. In these circumstances one can still envisage a "contractual" defense of religious group autonomy. One person may well consider another person's religious group to be fundamentally misguided, and yet each may be willing to accord the other recognition on equal terms.[31] To this one can add more generic defenses. The modern state has unparalleled resources at its disposal. It is both the most powerful guarantor of human rights and the greatest potential threat to civil liberty. To some extent it can be kept to its proper purpose by good institutional design, foremost of which is the idea of separated powers. The state can be held to account by engaged citizens acting through elections and their representatives. It can establish judicial processes for the vindication of fundamental rights. But it is ultimately a hierarchical coercive unit capable of bulldozing its way over minorities. Along with independent media, social groups have an important role to play in preventing such tyranny. They provide locations for the development of alternative ethics, critical of mainstream practices. And they can ultimately provide the critical mass of organized collective voice needed to face up to the otherwise overwhelming state. Religious groups represent the outstanding example of social groups robust enough to anchor opposition to the state.[32]

To this essentially negative argument can be added a more positive case. The processes of secularization have produced structural differentiation within society which enable individuals to join with different groups in different

---

31   Steven Smith, "The Jurisdictional Conception of Church Autonomy," in *The Rise of Corporate Religious Liberty*, ed. Micah Schwartzman, Chad Flanders, and Zoë Robinson (Oxford: Oxford University Press, 2016).

32   It is appropriate to refer here to the many international projects on the place of corporate religious freedom in the Jewish, Christian, and Muslim traditions, and in modern frameworks of democracy and human rights, led by John Witte, Jr. in his role as director of the Emory Center for the Study of Law and Religion. See, especially, the major collections coedited by Witte: *Christianity and Democracy in Global Context* (Boulder, CO: Westview Press, 1993); *Religious Human Rights in Global Perspective*, 2 vols. (The Hague: Martinus Nijhoff, 1996); *Proselytism and Orthodoxy in Russia: The New War for Souls* (Maryknoll, NY: Orbis Books, 1999); *Sharing the Book: Religious Perspectives on the Rights and Wrongs of Proselytism* (Maryknoll, NY: Orbis Books, 1999); *Christianity and Human Rights: An Introduction* (Cambridge: Cambridge University Press, 2010); *Religion and Human Rights: An Introduction* (Oxford: Oxford University Press, 2012); and *No Establishment of Religion: America's Original Contribution to Religious Liberty* (Oxford: Oxford University Press, 2012).

"spheres of justice."³³ The norms which govern family life are rightly different from those which govern the workplace, a community action group, a church, or a political party. The ability of persons to move between these spheres and enjoy distinctive combinations of multiple memberships without any one context becoming totalizing is the most basic social expression of civil liberty. It frees us up to enjoy each other's company in one context while leaving our disagreements in another dimension of life to one side. Civil society groups also provide schools for self-governance, enabling large numbers of people to "govern," in small ways to small extents, the lives of others. The cause of civil liberty is intertwined with the fate of autonomous civil society groups, among which Christian churches are paradigmatic. This is no mere theory; churches became vital spaces of public debate and resistance under Eastern European communism, catalyzing its eventual collapse.

Although medieval Christian peoples were governed by two main public institutions with their own bodies of law, those two bodies of positive law were themselves only branches of a single fundamental law, the law of nature, which was the representation of God's eternal decrees in terms accessible to all human beings. Christians had the added advantage of accessing the eternal law through the divine law of scripture. While there was tension in the reach and relationship of church and civil government, there was also an underlying harmony of purpose in theory, and a considerable intertwining in practice. The trope of a harmonious hierarchy of laws—law of God, law of nature and human law—remained dominant in English case law up to the mid-seventeenth century, and in a few areas such as family law much later still.

In modern times, which for purposes of political theory can be dated from Jean Bodin's (1530–1596) revolutionary account of state sovereignty and Hugo Grotius's (1583–1645) revolutionary restatement of natural law theory, the ultimate unity of law became inextricable from the legitimacy of the state. The Enlightenment which followed culminated in the formidable philosophical restatement of Immanuel Kant. As he so cogently argued, law is rendered morally necessary by our recognition that when human beings come into proximity, the way we necessarily affect and restrict each other's movements requires moral justification.³⁴ Once I start to assert control over objects in the material world, the conflict between our wills becomes even more intense. To put the

---

33 The term is taken from Michael Walzer, *Spheres of Justice: A Defense of Pluralism and Equality* (Oxford: Blackwell, 1985).

34 Patrick Capps and Julian Rivers, "Kant's Concept of Law," *American Journal of Jurisprudence* 63, no. 2 (2018): 259–94; and id., "Kant's Concept of International Law," *Legal Theory* 16 (2010): 229–57.

point as starkly as possible: from a Kantian perspective it is systemically unjust for churches and other religious groups to determine unilaterally how the interests of nonmembers in protection from COVID-19 infection are to figure in their decisions about collective worship. The only way of resolving this problem is to coordinate our wills under a common system of public laws based on the innate (natural) right of each human person. A system of public right must have separate and coordinate institutions of lawmaking, adjudication, and administration and execution. It must assert sovereignty over all people within a defined territory, and it must itself relate legally to other sovereign states in an inter-state system of coordination and dispute resolution with basic precepts of cosmopolitan law. In short, there is a moral imperative based ultimately on our recognition of the dignity of all human beings to conceive of law as a unity, created and sustained by the organs of the modern state. The German term *Rechtsstaat* captures this idea more accurately than approximate English equivalents such as "rule of law."

On such a view, fundamental or constitutional rights can only ever have presumptive status. They must remain potentially subject to being overridden by the imperatives of the national interest, and those imperatives cannot but be determined by the representatives of the entire nation. Any limitation of state jurisdiction in favor of the "autonomy" of a social group can only ever be a grant or recognition of lawmaking power subject to recall at any point if the group exercises its independence to the detriment of the public. Kant says this expressly in relation to the religious and military orders of late eighteenth-century Prussia.[35] The only type of autonomous normative system imaginable has to be territorially distinct, and even here it must be bound into an inter-state system of law. Thus, even if the Vatican has managed to sustain a claim akin to statehood in the international legal order, the Roman Catholic Church within any individual state is subject to its laws and legal forms. The device of the concordat mitigates the implications of this subordination by securing agreement on protected powers and liberties while preserving the form of a negotiated settlement between sovereign powers, but it cannot remove it entirely.

The unity of the modern law-state presents a challenge for accounts of religious group autonomy. On one hand, we may be persuaded that authority within society is plural, expressed through the collective life of distinct groups which gain their legitimacy directly from their members. On the other hand,

---

35   Immanuel Kant, *The Doctrine of Right*, General Remark B (AA 6:324), in *The Metaphysics of Morals*, ed. Lara Denis; tr. Mary Gregor (Cambridge: Cambridge University Press, 2017), 108.

the law-state holds the ring and asserts its own authority over all other collective entities and identities. For the great German jurist Otto Gierke (1841–1921), the desire to secure the political and legal significance of social groups led to a remarkable argument for their real personality.[36] Legal personality was neither a mere fiction nor a privilege to be conferred by the state but a matter of recognizing the dignity of humanity in its various collective expressions. Groups really are persons! As a pioneering legal historian, Gierke's work to retrieve indigenous German law, socially plural in contrast to the supposedly totalitarian and hierarchical tendencies of Roman rule, was influential on social and political theorists across Europe and the United States.[37] In the United Kingdom he found admirers in William Maitland, John Neville Figgis, Gerald Cole, and the early Harold Laski. In the case of Figgis, the linkage between social pluralism, civil liberty, and church autonomy became explicit.[38] In France the mantel was assumed by the "institutional" writers Maurice Hauriou, Georges Renard, and Joseph T. Delos. In the Netherlands, Abraham Kuyper was a key intellectual conduit, linking social pluralist thought to Reformed political theology.[39] And Kuyper struggled with the same fundamental problem: the state could not be described as sovereign, since it occupied one social sphere among many. At the same time, it enjoyed a certain supremacy on account of a distinct role in regulating the boundaries between the social spheres, protecting individuals from the abuse of power, and taxing all for the benefit of national unity.[40] In outcome, the "Calvinist constitution" was one which reconciled the supremacy of the state with the sovereignty of social spheres by asserting the subordination of churches to the law of the constitution, but not to the organs of the state. Although this was intelligible enough in relation to the executive

---

36 Otto von Gierke, "The Nature of Human Associations," in *The Genossenschaft Theory of Otto von Gierke: A Study in Political Thought*, ed. John D. Lewis (Madison: University of Wisconsin, 1935), Appendix C.

37 See Victor Muñiz-Fraticelli, *The Structure of Pluralism: On the Authority of Associations* (Oxford: Oxford University Press, 2014); and Jacob T. Levy, *Rationalism, Pluralism, and Freedom* (Oxford: Oxford University Press, 2015).

38 J. N. Figgis, *Churches in the Modern State* (London: Longmans, Green and Co., 1914).

39 Gierke's retrieval of the covenantal political thought of Johannes Althusius is important in this context, even if, as Jonathan Chaplin points out, Gierke read Althusius in a way which was not entirely congenial to Kuyper. See Jonathan Chaplin, *Herman Dooyeweerd: Christian Philosopher of State and Civil Society* (Notre Dame, IN: University of Notre Dame Press, 2011), 368, n. 91. On the seminal figure of Althusius, see Witte, *The Reformation of Rights*, chap. 3.

40 See Abraham Kuyper, "Calvinism and Politics," in his *Lectures on Calvinism* (Grand Rapids, MI: Eerdmans, 1931); discussion in Peter Heslam, *Creating a Christian Worldview* (Grand Rapids, MI: Eerdmans, 1998), 142–66.

and administrative branches, the relationship to a supreme legislature or the judicial branch was rather more obscure. The law-state relation was not ultimately resolved.[41]

As a result of developments in the judicial role in the later eighteenth century in which judges cast themselves as defenders of presumptive natural rights against Crown prerogatives, common law jurisdictions were considerably better placed to develop a law of social groups than were civilian ones.[42] Gierke was correct that the first and most important legal expression of group autonomy is its juridical personality. Although incorporation was a privilege enjoyed by custom only by the established church and later granted by Crown or Parliament, equivalent effects could be achieved by the device of the trust, unknown to civilian systems. Combined with the concept of office-holding— also ultimately derived from ecclesiastical paradigms—this enabled English courts in the eighteenth century to develop a law for legally tolerated religious congregations which secured a high degree of autonomy under ultimate judicial oversight.[43] Once it was also accepted that such congregations could effectively bind themselves into larger regional and national associations, a form of internal lawmaking was available to religious groups which provided a private law analogue to the public law of the established church.[44]

Language of "two kingdoms" or "sovereign spheres" naturally suggests a jurisdictional conception of religious group autonomy. There is some truth in the parallel with statehood in the sense that the internal law of religious groups can have a similar status to foreign law: effective within its domain, and to be proved as a fact before a court by the admission of expert testimony. But it has already been pointed out that the parallel with statehood is also unhelpful: religious groups do not control their property in the way that a state governs its territory. Moreover, the competence of a religious group is not parallel to that of the state, in the way that the competence of the British state parallels that of the United States. Rather, religious groups and states are concerned with distinctive subject matters, such that the business of one is not the business

---

41 Abraham Kuyper's intellectual successor, Herman Dooyeweerd (1894–1977), made progress with this problem in his discussion of "enkaptic interlacements" between the laws of church and state. See Chaplin, *Herman Dooyeweerd*, 246–54.

42 See Julian Rivers, "Natural Law, Human Rights and the Separation of Powers," in *The Cambridge Handbook of Natural Law and Human Rights*, ed. Tom Angier, Iain T. Benson, and Mark D. Retter (Cambridge: Cambridge University Press, 2023), 303–23.

43 I trace this development in Julian Rivers, *The Law of Organized Religions* (Oxford: Oxford University Press, 2010), 74–82.

44 This model received statutory expression in the legislation disestablishing the Anglican Church in Ireland and Wales. See Rivers, *The Law of Organized Religions*, 82–88.

of the other. Lawmaking organs of one should legislate only to govern internal matters, and courts of one entity should decline to hear cases concerning a subject matter properly belonging to the other. In the language of the Church of Scotland Act 1921, the contrast is between "spiritual matters" (doctrine, worship, government, and discipline) on one hand and "civil matters" on the other.

To some extent, the distinction between spiritual and civil makes perfect sense. The fact that the local priest has just delivered an unorthodox sermon discloses no cause of action in the civil courts; if I fall out with my employer, my remedy does not lie in church courts. But the underlying problem is that life cannot be carved up so neatly. The COVID-19 pandemic raised legal questions which fell squarely within both domains. And as those cases predictably demonstrate, when civil courts are faced with a matter which has both spiritual and civil dimensions, the tendency is for the latter concerns to predominate.

However, every now and then one can observe the reverse process in operation. On occasion, courts have been so impressed by the argument that the relationship between a religious minister and his or her organization is spiritual that they have concluded that it is not legal at all.[45] It must then be a purely voluntary arrangement which produces no enforceable rights on either side. This might not seem so very bad, since religious workers are often volunteers, but when the same logic is applied to questions of property, it has bizarre consequences. In recent English litigation concerning the control of a Sikh temple, the High Court and Court of Appeal both refused to determine which of two rival groups was the rightful owner. It took the Supreme Court to restore common sense. A civil court must be able to resolve a property dispute, even if it is required to explore the depths of unfamiliar and complex theological arguments to do so fairly.[46]

A jurisdictional view of religious group autonomy is unstable precisely because the binary opposition it appears to posit between spiritual and civil matters is untenable.[47] In classical canon law terms, it fails to account for the existence of *res mixta*: those matters which have a dual dimension. Religious liberty does not depend ultimately on being left alone by the state and its law. Instead, it requires the existence of distinctive bodies of civil law which protect the rights of self-government. In technical terms, these rights are powers not

---

45 See, for example, *Khan v Oxford City Mosque Society*, unreported, July 23, 1998. The development is discussed in Rivers, *The Law of Organized Religions*, 112–16.
46 *Khaira v Shergill* [2014] UKSC 33.
47 Steven Smith makes an important admission when he insists that the jurisdictional conception of church autonomy he professes to defend is not "absolute" and simply has a "stronger preemptive character" than a merits-based review. See Smith, "The Jurisdictional Conception of Church Autonomy," 27.

liberties: they enable religious groups to act with legal effect on others. They include the power to enter into legal relations with others (juridical personality), the power to form binding contracts, the power to acquire, hold, and dispose of property, and the power to sue and be sued for civil wrongs. The continuing relevance of long-standing doctrines of contract, tort, and property are an important part of any modern law of religious group autonomy.

Conceiving of religious group autonomy as the legal powers of self-government shows how it can have continuing relevance even in cases which concern both spiritual and civil matters. This point has numerous contemporary applications, for example in the ongoing discussions and development of vicarious liability for abuse within institutions. But the COVID-19 case law raises a different general problem: given that some sort of balancing of interests is inevitable in areas of overlap, how can the self-government of religious groups be integrated doctrinally with proportionality analysis?

5 Proportionality and the Self-Government of Religious Groups

We can take as a starting point the two COVID-19 judgments of the German Federal Constitutional Court.[48] Germany is, after all, the home of proportionality both historically and theoretically. The court refused to issue an injunction against the initial blanket ban on religious services in Hessen, but a fortnight later it found the restrictions in Lower Saxony unconstitutional to the extent that they made no provision for individual permissions to be granted if the religious group making the application could demonstrate to the regional authorities that it had put in place sufficient protective measures. The applicant mosque had gone to considerable lengths to enable Friday prayers to take place safely during Ramadan, and the high importance of religious liberty meant that the mosque should have the opportunity for gaining an administrative permission.

The directness and authority of the Court are clearly evident in the judgments. It makes its own decision about the validity of the legislative regimes introduced in Hessen and Lower Saxony, and it seems to have no inhibition in assessing the severity of the impact on religious believers or the costs to public health. This assumes some common public scale of values by which we can agree on the importance of spiritual acts in relation to common secular concerns. While the Court sought to protect collective religious liberty in the

---

48 Bundesverfassungsgericht, *Beschluss der 2. Kammer des Ersten Senats vom 10. April 2020* (1 BvQ 28/20); *Beschluss der 2. Kammer des Ersten Senats vom 29. April 2020* (1 BvQ 44/20).

narrower sense of the freedom of a group of believers to engage in common ritual acts, there is no suggestion of any religious self-government. Rather, the constitutional court positions itself as the mouthpiece or guardian of the constitution, which is a point of ethical unity between church and state.

This type of approach is vulnerable to the pressures of secularization. Since the importance of religious liberty depends on some recognition of the value of the religious acts at stake—celebrating the Mass, praying together—these are relatively easy to dismiss as idiosyncratic and lightweight in comparison with human life and health.[49] British judges applying proportionality analysis were rather more cautious about their ability to weigh the relevant interests. Two distinct strands can be seen to this caution. The more common—and this can also be found in COVID-19 cases in many other jurisdictions—is a degree of deference toward scientific assessment of the extent of the health risk and the various ways in which those risks may be mitigated. In the main case before the English Court of Appeal, the judges also directed attention to the accountability of the government to Parliament in what was ultimately a matter of political judgment.[50]

Elsewhere I have argued that these two types of judicial caution can be distinguished as deference to expertise and restraint in the face of superior legitimacy.[51] They apply particularly in relation to the final two stages of the proportionality test. When asking if a restriction on rights is the least necessary or involves minimal impairment, judges are often faced with questions of factual assessment and prognosis in areas of expertise which they may well lack. They are more likely to reach correct outcomes if they rely on experts. Given that their capacity to consider extensive depositions from expert witnesses is limited, evidence that the government has fulfilled that responsibility before concluding that a measure is necessary tends to show that it is, indeed, necessary. As for the final stage of analysis, when asking if a balance of interests or values is correct for the purposes of the law, a democratically accountable determination enshrined in primary legislation may well have more legitimacy than an individual judge's personal views. Taken to an extreme, deference and restraint have the effect of radically qualifying the final stages of proportionality review, turning it into something akin to "Wednesbury reasonableness"

---

49 See Julian Rivers, "The Secularisation of the British Constitution," *Ecclesiastical Law Journal* 14, no. 3 (2012): 371–99.

50 *R (Dolan) v Secretary of State for Health and Social Care* [2020] EWCA Civ 1605 at [86] and [90].

51 Julian Rivers, "Proportionality and Variable Intensity of Review," *Cambridge Law Journal* 65 (2006): 174–207.

(English law), or "rational basis review" (U.S. law). For this reason, such doctrines tend to be resisted by those preferring a more robust conception of constitutional rights, but their presence in case law and their underlying rationale seem undeniable.

Deference and restraint normally operate to reduce the intensity of judicial review, because they are applied by judges in relation to executive and legislative organs of the state. The concern from the perspective of religious group autonomy is that such doctrines further weaken an already subordinate position. They effectively encourage the court to side with the government and fail to do justice to the weaker religious minority. However, the same forms of argument can be used to incorporate a degree of self-government by religious groups into proportionality analysis. Religious groups have a form of expertise—theological and ecclesiological expertise—which judges do not possess. So long as they are sincere and plausible, the religious groups' assessments of the importance of various acts of collective worship have to be taken at face value. In practice, many courts did this when they accepted the testimony of individual claimants that important religious duties were at stake. As well as his main conclusion that the Scottish government had failed to demonstrate the necessity of complete closure of religious buildings, Lord Braid also held that the ministers had failed to appreciate the importance of gathering in person. Judges often pay lip service to the importance of restrictions on rights, but Lord Braid went further. After rebuking the minsters for assuming that "it doesn't really matter," he stated,

> While some people may derive some benefit from being able to observe on-line services, it is undeniable that certain aspects of certain faiths simply cannot take place, at all, under the current legislative regime: in particular, communion; baptism; and confession, to name but three. It is impossible to measure the effect of those restrictions on those who hold religious beliefs. It goes beyond mere loss of companionship and an inability to attend a lunch club.[52]

The idea that the weight of interference is "impossible to measure" might suggest that it has an absolute value, but the following sentence shows that it is really an admission of incompetence. The judge can only depend on the sincere testimony of the believer as to the spiritual significance of the prohibited acts. This may be very important—as important as eating and drinking.

---

52   *Philip*, [121].

By contrast, there was far less evidence that courts recognized the problem of political legitimacy. There is a considerable difference between a politician affirming that the right balance of interests requires places of worship to close and a religious leader coming to the same conclusion. The interest in religious self-government is an interest both in determining the significance of religious acts and an interest in religious groups' determining for themselves how those acts are to be carried out or reconceived in the face of threats to public health. Incorporating a principle of religious self-government into proportionality would have redirected attention to the following questions: To what extent have restrictions been negotiated with representatives of religious groups? To what extent do restrictions allow for choices to be made by religious groups in different modes of risk mitigation? Could restrictions take the form of duties to have policies along with guidance on the value of different risk-mitigation strategies? Where such processes work well, it becomes possible to replace substantive rule-based limits on religious activities, which attempt to be "correct," all things considered, with a minimum legal backstop below which no reasonable religious group should go. Religious groups, or their umbrella organizations, thus become trusted regulators alongside the state.

Tentative steps in this direction were already taken in the United Kingdom during the COVID-19 pandemic, although one suspects that the meetings hastily arranged between government representatives and religious leaders were as much about securing compliance as a genuine effort in dialogue. Models of partnership in reaching an agreed regulatory approach to matters of common concern are more associated with Tony Blair's "New Labour" ministry of 1997–2007,[53] but a recent attempt to reinvigorate them can be found in the report of the (Conservative) government's independent faith engagement adviser.[54] Here one finds calls for a new "proactive partnership" to include "regular roundtables with senior, serious and national faith leaders" and "consistent, quality faith literacy learning" for everyone on the public payroll.

This shows a better route forward than "most favored nation" approaches to free exercise alone. One suspects that in his desire to downplay the role of comparators, Justice Kavanaugh was struggling to reconcile his libertarian instincts with the egalitarian framing of *Smith*. This dissatisfaction with *Smith* is even more apparent in the recent opinions of Justices Samuel Alito and Neil

---

53   See Rivers, *The Law of Organized Religions*, 296–305.
54   Colin Bloom, *Does Government "Do God"? An Independent Review into How Government Engages with Faith*, Department for Levelling Up, Housing and Communities, Apr. 26, 2023, https://assets.publishing.service.gov.uk/government/uploads/system/uploads/attachment_data/file/1152684/The_Bloom_Review.pdf.

Gorsuch in *Fulton v City of Philadelphia*.[55] But if *Smith* is to be abandoned, more has to replace it than merely minimal state oversight. Straightforward recognition of a constitutional principle of religious group autonomy would indeed allow for a more open acknowledgment that the search here is for the absolute minimum of necessary regulation. But it should also result in attention being directed to internal governance and responsibility by religious groups—and this includes a shared public responsibility for the common good. One suspects that states which combine constitutional commitments to religious group autonomy with tolerant forms of historic religious establishment may find this combination somewhat easier to achieve.

6   Conclusion

The constitutional principle of religious group autonomy is present within many liberal democracies, but not securely so. The value of social pluralism is patent, but its reconciliation with modern unified systems of law problematic. Jurisdictional accounts do little to help the situation, being unattractive in theory and unworkable in practice. Paradoxically, they seem both to defend an unwarranted immunity for religious groups from legal oversight while also disempowering them. By contrast, conceiving of religious group autonomy as a power of self-government within the law holds out the hope of reconciling liberty with responsibility. In this chapter I have started to work out the implications of such an approach for proportionality-based assessments of religious-liberty restrictions in the context of pressing public interests. This analysis holds out hope that a similar approach may also be fruitful in other areas of unavoidable state-religion interaction.

Acknowledgments

I am most grateful to Kathleen Brady, Jonathan Chaplin, and Rafael Domingo for their insightful comments on an earlier draft.

---

55   *Fulton v City of Philadelphia* 593 U.S. _ (2021). (City's refusal to renew fostering services contract with Roman Catholic agency on account of the latter's refusal to certify same-sex couples is a breach of the Free Exercise Clause.)

CHAPTER 25

Obeying Conscience: The Commands and Costs of Resisting the Law

Jeffrey B. Hammond

1   Introduction

Conscience is making a comeback. To be sure, the working out of conscience is as old as Adam and Eve hiding from the Lord in the Garden of Eden after they ate the forbidden fruit.[1] Socrates drank the poisonous cup because his conscience would not relent to the demands of the elders of Athens.[2] And conscientious objection to war is no new thing—thousands of conscientious objectors have refused service in war, with objections to the Vietnam War the most resonant modern example.[3] Some people have even made refusing to take the COVID-19 vaccine a matter of religious conscience.[4]

Conscience is not new, but it is asserting itself as never before. And the exercise of conscience has become a calling card among conservative Christians (including conservative Protestants) to distinguish the demands of their faith from that which is more culturally conditioned. Christians like the photographer Elaine Huguenin,[5] the florist Barronelle Stutzman,[6] the football coach Joseph Kennedy,[7] and the baker Jack Phillips[8] have all taken stands, particularly on culturally fraught issues like marriage and public prayer. All have suffered significant personal consequences for refusing the demands of state and

---

1 See below, section titled "A Short Biblical Theology of Conscience."
2 See Plato, *Phaedo*, trans. David Gallop (Oxford: Oxford University Press, 2009).
3 See, for example, *Gillette v. United States*, 401 U.S. 437 (1971) (where the U.S. Supreme Court upheld the denial of petitioner's conscientious objection to the Vietnam War).
4 See Adelaide Madera, "COVID-19 Vaccines v. Conscientious Objections in the Workplace: How to Prevent a New Catch-22," *Canopy Forum*, Apr. 30, 2020, https://canopyforum.org/2021/04/30/covid-19-vaccines-v-conscientious-objections-in-the-workplace-how-to-prevent-a-new-catch-22/.
5 See *Elane Photography, LLC v. Willock*, 309 P. 3d 53 (N.M. 2013).
6 See, for example, *Washington v. Arlene's Flowers, Inc.*, 193 Wash. 2d 469 (Wash. 2019).
7 See *Kennedy v. Bremerton School District*, 142 S. Ct. 2407 (2022).
8 See *Masterpiece Cakeshop, Ltd. v. Colorado Civil Rights Commission*, 138 S. Ct. 1719 (2018).

federal law that otherwise would have compelled them to act in a way that, once done, would have left their very beings violated.

One should not think, however, that conscience and its exercise are limited to Christians who make grand gestures and bold stances for their faith. The otherwise anonymous Christians mentioned above, who have stepped out on legal ledges, sometimes to fall, for the demands of their faith (as they discern those demands) are nonexclusive examples of what it means to have and exercise a conscience. Some of these examples have discerned and deployed their consciences in wiser ways than others. Nevertheless, a sensitive conscience is available for every follower of Jesus, and deploying it is not meant solely for challenges the Christian might deem existential. It is a capacity to be honed and used in daily living. The well-developed conscience for the Christian is intimately tied to the Christian journey of sanctification.

A clarifying point is in order: religiously informed conscience is related to, but not the same as, free exercise of religion. It is common for these terms to be conflated.[9] Free exercise is both a constitutional category and a latticework of protections meant to *absolutely* protect internal beliefs and *contingently* protect outward acts.[10] Conscience, on the other hand, is the filter by which the person is motivated to believe or act or refrain from believing or acting in a certain way and for or against a particular end. What is unique about Stutzman, Phillips, and the others mentioned above is that they assessed their consciences and then made decisions based on those consciences, and what resulted were state and federal free-exercise cases. Conscience is the interior forum. Free exercise is the outer fight.

It is therefore important to continue to target and refine a distinctly Protestant view of conscience. This is not because Roman Catholic treatments of conscience are deficient. They are, however, *particularly focused*. Saint Thomas Aquinas, the fountainhead of Catholic theorizing on conscience, has emphasized the role of reason in determining the demands of conscience.[11] It is an

---

9   See Nathan S. Chapman, "Liberty of Conscience, Free Exercise of Religion, and the U.S. Constitution," in *Christianity and the Laws of Conscience: An Introduction*, ed. Jeffrey B. Hammond and Helen M. Alvaré (Cambridge: Cambridge University Press, 2021), 287; and Michael J. DeBoer, "Religious Conscience Protections in American State Constitutions," in ibid., 305.

10 See Cantwell v. Connecticut, 310 U.S. 296, 303, 304 ("Thus the [First] Amendment embraces two concepts—freedom to believe and freedom to act. The first is absolute but, in the nature of things, the second cannot be").

11 An important summary of Thomas's theorizing on conscience may be found in Cajetan Cuddy, OP, "St. Thomas Aquinas on Conscience," in Hammond and Alvaré, *Christianity and the Laws of Conscience*, 112.

important observation that should not be bypassed or glossed over. Unsurprisingly, though, a uniquely Protestant treatment of conscience will lift up revelation and spiritual leadership over against reason and calculation. Thus, this chapter continues to ask the question: what does conscience look and act like for a committed Christian whose bulwarks are the Bible and the "still, small voice" of the Holy Spirit?

Elsewhere,[12] I have argued that the hallmark of the redeemed conscience for a Protestant is the indwelling work of the Holy Spirit upon the Christian's heart, mind, and will to the end of fulfilling Christ's two greatest commands: those to love God and to love one's neighbor. In this chapter, I will expand upon that claim and will further demonstrate *how* the Spirit works on and innervates the believer's conscience so that she can fulfill the demands of God as she reads them in the Bible. But before that, this chapter will provide a brief sketch of the biblical theology of conscience, and in particular how important characters in the Bible have yielded to, or ignored, their consciences.[13]

This chapter will also explore the resources available in basic legal theory for the Protestant Christian to use in sifting, or discerning, which obligations or claims of human law are worthy of her conscience's attention and decision-making capacity. In brief, some human laws merely express the will of the lawmaker working out the conclusions of reason (*determinatio*) which the law-abiding Christian should have no problem obeying, while others centrally implicate the Christian's standing before God, and therefore summon all the resources of her conscience to determine if submission is required.

Finally, this chapter will explore the *conclusions of and actions taken upon* a conscientiously derived decision. Sometimes conscience demands that human law be resisted, because conscience has concluded that the law is deformed or unjust or makes a claim about reality that does not comport with reality as testified to in the Bible, as the Christian reads it.

This chapter is dedicated to my teacher Professor John Witte. Both in his law school courses in legal history and constitutional law, and in my work with him as a research assistant, Professor Witte taught me about the magisterial Protestant teachings on conscience, beginning with Martin Luther's famous (if partly apocryphal) declaration to the emperor at the Diet of Worms in 1520: "My conscience is captive to the Word of God. Thus I cannot and will

---

12   Jeffrey B. Hammond, "Toward a Theology of a Redeemed Conscience," in Hammond and Alvaré, *Christianity and the Laws of Conscience*, 152.

13   My previous work on conscience looked at it from a Reformed and evangelical perspective. While not discounting that approach, this chapter focuses more closely on what biblical theology has to say about conscience.

not recant, because acting against one's conscience is neither safe nor sound. Here I stand; I can do no other. God help me. Amen."[14] He taught me about the history of freedom of conscience claims in the Western legal tradition, and especially in the history of American constitutional law.[15] And he commissioned me to coedit a large volume on *Christianity and the Laws of Conscience*[16] in the Cambridge Law and Christianity Series that he edits.

2 A Short Biblical Theology of Conscience

According to New Testament scholar Grant Osborne, biblical theology is the "branch of theological inquiry concerned with tracing themes through the diverse sections of the Bible (such as the wisdom writings or the epistles of Paul) and then with seeking the unifying themes that draw the Bible together."[17] Biblical theology is conceptual in nature. To do biblical theology is to excavate and analyze concepts in the Bible that span several biblical texts, if not the entire corpus. In that vein, conscience is a thread of emphasis that runs throughout the Bible. In the Bible, conscience is the filter by which a person under God's scrutiny evaluates the choices before him, makes a choice, and then accepts the consequences of those choices.

Take, for instance, the parents of all humankind, Adam and Eve. As recorded in Genesis, the creation narrative has Adam first hearing God's express mandate—His law—not to eat of the special tree in the center of the Garden of Eden, lest he die (Genesis 2:16–17). Nevertheless, after considering the serpent's entreaty, "Did God really say ... ," Eve (first) and then Adam give way and eat the fruit from the Tree of Knowledge (Genesis 3:1–6, NIV). This failure by the couple is, I submit, ultimately a failure of conscience. Conscience was present, for Eve stopped to consider the serpent's question. She used her God-given

---

14 See detailed discussions in John Witte, Jr., *Law and Protestantism: The Legal Teachings of the Lutheran Reformation* (Cambridge: Cambridge University Press, 2002); id., *The Reformation of Rights: Law, Religion, and Human Rights in Early Modern Calvinism* (Cambridge: Cambridge University Press, 2007); and more recently id., *The Blessings of Liberty: Human Rights and Religious Freedom in the Western Legal Tradition* (Cambridge: Cambridge University Press, 2021).
15 See esp. John Witte, Jr., Joel A. Nichols, and Richard W. Garnett, *Religion and the American Constitutional Experiment*, 5th ed. (Oxford: Oxford University Press, 2022), esp. 60–66, 146–205.
16 Hammond and Alvaré, *Christianity and the Laws of Conscience*.
17 Pierre Gilbert, "On the Relationship between Biblical and Systematic Theology," *Direction* 49, no. 2 (2020): 178–93, at 181, quoting Grant Osborne, *The Hermeneutical Spiral*, rev. and exp. ed. (Downers Grove, IL: IVP Academic, 2006), 349.

power of reflection and reason to wonder if the course of action presented by the serpent would yield good or evil for her. She paused, rehearsed to the Tempter Yahweh's instruction, and reflected on whether or not God really did tell the couple not to eat of the forbidden tree. But she acted against the dictates of her conscience, because she ended up taking the fruit and eating it after agreeing with the Tempter's mistaken conclusions about the consequences of the forbidden fruit. It is in the pause for reflection, comparing the choice before her and the firm exhortation from her maker and the lie from the Tempter, that was the working out of Eve's defective conscience. Conscience was something to be listened to, but Eve didn't, and that failure to heed led to the first couple's temporal pain and ultimate demise.

The picture for Eve's mate, Adam, was much worse. Adam saw that Eve had been tempted and had disobeyed, and yet he cast his lot with hers and ate the fruit. Adam ignored his conscience screaming at him, which in this case was the conclusion of when fact—the fruit before him—and law—Yahweh's mandate—met. Adam rushed forward to be in league with his wife, flying by the certainty of what disobedience would mean to him. Adam had a conscience, but it was not robust and inclined to submit to the one who had created it.

Consider, too, the upstart Babylonian captives Daniel (Belteshazzar) and his friends, Shadrach, Meshach, and Abednego. These young men were hauled away to a foreign land and were pressed into their new king's service. These boys willingly served their new sovereign, but they had principled limits to their service. Daniel refused the sumptuous food served at the "training table" for the king's prospective officials in order to keep a plainer diet, and his choice benefitted him at the end of his training regimen (see Daniel 1). Daniel faced a double crisis of conscience. Daniel's insistence on vegetables and water was a matter of firm determination: "But Daniel resolved not to defile himself with the royal food and wine, and he asked the chief official for permission not to defile himself this way" (Daniel 1:8, NIV). But in order for Daniel to fulfill his conscience-informed principles, he needed the approval of the director of the king's training program. This official was reluctant, as he told Daniel, "I am afraid of my lord the king, who has assigned your food and drink. Why should he see you looking worse than the other young men your age? The king would then have my head because of you" (Daniel 1:10, NIV). How much resolve must it have taken for Daniel to risk not only his (and his friends') places in the training program and even their lives, but also the life of an official (though one that the Bible records as favorably inclined to Daniel because of God's intervention; see 1:9) who was just doing his job. Clearly, Daniel's principles would brook no compromise.

Conscience prioritizes faithful obedience over temporal conformity. Daniel and his friends could have acquiesced to the training regimen set out for them. They soberly chose not to, recognizing that forgoing "defile[ment]" with sumptuous foods meant obedience to Yahweh (Daniel 1:8, NIV). The young men appreciated the consequences of their resistance to the training regimen and chose obedience to an unseen god rather than obedience to an implacable king.

Shadrach, Meshach, and Abednego faced a similar crisis of conscience. These young men, who, like Daniel, were on the bureaucratic fast track, were faced with an existential choice. The king had enacted a law requiring obeisance to a ninety-foot-high golden statue (Daniel 3). These young men were loyal and willing servants of their king, not necessarily by choice, for their first choice surely would not have been to be forcibly removed from their homeland and pressed into a foreign government's administrative service. Rather, their loyalty was formed out of their character and the conviction that reverence for Yahweh meant rendering excellent service to their temporal sovereign even though they did not choose that service. The young men were condemned when their consciences made a seemingly rebellious response to an evil temporal law. But these young men were supernaturally saved from destruction. Amazingly, the fiery furnace did not consume them: "[not] a hair on their heads was singed; their robes were not scorched, and no smell of fire was on them." And even Nebudchadnezzar observed: "[for] ... the God of Shadrach, Meshach, and Abednego ... has sent his angel and rescued his servants! They trusted in him and defied the king's command and were willing to give up their lives rather than serve or worship any god except their own God" (Daniel 3:27, 28, NIV). The young men made a choice to defy the king, knowing that Yahweh could save them from the king's fiery wrath, but being resolute to defy the king even if Yahweh refused to save them and they burned up (see Daniel 3:17, 18).

Likewise, after he had risen to a high administrative position in Babylon, Daniel openly defied a law requiring religious homage to King Darius, concocted by Daniel's bureaucrat colleagues to entrap him. He threw open his shutter and prayed to Yahweh, notwithstanding the penalty for disobedience: a trip to the lion's den (Daniel 6). Daniel's conscience activated when fact—the prospect of his defiant praying to Yahweh—met law—Darius's royal decree that worship should be made to no one but Darius himself. It was in that moment of activated conscience that Daniel remembered his loyalty to a greater law and chose open refusal of temporal law with its swift and sure consequences, instead of craven disobedience to a law that did not have such immediate consequences and a lawgiver who could not be sensorily discerned.

Like his friends, Daniel was miraculously saved from condemnation by a force outside and greater than himself.

Both Daniel's and his friends' stories provide a nonobvious lesson about the working out of conscience. All four of these young men were unexpectedly saved from the death that human law required. In both the fiery furnace and the lion's den narratives, the king was happily surprised at the young men's rescue from otherwise certain destruction. No one should think, however, that their rescue is normative. These Yahweh followers exercised their consciences and were deliberately and altogether surprisingly saved from death by Yahweh. But they did not expect to be saved. They knew they might have to face the natural consequences of their temporal defiance.

Making a conscientious choice, sourced from conviction, could lead to disastrous consequences, even death. That Daniel and his friends were rescued, much like the *deus ex machina* of Greek drama, does not mean that everyone who makes a conscience-based choice to follow God's law will be similarly rescued. One should not expect to be saved from temporal consequences, even though an inscrutable God chose to redeem four young men from grotesque execution. Rather, the person making a conscience-informed choice should do so soberly, knowing that, more likely than not, devotion to the God of the Bible in the face of immense pressure will lead to retribution, persecution, and ostracization.

One final example in the Bible is, like that of Adam and Eve, about conscience gone awry. It is the man centrally responsible for Jesus's death, the high priest Caiaphas. As recorded in the Gospel of John, chapter 11, Caiaphas conspired with Israel's religious leaders to kill Jesus because they saw that Jesus's teaching and miracles, including raising Lazarus from the dead, were turning the people away from the control of the elites. The most pressing problem, of course, was that Jesus brought Lazarus back from death. Caiaphas could not reconcile his own anthropological and religious beliefs as a Sadducee—that there was no resurrection from the dead—with the fact that Lazarus had been dead for four days and had come back to life again only after Jesus said, "Lazarus, come out!" (John 11:43, NIV). If Christ had indeed resurrected his friend, then Caiaphas would seemingly have no choice but to put his faith in Jesus. But faith in Jesus would mean the end to Caiaphas's place of authority among the people, his finances, and the importance of his lineage. When confronted with fact—that Jesus raised Lazarus—Caiaphas effectively refused the truth staring him in the face and the only proper decision flowing from that truth. He refused the demands of his conscience—to put his faith in Christ (or at least not oppress him). That refusal— and the cascade of decisions flowing from it—was the genesis of the conspiracy that ultimately led to Caiaphas's condemnation of Christ, a key step toward his crucifixion. And ironically, what began with Lazarus's resurrection ended with Christ's own resurrection.

These biblical vignettes of conscience highlight an important truth about it: conscience involves both inclination and choice, and not always for the good. Adam and Eve were inclined to be enticed by the Tempter, and after considering his argument, they chose to disobey God's clear instruction. Daniel and his friends had a strong constitution before their tests, so when they faced their life-or-death choices, they unflinchingly chose obedience to Yahweh over easier choices to save their own necks. And before he faced the fact that Jesus had raised Lazarus from the dead, Caiaphas was a wealthy elite whose bedrock religious belief was that there was no resurrection. So, notwithstanding the indisputable evidence before him, Caiaphas made a choice that was reasonable to him: to eliminate the source of his dissonance.

3 What Is Biblical Conscience?

In essence, conscience is a monitor. It is a faculty of knowledge, discernment, and judgment, that compares a person's thoughts, words, and actions in light of that person's deeply held and firmly committed-to moral standards. Conscience does have a filtering function—everything that one thinks or does is poured through her conscience to see if it resonates with her previously staked-out ethical positions. But if conscience has a monitoring function, it also has a straightening function. If a person's spine is bent, then the person cannot walk straight. But once the backbone is righted, the person can both see what is in front of him and then take confident steps. Similarly, failing to heed the conclusion provided by conscience's monitoring function leads the person to speak distorting words and walk crooked steps. But that same conscience, once obeyed, empowers the person to see what is in front of him—that is, his world properly calibrated by his own ethical standards. And once corrected by conscience, the person can then walk confidently, with integrity, knowing that his actions are aligned with what he knows to be right.

The Bible seems to endorse the role of conscience as a monitor or a mirror. For example, in a famous extended passage on conscience, the Apostle Paul indicates that it can have intuitive knowledge of right and wrong whose provenance is separate from the principles of morality themselves. Paul explains:

> Indeed, when Gentiles, who do not have the law, do by nature things required by the law, they are a law for themselves, even though they do

not have the law. They show that the requirements of the law are written on their hearts, their consciences also bearing witness, and their thoughts sometimes accusing them and at other times even defending them.
ROMANS 2:14–15, NIV

The consciences of the law-abiding Gentiles were innate monitors. The moral demands of God's law were "written on their hearts" that "bore witness" to their actions—either praiseworthy, in following the law, or blameworthy in disobeying it. Notice the distinction that Paul makes: the demands of the law are separate from the Gentiles' hearts that both knew and kept those demands. Also notice that in "bearing witness," their consciences always told the truth about the actions they undertook as knowers of the law. That their consciences would cause their thoughts to sometimes accuse them must mean that those consciences were honest, not merely reflexively endorsing actions that happened to meet the requirements of the law.

Although conscience has monitoring and straightening functions, it is not necessarily an "all or nothing" proposition. A person can perfectly obey the demands of conscience and have no qualms about the resulting actions. Or a person can be confronted with a particularly troublesome dilemma—one that musters significant consequences to his career, reputation, or relationships—and can choose actions that his conscience is warning against. In that respect, the person "sears" his conscience against a robust application the next time such a harrowing dilemma is put to him. (See 1 Timothy 4:2, which speaks of "the insincerity of liars whose consciences are seared" [ESV]). It is true that if the person obeys his conscience after first disobeying it, this will have an effect of restoring him to moral wholeness. It is also true that if he disobeys his conscience in a particularly thorny situation, it will be incrementally harder to obey the next time hard circumstances confront him.

4   How the Spirit Works on a Christian's Conscience

In thinking about the role of the Spirit, some preliminary thoughts are in order. First, the Bible does not conflate any of the triune persons of God with a human's conscience. For example, in 1 Corinthians 4:4, Paul makes a case that he does not care that his spiritual charges in the Corinthian church might judge him for his work in sharing the gospel with them. He forthrightly states that "*my* conscience is clear" (emphasis added). Paul's conscience is his—he owns it, as it were. And it has rendered a preliminary verdict for him. The Spirit inspired Paul to record his experience with his conscience in this matter. But it was his conscience, and not the Spirit itself, that came to the moral conclusion about his own rectitude. Second, the passage in 1 Corinthians is instructive because it shows that Paul deployed his conscience for a particular purpose, in this case, doing the difficult discernment that he is free from any human judgment about his calling to evangelize and disciple the Corinthians.

Like Paul, the Apostle Peter held that conscience is a separate entity from direct supernatural intervention in the believer's life. For Peter, conscience is the inner critic that approves or condemns the soundness of the Christian's status before God. Take, for instance, 1 Peter 3. In this chapter, Peter mentions "conscience" twice—once as a vehicle of evangelistic readiness, and then, in receiving baptism, as a sign of sanctified purity. In both instances, that which is sought is a conscience that is clean and does not accuse the believer. The strong implication made by both of these instances in chapter 3 is that the Christian cannot have a clean conscience before an all-seeing God if she (a) does not have an "answer" to those who question about the "hope" concerning Christ that is within her; and (b) if her conscience has not first been cleansed through the washing of baptism. Nevertheless, that which provides hope—having an evangelistic answer to those seeking to know more about the Christian faith and submitting to the waters of baptism—comes with an implicit warning: the Christian should expect her conscience to be damaged if she is unprepared to contend for her faith. Likewise, Peter implies that one's gyroscope—one's conscience—cannot find true north absent submission to the waters of baptism.

Moral discernment would be a much easier enterprise if a Christian's conscience and the Holy Spirit were one. But if the Spirit were substituted for the Christian's own repository of values and the judgments that flowed from those values, there would be no need for the Bible to mention conscience as a separate entity. To be sure, the values and judgments "owned" by the Christian flow from the Spirit's own leading, guiding, and patiently *growing* of values, habits of mind, and traits of character that are in line with the Spirit's own character (see Galatians 5:22–23 listing the "fruit of the Spirit").[18] Yet that remodeled character is the believer's own to deploy in the humdrum of choice-worthy situations of everyday life.

---

18 I appreciate the insight of Timothy Keller, whose sermon on the passage about the fruit of the Spirit included the claim that the Spirit patiently grows His fruit in the believer's life. See Timothy J. Keller, "How to Change," Apr. 19, 1998, https://gospelinlife.com/?fwp_search=How%20to%20Change.

A person's conscience is separate from the Spirit who works upon that conscience. But now we must focus on the fact *that* the Holy Spirit works to renovate the Christian's conscience and *how* He does so.

Renovation, or sanctification, of the believer's thoughts, affections, inclinations, and even conscience, follows regeneration. Regeneration is that process of inner revelation and revolution whereby the person is supernaturally brought by the Spirit from a state of alienation from God to a place of faith in God and trust in Jesus's finished work upon the cross. Sanctification is the process whereby the Spirit of God, over the passage of time, progressively conforms the believer into the image of Jesus.[19] The Spirit's work of regeneration precedes His work of sanctification.

Regeneration is more of a fixed point. Sanctification is more of an ongoing work. The Spirit's work of sanctification, of making the believer holy, is a work of transformation. The Apostle Paul argues that this transformation is to a state of pure reflection of God's glory, and this transformative work is accomplished by the Spirit: "But we all, with unveiled face, beholding as in a mirror the glory of the Lord, are being transformed into the same image from glory to glory, just by the Spirit of the Lord." (2 Corinthians 3:18, NKJV). The Spirit sanctifies by prompting the believer to obey the words and example of Jesus. The Apostle Peter, for instance, greets his audience in 1 Peter 1:2 as those who live "through the sanctifying work of the Spirit, to obey Jesus Christ and be sprinkled with His blood."

Sanctification is a spiritual work of transformation. It must therefore be asked: how does the Spirit accomplish this work of transformation? But before transformation can begin, orienting the new believer to godly knowledge is first a work of regeneration. In the famous regeneration passage about God animating dry bones and turning a stony, unworkable heart into a soft, pliable heart of flesh, Ezekiel gives this insight: "I will put my Spirit in you and move you to follow my decrees and be careful to keep my laws" (Ezekiel 36:27, NIV). The person whose heart is not inclined toward God has no natural desire to follow God's ways, instructions, or principles. It takes a miraculous work of the Spirit to turn around a disoriented heart to one that earnestly desires to follow godly precepts. And it is only after that initial miraculous work is done that the ongoing work of transformation can proceed. This involves continuing instruction for the believer of God's purposes, decrees, and laws. Jesus, for example,

---

19   For a short article describing the multifaceted work of the Spirit in the life of the believer, including in regeneration and sanctification, see Chance Faulkner, "Five Works of the Spirit in the Life of the Believer," *The Gospel Coalition* (Canada), Sep. 1, 2020, https://ca.thegospelcoalition.org/article/five-works-of-the-spirit-in-the-life-of-the-believer/.

promised the Spirit as an "Advocate," "whom the Father will send in my name, [and who] will teach you all things and will remind you of everything I have said to you" (John 14:26, NIV). No transformation and following after God happens without true knowledge. And no true knowledge happens apart from Christ's own teaching. Christ's teaching is reinstituted and reinforced through the agency of the Spirit.

Another way that sanctification happens is through *cooperation*. Simply, for the believer to be changed into the image of Jesus, she must want to be changed and must cooperate with the way that the Spirit prompts and leads her. In Galatians 5, the Apostle Paul uses a very interesting metaphor to describe what cooperation with the Holy Spirit looks like: walking. "[W]*alk* by the Spirit, and you will not gratify the desires of the flesh" (Galatians 5:16, NIV, my emphasis added). He later observes, "if you are *led* by the Spirit, you are not under the law" (Galatians 5:18, NIV, my emphasis added). And later still, Paul wraps up his teaching about what a Spirit-filled life looks like by reminding the Galatians that "If we live by the Spirit, let us also *keep in step* with the Spirit" (Galatians 5:25, ESV, my emphasis added). All of these admonitions add up to the Christian's *purposeful obedience*—in refraining from the "works of the flesh," which Paul lists in this passage as "sexual immorality, impurity, sensuality, idolatry, sorcery, enmity, strife, jealousy, fits of anger, rivalries, dissensions, divisions, envy, drunkenness, orgies, and things like these" (Galatians 5:18–21, ESV). But that "keeping in step" or "walking" with the Spirit also means taking the actions necessary to cultivate the "fruit of the Spirit," which Paul defines as "love, joy, peace, patience, kindness, goodness, faithfulness, gentleness, [and] self-control" (Galatians 5:22–23, ESV).

We should understand this part of sanctification something like this: sanctification means obeying. Obeying means refraining from some actions (the works of the flesh) and doing others (those actions which lead to the cultivating of the fruit of the Spirit). As the Christian is progressively sanctified and thus grows in Christian maturity, that maturity will result in a conscience that is ever more refined to do the cooperative work of sanctification. Simply, the more the Christian progresses in sanctification, the more her conscience is attuned to make the decisions and take the actions necessary to stay on the path of sanctification.

5 Decision-Making Resources in the Law

Biblical theology helps the Christian see that conscience is a Bible-spanning concept and a basic constituent of God's people. The Holy Spirit is the agent that enlivens the Christian's conscience, and in the process of sanctification, the Christian cooperates with the Spirit to refine her conscience. Law is a background system of control that spars with conscience. It is therefore instructive to see how law interacts with conscience. This section will fix attention on three ways of seeing law—and how those lenses work with the person's conscience.

Law has a connection with conscience, although that connection is non-obvious and indirect. Much of law, maybe even most of it, is meant to fill in the blanks for a particular regulatory scheme that does not spark interest in or concern by the public. Simply, much of law is simply the working out of the rational will of the lawmaker, or *determinatio*.[20] *Determinatio* implies the good faith effort of the lawmaker to make the substance of a law fulfill the law's goals. Further, *determinatio* has much to do with the coordination function of law. So, to use a well-known example, if the goal is to have a system whereby traffic freely moves with a minimum of accidents, it is not necessarily an ethical problem that cars must be driven on the right-hand side of the road or that the speed limit is 35 miles per hour. Those realities exist because sides of the road and speed limits must be chosen, or else chaos will ensue.[21]

Determinatio implicates need. A side must be chosen, or else the goal (clean water, safe driving, buildings that stand) will be foiled. Conscience, however, implicates the self. It implicates the person's deepest-held values and innate sense of right and wrong. In making a conscientious choice, the person compares the demands of the law with what she knows to be right and wrong. However, it is hard to think of a situation in which a law that is rounded out by the technical, detail-oriented choices of the lawmaker implicates conscience.

---

20   The natural law philosopher John Finnis is the clearest contemporary expositor of *determinatio*. See his discussion of the topic in John Finnis, *Natural Law and Natural Rights* (Oxford: Oxford University Press, 1980), 284–89.

21   Finnis's own example is that of the lawmaker choosing the left-hand side of the road on which to drive and 70 miles per hour as the speed limit. Apart from these details, Finnis makes an important point that can be obscured when focusing on the fact that *determinatio* means that the lawmaker is making choices:
>   But there is also a sense in which (as the general theory claims) the rule of the road gets "all its normative force" ultimately from the permanent principles of practical reason (which require us to respect our own and others' physical safety) in combination with non-posited facts such as that traffic is dangerous and can be made safer by orderly traffic flows and limitation of speed, that braking distances and human reaction times are such-and-such, etc.

   Determinatio is not obviously, yet it is intimately, tied to the ultimate foundations of human law, that which Finnis calls "the permanent principles of practical reason." Ibid., 285.

Rather, for most laws, the law simply is, and the person should have no problem in obeying it.

But most laypersons do not have a strong sense of what it takes to make law. They do not consider that most law consists of mundane details and not dichotomous applied ethical puzzles. I contend that the vast majority of people in the United States and other Western countries give little thought to the deeper purposes that go into creating and enforcing law, and rather think of law in terms of the consequences that will come to them if they break it. These people reflexively are Austinian positivists.[22] In brief, the legal positivism coming from the nineteenth-century jurist and legal philosopher John Austin essentially sees law as a system of social control consisting of orders from a sovereign backstopped by the prospect of force. This is what law *is*. The lawmaker says, "Do x, but if you don't, your freedom will be limited or you will receive some other punishment." Most people accept this and the fact that it is a system of social control ultimately rooted in consequentialism. Obey the law and skirt the consequences. Break the law and suffer the consequences. And this form of consequentialism is a cousin to its intellectual forebear, utilitarianism; for Austinian positivism, at bottom, is perhaps not about gaining the "pleasure" that comes with obeying the law, but avoiding the pain that comes with disobeying it.

Those consequences can be significant: loss of freedom, loss of money, restrictions on one's business, and loss of reputation and concomitant branding as someone who breaks the law. Austinian positivism is a worldview that prizes, above all else, pliant citizens who willingly bend themselves to the expressed will of the lawmaker. It is a view of society that is top down and prizes the authority held by the lawmaker over against the lack of authority and agency held by citizens. If law is threats backed by force, then the number-one objective of someone with an Austinian worldview is not to have force applied to them. That must mean, of course, that that person obeys the law, whether they want to or not, and whether or not that law violates the person's most deeply cherished values that reflect their deepest and most authentic sense of self. For the Austinian positivist, it is more important to comply and keep regular order than to veer out of line and challenge a law that she thinks is unjust.

A view of law that focuses on *determinatio* trusts the lawmaker in fashioning law. A view of law that sees it as threats backed by force is apprehensive of

---

22 See, generally, John Austin, *Austin: The Province of Jurisprudence Determined*, ed. Wilfred E. Rumble (Cambridge: Cambridge University Press, 1995).

both law and those that enforce it. There is a third way, however. The person who takes this middle path can acknowledge the dual realities of the modern administrative state: that the lawmaker must have wide latitude to "fill up" the details of a regulatory scheme, and the citizen must be wary of certain laws that carry heavy punishments. The citizen knows not to murder because that crime carries the very real possibility of indefinite imprisonment or forfeiture of life. In this way, Austinian positivism has a chastening effect—keeping the citizen in line. The Christian should not lose sight that there is more than a hint of Austinianism in the Bible. The Apostle Paul's famous injunction about civil government—that the magistrate "does not bear the sword in vain" (Romans 13:4, NIV)—was, for Paul, a reason to obey the ruler. Compliance triggered by fear is the hallmark of the Austinian way.

But the middle way is to view submission to the law first as a matter of identity and deeply held values. For all of the recent famous cases mentioned at the beginning of this chapter, the person who bore the legal consequences of noncompliance is identified as a committed Christian pursuing whatever profession was the focus of the case. Jack Phillips, for example, is a baker and a "devout Christian."[23] Elaine Huguenin's identity is that of a "devout, practicing Christian," and secondarily a photographer; and the list goes on.[24]

The middle way views submission to legal authority primarily, but not exclusively, as a matter of identity and deeply held values. Jack Phillips refused to bake custom-designed cakes for homosexual weddings and transgender celebrations, but, presumably, he has not refused to comply with a myriad of other legal obligations required of him as a baker. Adhering to cleanliness standards, employment regulations, taxation requirements, and many other picayune regulatory mandates comprises the day-in-day-out stuff of being a baker, without any of which Phillips could not ply his trade.

However, the mundane laws governing the sanitary conditions of his bakery do not offend Phillips's conscience. It is, rather, laws that, according to him, compromise his identity as a Christian that have caused him to make conscientiously informed decisions to refuse service. His and other creators' identities

---

23   *Masterpiece Cakeshop*, 138 S. Ct. at 1724.

24   This phrase comes from a concurrence in the *Elane Photography* case, where Justice Richard C. Bosson writes that "Jonathan and Elaine Huguenot see themselves in much the same position as the students in Barnette. As devout, practicing Christians, they believe, as a matter of faith, that certain commands of the Bible are not left open to secular interpretation; they are meant to be obeyed." *Elane Photography*, 309 P. 3d at 78 (Bosson, J., special concurrence).

are conventional, traditionally conservative, and closely hewing to the values they find in the biblical text. They have identities whose foundation is a particular theological anthropology rooted in a creator God who ordained sexual complementarity and customary male-female marriage. For these creators, to be a Christian means to endorse (or at least not denigrate) traditional, conjugal marriage. For Phillips, Huguenin, and the others, to sell their goods or services in the context of a same-sex or transgender celebration would be to approve as true what their reading of the Bible—and, by extension, the demands of their religion—deem to be false. It would be, for them, to endorse with a beautiful creation, made with hours of careful labor and hard-won skill, that which their god has claimed to be anathema and diametrically opposed to that which their god has claimed to be good, as a matter of first principles.

For Phillips and others, to create artistic works to celebrate that which the Bible condemns is to compromise their Christian identities, and to compromise their Christian identities would be to compromise their *entire* identities. To compromise their entire identities is to live without integrity, and that they refuse to do.

The values/identity approach can be broken into a few general principles:

1. The Christian, in a sense, has a "dual" identity, but it is one based on priorities: Christian first and baker, photographer, florist second. The career identity informs the Christian identity and vice versa, but if there is ever a conflict, the Christian identity wins.
2. The approach is rooted in the Bible and considers as important those things that the Bible considers important: the human person, marriage, obedience, and sin, among other concepts. Conscience is not a "get out of jail free card" for any and all legal or moral obligations. In fact, the vast latticework of legal obligations the conscientious Christian will abide by as a matter of course and will not give a second thought to resisting. Conscientious disobedience is extraordinary and not routine.
3. To the extent that the person senses that her innermost, religiously informed, and religiously formed self is at stake, to that extent she will make conscientious decisions to refuse to do what the law demands. If, however, she perceives that what is most "core" about her *vis-à-vis* what the law demands is not at stake, she will not believe it necessary to make a conscientious decision.

One last point about the values/identity approach: one should not be naive and expect this way of thinking about conscience to be restricted to socially conservative Christians. This is a particular Protestant and personal approach. If the approach depends on the particular Christian's reading of the Bible (with the assistance of the Holy Spirit) for its most salient topics, themes, and instructions, followed by giving those instructions priority for practical obedience, then one should expect Christians who do not hew to a socially conservative worldview to find the values/identity approach attractive.

6 Actions Taken upon Conscientiously Derived Decisions

There are three possibilities for action after the Christian has made a conscience-based decision. The Christian may refuse to obey the legal mandate that, if obeyed, would violate her conscience. Or the Christian may ignore her conscience and obey the legal mandate. Or the Christian may initially refuse to obey the offending legal mandate but later relent and obey it.

The contemporary examples of Christian conscience set out in this chapter—Jack Phillips, Barronelle Stutzman, and Elaine Huguenin—have been of the first type, that is, of refusing to participate in the action mandated by existing law. And all three creators experienced significant consequences to their businesses and reputations for refusing to create an artifact that represented, to them, something false.

A couple of lessons can be drawn from the "resist first" approach—one that forthrightly engages conscience and, at the same time, steers close to an Austinian view of law, in that consequences of noncompliance are laid bare. First, the creators mentioned above have viewed success—or at least the absence of conflict with respect to their career or anything else—as not as important as obedience to the big-picture principles of what they believe the Bible teaches. They perceived the demands of integrity to be far more important than the relative temporal success brought by going along with mandates they despised.

Second, Christians who follow this "resist first" approach should expect their lives, after the decision to resist, to be much more difficult. It is not only that their professional lives likely will not flourish, but those lives will be beset with problems they might not have anticipated when they made the choice to resist. Take, for example, the most obvious problem: litigation. When the wedding creators chose not to make custom creations, those who were refused service did not quietly slink away. They believed that their actionable legal rights were violated, and they pressed those rights before courts and other enforcement bodies. Civil litigation is hard; it is burdensome; it creates stress and uncertainty in plaintiffs who file complaints and defendants who file answers. There are consequences to refusing to do what the mandates require, and it is not obvious that a person should expect to escape those consequences because she is convinced that her reasons for refusing are just or align with the resistor's religious beliefs. Crippling fines, loss of customers, much less loss of the business itself, family strife, and loss of peace, are just some of the repercussions that flow to the person who resists. No one wants this kind of fallout in their life. They invite it and should expect it, however, if they resist what the law demands. If they somehow escape life-altering aftereffects, they should count themselves fortunate.

It is important at this point to say a word about conscience's "sister" legal category, free exercise, and the escape valve in free exercise cases—the exemption. At the beginning of this chapter, I asserted that conscience and free exercise are related yet separate categories. Essentially, conscience is what motivates a Christian (or any other person spurred by moral scruples) to act or refrain from acting in light of a legal mandate. Free exercise, though, is the constellation of doctrines, found in the First Amendment of the U.S. Constitution, that gives a legal claim to religious bodies or persons to make a decision to do any number of religiously inspired actions that might or might not call for a religiously inspired exemption: participate in public worship,[25] refrain from paying for certain pharmaceuticals and medical devices in a for-profit company's health insurance plan,[26] and decide who may be employed as a minister by a church, among many other examples.[27]

Free-exercise claimants who press for an exemption from a generally applicable law essentially deny that they should suffer the consequences that flow from disobeying the law. These claimants hold that their religious practice or exercise is superior in type and priority to a law that applies to all—whether religious or not.

The Christian who takes a "refuse first" approach to conscience should not expect to get an exemption from the law's demands, and she should be ambivalent about receiving one. Biblical conscience is primarily about obeying the Bible's directives, as the Christian understands them. Conscience-based obedience has a distinct "in for a penny, in for a pound," flair to it. The conscientious Christian will soberly reflect on and internalize this prediction from Jesus: "If the world hates you, keep in mind that it hated me first" (John 15:18, NIV), and from Paul: "For it has been granted to you on behalf of Christ not only to believe in him, but also to suffer for him" (Philippians 1:29, NIV). The wedding creators discussed in this chapter have sought to be exempted from generally

---

25 See, for example, *South Bay United Pentecostal Church v. Newsom*, 141 S. Ct. 716 (Feb. 5, 2021) (granting, in part, an injunction against certain restrictions of in-person religious worship made by a state governor in light of the COVID-19 pandemic).

26 See *Burwell v. Hobby Lobby Stores, Inc., and Conestoga Wood Specialties Corporation, v. Burwell*, 573 U.S. 682 (2014).

27 See *Hosanna-Tabor Evangelical Lutheran Church and School v. Equal Employment Opportunity Commission*, 565 U.S. 171 (2012).

applicable laws on one ground or another. Jack Phillips should rejoice that the Supreme Court found that the hard edge of Colorado's antidiscrimination law should not come down on him.[28] That Elaine Huguenin and Barronelle Stutzman did not receive a pass from the consequences of their refusals should remind them (and everyone else) that conscientious obedience comes at a cost, one that should be counted (Luke 14:28).

Second, the Christian who obeys a questionable legal mandate chooses between two options. First, he might have justified to himself that the legal mandate does not implicate the core of his Christian faith. For example, with respect to the wedding-vendor cases, the Christian could view providing creative services for gay couples as a way of demonstrating Christian charity or acceptance. But, on the other hand, the Christian may have considered the consequences of disobedience to be too much to bear. This person lacks courage. For this Christian, the status quo and an undisturbed life are superior to stepping out and making their actions congruent with their beliefs.

But the most perplexing action to take in the face of the prompting of conscience is to first resist what the conscience believes to be an evil mandate and then later give into that mandate. The person who takes this route counts the cost of conscientious resistance and, after traveling on that road and experiencing the consequences of resistance, turns back and relents to the mandate. This is the route of rationalization—of justifying that going back on conscientious resistance, once made, will make for an easier life. This route does not start out as consequentialist, but it ends up there.

7 Conclusion

Christian conscience is venerable. It is as old as Adam and Eve. Conscience is cooperation between the Christian and the Holy Spirit, instantiated through the lifelong process of sanctification. Conscience is a faculty of chosen values and identity. Conscience is resistance to unpalatable legal demands, with a quiet determination to accept whatever consequences come with temporal disobedience. And ultimately, for the Christian, conscience is about having and maintaining a harmonious relationship with God.

---

28 From the biggest-picture perspective, Jack Phillips's case is certainly about him deploying his conscience to obey the tenets of his religion. However, the victory he won at the U.S. Supreme Court should be seen as narrow, reflecting the lack of evenhandedness and "neutrality" required of government enforcement authorities who adjudicate free-exercise claims. See *Masterpiece Cakeshop*, 138 S. Ct. at 1731, 1732.

PART 4

Faith, Law, and Family Historically and Today

∴

CHAPTER 26

The Legal Basis of the Sacramental Theology of Marriage

Philip L. Reynolds

For the past thirty-five years, John Witte has been writing on the history, theology, and law of marriage. His writings on this topic range from biblical and classical texts to the latest cases before American and European courts, with a special emphasis on the impact of the Protestant Reformation on Western marriage law.[1] I was privileged to be part of two major interdisciplinary projects that he codirected with Don Browning and Martin Marty, respectively—one on "Sex, Marriage, and Family and Religions of the Book," the second on "The Child in Law, Religion, and Society." As part of that work, John and I coedited a volume, *To Have and to Hold: Marrying and its Documentation in Western Christendom, 400–1600* (Cambridge University Press, 2007). With his patient encouragement, I also completed a hefty monograph: *How Marriage Became One of the Sacraments: The Sacramental Theology of Marriage from Its Medieval Origins to the Council of Trent* (Cambridge University Press, 2016).

That latter book focuses on how the doctrine of marriage as one of the sacraments of the New Law was constructed by medieval scholastic theologians. In retrospect, we can see the beginnings of the doctrine in anonymous collections of "sentences" compiled during the first quarter of the twelfth century, and it had acquired the de facto status of orthodoxy by the middle of the thirteenth century. Nevertheless, the doctrine was not formally defined as a dogma of the church until the sixteenth century, when the Council of Trent, responding to the Protestant reformers' rejection of Catholic sacramentalism in general and of the sacramentality of marriage in particular, determined that there were exactly seven named sacraments, no more and no less, and that one of these was matrimony: a sacrament in the fullest sense and in every respect.

---

1 See esp. John Witte, Jr., *From Sacrament to Contract: Marriage, Religion, and Law in the Western Tradition,* 2nd ed. (Louisville, KY: Westminster John Knox Press, 2012 [1997]); John Witte, Jr. and Robert M. Kingdon, *Sex, Marriage, and Family in John Calvin's Geneva* (Grand Rapids: Eerdmans, 2006); and John Witte, Jr., *Church, State, and Family: Reconciling Traditional Teachings and Modern Liberties* (Cambridge: Cambridge University Press, 2019).

My purpose in this chapter is to tease out a *legal argument* that runs through this theological development.[2] The argument preoccupied the prelates at Trent during the unusually fraught and protracted proceedings that were eventually settled in the decree *Tametsi* (1563). Looking back, however, we may find its seeds as early as the twelfth century. These seeds involved two things: a cluster of theological problems regarding the unusual composition of this particular sacrament; and the pastoral problem of clandestine marriages. A marriage was deemed clandestine when it was not contracted *in conspectu ecclesiae* (in the sight of the church), or *in facie ecclesiae* (before the church),[3] although what this condition required was not defined precisely until 1563.

The legal argument that I am teasing out in this chapter was a feature of theology, and not of canon law. After the marriage decretals of Pope Alexander III (reigned 1159–81), the results of which the theologians did their best to accommodate, medieval canon law contributed very little to the development of the sacramental doctrine of marriage.

1 Preliminary Observations

Scholastic theology emerged in the cathedral schools of northern Europe during the first quarter of the twelfth century. Among the traits that characterized this earliest scholastic theology were: an effort to systematize and to present essential theological truths in a readily accessible and watertight form; the posing and resolution of apparent inconsistencies in the textual traditions; a pragmatic emphasis, aimed at providing priests with the information that they needed for their ministry; and the harvesting of and reflection on more or less authoritative excerpts (*sententiae*) gathered chiefly from patristic writings but also from the work of recent and contemporaneous masters. The practice of collecting and reflecting on *sententiae* supplemented commentary on scripture, which was always the core of scholastic theology. As well as stirring up intellectual inquiry and debate, it paved the way for greater systematization.

Sacramental theology as an organized field of study and an apt topic for treatises emerged quickly in the context of the new scholastic theology, and the theology of marriage as one of the sacraments emerged concurrently with

---

2 The argument is a feature of Philip L. Reynolds, *How Marriage Became One of the Sacraments: The Sacramental Theology of Marriage from Its Medieval Origins to the Council of Trent* (Cambridge: Cambridge University Press, 2016) [hereafter, Reynolds, *One of the Sacraments*].

3 This phrase may originally or sometimes have meant "at the entry to a church."

this new sacramental theology.[4] It was designed to demonstrate that marriage was a valid Christian vocation while saving, nonetheless, the superiority of the celibate vocations, including those of the clergy in higher orders (subdeacons, deacons, and priests).[5] The theology also confirmed the clergy's legal and moral authority regarding the marriages of their parishioners.

The discipline of scholastic theology advanced considerably from around 1130 to the 1270s, as regards both its methodology and its knowledge base. The *quaestio*—a pair of plausible but mutually contradictory propositions in search of resolution—proved to be a much more powerful tool than the *sententia*. Theologians of the thirteenth and fourteenth centuries, informed by Aristotle and by Muslim and Jewish philosophy, were increasingly attracted to speculative inquiry, so that theology became the subtlest and most demanding of intellectual disciplines, presupposing many years of study. These developments coincided in northern Europe with the transition from cathedral schools to corporate universities, but few of the new universities during the thirteenth century had faculties of theology. (Paris was the most notable exception.) Scholastic theology during the thirteenth and fourteenth centuries was largely the province of the mendicant orders, especially the Dominicans and Franciscans: friars dedicated to preaching and confession. The friars practiced in their own houses of study the methods of teaching, study, and inquiry that had evolved in the urban schools.

The development of the sacramental theology of marriage went through three busy and highly productive periods, between which not much happened. The first period begins in the early twelfth century and culminates in Peter Lombard's *Sentences* (1158), in four books, which would prove to be the most successful and enduring textbook of theology.[6] The Lombard devoted most of the fourth book to the seven sacraments, with a treatise on the sacraments in general and then a treatise on each of the seven in turn. (Prior to Peter Lombard, it seems, no one had been counting!)[7] The last of these sacramental treatises, on marriage, is the longest, but the reasons for its length have less to do with theological considerations per se than with the many rules and regulations that marrying entailed.[8] The second busy period runs from the late twelfth century until about 1270. During this period, the sacramentality

---
4   Reynolds, *One of the Sacraments*, 291–361.
5   See Luke 20:34–35.
6   P. W. Rosemann, *The Story of a Great Medieval Book: Peter Lombard's Sentences* (Toronto: University of Toronto Press, 2013).
7   On the emergence of the idea of there being exactly *seven* sacraments, see Reynolds, *One of the Sacraments*, 21–28.
8   Peter Lombard, *Sent.* IV, dist. 26–42. Reynolds, *One of the Sacraments*, 422–36.

of marriage was the subject of highly technical theological inquiry. The third period is dominated by the Council of Trent (1545–63), although in retrospect one can find precedents in theological writings over the previous half century.

A major difference between the first and the second of these periods pertains to the tolerance for anomalies and inconsistencies. Twelfth-century theologians took these in stride. Indeed, the earliest extant statement identifying marriage as one of the sacraments (ca. 1125) presents this situation as an anomaly: "Whereas all the sacraments [including marriage] were instituted after sin and because of sin, marriage alone was also instituted before sin occurred, and not as a remedy, like the others, but as a duty."[9] Among the commonplaces of sacramental theology from around 1130 until the end of the twelfth century were (a) that the sacraments of the New Law, by definition, both signified and conferred special sacramental graces, and (b) that the sacrament of marriage, which was one of those sacraments, did not. Thirteenth-century theologians, on the contrary, were troubled by such anomalies and worked to resolve them. By 1250, most theologians agreed that marriage conferred a specific sacramental grace—a thesis that the canonists ignored for centuries. Thus, whereas twelfth-century theologians had regarded marriage as an integral but exceptional instrument within a sevenfold sacramental system, thirteenth-century theologians construed marriage as a species within the univocal genus of the sacraments of the New Law, also known as the sacraments of the church.

Two clarifications are in order before we proceed. First, when medieval writers spoke of the *sacrament* of matrimony, they were almost always referring to the act of getting married (that is, to the partners' mutual plighting of troth), and not to the consequent and life-long condition of being married. In this respect, the sacrament of marriage was comparable to that of baptism, which occurred momentarily at the font but established a life-long condition. Second, throughout the period under discussion, theologians as well as canonists assumed that marriage was wholly subject to ecclesiastical jurisdiction as regards its validity or invalidity.[10] Ecclesiastical authority alone, vested in bishops, councils, and popes, had both legislative and jurisdictional power over marriage: the power to determine the rules pertaining to validity, the diriment impediments, and so forth; and the power to determine through episcopal courts whether a particular marriage was invalid, so that the divorced partners would be free to marry others. The church courts even reserved the right to

---

9 *Cum omnia sacramenta*, ed. F. P. Bliemetzrieder, *Anselms von Laon systematische Sentenzen*, in *Beiträge zur Geschichte der Philosophie des Mittelalters* 18.2–3 (Münster: Aschendorff, 1919), 129.
10 Reynolds, *One of the Sacraments*, 33–51.

settle any secular consequences of a divorce, such as those pertaining to dowries. It should go without saying that this authority was not always respected, and that people in search of marital remedies sometimes sought relief from secular authorities. Uniformity was not a salient feature of medieval Europe, although the "clerical takeover" of marriage during this period was remarkably successful. In any case, such anomalies had no bearing on what the theologians taught about marriage.

2 A Hybrid Sacrament

As one of the seven sacraments of the New Law, marriage deserved to be celebrated in a church ritual, ideally with family members and other representatives of the community in attendance to witness the change of status taking place in their midst. Parish priests were supposed to oversee the process of marrying, and the ceremony of marriage was in itself a teaching opportunity. At the core of the church wedding, aside from the legal formalities, were the nuptial blessing and ritual acts of joining, such as the *dextrarum iunctio* (the priest's joining of the spouses' right hands). The popularity of the *dextrarum iunctio* in religious art as an image of marrying increased as the doctrine of marriage as one of the seven sacraments of the New Law became more deeply entrenched in the minds of the clergy and pious layfolk.[11]

Before *Tametsi*, however, the mutual agreement (*consensus*) of the spouses in the present tense, provided that there was no impediment of relationship, sufficed to make a valid and indissoluble marriage. No particular form of words was required, although some became customary. The record of witnesses might be necessary if the validity of a marriage became the subject of litigation, but witnessing was evidence that the act had occurred. It was not an integral component of the act itself. Hugh of Saint-Victor (d. 1141), in an early discussion of the perils of clandestinity, noted that the problem would go away if marriages had to be celebrated in church, but he conceded that the consensus of tradition ruled out that option.[12] One might speculate about the probable reasons for this resistance, which sharply distinguished Roman from Eastern Christianity, but that would be a topic for another essay.

The Fourth Lateran Council of 1215, in canon 51, prohibited clandestine marriages and declared that spouses who married clandestinely must make an

---

11   Ibid., 89–93.
12   Hugh of Saint-Victor, *De sacramentis christianae fidei* II.11.6, PL 176:488–494. Reynolds, *One of the Sacraments*, 398–400.

appropriate penance (*condigna poenitentia*). Although clandestine marriages were illicit and sinful, therefore, they were not invalid. The chief innovation of canon 51 was the extension of the reading of the banns, an Anglo-Norman practice that probably began in England, to the universal church. All parish priests were now required to announce a forthcoming marriage and, meanwhile, to conduct an inquiry to ascertain whether there was any impediment. (There were no precise details. Much was left to regional custom.) Priests who in any way connived in or failed to prevent clandestine marrying were to be suspended from office, for three years in the first instance.[13]

Professional theologians, therefore, had to accommodate the fact that this particular sacrament of the New Law, alone among the seven, could be validly performed without any prescribed verbal formula and even without the ministry of a priest. Theologians held that the nuptial blessing and ritual acts such as the joining of right hands pertained to the sacrament not *de necessitate* but only *de solemnitate*, like the priest's blessing of the water before the rite of baptism, and the mingling of a little water with the wine during the eucharistic rite.[14] The idea that the nuptial blessing or ritual joining of the couple was integral to the sacrament was always tempting, and some theologians tried to accommodate it, but it was too much at variance with accepted law and tradition to take root. Theologians might still argue that the absence of the ritual component meant that the sacrament was deficient in some sense—for example, that the sin of clandestinity was an obstacle to the reception of nuptial grace—but they were bound to accept that spouses who married clandestinely, provided that their *consensus* was authentic and that there was no impediment of relationship, were sacramentally bound together.

The validity of clandestine marriages was one of a cluster of anomalies pertaining to the unusually hybrid nature of the sacrament. The sacraments of baptism and Eucharist provided a model that theologians applied, *mutatis mutandis*, to the other five, but whereas baptism was only a symbolic washing, and Eucharist only a symbolic meal, sacramental marriage was a real marriage. Again, sacraments typically involved a priest's uttering of a prescribed sacred formula over some prescribed material stuff: bread and wine, or water, or chrism. The two components could be regarded as *verbum* (word) and *elementum* (stuff), respectively, according to an analysis that went back to Augustine, but scholastic theologians, well-versed in Aristotelian philosophy, preferred to think of them as form and matter. The hylomorphic analysis was more flexible

---

13 Reynolds, *One of the Sacraments*, 472–73.
14 Ibid., 592–99, especially 597 (on Thomas Aquinas).

than that of *verbum* and *elementum*, but even so, applying it to marriage was, at best, a stretch.

Most important of all, a salient feature of the sacraments, properly so called, was that the persons who received them did precisely that: their role was wholly receptive and passive. This is what was meant by saying that the sacraments performed their saving work *ex opere operato*—a scholastic phrase that the Council of Trent would include in its dogmatic statements on the sacraments. The agent was a ministering priest, and the recipients received the sacramental grace from a sacrament unerringly unless they put some obstacle in its way, such as an incompatible intention or a mortal sin. But in marriage, the recipients were also the agents of the sacrament. In effect, the spouses themselves were the ministers of this sacrament, although medieval theologians rarely spoke of the spouses as ministers. (The term would have implied that they were priests.)

Two Dominican theologians, Albertus Magnus (c. 1200–1280) and Thomas Aquinas (1225–1274), recognized to an unprecedented extent that marriage could be adequately explained as to its raison d'être and its rationale in political, merely human terms, prior to its special status as a sacrament. Here, the quotable experts were not Augustine and Gregory the Great but Aristotle and Cicero.

Albert and Thomas parsed marriage in terms of diverse branches of law. For example, Albertus Magnus claimed that marriage had undergone four historically cumulative "institutions," pertaining respectively to the natural law, to the Mosaic law, to the civil law (as embodied in the *Corpus Iuris Civilis*), and to the New Law of Jesus Christ.[15] And Thomas Aquinas proposed in the *Summa contra gentiles* that marriage was subject to three regimes: as the means of perpetuating the human species, it is an "office of nature," subject to the natural law; as the means of perpetuating the political community, it is subject to the civil law; and as the means of perpetuating the ecclesiastical community, it is subject to the governance (*regimen*) of the church.[16] There is no suggestion here, however, that marriage might be subject to multiple jurisdictions. As the superior court, canonical jurisdiction trumped secular jurisdiction over marriage.

---

15   Albertus Magnus, *IV Sent.* 26.14, q. 1, resp. For commentary, see Reynolds, *One of the Sacraments*, 699–700. Western theologians and canonists regarded the Justinianic corpus as the most authoritative embodiment of *civil* law.

16   Thomas Aquinas, *Summa contra gentiles* IV, cap. 78. For commentary, see Reynolds, *One of the Sacraments*, 715–17.

3 Marriage as Contract and Sacrament

In his *Scriptum* (his commentary on the *Sentences* of Peter Lombard), Thomas Aquinas distinguishes between the contract and the sacrament of marriage. Thomas characterizes the two components as material and spiritual, respectively. Thus, the sacrament of marriage presupposes what Thomas calls a "material contract." Assuming that every sacrament has analogous material and spiritual aspects, Thomas claims that the contract is related to the sacrament of marriage as ablution with water is related to the sacrament of baptism.[17] Every sacrament presupposes some natural or material entity that is raised to the spiritual level of a sacrament. It is because marriage is a contract, according to Thomas, and not because it is a sacrament, that it requires an agreement to be outwardly expressed in words or equivalent signs.[18] Thomas did not develop this theory extensively per se, but he used it as the key to explaining why the sacrament of marriage was peculiarly subject to positive legislation, and thus to changes regarding its sine qua non conditions, such as those pertaining to the impediments of age and relationship.[19] The purpose of such legislation, in his view, is to enhance the personal, familial, and political benefits of marriage.[20] The church's interests in such legislation are more elevated than those of merely secular political communities, but they are not essentially different. Construed as a contract, marriage is regulated by the commonwealth (the political community), which has the power to alter the preconditions required for valid contracts. Construed as a sacrament, marriage had been instituted once and for all by Jesus Christ, and only the "solemnities" (accidental ritual aspects) of the sacrament could be changed. Henceforth, theologians analyzed marriage in relation to two distinct domains, respectively contractual and sacramental, each illuminated by its own set of texts and theories. The sacrament presupposed the contract.

The contract-sacrament theory would prove to be the key that enabled the Council of Trent to rule that clandestine marriages would henceforth be invalid.[21] The Council regarded the writings of the medieval scholastic theologians as authoritative guides to doctrine, especially the *Summa theologiae* of Thomas Aquinas. Thomas had fallen silent before reaching the sacrament

---

17   Thomas Aquinas, *IV Sent.* d. 27, q. 1, a. 2, qu^a 1 [= *Suppl.* q. 45, a. 1], resp. & ad 1.
18   *IV Sent.* d. 27, q. 1, a. 2, qu^a 1 [= *Suppl.* q. 45, a. 1], resp.
19   *IV Sent.* d. 36, q. un., a. 5, [= *Suppl.* q. 58, a. 5], resp.
20   *IV Sent.* d. 40, q. un., a. 3 [= *Suppl.* q. 54, a. 3], resp.
21   André Duval, "Contrat et sacrement de mariage au concile de Trente," *La Maison-Dieu* 127 (1976): 34–63; and idem, "Le concile de Trente et la distinction entre le contrat et le sacrement de marriage," *Revues des sciences philosophiques et théologiques* 65 (1981): 286–94.

of marriage in his great *Summa*, but his extensive treatment of marriage in his early *Scriptum* would have been familiar to the theologians[22] at the Council through its inclusion in the *Supplementum* posthumously appended to the unfinished *Summa theologiae*. (The supplement was a reworking of material from the early *Scriptum*.) But the understanding of the contract-sacrament theory at Trent owed more to some sixteenth-century theologians than to Thomas himself—especially two doctors of Louvain, Adrian Florensz (the future Pope Hadrian VI, d. 1523) and Ruard Tapper (d. 1559), who had elaborated Thomas's theory. Both emphasized the power of a commonwealth (*res publica*) to regulate the nuptial contracts of its citizens.[23] Marriage without a valid contract, in their view, was like baptism without water. No theologian before 1563, however, had used this rationale to justify the invalidation of clandestine marriage.

4 Clandestine Marriage at the Council of Trent

Before 1563, most theologians held that marriages contracted clandestinely, other things being equal, were valid and insoluble. A few theologians were inclined to regard the nuptial blessing (with the joining of right hands) as a sacramental form, without which the union would be at best a valid contract. This opinion was not without appeal, for it was congruent with how clergy and layfolk imagined marriage as one of the sacraments of the church. Nevertheless, it was too much at variance with established legal and theological tradition to take root.

By the sixteenth century, however, the perennial anxiety about the perils of clandestine marriage had become febrile.[24] Churchmen, intellectuals, and orators, troubled by change and uncertainty, dreamed of an orderly political community rooted in marriage and the family, and they extolled the benign rule of the *paterfamilias*. Marriage, in their view, was fundamental to familial and civic well-being, whereas both clandestine marriages and marriages of minors without parental consent were subversive. Protestants criticized the church of Rome for accepting clandestine marriages as valid, but Catholic churchmen were no less troubled by them. To be sure, the fact that clandestinity made it easier for minors to marry without parental consent was part of the perceived problem. (These two issues, while separable in essence, were

---

22 Only a few of the bishops were qualified in theology, but many theologians were present at the Council as advisers to bishops.
23 Reynolds, *One of the Sacraments*, 907–15.
24 Ibid., 772–86.

initially intertwined during the proceedings of 1563. To the great indignation of the French, however, the council did not invalidate the marriages of minors without parental consent.) But that does not account for the dismay with which churchmen regarded clandestinely contracted marriages. The very term "clandestine" was pejorative.

Some writings on clandestine marriages during the half century before *Tametsi* illustrate how churchmen and theologians were thinking about the problem. The contributions of Johann Gropper (d. 1559) and Domingo de Soto (d. 1560) are especially revealing.[25] Gropper had a degree in law, and he was not a professional theologian. That did not prevent him from thinking deeply about theological problems, but his perspective on marriage was that of a concerned pastor and administrator. Domingo de Soto, in contrast, was a Dominican professor of theology with a distinguished chair at the University of Salamanca.

As assistant to Hermann von Wied, the reform-minded archbishop-elector of Cologne, Gropper organized the provincial council of Cologne in 1536. Clandestine marriage was on the agenda. Gropper regarded Cologne's decisions as merely provisional because he looked forward keenly to the long-awaited general council, which would surely take place soon. One outcome of the provincial council was Gropper's *Enchiridion christianae institutionis*: a practical manual of theology written to meet the needs of parochial clergy. It includes a treatise on the seven sacraments, with a section on each of the seven, including marriage. When the decrees of the council were published in 1538, Gropper's *Enchiridion* was appended anonymously, and it became conflated with the council's decisions. The prelates at Trent cited the section on marriage in the *Enchiridion* frequently during the deliberations of 1563, ascribing it to the provincial council.

Gropper discussed clandestine marriage at length. In his view, the abuse was a result of declining religious and civic standards: to the impiety and vulgarity of his own day. He looked back to a golden age when all marriages had been formally, liturgically, and splendidly celebrated. Gropper argued that a clandestinely contracted marriage was not really a sacrament but only a contract. As such, it was not necessarily insoluble. His reasoning was based on arguments not about the form or the essence of the sacrament, but about the intention of the participants. Spouses who married without the proper intentions befitting a sacrament would not receive the sacrament.[26]

---

25   On Johann Gropper's contribution, see Reynolds, *One of the Sacraments*, 759–72. On Domingo de Soto's, see ibid., 788–800.

26   Johann Gropper, *Enchiridion christianae institutionis in Concilio prouinciali Coloniensi editum* (Paris: Apud haeredes Mauricij à Porta, 1558), *De matrimonio* (= ff. 174r–192v). Reynolds, *One of the Sacraments*, 759–72.

Domingo de Soto wrote about the sacrament of marriage in his commentary on Book IV of Peter Lombard's *Sentences*, composed toward the end of his life.[27] He had attended the Council of Trent during the first of its three periods (1545–47) as a theologian appointed by the Holy Roman Emperor. He also led the Dominican theologians on behalf of their minister general and represented the theology faculty of Salamanca. He remarks in the commentary on the initial discussion of clandestine marriage at Bologna in 1547, although he had remained in Trent with the prelates loyal to the emperor. (Pope Paul III attempted to transfer the proceedings to Bologna on March 11, 1547, but there was too much opposition, and Paul's successor, Julius III, reconvened the council at Trent in 1551.) De Soto carefully discusses the theory that the nuptial blessing is the essential form of the sacrament, but he finds that it is too much at variance with the analysis of scholastic theological tradition, and he rejects it.[28]

As to the possibility of making clandestine marriage invalid, De Soto concedes that only a general council or the pope[29] can settle this matter definitively, but he argues that a clandestine marriage, however undesirable, must be valid because the agreement (*consensus*) of the spouses is sufficient. In no other sacrament is the action of the participants more essential and central than it is in marriage, he argues, or the action of an appointed minister more accidental and peripheral. Because the *consensus* of the recipients constitutes both the matter and the form of this sacrament, as Thomas Aquinas held, the sacrament is complete without the ministry of a priest, which is essential in the other six sacraments. De Soto concludes that marriages contracted clandestinely are valid and sacramental and can even confer nuptial grace.[30] Few professional theologians would have disagreed at that time.

At session 7 (March 3, 1547), the Council of Trent had defined the doctrine on the sacraments in general as well as the doctrines on baptism and confirmation in particular. There are exactly seven sacraments of the New Law, according to this definition: baptism, confirmation, Eucharist, penance, extreme unction, orders, and matrimony. No one may add to or subtract from this list. These sacraments were instituted by Jesus Christ, and they are necessary for salvation, for each sacrament contains the grace that it signifies and confers it *ex opere operato* on recipients who present no obstacle to such grace.[31]

---

27   Domingo de Soto, *In quartum librum Sententiarum*, 2 vols. (Salamanca, 1566–1579). Reynolds, *One of the Sacraments*, 788–800.
28   De Soto, *IV Sent*. 26.2.3. Reynolds, *One of the Sacraments*, 796–98.
29   The issue of conciliarism (whether supreme human authority over the church was vested in the pope or in a general council) was still unsettled: hence the disjunction.
30   De Soto, *IV Sent*. 28.1. Reynolds, *One of the Sacraments*, 798–800.
31   Reynolds, *One of the Sacraments*, 809–10.

It was at this point that the council moved to Bologna, where discussion of the sacrament of matrimony and of the reform of clandestine marriage began (April 26, 1547), but no decisions were reached at Bologna.[32] The council resumed in Trent in 1551, but discussion of the sacrament of matrimony had to wait until 1563.

Some clarifications about Tridentine procedures are in order here. First, the council distinguished systematically between decisions regarding dogma (*de dogmatibus*), which defined matters of faith, and decisions of discipline, or reform (*de reformatione*). The former were mostly expressed as condemnations anathematizing those who contradicted the doctrine. Because these canons were considered to be authentic judgments of truth, they were inalterable. Decisions about matters of discipline, on the contrary, were capable of being revoked or amended later. Second, we are remarkably well-informed about the deliberations of the council thanks to Angelo Massarelli, secretary to the council, who diligently recorded the proceedings. These *acta* were inaccessible until the 1880s,[33] but they are available today, together with related records and documents, in superb volumes published under the aegis of the Societas Goerresiana.[34]

The dogmatic canons and the decrees of reform regarding the sacrament of matrimony underwent four drafts, presented for discussion on July 20, August 7, September 5, and October 13, respectively. The last of these drafts was finally ratified on November 11 at the conclusion to session 24 (the penultimate session of the council).

The dogmatic canons did not present any serious difficulties and were settled quickly, but the decree of reform regarding clandestine marriages required lengthy discussion and brought to light profound and irreconcilable differences among the prelates.[35] The plan was to make clandestinity a diriment impediment. The proponents of invalidation outnumbered the opponents in the ratio roughly of five to two. Very few prelates changed sides, and the two camps remained stable throughout the discussion of the four drafts and at the conclusion of session 24. The division did not run entirely along regional or

---

32 Ibid., 810–17.
33 See Owen Chadwick, *Catholicism and History: The Opening of the Vatican Archives* (Cambridge: Cambridge University Press, 1978), 46–71.
34 *Concilium Tridentinum: Diariorum, actorum, epistularum, tractatuum nova collectio* (Friburgi Brisgoviae: Herder, 1901–). Volume 9, ed. S. Ehses, published in 1924, contains the proceedings of 1563.
35 Reynolds, *One of the Sacraments*, 896–982. I say "prelates" because as well as clerics holding office as bishops, archbishops, or patriarchs, some heads of religious orders and abbots of major monasteries were also included among the voting delegates.

provincial lines, but most of the opponents were Italians, and roughly half of the Italian prelates were opponents.

The opponents' case included three chief lines of argument. First, the invalidation of clandestine marriages was impossible because no merely human authority had the power to change the essence of a sacrament, which Jesus Christ himself had defined when he instituted the sacrament. Second, invalidation of the *persons* who could contract marriage was one thing; invalidation of the *manner* (*modus*) of marrying was quite another. There was precedent for changing the first aspect through positive law, but there was no precedent for changing the second aspect. Third, it was absurd to include the witnessing of an act within the definition of the act itself.

The proponents found their theological solution in the theory of marriage as a contract-sacrament. Just as baptism presupposed water, so the sacrament of marriage presupposed a material contract, which was regulated by the Christian commonwealth (*res publica christiana*). Consider what would happen, some proponents argued, if the wine offered on the altar changed into vinegar before the priest consecrated it. In that case, the consecration would not achieve transubstantiation—precisely *because* the essence defined as necessary for the sacrament remained unchanged. Just so, the proposed reform would invalidate the contract of marriage, preventing the sacrament, but it would "not touch the sacrament" (an oft-repeated phrase) by altering its conditions. No one contested the power of a commonwealth to include witnessing among the conditions for a valid contract.

Hitherto, theologians had used the analysis of marriage as a contract-sacrament to show why the rules determining who was capable of marrying whom could be changed by positive legislation. Now, the same analysis justified the invalidation of marriages contracted clandestinely: a major innovation (with the shift from persons to mode). The conditions for the validity of the contract were regulated by the Christian commonwealth, or *res publica christiana*, which had the power to change them.

These arguments did not appear in the decree of reform itself (*Tametsi*). We know about them from the *acta*, which should be studied in light of contemporaneous treatises prompted by the proceedings.

The initial word of the decree, *Tametsi* ("Although"), first appears in the second draft of the decree. Its appearance coincides with the excision of a dogmatic canon anathematizing those who held clandestine marriages to be invalid (namely, the Protestants), which had been in the first draft. To make this a matter of dogma obviously made little sense in the circumstances, and the canon was dropped. Thus, *although* the church has until now regarded clandestine marriages as valid, the decree explains, she has always abhorred them, and moral suasion has proved ineffective; and although the heretics were wrong to claim that clandestine marriages were already invalid, the church will render them invalid henceforth. The decree sets out all the conditions for a *bona fide*, ecclesiastical marriage, but the only strictly sine qua non condition is the presence of the parish priest or his delegate and of at least two other witnesses. The priest's essential role is that of chief witness, and not that of a liturgist or sacramental minister. The decree also states that the priest "shall either say, 'I join you together in marriage, in the name of the Father, the Son, and the Holy Spirit,' *or use other words according to the received rite of each province*" (my italics.) The fact that other words could be used instead of the recommended ones demonstrated to anyone who was theologically literate that this formula was not an essential sacramental form, which would have been universal and inalterable.

Clandestine marriages would henceforth be invalid, but not by their very nature or according to divine or natural law, as some had argued, but only as a result of new positive legislation. This was a very remarkable decision. The new legislation presupposed that the true church, headed by the bishop of Rome as the vicegerent of Jesus Christ, was not only the mystical body of Christ but also the Christian commonwealth, or *res publica christiana*. Without "touching" this sacrament, which, like the other six, Jesus Christ had instituted as a prolongation of his earthly ministry, the church as the *res publica christiana* had changed the conditions necessary for a valid *contract* of marriage.

CHAPTER 27

Law, Religion, and Education

Kathleen A. Brady

"Keep these words that I am commanding you today in your heart," Moses said of God's law, and "[r]ecite them to your children and talk about them when you are at home and when you are away, when you lie down and when you rise."[1] This teaching is "for our lasting good, so as to keep us alive," and "[i]f we diligently observe" it, "we will be in the right."[2] "Train children in the right way," Solomon later echoed, "and when old, they will not stray."[3] These words from the Jewish and Christian traditions reflect a common understanding among religious believers about the most fundamental purposes of education. Education has many functions, all would agree. It prepares children to live with others in society, succeed in the economy, and govern together in a shared polity, as today's scholars frequently emphasize. It also enables children to develop into independent adults capable of making their own decisions and taking responsibility for their own lives, others highlight. Its content has inherent value, increasing human understanding, developing human excellences, and driving human progress, others observe. From a religious perspective, however, the purposes of education go deeper and require more. Human flourishing has moral and spiritual components, and to teach a child well requires a broader perspective that embraces the full range of human goods. Education is, moreover, formative. It initiates each new generation into traditions of thought and practice that carry insights about right living, truths about human nature and ends, and the promise of connection to the divine source of all of these. Indeed, life itself, in all of its dimensions, depends upon these insights and connections, and parents bear the primary responsibility to ensure the transmission of this wisdom.

For a century American constitutional law has recognized robust parental rights to direct the education and upbringing of their children, especially their religious education, but this framework has come under deepening attack. Scholars have argued that the requirements of civic education in a democracy place significant restrictions on these rights when parents make educational

---

1 Deuteronomy 6:6–7 (New Revised Standard Version).
2 Deuteronomy 6:24–25.
3 Proverbs 22:6.

choices that limit the exposure of their children to alternative points of view or consideration of different value systems. Others have argued that exposure and engagement with ideological diversity is essential for children to develop and express their own views and that children should play a greater role in making decisions about the type and scope of their education even when parents disagree. Scholars advocating child-centered perspectives have frequently called for the dramatic curtailment, reconceptualization, and even abandonment of parental rights in favor of approaches that prioritize children's rights and interests. Much of this scholarship has been critical of the educational practices of conservative religious believers, including homeschooling, separatist religious schools, and demands for exemptions from curriculum requirements in public schools. These practices have been condemned as harmful to both children and society alike.

In this chapter, I engage some of these critiques in light of John Witte's important historical work on the family in Western thought. The family, Witte has argued, can be conceived of as a multidimensional sphere, with natural goods and functions at one pole; social, economic, communicative, and contractual dimensions in the middle; and spiritual aspirations and ideals at the other pole, binding the rest together.[4] Children's interests and rights have had an important place in Western constructions of the family sphere, as have civic concerns, but these have also been integrated with other important concepts. These include parental duties that complement parental rights, and reciprocal rights and duties of children. Likewise, the health of human society depends upon the protection of the family and its mutually supportive relationships from state encroachment, even as families also depend upon the aid of other institutions, including both church and state.

Critics of America's constitutional framework frequently argue that expansive parental rights subsume children, hiding their needs and interests in a mythical private family unit and turning them into instruments of parental desires and objectives. They view their work as recovering the child and their rights. Witte's scholarship affirms the importance of children's rights, but it uncovers much more nuance from the Western tradition. Parents and children share interlocking rights and duties, and they form parts of multiple communities that must respect human autonomy while also making room for the capacity and desire of human persons to seek the truth, live rightly, and reach for the source of these human goods. There must be limits on parental rights where they compromise essential needs of children and vital interests

---

4 John Witte, Jr., *Church, State, and Family: Reconciling Traditional Teachings and Modern Liberties* (Cambridge: Cambridge University Press, 2019), 14–15, 186.

of the larger society, and Witte's work helps us to see where these limits might be drawn. However, he also points us to the promise of greater cooperation among parents, religious communities, and the state. Notwithstanding America's diversity, conservative religious believers share with others many of the same values, concerns and goals for children, and true partnerships between parents and government actors will go much further toward meeting the needs and interests of children than will competitive relationships or isolated efforts.

1   Parental Rights under Current Constitutional Law

A century ago, in *Meyer v. Nebraska*, the Supreme Court recognized a constitutional right of parents to direct the education of their children and tied this right to a "corresponding" "natural duty."[5] The *Meyer* Court struck down a state law that prohibited the teaching of foreign languages to children in schools before they had graduated from the eighth grade. The Court recognized that the state may "do much" to promote the intellectual, moral, and civic education of children, including adopting reasonable regulations for all schools,[6] but this law was "arbitrary and without reasonable relation" to any legitimate goals.[7] Education in a foreign language is not harmful to children, and the state had other ways to promote the assimilation of immigrants into American society.[8] The Court contrasted the Constitution's protection for parental rights to Plato's ideal commonwealth, where children were held in common to "submerge the individual and develop ideal citizens."[9] Two years later, in *Pierce v. Society of Sisters*, the Court struck down a state law requiring all students between the ages of eight and sixteen to attend a public school.[10] The Court repeated that parents have a constitutional right "to direct the upbringing and education of children under their control,"[11] and while the state may reasonably regulate all schools,[12] it may not seek to "standardize its children by forcing them to accept instruction from public teachers only."[13] "The child is not the mere creature of the State," the Court said famously, and "those who nurture him and direct his

---

5   262 U.S. 390, 400 (1923).
6   Ibid., 401–02.
7   Ibid., 403.
8   Ibid.
9   Ibid., 402.
10 268 U.S. 510, 530, 536 (1925).
11 Ibid., 534–35.
12 Ibid., 534.
13 Ibid., 535.

destiny have the right, coupled with the high duty, to recognize and prepare him for additional obligations."[14]

Almost fifty years later, in *Wisconsin v. Yoder*,[15] the Court drew on *Pierce* to articulate especially strong protections where state regulation would interfere with the religious upbringing and education of children. *Pierce* "stands as a charter of the rights of parents to direct the religious upbringing of their children," the Court stated.[16] The Constitution protects the "primary role of the parents in the upbringing of their children,"[17] and "when the interests of parenthood" are combined with a burden on religious exercise, more than a reasonable exercise of state power is required to justify state interference.[18] Heightened scrutiny applies instead, and the state must show that its restrictions are necessary to achieve "interests of the highest order."[19] The *Yoder* Court held that Wisconsin may not require Amish parents to send their children to school beyond the eighth grade. The Amish have their own traditions for preparing adolescents for the community's simple life of farming and related work,[20] and replacing two years of high school with this informal vocational education would not endanger the physical or mental health of Amish children,[21] threaten the public peace, safety, or order,[22] impede the ability of Amish youth to develop into responsible democratic citizens,[23] or prevent them from becoming self-reliant members of society, even if they choose to leave the Amish community in the future.[24] On the other hand, forcing Amish children to attend high school would undermine their integration into the Amish community and expose them to competing "worldly influences,"[25] with the effect of "influenc[ing], if not determin[ing], the[ir] religious future"[26] and potentially destroying the community's way of life.[27]

---

14   Ibid.
15   406 U.S. 205 (1972).
16   Ibid., 233.
17   Ibid., 232.
18   Ibid., 233.
19   Ibid., 215.
20   Ibid., 211–12, 222–24.
21   Ibid., 230.
22   Ibid.
23   Ibid., 221–27.
24   Ibid., 221–25.
25   Ibid., 210–12, 217–18.
26   Ibid., 232.
27   Ibid., 218–19.

To the dissent's objection that Amish children may want to become pianists, astronauts, or oceanographers one day and should have the right to be heard,[28] the majority responded that the issue of the children's desires is not before the Court.[29] Even if it were, the majority continued, recognition of an independent right like this would "call into question" parental prerogatives recognized by the Court and "give rise to grave questions of religious freedom."[30] The dissent drew a disparaging picture of Amish parents "harness[ing]" potentially unwilling children "to the Amish way of life" with the effect of "truncat[ing]" their education and "stunt[ing] and deform[ing]" their entire lives.[31] Three justices concurring in the majority opinion explained that they were not convinced that Amish children would be "intellectually stultified or unable to acquire new academic skills later," should they choose to leave the Amish community.[32] The majority also drew a more flattering picture. The Amish community's "idiosyncratic separateness exemplifies the diversity we profess to admire and encourage,"[33] the Court stated, and we cannot "assum[e] that today's majority [culture] is 'right' and the Amish and others like them are 'wrong.'"[34]

In each of these cases, the Court tied parental rights to direct the education of children to corresponding duties. *Yoder* echoed *Pierce* that parents have "the right, coupled with the high duty, to recognize and prepare [children] for additional obligations."[35] In additional cases addressing parental rights more broadly, the Court has repeated time and again that "the custody, care and nurture of the child reside first in the parents, whose primary function and freedom include preparation for obligations the state can neither supply nor hinder."[36] The Court in *Yoder* recognized that these additional obligations "must ... include the inculcation of moral standards[] [and] religious beliefs,"[37] and the heightened protection it afforded for religious education reflects the value that the First Amendment places on religious pursuits.

---

28   Ibid., 242, 244–46 (Douglas, J., dissenting).
29   Ibid., 231 (majority opinion).
30   Ibid.
31   Ibid., 245–46 (Douglas, J., dissenting).
32   Ibid., 240 (White, J., with Brennan and Stewart, JJ, concurring).
33   Ibid., 226 (majority opinion).
34   Ibid., 223–24.
35   Ibid., 233 (quoting Pierce v. Soc'y of Sisters, 268 U.S. 510, 535 (1925)).
36   Prince v. Massachusetts, 321 U.S. 158, 166 (1944); see also Troxel v. Granville, 530 U.S. 57, 65–66 (2000) (plurality opinion) (quoting *Prince*); Bellotti v. Baird, 443 U.S. 622, 638 (1979) (quoting *Prince*); Quilloin v. Walcott, 434 U.S. 246, 255 (1978) (quoting *Prince*); Stanley v. Illinois, 405 U.S. 645, 651 (1972) (quoting *Prince*); Ginsberg v. New York, 390 U.S. 629, 639 (1968) (quoting *Prince*).
37   *Yoder*, 406 U.S. at 233.

The *Yoder* Court suggested that one basis for these corresponding rights and duties is the natural interest and affection of parents for their children. "The history and culture of Western civilization reflect a strong tradition of parental concern for the nurture and upbringing of their children," the Court observed.[38] In other cases addressing parental rights to custody and care more broadly, the Court has similarly observed that "historically [the law] has recognized that natural bonds of affection lead parents to act in the best interests of their children."[39] The Court has further explained that the law presumes that "parents possess what a child lacks in maturity, experience, and capacity for judgment."[40] These views have supported a general presumption that parents act in the best interests of their children.[41] This is not always the case, and all states make exceptions for cases of abuse and neglect.[42] The Court has also made clear that states may reasonably regulate all schools, and even when religious exercise is impinged, states may intervene to protect the physical and mental health of children and ensure that they have adequate training to become independent and self-reliant adults. The Court has also recognized that children have constitutional rights that sometimes place limits on parental authority. For example, a child has a constitutionally protected interest in avoiding unnecessary institutionalization for mental health care, and this right requires the involvement of a neutral decision maker when parents seek care at a state institution.[43] In general, however, the Court envisions parents as the primary protectors of their children's interests, and the supportive bonds of the parent-child relationship as essential means to promote the growth of the child into maturity and independence.[44] Unless there are specific problems of a pressing nature, American constitutional law views "the family as a unit with broad parental authority over minor children,"[45] a "private realm" which the state generally "cannot enter."[46]

---

38   Ibid., 231–32.
39   Parham v. J.R., 442 U.S. 584, 602 (1979). The Court cited, in support, William Blackstone's *Commentaries on the Laws of England* and James Kent's *Commentaries on American Law*. See also *Troxel*, 530 U.S., 68 (quoting *Parham*).
40   *Parham*, 442 U.S., 602; *Troxel*, 530 U.S., 68 (quoting *Parham*).
41   *Parham*, 442 U.S., 604; *Troxel*, 530 U.S., 68.
42   *Parham*, 442 U.S., 602–03.
43   Ibid., 606–07. The Court has also struck down notice and consent rules unduly burdening a minor's then-protected right to an abortion. See Bellotti v. Baird, 443 U.S. 622 (1979); Planned Parenthood v. Danforth, 428 U.S. 52 (1976).
44   See *Bellotti*, 443 U.S., 638–39.
45   *Parham*, 442 U.S., 602.
46   Prince v. Massachusetts, 321 U.S. 158, 166 (1944); see also *Troxel*, 530 U.S., 68–69 (stating that "so long as a parent adequately cares for his or her children (i.e., is fit), there will

2 Critiques of Parental Rights

While the Court has consistently upheld strong protections for parental rights, particularly where the religious upbringing and education of children is involved, scholarly attacks on the Court's precedents have increased and deepened. While these attacks are varied, a number of common critiques have emerged. Some of these would entail the dramatic curtailment of parental rights or even their abandonment altogether.

One long-running critique focuses on the state's interest in civic education. The Court's decisions have consistently left room for governments to require at least a minimum of civic education for all children. The state may "do much" to "improve the quality of its citizens," the Court stated in *Meyer*,[47] and in *Pierce*, the Court allowed for reasonable regulation of all schools, including requiring "studies plainly essential to good citizenship."[48] While the Free Exercise Clause may limit the state's regulatory reach when religious education is involved, the *Yoder* Court recognized that states have pressing interests in preparing students to be responsible, law-abiding and self-sufficient adults capable of participating effectively in democratic self-government.[49] According to the Court, the objection of Amish parents to formal schooling after the eighth grade did not endanger these interests: "[t]he independence and successful social functioning of the Amish community" has a track record in the United States of more than two centuries, the Court observed.[50]

Scholars who have emphasized the importance of civic education in a democracy have disagreed about how extensive this education must be and what it entails. For some scholars, the self-sufficiency, respect for the law, and willingness to coexist peacefully with others that the Amish demonstrated is enough.[51] However, other scholars would require more than what the *Yoder* Court envisioned. Citizenship in a liberal democracy requires toleration, mutual respect, and the ability to deliberate thoughtfully about public affairs, they argue, and cultivating these virtues in each new generation is not possible

---

        normally be no reason for the State to inject itself into the private realm of the family to further question the ability of that parent to make the best decisions concerning the rearing of that parent's children").

47   Meyer v. Nebraska, 262 U.S. 390, 401 (1923).
48   Pierce v. Soc'y of Sisters, 268 U.S. 510, 534 (1925).
49   Wisconsin v. Yoder, 406 U.S. 205, 221–27 (1972).
50   Ibid., 226–27.
51   See William Galston, "Civic Education in the Liberal State," in *Liberalism and the Moral Life*, ed. Nancy L. Rosenblum (Cambridge, MA: Harvard University Press, 1989), 89, 98–99.

without exposure to alternative perspectives and ways of life,[52] critical thinking and the ability to deliberate about value systems that are different from one's own,[53] and a willingness to engage in public debate in terms that others can reasonably understand and accept.[54] The Court in *Yoder* was wrong to excuse the Amish from Wisconsin's compulsory education rules.[55] Separatist informal education that limits the exposure of children to other ways of life and obstructs deliberation about diverse value systems leaves future citizens without the virtues and habits essential for liberal democracy. There are similar problems with homeschooling[56] and with allowing parents to opt out of curricula designed to promote critical thinking and acquaint children with diversity.[57] These scholars do not necessarily challenge the concept of parental rights, including the assumption that parents care about their children deeply and should have opportunities to inculcate the values and beliefs that are important to them.[58] However, they tend to view these rights as autonomy rights that must yield to state imperatives.[59]

---

52 Stephen Macedo, *Diversity and Distrust: Civic Education in a Multicultural Democracy* (Cambridge, MA: Harvard University Press, 2000), 160, 201; Amy Gutmann, "Civic Education and Social Diversity," *Ethics* 105 (1995): 557–79, at 561; see also Martha Albertson Fineman and George Shepherd, "Homeschooling: Choosing Parental Rights Over Children's Interests," *University of Baltimore Law Review* 46 (2016): 57–106, at 74.

53 Macedo, *Diversity and Distrust*, 239–40; Gutmann, "Civic Education and Social Diversity," 573–74, 575, 578; see also Amy Gutmann, *Democratic Education* (Princeton: Princeton University Press, 1987), 39–40, 44.

54 Macedo, *Diversity and Distrust*, 11, 169–72; Amy Gutmann and Dennis Thompson, *Democracy and Disagreement* (Cambridge, MA: Harvard University Press, 1996), 55–57. This is the requirement of public reason articulated most famously by John Rawls. See John Rawls, *Political Liberalism* (New York: Columbia University Press, 1993), 212–54; id., *Justice as Fairness: A Restatement* (Cambridge, MA: Harvard University Press, 2001), 89–94; and id., "The Idea of Public Reason Revisited," *University of Chicago Law Review* 64 (1997): 765–807. For Rawls, this requirement applies only to public debate and decision-making about constitutional essentials and matters of basic justice, but for others, the demands of public reason extend to public debate and decision-making more broadly.

55 Macedo, *Diversity and Distrust*, 208; Stephen Macedo, "Liberal Civic Education and Religious Fundamentalism: The Case of God v. John Rawls?," *Ethics* 105 (1995): 468–96, at 488; and Gutmann, "Civic Education and Social Diversity," 570.

56 Fineman and Shepherd, "Homeschooling: Choosing Parental Rights Over Children's Interests," 98.

57 Macedo, *Diversity and Distrust*, 201–02; and Gutmann, "Civic Education and Social Diversity," 571–72.

58 Macedo, *Diversity and Distrust*, 101, 237, 241–42, 244–45; Gutmann, *Democratic Education*, 43; and Gutmann, "Civic Education and Social Diversity," 575.

59 Macedo, *Diversity and Distrust*, 244; Gutmann, "Civic Education and Social Diversity," 575; see also Fineman and Shepherd, "Homeschooling," 106 (arguing for the prohibition

Another critique that is sometimes combined with the first emphasizes the importance of the child's own interest in autonomous decision-making. Education must prepare children to make their own life choices as adults, including their own decisions about the beliefs and values they will hold.[60] At a minimum, this requires that students be exposed to new ideas and experiences so that they can learn to reflect about different ways of life and exercise meaningful choice in the future.[61] It also requires training in skills that will allow children to choose among careers in an increasingly competitive economy.[62] The decision of Amish parents to remove their children from school after the eighth grade thwarts their autonomy interests.[63] So does homeschooling by conservative Christian parents who use home-based education to limit their children's experiences and maximize the likelihood that they will stay within their parents' faith communities.[64] Some sectarian private schools are designed to do the same thing.[65] Those who share this perspective often recast children's interests as rights which the state has a duty to recognize and protect.[66]

A variation on this child-centered perspective emphasizes the interest of children in exercising their agency in the present. Even while they are still dependent on adults, children have a growing capacity for expressing their own ideas, developing their own values and identities, and engaging with the

---

of homeschooling, which pits parental "expressive" rights against the interests of both children and the state).

[60] Elizabeth Bartholet, "Homeschooling: Parent Rights Absolutism vs. Child Rights to Education & Protection," *Arizona Law Review* 62 (2020): 1–80, at 6, 57; and James G. Dwyer, "The Liberal State's Response to Religious Visions of Education," *Journal of Catholic Legal Studies* 44 (2005): 195–231, at 211–12.

[61] Bartholet, "Homeschooling," 6, 57; Dwyer, "The Liberal State's Response," 212; see also Fineman and Shepherd, "Homeschooling," 98 (arguing for a prohibition on homeschooling because children need exposure to alternate views so that they have "the ability as adults to assess and eventually choose for themselves among competing values").

[62] Bartholet, "Homeschooling," 3–4, 14, 57; and Fineman and Shepherd, "Homeschooling," 63.

[63] James G. Dwyer, "Parents' Religion and Children's Welfare: Debunking the Doctrine of Parents' Rights," *California Law Review* 82 (1994): 1371–1447, at 1386; and Fineman and Shepherd, "Homeschooling," 91.

[64] Bartholet, "Homeschooling," 6; and Fineman and Shepherd, "Homeschooling," 98, 106.

[65] Bartholet, "Homeschooling," 78; James G. Dwyer, "Changing the Conversation about Children's Education," in *Moral and Political Education: Nomos XLIII*, ed. Stephen Macedo and Yael Tamir (New York: New York University Press, 2002), 314–56, at 336.

[66] Bartholet, "Homeschooling," 58, 80; see also Dwyer, "Parents' Religion and Children's Welfare," 1374–77.

larger world.⁶⁷ They also have present interests in exposure to new ideas to promote curiosity, creativity, and intellectual development.⁶⁸ Children are equal with adults in dignity and moral worth, these scholars argue, and their own decisions require respect even when children are not fully autonomous and even if their views will not ultimately prevail.⁶⁹ This means a voice for the child in their education⁷⁰—perhaps, for some, even a decisive one.⁷¹ It also means restrictions, if not prohibitions, on homeschooling, especially where parents seek to shield their children from beliefs and values that are different from their own.⁷² It means, further, oversight of all schools so that children's present interests are met,⁷³ as well as limitations on the ability of religious parents to opt their children out of objectionable aspects of public education.⁷⁴

Those who emphasize the autonomy and agency interests of children tend to be the strongest critics of robust parental rights. Today's constitutional framework instrumentalizes children and treats them like a form of property that parents have a right to control and use for their own purposes, including their own religious purposes, a number of scholars have argued.⁷⁵ The Court's decisions in *Meyer* and *Pierce* and the framework built upon them have roots in a patriarchal property-based understanding of the parent-child relationship that couples autonomy rights of adults with possession of children.⁷⁶ Scholars

---

67   Barbara Bennett Woodhouse, *Hidden in Plain Sight: The Tragedy of Children's Rights from Ben Franklin to Lionel Tate* (Princeton: Princeton University Press, 2008), 35–36; Anne C. Dailey and Laura A. Rosenbury, "The New Law of the Child," *Yale Law Journal* 127 (2018): 1448–1537, at 1451; and Anne C. Dailey and Laura A. Rosenbury, "The New Parental Rights," *Duke Law Journal* 71 (2021): 75–165, at 100–01.
68   Dailey and Rosenbury, "New Law of the Child," 1451, 1493.
69   Woodhouse, *Hidden in Plain Sight*, 40–41; Samantha Godwin, "Against Parental Rights," *Columbia Human Rights Law Review* 47 (2015): 1–83, at 36, 39, 52–53; see also Dailey and Rosenbury, "New Law of the Child," 1451–52 (stating that "[o]ur approach takes seriously the idea of children as individuals in their own right, worthy of respect, even as they are dependent in varying ways upon the adults in their lives").
70   Barbara Bennett Woodhouse, "Speaking Truth to Power: Challenging 'The Power of Parents to Control the Education of their Own,'" *Cornell Journal of Law and Public Policy* 11 (2002): 481–501, at 488, 501; see also Woodhouse, *Hidden in Plain Sight*, 38.
71   Godwin, "Against Parental Rights," 49–50.
72   Dailey and Rosenbury, "New Law of the Child," 1453, 1522–23; and Dailey and Rosenbury, "New Parental Rights," 128–35.
73   Dailey and Rosenbury, "New Law of the Child," 1522.
74   Ibid., 1495–96.
75   Dwyer, "Parents' Religion and Children's Welfare," 1405; Godwin, "Against Parental Rights," 30, 38; Barbara Bennett Woodhouse, "'Who Owns the Child?': *Meyer* and *Pierce* and the Child as Property," *William & Mary Law Review* 33 (1992): 995–1122, at 1114–15.
76   Woodhouse, "'Who Owns the Child?,'" 997, 113–15; see also Barbara Bennett Woodhouse, "Hatching the Egg: A Child-Centered Perspective on Parents' Rights," *Cardozo Law Review*

have also described parental rights as a form of "child coverture," hiding and subsuming the child and their own voice and interests within the privacy of a unitary family.[77] At best, the interests of parent and child are assumed to align when, in fact, they often do not.[78] Some of these critics retain the concept of parental rights but dramatically curtail them. Parental rights are autonomy interests, and when they conflict with the child's own autonomy interests, the child's interests prevail.[79] Parental rights have also been reconceptualized in a variety of ways. Parental rights have been reimagined as fiduciary responsibilities to vindicate the rights of the child[80] or as relational rights that are limited by the child's independent interests and agency.[81] A number of scholars have rejected the idea of parental rights altogether, replacing it with other concepts like a trusteeship[82] or a "child-rearing privilege."[83] In all of these new models, the child's own rights become paramount, prevailing over parental liberty interests when there is a conflict, much the way that parental rights have traditionally prevailed over the interests of the child. The educational practices of conservative religious communities that are often used to illustrate these new frameworks become examples of dominion and control that deprive children of the opportunities and resources they need to develop into independent persons with their own interests and life goals.

3 What These Critiques Uncover and What They Miss

In his scholarship on the family, Witte develops a model of the family as a multidimensional sphere or globe with natural, social, economic, communicative, contractual, and spiritual dimensions.[84] The relationship between parents and children spans these dimensions, and like other aspects of the family, it

---

14 (1993): 1747–1865, at 1809 (describing a "legal tradition of possessive individualism" that treats the child as a possession under parental control).
77 Dailey and Rosenbury, "New Parental Rights," 90–96.
78 See Dwyer, "Changing the Conversation about Children's Education," 327, 329; and Dailey and Rosenbury, "New Parental Rights," 77.
79 Bartholet, "Homeschooling," 57; and Dailey and Rosenbury, "New Law of the Child," 1452.
80 Barbara Bennett Woodhouse, "A Public Role in the Private Family: The Parental Rights and Responsibilities Act and the Politics of Child Protection and Education," *Ohio State Law Journal* 57 (1996): 393–430, at 394–95; see also Godwin, "Against Parental Rights," 82.
81 Dailey and Rosenbury, "New Parental Rights," 85.
82 Barbara Bennett Woodhouse, "The Dark Side of Family Privacy," *George Washington Law Review* 67 (1999): 1247–62, at 1256.
83 Dwyer, "Parents' Religion and Children's Welfare," 1374.
84 Witte, *Church, State, and Family*, 14–15, 186.

interacts with the religious, political, and civic institutions that make the family not only multidimensional but also multi-institutional.[85] Critics of the Court's precedents are not wrong to emphasize children's interests and rights, Witte would agree.[86] They are also not wrong to explore the connection between the education of children and the needs of society. The interests of children have always had a central place in Western constructions of the family, and the Western tradition has recognized children's rights since the Middle Ages.[87] Civic concerns also weave in and out of Western constructions of the family.[88] However, much is missing from modern critiques that Witte's wide-ranging exploration of Western philosophical, religious, and legal thought on the family uncovers. Witte's work offers a deeper understanding of the roots of our constitutional tradition, greater attention to important elements of the Court's decisions that critics tend to overlook, and a fuller picture of the many values and considerations at stake when states, families, and religious communities clash—and cooperate—over the education of children.

At the bottom of the family sphere, Witte explains, is the natural pole that anchors the family in the natural goods of family life as well as the natural inclinations, instincts, and affections that underlie the family form.[89] These natural inclinations include the strong natural attachments and affections of parents for their children that the Court has cited as a basis for recognizing the primary role of parents in the upbringing of their children. The natural pole also includes the natural law reasoning that Western theorists have long used to develop ideals and rules for the family based on human nature, conscience, experience, rational reflection, custom, and tradition.[90] Children are born fragile and dependent, and the parents who have given them life and have a natural affection for them have duties to care for them, assist their growth and development over time, and prepare them for independent lives as adults.[91] These parental duties give rise to parental rights, the Western tradition has long taught,[92] and beginning in the Middle Ages, the church also recognized children's rights corresponding to the duties held by parents and, in their absence,

---

85   Ibid., 9, 198–200, 226.
86   Witte defends the idea of children's rights against conservative religious critics in chapter 8 of *Church, State, and Family*.
87   Ibid., 256–66.
88   The discussion below touches on just a few of these connections.
89   Witte, *Church, State, and Family*, 14, 186.
90   Ibid., 189, 196.
91   Ibid., 4–7.
92   Ibid., 44, 64–69, 220, 259–61.

by church and state authorities in their place.⁹³ This interlocking matrix of natural rights and duties between parents and children endured as a staple of the Western tradition through the early modern period in both Protestant and Catholic thought,⁹⁴ and it was carried through the Enlightenment by many theorists, including those strongly critical of traditional Christianity.⁹⁵ It also became part of both the civil and common law traditions, including the Anglo-American legal tradition that shaped the Court's approach to parental rights.⁹⁶ Parents have duties to care for, nurture, and educate their children, and corresponding rights to direct their upbringing.⁹⁷ Children have rights to the care that parents are obligated to provide as well as duties to care for parents when they become aged and unable to care for themselves.⁹⁸ Parental rights and duties are exercised in the context of supportive institutions, including both church and state, and religious and governmental authorities also step in to protect children when necessary.⁹⁹ When the Supreme Court has spoken of the connection between parental rights and duties, it is drawing on this tradition, just as it is when it rests parental rights on the natural affection of parents for their children and the assumption that parents best know the needs and interests of their children.

Critics of the Court's protections for parental rights generally envision these rights as autonomy rights that serve the interests of parents but often only incidentally the interests of their children.¹⁰⁰ Religious education, in particular, becomes an exercise or expression of the parents' faith and, as such, something that can come at the expense of children who may have different views or no opportunities to develop their own. For many critics, natural attachments also become suspect. The intuition that our children belong to us or are, in some way, an extension of ourselves is fundamentally egotistical.¹⁰¹ Children are treated like property and instrumentalized for their parents' own purposes.

---

93   Ibid., 220, 259–61.
94   Ibid., 6–7.
95   Ibid., 7, 261–65, and chap. 6.
96   Ibid., 261–66.
97   Ibid., 220–21, 265–66.
98   Ibid.
99   Ibid., 9, 14, 198–99, 220, 260–61, 354–55, 356–57.
100 Anne Dailey and Laura Rosenbury have put this point starkly: "Although parental rights may indirectly further children's interests, they are a circuitous and unreliable means of doing so. Parental rights construct children predominantly as objects of control, rather than as people with values and interests of their own." Dailey and Rosenbury, "New Law of the Child," 1471.
101 See Dwyer, "Changing the Conversation about Children's Education," 325–27; and Godwin, "Against Parental Rights," 30–31, 48–49.

However, these arguments oversimplify the tradition of parental rights. The intuition that our children belong to us is part of what gives rise to parental affections, and these affections can be deeply sacrificial.[102] Parents naturally strive to give their children a better future and more possibilities than they have had. "Children are, in the end, what men and women live for," a lawyer for the Society of Sisters in the *Pierce* case wrote in his brief.[103] "All that we missed, lost, failed of, our children may have, do, accomplish in fullest measure."[104] This is not an expression of egotism or exploitation, as some critics have argued,[105] but a powerful other-regarding instinct. To be sure, this instinct comes with risks that parents may confuse their own desires with those of their children, and all parents must learn, sometimes painfully, to adjust their dreams for their children to their children's own dreams for their future. However, parental failures and imperfections do not fundamentally change the nature of the parental attachments that provide an important basis for recognizing parental rights.

A property-based view of parental rights also misses the context of these rights in a larger constellation of parental duties and children's rights. The Court has never envisioned parental rights in isolation. In *Meyer*, *Pierce*, and *Yoder* and numerous other cases, the Court has tied parental freedoms to parental responsibilities. Parents have duties that match their natural affections, and their love and care for their children lead them to understand their children and their needs best. Parents are not perfect and will often fall short of their best intentions, and multiple supportive institutions have long played an assisting role in child-rearing. However, it is too simplistic to see parental rights as ownership rights, and foolish to minimize the value of parents' strong interests in their children. It is also too simplistic to see parental rights as a form of coverture that silences the voices of children and subsumes them into the mythical private family unit. Parental rights correspond to parental duties to help children develop their own voices over time and to grow into independent and responsible adults. Very few parents want slavish children or stunted adults. Indeed, parents are usually best positioned to defend their child's voice when others, including well-meaning bureaucracies, cannot hear it. The privacy that the law affords families is designed to strengthen the ability

---

102   Witte, *Church, State, and Family*, 55 (discussing the work of Aquinas).
103   Woodhouse, "'Who Owns the Child?,'" 1102, quoting the brief written by William Dameron Guthrie. Guthrie also wrote an influential amicus brief in *Meyer v. Nebraska*, 262 U.S. 390 (1923). Ibid., 1077–79.
104   Ibid., 1102.
105   Ibid., 1103.

of parents to care for their children and to defend against encroachments that may be well-intentioned but lack the unique perspective and concern that parents have. The best interests of the child will always be specific to the child, and in general no one knows their children better than parents.

Critics of strong parental rights also often reject the idea of natural law and natural rights. The claim that parental rights have a basis in natural rights is just a naked assertion, a form of fiat without justification, some have suggested.[106] The Court's rules do not correspond to anything essential about the world or human realities, others have argued.[107] They are just the creations of positive law. However, these dismissals are again too facile. The Court's embrace of parental rights and the related natural rights tradition draws upon centuries of reasoning about human nature and experience, and the Court's opinions participate in this reasoning and extend it. Critics are correct that Western history also includes the concepts of patriarchy and coverture, but Witte argues convincingly that these concepts "obscured the[] ideals" of Western teaching rather than represented them.[108] Reciprocal rights and duties between parents and children is a very different concept than paternal ownership and dominion. Authority is for the benefit of the child, not at their expense.

Of course, the law must not ignore the imperfections of parents and their more serious failures, and it never has. As Witte explains, the social dimension of the family includes the many institutions that have long supported the family and stepped in where parents abandon, neglect, or abuse their children.[109] The family is both multidimensional and multi-institutional.[110] Religious communities have long played this supportive role, including through the operation of religious schools and other programs designed to benefit children and the family more broadly.[111] So have other voluntary associations and charities, neighborhoods and informal social networks, and professions of many kinds.[112] The state also has a vital role, but Witte cautions that its role must be to aid parents and other institutions, not supplant them.[113] The state cannot replace parental love and the unique perspectives that parents have about

---

106 Dwyer, "The Liberal State's Response to Religious Visions of Education," 219; see also Fineman and Shepherd, "Homeschooling," 91–92.
107 Dailey and Rosenbury, "New Law of the Child," 1467, 1474; and Dailey and Rosenbury, "New Parental Rights," 106.
108 Witte, *Church, State, and Family*, 371.
109 Ibid., 9, 14, 198–99, 220, 260–61, 354–55, 356–57.
110 Ibid., 9, 198–200, 226.
111 Ibid., 354–55.
112 Ibid., 9, 14–15, 197–200, 356–57.
113 Ibid., 356–57, 369.

their children's needs, and it must respect the different religious beliefs and value systems that are nourished by a free society.[114]

The strongest critics of expansive parental rights tend to pit the interests of parents and children against one another and assume that the state will often be the better judge of what is best for the child. The state becomes the guarantor of the child's future autonomy and the protector of the child's present agency, voice, and diverse interests and values. Disputes between parents and children become battles where parents naturally, but problematically, seek to align their children's views with their own, while children seek to define their own lives. But this is a caricature. Parents are not so inclined to stifle their children's individuality that they cannot be trusted with broad authority over their children's education and upbringing. Most parents listen to their children's developing voices and perspectives, although, as the Court has recognized, generally "parents possess what a child lacks in maturity, experience, and capacity for judgment."[115] Critics are particularly troubled by the decisions of conservative religious parents to seek educational environments that limit their children's exposure to conflicting value systems in order to ensure that they remain within the parents' faith communities. Of course, these parents do not necessarily seek to control other aspects of their children's lives or developing interests, but there is also little risk that they will be able to fully seal their children's religious world off from the larger culture, unless they also imprison them within the home (and take away their electronics). Children will see and meet others in a variety of contexts, including in the marketplace and on the playground. There is also no danger that parents can prevent adolescents from questioning their beliefs and values, or from leaving the community when they become adults. On the other hand, if parents are prevented from educating their children in tight-knit, cohesive religious settings, the thick normative worlds that open up to children in these contexts may no longer be an option for them to consider. As the Court noted in *Yoder*, requiring Amish children to attend high school "influence[s], if not determine[s], the religious future of the child"[116] and, indeed, the options available for others to consider. Moreover, deep grounding in a particular belief system may enhance the depth of later engagement with other ideas and open up lines of thought one might not otherwise develop.

---

114 Ibid., 358, 365.
115 Parham v. J.R., 442 U.S. 584, 602 (1979); and Troxel v. Granville, 530 U.S. 57, 68 (2000) (quoting *Parham*).
116 Wisconsin v. Yoder, 406 U.S. 205, 232 (1972).

Today's critics also tend to overlook the communicative dimension of the family that strong protections for parental rights recognize and safeguard. This dimension includes the vital role that parents play in transmitting values and beliefs to new generations and the mutually supportive bonds and relationships between family members.[117] "[P]rivate daily communications" fall within this dimension, Witte explains, referencing the intimacy of the parent-child relationship and other relationships among family members.[118] Most scholars recognize that this intimate relationship benefits the child,[119] but they downplay the risks to this relationship where governments intervene in disputes between parents and children over divergent beliefs and values or second-guess parental decision-making more generally. They also downplay the risks that this intervention will disrupt the vital role that families play in transmitting values to future generations.

These scholars also miss the connection between strong family relationships of trust and mutual support and the civic interests that they value. The family benefits from state support, but stable, flourishing families are also essential to the health of societies. The family is "the foundation of society," "a kind of school of deeper humanity," the Catholic Church has taught, as Witte has observed.[120] For early modern Protestants, Enlightenment theorists, and common law jurists alike, Witte explains, the family was "the first school of love and justice, nurture and education, charity and citizenship, discipline and production."[121] Protecting the privacy of the family and minimizing intrusions into its relationships is designed, in part, to strengthen the bonds of care and trust that nourish not only the child but also the society more broadly. Scholars who argue that parental rights must yield to hefty demands of civic education often fail to consider the ways in which these demands might erode as well as advance civic interests. Indeed, significant intrusion into the educational choices of parents, especially when religious interests are impinged, is likely to generate civic distrust and undermine civic stability rather than strengthen tolerance and mutual respect.

It is, however, the spiritual dimension of the family that critics of expansive parental rights both miss and misunderstand the most. Descriptions of parental rights as liberty interests that pose potential risks to the state and

---

117 Witte, *Church, State, and Family*, 214–15.
118 Ibid., 14, 186.
119 This includes some of the strongest critics of expansive parental rights. See Dailey and Rosenbury, "New Parental Rights," 81, 112–13; and Godwin, "Against Parental Rights," 56–57.
120 Second Vatican Council, *Gaudium et Spes: Pastoral Constitution on the Church in the Modern World* (1965), sec. 52, discussed in Witte, *Church, State, and Family*, 224–25.
121 Witte, *Church, State, and Family*, 368.

to children who may want to make different choices leave out the most vital information about what is at stake for religious parents. Parents do not view the religious education of their children as an egotistical endeavor to replicate their own religious choices and preferences, creating "puppets of [their] wishes."[122] Rather, they view it as the fulfillment of their highest duty to their children. For the believer, their faith tradition discloses essential truths about human nature, purposes, and ends, and these truths make full human flourishing possible. Religious traditions connect human persons to the divine source of all that exists and support life in all its dimensions. Teach your children God's law, Moses says, so that they "will be in the right" and live.[123] God, and his teaching and commandments, are a vital part of the parent-child relationship, informing it and directing it to the child's benefit. "[W]hat does ... God desire" of the marital covenant, the prophet Malachi asks.[124] "Godly offspring."[125] Witte offers this gloss: the procreation, care, and education of children are "a sharing with God in the creation and nurture of a new image-bearer and a new covenant-follower of God on earth."[126] They participate in God's creative love and care for humanity.[127] For the religious believer, then, religious education is the deepest and most significant act of parental love, the supreme reflection of the affection parents naturally have for their children. As the Court in *Yoder* recognized, the First Amendment respects this parental drive and desire with the strongest protection.[128]

Thus, the religious beliefs of parents and children alike are more than simply personal preferences or choices. They reflect the capacity and desire of humans to seek the truth, live rightly, and reach for the divine source of all human goods. It is natural for parents to want to pass on what they understand about these matters to their children and to view this education as among the most important of their children's present and future interests. Critics of expansive parental rights seek to highlight and elevate the interests of children, but this spiritual interest is often missing and, with it, the value of religious education. Of course, not everyone has religious beliefs or assigns value to religious education, but the First Amendment protects the views and practices of those who do and the many different paths they choose.

---

122 Dailey and Rosenbury, "New Parental Rights," 101.
123 Deuteronomy 6:24–25.
124 Malachi 2:15.
125 Ibid.
126 Witte, *Church, State, and Family*, 231.
127 Ibid., 258–59 (discussing Aquinas's teaching and glossing Matthew 7:9–12).
128 Wisconsin v. Yoder, 406 U.S. 205, 233–34 (1972).

But if religious beliefs cannot be reduced to mere choice or human agency, they also inescapably involve choice. No one can be forced to believe, and effective education can never be the "indoctrination" that many of the scholars discussed here fear.[129] Religious education begins as formation within a tradition, but the child must eventually choose to remain within that tradition or reject it. If they stay within it, they will become part of a continuing process of renewal and revitalization. Religious traditions are never static. They cannot survive without the formation of new generations in the beliefs and practices of the past, but they will not thrive if these new generations do not embrace the tradition as their own and continually develop it in light of new challenges and circumstances, including new ideas in the surrounding culture. Conservative Christian parents who homeschool or choose other forms of separatist education for their children may appear from the outside to be rigid and resistant to change, but many of them are trying something new.[130] While they may wish otherwise, they cannot keep their children from eventually doing the same. It is, however, another caricature to view conservative religious believers as puppeteers of passive children. The religious parent who wants for their children what they have "missed, lost, [or] failed of"[131] naturally wants most earnestly for their child a deeper faith, more profound insights, and a straighter path. None of this can be forced, and the way forward is not always clear. Parents understand this, and they know that while they can influence, they can never control.

4   The Multi-institutional Family

As with all rights, there must be limits on parental rights. Parents should be given the primary responsibility for the care and education of their children, but their authority cannot be absolute. These limits, however, must be

---

129   Bartholet, "Homeschooling," 5; Dwyer, "Parents' Religion and Children's Welfare," 1445; Martha L. A. Fineman, "Taking Children's Interests Seriously," in *Child, Family, and State: Nomos XLIV*, ed. Stephen Macedo and Iris Marion Young (New York: New York University Press, 2003), 234–242, at 240.
130   The recognition of homeschooling in most states is a relatively recent phenomenon, and the number of homeschooling families has grown dramatically in recent decades. See Bartholet, "Homeschooling," 8–9, 37–38. See, generally, James G. Dwyer and Shawn F. Peters, *Homeschooling: The History and Philosophy of a Controversial Practice* (Chicago: University of Chicago Press, 2019).
131   Woodhouse, "'Who Owns the Child?,'" 1102 (quoting William Dameron Guthrie's brief for the Society of Sisters in *Pierce v. Society of Sisters*, 268 U.S. 510, 530 (1925)).

narrow, and they must reflect the traditional assumption that parents love and know their children best. They must also respect the position of parents who consider a religious education to be among their children's most important interests and their own highest duties.

Certainly parents must not be allowed to abuse or neglect their children.[132] Some critics of homeschooling have argued that homeschooling has been used as a haven for parents who neglect or abuse their children, and there is evidence that this occurs.[133] However, the extensive restrictions or prohibitions that some have advocated are not necessary to address this problem. More narrowly tailored rules directed at known or suspected abusers can protect children's interests while respecting the desire of many parents to homeschool. Where homeschooling is a religious choice as it often is, sweeping restrictions also do not respect the free-exercise concerns at stake. Where general parental rights are combined with an infringement on religious exercise, the *Yoder* Court made clear that heightened scrutiny applies.[134] While the Court no longer applies strict scrutiny whenever the government substantially burdens religious exercise, as it once did, it has reaffirmed its decision in *Yoder*.[135] Protecting children from abuse and neglect is surely a compelling state interest, but the government must show a tight connection between this objective and its rules. A ban or extensive restrictions would not even pass a much lower standard of review.

The Court has also recognized that governments can act to ensure that the educational choices of parents provide children with basic knowledge and skills and sufficient training to prepare them to function as independent, self-sufficient adults capable of engaging effectively in democratic self-government.[136] These requirements might include, for example, studies on U.S. history and government.[137] However, the hefty requirements for civic education that many scholars propose go beyond what is necessary to meet these basic goals. Exposure to and consideration of alternative belief systems in a school setting is not necessary to cultivate tolerance and mutual respect for one's fellow citizens or to exercise political judgment in a democratic polity. America's experience before the advent of compulsory education belies these

---

132 See Parham v. J.R., 442 U.S. 584, 602 (1979).
133 Bartholet, "Homeschooling," 14–20; see also Woodhouse, "Speaking Truth to Power," 488–90 (giving a deeply troubling example).
134 Wisconsin v. Yoder, 406 U.S. 205, 215, 233–34 (1972). See discussion *supra* notes 17–19 and accompanying text.
135 Employment Div. v. Smith, 494 U.S. 872, 881 (1990).
136 See discussion *supra* notes 6, 12, 21–24, 48 and accompanying text.
137 See *supra* note 48 and accompanying text.

scholars' claims to the contrary. Nor does the give and take necessary for democratic self-government require citizens to conduct public affairs in terms that all can be expected to understand and accept. Consensus can be found among those who approach problems from very different perspectives and value systems, and exposure to opposing views in public debate and decision-making can shift one's perspectives over time. Indeed, adopting educational requirements that ignore the concerns of religious traditionalists is probably more likely to undermine civic trust and cooperation than to advance them.

Limits would also be appropriate where the educational choices of parents truly risk stunting their children's intellectual or emotional development so that their ability to make their own independent decisions as adults is compromised. A commitment to religious freedom means protecting the right of all citizens to make their own religious decisions, and the *Yoder* Court has also appropriately allowed for state intervention to protect the physical and mental health of children.[138] However, critics overstate the risks associated with the separatist choices of America's religious conservatives. Homeschooled children are not generally sealed off from the larger world. They go to churches and stores, and they encounter other children on playgrounds, sports teams, and other clubs and extracurricular activities. Likewise, Amish children are not unaware of different ways of life in the world around them. It is possible to imagine forms of education that would stunt the normal development of children, or parents who would try to lock their children away from the modern world altogether. However, broad prohibitions or restrictions based on sweeping assumptions without specific evidence of an actual problem are not justified. Broad restrictions would also require more than the assumption made by some scholars that homeschooling parents will not abide by less restrictive rules.[139] Proposals for presumptive bans on homeschooling that would make exceptions for secular but not religious needs are especially problematic because they would discriminate against religion in violation of the Free Exercise Clause.[140]

---

138   See *supra* note 21 and accompanying text.
139   Bartholet, "Homeschooling," 73–74; see also Fineman and Shepherd, "Homeschooling," 98–99 (arguing that impracticable monitoring by government officials would be necessary to ensure compliance).
140   For such proposals, see Bartholet, "Homeschooling," 72–73; Dailey and Rosenbury, "New Parental Rights," 130. The Court has held that the government violates the Free Exercise Clause where it has established a mechanism for individualized exceptions to a rule but denies a religious exception without justifying its denial as the least restrictive means of achieving a compelling state interest. Fulton v. City of Philadelphia, 141 S. Ct. 1868, 1877,

While some limits on parental rights are essential, for most children the greater promise will come from cooperative relationships between parents and the state. In earlier periods of Western history, religious and state authorities often worked closely together to support families,[141] but in pluralistic societies that embrace religious freedom, this type of close integration between church and state is no longer possible or desirable. Cooperative relationships between parents and governments must also make space for the many different belief systems that parents may hold. However, true partnerships that recognize both the principal responsibility of parents for their children and the resources that the state may be able to offer hold great promise for improving the lives of children, much greater promise than adversarial relationships or isolated efforts.

While critics of strong parental rights often highlight what they believe to be the most egregious forms of parental misconduct, they also describe many lesser shortcomings, including a number that most parents will recognize in themselves. Parents want what is best for their children, but they act with imperfect information. They are tempted to assume that their desires match their children's needs even if they do not, and while they usually listen to their children's voices, they may have trouble fully understanding what they have to say. They also face challenges that confound us all, even experts they may go to for help and guidance. None of this means that courts should abandon the presumption that parents act in the best interests of their children or that governments should substitute their own judgments for those of parents. Nor does this mean that governments should intervene to give effect to the child's voice when children disagree with parents who are well-intentioned and doing their best to act in their children's interests. State actors are imperfect too, and generally they do not love and know the child as well.

However, the imperfections of both parents and state authorities alike do mean that there is great benefit from cooperative relationships that combine the unique concern and perspectives of parents with the resources and expertise that governmental officials can offer. As Witte observes, parents already benefit from the support of many different types of formal and informal associations and relationships, including religious communities, neighborhoods, civic groups, and professionals of all sorts. Governments, in particular, play a substantial role in supporting the educational responsibilities of parents, including through the operation of public schools and the provision of

---

1881–82 (2021); Church of the Lukumi Babalu Aye, Inc. v. City of Hialeah, 508 U.S. 520, 537–38 (1993); Employment Div. v. Smith, 494 U.S. 872, 884 (1990).

141 Witte, *Church, State, and Family*, 9, 198.

resources to private schools, including increasingly religious schools.[142] However, in these relationships, governments often assume a directive role, setting curriculum standards and other requirements with little direct involvement from the families they serve. They also miss opportunities to partner with parents in meeting the challenges that students face. Today these challenges are serious and growing, including achievement gaps exacerbated by pandemic learning loss affecting all students,[143] harms associated with social media use,[144] increasing adolescent depression and sexual assault,[145] and the psychological toll of a culture of violence that has every school child drilling for a mass shooting.

As America's culture wars grind on, it can seem like productive partnerships are unrealistic. In the public-school setting, school officials and parents have increasingly battled over issues like racial justice and the treatment of children exploring their sexual orientations and gender identities. There is also significant suspicion among outsiders about the agendas and educational adequacy of the private educational choices of America's most conservative religious communities. In return, these groups are naturally suspicious of government intervention. However, most parents and educational officials still share important basic norms, including the value of each child and their educational development and emotional health. Productive partnerships can start with shared concerns and transparent efforts to provide parents with information and resources that may be of benefit to them and their children. Parents should be free to act upon this information as they see best. Combining the expertise of state actors with the unique experience of parents in a way that respects America's different faith traditions will lead to better outcomes for children. It also leaves room for our knowledge about what is beneficial for children to grow and develop. Additionally, truly cooperative partnerships can help to diffuse tensions over time and make it possible to address challenges that involve deeply divisive issues.

---

142   Beginning in the 1980s, the Court began loosening its Establishment Clause restrictions on aid to religious schools, and now under the Free Exercise Clause the Court is expanding the contexts in which aid must be available on an equal basis with secular schools. For the Court's most recent decisions, see Carson v. Makin, 142 S. Ct. 1987 (2022) and Espinoza v. Mont. Dep't of Revenue, 140 S. Ct. 2246 (2020).
143   National Center for Education Statistics, "National Assessment of Educational Progress (NAEP) Long-Term Trend Assessment" (2023).
144   U.S. Surgeon General's Advisory, "Social Media and Youth Mental Health" (2023).
145   Centers for Disease Control and Prevention, "Youth Risk Behavior Survey: Data Summary & Trends Report 2011–2021" (2023).

Efforts should also be made to accommodate parents who object to specific aspects of public-school curricula on religious grounds. Families are moral and religious communities that play an essential role in transmitting values to the next generation. Schools are moral communities as well, even public schools, and they also play a vital role in passing down social and civic values to future generations. In public schools, these values should be broadly shared principles that most families can agree upon, and parents should have an important role in determining what these values are. However, not all families will agree on the values that are chosen, and America's most conservative religious parents may find themselves outside of whatever consensus is reached. Some may leave for private religious schools or choose to homeschool their children, but many may not be able to or want to. Critics of expansive parental rights have frequently opposed accommodations that would allow parents to opt children out of material such as sex education and deliberation about different belief systems.[146] However, making accommodations that are feasible and do not compromise basic educational goals is the better course. Accommodations respect religious liberty and preserve the pluralism that enriches America's moral and religious landscape. As the Court in *Yoder* reminded, we may be sure where truth lies, but we may be wrong, and America's dissenting religious groups preserve ways of life that we may one day find valuable.[147] School officials can begin by trying to explain to parents the reasons for their educational programs. Parents may have misunderstood the purposes or content of these programs or the effect they are likely to have on their children, and it may be possible to make easy adjustments to satisfy their concerns. However, when impasses are reached, accommodations should be made wherever possible. Accommodations not only respect religious freedom but also build civic trust and protect the willingness of all parties to work together to advance the many common values they do have.

In the context of homeschooling, in particular, there is significant room for partnerships that would advance the interests of children, address many of the concerns of critics, and respect the concerns of parents. Critics argue that homeschooled children are isolated socially and intellectually, cut off from other children and ways of life. In reality, most homeschooled children meet other children in a variety of contexts, such as at church, in homeschooling

---

146 Macedo, *Diversity and Distrust*, 157–60, 201–02; Gutmann, "Civic Education and Social Diversity," 570–72; see also Dailey and Rosenbury, "New Law of the Child," 1496 (writing critically of laws that allow parents to withdraw their children from classes in sex education).

147 Wisconsin v. Yoder, 406 U.S. 205, 223–24 (1972).

co-ops, in the marketplace, and through formal and informal youth activities. However, more could be done to give homeschooled children access to additional academic and extracurricular opportunities. For example, public schools could make it easier for homeschooled children to take public-school classes or participate in after-school activities. Not all parents would be interested in these opportunities, but some would, especially if they believe that these are genuine efforts to benefit their children without undermining their belief systems. Partnerships like these would also benefit others as well by promoting mutual understanding and respect among groups of future citizens with very different ways of looking at the world. Moreover, where there is a track record of successful partnerships, homeschool communities might be less resistant to forms of regulation that could improve the educational experiences and outcomes of their children.

5 Conclusion

Critics of robust constitutional protections for parental rights often pit these rights against the interests and rights of children and the demands of liberal democracy. Parental rights certainly have limits, but critics tend to overlook the many ways that they complement and vindicate the rights of children and strengthen the larger civic community. Both parental rights and children's rights have been essential features of Western constructions of the family, Witte has argued, and they are related. So have mutually supportive relationships between families and the communities and institutions around them. The greatest promise for improving the lives and education of children involves the cooperation of all these entities in ways that recognize the primary role of parents in raising their children, the inherent pluralism of free societies, and the expertise that state officials and other professionals can offer.

CHAPTER 28

Christianity, Child Well-Being, and Corporal Punishment

Marcia J. Bunge

1 **Introduction**

Although many legal strides have been made around the world over the past one hundred years regarding child protection and children's rights, children face a host of ongoing and newly emerging challenges.[1] Children make up approximately one-third of the human population, and in countries rich and poor, many experience poverty, malnutrition, maltreatment, and a lack of adequate education and health care. Although not always in the news or public awareness, the enormous needs of children and their families are evident around the world. They struggle to meet even their basic needs under difficult circumstances, whether living in poor or prosperous countries or fleeing political unrest or environmental disasters. In addition to such ongoing challenges, new ways of exploiting children through social media and corporate marketing contribute to global increases in childhood depression, anxiety, and self-destructive behaviors.

Secular and religious initiatives, including many by diverse Christian communities and organizations worldwide, have sought to address these and other challenges. Although Christians differ in a host of ways, whether theologically, culturally, or politically, several biblical passages undergird their shared commitments to children, including mandates to love the neighbor and to seek justice for the poor and the orphan. The book of Isaiah, for example, provides a vision of all children flourishing that aligns with a host of Christian commitments to children. The book begins with the plea, "Cease to do evil, learn to do good; seek justice, rescue the oppressed, defend the orphan, plead for the

---

1 For a brief introduction to strides and challenges, see Michael Freeman, "Children's Rights Past, Present, and Future: Some Introductory Comments Michael Freeman," in *The Future of Children's Rights*, ed. Michael Freeman (Leiden: Brille, 2014), 3–15.

widow" (Isaiah 1:16–17), and woven throughout the text is a powerful vision of all children experiencing peace, well-being, and wholeness—*shalom*.[2]

Furthermore, Christian communities and organizations recognize that addressing such challenges requires collaboration and cultivating creative alliances across lines of difference. There can be no easy fix, since promoting child protection and well-being involves attending to a host of political, cultural, economic, educational, legal, medical, religious, and environmental factors. For example, Christians have worked across religious, secular, and political lines to address disaster relief, child marriage, the lack of educational opportunities for girls and the poor, and the global sex trafficking of minors.[3] Child-focused Christian organizations, such as Viva Network, World Vision, and Compassion International, attract faith leaders from diverse branches of the church who hold differing theological views, such as about biblical interpretation, yet effectively work together to address the needs of children. The World Council of Churches has also worked together with UNICEF and other child-focused secular agencies to develop common statements and practical strategies regarding child well-being and children's rights.

Given such creative global coalitions and shared Christian commitments to children, it is puzzling and troubling that Christians in the United States are not more effectively working together to address the tremendous challenges that many children and families in this prosperous country continue to face. For example, Christians left and right have not been able to get past disagreements about abortion and reproductive rights to work together to ensure that all children in the U.S. have clean water and air, housing, equal access to educational opportunities, or health care. All countries in the world have ratified the 1989 United Nations Convention on the Rights of the Child (CRC) except

---

2 All biblical passages quoted in this chapter are taken from the New Revised Standard Version (NRSV). Isaiah declares, "Great shall be the prosperity [*shalom*] of your children" (54:13). For more on Isaiah's vision, see Jacqueline E. Lapsley, "'Look! The Children and I Are as Signs and Portents in Israel': Children in Isaiah," in *The Child in the Bible*, ed. Marcia J. Bunge (Grand Rapids: Eerdmans, 2008), 82–102.

3 Although he does not directly address children or children's rights, Allen D. Hertzke shows how an unlikely and highly diverse alliance of Jews, Roman Catholics, American evangelicals, and other activists and religious leaders came together across lines of difference to address religious and other forms of persecution, sparking a global human rights movement that has championed other human rights cases, including sex trafficking. See Allen D. Hertzke, *Freeing God's Children: The Unlikely Alliance for Global Human Rights* (Lanham, MD: Rowman & Littlefield, 2004), 3.

the U.S. Even though various denominations and highly respected scholars, including John Witte, Jr., have taken seriously critiques of the CRC and have persuasively argued that it is worthy of qualified ratification,[4] some politically conservative Protestants and a few Catholics and Orthodox Christians still fear that its ratification or even the acceptance of selected children's rights might threaten religious liberty and erode parental authority and rights.

Furthermore, although sixty-five countries have now banned the corporal punishment of children in all settings,[5] this practice is legally and politically tolerated in the U.S. All fifty states permit parents to utilize corporal punishment provided the force is determined to be "reasonable," and several states still permit corporal punishment in schools.[6] Only twenty-seven states ban corporal punishment in public schools, and only two states have laws specifically prohibiting corporal punishment in private schools. Throughout the U.S., regulations are lax regarding homeschooling. Some Christians strongly support laws that permit corporal punishment, others actively seek to repeal them, and still others ignore the issue altogether despite risks to children. Medical risks of corporal punishment include using excess force, and 28 percent of children in the U.S. are hit so hard that they receive injuries.[7] In schools that permit physical punishment, teachers disproportionately punish boys, Black

---

4 See his chapter on "Why Suffer the Children? Overcoming the Modern Church's Opposition to Children's Rights," in John Witte, Jr., *Church, State, and Family*, 238–73. See also Kathleen Marshall and Paul Parvis, *Honouring Children: The Human Rights of the Child in Christian Perspective* (Edinburgh: Saint Andrews Press, 2004); and John Witte, Jr. and Don S. Browning, "Christianity's Mixed Contributions to Children's Rights: Traditional Teachings, Modern Doubts," in *Children, Adults, and Shared Responsibilities: Jewish Christian, and Muslim Perspectives*, ed. Marcia J. Bunge (Cambridge: Cambridge University Press, 2012), 272–91.

5 See the progress report on the End Corporal Punishment website, https://endcorporalpunishment.org/.

6 For statistics on corporal punishment, see the Office for Civil Rights in the Department of Education. For a summary of statistics updated March 2023, see https://ocrdata.ed.gov/assets/downloads/Corporal_Punishment_Part4_Updated.pdf.

7 Victor I. Vieth, "Augustine, Luther, and Solomon: Providing Pastoral Guidance to Parents on the Corporal Punishment of Children," *Currents in Theology and Mission* 44 (Jan. 2017): 32, citing Vincent J. Felitti and Robert F. Anda, "The Relationship of Adverse Childhood Experiences to Adult Medical Disease, Psychiatric Disorders and Sexual Behavior: Implications for Healthcare," in *The Impact of Early Life Trauma on Health and Disease: The Hidden Epidemic*, ed. Ruthe A. Lanius, Eric Vermeten, and Clare Pain (Cambridge: Cambridge University Press, 2010), 78.

students, Indigenous children, and children with disabilities.[8] Cases of abuse and neglect are also documented among homeschooled children.[9]

The lack of a united efforts to address the corporal punishment of children in the U.S. is especially heartbreaking, given its widespread use and the now well-established evidence that physical punishment is not only ineffective but also harmful to children's development.[10] The UN Committee on the Rights of the Child, which oversees the CRC, defines "corporal" or "physical" punishment as "any punishment in which physical force is used and intended to cause some degree of pain or discomfort, however light."[11] Most instances of corporal punishment occur in the home by parents or caregivers. UNICEF estimates "about 6 in 10 children worldwide (almost 1 billion) between the ages of 2 and 14 are subjected to physical (corporal) punishment by their caregivers on a regular basis,"[12] and 75 percent of children between the ages two and four are regularly subjected to physical punishment by their caregivers.[13] Although physical

---

8   Mark Keierleber, "'It's Barbaric': Some US Children Getting Hit at School Despite Bans," *Guardian*, May 19, 2021, https://www.theguardian.com/education/2021/may/19/us-children-corporal-punishment-schools. Keierleber cites the lengthy report by the U.S. Government Accountability Office on "Discipline Disparities for Black Students, Boys, and Students with Disabilities" (March 2018).

9   See "Some Preliminary Data on Home School Child Fatalities," https://www.hsinvisiblechildren.org/commentary/some-preliminary-data-on-homeschool-child-fatalities/.

10 See the many evidence-based and widely respected studies that demonstrate the ineffectiveness and harms of physical punishment, including spanking, such as: Elizabeth T. Gershoff and Andrew Grogan-Kaylor, "Spanking and Child Outcomes: Old Controversies and New Meta-Analysis," *Journal of Family Psychology* 30, no. 4 (2016), 453–69; E. T. Gershoff et al., "The Strength of the Causal Evidence Against Physical Punishment of Children and Its Implications for Parents, Psychologists, and Policymakers," *American Psychologist* 73 (2018), 626–38; E.T. Gershoff et al., "Strengthening Causal Estimates for Links between Spanking and Children's Externalizing Behavior Problems," *Psychological Science*, 29 (2018), 110–20; and J. Ma et al., "Associations of Neighborhood Disorganization and Maternal Spanking with Children's Aggression: A Fixed-Effects Regression Analysis," *Child Abuse & Neglect* 76 (2018), 106–16.

11 UN Committee on the Rights of the Child (CRC), "General Comment No. 8 (2006): The Right of the Child to Protection from Corporal Punishment and Other Cruel or Degrading Forms of Punishment (Arts. 19; 28, Para. 2; and 37, inter alia)," Mar. 2, 2007, CRC/C/GC/8, https://www.refworld.org/docid/460bc7772.html.

12 UNICEF, *Hidden in Plain Sight: A Statistical Analysis of Violence against Children* (New York, 2014),165–66. https://data.unicef.org/resources/hidden-in-plain-sight-a-statistical-analysis-of-violence-against-children/.

13 UNICEF, "A Familiar Face: Violence in the Lives of Children and Adolescents," 2017, https://data.unicef.org/resources/a-familiar-face/.

punishment takes many forms, including choking, burning, or whipping children, the most common form in the U.S. and around the world is spanking and hitting children with a bare hand.[14] Although most states and individuals reject extreme forms of corporal punishment and understand their harms to a child's mental, emotional, physical, and spiritual well-being, spanking is still widely used and accepted, and most American parents spank their children (especially those ages 2 to 7).[15]

Decades of research now clearly and consistently link physical punishment, including spanking, to risks of harm to children, and this research has prompted the emergence of many effective parenting programs that reject spanking and offer parents and caregivers alternatives. Studies that bracket out extreme forms of physical punishment and focus specially on spanking find that it is ineffective and associated with multiple risks, including impaired cognitive ability, low self-esteem, mental health problems, weaker relationships to parents, weaker moral internalization, an increased likelihood of aggressive behavior and substance abuse, and an increased risk for physical abuse.[16] Spanking also increases the likelihood of antisocial behavior and mental health problems in adulthood and even "small effects can translate into large societal impacts."[17] In the light of the overwhelming evidence, social scientists, psychologists, physicians, social workers, and child advocates are calling for the end of spanking and other forms of corporal punishment in all settings, without exception, including the home. They are also offering parents and caregivers positive and effective educational programs that promote creative and compassionate alternatives to physical punishment.[18]

---

14   UNICEF, *Hidden in Plain Sight*, 101.
15   Rates of spanking in the U.S. have recently been declining in some areas but vary across the county. David Finkelhor et al., "Corporal Punishment: Current Rates from a National Survey," *Journal of Child and Family Studies* 28 (2019): 1991–97; and E. T. Gershoff et al., "Longitudinal Links between Spanking and Children's Externalizing Behaviors in a National Sample of White, Black, Hispanic, and Asian American families," *Child Development* 83 (2012): 838–43.
16   For the most complete analyses of outcomes associated with spanking see Gershoff and Grogan-Kaylor, "Spanking and Child Outcomes."
17   Ibid., 465.
18   See Elizabeth T. Gershoff, Shawna J. Lee, and Joan E. Durrant. "Promising Intervention Strategies to Reduce Parents' Use of Physical Punishment," *Child Abuse & Neglect* 71 (2017): 9–23. The authors find that culturally competent parent education as well as the use of evidence-based practices that promote alternatives to physical punishment can support caregivers seeking to change harmful parenting practices. See also Joan E. Durrant, *Positive Discipline in Everyday Parenting*, 4th ed. (Stockholm: Save the Children Sweden, 2006) and other resources available on the website of the highly effective and internationally

If the social-scientific evidence about the harms of physical punishment, including spanking, is now so compelling, and if parents and caregivers can find plenty of resources that promote effective alternatives to physical punishment, then why have more Christians not come together to help stop this practice in their homes and in the U.S.? Why do some Christians still actively support it? Why do some warn of its dangers yet still permit spanking as a last resort? Why are still many more simply silent? In the face of children's suffering, why are Christians—whether right or left, conservative or liberal—who share strong commitments to child well-being neglecting to speak out in their congregations and the public square against corporal punishment in schools or the home? After all, Christians have shown that they can be strong and united advocates for children and marginalized groups around the world. They can critique the practice of child marriage and sex trafficking here and abroad, but why not the practice of spanking and hitting children in their own homes?

In addition to widespread acceptance of spanking in American culture, one clear and major obstacle within the church itself to working together to end physical punishment in all settings is widespread yet narrow assumptions about children and obligations to them built on selected passages or narrow interpretations of the Bible. Thus, one important way for Christians to move forward is not only by recognizing the harms of corporal punishment and offering alternative parenting practices but also by critically examining their assumptions about children and looking more closely at wisdom from the Bible and the Christian tradition. Indeed, as child advocates and faith leaders are finding, when Christians are presented with scientific evidence of the harms of spanking and, at the same time, are given an opportunity to reflect on this evidence in relationship to their religious beliefs, spiritual practices, and interpretations of the Bible, their attitudes change, and they are more likely to avoid or at least to consider avoiding spanking their children.[19]

In line with these findings, this chapter aims to motivate and empower more Christian individuals and organizations to help end the corporal punishment

---

recognized program developed by Durrant called Positive Discipline in Everyday Parenting, https://pdel.org.

19 See, for example, Cindy Miller-Perrin and Robin Perrin, "Changing Attitudes about Spanking among Conservative Christians Using Interventions That Focus on Empirical Research Evidence and Progressive Biblical Interpretations," *Child Abuse & Neglect* 71 (2017): 69–79. For more on the role of religion in cases of corporal punishment and the significance of sensitivity to the religious worldviews of parents, see Victor I. Vieth, "From Sticks to Flowers: Guidelines for Child Protection Professionals Working with Parents Using Scripture to Justify Corporal Punishment," *William Mitchell Law Review* 40, no. 3 (2014): Article 3, https://open.mitchellhamline.edu/wmlr/vol40/iss3/3.

of children in all settings by reflecting on and expanding the church's vision of children and commitments to them. The chapter highlights examples of shared commitments and collaborative contributions to child well-being among Christians, outlines their diverging opinions on the corporal punishment of children, and then provides biblical and theological grounds for rejecting corporal punishment.

Building specifically on biblical perspectives about children's vulnerabilities, strengths, and agency and about discipline, discipleship, and limits of parental authority, the chapter claims that physical punishment of children is inconsistent with central Christian conceptions of and commitments to children. By outlining areas of existing agreement and robust biblical and theological grounds for banning corporal punishment in all settings, the chapter shows how diverse and sometimes polarized Christian denominations and faith-based organizations could widen their common ground and work together more effectively to protect children and promote their well-being. In this way, Isaiah's powerful vision of *shalom* for children might be more fully realized both in households and in the larger society.

Although this chapter focuses on the U.S. and Christian grounds for rejecting the corporal punishment of children, it has implications for any secular or religious child advocacy groups that seek to reduce spanking and corporal punishment. For example, the chapter could be used as a resource in any program that includes Christian participants. Furthermore, since over 80 percent of the world's population self-affiliates with a religious tradition, and corporal punishment is a worldwide problem, this chapter encourages child advocates to couple scientific evidence against corporal punishment with cultural sensitivity and attention to the religious beliefs and practices of the communities they are seeking to serve. Finally, the chapter can be a springboard for faith leaders and child advocates from diverse religious traditions to search for and emphasize not only scientific but also religious and spiritual grounds for ending corporal punishment in their faith communities.

2 Common Commitments and Areas of Cooperation

Although Christians in the United States have highly diverse understandings about many issues, they understand that children are vulnerable and in need of protection, and they share a commitment to addressing urgent needs of children. They take seriously biblical mandates to love the neighbor and to care for the poor, sick, and hungry, including children. Even though Christians might disagree about biblical interpretation, the relation between science and religion, or the role of the state in educating and protecting children, many Christian denominations and individuals can and have worked together locally and globally to address the needs of children and families by offering, for instance, disaster relief, food, shelter, health care, job training, and education. Furthermore, Christian denominations and faith-based organizations often work across many lines of difference to coordinate their efforts, and many programs initiated by Christians—such as Bread for the World, World Vision, Mennonite Disaster Service, Lutheran Social Services, Lutheran World Relief, and Catholic Relief Services—are widely respected by secular and faith-based organizations alike.

In addition to emphasizing their responsibility to address urgent needs of children here and abroad, Christians in the U.S. across the political and ecclesial spectrum also affirm the importance of the family for protecting, ensuring the well-being of, and nurturing the faith of children. They understand that children are developing and need guidance, and that parents should provide for their children's needs and play a central role in their physical, intellectual, moral, and spiritual formation. Many Christians, like Jews, refer to the famous lines from Deuteronomy when encouraging parents to talk about faith with their children: "You shall love the Lord your God with all your heart, and with all your soul, and with all your might. Keep these words that I am commanding you today in your heart. Recite them to your children and talk about them when you are at home and when you are away, when you lie down and when you rise (6:5–7)." Christians also emphasize that the church should support families in this task, and thus churches across the country typically welcome families, offer a host of religious education and youth programs, and provide material and financial support for families in need.

Diverse denominational and nondenominational Christians also believe that strong family life serves not only children but also the larger society. The Roman Catholic Church, for example, strongly affirms the primacy of the family, claiming it is a divine institution and the basic unit of society, where children can fully and properly develop and appropriate important values, such as justice, that also help them contribute to the common good. As Pope Francis stated, "The family remains the basic unit of society and the first school in which children learn the human, spiritual, and moral values which enable them to be a beacon of goodness, integrity, and justice in our communities."[20]

---

20 Pope Francis, "Address of Pope Francis, Apostolic Journey of His Holiness to Seoul on the Occasion of the 6th Asian Youth Day," Aug. 16, 2014, https://www.vatican.va/content/francesco/en/speeches/2014/august/documents/papa-francesco_20140816_corea-leader-apostolato-laico.html.

Catholic social teaching also emphasizes that children are a gift, and that the family is the place where children learn "their first and most important lessons of practical wisdom" and "a divine institution that stands at the foundation of life of the human person as the prototype of every social order."[21]

Certainly, in the light of mounting evidence of child sexual abuse cases not only in the Roman Catholic Church and the Southern Baptist Convention but also other churches and organizations that work with children and youth (such as schools and sports facilities), the church has clearly failed children, and more churches are finally paying serious attention to preventing child abuse within their walls. Local congregations and national church bodies have a host of resources available to create substantive child-protection guidelines and policies.[22] Christians are also working across religious and secular lines to find more effective ways not only to prevent but also to recognize and respond to child abuse. For example, churches are learning from and working with highly respected secular organizations, such as the Zero Abuse Project,[23] and religiously affiliated projects, such as the Jewish organization Sacred Spaces.[24] This work of child protection within the church slowly includes helping the church respond to the abuse and murder of Indigenous children in residential schools in the United States and Canada and around the world. For example, in response to calls for action that came out of Canada's Truth and Reconciliation Commission, Canadian churches are working with others to eliminate sexual abuse in the church and to ban laws that permit corporal punishment.[25]

---

21 See Pontifical Council for Justice and Peace, *Compendium of the Social Doctrine of the Church*, 210–11. See the entire section in the *Compendium* on "The Family, the Vital Cell of Society": https://www.vatican.va/roman_curia/pontifical_councils/justpeace/documents/rc_pc_justpeace_doc_20060526_compendio-dott-soc_en.html.

22 See, for example: Joy Thornburg Melton, *Safe Sanctuaries: Reducing the Risk of Child Abuse in the Church* (Nashville: Discipleship Resources, 1998); Jeanette Harder, *Let the Children Come: Preparing Faith Communities to End Child Abuse and Neglect* (Scottdale, PA: Herald Press, 2010); Boz Tchividjian, *Protecting Children from Abuse in the Church* (Greensboro, NC: New Growth Press, 2013); and Boz Tchividjian and Shira M. Berkovits, *The Child Safeguarding Policy Guide for Churches and Ministries* (Greensboro, NC: New Growth Press, 2017)

23 https://www.zeroabuseproject.org/.

24 https://www.jewishsacredspaces.org/.

25 For an introduction to these efforts, see *Decolonizing Discipline: Children, Corporal Punishment, Christian Theologies, and Reconciliation*, ed. Valerie Michaelson and Joan E. Durrant (Winnipeg: University of Manitoba Press, 2020). See also Valerie Michaelson, "A Decolonial Approach to Formation and Discipline," in *Child Theology: Diverse Methods and Global Perspectives*, ed. Marcia J. Bunge (Maryknoll, NY: Orbis Books, 2021), 172–89.

3 Areas of Disagreement Regarding Physical Punishment

Although nondenominational and denominational Christians alike affirm the significance of parents and the family for child well-being and understand the need for child protection within the walls of the church, they generally neglect to address the tremendous problem in the United States of child neglect and abuse in the home. Most cases of child abuse and neglect occur in the home. Approximately seven million child-abuse cases are reported each year in the U.S., and 90.6 percent of the victims are maltreated by one or both parents.[26] Approximately five children die each day because of abuse, and 80 percent of fatalities involve a parent. However, few churches speak, teach, or preach about injustices that children experience at home, including physical punishment.

Furthermore, although conservative Protestants helpfully honor the importance of parenting and bringing up children in the faith, many affirm a parent's right to spank their children. Some strongly advocate its use, while others consider it a last resort. Conservative Protestants in general are more likely than other parents to support and practice physical punishment.[27] Those who actively support a parent's right to use corporal punishment incorporate methods of spanking children into their books about Christian parenting, child rearing, and discipline. Some of the more extreme yet highly visible conversative Christian approaches to parenting allow and, in some cases, even encourage the corporal punishment of children with the "rod" as part of "disciplining." Even though other conservative Christians have moved further away from the practice of spanking, they still leave the door open for spanking as a last resort. For example, the organization Focus on the Family and its founder, James Dobson, have paid attention in important and positive ways to strengthening families, child development, and faith formation. They do not equate discipline with punishment and absolutely and clearly reject child abuse. Nevertheless, Dobson's popular book, *The New Dare to Discipline,* and the Focus on the Family website still allow spanking as a last resort.[28] Parenting books by conservative Christians are so widespread in social media that

---

26   See these and other statistics on child abuse and neglect: The American Society for the Positive Care of Children, https://americanspcc.org/child-maltreatment-statistics.
27   John P. Hoffman, Christopher G. Ellison, and John P. Bartkowski, "Conservative Protestantism and Attitudes toward Corporal Punishment," *Social Science Research* 63 (2017): 81–94.
28   See *The New Dare to Discipline* (Carol Stream, IL: Tyndale Momentum, 2018) and several references to spanking on the Focus on the Family website, including "How to Spank: To Spank or Not to Spank," https://www.focusonthefamily.com/parenting/to-spank-or-not-to-spank/.

many Christians and non-Christians alike assume that Christian parenting and Christian approaches to discipline involve physically punishing children.

Whether they rigorously support spanking or consider it a last resort, conservative Protestants often refer to a narrow range of biblical texts to support their position, and they end up with narrow theological understandings of children and child-parent relations. For example, they tend to paraphrase and interpret selected passages from Proverbs, such as "Folly is bound up in the heart of child, but the rod of discipline drives it far from him" (22:15), as providing a mandate for spanking their children. They also cite a passage in Ephesians that refers to "the discipline and instruction of the Lord" (6:4). Based on such passages, the role of parents is primarily understood as teaching and disciplining, and the role of children as learning and obeying. Conservative Protestants also tend to emphasize the authority of parents and parental rights, and they believe that obedience to parents cultivates obedience to God. Few resources talk about the limits of parental authority or the capacity of parents to sin or harm their children. In addition, some conservative Protestants stress that children are prone to egocentrism and sinfulness, and parents must therefore shape or even "break" their will because, if left to their own devices, children will defy their parents and God.[29]

For various reasons, the Roman Catholic Church and mainline Protestant churches have not aggressively challenged the practice of corporal punishment in the home, and they are less vocal about how parents should raise their children than highly visible conservative Protestant approaches. Some of the most highly respected approaches to faith formation in mainline churches, such as Godly Play,[30] certainly help parents have a deep respect for children, their questions, and spiritual life. Yet parenting workshops and resources are less widely available or promoted among mainline churches. Liberal Protestant churches are vocal about social and environmental injustices and child abuse in the church but strangely silent about injustices against children and child maltreatment in the family.

Given the visibility of narrow yet popular religiously conservative conceptions of children, parenting, discipline, and faith formation, and the absence of more intentional conversations about parenting in many mainline congregations, other parents make assumptions about what "Christian parenting"

---

29 C. Miller-Perrin and R. Perrin, "Changing Attitudes," 71.
30 Founded by Jerome W. Berryman. For more information and resources, see the Godly Play Foundation website (https://www.godlyplayfoundation.org/) and books by Jerome Berryman, including *Godly Play: An Imaginative Approach to Religious Education* (San Francisco: HarperSanFrancisco, 1991).

and "raising children in the faith" mean and want nothing to do with it. These parents might baptize their children but then step back completely, presuming that Christian parenting is coercive, even harmful.

Even more tragically, when parents and faith leaders religiously justify or simply ignore child maltreatment, however "mild," children can experience not only physical, emotional, mental, and intellectual but also spiritual harm. Thirty-four major studies, involving more than nineteen thousand abused children, demonstrate that even though religion and spirituality can play a positive role in coping with traumatic events, many children who are maltreated experience spiritual struggles or a loss of faith.[31]

4 Robust Theological Conceptions of and Commitments to Children

Thus, we see many branches of Christianity—whether right or left, conservative or liberal, whether they encourage spanking or say nothing at all about it—ignoring the dangers of corporal punishment for child well-being and neglecting to speak out against laws that allow corporal punishment in the home and other settings.

One important way that Christians can find stronger common ground for promoting child well-being and rejecting corporal punishment is by expanding their conceptions of and corresponding commitments to children. More robust and biblically based conceptions of children (also called theologies of childhood) strengthen adult-child relationships and empower the whole church to reject corporal punishment and help all children thrive.[32]

As we have seen, even though Christians might differ theologically and in their parenting practices, they already share at least two important conceptions of children and obligations to them. First, they understand that children

---

31 Donald F. Walker et al., "Changes in Personal Religion/Spirituality During and After Childhood Abuse: A Review and Synthesis," *Psychological Trauma: Theory, Research, Practice and Policy* 1 (2009): 130–45.

32 This section on theological conceptions of and commitments to children builds on several articles I have written on theologies of childhood, including "The Significance of Robust Theologies of Childhood for Honouring Children's Full Humanity and Rejecting Corporal Punishment," in Michaelson and Durrant, *Decolonizing Discipline*, 108–22. See also "Conceptions of and Commitments to Children: Biblical Wisdom for Families, Congregations, and the Worldwide Church," in *Faith Forward: Launching a Revolution through Ministry with Children, Youth, and Families*, vol. 3, ed. David M. Csinos (Lake Country, BC: Wood Lake, 2018), 94–112; and "The Vocation of the Child: Theological Perspectives on the Particular and Paradoxical Roles and Responsibilities of Children," in *The Vocation of the Child*, ed. Patrick McKinley Brennan (Grand Rapids, MI: Eerdmans, 2008), 31–52.

are vulnerable, and therefore adults have a responsibility to protect them and address their needs. Second, they view children as developing and in need of guidance, and therefore parents, caregivers, and other caring adults have a responsibility to guide children, nurture their faith, and educate them. These two biblical perspectives alone provide Christians ample grounds for protecting children and rejecting physical punishment. After all, if Christians agreed that they are to protect and seek justice for the most vulnerable, including children, then why would they not seek to protect all children from any form of physical harm and provide the basic security they need to thrive? Furthermore, if Christians understood that children are still developing and that adults are called to instruct, guide, and bring them up in the faith, helping them to love God and neighbor, and if they would not strike an adult as a way to teach love of neighbor, then why would they strike a child? Even without knowing the scientific evidence, does it not make common sense that physically punishing children thwarts learning and impedes their capacity to internalize central Christian values of love and justice? What positive role could spanking possibly play in bringing up children in the faith and nurturing their moral and spiritual development?

Even though these two central Christian perspectives about children's need for protection and guidance are important, by critically and more closely examining the Bible and Christian tradition, Christians discover several additional perspectives that provide a stronger vision of children's full humanity. These additional perspectives help the church view children not only as vulnerable and developing and thereby in need of protection and instruction but also as fully human persons with unique strengths and capacities who enrich and contribute to communities and deserve to be heard and respected.

Here are just two additional biblically based perspectives that provide the church with a more holistic and full-bodied understanding of children and obligations to them.

First, the Bible and Christian tradition emphasize that children are whole and complete human beings who are made in the image of God. Thus, adults are to treat children, like all persons, with dignity and respect. Respect for the equal worth of people, including children, is built on one of the most foundational conceptions of human beings in both Judaism and Christianity: All human beings are made in the image of God and possess a fundamental God-given equality. This conviction is based on Genesis 1:27, which states that God made all human beings in "the image of God." Thus, all children, like all adults—regardless of race, gender, age, socioeconomic status, sexual orientation, or any other difference—are made in God's image, have intrinsic value, and are equally worthy of dignity and respect. Although we might consider it self-evident that infants and children are human beings, in many places and times, including in various contexts today, many children are not considered fully human. Children have been perceived and mistreated as ignorant, a parent's property, or economic burdens. They have been exploited as gullible consumers, sex objects, or child soldiers. Yet from the beginning of the church, theologians have emphasized the full equality and intrinsic value of all persons, including infants and children. In the third century, for example, Cyprian wrote that all people, even infants, are "alike and equal since they have been made once by God." All share a "divine and spiritual equality."[33]

The perspective that children are made in God's image and are therefore to be treated as worthy of dignity and respect provides powerful grounds for Christians to reject corporal punishment in all settings. With this perspective, how could anyone bracket out some groups of children—whether two to four years, two to twelve, or any other age outlined in civil law or some Christian parenting resources—for corporal punishment when we do not consider such punishment appropriate for adults? In what way would spanking children, slapping their hands, or giving them "two smacks max" as a form of discipline convey to them their full humanity and dignity and our respect for them as fully human and made in the image of God? After all, if one hits an adult, we call it assault. If one strikes a partner, we call it domestic violence. Why dismiss hitting or spanking vulnerable infants and children who are made in God's image and have intrinsic worth as mild discipline or as a parent's right?

Second, the Bible also claims that children are models of faith for adults, spirit-filled, and endowed with strengths, gifts, and talents to contribute to their families and communities now and in the future. Thus, adults do not just teach children. From a biblical perspective, adults are to listen to and learn from them, honor their current relationship with God and their contributions to families and communities, and provide them with an excellent education so that they can continue to cultivate their gifts and talents and contribute to the common good, both now and in the future. The Bible depicts children and young people in striking and even radical ways as models of faith, positive agents of change, and prophets, such as in the stories of the boy Samuel (1 Samuel 2–4) and the young David (1 Samuel 17). In all three synoptic gospels, Jesus identifies himself with children and lifts them up as paradigms of receiving the reign of God, saying, "Truly I tell you, whoever does not receive the kingdom of God as a little child will never enter it" (Mark 10:13–16). The Bible also depicts children as Spirit-filled. As theologians across branches of Christianity,

---

33   Cyprian, Letter 64.3; in *Letters*, trans. Sister Rose Bernard Donna (Washington, DC: Catholic University of America Press, 1964), 217–18.

including the Pentecostal theologian Amos Yong, remind the global church: God's Spirit is not limited by a person's age; it is already working in children and young people.[34] Biblical passages depict children and infants praising God (Psalms 8:2; Matthew 21:15). As the book of Acts declares, God's Spirit will be poured out "upon all flesh, and your sons and your daughters shall prophesy, and your young men shall see visions" (Acts 2:17; cf. Joel 2:28–32). In these and other ways, the Bible depicts children as Spirit-filled, models for adults, positive agents of change, prophets, and endowed with gifts and talents.

This conception of children with its corresponding responsibility for adults to listen to, learn from, and recognize the contributions of children strengthens adult-child relationships and empowers child advocacy in a host of ways. For example, by listening more carefully to children, adults cultivate more meaningful and mutually rewarding conversations with them. By recognizing children's strengths, adults more intentionally honor the ways that children and young people already enrich familial and community life. By realizing that the Holy Spirit is already moving in children's lives, adults pay more attention to their ethical and spiritual questions and are more open to listening and learning from their experiences. In these ways and more, this perspective deepens respect for children and creates stronger adult-child bonds. Adults are thereby more likely to listen to, delight in, and advocate for children and less likely to physically harm, disrespect, or simply dismiss them.

Robust Christian understandings of children that incorporate the above four and other biblically based conceptions of children greatly strengthen commitments to and relationships with them. Full-bodied theologies of childhood help Christians see children in a multifaceted and paradoxical light. Children are developing in need of guidance and protection yet also fully human and worthy of dignity and respect. They are vulnerable and in need of protection and guidance yet also endowed with strengths and insights that contribute to our daily lives. Holding together and attending to these four and other important perspectives helps adults cultivate closer and more meaningful relationships with children in their midst and empowers stronger advocacy with and on behalf of all children. As Christian theologians around the world pay greater attention to the vulnerabilities and strengths of children, they are developing an increasing number of robust theologies of childhood as well as child-attentive theologies that, like Black, feminist, and other liberation theologies,

---

34   See Amos Yong, "Children and the Spirit in Luke and Acts," in Bunge, *Child Theology*, 108–28.

reexamine central Christian doctrines and practices in the light marginalized groups—in this case children.[35]

5 The Teachings and Example of Jesus

Robust theologies of childhood are also in line with the teachings and example of Jesus. Jesus taught his disciples and followers to love God with all your heart, soul, mind, and strength and to love your neighbor as yourself (Mark 12:30–31), and he clearly included children as our neighbors. At a time when children occupied a low position in society, and child abandonment was not a crime, the gospels portray Jesus as blessing, welcoming, touching, and healing children.

If we look closely at just a few of the verbs used to describe Jesus's interactions with children, we see his warm, compassionate, and respectful engagement. He blesses, heals, and takes children up in his arms. Furthermore, he equates welcoming a child in his name to welcoming himself and the one who sent him, claiming "Whoever welcomes one such child in my name welcomes me" (Matthew 18:1–5; Mark 9:37).[36] Here the Greek word for "welcomes" or "receives" (δέχομαι; dechomai) can mean "warmly receptive or welcoming" or "receptive with a high level of involvement."

In addition, Jesus rebukes those who turn them away and even lifts children up as models of faith. When children are brought to Jesus so that he might bless and pray for them, the disciples try to stop them, but Jesus rebukes the disciples, saying, "Let the little children come to me, and do not stop them; for it is to such as these that the kingdom of heaven belongs" (Matthew 19:14). In another passage found in all three synoptic gospels, Jesus uses a strong word meaning "cause to stumble" or "offend" and related to the English word for "scandal" (σκανδαλίσῃ, skandalisē) when he says, "If any of you *put a stumbling block* [σκανδαλίσῃ] before one of these little ones who believe in me, it would be better for you if a great millstone were hung around your neck and you were thrown into the sea" (Mark 9:42; cf. Luke 17:2; Matthew 18:6).

---

35 For an introduction to the specific task of child-attentive theologies, including child liberation theologies, see Marcia J. Bunge and Megan Eide, "Strengthening Theology by Honoring Children," in Bunge, *Child Theology*, XIII–XXV; Craig Nessan, "Attending to the Cries of Children in Liberation Theologies," in Bunge, *Child Theology*, 1–20; and the work of R. L. Stollar, including *The Kingdom of Children: A Liberation Theology* (Grand Rapids, MI: Eerdmans, 2023).

36 For other relevant passages, see Mark 9:33–37 and 10:13–16; Luke 9:46–48 and 18:15–17; and Matthew 18:1–5, 19:13–15, 11:25, and 21:14–16.

Furthermore, we find no biblical accounts of Jesus striking an adult, let alone a child, or commanding or teaching his followers to physically punish their children. Rather, his teaching and actions consistently reflect compassion for others, including children and the marginalized. Even if not all of Jesus's words and actions were recorded, one cannot imagine Jesus slapping, striking, or spanking a child or encouraging his followers to do so. Who knows of any images, paintings, noncanonical texts, or stories of Jesus spanking or hitting children?

It is also noteworthy that physical punishment does not appear in the New Testament picture of discipleship. Jesus never recommends hitting, spanking, or physically punishing oneself or others as a way to be a faithful follower or to love God and the neighbor. Rather, he calls his followers to be close to him and to be like him. Furthermore, the activities and practices Jesus carries out and encourages his disciples to emulate are loving others (including one's enemies), repenting, forgiving, praying, serving the poor, fasting, caring for and healing the sick, washing one another's feet, being humble, attending to the Word of God, and spreading the good news.[37]

6 Biblically Based, Christ-Centered Notions of Discipline and Discipleship

A robust understanding of commitments to children, Jesus's teachings and actions, and a closer reading of additional biblical texts help to clarify for Christians what discipline and discipleship might properly mean in relationship to child-rearing and physical punishment. As noted above, Christians debates about child-rearing often refer to the notion of discipline and the passage in Ephesians on "the discipline and instruction of the Lord" (6:4). However, Christians interpret discipline in a variety of ways. As we have seen, some conservative Protestants strongly link discipline with physical punishment. Others offer a broader view of discipline yet still consider spanking to be part of a parent's "discipline toolkit," even if only as a last resort.[38] Given this close and

---

37 For reflections directly on child abuse and Jesus's teaching, see Victor I. Vieth, *On This Rock: A Call to Center the Christian Response to Child Abuse on the Life and Words of Jesus* (Eugene, OR: Wipf & Stock, 2018).

38 See "Biblical Discipline: A Full Toolkit for Parents," on the Focus on the Family website. Here, discipline is not defined as punishment, yet spanking still has a place in a parent's "discipline toolkit" as a "last resort, done to capture attention and create clear understanding so that a particular behavior doesn't happen again": https://www.focusonthefamily.com/parenting/building-your-discipline-toolkit-from-a-biblical-perspective/.

common connection between discipline and physical punishment, some liberal and mainline Christians avoid the term altogether, yet in the process they sometimes shy away from more intentionally emphasizing the responsibility of parents to help nurture children's spiritual development in their daily lives.

Thus, clarifying the meaning of "discipline" and "discipleship" is important not only for conservative or evangelical but also for liberal or mainline Christians. Furthermore, clarifying the meaning of these highly contested terms is another important way to empower Christians across the ecclesiastical and political spectrum to come together with the shared goal of rejecting physical punishment in all settings, including the home.[39] By reflecting more deeply on the meaning of "discipleship" and "discipline," Christians can also think together in fresh and creative ways about positive faith formation and parenting practices that exclude spanking and any other form of physical punishment, as many parents and faith leaders are doing.[40]

In the English translations of the Bible, words for "discipline" and "discipleship" are translations of various Greek terms. When we examine more carefully their meanings in specific New Testament passages, we find some surprises. They have nothing to do with corporal punishment. Rather, as we see both in the Bible and in testimonies of positive faith formation experiences past and present, "discipleship" and the "discipline of the Lord" are cultivated by following Jesus's command to love and serve the neighbor (which refers to all persons, including one's enemies) and by carrying out central spiritual practices such as worshipping, praying, forgiving, and reading the scriptures.

The Greek word for "disciple" is μαθητής (*mathētēs*), and it refers broadly to a student, pupil, learner, or adherent of a particular leader or movement. In the gospels, we see Jesus calling his disciples to learn from him, to be in relationship to him, and to heal, preach, love, and forgive. "Learn from me," he says, "for I am gentle and humble in heart, and you will find rest for your souls" (Matthew 11:29). Jesus appoints twelve disciples "to be with him, and to be sent out to proclaim the message" (Mark 3:14). In Luke, after healing all who were trying to touch him, Jesus preaches to a great crowd of disciples, teaching them to "love your enemies, do good to those who hate you" (Luke 6:27). Jesus later

---

39 This section on discipline and corporal punishment builds on Marcia J. Bunge, "Rethinking Christian Theologies of Discipline and Discipleship," in Michaelson and Durrant, *Decolonizing Discipline*, 152–60.

40 See, for example, the work of Charlene Hallett and Ashley Stewart-Tufescu, who are facilitators for the Positive Parenting in Everyday Life program, including their coauthored chapter "Walking the Path toward Reconciliation: One Mother's Transformative Journey from Parenting with Punishment to Parenting with Positive Discipline," in Michaelson and Durrant, *Decolonizing Discipline*, 161–72.

powerfully states, "A disciple is not above the teacher, but everyone who is fully qualified [or "fully trained"] will be like the teacher" (Luke 6:40). Becoming a disciple of Jesus involves following him and being in relationship or fellowship with him. As Paul writes to the Corinthians, God is calling them "into the fellowship of his Son, Jesus Christ our Lord" (1 Corinthians 1:9).

Given this notion of disciple and discipleship, what can we learn further about the concept of discipline in the New Testament? None of the teachings or sayings of Jesus in the gospels refer to "discipline." References to "discipline" are found only in some letters of the New Testament, where the word is often a translation of the Greek word παιδεία (*paideia*), which cannot be responsibly translated as "physical punishment."

Paideia is a Greek term that generally refers to instruction, training, education, upbringing, or guidance.[41] *Paideia* has been used in ancient Greek philosophy and even at some liberal arts colleges today to speak about the kind of wide-ranging education that can lead to excellence, virtue, and contributions as a citizen.[42] Thus, for the ancient Greeks and for thinkers past and present, *paideia* refers to a broad and holistic education that includes training in moral, physical, and intellectual life. Even though some ancient Greeks did physically punish children as part of their upbringing, *paideia* is not a term that can be translated or understood as physical punishment but is much more closely associated with well-rounded understandings of education, formation, and training.

In the often-quoted passage from Ephesians 6:4, for example, the word translated as "discipline" is *paideia*, and it is used in the phrase, "discipline of the Lord." Here, "discipline and instruction," especially "discipline and instruction in the Lord," cannot be equated with physical punishment. Furthermore, this passage even begins with a warning not to provoke children to anger or exasperate them. "Do not provoke your children to anger but bring them up in the discipline [*paideia*] and instruction [*nouthesia*] of the Lord" (Ephesians 6:4).

Colossians also warns parents not to provoke their children "or they may lose heart" (Colossians 3:21), and this text and others address the qualities of those who find new life in Christ. The Greek verb used in 3:21 is ἀθυμῶσιν

---

41 See the entry for *paideia*, for example, in F. Wilbur Gingrich and Frederick W. Dancker, *A Greek-English Lexicon of the New Testament and Other Early Christian Literature*, 2nd ed., rev. and augmented from Walter Bauer's 5th ed., 1958 (Chicago: University of Chicago Press, 1979).

42 Luther College, a liberal arts college in Decorah, Iowa, for example, uses the word *paideia* as the title of a signature offering in its general education program. See "Paideia," Luther College, https://www.luther.edu/academics/approach-to-academics/paideia.

(*athymōsin*), and other translations of the passage include "lest they become discouraged" or "disheartened." In Colossians, the warning not to provoke children to anger is preceded by a long description of the new life in Christ and the admonition to "clothe yourselves with compassion, kindness, humility, meekness, and patience," and, "above all," to "clothe yourselves with love, which binds everything together in perfect harmony" (Colossians 3:12,14). In Paul's letter to the Galatians, he also speaks of being "clothed with" and unified in Christ (Galatians 3:26–27). He describes the fruit of the Spirit as "love, joy, peace, patience, kindness, generosity, faithfulness, gentleness, and self-control" (Galatians 5:22–23), and he warns: "If anyone is detected in a transgression, you who have received the Spirit should restore such a one in a spirit of gentleness" (Galatians 6:1).

The noun *paideian* is used in 2 Timothy to speak of "training in righteousness" (2 Timothy 3:16), and here, too, there is no reference to physical punishment. Rather, the passage emphasizes that "training in righteousness" takes place by studying scripture. "All scripture is inspired by God and is useful for teaching, for reproof, for correction, and for training [*paideian*] in righteousness" (2 Timothy 3:16). The Greek word translated as "for correction" in this passage is ἐπανόρθωσιν (*epanorthōsin*), which refers to restoring to an upright state or straightening of the conduct of one who is crooked.

Some references to "self-discipline" or "self-control" can also be found in New Testament letters in relation to both discipleship and leadership, and they are translations of other Greek terms. For example, Titus 1:8 uses the Greek adjective ἐγκρατῆ (*enkratē*), translated as "self-disciplined," "disciplined," or "temperate," to help describe one of the important qualities of a church leader, along with "hospitable," "a lover of goodness," "upright," "devout," and "prudent" (also translated as "sensible"). In 2 Timothy, self-discipline and love are contrasted with cowardice: "For God did not give us a spirit of cowardice, but rather a spirit of power and of love and of self-discipline [σωφρονισμοῦ (*sōphronismou*)]" (2 Timothy 1:7).

The only passage in the New Testament that appears to link discipline (*paideia*) with suffering and possibly punishment are a few verses in Hebrews (12:5–9) that quote directly from Proverbs.[43] Here the author of Hebrews speaks of the "discipline [*paideias*] of the Lord" and quotes Proverbs 3:11–12. However,

---

43 For further discussion of Proverbs and Hebrews 12, see William Morrow, "What Do We Do with Proverbs?," in Michelson and Durrant, *Decolonizing Discipline*, 93–107. For an expansive interpretation of Proverbs as a whole, see William P. Brown, "To Discipline without Destruction: The Multifaceted Profile of the Child in Proverbs," in *The Child in the Bible*, 63–81.

in these passages of Hebrews, the author is not speaking about training or teaching children, and the one here who disciplines is not parents but God. As we learn from many biblical scholars, the author of Hebrews is addressing early Christians who have experienced persecution. The author acknowledges their suffering and encourages them to keep the faith. Although this text has much to say about enduring suffering and God's action in the world, this passage does not prescribe the corporal punishment of children.

Given even this brief exploration of discipleship, discipline, and Jesus's own teachings and example, Christians have ample biblical support to reject physical punishment, including spanking, as a proper form of Christ-centered discipline. Although some Christians have spanked or physically punished their children to "discipline" them or help them become disciples, the primary and biblically based spiritual practices encouraged by Jesus and among diverse forms of Christianity around the world, past and present, for becoming or raising disciples do not include physical punishment. Rather, among the most central practices are loving others, praying, repenting, forgiving, studying the Word of God, worshipping together, sharing bread and wine in remembrance of Jesus, being baptized, spreading the good news, and serving those in need.

Such spiritual practices, which are deeply rooted in the Christian tradition, are also the focus of several contemporary studies of healthy spiritual development and faith formation. For example, prominent social-scientific studies of the spiritual and religious lives of children and teenagers do not indicate that physical punishment promotes healthy child development or spiritual growth. Rather, social scientists who have studied Christian families and faith communities point to other factors that help children grow and develop in their faith and cultivate a larger sense of purpose, such as worshipping, praying, caring for others, and talking about faith at home and in their faith communities.[44] Respected religious educators who have developed faith formation programs and resources for the church say nothing about corporal punishment, focusing instead on cultivating warm and caring child-adult relationships, talking

---

44 See, for example, Christian Smith and Melinda L. Denton, *Soul Searching: The Religious and Spiritual Lives of American Teenagers* (Oxford: Oxford University Press, 2005); Robert Wuthnow, *Growing Up Religious: Christians and Jews and Their Journeys of Faith* (Boston: Beacon Press, 1999); Eugene C. Roehlkepartain et al., eds., *The Handbook of Spiritual Development in Childhood and Adolescence* (Thousand Oaks, CA: Sage, 2006); and Karen M. Yust et al., eds., *Nurturing Child and Adolescent Spirituality: Perspectives from the World's Religious Traditions* (Lanham, MD: Rowman & Littlefield, 2006). See also the resources and ongoing studies of the Search Institute, https://searchinstitute.org/.

about faith, and carrying out spiritual practices with children and youth in the home and congregation.[45] When young people themselves are asked to reflect on experiences that positively shaped their spiritual or moral development, they do not mention spankings. Rather, most of them talk about positive role models and experiences such as participating in service projects, belonging to a warm and supportive faith community, leading worship, attending summer camps, praying with others, and talking about life's joys and struggles with parents, mentors, or friends. Such practices—not physical punishment—nurture faith, cultivate a rich emotional, moral, and spiritual vocabulary, create meaningful relationships with adults, and help children flourish.

Even if one believes that corporal punishment truly does no harm, what positive role could it possibly play in nurturing a child's spiritual development? Do adults who were physically punished as children talk about it as one of the most powerful and positive ways that they deepened their faith or connected more deeply with their parents? As testimonies of children who have been spanked, memories of adults who were physically punished as children, and the research of social scientists clearly show, physical punishment is much more likely to promote fear and anger, breed shame and resentment, and erode self-esteem and parent-child relationships.[46]

---

45 Additional resources on the spiritual development and faith formation of children in Christian communities include Merton P. Strommen and Richard Hardel, *Passing on the Faith: A Radical New Model for Youth and Family Ministry* (Winona, MN: St. Mary's Press, 2000); Kara Powell, Brad Griffin, and Cheryl Crawford, *Sticky Faith: Youth Worker Edition* (Grand Rapids, MI: Zondervan, 2011); John Roberto, Kathie Amidei, and Jim Merhaut, *Generations Together: Caring, Praying, Learning, Celebrating, and Serving Faithfully* (Naugatuck, CT: LifelongFaith Associates, 2014); Vern Bengtson, *Families and Faith: How Religion Is Passed Down across Generations* (New York: Oxford University Press, 2013); and Catherine Stonehouse and Scottie May, *Listening to Children on the Spiritual Journey: Guidance for Those Who Teach and Nurture* (Grand Rapids, MI: Baker Academic, 2010). For more about the spiritual lives of children and adolescents generally, see, for example, S. Cavalletti, *The Religious Potential of the Child* (New York: Paulist Press, 1983); Robert Coles, *The Spiritual Life of Children* (Boston: Houghton Mifflin, 1990); and David Hay and Rebecca Nye, *The Spirit of the Child* (London: Fount, 1998).

46 For concise, compelling, and accessible introductions to social-scientific research on the harms of corporal punishment and on the perspectives of children who have been physically punished, see the following chapters in Michaelson and Durrant, *Decolonizing Discipline*: Joan E. Durrant, "'I Was Spanked and I'm OK': Examining Thirty Years of Research Evidence on Corporal Punishment," 23–25; and Bernadette J. Saunders, "Corporal Punishment: The Child's Experience," 36–50.

7 Children's Growing Moral Capacities and the Limits of Parental Authority

The church can also work together to advance its child-protection efforts by building on biblically informed perspectives on children, discipline, and discipleship to expose and dispel a narrow and destructive view of children that is widely and falsely assumed by religious and secular groups alike to be central to Christian parenting. This is the notion that children are primarily sinful and disobedient and that therefore a primary duty of parents is to assert their authority, ensure that their children obey them, and, if necessary, "break their wills" by spanking them or physically punishing them with their hand or a "rod." Conservative Protestants are more likely to express this view, and they justify it primarily by referring to selected passages in Proverbs. Although studies find that conservative Christians do not abuse children at higher rates than other parents, they are more likely to spank or slap their young children.[47] Furthermore, focusing on children almost exclusively as sinful has warped Christian approaches to children and led in some cases to child abuse and even death.

By referring primarily to Proverbs to justify their actions, Christians who rigidly hold this view neglect the rich and robust conceptions of children and corresponding obligations to them that we find in the Bible, as outlined above. Those who focus primarily on children's sin also end up with distorted notions of children's growing development and parental authority. They also overshadow Jesus's central message of loving God and loving your neighbor as yourself with flat and negative notions of children and inflated and dangerously naïve views of parents.

The Bible and the Christian tradition do emphasize that children are moral agents with growing capacities and responsibilities, and that adults should seek to model for them compassion and accountability and cultivate practices and patterns of mutual confession, forgiveness, and renewal both at church and in the home. Connected to this perspective is an understanding that human beings have the capacity to harm themselves or others. In biblical language, they sometimes sin against themselves or others. As Paul wrote, all are "under the power of sin," and "there is no one who is righteous, not even one" (Romans 3: 9–10; cf. 5:12).

---

47 See Christopher G. Ellison, "Conservative Protestantism and the Corporal Punishment of Children: Clarifying the Issues," *Journal for the Scientific Study of Religion* 35, no.1 (1996): 1–16; and Christopher G. Ellison, J. P. Bartkowski, and Michelle Segal, "Do Conservative Protestant Parents Spank More Often? Further Evidence from the National Survey of Families and Households," *Social Science Quarterly* 77, no. 30 (1996); 663–73.

Although the word "sin" might seem like an outdated or harsh and judgmental concept, in the Bible and the Christian tradition, sin is a common translation for Greek and Hebrew words (*chatá* and *ἁμαρτία/hamartia*) for "missing the mark" or "going astray," and sin refers to various ways that human beings fail to love God, others, and even themselves. Furthermore, in Jesus's teachings and the Christian tradition, recognition of sin is consistently coupled with the importance of repentance, forgiveness, love, and renewal.

Building on biblical wisdom, Christian theologians who have reflected seriously on sin do not focus on children's sin but rather speak of sin in relationship to life's harsh realities and injustices and underscore two related points about the human condition generally. On one hand, many theologians claim that all people are born in a "state of sin"; they live in a world that is not what it ought to be. Their families are not perfectly loving and just; social institutions that support them, such as schools and governments, are not free from corruption; and the communities in which they live, no matter how safe, have elements of injustice and violence. On the other hand, theologians also claim that human beings, as individuals, possess moral capacities and responsibilities and that adults, and even children as they develop and grow, sometimes carry out sinful, harmful actions. Social scientists and educators also recognize that as children and young people develop, they can recognize unfair and unjust treatment directed to them, whether by other children or by adults. Furthermore, children and young people can also act in ways that are unjust and harmful to themselves or others, and thus bear some degree of responsibility for their actions.[48]

This broader notion of sin is not a rationale for physically punishing children, and it helps expand our understanding and appreciation of children's growing moral sensibilities and the need to play a positive role in helping them cultivate a conscience and appropriate important Christian virtues and values, including love and justice. A proper understanding of sin coupled with sensitivity to children's needs, vulnerabilities, and development helps adults recognize children's agency and their growing capacities to both help and harm. Attention to their agency, drive toward autonomy, risk-taking, and experimentation also corrects a simplistic view of children as pure and innocent. Such a naïve view leaves no room for appreciating a child's own growing moral agency

---

48 See the work by developmental psychologist William Damon, including *The Moral Child: Nurturing Children's Natural Moral Growth* (New York: Free Press, 1988); and the book by educator Vivian Gussin Paley, *You Can't Say You Can't Play,* repr. ed. (Cambridge, MA: Harvard University Press, 1993).

and levels of accountability or for talking to children about the impact of the actions of both adults and children on others.

A broader understanding of wrongdoing or sin also gives parents, caregivers, and mentors a language to talk with children about human mistakes and shortcomings—whether their own or those of others—as well as ethical responsibilities and the lifelong importance of having compassion for themselves and others. Since children, as they grow, both experience the harms caused by others and at times cause harm to others, adults can help children by modelling for them compassion and accountability and by cultivating meaningful and mutual practices at home and in their faith community of accountability, forgiveness, and renewal. Adults teach children much about humility and accountability and create deeper connections with children when they can say to children, "I'm sorry. I made a mistake." Sadly, some parents are reluctant to apologize.[49]

In this way and others, a robust language of sin also corrects inflated notions of parental authority, thereby helping to protect children. Grounded in this broad and biblically informed notion of sin, serious theologians throughout the Christian tradition have addressed the nature and limits of parental authority. From a biblical and Christian perspective, one's ultimate authority is God, not one's parents. Several biblical stories depict the shortcomings and wrongdoings of parents and family members who harm children or demand absolute obedience to themselves instead of God.

Theologians across Christian denominations who honor parents and the family while also acknowledging the limits of parental authority also express the need for the church and civil authorities to protect children from unjust and harmful actions of parents, caregivers, and other family members. For example, the sixteenth-century reformer Martin Luther, whose ideas sparked the Reformation and continue to shape Protestant views of the family today, honored parents but also recognized their shortcomings and the need at times for church and state to intervene. Luther was a parent himself and a strong advocate of protecting and providing education for all children. He and his wife, Katharina von Bora, raised ten children, and he wrote movingly about the vocation of parents and the responsibilities of educating children and raising them in the faith. He wrote the *Small Catechism* for use in the household, encouraged parents to train children "with kind and agreeable methods"

---

49 J. Ruckstaetter et al., "Parental Apologies, Empathy, Shame, Guilt, and Attachment: A Path Analysis," *Journal of Counseling and Development* 95, no. 4 (2017): 389–400.

instead of "beatings and blows," and wrote about how the daily and seemingly mundane tasks of parenting, such as washing diapers, are sacred.[50]

Although he honored the vocation of parenting, Luther realized that parents are not perfect and can sometimes neglect their children, be unjust, and even become tyrants. He also recognized that parental authority is always limited, never absolute, because a child's ultimate loyalty and obedience is to God. "Parental authority is strictly limited," he says; "it does not extend to the point where it can wreak damage and destruction to the child, especially to its soul." Parental authority is for "building up," not "for destroying."[51] His view of the family is also intimately connected to his view of church and state. Luther emphasized the role of three estates—the household, the church, and the political state—to help secure peace and build societies in which all might thrive. He understood that parents, pastors, and political leaders all carry out particular roles and responsibilities that serve the common good and help individuals, families, and societies flourish. In cases of child abuse or maltreatment in the household, the church and state can and should intervene to protect children.

Attention to the limits of parental authority found in the Bible and Christian theology align with warnings raised by legal experts today about the risks to children of overprotecting parental rights. This is true in cases in which parents who harm their children or face possible child abuse charges seek to justify their actions based on their religious beliefs. Highly respected scholars, such as Robin Fretwell Wilson, also warn the state and policy makers to take seriously the risks to children and women of ceding authority for family disputes to religious bodies.[52] As she states, and as almost everyone can clearly see, "Religious communities are not immune from family violence."[53]

Given these realities and theological and legal warnings about the limits of parental authority, faith leaders should work more intentionally with civic authorities and policy makers to address the problem of lax or nonexistent laws regarding the corporal punishment of children in religiously affiliated private schools or in their own homes. They should also open their eyes to the

---

50   Martin Luther, *The Large Catechism of Dr. Martin Luther, 1529*, in *The Annotated Luther, Study Edition*, ed. Kirsi Stjerna (Minneapolis: Fortress, 2016), 309–10; and *The Estate of Marriage* (1522), in *Luther's Works* (LW), ed. Jaroslav Pelikan and Helmut Lehmann (St. Louis: Concordia Publishing House, 1955–86), 45:40–41.

51   Luther, *That Parents Should Neither Compel nor Hinder the Marriage of Their Children, and That Children Should Not Become Engaged without their Parents' Consent* (1524), LW 45:386.

52   Robin Fretwell Wilson, "The Perils of Privatized Marriage," in *Marriage and Divorce in a Multicultural Contexts: Multi-Tiered Marriage and the Boundaries of Civil Law and Religion*, ed. Joel A. Nichols (Cambridge: Cambridge University Press, 2012), 253–83.

53   Ibid., 283.

realities of child maltreatment, abuse, and neglect in families. Although we are rightly outraged by child abuse and seek to protect children from strangers, pastors, teachers, or coaches, the most common perpetrators are relatives.

8   Conclusion

Building on theological and biblically based perspectives on children, the chapter has shown that the physical punishment of children is inconsistent with central Christian conceptions of and commitments to children. A robust understanding of children honors children's full humanity, reflects the teaching and actions of Jesus, cultivates a Christ-centered and nonviolent understanding of discipline and discipleship, and acknowledges the limits of parental authority. Grounded in this larger vision, Christians are well-equipped and empowered to reject all forms of physical punishment of children, even spanking or other so-called mild forms, in their homes and faith communities, and to advocate for laws prohibiting corporal punishment in all settings.

The time is ripe for Christians to move beyond polarization and help end the physical punishment of children. Christians have proven they can work across lines of difference to promote positive change for children, and a host of partners would support and collaborate with them in ending corporal punishment. Social scientists have provided clear evidence of the harms of corporal punishment, including spanking. Pediatricians, child psychologists, and neuroscientists have revealed the unique vulnerabilities and amazing capacities of infants and children and the importance of warm and caring relationships for ensuring their healthy physical, emotional, ethical, spiritual, and intellectual development. Several child-focused secular and religious organizations fully support the UN Convention on the Rights of the Child, and scholars, theologians, and legal experts have shown how these rights are in line with Christian beliefs about the integrity and inherent dignity of all persons. Positive parenting programs are already in place. Multidisciplinary teams of child protection professionals are becoming more aware of the positive role that religion can play in child well-being. Since some Christian organizations already deem spanking a last resort, as they become increasingly aware of children's vulnerabilities, the risks of spanking, and scriptural wisdom, they might eventually reject spanking in all situations. Theologians around the world are also becoming less adult-centered and more child-attentive, thereby offering fresh interpretations of Christian doctrines and practices that honor children's full humanity.

When one considers the host of challenges children face today, encouraging the church to help end corporal punishment in all settings might seem like a minor step. However, if Christian parents and caregivers understand the risks of corporal punishment, recognize its inconsistency with Christian commitments to children, and take up positive parenting practices that avoid physical punishment, then they will help end children's suffering and foster their children's flourishing. In this way, Christian families and organizations could also become a beacon of justice for the wider community, helping all children experience genuine *shalom*.

CHAPTER 29

To Ratify or Not to Ratify the UN Convention on the Rights of the Child: Gains and Losses

Mariela Neagu and Robin Fretwell Wilson

1   Introduction

The UN Convention on the Rights of the Child (CRC)[1] is the most widely ratified human rights instrument in the world.[2] Indeed, since its adoption in 1989, it has been ratified by every country in the world—with the sole exception of the United States.[3] It comes as a great surprise to many who are not human rights experts to learn that the U.S. stands apart from the world in not ratifying the CRC. The United States hosts the United Nations, the organization which adopted the CRC. Across the world—or at least in countries which are democratic or where people strive for a fair society—the U.S. is largely perceived as the land of freedom and home to human rights.[4] Moreover, as John Witte explains, "American human rights lawyers and nongovernmental organizations (NGOs) were among the principal architects of [the CRC] and have been the most forceful for children's rights at home and abroad."[5] But what does the U.S. failure to ratify the CRC mean for its policies, internally and internationally, and ultimately for the children of the United States?

---

1   Convention on the Rights of the Child, New York, Nov. 20, 1989, 1577 U.N.T.S. 3, https://www.unicef.org/child-rights-convention/convention-text [hereafter CRC].
2   The significance of ratification cannot be understated. Ratification means that a signatory agrees to be bound by the treaty. Ratification, https://ask.un.org/faq/14594. By contrast, signing the CRC means that the United States has expressed "willingness … to continue the treaty-making process." "It also creates an obligation to refrain, in good faith, from acts that would defeat the object and the purpose of the treaty." Arts.10 and 18, Vienna Convention on the Law of Treaties 1969.
3   Status of Ratification by Country, https://indicators.ohchr.org/.
4   Jonathan Todres, "Incorporating the CRC and Its Optional Protocols in the United States," in *Incorporating the United Nations Convention on the Rights of the Child into National Law*, ed. Ursula Kilkelly et al. (Cambridge, UK: Intersentia, 2021), 123–44.
5   John Witte, Jr., *Church, State, and Family: Reconciling Traditional Teachings and Modern Liberties* (Cambridge: Cambridge University Press, 2019), 238.

This chapter examines the genesis and importance of the CRC and the controversy around it in the United States, and suggests that the standard explanations for the U.S. nonratification are oversimplified. We note that both the European Union (EU) and the United States are federalist systems, and that the EU itself has ratified some instruments and not others, while U.S. cities and local governments have embraced some UN conventions. We then note that decisions surrounding the welfare of children are guided by the best interests of children in both the United States and EU countries. We illustrate that choosing how best to protect children in the United States and elsewhere is context dependent and that substantively divergent decisions can nonetheless serve the best interests of children. We ground this discussion by looking at one of the most vulnerable groups in any society: children who cannot be raised by their families of origin, whether they are in foster care or have been adopted. We conclude by applauding Professor Witte's long-running contributions to our comparative understanding of institutions supporting the family and the welfare of family units—for which children and vulnerable persons are better off.

2 Genesis and Importance of the CRC

By the adoption of the CRC,[6] children's rights acquired a date and a place of birth: New York, November 20, 1989. The CRC resulted from a decade of debates, negotiations, and compromises in which the nations of the world participated. It reflects, in many ways, the "wisdom of the crowd." Importantly, the CRC came after two world wars, in which thousands of children were victims of the most horrendous atrocities.[7] While some see the CRC as birthing children's rights, the idea of rights for children is decades older. Children's rights are often linked to scholars such as Eglantyne Jebb[8] and Janusz Korczak.[9] Indeed, the

---

6 CRC. See also "The United Nations Convention on the Rights of the Child," R40484, Congressional Research Service (July 15, 2015).
7 Many countries in the developed world had practices that mistreated children, often the children of poor or unmarried mothers. These range from Switzerland's *Verdingkinder,* meaning contracted-out children, to Ireland's export of children for adoption, to orphan trains in the United States. See Ursula M. Baer, "Switzerland's Apology for Compulsory Government-Welfare Measures: A Social Justice Turn?," *Social Justice* 43, no. 3 (2016): 68–90; and Jeanne F. Cook, "A History of Placing-Out: The Orphan Trains," *Child Welfare* 74, no. 1 (Special Issue, Jan./Feb. 1995):181–97, https://www.jstor.org/stable/45399030. Ibid.
8 Eglantyne Jebb, https://en.wikipedia.org/wiki/Eglantyne_Jebb.
9 Janusz Korczak, https://en.wikipedia.org/wiki/Janusz_Korczak.

concept of children's rights has roots in the U.S. decades prior to the drafting and negotiation of the CRC.[10]

Over decades of implementation, the CRC has contributed to bettering the lives of many children. The CRC has fostered policies that treat children as human beings, worthy of respect and a dignified life. Principal among these innovations is the notion of children's voice. The norm at stake is crucial: essentially, a dialogue with the child on matters that affect her life, an approach that treats children with respect, bearing in mind limitations, such as age and maturity.

Although the first call to give children special protection was adopted in Geneva in 1924,[11] followed in 1959 by the UN Declaration on the Child,[12] these revolved around children's well-being and protection. These declarations did not adopt "dignity rights,"[13] such as the child's right to *both* express their views on matters which affect their lives *and* have their views be given due weight, contained in Article 12 of the CRC.[14]

Other provisions that make the CRC unique are the articles related to children's identity. Children are regarded as members of the families they are born into.[15] The CRC celebrates every child as an individual by asking states to protect their individual characteristics.[16] Articles 7 and 8 provide that children have the right to know and preserve their identity (name and nationality) and their family relations.[17] Article 9 of the CRC protects children from separation from their parents against the parents' will, unless separation is in the child's best interest.[18] Despite nonratification, the U.S. has long had practices that reflect these norms. For example, there has been a movement to open adoptions, although such arrangements are not enforced in the U.S. By contrast, some European countries allow for practices of anonymous birth ('*sous x*') or baby boxes, which have been criticized by the UN Committee on the Rights of the Child.[19]

---

10 Martin Guggenheim, *What's Wrong with Children's Rights* (Cambridge, MA: Harvard University Press, 2007).
11 Witte, *Church, State, and Family*, 238.
12 UN Declaration on the Rights of the Child (1959), https://archive.crin.org/en/library/legal-database/un-declaration-rights-child-1959.html.
13 Ibid.
14 CRC, Article 12.
15 Ibid., Articles 9 and 10.
16 Ibid., Articles 7 and 8.
17 Ibid.
18 Ibid., Article 9.
19 Sophia Jones, "U.N. Committee Calls for an End to Centuries-Old Practice Of 'Baby Boxes,'" N.P.R. (Nov. 26, 2012), https://www.npr.org/sections/thetwo-way/2012/11/26/165942545/u-n-committee-calls-for-an-end-to-centuries-old-practice-of-baby-boxes.

Continuity with one's family of origin is prized under the CRC. In many countries, including welfare states (Europe and North America), children end up in care not as a result of child abuse but because of poverty and a lack of support to prevent them from entering care. If children cannot be raised by their family, Article 20 gives them the right to special protection and care of the state (foster care, adoption, or suitable institutional care), requiring that "due regard shall be paid to the desirability of continuity in a child's upbringing and to the child's ethnic, religious, cultural and linguistic background."[20]

Other guarantees include:
- the right to "form [] his or her own views" and "the right to express those views freely";
- the "right ... to seek, receive and impart information ... of all kinds";
- the "right ... to freedom of thought, conscience and religion";
- the "rights ... to freedom of association and to freedom of peaceful assembly";
- the right to "his or her privacy, ... or correspondence"; and
- the right to "mass media" and "access to information and material ... aimed at the promotion of his or her social, spiritual and moral well-being."[21]

These child-centric guarantees are tempered by "the strong presumption of the CRC, stated in Articles 5 and 27, that the state must respect the rights and duties of parents to provide direction to their children in exercising all of their rights, including freedom rights."[22]

Of course, under the Due Process Clause in the 14th Amendment to the U.S. Constitution, parents are entitled to the custody and care of their children, free from state interference, absent a risk of harm to their the child.[23] Some read these guarantees as unfettered, but they are not: they are bounded by risk to the child.[24] State interference varies between states and sometimes within the same country, as in the United States.[25]

The CRC and other conventions exert a powerful norming force on questions of child welfare. This happens in two ways: countries adopt laws informed by the CRC, and decisions affecting child welfare in countries that have ratified

---

20 CRC, Article 20, ¶ 3.
21 Ibid.
22 Witte, *Church, State, and Family*, 249.
23 See Robin Fretwell Wilson and Shaakirrah Sanders, "By Faith Alone: When Religion and Child Welfare Collide," in *The Contested Place of Religion in Family Law*, ed. Robin Fretwell Wilson (Cambridge: Cambridge University Press, 2018), 344–45.
24 Ibid.
25 Neil Gilbert, Nigel Parton, and Marit Skivenes, eds., *Child Protection Systems: International Trends and Orientation* (New York: Oxford University Press, 2011).

the CRC are made in the shadow of the CRC's provisions. Let's consider each in turn.

First, the laws themselves. Within Europe, countries make their own policies in family law and in child protection that reflect their individual cultural identities. Yet these laws reflect the provisions of the CRC.[26] In the 1990s, the decade of the ratification of the CRC, most welfare states started to revise their legislation, policies, and practices around children in state care to ensure that these complied with the CRC.[27] The CRC—and the European Human Rights Convention (EHRC),[28] discussed next—provides a framework around which legislation and policies are constructed to promote human rights values across the region and, in some cases, to protect families from invasive state interference. Thus, most child protection policies in Europe are shaped by concepts animating the CRC, such as protection from harm, the best interests of the child, and the child's right to be heard. However, the evidence from ratifying countries to support such concerns is broadly missing.

Second, the CRC and other conventions shape outcomes. European countries are compelled to respect the European Human Rights Convention (EHRC),[29] which itself protects the right to family life against state invasive policies or practices and gives the right to a fair trial.[30] The judges of the European Human Rights Court draw on the CRC when examining possible breaches of the EHRC in cases involving children.[31] Norway, for example, has been asked to review its practice of removing children swiftly from their families without providing services to the family.[32] Most countries in Europe, in contrast to Norway, have a significantly higher threshold for removing children. The majority of the children in care across European nations are not placed for adoption but

---

26   Géraldine Van Bueren, *Child Rights in Europe: Convergence and Divergence in Judicial Protection* (Strasbourg: Council of Europe, 2007).
27   Gilbert et al., 25.
28   The European Convention on Human Rights, 1950, https://www.echr.coe.int/documents/convention_eng.pdf.
29   Convention for the Protection of Human Rights and Fundamental Freedoms, Sep. 3, 1953, https://www.echr.coe.int/Documents/Convention_ENG.pdf (hereafter EHRC).
30   Van Bueren, *Child Rights in Europe*.
31   Ursula Kilkelly, ed., *The Child and the European Convention on Human Rights*, 2nd ed. (London: Routledge, 2017).
32   Saadet Firdevs Aparı, "Norway's Child Welfare Agency Comes under Fire," May 26, 2022, https://www.aa.com.tr/en/europe/norway-s-child-welfare-agency-comes-under-fire/2597801.

are put in foster or residential care, maintaining their identity and according with their right to stay in contact with their families.[33]

Still, the two conventions—the EHRC and CRC—provide a framework around which legislation and policies are constructed to promote human rights values across the region and, in some cases, to protect families from invasive state interference. Most child protection policies in Europe are shaped by the CRC and, hence, by concepts such as protection from harm, the best interests of the child, or the child's right to be heard. All U.S. states currently express their child protection policies primarily in terms of the best interests of the child.[34]

3 The Ratification Controversy

In many ways, the ratification controversy stems from politics. The CRC is seen as part of a movement to bring international law to bear on U.S. domestic law.[35] Like the U.S. decision not to ratify the Convention on the Elimination of All Forms of Discrimination against Women (CEDAW)—ratified by 185 countries since its adoption by the United Nations in 1979[36]—"American exceptionalism" and the U.S. commitment to going it alone, or "unilateralism," surely have contributed.

The U.S. attitude toward international human rights law, particularly "the positive nature of rights,"[37] also helps to explain why the U.S. has not ratified the CRC. We could imagine that ratification might hold some appeal to social conservatives *if* pitched as a device to protect families from state interference. But children's rights in the U.S. are still nascent. As one barometer: it was worthy of remark that the U.S. Supreme Court, in its landmark same-sex marriage

---

33 Gilbert et al., *Child Protection Systems*.
34 See, for example, Robin Fretwell Wilson, ed., *Reconceiving the Family: Critique on the American Law Institute's Principles of the Law of Family Dissolution* (Cambridge: Cambridge University Press, 2006); and Jennifer Wolf, "Child's Best Interest in Custody Cases," Jun. 23, 2021, https://www.verywellfamily.com/best-interests-of-the-child-standard-overview-2997765.
35 See Robin Fretwell Wilson, "Family Law Isolationism and 'Church, State, and Family,'" *Journal of Law and Religion* 34 (2019): 490–95.
36 Hannah Elizabeth Kington, "Why Has the United States Never Ratified the UN Convention on the Elimination of All Forms of Discrimination against Women?," Honors College Capstone Experience/Thesis Projects, Western Kentucky University, 2009, https://digitalcommons.wku.edu/cgi/viewcontent.cgi?article=1159&context=stu_hon_theses.
37 Guggenheim, *What's Wrong with Children's Rights*, 14.

decision, *Obergefell v. Hodges*, invoked the interests of children in their parents' marrying.[38]

The CRC has been opposed by religious groups and social conservatives opposed to government intervention in the family, as John Witte aptly shows in his work. CRC skeptics see the family as a private domain outside the government's reach. Witte probes critics' fear that freedoms granted children in the CRC would restrict the authority of parents to shape and mold their children.

Since the publication of Witte's volume *Church, State, and Family*, the question of children's rights has gotten increasingly bogged down in the culture war and political identity.[39] The entwining of children's rights with the culture war in the United States can only make ratification an even harder sell.

Family law developments, such as the rise of parental rights and fathers' rights, have also helped to stall ratification. In *What's Wrong with Children's Rights?*, Martin Guggenheim undertakes a thorough analysis of U.S. attitudes toward children's rights and the conceptual barriers that hinder the implementation of children's rights. The conundrum of children's rights versus parents' rights continues to divide lawyers in the U.S.,[40] creating a barrier to ratification. Ideological opposition to what it might mean to give prominence to children's voices, as Article 12 does, has also played a role. Hearing children's views is seen by some as diminishing adult authority. Critics worry that "categorically stated children's rights" will not bend to the presumption that the CRC's guarantees are read together with the rights of parents to direct the custody and care of their children over time.[41]

In sum, in the United States, children's voices and their relational or identity rights, which are enshrined in the CRC, are not regarded as important as they would be in countries which take the CRC as the bedrock of their child protection and adoption legislation. These observations form part of the received wisdom about nonratification of the CRC by the United States.

Often overlooked, however, are the structural difficulties with ratification. Ratification of the CRC—*if* binding on the political units within the ratifying country—is especially hard for a federalist system. In the U.S. federalist system, many areas of policy—not the least of which are domestic relations—are in the control of state legislatures. States are often lauded by jurists as

---

38 Obergefeld v. Hodges, 567 U.S. 644, 667 (2015). "A third basis for protecting the right to marry is that it safeguards children and families and thus draws meaning from related rights of childrearing, procreation, and education."
39 Phillip Elliott, "Most Parents Don't Like School Culture Wars, New Polling Shows," *Time*, Jan. 25, 2023, https://time.com/6250139/parents-school-culture-wars-polling/.
40 Ibid.
41 Witte, *Church, State, and Family*, 249.

laboratories of experimentation. In Justice Louis D. Brandeis's famous articulation, "It is one of the happy incidents of the federal system that a single courageous state may, if its citizens choose, serve as a laboratory; and try novel social and economic experiments without risk to the rest of the country."[42]

As we show in Part 4, below, U.S. states have adopted radically different approaches on just one child welfare question: the placement of children for adoption by private adoption agencies. They do this under their respective sovereignty as lawmakers protecting the general welfare of citizens in each of the fifty states. This means that the construction of U.S. family law is bottom-up—unlike, say, in a country with a federal family law system, like Australia. We can best think of family law in the United States as fifty-plus sets of positive law enacted by fifty states, the District of Columbia, and U.S. territories, as well as the sovereign Indian nations within the U.S. Of course, no unifying treaty like the EHRC is being discussed in the United States. In this sense, perception and reality diverge.

As the next part shows, the norms at stake in the CRC—that children should be treated with respect and should be consulted on matters affecting their welfare, when sufficiently mature—are well established in U.S. law.[43]

4 The Ratification Controversy Is Oversimplified: Decisions Are Guided by Best Interests of Children Everywhere

As authors, we are divided on how critical it is for the U.S. to ratify the CRC. For one of us, the ideal would be for the U.S. not to reject ratification but to engage in dialogue and consider ratification with reservations. Many countries have done this, recognizing the specific identity of the country and joining the dialogue table at Geneva. For the other of us, ratification is less important than having U.S. states incorporate key principles of the CRC into their own laws.

Nonetheless, we agree as authors that on substantive family law questions, governments in good faith can adopt very different structures and still serve the welfare of children, as the next part makes concrete. For both of us, the CRC serves as a valuable repository of theory and best practices that can underpin and inform laws, practice, and thinking about children. We believe the ratification controversy is overstated in two respects: there are structural similarities between the EU and U.S. that are often not teased out, and there are similarities in the conceptual foundations of child welfare laws in the U.S. and Europe.

---

42 New State Ice Co. v. Liebmann, 285 U.S. 262 (1932).
43 Wilson, "Family Law Isolationism and 'Church, State, and Family,'" 491.

First, structurally: the EU and the U.S. are both federalist systems. Europe is not a single federal entity. Member countries make their own policies in family law and child protection that reflect their individual cultural identities and commitments. In this way, the EU is more like the U.S. than not. U.S. states are the analogue to countries in Europe. We can thus think of the CRC ratification as fifty states not having ratified the CRC. Nothing prevents U.S. subunits from embracing the CRC's norms and making them part of domestic law, much as U.S. cities and states have done with CEDAW.[44]

Importantly, the European Union has not ratified the CRC either, even as all member states have. Of course, the EU was initially only an economic union, and now it has expanded its areas of influence. However, the EU has ratified the UN Convention for Persons with Disability, which is a more recent convention than the CRC. This Convention resembles the CRC in many ways because it contains both political and economic rights for disabled persons.

The U.S. has ratified other treaties—notably those on human trafficking, given effect in the U.S. federal human trafficking laws—suggesting that non-ratification of the CRC may come from the CRC's breadth. The CRC touches nearly every experience of family life, and its ratification, *if* binding, would implicate the states' regulation of the general welfare of persons in countless domains.

We note again that the CRC does not form the basis for taking decisions of countries to court. It has no implementation mechanism. Instead, in Europe the CRC gains its force from a collateral treaty, the EHRC. The EHRC can issue binding decisions, much as the U.S. Supreme Court can do with respect to U.S. states.

Second, conceptually: the CRC is best thought of as a source of authority for best practices. The CRC may serve as a base for soft law or shaming of countries. The UN prepares country reports, which help move countries to better protect children's rights. In this regard, the ratification question carries far more importance in the minds of lawmakers and the public than we would predict actual ratification would have.

Consider just one of the CRC's prized tenets—children's voices. These are given effect in the U.S. through various devices. When states do intervene in a family, or the parents are not aligned in a custody matter, some states permit the child to have appointed counsel.[45] Children have guardians *ad litem*

---

44 Cities for CEDAW, http://citiesforcedaw.org/.
45 Melissa Kucinski, "Why and How to Account for the Child's Views in Custody Cases," *Family Advocate* 43 (May 10, 2021).

appointed in child welfare matters in most, if not all, states in the U.S.[46] Judges will solicit children's views, often in camera, to protect the minor's privacy.[47] None of this means that the court *must* follow the child's views, only that the resulting decision is best informed by children themselves when they are of sufficient maturity to express a reasoned view.

In the United States, decisions about child custody are guided by the best interests of the child in all fifty states.[48] In states that give content to best-interest determinations through the primary caretaker or other standard, those laws have been explained in terms of the best interests of the child.[49]

In Europe, most countries are exploring, beyond ratification, stronger ways to implement the CRC by incorporating its provisions into domestic law. Between the European drive to incorporate the CRC and the U.S. reluctance to ratify it sits the UK, a country which has ratified the CRC but has not incorporated it into law. Explaining the government position to the Joint Committee on Human Rights, Edward Timpson (then the Minister of State for Children and Families at the Department for Education) stated that "there was no 'block' upon incorporation, but rather that the position of the Government is that it was confident that the laws and policies that ... [the Government] ... has in place already are strong enough to comply with the Convention."[50]

While Wales and Scotland draw on children's rights in their policies for children, Westminster has opposed Scotland's attempt to incorporate the CRC into its domestic law.[51] As in the U.S., the idea exists that children's rights are "a scary set of tenets or concepts,"[52] and it is possible that the very idea of rights worries governments. In the UK, such concerns are surprising, given that

---

46   Gilbert et al., *Child Protection Systems*.
47   Kucinski, "Why and How to Account for the Child's Views in Custody Cases."
48   Wilson, *Reconceiving the Family*.
49   Robin Fretwell Wilson, "Trusting Mothers: A Critique of the American Law Institute's Treatment of De Facto Parents," *Hofstra Law Review* 38 (2010): 1103–89.
50   John Dunford, "Children and Young People's Guide: Review of the Office of the Children's Commissioner" (England, 2010), https://assets.publishing.service.gov.uk/government/uploads/system/uploads/attachment_data/file/626561/DfE-00573-2010.pdf.
51   Scottish Government, Supreme Court Judgement: Statement by Deputy First Minister John Swinney, Oct. 6, 2021, https://www.gov.scot/publications/deputy-first-minister-john-swinney-statement-supreme-court-judgement-6-october-2021/.
52   House of Lords, House of Commons Joint Committee on Human Rights, "The UK's Compliance with the UN Convention on the Rights of the Child: Eighth Report of Session 2014–15," p. 12, https://publications.parliament.uk/pa/jt201415/jtselect/jtrights/144/144.pdf ("Dr Atkinson, the outgoing Children's Commissioner ... said that she did not necessarily favour full incorporation of the CRC as it would 'probably take up too much parliamentary time and not necessarily be realised.' She suggested an incremental process: What you do—almost by stealth, setting precedents from the High Court and Supreme Court

children's capacity to make decisions with regard to their life outside parental competence is regulated by the so-called Gillick competence,[53] by which professionals can assess whether a child (under sixteen) can make relevant decisions about their medical care. This predates the adoption of the CRC and is by no means the outcome of ratifying the CRC.

As we explain in the next part, choosing how to serve the best interest of a child is culturally and contextually dependent. Many different good-faith decisions can be made, all serving the welfare of children.

5 Making These Observations Concrete: Children in Care

In the U.S. and Europe, there is a basic philosophical difference over how best to care for children when their family of origin cannot do so. In the U.S., adoption is often regarded as the ideal type of placement because it gives children stability.[54] Thus, the core concepts around which the child protection system in the U.S. is constructed are safety and permanency, with a drive toward adoption. In child protection systems in continental Europe (the UK is an exception), adoption is regarded as a measure of last resort because blood ties and identity rights are seen as more important, or the bar for removing parental responsibility is higher.[55] But even in EU countries where adoption occupies a privileged position, adoption serves only a small proportion of the children taken into care.

Instead of focusing on permanency and adoption, countries that adopt a children's rights approach aim to achieve continuity and stability in a child's upbringing, both of them being conditions for good development.[56] In practice,

---

benches—is nibble away. You get people to recognise that the rights of the child are not a scary set of tenets or concepts, but inherent in a civilised society.").

53 The standard used in England and Wales to decide whether a child (a person under sixteen years of age) is able to consent to their own medical treatment, without the need for parental permission or knowledge: https://en.wikipedia.org/wiki/Gillick_competence.

54 W. Bradford Wilcox and Robin Fretwell Wilson, "Bringing Up Baby: Adoption, Marriage, and the Best Interests of the Child," *William & Mary Bill of Rights Journal* 14 (2006): 883–908.

55 Kenneth Burns, Tarja Pvsv, and Marit Skivenes, eds., *Child Welfare Removals by the State: A Cross-Country Analysis of Decision-Making Systems* (Oxford: Oxford University Press, 2017); and June Thoburn and Brigid Featherstone, "Adoption, Child Rescue, Maltreatment, and Poverty," in *The Routledge Handbook of Critical Social Work*, ed. Stephen A. Webb (London: Routledge, 2019), 401.

56 American Academy of Pediatrics, Committee on Early Childhood, Adoption & Dependent Care, "Developmental Issues for Young Children in Foster Care," *Pediatrics* 106, no. 5

this is translated into child protection systems with more residential and foster care (for example, in Germany, Italy, and Spain). Such approaches address care in comprehensive and relational ways (for example, the social pedagogy approach in Germany),[57] achieving stability through continuity rather than placement of children with foster families, which often leads to separation of siblings.[58] Residential care can be a force for keeping siblings together.

Again, contrast the U.S. During the 1990s, there was an increasing focus on child safety and adoption.[59] In 1997, the U.S. enacted the Adoption and Safe Families Act (ASFA).[60] This legislation has elements that mirror CRC concepts, such as being guided by the best interest of the child or the fact that children should have lawyers or guardians *ad litem* representing their views.[61]

The U.S. has also pursued, for decades, intercountry adoption of children[62] (particularly babies) in the aftermath of war or other circumstances of upheaval or political instability, a trend which started after World War II. This trend is almost entirely excluded by Article 21(b) of the CRC.[63]

In short, structurally, the two systems for caring for children are different in the U.S. and Europe. We elaborate on them below with examples and then ask the obvious: can anyone say with certainty *ex ante* which better serves the interest of children as a group or individually?

5.1 *Romania*

A revealing way to explain these differences and their impact on children is to look at Romania's child protection policy and politics after the collapse of

---

(2000); n45–50, https://doi.org/10.1542/peds.106.5.1145. To be sure, adoption may give continuity to infants who are adopted. With older children in the care of the state, foster care with an ongoing connection to the child's family of origin may give greater continuity. Of course, open adoption can give continuity with a child's family of origin.

57   Jessica Kingsley, "Social Pedagogy and Working with Children and Young People," *The British Journal of Social Work* 42 (Jun. 2012): 799–801, https://doi.org/10.1093/bjsw/bcs078.

58   Nicole Weinstein, "One in Three Children in Care Separated from Their Siblings, Research Finds," *Children & Young People Now*, Jan. 30, 2023, https://www.cypnow.co.uk/news/article/one-in-three-children-in-care-separated-from-siblings-research-finds.

59   Guggenheim, *What's Wrong with Children's Rights*, 10.

60   Adoption and Safe Families Act, https://www.govinfo.gov/content/pkg/BILLS-105hr867enr/pdf/BILLS-105hr867enr.pdf.

61   Gilbert et al., *Child Protection Systems.*

62   Judith Gibbons and Karen Smith-Rotabi, eds., *Intercountry Adoption: Policies, Practices, and Outcomes* (London: Routledge, 2012); and Michael W. Ambrose and Anna Mary Coburn, "Report on Intercountry Adoption in Romania" (2001), https://pdf.usaid.gov/pdf_docs/PNACW989.pdf.

63   UNICEF, International Child Development Centre, "Intercountry Adoption," 1998, https://www.unicef-irc.org/publications/102-intercountry-adoption.html.

the communist regime in 1990. Not long after the adoption of the CRC, images of malnourished children in institutions in Romania[64] shocked viewers all over the world just days after the execution of the country's dictator, Nicolae Ceausescu. These images attracted an unprecedented volume of international aid from all Western European countries and an equal interest in children for adoption. Soon, Romania was regarded as "the last reservoir of Caucasian babies,"[65] a phrase which illustrates how children were marketed through corrupt intercountry adoption practices.[66]

Although Romania ratified the CRC as early as 1990, Article 21(b), according to which intercountry adoption may be a solution for children who cannot be adopted or looked after in a suitable manner in their country of origin, was mistranslated in the official publication of Romania's law journal.[67] Between 1997 and 2001, Romania became one of the largest suppliers of children in the world after Russia and China, with thousands of children leaving the country, some with forged documents[68] (mainly to the U.S. and economically developed European countries) through an intrinsically flawed and corrupt system.[69] However, when Romania started to reform its child protection system (a condition for the country's accession to the European Union) with support from international donors (the European Union, USAID, and others), the pressure from the adoption lobby groups (adoption agencies, law firms, and prospective adoptive parents) reached the U.S. Congress and the highest decision-making levels in the two countries, with Romania's accession to NATO being threatened.[70]

The EU claimed that Romania's international adoption system allowed for decisions which were not in the best interests of children,[71] while the claims of the American pro-adoption lobby were "misguided since they fail to take proper account of these international obligations" and "flawed, not least

---

64   Mariela Neagu, *Voices from the Silent Cradles: Life Histories of Romania's Looked After Children* (Bristol, UK: Policy Press, 2021).
65   Gail Kligman, *The Politics of Duplicity: Controlling Reproduction in Ceausescu's Romania* (Berkeley: University of California Press, 1998).
66   Ambrose and Coburn, "Report on Intercountry Adoption in Romania."
67   Mariela Neagu, "Children by Request: Romania's Children between Rights and International Politics," *International Journal of Law, Policy and the Family* 29, no. 2 (2015): 215–36.
68   Sue Lloyd-Roberts, "Romania—Buying Babies," BBC Newsnight, Mar. 1, 2000, https://www.youtube.com/watch?v=IQKttELI5-U.
69   IGAIA (Independent Group for Analysis of Inter-country Adoption), "Re-Organising the International Adoption and Child Protection System," 2002.
70   Tom Gallagher, *Romania and the European Union: How the Weak Vanquished the Strong* (Manchester: Manchester University Press, 2009).
71   Neagu, *supra* note 67, at 215–36.

because they rely on a distorted notion of what constitutes 'abandonment' and the status of 'orphan.'"[72] The European Commission appointed an independent panel of high-level experts from five different European countries to advise the government of Romania in drafting its Children's Rights Act and its Adoption Law, ensuring their compliance with the CRC.[73] The new legislation excluded intercountry adoption almost entirely, as it was not regarded as a child protection measure. Children who were not adopted were protected in foster care or in children's homes. Romania's children became subject to opposing ideological views, with the EU advocating for the protection of children against corrupt practices, while other countries advocated primarily for the interests of their citizens (as prospective adoptive parents), or the interests of adoption agencies. This led to ideological war between EU and the U.S. At the same time, UNICEF, the agency providing humanitarian aid for children, took a more ambiguous position, which supported intercountry adoption of children who are not being raised in a family environment, stating that long-term state care should not be preferred to a permanent family. The difference of opinion between the two approaches became obvious when the U.S. State Department organized an expert dialogue with the members of the EU Independent Panel.[74]

This dialogue highlighted the U.S. approach to children's welfare to ensure children's safety and stability through "permanent" families (that is, adoption).[75] Europe took a holistic approach, which included special care outside families, with due regard being paid to other rights, including identity rights and the child's right to be heard. The case of two Italian couples, who adopted two girls from a charitable children's home in Romania without meeting them, illustrates the importance of listening to the children.[76] The charity where the girls were placed took the case to the European Court of Human Rights.[77] The girls, age ten when the adoption agency lawyers went to collect them from the children's home, and age thirteen at the time of the EHRC decision, were allowed to stay in the children's home because "their interests lay in not having imposed upon them against their will new emotional relations with

---

72   Andrew Bainham, "The Politics of Child Protection in Romania," *International Journal of Children's Rights* 17 (2009): 527–42, https://doi.org/10.1163/092755609X12466074858754.
73   Neagu, *supra* note 67.
74   Roelie Post, *Romania: For Export: Only the Untold Story of the Romanian "Orphans"* (St. Anna Parochie, Netherlands: Hoekstra, 2007).
75   Jill Duerr Berrick, *The Impossible Imperative: Navigating the Competing Principles of Child Protection* (New York: Oxford University Press, 2017).
76   Van Bueren, *supra* note 26.
77   Post, *Romania: For Export*.

people with whom they had no biological ties and whom they perceived as strangers."[78]

Beyond being an example of the child's right to be heard, this decision points out indirectly the weakness of the Hague Convention on Protection of Children and Co-operation in Respect of Intercountry Adoption[79] (an international private law convention regarded as an ethical standard for intercountry adoption procedures) which does not require a pre-adoption placement, a standard practice in domestic adoption. Perhaps the most significant weakness of child protection systems is the insufficient capacity to listen to children and the lack of mechanisms, trusted by children, for children to report when things go wrong while they are in any type of care. This is particularly challenging for child protection systems which rely largely on foster care placements. Reflecting on her journey in care in the U.S., a woman who had been through dozens of placements after her adoption failed concluded that nobody really listened to her,[80] a statement which is in stark contrast with the fundamental question in moral philosophy, "what are you going through?"[81] After all, moral philosophy and its fundamental principle of viewing humans as ends in themselves is a bedrock of the human rights conventions, including the CRC.

Beyond its philosophical underpinnings, the CRC is old enough to be investigated as to how it has worked in practice. One of the authors has worked with CRC both in policy and in research with Romanian-born children and young people who grew up in state care. Her study[82] is based on the analysis of forty life histories of Romanian-born young people in their twenties who grew up in different types of care: children's homes, foster care, and adoption, including international adoption. These reflective narratives provide insights about how children perceive different types of care and about how care can interfere with children's identity formation. The study suggests that the quality of care (highest in domestic adoption but not in international adoption) was closely linked to quality of life in adulthood. Although stigmatization was reported in all types of placement, having parents or caregivers who listened to them was an important protective factor during their childhood. Interestingly, those who

---

78 Pini and others v. Romania, nos. 78028/01 and 78030/01, judgments of Jun. 22, 2004, ECHR.
79 Convention of 29 May 1993 on Protection of Children and Co-operation in Respect of Intercountry Adoption, https://www.hcch.net/en/instruments/conventions/full-text/?cid=69.
80 Jennifer Brown, Shannon Najmabadi, and Olivia Prentzel, "Failed Twice: Colorado Foster Kids Who Are Adopted Often End Up Back in the Child Welfare System," *Colorado Sun*, Nov. 14, 2022, https://coloradosun.com/2022/11/14/colorado-failed-adoptions-foster-kids-welfare/.
81 Simone Weil, *Waiting for God* (London: Routledge, 2009).
82 Kington, "Why Has the United States Never Ratified."

were not happy in their foster care placements but who had social workers who took them seriously and helped them go to other placements (kinship care, residential care, or guardianship), had smoother transitions to adulthood compared to those who stayed in unhappy foster care placements.[83] These findings support the CRC, particularly the importance of Article 12 on the child's right to be heard.

Furthermore, the study found that intercountry adoption was the most radical intervention in a child's identity, and the interviewees in that group struggled most in adulthood in their relationships with their adoptive parents, in navigating between two cultures, and in their personal and professional lives. This was in stark contrast with young people who had a similar start in childhood but who were adopted in Romania. Those adopted in Romania, whose adoption did not imply such a profound change of their habitat, were all in good relationships with their adoptive parents, irrespective of conflicts some had during adolescence with their adoptive parents. They were all supported to attend university, and at the time of the interview they had all experienced at least one healthy romantic relationship. The reunion with their birth families (when it took place) did not change the quality of the relationship they had with their adoptive parents and adoption did not constitute a barrier to achieving flourishing lives in adulthood. While intercountry adoption in Romania had been contested because of its endemic corrupt practices, these findings suggest its complexity and impact on young people in the long run. Had Romania respected the letter of Article 21(b), hardly any of its children would have left the country. Moreover, research indicates that this is a common outcome and that many intercountry adoptees struggle with significant mental health issues.[84]

In an increasingly interconnected world, intercountry adoption has plummeted constantly since 2004. This is due not only to countries developing their child protection systems but also to increased awareness and evidence about its use to disguise human trafficking—as well as poor practices such as rehoming, citizenship issues, or poor-quality home studies in the receiving countries, including the U.S.[85] In 2020, the Netherlands (a receiving country and home to the Hague Convention, which regulates intercountry adoption) suspended

---

83   Ibid.
84   Anders Hjern, Frank Lindblad, and Bo Vinnerljung, "Suicide, Psychiatric Illness, and Social Maladjustment in Intercountry Adoptees in Sweden: A Cohort Study," *The Lancet* 360 (2002): 443–48.
85   Susan Jacobs and Maureen Flatley, "The Truth about Intercountry Adoption's Decline," *The Imprint: Youth & Family News*, Apr. 23, 2019, https://imprintnews.org/adoption/the-truth-about-intercountry-adoptions-decline/34658#0.

adoptions from abroad, and voices of grown-up intercountry adoptees played a major role in influencing that decision.[86] Moreover, in September 2022 the United Nations issued a statement asking states to prevent and eliminate illegal intercountry adoptions.[87] All these actions suggest that the concerns expressed by countries while negotiating the CRC article related to intercountry adoption were justified.[88]

5.2 The U.S. Preference for Adoption by Private Agencies

In the United States, it can be really hard to free children for placement. The Adoption and Safe Families Act (ASFA) strives for reunification, as we note above. Under ASFA, "states must file a petition to terminate parental rights and concurrently, identify, recruit, process and approve a qualified adoptive family on behalf of any child, regardless of age, that has been in foster care for 15 out of the most recent 22 months."[89]

States vary wildly in the proportion of children in foster care who ultimately are freed for adoption by termination of parental rights (TPR).[90] Within the first five years in foster care, the proportion of children freed for adoption ranges from 9 percent to 44 percent.[91] When we look at the midrange between fifteen and twenty-two months under ASFA—seventeen months—the proportion of children freed for adoption ranges from 16 percent to 89 percent.[92] When children exit foster care before seventeen months, their experiences also vary: "77 percent exit to a parent or relative's care (either with or without guardianship)."[93] For some children (Native Americans), kinship placement is mandated by statute.[94] The percentage of foster children adopted by a non-relative increases after the seventeen-month mark. One quarter will reunite with their parent or exit to care by a relative, while 47 percent will leave to

---

86 Cinta Zanidya, "International Adoption in the Netherlands: 'Not a Fairytale,'" The Groningen Observer, Feb. 10, 2022, https://groningenobserver.com/international-adoption-in-the-netherlands-not-a-fairytale/.

87 The Office of the High Commissioner of Human Rights, "Illegal Intercountry Adoptions Must Be Prevented and Eliminated: UN Experts," U.N. Press Release, HCHR, Sep. 29, 2022, https://perma.cc/44W8-F75B.

88 UNICEF, " Intercountry Adoption."

89 "Summary of the Adoption and Safe Families Act of 1997," Adoption in Child Time, Mar. 10, 2018, https://adoptioninchildtime.org/bondingbook/summary-of-the-adoption-and-safe-families-act-of-1997-pl-105-89.

90 Ibid.

91 Ibid.

92 Ibid.

93 Ibid.

94 Indian Child Welfare Act (ICWA) of 1978, 25 U.S.C. 1902 (2016).

a permanent adoption.[95] Sadly, the fortunes of children vary by race.[96] This variability in approach among the states illustrates that the U.S. has fifty-plus different child welfare systems.

Four other concrete policy examples illustrate just how difficult it would be to bring conformity among the states in approaches to caring for children in need of families. First, in a handful of states, birth mothers have the ability to guide the placement of their children with adoptive families, by law.[97] In other states, this phenomenon occurs in practice, if not by law.[98]

One of us, Wilson, is adopted. As she recently explained:

> A birth mother who feels unable to raise a child should be able to have confidence that if she chooses adoption, the child will be raised in a family that provides the best opportunities.
>
> I have no idea what considerations my birth mother had to take into account when deciding to give me up for adoption. But I can say this: as a mother myself, I know it must take incredible courage to break the bond with one's child. When a birth mother comes to this difficult juncture, we need to do all that we can to respect and honor her wishes.

---

95 "Summary of the Adoption and Safe Families Act of 1997."
96 Ibid. ("White and multiracial children are more likely than children of other races to experience TPR, while Asian and Hispanic children are most likely to have TPR occur within 17 months.")
97 See, for example, S.C. Department of Social Services, Human Services Policy & Procedures Manual § 401.17 ("The Department will respect birth parent preferences in the selection of an adoptive family in so far as they are in the best interest of the child involved."); Arizona Administrative Code § 21–5–409 ("The adoption agency may advise the parent that it will use the entity's best efforts to honor any placement preferences the birth parent may have, to the extent such preferences are consistent with the best interests of the child."); and Robin Fretwell Wilson, "Opinion: How to Make Adoption Easier in Utah—And Everywhere Else, *Deseret News*, Feb. 15, 2023, https://www.deseret.com/2023/2/15/23599709/adoption-expenses-agencies-placement-utah.
98 See, "Finding a Family," American Adoptions, https://www.americanadoptions.com/pregnant/finding-a-family-for-your-baby. Note that under the Multi-Ethnic Placement Act (MEPA), state child welfare agencies and contractors involved in adoption or foster care placements or child welfare agency contracts must use diligent recruitment efforts. MEPA established that a MEPA violation also violates of Title VI. Title VI and Title IV prohibit race matching. MEPA and Title VI do not address discrimination on the basis of religion, age, gender, culture, or any other characteristic. On religious matching, see, generally, Laura J. Schwartz, "Religious Matching for Adoption: Unraveling the Interests Behind the 'Best Interests' Standard," *Family Law Quarterly* 25 (1991): 171–92, https://www.jstor.org/stable/25739869.

Some states allow birth mothers to express preferences and guide the placement of a child being relinquished for private adoption. Adoption agencies are allowed and encouraged to follow the good-faith wishes of the birth mother as to optimal placement.[99] Allowing a birth mother to direct, insofar as it is possible, the placement of a child in a family that makes sense to her can be a novel way of helping mothers make the difficult choice to relinquish a child. The CRC would seem to support allowing birth mothers to express their wishes as a device to ensure family connection.

Second, open adoption, where the birth mother can remain in contact with the adopted child and adoptive family, is very common in the U.S.[100] It is a voluntary situation but is often employed, and maintains the child's connection to her heritage and roots. But it is not enforced anywhere, as we note above.

Third, adoption agencies actively encourage adoption from foster care, with an emphasis on adoption of siblings.[101] This aims to maintain continuity and some connection to the family of origin.

Finally, adoption, more than foster care, is predominantly facilitated in the U.S. by private rather than public entities. As one example, in Utah in 2019, the most recent national adoption data available indicate that 1,281 children were adopted. Almost half of those adoptions were facilitated by private adoption agencies.

Some states allow contracting adoption agencies to follow their religious convictions in placement. Other states say agencies may not make distinctions in placement, which has hastened the closure of religious agencies in some states.[102] The United States Supreme Court in *Fulton v. City of Philadelphia* held that government refusals to contract with religious agencies violated First Amendment guarantees of free exercise of religion if the government has

---

99 See, for example, "How to Give My Baby Up for Adoption—7 Steps," Adoption Network, https://adoptionnetwork.com/birth-mothers/adoption-planning-guide/adoption-process-for-birth-mothers/.
100 "What is Open Adoption?," Gladney Center for Adoption, Jul. 3, 2017, https://adoption.org/what-is-open-adoption. "According to Creating A Family (www.creatingafamily.org), closed domestic adoptions only make up 5% of adoptions that take place. 40% of adoptions are mediated and 55% of those adoptions are open. The percentage of adoption agencies that offer open adoption has also increased to 95%." https://www.birthmotherschoice.com/2017/10/20/what-is-open-adoption/.
101 See, for example, https://bethany.org/help-a-child/adoption/us-foster-care-adoption.
102 "Solomon's Decree: Conflicts in Adoption and Child Placement Policy," The Cato Institute, https://www.cato.org/events/solomons-decree-conflicts-adoption-child-placement-policy; *A Matter of Conviction: Moral Clashes Over Same-Sex Adoption*, 22 BYU J. PUB. L. 475 (2008).

discretion to make exceptions for contractors and refuses to do so for a religious agency.¹⁰³

The distinction between state agencies and private contractors that form the backbone of the U.S. adoption and foster system is an important distinction. The CRC, if ratified and binding, would reach state actors but not private companies. Private citizens and organizations rarely qualify as state actors. "Numerous private entities in America obtain government licenses, government contracts, or government-granted monopolies."¹⁰⁴ Those arrangements do not transform such an entity into a state actor, as the U.S. Supreme Court's "many state-action cases amply demonstrate."¹⁰⁵

Further, being highly regulated by the government "does not by itself convert [private] action into that of the State for the purposes of the Fourteenth Amendment."¹⁰⁶ Nor does the receipt of public funding, even if it constitutes the bulk of an organization's operating expenses.¹⁰⁷ "Nor does combining the two factors; being highly regulated *and* publicly funded does not make a private organization's actions government actions."¹⁰⁸

The importance of adoption has leapt in the United States after *Dobbs v. Jackson Women's Health Organization*¹⁰⁹ overturned *Roe v. Wade*. U.S. states may now regulate abortion without federal oversight, a fact that has created a patchwork of differing regimes across the country. After *Dobbs*, it's likely that the number of adoptions in the U.S. will increase in the coming years.¹¹⁰

Now, it is self-defeating for the adoption placement system as a whole to turn away an otherwise qualified couple. And it is equally self-defeating for

---

103   Fulton v. City of Philadelphia, (Slip Opinion) October Term, 2020.
104   Manhattan Cmty. Access Corp. v. Halleck, 139 S. Ct. 1921, 1932 (2019).
105   Ibid.
106   Blum v. Yaretsky, 457 U.S. 991, 1004 (1982) (quoting Jackson v. Metro. Edison Co., 419 U.S. 345, 350 (1972)); accord, *Manhattan*, 139 S. Ct. at 1932 ("New York State's extensive regulation of MNN's operation of the public access channels does not make MNN a state actor").
107   See *Blum*, 457 U.S. at 1011 (holding that a nursing home that accepted "substantial funding" from the state was not a state actor); accord Rendell-Baker v. Kohn, 457 U.S. 830, 840 (1982) (holding that a private school's "receipt of public funds does not make the discharge decisions acts of the State").
108   Douglas Laycock et al., "The Respect for Marriage Act: Living Together Despite Our Deepest Differences," *University of Illinois Law Review* (forthcoming, 2023).
109   597 U.S. ___ (2022).
110   Abortions have plummeted, but it is too soon to know whether adoptions have increased. Compare Kelsey Butler, "Legal Abortions in US Down 5,000 Per Month Since the End of Roe," *Bloomberg News*, Apr. 11, 2023 ("In the six months since the US Supreme Court overturned Roe v. Wade, there were 5,377 fewer abortions on average per month, according to a new report.").

the adoption placement system as a whole to close adoption agencies that are serving otherwise qualified couples.

Both gay couples and traditionally religious families represent a sizable fraction of all those who adopt.[111] We do not want to drive faith-based agencies from this space. They are extremely valuable in the placement of children into loving families. Protecting the vulnerable is not only a Christian commitment but is shared, to our knowledge, by virtually every faith tradition. One obvious solution: place all the adoption agencies that serve a state's residents—whether birth mothers or prospective adoptive parents—into a consortium. Every qualified prospective family will know that there is an agency available to serve them. This consortium then guarantees every perspective adoptive family the respect they deserve.

If one wants to understand the continued and deep isolationism of U.S. family law, it *ironically* stems from the fact that the states themselves stake out very different substantive approaches to difficult questions, acting as laboratories of experimentation.[112]

5.3   Brief Synopsis

As this part of our chapter shows, countries have substantive differences in how they structure their systems to care for children when their families of origin cannot. It is difficult to say that one structure is necessarily superior to another, given the many contextual and cultural factors that shape such systems and lead countries to adopt them. Importantly, particular approaches may be better for particular types of children: infants, sibling groups, children removed from a family of origin by reasons of abuse, children removed from a family of origin for reasons of neglect, and other ruptures.

Empirically, over time, we might learn that foster care can accommodate more children or that children fare better in group placements rather than individual adoptions. But absent that empirical basis, it is difficult to say *ex ante* that one approach—adoption or foster care—is less valid than the other. It seems that countries and governments should be able to decide where the emphasis should be placed.

---

111 "Who Adopts the Most?," Gladney Center for Adoption, https://adoption.org/who-adopts-the-most. Of course, gay couples may be religious and religious communities include LGBT members.

112 See Wilson and Sanders, "By Faith Alone: When Religion and Child Welfare Collide," 344–45.

6 Conclusion: John Witte's Fitting Legacy

Extending our comparative understanding of how to promote family welfare is a fitting legacy for someone of John Witte's stature and influence. The ratification debate over whether to embrace the CRC is only one domain in which his work has added to a nuanced appreciation of what is at stake.

The CRC provides important tenets for policy makers and practitioners in how to think about children's needs beyond the basics of being fed and clothed. One of the reasons the CRC has enjoyed such wide ratification is the extensive negotiations that took place among delegations from all over the world for about ten years. Its concepts are derived from what makes us dignified humans.

In many ways, the CRC has passed the test of time. We have ample evidence that when the spirit of the CRC has been followed, it has guided practitioners and policy makers in making decisions for children which contributed to better childhoods—implicitly improving their chances of becoming healthy and active citizens.[113] In an equitable world, the CRC should be regarded as a moral tool and not an ideological one, to guide us to improve the lives of children and lay the foundations for healthier future societies.

This is important for all countries but even more for countries with declining birth rates and aging populations where children are an increasingly scarce and precious asset, and where children's mental health has become a public health concern.[114]

---

113   Kington, "Why Has the United States Never Ratified."
114   Organization for Economic Co-operation and Development, "Children and Young People's Mental Health in the Digital Age," Sep. 29, 2022, https://www.oecd.org/els/health-systems/Children-and-Young-People-Mental-Health-in-the-Digital-Age.pdf.

CHAPTER 30

Faith-Based Family Law Arbitration in Secular Democracies—Is the End Near?

Michael J. Broyde

1   Introduction

For nearly a century, the sunlight of the Federal Arbitration Act (FAA) has encouraged the growth of religious alternative dispute resolution. Many scholars and politicians, however, take offense to the existence and authority of religious tribunals under the FAA paradigm.[1] This chapter endeavors to explore and critique the challenges these opponents pose, and thereafter delineate the grander virtues of religious arbitration. In its first part, the piece reviews the history of religious arbitration and, in its second, it discusses the three pending challenges to religious arbitration: two are frontal arguments that religious arbitration needs to cease, and one is an attempt to deeply limit its authority in the family law context. Finally, this chapter discusses the grander virtues of religious arbitration and offers concluding thoughts.

However, before embarking on substance, I want to take heed of the purpose of this volume and offer some words of tribute to my close colleague and dear friend, Professor John Witte, Jr. I have worked with John at the Center for the Study of Law and Religion at Emory Law School for more than thirty years. Although John has no deep interest in either arbitration law or religious arbitration, I must say that he was instrumental in my becoming an expert in the field. This is not surprising for three reasons. First, John is a scholar's scholar. He watches so many fields within law and religion so as to gain a deep appreciation for the importance of all fields. Second, he is himself a prodigious scholar whose interests are actually quite diverse. Third, unlike many scholars, John is a stellar administrator—he organizes and arranges journals, books, conferences, and events on all topics, large and small.

For such an outstanding scholar and administrator, he is an astonishingly nice human being. He never misses a chance to be kind to all of the Lord's

---

1   For further explanation, see my book, Michael J. Broyde, *Sharia Tribunals, Rabbinical Courts, and Christian Panels: Religious Arbitration in America and the West* (Oxford: Oxford University Press, 2017), chaps. 8 and 9.

creatures, great and small. Being one of those small creatures around him, I am grateful. All tributes to him are earned by his kind deeds and superb scholarship.

2 American Pluralism through Private Law

Like all Americans, the faithful engage in mundane commerce within and outside their communities. So, too, are the faithful often embroiled in family disputes over their mundane interpersonal dealings.[2] But unlike other Americans, the faithful occupy a unique position in American jurisprudence. Namely, the legal system treats religious parties cautiously, and courts are often unwilling or incapable to involve themselves in religious disputes.[3] The anthem of separation between church and state is a frequent citation,[4] and as a result, judges developed the "neutral principals of law" doctrine to justify their tentative hand on religiously influenced disputes.[5] Relying on civil rulings based on neutral principles, or "objective, well established concepts of law," courts soothe concerns that adjudicating religious disputes "would impermissibly contravene prevailing interpretations of the Establishment Clause."[6] However, the inconsistent legal treatment of faith-based tribunals jeopardizes the rights of coreligionists to the free exercise of religion. Whether courts are willing to address them or not, such matters represent genuine disputes between individuals and organizations that must be resolved if people are to exist and function together in society. It is thus important to realize that these kinds of conflicts *will* get resolved.[7] The critical question is whether society wants such matters dealt with internally by religious authorities without any legal oversight.[8]

---

2 Ibid., 42; and Michael A. Helfand and Barak D. Richman, "The Challenge of Co-Religionist Commerce," *Duke Law Journal* 64 (2015): 769–822, at 771.
3 Helfand and Richman, "The Challenge of Co-Religionist Commerce," 771.
4 Ibid., 769 n. 10: "Although the reasons for this constitutional restriction vary, most scholarly treatments contend that the Establishment Clause erects structural or jurisdictional barriers to courts' ability to interfere with the authority of religious institutions to govern religious life.".
5 *Encore Prods., Inc. v. Promise Keepers*, 53 F. Supp. 2d 1101 (D. Colo. 1999): "'Neutral principles' are secular legal rules whose application to religious parties or disputes do not entail theological or religious evaluations" (citing *Jones v. Wolf*, 443 U.S. 595 [1979]).
6 Helfand and Richman, "The Challenge of Co-Religionist Commerce,"773.
7 Michael J. Broyde, "Faith-Based Arbitration Evaluated: The Policy Arguments for and Against Religious Arbitration in America," *Journal of Law and Religion* 33, no. 3 (2018): 340–89, at 370.
8 Ibid., 370.

Coreligionists engaged in secular activities walk a tightrope when drafting contracts: they must incorporate enough faith-based concepts to fully define contractual expectations, but the more religion they insert, the more civil courts fear enforcing agreed-to sanctions.[9] Rather than pass faulty judgment and risk unconstitutional decision-making, civil judges often mishandle and misinterpret coreligionist contracts, administering insufficient justice for all parties.[10] Even sidestepping the Establishment Clause problem by incorporating religious doctrine into contracts by general reference, but without spelling out the specific doctrines to which the parties have agreed, also fails to serve justice. In secular conflicts, courts struggle with whether to include context, or parole evidence, when interpreting ubiquitous contracts; meanwhile, courts nearly always prefer strict textual interpretations of religiously influenced contracts.[11] Where extrajudicial regulatory practices fail, the faithful require secular enforcement of contracts that allow for religious tribunals.

Constitutional jurisprudence also fails to resolve coreligionist disputes where faith meets the secular world. Free exercise jurisprudence, for instance, requires a "separation of religion from power"—an artificial delineation directly shaped by the West's unique post-Reformation history.[12] However, an international comparative analysis of religion reveals that many cultures regularly mix faith, law, and politics—a combination too spicy for our American constitutional jurisprudence to handle. Under American law, a religious group would be required to "recognize itself, and articulate this self-recognition, within the terms of liberal national discourse. Religious sensibilities that do not yield to such protocols of legibility cannot be heard in the public domain."[13] Such a consensus model assumes that religious minority communities will follow the integrationist model of American Catholics by assimilating into predefined and nationalistically minded "democratic mores."[14] The state expects the religious to view holy texts as historical objects and for the faithful to abide

---

9   See Michael J. Broyde and Alexa J. Windsor, "In Contracts We Trust (and No One Can Change Their Mind)! There Should Be No Special Treatment for Religious Arbitration," *Pepperdine Dispute Resolution Journal* 21 (2021):1–41, at 17–19 (an example as to how this plays out within the kosher industry).
10 Ibid.
11 Broyde, *Sharia Tribunals,* 43.
12 Silvio Ferrari, introduction to *Routledge Handbook of Law and Religion,* ed. Silvio Ferrari (London: Routledge, 2015).
13 Saba Mahmood, "Secularism, Hermeneutics, and Empire: The Politics of Islamic Reformation," *Public Culture* 18, no. 2 (2006): 323–47, at 328 n.10.
14 Charles Taylor, "Why We Need a Radical Redefinition of Secularism," in *The Power of Religion in the Public Sphere,* ed. Eduardo Mendieta and Jonathan VanAntwerpen (New York: Columbia University Press, 2011), 36.

by civil authorities' tolerance of their practices. Seemingly, this citizen must be a member of the nation first, and the religious community second.

To be sure, secular tolerance is a weak foundation upon which to build predictable expectations. Religious minorities who wish to organize their private and public lives to align with their beliefs have instead turned to the private law wheelhouse, an avenue well-traveled by private businesses throughout the past century.

Modern religious arbitration is an American legal reality. "Biblically based" forums designated by arbitration agreements are enforceable in several jurisdictions.[15] Consider, for example, the Beth Din of America, a religious arbitration forum that "obtain[s] Jewish divorces, confirm[s] personal status and adjudicate[s] commercial disputes stemming from divorce, business and community issues."[16] The Beth Din operates in most states and addresses around four hundred family law matters per year as well as around one hundred commercial disputes.[17] Indeed, the Jewish extrajudicial process earned respect from the American judiciary despite its procedural differences:[18] "the Beth Din method of arbitration has the imprimatur of our own judicial system, [and is] a useful means of relieving the burdens of the inundated courts dealing with civil matters."[19]

The benefits and pitfalls of commercial extralegal arbitration for the religious can also be seen in the Christian and Muslim context. Christian Conciliation, as implied in the name, prioritizes *conciliation*—a trait that defies the American adversarial process.[20] Following Jesus's admonition to legal jurists,[21] Christian dispute resolution focuses on negotiation, an introspective

---

15 Broyde, *Sharia Tribunals*, 16–17.
16 Abdul Wahid Sheikh Osman, "Islamic Arbitration Courts in America & Canada?," *Hiiraan Online*, 2005, https://www.hiiraan.com/op/eng/2005/dec/Prof_Abdulwahid211205.htm; and see Broyde, *Sharia Tribunals*, 14–16.
17 Nicholas Walter, "Religious Arbitration in the United States and Canada," *Santa Clara Law Review* 52 (2012): 501, at 521.
18 See generally Michael J. Broyde, "Jewish Law Courts in America: Lessons Offered to Sharia Courts by the Beth Din of America Precedent," *New York Law School Review* 57 (2013): 287–311.
19 *Mikel v. Scharf*, 85 A.D.2d 604 (App. Div. 1981) (affirming reward granted by religious tribunal); *Meshel v. Ohev Sholom Talmud Torah*, 869 A.2d 343 (D.C. 2005) (permitting religious arbitration within Beth Din to continue).
20 Michael A. Helfand, "Arbitration, Transparency, and Privatization: Arbitration's Counter-Narrative: The Religious Arbitration Paradigm," *Yale Law Journal* 124 (2015): 2994–3051, at 2997.
21 Matthew 23:23 ("Woe to you, teachers of the law ... you have neglected the more important matters of the law—justice, mercy, and faithfulness").

examination of one's own interests, and then the conflict between individual interests and the greater good.[22] In other words, the goal is to repair the relationship between the parties rather than to decide a winner or a loser.[23] Lawsuits between Christians are discouraged until other gospel-based processes have been exhausted.[24] Groups like the Christian Dispute Resolution Professionals, Inc. and Peacemaker Ministries espouse this mentality, even in realms as diverse as insurance disputes, employment disputes, and personal injury, ensuring alternative avenues for dispute resolution based on religious texts and values.[25]

Peacemaker Ministries, the largest Christian arbitration organization in the United States, conducts on average one hundred conciliations and arbitrations a year while certifying around one hundred and fifty conciliators.[26] The founder of Peacemaker Ministries, Ken Sande, has highlighted the values of an alternative, restorative justice by referencing an estate fight within a mourning family.[27] The clash involved six siblings, one of whom, Frank, was mentally ill and lived in a farmhouse on the property in dispute. A trust had been established for his care upon the death of the parents, while the farmhouse was deeded to the other five siblings. When the moment came, the five siblings wished to sell the farmhouse immediately, evicting Frank. When they told him, he was terrified to leave the only home he had ever known. Heated arguments over the farmhouse culminated in Frank nearly assaulting his siblings with a baseball bat.

After a call to a pastor to reach a consensus, stop any violence, and avoid litigation over the property, the family prayed over how to honor God, respect their parents' wishes, and treat one another "in a way that shows the power of gospel in each of [their] lives."[28] Ultimately, the solution the family reached was distinct, and, in fact, more kind, than anything a civil court would have decided:

---

22 R. Seth Shippee, "'Blessed Are the Peacemakers:' Faith-Based Approaches to Dispute Resolution," *ILSA Journal of International & Comparative Law* 9 (2002): 237–59, at 242.

23 Judith M. Keegan, "The Peacemakers: Biblical Conflict Resolution and Reconciliation as a Model Alternative to Litigation," *Journal of Dispute Resolution* (1987): 11–25, at 12.

24 Relational Wisdom 360, *Handbook for Christian Conciliation*, 11 (citing Matthew 18:15–20 and 1 Corinthians 6:1–8), https://rw360.org/wp-content/uploads/2019/04/Handbook-for-Christian-Conciliation-v5.3-4-23-19.pdf.

25 Relational Wisdom 360, rw360.org.

26 Broyde, *Sharia Tribunals*, 17; "Frequently Asked Questions," Peacemaker Ministries, http://peacemaker.net/icc-frequently-asked-questions/; and Walter, 521.

27 Sande, "Turning Assault into Reconciliation," Relational Wisdom 360 (Jan. 2015), https://rw360.org/2015/01/11/turning-assault-reconciliation/.

28 Ibid.

"Frank," he [his brother] went on, "in appreciation for all you did for Mom, we want to give you this gift. It is an agreement we have all signed that gives you a life estate in the farmhouse. That means you will be able to stay there as long as you live. We found a buyer who is willing to purchase the rest of the farmland. Ownership of the house will eventually pass to our children. But as long as you want to live there, we want you to know that it is your home.[29]

To a civil court, Frank was clearly in the wrong. But costly, adversarial solutions would have only shattered the family further. It is not surprising that "instead of learning where they need to change and how they can avoid similar problems in the future, many parties [in an adversarial process] leave a courtroom holding even more tightly to their harmful values and opinions."[30] Christian Conciliation was an alternative, discouraging adversarial contention and encouraging confessionals on "matters of the heart" between parties[31]—a values structure which can resolve a wide variety of seemingly secular conflicts.[32]

To further drill down into the oft mundane nature of religious disputes settled in arbitration, one can look to Islamic courts adhering to sharia. Islamic Courts operate on a smaller scale because of community structures in America,[33] theological conflicts over whether sharia can operate in non-Islamic jurisdictions,[34] and racism from outside the community.[35] Despite these challenges, however, sharia tribunals have built positive precedential

---

29   Ken Sande, *The Peacemaker: A Biblical Guide to Resolving Personal Conflict* (Grand Rapids, MI: Baker Books, 2004), 17–20.
30   Ken Sande, "Danger of 'Good' Advocacy," Relational Wisdom 360, https://rw360.org /2022/06/17/the-dangers-of-good-advocacy/.
31   Relational Wisdom 360, *Handbook for Christian Conciliation*, 9.
32   Ibid., 6–7. One example of a successfully solved conflict is as follows: "The owner of a house accused a builder of doing defective work, an employee claimed that she was improperly fired from her job, the owners of a business could not agree on how to divide its assets, a church was being torn apart by doctrinal and personality conflicts, a partner in an oil and gas development venture believed he had been defrauded, a patient alleged that a doctor had performed surgery improperly, the birth mother of a child wanted to reverse an adoption, an author claimed that a publisher had broken a contract to publish his book, a husband and wife were struggling with an impending divorce, two ranchers disagreed on road right-of-way, a company claimed that its competitor's product infringed on its patent, a divorced couple disagreed constantly over child support and visitation."
33   Michael J. Broyde, "Shari'a and Halakha in North America: Faith-Based Private Arbitration as a Model for Preserving Rights and Values in a Pluralistic Society," *Chicago-Kent Law Review* 90 (2015): 111.
34   Broyde, *Sharia Tribunals*, 20.
35   Osman, "Islamic Arbitration Courts in America & Canada?"

support in civil courts in recent years.³⁶ While Islamic arbitration agreements are a recent development, courts generally respect the mutual consent of the parties to use Islamic principles and institutions in their private disputes.³⁷

Sharia procedural requirements, while impossible in a civil courtroom, can comply with Islamic dispute resolution. For example, under Islamic law, roles and titles in a case are fluid, determined by the strength of a claim. The claimant "is the party whose claim is deemed weaker and who needs to present additional evidence to support his case."³⁸ Meanwhile, the defendant's position is seen as stronger, benefited by presumptions or evidence. A first step of litigation is settling who takes which role.³⁹ That said, the claimant does not need "to produce all relevant evidence in order to satisfy a prima facie standard," and, under Islamic evidentiary rules, they may shift "the burden onto the defendant, forcing the hand of what might otherwise be a complacent corporation."⁴⁰

Interestingly, Islamic tribunals in the United States offer an opportunity for Muslims to revive the pluralistic ethos of pre-Ottoman imperial sharia. In fact, there is a new, developing Islamic jurisprudence, *Fiqh al-aqalliyyat*, or sharia for Muslims living in non-Muslim nations, in which rules shift and adapt to the reality of living through a diaspora. This is a historical anomaly rooted in the Ottoman consolidation of power, codification by European powers, and internal movements towards modernization (which often followed European trends in common law).⁴¹ Under the *Fiqh* paradigm, adaptations are made which otherwise may not be allowed under Islamic law.⁴² *Fiqh* offers an alternative for Muslims to coexist with secular, democratic nations while not violating tenets of their faith. Thus, we see a development contrary to the postcolonial perception of Islam as an unmoving, "unchangeable set of norms that is binding upon all Muslims."⁴³ To regain a dynamic jurisprudence, many Islamic arbitration tribunals today also operate using a procedural posture called *tahkim*, which

---

36 *Jabri v. Qadurra*, 108 S.W.3d 404 (Tex. App. 2003); and *Abd Alla v. Mourssi*, 680 N.W.2d 569 (Minn. Ct. App. 2004).
37 Compare Cynthia Brougher, *Application of Religious Law in U.S. Courts: Selected Legal Issues* (Washington, DC: Library of Congress, Congressional Research Service, 2011), 3.
38 Michael A. Helfand, "Religious Arbitration and the New Multiculturalism: Negotiating Conflicting Legal Orders," *New York University Law Review* 86 (2011): 1231, at 1265–66.
39 Ibid..
40 Ibid.
41 Rabea Benhalim, "The Case for American Muslim Arbitration," *Wisconsin Law Review* (2019): 531–92, at 562–63.
42 Ibid., 532.
43 Ibid., 540.

typically involves a flexible, less law-based arbitral process.[44] These decisions, rather than bound by precedent, are grounded in *maslahah*, or equitable, pragmatic policy.[45]

The United States has a great diversity of Muslims and, commensurately, greater representation from all jurisprudential schools of Islamic law.[46] This means that, "unlike most Muslim-majority countries, ... there is freedom for robust differences of opinion on the correct application of Islamic law."[47] Diversity, and *tolerance* of diversity—both religious and ethnic—may return some of the dynamism of early Islamic law. Furthermore, the lack of historical conflict in the United States between branches of Islamic jurisprudence—say, between Sunni and Shi'a Muslims—creates a neutral space for cooperation and collaboration. U.S. laws on personal status, dominated by the equality ethos, could influence future conversations between Islamic jurists and encourage modernization.

Consider the role of women in Islamic arbitration, for instance. *Hanafi* scholars allow female arbitrators where disputes directly relate to women or involve property, whereas "some *Maliki* and *Zahiri* scholars permit women to serve as judges, and therefore they may serve as arbitrators in some circumstances."[48] In America, where our Muslim population is disproportionally well-educated,[49] sophisticated women could thus ostensibly forum-shop between Islamic schools of jurisprudence—not only to benefit themselves within a given dispute, but to push modern Islamic Law toward doctrinal preferences which more favorably support women.[50]

The goal of religious dispute resolution is not merely—or perhaps even primarily—to reach the most accurate, formally legalistic resolution of a dispute. Instead, religious arbitration processes seek to promote fairness, reconciliation, acknowledgment of wrongdoing, and the establishment of equitable and peaceful relations between disputants. Within this framework, the inclusion of lawyers and other counselors is often seen as counterproductive, given that the goal is not to enable each party to press its rights to the furthest extent of the law, but to help each litigant fulfill his or her religio-legal and moral obligations to others. Indeed, some religious arbitration tribunals

---

44 Broyde, "Faith-Based Arbitration Evaluated," 353.
45 Ibid.
46 Benhalim, "The Case for American Muslim Arbitration," 547.
47 Ibid., 557.
48 Ibid., 573–74.
49 Ibid..
50 Ibid.

proscribe the involvement of lawyers in direct contradiction to the legal framework for arbitration established by many secular law regimes.

Alternative dispute resolution (ADR) is not limited to Abrahamic-influenced extrajudicial tribunals. Rather, it provides opportunities for conflict resolution within "encapsulated communit[ies] within a larger constitutional regime."[51] While I will limit my analysis of these models to focus on religious entanglement and arbitration, it is important to draw attention to the widespread appeal of choice of law and choice of forum for affinity communities whose expectations are misaligned with U.S. civil court priorities and values. The Navajo Nation is one such example, infusing their dispute resolution processes with corporate, collective ideals of justice, rather than the individualistic, rights-based model of the U.S. legal regime.

Ultimately, people who choose to arbitrate based on religious or cultural laws are choosing their set of laws precisely because it offers something that the secular world or dominant legal regime cannot.[52] If their intent is to have a neutral observer picked for them with formal legal training, or with the legal priorities of fairness and common law, they can look to courtrooms in every municipality in the country.[53] Instead, the unique inability for affinity groups, including the religious, to articulate their expectations through secular language necessitates arbitration clauses to overcome the problems associated with incorporating alternative (religious) values into contracts. These arbitration clauses—directing parties to settle through religious tribunals using religious laws—have allowed religious minority groups to access justice that would otherwise be mishandled by judges within civil courts. While abuses do occur—and where they do, they ought to be condemned—such power abuses are not unique, but inherent to the current state of American contract law.

In the next section, I explore the critiques of religious arbitration born out of reference to these abuses, and argue that robust arbitration law allows for the proliferation of alternative value communities, while defending against the use of religion as a weapon against the greater equality project of the United States.

---

51 Edo Banach, "The Roma and the Native Americans: Encapsulated Communities within Larger Constitutional Regimes," *Florida Journal of International Law* (2001–02): 353–95.
52 Broyde, "Faith-Based Arbitration Evaluated," 355.
53 Ibid.

3 Problems Confronting Religious Arbitration: Three Issues

Religious arbitration and its enforcement always stir discontent. From the *New York Times*[54] to the *Yale Law Journal*,[55] writers have expressed fear that religious arbitration coerces people to obey religious law, establishes national religions, or otherwise interferes with popular freedom.

Three challenges have coalesced within the past few years.

The first challenge is typified by the recent decision in *Bixler v. Scientology*. There, the California Appellate division allowed parties to back out of an arbitration agreement to a religious tribunal on religious freedom grounds.[56] Essentially, the *Bixler* court created a new exit right to contracts and a new doctrine in federal arbitration law, applicable only to cases of religious dispute resolution. The second challenge is the expansion of the state action doctrine by way of reverse-entanglement arguments positing that state enforcement of religious arbitration is the constitutional equivalent of enforcement of religion.[57] The third challenge is the possible application of the recently passed Ending Forced Arbitration of Sexual Assault and Sexual Harassment Act (EFASASH) of 2021,[58] which ends binding predispute arbitration agreements on matters of sexual assault or sexual harassment and maybe many divorce matters as well. I address all three seriatim.

4 Religious Right to Exit Contract

In *Bixler*, former Church of Scientology members sued the institution along with a powerful leader who had allegedly raped and sexually harassed them

---

54 The *New York Times* ran a series of three front-page articles about arbitration, one of which focused on religious arbitration; see Jessica Silver-Greenberg and Robert Gebeloff, "Arbitration Everywhere, Stacking the Deck of Justice," *New York Times DealBook*, Oct. 31, 2015, http://www.nytimes.com/2015/11/01/business/dealbook/arbitration-everywhere-stacking-the-deck-of-justice.html.

55 Sophia Chua-Rubenfeld and Frank J. Costa Jr., "The Reverse-Entanglement Principle: Why Religious Arbitration of Federal Rights Is Unconstitutional," *Yale Law Journal* 128 (2019): 2087–121. See also Skylar Reese Croy, "In God We Trust (Unless We Change Our Mind): How State of Mind Relates to Religious Arbitration," *Pepperdine Dispute Resolution Law Journal* 20 (2020): 120–47.

56 *Chrissie Bixler et al. v. Scientology and Danny Masterson*, No. B310559 (Cal. Ct. App. 2022), *cert denied*. The California Supreme Court declined to grant review of the case, and it was ordered as not for publication.

57 Chua-Rubenfeld and Costa, "The Reverse-Entanglement Principle."

58 S.2342, 117th Congress 2022.

while they were members. An arbitration clause within the contracts they signed to become church members required all claims or controversies to be resolved via the procedures of the church's Ethics, Justice and Binding Religious Arbitration system.[59] Citing a minister from the church, the former members argued that "[t]he justice codes and procedures are an inherent part of the religion, and are derived from our core beliefs."[60] The Church of Scientology argued—and the lower court agreed—that the civil court risked violating the Entanglement Clause if they were to make the determination as to whether alternative dispute resolution is a key tenet of the Church of Scientology.[61] In essence, the Church of Scientology sought the binding power of contract combined with the heightened inscrutability of religious practices to compel arbitration.

The California Court of Appeals, however, ruled against the church. The court relied on the petitioners' completely unfettered constitutional right to change religions,[62] interpreting this case as balancing "petitioners' right to leave a faith *and* Scientology's right to resolve disputes with its members without court intervention."[63]

In my view, this analysis is disingenuous to the actual problems presented by the case. A religiously based contract should not be treated any differently than a secular contract, and a neutral contractual analysis of the case would be sufficient to prevent abuse and defend constitutional rights to free exercise. Indeed, contracts can always be broken; contract enforcement is distinguishable from the government's coercive control over its citizenry.[64] The price for breaking a contract, limited by general contract law, still allows for an individual to convert to a new religion while honoring previous agreements.[65]

It is a simple fact of modern life that Americans regularly sign away their rights, both statutory and constitutional. Indeed, the duel between contractual freedom and judicial authority has shaped the past century of American

---

59 *Bixler*, 11.
60 Ibid., 15.
61 Ibid., 21–22.
62 Ibid., 33.
63 Ibid., 35.
64 Broyde and Windsor, "In Contracts We Trust," section III.A. The restraints on a person's freedom of conscience by contractual obligation is easily distinguishable from the free-exercise restraint on conscience, where the government, using its full coercive power, sends people to be killed or jailed. See, *Welsh v. United States*, 398 U.S. 333 (1970) and its progeny for free conscience claims at their zenith.
65 Ibid.

jurisprudence.[66] Judges, loathe giving authority and legitimacy to the noninitiated, fought and ruled against extrajudicial arbitration for decades.[67] But under the FAA and derivative state laws, the paradigm is now procedural due process,[68] and courts apply a high level of deference to alternative dispute awards. In fact, the Supreme Court has stated time and time again that arbitration clauses are to be treated no differently than any other contractual clause.[69] Exit rights to arbitration clauses are narrow and narrowing, and those few exit rights almost entirely rely on unconscionability where fraud is not present.[70] Instead of a heavier reliance on unconscionability to undercut abusive contracts, the *Bixler* court created a religious exit right to contract law specifically where signors incorporate religion into their agreements.

The *Bixler* court's decision to put religious free exercise on a pedestal runs counter to the long American tradition of rights waiver through contract. It would be preferable, I have argued elsewhere, for courts to conduct a classic unconscionability analysis instead of inventing a new *religious* exit right to contract law.[71]

Religious arbitration must echo the norms of secular arbitration, otherwise civil courts will refuse to enforce an award.[72] Now, admittedly, FAA's policy of favoritism toward arbitration has weakened unconscionability somewhat as a contract defense claim, since arbitration itself is never unconscionable. The lax standards for "knowing" what rights one is waiving away at the time of contracting lead to the textbook case: a party, not knowing what they are getting themselves into or later wishing for different terms, binds themselves inextricably to harsh terms that will produce a manifest injustice.[73] However, such abuse is not limited to religious arbitration agreements. To prohibit religious arbitration on free exercise grounds would not lower the thresholds for an unconscionability claim or repudiate an expansive severability doctrine. This is further support for the contention that contract abuse should be met with a contract defense, not by elevating or prohibiting religious contracts.

---

66 Broyde and Windsor, "In Contracts We Trust," 4–9.
67 Ibid.
68 Broyde, *Sharia Tribunals*, 145–46.
69 Chua-Rubenfeld and Costa, "The Reverse-Entanglement Principle," 2087.
70 See Broyde and Windsor, "In Contracts We Trust," section III.A.
71 "Contract Law Should be Faith Neutral," NYU Annual Survey of American Law, forthcoming.
72 Broyde, *Sharia Tribunals*, 150: "Arbitral tribunals must accept that secular courts will be powerless to enforce their awards unless they satisfy the minimal technical requirements set by the secular law arbitration framework."
73 Broyde, "Faith-Based Arbitration," 351.

When judges ignore neutral principles and bypass the unconscionability defense in scrutinizing religious contracts, they often reach wrong decisions because they do not, and cannot, understand the religious issues they implicate. And this is to be expected—after all, for courts to be fully conversant with the religious content would tread upon religious freedom and establishment concerns. Consider, for example, judicial treatment of Islamic *mahr* agreements[74] and Jewish *ketubah* contracts in the family law context,[75] or the *heter iska* in commercial settings.[76] In these cases, different courts often reach demonstrably inconsistent results and issue rulings that respond poorly to litigants' actual needs and interests.[77]

Even when armed with the subjective unconscionability defense, courts have a poor track record of recognizing the various forms of pressure that religious communities exert to get individuals to agree to arbitrate disputes. Traditional Jewish law, for instance, maintains that Jews are obligated to resolve their disputes with coreligionists in rabbinic courts.[78] Jewish litigants that refuse to appear before a rabbinic tribunal when summoned may be subject to a *seruv*, a public declaration that such parties are in contempt of court. The practical ramifications of a *seruv* vary widely from community to community, but can include exclusion from participation in religious services, denial of the rights and privileges of membership in the Jewish community, and expulsion of one's children from private religious schools. Additionally, other members of the Jewish community might refuse to engage in business with the subject of a *seruv*, thus dealing real economic consequences.

For a court to properly evaluate the degree to which communal pressure and formal religious doctrines—like the rabbinic *seruv*—unduly coerce parties to agree to arbitrate disputes in religious forums requires examining and judging a community's religious values.[79] Not only is there good reason to think that courts are simply bad at such determinations, but, under religious freedom

---

74 See *Hibibi-Fahnrich v. Fahnrich*, no. 46186/93, WL 507388 (1995); see also *In re Marriage of Dajani*, 129 Cal. App. 2d 1387 (1988); *In re Marriage of Obaidi*, 154 Wash. App. 609, 616 (Wash. Ct. App. 2010).

75 See *In re Marriage of Goldman*, 554 N.E.2d 1016 (1990). See also *Koeppel v. Koeppel*, 138 N.Y.S. 2d 366 (1954); and *Avitzur v. Avitzur*, 446 N.E.2d 138 (1983).

76 See *IDB v. Weiss & Wolf*, NYS Sp. Ct. 1984, NYLJ 2/4/85, 14; *Bank Leumi Trust Co. of New York v. Morris Spitzer*, NYS Sup. Ct. 9/18/86 no. 017734/1986; and *Bollag v. Dresdner*, 495 NYS 2d 560 (1985).

77 See, for example, *Presbyterian Church v. Mary Elizabeth Bull Hull Memorial Presbyterian Church*, 393 U.S. 440 (1969).

78 Broyde, "Faith-Based Arbitration," 355.

79 Ibid., 359.

doctrines, they may be barred from doing so. By default, this leaves vulnerable parties unable to seek redress through the courts for reasons that existing legal frameworks for arbitration anticipate.

5 State Action and Reverse Entanglement

Where secular authority is required to civilly enforce the decisions of faith-based tribunals, some raise concerns of religious entanglement with government in violation of the First Amendment Establishment Clause. Where contract law allows for unintended waivers of federal rights through choice of law and forum doctrines in arbitration, some see the interference with the First Amendment Free Exercise Clause. Further, where a party has unilateral input on choice of law and forum, some worry that parties may effectively shop for favorable arbiters who guarantee victory ahead of any conflict. These perceived power imbalances and harbingers of discrimination are the subject of a recent article in the *Yale Law Journal*, and others, creating a reverse-entanglement doctrine to end secular enforcement of decisions by religious arbitration tribunals.[80] The heart of the claim is as follows: if a party to a faith-based conflict seeks secular enforcement of a settlement, civil courts risk unconstitutionally violating religious establishment by enforcing a religious tribunal's rulings.

To illustrate the state action expansion under reverse entanglement, I offer a hypothetical: You are an Orthodox Jew, and you enter a marriage with your Orthodox Jewish spouse. Both of you agree to live by the faith and sign a prenuptial agreement that selects not only Jewish law to serve as the rules of decision but also a suitable (beth din) rabbinical tribunal to arbitrate any disputes. Further, you both sign a prenuptial agreement which requires that any children of the union must be raised within the Orthodox Jewish faith, and, as required by the prenuptial agreement, one spouse will provide for the other.[81]

Fifteen years and three children later, you convert from Judaism to a different religion, and you file for divorce, citing irreconcilable differences. Under state law, you would likely pay less in spousal and child support fees and could perhaps nullify any religious requirements from the custody agreement. However, that fifteen-year-old prenuptial agreement requires a beth din to adjudicate any disagreements or marriage-related challenges. There, fault in divorce

---

80 Chua-Rubenfeld and Costa propose the reverse-entanglement principle as a sword and shield against civil rights violations within extrajudicial religious tribunals. A similar but related argument can be found in Broyde and Windsor "In Contracts We Trust."
81 *Marcovitz v. Bruker*, [2007] 3 S.C.R. 607 (Canada).

may be considered, and Jewish jurisprudence might consider you to be breaching the prenuptial agreement as well as duties of the faith, for which Jewish law will penalize you.

You don't like your chances under Jewish law. So, you go to a secular court and demand that it handle the divorce. You argue that if the secular court were to enforce your prenuptial agreement and the associated arbitration clause, it would violate the First Amendment Establishment Clause. The prior agreement does not matter; the prior fifteen years of contractual compliance does not matter; the nonviolation of the contract by the other party does not matter.

To be sure, this dispute *will* be resolved, and regardless of the outcome, someone *will* be disappointed. The legal quandary is over *who ought to be disappointed*: the party adhering to the contract or the party with a change in position. The proponents of the new reverse-entanglement principle, advocating for the prohibition of religious-contract enforcement, silence altogether the option for religious arbitration *that the parties agreed to in advance of conflict*.[82] They would thus submit that the *only* answer to the "who is disappointed" question is that the previous meeting of the minds must be void—the party who abides by the contract must lose. In a situation where the contract is legitimate, not void nor voidable for abuse or error, this result is counter to a variety of American legal tenets.

Based on a novel interpretation of the now-discarded Establishment Clause of *Lemon v. Kurtzamn* (1971), reverse entanglement would apply the state-action doctrine to the civil enforcement of private, secular agreements between coreligionists who consent to faith-driven dispute resolution. If a party to a faith-based conflict seeks secular enforcement of a settlement, civil courts risk unconstitutional religious establishment by enforcing a religious tribunal's rulings. As a sword, the principle cuts out the civil enforcement of faith-based dispute resolution within the sphere of secular conflicts. As a shield, it protects minorities from contractual power imbalances and limits lay exposure to religious law and values. Reverse entanglement creates a firm boundary between the religious and the secular by prohibiting civil enforcement of faith-influenced contractual obligations.

This is not an entirely new argument. Since the 1990s, academics and politicians, concerned by Supreme Court deference to arbitration, have launched a multipronged attack against arbitration and enforcement.[83] One such prong applies the state-action doctrine to arbitration award enforcement, tying in

---

82   Chua-Rubenfeld and Costa Jr., "The Reverse-Entanglement Principle."
83   Sarah Rudolph Cole, "Arbitration and State Action," 2005 *BYU Law Review* 1 (2005): 1 n.2.

constitutional due process in procedure to the arbitration process.[84] Thus far, however, every federal court has rejected the application of state action to contractual arbitration.[85]

Similar to the religious-exit right conjured by the *Bixler* court, reverse entanglement fails to solve its main fear: contractual abuse. What it does do, however, is isolate and in some cases eliminate religious arbitration entirely. Religious minorities would face a Catch-22: Current jurisprudence discourages them from outlining religious concepts within contracts,[86] but where coreligionist commerce must occur, the legitimacy of religious tribunals to resolve disputes would be at risk. Interpreting civil enforcement of religious arbitration as state establishment of religion only tightens the thumbscrews for religious minority groups and ignores the historical *de minimis* entanglement between church and state, which has always been tolerable under the Constitution.[87]

For a viable use of the state-action doctrine to limit arbitration abuse, I again argue for unconscionability as a solution. Unconscionability can even be strengthened by the state-action doctrine. Instead of expanding the interpretation of *Shelley v. Kraemer*,[88] the linchpin behind reverse entanglement, from enforcement of racial covenants to include the enforcement of religious agreements, I propose a reinterpretation. When examining the state's role in arbitration enforcement, the crux of the *Shelley* decision was the control exerted on nonparties to the contract—that future buyers and sellers of a home with a racial covenant are forced to adhere to terms to which they never assented. I propose a contractual privity model when determining whether an arbitration agreement, through civil court enforcement, constitutes a state action.

---

84 Sarah Rudolph Cole, "Arbitration and the *Batson* Principle," *Georgia Law Review* 38 (2004): 1145; Jean R. Sternlight, "Rethinking the Constitutionality of the Supreme Court's Preference for Binding Arbitration: A Fresh Assessment of Jury Trial, Separation of Powers, and Due Process Concerns," *Tulane Law Review* 72 (1997): 1–100; see Edward Brunet, "Arbitration and Constitutional Rights," *North Carolina Law Review* 71 (1992): 81 (Part III proposes how to increase constitutional rights in arbitration and on review).

85 For an expansive list of federal cases rejecting the application of state action to contractual arbitration, see Michael J. Broyde and Alexa J. Windsor, "Contract Law Should Be Faith Neutral: Reverse Entanglement Would be Stranglement for Religious Arbitration," NYU *Annual Survey of American Law* 79 (2023), 17–87.

86 Broyde, "Faith Based Arbitration," 367–68.

87 *Lemon v. Kurtzman*, 403 U.S. 602, 614 (1971) ("Judicial caveats against entanglement must recognize that the line of separation, far from being a 'wall,' is a blurred, indistinct, and variable barrier depending on all the circumstances of a particular relationship."); and John Witte, Jr., Joel A. Nichols, and Richard W. Garnett, *Religion and the American Constitutional Experiment*, 5th ed. (Oxford: Oxford University Press, 2022), 163.

88 *Shelley v. Kraemer*, 334 U.S. 1 (1948).

Arbitration clauses have proliferated throughout the past decades, and, with this growth, concern for the effective vindication of statutory and constitutional rights has flourished. As a solution to this concern, litigators and academics alike have advanced the theory that, where a court enforces an arbitration clause or award, that court is performing a state action.[89] Where state action is found, the vindication of constitutional protections and rights is required by the courts. Such protections normally do not apply between nongovernmental actors, but by asking courts to enforce private agreement, state action would bind them to apply constitutional limitations to private parties and private conflicts. Such a mix between constitutional protection and individual liberties is, however, a tall order. Requirements like procedural due process, meant to prevent governments from making arbitrary or capricious decrees, would severely limit the functionality of private businesses and the efficiency of dispute resolution.[90]

Originally within the private contract sphere, the state-action doctrine forbade the civil enforcement of racial covenants within property law. While *Shelley* was a consolidation of two cases, the relevant facts were the same: a racial minority family moved into a home within a neighborhood governed by racially restrictive covenants, and members of the neighborhood sought civil courts to evict the families. In the *Shelley* case, specifically, there were many problems with the covenant in question: not all members of the neighborhood had signed on, the covenant was deemed inactive without the proper number of signatures, African Americans already lived within the community (and had refused to sign on), and neither the Shelleys nor the seller of the property were informed of the covenant until after the purchase.[91]

The Supreme Court found that civil enforcement of such a covenant would cause the state to violate the Equal Protection Clause of the Fourteenth Amendment. The Court identified the clear intent of the Fourteenth Amendment drafters: "[I]t is clear that the matter of primary concern was the establishment of equality in the enjoyment of basic civil and political rights and the preservation of those rights from discriminatory action on the part of the States based on considerations of race or color."[92] Without support "by the full panoply of state power, petitioners [Shelleys] would have been free to occupy the properties in question without restraint."[93] Any action, demanded of the

---

89   Chua-Rubenfeld and Costa, "The Reverse-Entanglement Principle."
90   Cole, "Arbitration and State Action," 6 n.18.
91   Ibid.
92   *Shelley*, 1186.
93   Ibid., 1183.

state by an individual, "which results in the denial of equal protection of the laws to other individuals," was verboten.[94]

Today, state-action jurisprudence is a "conceptual disaster area;"[95] its application has been described as "a torchless search for a way out of a damp echoing cave."[96] There is no single test to identity where a private actor's actions transcend to state action.[97] Where tests exist, the Supreme Court has defined the circumstances of their use narrowly,[98] and, furthermore, circuit courts apply these tests haphazardly to dissimilar fact patterns.[99] *Shelley* was decided in the post-World War II period, a time when American society grappled with its moral victory against the Nazis and its own discriminatory policies at home.[100] One can see how the social context of the era encouraged the Court to act expansively against racial discrimination and punitively against racist private law. Further, the application of the covenant in *Shelley* was against the wishes of both the buyer and seller of the home, and instead was the vindication of contractual rights granted to parties outside the agreement—a factor the Court likely considered when overturning the lower court's enforcement of the covenant.[101]

Even where private parties rely on statutory schemes and make use of the judicial system to vindicate their rights, the Court is hesitant to find state action outside of racial animus.[102] To entangle a conflict and its resolution with the state is not enough for it to be attributed as an action of the state.[103] Instead, to find state action in entanglement, the Court requires "significant encouragement, either overt or covert" by the state: "[m]ere approval or acquiescence of

---

94 Ibid., 1185.
95 Charles L. Black Jr., "Foreword: 'State Action,' Equal Protection, and California's Proposition 14," *Harvard Law Review* 81 (1967): 69, at 95.
96 Ibid.
97 *Brentwood Acad. v. Tenn*, 531 U.S. 288, 294 (2001).
98 For an outline of seven distinct tests for state action application, see Julie K. Brown, "Less Is More: Decluttering the State Action Doctrine," *Missouri Law Review* 73 (2008): 561–81, at 565–68.
99 Ibid., see section "D. Circuit Courts' Application of State Actor Determinative Tests," 568–72.
100 Alexis Clark, "Returning from War, Returning to Racism," *The New York Times*, Jul. 2020, https://www.nytimes.com/2020/07/30/magazine/black-soldiers-wwii-racism.html.
101 Cole, "Arbitration and State Action," 10 n.43.
102 Ibid., 15; and *Flagg Bros. v. Brooks*, 436 U.S. 149 (1978); *Lugar v. Edmonson Oil Co.*, 457 U.S. 922 (1982).
103 Cole, "Arbitration and State Action," 19 (citing and interpreting *American Manufacturers Mutual Insurance Co. v. Sullivan*, 526 U.S. 40, 51 (1999), which held that a private party's decision to withhold workers' compensation payment under a Pennsylvania regulatory scheme was insufficient for a finding of state action in the deprivation of payment).

the State is not a state action."[104] Under the FAA, the state authorizes, but does not require, the use of arbitration, and courts are involved only at the start of the dispute (to stay litigation and compel arbitration) and at the end of the dispute (to enforce an award or handle an appeal of that award).

Dispute resolution is "neither a traditional nor [an] exclusive state function."[105] But even if we accepted dispute resolution as a traditionally public function of the courts, it is not one exclusively held by the courts.[106] The extrajudicial nature of arbitration distinguishes it from civil court resolution. After all, the parties, through an arbitration clause, delegate power to the arbitrator to resolve their disputes. This delegation of authority is easily distinguished from the government's delegating authority to a power company or to an agency conducting elections.[107]

The concept of reverse entanglement proposes a new avenue for state action—it argues that any enforcement of religious agreements would be an undue entanglement with religion, and, therefore, any religious arbitration enforcement by civil courts is an Establishment Clause violation. Prohibition on excessive entanglement between religion and government was originally a separate criterion of the *Lemon* test,[108] but today the entanglement analysis is tempered by the requirement for the court to find that the government advances a particular religion for there to be a constitutional violation.[109]

The recent Supreme Court case of *Carson v. Makin* makes it absolutely clear that a court will refuse to support a principle that maintains that it is *never* constitutional to withhold a privilege to the religious that is otherwise provided to others.[110] There, the court stated, "[i]n particular, we have repeatedly held

---

104 *Sullivan*, 22.
105 Cole, "Arbitration and State Action," 48 (citing *Flagg Bros.*).
106 *Flagg Bros.*, 160 (where a warehouse sold items in unpaid storage in accord with state statute: "The challenged statute itself provides a damages remedy against the warehouseman for violations of its provisions. This system of rights and remedies, recognizing the traditional place of private arrangements in ordering relationships in the commercial world, can hardly be said to have delegated to Flagg Brothers an exclusive prerogative of the sovereign."); Cole, "Arbitration and State Action," 48 ("Like debtors and creditors, employees and consumers have myriad options, from mediation to arbitration and beyond, to resolve their disputes. That negotiating alternatives to arbitration at the beginning of a contractual relationship would be difficult would be irrelevant to a court, as it was immaterial to the Court in Flagg."); see also Cole, "Arbitration and State Action," 48n1.
107 Cole, "Arbitration and State Action," 46; *Flagg Bros.*, 158–60.
108 *Lemon* (a legal examination to determine whether a government action violated the Establishment Clause of the Constitution).
109 *Agostini v. Felton*, 521 U.S. 203 (1997); and Witte, Nichols, and Garnett, *Religion and the American Constitutional Experiment*, 163.
110 20–1088, 596 U.S. ___ 2022.

that a State violates the Free Exercise Clause when it excludes religious observers from an otherwise available public benefit."[111] *Carson* held that the state cannot fund all private schools other than religious schools; it could abolish funding for private schools entirely, but it could target religious private schools directly. Similarly, a state cannot permit adjudication through any arbitration the parties want other than religious arbitration.

Acknowledging that the United States weighs free exercise rights heavily when balancing the equities of a case, proponents of the reverse-entanglement principle look to the French system of secularism and its prioritization of neutrality of public life.[112] But the problems French secularism seeks to solve are inherently different than the ones American secularism prioritizes, and to apply a French model to an American legal problem is counterintuitive and detrimental to religious minority groups. To outlaw religious tribunals or to treat them differently than other tribunals, based on international law, reconciliation, privacy, or otherwise, is to enforce a French style of secularism— to force religion into privacy and to smother its expression in public life. In contravention of the current, neutral treatment of religion by courts, the reverse-entanglement principle attempts to prohibit religious arbitration by declaring enforcement of such arbitration awards as the establishment of a religion by the U.S. government.

Why expand state-action doctrine to forbid things far less pernicious than racially exclusionary covenants? Why allow civil courts to prohibit the enforcement of faith-based extrajudicial tribunals which would otherwise be allowed, but not for its religious nature? No, my position is that clauses allowing religious choice of law or forum remain in the substantive law sphere and maintain equal juridical oversight as similarly situated nonreligious contracts. Deeming a court's enforcement of an arbitration award under the state-action doctrine would have a rippling effect that would cripple arbitration jurisprudence entirely.

To understand this point, consider the case of international commercial arbitration. If the choice of law indicates French law as the dispute resolution paradigm, all American rights are waived. If choice of law indicates an Alabama law paradigm, and the forum and conflict occur in California, then California state rights are waived. There is no difference between using another nation's legal rules to resolve disputes and using Jewish law or Catholic canon

---

111   Ibid., 7.
112   Arthur Kutoroff, "First Amendment versus Laicite: Religious Exemptions, Religious Freedom, and Public Neutrality," *Cornell International Law Journal* 48 (2015): 247–78.

law to resolve disputes, so long as the agreement signed fits within the validity requirements of contract law.

Elsewhere, I have called for a new application of the state-action doctrine within arbitration law to limit enforcement of agreements on parties outside of contractual privity. *Shelley*, the linchpin case for state action, can easily be read as prohibiting the enforcement of any problematic covenants which might bind new buyers and sellers to an encumbered property rather than the prohibition on enforcement of racial covenants only. One could postulate a case where a covenant in property seeks to control the behavior of subsequent property buyers—those without a say in writing the agreement but bound by the mutual assent of folks they may have never met. Such a covenant ought to be limited to only the signers even if there is an arbitration provision. That would be both good and necessary. By limiting the contractual universe to the signers, unconscionability can then be raised to challenge any agreements which seek primarily to control interactions with outside parties. To our topic here, unconscionability can address the problems of alternative dispute resolution identified by its opponents, while defending the right of the faithful to choose alternative avenues of justice.

Despite the torts interpretation of privity as a limit to redressing harm,[113] I believe that nonprivity should still evoke higher scrutiny from the courts through classic unconscionability analyses. Contracts which contain alternative dispute resolutions ought to address only the universe of interactions between signers, *not* the relationship between a signer and others.

Consider *Bixler* once more. The plaintiffs alleged that under the laws of Scientology, members cannot report crimes to the police, as the report to authorities would be considered a "high crime" and likely subject to punishment.[114] The claims against Scientology consist of *crimes*[115]—crimes that, if the arbitration agreement were enforced by the court, would impact the ability of the police to prevent crimes and the courts from punishing crimes. Such contractual conditions which control and impact the relationship and actions toward a third, nonprivy party, ought to have a higher level of scrutiny with

---

113 *Winterbottom v Wright (1842) 10 Mees & W 109, 152 Eng Reprint 402.*
114 *Bixler*, 4–5.
115 *Bixler*, 5–6 ("[C]ollectively plaintiffs allege Scientology's agents committed the following acts against them: surveilled them, hacked their security systems, filmed them, chased them, hacked their email, killed (and attempted to kill) their pets, tapped their phones, incited others to harass them, threatened to kill them, broke their locks, broke into their cars, ran them off the road, posted fake ads purporting to be from them soliciting anal sex from strangers, broke their windows, set the outside of their home on fire, went through their trash, and poisoned trees in their yards.").

stronger defense against enforcement available. As crimes like stalking, vandalism, harassment, theft, and abuse are violations which demand response from law enforcement—and the goal of the arbitration agreement in *Bixler* was seemingly to silence those crimes—the contract should rightly be scrutinized. But this is not the case for many contracts between religious parties seeking redress in religious tribunals—nor is the First Amendment needed to regulate arbitration of matters that are crimes.

Reverse entanglement rests its laurels on expanding *Shelley*'s state-action doctrine to religious tribunals. The principle is violated when a civil court enforces an extrajudicial faith-based tribunal decision as the court is de facto establishing religion. Therefore, any choice-of-law-or-forum clause which implicates religious values is treated as void, no matter the length of adherence to contract, consensus of the parties, or validity of the assent. There are some activities—like dueling—that society sets forth as prima facie unacceptable, no matter how genuinely the parties consent or how expertly and intelligibly the contract is written. Reverse entanglement would seek to add religion outside the home to that list of socially unacceptable activities.

6 Ending Forced Arbitration of Sexual Assault and Sexual Harassment Act and Its Implication for Family Arbitration

The recently passed Ending Forced Arbitration of Sexual Assault and Sexual Harassment Act (EFASASH) of 2021[116] poses serious challenges to all family law arbitration. Though the challenges are less related to the religious discussion up to this point, since they do not focus on religious arbitration—although if expansively applied, the law could end almost all family arbitrations.

EFASASH allows parties who have signed a binding prenuptial arbitration agreement governing any disputes they might have in the event of divorce to argue that they should not be compelled into arbitration in cases where the marriage ended due to any act of sexual harassment. More specifically, a pre-dispute binding arbitration will not be enforced if the agreement applies to "a dispute relating to conduct that is alleged to constitute sexual harassment under applicable Federal, Tribal, or State law." The use of the term "relating to conduct"—more than saying "the dispute is *about*"—will be more broadly interpreted to include all sorts of other cases. Indeed, it takes more imagination

---

116 S.2342, 117th Congress 2022.

to construct an "end of marriage" case that does not touch on such conduct than one that does.

EFASASH—at least in the area of sexual assault and harassment—returns us to law that predates the FAA itself. As a member of the New York Court of Appeals in 1914, Justice Benjamin Cardozo discussed his concerns about arbitration, noting:

> In each case ... the fundamental purpose of the contract [of arbitration] is the same—to submit the rights and wrongs of litigants to the arbitrament of foreign judges to the exclusion of our own.... If jurisdiction is to be ousted by contract, we must submit to the failure of justice that may result from these and like causes. It is true that some judges have expressed the belief that parties ought to be free to contract about such matters as they please. In this state the law has long been settled to the contrary. The jurisdiction of our courts is established by law, and is not to be diminished, any more than it is to be increased, by the convention of the parties.[117]

Cardozo was not alone. In fact, most Western legal systems were initially hostile to ADR forums operating apart from the state-sponsored justice system and resolving conflicts in accordance with substantive and procedural values different from those embraced by the law.[118] Giving parties the ability to govern their own agreements, *including* allowing them to agree to choice-of-law and choice-of-forum provisions, made opponents of ADR, including Cardozo, uneasy.

To see why, consider the following case from the narrow Orthodox Jewish universe. A couple is married in an Orthodox Jewish ceremony, and they sign the standard prenuptial agreement commonly used in the Orthodox community. The agreement directs that the husband give and the wife receive a Jewish divorce, and that they submit all other matters in dispute to the same rabbinical court.[119] The agreement that the parties sign says explicitly that "The Beth Din of America may consider the respective responsibilities of either or both of the parties for the end of the marriage, as an additional, but not exclusive, factor in determining the distribution of marital property and maintenance."[120]

---

117 *Meacham v. Jamestown, J. & C. R. Co.*, 105 N.E. 653, 655 (N.Y. 1914) (Cardozo, J., concurring) (internal citation omitted).
118 See Steven C. Bennett, *Arbitration: Essential Concepts* (New York: ALM, 2002), 12–13.
119 For an example of this, see https://theprenup.org/the-prenup-forms/.
120 Such a clause is exactly in 11:C of the standard agreement found in note 119.

This gives the party at fault every reason to work as hard as they can to remove the matter from the jurisdiction of the rabbinical court. Although EFASASH— designed mostly with employment as its focus[121]—makes it clear that only the victim, and not the harasser, can opt out of the arbitration agreement,[122] one can see that, in the context of a family law dispute, the statute seems to allow either party to void an arbitration agreement when they both allege conduct that constitutes sexual harassment.

Indeed, as others have pointed out,[123] EFASASH does not define the term "sexual harassment" at all. At the very least, it includes pregnancy, sexual orientation, and almost all gender-driven distinctions. It does not seem far-fetched to imagine that an effect of the statute will be to undermine the functional validity of all arbitration clauses in prenuptial agreements, since an allegation of sexual harassment, even if not proven, is enough to end such agreements.[124] Frankly, it is almost ridiculously easy to weave such allegations into almost any divorce papers. This effective return to the pre-FAA norms of a century ago in the area of family law might thus very well result in a government that can restrict all arbitration in the area of family law and, incidentally, restrict religious arbitration as well.

7   Conclusion

Alternative dispute resolution allows minority religious communities to exercise different values from the values prioritized within the secular legal system. Arbitration creates a haven for free exercise of religion within religious minority communities. To shut down this avenue would be a violation of religious liberty, in spirit even if not in law. A religious-arbitration clause should be no different than a choice-of-law clause mandating Spanish, Belgian, Israeli—or any other nation's—law as the guideline for dispute resolution. To

---

121   See David Horton, "The Limits of the Ending Forced Arbitration of Sexual Assault and Sexual Harassment Act," *Yale Law Journal Forum*, https://www.yalelawjournal.org/forum/the-limits-of-the-ending-forced-arbitration-of-sexual-assault-and-sexual-harassment-act.
122   See section (a) of the act.
123   Sandra Sperino, "Escaping Arbitration and Class Action Waivers for Harassment Because of Pregnancy, Sexual Orientation or Gender Identity" (forthcoming article).
124   It is not inconceivable that, even if the primary purpose of many of these agreements is to ensure that a Jewish divorce is given and received, a situation could arise where a husband, who is withholding a Jewish divorce, would use this clause to invalidate these agreements with an allegation of sexual harassment.

specifically outlaw a religious-arbitration clause and not secular ones, both of which may involve waivers of federal rights, ought to be understood as a state action inhibiting free exercise.

Commitments to religious liberty and religious disestablishment require liberal states to give religious arbitration the benefit of the same legal protections offered to nonreligious dispute resolution generally. If society wishes to enable and encourage citizens to utilize private dispute resolution forums rather than state courts to resolve litigious conflicts, then it must do so by putting both religious and nonreligious arbitration mechanisms on equal footing. Any other result would amount to a governmental attempt to disestablish religion in favor of irreligion, a serious constitutional problem in the United States.

Not all jurisdictions maintain the kind of strict establishment limits that exist in the United States, nor are such restrictions on states' privileging of religion over nonreligion, or religion over irreligion, strictly necessary from a standard liberal perspective. Modern Western nation-states have adopted a range of different approaches to this issue. On one hand, there is American-style neutrality, and on the other, as in the United Kingdom, there is freedom of religion alongside an official state church. There is also, of course, the affirmative secularism and public hostility toward religious practice seen in countries like France. In many cases, including the United States, these commitments are products of unique historical experiences.[125] To expand the state-action doctrine, to enhance religious exit rights, or to outright ban religious tribunals from the legal realm of alternative dispute resolution would be to adopt a decidedly non-American stance against religious pluralism.

---

125   See, generally, Stephen V. Monsma and J. Christopher Soper, *The Challenge of Pluralism: Church and State in Five Democracies* (Lanham, MD: Rowman & Littlefield, 2009).

CHAPTER 31

Cosmic Disorder: Angelic Rebellion, the Sin of Sodom, and the Epistle of Jude

Charles J. Reid Jr.

1   Introduction

I am both humbled and honored to have been asked to contribute to this volume dedicated to the life and career of John Witte. I have had the great good fortune of knowing John for more than thirty years. Our time together goes back to 1991, when I joined the Emory Law School community as Harold Berman's research associate in law and history. John was then a young faculty member, having previously served as Hal Berman's research associate.

We quickly bonded over shared interests. Both of us alike took great delight in legal history, understood broadly to encompass the ancient, medieval, and modern worlds. John was an excellent classroom teacher, and I saw him as a role model. Finally, also, we shared the same mentor—Harold Berman—a true giant among scholars and someone who could simultaneously be demanding in his expectations, effusive in his praise, and excited and enthusiastic in his inquisitiveness.

John's scholarly accomplishments are manifold. This chapter is dedicated to John and intended to examine an aspect of religious and legal history to which he has devoted considerable attention—the history of marriage and sexuality. His breadth and range of scholarship in this field are vast and impressive. One might begin by looking at his book *From Sacrament to Contract; Marriage, Religion, and Law in the Western Tradition*, originally published in 1997 and published in a revised and expanded second edition in 2012.[1] The second edition, in particular, is rich in its discussion of the scriptural and patristic foundations of marriage, while still retaining its forceful and streamlined character. In an age in which marriage is being reconceived in important ways, John's contribution to the debate continues to give us a sense of rootedness, place, and

---

1   John Witte, Jr., *From Sacrament to Contract: Marriage, Religion, and Law in the Western Tradition*, 2nd ed. (Louisville, KY: Westminster John Knox Press, 2012).

purpose. Yet John also knows that "we must not cling too dogmatically to an ideal form of household."²

If *From Sacrament to Contract* is the broad sweeping vista, the panoramic view of the history of marriage, then *Sex, Marriage, and Family in John Calvin's Geneva*, coauthored with Robert Kingdon, is a detailed and focused portrait of an important moment in time—that period in the mid-sixteenth century when John Calvin—lawyer, reformer, theologian, and civic leader—sought to build a godly community deep in the fastnesses of the Alps.³ The book is a study of theology and law, enriched by a number of primary-source documents. Thus, one finds, in the chapter titled "Honor Thy Father (and Thy Mother)," a discussion of the significance Calvin assigned to parental consent to marriage,⁴ followed by a number of translated documents, chiefly records of judicial proceedings.⁵ This pattern of organization is repeated throughout the work, with the effect that the reader has been given a nearly encyclopedic introduction to the richness and range of issues that must have vexed this community of devoted and earnest believers.

The Sins of the Fathers: The Law and Theology of Illegitimacy Reconsidered examines a great and tragic paradox of the Western religious and legal orders.⁶ And that is the imposition of legal disabilities on children for the mere status of their birth. There is an instinctive unfairness to such consequences. It offends against what we think of as consistent standards of personal accountability. In religion, when an individual sins, he or she is held to account by the threat of divine punishment. In law, when we have an automobile accident, and it is our fault, the law of torts will find us liable for the injuries we cause. Sexual morality, however, is different. The ideals of chastity, marriage, and monogamy have been traditionally enforced by declaring the offspring of nonconforming relationships illegitimate and unworthy of a whole array of social, psychological, and material benefits. Great literary figures have offered their veiled and indirect criticism of this arbitrary legal and social shunning through the characters they have created—one thinks of Leo Tolstoy's Pierre Bezukhov, the awkward,

---

2   Ibid., 329.
3   John Witte, Jr. and Robert M. Kingdon, *Sex, Marriage, and Family in John Calvin's Geneva: Courtship, Engagement, and Marriage* (Grand Rapids: Eerdmans, 2005).
4   Ibid., 164–82.
5   Ibid., 183–201 (also included in the materials are several excerpts of Calvin's commentary on select passages of scripture).
6   John Witte, Jr., *The Sins of the Fathers: The Law and Theology of Illegitimacy Reconsidered* (Cambridge: Cambridge University Press, 2009).

excitable, warm-hearted protagonist of *War and Peace*, and Henry Fielding's resourceful adventurer Tom Jones.[7]

John Witte's criticism of the system is more direct. Biblical faith demands inclusion, not exclusion—mercy, not harshness.[8] The old legal disabilities caused enormous suffering and should be abolished in their entirety. Nevertheless, society should not thereby abandon marriage as the best, most appropriate vehicle for the raising and nurturance of children and should find ways to promote its continuance and success.[9]

Finally, there is *The Western Case for Monogamy Over Polygamy*.[10] It is not self-evident that Western society should have opted for monogamy in the first place. The leaders of the Hebrew nation, from which the West derives its holy book, were polygamists. One thinks of Jacob, married simultaneously to Rachel and Leah; and King David and his many wives and consorts; and King Solomon with his vast harem, numbering in the hundreds. It could have turned out differently. Professor Witte, however, makes it clear that we should be happy that it did not. In intimate matters, he persuasively argues, "there is something intuitively more attractive in being with one other person, not two or more."[11]

These works are accomplishments, monuments really, to a keen and continuing interest—indeed a lifetime of interest—in the theological, social, and legal foundations of marriage. This chapter in biblical exegesis is intended as an homage—a tribute—to this life of scholarly achievement. Bravo, John! Congratulations! I hope you enjoy my small contribution.

2   The Problem Stated

In an article I published in 2019, I made the case that the Catholic Church's teaching on same-sex relationships had evolved in some significant ways in the two centuries between 1820 and 2020, and that in recent years the door had been opened, at least a little way, in the direction of reconsidering some ancient proscriptions.[12] Thus, I pointed to a statement by Cardinal Reinhard Marx of Munich-Freising, who said, "You cannot say that a long-term

---

7   Henry Fielding, *The History of Tom Jones, a Foundling* (London: A. Millar, 1749).
8   Witte, *Sins of the Fathers*, 175.
9   Ibid., 182–84.
10 John Witte, Jr., *The Western Case for Monogamy Over Polygamy* (Cambridge: Cambridge University Press, 2015).
11 Ibid., 463–64.
12 Charles J. Reid Jr., "Same-Sex Relations and the Catholic Church: How Law and Doctrine Have Evolved, 1820–2020," *Journal of Law and Religion* 34 (2019): 210–44, at 234–41.

relationship between a man and a man, who are faithful, is nothing. That it has no worth."[13] Similarly, I noted remarks by Bishop Johan Bonny of Antwerp, who "called upon the church to recognize 'the kind of interpersonal relationship that is also present in many gay couples.... The Christian ethic is based on lasting relationships where exclusivity, loyalty, and care are central to each other.'"[14]

The pace of such statements has accelerated since I wrote my study in 2019. Thus, in February 2022, Cardinal Jean-Claude Hollerich declared, regarding the Catholic Church's traditional teaching on same-sex relations: "I believe that the sociological scientific foundation of this teaching is no longer correct."[15] Similarly, Cardinal Robert W. McElroy of San Diego has called for the "radical inclusion" of LGBT persons in the life of the church. Writing in the Jesuit journal *America*, Cardinal McElroy declared: "It is a demonic mystery of the human soul why so many men and women have a profound and visceral animus toward members of the L.G.B.T. communities."[16] Cardinal McElroy went on to argue for a reevaluation of a Catholic theology that focused "disproportionately upon sexual activity" and that neglected the depth and quality of interpersonal relationships.[17]

Finally, Pope Francis himself added to this line of development in an interview with the Associated Press in January 2023. He stated that "[b]eing homosexual isn't a crime."[18] He was aware, he said, of bishops who thought differently, "[b]ut he attributed such attitudes to cultural backgrounds and said that bishops in particular need to undergo a process of change to recognize the dignity of everyone."[19] One observer noted: "Those remarks were one more instance of Francis's incremental approach toward acceptance of gay people,

---

13 Ibid., 238, quoting Sarah McDonald, "Cardinal Marx: Society Must Create Structures to Respect Gay Rights," *National Catholic Reporter*, Jun. 28, 2016.
14 Reid, "Same-Sex Relations," 238, quoting John A. Dick, "Belgian Bishop Advocates Church Recognition of Gay Relationships," *National Catholic Reporter*, Dec. 30, 2014.
15 Elise Ann Allen, "Top European Cardinals Want Changes on Homosexuality, Priestly Celibacy," *Crux*, Feb. 4, 2022. See also Christopher White, "Top Synod Cardinal: Church Should Change Attitude, Not Teaching, on Gay Relationships," *National Catholic Reporter*, Aug. 26, 2022, indicating Cardinal Hollerich moderated his previous call for a reversal of church teaching.
16 Robert W. McElroy, "Cardinal McElroy on 'Radical Inclusion' for L.G.B.T. People, Women, and Others in the Catholic Church," *America*, Jan. 24, 2023.
17 Ibid.
18 Nicole Winfield, "The AP Interview: Pope Says Homosexuality Not a Crime," Associated Press, Jan. 25, 2023.
19 Ibid.

which has involved expressing compassion for them and support for them in civic matters, while leaving aside the Church's stern teaching."[20]

Plainly, there is a movement within the Catholic Church in favor of the acceptability of same-sex relationships. But it is commonly said in response that the church is not a democracy, it should not be subject to the winds of change, that its teaching is unchanging and infallible, and that whatever Cardinal Hollerich or Cardinal McElroy might think, the acts associated with same-sex relations remain wrong, immoral, and intrinsically disordered.

Embedded in this summary of objections I have just reproduced lies a host of theological assumptions. And a short chapter like this one, published in a collection as a tribute to a friend, is not the appropriate venue for disentangling these many assumptions. Still, these assumptions rest, in part, on a scriptural foundation. Same-sex acts are wrong because they are regarded as such in scripture.

This chapter is intended as an exploration of these scriptural foundations. But we must be selective. Let us therefore confine ourselves to the New Testament. There are two passages in letters we know to be authentic to Paul that treat the issue of same-sex relations.[21] In Romans 1:24–27, we find Paul denouncing idolaters who "exchanged the glory of the immortal God for the likeness of an image of mortal man or of birds or of four-legged animals or of snakes,"[22] and who, because of their idolatry, were "handed ... over to degrading passions. Their females exchanged natural relations for unnatural and the males likewise gave up natural relations with females and burned with lust for one another" (vv. 26–27) In 1 Corinthians, furthermore, we find Paul writing: "Do not be deceived. Neither fornicators, nor idolaters nor adulterers, nor men who have sex with men, nor thieves, nor the greedy, nor drunkards, nor slanderers, nor robbers will inherit the kingdom of God" (6:9–10). Finally, there is

---

20 Paul Elie, "Pope Francis Speaks Out on Homosexuality—and Further Angers Traditionalists," *The New Yorker*, Jan. 27, 2023. See also Benoit Nyemba and Sonia Rolley, "As Pope Francis Visits Congo, LGBT+ Activists Cheer for Perceived Ally," Reuters, Feb. 1, 2023. The article notes that an African LGBT campaigner stated, regarding the pope's message, "'We think it will change the perception of all the religious people in our countries who think that when you are homosexual, you are to be slaughtered, to be dehumanised, you are devils.'"

21 And there is 1 Timothy 1:9–10, but since 1 Timothy is probably second century, and its usage is clearly derivative of these earlier sources, there is no need to give it any independent discussion.

22 Romans 1:23. Unless otherwise noted, translations of Bible verses are from the version found on the website of the United States Conference of Catholic Bishops, https://bible.usccb.org/bible.

2 Peter 6–7, which mentions God's destruction of Sodom and Gomorrah and God's rescue of Lot, and speaks allusively of sexual immorality.

All of these passages pose challenges to translators and commentators, and each one deserves its own separate treatment. Alas, there is not space enough in this chapter to attempt such an explication, nor shall I try. I shall confine myself rather to a fourth New Testament passage, a seemingly harsh condemnation of same-sex activity found in the Epistle of Jude. There we find a passage that is conventionally translated: "Just as Sodom and Gomorrah and the surrounding cities, which likewise acted immorally and indulged in unnatural lust, serve as an example by undergoing a punishment of eternal fire" (v. 7).

The purpose of this chapter is to come to a clearer understanding of this passage from the Epistle of Jude. I seek to ascertain whether the standard translation of this passage is actually an accurate one. I also hope simultaneously to obtain a more precise appreciation of its normative dimension. For Catholics know that not every word of scripture is binding in precisely the same way. Thus, we find at the conclusion of the Gospel of Mark this assurance about the followers of Jesus: "They will pick up serpents and if they drink any deadly thing, it will not harm them" (16:18). Yet it is the case that Catholics are not snake handlers, nor likely to become snake handlers. A passage like this one is taken metaphorically, not literally, as symbolic of a triumph over the twin threats of grave evil and death. So we must confront the question: What is the meaning of Jude's condemnation?

The next section of this chapter seeks to understand the authorship and purpose of the Epistle of Jude. To call its origins obscure might amount to a bad pun, but it also fairly describes the reality of our state of knowledge. Still, I shall examine the relevant scholarship on these issues, since that will have some bearing on what follows. The section thereafter conducts a close investigation of the Greek text of Jude 7, the passage in which the sin of Sodom is discussed. The chapter then situates the passage within a larger literary and social milieu and is specifically focused on how the sin of Sodom was understood around the time of Jude's composition. The final section addresses the theological dimension of the text: How should a contemporary reader make sense of the passage? Must it be read as a prohibition? And, if so, what exactly is being prohibited? Or should it be fitted within some larger interpretive framework?

3   Date, Place, and Purpose

The letter as it comes down to us is said to have been written by "Jude, a slave of Jesus Christ and brother of James" (v. 1). It consists of a single chapter and twenty-five verses. It condemns a faction within the community it addresses. They have been infiltrated by enemy agents who have succeeded in subverting their good morals and their decency (v. 4). Followers have thus been led astray and now "defile the flesh, scorn lordship, and revile glorious beings (v. 8)." "They followed the way of Cain, abandoned themselves to Balaam's error for the sake of gain, and perished in the rebellion of Korah (v. 11)." "These people are complainers, disgruntled ones who live by their desires; their mouths utter bombast as they fawn over people to gain advantage (v. 16)." Their alleged sexual transgressions add one more item to this already lengthy indictment.

Who was Jude, and about whom were these condemnations uttered? One might begin with the *Anchor Bible Commentary on Jude*, written by Bo Reicke and published in 1964. Reicke makes much of the salutation. If Jude was James's brother, Reicke speculates, and James was Jesus's brother, then Jude was also among Jesus's brothers, as attested in the Gospels of Matthew and Mark.[23] And the figure of Jude, though obscure today, was sufficiently prominent, according to one ancient account, to have attracted the Emperor Domitian's attention.[24] While it is highly unlikely that the epistle was drafted by Jesus's brother, this background indicates that it is probable that an anonymous author assumed the name of Jude for the authority it conferred.[25]

Jerome Neyrey, author of the second edition of the *Anchor Bible* commentary on Jude, published in 1993, accepts Reicke's conjectures regarding authorship.[26] Regarding the place of composition, Neyrey thinks the letter was likely written either in Alexandria or in Palestine.[27] It was composed in sophisticated Greek, suggestive of a place of learning, like Alexandria, but its ready use of Jewish themes evinces proximity, even familiarity, with neighboring Jewish communities.[28] Neyrey thinks that there are reasons to favor "an early-second-century date," but the evidence on this point is lacking in firmness.[29] Jörg Frey, in his magisterial study of the letter, develops some of these themes. Writing in italics for emphasis, Frey described the author "as a relatively well-educated,

---

23 Bo Reicke, *The Epistles of James, Peter, and Jude* (Garden City, NY: Doubleday, 1964), 190–91. See Matthew 13: 55; and Mark 6: 3.
24 Richard Bauckham, *Jude and the Relatives of Jesus in the Early Church* (London: Bloomsbury, 2015), 94–106.
25 Reicke, *The Epistles of James, Peter, and Jude*, 191.
26 Jerome H. Neyrey, *2 Peter, Jude: A New Translation with Introduction and Commentary* (New York: Doubleday, 1993), 30–31.
27 Ibid., 29–30.
28 Ibid., 30.
29 Ibid.

Hellenistically influenced Jewish Christian."[30] Regarding date and place of composition, however, Frey declares simply that "the text allows little more than speculation."[31]

Richard Bauckham, on the other hand, has a very different understanding of the text's origins.[32] To Bauckham, the author of the Epistle was Jude, the actual brother of the Lord. Bauckham does not think this idea far-fetched, even if one wanted to assign a date of composition late in the first century. Thus, Bauckham hypothesizes: Suppose Jude was Jesus's youngest brother, born around 10 CE. He could have written this text even as late as the closing decade of the first century, when he would have been eighty years old.[33] The milieu in which Jude operated was almost certainly Palestinian, and the target of his denunciation a group of wandering charismatics who preached a kind of divinely inspired libertinism.[34] Bauckham's is an imaginative reconstruction, but every point he makes is backed by at least some bits of evidence.

Just as vigorously, however, John Gunther has stated the case that the epistle must be an Alexandrian product.[35] The author's Greek was too good for a native Judean like Bauckham's Jude.[36] The author, furthermore, was immersed in the Jewish apocryphal literature—like 1 Enoch and the Assumption of Moses— and such texts were "unusually popular in Egyptian Christian circles."[37] The libertine practices the author attacked were known in Alexandrian circles.[38] Even his choice of metaphors—"reefs or sunken rocks"—made more sense for a coastal Alexandrian readership than a Palestinian one.[39] The likely date of composition for Gunther thus became the early second century, when a "post-apostolic generation" had succeeded to leadership positions.[40]

The Finnish scholar Lauri Thurén, finally, casts doubt upon many of the common assumptions undergirding the scholarship on Jude.[41] What is rhetorical

---

30   Jörg Frey, *The Letter of Jude and the Second Letter of Peter: A Theological Commentary*, trans. Kathleen Ess (Waco, TX: Baylor University Press, 2018), 29.
31   Ibid., 32.
32   Richard J. Bauckham, *Jude, 2 Peter* (Waco, TX: Baylor University Press, 1983).
33   Ibid., 15.
34   Ibid., 11–12.
35   John J. Gunther, "The Alexandrian Epistle of Jude," *New Testament Studies* 30 (1984): 549–62.
36   Ibid., 550–51.
37   Ibid., 550.
38   Ibid., 554–55.
39   Ibid., 551.
40   Ibid., 556.
41   Lauri Thurén, "Hey Jude! Asking for the Original Situation and Message of a Catholic Epistle," *New Testament Studies* 43 (1997): 451–65.

convention in Jude, Thurén asks, and what is reality? In particular, Thurén sees a formulaic quality to the denunciations found in Jude. "In antiquity, and also in Early Jewish and Christian texts, an overstated and stereotypical portrayal of the adversaries was so normal that it was known and accepted by both partners of communication."[42] The name-calling and the accusations of sexual license, in other words, may be more ritualistic than real. What Thurén leaves to the reader, however, is greater uncertainty: we should be cautious about taking the epistle literally; its many denunciations may not reflect the actual practices of those so denounced; and thus its historical particularities "remain[] inaccessible for us."[43] What a challenge! What, therefore, can we safely conclude about the date, place, and purpose of the Epistle of Jude? I am inclined toward a probable date late in the first or early in the second century, but I remain open to the possibility that the work was composed in either Palestine or Alexandria. The author's easy use of Jewish sources suggests an audience probably quite familiar with if not immersed in Jewish apocalypticism. There is also little doubt that the letter was written to answer some dispute internal to the community of believers, even if the literal charges of libertinism must be taken *cum grano salis*. With these cautionary words, we should consider the language of Jude 7.

4 Jude Verse 7

In Greek, Jude 7, reads: "Hōs Sodoma kai Gomorra kai hai peri autas poleis kai homoion tropon toutois ekporneusasai kai apelthousai opisō sarkos heteras, prokeintai deigma puros aioniou diken hupechusai." Discussion of the word *hōs*—"just as"—will be deferred. What we should focus on first are the place names—Sodom and Gomorrah. The fate of these two cities is told in Genesis 19. God had passed judgment on the two cities, and, having listened to Abraham plead on behalf of the inhabitants of these locations, had sent two angels to extract Lot, Abraham's nephew, and Lot's family before sending down consuming fire (19:1). Lot offered the two angels—who had appeared in the form of men—hospitality, providing them with meals, offering them a place to stay the night (19:2–3). That evening, Lot's home was surrounded by the male inhabitants of Sodom, who insisted upon raping the two visitors (19:4–5). To calm the crowd, Lot offered them the chance to sleep with his daughters (19:7–8), but the mob refused the invitation and instead stormed Lot's home

---

42 Ibid., 458.
43 Ibid., 464.

(19:9). The angels then miraculously intervened by striking the unruly crowd blind (19:11). The angels subsequently helped Lot and his two daughters escape (19:15–17), while the cities were burned in sulphuric flames (19:24–25 and 28).

What was the sin of Sodom? To describe this transgression, Jude's Greek used two verbs, *ekporneusasai* and *apelthousai*. Let's examine first *ekporneusasai* (*ekporneu*) which has a close connection with *porneu*, to prostitute oneself.[44] Thus one reads in Herodotus: "All the daughters of the common people of Lydia ply the trade of prostitutes" (*porneuontai*).[45] It is similarly related to the noun *porneia*, whose first meaning was also "prostitution,"[46] and which was applied not only to women but also to men.[47] Looseness, casualness, a lack of restraint and decency, were the associations clustered around both words.[48] The Gospel of Matthew recorded Jesus as permitting divorce on the basis of *porneia* (Matthew 5:32 and 9:19), which has been interpreted as meaning sexual activity by the woman with someone not her husband after she has been betrothed or married.[49] The verb *ekporneu*, on the other hand, occurs much less frequently, recorded chiefly in the Septuagint.[50]

If *ekporneusasai* can be translated as illicit sexual activity, what of the verb *apelthousai*? It is derived from the irregular verb *aperchomai*, which might mean "to go away from, depart."[51] Thus, some of Jesus's disciples departed from his side because they failed to comprehend his eucharistic instructions (John 6:66). In at least one instance in the New Testament, the verb was used in association with a kind insane or furious departure. The verb thus figures in the story of the Gadarene swine. The wicked spirits Jesus expelled from a pair of

---

44 Henry George Liddell and Robert Scott, *A Greek-English Lexicon*, 9th ed (Oxford: Oxford University Press, 1978), 1450.
45 Herodotus, *Histories* 1.93 (=Herodotus, *The Histories*, vol. I, trans. A. D. Godley, Loeb Classical Library, rev. ed. [London: Heinemann, 1926], 122–23).
46 Liddell and Scott, *Greek-English Lexicon*, 1450.
47 Demosthenes, 19.200 (=Demosthenes, *De Corona, De Falsa Legatione XVIII, XIX*, trans. C. A. Vince and J. H. Vince, Loeb Classical Library, rev. ed. [London: Heinemann, 1939], 372–73).
48 [66] Aaron Milavec, *The Didache: Faith, Hope, and Life of the Earliest Christian Communities, 50–70 CE* (Mahwah, NJ: Paulist Press, 2003), 134.
49 David Janzen, "The Meaning of *Porneia* in Matthew 5:32 and 9:19: An Approach from the Study of Ancient Near Eastern Culture," *Journal for the Study of the New Testament* 80 (2000): 66–80, at 72. See also Phillip Sigal, *The Halakhah of Jesus of Nazareth According to the Gospel of Matthew* (Atlanta, GA: Scholars Press, 2007), 118 (Jesus regarded divorce as something that should be confined to grave sins, such as *porneia*).
50 Liddell and Scott, *Greek-English Lexicon*, 518. See, for example, Septuagint Genesis 38:24.
51 Liddell and Scott, *Greek-English Lexicon*, 187.

demoniacs abruptly departed their victims and entered a herd of swine, causing them to stampede over a cliff and drown (Matthew 8:32).

Taken collectively, the two verbs carry the connotation of lewd, pornographic movement, tinged with at least a little insanity, drawn simultaneously to something grotesquely illicit, and withdrawing from the good, the decent, and the morally appropriate. So if that is the action the verbs *ekporneusasai* and *apelthousai* are meant to convey, then what is the object of these two verbs?

It is *sarkos heteras*—"strange flesh." A few words about each term. *Sarx*, meaning flesh, is an ancient term.[52] This noun was used without significant connotations, for instance, in the *Odyssey*, to describe a wound Odysseus suffered when a wild boar tore his "flesh" (*sarkos*).[53] When Prometheus made sacrifice to Zeus in Hesiod's *Theogony*, he placed "the meat" (*sarkas*) on top of the animal's skin before offering it to the god.[54] Epicurus, furthermore, imparted to the word a philosophical dimension, corresponding with his materialist account of pleasure and pain.[55]

With the New Testament, moreover, *sarx* assumed a theological role. Thus, the Gospel of John spoke of the Incarnation as "The Word of God became flesh (*sarx*), and dwelt among us" (1:14). Later in John, Jesus described himself as "flesh" (*sarx*) given "for the life of the world" (6:51). But if *sarx* could be sacred, it also assumed a sexual dimension in New Testament texts. Thus, the Gospel of Mark declared that married couples were no longer two "but one flesh"—*alla mia sarx* (10:8)). And as for Paul, although he employed *sarx* in morally neutral ways that would have been familiar to the readers of the *Odyssey* or Hesiod, he also made use of the expression to signify human fallenness,[56] or even to juxtapose the temptations of the flesh with the necessity of resistance.[57]

If *sarx* was flesh, often understood with carnal overtones, then what of *heteras*? It is a form of the adjective *heteros*, and its primary meaning is "one or

---

52   Liddell and Scott, *Greek-English Lexicon*, 1585.
53   *Odyssey* 19:450.
54   Hesiod, *Theogony*, 538.
55   Elizabeth Asmis, "Psychology," in *The Oxford Handbook of Epicurus and Epicurianism*, ed. Phillip Mitsis (Oxford: Oxford University Press, 2020), 189, 206.
56   Galatians 5:16–17. See also Douglas Moo, *A Theology of Paul and His Letters: The Gift of the New Realm in Christ* (Grand Rapids: Zondervan, 2021), 453 (further developing the language from Galatians).
57   1 Corinthians 5:5; and 1 Corinthians 5:16. See also Dale B. Martin, *The Corinthian Body* (New Haven: Yale University Press, 1995), 173: "The battle being waged in the body of the sexual offender in 1 Corinthians 5 is a microcosm of the battle between Pneuma and Sarx being fought throughout the world."

the other of two."⁵⁸ A secondary meaning is "of another kind, different."⁵⁹ Plato used the adjective to distinguish between "opinion" and "true knowledge."⁶⁰ Odysseus availed himself of the word when describing his frantic, racing thoughts while trapped in the Cyclops's cave.⁶¹ "Alternatives," "choices," "differences," "divergences"—these words represent the linguistic range of *heteros*.

So the men of Sodom feverishly pursued alien flesh? Is that how we should render verse seven? I will answer that question in the final section of this chapter. But for the moment, let us return to the word *hōs*, which I initially deferred. It is used as a correlative conjunction to introduce verse seven, tightly joining it to the action found in verse six. And in verse six we find: "The angels too, who did not keep to their own domain, but deserted their proper dwelling, he has kept in eternal chains, in gloom, for the judgment of the great day."⁶²

This is a controversial passage. No less an authority than Saint Jerome wrote that there were some who believed that the Epistle of Jude should not be counted within the New Testament on the basis of this passage, though Jerome maintained that wide acceptance and long use justified Jude's continued inclusion.⁶³

Why the reluctance to count Jude as scripture? The passage was not only a reference to but seemed to take as scriptural truth a story found in the first book of Enoch widely known as the "Rebellion of the Watchers."⁶⁴ The Enochic material is itself fairly exotic. It is a sprawling work that took shape gradually over a sprawling chronology extending from the third century BCE to the first century CE.⁶⁵ It was written originally in Aramaic—it is possible that the author of Jude would have known the Aramaic version—but the text "has been preserved only in a fifth-to-sixth-century CE Ethiopic (Ge'ez) translation of an intermediate Greek translation."⁶⁶ While a number of early Christian

---

58   Liddell and Scott, *Greek-English Lexicon*, 702.
59   Ibid.
60   Plato, *Meno*, 97D.
61   *Odyssey* 9:302.
62   Jude 6.
63   Nicholas J. Moore, "Is Enoch Also among the Prophets? The Impact of Jude's Citation of 1 Enoch on the Reception of Both Texts in the Early Church," *Journal of Theological Studies* 64 (2013): 498–515, at 500.
64   George W. E. Nickelsburg, *1 Enoch 1: A Commentary on the Book of 1 Enoch, Chapters 1–36; 81–108* (Minneapolis: Fortress Press, 2001), 165.
65   Ibid., 1.
66   Ibid.

writers took Enoch seriously,[67] it gained canonical status only in the Ethiopian Church.[68]

The portion of 1 Enoch that particularly attracted the attention of the author of Jude concerned the fate of those angels who rebelled against God's ordering of the world. These angels made a brief appearance in Genesis 6:1–2, which states merely that angels once descended to earth, mated with human women, and produced a race of giants.

"The Rebellion of the Watchers," which begins at 1 Enoch 6, embellishes this story by telling us, for instance, that this traitorous band of angels were some two hundred in number,[69] and that they not only mated with human women but taught them sorcery (7:1), and that the "great giants" borne by the women (7:2) "began to kill men and devour them" (7:4). Other angels taught men how to fashion weapons of war (8:1) and spread "much godlessness upon the earth" (8:2). In desperation, "the earth brought forth an accusation" (7:6). The archangels Michael, Sariel, Raphael, and Gabriel then responded by suppressing the rebellion. God finally condemned the angelic ringleaders to subsist forever in the darkened dungeons of hell (10:4–25).

It is this story, and most especially the condemnation that comes at its conclusion, that the author of Jude meant to juxtapose to the destruction of Sodom and Gomorrah. That is the purpose of *hōs*. The use of this correlative conjunction draws tight the connection between the action in the two verses. In each instance, sexual boundaries were transgressed, and divine judgment and annihilation were the consequences. We shall return to the theme of transgressing boundaries, but let us first explore the meaning of the sin of Sodom in the Hebrew scriptures and as understood by Jude's rough contemporaries.

5   The Sin of Sodom

The sin of Sodom has been the subject of interpretation nearly from the beginning of the Hebrew tradition. Disobedience, disloyalty, indifference to God's law, and the abandonment of justice—these are the predominant themes the Hebrew prophets strike in describing the sins of Sodom.

---

67   Such as Tertullian. See David R. Nienhaus, *Not by Paul Alone: The Formation of the Catholic Epistle Collection and the Christian Canon* (Waco, TX: Baylor University Press, 2007), 40.

68   Leslie Baines, "Enoch and Jubilees in the Canon of the Ethiopian Orthodox Church," in *A Teacher for All Generations: Essays in Honor of James C. VanderKam*, ed. Eric F. Mason (Leiden: Brill, 2012), 2:799–818, at 801.

69   1 Enoch 6:5 (I am following the translation by George W. E. Nickelsburg and James C. VanderKam, *1 Enoch: The Hermeneia Translation* [Minneapolis: Fortress Press, 2012], 24).

Thus, the opening verses of Isaiah, anticipating the coming destruction of the Kingdom of Judah, compared the Jerusalem that the prophet knew to Sodom and Gomorrah (Isaiah 1:9–23). Judah's "princes are rebels" 1:22), who are "all greedy for presents and eager for bribes" (1:23). Called to "be just to the orphan [and] plead for the widow" (1:17), the rulers denied their responsibilities and now must face destruction (1:24). In Jeremiah, faithless, lying prophets "strengthen the hands of the wicked" and "are all like Sodom" (Jeremiah 23:14). Finally, Ezekiel catalogued the sins of Sodom: "pride, gluttony, calm complacency; ... They never helped the poor and needy. They were proud and engaged in loathsome practices before me, and so I swept them away" (Ezekiel 16:49–50). "The plight of the poor," and their neglect, one commentator has observed, justified for the author of Ezekiel, the destruction of Sodom.[70] There is a sexual component to Ezekiel 16, a powerful component, but it is focused on adultery, promiscuity, and abandonment, not on same-sex relations.[71]

Composed around the year 180 BCE,[72] the book of Sirach, for its part, described the sin of Sodom as that of pride: "[God] did not spare the neighbors of Lot, abominable in their pride. He did not spare the doomed people, dispossessed because of their sin" (16:8–9). In the book known as the Wisdom of Solomon, one encounters two references to Sodom, the first being its destruction because of the sins of the "wicked" (10:6), the second attributing its devastation to the Sodomites' "grievous hatred" of the guests who had arrived in their midst (19:13). "[V]iolent thunderbolts," it was recorded, did the damage.[73]

In none of these early texts was sexual transgression made the basis of Sodom's destruction. The same can be said for the Gospel texts. Thus, in both Matthew and Luke the destruction of Sodom is mentioned as evidence of God's sovereignty and his implacable judgment. Thus: "It will be the same as it was in Lot's day: people were eating and drinking, buying and selling, planting and building, but the day Lot left Sodom, it rained fire and brimstone from

---

70   J. David Pleins, *The Social Visions of the Hebrew Bible: A Theological Introduction* (Louisville, KY: Westminster John Knox Press, 2001), 337. See also Paul M. Joyce, *Ezekiel: A Commentary* (New York: T & T Clark, 2007), 133: "It is noteworthy that the sin of Sodom is not defined overtly in relation to sexual morality."

71   Peter Enns, *Exodus Retold: Ancient Exegesis of the Departure from Egypt in Wis. 15–21 and 19:1–9* (Atlanta, GA: Scholars Press, 1997), 25; Gail Corrington Streete, *The Strange Woman: Power and Sex in the Bible* (Louisville, KY: Westminster John Knox Press, 1997), 99; John Hill, *Constructing Exile: The Emergence of a Biblical Paradigm* (Eugene, OR: Cascade Books, 2020), 34–35.

72   John E. Rybolt, "Sirach," in *The Collegeville Bible Commentary: Old Testament*, Dianne Bergant (Collegeville, MN: Liturgical Press, 1992), 722.

73   Ernest G. Clarke, *The Wisdom of Solomon* (Cambridge: Cambridge University Press, 1973), 127.

heaven and it destroyed them all."[74] Perhaps the narrators of these Gospels assumed that their readership knew the reasons for Sodom's demolition, but it goes without explanation in the texts.

The rabbinic commentary similarly deemphasized the sexual dimensions of the sin of Sodom. The crime of Sodom is thus seen variously as violence,[75] corruption, blasphemy, and bloodshed.[76] As Steven Greenberg has put it: "Among the early rabbinic commentators, the common reading of the sin of Sodom was its cruelty, arrogance, and disdain for the poor. The sages of the Babylonian Talmud also associated Sodom with the sins of pride, envy, cruelty to orphans, theft, murder, and perversion of justice."[77] Sodom's miserliness toward the poor was the focus of rabbinic stories that laid stress on the city's extraordinary wealth and copious "natural resources" and its refusal to share with the needy and oppressed.[78] The insistent sexual demands of the mob that confronted Lot and his angelic visitors was understood as a particular manifestation of the breach of "the ancient law of hospitality" that was the Sodomites' real offense.[79]

Still, a parallel tradition focused on the sexual appetites of the residents of Sodom developed alongside this body of material, and it was well-established by the first century of the Christian era. The book of Jubilees, which dates probably to the years between 175 and 124 BCE,[80] blamed the destruction of Sodom on sexual sins ("fornication, impurity, and corruption/abomination" [20:5]), although these offenses were not further specified.[81] The same passage also ambiguously mentioned the "giants" who had been spawned by angelic-human coupling, although the point remained otherwise undeveloped.

---

74   Luke 17:28–30. Compare Matthew 11:23–24: "And as for you, Capernaum, would you be raised as high as heaven? You shall be flung down to hell. For if the works of power done in you had been done in Sodom, it would have remained till this day. Only I tell you that it will be more bearable for Sodom on judgement day than for you."
75   J. A. Loader, "The Sin of Sodom in the Talmud and Midrash," *Old Testament Essays* 3 (1990): 231–45, at 235.
76   Ibid., 239–40.
77   Steven Greenberg, *Wrestling with God and Men: Homosexuality in the Jewish Tradition* (Madison: University of Wisconsin Press, 2004), 65.
78   Ibid.
79   Ibid. See also Eliezar Segal, "A Funny Thing Happened on My Way to Sodom," *Journal for the Study of Judaism* 45 (2014): 103–29, at 126, use of the Hellenistic typos of the "clever slave" as a rabbinic subversive device to explore "the morally topsy-turvy world of Sodom."
80   James C. VanderKam, *A Commentary on the Book of Jubilees*, vol. I, *Chapters 1–21* (Minneapolis, MN: Fortress Press, 2018), 37–38.
81   VanderKam, *Commentary on the Book of Jubilees*, 613.

Another early set of texts are the so-called Testaments of the Twelve Patriarchs, which, aside from a few Christian interpolations, can largely be dated, like Jubilees, to the second century BCE.[82] True to their title, the document purports to be a set of written reflections in chronological order, from oldest to youngest, by each of Jacob's sons, addressed in turn to their progeny. The "Rebellion of the Watchers" features prominently in the first of these testaments, that of Reuben. Warning his offspring, Reuben allegedly wrote, misogynistically, that "women are evil."[83] Women, the author continued, bore at least partial responsibility for the angels who broke the cosmic order by having sex with them. "For it was thus that they charmed the Watchers.... As they continued looking at the women, they were filled with desire for them" (Reuben 5:6)

Sodom was also mentioned several times in the testaments. In the Testament of Levi, the sin of Sodom is described as sleeping with "gentile women" (Levi 14:6). The Testament of Benjamin declared that the sin of Sodom was promiscuity: "you will be sexually promiscuous like the promiscuity of the Sodomites, and will perish, with few exceptions. You shall resume your action with loose women" (Benjamin 9:1).

But the sin of Sodom also came to be associated with the Rebellion of the Watchers. Thus, in the Testament of Naphtali, the Rebellion of the Watchers and Sodom are discussed in close proximity. "Sun, moon, and stars do not alter their order," Naphtali warned, and neither should they who worship the true God (Naphtali 3:2). Naphtali went on: "[D]o not become like Sodom, which departed from the order of nature. Likewise, the Watchers departed from nature's order" (3:5). For Sodom was the scene of "every lawlessness" (4:1). The author of the Testament of Gad, finally, warned his readership: "Do not become like Sodom, which did not recognize the Lord's angels and perished forever" (Gad 7:1).

These texts have drawn the focus of commentators. Weston Fields admitted that the question of "hetero- or homosexual relations is ambiguous," but he added: "The ambiguity, however, is probably only apparent; the Sodomites seem to have become proverbial for homosexual relations in an early period."[84] William Loader, furthermore, noticed the relationship of the Sodom texts and the Rebellion of the Watchers, but he drew the following lesson: "as the angels

---

82 H. C. Kee, "Testaments of the Twelve Patriarchs (Second Century BC)," in *The Old Testament Pseudepigrapha*, vol. I, *Apocalyptic Literature and Testaments*, ed. James H. Charlesworth (Garden City, NY: Doubleday, 1983), 775–828, at 777–78.
83 Testament of Reuben 5:1. Subsequent textual references are in parentheses.
84 Weston W. Fields, *Sodom and Gomorrah: History and Motif in Biblical Narrative* (Sheffield: Sheffield Academic Press, 1997), 182.

sinned by denying their created order of being ... so the men of Sodom similarly perverted their created order by engaging in sexual relations with men."[85]

Michael Carden, on the other hand, has argued that associations like the ones drawn by Fields and Loader misunderstand the texts. "[N]one of these passages," Carden wrote, referencing the Testaments, clearly indicate an association with same-sex relations."[86] The sexual offense at issue in the Testaments was something else altogether: "It is the crossing of the human/angelic boundary due to *porneia* that provides the basis for the parallels between the Watchers and Sodom."[87] This is an absolutely essential point, and one to which I shall return with regard to the Epistle of Jude.

By the time one arrives at the age of Philo of Alexandria (ca. 20 BCE—ca. 50 CE), however, the Sodom account was being unambiguously interpreted as involving same-sex sexuality, at least in some circles.[88] Philo's account blended together some of the themes we have already reviewed along with the subject of gay sex. Sodom "was brimful of innumerable inequities, particularly such as arise from gluttony and lewdness."[89] The land was "deep-soiled and well-watered," but the Sodomites poured their wealth and energy into forbidden luxury, most especially same-sex relations.[90] Thus, "men mounted males without respect for the sex nature which the active partner shares with the passive."[91] For this reason, God chose to wipe Sodom from the earth, using as his instrument "a great rain, not of water but fire."[92]

Flavius Josephus (ca. 37 CE—ca. 100 CE), the former Jewish/Roman general turned Roman spokesperson for Jewish causes, synthesized the rabbinic and the

---

85 William Loader, "Homosexuality and the Bible," in *Two Views on Homosexuality, the Bible, and the Church*, ed. Preston Sprinkle (Grand Rapids, MI: Zondervan, 2016), 17, 26. See also J. A. Loader, *A Tale of Two Cities: Sodom and Gomorrah in the Old Testament, Early Jewish, and Early Christian Traditions* (Kampen, the Netherlands: J. H. Kok, 1990), 82, writing, regarding the Testaments, that "the changing of its order by Sodom can only refer to the homosexual aspirations of the Sodomites." Both William Loader and J. A. Loader appear to be guilty of assuming what they wished to prove.

86 Michael Carden, *Sodomy: A History of a Christian Biblical Myth* (London: Equinox, 2004), 57.

87 Ibid., 58.

88 Louis Crompton, *Homosexuality and Civilization* (Cambridge, MA: Belknap Press of Harvard University Press, 2003), 136.

89 Philo, *On Abraham*, 133 (= Philo, vol. 6, trans. F. H. Colson, Loeb Classical Library, [Cambridge, MA: Harvard University Press, 1935]), 69.

90 Ibid., 133–34 (= Philo, 69).

91 Ibid., 135 (= Philo, 71).

92 Ibid., 138 (= Philo, 71, 73).

Philonic traditions when he discussed the crimes of Sodom.[93] The Sodomites so thoroughly "hated foreigners and declined all intercourse with others," that God passed judgment on them for this reason alone.[94] But when the angels visited Sodom to rescue Lot and his family, "the Sodomites, on seeing these young men of remarkably fair appearance whom Lot had taken under his roof, were bent only on violence and outrage to their youthful beauty."[95] Angered at these "atrocities," God responded by repeating his condemnation,[96] and laying waste to the city.[97]

6 Jude Verse 7: Meaning and Implications

We have now developed several strands of thought. There is the association with Sodom and Gomorrah. There is in Jude 7 the language of sexual desire if not incipient sexual violence. There is also the association of verse seven, through the correlative conjunction *hōs*, with verse six and the Rebellion of the Watchers. There is, as well, the variable meanings, by generations of Jewish commentators, imputed to the sin of Sodom. Then, at last, there is the cosmic disorder of angelic/human sexual intercourse depicted in the Rebellion of the Watchers. How have scholars assembled these pieces? How should we?

There was a time when Jude 7 was treated unproblematically as representing just one of several biblical condemnations of gays and gay sex. One might thus consult *The Interpreter's Bible*, where we find the "exposition" portion of the commentary noting that while the angels in verse six were "guilty of vice," "Sodom and Gomorrah are guilty of homosexuality."[98] To reinforce the point, the commentator added: "The punishment is still evident in the residual ruins of those cities which may be seen to this day. The fires of that Gehenna are still burning."[99] Nor is *The Interpreter's Bible* alone. A similar reading can be found

---

93 Louis H. Feldman, *Josephus's Interpretation of the Bible* (Berkeley: University of California Press, 1998), 264–65.

94 Josephus, *Jewish Antiquities*, 1.194–95 (= Josephus, *Jewish Antiquities*, trans. H. St. J. Thackeray, Loeb Classical Library [Cambridge, MA: Harvard University Press, 1930], 1:97.

95 Ibid., 1.200–201 (= Josephus, 1:99).

96 Ibid., 1.202 (= Josephus, 1: 99). See also Martti Nissinen, *Homoeroticism in the Biblical World: A Historical Perspective* (Minneapolis, MN: Fortress Press, 1998), 94, seeing in Josephus's account of "the Sodomites' attempt to rape the men ... pederastic elements."

97 Josephus, *Jewish Antiquities*, 1.203–04 (= Josephus, 101).

98 *The Interpreter's Bible* (Nashville, TN: Abingdon, 1957), 12:328.

99 Ibid.

in *The Broadman Bible Commentary*, though it requires connecting the commentary on Jude with the commentary on Genesis 19.[100]

In 1968, the Jesuit scholar Thomas W. Leahy proposed, in the *Jerome Biblical Commentary*, to link verses six and seven in a single interpretive framework and to suggest that the offense committed by the residents of Sodom had nothing to do with same-sex relations, but instead involved something radically different: "As the angels sought out creatures of another order of being (women), so the Sodomites sought out angels."[101] Nothing, however, came of this suggestion. Its larger implications went unexplored. Thus, twenty-two years later, in 1990, Jerome Neyrey could write, regarding the same passage in the second edition of the *Jerome Biblical Commentary*, that: "[Another] example emphasizes not so much a fall from grace as simply crime and punishment: Sodom indulged in the worst vices (homosexuality—'going after other flesh' [Gen. 19: 4–8)—and fornication)."[102]

Change, when change came, arrived from outside the company of biblical scholars. One might begin with Derrick Sherwin Bailey (1910–1984). A review of his life story in the *Oxford Dictionary of National Biography* suggests that Bailey had a most conventional upbringing and family life. The son of a railway signalman, Bailey worked in the insurance industry before pursuing a career in the ministry in his early thirties. He married, had two children, and earned a PhD from the University of Edinburgh.[103] He developed an interest in sexual ethics, and in 1955 published *Homosexuality and the Western Christian Tradition*.[104]

---

100 Thus, one must compare Ray Summers, "Jude," *The Broadman Bible Commentary* (Nashville, TN, 1972), 12:232, 237, with Clyde T. Francisco, "Genesis," in *The Broadman Bible Commentary*, rev. ed. (Nashville, TN: Broadman, 1973), 1:177 ("The request of the men of Sodom that they *know* the visitors was probably a demand for homosexual activities. Thus, the term 'sodomy' found its origin"). Such an interpretation persists in some circles. See, for instance, Brian Neil Peterson, "Identifying the Sin of Sodom in Ezekiel 16: 49–50," *Journal of the Evangelical Theological Society* 61 (2018): 307–20.

101 Thomas W. Leahy, SJ, "The Epistle of Jude," in *The Jerome Biblical Commentary*, ed. Raymond Brown et al. (Englewood Cliffs, NJ: Prentice-Hall, 1968), vol. 2, *The New Testament*, 379.

102 Jerome H. Neyrey, "The Epistle of Jude," in Brown et al., *The New Jerome Biblical Commentary*, 918. Regarding the angels of verse 6, Neyrey wrote: "They too fell from grace, from heaven to hell, from light to gloom." No effort was made to connect verses six and seven.

103 Matthew Grimley, "Bailey, Derrick Sherwin," *Oxford Dictionary of National Biography*, Oct. 4, 2012, doi https://doi.org/10.1093/ref:odnb/101207.

104 Derrick Sherwin Bailey, *Homosexuality and the Western Christian Tradition* (Hamden, CT: Archon Books, 1975) (reprint of 1955 edition).

In this book, he sought to refocus interpretation of Jude 7 and to identify its importance in large and ongoing debates over public policy. "Jude," Bailey asserted, "does not ascribe the punishment of the Sodomites to the fact that they proposed to commit homosexual acts *as such*; their offense was rather that they sought to do so with 'strange flesh'—that is, with supernatural, non-human beings."[105] His very conventionality aided him in making his case,[106] and Bailey soon found himself playing an instrumental role in the Wolfenden Commission's recommendation that English law should decriminalize homosexual acts between consenting adults.[107]

John McNeill was a Jesuit priest and a trained moral theologian who had begun cautiously to explore, at the end of the 1960s, the ethical dimensions of same-sex relations.[108] He was also a gay man who would subsequently be expelled from the Jesuit order, serve in 1987 as Grand Marshal of the New York City pride parade,[109] and, late in life, marry his long-time companion.[110] Writing about Jude 7 in 1976, McNeill drew out the significance that Thomas Leahy, in the *Jerome Biblical Commentary*, had missed: "Once again, the homosexual element is only incidental; the emphasis is upon the sexual incompatibility of the angelic and human orders rather than upon any particular type of coitus between persons of the same sex."[111]

Four years later, the Yale University historian John Boswell revisited Jude 7 in his pathbreaking book, *Christianity, Social Tolerance, and Homosexuality*.[112] Boswell was a religious believer, having converted to Roman Catholicism in

---

105 Ibid., 16.
106 Grimley, "Bailey."
107 Brian Lewis, *Wolfenden's Witnesses: Homosexuality in Postwar Britain* (Houndsmill: Palgrave Macmillan, 2016), 233–34; Graham Willet, "The Church of England and the Origins of Homosexual Law Reform," *Journal of Religious History* 33 (2009): 418–34, at 424, 430–34; Michael Wilson, "From Sherwin Bailey to Gay Marriage: Some Significant Developments in Christian Thought Since 1955," *Modern Believing* 54 (Jul. 2013): 201–12.
108 James P. McCartin, "The Church and Gay Liberation: The Case of John McNeill," *U.S. Catholic Historian* 34 (2016): 125–41, at 129–31.
109 "Dignity USA Mourns Death of John J. McNeill, Celebrates Life of Seminal Figure in LGBT Catholic Movement," Sep. 23, 2015, https://www.dignityusa.org/civicrm/mailing/view?reset=1&id=468.
110 Elaine Woo, "Rev. John McNeill Dies at 90; Gay Priest, Author Expelled by Jesuits," *Los Angeles Times*, Sep. 29, 2015; and Margalit Fox, "John McNeill, 90, Priest Who Pushed Catholic Church to Welcome Gays, Dies," *The New York Times*, Sep. 26, 2015.
111 John J. McNeill, *The Church and the Homosexual*, 3rd ed. rev. and expanded (Boston, MA: Beacon Press, 1988), 71.
112 John Boswell, *Christianity, Social Tolerance, and Homosexuality: Gay People in Western Europe from the Beginning of the Christian Era to the Fourteenth Century* (Chicago: University of Chicago Press, 1980).

his middle teens.[113] He died tragically of the complications of AIDS at the age of forty-seven.[114] His book won the American Book Award for history in 1981,[115] although its thesis, that "only in the twelfth and thirteenth centuries [did] Christian writers formulate[] a significant hostility toward homosexuality," was and remains controversial.[116] Regarding Jude 7, Boswell observed that "there is no hint of homosexuality."[117] "'[S]trange flesh' hardly suggests homoeroticism."[118] For Boswell, as it had been for Bailey and McNeill, the passage was all about the forbidden crossing of the human/angelic barrier.[119]

This interpretation of Jude 7 has now won widespread but hardly unanimous acceptance among biblical scholars. Jörg Frey expressly rejects the homosexual reading of Jude 7 as improbable and prefers to read the passage as the Sodomites seeking to reverse the order of creation by chasing after sexual relations with another kind of being—angels.[120] Duane Frederick Watson noticed the close connections between verses six and seven and wrote regarding them: "In both cases God's order is broken and the message is that breaking God's established order [i.e., by transgressing the angelic/human boundary] leads to punishment of eternal fire."[121] Richard Bauckham has taken a similar position in two different academic venues,[122] as have a number of other scholars.[123]

---

113 Patricia Boswell, "John Boswell's Faith Lit Up a Generation," *Christian Century*, Apr. 7, 2022.
114 David W. Dunlap, "John E. Boswell, Historian of Medieval Gay Culture, Dies," *The New York Times*, Dec. 25, 1994.
115 "Paperbacks: New and Noteworthy," *The New York Times*, Jul. 19, 1981.
116 Matthew Kuefler, "The Boswell Thesis," in Kuefler, ed., *The Boswell Thesis: Essays on Christianity, Social Tolerance, and Homosexuality* (Chicago: University of Chicago Press, 2005), 2.
117 Boswell, *Christianity, Social Tolerance*, 97.
118 Ibid.
119 Ibid. See also Mark D. Jordan, *The Invention of Sodomy in Christian Theology* (Chicago: University of Chicago Press, 1997), 32, taking a more cautious view of Jude 7, stating only that "it [does not] necessarily refer to same-sex copulation."
120 Frey, *Letter of Jude*, 91.
121 Duane Frederick Watson, *Invention, Arrangement, and Style: Rhetorical Criticism of Jude and 2 Peter* (Atlanta, GA: Scholars Press, 1988), 53.
122 Richard J. Bauckham, "Jude," in *Harper's Bible Commentary*, ed. James Luther Mays et al. (San Francisco: Harper, 1988), 1298; and Bauckham, *Jude, 2 Peter*, 54.
123 See, for instance, David Seal, *Jude: An Oral and Performance Commentary* (Eugene, OR: Wipf & Stock, 2021), 45–46; David R. Nienhaus and Robert W. Wall, *Reading the Epistles of James, Peter, John, and Jude as Scripture: The Shaping and Shape of a Canonical Collection* (Grand Rapids, MI: Eerdmans, 2013), 231; Richard Kugelman, *James and Jude* (Wilmington, DE: Michael Glazier, 1980), 91.

Other scholars, however, are ambivalent regarding this interpretation,[124] or continue to reject it.[125] Dr. Robert A. J. Gagnon of Houston Christian University concedes that Jude 7 is ambiguous but says that the reference to Sodom and Gomorrah "probably refers to homosexual acts."[126] James De Young, professor of New Testament at Western Seminary in Portland, Oregon, has taken a position similar to Gagnon's, asserting that the men at Sodom perceived that they were pursuing "a same-gender relationship," and that "Jude simply continues a tradition that arises from the event of Sodom's destruction."[127]

There are strong reasons to side with those who understand Jude 7 as a condemnation of the unspeakable sin of violating one's human nature to seek relations with angelic beings, and equally strong reasons to reject those who maintain that the verse pertains to the immorality of homosexual acts.

This position is justified by bearing in mind that Jude is saturated in Jewish thought.[128] As such, the author of Jude would have conceived of the sin of Sodom in terms far broader than homosexual activity. His conception would have embraced all of the interpretive possibilities we reviewed above. The sin of Sodom was an act of consummate and comprehensive wrong-doing, and Jude's author would have seen it that way.

---

124 Grant Osborne reads Jude 7 as condemning "homosexuality," although he concedes that a number of scholars now interpret the text as involving forbidden human-angelic intercourse. Grant R. Osborne, *Cornerstone Biblical Commentary: James, 1–2 Peter, Jude* (Carol Stream, IL: Tyndale House, 2011); Michael Green, *2 Peter and Jude: An Introduction and Commentary* (Downers Grove, IL: Intervarsity Press, 2009), 193 ("The men of Sodom and Gomorrah engaged in homosexuality; that was unnatural. But Jude may mean that just as the angels fell because of their lust for women, so the Sodomites fell because of their lust for angels").

125 See, for example, Neyrey, *2 Peter, Jude*, 61.

126 Robert A. J. Gagnon, *The Bible and Homosexual Practice: Texts and Hermeneutics* (Nashville, TN: Abingdon, 2001), 87–88. Gagnon reasons that although it was possible that the residents of Sodom crossed the angelic/human boundary, they would have thought themselves pursuing sex with other men, since the angels visited Sodom in the form of men.

127 James B. De Young, *Homosexuality: Contemporary Claims Examined in Light of the Bible and Other Ancient Literature and Law* (Grand Rapids, MI: Kregel, 2000), 222. The Episcopal theologian Tobias Haller, on the other hand, reads Jude 7 as obliquely supporting same-sex marriage, since the text counsels that parties should seek to couple with those who are similar to themselves and not different in kind. Tobias Stanislas Haller, *Reasonable and Holy: Engaging Same-Sexuality* (New York: Seabury, 2009), 29.

128 See, for instance, E. Earle Ellis, *Prophecy and Hermeneutic in Early Christianity: New Testament Essays* (Eugene, OR: Wipf & Stock, 2003) (reprint of 1978 edition), 226: "Jude's writing ... is a midrash on the theme of judgment"). See also Darian Lockett, *An Introduction to the Catholic Epistles* (London: Continuum, 2012), 87, developing Jude as midrash; and J. Daryl Charles, *Literary Strategy in the Epistle of Jude* (Scranton, PA: University of Scranton Press, 1993), 145–62 ("Jewish-Tradition Material in Jude").

The author of Jude, furthermore, was preoccupied with angels, and he expected his audience to have shared his enthusiasm. The Rebellion of the Watchers involved an unspeakable transgression—perhaps the very worst sin any created being could commit—the crossing by carnal coupling of the angelic/human barrier. This was a subject of 1 Enoch, which was plainly Jude's source for verse six, but it was a horror that was widely shared in the Jewish milieu which produced Jude. The Testaments of the Patriarchs attest to its dreaded nature.

This reading is reinforced by Jude's other references to angelic beings. In verse nine, we encounter a legend, taken from the Assumption of Moses,[129] that the Archangel Michael and the devil contended for the body of Moses, with Michael finally prevailing.[130] And in verse eight, the verse that immediately follows the verse we are concerned with, we find Jude condemning those troublemakers who have fractured the community because of the casual way they have despised and detested angels.[131]

Angels, and the respect owed to them as cosmologically superior to humankind, were among Jude's principal concerns. Thus, a recent commentator has asserted that the letter was written expressly to "highlight the role and power of the angelic realm."[132] And this engrossment with angels is entirely consistent with Jude's Jewish context. Angels permeated the pseudepigraphic literature that Jude's author knew and expected his readers to know.[133] By acting as they did, both the rebellious Watchers and the Sodomites violated "the divinely established order of the cosmos."[134] And verses six and seven stood as warnings to those who regarded God's holy order with contempt.

---

129   Ryan E. Stokes, "Not Over Moses' Dead Body: Jude 9, 22–24, and the Assumption of Moses in Their Early Jewish Context," *Journal for the Study of the New Testament* 40 (2017): 192–213.
130   Jude 9.
131   Jude 8.
132   Chad Pierce, "Apocalypse and the Epistles of 1, 2 Peter, and Jude," in *The Jewish Apocalyptic Tradition and the Shaping of New Testament Thought*, ed. Benjamin E. Reynolds and Loren T. Stuckenbruck (Minneapolis, MN: Fortress Press, 2017), 318.
133   There was a "flourishing of traditions about angels" at the time Jude was composed. Annette Yoshiko Reed, *Demons, Angels, and Writing in Ancient Judaism* (Cambridge: Cambridge University Press, 2020), 5. Indeed, first century CE rabbis were alarmed at the proliferation of angels: "[M]ost disturbing of all to the Rabbis was the 'population explosion' of angels to the point that they nearly overwhelmed the Creator Himself": Morris Margolies, *A Gathering of Angels: Angels in Jewish Life and Literature* (New York: Ballantine Books, 1994), 77.
134   John Dennis, "Cosmology in the Petrine Letters and Jude," in *Cosmology and New Testament Theology*, ed. Jonathan T. Pennington and Sean M. McDonough (London: T & T Clark, 2008), 169.

When we read Jude, in other words, we should approach the text with a sense of wonder at the strangeness of it all. Jude does not move in a thought-world at all like our own. It is a world where the supernatural is all around, nearly tangible, not quite visible, but clearly felt. If we let this Jude speak to us, in his own voice, and not listen to only what we want to hear, we will discover something sacred, something marvelous, and something that is of no utility whatever in the culture war. And that is a good thing.

Counting My Blessings: A Response

John Witte, Jr.

What a joy to read this magnificent volume, *Faith in Law, Law in Faith*. I am honored and humbled by this gift and admire and appreciate the deep erudition and generosity of the contributors. These thirty-one elegant chapters are lovely blessings of friendship to cherish. They hold learned insights to ponder. And they attest powerfully to the robust solidarity and fellowship that the international guild of law-and-religion scholars has built across multiple confessions and professions over the past half century.

This guild now embraces some fifteen hundred scholars around the globe—jurists, theologians, historians, ethicists, philosophers, anthropologists, sociologists, and other specialists—many of them gathered in some fifty institutes of law and religion on five continents. These diverse scholars are studying the religious dimensions of law, the legal dimensions of religion, and the interaction of legal and religious ideas and institutions, methods and practices—historically and today, in the West and well beyond. These scholars believe that, at a fundamental level, religion gives law its spirit and inspires its adherence to ritual, tradition, and justice. Law gives religion its structure and encourages its devotion to order, organization, and orthodoxy. Law and religion share such ideas as fault, obligation, and covenant and such methods as ethics, rhetoric, and hermeneutics. Law and religion also balance each other by counterpoising justice and mercy, rule and equity, discipline and love. It is this dialectical interaction that gives these two disciplines and two dimensions of life their vitality and their strength. Without law at its backbone, religion slowly crumbles into shallow spiritualism. Without religion at its heart, law gradually crumbles into empty, and sometimes brutal, formalism.

This is the field of interdisciplinary study that I have had the privilege of working in for the past forty plus years. In college, my charismatic philosophy professor H. Evan Runner taught me to look for the religious sources and commitments implicit or explicit in historical and modern ideas and institutions, including those of law, politics, and society. My great law school mentor and later longstanding colleague, Harold J. Berman, taught me to map the shifting belief systems at the heart of the evolution and revolutions of the Western legal tradition. Early collaborators in our Center projects, particularly the wonderful trio of University of Chicago professors Don Browning, Jean Elshtain, and

Martin Marty, showed me how to navigate the "sea of metaphors" on which fundamental ideas and institutions inevitably float.

By trial and error, I have gradually translated all this early instruction into a three-dimensional method of studying law and religion. First, I try to keep three "r's" in mind—*retrieval* of the religious sources and dimensions of law in the Western tradition, *reconstruction* of the most enduring teachings of the tradition for our day, and *reengagement* of a historically informed viewpoint with the hard legal and religious issues that now confront church, state, and society. Second, I try to bear in mind three "i's." Much of my work is *interdisciplinary*, bringing the wisdom of religious traditions into conversation with law, the humanities, and the social and hard sciences. It is *international* in situating American and broader Western debates over legal issues within a comparative historical and emerging global conversation. And my work is *interreligious* in comparing the legal teachings of Catholicism, Protestantism, and Orthodoxy, sometimes those of Judaism, Christianity, and Islam, and occasionally those of Abrahamic, Asian, and Indigenous faith communities.

Finally, three "f's" feature in this work—the three things that people will die for: their *faith*, their *freedom*, and their *family*. I have written at length on cardinal issues of religion, human rights, and religious freedom from biblical times to today. I have used the same wide canvas to sketch pictures of the evolving law and theology of sex, marriage, family, and children in the Western tradition, including troubling issues like polygamy and illegitimacy, and newly charged issues like same-sex marriage and children's rights. I have focused on the *drei Stände*, as Martin Luther called them—the three "estates" of church, state, and family that have been cornerstones of Western civilization. I have written at length on the influences of the sixteenth-century Protestant Reformations on law, politics, and society in Western Europe and the Americas. And I have been working of late on broader global patterns of Christianity and law, theology and jurisprudence, as part of a collegial effort to build a new library of books on the interaction of law with each of the axial world religions. It has been a glorious run, though more remains to be done.

It is greatly rewarding to see how this work has been embraced and extended in the hands of the thirty-three scholars who have shared their talents so generously in these pages. It warms this old law professor's heart to see chapters from three of my former students who are now distinguished scholars. And it is a joy to see chapters from so many friends with whom I have had the privilege to work on various projects and publications of our Center for the Study of Law and Religion at Emory.

By way of response, permit me to focus briefly on each contributor to this volume and say a word about my interactions with them and about their work and its place in the field of law and religion. This will allow me to express my gratitude not only for each contributor but also for the solidarity and fellowship that have long inspired our international guild. The work of these contributors helps to map a good bit of the modern field of law and religion.

My first and most profound thanks go to the trio of editors—Rafael Domingo, Gary Hauk, and Timothy Jackson—for their initiative in assembling this volume while contributing their own lovely chapters.

Rafael Domingo, a distinguished Catholic Spanish jurist and legal historian, came to Emory in 2012 after serving as a Strauss Fellow at New York University working with the Jewish law-and-religion sage Joseph Weiler. Rafael joined our Center as the Francisco de Vitoria Senior Fellow, later adding the title of Spruill Family Professor of Law and Religion. We soon became close collaborators in a long series of books and research projects on law and Christianity. Rafael brilliantly integrated his scholarly expertise on classical Roman law, Catholic theology, and the Christian *ius commune* into a robust new theory of global law and religion and an impressive call for a respiritualization of law and the legal profession. He has published signature monographs on *The New Global Law* (Cambridge, 2010), *God and the Secular Legal System* (Cambridge, 2016), *Roman Law* (Routledge, 2018), *Derecho y Trascendencia* (Aranzadi, 2023), and *Law and Religion in a Secular Age* (Catholic University of America, 2023). He coedited five volumes in our Center's series on "Great Christian Jurists in World History,"[1] and the two of us coedited two anthologies: *Christianity and Global Law* (Routledge, 2020) and *The Oxford Handbook of Christianity and Law* (Oxford, 2023). Rafael also translated several of my writings into Spanish, including *Raíces protestantes del Derecho* (Aranzadi, 2023), which he has published in a new Spanish book series that we are coediting. In 2023, Rafael returned to his beloved homeland and alma mater at the University of Navarra to take up the next phase of his work and to care for his aging parents. For this volume, he has written a deeply insightful chapter that explores my life and work as a Christian jurist and analyzes my use of relational, biographical, and jurisprudential perspectives to engage themes of law and religion. With typical ingenuity and imagination, Rafael also challenges me to expand and improve

---

1 Rafael Domingo and Javier Martínez Torrón, *Great Christian Jurists in Spanish History* (Cambridge: Cambridge University Press, 2016); Olivier Descampes and Rafael Domingo, eds., *Great Christian Jurists in French History* (Cambridge: Cambridge University Press, 2019); Orazio Condorelli and Rafael Domingo, eds., *Law and the Christian Tradition in Italy: The Legacy of the Great Jurists* (London: Routledge, 2020); M. C. Mirow and Rafael Domingo, eds., *Law and Christianity in Latin America* (London: Routledge, 2021); and Franciszek Longchamps de Bérier and Rafael Domingo, eds., *Law and Christianity in Poland: The Legacy of the Great Jurists* (London: Routledge, 2023).

my work on law and Christianity, offering several arresting tripartite themes to take up.

Gary S. Hauk has been a stalwart friend for nearly four decades. I first met him when he served as a reference librarian at Emory while he was finishing his doctorate in ethics, and he introduced me to the fabulous collection of Protestant Reformation incunabula at Pitts Theology Library. Since then, Gary has provided great leadership as secretary of Emory University, chief of staff to four Emory presidents, and university historian. He produced several beautifully crafted and illustrated histories of Emory University, Candler School of Theology, and our Center for the Study of Law and Religion, edited collections of presidential papers and faculty essays, and produced interviews and videos for the archives.[2] We worked together over the years to bring a number of luminaries to our Center's lecterns, including President Jimmy Carter, Archbishop Desmond Tutu, Chief Rabbi Lord Jonathan Sacks, and His Holiness the 14th Dalai Lama. I was privileged to coedit a book with Gary on *Christianity and Family Law* (Cambridge, 2017) and to have him coedit my volume on *Faith, Freedom, and Family* (Mohr Siebeck, 2021). Gary's chapter in this volume captures the forty-year story of our Law and Religion Center, fueled by the interdisciplinary energy and ambitions of the Emory administration and faculty. Institutional histories of law-and-religion faculties and centers around the world today are an increasingly important part of the field of law-and-religion study.

Timothy P. Jackson has been a fine partner in our Center's work, and a master interlocutor at our project roundtables on "Christian Jurisprudence," "The Pursuit of Happiness," "Sex, Marriage, and Family," and "The Child in Law, Religion, and Society." Tim came to Emory in 1995, fresh from teaching religion and philosophy at Stanford. He has explored the meanings and measures of love and charity, sanctity and dignity, justice and mercy in the Western tradition and beyond. Jesus, Lincoln, and King have been perennial touchstones in his work, but his scholarly ken ranges from the pre-Socratics to the postmoderns, from the depths of philosophy and theology to the heights of literature and art. As a senior fellow in our Center, he produced a trio of pathbreaking

---

2   See esp. Gary S. Hauk, *A Legacy of Heart and Mind: Emory Since 1836* (Atlanta: Bookhouse, 1999); id., *Reason and Revelation Joined: Candler at One Hundred* (Atlanta: Candler School of Theology, 2014); id., *Emory as Place: Meaning in a University Landscape* (Athens: University of Georgia Press, 2019); id., *Forty Years of Law and Religion at Emory* (Atlanta: Center for the Study of Law and Religion, 2023). See also Gary S. Hauk and Sally Wolff King, eds., *Where Courageous Inquiry Leads: The Emerging Life of Emory University* (Atlanta: Emory University, 2010).

monographs on agape—*Love Disconsoled* (Cambridge, 1999), *The Priority of Love* (Princeton, 2003), and *Political Agape* (Eerdmans, 2015)—as well as two anthologies: *The Morality of Adoption* (Eerdmans, 2005) and *The Best Love of the Child* (Eerdmans, 2011).[3] His most recent work includes searching meditations on anti-Semitism and the Holocaust,[4] as well as trenchant explorations of religion, science, and bioethics for a forthcoming title, *Faith in Science?* Tim's learned chapter in this volume takes up the great dialectic of law and love, *nomos* and *agape*, from the ancient Greeks to modern times, ending with provocative suggestions about the role of the Christian sacraments in mediating and elevating this dialectic.

I am deeply grateful for the five additional chapters in Part 1, alongside those of Rafael Domingo and Gary Hauk, that assess my scholarship on different themes. In the opening chapter, Welsh jurist and Anglican theologian Norman Doe offers a sweeping analysis of my scholarly contributions. He uses his trademark gifts of biography and intellectual history to trace the roots and routes of my scholarship and to situate it within the global field of law and religion. Norman is the world's leading scholar of comparative church law, with a series of pathbreaking titles on Anglican law, comparative Anglican-Catholic canon law, and Christian laws altogether, as well as other Abrahamic laws and their interactions with secular legal systems.[5] Church laws, he has shown, have long been essential parts of the Western legal tradition, providing balance to secular state laws and alternative forums for implementing law, religion, and morality. Today, Norman argues, church laws form the backbone of Christian ecclesiology and ecumenism; they are the sturdy instruments of both denominational identity and Christian unity on many matters of public and private spiritual life. Christian and other faith-based legal systems that Norman has so

---

3   See also Timothy P. Jackson, "Martin Luther King, Jr. (1929–1968)," in John Witte, Jr. and Frank S. Alexander, eds., *The Teachings of Modern Protestantism on Law, Politics, and Human Nature* (New York: Columbia University Press, 2007), 331–73.

4   See esp. Timothy P. Jackson, *Mordecai Would Not Bow Down: Anti-Semitism, the Holocaust, and Christian Supersessionism* (Oxford: Oxford University Press, 2021).

5   See esp. Norman Doe, *The Legal Framework of the Church of England* (Oxford: Oxford University Press, 1996); id., *Canon Law in the Anglican Communion* (Oxford: Oxford University Press, 1998); id., *The Law of the Church in Wales* (Cardiff: University of Cardiff Press, 2002); id., *An Anglican Covenant: Theological and Legal Considerations for a Global Debate* (Canterbury: Canterbury Press, 2008); id., *Law and Religion in Europe* (Oxford: Oxford University Press, 2011); id., *Christian Law: Contemporary Principles* (Cambridge: Cambridge University Press, 2013); id., *Comparative Religious Law: Judaism, Christianity, Islam* (Cambridge, 2018).

ably analyzed remain part of the core curriculum of the modern study of law and religion.[6]

Twenty plus years ago, I joined Norman and his collaborators Mark Hill and Dick Helmholz on the editorial board of the flagship *Ecclesiastical Law Journal*. The four of us, together with Rafael Domingo and Gary Hauk, also built up the Cambridge Studies in Christianity and Law book series commissioned by our Center, and we collaborated on ambitious books on Magna Carta, great Christian jurists in English history, Christianity and natural law, and Christianity and criminal law.[7] Norman further edits the Routledge Law and Religion Series that has published several more of our Center's volumes, and he graciously invited me recently to join him as coeditor of *Brill Research Perspectives on Law and Religion*.

Dick Helmholz is the world's leading historian of medieval law, particularly medieval Catholic canon law and its influence on civil law and common law before and after the Protestant Reformation. He has written seminal texts on medieval family law that have inspired and instructed me and two generations of other legal historians.[8] He has published definitive histories of English ecclesiastical law and its jurists, a poignant study of "the spirit of classical canon law," and several major volumes on religious and canonical sources of Magna Carta, constitutional law, judicial review, criminal law and procedure, and more.[9] It

---

[6] See Norman Doe, ed., *Church Laws and Ecumenism: A New Path for Christian Unity* (London: Routledge, 2021); and John Witte, Jr., "Law at the Backbone: The Christian Legal Ecumenism of Norman Doe," *Ecclesiastical Law Journal* 24 (May 2022): 194–208. See also the chapters herein by Mark Hill on Anglican ecclesiastical law and Michael Broyde on Jewish law and faith-based arbitration.

[7] See Norman Doe, "The Still Small Voice of Magna Carta in Christian Law Today," in Robin Griffith-Jones and Mark Hill, eds., *Magna Carta: Religion and the Rule of Law* (Cambridge: Cambridge University Press, 2015), 248–66; Norman Doe, "Richard Hooker: Priest and Jurist," in Mark Hill and R. H. Helmholz, eds., *Great Christian Jurists in English History* (Cambridge: Cambridge University Press, 2017), 115–38; Norman Doe, ed., *Christianity and Natural Law: An Introduction* (Cambridge: Cambridge University Press, 2017); and Mark Hill, R. H. Helmholz, Norman Doe, and John Witte, Jr. eds., *Christianity and Criminal Law: An Introduction* (London: Routledge, 2020).

[8] See esp. R. H. Helmholz, *Marriage Litigation in Medieval England* (Cambridge: Cambridge University Press, 1974); and id., *Roman Canon Law in Reformation England* (Cambridge: Cambridge University Press, 1990).

[9] See, for example, R.H. Helmholz, *The Oxford History of the Laws of England Volume 1: The Canon Law and the Ecclesiastical Jurisdiction 597 to the 1640s* (Oxford: Oxford University Press, 2004); id., *Canon Law and the Law of England* (London: Hambledon Press, 1987); id., *The Profession of the Ecclesiastical Lawyers: An Introduction* (Cambridge: Cambridge University Press, 2019); id., *The Spirit of Classical Canon Law* (Athens: University of Georgia Press, 2010); and id., "Magna Carta and the *Ius Commune*," *University of Chicago Law Review* 66 (1999): 297–371.

was Dick who invited me to my first international academic conference—a 1989 roundtable at Trinity College Dublin on canon law in Protestant lands.[10] Since then, we have shared many roundtables and lecterns at the University of Chicago, Emory, the Inns of Court, and elsewhere, including a memorable event celebrating a Festschrift for him.[11] Dick has contributed a dozen elegant chapters to our Center's commissioned books on law and religion, legal history, and Christian jurisprudence. He always submits his chapters early, exactly fit to purpose, and without a speck of work to do for the editor. I am immensely grateful for his chapter herein. He commends my use of biographical narratives to recount the history of ideas and institutions and my willingness to be "surprised" by what a careful reading of primary sources can reveal, sometimes contrary to fashions in studying the history of faith, freedom, and family. Among other things, Dick taught me to look for both surprising continuity and discontinuity in the development of legal ideas and institutions, including, notably, the ongoing influence of medieval scholasticism and canon law in the Western legal tradition well after the Protestant Reformation and the Enlightenment. This latter theme recurs in the later chapters herein by Samuel Bray and Mathias Schmoeckel.

Nicholas Wolterstorff is a giant in the world of philosophy. As a young Calvin College student, I learned a great deal from him and his writings. Since then, it has been a great privilege to work with him intermittently on Christian jurisprudence themes and to welcome him to our Center lecterns and roundtables. Nick has written voluminously on the philosophy of religion, political theology, Christianity and education, aesthetics and liturgy, and more.[12] His brilliant and original work on justice and human rights has proved especially influential in the field of law and religion—from his early title *Until Justice and Peace Embrace* (Eerdmans, 1987) through to his later trio of masterworks, *Justice: Rights and Wrongs* (Princeton, 2008), *Justice in Love* (Eerdmans, 2011), and *Journey Toward Justice* (Baker, 2013). Nick has parried both Christian skeptics who view human rights as betrayals of Christianity, and secular skeptics who view religious theories and claims of rights as betrayals of liberalism. He demonstrates cogently that human rights and religious freedom in the Western tradition have deep biblical and classical roots, and they remain sublime divine gifts for humans to express their love for God, neighbor, and self and to honor the image of God that all of us bear. Nick's chapter herein distills some

---

10   R. H. Helmholz, ed., *Canon Law in Protestant Lands* (Berlin: Duncker & Humblot, 1992).
11   Troy L. Harris, ed., *Studies in Canon Law and Common Law in Honor of R. H. Helmholz* (Berkeley, CA: The Robbins Collection, 2015).
12   See the link online to his main writings at "Nicholas Wolterstorff Books."

of his theory of rights and shows the compatibility between his philosophical approach and my historical approach to the topic. He generously comments on the distinctive form—the "inscape"—of my historical, constitutional, and comparative work on these themes. In a day when so many scholars have derided human rights as a species of Western imperialism, Christian chauvinism, and corrosive individualism, Nick's robust defense of rights is a welcome voice in the world of law and religion.

Helen Alvaré, chaired law professor at George Mason University, is a courageous Catholic scholar who has ably and amply defended religious freedom, sexual responsibility, family integrity, and the rights of children, both born and unborn. Helen's wide-ranging expertise on these vital topics has earned her regular audiences with officials in the Vatican, the United Nations, and the United States Conference of Catholic Bishops. But her work has also put her in sharp competition with many leading scholars of religious freedom, feminist jurisprudence, and sexual liberty who take contrary stands on these central topics. Defying liberal feminist caricatures, Helen lifted up the diverse voices of spiritual women in a beautiful 2012 collection, *Breaking Through: Catholic Women Speak for Themselves*, to illustrate the various ways that women of faith have met their multiple callings and challenges in church, state, economy, and society.[13] She followed up with two powerful monographs: *Putting Children's Interests First in Family Law and Policy* (Cambridge, 2017) and *Religious Freedom After the Sexual Revolution* (Catholic, 2022). I first met Helen in 2004, when she responded to a lecture on family law history I delivered at Catholic University of America. She has been a generous reviewer of my scholarship in this field ever since, and a powerful contributor to our Center's projects, publications, and public events.[14] Helen's chapter in this volume takes the full measure of my writing about sex, marriage, family, and children, and she kindly commends several features of this effort. The topics of faith, freedom, and family that have occupied both of us over the years remain central but fiercely contested in the modern study of law and religion.

---

13   See, for example, Helen M. Alvaré, "Christianity and Family Law," in John Witte, Jr. and Rafael Domingo, eds., *Oxford Handbook of Christianity and Law* (Oxford: Oxford University Press, 2023), 434–66; and id., "The Enduring Institution: The Law of Marriage in the West," *Law and Liberty* (October 7, 2012) (review of John Witte, Jr., *From Sacrament to Contract: Marriage, Religion, and Law in the Western Tradition*, 2nd ed. (Louisville, KY: Westminster John Knox Press, 2012), https://lawliberty.org/book-review/the-enduring-institution-the-law-of-marriage-in-the-west/.

14   See, for example, Helen M. Alvaré, "Religious Freedom versus Sexual Expression: A Guide," *Journal of Law and Religion* 30 (2015): 475–95.

Distinguished Cambridge political theorist Jonathan Chaplin has been a keen and trenchant reviewer of my work for nearly three decades.[15] Jonathan and I were schooled in the same broad Calvinist tradition with its focus on ordered liberty, structural pluralism, covenant fidelity, constitutional democracy, human rights, rule of law, and the need for public and private religious reasoning about fundamentals. He has written definitive works on political theory and on religion and politics in reflection of this heritage, especially his monograph, *Herman Dooyeweerd: Christian Philosopher of State and Civil Society* (Notre Dame, 2016), which is the best single-volume analysis of this complex Dutch Calvinist thinker.[16] In a recent lengthy review of my 2019 volume, *Church, State, and Family*, Jonathan did me the great kindness of sifting out and systematizing the basic political theory and Calvinist world view he saw at work in that book and in my earlier works on family law. He pointed out my basic (Calvinist) assumptions about the limited ambit and remit of political power, the "sovereignty" of the spheres of the church and the family vis-à-vis each other and the state, and the necessary constitutional and cultural conditions to ensure proper institutional checks and balances on family, church, and state authorities alike. In his welcome chapter herein, Jonathan goes further, both in documenting my historical retrieval of "Protestant political thought" and in showing how these earlier teachings, particularly (neo-) Calvinist formulations, continue to inform my analysis of modern legal issues of human rights, religious freedom, and church-state relations. Jonathan's chapter and earlier reviews will guide me as I try my hand at more systematic and normative work in the years ahead.

On reading the seven chapters in Part 1, I could not help but remember Hal Berman's words, thirty years ago, in response to a Festschrift conference we had organized for his seventy-fifth birthday: "I now understand much better

---

15 See, for example, Jonathan Chaplin, "Book Review of John Witte, Jr. and Johan D. Van der Vyver, eds., *Religious Human Rights in Global Perspective*, 2 vols.," *Studies in Christian Ethics* 10 (1997): 138–42; and id., "The Role of the State in Regulating the Marital Family," *Journal of Law and Religion* 34 (2019): 509–19 (review of John Witte, Jr., *Church, State, and Family: Reconciling Traditional Teachings and Modern Liberties*). See also his recent fine essay in response to a symposium that our Center commissioned: Jonathan Chaplin, "Whose Liberalism, Which Christianity?" *Notre Dame Law Review* 98 (2023): 1697–720.

16 See also Jonathan Chaplin, *Faith in Democracy: Framing a Politics of Deep Diversity* (London: SCM Press, 2021); id., *Talking God: The Legitimacy of Religious Public Reasoning* (London: Theos, 2008); Jonathan Chaplin and Gary Wilton, eds., *God and the EU: Faith in the European Project* (London: Routledge, 2015); and Jonathan Chaplin and Robert Joustra, eds., *God and Global Order: The Power of Religion in American Foreign Policy* (Waco, TX: Baylor University Press, 2010).

what I have been trying to do these past several decades."[17] At the time, that rang false to my youthful ears; how could this great scholar not know what he was doing? Thirty years on, I understand Hal's sentiment better. For many of us, scholarship is a process of discovery and experimentation, not mechanical execution of a predetermined writing plan or rigid proof of an immutable thesis. Legal and historical scholarship in particular "entails a lot of artistry, and ... practicing," in Rafael Domingo's apt phrase—letting the sources and archives guide your pen, even if much of what you write ends up in the junk folder by the time a book goes to press. My junk folder is pretty full!

The nine chapters in Part II, including Timothy Jackson's chapter on law and love already referenced, take up different topics of faith and law viewed in biblical and theological perspectives.

I am honored by the opening chapter by my great Heidelberg friend and Protestant übertheologian Michael Welker. I first met Michael at a conference in 1998 and was struck by his clarion call for a theology that was "serious," "truth-seeking," "existentially grounded," and "comprehensible," with studied "competence in social and cultural criticism," and a sturdy willingness to engage "the burning questions that our contemporary cultures and societies pose."[18] In the quarter century since then, the two of us have collaborated on several major projects that included theological and legal themes. We have lectured and moderated roundtables together at Heidelberg and Emory, and have edited, reviewed, translated, and published each other's work. I have learned so much from Michael's brilliant sixty plus volumes on law, justice, and mercy in the Bible; on the power of trinitarian theology for modern life and law; on the wisdom of multidimensional theories of legal, political, and social life; and much more.[19] These themes feature in his pithy chapter in this volume, and more expansively in his recent lengthy review of my *Faith, Freedom, and Family*. Michael mercifully found much to commend in that volume and earlier work, while properly criticizing my continued uncritical engagement with historical theories of natural law and natural rights; one of these days I will need to think through my position on natural law.[20] But Michael forgave my failures enough to recommend me for an honorary doctorate in theology as well as for t

---

17   The Festschrift was published as Howard O. Hunter, ed., *The Integrative Jurisprudence of Harold J. Berman* (Boulder, CO: Westview Press, 1996).
18   Michael Welker, "Is Theology in Public Discourse Possible Outside Communities of Faith," in Luis Lugo, ed., *Religion, Pluralism, and Public Life: Abraham Kuyper's Legacy for the Twenty-First Century* (Grand Rapids: Eerdmans, 2000), 110–22.
19   See the immense collection: https://michael-welker.com/en/.
20   See Michael Welker, "A Magnum Opus Discussed: *Faith, Freedom and Family: New Studies in Law and Religion* by John Witte, Jr.," *Journal of Law and Religion* 38 (2023): 108–17.

he James Pennington Prize and Lectureship from the University of Heidelberg. I once had occasion to be with Cardinal Joseph Ratzinger shortly before he became Pope Benedict XVI. Not quite knowing what to say to this giant hierarch on a chance meeting, I asked him whom he judged to be the three greatest German theologians at work in his day. Michael Welker was one of the three.

David VanDrunen is a powerful and prolific Protestant systematic theologian and ethicist at Westminster Seminary California. Trained in law as well, he has written a dozen superb books on political theology in which he explores the place of creation order, natural law, covenant teachings, moral realism, two-kingdoms ontologies, and other themes in biblical, medieval, and early modern Protestant texts. He also expounds on the enduring power of these teachings for modern churches, states, and societies alike.[21] David has inevitably faced criticism from both Calvinist insiders who resist discussions of (unredeemed) nature and secular outsiders who eschew theological arguments for public life and law. But he has deeply mined the relevant biblical texts to show the biblical provenance and promise of at least some natural law teachings. And he has developed a highly original argument about the place of the Noahide covenant in law, politics, and society—complementing and amplifying the creative work on the Noahide covenant by seventeenth-century English jurist John Selden and contemporary Jewish philosopher David Novak.[22] I have had the privilege of watching David VanDrunen develop this complex political theology over the past twenty-five years and discussing it with him as a guest in his seminary and as his host in our Center. In his chapter herein, he takes up the themes of covenantal politics and marital covenants that have long occupied me. He shows both the promise of covenant thinking for the modern state and family, but also the increasing limits of that logic in this secular age "after Christendom." The role of covenant as a rhetorical and conceptual bridge between law and religion nonetheless holds ample promise. It's not accidental, for example, that many of the major international human rights documents today are called "covenants."

---

21 See esp. David Van Drunen, *Natural Law and the Two Kingdoms: A Study in the Development of Reformed Social Thought* (Grand Rapids: Eerdmans, 2010); id., *Divine Covenants and Moral Order: A Biblical Theology of Natural Law* (Grand Rapids: Eerdmans, 2014); and id., *Politics after Christendom: Political Theology in a Fractured World* (Grand Rapids: Zondervan Academic, 2020).

22 David Novak, *Natural Law in Judaism* (Cambridge: Cambridge University Press, 2008); on Selden, see John Witte, Jr., *Faith, Freedom, and Family: New Essays on Law and Religion,* ed. Norman Doe and Gary S. Hauk (Tübingen: Mohr Siebeck, 2021), 177–98 (chapter on "The Integrative Christian Jurisprudence of John Selden").

M. Christian Green was one of our Center's top early law-and-religion graduates and went on to do a doctorate in ethics at the University of Chicago. As my research assistant at Emory, Christy did remarkable excavations—before the internet—of massive lodes of primary sources that have long fed my work on religious freedom and human rights and enabled us to publish several works together.[23] I was privileged to join Don Browning and Jean Elshtain on her dissertation committee, and watched her also research with equal industry various issues of marriage and family life, producing a marvelous study of fatherhood from biblical times to today. While teaching at Chicago, Harvard, and Emory, she has also done formidable service in the international law-and-religion guild, including notably as a leader of the African Consortium of Law and Religion Studies. Christy has remained a vital player in our Center for nearly three decades and now serves as senior editor for the *Journal of Law and Religion*.[24] She has been keenly interested in questions of what she calls "bystander indifference" to crimes, tragedies, and natural disasters, as well as generational complacency in facing ongoing existential dangers like global warming, world poverty, environmental degradation, and massive health-care disparities. In her incisive chapter herein, she uses the New Testament parable of the Good Samaritan to ground her call for individual and collective empathy and energetic engagement with the needs of others. She practices what she preaches: I remember her assembling a whole vanload of her Harvard Divinity School students to give aid to the many victims of Hurricane Katrina that had devastated her home state of Louisiana, and then commissioning these

---

23   See, for example, John Witte, Jr. and M. Christian Green, "The American Constitutional Experiment in Religious Human Rights: The Perennial Search for Principles," in Johan D. van der Vyver and John Witte, Jr., eds., *Religious Human Rights in Global Perspective: Legal Perspectives* (Dordrecht: Martinus Nijhoff, 1996), 499–559; id., "Religious Freedom, Democracy, and International Human Rights," *Emory International Law Review* 23 (2009): 583–608; id., "Religion," in Dinah Shelton, ed., *The Oxford Handbook of International Human Rights Law* (New York: Oxford University Press, 2013), 10–31; id. "Freedom, Persecution, and the Status of Christian Minorities," in Lamin Sanneh and Michael J. McClymond, eds., *The Wiley-Blackwell Companion to World Christianity* (Malden, MA: Wiley Blackwell, 2016), 330–49; and id. "Religious Freedom, Democracy, and International Law," in Timothy S. Shah, Alfred Stepan, and Monica Duffy Toft, eds., *Rethinking Religion and World Affairs* (New York: Oxford University Press, 2012), 104–24. See also John Witte, Jr. and M. Christian Green, eds., *Religion and Human Rights: An Introduction* (Oxford: Oxford University Press, 2012); John Witte, Jr., M. Christian Green, and Amy Wheeler, eds., *The Equal Regard Family and its Friendly Critics: Don S. Browning and the Practical Theological Ethics of the Family* (Grand Rapids: Eerdmans, 2007); and Don S. Browning, M. Christian Green, and John Witte, Jr., eds., *Sex, Marriage, and Family in World Religions* (New York: Columbia University Press, 2006).

24   https://mchristiangreen.com/vitae-2/.

students to write reflective essays on this experience which she wove into a lovely anthology.

Patrick Brennan and William Brewbaker have contributed a highly innovative and learned chapter to this volume. Patrick has been a longstanding friend; his Berkeley law professors John Noonan and Jack Coons introduced us in 1998. Since then, Patrick has hosted several lectureships for me at Arizona State, Catholic University, and Villanova University, and he played starring roles in our Center's projects on "Christian Jurisprudence" and "The Vocation of the Child."[25] He has written brilliantly on issues of liberty, equality, sovereignty, authority, conscience, criminal law, and religious freedom—all central topics in the study of law and religion.[26] Patrick brought a good deal of this learning to bear on his signature title *Christian Legal Thought: Materials and Cases* (Foundation, 2017), coauthored with Bill Brewbaker. Bill is a more recent friend of mine who has contributed ably to our Center's projects. He has made creative use of biblical and theological concepts of creation and vocation, law and love, justice and mercy to adumbrate a Christian jurisprudence.[27] In their chapter herein, Patrick and Bill take up the familiar Protestant doctrine of "the uses of the law." The sixteenth-century reformers used this doctrine to respond to various radicals in their day who saw in new Protestant teachings of free grace a license to be a law unto themselves. Even though law was not a pathway to salvation, the reformers responded, the laws of nature, church, and state alike have ongoing civil, theological, and pedagogical uses in this life, and need to be obeyed. Having documented the echoes of this doctrine in the Protestant tradition, I have flirted with its possible applications in modern criminal law, family law, and human rights law. Bill's Protestant leanings incline him to think

---

25   See, for example, Patrick M. Brennan, "Jacques Maritain (1882–1973)," in John Witte, Jr. and Frank S. Alexander, eds., *The Teachings of Modern Catholicism on Law, Politics, and Human Nature* (New York: Columbia University Press, 2007), 106–80; and Patrick M. Brennan, ed., *The Vocation of the Child* (Grand Rapids: Eerdmans, 2008). See also his review of my *From Sacrament to Contract:* Patrick M. Brennan, "Of Marriage and Monks: Community and Dialogue," *Emory Law Journal* 48 (1999): 689–732. I was privileged to include a foreword to his early masterpiece: John E. Coons and Patrick M. Brennan, *By Nature Equal* (Princeton: Princeton University Press, 1999), XVII–XXIV.

26   See esp. Patrick M. Brennan, *Civilizing Authority: Society, State, and Church* (Lexington, KY: Lexington Books, 2007); and Patrick M. Brennan, H. Jefferson Powell, and Jack L. Sammo, *Legal Affinities: Explorations in the Legal Form of Thought* (Durham, NC: Carolina Academic Press, 2014).

27   See, for example, William Brewbaker, "Found Law, Made Law and Creation: Reconsidering Blackstone's Declaratory Theory," *Journal of Law and Religion* 22 (2006): 255–88; and id., "Theory, Identity, Vocation: Three Models of Christian Legal Scholarship," *Seton Hall Law Review* 39 (2009): 17–61.

I am "mostly right" to develop this idea; Patrick's Catholic philosophy finds this idea "mostly wrong." The two of them offer learned critiques of what I have written, and suggest alternative concepts like friendship and fellowship, if not charity and love, to drive humans to be law-abiding. These insights have left me with a great deal to ponder, and they have given law-and-religion scholars a novel contribution to ongoing questions about the nature, purpose, and end of law.

Samuel Bray, chaired professor at Notre Dame Law School, tells a wonderfully counterintuitive story about the influence of the Roman Catholic intellectual tradition on the common law. "Counterintuitive" because Anglo-American common lawyers and philosophers were notorious for their anti-Catholicism until well into the twentieth century, purportedly leaving Roman Catholicism to influence only the civil law and canon law traditions on the Continent. Indeed, when the seventeenth-century English judge Sir Matthew Hale wrote famously that "Christianity is part of the common law," he had Anglican Christianity in mind, not the teachings of Rome.[28] And while John Locke in 1689 presciently advocated religious toleration, he specifically excluded Roman Catholics from the ambit of religious liberty; so did Parliament until finally granting limited toleration to Catholics in 1829.[29] Even so, Sam shows that English common lawyers—before and after the Reformation—drew deeply on their Catholic intellectual and legal inheritance. They conversed with historical and contemporaneous Catholic sources, and they generated several legal ideas that self-consciously added to that Catholic inheritance. Sam has the outlines of a marvelous book in this chapter, which I hope he will write. This is the kind of scholarship that his readers have come to expect from him. He is a brilliant textualist, having prepared, among many other projects, a new translation of the first part of Genesis,[30] an exquisite new annotated edition of the 1662 Book of Common Prayer,[31] and a source-rich history of equity on both sides of the Atlantic.[32] A dozen years ago, the great Stanford Law School professor and federal judge Michael McConnell introduced me to Sam, his

---

28 See sources in Stuart L. Banner, "When Christianity Was Part of the Common Law," *Law and History Review* 16 (1998): 27–62.

29 John Locke, *Letter Concerning Toleration* (1689), in *The Works of John Locke*, 12th ed., 9 vols. (London: Rivington, 1824), 5:1–58, at 47.

30 Samuel L. Bray and John F. Hobbins, *Genesis 1–11: A New Old Translation for Readers, Scholars, and Translators* (Wilmore, KY: Glossahouse, 2017).

31 Samuel L. Bray and Drew N. Keane, eds., *The 1662 Book of Common Prayer International Edition* (Westmont, CA: IVP Press, 2021).

32 See, for example, Samuel L. Bray and Paul B. Miller, "Christianity and Equity," in Witte and Domingo, *Oxford Handbook to Christianity and Law*, 389–405; id., "Getting Into Equity,"

former judicial clerk, and I have admired and appreciated Sam's lavish learning and steady leadership in our Center's projects and fellowships since then. Particularly his work in Anglo-American legal history and on the historical and contemporary applications of equity jurisprudence are vital contributions to the field of law and religion.

Mathias Schmoeckel, a leading legal historian at the University of Bonn, tells a comparable story about the place of the medieval *ius commune* in Protestant lands on the European continent. That story, too, is counterintuitive. After all, Martin Luther is (in)famous for burning the medieval canon law books at the city gates of Wittenberg and rejecting Roman law as "pagan learning" that had no place in the Bible-based communities born of the Reformation.[33] But Mathias documents clearly that the Protestant jurists and moralists who structured the new legal systems of Protestant churches and states drew heavily on the medieval Catholic canon law and civil law jurisprudence that they knew. Yes, they reformed some of this legal inheritance to reflect the new Protestant teachings, but Reformation jurists treated the sophisticated law and jurisprudence of Christianized Rome and medieval Christendom as a rich repository of natural law and Christian wisdom—a position that Luther and other early Protestant theologians ultimately accepted. Mathias is the world's ranking expert on the Protestant Reformation and law, and he has written brilliant volumes on the German, Swiss, and French reformations that he samples in his chapter with case studies of Wittenberg, Basel, and Bourges.[34] He has also published learned titles on canon law, criminal law, family law, procedural law, legal codification, and the law of notaries, and recently coedited an outstanding six-volume series documenting the influence of medieval canon law on European legal culture.[35] I was privileged to get to know Mathias twenty plus years ago, when we met annually for a project on "concepts of law," directed by

---

Notre Dame Law Review 97 (2022): 1763–99; Samuel L. Bray, "The System of Equitable Remedies," UCLA *Law Review* 63 (2016): 530–94.

33 See John Witte, Jr., *Law and Protestantism: The Legal Teachings of the Lutheran Reformation* (Cambridge: Cambridge University Press, 2002), 53–70.

34 See esp. Mathias Schmoeckel, *Evangelischen Kirchenrecht: Grundlagen und Grundfragen* (Tübingen: Mohr Siebeck, 2023); and id., *Das Recht der Reformation* (Tübingen: Mohr Siebeck, 2014).

35 See, for example, Mathias Schmoeckel et al., eds. *Der Einfluss der Kanonistik auf die europäische Rechtskultur,* 6 vols. (Cologne: Böhlau Verlag, 2009–20); Mathias Schmoeckel and Werner Schubert, *Handbuch zur Geschichte des deutschen Notariats seit der Reichsnotariatsordnung von 1512* (Baden-Baden: Nomos, 2012); Mathias Schmoeckel, *Erbrecht,* 6th ed. (Baden-Baden: Nomos, 2020); id., *Kanonisches Recht: Geschichte und Inhalt des Corpus Iuris Canonici* (Munich: C. H. Beck, 2020); and id., *Die Jugend der Justitia: Archäologie der Gerechtigkeit im Prozessrecht der Patristik* (Tübingen: Mohr Siebeck, 2013).

our mutual friend, Michael Welker. Since then, Matthias and I have lectured and written together,[36] contributed to each other's books and conferences, served together on the editorial board of the *Zeitschrift der Savigny-Stiftung*, and enjoyed wonderful fraternity and friendship. My wife, Eliza, and I remember with special delight an evening we spent with Mathias and his father at Mathias's home outside of Bonn, touring his glorious multi-acre garden that is as elegantly manicured as his scholarship.

Mark Hill, KC, too, has been a dear friend and invaluable collaborator for the past quarter century. Together with Norman Doe,[37] Mark has led the global study of Anglican ecclesiastical law and its place within other Christian legal systems. His impressive *Ecclesiastical Law*, 4th ed. (Oxford, 2018) is the standard text used by church law scholars and practitioners throughout the British Commonwealth and worldwide Anglican Communion. For many years, Mark presided over the Ecclesiastical Law Society in the United Kingdom and in that capacity edited the *Ecclesiastical Law Journal*, a Cambridge University Press imprint, and produced several other volumes on church law and theological jurisprudence.[38] Mark and Dick Helmholz edited the first of our Center's series on "Great Christian Jurists in World History," an excellent anthology on *Great Christian Jurists in English History* (Cambridge, 2017). In recent years, Mark has taken leadership roles in the International Consortium of Law and Religion Studies and has traveled around the world, especially in the Global South, to speak and spearhead projects on law and religion, religious freedom, constitutional reforms, and human rights. For all this globe-trotting, however, Mark has remained a dedicated and much sought-after barrister in secular courts in the United Kingdom and a formidable ecclesiastical judge and advocate in church courts. And he has always made time for my colleagues and me—collaborating with our Center on various projects and events, contributing learned articles to our publications, reviewing and blurbing my books, and graciously

---

36 See, for example, Mathias Schmoeckel and John Witte, Jr., eds., *Great Christian Jurists in German History* (Tübingen: Mohr Siebeck, 2020); and id., "Christianity and Procedural Law," in Witte and Domingo, *Oxford Handbook of Christianity and Law*, 376–88.

37 See Frank Cranmer, Mark Hill, Celia Kenney, and Russell Sandberg, eds., *The Confluence of Law and Religion: Interdisciplinary Reflections on the Work of Norman Doe* (Cambridge: Cambridge University Press, 2016).

38 See, for example, Mark Hill and A. K. Thompson, eds., *Religious Confession and Evidential Privilege in the 21st Century* (Sydney: Shepherd Street Press, 2023); Mark Hill, Russell Sandberg, and Norman Doe, eds., *Religion and Law in the United Kingdom* (Alphen aan de Rijn: Kluwer, 2021); Hill et al., *Christianity and Criminal Law;* and Hill and Helmholz, *Great Christian Jurists in English History*.

opening lectureships to me throughout the United Kingdom.[39] A particularly memorable occasion he made possible was the privilege to preach from Richard Hooker's pulpit in the Temple Church, a rare treat for this mere lawyer and a Calvinist at that.

Brandon Paradise offers the world of law and religion a rare combination of deep training in Orthodox Christian theology, modern American constitutional law, and critical race theory. The Orthodox sage John McGuckin introduced us some fifteen years ago, when Brandon first began teaching law at Rutgers Law School, and I have learned from his work ever since, particularly during his early visits to our Center and more recently during his tenure as a McDonald Senior Fellow. Brandon has courageously pushed back against the anti-Black animus of some Christian theologies as well as the antireligious animus of some critical race theories. He has called us all to remember the powerful example of civil and human rights advocated by the *Reverend* Dr. Martin Luther King Jr. and fostered by the Black churches, which remained committed to the truth of scripture, the essential role of faith in law and politics, and the critical values of discursive community.[40] Brandon has also held out the powerful witness of Orthodox theology and church life for engaging and, where needed, reforming liberalism's cardinal commitments to democracy, constitutional order, rule of law, and protection of human rights.[41] He and Center Senior Fellow Terri Montague recently organized a marvelous forum on all these themes, featuring Brandon's old professor Cornel West as well as Bernice King, MLK's daughter and an early graduate of our Center. In his chapter herein, Brandon ably interweaves his innovative account of Christianity, race, law, and liberalism with some of the main themes of law and religion that he finds in my writings. His distinctive voice and perspective are refreshing contributions to the study of law and religion.

Part III of this volume features nine learned chapters on the history, theory, and law of human rights and religious freedom. These topics have attracted by far the largest body of scholarship in the field of law and religion. All nine chapters add keen and original insights to the literature. As we saw in

---

39 See, for example, Mark Hill, "Christianity and Human Rights Law," in Witte and Domingo, *Oxford Handbook of Christianity and Law*, 593–604.

40 See, for example, Brandon Paradise, "How Critical Race Theory Marginalizes the African-American Christian Tradition," *Michigan Journal of Race and Law* 20 (2014): 117–211; id., "Racially Transcendent Diversity," *University of Louisville Law Review* 50 (2012): 415–89; and id., "Confronting the Truth: The Necessity of Love for Justice," *Journal of Law and Religion* 37 (2022): 230–43.

41 See, for example, Brandon Paradise and Fr. Sergey Trostyanskiy, "Liberalism and Orthodoxy: A Search for Mutual Apprehension," *Notre Dame Law Review* 98 (2023): 1657–98.

discussing Nicholas Wolterstorff's chapter, the historical roots and routes of human rights and religious freedom, and their constitutional and cultural legitimacy in late modern societies, are all highly contested among scholars today, and these topics have attracted a small library of interdisciplinary literature. An even larger library has grown to address the historical origins and modern interpretations of the First Amendment religious freedom guarantees and accompanying statutes in the United States. The rapidly expanding religious freedom jurisprudence of individual European national courts and the pan-European courts in Strasbourg and Luxembourg has attracted a growing body of new scholarship, too, on both sides of the Atlantic, as has the work of high national courts in the Middle East (especially in Israel) and the Global South (especially in India, South Africa, and Chile). Since the 1980s, UN special rapporteurs, national state departments, and NGOs have issued detailed surveys of the state of human rights and religious freedom around the world and have documented the alarming rise in religious persecution in the new millennium. These reports, too, have attracted a great deal of commentary by law-and-religion scholars from various disciplines.

Distinguished Catholic jurist Andrea Pin, newly chaired professor at the University of Padua, has written with depth and vigor on the ultimate foundation of human rights in the idea that all humans are created in the image of God, and by virtue of that status enjoy an inherent human dignity. In a series of articles and forthcoming books, Andrea has compared various Christian, Jewish, and Muslim concepts of human dignity and their impact on local law and human rights protections in Europe, the Middle East, and the Americas.[42] He is expanding this work to take up new questions about human dignity, identity, and responsibility born of the AI revolution. His writings also include exquisite studies of comparative constitutional law, competing theories of rule of law, and contested questions about the place of Muslims and sharia in Europe.[43]

---

42 See, for example, Andrea Pin, "Arab Constitutionalism and Human Dignity," *George Washington University International Law Review* 50 (2017): 1–67; id., "Balancing Dignity, Equality, and Religious Freedom: A Transnational Topic," *Ecclesiastical Law Journal* 19 (2017): 292–316; id., "Religions, National Identities, and the Universality of Human Rights," *Oxford Journal of Law and Religion* 3 (2014): 419–39; id., "Catholicism, Liberalism, and Populism," *Brigham Young University Law Review* 46 (2021): 1301–28; and id., "AI, the Public Square, and the Right to be Ignored," in Jeroen Temperman and Alberto Quintavalla eds., *Artificial Intelligence and Human Rights* (Oxford: Oxford University Press, 2023), 177–94.

43 Andrea Pin, *The Legal Treatment of Muslim Minorities in Italy: Islam and the Neutral State* (London: Routledge, 2016); id., *Il diritto e il dovere dell'uguaglianza : problematiche attuali di un principio risalente* (Naples: Editoriale scientifica, 2015); and id., "The Inevitability of Precedent," *The Italian Review of International and Comparative Law* 2 (2022): 246–62.

All these are core topics of the law-and-religion field, and they all feature in his learned chapter in this volume. Andrea has been a wonderful friend to me and my family since we met some fifteen years ago, and he has been a highly productive senior fellow in our Center. He has contributed generously to our courses, conferences, and publications, and expertly translated several of my writings into Italian. He has hosted Eliza and me in the glorious cultural capitals of Padua, Venice, Milan, Rome, and Florence, opening wonderful forums to me, and introducing valuable conversation partners throughout Italy. In recent years, we have written together on the religious freedom jurisprudence of the European Court of Human Rights and the Court of Justice of the European Union, and I have learned much from his insider views as a European lawyer and a devout Catholic. We are now embarked on a book-length study comparing European and American religious freedom jurisprudence.[44]

David Little has pioneered the study of religion, human rights, and religious freedom during sixty-five years of distinguished scholarly work at Yale, Harvard, and Georgetown Universities, the University of Virginia, and the United States Institute of Peace. He has traced cardinal human rights principles from antiquity to today—with a special focus on the prescient contributions of Protestants like his heroes John Calvin and Roger Williams to modern ideas of human rights. He has written astutely on the many vexed questions arising under the First Amendment religion clauses. And he has charted the religious sources and dimensions of modern human rights, particularly the international instruments protecting freedom of thought, conscience, and belief, freedom from religious hatred, incitement, and discrimination, and the rights to religious and cultural self-determination.[45] His most recent work makes a compelling argument that the ultimate *Grundnorm* of human rights lies in the natural right of self-defense, which historical writers and international human rights documents alike take as axiomatic. David has been a wonderful friend and collaborator in our Center's projects since the early 1990s.[46] We have

---

44   Andrea Pin and John Witte, Jr., *Le origini e il futuro della libertà religiosa in Europa e negli Stati Uniti* (Milan: Il Mulino, 2024).

45   See the lengthy bibliography and assessment of his work in Sumner B. Twiss et al., eds., *Religion and Public Policy: Human Rights, Conflict and Ethics* (Cambridge: Cambridge University Press, 2015). See also David Little, *Essays on Religion and Human Rights: Ground to Stand On* (Cambridge: Cambridge University Press, 2015).

46   See, for example, David Little, "Studying 'Religious Human Rights': Methodological Foundations," in John Witte, Jr. and Johan D. Van der Vyver, eds., *Religious Human Rights in Global Perspective: Religious Perspectives* (The Hague: Martinus Nijhoff, 1996), 45–78; and id., "Religion, Human Rights, and Public Reason," in Witte and Green, *Religion and Human Rights*, 135–54.

lectured for each other, appeared together in several public conferences and panels, and reviewed each other's work.⁴⁷ It was a special privilege to keynote the Festschrift conference for him on his retirement from Harvard Divinity School.⁴⁸ David is an erudite reader and trenchant critic; to send a manuscript to him for commentary is to know the true meaning of "fear and trembling." I have learned so much from our lengthy exchanges over the years. In his chapter herein, he returns with fresh insights and sources to tell more of the story of the history of rights in the later medieval era and in the Calvinist Reformation, showing the continuity with, if not dependence of, Calvin and the early Calvinists on late medieval nominalist and conciliarist views of rights and religious freedom.

Leading German church historian Jan Stievermann is, perhaps ironically, one of the world's best historians of early American religion. While he has also written on European church history, he has made two pathbreaking contributions to the study of law and religion in American history. The first was in preparing, together with Reiner Smolinski and a team of other scholars, a critical edition of the ten-volume *Biblia Americana* by Puritan leader Cotton Mather. This is the most important publication on American colonial religious history since *The Works of Jonathan Edwards,* and it was little known let alone read before the arduous efforts of the *Biblia* team to bring it to light. Mather's massive learning, including notably on themes of law and religion, pulses throughout this encyclopedic biblical commentary. Jan follows Mather every step of the way, offering keen annotations on the text, and separate commentaries, articles, and books on Mather's contributions.⁴⁹ His excellent chapter herein on Mather's teachings on religious freedom and other liberties is one of many examples of the riches available to scholars of law and religion who

---

47   See, for example, David Little, "Review Essay: Religion and Justification of Rights Discussed," *Journal of Law and Religion* 38 (2023): 141–57 (Review of Witte, *Faith, Freedom and Family* and John Witte, Jr. *The Blessings of Liberty: Human Rights and Religious Freedom in the Western Legal Tradition* (Cambridge: Cambridge University Press, 2021); John Witte, Jr., "Review Essay: Law, Religion, and Human Rights in David Little's Thought," *Journal of Law and Religion* 32 (2017): 197–201.

48   John Witte, Jr., "David Little: A Modern Calvinist Architect of Human Rights," in Twiss et al., *Religion and Public Policy*, 3–23.

49   See, for example, Jan Stievermann, *Prophecy, Piety, and the Problem of Historicity: Interpreting the Hebrew Scriptures in Cotton Mather's Biblia Americana* (Tübingen: Mohr Siebeck, 2016); id., "Admired Adversary: Wrestling with Grotius the Exegete in Cotton Mather's *Biblia Americana* (1693–1728)," *Grotiana* 41 (2020): 198–235; and id., "The Debate over Prophetic Evidence for the Authority of the Bible in Cotton Mather's *Biblia Americana*," in *The Bible in American Life*, ed. Philip Goff et al. (New York: Oxford University Press, 2017), 48–62.

take up the *Biblia*. And the chapter adds further nuance to and appreciation for the Puritan sources of American constitutionalism. Jan's second major contribution involves James W. C. Pennington, who escaped from slavery and became a powerful Presbyterian preacher and the leader of the world abolitionist movement before the American Civil War. Jan is leading the way in the reappraisal of Pennington as a major antebellum abolitionist and reformer, who even received an honorary doctorate from the University of Heidelberg and, it turns out, had been the first Black person ever to study at Yale. With his Heidelberg colleagues, Jan established the Pennington Prize and Lectureship at Heidelberg, yielding a series of volumes on Pennington.[50] Jan and Michael Welker kindly nominated me for that prize and lectureship, and I have made Pennington's remarkable odyssey a central chapter in my ongoing history of Calvinism and rights.[51] The two of them also commended me for an honorary doctorate in theology from Heidelberg; Jan's beautiful *laudatio* will long serve me as a talisman against self-doubt.

Joel A. Nichols, chaired professor and long-serving dean at the University of St. Thomas Law School, in Minneapolis, was a brilliant student and graduate of our Center. Already as a student, his research and scholarly gifts were on full display as he published a prize-winning article on covenant marriage and a lengthy study of international religious freedom norms governing proselytizing.[52] He has continued to write about domestic and international religious freedom, and has joined me as a coauthor of the last three editions of *Religion and the American Constitutional Experiment* (5th ed. Oxford, 2022) and a few related articles.[53] He also directed a superb comparative project for our

---

50   Jan Stievermann, ed., *The Pennington Lectures, 2011–2015* (Heidelberg: Universitätsverlag Winter, 2015); Jan Stievermann et al., eds., *James W. C. Pennington: Essays Toward Rediscovering a Great African American Intellectual and Reformer* (Oxford: Oxford University Press, forthcoming).

51   See, for example, John Witte, Jr. and Justin L. Latterell, "Between Martin Luther and Martin Luther King: James Pennington and the Struggle for 'Sacred Human Rights' Against Slavery," *Yale Journal of Law and Humanities* 31 (2020): 205–71.

52   Joel A. Nichols, "Louisiana's Covenant Marriage Law: A First Step Toward a More Robust Pluralism in Marriage and Divorce Law?" *Emory Law Journal* 47 (1998): 929–1001; and id., "Mission, Evangelism, and Proselytism in Christianity: Mainline Conceptions as Reflected in Church Documents," *Emory International Law Review* 12 (1998): 563–650.

53   John Witte, Jr. and Joel A. Nichols, introduction to John Witte, Jr. and Eliza Ellison, eds., *Covenant Marriage in Comparative Perspective* (Grand Rapids: Eerdmans, 2005), 1–25; id., "The Frontiers of Marital Pluralism," in Joel A. Nichols, ed., *Marriage and Divorce in a Multi-Cultural Context: Multi-Tiered Marriage and the Boundaries of Civil Law and Religion* (Cambridge: Cambridge University Press, 2011), 357–78; id., "Who Governs the Family? Marriage as a New Test Case of Overlapping Jurisdictions," *Faulkner Law Review* 4 (2013):

Center on plural forms and forums of family law, yielding a signature work, *Marriage and Divorce in a Multi-Cultural Context* (Cambridge, 2011). Joel has been uncommonly generous to me and my family: every Christmas since his first year at Emory, he has sent us a delicious box or two of pears as a token of ongoing friendship and fraternity; "the Nichols pears" are now a staple of our family's Yuletide cheer. In his chapter herein, Joel has returned to his southern roots, taking up anew his pathbreaking research on the colonial history of religious liberty in Georgia. He shows the surprisingly robust religious pluralism and religious liberty in this young colony, and punctures deftly the stereotype of colonial Georgia as a mere dumping ground for transported debtors and felons.

In a long series of volumes beginning in 1987, Daniel L. Dreisbach, of American University, has brilliantly illuminated the religious sources of American law and politics and the religious character of many of America's founders. Not only famous founders like George Washington, Thomas Jefferson, and John Adams but also forgotten founders like Jaspar Adams, Benjamin Rush, and Oliver Ellsworth come to light and life in Daniel's volumes. He documents in detail the founders' dependence on the Bible and on basic Christian moral teachings in creating the new constitutions, statutes, and cases of the young American republic.[54] A careful textualist, Daniel has also assembled a wonderful collection of primary sources showing the founders' diverse teachings on liberty of conscience and religious freedom; he also published a definitive study of the origins and meanings of the famous metaphor of "a wall of separation between church and state" and the varying applications of that phrase first by Thomas Jefferson and then by Supreme Court opinions citing Jefferson.[55] Daniel has been a go-to resource and critic for me for the past thirty years, offering valuable commentary on my early efforts to map First Amendment history and Supreme Court case law. He also coedited our Center's commissioned volume

---

321–49; and id., "'Come Now Let Us Reason Together': Restoring Religious Freedom in America and Abroad," *Notre Dame Law Review* 92 (2016): 427–50.

54 See, for example, Daniel L. Dreisbach, *Reading the Bible with the Founding Fathers* (Oxford: Oxford University Press, 2016); id., *Religion and Politics in the Early Republic* (Lexington: The University Press of Kentucky, 2015): Daniel L. Dreisbach and Mark D. Hall, eds., *Faith and the Founders of the American Republic* (Oxford: Oxford University Press, 2014); Daniel L. Dreisbach and Mark D. Hall, eds., *The Forgotten Founders on Religion and Public Life* (Notre Dame, IN: University of Notre Press, 2009); and Daniel L. Dreisbach, Mark D. Hall, and Jeffry H. Morrison, eds., *The Founders on God and Government* (Lanham, MD: Rowman and Littlefield, 2004).

55 Daniel L. Dreisbach, *Thomas Jefferson and the Wall of Separation Between Church and State* (New York: NYU Press, 2002); and Daniel L. Dreisbach and Mark D. Hall, eds., *The Sacred Rights of Conscience* (Indianapolis: Liberty Fund, 2009).

on *Great Christian Jurists in American History* (Cambridge, 2019). His learned chapter herein revisits the history, judicial interpretation, and political manipulations of the "wall of separation" metaphor, and very kindly weaves together and commends my efforts to map the various meaning and uses of this metaphor in Western history and American constitutional thought.

Mark A. Noll has long been America's leading Evangelical church historian and commentator, producing thirty books and hundreds of articles while teaching two generations of students at Wheaton College and the University of Notre Dame. He has documented beautifully the anchoring role of the Bible in American law, politics, and culture from early colonial days into the twentieth century.[56] But he has also lamented the decline of America's "Bible civilization" after World War I, and the growing "scandal of the Evangelical mind" as twentieth-century American Protestants gradually lost their distinct epistemological grounding in scripture, tradition, reason, and experience, and their traditional aspiration to educate themselves to find their Christian vocation in all walks of life, including in the legal profession.[57] Mark's *America's God* (Oxford, 2002), *In the Beginning Was the Word* (Oxford, 2015), and *America's Book* (Oxford, 2022) are must-reads for anyone serious about American religious history. In recent writings, he has also taken up the history of Protestantism in the Americas, Europe, and Africa, and has been in the vanguard of scholars now working on world Christianity. Mark has been a wonderful friend to me over many years, always sending encouraging notes and materials, commenting on my manuscripts, reviewing my books, and opening doors to me. He provided a magisterial introduction to our Center volume on *Modern Protestant Teachings on Law, Politics, and Human Nature* (Columbia, 2007), and contributed other valuable writings to our projects.[58] In his chapter herein, Mark shows how the United States Supreme Court's separatist interpretation of the First Amendment in the mid-twentieth century hastened the decline of the value and use of the Bible in public schools and public life altogether. The Supreme Court's recent First Amendment cases have been more accommodating of public expressions of religion, to the delight of some and the dismay of others.

---

56 See a full listing of his writings here: https://history.nd.edu/assets/47887/.
57 See Mark A. Noll, *The Scandal of the Evangelical Mind* (Grand Rapids: Eerdmans, 1994); and id., *America's Book: The Rise and Decline of a Bible Civilization, 1794–1911* (Oxford: Oxford University Press, 2022).
58 See, for example, Mark A. Noll, "Introduction to Modern Protestantism," in Witte and Alexander, eds., *The Teachings of Modern Protestantism*, 1–28; and id., "The Gift of *Sola Scriptura* to the World," in John Witte, Jr. and Amy S. Wheeler, eds., *The Protestant Reformation of the Church and the World* (Louisville, KY: Westminster John Knox, 2018), 23–46.

First Amendment religious freedom is also at the heart of the expertise of my distinguished friend and Georgia neighbor, Nathan Chapman. Trained in both law and theology at Duke University, and then in religious liberty at Stanford, Nathan has emerged as a great leader of the next generation of law and religion scholars and teachers. He has published several definitive articles on First Amendment history and jurisprudence, as well as on broader American constitutional questions, such as due process and sovereign immunity.[59] He and his mentor, Michael McConnell, have published a brilliant book, *Agreeing to Disagree: How the Establishment Clause Promotes Religious Pluralism and Protects Freedom of Conscience* (Oxford, 2022). Nathan has also embarked on several studies engaging deep questions of political and legal theology, and the place of Christian ideas and institutions in post-Christian liberal societies—topics that we have pondered together during several long and enjoyable hikes.[60] I have admired Nathan's refined organizational and mentorship skills, as he has worked to foster fellowship and mutual encouragement for law-and-religion scholars and Christian jurists around the nation. His chapter herein, like his recent lengthy review essay of my coauthored *Religion and the American Constitutional Experiment*,[61] is typically astute and generous in assessing my efforts to build an integrative principled approach to the First Amendment. Nathan goes well beyond me in applying that approach to assess the constitutional limits on government religious speech. He argues for a novel "threat-of-discrimination" approach, in place of the less satisfying separatist, coercion, history, or endorsement approaches of the United Supreme Court.

University of Bristol jurist and legal philosopher Julian Rivers is, alongside Norman Doe and Mark Hill, one of the pioneers of the modern study of law and religion in the United Kingdom. The three of them, along with Dick Helmholz, built up the *Ecclesiastical Law Journal*. Julian also founded and now

---

59 See, for example, Nathan S. Chapman and Michael W. McConnell, "Due Process as Separation of Powers," *Yale Law Journal* 121 (2012): 1672–807; Nathan S. Chapman, "Due Process Abroad," *Northwestern University Law Review* 112 (2017): 377–452; id., "Disentangling Conscience and Religion," *University of Illinois Law Review* (2013): 1457–501; and id., "Forgotten Federal-Missionary Partnerships: New Light on the Establishment Clause," *Notre Dame Law Review* 96 (2020): 677–747.

60 See, for example, Nathan S. Chapman, "'The Arc of the Moral Universe': Christian Eschatology and U.S. Constitutionalism," *Notre Dame Law Review* 98 (2023): 1439–68; id., "Christianity and Crimes Against the State," in Hill et al., *Christianity and Criminal Law*, 153–69; and id., "The Weight of Judgment," in Hill et al., *Christianity and Criminal Law*, 332–48.

61 Nathan S. Chapman, "American Religious Liberty Without (Much) Theory," *Journal of Law and Religion* 38 (2023): 126–40 (review of John Witte, Jr., Joel A. Nichols, and Richard W. Garnett, *Religion and the American Constitutional Experiment*, 5th ed. (Oxford: Oxford University Press, 2022)).

edits the *Oxford Journal of Law and Religion*. These are the two leading law-and-religion journals in the British Isles. I have long admired Julian's elegant and crystal-clear contributions to law-and-religion scholarship, including wonderful chapters on the biblical, historical, and jurisprudential dimensions of equality that he contributed to our Center's recent publications.[62] He has also written insightfully on several core topics in law and religion—natural law, human rights, religious establishments, church-state relations, freedom of expression, and constitutional theory, drawing on Anglo-American, European, and international jurisprudence alike. I have admired his courage in standing up for the place of (the Christian) faith in the secular academy, and his defense of religious freedom as a necessary foundation and feature of constitutional order. His weighty monograph *The Law of Religious Organizations: Between Establishment and Secularism* (Oxford, 2010) is a sterling defense of religious freedom and a call for better balancing of competing rights claims. Julian extends and updates that book's main argument in his chapter herein; he defends the corporate religious freedom of the church on historical, philosophical, and constitutional grounds, but also illustrates how British, German, and American courts alike have wavered in their definition and defense of this ur principle, not least during the COVID-19 public health crisis.

Faulkner University law professor Jeffrey B. Hammond was also one of our Center's early prize students, who has gone on to a fine teaching career focused on legal and theological dimensions of health law, bioethics, religious liberty, and legal philosophy.[63] During his time at Emory, Jeff did wonderful research on the first edition of my *Religion and the American Constitutional Experiment*. He also collaborated with my Center colleague Abdullahi An-Na'im on a substantial study on religion, culture, and human rights in Africa[64] and worked on Harold J. Berman's epic series on *Law and Revolution*. Jeff has been a notably faithful alumnus and senior fellow in our Center over the past two decades, participating actively in our conferences and projects. He was kind enough to

---

62 See, for example, Julian Rivers, "Christianity and the Principle of Equality in International Law," in Rafael Domingo and John Witte, Jr., eds., *Christianity and Global Law* (London: Routledge, 2020), 231–50; and id., "Christianity and Equality," in Witte and Domingo, *Oxford Handbook of Christianity and Law*, 777–88.

63 See, for example, Jeffrey B. Hammond, "The Minimally Conscious Person: A Case Study in Dignity and Personhood and the Standard of Review for Withdrawal of Treatment," *Wayne Law Review* 55 (2009): 821–900; and id., "Protestant Legal Theory: Apology and Objections," *Journal of Law and Religion* 32 (2017): 86–92.

64 Abdullahi Ahmed An-Na'im and Jeffrey B. Hammond, introduction to Abdullahi A. An-Na'im, ed., *Cultural Transformation and Human Rights in Africa* (London: Zed Books, 2002).

invite me to an excellent symposium that he organized on "Overlapping Jurisdictions: What Role for Conscience and Religion," to which he made a learned contribution on contract, covenant, and conscience.[65] He coedited a superb study commissioned by our Center on *Christianity and the Laws of Conscience* (Cambridge, 2021). In his chapter herein, Jeff explores the biblical foundations and theological calculus in making claims of conscience. He then uses recent religious freedom cases to illustrate how a religiously informed conscience sometimes compels parties to seek exemptions from compliance with state prescriptions or proscriptions, sometimes at significant cost to their livelihoods and social standing. The questions of religious exemptions and accommodations from general state laws are heated topics of dispute these days in law-and-religion and broader constitutional scholarship.

Part IV of this volume gathers six excellent chapters, by old friends and new, that illustrate a few of the challenging issues of sex, marriage, and family that have long occupied law-and-religion scholarship. The marital family is humanity's oldest and most essential social institution, whose various different forms and norms reflect both spiritual and secular dimensions. Marriage is not only a sacrament and covenant celebrated in special liturgies and ceremonies; it is also a contract and civil status that imposes rights and duties of spousal support and protection, and of parental nurture and education. Spouses, churches, and states have all set basic rules, procedures, and expectations for the proper formation, maintenance, and dissolution of the marital family, and for the proper care, nurture, and education of children. These overlapping dispensations often come into sharp tension in cases of spousal or child neglect or abuse, household conflict or divorce, or with death and inheritance disputes. Today, parents, state officials, and children with growing moral agency often need to sort out whose authority or interests take precedence in disputes. All these topics and more are at the center of the field of law and religion not only in Western lands but throughout the world.[66]

My distinguished Emory colleague and friend Philip L. Reynolds has been a wonderful senior fellow in our Center for more than two decades. He was a leading participant in two major Center projects on "Sex, Marriage, and Family" and "The Child in Law, Religion, and Society." He directed the Center's major project on "The Pursuit of Happiness." He edited a superb title on first millennium sources for our book series on "Great Christian Jurists in

---

65   See in this symposium: Jeffrey B. Hammond, "Conscience as Contract, Conscience as Covenant," *Faulkner Law Review* 4 (2013): 433–44.
66   See Browning et al., eds., *Sex, Marriage and Family in World Religions*.

World History."⁶⁷ Throughout his time at Emory, he was a master interlocutor and presenter at numerous Center roundtables, classes, and public conferences. But it is especially his books, coming out of these projects, that will long edify the law-and-religion field. His early work, *Marriage in the Western Church* (Brill, 1994), offered a brilliant account of first-millennium theological and legal teachings on marriage before and after the Christianization of the Roman Empire. The two of us coedited *To Have and to Hold: Marrying and its Documentation in Western Christendom, 400–1600* (Cambridge, 2007). But most important is Philip's definitive history, *How Marriage Became One of the Sacraments* (Cambridge, 2018), a thousand-plus-page account that traces the idea of the marital sacrament from Saint Paul's *mysterion* of marriage (Ephesians 5:32) to the 1563 Decree Tametsi of the Council of Trent that finally settled the theology and law of marriage as a sacrament. Philip's chapter herein gives us a small taste of this latter masterwork in showing the interweaving of theological and legal arguments about the marital sacrament in the High Middle Ages.

Kathleen A. Brady has been a pivotal Catholic jurist working skillfully at the clogged intersections of church, state, family, and school. The great judge John T. Noonan Jr. strongly recommended Kathleen to serve as a senior fellow in our Center, and with her dual training in law and religion at Yale she has long proved to be a wonderful conversation partner. Even while teaching for a time at Villanova Law School and enjoying a fellowship at Princeton University, she continued her fellowship at our Center. She has played a crucial role in back-to-back Center projects on Christian jurisprudence, offering keen insights from the Catholic tradition to a deep conversation with a score of Catholic, Protestant, and Orthodox scholars. For one of those projects, she wrote a brilliant prize-winning book, *The Distinctiveness of Religion in American Law* (Cambridge, 2015) to counter the growing efforts in the academy to abolish religious freedom as a special category. She has since published several more articles defending the historical and constitutional place of religious freedom in the American constitutional order, the values of accommodating sincere religious claims, and the need for church autonomy in fundamental questions of polity, property, and social services.⁶⁸ In her fine chapter herein, Kathleen

---

67   Philip L. Reynolds, ed., *Great Christian Jurists and Legal Collections in the First Millennium* (Cambridge: Cambridge University Press, 2019).
68   See, for example, Kathleen A. Brady, "The Distinctiveness of Religion: An Introduction and Response to Readers," *Journal of Law and Religion* 32 (2017): 518–22; id., "Catholic Liberalism and the Liberal Tradition," *Notre Dame Law Review* 98 (2023): 1469–96; id., "Religious Freedom and the Common Good," *Loyola University Chicago Law Journal* (2018): 137–64; id., "Religious Accommodations and Third-Party Harms: Constitutional Values and Limits," *Kentucky Law Journal* 106 (2018): 717–50; id., "Independent and Overlapping:

tackles several vexed questions of parental and children's rights in education, finding traction in Catholic subsidiarity doctrine as well as my multidimensional view of the family to argue strongly for the priority of parental rights in the education of their minor children.

Marcia J. Bunge, a leading Christian ethicist, has published definitive works on the unique place of the child in the Bible, in the Christian tradition, and in various world religions.[69] Marcia and I share a deep appreciation for Martin Luther's signature emphasis on the need for education of both boys and girls to equip them for their distinct Christian vocation. We also shared a great mentor in the late Don Browning, the dean of interdisciplinary family studies at the University of Chicago, who brought us together for projects both at Chicago and in our Center at Emory.[70] Marcia has been a champion of children's rights and has defended an ethic of "childism" that takes better account of each child's evolving moral agency and growing independence from parents, teachers, and other authority figures. In her chapter herein, Marcia offers a robust critique of corporal punishment of children on biblical, moral, and utilitarian grounds. As a jurist and amateur theologian, I find her argument altogether convincing. If the law prohibits an adult person from striking a fellow adult with impunity, even though that victim is capable of self-defense and private redress, why should an adult be able to strike a child with impunity, especially when many children cannot defend themselves or turn to others for help? Why pick out one Old Testament Proverb as an enduring command for modern parents—"He who spares the rod hates his son" (Proverbs 13:24)—while ignoring many other actual Mosaic commands about parenting, including violent ones

---

Institutional Religious Freedom and Religious Providers of Social Services," *Loyola University Chicago Law Review* 54 (2022): 683–757; and id., "COVID-19 and Restrictions on Religious Worship: From Nondiscrimination to Church Autonomy," *Fides et Libertas* (2021): 23–41.

69 See esp. Marcia J. Bunge, ed., *The Child in Christian Thought* (Grand Rapids: Eerdmans, 2001); Marcia J. Bunge, Terence Fretheim, and Beverley Roberta Gaventa, eds., *The Child in the Bible* (Grand Rapids: Eerdmans, 2008); Marcia J. Bunge, ed., *Children, Adults, and Shared Responsibilities* (Cambridge: Cambridge University Press, 2012); and Don S. Browning and Marcia J. Bunge, eds., *Children and Childhood in World Religions* (New Brunswick, NJ: Rutgers University Press, 2009).

70 See, for example, Marcia J. Bunge, "The Vocation of the Child: Theological Perspectives on the Particular and Paradoxical Roles and Responsibilities of Children," in Brennan, ed., *The Vocation of the Child,* 31–52; and id., "Communicating Values by Honoring Families and the Full Humanity of Children: Lessons from Robust Theologies and Detrimental Developments Among Protestants," in John Witte, Jr., Michael Welker, and Stephen Pickard, eds., *The Impact of the Family on Character Formation, Ethical Education, and the Communication of Values in Late Modern Pluralistic Societies* (Leipzig: Evangelische Verlagsanstalt, 2022), 105–26.

like: "Whoever strikes his father or his mother shall be put to death" (Exodus 21:15)? Like Marcia, I find more authoritative Jesus's statement: "'Suffer the little children to come unto me.' ... And he took them up in his arms, put his hands upon them, and blessed them" (Matthew 19:13–15). That strikes me as the better way of offering firm and loving nurture and discipline of children.

Robin Fretwell Wilson, chaired professor of law at the University of Illinois, has done remarkable work over the past three decades trying to mediate claims of religious freedom and sexual liberty at a time of growing family fragility. She has warned about the dangers of abolishing traditional state marriage and family laws too quickly without providing sturdy legal protections for women, children, the elderly, and the impoverished.[71] She has also warned about the vulnerabilities of these same parties, especially children, in various faith-based family law systems that have gained attractiveness and independence as state family laws have thinned.[72] Both before and after the 2015 *Obergefell* case established the right to same-sex marriage in the United States, Robin has charted creative constitutional and political pathways to accommodate if not reconcile competing views of traditional marriage and the rapidly escalating claims of LGBTQ+ liberty. Her trio of books on point bring a variety of authors and perspectives together in creative dialogue.[73] Robin has always found time to contribute to our Center's projects and public forums and was kind enough to present me with an award for my work on family law. In the chapter herein, Robin teams up with Mariela Neagu of Oxford University to revisit the question of whether the United States gains or loses by becoming the last country in the world to ratify the 1989 UN Convention on the Rights of the Child. After rehearsing the history of the Convention, its impact in illustrative countries that have adopted it, and the main arguments against ratification by the United States, the two authors recommend ratification by the United States and concomitant legal reforms that provide much better protections and provisions for children.

---

71 See, for example, Robin Fretwell Wilson, ed., *Reconceiving the Family: Critical Reflections on the American Law Institute's Principles of the Law of Family Dissolution* (Cambridge: Cambridge University Press, 2006).

72 Robin Fretwell Wilson, "The Perils of Privatized Marriage," in Nichols, *Marriage and Divorce*, 253–83.

73 William N. Eskridge Jr. and Robin Fretwell Wilson, eds., *Religious Freedom, LGBT Rights, and the Prospects for Common Ground* (Cambridge: Cambridge University Press, 2019); Robin Fretwell Wilson, ed., *The Contested Place of Religion in Family Law* (Cambridge: Cambridge University Press, 2018); and Douglas Laycock, Anthony Picarello, and Robin Fretwell Wilson, eds., *Same-Sex Marriage and Religious Liberty* (Lanham, MD: Rowman & Littlefield, 2008).

Michael J. Broyde, a distinguished rabbi and scholar of Jewish law, has been my dear friend and collaborator for more than thirty years. We have worked intensely together to build up our Center's Abrahamic conversation on law and religion, and we have run several major projects on the fundamentals of faith, freedom, and family.[74] Michael has been like a brother to me, offering wise counsel, loving pastoral care, and valuable critique of my scholarship and administrative efforts. He has also been a wonderful bridge builder between his Jewish world and my Christian world. Michael admired my parents for resisting the Nazi occupation of the Netherlands and rescuing European Jews through the underground in World War II. He also appreciated my interest in the Hebrew Bible and Talmud and has fed me valuable sources and introduced me to wonderful scholars like David Blumenthal, David Novak, and Elliot Dorff, who have contributed vitally to our Center projects. Michael has long been involved as a judge on the Beth Din in New York, arbitrating family, commercial, and other disputes for voluntary Jewish participants. In recent years, he has defended this form of alternative dispute resolution, most notably in his pathbreaking *Sharia Tribunals, Rabbinical Courts, and Christian Panels: Religious Arbitration in America and the West* (Oxford, 2017). Since then, however, Michael shows in his chapter herein, the place of faith-based legal systems and procedures in liberal democracies has become ever more tenuous, even though corporate religious freedom and autonomy have been strengthened in recent cases both in the United States and Europe. Michael makes a strong case for both continuing and self-regulating this religious arbitration, particularly for minority religious communities whose norms and habits depart from the cultural mainstream. This is a shrewd warning for majority Christians in America today, who might soon find themselves in a comparable minority status and with a need to protect themselves in a growing secular age.

---

74 See, for example, Michael J. Broyde, "Religious Edicts, Secular Law, and the Family," *Journal of Law and Religion* 34 (2019): 496–503 (review of Witte, *Church, State, and Family*); id., "Law, Economy, and Charity," in Jürgen von Hagen et al. eds,. *The Impact of the Market on Character Formation, Ethical Education, and the Communication of Values in Late Modern Pluralistic Societies* (Leipzig: Evangelische Verlagsanstalt, 2020), 115–32; id., "The Covenant-Contract Dialectic in Jewish Marriage and Divorce Law," in Witte and Ellison, *Covenant Marriage*, 53–69; and id., "Proselytism and Jewish Law: Inreach, Outreach, and Jewish Tradition," in John Witte, Jr. and Richard C. Martin, eds., *Sharing the Book: Religious Perspectives on the Rights and Wrongs of Proselytism* (Maryknoll, NY: Orbis Books, 1999), 45–60. See also Michael J. Broyde, ed., *Marriage, Sex, and Family in Judaism* (Lanham, MD: Rowman & Littlefield, 2005); Michael Broyde and John Witte, Jr., eds., *Human Rights in Judaism: Cultural, Religious, and Political Perspectives* (New York: Jason Aronson, 1998).

Charles J. Reid, an erudite legal historian at St. Thomas Law School, is also a longstanding friend and coworker. We shared a mentor in Harold J. Berman and friendship with Judge John T. Noonan Jr., about whom Charles has written insightfully.[75] Charles has made major contributions to the history of family law and human rights, particularly in unearthing influences of medieval Catholic theological and canon law on the Western legal tradition.[76] He has been a wonderful collaborator on several of our Center's projects and contributed a number of incisive chapters to our volumes.[77] He has also been a valuable adviser to me in negotiating and translating arcane texts and topics in medieval canon law and civil law that he knows so well. Those exquisite textual skills are on full display in Charles's remarkable chapter herein on. Same-sex desire, intimacy, and relationships in the Bible and the ancient world have become highly contested topics in the past two generations, as theologians and jurists have faced the growing pressure to recognize same-sex liberties and marriages in churches and states alike. Various proof texts in the Bible and Apocrypha have been subject to intense new exegetical battles. Charles joins this heated discussion with a learned new reading of the Letter of Jude, eruditely parsing every word in this letter and comparing them to other biblical and apocryphal texts. This is a novel and innovative contribution that jurists and theologians will need to take into account.

Here, then, in these thirty-one chapters, readers are treated to exquisite illustrative treatments of many of the most pressing topics in the ever-expanding field of law-and-religion study.

– Mapping the modern field of law and religion, the various methods and disciplines employed in its cultivation and expansion, and the various institutions, fellowships, and publications that have developed for this study over the past half century;

---

75 See, for example, Charles J. Reid Jr., "John T. Noonan, Jr.: Catholic Jurist and Judge," in Dreisbach and Hall, *Great Christian Jurists in American History*, 208–29; and id., "Judge John T. Noonan, Jr. v. Joe Arpaio," *University of St. Thomas Law Journal* 17 (2022): 993–1008.

76 See, for example, Charles J. Reid Jr., *Power over the Body, Equality in the Family: Rights and Domestic Relations in Medieval Canon Law* (Grand Rapids: Eerdmans, 2004); id., "Thirteenth-Century Canon Law and Rights: The Word *Ius* and Its Range of Subjective Meanings," *Studia Canonica* 30 (1996): 295–342; and id., "The Canonistic Contribution to the Western Rights Tradition: An Historical Inquiry," *Boston College Law Review* 33 (1991): 37–92.

77 See, for example, Charles J. Reid Jr., "Thomas Aquinas (1225–1274)," in Condorelli and Domingo, *Law and the Christian Tradition in Italy*, 98–127; id., "The Rights of Children in Medieval Canon Law," in Brennan, *The Vocation of the Child*, 243–265; and Charles J. Reid Jr. and John Witte, Jr., "In the Steps of Gratian: Writing the History of Canon Law in the 1990s," *Emory Law Journal* 48 (1999); 647–88.

- Individual and corporate religious freedom: viewed in domestic, regional, and international legal systems; analyzed in historical, jurisprudential, and theological perspectives; and reflected in principles like liberty of conscience, free exercise of religion, religious pluralism and equality, separation of religion and state, and the establishment or disestablishment of religion by state law;
- Law, religion, and human rights more generally, including historical and philosophical contributions of Christian and other faiths to the cultivation and abridgement of various rights and liberties; the interactions of religious rights and other claims of liberty and the means of brokering conflicts; and the protection of specific rights of spouses, parents, and children sometimes by, and sometimes against, religious and state authorities;
- The law and theology of "mixed institutions," particularly marital families but also schools and charities, each with spiritual and temporal dimensions and each subject to the contesting jurisdictional claims of churches, states, and the parties within each of these primal institutions;
- Church law and other faith-based legal systems, and their foundational roles in the development of the Western legal tradition; their structural role in building religious communities and bolstering their claims to religious autonomy; their bridging role in building interdenominational, if not interfaith dialogue, cooperation, and common causes for the common good; and their adjudicative role in brokering disputes among the voluntary faithful;
- The influences of theology and religious ideas on law and legal thought: their shaping influence on canon law, civil law, and common law systems historically and today; and their vital contributions to many fundamental questions concerning the nature, purpose, and uses of law and authority, the mandates and limits of rule and obedience, the rights and duties of officials and subjects, the care and nurture of the needy and innocent, the justice and limits of war and violence, the nature of fault and the means of punishing it, the sources of obligations and the procedures for vindicating them, the origins of property and the means of protecting it, the dignity and equality of all human beings, and the balance of justice and equity, law and love.

Many other sectors of the field of law and religion have also commanded scholarly attention of late: natural law theory; comparative legal and religious professionalism; comparative hermeneutics and semiotics in parsing authoritative legal and religious texts; the roles of religious and moral arguments in secular law; and the place of ritual and ceremony in the enactment of law and politics. Christian and Jewish scholars have been among the leaders in this study in the past half century, but happily there are growing scholarly guilds studying law and religion in Islam, Buddhism, Hinduism, Confucianism, and various Indigenous traditions, too. Scholars from these various religious and legal traditions have already learned a great deal from each other and have cooperated in developing richer understandings of sundry legal, religious, and political subjects. This comparative and cooperative interreligious inquiry into fundamental issues of law, politics, and society needs to continue—especially in our day of increasing interreligious conflict and misunderstanding, and especially as the world struggles to discover proper, responsible, and effective legal constraints on religious fundamentalism and extremism.

What a blessing it has been to be part of this global enterprise. I have been privileged to work with tens of thousands of scholars, fellows, students, readers, and audience members around the world, and to publish with wonderful editors at Cambridge, Oxford, Columbia, Eerdmans, Routledge, Westminster John Knox, Mohr Siebeck, Evangelische Verlagsanstalt, Chr. Kaiser, China Legal Publishing House, and other presses. My colleagues and I have been tremendously blessed by several foundations that have entrusted us with their generous benefaction—most notably the McDonald Agape Foundation, The Pew Charitable Trusts, the Lilly Endowment, the Ford Foundation, the Henry Luce Foundation, and the John Templeton Foundation, and several generous individual benefactors, notably Dorothy Beasley, Jean Bergmark, Charlotte McDaniel, Cary Maguire, Gonzalo Rodriguez-Fraile, and Brent Savage.

Little of this work in law and religion would have been possible without the rock-solid support and encouragement of the Emory University leadership, particularly in the early years. I am especially grateful to our Center founders President James T. Laney and Professor Frank S. Alexander, both still beloved friends today. Way back in 1982, the two of them established a prototype program in law and religion, and then persuaded Hal Berman to move from Harvard to Emory in 1985. I came as Berman's research fellow and was appointed two years later as program director and then as law professor. Early on, Frank, Hal, and I collaborated closely to build up the work in law and religion with Jim Laney's blessing and support, and with several early foundation grants. In those early years, we also had vital support from successor Emory presidents William M. Chace and James W. Wagner, provosts Billy E. Frye and Rebecca S. Chopp, as well as stalwart deans Howard O. Hunter, Thomas C. Arthur, and Robert A. Schapiro in the Law School, and deans James L. Waits, Kevin R. LaGree, Russell E. Richey, and Jan Love in the Theology School. Several core Emory faculty have also been essential allies over the years, especially Emory colleagues and friends Robert Ahdieh, Abdullahi An-Na'im, Thomas C.

Arthur, David Bederman, David Blumenthal, Robert Franklin, Rich Freer, Jon Gunnemann, Peter Hay, Mark D. Jordan, Michael Perry, Brent Strawn, Steven M. Tipton, and Johan van der Vyver, plus the Emory contributors to this volume: Michael Broyde, Rafael Domingo, Christy Green, Gary Hauk, Timothy Jackson, and Philip Reynolds.[78]

What makes organizations like our Center for the Study of Law and Religion thrive are the professionals who work behind the scenes, often harried and unheralded, but vital to the effort. My wife, Eliza Ellison, remarkably, carried much of the Center's administrative load on her own for more than a decade before the powerful trio of April Bogle, Anita Mann, and Amy Wheeler joined us in 2000. Amy has been with the Center since then and has become my indispensable chief of staff. We had wonderful new colleagues join us in key administrative leadership over the years, including Silas Allard, John Bernau, Christy Green, Justin Latterell, Shlomo Pill, Audra Savage, and Sara Toering. Our Center's new executive director, Whittney Barth, appointed in 2022, has already taken superb command of the daily administration, much to my relief and admiration.

What makes life worth living, however, is above all a loving, faithful family. I was much blessed to have wonderful parents, John and Gertie Witte, who met in the underground during the Nazi occupation of the Netherlands and later emigrated to Canada, with shirts on their backs, two suitcases in hand, and their first baby in their arms. By dint of hard work and deep faith, they built a beautiful life in our simple home, marked by piety, discipline, industry, sacrifice, loyalty, love, hospitality, gratitude, humor, and joy—virtues and values that they instilled in all their children. I was also much blessed to have three wonderful older sisters Ria, Gertie, and Jane, and their eventual spouses, Obie, John, and Norm, and all their children and grandchildren. Our family adopted a lovely but severely handicapped brother, Robert, who died in 1980 at the age of sixteen. My adult life has been overwhelmingly blessed by the love of my life, Eliza, our two wonderful daughters, Hope and Alison, their loving husbands, Justin and Samuel, and our five wonderful grandchildren, Baylor, Alina, Jubilee, Elet, and Gemma. Family and faith have always come first in my life. I would not be who or what I am today without the love of my family and the love of a gracious God who has blessed us all so richly. May it long continue!

---

78 For this early history, see Hauk, *Forty Years of Law and Religion at Emory;* and John Witte, Jr., "A Tribute to Frank S. Alexander," *Journal of Law and Religion* 35 (2020): 193–97.

Index of Scriptural References

- This index includes references to Old and New Testaments Bible books and verses, deuterocanonical books/apocrypha, and Old Testament pseudepigrapha.
- Old and New Testament Bible books are listed in canonical order.
- Page references in **bold type** indicate a more in-depth treatment.

Old Testament

Genesis
  1:27   36, 219, 552
  1:28   49, 163
  2–   149
  2:16–17   219, 482
  2:20–25   163
  3:1–6   482
  3:1–7   219
  6:1–2   627
  8:21–9:17   154
  8:21–22   154
  8:22   158
  9:1   163
  9:6   155
  9:7   163
  9:8–9   154
  9:10   154
  9:13   154
  9:17   154
  12–   154
  14–   152
  14:8–16   152
  14:21   152
  14:22–24   152
  15–16–   154
  15:17   160
  16:2   49
  18–19–   152
  19–   633
  19:1   623
  19:2–3   623
  19:4–5   623
  19:4–8   633
  19:7–8   623
  19:9   624
  19:11   624
  19:15–17   624
  19:24–25   624
  19:28   624
  20   155, 160, 162
  20:3–7   160
  20:9   160
  20:11   160
  21   155, 156, 157, 162
  21:22–23   161
  21:23–24   154
  21:23   156
  21:25–31   156
  21:31–32   154
  21:31   161
  21:33   161
  24:27   219
  26–   155, 156, 157
  26:28–31   154
  26:29   156

Exodus   223
  1:17   161
  15:11–13   218–219
  15:13   219
  18–19–   361
  18:21   161
  19:5   156
  19:6   361
  20–23–   138
  20:1–4   219
  20:22–21:11   142
  21:1–11   141
  21:12–14   139
  21:15   667
  21:23–25   139
  22:20–23:12   141
  22:20   156
  23:13ff.   142

Leviticus
  19.2   219, 223

Deuteronomy 156
  6:5–7 547
  6:6–7 515, 515n1
  6:24–25 515, 515n2
  25:17–18 162
  25:17–19 161

Joshua
  2:4–12 221
  24:2 160

1 Samuel
  2–4– 553
  5:3 156
  8:7 362
  17– 493

1 Kings
  11:17 156

1 Chronicles
  11:3 156

2 Chronicles
  15:12–14 156
  15:13 156
  23:3 156
  23:16 156

Job
  10:12 219

Psalms
  8:2 554
  9:7–9 220
  9:18 220
  33 220
  42:8 221
  146:6–9 220
  146:10 220

Proverbs 562
  3:11–12 559
  13:24 666
  22:6 515, 515n3
  22:15 550

Isaiah 220
  1:9–23 628
  1:16–17 540–541
  1:17 628
  1:22 628
  1:23 628
  1:24 628
  5:5–6 413
  16:5 221
  42:6 222
  51:6 220
  51:8 220
  54:13 541n2
  63:7 219

Jeremiah
  23:14 628

Ezekiel
  16:49–50 628
  36:27 489

Daniel
  1– 483
  1:8 483, 484
  1:9 483
  1:10 483
  3– 484
  3:17 484
  3:18 484
  3:27 484
  3:28 484
  6– 484
  12:13 221

Hosea
  6:6 221

Joel
  2:28–32 554
  3– 146, 147

Micah
  3:11 221

Malachi
  2:14 149

New Testament

Matthew 621
  5:13–16 223

INDEX OF SCRIPTURAL REFERENCES 675

Matthew (*cont.*)
   5:32   624
   8:32   625
   9:19   624
   11:23–24   628–629, 629n74
   11:29   557
   13:24–30   367
   16:18–19   157
   18:1–5   555
   18:6   555
   19–14–   555
   19:13–15   667
   19:16–22   222
   21:15   554
   22:21   26
   23:23   136, 137, 138, 140, 143
   25:45   177
   26:52   340
   27:46   227
   28:19   35

Mark   621
   3:14   557
   3:25   425n27
   9:37   555
   9:42   555
   10:8   625
   10:13–16   553
   12:17   26
   12:30–31   555
   16:18   620

Luke
   6:27   557
   6:40   558
   10:25–28   165, 165n1
   10:29   165, 165n2
   10:31–38   166
   14:23   364
   14:28   497
   17:2   555
   17:28–30   628–629, 629n74
   20:24   26
   22:24   227

John
   1:14   625
   6:51   625
   6:54–56   232
   6:66   624
   8:32   299, 299n37
   11:25   223
   11:43   485
   13:34   172
   14:6   299n35, n40
   14:26   490
   15:18   496
   16:13   299, 299n36
   18:37   299, 299n38
   18:38   299, 299n39

Acts   369
   2–   146, 147
   2:17   554

Romans
   1:23   619, 619n22
   1:24–27   619
   2:14–15   486
   2:20   145
   3:9–10   562
   3:20   230
   3:23–24   231
   5:12   562
   7:12   145
   7:14   145
   8:2   145
   9–11   137
   13   337, 362, 363, 371
   13:1–2   341
   13:4   157, 493

1 Corinthians
   1:9   558
   4:4   487–488
   6:9–10   619
   13:6   299n40
   15:56   145

2 Corinthians
   3:18   489

Galatians
   3:10   186
   3:24   186
   3:26–27   559
   3:27–28   78
   5–   490
   5:18–21   490
   5:18   490
   5:22–23   488, 490, 559

Galatians (*cont.*)
   5:25   490
   6:1   559
   6:2   222

Ephesians
   4:11   157
   5:22–33   163
   5:24–25   78
   5:32   665
   6:4   550, 556, 558

Philippians
   1:29   496
   4:8   82

Colossians
   3:12   559
   3:14   559
   3:21   558–559

1 Thessalonians
   4:1–7   221

1 Timothy
   1:9–10   619*n*21
   4:2   487

2 Timothy
   1:7   559
   3:16   559

Titus
   1:8   559

Hebrews   559–560
   12:5–9   559

1 Peter
   1:2   489
   1:13–16   221
   3–   488

2 Peter
   6–7   620

1 John
   4:19   234

Jude   621–622, 623–625, 631
   1   620
   4   621
   7   620, 623, **632–638**
   6   626, 626*n*62, 632, 633, 633*n*102, 637
   8   621, 637
   9   637
   11   621
   16   621

Revelation
   9–   359, 364

Deuterocanonical books/ apocrypha

Sirach
   10:6   628
   16:8–9   628
   19:13   628

Old Testament Pseudepigrapha

1 Enoch   622, 626–627, 637
   6–   627
   6:5   627*n*69
   7:1   627
   7:2   627
   7:4   627
   7:6   627
   8:1   627
   8:2   627
   10:4–25   627

Jubilees   630
   20:5   629

Testaments of the Twelve Patriarchs

Testament of Benjamin, 9:1   630

Testament of Gad, 7:1   630

Testament of Levi, 14:6   630

Testament of Moses/Assumption of Moses   622

Testament of Naphtali
   3:2   630

3:5   630
4:1   630

Testament of Reuben (Old Testament Pseudepigrapha/Testaments of the Twelve Patriarchs)
   5:1   630, 630n83
   5:6   630

Index of Titles

— Page references in **bold type** indicate a more in-depth treatment.

Ad conditorem (papal bill, Nicholas III)   61
America (Jesuit journal)   618
American Freedom and Catholic Power (Paul Blanshard)   402
Anchor Bible Commentary on Jude (Bo Reicke, Jerome Neyrey)   621
Antitribonien ou discours d'un grand et renomme iurisconsulte de notre temps sur l'estude des loix (François Hotman)   262, 265
Apology (John Jewel)   244
The Art of Happiness: A Handbook for Living (Dalai Lama)   127

The Best Love of the Child: Being Loved and Being Taught to Love as the First Human Right (Timothy Jackson)   129
Biblia Americana (Cotton Mather)   358–359, 361, 364, 367, 658
A Bill Establishing a Provision for Teachers of the Christian Religion (Patrick Henry)   371
The Blessings of Liberty: Human Rights and Religious Freedom in the Western Legal Tradition (John Witte, Jr.)   14, 51, **53, 54, 55, 65–66**, 119, 194*n*54, 195
Book of Common Prayer (1662)   244
Brethren Dwelling in Unity (Cotton Mather)   366
Brill Research Perspectives on Law and Religion (series)   644
The Broadman Bible Commentary (Clifton J. Allen)   633

Cambridge Studies in Law and Christianity Series   13, 25, 32, 482, 644
Canones Apostolorum   253
The Canopy Forum (online journal, CSLR)   25, 130
A Christian Europe: Passages of Exploration (Joseph Weiler)   144
Christianity and Democracy in Global Context (John Witte, Jr.)   27, 118
Christianity and Family Law (John Witte, Jr., Gary Hauk)   26–27, 29, 642

Christianity and Global Law (John Witte, Jr., Rafael Domingo)   27, 641
"Christianity and Human Rights: Past Contributions and Future Challenges" (John Witte, Jr., Justin Latterell)   293*n*12
Christianity and Human Rights (John Witte, Jr., Frank Alexander)   28, 45–46
Christianity and Law: An Introduction (John Witte, Jr., Frank Alexander)   28, 122
Christianity and the Laws of Conscience (Jeffrey B. Hammond, Helen M. Alvaré)   482, 664
Christianity, Social Tolerance, and Homosexuality (John Boswell)   634–635
Chronica (Philipp Melanchthon, Johannes Carion)   255
The Church: Towards a Common Vision (World Council of Churches, Faith and Order Commission). *See* Common Vision
Church, State, and Family: Reconciling Traditionala Teachings and Modern Liberties (John Witte, Jr.)   15, 29, 51, 55, 77, 82, 87, 105, 108, 574
Commentaria in consuetudines ductus Burgundiae (Barthélemy de Chasseneuz)   264
Commentaries on the Constitution (Joseph Story)   419, 420
Commentarii in consuetudines parisienses (Charles Dumoulin)   264–265
Commentary on the Psalms (John Calvin)   337
Commentary on Romans (John Calvin)   336
Common Vision (Faith and Order Commission, World Council of Churches)   11, 272
  on church membership   275
  on church property and finance   281–282
  on church, state, and society   282–283
  on doctrine and worship   278–279
  on ecclesiastical governance   277
  on ecumenical relations   280–281

INDEX OF TITLES 679

on ordained ministry 276
on principles of Christian law 283–286
purpose and mission of 273–274, 275
on religious freedom 282–283
on rites of passage 279–280
Confessio Augustana 253
Corpus iuris canonici 40, 45, 257, 263, 266
  See also canon law [Index of Subjects]
Corpus iuris civilis 257, 262, 266, 507
Critique of Practical Reason (Immanuel Kant) 224
Critique of Pure Reason (Immanuel Kant) 224

Declaration of Gentlemen (Cotton Mather) 355–357, 363
Decretum Gratiani 252, 254, 263
De Dignitate Hominis (Pico della Mirandola) 312
Defensio interpretum iuris civilis (Bonifacius Amerbach) 261
De Institutionae historiae universae (François Baudouin) 269
De iure belli ac pacis libri tres (Hugo Grotius) 268
De laudibus legum Angliæ (John Fortescue) 246
De origine iuris Germanici (Hermann Conring) 268
De sacris Ecclesiae ministeriis & beneficiis libri octo (François Le Douaren) 264
Dictatus Papae (Gregory VII) 267
Didache 287
Digest of Roman Law (Justinian I) 467
A Discourse Concerning Unlimited Submission and Non-Resistance to the Highest Powers (Jonathan Mayhew) 371
A Dissertation on the Canon and Feudal Laws (John Adams) 371

Ecclesiae Gallicanae in schismate status (Pierre Pithou) 264
Ecclesiastical Law Journal 13, 644, 662
Eleutheria (Cotton Mather) 359, 365, 368
The Embarrassment of Riches (Simon Schama) 55–56
Emory Studies in Law and Religion (series) 13
Enchiridion christianae institutionis (Johann Gropper) 510

"The English Lawyer" (John Dodderidge) 247
The Equal Regard Family and Its Friendly Critics (John Witte, Jr. et al.) 82
Essential Rights and Liberties of Protestants (Elisha Williams) 371
Eudemian Ethics (Aristotle) 218
Exiit (papal bull, Nicholas III) 60, 61
Exsurge Domine (papal bull, 12 December 1520) 252

Faith, Freedom, and Family: New Essays on Law and Religion (John Witte, Jr.) 17–18, 48, 51, 55, 120, 642
Faith and Order: The Reconciliation of Law and Religion (Harold Berman) 137–138
Family Transformed: Religion, Values, and Society in American Life (John Witte, Jr., Steven Tipton) 77, 81
Foundations of Modern Political Thought (Quentin Skinner) 340n55, 342
Francogallia (François Hotman) 265, 343
From Sacrament to Contract (John Witte, Jr.) 14, 29, 55, 71–72, 76, **615–616**

Georgia Gazette 384, 389
God's Joust, God's Justice (John Witte, Jr.) 14, 51, 55
Groundwork of the Metaphysics of Morals (Immanuel Kant) 223–224

The History of the Common Law of England (Matthew Hale) 242
Homosexuality and the Western Christian Tradition (Derrick Sherwin Bailey) 633–634
How Marriage Became One of the Sacraments: The Sacramental Theology of Marriage from its Medieval Origins to the Council of Trent (Philip Reynolds) 128, 501, 665

Institutes of the Christian Religion (John Calvin) 171–172, 337
The Interaction of Law and Religion (Harold Berman) 116
The Interpreter's Bible (Abingdon Press) 632

Jerome Biblical Commentary (Thomas W. Leahy) 633, 634

Journal of Church and State 13
Journal of Law and Religion 13, 25, 123, 124, 127, 290
The Judgments of God upon the Roman Church (Drue Cressener) 359

Ein kurtzer und nützlicher Process ("A short and useful trial," Joachim Gregorii von Pritzen) 259

Law and Language: Effective Symbols of Community (Harold Berman) 39–40
Law and Protestantism: The Legal Teachings of the Lutheran Reformation (John Witte, Jr.) 14, 28, 55
Law and Revolution (Harold Berman) 39, 116, 663
Laws of Ecclesiastical Polity (Richard Hooker) 244, 248n60, 412
The Laws (Plato) 215
The Legal Teachings of the Lutheran Tradition (John Witte, Jr.) 55
Leges Visigothorum (Pithou) 266
Legum Romanarum et mosaicarum collation 263
"Letter from Birmingham Jail" (Martin Luther King Jr.) 201–202
Liber Sextus 263
Les libertez de l'eglise gallicane (Pierre Pithou) 263–264
Loci communes (Philipp Melanchthon) 258

Magnalia Christi Americana (Cotton Mather) 360
Malachi (Cotton Mather) 369
Manuductio ad Ministerium (Cotton Mather) 368–369
Marriage, Religion, and Law in the Western Tradition (John Witte, Jr.) 55
Marriage in the Western Church: The Christianization of Marriage During the Patristic and Early Medieval Periods (Philip Reynolds) 128, 665
Methodus ad facilem historiarum cognitionem (Jean Bodin) 269
"The Mode of Education, Proper in a Republic" (Benjamin Rush) 422
Modern Christian Teachings on Law, Politics, and Human Nature (John Witte, Jr., Frank Alexander) 122

The Morality of Adoption: Social-Psychological, Theological and Legal Perspectives (Timothy Jackson) 129
Mordecai Would Not Bow Down: Anti-Semitism, the Holocaust, and Christian Supersessionism (Timothy Jackson) 129

The New Dare to Discipline (James Dobson) 549
A New Reformation of Rights: Calvinist Contributions to Modern Human Rights (John Witte, Jr.) 51
New York Times 599
The Nicomachean Ethics (Aristotle) 217
Ninety-Five Theses (Martin Luther) 241

"Obligation: A Jewish Jurisprudence of the Social Order" (Robert Cover) 64
Odyssey (Homer) 625
On Charity & Justice (John Witte, Jr.) 181
Oxford Dictionary of National Biography 633
The Oxford Handbook on Christianity and Law (John Witte, Jr., Rafael Domingo) 29–30, 641
Oxford Journal of Law and Religion 663

Paraphrase and Notes on the Epistles of St. Paul (John Locke) 362–363
Parentator (Cotton Mather) 366–367, 368
Poetics (Aristotle) 56
Political Theology (journal) 290
The Power of Giving Law to the Consciences of Men in Disputable Matters (Cotton Mather) 364
The Principles of Canon Law Common to the Churches of the Anglican Communion (Anglican Communion Legal Advisors Network) 284

Quo elongati (papal bill, Gregory IX) 60

Ratio Disciplinae (Cotton Mather) 369
The Reformation of Rights: Law, Religion, and Human Rights in Early Modern Calvinism (John Witte, Jr.) 14, 28, 51, 55, 351
Religion and the American Constitutional Experiment (John Witte, Jr. et al.) 51, 55, 123, 351, 659, 662, 663

INDEX OF TITLES

Religious Human Rights in Global Perspective (John Witte, Jr. et al.)   118
Rights of Magistrates (Theodore Beza)   344
Routledge Series on Law and Religion   25, 32, 644

Sachsenspiegel ("Mirror of the Saxons," Eike von Repgow)   257–259, 260
Scriptum (Thomas Aquinas)   508, 509
Sentences (Peter Lombard)   503, 508, 511
Sex, Marriage, and Family in John Calvin's Geneva (John Witte, Jr., Robert Kingdom)   28, 55, 616
Sex, Marriage, and Family in the World Religions (John Witte, Jr. et al.)   79–80
The Sins of the Fathers: The Law and Theology of Illegitimacy Reconsidered (John Witte, Jr.)   14–15, 24, 29, 55, 75, 82, 616–617
Small Catechism (Martin Luther)   564–565
Statement of Principles of Christian Law Common to the Component Churches (Panel of Experts in Christian Law)   283, 285–286
Summa contra gentiles (Thomas Aquinas)   507
Summa Theologiae (Thomas Aquinas)   242, 508
Supplementum (to *Summa Theologiae*, Thomas Aquinas)   509

The Teachings of Modern Christianity on Law, Politics, and Human Nature (John Witte, Jr.)   32
Theogony (Hesiod)   625
"'There but for the Grace': The Ethics of Bystanders to Divorce" (M. Christian Green)   170
To Have and to Hold: Marrying and Its Documentation in Western Christendom, 400–1600 (John Witte Jr., Philip Reynolds)   72, 83, 127, 501, 665
Toward an Islamic Reformation: Civil Liberties, Human Rights and International Law (Abdullahi Ahmed An-Naim)   120
Treatise of the Nature of Laws in General and Touching the Nature of Law (Matthew Hale)   242
Two Treatises on Government (John Locke)   363
The Tyranny of Merit (Michael Sandel)   320

Vindication of Liberty against Tyrants (Philippe Mornay)   344, 347

War Against the Idols (Carlos Eire)   340n55
War and Peace (Leo Tolstoy)   617
The Western Case for Monogamy over Polygamy (John Witte, Jr.)   15, 29, 48–49, 55, 200, 617
"What Christianity Offers to the World of Law" (John Witte, Jr.)   38
What's Wrong with Children's Rights? (Martin Guggenheim)   574

Yale Law Journal   599, 603

Index of Persons

- The Index of Persons includes names of persons and human characters. Deities and other nonhuman beings are included in the Index of Subjects.
- Page references in **bold type** indicate a more in-depth treatment of the person.

Abbott, Lyman   124
Abednego (Jewish man in Book of Daniel)   483, 484
Abimelech (King of Gerar)
   covenants with Abraham and Isaac   **154–156**, 157, 159, 160, 161
   fear of God   160–161, 162
   taking Sarah   160, 162n27
Abraham   49, 162n27
   Abrahamic covenant   92, 160
   covenant with Abimelech (King of Gerar)   **154–156**, 157, 159, 160, 161
   king of Sodom/Sodom and   152, 623
   See also Lot
Ackerman, Bruce   211
Adam and Eve   479, 482–483, 485, 486, 497
Adams, John (President of the United States, 1797–1801)   32
   on Jefferson   397
   proclamation of days of prayer, fasting, and thanksgiving   391, 398
   on religion and moral citizenry as basis for freedom and successful republics   416–417, 418, 419, 422, 423, 424, 433
   on resistance against tyrants   371
   on slender church establishment   416, 418, 433
Aetios, Fr. (Dimitrios Nikiforos, Grand Ecclesiarch, Ecumenical Patriarchate of Constantinople)   286
Albertus Magnus   507
Alexander III (pope, r. 1159–1181)   502
Alexander, Frank   28, 32, 115–116, 122, 196, 671
Alito, Justice Samuel   477–478
Allard, Silas W.   123, 672
Almain, Jacques   331
Alsted, Johann Heinrich   241
Althusius, Johannes   32, 33, 89
   on integrative jurisprudence   440

   on political covenants   151
   on "symbiotic association"   92–93, 110
Alvaré, Helen   295, 646
Ambrose of Milan, Saint   467n28
Amerbach, Bonifacius   261
Amos, Andrew   246
Amos (prophet)   117
Andros, Sir Edmund (Governor of the Dominion of New England, 1674–1863)   355, 356, 357, 360
An-Naim, Abdullahi Ahmed   119–120, 125, 663
Anne (Queen of Great Britain and Ireland, r. 1702–1714)   357, 365
Apel, Johann   43
Aristotle
   on friendship   211
   on happiness   216–217, 222
   on marriage   507
   on relation between law and faith   214, 215–218, 222, 233
   as source of inspiration for 13th and 14th century theologians   503, 507
   as source of inspiration in common law   241–242, 247, 248n60
   on storylines in fiction   56
   on virtue   215
Asa (King of Judah, r. c. 913–873 BCE)   156
Atkinson, Maggie   577–578n52
Augustine, Saint   32, 246
   on law/justice and loves   193, 211
   on reason and revelation   248
   on sacraments   506, 507
   on unjust law   201
Austin, John   198, 199, 200, 492–493

Backus, Isaac   417, 418
Bacon, Roger   242
Bailey, Derrick Sherwin   633–634
Balaam   621
Baldus de Ubaldis   261
Bancroft, George   420

INDEX OF PERSONS 683

Baron, François-Éguinaire 262
Barrett, Justice Amy Coney 458
Bartholomew I (Archbishop of
    Constantinople, Ecumenical
    Patriarch, 1991–present) 271,
    283, 286
Barth, Whittney 130, 672
Bartolus de Saxoferrato 261
Bauckham, Richard 622, 635
Baudouin, François 265, 269
Becket, Saint Thomas (Archbishop of
    Canterbury, 1162–1170) 467
Becon, Thomas 84
Beecher, Lyman 421
Bellah, Robert 126
Bell, Derrick 297, 301
Berman, Harold
    on "communification" 213
    law and religion scholarship of,
        on integrative jurisprudence 34, 440
        on interaction/relation between law
            and religion 7, 22, 116, 309
        legal historical method 138
        on "weightier matters of the
            law" 136, 137, 138, 143
    as mentor of and source of inspiration
        for JW 4–5, 18, 116, 136, 615,
        639, 671
    publications on scholarship of 33, 50
    on purpose of human law 234
    religious background 37, 137
    scholarly career and reputation 116, 137,
        647–648
    sources of inspiration 4
    works 39–40, 116, 136, 663
Bernau, John 130, 131, 672
Bernstein, Anita 125
Berryman, Jerome W. 550n30
Beza, Theodore
    on church-state separation 93
    on covenants 151, 345, 346
    on First and Second Table
        violations 344, 346
    on protection of people's rights by
        governments 345, 356
    on right of self-defense and
        revolution 343, 344, 345, 346,
        347, 349
    as source of inspiration for JW 32, 89

Black, Justice Hugo L. 395, 402
Blackstone, William 32, 247, 520n39
Blair, Tony (Prime Minister of the United
    Kingdom, 1997–2007) 477
Blanshard, Paul 402
Blumenthal, David 119, 125, 668, 672
Bodin, Jean 269, 327, 343, 469
Boehmer, Justus Henning 254, 259
Bohatec, Josef 336
Bonhoeffer, Dietrich 145–146
Boniface (pope, r. 607) 359
Bonny, Johan (Bishop of Antwerp, 2009–
    present) 618
Borgia, Cesare 226
Bosson, Justice Richard C. 493n24
Boswell, John 634–635
Bracton, Henry de 245
Bradstreet, Simon 360
Brady, Kathleen A. 461n15, 665–666
Braid, Lord Peter **463–466**, 476
Brandeis, Justice Louis D. 575
Bray, Samuel 652–653
Brennan, Patrick McKinley 193, 651–652
Brewbaker, William 185, 193, 651–652
Browning, Don S. 28, 125, 168, 170, 171, 501,
    639, 650, 666
Brown, Robert E. 363, 363n20
Broyde, Michael J. 119, 125, 668, 672
Brunnemann, Johannes 268
Brunner, Emile 32
Bucer, Martin 84
Bugenhagen, Johannes 251
Bulloch, Archibald 386
Bunge, Marcia J. 666–667
Burgh, James 413
Burnet, Gilbert 246
Bush, George W. (President of the United
    States, 2001–2009) 180

Caiaphas (Jewish high priest) 485–486
Cain 621
Cal
Calamy, Edmund 366
Callender, Elisha 354
Calvin, John
    on bystander ethics 171–172
    as Christian jurist 31
    on church and state 93, 338–339
    contradictions in thought 42

Calvin, John (*cont.*)
    educational background   336, 336*n*36
    on equity   336–337, 338
    on First and Second Table enforcement
        and violations   338, 339, 342
    on marriage   78, 150, 616
    on natural law   91, 336–337
    on natural reason   337–338
    on natural rights   336, 343, 349
    political involvement   42, 338
    on religious freedom and human
        rights   41–42
    on representative governments vs.
        monarchies   338–339, 341
    on revolution   338, 341, 342, 343
    on right of self-defense   335–336,
        340–341, 343, 349
    on sin   187, 187*n*18
    sources of inspiration   336, 336*n*36, 337,
        338, 339, 340*n*55
    works by JW/JW on   32, 33, 41–42
    on worthy and unworthy poor   177
    See also Calvinism/Calvinists [Index of
        Subjects]
Campbell, Alexander   421
Cantiuncula, Claudius (Claude
    Chansonette)   261
Capito, Wolfgang   43
Carden, Michael   631
Cardozo, Justice Benjamin   414, 612
Carion, Johannes   255
Carter, Jimmy (President of the United States,
    1977–1981)   27, 31, 114, 117, 118,
    121, 129, 642
Carter, Stephen L.   405–406
Catherine of Siena, Saint   31
Cavadini, John   236, 247, 248
Ceausescu, Nicolae (President of Romania,
    1974–1989)   580
Chansonette, Claude (Claudius
    Cantiuncula)   261
Chaplin, Jonathan   471*n*39, 647
Chapman, Nathan   662
Charles I (King of England and Ireland, r.
    1625–1649)   356
Charles II (King of England, Scotland, and
    Ireland, r. 1660–1685)   352, 354
Charles V (Holy Roman Emperor, r. 1519–
    1556)   335

Chase, Justice Samuel   202
Chasseneuz, Barthélemy de
    (Chassaneus)   264
Chopp, Rebecca S.   121, 671
Chrysostom, Saint John   32
Cicero   507
Clarendon, Earl of (Edward Hyde)   246
Clinton, Bill (President of the United States,
    1993–2001)   179, 181
Clovis (King of the Franks, r. 481–511)   265
Cohen, Leslie   119
Coke, Sir Edward   32, 237, 238, 238*n*18, 245,
    246, 247
Cole, Gerald   471
Coleman, Major   124
Coler, Matthias   259
Colwell, Ernest Cadman   115
Connan, Francois de   262
Conring, Hermann   259, 267–268
Constantine the Great (Roman Emperor, r.
    306–337)   359, 411
Cooper, J. F.   352
Cotton, John   354, 367
Cover, Robert   64–65
Cranmer, Thomas   32, 243*n*39
Cressener, Drue   359
Cujas, Jacques   260*n*35, 262
Cyprian, Saint   553

Dailey, Anne   524*n*69, 527*n*100
Dalai Lama   114, 126–127, 642
Daniel (prophet)   342, **483–485**
Darius (King of Babylon)   484
David (King of Israel, fl. c. 1000 BCE)   156,
    362, 553, 617
Delos, Joseph T.   471
Delsol, Chantal   310
Deneen, Patrick   319
Descartes, René   62
De Young, James   636
Dobson, James   549
Dodderidge, Sir John   247
Doe, Norman
    on church law   287, 643–644, 654, 662
    works/editorships   25, 28, 29, 32, 48
    workshops   286
Domingo, Rafael   112, 122, 131, 641–642, 644
Domitian (Roman emperor, r. 81–96)   621
Dooyeweerd, Herman   5, 18, 32, 111, 179

INDEX OF PERSONS 685

Dorff, Elliot   668
Dreisbach, Daniel L.   660–661
Dumoulin, Charles   260n35, 263, 264–265
Duns Scotus, John   58, 241
Dupré, Catherine   312–313
Dürig, Günter   143
Durrant, Joan E.   544–545n18
Dwight, Timothy   421

Eberlin von Günzburg, Johann   43
Edward VI (King of England and Ireland, r. 1547–1553)   360
Eike von Repgow   257–258
Einstein, Albert   31
Eire, Carlos   340n55
Eisermann, Johannes   47n26, 174–175
Ellesmere, Lord Chancellor (Thomas Egerton)   239, 247
Ellis, Henry (Governor of Georgia, 1758–1760)   384–385
Elshtain, Jean Bethke   27, 126, 168, 172–173, 639
Epicurus   625
Erasmus, Desiderius   261
Eustachius a Sancto Paulo (Eustache Asseline)   241
Eve. *See* Adam and Eve
Ezekiel (prophet)   149

Fielding, Henry   617
Fields, Weston   630, 631
Figgis, John Neville   471
Fineman, Martha   125, 128
Finnis, John   491n20–21
Fivush, Robyn   125
Flavius Josephus   631–632
Floyd, George   140
Foege, William   129
Foster, Frances Smith   125
Foucault, Michel   169
Francisco, Clyde T.   633n100
Francis (pope, r. 2013–present)
  on canon/church law   272, 286
  on family   547
  on homosexuality   618–619, 619n20
Francis, Saint   60
Frey, Jörg   621–622, 635
Frink, Samuel   383–384, 384n67,n71, 385
Fukuyama, Francis   316

Fuller, Millard   128

Gagnon, Robert A. J.   636
Gaius   258
Gallaudet, Thomas   421
Gandhi, Mahatma   303, 304
Garfield, James A.   431
Garnett, Richard   123, 440
Gelasius I (pope, 492–496)   466
Genovese, Kitty   171
George II (King of Great Britain and Ireland, r. 1727–1760)   378, 380, 381
Gershom ben Judah, Rabbi   49
Gerson, Jean   241, 331, 333
Gierke, Otto   471–472
Gingrich, Newt   179
Ginsburg, Justice Ruth Bader   458
Glendon, Mary Ann   167n4, 183
Godefroy, Denis   262
Göde, Henning   253
Goldfeder, Mark   131
Goodman, Christopher   151
Goodman, Lenn E.   300–301
Gorsuch, Justice Neil   477–478
Grafton, Anthony   240n26
Gratian   32, 252–253, 254, 262
Greenawalt, Kent   126
Greenberg, Steven   629
Greene, Jamal   203–204, 206
Green, M. Christian (Christy)   124, 125, 650–651
Gregory I (Gregory the Great, pope, r. 590–604)   507
Gregory VII (pope, r. 1073–1085)   267, 467
Gregory IX (pope, r. 1227–1241)   60
Gropper, Johann   510
Grosseteste, Robert (Bishop of Lincoln, 1235–1253)   242
Grossi, Paolo   309
Grotius, Hugo   32, 245
  on canon law   44
  on natural law   47, 268, 469
Grumbach, Argula von   43
Guggenheim, Martin   574
Gunnemann, Jon   228, 672
Gunther, John   622
Gunton, Colin   212
Gyatso, Tenzin (14th Dalai Lama)   114, 126–127, 642

Habermas, Jürgen 25, 293, 324
Hadrian VI (pope, r. 1522–1523) 509
Hagar (wife of Abraham) 49
Hale, Sir Matthew 237, 242, 246, 247
Hall, David 352
Haller, Tobias 636n127
Hallett, Charlene 557n40
Hamburger, Philip 441
Hamilton, Alexander 420
Hammond, Jeffrey B. 663–664
Hampshire, Stuart 209
Hampton, Stephen 243n38
Hand, John 428
Hart, David Bentley 298–299n34
Hart, H.L.A. 199, 200
Hauerwas, Stanley 295
Hauk, Gary S. 29, 48, 77, 642, 644
Hauriou, Maurice 471
Hehir, Bryan 27
Heiminsfeld, Melchior Goldast von 260
Helmholz, R.H. (Dick) 28, 29, 206n108, 236, 644–645, 662
Hendrix, Scott 232
Henry II (King of England, 1154–1189) 467
Henry VIII (King of England, r. 1509–1547) 49, 84
Henry, Patrick (Governor of Virginia, 1776–1779/1784–1786) 371, 417–418
Hertzke, Allen D. 541n3
Hesiod 625
Hill, Mark 13–14, 29, 644, 654–655, 662
Hittinger, Russell 208n117
Hobbes, Thomas 59, 63, 173, 198, 203, 327
Hogue, Carol M. 125
Holifield, Brooks 125, 228
Hollerich, Jean-Claude (Archbishop of Luxembourg, 2011–present) 618, 619
Holmes Jr., Oliver Wendell 198, 200, 203, 204, 205, 206
Home, Henry (Lord Kames of Scotland) 84
Hooker, Richard 32, 244, 248, 412
Hopkins, Gerard Manley 52, 52n3–4
Hosea (prophet) 149
Hostiensis 32
Hotman, François 257, 262, 263, 265, 343
Hugh of Saint-Victor 505
Huguenin, Elaine 479, 493, 494, 495, 497
Hus, Jan 334, 349

Hutchison, Anne 364

Irnerius 255, 262
Isaac 154–155, 156, 157, 159
Isaiah (prophet) 149
Isidore of Seville, Saint 31

Jackson, Andrew (President of the United States, 1829–1837) 420
Jackson, Timothy P. 125, 128–129, 315n18, 642–643
Jackson, William 428
Jacob 617
James I/VI (King of Scotland, r. 1567–1625/ King of England, and Ireland, r. 1603–1625) 237, 243n38, 327
James II (King of England, Scotland, and Ireland, r. 1685–1688) 354, 355
James (brother of Jesus) 621
Jebb, Eglantyne 569
Jefferson, Thomas (President of the United States, 1801–1809) 32
  Baptists and 371, 397–399
  letter to Danbury Baptists 398, 400–402, 409
  on church-state separation 371, **397–403**
  controversies/religious proclamations by Jefferson 399–400
  "wall of separation" 395, 398, 399, 400, 402, 407, 408, 409, 410, 411, 660
  Declaration of Independence (1776) 355
  and/on First Amendment 400, 402
  as governor of Virginia 397, 399, 400, 417
  on religion and republicanism 418–419
  religiosity of 397, 398, 400
  on religious freedom/liberty 397, 398
  on religious speech, symbols, and proclamations 397, 398, 400n19, 445, 447
  Second Inaugural Address 400n19
  on unalienable rights 429
Jeremiah (prophet) 149
Jerome, Saint 626
Jesus Christ
  on children/childhood 553, 555–556
  on corporal punishment 556, 560
  crucifixion of 145–146, 222, 227, 299
  on disciples 557–558, 624

INDEX OF PERSONS 687

    on divorce 624
    in Good Samaritan story 165–166
    holiness of 221–222, 223
    obedience to 489
    on relation between law and faith 226, 228
    on religious coercion and religious tolerance of 364, 367
    resurrection of 146, 223
    revelation of 236
    Second Coming 370
    on self-defense 340
    on truth 299
Jewel, John (Bishop of Salisbury, 1559–1571) 243n39, 244
Joash (King of Judah, r. c. 836–796 BCE) 156
John XXII (pope, r. 1316–1334) 60–61
John Paul II (pope, r. 1978–2005) 27, 29, 31, 117
Johnson, Luke Timothy 28, 125
Jordan, Mark D. 125
Joseph 361
Jude (slave or brother of Jesus Christ) 620, 621, 622
    See also Jude [Index of Scriptural References]
Julius III (pope, r. 1550–1555) 511
Justinian I (Byzantine emperor, 527–565) 255, 467, 507n15
Justus Jonas the Elder 253

Kant, Immanuel 319
    on dignity 312, 313, 314
    on personal autonomy 225
    on relation between law and faith 214, **223–227**, 233, 469–470
Katharina von Bora 564
Kavanaugh, Justice Brett 458, 459, 477
Keckermann, Bartolomeus 241
Keller, Timothy 488n18
Kelsen, Hans 21–22, 31
Kennedy, Joseph 479
Kennedy, Justice Anthony 451
Kennedy, Rick 355, 361
Kepler, Johannes 240n26
Kierkegaard, Søren 214, 224, 226–227
King, Bernice 124, 290, 655
Kingdom, Robert 616
Kingdon, Robert 48, 616

King Jr., Martin Luther
    on America's Christian foundation 117
    Black freedom movement 289
    as Christian jurist 31
    on civil and human rights 655
    continuation of legacy by daughter 123
    noninstrumental view of law of 201–202
    on truth and love 291, **302–305**
    works by JW/JW on 32
Kisch, Guido 261
Kling, Melchior 43, 253, 254, 258–259
Komline, David 421
Koppelman, Andrew 449–450
Korah (son of Izhar) 621
Korczak, Janusz 569
Krawietz, Werner 136
Kuyper, Abraham (Prime Minister of the Netherlands, 1901–1905)
    on church-state separation 96
    on common grace 182, 196
    on development of humanity/human life 197
    on impact of Calvinism on America 95
    on Industrial Revolution 178
    on natural rights 181–182
    on political pluralism/federalism 110–111
    on poverty/poverty relief 177–178
    on protection of liberties and rights 98
    on religious freedom and confessional pluralism 96
    on (sphere) sovereignty 37, 178, 179, 471–472
        associational liberty 95, 104–105, 110, 111, 111n84
        sovereignty of God 196, 197
        state sovereignty and authority 96, 111, 471
    on state "perfectionism" 91
    works by JW/JW on 6, 18, 20, 32, 33, 135, 177–178

Lactantius 32
Lagus, Konrad 259
Lancaster, Joseph 421
Lancilotti, Giovanni Paolo 267
Laney, James T. 114, 116, 120, 671
Langton, Stephen (Archbishop of Canterbury, 1207–1228) 467
Laski, Harold 471

Latterell, Justin   123, 131, 293n12, 672
Laycock, Douglas   126
Lazarus   485–486
Leah (wife of Jacob)   617
Leahy, Thomas W.   633, 634
Le Douaren, François   263, 264, 265
Legge, Dominic   205
Leibniz, Gottfried Wilhelm   23
Lewis, David V.   302
Linck, Wenceslaus   43
Lincoln, Abraham (President of the United States, 1861–1865)   425n27
Little, David   28, 657–658
Lizet, Pierre   264
Loader, J.A.   631n85
Loader, William   630–631, 631n85
Locke, John
   on authority of rulers   362–363
   on equality   325
   on natural (subjective) rights   59, **63–65**, 327, 344, 368
   on proselytization   451
   on protection of property   201n86
   on self-defense   331
   social contractarian analysis   203
Lombard, Peter   32, 503, 508, 511
Lonergan, Bernard   208, 211
Lot   620, 623–624, 628, 629, 632
Lothar III of Supplinburg (Holy Roman Emperor, r. 1133–1137)   255
Luhmann, Niklas   135
Lushington, Stephen   247
Luther, Martin
   on canon law/papal authority   41, 252–253, 254, 257, 653
     burning of papal/canon law books   40, 251, 252, 653
     Catholic sacraments   230
     papal dispensation   41
     rejection of *imitatio Christi*   224
   on conscience   481–482
   on cross of Christ   145–146
   on despair and blasphemy   224, 225, 226
   excommunication of   251, 252
   on freedom of Christians   90, 226
   on human sovereignty   225
   on Jews   233n43
   on jurists   10, 31, 40–41
   on marriage/marital law   150, 232, 254
   on mutual connection between rights and duties   318
   on parenting/parental authority   564–565
   on polygamy   49
   as "Protestant pope"   41
   reduction of New Testament Christianity   224, 226
   on relation between law and faith   214, 224–226, 227, 233, 252
   on resistance and right of self-defense   335
   on Roman law   254, 256, 257
   on salvation by faith alone (*sola fide*)   226, 252
   on Saxon law   257–258, 259
   on sin   187
   on three estates (household, church, political state)   565, 640
   total depravity doctrine   174, 225
   works by/JW on   32, 41, 42–43, 233

McConnell, Michael   17, 652, 662
McCrudden, Christopher   310, 312
MacCulloch, Diarmaid   248n60
McDermott, Scott   241
McDonald, Alonzo L.   121–122
McElroy, Robert W. (Bishop of San Diego, 2015–present)   618, 619
Machen, J. Gresham   431–432
McKenzie, Robert Tracy   420
McNeill, John   634
Madison, James (President of the United States, 1809–1817)
   on religious freedom/disestablishment of Church of England   389, 402, 417–418, 431
   on religious speech, symbols, and proclamations   445, 447
   works by JW/JW on   32
Maffei, Domenico   261
Mair, John   332, 336, 336n36
Maitland, William   471
Malachi (prophet)   149, 532
Malik, Charles   314
Maloy, J.S.   352
Mann, Horace, on Bible reading and republican values   **422–425**, 426, 428, 430, 433

INDEX OF PERSONS 689

Mansfield, Lord (William Murray)   247
Marisco, Adam de (Adam Marsh)   242
Maritain, Jacques   27, 31, 32, 209, 296–297
Marquardt, Elizabeth   170
Martha (sister of Lazarus)   223
Marty, Martin E.   118, 125, 126, 129, 501, 640
Marx, Reinhard (Archbishop of Munich and Freising, 2008–present)   617–618
Mary II (Queen of England, Scotland, and Ireland, r. 1689–1694)   355, 357
Massarelli, Angelo   512
Mateus, Odair   285
Mather, Cotton
  on Catholics   368n33
  on church-state separation   353
  on civic rights of nonconforming Protestants   365
  on Congregationalism   357, 363, 365, 369
  covenant theology of   353, 361
  definition of Protestantism   369
  in/on Glorious Revolution   355–356, 357
  ordination sermon   354
  on piety   370
  on political liberty   353
  on/and Protestant liberty   **358–363**
  on religious coercion   363, 364, 366, 368
  on/and religious freedom and liberty of conscience   354, **363–370**
  reputation   353
  on resistance   353, 354, 355, 356, 357
  on slave trade/slavery   353
  works   358, 658
Mather, Increase   357, 366, 367
Mather, Richard   354
Matthews, Stanley   431, 432
Mayhew, Jonathan   371
Melanchthon, Philipp   32, 43
  on canon law   253
  on criminal punishment   187n18
  on natural law   174, 268
  on resistance and right of self-defense   335
  on Roman law   255–257, 258, 261, 262
  on Saxon law   258, 259
Menn, Stephen   217
Mercer, Jesse   391n107, 392, 392n111
Mercer, Silas   388, 390, 391n107, 392

Meshach (Jewish man in Book of Daniel)   483, 484
Micah (prophet)   117
Middlekauff, Robert   356
Milton, John   49, 89, 151
Montague, Terri   123, 290, 655
More, Sir Thomas   33, 240, 246
Mornay, Philippe du Plessis
  on covenants with God vs. rulers   346
  on First and Second Table violations   344, 346
  on freedom/liberty   344
  on protection of people's rights by governments   345
  on right of self-defense and revolution   343, 344, 345–346, 347, 349
Moses
  on educating children   515, 532
  Eike von Repgow vs.   257–258
  eudaimonism and   222
  Mosaic covenant   156–157
  Mosaic government   214, 361–362, 363
  on relation between law and faith   218–221, 226, 228
  See also Mosaic law [Index of Subjects]
Moyn, Samuel   59n17, 210
Müller, Wolfgang P.   128
Murner, Thomas   261
Mutua, Athena   301n47

Nasr, Seyyed Hossein   127
Neagu, Mariela   667
Nebudchadnezzar (King of Babylon)   484
Neibuhr brothers   320
Neuhaus, Richard John   27
Newsom, Carol   228
Neyrey, Jerome   621, 633
Nicholas III (pope, 1277–1280)   60–61
Nicholas of Cusa   331
Nichols, Joel A.   123, 440, 659–660
Niebuhr, H. Richard   172
Niebuhr, Reinhold   32
Nietzsche, Friedrich   214, 225–226, 227, 233
Nikiforos, Dimitrios, (Fr. Aetios, Grand Ecclesiarch, Ecumenical Patriarchate of Constantinople)   286
Noah   154–155, 156, 157, 162–163

Noll, Mark A.   661
Noonan Jr., John T.   118, 211, 665
    on channeling and teaching functions of law   **198–201**
Novak, David   28, 126, 668
    on intrahuman covenants   152n10, 156, 161

O'Connor, Justice Sandra Day   448
O'Donovan, Joan Lockwood   65
Oekolampadius, Johannes   260–261
Oldendorp, Johann   33, 43, 248, 254
Osborne, Grant   482, 636n124
Ozment, Steven   4

Paradise, Brandon   655
Parkinson, Patrick   295
Parsons, Talcott   135
Paul III (pope, r. 1534–1549)   511
Paul, Saint   482
    on carnal temptation   625
    church law and   287
    citation in legal cases/jurisprudence   245
    on civil government   363, 493
        resistance against   363
        rights enforcement by governing authorities   336, 337, 341
    on conscience   **486–488**, 489, 490, 496
    on cross of Christ   145–146
    on disciples   558
    on divine love (*agape*)   222
    on fruit of the Spirit   559
    on Jews and Christians   137
    on marriage   29, 162–163
        women in marriage   77–78
    Protestants and theology of   145
    on relation between law and faith   214, 222, 223
    on same-sex relations   619
    on sin/knowledge of sin   230–231, 562
    on virtues   82
Pennington, James W.C.   659
Penn, William   368
Perry, Michael J.   28, 672
Peter of Andlau   260
Peter, Saint   243, 340, 488, 489
Philip II (King of Spain, r. 1556–1598)   47
Phillips, Jack   479, 480, 493–494, 495, 497, 497n28
Philo of Alexandria   631, 632

Phips, William   360
Pico della Mirandola   312, 319
Pilate, Pontius   299
Pill, Shlomo   131, 672
Pin, Andrea   656–657
Pithou, François   263, 266
Pithou, Pierre   263–264, 266
Plato   248n60, 626
    on ideal commonwealth   517
    on relation between law and faith   214, 215–216, 218, 219, 223, 228, 233
Plowden, Edmund   237, 237–238n14, 247
Posner, Richard   48
Powell, Jefferson   198
Preston, John   242n32
Pritzen, Joachim Gregorii von   259
Purcell, John Baptist (Bishop of Cincinnati, 1833–1883)   421

Rachel (wife of Abraham)   617
Rahab (prostitute in Joshua, 2)   221
Rauschenbusch, Walter   124
Rawls, John   203
    on dignity   312–313
    on justice as fairness   22
    on place of religion in public sphere   317
    on public reason in marriage and family life   25
    on religious discourse in political, economic, and legal contexts   229, 324
    on religious values in democratic deliberation   293
Raymond of Peñyafort   32
Raz, Joseph   316
Reagan, Ronald (President of the United States, 1981–1989)   438, 450
Rebuffe, Pierre   262
Reed, Justice Stanley F.   395
Rehnquist, Justice William H.   396, 403
Reicke, Bo   621
Reid Jr., Charles J.   58, 669
Renard, Georges   471
Reynolds, Philip L.   72, 83, 125, **127–128**, 228, **664–665**
Rittershausen, Konrad   266–267
Rivers, Julian   662–663
Robert ("Ponkie", adopted brother of JW)   14, 23, 320, 672
Roberts, Chief Justice John   203, 210, 458

Robitscher, Jonas   115
Romero, Oscar (Archbishop of San Salvador, 1977–1980)   31
Rorty, Richard   293
Rosenbury, Laura   524n69, 527n100
Rosen, Michael   314
Rosenstock-Huessy, Eugen   4
Rosenthal, A. M.   171
Runner, H. Evan   3, 639
Rush, Benjamin   422, 423, 660

Sacks, Lord Jonathan (Chief Rabbi of the United Hebrew Congregations of the Commonwealth, 1991–2013)   127, 320–321, 323, 642
St. German, Christopher   240–241
Samuel (prophet)   553
Sande, Ken   594
Sandel, Michael   320
Sarah (wife of Abraham)   49, 160, 162n27
Saul (King of Israel, fl. 11th c. BCE)   362
Savage, Audra   124, 672
Savigny, Friedrich Carl von   21, 257, 270, 440
Scalia, Justice Antonin   448
Schama, Simon   55
Scheurl, Christoph   253
Schmitt, Carl   325
Schmoeckel, Mathias   33, 645, 653–654
Schneidewin, Johannes   43
Schori, Katharine Jefferts (Presiding Bishop of the Episcopal Church, 2006–2015)   127
Schürpf, Hieronymus   253–254, 259
Schwarz, Ignaz   268
Selden, John   32, 33, 158n21, 242n36, 245, 649
Servetus, Michael   42, 338
Shadrach (Jewish man in Book of Daniel)   483, 484
Sharpton, Al   140
Sichardus, Johannes   261
Simons, Menno   412
Skinner, Quentin   340n55, 342–343, 344, 348
Smolinski, Reiner   658
Socrates   226, 479
Sodom, King of   152
Solomon (King of Israel, r. c. 970–931 BCE)   362, 515, 617
Soloveitchik, Rabbi Joseph   313
Soto, Domingo de   510, 511
Sotomayor, Justice Sonia   396

Stackhouse, Max   135
Stanwood, Owen   358n13
Stevens, Justice John Paul   396
Stevens, William Bacon   392n111
Stewart, Justice Potter   395, 411
Stewart-Tufescu, Ashley   557n40
Stievermann, Jan   658–659
Stillingfleet, Edward   245
Stintzing, Roderich von   269
Story, Justice Joseph   32, 247, 419, 420, 428, 440
Strauss, Leo   327
Strawn, Brent   228, 672
Strayer, Joseph R.   230n39
Stryk, Samuel   268
Stutzman, Barronelle   479, 480, 495, 497
Suárez, Francisco   242, 243n38, 245–246, 248
Sullivan, Justice John Joseph   428
Summers, Ray   633n100
Surgant, Johann Ulrich   261

Tapper, Ruard   509
Thomas Aquinas, Saint   241, 337
   as Christian jurist   31
   on conscience   480
   on divine law   23
   on friendship   185, 211–212
   on marriage   507, 508–509, 511
   on natural law   47, 440
   on rights   58
      natural rights   333–334
      subjective rights   62, 205n102
   works by JW/JW on   32
Thomasius, Christian   259, 267
Thomassin, Louis de   262
Thurén, Lauri   622–623
Tierney, Brian   28, 63, 309, 348
Timpson, Edward   577
Tipton, Steven M.   77, 81, 123, 228, 672
Tiraqueau, André   262
Tocqueville, Alexis de   95
Toering, Sara   123–124
Tolstoy, Leo   616
Trump, Donald (President of the United States, 2017–2021)   180
Tuininga, Matthew J.   124
Tutu, Desmond (Archbishop of Cape Town, 1986–1996)   27, 28–29, 114, 117, 118, 642

Ulpian (Roman jurist, d. 223 or 228 CE)   62

Van der Vyver, Johan D.   118
VanDrunen, David   649
Vaughan, Chief Justice John   245–246, 247
Vercingetorix (Gallic king, d. 46 BCE)   265
Vermeule, Adrian
    on determination in application of
        natural law   104n61
    on individual rights and/vs. right
        of government/common
        good   112n89, 204–206
Villey, Michel   60, 61–63, 309
Vitoria, Francisco de   32

Waite, Morrison R.   401
Waldron, Jeremy   325
Wang, Eric   124
Washington, George (President of the United
    States, 1789–1797)   398, 418,
    420
Watson, Duane Frederick   635
Weiler, Joseph   122, 136, 144, 325, 641
Weimer, Adrian   352
Welker, Michael   30, 131, 648–649
Wesenbeck, Matthaeus   253, 259
West, Cornel   290, 655
Weyhe, Eberhard von   253, 266
Whall, Thomas   424
Whitefield, George   378, 379–380
Whitehead, Alfred North   135
Wied, Hermann von (Archbishop-elector of
    Cologne, d. 1552)   510
Wieseltier, Leon   204n96
Willard, Emma   421
William of Auvergne (Bishop of Paris,
    1228–1249)   242
William of Ockham   241
    on rights   58
        natural subjective rights   60, 61–63,
            66, 330
        right of self-defense   331, 334
William of Orange (King of England,
    Scotland, and Ireland, r.
    1689–1702)   355, 357
Williams, Elisha   371
Williams, Roger   364, 367, 368, 412–413
Wilson, Robin Fretwell   565, 667
Winship, Michael   352

Witte, Jr., John
    career   6, 30, 113–114, 115, 116, 120, 271,
        293, 615
        See also Center for the Study of Law
            and Religion (CSLR) [Index of
            Subjects]
    educational background   3–4, 37, 39, 53,
        196, 645
    family background and youth   3, 18,
        23–24, 113, 129, 271, 319–320,
        672
    mentorships   123–124, 148, 372
    prizes, awards, honorary doctorates, and
        distinguished titles   6, 16–17,
        35, 114, 648–649, 659
    public lectures and (roundtable)
        conferences   6, 13, 27, 47, 118,
        122, 642, 645
    religious background/religiosity of   3, 18,
        19–21, 23, 37, 54, 148, 271, 296
    scholarship and methodologies   9–12, 18,
        195, 271, 290, 293
        biographical approach   30–33
        integrative approach to law   440
        interdisciplinary approach   79–81
        law and religion in thought of
            JW   6–9
        metaphors   21, 35
        sources of inspiration and
            mentors   4–6, 18, 20, 37, 83, 89,
            95, 639, 666
            See also Berman, Harold;
                Dooyeweerd, Herman; Kuyper,
                Abraham
        sponsors/benefactors   671
        stewardship, discipline,
            accessibility, influence, and
            engagement   9–10, 18, 129
        triads   9, 23, 24, 35, 120,
            640
            three "I's" (interdisciplinary,
                international,
                interreligious)   9, 640
            three "R's" (retrieval,
                reconstruction,
                reengagement)   9, 24, 640
    skills and reputation,
        "fundamental intuition"   21–24
        leadership   12–13, 37, 120

Witte, Jr., John (*Cont.*)
professional collaboration and friendships   4, 13–14, 120, 128, 135
scholarly and personal virtues   34, 37, 39, **81–85**, 129, 590–591, 615
self-identification as scholar   8–9, 195, 325
works   13, 17–18, 24, **26–30**, 32–33, 48, 51
editorships   13, 25, 32, 654
forthcoming studies   29, 30, 37–38
number of   289
publishers   671
reception and reviews   14–15, 18
See also under [individual works in Index of Titles]; [individual topics in Index of Subjects]
translations   13, 24, 33, 641
Wolterstorff, Nicholas   3, 91*n*12, 196, 645–646, 656
Woodruff, George   116
Woodruff, Robert   116
Wright, James (Governor of Georgia, 1760–1776)   385
Wyclif, John   334

Yong, Amos   554

Ziegler, Caspar   267
Zubly, John J.   375, 377, 384–385

Index of Subjects

- In addition to subjects the Index of Subjects includes references to groups of people, nonhuman beings, institutions, geographical places, court rulings, acts, projects, and events. Names of persons and human characters are included in the Index of Persons. Book, article, and journal titles are included in the Index of Titles. Scriptural references are included in the Index of Scriptural references.
- The abbreviation 'JW' refers to John Witte, Jr.
- Page references in **bold type** indicate a more in-depth treatment of the subject.

abortion   74, 82, 228, 520n43, 541, 587, 587n110
Abrahamic covenant   92, 160
absolutism
   in France   343, 354, 358
   of House of Stewart/in England   352, 355, 356, 357, 358n13, 360
   of papacy   359
ACLU (American Civil Liberties Union)   402
Act of Toleration (England, 1691)   357, 365
Adamic covenant   92
Administrative Procedure Act (United States, 1964)   206
adoption
   adoption agencies (state and private)   575, 581, 586–588
   adoption lobby groups   580
   by gay couples   588
   children's perception of   582, 583, 584, 585
   children's say/right to be heard   581
   child safety and   578, 579, 581
   continuity/permanency   579n56, 581, 586
   corruption and   580, 581, 583
   in Europe   569n7, 578, 579, 581
      Netherlands   583–584
      Romania   579–584
   identity (rights) and   578, 581, 583, 586
   intercountry   569n7, 579, 580, 581, 582, 583–584
   legal cases/court rulings   581–582, 587
   open adoption   570, 586, 586n100
   selection of adoptive families   584, 585–586, 585n97,n98
   in United States   578, 579, 581, **584–588**
Adoption Law (Romania, 2012)   581

Adoption and Safe Families Act (ASFA, United States, 1997)   579, 584
adultery   78, 628
Africa, religious family law in   125
African American Christianity   289, 293, 294
   See also King Jr., Martin Luther [Index of Persons]
Afrikaners   159n23
agape (unconditional/divine love). See love
Alexandria   621, 622, 623
alms/alms giving   175, 177, 178
   See also charity
alternative dispute resolution   598, 612, 613
   See also arbitration
Amalek (enemy nation of Israelites)   162
America. See United States
American Civil Liberties Union (ACLU)   402
American Civil War (1861–1865)   391
American Revolution (1765–1783)   66, 310, 328, 350, 376, 385
Americans United for Separation of Church and State   402–403
American War of Independence (1775–1783)   376
Amish, education   518–519, 521, 522, 530, 535
Anabaptists   66, 89, 387, 411–412, 411n56
angels
   crossing of angelic/human boundaries   629, 631, 632, 634, 635, 636n124,n126, 637
   power/authority of   637, 637n133
   rebelling/Rebellion of the Watchers   626, 627, 630–631, 632, 633, 635, 637
Anglican Church/Church of England
   British as blessed and privileged by God   358

INDEX OF SUBJECTS 695

Anglican Church/Church of England (*cont.*)
  canons/church law 240, 244, 274, 284
  Catholic influences in 237, 239, 240, 244, 355
  dissenters/nonconfirmists 354, 360, 365–366, 368, 383–385, 412
    See also Anabaptists; Baptists; Congregationalists; Presbyterian Church/Presbyterians; Puritans; Quakers; Unitarians
  establishment/disestablishment in American colonies 365–366
    Georgia 373, 374, 378, 379, 380, 381–388, 393–394
    Massachusetts 354–355, 365, 368
    South Carolina 374
    Virginia 374, 389, 402, 417
  High Church 354, 365
  influences of reformers on Anglican theology 84
  Low Church 359, 366
  natural law in 47
  organization 276, 277
  payment of ministers 378–379, 382
  on polygamy 49
  reestablishment of (1660–1662) 354
  role in education 379
  sacraments/rites of passage 232, 280
  on same-sex marriage 280*n*42
  on spiritual and temporal authority of monarchs/princes 91–92
  works by/JW on JW 88
  worship 279
Anglican Communion 277, 284, 365
Anglican Communion Legal Advisors Network 284
Anglican Consultative Council 284
Anglo-American legal tradition/law
  contracts in 199
  criminal law in **188–191**
  parental rights and duties in 527
  See also common law
Antichrist/Antichristian tyranny 354, 358–359, 360, 364, 365
apartheid/apartheid laws (South Africa) 28, 117, 118, 193
apelthousai (term/definition) 624–625
apodictic law 141
Apollo (Olympic god) 215

Apostles' Creed 244
Apostolic Palace (Rome) 285
arbitrary rule/force 346, 356
  self-defense against arbitrary abuse 329–330, 331, 332, 334
arbitration
  arbitration abuse 605
  commercial/private 593–594, 609–610
  extrajudicial nature of 608
  free exercise of religion and 613–614
  religious vs. nonreligious 592–593, 598, 609–610, 614
  secular/civil enforcement of 604–605, 609
    crimes 603, 604, 605, 610–611
  See also religious arbitration
Aristotelian philosophy/scholasticism 241, 506
  See also Aristotle [Index of Persons]
Articles of Religion (England) 240
Articles of Union (1707) 464
ASFA (Adoption and Safe Families Act, United States, 1997) 579, 584
Asian law and religion scholars 12
assembly, free. *See* associational freedom/liberty
associational freedom/liberty 104–110, 183, 409
  associational autonomy 107, 108*n*74, 109
  associational rights,
    individual vs. 105–106, 105*n*67
    JW on 106, 106*n*70, 107
  Calvinists on 183
  Kuyper on 95, 104–105, 110, 111, 111*n*84
  political pluralism vs. 110
  state authority and 107–108
Asylum for the Education of Deaf and Dumb Persons (CT) 421
Athanasian Creed 244
Austinian positivism 492–493
Australia 167, 235, 575
autonomy
  of law 137, 140, 294, 295
  lawlessness of 233
  personal autonomy/self-determination 225, 316
  parents vs. children 523, 524–525, 527–528, 530
  See also church autonomy; religious autonomy; sovereignty

of social groups   470
theonomy vs. personal   224, 225, 226

Babylon   483, 484
baptism   230–231, 233, 511
   Eucharist and   280
   rites of passage   279, 280, 506
   sacrament of marriage compared to   504, 506, 508, 513
Baptist Association of Danbury (CT)   398, 400–402, 409
Baptists
   authority and governance/organization   276, 277
   Black Baptist churches   376
   child sexual abuse   548
   in Georgia   376, 388, 390, 392, 392n112, 394
   on natural law   47
   persecution of   366
   rites of passage   280
   support to Jefferson/on church-state separation   371, 388, 397–399
   letter by Jefferson to Danbury Baptists   398, 400–402, 409
   tax exemptions   369
Baptist World Alliance   277
Basic Law of the German Federal Republic (1949)   314
bastards. *See* nonmarital children
BeltLine (community development project, Atlanta)   123
Beth Din of America (religious/Jewish arbitration forum)   593, 612
Bible, Greek terminology/text   557–559, 563, 620, 623, 624–625
Bible reading
   in public schools (United States)   415–416, 421, 442
      Catholic protest against use of Protestant Bible   422, 424, 426, 427
      legal cases/court rulings   415, **424–433**, 436, 442
      sectarian vs. nonsectarian/secular function of   421, 422, 424, 425, 426, 427, 428, 429, 432
Biblical law   138, 143
   See also faith; justice; mercy; "weightier matters of the law"

biblical theology   482
bicameral governments   362
Bill of Rights (England, 1689)   357
births
   anonymous births   570
   marital childbearing   76
   nonmarital births   14, 23, 74, 75, 78, 82, 84, 85, 319–320, 616–617
Bishop of Rome, jurisdiction in England   237, 238
Black freedom movement   289
   See also King Jr., Martin Luther [Index of Persons]
Bladensburg cross (war memorial)   447
blasphemy   93n23, 97, 153, 189, 224, 226, 629
blood vengeance   139
Bologna, Council of Trent sessions in (1547)   511, 512
Bologna, Concordat of (1516)   263
Book of Common Prayer   442
Book of the Covenant   138, 139–140, 142
   See also Exodus [Index of Scriptural References]
Bosnia   168
Boston. *See* Glorious Revolution
Bourges   252, 263, 265
Bread for the World (Christian aid agency)   547
British Protestants
   as blessed and privileged by God   358
   See also Anglican Church/Church of England
Buddhism   20, 126
Burgundy   264
bystanders, charitable   167, 168, **169–172**, **181–183**

California   167, 438
California Court of Appeals, *Bixler v. Scientology* (No. B310559 (Cal. Ct. App. 2022))   **599–601**, 605, 610–611, 610n115
Calvinism/Calvinists
   on charity   181–183
   on constitutions/constitutional rights   89, 182, 183
   in France   341, 342, 343–344, 349, 377
   on human rights   14, 41
   on human sinfulness   94
   on matrimonial law   48

on religious freedom   14, 41, 96
on resistance and revolution   327–328, **335–342**, 343, 348
on right of self-defense   328, 329, 335–336, 340–341, 343, 345–346
See also Calvin, John [Index of Persons]
on state authority   88, **89–94**, 96
works by/JW on   88, 89, 182
Calvin Theological Seminary (Grand Rapids, MI)   124
Calvin University (Grand Rapids, MI)   3–4, 196, 645
Cambridge Platform (1648)   352
Cambridge University   241
Cambridge University Press   25, 127
Canada   3, 111n84, 113, 167, 548, 672
Candler School of Theology (Emory University)   118, 127, 228, 642
canon law
 amendment of   45
 in Anglican Church   240, 244, 284
 authority of   252
 as basis for church law   283
 civil law and/vs.   267
 as custom   44–45
 European legal system and   39, 44
 in France   262–264
 inherent qualities of   266–268
 language use for   240
 natural subjective rights and   66
 Protestants on/Protestant application of   **43–45**, 251–252, 253, **266–268**, 653
  burning of canon law books by Luther   40, 251, 252, 653
 Roman law and/vs.   256–257, 267
 See also *ius commune*
Canons of 1604 (England)   240
Canterbury   244
capital punishment   231
Cardiff Law School   16, 284
cardinal virtues   218, 222, 223
Carter Center (Atlanta)   116, 118–119
casuistic law   141
Catholic Church/Catholics
 authority and governance/organization   276, 466–467
 baptism   280
 church autonomy   466–467
 reforms   467

religious freedom in   46
rites of passage   280
See also Roman Catholic Church/Roman Catholics
sexual abuse   126
in United States   420, 421, 592
 Cincinnati   427
 Georgia   373, 376–377, 378, 380, 386, 394
 Maine   426
 Massachusetts   424
 worship   279
Catholic intellectual tradition
 eight theses of (Cavadini)   247–248, 247–248n58
 influence on common law. *See* common law
 on integration of reason and revelation   236, 247–248n58, 248
 on natural law   47
 term/definition   235–236
catholicity
 meaning of   244, 244n49
 Roman vs. non-Roman claims on   243
Catholic Relief Services (relief program, United States)   547
Catholic social teaching (term/definition)   235
CEDAW (Convention on the Elimination of All Forms of Discrimination against Women)   573, 576
celibacy   43, 231, 232, 287
Center for the Study of Human Rights (Columbia University)   120
Center for the Study of Law and Religion (CSLR, Emory University)
 conferences   118, 126, 127, 130
 digital publishing/scholarship   25, 129–130
 faculty/staff   122–123, 127–129, 130, 590, 642, 671–672
  leadership by JW   6, 18, 113, 114, 116, 130, 131
 funding and expansion   120–122, 671
 origins/history   114, 642
 projects/areas of research   124–125, 126, 127, 128, 131, 501, 664
 reorganization   129–131
 See also Law and Religion Program (Emory University)

vision   131–132
Centre for Law and Religion (Cardiff Law School)   16, 284
ceremonial Deism   436, 442, 448, 450
charity
  charitable bystanders   167, 168, **169–172**, 181–183
  "charitable choice provisions" (Clinton)   179–180
  distortion by sin   174
  family as first source of   176
  government spending and charitable giving   179–180
  justice and   172–174
  limits to private   175
  natural rights and   182
  Protestant Reformers on   **174–178**
  redemptive charity   176–177
  responsibility to protect/to be charitable   168, 171, 172, 173, 175, 178, 182
  spiritual efficaciousness of   176, 213*n*142
  works by/JW on   174–177, 181–183
  "worthy"/"deserving" vs. "unworthy"/"undeserving" of assistance   175, 176, 177, **179–181**
Charter of Georgia (1732)   377–378, 386
child abuse and neglect
  child (sexual) abuse in church   126, 548, 550
  exploitation of children   540
  loss of faith/spiritual struggle and   551
  See also child protection and welfare; corporal punishment of children
  state intervention   520, 529, 534
  statistics (United States)   549
childbearing. *See* births
childhood
  theologies of   **551–555**
    teachings and example of Jesus   555–556
"The Child in Law, Religion, and Society" (project by JW/CSLR)   125, 128, 501, 664
child marriage   509–510, 545
child protection and welfare   546
  care of children (out of family of origin), causes of entering care   571

  perception of different types of care by children   582–583
  See also adoption; children's homes/residential care; foster care
  United States vs. Europe   578–579
Christian commitment to   540–541, 546–547, 549, **551–554**, 562, 564, 566
  child-focused Christian organizations   541, 547
  cooperation with secular organizations   548, 564, 566
Indigenous children   548
intervention by church and/or state   564, 565–566, 571, 572–573, 576
law and policy making,
  Europe   572, 573, **575–578**
  United States   573, **575–578**
right of children to be heard/consulted   575, 576–577, 578, 581–582
in Romania   **579–584**
See also child abuse and neglect; children's rights; corporal punishment of children
in United States   541
children
  children's sin   562–564
  contracted-out children (*Verdingkinder*, Switzerland)   569*n*7
  equality of   552–553
  mental health/depression   520, 540, 551
  as models of faith for adults/Spirit-filled children   553–554, 555
  as moral agents/growing moral capacities of   562, 563
  nonmarital   14, 23, 74, 75, 78, 82, 84, 85, 616–617
  percentage of world population and spread   540
  sexual orientation and gender identity   537
children's homes/institutional care   571, 573, 579
  in Romania   580, 581, 583
children's rights
  culture war and   574
  dignity rights   570
  identity rights   570, 573, 574, 578, 581, 583, 586

INDEX OF SUBJECTS 699

children's rights (cont.)
  JW on 516–517, 574
  (natural) rights and duties between
      parents and children 516–517,
      520, 526–527, 529, 574
  parental vs. children's autonomy 523,
      524–525, 527–528, 530
    limiting parental authority 520, 574
  right to be consulted/heard 570
    choosing education 516, 518–519,
      523–524, 530
    on matters affecting welfare 575,
      576–577, 578, 581–582
  See also child protection and welfare; UN
      Convention on the Rights of the
      Child
Children's Rights Act (Romania, 2005) 581
child welfare. See child protection and
    welfare
China 580
Christian civilization, four components
    of 310
Christian Conciliation 593, 595
Christian Dispute Resolution Professionals,
    Inc. 594
Christian identity, compromise of 19, 145,
    228, 494–495
Christianity
  definition (JW) 26
  future of 325
  influences on democracy 27
Christianity, community, culture triad 35–
    36, 38
"Christianity and Democracy in Global
    Context" (conference, Center for
    the Study of Law and Religion,
    Emory University) 118
"Christianity, Law and Racial Justice:
    Shaping the Future" (symposium
    project) 290
Christianity and law (relation/
    interaction) 24–27
  from a biographical perspective 30–33,
    37
  from a jurisprudential perspective 34–
    35, 37, 38
  from a relational perspective 37
    forthcoming studies by JW 29
    works by JW/JW on 27–30

interdisciplinary learning 147
  See also "weightier matters of the law"
  in modern pluralistic societies 34, 38
  time vs. spirituality dimension 26
Christianity, race, and law (emerging
    discipline/interaction) 289–291
  rights, power, and truth in,
    integration of truth and political
      discourse 299–300
    rejection of epistemic
      relativism 298–299
    robust inclusive debate vs. standpoint
      theory 300–302
Christian jurisprudence 136, 145, 215, 230
Christian jurists 10, 30–33
Christian law
  church law vs. 273
  development of common principles
    of Christian law (Common
    Vision) 283–286
  origins 272
  purpose of 271–272
  See also church law; Common Vision
    [Index of Titles]
Christian law and religion scholarship/
    scholars
  Catholic-Protestant debates (Reformation/
      Counter-Reformation) 240–243
  Christian law and religion scholarship,
    JW on five responsibilities/ethics
    of 9–10
  inter-Christian and interfaith
    dialogue 11–12
  intuition and 21–22
  JW on 290, 639
  quality and integrity of legal
    scholarship 137
  race and law scholarship 289–290, 294,
    298
  scholasticism as theological method 239
Christology 136, 145
Christophobia 136, 144–145
church authority and governance 276–277,
    349
  abuse of authority 94, 333, 364
  charitable responsibilities 178
  church discipline and conflict
    resolution 277–278
  jurisdiction 464

public/state vs. church authority 89–90, 93–94
See also church autonomy; church law; church-state relations; church-state separation
church autonomy 408
  Catholic Church 466–467
  during COVID-19 pandemic **455–457**, 462, 464, 465, 474
  in Scotland 464, 465
  See also religious autonomy
church discipline 277–278
Church of England. *See* Anglican Church/Church of England
church finance
  church fees 282, 384, 385, 386
  church taxes 369, 382, 388–389, 417, 420
  property 281–282
Church of Jesus Christ of Latter-day Saints 48
church law
  Christian law vs. 273
  development of common principles of Christian law 273–274, **283–287**
  JW on 287–288
  unity in. *See Common Vision* [Index of Titles]
church membership 274, 275
Church of Scientology, religious arbitration of sexual harassment case **599–601**, 605, 610–611, 610n115
Church of Scotland Act (1921) 464, 473
church-state relations 292
  Calvin on 338–339
  in Georgia 373, **380–383**, 386–387, 388, 390, 394
  in New England 352, 364, 395
  Puritans on 352
  See also church-state separation
church-state separation 349, 591
  Common Vision on 282
  concept 408–410
  education and 395–396
  JW on 364, 407, **408–411**, 414, 435, 441
  Kuyper on 96
  liberty of conscience and 409, 441
  Mather on 353
  origins 466–467
  Puritans on 93, 96, 352

See also Baptists; First Amendment to the United States Constitution; Jefferson, Thomas [Index of Persons]
  tax support as compromise for 420
  under Jefferson 371, **397–403**
  controversies 399–400
  "wall of separation" 395, 398, 399, 400, 402, 407, 408, 409, 410, 411, 660
  violation of 180
  "wall of separation"–metaphor 396, 399, 400, 401–403, 404, 660
Cincinnati Bible War (1869–1870) 427, 431
Cincinnati Board of Education 427
citizenship 368, 521–522
civic education 515, 521–522, 526, 531, 534
  See also public schools
civic friendship 211–212
civil law 251
  canon law and/vs. 267
  divine (moral) law and/vs. 190, 191, 192–193, 469
  educational use of 192, 193, 198
  See also Anglo-American legal tradition/law; French law; German law; *ius commune*; Roman law; Saxon law
civil liberty 457, 461, 466, 468, 469, 471
civil rights, human vs. 300n41
clandestine marriage 502, 505–507
  Council of Trent on 508–509, **510–514**
Clarendon Code (England, 1661–1665) 354
clergy
  clerical immunity 43
  payment of 264, 282, 378–379, 382
  in public office 282, 408
  See also ordained ministry/ministers
CLS (critical legal studies) 292, 295
Code of Canon Law (1983) 274
College of Bishops (Roman Catholic Church) 277
Colloquium of Anglican and Roman Catholic Canon Lawyers 271, 284
Cologne, Provincial Council of (1536) 510
Colorado 497
commercial arbitration 593–594, 609–610
Committee on Social Thought (University of Chicago) 115
common good
  Catholic vs. Protestant views on 212

friendship and 212, 213
individual rights and/vs. 112n89,
    204–206, 208–209
  JW on 185, 207, 208, 210–211
  neutrality on 210–211
common grace 182, 196
common law (Anglo-American law)
  Catholic influence on,
    Catholic-Protestant scholarly debates/
      conversed influence **239–243**
    generated influence 238, **243–248**
common law (Anglo-American law) (*cont.*)
    inherited influence 238–239
  definition 235
  influence of *ius commune* on 236–237
  ius gentium 211, 296n27
  origins/development of 237, 238
  See also Anglo-American legal tradition/
    law; *ius commune*
common schools. *See* public schools
"communification" (Berman) 213
communion (*koinonia*) 275
community, Christianity, community, culture
    triad 35–36, 38
Company of Vintners (London) 245
"compassionate" conservatism (George W.
    Bush) 180
Compassion International (Christian
    organization, United States) 541
conciliarism/conciliarists
  on church and state authority 333, 339
  objectives of 334
  on right of self-defense 331–332,
    335–336, 348, 349
Concordat of Bologna (1516) 263
Confederation Congress (1787) 418
confession 280
confessional pluralism 96
  See also religious pluralism
confirmation 233, 279, 511
conflict resolution (within churches) 277–
    278
  See also religious arbitration
Confucianism 20
Congregationalists
  authority and organization 276, 277
  in Georgia 375, 381
  Mather on Congregationalism 357, 363,
    365, 369

  in New England 369
    Connecticut 397
    Massachusetts 354–355, 357,
      363–364, 365, 397
    in New York 421
    in Ohio 421
  Puritans and 354–355
Connecticut 397, 417
conscience
  conscientious objection from military
    service 387, 390
  creation, covenant, conscience triad 36,
    38
  interaction with law/lawmakers **491–
    495**
  obedience/disobedience to 486, 487
  origins and concept 479–480
  role and functions of 486–487
  See also liberty of conscience; religious
    conscience
Conscious Development Foundation (United
    States) 121
Constance, Council of (1414–1418) 334
constitutional courts (concept) 31
constitutionalism 349
  American,
    common good constitutionalism
      210
    New England 353
    origins 94, 352, 370
    religious freedom/liberty and 51,
      435, 441
  European 313
constitutional rights and freedoms 183
  in Europe 457
  See also associational freedom/liberty;
    freedom of speech; religious
    freedom/liberty
  status of 470
constitutions
  as divinely modeled covenants 182
  European Union 144
  Georgia **385–393**, 417
  New England 353, 371, 416, 417
  recognition of God in 96
Constitution of the United States (1788) 210,
    389
  commentaries on 419, 420
  constitutional principles 95–96

formative impact of Puritanism and
Calvinism on 94, 95, 352, 370
See also First Amendment to the
Constitution of the United States;
Fourteenth Amendment to the
Constitution of the United States
Tenth Amendment 110
"Contract with America" (legislative agenda,
Republican Party, 1994) 180
contracts/contract law 199, 598, 603
coreligionist contracts 592
covenants vs. contracts 36, 152–153, 163,
182
religious right to exit contract **599–603**,
605, 610–611
Convention on the Elimination of All Forms
of Discrimination against Women
(CEDAW) 573, 576
conversion 180, 277, 360, 423, 603
corporal punishment of children
alternatives to 544–545, 544–545*n*18
at schools 542–543, 545
ban on 542, 548
Biblical interpretation 545–546, 550,
556–561, 562
by parents 542, 545
Christian views/practices 545, 550, 566
conservative Protestants 549–550,
556, 562
Roman Catholics 550
definition 543
forms of punishment 544
groups/type of children most
punished 542–543, 548, 553
ineffectiveness and harm 543, 544, 551,
560, 561, 566
Jesus Christ on 556, 560
link with discipline/discipleship 549,
550, 553, 556, 560
permission and acceptance in US 542,
543, 545, 549, 551
rejection of 546, 551, 560, 566
See also child protection and welfare;
spanking
statistics 543
corpus Christianum 89
Corpus Christi (TX) 438
corruption
in adoption (Romania) 580, 581, 583

in Sodom 629
Council of Constance (1414–1418) 334
Council of Trent (1545–1563) 45, 128, 241,
504
Bologna sessions 511, 512
on marriage/clandestine marriage 128,
501–502, 504, 508–509, **510–514**
on sacraments 507, 511
Counter-Reformation 355
Catholic-Protestant scholarly
debates 240–243
Court of Common Pleas (England) 239,
245, 246
Eyston v. Studd (2 Plowden 459; 75 ER 688,
1574) 247
Court of Exchequer Chamber
(England) 245
Court of International Trade (New York) 123
Court of King's Bench (England) 239, 242
Thomas v. Sorrell (1673, EWHC (KB)
J85) 245–247
court rulings. *See under individual courts*
coutumes (France) 264–265, 266
covenants
concept and characteristics of 148,
150–151
contracts vs. covenants 36, 152–153, 163,
182
creation, covenant, conscience triad 36,
38
divine-human covenants 92, 150, 151, 154,
160, 345, 361
violation of 149, 346–347
history/origins 148
intrahuman covenants 92, **151–154**, 157,
159, 160, 161
Mosaic 156–157
new covenant 148, 157
Puritan covenant theology 92–93, 94,
352, 361, 370
racially restrictive covenants 605–607,
609, 610, 611
right of self-defense and 328
sacraments vs. 14
See also marital covenants; Noahic
covenant; political covenants; Ten
Commandments/Decalogue
social covenants 92–93
treaties vs. 161

covenants (*cont.*)
    works by/JW on   20, 92, 93, 148, **149–151**, 157
COVID-19 pandemic   179, 181
    civil vs. spiritual dimensions   473
    conscientious objection against vaccination   479
    legal cases/court rulings   455–456, 457, 474
        German Federal Constitutional Court   474–475
        Scotland   456, 461, **463–466**
        secular vs. religious cases   458, 459, 460, 461
        United Kingdom   456, **461–466**, 475
        US Supreme Court   97, 456, **458–461**
    religious/church autonomy and   **455–457**, 462, 464, 465, 474
    restrictions on collective worship   455, 459, 460, 462, **463–466**, 470, 496*n*25
    scholarship during   130
CRC. *See* UN Convention on the Rights of the Child
creation   20
    creation, covenant, conscience triad   36, 38
crimes, civil enforcement of arbitration   610–611
criminal law
    contemporary (Anglo-American) vs. Protestant Reformed uses of law   188–191
    purposes/functions of   188–189, 190, 191
    works by JW   13, 29
critical legal studies (CLS)   292, 295
critical race theory (CRT)   289, 292
    on nature/ideal of law   294, 295, 300
    on/and (moral) truth   290, 297–298, 298*n*34, 301, 302, 303, 304
    on power   291
        impact of politics and power on formation and application of rights   299–300
    on racial justice/injustice   300, 301
    role of African American Christian tradition in   293, 294
    on value of rights   295, 296
cross of Christ   145–146, 147
    public display of   437, 447–448, 450, 451

CRT. *See* critical race theory
crucifixion of Jesus Christ   145–146, 222, 227, 299
CSLR. *See* Center for the Study of Law and Religion (Emory University)
culture, Christianity, community, culture triad   35–36, 38
culture war (United States)   574
custody
    best interest of children   577
    children's right to be consulted/heard   576
    parental rights of   519, 520, 571, 574
    religious arbitration   603
Cyclops   626

Danbury Baptists, letter from Jefferson to   398, 400–402, 409
Darwinism   228, 321
Decalogue. *See* Ten Commandments/Decalogue
Declaration of the Rights of the Inhabitants of the Commonwealth of Massachusetts (1780)   417
Deistic rationalism   224
Delaware   417
democracy
    American democracy   224
    importance of civic education for   521–522, 526, 534
    influences of Christianity on   27
    pluralism vs. secularism in   293*n*12
    religion and moral citizenry as basis for republican   416, 417, 418, 420, 425, 426, 430, 431, 432–433
    See also representative democracy/government
    works by JW   118
democratic republicanism, moral calculus/logic of   416, 418, 420, 425, 426, 430
depravity, total depravity doctrine (Luther)   174, 225
despair   225, 226, 233
determinatio (rational will of lawmakers)   491, 491*n*20–21, 492
dextarum iunctio (ritual act of joining spouses' right hands)   505
Dharamsala (India)   126
Diet of Worms (1520)   481–482

digitalization publishing/scholarship 129–130
dignity. *See* human dignity
disabled persons 576
disciples 557–558
discipline/discipleship
  church discipline 277–278
  definition/meaning 557–558
  link of corporal punishment with 549, 550, 553, 556, 560
  New Testament on discipline 558–560
discipline/discipleship (*cont.*)
  self-discipline/self-control 559
discrimination. *See* racial discrimination; religious discrimination
discrimination
  racial 202, 607
  religious 452–454, 456, 459, 461
disestablishment of religion
  in Constitution of the United States 391–392
  history and traditional understanding of 442, 444
  See also Anglican Church/Church of England; Establishment Clause
dispute resolution, alternative 598, 612, 613
  See also arbitration
Dissenters (from Anglican Church) 354, 357, 358, 360, 365–366
  in Georgia 373–374, 377, 380–381, 394
  disputes between Anglicans and Dissenters 383–385
  See also Anabaptists; Baptists; Congregationalists; Presbyterian Church/Presbyterians; Puritans; Quakers; Unitarians
divine grace 221, 225
divine law, during Middle Ages 23
divine love (*agape*). *See* love
divine (moral) law
  civil law and/vs. 190, 191, 192–193, 469
  uses of. *See* uses of the law
divine order 36
divorce
  bystander concept and 170
  ecclesiastical vs. secular jurisdiction 504–505
  evolution in lawmaking and cultural transformation 73, 74, 163, 170

Jewish arbitration agreements 603–604, 611, 612–613, 613*n*124
no-fault divorce 170, 232
polygamy as alternative for 49
reintroduction of 257
doctrine (concept) 278–279
Dominicans 503
dualism 138
Due Process Clause (Fourteenth Amendment to the Constitution of the United States) 571
Duke Divinity School (Durham, NC) 228
Dutch Reformed Christianity/Dutch Reformed Church 96, 196
  Afrikaans versions of 159*n*23
Dutch Republic 110
  See also Netherlands, the
Dutch Revolt (c. 1566/68–1648) 350
duties, intertwinement of rights and 318

Ebenezer (GA) 374–375, 385
ecclesiastical authority. *See* church authority
ecclesiastical law. *See* canon law
Ecclesiastical Law Society (London) 284
ecclesiology 272–273, 286–287, 288
ECHR. *See* European Court of Human Rights
economic recession 180, 181
ecumenism/ecumenical dialogues
  ecumenical approach of JW/JW on 11–12, 20, 21, 78–79
  See also Common Vision [Index of Titles]
Edict of Nantes (1685) 365
education
  Amish 518–519, 521, 522, 530, 535
  children's rights in choosing 516, 518–519, 523–524, 530
  church-state separation and 395–396
  foreign language education 517
  Free Exercise Clause and 521, 535
  in Georgia 379–380, 387, 393
  homeschooling 522, 523, 524, 533, 533*n*130, 534, 535, 538–539, 542
  importance of civic education for democracy/society 521–522, 526, 534
  parental rights in directing 515–516, 531–532, 534, 538
    legal cases/court rulings 517–518, 521
    scholarly critiques **521–533**

INDEX OF SUBJECTS 705

purpose and functions of 515
religious education 421, 531–533, 534, 535
role of state in upbringing and 529–530, 531, 534, 536–537
See also homeschooling; public schools
EFASASH (Ending Forced Arbitration of Sexual Assault and Sexual Harassment Act, 2021) 599, **611–613**
Egypt 142–143, 162
EHRC (European Human Rights Convention) 572–573
ekporneusasai (term/meaning) 624, 625
"Eleutherians" (Mather), "Idumeans" vs. 359–360
Emory College (Atlanta, GA), Department of Religion 119
Emory School, Harvard and Duke school vs. 228
Emory University (Atlanta, GA) 6, 39, 113, 642
  Emory Law School 115, 116, 118, 120
  See also Center for the Study of Law and Religion (CSLR)
employment, secular employment vs. employment by God 456
Ending Forced Arbitration of Sexual Assault and Sexual Harassment Act (EFASASH, 2021) 599, **611–613**
endorsement of religion/endorsement test 434, 436–437, **445–449**, 453
England 44, 362
  autonomy for legally tolerated religious congregations 472
  post-Reformation 359–360
  revolutionary movements 327, 335
  See also Anglican Church/Church of England; common law; United Kingdom
English Civil War (1642–1651) 356
English Reformation, Catholic-Protestant scholarly debates **240–243**
Enlightenment
  humanism and 224, 226
  human rights and 29, 46, 59, 66, 310, 327
  ideal of law 292, 294, 300
  individualism and 62
  marriage law and 73, 74

natural subjective rights and 63–65, 327, 368
parental and children's rights/duties 527
revolutionary thought and 348, 469
Entanglement Clause 600
Episcopal Church 127, 137, 374, 389, 394
episcopal governance 243, 276, 412
equality/inequality
  of children 552–553
  friendship and 213
  New Testament on human 46
  See also racial subordination; religious equality; social equality
Equal Protection Clause (Fourteenth Amendment to the US Constitution) 606
equity 336–337, 338
eros 218, 232
Establishment Clause (First Amendment to the US Constitution)
  Free Exercise Clause vs. 180, 458
  on government religious speech 435, 438, 443
  endorsement of religion 434, 436–437, **445–449**, 453
  nonspeech specific approaches 444–445
  proselytization 451
  religious speech tests 434, 436–437, 443–449, 452–454
  taking position on religious questions 449–451
  interpretation of 591
  jurisprudence 93, 99–100, 99n44, 102, 180
  JW on 99–100, 102
  meaning 99–100
  on public use of religious symbols 436, 437, 438, 442, 453
  violations/sidestepping of 102
    Bible reading in public schools 415, 442
    government religious speech 444–445, 452
    religious contract/arbitration enforcement 592, 603, 604, 608
eternity clause/guarantee (German law) 143

ethics
  charitable bystanders 168, 169–172, 181–183
    See also Good Samaritan
Eucharist 232–233, 279, 280, 506
eudaimonism 215, 221, 222, 230
Europe
  family and child protection law/policy making in 572–573, 575–578
  fundamental constitutional rights in 457
  polygamy in 48, 49
  religious freedom/liberty in 101–102
  revolutionary movements in 328, 329
European Constitution 144
European Court of Human Rights (ECHR) 572, 576
  Pini and others v. Romania (78028/01, 78030/01, Jun. 22, 2004, ECHR) 581–582
European Human Rights Convention (EHRC) 572–573
European Union
  on child protection and adoption regime in Romania 580–581
  federalist structure of 576
  ratification of conventions 569, 576
euthanasia 226, 311, 314, 316
Exclusion Crisis (1679–1681) 356
excommunication 43, 251, 252

FAA (Federal Arbitration Act) 590, 599, 601, 608, 612, 613
faith 222
  faith formation 560–561
  reason and 236, 236n6, 247–248n58, 248
  salvation by faith alone (*sola fide*) 226, 252
  as "weightier matter of law" 138
"Faith-Based Family Laws in Pluralistic and Democratic States" (project, CSLR) 125
faith, freedom, family triad 23, 640
"faith in law, law in faith" 22
Faith and Order Commission (World Council of Churches) 273, 285
  See also *Common Vision* [Index of Titles]
family disputes
  arbitration 581, 599, 611–613
  sample cases 594–595

family/family life
  importance of strong family life 547–548
  multi-institutional family 533–539
  right to 571, 572, 573, 574
  secular meaning of 322–323
  transformation of family life 74
  works by/JW on 516, 525–526, 529
family law/teachings
  charitable responsibilities of family 176, 178
  family norms 69, 75
  freedom and 322
  lawmaking,
    Africa vs. the West 125
    Western 71, 73, 572, 575
  multidimensional rights and duties of marital family 105
  protection of family 322–323, 573, 574
  religion/faith and,
    historical presentation of sex, marriage, and family 71–72, 73–74, 76, 516
    influence of religion on family law and culture 76–79
  secular meaning of 322–323
  See also children's rights, parental authority; marriage law; parental rights
  state action/intervention 87, 571, 573, 574
  works by JW/JW on 15, 29, 55, 69–70, 76–77, 105, 320, 516
    faith, freedom, and family triad 23, 640
    new projects 124–125
    scholarly approach and virtues of JW 32, 37, 71, 78–85, 322
family relations/ties
  adult-child relationships 551, 554, 560, 561
  communication and trust 531
  consequences of breaking 82
  JW on 531
  social welfare and 74
fear of God 160–161, 161–162, 163, 224
Federal Arbitration Act (FAA) 590, 599, 601, 608, 612, 613
federalist systems, ratification of conventions in 574–575
Federation Press 32

INDEX OF SUBJECTS 707

Fieldstead Institute 121
fiqh (Islamic jurisprudence) 596
First Amendment to the US Constitution
        (1791) 56
    constitutional status of religion in 101
    Free Speech Clause 436
    historical context of 396, 399, 402, 434
    JW on 99–100
    prohibition of religious
        establishment 415
    religion clauses 99–100, 435, 440, 443,
        452
    See also Establishment Clause; Free
        Exercise Clause
    separation of church and state 400–401,
        403, **404–406**, 409, 410, 419
First Continental Congress (1774) 385
First Table of Mosaic Law 338, 342, 344,
        346, 367
Florida 167, 377
Focus on the Family (fundamentalist
        Protestant organization) 549,
        556n38
forced conversion 360
Ford Foundation (New York) 121, 125
foster care
    children's perception of 582–583
    in Europe 572–573, 578–579
        Romania 581, 582–583
    in United States 584–585, 586
foundlings 570
Fourteenth Amendment to the US
        Constitution (1868) 415, 587
    Due Process Clause 571
    Equal Protection Clause 606
Fourth Lateran Council (1215) 505–506
France 358, 391
    absolutism in 343, 354, 358
    Calvinists/Huguenots in 341, 342,
        343–344, 349, 377
    canon law in 262–264
    nationalism 266
    reception of *ius commune* in Protestant
        Reformation 252, **261–266**,
        269
    revolutionary movements in 327, 335
    secularism in 609, 614
Franciscans 60–61, 503
Franks 265

free assembly/association. *See* associational
        freedom/liberty
freedom of choice 36, 226
freedom/liberty
    in family law 322
    governmental protection of subjective
        rights of 96, 101–102, 205, 336, 338,
        345, 348, 356
    JW on 96n36, 207, 315, 321
    See also associational freedom/liberty;
        constitutional rights and freedoms;
        freedom of speech; political
        freedom/liberty; religious freedom/
        liberty
    subjective rights of freedom and/vs.
        common good 205
freedom of speech 101, 183, 344, 436
Free Exercise Clause (First Amendment to
        the US Constitution) 586–587
    aid to religious schools 537n142
    on education 521, 535
    Establishment Clause vs. 180, 458
    meaning 99–100
    violations of 93, 437, 478n55, 586–587,
        603, 609
free exercise of religion 409, 600, 609
    arbitration and 613–614
    legal cases/court rulings/
        jurisprudence 480, 586–587, 592,
        601
    See also education
    strict scrutiny v. rational basis
        cases 458–459, 460
    religious conscience and/vs. 480, 496,
        497n28, 600n64
Free Speech Clause (First Amendment to the
        US Constitution) 436
French language 266
French law 263, **264–266**
French Revolution (1789–1799) 310, 312,
        319, 397
friendship
    Aristotle on 217
    civic friendship 211–212
    common good and 212, 213
    human equality and 213
    JW on 185
    purpose of 185–186, 211
    Thomas Aquinas on 185–186, 211–212

fundamental rights
  concept and origins   143
  in Europe   457
  presumptive status of   470
  revolution to protect   327–328, 339
funerals   280, 384
FUNVICA Foundation   121

Gabriel (archangel)   627
Gadarene swine (story)   624–625
Gage County (NE)   428
Gallic Church   263
Gauls   265
gay couples/relations
  adoption by   588
  Catholic doctrine   617–619
  condemnation in Old Testament   631, 632, 636, 636n124
  See also same-sex marriage/relations
gender equality   77
gender identity, children and   537
General Assembly Act (Scotland, 1592)   464
General Court (Massachusetts)   355
Geneva   42, 338
Genevan Reformation/Genevan Church   42, 78
  marriage contracts in   48, 83
  See also Calvinism/Calvinists
genocides   168, 169, 170
Gentiles   162, 222, 367, 486–487, 630
Georgia
  1785 Act   388–389, 390, 393
  Anabaptists in   387
  Baptists in   376, 388, 390, 392, 392n112, 394
  Catholics in   373, 376–377, 378, 380, 386, 394
  Charter (1732)   377–378, 386
  church-state relations   373, 380–383, 386–387, 388, 390, 394
  Congregationalists in   375, 381
  conscientious objection from military service in   387, 390
  education in   379–380, 387, 393
  establishment of Anglican Church in   373, 374, 378, 379, 380, 381–383, 393–394
    church fees   384, 385, 386
    disputes with Dissenters   383–385
    organization   382–383, 387–388

  financial government support for religion   378–379
  haven for persecuted/dissenting groups   377–379, 381
  Jews in   374
  land grants   375, 377, 379, 393
  liberty of conscience in   373, 378, 381, 386, 392, 394
  Lutherans (Salzburgers/Moravians) in   374–375, 379, 381, 385
  marriage in   379, 384–385
  Methodists in   376
  parishes in   382–383, 387
  Protestant Dissenters in   373–374, 377, 380–381, 394
    disputes with Anglicans   383–385
  Quakers in   376, 378, 387, 390
  religious equality in   377, 378, 380, 394
  religious freedom/liberty in   373, 378, 383, 386, 389, 391–392, 393, 394
  religious history   373–377
  religious pluralism in   **373–376**, 378, 386, 390
  revolutionary sentiment in   385
  as royal colony   380–385
  Scottish Presbyterians in   375
  Sunday peace/rest in   383
  taxation in   387, 388–389
Georgia Baptist Association   388
Gerar (Biblical Philistine city-state)   160, 161, 162, 162n27
German Federal Constitutional Court, COVID-19 rulings   474–475
German law   143, 268, 471
Germany   214
  canon law in   44
  child protection in   579
  impact of Lutheran theological ideas on secular laws   14
  rise of universities   249
giants   627, 629
Gillick-competence   578, 578n53
globalization/global markets   320–321
global law   12, 29, 122, 641
Glorious Revolution (New England, 1688–1689)   353, 355–356, 357, 358n13, 363
God
  fear of   160–161, 161–162, 163, 224
  holiness of   218–219, 221, 222, 223, 224

INDEX OF SUBJECTS

imitatio Dei   223, 224, 226, 227
  obedience to   222, 225, 483, 486
  recognition in constitutions   96
  secular employment vs. employment by   456
  sovereignty of   91
  as *Übermensch*   226
Godly Play Foundation (Ashland, KS)   550
gods, Aristotle and Plato on   217–218
Gomorrah   620, 623, 627, 628, 632, 636
good law   145–146, 269, 443
Good Samaritan story   **165–169**
  bystander ethics in   169–172
  in contemporary sociopolitical sphere   181–183
  "Good Samaritan" laws/duty to rescue   167
  "Good Samaritan" states   167, 172–173, 175, 178, 182
  JW on   168, 171
  lawyer in   165–166
  priest and Levite in   166, 172, 182
good, the/goodness   215–216, 224
  in Moses and the Prophets   218
  Plato vs. Aristotle on   215–216, 217, 218
good will   223–224, 225
good works   176, 190–191, 192, 192n44, 252, 295
government authority. *See* state authority
government religious speech. *See* religious speech and proclamations (by government)
governments
  protection of subjective rights of freedom   96, 101–102, 205, 336, 338, 345, 348, 356
  See also monarchies/monarchial rule; republics; state
government spending
  direct support to religion (Georgia)   378–379
  relation between charitable giving and   179–180
grace   21, 196, 221, 224, 225
Graduate Institute for the Liberal Arts (ILA, Emory University)   115
gratitude   144, 223
Great Commandment, Good Samaritan ethics and   **169–172**
great flood   154, 155n15, 163

Great Recession (2008)   180
Greece   214
Greek cardinal virtues   217, 218, 223
Greek eudaimonism   215, 221
Greek (language), Bible   557–559, 563, 620, 623, 624–625
Greek philosophy/philosophers   80, **215–218**, 221, 222, 223, 558
guardians *ad litem*   576, 579
guilds   177

Habitat for Humanity (NGO, Atlanta, GE)   129
Hague Convention on Protection of Children and Co-operation in Respect of Intercountry Adoption (1993)   582, 583
Halle (Germany)   267
Hanafi scholars   597
Hanover, House of   366
happiness
  Aristotle on   216–217, 222
  in Christian ethics   223
  "happiness project" (CSLR)   127, 233, 664
  holiness vs.   218
  pursuit of   127, 233
  sanctification and   222
hard sciences, humanities and/vs.   9, 117, 640
Harold J. Berman Library (CSLR, Emory University)   120
Harvard Divinity School   130, 228, 650
Harvard Law School   4, 6, 18, 39, 116
Haskins Medal   128
health care, law, religion and   131
Hebrew republicanism   361
hendiadys   220
Henry Luce Foundation (New York)   121, 671
heresy   42, 62, 264, 267
hesed (unfailing love)   220–221
Hessen (Germany)   474
Hinduism   20
historical writing   55–56
history, law and   21
holiness
  of God   218–219, 221, 222, 223, 224
holiness (*cont.*)
  happiness vs.   218
  of Jesus Christ   221–222, 223
  sanctification and   222

Holocaust   168
Holy Communion   233, 280
holy orders   231–232
Holy Spirit
    conscience and role of   138, 481, **487–491**, 497
    (power) as Spirit of justice   136, 144, 145, 146, 147
holy will, human will vs.   224, 227
homeschooling
    abuse and neglect in cases of   534, 542
    isolation/limited exposure to alternative views   522, 523n61, 524, 538–539
    motivations for   523, 533
    prohibition/restrictions on   523n59,n61, 524, 534, 535
    recognition of   533n130
homo religiosus, homo Christianus vs.   20
homosexuality   618–619, 630–631, 633, 636, 636n124
    See also gay couples/relations; same-sex marriage/relations
Hong Kong   13, 121, 169
hope   222
hōs (term/meaning)   623, 627, 632
house purchases, racially restrictive covenants   605–607, 609, 610, 611
Huguenots   341, 342, 343–344, 349
human dignity
    children's dignity rights   570
    constitutional/secular vs. religious understanding   311, **313–315**, 321
    historical development/evolution of   312, 314
    in human rights debate   312
    inviolability of human   143–144
    in modernity/postmodernity   312, 314
    religion vs.   223, 312, 321
    sanctity and/vs.   314–316
human flourishing   209n119, 215, 217, 219
human freedom/liberty. *See* freedom/liberty
humanism, Enlightenment and   224, 226
humanities, hard sciences and/vs.   9, 117, 640
humanity, development of   197
human law, friendship as purpose of   185–186, 211

human nature, in legal history   40–42
human rights
    advocacy of   52
    Christianity and   14, 28–29, 197
        Bible on human rights   143–144
        Protestant Reformation/Calvinism and   14, 41–42, 66
        role of Christian lawyers   10–11, 31
    civil vs.   300n41
    human dignity and   312
    intellectual historical perspective on   53, 58
    Islam and   120
    legal perspective on,
        human rights in legal history   45–47, 53, 58
        intellectual vs. legal historians   58
        legal rights and/vs. human rights   53, 99
        uses of law and vindication of   185, 190–191, 192n44, 202, 209, 295
    origins of   29, 46, 54, 197–198
        Enlightenment   29, 46, 59, 66, 310, 327
    philosophical perspective on   29, 52–53, 58, 67, 207–208
    in political discourse and   198, 296–297, 298, 299–300, 299n41
    religion and,
        place of religion in (creation of)   46, 54–55
        religious freedom and human rights   14, 18, 56, **65–68**, 207
        respect of human rights by religions   77
        theological and philosophical critic   207–208
    See also natural rights
    term and definition/concept   59, 59n18
        natural rights vs.   59
        subjective vs. objective rights   59, 65
    violations and rights claims   57, 194, 211
    works/studies by JW   45–46, 51, 53, 65, 98–99, 118
        centrality of religion in work   54–55
        polemical significance of work   57–60
        rhetorical form of work   55–57

INDEX OF SUBJECTS 711

Human Rights Act (UK, 1998)   463
human rights movements   541*n*3
Human Rights Watch/Africa (Washington, DC)   120
human sovereignty   225
human trafficking   576, 583
human will   223–227

identity
  children's identity rights   570, 573, 574, 578, 581, 583, 586
  Christian   19, 145, 228, 494–495
idolatry   156, 160, 346, 359
"Idumeans" (Mather)   359, 362, 363
ILA (Graduate Institute for the Liberal Arts, Emory University)   115
illegitimacy/"illegitimacy" laws   75, 78, 82
illegitimate children. *See* nonmarital children
Illinois Supreme Court   428
imitatio Dei/imitatio Christi   223, 224, 226, 227, 232
imperialism   358, 365
Independent Presbyterian Church (Savannah, GA)   375
India   126, 246
Indigenous people/traditions   20, 78, 548
individualism
  in Anglo-American world   167
  causes of   62, 90
  in handling sex, marriage, and parenting   73, 74
  liberalism and/vs.   316
  overcoming   222
  possessive   65, 67
  of rights   67
  social   64–65
individual rights
  associational vs.   105–106, 105*n*67
  Catholic vs. Protestant views on   212
  right of government/common good and/vs.   202–207, 208–209
industrialization   177–178
institutional authority   90–91
institutional care (for children). *See* children's homes
integrative jurisprudence   137, 440–441, 445, 454

interdisciplinary teaching/scholarship   114, 115–116, 118, 119, 121, 129, 131
international human rights law   168
internet   169
interreligious dialogues   12, 21
Iran   169
Ireland   472*n*44, 569*n*7
Islam   19, 49, 120, 125
Islamic arbitration (United States)   595–597, 602
Islamic jurisprudence (*fiqh*)   596
Islamic law. See *sharia*
Islamophobia   126
Israel   143, 157, 162, 214, 220
Italy   255, 579
ius commune (classic sources of canon and civil law)   44, 251
  importance of Roman and canon law in   269
  influence on common law   236–237
  reception in Protestant Reformation, amalgamation   266–268
  at University of Basel   252, 260–261
  in France   252, 261–266, 269
  in Wittenberg   252–260
ius gentium (international common law)   211, 296*n*27
ius ("law," term)   23, 204, 206
ius particulare (local legal traditions)   251

Jericho   166
Jerusalem   628
Jewish arbitration (United States)   593, 602
  divorce   603–604, 611, 612–613, 613*n*124
Jewish law and religion scholarship/scholars   12
Jewish philosophy   503
Jews   166, 222, 427
  antisemitic   226
  blame for spreading COVID-19   455
  on child protection/children's needs   547
  in Cincinnati   427
  in Georgia   374
  on happiness   221
  Luther on   233*n*43
Jim Crow laws (America, late 19th/early 20th c.)   193

John Templeton Foundation (West Conshohocken, PA)   127
Joint Committee of Human Rights (House of Lords, House of Commons, UK)   577, 577n52
Judah, Kingdom of   628
Judaism   19
  eudaimonism and   222
  human rights and   29
  Jewish law   119, 367
  polygamy in   48–49, 75
  religious uniformity in   367
judgments *See under individual courts*
Judy and Michael Steinhardt Foundation (New York)   121
jurisprudence
  integrative   137, 440–441, 445
  Islamic (*fiqh*)   596
  sacramental   **228–233**
jurists
  Christian   10, **30–33**
  Martin Luther on   10, 31, 40–41
  training of   137
jury (English law)   238
justice
  charity and   172–174
  as driving force of law   30, 302
  as fairness   22
  love and   36, 220, 303
  natural law as basis for   440
  rights and   298, 299–300
  See also racial justice
  social   131, 289
  as "weightier matter of law"   138, 139–140

King Center (Atlanta)   124
King James Bible   415, 420, 421, 424, 425, 426, 427, 428, 432
Kirchenordnungen (Protestant Reformation)   251

Lambeth Conference   277, 284
land grants (Georgia)   375–376, 377, 379, 393
last rites   230, 231
Latin language   240, 266
law (*nomos*)
  autonomy of   137, 140, 294, 295
  concept/understanding of, narrow vs. broad   291–292
  definition   26
  driving forces of   30, 291, 297, 298, 301, 302, 304
  hierarchy of   469
  instrumental vs. noninstrumental understanding of   184–185, 202, 204
  most important matters of law. *See* "weightier matters of the law"
  objectivity of   292, 294, 295, 300
  origins/history of   21, 26
  reason (*nous*) vs.   218
  science of law   22, 199, 201
  See also Christianity and law (relation/interaction); law and religion (relation/interaction); uses of the law
  systematic and systemic stability of   140, 141
  unconditional love (*agape*) and/vs.   214, 232, 643
Law and Judaism Program (Center for the Study of Law and Religion, Emory University)   119
law, liberty, love triad   36–37, 38
lawmakers
  conscience and   **491–495**
  rational will of (*determinatio*)   491, 491n20–21, 492
law and religion (relation/interaction)
  cross-fertilization and learning effect   7, 132, 136, 137–138, 147
  in non-monotheistic religions   126–127
  origins and evolution of thought,
    contemporary   309–310
    early Christian   214, **221–223**
    future   126
    late Christian/post-Christian   23, 28, 214, **223–228**
    modernity/postmodernity vs. previous ages   309–310
    pre-Christian   22–23, 214, **215–221**, 222
  religious values in law   101, 295, 297, 300
  See also Christianity and law
  streams of thought   6–8

INDEX OF SUBJECTS 713

law and religion (relation/interaction) (*cont.*)
    dialectical interaction of law and religion 6–7, 18, 639
    juridical character of religion 7, 18
    religiosity of secular laws 7, 18, 317
    tensions and harmony between 8, 10, 117, 469
    Western and non-Western Christian understandings 11–12, 26
    works by JW/JW on 6–8, 17–18, 132, **291–293**, 310–311, 317, 319
Law and Religion Program (Emory University) 114, 115, 116, 118, 119
    See also Center for the Study of Law and Religion (CSLR)
law and religion studies 16, 115–116, 117
    See also Center for the Study of Law and Religion
lawyers
    in Good Samaritan story 165–166
    Protestant 42–43, 254, 260
    See also Christian jurists
legal cases, *See under individual courts*
legal history
    canon law in 43–45
    human nature in 40–42
    JW on 310–311, 315
    natural/human rights in **45–47**, 53, 58
legal positivism 44–45, 492–493
legal rights, human and/vs. 53, 99
Levites 166, 172, 182
Lex Salica (ancient Frankish civil law code) 265
lex talionis 139
LGBTQ persons 15, 73, 618
liberalism
    individualism and/vs. 316
    JW on 209–210, 318–319
    liberal pluralism 228
    moralization of modern liberal societies 30
    neutrality of 190
    religion and 317, 318
libertarianism 167, 180, 209, 209*n*119
liberty of conscience 399, 407, 440
    church-state separation and 409, 441
    in Georgia 373, 378, 381, 386, 392, 394
    as native right 354, 368
    protection of 364, 409
    See also religious conscience

in US Constitution/Founding Fathers on 392, 409, 660
liberty, law, liberty, love triad 36–37, 38
Lilly Endowment 121, 131, 671
local legal traditions/law (*ius particulare*) 251
London 244, 285
Lord's Supper 280
Los Angeles 438
Lotharian Legend (theory, Philipp Melanchthon) 255
Louisiana 167–168*n*5, 650
love
    as expression of truth 303
    justice and 36, 220, 303
    King on **302–305**
    law, liberty, love triad 36–37, 38
    of neighbor 168, 174, 176, 180, 222, 234, 318, 368, 546, 557, 562
    unconditional/divine (*agape*) 182, 214, 222, 291, **302–305**, 643
        law (*nomos*) and/vs. 214, 232, 643
    unfailing love (*hesed*) 220–221
Lower Saxony (Germany) 474
Lutheran Church
    church law 274
    mission/goals 274
    organization 276
    rites of passage 280
    worship 279
Lutheranism/Lutherans
    on authority and freedom 90, 91–92
    in Georgia (Salzburgers/Moravians) 374–375, 379, 381, 385
    impact on secular laws 14
    on natural law/natural rights 47, 335
    on poverty and charity 176
    on resistance, revolution, and self-defense 328, 335
    on sacraments 230, 232
    See also Luther, Martin [Index of Persons]
    works by JW/JW on 14, 88, 230
Lutheran Social Services 547
Lutheran World Federation (Geneva) 277
Lutheran World Relief (international NGO) 547

McDonald Agape Foundation 25, 121–122
Magna Carta (1215) 56, 66, 356, 467

Maine Judicial Supreme Court, *Donahue v. Richards* (38 Me. 379 (1854)) 426
Maliki scholars 597
malum in se/malum prohibitum 245
marital covenants
    justification/legitimacy of 163
    marriage as contract vs. covenant 150, 163, 508–509
    marriage as sacrament vs. covenant 14, 232
    origins/foundation 162–163
    political vs. 163
    recognition in American states 150
    works by JW/JW on 149–151, 153, 162
marriage/marriage law
    clandestine marriage 502, 505–507, 508–514
    Enlightenment and 73, 74
    in Georgia 379, 384–385
    impediments to marriage 84, 505, 506
    jurisdiction/authority,
        ecclesiastical vs. secular/civil 73–74, 504–505, 507, 508
        state authority/interference in 87, 108, 199–200
    (legal) equality between all forms of 15
    marriage contracts/settlements 73–74, 83, 322
    marriage as covenant. *See* marital covenants
    marriage licenses 74–75, 199, 384–385
    of minors/parental consent 509–510, 545, 616
    in natural law 149
    Old Testament on 149
    origins of 162–163
    plural/polygamous marriage. *See* polygamy
    redefinition of marriage 200
        See also polygamy; same-sex marriage/relations
    religion and,
        Protestant theology 45, 150, 254, 257
        religion shaping law 73, 124, 150
    as sacrament 128, 232, 501, 502–504
        compared to other sacraments 504, 506–507, 508, 513
        hybrid sacrament 505–507
        sacrament of New Law 501, 504, 505, 507
    same-sex marriage. *See* same-sex marriage/relations
    See also divorce; family law/teachings; marital covenants; nonmarital children; sex; wedding ceremonies/rites of passage
    women's status/relation between sexes 77–78, 83, 150
    works by JW/JW on 29, 55, 69–70, 71–76, 79–81, 82–83, 105, 127–128, 322, 501, 615–617
Maryland 417
maslahah (equitable, pragmatic policy) 597
Massachusetts 362
    Charter of Massachusetts 355, 356, 357–358, 364
    Congregationalism in 354–355, 357, 363–364, 365, 397
    Council of Assistants 355, 357
    duty to rescue in 167
    General Court 355
    integration into New England and royal governorship 355, 356, 357
    political autonomy 355, 357
    public education in 421, 424
    reform of church polity 368
Massachusetts Bay 241, 354, 363
Massachusetts Body of Liberties 352, 355, 356
Massachusetts Constitution (1780) 371, 417, 420, 431
    JW on 416, 430, 433
Massachusetts Declaration of Rights (1780) 425, 428
Massachusetts Police Court 430
    Commonwealth v. Cooke (7 Am. Law Register 417, 1859) 425–426
Massachusetts State Board of Education 422
matrimony/matrimonial law. *See* marriage/marriage law
medical care, children's right to be heard 578
Medieval Academy of America (Boston, MA) 128
Mennonite Disaster Service 547

mental health (of children)   520, 540, 551
MEPA (Multi-Ethnic Placement Act, US)   585*n*98
mercy   138, 140–142, 166
   natural law vs. laws of mercy   141
   See also Good Samaritan
metaphors   21, 35, **403–406**
   See also "wall of separation"–metaphor
Methodist Church/Methodists   277, 280, 376, 421
Michael (archangel)   627
Michigan Supreme Court, *Pfeiffer v. Board of Education* (118 Mich. 560 (1898))   427–428
military service, conscientious objection from   387, 390
Minnesota   167
mishpat (justice)   220
   See also justice
modernity
   dignity awareness in   312, 314
   JW on   318, 319
   relation between law and Christianity in previous ages vs.   309–310
modern positivism   440
Mohr Siebeck   25, 32
monarchies/monarchial rule
   Calvin on   338–339, 341
   representative governments vs.   338–339, 340, 362
   spiritual and temporal authority of   91–92, 362
monogamy   15, 48, 50
monotheism   221
morality
   moral duties   318
   moralization of modern liberal societies   30
   moral teaching at public schools   419
   private   189
   religion and moral citizenry as basis for successful republics   416–417, 418, 419, **422–424**, 426, 427, 428, 430, 431, 432–433
moral law. *See* divine (moral) law
"Moral and Spiritual Formation of Children" (seminar, Elizabeth Marquardt)   170

moral truth, critical race theory on/and   290, 296, 297–298, 298*n*34, 301, 302, 303, 304
Moravians   374, 375
Mormons   49, 401
mortality   231
Mosaic covenant   156–157
Mosaic government   213, 361–362, 363
Mosaic law   146, 355
   marriage in   149–150
   Saxon law vs.   257–258
   See also Ten Commandments/Decalogue
mosques, religious autonomy and   463, 474
Multi-Ethnic Placement Act (MEPA, US)   585*n*98
multi-institutional family   **533–539**
Muslim law and religion scholarship   12
Muslim philosophy   503

narratives   56–57
nation-state   230, 230*n*39
NATO   580
natural law   195, 197
   in Catholic doctrine   47
      Thomas Aquinas   47, 440
   as fundamental law   469
   laws of mercy vs.   141
   marriage in   149
   positive law, religious liberty, and   452
   Protestant Reformation and   47, 239, 268
      Calvin   91, 336–337
      Hugo Grotius   47, 268, 469
      Melanchthon   174, 268
   reason and   174
natural rights
   Calvin on   336, 343, 349
   charity and   182
   human persons as embodiment of   208
   human rights vs.   59
   in legal history   45–47, 53, 58
   Lutherans on   335
   natural subjective rights   59, 60, 61, 333
      Enlightenment and   **63–65**, 66, 327

natural rights (*cont.*)
    Locke on   59, **63–65**, 327, 344, 368
    origins of   66
    right of self-defense and   334, 348
    William of Ockham on   60, **61–63**, 66, 330
    parental rights and   526–527, 529
    representative government and   349
    See also human rights
    term and taxonomy   59, 59n18
    Thomas Aquinas on   333–334
Navajo Nation   598
Nazis/Nazi laws   193, 226
Nebraska Supreme Court, *State ex. rel. Freeman v. Scheve* (65 Neb 853 (1902))   428
neighbor
    definition   165, 166, 168
    love and charity for   168, 174, 176, 180, 222, 234, 318, 368, 546, 557, 562
    responsibility for/helping   171, 182, 183
    See also bystanders, charitable
Neo-Calvinism   88, 89, 95, 111, 647
    See also Kuyper, Abraham [Index of Persons]
Neo-Thomism   59, 60, 62, 208n17
Netherlands, the
    adoption in   583–584
    industrialization in   177–178
    Mornay in   347
    revolutionary movements in   327, 335, 349
New England
    constitutionalism/constitutions   353, 371, 416, 417
    duty to rescue in   167
    governorship of Edmund Andros   355, 356, 357, 360
    history   360
    integration/Anglicization of colonies   354–355, 365
    persecution of Baptists in   366
    See also Connecticut; Massachusetts
New England Puritanism/Puritans   151
    on church-state relations   352
    congregationalism and political autonomy   354–355, 357, 363–364, 369
    on covenants   352
    evolution of   371
    JW on   351–352
    on resistance and revolution   353, 354, 355, 356, 357
    See also Mather, Cotton [Index of Persons]
New England Way   352, 354, 357, 367, 369
New Hampshire   417
New Haven   421
New Jersey   415
New Jersey Supreme Court, *Doremus v. Board of Education* (5 NJ 435 (N.J. 1950) 75 A.2nd 880)   429–430, 430n36
New Law, marriage as sacrament of   501, 504, 505, 507
New Testament
    on discipline   558–560
    on human equality   46
    on meaning of Christianity   225, 226
    nomos in   222
    on nonviolence   345
    political covenants and   157
    reduction of New Testament Christianity   224, 226
    on same-sex relations   619–620
    See also Jude [Index of Scriptual References]
New York City   421
New York Court of Appeals, *Meacham v. Jamestown, J. & C.R.Co.* (105 N.F. 653, 655 (N.Y. 1914))   612
Nicene Creed   244
Nigeria   235
Noahic covenant   155n15
    as foundation for marital covenants   162–163
    as foundation for political covenants   154–155, 156, 157
nominalism   62–63
nomos. *See* law
"A Non-Christian Europe: Is It Possible?" (lecture, Joseph Weiler)   144
Nonconfirmists. *See* Dissenters
nonmarital children
    adoption and parenting of   14, 23, 82
    care responsibility for   85
    legal disabilities of   616–617
    treatment and suffering/punishment of   74, 75, 84, 319–320
    well-being of   75, 78, 84
    works by JW/jw on   14, 23, 75, 82, 85, 616–617
nonmonotheistic religions   126–127

nonviolence   303, 345
norms and values
    civil law and/vs. divine moral law   192–193
    family norms   69, 75
    See also morality; religious values
Northwest Ordinance (1787)   418, 427, 428
Norway   572
nous. See reason (nous)/reasoning
nuptial blessing   505, 506, 509, 511

oaths/oath taking   154, 159, 161, 163, 222, 378, 380, 387, 390
    affirmation vs.   378
    in courts   222
    in Georgia   378, 380, 387, 390
    international treaties/covenants   163
    for intrahuman covenants   154, 159, 161
    See also covenants
Oath of Supremacy   237, 238
obedience
    See also conscience
    to conscience   486, 487
    to God   222, 225, 483, 486
    to Jesus Christ   489
objective rights   59, 65
Occasional Conformity Act (England, 1711)   365
Odysseus   625, 626
Ohio   376, 421, 427
Old Testament
    covenants in   153, **154–157**, 158
    on marriage   149
    on same-sex relations   628, 630–631, 634, 636, 636n127
    Saxon law and/vs.   257–258
optimism   420
ordained ministry/ministers   275–276
    payment of ministers   378–379, 382
"orderly federalism" (Kuyper)   110
orphans   175, 540, 569n7, 581, 628
Orthodox Christianity/Orthodox Church
    authority, governance, and organization   276
    democracy and   27
    law and religion in   26
    membership conditions   275
    natural law in   47
    rites of passage   280
    worship   279

Overton Park   206
ownership. See possession
Oxford University Press   25

paideia/paideian (term)   558–559
Palestine   621–623
Panel of Experts in Christian Law   271, 283
papal authority   252, 359
    See also canon law
papal dispensation   41, 43
papal lawbooks (*Corpus iuris canonici*)   40, 251, 252, 653
parental authority
    children as models of faith for parents   553–554, 555
    children's growing development and   562
    limits on   520, 546, 564–566, 574
    parental vs. children's autonomy   523, 524–525, 527–528, 530
    See also corporal punishment of children
    state intervention   564, 565–566, 571, 572–573, 576
parental rights and duties
    child protection and guidance   547, 552
    in Convention on the Rights of the Child   571
    cooperation between parents and state   536–537, 539
    corporal punishment   549, 553
    See also corporal punishment of children
    custody   519, 520, 571, 574
    directing education and upbringing   515–516, 532–533, 534, 538, 564
    JW on   526–527, 529
    legal cases/court rulings,
        on education   517–518, 521, 528, 530, 534, 538
        on upbringing   518, 519–520, 528, 530, 534, 538
    limits on   533–534, 536
    (natural) rights and duties between parents and children   516–517, 520, 526–527, 529, 574
    overprotection of   565
    property-based view of   524, 527, 528
    scholarly critiques of   **521–533**
    state intervention   564, 565–566, 571, 572–573, 576
    termination of   584

parenting
  individualism in 74
  influence of religion on 77
  mistakes and apologizing 564
  of nonmarital children 23, 82
  parental failures/imperfection 528, 529, 565
  positive parenting practices 557, 566, 567
  See also family law/teachings
  views of different branches of Christianity on 551–552
Paris 243, 264
Parlement of Paris 264, 265
Parousia 223, 367
paternalism/patriarchy 73, 75, 529
  political paternalism 332, 347
  religious paternalism 338, 346, 349
Peacemaker Ministries (Christian arbitration organization, US) 594
penance 231
Pennsylvania 375, 415, 422
people of color 300, 301, 303
perfection 225
persecution 365, 366, 367, 378
personal and social freedom/liberty 90–91
Personal Work and Responsibility Act (US, 1996) 180–181
The Pew Charitable Trusts 121, 671
Pew Research Center 455
philosophy/philosophers
  Greek 80, **215–218**, 221, 222, 223, 558
  on human rights 52–53, 58, 67
piety 370
Pilgrims 224, 225
pistis. *See* faith
pluralism
  JW on 291
  secularism vs. 293*n*12, 614
  See also political pluralism; religious pluralism
pluralist societies 34, 109, 300, 538
  relation between Christianity and law in modern 38
  role of institutions in 131
plural marriage. *See* polygamy
police 169
political association. *See* political covenants
political authority 90, 100, 110–111, 349
  See also state authority

political covenants **154–162**, 346
  contemporary 157, **159–162**
  divine-human 149, 150, 151, 154, 158
  intrahuman 154–156, 159
  marital vs. 163
  new covenant vs. 157
  in Old Testament 153, **154–157**, 158
  origins/history 156, 157, 158
  Protestant Reformed view 150–151, 157–159
  Puritan 92–93, 94, 352, 361, 370
  religious freedom/liberty and 151, 158
  See also Noahic covenant, Mosaic covenant
  in United States 161
  works by JW/JW on 149, 150–151, 153
political equality 103
political freedom/liberty 42, 353
political participation 91, 209*n*119
political pluralism 95–96, 110
political science, theology and 228
politics/political theory
  (human) rights in political discourse 198, 296–297, 298, 299–300
  Protestant political thought, in Calvinism 88, **89–94**
  works/studies by JW 87
polygamy
  as alternative for divorce 49
  criminalization of 401
  in Europe 48, 49
  in Hebrew Bible/Judaism 48–49, 75
  in Islam 49
  legalized 202–203
  origins of 80
  polygamous unions/marriage 200, 202, 210, 322
  in United States 48
  Western monogamy vs. 15
  women's rights 48, 75
  works by JW/JW on 48, 49–50, 75, 80, 200–203, 322, 617
polytheism 160
poor-relief laws/theology 173, 175, 177
popery 354, 357, 358
porneia (prostitution) 624, 631
"Positive Discipline in Everyday Parenting" (program, Joan Durrant) 544–545*n*18, 557*n*40

INDEX OF SUBJECTS 719

positive law 91, 441, 442, 443, 445,
    452, 469
possession
  property vs. 259
  right of 60–61
postmodernity
  dignity awareness 314
  future of religion in 320, 325
  JW on 318
  relationship between law and Christianity
    in previous ages vs. 309–310
poverty
  children entering care due to 571
  disdain for the poor 628, 629
  family relations/ties and 82
  Franciscan 60–61
  See also charity
  spiritual idealization of 176
  voluntary 176
  "worthy"/"deserving" vs.
    "unworthy"/"undeserving" of
    assistance 175, 176, 177, **179–181**
power
  as driving force of law and racial
    issues 291, 297, 298, 301, 302
  unequal power relations 291, 301
Pragmatic Sanction (Bourges, 1438) 263
prayer
  before legislative sessions 434, 436, 443,
    450–451
  day of payer 447
  ecumenical 446
  Friday 474
  national 450
  praying in public 437, 479
  school prayers 395–396, 403, 436
Prayer for All Sorts and Conditions of
  Men 244
prenuptial contracts/agreements 73,
    603–604, 611, 612, 613
Presbyterian Church/Presbyterians 159, 277,
    279, 280, 365
pride 628, 629
pride parades 634
priests
  in Good Samaritan 166
  payment of 264, 378–379, 382
Princeton University 121, 124
private schools, public funding of 609
Progressivism 204

Prometheus 625
property 83, 259, 281–282, 331, 473
proportionality analyses/tests 474–475
proselytization 451
prostitution (*porneia*) 624, 631
protection, responsibility to protect/be
  charitable 168, 171, 172, 173, 175,
    178, 182
Protestant Episcopal Church (United
  States) 374, 389, 394
Protestantism/Protestants
  claims on catholicity 243
  (classic) Protestantism and law 28
  on corporal punishment of
    children 549–550, 556, 562
  definition (Mather) 369, 370
  democracy and 27
  on integration of reason and
    revelation 236
  persecution of Protestants 365
    See also Huguenots
  political thought 88
  on revolution 327–328, 329, 348
  See also Anglican Church/Church of
    England; Calvinism/Calvinists;
    Lutheranism/Lutherans
  on theology of Saint Paul 145
Protestant lawyers 42–43, 254, 260
Protestant liberty **358–363**
Protestant Reformation. *See* Reformation
Protestant Reformism/Protestant Reformed
  tradition 20
Protestants and Other Americans United
  for the Separation of Church and
  State (separationist advocacy
  organization) 402–403
Provincial Council of Cologne (1536) 510
prudishness 73, 75
Prussia 470
public authority. *See* state authority
public health 131
Public Health (Control of Disease) Act
  (UK, 1984) 463
public punishment/trial 258, 259
public schools
  Bible reading in 415–416, 421, 422,
    424–433, 436, 442
  common schooling vs. church
    establishment 424
  corporal punishment at 542–543

720 INDEX OF SUBJECTS

display of religious symbols at   442–443
government sponsored speech in   434, 436
in Massachusetts   421, 424
moral teaching at   419
objections to curricula on religious grounds   538
Quakers and   421
replacing colonial educational structures   421
requirement for attending   517–518
school prayers in   437–438
punishment   139, 319–320
See also corporal punishment
Puritan Revolution   350
Puritans   224
Congregationalists and   354–355
covenant theology   92–93, 94, 352, 361, 370
on divine grace   225
formative impact on America   94, 95
on rights   371
See also Mather, Cotton [Index of Persons]; New England Puritanism/Puritans
on state authority and religious freedom   96
works by JW/JW on   88, 351, 370–371

Quakers
in Georgia   376, 378, 387, 390
public schools and   421
suppression of   364, 366
Quebec   167
Queens' College (Cambridge University)   241

R2P (responsibility to protect)   168
rabbinical court. *See* Jewish arbitration
race. *See* Christianity, race, and law (emerging discipline/intersection); critical race theory
racial discrimination   202, 607
racially restrictive covenants   605–607, 609, 610, 611
racial justice   290, 298, 300
political discourse and   301

power and interests as driving force in racial issues   291, 297, 298, 301, 302, 304
privileging perspectives of people of color in addressing   300, 301, 303
See also critical race theory
racial power   294, 297, 298, 299
racial subordination   294, 295, 298, 300, 301, 304
racism   140, 201–202
Ramadan   474
rape   78, 623
Raphael (archangel)   627
rational basis review (U.S. law)   476
rationalism
Deistic   224
rational will of lawmakers (*determinatio*)   491, 491n20–21, 492
realism   420
reason (*nous*)/reasoning
compatibility with religion   80, 227
law vs.   218
natural law and   174
revelation/faith and   236, 236n6, 247–248n58, 248
Rechtsstaat (term)   470
Reformation
Catholic-Protestant scholarly debates   240–243
as cause of individualism   62, 90
on charity   173, 174–178
contribution to transformation of law and legal theory   28, 37, 43, 89
first two centuries of   240–241
on marriage   150
natural law and   47, 239, 268
on political covenants   150–151, 157–159
post-Reformation England   359–360
purpose of   224
reception of *ius commune* in   251–252, 269–270
amalgamation   266–268
at University of Basel   252, 260–261
in France   252, 261–266, 269
in Wittenberg   252–260
reformation and repurposing of law   251

INDEX OF SUBJECTS 721

Reformation (*cont.*)
  on sacraments 501
  See also Calvinism/Calvinists;
      Lutheranism/Lutherans
  theology 186
Reformed churches, organization 277
Reformers
  on canon law 43–45, 251–252, 253,
      266–268, 653
  human nature of/as human beings 40
  influence on Anglican theology 84
  little-known 43
  See also Calvin, John [Index of Persons];
      Luther, Martin [Index of Persons]
regeneration 489
relativity theory 31
religion
  centrality in (creation of) human
      rights 46, 54–55
  compatibility with reason 80, 227
  concept 292
  dimensions of 7–8, 321
  endorsement of/endorsement test 434,
      436–437, **445–449**, 453
  establishment by/status in law 101, 395
  See also church-state relations
  future of 320, 325
  human dignity and/vs. 223, 312, 321
  influence on family law 76–79
  protection of 67–68
  See also law and religion (relation/
      interaction); religious autonomy;
      religious freedom/liberty
religion clauses (US Constitution). *See*
      Establishment Clause; Free Exercise
      Clause
religious arbitration
  abuse of 601, 603–604
  challenges of,
    application of Ending Forced
        Arbitration of Sexual Assault and
        Sexual Harassment Act 599,
        611–613
    expansion of state action by reverse
        entanglement arguments 599,
        603–611
    religious right to exit contracts 599–
        603, 605, 610–611
  Christian arbitration 593–594

commercial arbitration 593–594,
    609–610
conversion and 603
divorce 603–604, 611, 612–613,
    613*n*124
goal of 597–598
nonreligious vs. 614
religious arbitration clauses 613–614
sample cases 594–595
secular enforcement of decisions 603,
    604, 605, 610–611
See also Islamic arbitration; Jewish
    arbitration
in seemingly secular conflicts 592, 595,
    595*n*32
religious associations 97, 105, 106, 106*n*70,
    108, 109
See also associational freedom/liberty
religious autonomy
  COVID-19 and **455–457**, 462, 464, 465,
      474
  British rulings 456, **461–466**, 475
  German rulings 474–475
  Scottish rulings 456, 461, **463–466**
  US Supreme Court rulings 97, 456,
      458–461
  proportionality and 474–475
  religious group autonomy 455, 456–457,
      461, 463, 476, 478
  origins and nature **466–474**
  self-government **473–477**, 478
  See also church autonomy
  "two kingdoms"/"sovereign spheres"
      doctrines 150, 467, 472
religious coercion 363, 364, 366, 368, 371,
    411, 435
See also endorsement of religion/
    endorsement test
religious conscience
  Biblical theology **482–487**, 496
  conscientiously derived decisions 411,
      495–498
  court rulings/legal cases 479–480,
      493–494, 495
  free exercise of religion and/vs. 480, 496,
      497*n*28, 600*n*64
  JW on 481
  Protestant 480–481
  role of Holy Spirit 481, **487–491**, 497

Roman Catholic   480
values/Christian identity approach   493–495
religious discrimination   452–454, 456, 459, 461
religious education   531–533, 535
  See also homeschooling
religious education/schools
  government resources to   536–537, 537n142
  public funding of   609
religious equality   96
  conflicts with competing equality claims   102–103, 442, 452, 453
  in Georgia   373, 376–377, 378, 380, 394
religious freedom/liberty
  in America/United States   95, 97, 99, 614
    Georgia   373, 378, 383, 386, 389, 391, 391–392, 393, 394
    Jefferson on   397, 398
    principles of American religious liberty   407–408, 441, 441–442, 443
  in Catholic Church   46
  compared to other freedoms   101
  ecumenical view on   282–283
  essential rights and liberties   407
  in Europe   101–102
    United Kingdom   614
  human rights and   14, 18, 56, 65–68, 207
  origins and historical/traditional understanding of   333, 443, 444, 447, 454
  political covenants and   151, 158
  in Protestantism   334
    Calvin on religious liberty   41–42, 337
    contribution of Protestant Reformation   14, 66
    Mather on Protestant liberty   354, 363–370
    Protestant liberty   358–363
  same-sex marriage/relations and   15
  state authority and   96–104, 229
    JW on   97, 99–101
    protection of religious freedom   97, 101–102, 339, 440
    treatment from different perspectives, advocacy   52
    intellectual history   53
    legal history   53
    philosophy   52–53
  violation of   57, 435
  works/studies by JW   51, 54–55, 65, 120, 207
    genre of work   52–53
    polemical significance of work   57–60
    rhetorical form of work   55–57
religious groups, self-government   473–477, 478
religious holidays   391, 398, 399, 400
religious neutrality. See First Amendment to the US Constitution
religious pluralism   416, 432, 446, 449–450, 453, 454
  in Georgia   373–376, 378, 390, 394
religious speech and proclamations (by government)
  constitutional vs. unconstitutional/coercive vs. noncoercive   436, 438, 442
  court rulings/jurisprudence   442, 444, 448
  Establishment Clause on   435, 438, 443
    endorsement of religion   434, 436–437, 445–449, 453
    non-speech specific approaches   444–445
    proselytization   451
    religious speech tests   434, 436–437, 443–449, 452–454
    taking position on religious questions   449–451
  historical and traditional understanding of   443, 444–445, 446–447
  by Jefferson   398, 399–400, 400n19
  JW on   441–442, 443
  before legislative sessions   434, 436
  at public schools   434, 436
  secular-purpose requirement   444
  See also Bible reading; religious symbols/displays; school prayers
religious speech tests (US Supreme Court)
  coercion test   452
  endorsement test   434, 436–437, 446–449, 453
  purpose-and-effects test   444
  threat-of-discrimination test   452–454

religious symbols/displays
    government-sponsored   434, 436, 451, 453
        court rulings/jurisprudence   437, 443,
            447–448, 453
        endorsement test   434, 436–437,
            446–449, 453
        on war memorials   437, 450
religious tolerance   366–367, 368n33, 373,
    386
religious uniformity   367
religious values
    incorporation in/influence on law   101,
        295, 297, 300, 318
    objectivity of   185
representative democracy/government
    monarchy vs.   338–339, 340, 362
    natural rights and   349
republics/republicanism   361
    religion and morality in citizenry as
        basis for successful   417, 418, 419,
        422–424, 426, 427, 428, 430, 431,
        432–433
    See also state
rescue/rescuers. *See* bystanders, charitable
residential care (for children). *See* children's
    homes; foster care
resistance
    Calvinists on   327–328
    Lutherans on   335
    New English Puritan thought on   353,
        354, 355, 356, 357
    See also revolution; self-defense, right to
responsibility to protect (R2P)   168
Restoration. *See* Stuart Restoration
"Restoring Religious Freedom" (project,
    CSLR)   131
resurrection   146, 223
revelation, reason and   236, 236n6,
    247–248n58, 248
revenge   139
reverse entanglement principle (religious
    arbitration)   599, **603–611**
revolution
    Calvinists on   328, **335–342**, 343, 344, 348
    definition   335
    JW on   328, 348
    Lutherans on   328
    origins of revolutionary thought   348
    Protestant logic of   327–328, 329, 348

revolutionary sentiment in Georgia   385
role of First Table in   344
See also resistance; self-defense, right to
to protect fundamental rights   327–328,
    339
revolutionary movements
    in America   328, 329, 335
    in Europe   327, 328, 329, 335
right conflicts, individual rights and/vs.
    right of government/common
    good   202–207, 208–209
righteousness (*tsedaqah*)   220
rights
    abstract   195
    bottom-up approach to   207
    definition   207
    friendship and   211–213
    "good" vs. "bad"   195
    grounding in truth and justice   298,
        299–300
    individualism of   67
    individual rights and/vs. right of
        government/common good   202–
        207, 208–209
    intertwinement of duties and   318
    JW on   295–296, 296n27, 299, 327
    meaning of   327
    protection of   95, 98, 336, 337, 338, 345,
        348, 356, 368
    recognition of   207
    rights claims   194, 318
    rights "literacy"   98, 99
    rights talk in political discourse   198,
        296–297, 298, 299–300
    See also human rights
    value of   295–296
rites of passage   279–280
Robert W. Woodruff Professorships   114,
    115, 116
Roman Catholic Church/Roman Catholics
    authority and governance/
        organization   89–90, 276–277
    claims on catholicity   243
    on democracy   27
    on family   547–548
    JW on   20
    on resistance and revolution   328
    See also canon law; Catholic Church/
        Catholics

sexual child abuse 548
(view on) corporal punishment of children 550
Roman Empire 359
Romania
    adoption from/in 579–584
    child protection policy 579–584
    foster care 581, 582–583
    implementation of CRC 580, 581, 582
Roman law
    authority of 256, 261, 262, 267
    canon law and/vs. 44, 146, 256–257, 267, 467
    in France 261–262, 265, 266
    Luther on 254, 256, 257
    Melanchthon on 255–257, 258, 261, 262
    Protestant application of 266–268
    Saxon law and/vs. 259, 260
    subjective rights in 330–331
    teaching of 261
Rouen (France) 243
Round Hill School (Northampton, MA) 421
Russia 168, 580
Russian Orthodox Church 137
Rwanda 168

Sabbath observance 97
sacraments
    covenants/contracts vs. 14
    JW on 230
    marriage vs. other 506–507
    of the New Law (sacraments of the church) 501, 504, 505, 507, 511
    Protestant reformation on 501
    Roman Catholic 230
    sacramental jurisprudence 228–233
    sacramental theology 502, 504
    See also baptism; confirmation; Eucharist; marriage/marriage law
    Ten Commandments vs. 230, 233
sacramentum (term) 23
Sacred Spaces (Jewish organization) 548
St. Bartholomew's Day Massacre (August 24, 1572) 265, 343
saints, invocation and adoration of 237
salvation
    by faith alone (*sola fide*) 186, 226, 252
    sacraments and 511

Salzburgers (Lutherans from Salzburg in Georgia) 374–375, 379, 381, 385
same-sex marriage/relations 634
    in Anglican Church 280n43
    association with Sodom and Gomorrah 632, 636
    in Catholic Church 478n55, 617–619, 634
    ethical dimensions of 634
    fundamental right to 202, 210
    legal cases/court rulings,
        Masterpiece Cakeshop v. Colorado Civil Rights Commission (584 U.S. – (218)) 479, 493–494, 497, 497n28
        Obergefell v. Hodges (576 U.S. 644 (2015)) 200, 202, 203, 210, 573–574, 574n38
    New Testament on 619–620
        See also Jude [Index of Scriptual References]
    Old Testament on 628, 630–631, 634, 636, 636n127
    recent lawmaking 73, 200, 280n42
    religious freedom and 15
sanctification 222, 489–490
sanctity, dignity and/vs. 314–316
Sariel (archangel) 627
sarkos heteras (term/meaning) 625
sarx (term/meaning) 625–626
satellite communication 169–170
Savannah (GA)
    Black Baptist Church in 376
    education in 379
    establishment of Church of England in 383
    religious pluralism in 374–375
Saxon law
    benefits of 259–260
    Luther on 257–258, 259
    Melanchthon on 258
    Old Testament and/vs. 257–258
    Roman law and/vs. 259, 260
Saxony 266
Scandinavia 14, 44
Schism Act (Established Church Act, England, 1714) 365
scholarship/scholars. See Christian law and religion scholarship/scholars

INDEX OF SUBJECTS

scholastic theology, history and evolution of   502–503
school prayers   396, 403, 434, 436, 437–438, 443
Scotland
  canon law in   44
  children's rights policy   577
  COVID-19 court rulings/cases   456, 461, 463–466
  revolutionary movements in   327, 335, 349
Scottish National Covenant (1638)   159
Scottish Presbyterian Church/Scottish Presbyterians (Georgia)   375
Scottish Reformation   349
scripture, illegitimacy vs.   82
Second Coming of Christ   370
Second Continental Congress (1775)   385, 386
Second Table of Mosaic Law   368
Second Vatican Council (1962–1963)   27, 46, 208n117
sectarian religion and worship
  Bible reading at public schools and   424, 425, 426, 427, 428, 429, 432
  endorsement of sectarian religion   448–449
secular conflicts, religious arbitration in   592, 595, 595n32
secular employment, employment by God vs.   456
secularism   411
  American vs. French   609, 614
  pluralism vs.   293n12, 614
  secular legacy of Christianity   317–320
  secular-purpose requirement   444
  secular values   185
secularization   36–37, 310, 314, 468–469
secular law
  religious contribution to   7, 14, 319
  role of Christian lawyers in   10
self-consciousness   223
self-defense, right of
  against arbitrary force/abuse   329–330, 330n11, 331, 332, 334
  Calvinists on   328, 329, 335–336, 340–341, 343, 345–346
  canonists on   330–331, 334
  conciliarists on   331–332, 335–336, 348, 349

covenants and   328
JW on   327, 328–329
logic of self-defense   329–334
Lutherans on   335
meaning of   329
origins   330
See also resistance; revolution
subjective natural rights and   334, 348
self-discipline/self-control   559
self-government
  of religious groups   473–477, 478
  See also religious autonomy
separation of church and state. See church-state separation
separatist informal education. See homeschooling
September 11   126, 181
seruv (Jewish declaration of being in contempt of court)   602
sex
  historical association between religion and sex   71, 73, 74, 75–76
  individualism and   73, 74
  nonmarital   73
  sexual dimensions of sin of Sodom   623, 628, **629–632**, 633, 634, 635
  sexual morality/immorality   616, 616–617, 620, 627, 628, 629
  works by JW/JW on   69–70, 71, 76, **79–81**, 82, 84, 616–617
"Sex, Marriage, and Family and the Religions of the Book" (project by JW/CSLR)   124–125, 501, 664
sexual assault and abuse
  of children   126, 548, 550
  enforcement of arbitration   611–613
  sex trafficking   541n3, 545
  sexual harassment (definition)   613
sexual revolution   75
sharia (Islamic law)   49, 120, 596
sharia councils   99n42, 108n74
Sikh temples   473
sin
  Calvin and Luther on   187, 187n18
  charity distorted by   174
  children and   562–564
  corporal punishment and   563
  law under power of   145–146

Saint Paul on   230–231, 562
See also Sodom
structural   94
talking about   564
term/definition   563
Sinai   157
slavery/slave laws   141, 142, 143, 144, 193, 201, 228, 353
slender church establishment   416, 418, 431, 433
smartphones   169
social assistance
See also charity
"worthy"/"deserving" vs. "unworthy"/"undeserving" of   175, 176, 177, **179–181**
social covenants   92–93
social equality/inequality
religious vs.   103
role of law and religion in   131
social justice   131, 289
social media   169, 183, 540
Social Science Research Network   121, 125
social services   180
social welfare   178, 180
family relations and   74
reforms (US)   181
rights to   183
"worthy"/"unworthy" for assistance/"no fault of their own"   175, 176, 177, 178–181
Societas Goerresiana   512
society, sovereignty, society, solidarity triad   37, 38
Society for Establishing a Free School (New York City)   421
Society for the Law of the Eastern Churches   272
Society for the Propagation of the Gospel in Foreign Parts (SPG)   378–379, 382
Sodom   162, 620, 623, 626, 627
association with homosexuality/same-sex relations   632, 636
sin of   624, **627–632**
disdain for the poor   628
sexual dimensions of   623, 628, **629–632**, 633, 634, 635
sodomy   48
sola fide (salvation by faith alone)   186, 226

solidarity, sovereignty, society, solidarity triad   37, 38
South Africa   117, 159*n*23
South Carolina   374, 377, 378
Southern Baptist Convention   548
sovereignty
of God and Jesus Christ   20, 91
human   225
of law   137
popular   349–350
See also autonomy
sovereigns as serving agents to the people   345
sovereignty, society, solidarity triad   37, 38
sphere sovereignty (Kuyper)   104, 111, 178, 179, 471–472
of state   332, 469, 470–471
See also state authority
Soviet Union   117
Spain   358, 377, 378, 579
spanking
acceptance in US   545
alternatives to   544–545
Christian views/practices   551, 552, 553, 556, 560, 562
ineffectiveness and harm   544, 545, 552, 553, 561, 566
parent's right to/as last resort   549, 553, 556*n*38
rates of spanking in US   544*n*15
SPG (Society for the Propagation of the Gospel in Foreign Parts)   378–379, 382
sphere sovereignty (Kuyper)   104, 111, 178, 179, 471–472
Spirit-filled children   553–554, 555
spiritual authority (of monarchs/princes)   91–92
state
Christian welfare state   175
"Good Samaritan" state   167, 172–173, 175, 178, 182
"mutual service" between religious and political authorities   100
relation with church. *See* church-state relations; church-state separation
rise of modern nation-state   230, 230*n*39
state authority

INDEX OF SUBJECTS

abuse of authority   94, 109, 333
associational autonomy/freedom
    and   107–108, 109
    Calvinism on   89–94, 96
    church vs.   89–90, 93–94
    See also church-state relations; church
      state-separation
    in education and upbringing of
      children   529–530, 531, 534,
      536–537
    cooperation between parents
      and   536–537, 539
    state intervention   571, 573, 574
    JW on   86–88, 90, 91–92, 93, 94, 95, 97
    lawmaking by/jurisdiction of states
      86–88, 89–90, 93–94, 349
    in marriage/marriage law   87, 108,
      199–200
    protection of subjective rights of
      freedom   96, 101–102, 205, 336,
      338, 345, 348, 356
    religious freedom and   96–104, 229
    scope of   94, 102
    vertical distribution of authority   110–111
Statute for Religious Freedom
    (Virginia)   418
Stoicism/Stoics   62
Stuart, House of, absolutism of   92, 352, 354,
    355, 356, 357, 358n13, 360
subjective rights   205
    Christian contribution to   210, 330
    JW on   205n102, 209
    objective vs.   59, 65
    origins   327, 330, 333
    positive vs. natural   59, 60, 61
    in Roman law   330
    See also natural rights
suicide, assisted   314, 316
Sunday peace/rest   383
Superior Court of Cincinnati   427
Supreme Court of Illinois, *People ex rel. Ring
    v. Board of Education* (245 Ill. 334,
    92 N.E. 251)   429, 429n34
Supreme Court of New Mexico, *Elane
    Photography v. Willock* (309 P. 3d 53
    (N.M. 2013))   479, 493, 493n24
Supreme Court of the United Kingdom,
    Khaira v. Shergill ([2014] UKSC
    33)   473, 473n46
Supreme Court of the United States

cases,
    Abington School District v. Schempp
      (374 U.S. 203 (1963))   396, 415, 424,
      427, 429, 430, 432, 442n31
    *American Legion v. American
      Humanist Association* (588 U.S.
      ___ (2019)/139 S.Ct. 2067, 204
      (2019))   437, 447–448, 453
    Bixler v. Scientology (143 S.Ct. 290
      (2022)). *See* California Court of
      Appeals
    Calder v. Bull (3 U.S. (3 Dall.) 386
      (1798))   202
    *Calvary Chapel Dayton Valley v. Steve
      Sisolak* (591 U.S. ___ (2020))   459
    Cantwell v. Connecticut (310 U.S. 296
      (1940))   409n44
    Carson v. Makin (596 U.S. ___
      (2022))   608–609
    *Dobbs v. Jackson Women's Health
      Organization* (597 U.S.___
      (2022))   587
    Doremus v. Board of Education (342,
      U.S. 429 (1952))   415, 429–430,
      430n36
    Employment Division v. Smith (494 U.S.
      872 (1990))   458–459, 460, 461,
      477–478
    Engel v. Vitale (370 U.S. 421, 429
      (1962))   442
    Everson v. Board of Education (330, U.S.
      1 (1947))   395, 396, 402, 403, 410
    Flagg Bros. v. Brooks (436 U.S. 149
      (1978))   608n106
    Fulton v. City of Philadelphia (593 U.S.–
      (2021))   478, 586–587
    Kennedy v. Bremerton School District
      (142 S.Ct. 2407 (2022))   437–438
    Lemon v. Kurtzamn (403 U.S. 602
      (1971))   604, 608
    McCollum v. Board of Education (333
      U.S. 203 (1948))   395–396
    *Masterpiece Cakeshop v. Colorado Civil
      Rights Commission* (584 U.S. –
      (2018))   479, 493, 497, 497n28
    Meyer v. Nebraska (262 U.S. 390, 400
      (1923))   517, 521, 524, 528
    Obergefell v. Hodges (576 U.S. 644
      (2015))   200, 202, 203, 210,
      573–574, 574n38

cases, (cont.)
   Parham v. J.R. (442 U.S. 584 (1979))   520, 520n39
   Pierce v. Society of Sisters (268 U.S. 510 (1925))   517–518, 519, 521, 524, 528
   Prince v. Massachusetts (321 U.S. 158 (1944))   520, 520–521n46
   Reynolds v. United States (98 U.S. 145 (1879))   401–402
   Roe v. Wade (410 U.S. 113 (1973))   587, 587n110
   Shelley v. Kraemer (334 U.S. 1 (1948))   605–607, 610, 611
   Tandon v. Newsom (593 U.S. (2021))   458n8, 460
   Vidal v. Girard's Executors (43 U.S. 127 (1844))   428–429, 429n34
   Wallace v. Jaffree (472 U.S. 38 (1985))   403
   Wisconsin v. Yoder (406, U.S. 205 (1972))   518, 519–520, 521–522, 528, 530, 534, 535, 538
   COVID-19 rulings   97, 456, **458–461**
   endorsement/religious speech tests   434, 436–437, **443–449**, 453
   Establishment Clause jurisprudence   93, 99–100, 102, 180
   Free Exercise Clause jurisprudence   93, 180, 437, 586–587, 608–609
   on parental rights and duties   527
   on (protection of) religious freedom   97, 441
   See also Free Exercise Clause
surveillance systems/technologies   169
Switzerland   569n7
"symbiotic association" (Althusius)   110
Syria   168, 169

tahkim (Islamic arbitration procedure)   596–597
Talmud   287, 629
Tametsi (decree on clandestine marriage, 1563)   502, 505, 510, 513–514
taxation
   church taxes   369, 382, 388–389, 417, 420
   in Georgia   387, 388–389
   separation of church and state and   408
   tax exemptions   43, 369
   tax increases   356, 364

tax reductions   180
tax support to churches   420
Tea Party movement (US)   180
Ten Commandments/Decalogue   219, 223
   authority of   258, 336
   enforcement and violations of First and Second Table   336, 338–339, 342, 344, 346, 367–368
   fundamental religious and civil rights in   46
   JW on   186, 230
   morality and   427
   public display of   436, 443
   Roman law and   255
   seven sacraments vs.   230, 233
   under state control   338
Tenth Amendment to the US Constitution (1791)   110
terrorism   181
Thanksgiving   445, 447
theological virtues   222, 223
theology
   law and   136
   political science and   228
   scholastic   502–503
theonomy   233
   personal autonomy vs.   224, 225, 226
"The Pursuit of Happiness" (project, CSLR)   127, 233, 664
Thomas v. Sorrell (1673/4, EWHC (KB) J85)   245–247
three estates (household, church, political state)   565, 640
Torah   92, 219, 222
Tories   365
tort law   191, 192
treaties, covenants vs.   161
Tree of Knowledge   482–483
Trent, Council of. See Council of Trent
triads
   Christianity, community, culture   35–36, 38
   creation, covenant, conscience   36, 38
   faith, freedom, family   23, 640
   law, liberty, love   36–37, 38
   sovereignty, society, solidarity   37, 38
   three "I's" of JW (interdisciplinary, international, interreligious)   9, 24, 640

three "R's" of JW (retrieval, reconstruction, reengagement)   9, 24, 640
use by JW   9, 23, 24, 35, 120
Trinitarian Protestants   357
Trinitarian theology   145
Trinity   35, 37, 338
triumphalism   291
Troy Female Seminary   421
truth
   critical race theory on/and   290, 297–298, 298n34, 301, 302, 303, 304
   as driving force of law   302
   existence of   298–299
   grounding rights in fundamental truths   298, 299–300
   JW on   296
   King on   302–305
   in law and religion   296
   love and justice as expressions of truth   303
   nonviolence and   303
   perceptions of   302–303
Truth and Reconciliation Commission (Canada)   548
tsedaqah (righteousness)   220
Tudor, House of   92
turf wars   90
two-kingdoms doctrine   150, 467, 472
tyranny/tyrants   327, 328, 329, 344, 345, 346, 347
   Antichristian   354, 358–359, 365

Ukraine   168
UN Committee on the Rights of the Child   543
   See also UN Convention on the Rights of the Child
unconscionability   605
UN Convention for Persons with Disability   576
UN Convention on the Rights of the Child (CRC, 1989)   566
   Art. 5   571
   Art. 7   570
   Art. 8   570
   Art. 9   570
   Art. 12   570, 574, 583
   Art. 20   571
   Art. 21(b)   579, 580, 583

   Art. 27   571
   enforcement of   576
   implementation in Europe   572, 577
      Romania   580, 581, 582
   JW on   542, 568, 589
   origins/history   569–570
   overview of rights   571
   ratification/ratification controversy   542–543, 568–569, 568n2, 573–578, 587, 589
   uniqueness of   570
UN Declaration on the Child   570
UNICEF   541, 543, 581
Unitarians   421, 423
United Kingdom
   COVID-19 judgments   456, 461–466, 475
   freedom of religion   614
   "Good Samaritan" laws in   167
   implementation of CRC in   577–578, 577–578n52
United States   351
   adoption in   578, 579, 581, **584–588**
   child welfare laws and policy in   575–578
   church-state relations. *See* church-state separation
   common law in   235, 249
   divorce in   170
   early American revolutionary movements   328, 329, 335
   federalist structure of   576
   "Good Samaritan" laws in   167
   libertarianism in   167n4
   motto of   438
   political covenants in   161
   polygamy in   48
   ratification of conventions   568–569, 573, 587
      See also UN Convention on the Rights of the Child
   as religious country   117, 161–162
   religious freedom in. *See* religious freedom/liberty
   secularism in   293n12, 609, 614
   See also Constitution of the United States; Supreme Court of the United States
United States Bill of Rights (1789)   67, 77
United States Declaration of Independence (1776)   127, 355, 386, 422

Universal Declaration of Human Rights
 (1948)   31, 168, 314, 315
universities, origins/history   503
University of Basel
 reception of *ius commune* in Protestant
  Reformation   252, 260–261
 rejection of canon law   256
University of Heidelberg   35
University of La Sapienza   31
University of Notre Dame   236
University of Salamanca   510, 511
University of Southern Carolina   121
upbringing
 continuity in   571
 parental rights in directing   515–516
  legal cases/court rulings   518, 519–520
  scholarly critiques   521–533
  role of state in education and   529–530,
   531, 534, 536–537
 state intervention   571, 573, 574
USAID   580
US Civil Rights Act (1964)   194, 201
US Department of Housing and Urban
 Development   123
use, right of   60–61
uses of the law (Protestant Reformed
 doctrine)   186–189
 channeling/nudging function   199, 200
 civil use   186–187, 188, 191, 295
 contemporary (Anglo-American) criminal
  law and/vs.   188–191
 divine moral law and/vs. civil law   190,
  191, 192–193, 469
 educational use/teaching function   187,
  188, 189, 191, 198, 199, 200, 295
 friendship and   211–213
 moral use   187
 policeman approach to law/public order
  by threat   198–199, 205–206, 210
 role of state   190, 190n33, 191
 as science of power   199, 201
 theological use   187, 188, 188n26, 189, 191,
  295
 vindication of human rights and   185,
  190–191, 192n44, 202, 209, 295
 works by JW/JW on   185, 186–211, 295,
  296
  Catholic critiques and points of
   agreements   198–211
  historical survey   186, 195

Protestant endorsement and
 critiques   191–198

Valois, House of   343
Vatican   470
Verdingkinder (Switzerland)   569n7
Vermont   167, 417
Vietnam War (1955–1975)   479
Virginia   371
 constitution   417
 establishment/disestablishment of
  Church of England in   374, 389,
  402, 417, 420
 religious freedom/liberty in   397, 418
 religious proclamations in   399, 400
 under Jefferson   397, 399, 400, 417
Virginia Declaration of Rights   389
virtues
 Aristotle on   215
 cardinal   218, 222, 223
 theological   222, 223
Viva Network (international child-focused
 charity)   541
Voting Rights Act (US, 1965)   194
Vrije Universiteit (Amsterdam)   5

Wales   462, 472n44, 577
"wall of separation"–metaphor (church-state
 relations)   396, 399, 400, 409, 660
 influence on/appearance in American
  jurisprudence   400, 401–403, 407,
  410
 JW on   396, 406–414
 trouble of use in law   404–406
war memorials, religious symbols on   437,
 447–448, 450
Washington (state)   167
wedding ceremonies/rites of passage   505–
 506, 509, 511, 514
Wednesbury reasonableness (English
 law)   475–476
"weightier matters of the law"
 (Berman)   136, 137–138
 Biblical/theological perspectives on   136,
  138–144
  faith   142–144
  justice   138, 139–140
  mercy   140–142
 lessons to be learned from   147
 See also faith; justice; mercy

INDEX OF SUBJECTS 731

Western law and religion scholarship/
  scholars   11–12
  See also Christian law and religion
    scholarship/scholars
Western legal system   137, 140
  See also common law
Whig Party/Whig ideology   352, 356, 358,
    358*n*13, 366
Whig theory/theorists   353, 356, 358, 361,
    366, 413
white Christian nationalism   351, 354–355
Wisconsin   167
wisdom   438
Wittenberg/Wittenberg University   214, 224
  reception of *ius commune* in Protestant
    Reformation   252–260
Wolfenden Commission (UK)   634
women
  abuse of   78
  desire of rebelling angels for   630, 633,
    636*n*124
women's rights   46
  in Christianity   77–78
  polygamy and   48, 75
  property rights   83
works, role of own works in justification   186

World Communion of Reformed
    Churches   277
World Council of Churches
  11th Assembly (2022)   11, 286
  child protection   541
  See also *Common Vision* [Index of Titles]
World Methodist Council   277
World Vision (Christian aid
    organization)   541, 547
World War II   138, 312, 314
Worms, Diet of (1520)   481–482
worship   142
  COVID-19 restrictions on collective
    455, 459, 460, 462, **463–466**, 470,
    496*n*25
  forms of   279
Wrightsborough (GA)   387

Yale Divinity School   121
Yale Law School   4, 64
Year Books (medieval England)   238
Yugoslavia   168

Zahiri scholars   597
Zero Abuse Project (US)   548
Zeus   215, 625